PAINTING FOR PROFIT

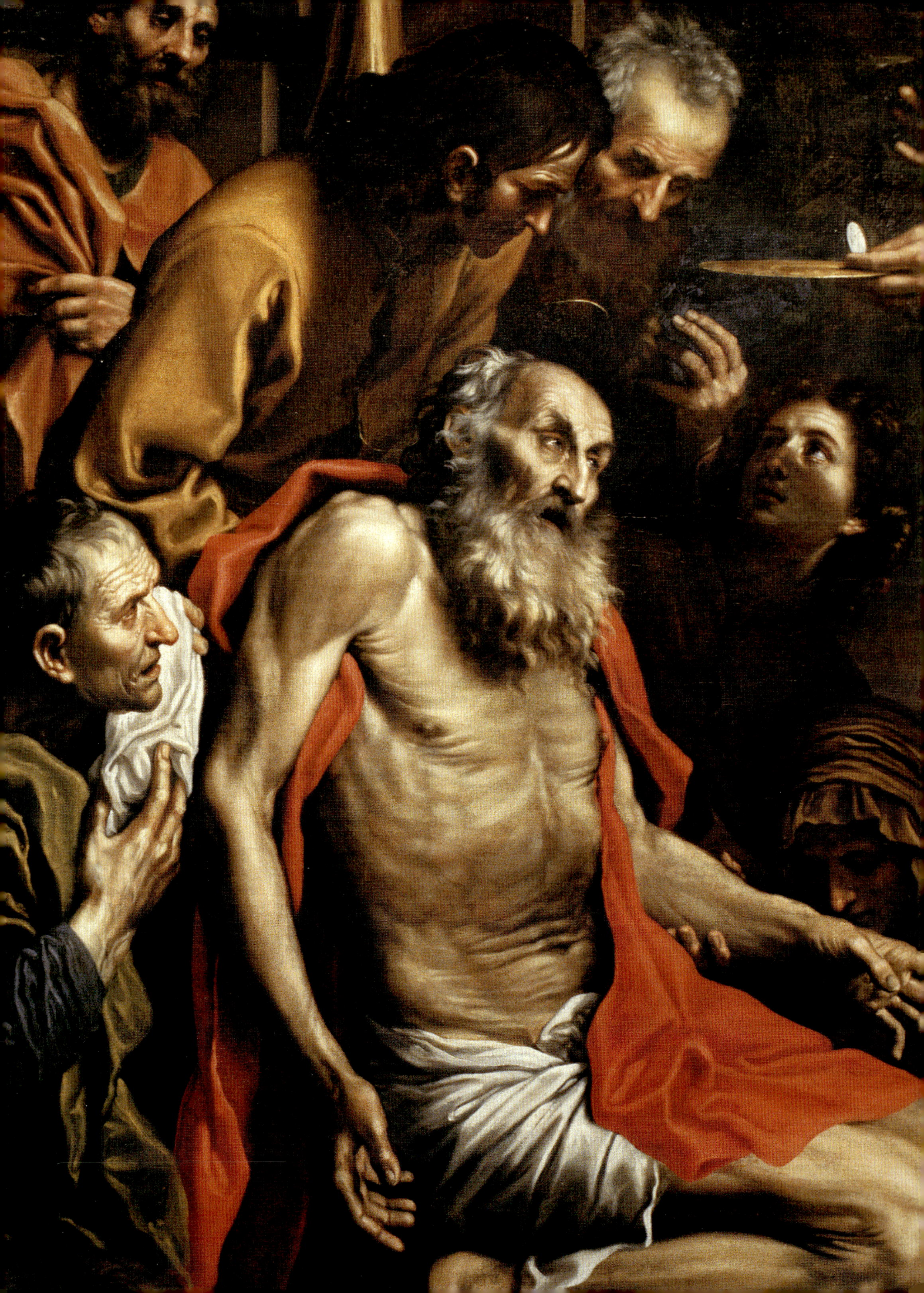

Painting for Profit

THE ECONOMIC LIVES OF SEVENTEENTH-CENTURY ITALIAN PAINTERS

RICHARD E. SPEAR AND PHILIP SOHM

*With Contributions by Renata Ago,
Elena Fumagalli, Richard A. Goldthwaite,
Christopher R. Marshall, and Raffaella Morselli*

YALE UNIVERSITY PRESS ~ NEW HAVEN AND LONDON

Matthew Sohm translated the essays on
Bologna, Florence, and the Five Industrious Cities

Designed by Sarah Faulks

Printed in China

Library of Congress Cataloging-in-Publication Data
Spear, Richard E., 1940-
Painting for profit : the economic lives of seventeenth-century Italian painters / Richard E. Spear and Philip Sohm. – Rome: setting the stage / Richard E. Spear – Naples / Christopher R. Marshall – Bologna / Raffaella Morselli – Florence / Elena Fumagalli – Venice / Philip Sohm – Five industrious cities / Renata Ago – The painting industry in early modern Italy / Richard A. Goldthwaite.
p. cm.
Includes bibliographical references and index.
ISBN 978-0-300-15456-6 (cl : alk. paper)
1. Painters–Italy–Economic conditions–17th century. 2. Painters–Italy–Social conditions–17th century. 3. Painting–Economic aspects–Italy–17th century. 4. Art and society–Italy–History–17th century. I. Sohm, Philip L. (Philip Lindsay), 1951- II. Title.
ND616.S64 2010
338.4'7759509032–dc22
2009054056
A catalogue record for this book is available from The British Library

Frontispiece: Domenichino, *Last Communion of St. Jerome*, detail, 1612–14. Oil on canvas, 419 × 256 cm. Pinacoteca Vaticana.

Contents

Tables

Acknowledgments

Many debts were incurred during the research and writing of this book. The authors are particularly grateful to the Clark Art Institute, which sponsored a colloquium in 2004 that brought the team together from Australia, Canada, Italy, and the U.S.A. to Williamstown for two days of productive discussions and planning. Special thanks are owed to Gillian Malpass of Yale University Press for her unwavering support of our project, to Nancy Marten for her exceptionally acute eye as our copy-editor, and to Sarah Faulks for her sensitive design of our book. The authors also acknowledge the generous institutional support and assistance received from many colleagues and friends:

Richard Spear: the Bogliasco Foundation/Liguria Study Center, the Rockefeller Foundation/Bellagio Study Center, Patrizia Cavazzini for her invaluable help with countless issues, Joseph Connors, Belinda Granata, Ann Sutherland Harris, Peter Lukehart, Francesco Petrucci, Louise Rice, James Ryan, Erich Schleier, Donatella Sparti, and above all Athena Tacha for her loving and intellectual presence.

Philip Sohm: Social Sciences and Research Council of Canada, Bernard Aikema, Olivier Bonfait, Linda Borean, Sybille Ebert-Schifferer, Elizabeth Griffith, Bernice Iarocci, Maria Loh, Peter Lukehart, Colin Murray, Athena Tacha, and Jonathan Unglaub.

Elena Fumagalli: Giovanni Pagliarulo, Riccardo Spinelli, Frank Dabell for his important help, and especially Patrizia Cavazzini for her generous support.

Richard Goldthwaite: Gian Mario Cao, Pamela Long, Neil De Marchi, Kent Lydecker, and Jonathan Nelson.

Raffaella Morselli: Gian Piero Cammarota, Andrea Emiliani, Marcello Fantoni, the late Luigi Spezzaferro, Maria Cristina Terzaghi, Alessandra Ruggiero and Lucie Esposito for their important help, and particularly Roberta Piccinelli for continuing assistance.

Preface

RICHARD E. SPEAR

The genesis of this book was an idea of Philip Sohm. After reading my monograph on Guido Reni (1997) with chapters dedicated to money and marketing strategies, he suggested that we adopt the socio-economic approach I had taken and expand it to encompass all of seventeenth-century Italian painting. The proposal was attractive, especially because so little has been published about the economic lives of Italian baroque painters. Moreover, those few historians who have investigated Italian baroque art from an economic perspective, including Francis Haskell in his pioneering *Patrons and Painters* of 1963, typically have focused on patronage whereas our interest was the artist. Yet it was a dauntingly ambitious idea, even if we limited our study to painting, which seemed reasonable because the economic bases of architecture and sculpture were so vastly different.

We nevertheless feared that even to investigate just the painters would require our two lifetimes. Accordingly, we decided to invite a team of collaborators and to focus our study on the major artistic centers that were different economically and politically, with the intention of maximizing opportunities to compare our findings.[1] We asked three art historians to work with us because the questions we were posing, as outlined in the Introduction, tend to differ from those of interest to many economic historians, who usually are more concerned with the place of art in a national economy than with the artist and his or her work. To broaden our perspective, however, we invited two more scholars to join us: Renata Ago, a social historian who specializes in social economics, and Richard Goldthwaite, the economic historian who largely initiated economic analysis of Italian Renaissance art.

Research on the economics of seventeenth-century Netherlandish art, pioneered by the late Michael Montias, has been exceptionally fruitful. While it inspired our work, we generally resisted temptation to compare our data with what Montias and other economic and art historians of Northern art have discovered (some of their publications are cited and discussed below). We resisted the temptation for two reasons. Most importantly, the social and economic conditions of seventeenth-century Italy (which itself was anything but homogeneous, as this book shows) and northern Europe were far too different to allow simple comparisons. To make them properly, which is our second reason, would have required a separate, lengthy study.

Our book is organized by city with many similar questions posed across the essays, yet inevitably there are differences in the material covered, whether because of the nature of the data available or because, as in the case of Florence with its dominant court structure, a particular focus was called for and space did not allow much further discussion. Effort has been made nonetheless to facilitate comparisons, for example by tabulating data on altarpieces, the most lucrative of commissions, for all five cities.[2]

The number of pages allocated to Rome requires explanation. Primarily because Rome was the center of seventeenth-century Italian art and provides the richest documentation, it merits extra attention. Additionally, we decided to use the essay on Rome as an essential complement to the Introduction: to have it set the stage for the rest of the book by opening issues that pertain to all of the cities (for instance, artistic competition and the ways painters earned extra money) and to have it include data—such as prices of consumer goods, the costs of artists' materials, and the comparative values of the genres of painting—which if discussed in every essay would have been unduly repetitive.

Unless indicated otherwise, we generally have relied on Angelo Martini's still unsurpassed *Manuale di metrologia* (1883) to work our way through the difficult maze of seventeenth-century Italian and European exchange rates.[3] Although the data we compiled on original prices of seventeenth-century Italian paintings are too extensive to be included in their entirety here, a significant portion of what we found will become available on a database under development with the Getty Research Institute.[4]

We realize that a book of this ambition has many lacunae. Our purpose, however, was not to write a comprehensive history, but to widen Vasari's view that money matters by showing that to neglect it as a motivating factor in painters' lives can leave a big gap in our understanding of art history.

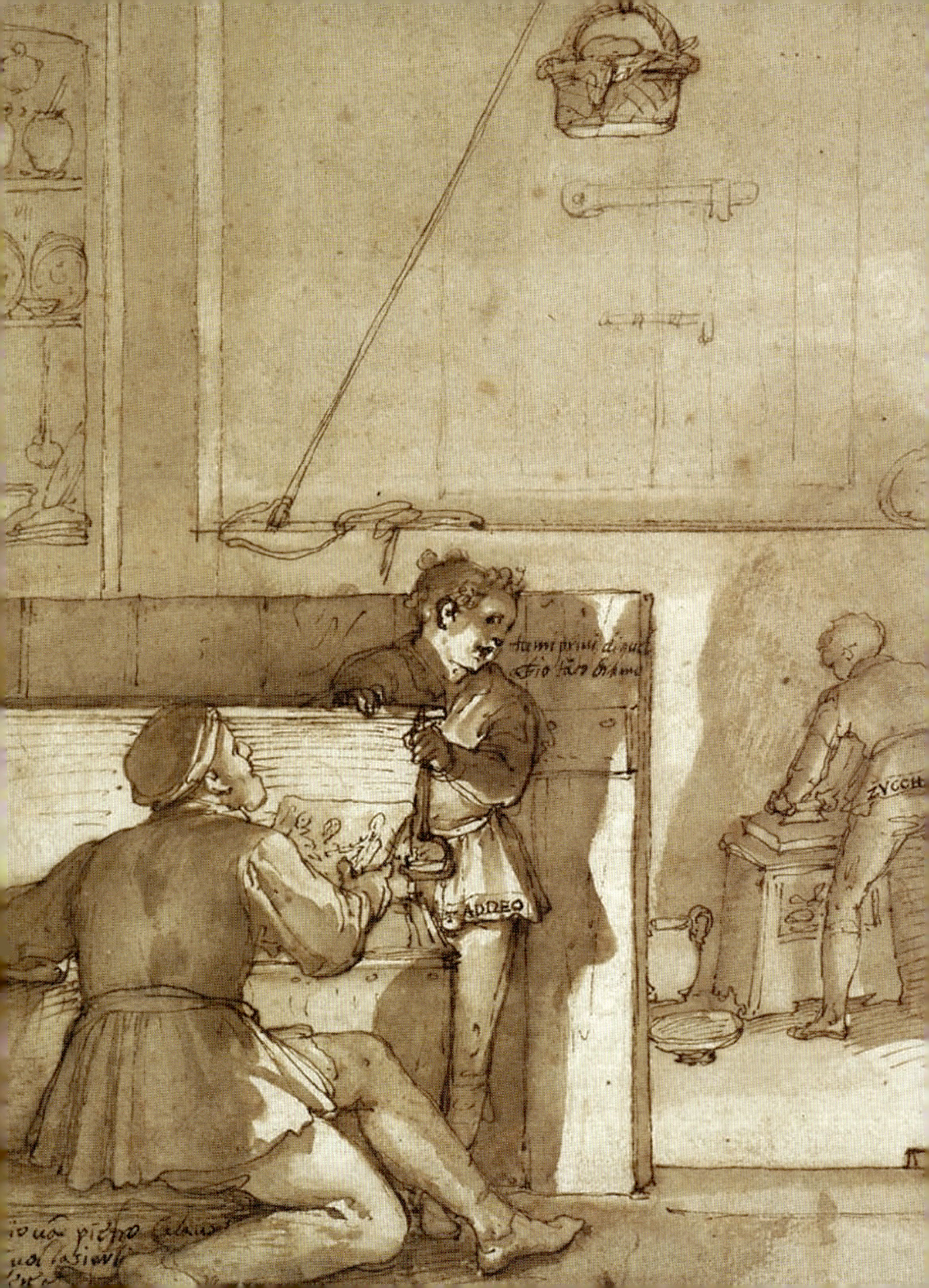

ADDEO
ZVCCH

Introduction

PHILIP SOHM

This book is full of numbers. Its challenge is to decide what those numbers signify and how to decode the language of money. We hoped to show how ducats and scudi tell many stories about how painters lived and worked, how they perceived themselves within a professional and commercial community, how they were perceived by those outside that community, and what they did to advance themselves or merely to survive. Money shaped the material world of painters, and in the pursuit of money painters shaped the pictorial worlds. Did money inspire, liberate, or corrupt? In trying to answer these and other questions, we relied on various types of sources. There are those written by the painters themselves—letters, testaments, legal disputes, diaries—and, most pertinently, account books kept by painters in Venice, Bologna, and Florence: Paolo Farinati (1573–1606) and Tiberio Tinelli (1618–33); Guercino (1629–66), Giacomo Alboresi, and Marcantonio Franceschini; Andrea Boscoli (1589–1600 and 1606), Domenico and Valore Casini (1616–32), and Antonio Franchi (1683–1704).[1] Then there are those contemporary sources written about painters, either as unpublished notes (Giulio Mancini and Richard Symonds) or codified in art biographies. The most useful biographies were written by fellow painters (Giovanni Baglione, Carlo Ridolfi, Giovanni Battista Passeri, and Raffaelle Soprani), an art curator (Filippo Baldinucci), an economist and art collector (Lione Pascoli), and historians with archival or antiquarian interests (Carlo Cesare Malvasia and Giovanni Pietro Bellori). And then, finally, there are the legal documents that record business transactions (contracts and payments), legislation by guilds and academies, censuses, and residential rental and ownership records.

The state of research today on the economic lives of Italian painters resembles research on patronage studies just before Francis Haskell's pioneering *Patrons and Painters* (1963), when troves of documentation about patronage lay scattered in diverse publications on individual patrons or painters without, however, any serious synthetic study. Today economic data on seventeenth-century Italian painters have reached a critical mass, but with few recent exceptions (notably Richard Spear, Olivier Bonfait, Guido Guerzoni, and Patrizia Cavazzini) their analysis remains fragmented and episodic, and mostly restricted to individual painters, their products and production, costs and profits, incomes and overheads. With the exception of Bologna, no cohesive overview of local practices has been attempted. We know little or nothing about diachronic trends (how, for example, prices and production changed over a century, and how supply and demand operated within the art world). We are also ignorant of local economic conditions in one city and how they differed from those in other cities, as we are too about how those differences might have encouraged emigra-

Facing page: detail of Fig. 1

tion and immigration. In 2003, after reviewing an important group of essays on the Italian art market, Richard Goldthwaite concluded that "studies of particular entrepreneurial artist-producers do not lead to generalizations about the industry; studies of the art market in one city make no comparisons with markets in other cities of the same period. And a sense of change over time is notably absent."[2]

Unlike some multi-authored books, ours germinated from a common agenda that we developed collectively first online and then in person (courtesy of the Clark Art Institute). We agreed to analyze the economics of production, marketing, and sales taken from the painter's point of view rather than the collector's or patron's. We wanted to know how prices were set, and how prices might affect or reflect a painting's subject, size, number of figures, speed of execution, costs of production (notably materials, labor, and rent), style, and the age and status of the painter. How, we wondered, did sales techniques (bargaining, discounting, and gifting) and marketing venues (shops, dealers, and lotteries) influence painters' incomes? While they earned most of their income from the sale of paintings (paid in cash, by barter, or with honors and sinecures), some also relied on salaries and wages, and others enjoyed ancillary incomes from appraisal fees, copy and restoration work as well as miscellaneous investments. Not all of these topics are discussed in each essay. Because Rome provided us with a disproportionate wealth of material in certain areas, especially the costs of running a studio, we delegated these topics to Spear. In this way (and others), Rome serves as a second, more extensive introduction. Renata Ago's essay on "Five Industrious Cities" examines the socio-economic world of seicento Italy in general. It reviews such topics as socio-economic stratifications; domestic budgets; professional associations such as guilds, colleges, and academies; incomes of different trades and professions; professional incomes, investments, and expenses; and market demand for luxury goods.

No author and source citations are given in this Introduction for material that is documented and discussed elsewhere in the book. For example, any unreferenced observation about Bologna should be credited to Raffaella Morselli, whose essay the reader should consult for further information. For those facts and claims that are referenced, the reader can assume that these are my contributions and are not found elsewhere in the book.

Economic history is ridden with numeric complexities: non-standardized local currencies; gold and silver currencies whose value drifted as New World metals flooded Europe and then receded; concealed or non-monetary payments; and costs of living that varied city by city. While trying to address some of these problems, we agreed to accept certain limitations. All figures have been left in the local currency without regard for its shifting value. The Roman silver scudo was the most stable currency with little or no change through most of the century. By contrast, the Florentine gold scudo lost 20 percent of its value against the Roman scudo, the Venetian ducat lost 28 percent, the Bolognese scudo di cambio lost 32 percent, and the Neapolitan silver ducat lost 35 percent. Those readers who want to convert currencies for the sake of comparison are referred to Table 30 in Ago's essay.

Artistic Value: The Ethics and Psychology of Money

Most painters did not have the inclination, education, or luxury of time to philosophise about "value," an elitist idea like "art" itself, which elevates intangible qualities such as beauty, creativity, and expression over the material and tangible. For painters of still lifes and *madonninas*, sold at low standardized prices, production took precedence over ideation. Paintings of this sort were priced like other commodities and sold in various shops, often (oddly) in barbershops and other ad hoc spaces.[3] Salvator Rosa, who reluctantly specialized in those pictorial genres that these merchants wanted (landscapes and battle scenes), noted that "hunger . . . domesticates painters and reduces them to working for barbers."[4] At the opposite end of the socio-economic scale, where painters worked on commission for the noble and wealthy, value (and hence prices) became a signifier of intangibles—a painter's talent, a painting's beauty—that led to huge price differentials.

How economic and artistic values were related, if at all, is a question with a history that became a matter of some urgency amongst writers during the mid-sixteenth century. Michelangelo, whose commercial practices and ideas challenged opinions about value, was a pivotal figure. Francisco de Hollanda credited him with an economic revaluation of art, hoping to export his concept of high-value art to Portugal. In the *Diálogos em Roma*, avowedly a recollection of conversations in Rome in 1538, Hollanda asks Michelangelo what he means by "value." Michelangelo responds that value cannot be set by "anyone" but only by those with judgment. At this point in time, at least from Hollanda's Portuguese perspective, value was still understood as pro rata: "As for me, I give the highest price for the work done by a great painter, even if he has spent little time over it. . . . And I value very little that which an unskilled painter has painted in many years of work, however much they call him a painter."[5] Hollanda ascribed the artistic success of painters in Italy to their generous remuneration: "One great reason why one can paint only in Italy and nowhere else consists in the salaries and prices that painters receive here."[6]

Vincenzo Borghini, the first director of the Accademia del Disegno, rejected Hollanda's popular belief that artistic and economic value were directly correlated.[7] Like Hollanda, he did so by dismissing an antiquated notion held by "our elders or ancestors" that the value of art could be quantified by size or time, pro rata work that "we call weigh and pay." He then turned to a new misapprehension that arose from the cult of artistic genius, the so-called "triumph of the laurel," which owes its popularity to Michelangelo as much as to any other artist. Borghini accepted the premise that artistic quality should determine the price. So prevalent had this expectation become, he observed, that now many people believe that a high price indicates high quality, that "from the smoke many argue the existence of fire." A false syllogism arose from these beliefs: since a well-made figure should be appraised at a high price, any expensive painting proves its artistic value with its price. If a painting is expensive, it must be great art. Borghini found this syllogism to be "a dangerous thing" because of its abuse of logic, obviously, but he also worried that it allowed people with money to determine what is good artistically (as if it were not always so).

When Guido Reni claimed to be a better painter than Guercino because his paintings cost more, it sounds as if Reni had fallen prey to Borghini's syllogism. Times had changed. Reni might have been motivated by his gambling debts and fragile ego, but his statement can also be taken as a sign of how attitudes toward money had evolved between the mid-sixteenth and mid-seventeenth centuries.[8] There remained idealists during the seventeenth century, like the sour culture critic Antonio Lupis, who mocked this value system: "Today so many people value paintings according to their price."[9] Painters, however, commonly thought of their reputations in terms of price as much as art. Ludovico Carracci initiated price increases in late sixteenth-century Bologna, and Malvasia approved because he understood money as a symbolic currency. Art itself had been revalued; prices rose because the Bolognese finally grasped the high value of art. Wanting to explain why Ciro Ferri was charging about five times as much as local painters in Bergamo, David Brembati wrote that "this painter is truly one of the best to be found in Italy today, and he knows it and would like to be known by others for the prices he commands."[10]

The cultured elite writing theory accepted the argument that quantifiable criteria such as materials, size, or time were the wrong criteria by which to value art because they reduced it to a craft and commodity. The reality behind their theorizing, however, tells a different story, one that is the subject of this book. Yes, some artists like Bernini and Cortona benefited from the Michelangelo legacy and attained great wealth based on recognized originality and creativity. Patrons and collectors were willing to pay hefty premiums to own or display their work. Most artists, however, were subject to the constraints of the marketplace and accepted quantified prices based on such supposedly demeaning criteria as size. And looking further down the economic ladder, many still accepted standard payments simply by unit produced, and some even worked on the basis of low daily wages, as if they were masons or other skilled craftsmen.

~

The entrepreneurial society where painters engaged in business was etched with psychological complexities that affected their lives and work. How painters manipulated and traumatized their competitors can be introduced through Baldinucci's story of the Florentine Carlo Dolci and the Neapolitan Luca "fa presto" Giordano. Sweet, gentle, insecure Dolci spent such care on his paintings, Baldinucci tells us, that Giordano warned him, "If you continue to paint in this way, to invest so much time in executing your works . . . you will certainly die of hunger." He did not die of hunger, but these words, spoken in jest, precipitated a psychological and physical crisis. When Dolci showed his final work, an *Adoration of the Magi*, to the Granduchessa Vittoria, she pulled out a painting by Giordano and praised it lavishly: "What do you think of this work, Carlo? Would you ever believe that it was done, as it truly was, in just a few days?" Dolci, churning with "dark thoughts," started to undergo strange changes. "With a false understanding of himself," he fixed upon the idea that there was no painter in the world who was more unworthy than himself. Growing paler and more emaciated, he finally died of shame and remorse.

Dolci was a slow painter but he set his prices high: "200 scudi for each [portrait] but he works six months on one," wrote Nicodemus Tessin the Younger while visiting Florence in 1674.[11] Their value continued as collectibles, at least in Venice where a painting of a child by Dolci was assigned one of the highest prices (300 ducats) in the Correggio collection, second only to one by Rosa (500 ducats).[12] Giordano targeted another slow and patient Florentine. Baldassare Franceschini (called Volterrano) procrastinated in completing a prestige altarpiece for S. Maria della Salute in Venice because (according to the art dealer Paolo del Sera) "such extreme finish takes a long time." Learning of this situation, Giordano did "a Tintoretto turn" (to use Sera's phrase) and quickly painted an unsolicited replacement, placed it on the altar, and offered it at a discount price (200 ducats, compared with the 720 ducats that Franceschini would have received). The procurators of the Salute accepted, and Franceschini took yet another step toward penury. Despite Sera's patriotic promotion of Franceschini in Venice—he told Cardinal Carlo de' Medici in 1662 that "our Volterrano" was the best contemporary painter in Venice—and despite his high prices—"one must pay 100 scudi for a head with two hands"—Franceschini "struggled to support a wife and child or two" because of his diligent habits.

These two stories of Dolci and Volterrano, one fictionalized and the other reliably documented, reveal various economic phenomena: that Giordano was a cunning manipulator of people, discouraging the competition and enticing patrons by unorthodox means; that styles and techniques had financial consequences; and that regional artistic rivalries were personalized by biographers and rendered in economic terms.

Because poverty was a fact of life for so many painters, a fear of poverty held many prosperous painters in its grip. Some were more susceptible than others, but so many stories circulated in biographies (and presumably on the streets) about loss of income and loss of financial security that one senses a miasma of anxiety about money. "I paint to live and help my poor parents," wrote the Perugine Gian Domenico Cerrini in 1666, adding that "out of necessity I make many paintings just to live and bear my essential living expenses."[13] The prosperous minority had only to look at the struggling majority to realize how precarious their own lives were. Psychoses developed. Perugino, having been born poor, lived with "the fear of poverty constantly before his eyes."[14] His art suffered since he undertook work solely to earn more money. "He would have sold his soul for money," Vasari concluded. Avaricious Pintoricchio died after losing 500 gold ducats. Agostino Carracci was once denied an opportunity to earn a "high salary," grew melancholy as a result, and "finally fell into a state of deep dejection."[15] His brother Annibale plunged into a debilitating depression after he received a unexpectedly meagre payment from Odoardo Farnese. Money, in other words, could become a psychological pathogen even for successful painters.

~

By the late sixteenth century, two conflicting views about the monetary motivations of artists coexisted. Pragmatists like Vasari accepted the fact that artists struggled to earn a living and in that struggle their art suffered:

> We rightly admire the celebrated artists of the past who created great work, knowing their prize would be a happy life and a generous reward. How much more, then, should we praise and exalt those rare men of genius who create priceless work and who live not merely unrewarded but in circumstances of wretched poverty. It is undeniably true that if the artists of our own time were justly rewarded they would produce even greater works of art, far superior to those of the ancient world. Instead, the artist today struggles to ward off famine rather than to win fame, and this crushes and buries his talent and obscures his name.[16]

Poverty perverts art. According to one of Vasari's most compelling (and true!) stories, Raffaellino del Garbo overextended himself so as to "ward off famine . . . [he] crushes and buries his talent and obscures his name."[17] Forced to support his family, he accepted commissions "at diminished prices and thus [his painting] became constantly more degenerate." Francesco Albani was a modern Raffaellino. After his brother's death left him massively indebted, Albani maximized profits by producing a multitude of small formulaic paintings, working "more from necessity than from genius, more for money than for glory."[18]

Vasari can be credited with establishing the starving artist as a narrative cell in art biography. But for every poor artist in Vasari's *Lives*, there were many more unknown painters who merely subsisted, living marginal and uncelebrated lives. Vasari, however, was concerned not with the forgotten multitude but with those who might have achieved greater results if they had not had to struggle for money. There are two kinds of artists, Vasari claimed: those whose "rare intellects" transcended money and those "hapless intellects" whose creativity was stultified by a lack of money. Raffaellino clearly fell into the latter category. So did the talented Brusasorci, who was so risk adverse that he never dared to leverage himself out of poverty by attempting more adventurous work.[19] Which kind was Vasari? Neither. In fact, his life disproves his thesis. By any historical measure (our own or that of his contemporaries), Vasari succeeded artistically as an architect, courtier, critic, historian, and entrepreneur. As a painter, and it was through his painting that Vasari acquired much of his wealth, we rank him as low as the younger generation did who retrospected his work shortly after his death. Money for him was an incentive, even inspirational, just as he claimed, but insufficient to become a painter to rival antiquity. It inspired an awesome rate of production, but not a concordant quality of art. Vasari was in good company during the later sixteenth century. Like Neri di Bicci (the richest painter in late fifteenth-century Florence), and like Federico Zuccaro, Giuseppe Cesari d'Arpino, and others a generation later, Vasari capitalized on a technique, studio organization, and social network that enabled him to become conspicuously rich.[20]

"I—thank God—do not need to beg my bread with toil. I am therefore not forced by necessity to corrupt art and part with my works for a piece of bread from whoever wishes to pay me for them."[21] When in 1591 Gregorio Comanini attributed these words to the painter Ambrogio Figino, he acknowledged the realities of poverty without glamorizing its benefits. Is it better for a painter to be "comfortable and rich or poor and needy"?[22] Mancini posed and answered this question by affirming the practical benefits of comfort for artists. Money liberates artists from the tyranny of production at the expense of quality. The portraitist and biographer Ridolfi, who knew the importance of money from living many years without much, dismissed those who glorified poverty: "Some people believe that virtue must always remain wrapped in rags."[23]

Vasari, Comanini, Mancini, and Ridolfi were pragmatists. On the other side stood the idealists who believed that money corrupts and poverty purifies. They took Protogenes as their model for the artistic virtues of poverty. Poor by choice and thus an artistically pure artist, Protogenes was the Diogenes of the art world. A diligent perfectionist, he remained poor because he refused to sacrifice quality or increase quantity simply to earn money. He even undernourished himself "so as not to thicken his intelligence."[24] This self-purifying Protogenes was thus characterized in Hollanda's dialogues, with an intentional nod to the latter-day puritan Michelangelo. Michelangelo's tattered clothing, casual hygiene, humble furniture, and intermittent nourishment took on mythic status.[25] He could afford better, but he refused the usual comforts that great wealth could bring him. "Although he became very rich, he lived like a poor man."[26] Michelangelo was conspicuously wealthy, as Rab Hatfield's meticulous study shows, but this had little effect on his self-image: "I am a poor fellow, and of little worth, plodding along in that art which God has assigned to me, in order to prolong my life as long as I can."[27] Poverty forced many artists to live this way, but Michelangelo chose it for himself—the ascetic aesthete—or forced it on himself by an intractable miserliness.

Hollanda's Protogenes originated with Pliny the Elder, but Hollanda gave greater importance to Protogenes' self-abnegation than other later interpreters of Pliny (Carlo Dati and Franciscus Junius, for example). The self-denying Protogenes was enriched with further detail in the seventeenth century. Rosa has him eating only leguminous plants while at work, just enough to quiet his stomach but not enough to quench his inspiration.[28] In a further embellishment of the Protogenes myth, Antonio Lupis claimed in *Il chiaro scuro di pittura morale* (Venice, 1685) that Protogenes spurned affluence and chose to live in "a rustic hut with a little garden," thereby embodying "the richness of poverty."[29] (Lupis thematically juxtaposed Protogenes with Reni, the exemplar of "the misery of riches" because he was showered with gold like Danäe.) Protogenes shadowed Annibale Carracci and his contemporaries. Annibale seemed to be, noted Malvasia, "frightened and ashamed" of money and disdained gold and fancy clothes, unlike his brother Agostino. "What ineffable restraint in a mind more disciplined and composed than could ever be boasted of by ancient philosophy!"[30]

Idealists took the mercenary painter as complicit with a materialist culture that values wealth and luxurious display over beauty. Money, according to this view, corrupts the intellect. The financial security of Sebastiano del Piombo's papal office made him a lazy painter.[31] "The comforts of life are an obstacle to those who seek to advance [their art]," claimed Federico Barocci, then one of Rome's highest priced painters.[32] Charles Le Brun was an overpaid underachiever, according to Lorenzo Magalotti, who held that after Le Brun received an annual stipend of 10,000 scudi from Louis XIV, he produced only inferior works.[33] Bellori and Rosa believed that worldly success as a painter corrupts artists and leads to artistic decline.[34] (Rosa never reconciled his views as a satirist with his economic success as a painter.)

According to the painter and pedagogue Giovan Battista Armenini, Perino del Vaga feared poverty so much (and so unnecessarily) that he exploited painters who actually were poor and were willing to work for substandard wages: "This sort of mad avarice became common and young artists are now paid by the day just as though they were wretched peasants."[35] The exploitation of cheap labor preceded Perino and continued into the seventeenth century. A pragmatist would take Perino's economic strategy as an inventive capitalist solution to the growing competition from younger painters. A moralist like Armenini, however, gave Perino's practice psychological and moral defects—greed and unprincipled commerce—that resulted in artistically inferior work, "smearing" the walls of "the most beautiful and most famous buildings."

Writing in 1612, the Bolognese painter, critic, and historian Francesco Cavazzoni also reflected on the temptations of money.[36] Quoting Petrarch—"Povera e nuda vai Filosofia, dice la turba al vil guadagno intesa"—he explained why contemporary art had declined. In antiquity, he claimed erroneously, only the nobility were allowed to practice the art of painting because they would have no financial needs that might sully their art, "and the greatest shame is that painters today let themselves perish in the mouths of that horrible monster, ambition." Poverty is not so much a lamentable precondition that determines choice but, as the fable of Protogenes suggests, a condition to overcome. Giampaolo Lomazzo believed that patrons with both taste and money were rare in those days (1589) and that consequently "the painter prostitutes his studio making everything for greed."[37] Virtuous poverty or decadent prosperity? Moralists, like other idealists, insisted that a choice always exists and that prostitution, whether selling one's talent or one's body, was the wrong choice.

Many critics of late sixteenth-century painting (Borghini in 1584, Lomazzo in 1589, Comanini in 1591, Armenini in 1584, Cavazzoni in 1603) understood their culture as one degraded by the pursuit of money, where "in our age . . . avarice overflows all bounds."[38] By the early seventeenth century, it seemed to many painters and critics that the greatest masters had died (Leonardo, Raphael, Correggio, Michelangelo, and Titian) and that art had languished into its "old age," to use Mancini's revealing metaphor. They wrote as modern-day Plinys looking back at a lost golden age and identifying artists' avarice and patrons' love of luxurious materials as a principal cause for decline. In 1637 Franciscus Junius did as well but turned to Petronius Arbiter for further explanation: "Doe not wonder therefore that picture is lost, seeing all the gods and men think a lumpe of gold better than all that Apelles and Phydias a couple of doting Grecians have made."[39]

Skillful entrepreneurs like Zuccaro and Arpino managed to leverage the reputation of "art" into personal wealth, but within the moralists' frame of reference their wealth tainted their art. Zuccaro defended his brother Taddeo against Vasari's charges of "rapacious avarice" and the exploitation of "young strangers who are always to be found in Rome, and who go about working by the day in order to learn and to gain their bread."[40] Zuccaro responded in the margins of his copy of Vasari's *Vite* that the accusation was true only of Vasari's practice as a painter.[41] Yet in the 1590s, some Romans believed that Federico, like Taddeo, was motivated only by money and an extravagant lifestyle, and that for this reason he always charged "excessive prices."[42] Whether Federico felt artistically compromised by his wealth is doubtful, although one wonders whether the many public criticisms of his painting might not have had some economic envy behind them. When he painted a visual biography of Taddeo's life in his Roman palace, he chose as his subject his brother's poverty and hardship as a youth as if to defend his own wealth by Taddeo's hard work (Fig. 1). "In truth," Vasari concluded in his life of Taddeo, "Federigo will be heir to the talents of Taddeo no less than to his property." One may also sense a guilty ambivalence on Federico's part about his "great big palace" (*palazzotto*), as Grazioso Graziosi labelled it in 1593, when Federico called it his "doghouse" (*tugurio*) on the Pincio.[43] By one account that proved to be close to the truth: "It will easily be the ruin of his sons."[44]

Mannerism and greed, where wealth is often taken as a sign of successfully enacted greed, became a clear backdrop for seventeenth-century painters with biographical aspirations. Rosa best embodies the inner conflicts brought by money to art. He understood himself as a pure artist, working only for his art and without financial motives, and he wanted others to think of him in this way so that no one would misclassify him as a greedy Mannerist, a shabby Bambocciante, or some other materialist. When he wrote to Antonio Ruffo that "I do not paint to enrich myself but only for my own satisfaction and only when I am transported by inspiration," Rosa was telling a partial truth.[45] At that time he had not been painting for at least two months, a fallow period that would continue for another three months or more, but as he confessed to his close friend Ricciardi, he was forced to stop for medical reasons (including trouble with his eyesight) and not necessarily for a lack of inspiration.[46] Rosa represented himself to Ruffo as an inspirationalist, not in a confessional mode as he did with Ricciardi, nor simply as a matter of explanation, but as a means of manipulation. He wanted more money from the notoriously stingy Ruffo and adopted a clever self-marketing strategy to achieve his goal. By appealing to this particular public persona for artists, he reassured Ruffo of the purity of his motives and the transcendence of his art. By denying any mercenary motive, he hoped to loosen Ruffo's purse strings.

Demography, Chronology, and Geography

How many painters were working in Italy during the seventeenth century? This is one of many basic socio-economic questions that art historians have not answered, and with good reason. First, our data come from different kinds of documentary sources that result in varying population figures: civic censuses like the Roman *stati d'anime* and Venetian *decime*, guild and academy enrolments, artist biographies, and personal estimates. Not only are the data inconsistent for a single city, but those inconsistencies are compounded when comparing different cities. Second, there is the problem of defining what is meant by "painters." In Renaissance Venice, the painters' guild distinguished between figure painters (*pittori*) and decorative painters (*dipintori* or, in its Venetian form, *depentori*). Florentine censuses maintained this distinction into the seventeenth century. It would be convenient to say that our book concerns only *pittori*, but by this date one could be a *pittore* without painting figures. The new genres of landscape, cityscape, still life, and animals, as well as the growing fame of many *quadraturisti*, meant that the human figure was no longer the sole measure of art. By the mid-seventeenth century, the legal nomenclature of *pittori* and *dipintori* in Venice and Florence defined socio-economic status and artistic aspiration: *dipintori* were craftsmen, tradesmen, and poorer; *pittori* practiced a liberal art and were richer. When the wealthier Venetian *pittori* formed a *collegio* that excluded *dipintori*, they claimed that the craft and trade of decorative painting demeaned the liberal art of figure painting. In Genoa the distinction between those painters who engaged in commerce and those who (supposedly) did not became a key test for admission to the nobility.[47]

Demography, when it is expressed as painters per capita, will tell us something about the vitality of the local market in comparison with others. Cities in Flanders and Holland with more than 1 percent painters per capita were net exporters of paintings, the accepted assumption being that higher ratios produced more surplus stock available for export. In Italy, where no city had more than 1 percent painters per capita (much less any near the rate of 1.3 to 2.4 percent of some northern cities) and where the art market differed in so many other ways, this assumption would need more revision than the data from our study allow. From the examples recently collected by Neil De Marchi and Louisa Matthew, it may be true that the city with the highest per capita rate (Rome) was the largest exporter.[48] Venice and Naples were probably close behind, probably because the former was a major international trade center and the latter had unparalleled ties to Spain, the largest market for small mass-produced paintings destined for the Americas. Bologna, with a large per capita population second only to Rome, apparently did not engage in mass exports although it rivalled Rome in producing luxury high art for export, at least judging from the numbers of seventeenth-century Bolognese paintings found in Italian and French collections.

In a European context, Italy exported old masters more than moderns and were net importers of painters; that is, more painters emigrated to Italy for work than Italians emigrated from Italy. With the highest per capita rate in Italy, Rome probably had the highest rate of foreign exchange of goods and talent. Rome is "where you go to get rich," a Milanese patron was told in 1625 to explain why a 250 scudo altarpiece by Giovanni Battista Crespi (Cerano) would cost 500 scudi if it were commissioned in Rome.[49] The price differential was not so extreme in reality—the doubled price is more for rhetorical emphasis—but prices were indeed higher and known to be higher in Rome, and these could have attracted painters to the city.

By two accounts, there were 190 painters in Rome in 1634 and about 200 in 1665, a per capita rate of about 0.19 percent (for general population figures for each city, see Table 32 in Ago's essay). The *stati d'anime* of 1619 for two parishes where painters traditionally clustered indicate a rate of 0.29 percent. The Campo Marzio census of 1656, admittedly limited to one area of Rome with a population of 15,543, identified 100 painters or an astonishing per capita rate of 0.64 percent. No other Italian center could rival these numbers. Smaller art centers might produce anomalous results, but if Verona (0.07 percent), Milan (0.075 percent), Brescia (0.1 percent), and Genoa (0.15 percent) are typical, then Rome remains secure in its premiere position.[50] The census of 1632 in Florence records 68 *pittori* (enumerated separately from the six *dipintori*) in a population of 66,056, a per capita rate of 0.1 percent. The per capita rate was almost two-thirds higher in Bologna, about 0.166 percent. In Venice after the plague of 1630–31, the Provveditori alla Sanità recorded 80 painters living in 1633, rising to 92 in 1642. With the general population in Venice rising from 102,307 in 1633 to 120,307 in 1642, the proportion of painters remained at a steady per capita of 0.078 percent and 0.076 percent respectively. In 1696, 180 painters paid taxes to the Collegio de' Pittori, nearly doubling the per capita rate to 0.13 percent.

Demography by number of registrants in a guild or academy is unreliable for various reasons. Many painters avoided registration in their guild or academy, especially when no obvious advantage was accrued (and if they could get away with it). Censuses cannot be as easily manipulated, nor was there a strong motive to do so, and thus deviations were much smaller, probably the result of clerical error or multiple trades. Only half of Florence's painters as recorded by census were registered with the Accademia del Disegno, or about 0.05 percent per capita. Like Florence, Venice in the late seventeenth century also had an inscription rate in the Collegio of about 1 : 2 of all eligible painters.

The divergent demographic rates for painters in Rome reveal a massive but hidden substratum that Spear aptly calls "the vanished." Using Baglione's *Vite de' pittori, scultori ed architetti* (1642) as an indicator of high-art painters, those whose lives and works are worthy of biography, the per capita rate in Rome was only 0.008 percent. Using Bernini's global estimate, it was 0.2 percent. The census, however, makes no distinctions between high or low art, and there we find the rate rocketing to 0.83 percent or more. In other words, those painters fortunate enough to be inscribed into art history were merely the tip of the iceberg. Most painters, those whom Pietro da Cortona and Giovanni Domenico Ottonelli called the "dregs" (*infimi*), churned out the cheap, anonymous, and crude paintings that are known only through inventories of modest, middle-class collections and today's low-end auctions. Others slaved in anonymity as studio assistants for painters with name recognition.

Peter Lukehart published a remarkable testimony by one of these forgotten painters, a certain Giovanni Gerolamo Zafferino, who was charged with theft in 1581. While bringing his two hats to be cleaned at a monastery, a monk noticed him running to find a spot to urinate and assumed him to be a thief. Zafferino explained this undignified situation by referring to the poverty of painters: "I have little money and few articles of clothing, about five shirts and ten handkerchiefs. . . . I have a few pennies, and sometimes I live on only a baiocco's worth of bread all day. By the end of the month I have spent everything I have earned on food and clothing." The hardships of poor painters like Zafferino are captured in the visual biography of Taddeo Zuccaro, where his brother Federico shows him employed as a household servant grinding colors, unable to study the drawings that his master kept in a trunk (Fig. 1).[51]

~

Art historians organize and restrict their material temporally and geographically. There are good reasons for this, especially in monographic studies of individual artists or thematic studies of style and patronage, but what about the economics of art? Turning first to the question of chronology, we need to ask if the seventeenth century is a justifiable time frame, or if its neutrality is just a matter of convenience. Hiding behind the "seventeenth century" is the "Baroque," whose chronological boundaries are disputed but definitely spill over both sides of the seventeenth century. At least a period defined by a style, even one now discredited as a unifying period style, is a less arbitrary slice of time than simply a century. But does it have any validity for economics in general and the economics of art in particular? Contemporary perceptions as well as the economic data suggest that it does. Ago notes that the traditional label used by economic historians—"the crisis of the seventeenth century"—is misleading for various reasons. First, it flattens out peaks and valleys into a general economic stagnation and does not take into account mitigating systemic improvements. Second, it conceals the origins of economic instability in the 1570s when supply and demand fluctuations started. And third, economic instability in the seventeenth century was valid only in comparison with earlier periods. In reality, economic consistencies are also documented, especially those that benefited laborers, craftsmen, and tradesmen: wealth became more evenly distributed across the different income brackets, and wages outpaced prices of essential commodities thus lowering the cost of living. The purchasing power of master masons as measured by bread rose from the turn of the century to the 1640s by about 30 percent in Rome, 35 percent in Florence, and 60 percent in Naples and Venice, although this increase was partly generated by a drop in population following the plagues of 1630–31 and a consequent drop in demand.

As for the art economy, at least from the consumer's point of view, prices were rising rapidly. In 1580 the Venetian Senate tried to remedy the escalating cost of state portraits by imposing price controls, ineffectively as it turned out. At about the same time, according to Malvasia, Ludovico Carracci revolutionized prices in Bologna by redefining the social status of painters, how they should live and act, and hence how they should be paid:

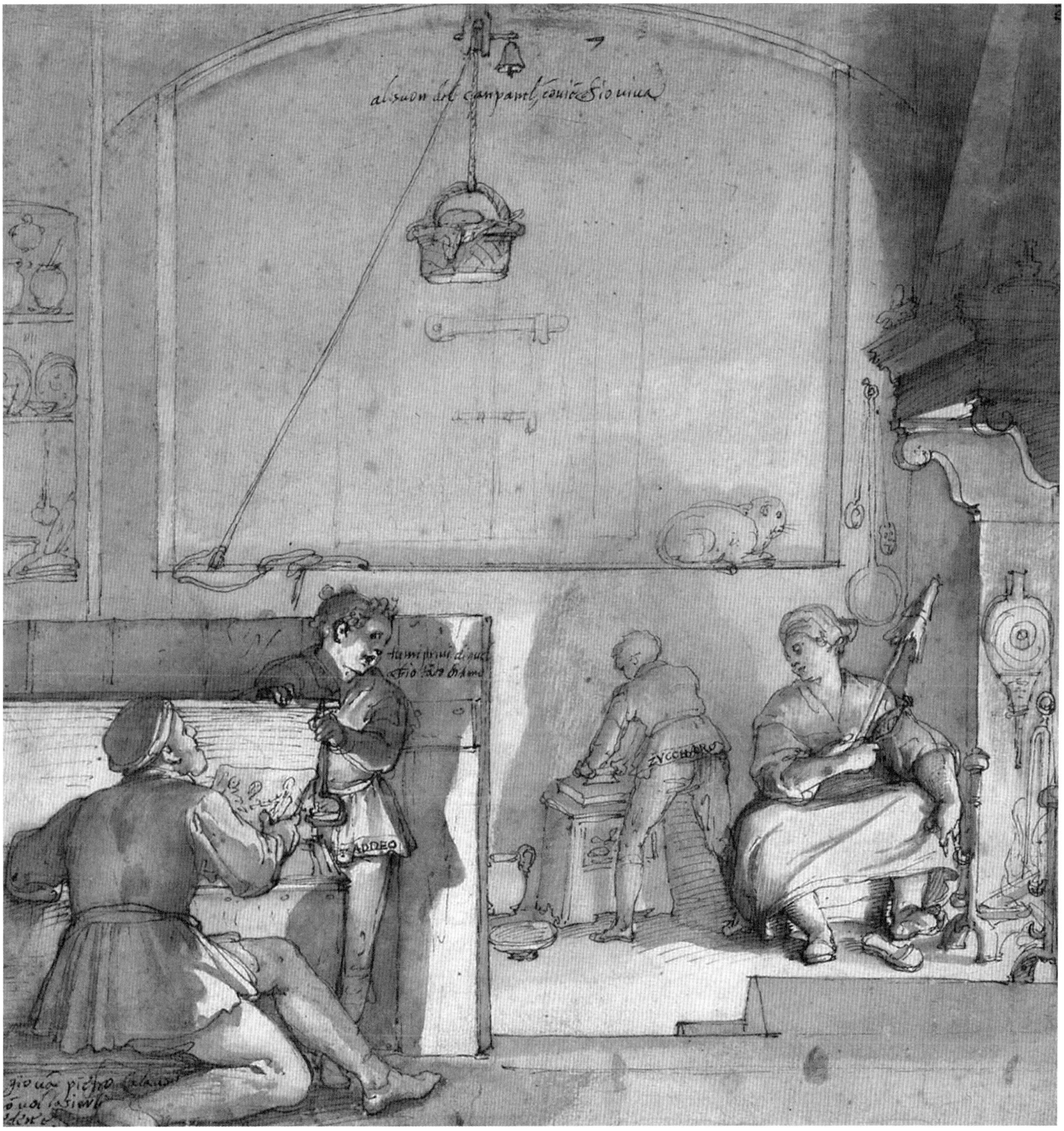

1 Federico Zuccaro, *Taddeo in the House of Giovanni Piero Calabrese*, ca. 1595. Pen and brown ink, brush with brown wash, over black chalk, 27.5 × 26.6 cm. J. Paul Getty Museum, Los Angeles.

> And since [Ludovico Carracci] also dressed in a noble fashion, usually in silk, and in the winter, wore a coat lined with lynx, and was always attended by a large crowd of students, he looked like a prince. He raised his prices even before Guido did.[52]

Malvasia asserted Ludovico's precedence over Guido in this pricing revolution in order to correct Bellori, who claimed that "concerning prices one can say that Reni rewarded painting not only at home and in Lombardy but in all of Italy where prices were too low and buyers were accustomed to the lowest prices."[53] Sometime between 1672 and 1689, Bellori returned to the subject of inflation in the late seventeenth century, this time ascribing it to Carlo Maratta (a claim analyzed in detail in Spear's essay). For Malvasia, inflation provided evidence of artistic progress. It proved that *la felsina pittrice* had entered a golden age after a fallow period during the mid- and late sixteenth century.

In a little-known but all-knowing tract on modern culture, *Il Scoprimento del mondo umano* (1696), the social satirist Angelo Seravalli turned the tables on Malvasia's and Bellori's positive views of inflation, and presented inflation as evidence of cultural decadence. In a section titled "Inflation of prices of paintings made by modern painters," he identified two primary culprits, Rubens and Reni.[54] They wanted greater wealth, Seravalli claimed, and adopted different means to acquire it. In order to escape the "old tariffs" in Italy, Rubens returned to Flanders where he accumulated "that monstrous wealth known throughout Europe." Reni stayed in Italy and changed the system by refusing to "spread the colors onto the canvas before he saw the canvas gilded with the zecchini of the purchaser." Seravalli imagined that if the old masters of the sixteenth century could see the abusive increases of prices commanded by modern masters, they would be shocked by their greed and by the distance between artistic and economic value. The moderns may have "a richness of charming colors" but they lack "the mastery of design" that made the ancients superior, and yet the moderns are disproportionately rewarded.[55]

In an imaginary dialogue between Andrea del Sarto, Correggio, and Annibale Carracci, Seravalli has them complain about the high prices paid to Cortona and Giordano for their palace ceilings. Carracci laments about the pittance he received for the Farnese ceiling, a mere 600 fiorini. "Quiet!" Correggio responds. "Do you know how much I received for my famous cupola in Parma? A sack of quattrinacci so heavy that it nearly killed me to carry home, while Giordano now gets sacks of silver for doing much less on a cupola in Florence." Sarto intervenes: "And what about my famous painting that is called the Madonna del Sacco because I was paid just three sacks of grain?" "The greed of the moderns," Carracci agrees, "has made them mercenaries and servants to money. How much greater will our fame shine in the future because of our incorrupt parsimony."

Moralizing aside, was Seravalli correct in asserting that the price of paintings rose continuously during the seventeenth century? And what about Bellori and Malvasia, both of whom Seravalli cited? Were they claiming inflation as economic proof of their ameliorative histories of art, where the artistic merit of Ludovico Carracci, Reni, and Maratta is seen to be financially rewarded? In other words, should we read their statements as evidence for economic history or art history? Antoine Schnapper has documented an inflation of prices and an increase in the wealth of French painters during this period.[56] And Karen Serres is working on a remarkable case study involving civic group portraits in Paris where the usual variables of patron, size, and subject are absent, leaving mainly temporal change to explain rising prices.[57]

We have not yet found a comparable controlled study for Italy where so many price-sensitive factors can be eliminated. Preliminary studies that use aggregate prices for paintings of different sizes, subjects, and locations have been made by Bonfait and Morselli for Bologna, Marshall for Naples, and Spear for Rome.[58] Bonfait argued that Malvasia was indeed right. Prices in Bologna rose dramatically between 1590 and 1640 (stabilizing by mid-century) not in response to greater demand or inflationary trends in general, but because the status of art and artists had risen where, as Malvasia wrote, now painters wanted to be called *signore* and not *messer* as they were previously known. Morselli has confirmed Bonfait's findings.

Christopher Marshall, who reappraises his earlier conclusions on Neapolitan prices, concludes here that (after such variables as currency fluctuations are removed) prices rose significantly only in the early seventeenth century with the transforming visit by Caravaggio in 1606. Not only did Caravaggio introduce a new and enduring artistic idiom to Naples, one that eventually became identified as a civic style, but with the 400 ducats that he received for the *Seven Acts of Mercy* (Pio Monte della Misericordia, Naples), he also set a new standard for altarpiece prices, nearly four times higher than previous ones. Unlike the immediate artistic influence that Caravaggio wielded in Naples, economically the effects became manifest only in the 1620s and 1630s when painters in Naples began to receive payments of "truly baroque figures," as Marshall puts it. By 1640 prices plateaued, even for those painters most in demand (Stanzione and Ribera), until the plague of 1656 when they dropped and remained lower for the remainder of the century, although still at par with most other goods and services.

Evidence for price inflation in Rome is inconclusive. Spear confirms that Maratta indeed commanded higher prices and that as a result his pupils also enjoyed a financial boost, but he hesitates in affirming Bellori's categorical statement that prices of paintings rose generally in the late seventeenth century. Spear questions whether the example of Maratta should be extrapolated to all Roman paintings because most economic studies show wages and prices remaining stable during the late seventeenth century. Star painters do set new standards and pull up others in a rising tide, but Rome was a larger and more complex art market than other cities and could more easily sustain such epiphenomena as Maratta and his followers.

Data for Florence are also inconclusive. Changes in the Medici stipends, dropping from the time of Francesco I to Ferdinand I, can have the same net effect on painters' incomes as lower demand (and lower prices) of a market-driven deflation. What we do not know is whether prices for paintings bought or commissioned outside of the Medici court also dropped or (possibly) rose in compensation. Prices rose during the second half of the seventeenth century, as a consequence of Antonio Giusti's high fees according to Giovan Camillo Sagrestani (1660–1731); Elena Fumagalli finds confirmation of this in the larger patrimonies left by fresco painters while admitting that insufficient evidence precludes firm conclusions.

In Venice and the Veneto from 1580 to 1660, prices remained remarkably steady, wavering between 15 and 16 ducats per square meter for paintings in churches and public buildings. In the 1660s average prices jumped by 66 percent and levelled off in the range of 24 to 27 ducats per square meter until in 1710, when prices doubled. As in Rome, Naples, and Bologna, these three moments of inflation correspond with the emergence of star painters who commanded trendsetting high prices (Palma Giovane in the 1580s, Antonio Zanchi and Pietro Liberi in the 1660s, and Sebastiano Ricci and Giovanni Antonio Pellegrini in the 1710s).

Despite the similar causes adduced for rising prices, our conclusions differ concerning the timing and extent of inflation. This might be the result of different methodologies or different degrees of caution in using statistical evidence or even (as in the case of Florence) the different kinds of data available for analysis. Where we agree, unequivocally, is that chronology is a weak force (to borrow a term from physics) in explaining any particular price, at least compared to the strong forces of an artist's reputation, the patron's or collector's socio-economic status, the subject of the painting, its size, compositional complexity, and medium. The prices summarized in tables in each section, because they are arranged chronologically, invite (and frustrate) the reader to try to identify temporal patterns. But, even after variables such as subject genre or painting type (altarpiece, mural fresco, etc.) are removed from the equation, it remains clear that the particular circumstances of a painting's commission or purchase explain variations in prices more consistently than when in the century it was made.

~

Like pictorial styles, the economy of painting varied regionally because the production and marketing of art tended to be local. Guilds and academies regulated or, at least, sometimes intervened in the pricing and commercial conduct of painters, and in turn were regulated by local polities. Geographic divisions may have a greater inherent logic than chronological divisions, but they too carry problems of their own. We define "painting in Florence," for example, as any painting done in Florence, whether by a native-born or trained Florentine, a resident expatriate, or a transient foreigner. If it was painted in Florence, then it is the subject of painting in Florence. The problem with this catholic definition, however, is that painters were born and trained in particular places, developed their artistic idiom and commercial practices in that city, and carried them to new locations when they travelled.

The phenomenon of the travelling painter, not new to the seventeenth century but more common and more international in scope, poses interesting questions about economic exchanges. What were the artistic and economic benefits of relocating? How did painters adapt to their new markets or reshape them? Did Venice, for example, attract painterly artists because there was a local and international market for the style inherited from Titian, Tintoretto, Veronese, and others? Were immigrants to Venice positioning themselves strategically in financial terms within a fertile market, or were they finding a comfortable and understanding home for their stylistic language, or both? Besides finding higher prices or more employment, traveling to a new city had other economic benefits. Marco Boschini accused Giordano of emigrating for profit because it brought a unique marketing opportunity:

"Painters often enjoy complaining to each other about those who come to Venice for profit and introduce many copies of their work, presenting them as if they were originals."

Foreign painters concentrated in Rome and Venice, having spotted a market niche for genre and landscape painting. The Campo Marzio census of 1656 identified 55 percent of the painters in Rome as Italian, 20 percent as French, and 20 percent as Flemish. Martinioni and Boschini identified half of the painters working mid-century in Venice as foreign. Foreigners flooded into Rome because of its reputation as a repository of ancient and modern art, and because the demand for paintings was the greatest there. Venice, besides being a major trading center with northern Europe, might also have drawn such high levels of immigration because of the republic's legendary political and intellectual freedoms. Rome allowed Flemish and Dutch painters to opt out of the Accademia di S. Luca and establish their own "academy" (the Schildersbent or Bentvueghels). Florence seems to have been the most closed. Foreigners there faced an unsympathetic reception by painters, collectors, and patrons, unless they had been invited by the Medici or were superstars like Giordano, in which case they were paid better than local painters. A Medici invitation may have assured better payment, but in the opinion of Angelo Michele Colonna, who was well positioned to make the comparison, the Medici court "is reputed to treat painters better than all the other [courts], but it seems the opposite to me." As for Naples, although many foreigners prospered there, visiting star painters (Reni, Domenichino, and Lanfranco, for example) faced a hostile and sometimes murderous clique.

One reason for dividing this book into cities, besides the obvious one of convenience (drawing on the expertise of scholars who have specialized in those areas), was to test out the hypothesis that there were economic benefits to be gained by working in one city instead of another. To reduce the question to its most basic form, was Rome really "where you go to get rich"? Could Cerano really have sold his 250 scudo altarpiece made in Milan in 1625 for 500 scudi if he lived in Rome, as his Milanese patron predicted? Examples cited by Fumagalli, comparing prices of cupola and palace frescoes in Rome and Florence, suggest that he could. The French painter Reynaud Levieux certainly did, increasing his prices (per square meter) by 25 to 50 percent when he moved to Rome in 1676.[59] And when the Bolognese painter Domenico Canuti was asked to bid for the commission of an altarpiece in Vicenza, his price of 570 ducats was almost three times higher than the 200 ducats given by the expensive Zanchi and by an even higher factor than Liberi's (145 ducats) and Giulio Carpioni's (80 ducats).[60]

Disparity in prices created market imbalances and could produce local realignments to compete with higher prices abroad. In 1637 Giulio Rospigliosi worried that Cortona might "bring back here [to Rome] the prices prevailing in Bologna." The cardinals at St. Peter's had similar concerns. When they were tempting Reni back to Rome with a hefty sum, they considered disguising the payment (1,600 scudi instead of the customary 1,000) so that "the other painters will not feel encouraged to make similar claims." In Naples, Reni's high prices produced professional resentment amongst painters who evidently could not (or did not know how to) leverage Reni's rates to produce a rising tide that they could all ride, but then Neapolitan painters were conspicuously hostile toward foreigners who picked up prestige commissions.

One would expect that prices in rich, competitive art centers would be higher than in small towns. In France, where center and periphery had real political and economic meaning, prices in Paris and the provinces remained at parity until mid-century when prices began to rise much faster in Paris.[61] On the other hand, a study of altarpiece prices in fifteenth- and early sixteenth-century Italy claims that "relatively low prices were paid in the areas long recognised as central to the development of Renaissance painting."[62] This conclusion, however, was based on a small set of data. The data presented in the essay on Venice below show mixed results where some regional cities averaged higher prices than Venice (Bergamo, Brescia, and Treviso) and others lower (Padua, Vicenza, Udine, and Verona). When Bergamesque patrons wanted cheaper painters, they turned to the locals. In this and other cases, travelling pays. When Guercino relocated from Cento to Bologna after Reni's death freed up the premiere spot, he raised his prices, and with an increase in production too, his annual income rose markedly.[63] Conversely, when Domenichino relocated from center to periphery in 1618, he was paid far more than he had ever earned in Bologna or Rome.

Market Value: Gifting, Negotiation, and Adjudication

The market value of a painter's work was established, according to Mancini and Giovanni Domenico Peri, by negotiation and by experts. Mancini believed that the economic value of art, like artistic value, is neither stable nor objective, nor inherent to the works themselves.

Instead, prices are negotiated individually and rest on a variety of incommensurate factors, including the fame and reputation of the artist, the status and wealth of the patron or collector, and the amount of time that the artist needed to produce the work. What Mancini meant when he wrote that painting is not "a necessary thing but one for pleasure," and hence does not have a "determined price," can be more fully understood by reading a frequently reissued book on commerce by Peri, first published in 1639 or nearly 20 years after Mancini's manuscript started circulating. Peri defined two kinds of goods, "those necessary for life" such as bread, wine, and salt, and those "for comfort or ornament and delight such as brocades, velvets, tapestries, paintings, sculpture, gems, and the like."[64] Prices of essential goods are tied to the true costs of production and distribution, and should be controlled by the state or prince "for the public good." For these reasons, they will show less variety than prices of luxury goods, whose purchase is discretionary and whose high prices are set by "great men and women" competing for rare quality works.

Of the three pricing mechanisms—gifting, negotiation, and adjudication—famous painters in high demand would benefit most from the first, both financially and socially. In his negotiations with Francesco I d'Este for a portrait, Niccolò Renieri resisted requests to set a price before the painting's completion: "In dealing with great princes he finds that it is better not to set a fixed price."[65] Gifting, in other words, works well with "men of great talent and generosity," as Mancini put it, who will pay not only what the painting is worth but what they themselves are worth.[66] He does not say so directly, but the context for his discussion of gifting acknowledges that it, too, was a type of negotiation, one that disguises its commercial aspect behind social codes. This fiction was especially useful for Genoese painters who, aspiring to the nobility, had to prove that they did not earn a living by retail trade or manual labor.[67] It was a difficult proof since both conditions were generally prerequisites for painters. The Genoese artist Giovanni Battista Paggi, who was already a member of the nobility, defended painting against the charges of it being a "manual art . . . servile and mercenary."[68] Agreeing with the position held by his noble peers, Paggi argued that negotiated prices for paintings demeaned the status of painting in general: "If one sets a price for a painting from a painter as if [one were ordering] a coffer from a carpenter, it makes it plebeian because that is what common shopkeepers do who wear smocks." A painter who agrees to be paid by the day, Paggi continued, is no better than a stonemason. Gifting avoided these class associations under the guise of an exchange between equals. It acknowledged a noble belief system that money soils the purity of art, even though in reality painters became rich, famous, and noble through the commerce of art.

If a painting was not gifted, painter and buyer arrived at an agreed-upon price, sometimes with the help of experts. The term "negotiation" civilizes what must really have been bargaining and haggling. Whatever its name, it was a market transaction where the terms of production and recompense were made explicit, where painting was treated like other commodities.

Most prices outside of Florence and Genoa were negotiated beforehand. Contracts typically specified the subject, and sometimes the number and identity of figures; the size; the costs that will be paid separately, normally including ultramarine, canvas, and stretcher; the schedule for payment (Ludovico David claimed that painters expected a deposit of at least one-quarter of the full price) and any penalty for late work; and finally (and less frequently) attempts were made to control artistic quality by requiring a sketch and by specifying the conditions of production, whether the painting can be autograph or studio.[69]

Because painters typically served as their own agents, whether selling to a dealer, collector, or patron, negotiations took on a psychological or interpersonal dynamic. Artemisia Gentileschi, for example, proved herself to be a shrewd negotiator when she reminded Antonio Ruffo that "you will find the spirit of Caesar in this soul of a woman."[70] She did not want him to typecast her as a submissive woman, allowing men to manage her financial matters, as Sofonisba Anguissola did. Public performance—including clothes, residence, studio, personal hygiene, and social manners—could affect the price of a painting as much as the material, visual, or reputational qualities. Painters' residences were sites for making money, not just in the literal sense as places of production, but as places of public presentation and financial negotiation.

~

Contracts record the results of negotiations—who set which criteria, how payments were to be made—but the negotiation process itself remains opaque, being generally verbal and hence lost to history. There are, however, examples of epistolary negotiations that convey the psychological textures of business transactions, putting a face to numbers as it were. One case will be summarized here.[71] It involves a now lost altarpiece of *St. Anthony Kneeling before the Christ Child* in

SS. Faustino e Giovita, Vicenza. On 8 January 1671, Giovanni Giamberlanno, the father-confessor charged with its commission, tendered two offers through two intermediaries to the Venetian painters Zanchi and Liberi. The subject, the size of the altarpiece, the number of figures, and the price were specified. Zanchi responded first. He quoted two prices, 120 ducats for a St. Anthony *in gloria* or 150 ducats if Giamberlanno preferred a narrative from the saint's life. Giacomo Romanello (one of Giamberlanno's agents in Venice) called these prices "exorbitant" (actually they were low both for Zanchi and for Venice) and advised Giamberlanno to contact Carpioni instead, a talented local who was reliably cheaper than the top-tier painters living in Venice. (Giamberlanno did so one year later for a different altarpiece and indeed paid less.)

Liberi's response arrived two days later and was more complicated. He was known as a more expensive painter, or at least one with a more restrictive pricing practice, and Francesco Salesà (another of Giamberlanno's agents) acknowledged this market reality when he proposed to Liberi a price of 200 ducats or 33 percent higher than Zanchi's "exorbitant" price rejected by Romanello. From Liberi's point of view, however, 200 ducats would not pay for enough figures to fill the space required. He offered to throw in a free *putto* or two, but the only real remedy was another 100 ducats. Liberi wanted Salesà to believe that he priced paintings by the number of figures. The reason he gave this misleading impression was to create an artistic problem that could only be solved with extra money. The size of the altarpiece could not be reduced so the number of figures must be increased in order to avoid a compositional void. Guercino faced a similar problem with patrons whose purses were smaller than his canvases. In his study on Guercino's *prix fixe*, Spear reminds us that the empty spaces in some of Guercino's later paintings should be interpreted not (or not solely) as an artistic expression or as a kind of late style but as the product of underfunding.[72]

Anticipating difficulties with his proposal to pay for extra figures, and perhaps hoping to leverage those 100 extra ducats by other means, Liberi offered an unattractive discount solution. For only 100 ducats, Liberi would complete a painting of St. Anthony

> because now, just now, I happen to have one already almost finished. . . . I was making it for the Procurator Dolfin, who died and left me with this painting that is the same size as yours except for the height, which is one-quarter taller but it can be cut to accommodate your altarpiece. . . . I can have it in your hands in three or four days after I make some final touches.

Evidently this offer appealed to Salesà and Giamberlanno. Having hooked them, Liberi started reeling them in. He proposed to show them "a little sketch" as a further enticement, but in making the sketch he realized that the quoted 100 ducat price was in fact too low. Out of respect for Salesà, or so Liberi claimed (painters often appealed to honor when it came to money), he wouldn't raise the price by more than 20 ducats. Just 20 ducats and some marzipan by the end of Carnevale and a quarter of veal by Easter, just like the one he received last year: "I never had such good veal as the one you sent me last Easter."

Salesà did not like any of this. His counterproposal involved a new painting, not a recycled one, for just 80 ducats. Liberi's tone on 27 January was strategically admonished: "I am content to accept 80 ducats since the painting is almost finished and it seems that I will have little work to complete it, but if I have to start anew, 80 ducats is too little, even for brothers like us. . . . Send me the 80, but by God 60 is too little money." This worked. Three days later Liberi was awaiting receipt of the "holy marzipan" that would bring him grace, peace, and tranquility. Barter, as Liberi knew, was a means to give a cash-strapped patron more room for negotiation. It was also an occasion for intended or unwitting levity. Domenico Tintoretto received five sacks of flour for his figure of St. Scholastica, probably weighing as much as herself as if the payment were a scholastic code.[73] Rosa once received cheese worth 100 scudi, enough to become a *formaggiaio*.

Nearly a month later (21 February) Liberi announced that

> the St. Anthony is sketched, and by this Holy Week I will have put my name on it, as you desired, although I try to avoid doing so whenever possible, but out of affection for you I will do so, but by God 60 ducats is too little, much too little by God, and you must let me write this above my name that for anyone else it would cost 100 scudi.

He tried to leverage an extra 20 ducats in two ways: by claiming a higher value since he had just agreed to sign the painting (avowedly contrary to his usual practice), and by applying extortionate pressure since he proposed to add a note above his signature threatening to unmask Salesà as a cheapskate unless he paid more money. Unexpectedly, a month later Salesà raised his offer to 100 ducats. This kind of last minute bargaining, when accompanied by delays, was not uncommon. As one art agent explained to Francesco I d'Este as he waited impatiently for Renieri to finish a portrait, "painters often try to raise the value of a work by delaying its completion."[74] Whatever Liberi's motives, however, the *deus ex machina* to this convoluted story was a nude woman, a painting of *Venus* that Liberi offered to give Salesà. One month later, on 26 March, Liberi claimed that "the St. Anthony will be finished today or tomorrow." Two days later "disaster" struck. Just as Liberi was giving the painting its final touches and laying on the varnish,

> a sponge wiped away a lot of the colors leaving the flesh untouched, fortunately. This disaster, however, will have brought some good because I will now also retouch the flesh and the painting will be more finished.

Giamberlanno had ignored Liberi's warning that 200 ducats would not buy enough figures for a well-composed painting, and when Romanello first saw the nearly finished altarpiece in April, he indeed found it vacant and unpleasant:

> It is not one of his beautiful works. St. Anthony is on his knees, and there is the Christ Child who appears without a gloria of angels, and there is no place, buildings or otherwise, where he sleeps, so that I want to say that it's very thin and simple. True, the painting is only sketched and when he finishes it he will add something.

Romanello concluded: "Please don't tell signor Salesà that I made these comments because I don't want the Cavaliere [Liberi] to be unhappy with me, since one doesn't express this kind of criticism amongst painters." The Venetians were less discreet than Romanello. When, by Liberi's own account, the altarpiece was publicly displayed before being shipped to Vicenza, "The improvident cried and shouted. I intended that the figure of St. Anthony would have some spirited twisting, but alas I deceived myself. They [the Venetians] would see it as mangled and badly painted, and thus they raised their clamor."

For those who want art purified of lucre, the Liberi correspondence casts him in an unflattering light: an opportunist who sacrificed his art to snag some money, a dissembler of cunning humility. In reality, however, many painters adjusted their styles to fit the patron's pocketbook as Giordano's "three brush" policy shows (discussed below). Zanchi, in a later negotiation with Giamberlanno, warned him that his bid of 200 ducats for an altarpiece was reasonable, and that if they tried to pay him 30 or 40 ducats less, "you'll end up having a mess." A week later Zanchi decided it would take 300 ducats, not 200, and that if anyone were to agree to paint it for 200 ducats, "they will make a mess of it."

This kind of pressure, where painters promise better quality for better pay, was not uncommon. Artemisia Gentileschi tried to extract more money this way from the skinflint collector Ruffo: "But I can tell you for certain that the higher the price, the harder I will strive to make a painting that will please Your Most Illustrious Lordship."[75] Giamberlanno, however, ignored Zanchi's appeal and instead made a counteroffer of 150 ducats, at which point Zanchi decided that, yes, actually, he could paint it for 200 ducats as originally agreed. Like any bazaar marketeer, Liberi and Zanchi quoted high at the beginning in order to create a bargain later. Many Venetians did this, and according to Artemisia, this too was "the custom in Naples, where they ask thirty and then give it for four."

In his negotiations with Giamberlanno, Zanchi applied the bargaining strategy of comparative pricing: "Zanchi cannot do it for less than 200 ducats and [as proof] he showed me another altarpiece that he made for Bergamo, which he made for 200 ducats or more, which is a good price but then it is true that he made it with every diligence and it is a divine thing." This was a common practice. Cortona pointed to Lanfranco and Sacchi to explain why his fee of 7,900 scudi for mosaics in St. Peter's was reasonable. Palma Giovane told the governors of the Duomo in Salò that 300 scudi was a fair price for his *Annunciation* (Fig. 2) because he had been paid 200 scudi for the *Madonna and Child with Donor* (Fig. 3).

And the price was indeed fair. The *Annunciation* is about five times larger than the *Madonna and Child with Donor* (630 × 430 cm compared with 297 × 187 cm) and has many more figures set in a complex scenography. Buyers could also benefit from comparative pricing, as did Stefano Conti when he convinced Gregorio Lazzarini to accept only 75 ducats (Lazzarini wanted 100) by telling him that Antonio Bellucci had agreed to this fee.

Comparative pricing recognized an external measure—market value or whatever the market will bear—which operated (in part) on the principle of supply and demand. Painters could manipulate these external measures for their own benefit, first by choosing comparative examples that were smaller or compositionally simpler, and second by always quoting the highest priced example. Painters also recognized that they could benefit financially by intervening with supply and demand, either unscrupulously as did Perino del Vaga by increasing production and lowering quality when faced with "that rabble of artisans," or inadver-

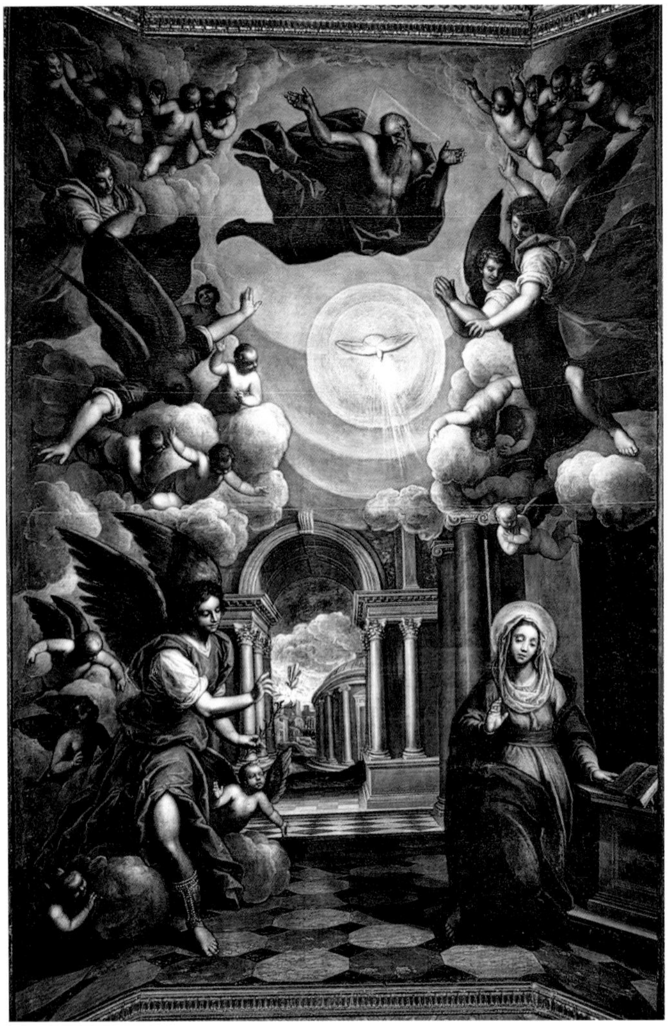

2 Palma Giovane, *Annunciation*, 1628. Oil on canvas, 630 × 430 cm. Duomo, Salò.

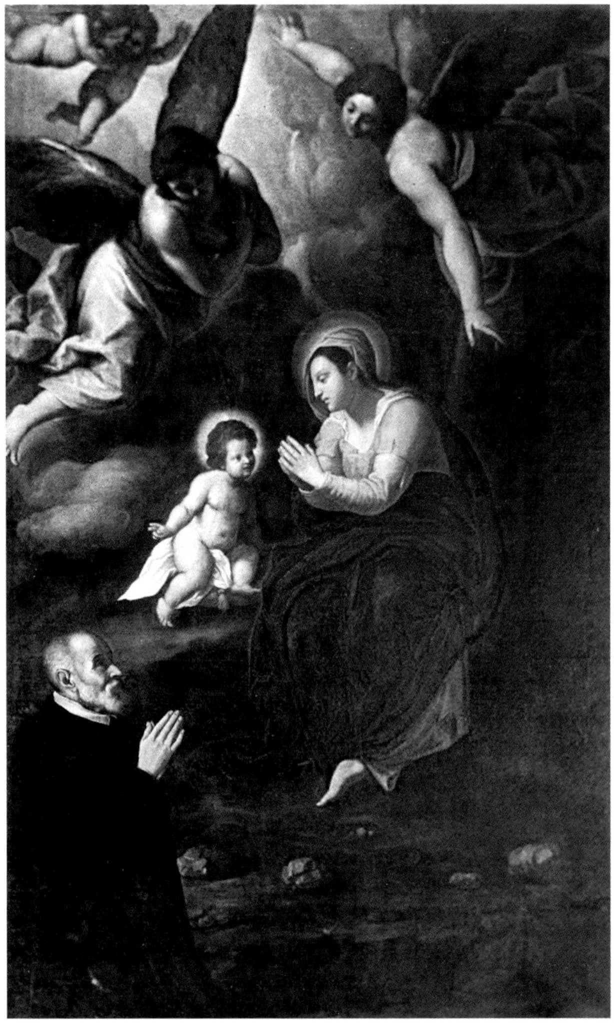

3 Palma Giovane, *Madonna and Child with Donor*, 1609. Oil on canvas, 297 × 187 cm. S. Lorenzo in Sant'Agostino, Reggio Emilia.

tently as did Ferri who (according to Angelo Doni in 1685) spent so much time painting frescoes in Florence that he could not satisfy the demand for his canvases, resulting in a "daily increase in price." According to Malvasia, Reni's practice of turning away commissions "was commonly judged to be . . . a shrewd device for making his works more desired and consequently more esteemed because they were so difficult to obtain." Palma Giovane, on the other hand, flooded the market with his paintings, resulting in a lower demand and lower prices.[76]

~

Mancini and Peri recognized the occasional need for "experts" to price paintings. When negotiations failed, or when the product or payment failed to meet expectations, either party could initiate a formal appeal through prescribed legal channels. Judicial reviews could be, and often were, also agreed upon by painter and patron from the start as the means to determine the price when the painting was finished.[77] In Bologna, contracted prices were common, but judging from the number of legally sanctioned experts (46 of them, although for most it was only occasional employment), there must have been some considerable demand for adjudication. In Florence, where predetermined pricing was rarer and painters practiced a kind of institutionalized gifting, reviews were more frequent. The Accademia del Disegno set up a procedure that included a review board of member painters. According to Apollonio Bassetti, secretary to Cosimo III, Ferri did not want to set a price beforehand: "He's never done that, nor does he want to do it now." Just how frequent the practice was can be gauged from Franchi's account book, 1683–1709. In Venice the magistrates in the Giustizia Vecchia delegated the responsibility to painters.[78] Unfortunately, it is not always clear what exactly about a painting is being adjudicated. Is it the size, the number of figures, or some other tangible or quantifiable element, or is it artistic quality? In one case when Antonio Aliense appraised a painting by Domenico Bruni, he concluded that the perspective and proportions of the original design had been improved, and consequently Aliense recommended that 100 ducats (i.e., 33 percent) be added to its value:

> There are also gilded arabesques and flower vases on pedestals and other things that show greater effort and augment the work's beauty. Consequently, it seems in my mind that all the aforementioned constructions are worth 100 ducats more than they would have been worth if the work had followed the preliminary design. And, as the above work is presented, I estimate that it cannot be worth less than 400 ducats.[79]

Conflicts of interest naturally shadowed the adjudication process. Count Teodoro Sangiorgio objected to setting the price of Tintoretto's Gonzaga cycle after the fact because "every profession supports its own."[80] He was right. Usually appeals went against the patron, which is hardly surprising since the adjudicators were fellow painters. The Collegio dei Notai in Verona agreed to have Santo Prunato's *Presentation in the Temple* (Palazzo del Comune, Verona) adjudicated by two painters, one nominated by the Collegio, the other by Prunato.[81] The Collegio appointed Biagio Falcieri, despite the fact that he was godfather to Prunato's first-born son.[82] Prunato named Simone Brentana as his representative, possibly with assurances that he would subsequently benefit from a commission for the same cycle of paintings, as indeed he did. Unsurprisingly, Falcieri and Brentana ruled in favor of Prunato's claimed fee of 170 ducats.

The most generous settlement on record in Venice came in 1652 after Francesco Ruschi completed an altarpiece of the *Madonna and Child with Sts. Francis, Helen, and Matthew* (Fig. 4) for Francesco Morosini.[83]

Morosini wanted to pay only 100 ducats for this large painting (13 square meters), perhaps annoyed by the eight-year delay in its production, and Ruschi refused anything less than 300. One of the two adjudicators appointed by the Procuratore de Supra, Sebastiano Mazzoni, tried to insult Morosini (Mazzoni was famous for his satiric poetry) by setting the price at 900 ducats. The second adjudicator, Ermanno Stroifi, recommended 550 ducats, and that became the final settlement, a record at that time. As one of the costliest altarpieces in Venice, whether measured in ducats or ducats per square meter, it allowed Ruschi to leverage high prices for his altarpieces in the future. In 1661, nine years after his settlement with the Morosini, presumably by using a strategy of comparative pricing that Palma Giovane, Cortona, and Zanchi had successfully deployed (to name only a few already discussed above), Ruschi negotiated prices for two altarpieces of comparable format but a third the size (Fig. 5). Using size as a measure of value, the two prices (40 and 50 ducats per square meter) neatly frame the uncommonly high standard set by the Morosini altarpiece (43 ducats per square meter).

The one case of a valuation that resulted in a lower price involves a votive altarpiece in S. Maria della Salute, Venice (Fig. 6). Bernardino Prudenti was virtually unknown, then and now, but managed to snare this prestige commission in 1631 soon after the end of the plague. He allegedly painted it in four days, despite its enormous size of about 49 square meters, for a celebratory procession.[84] When it came time to appraise its value seven years later, a delay possibly caused by a need for Prudenti to complete the work after his four-day stint, two painters decided on a fee of 600 ducats plus expenses for ultramarine blue and canvas. Prudenti objected, despite the fact that no altarpiece in Venice had ever commanded such a lofty sum, and ended up with 350 ducats.[85]

~

Painters were inventive promoters and marketeers of their work. Rosa used prints to announce and advertise paintings not yet painted. Lotto and Renieri sold paintings by lottery. Giordano did a "Tintoretto turn," as del Sera called it at the time, with a sneak preemptive gift. Painters everywhere sold works illegally on the streets or in unauthorized shops or circumvented the laws by displaying their work for publicity.[86] They followed the dictates of supply and demand and changed their specialties (Antonio Bracciolini) or their locales (Pietro Tempesta) to fill a market niche. They also marketed themselves. In 1683 Niccolò Cassana wanted to place a self-portrait in the Medici collection and sought the help of Matteo del Teglio, a Florentine agent who agreed to write to Cosimo III de' Medici: "I want to quiet an ambitious painter here [in Venice] who cannot be calmed with reason, however good.

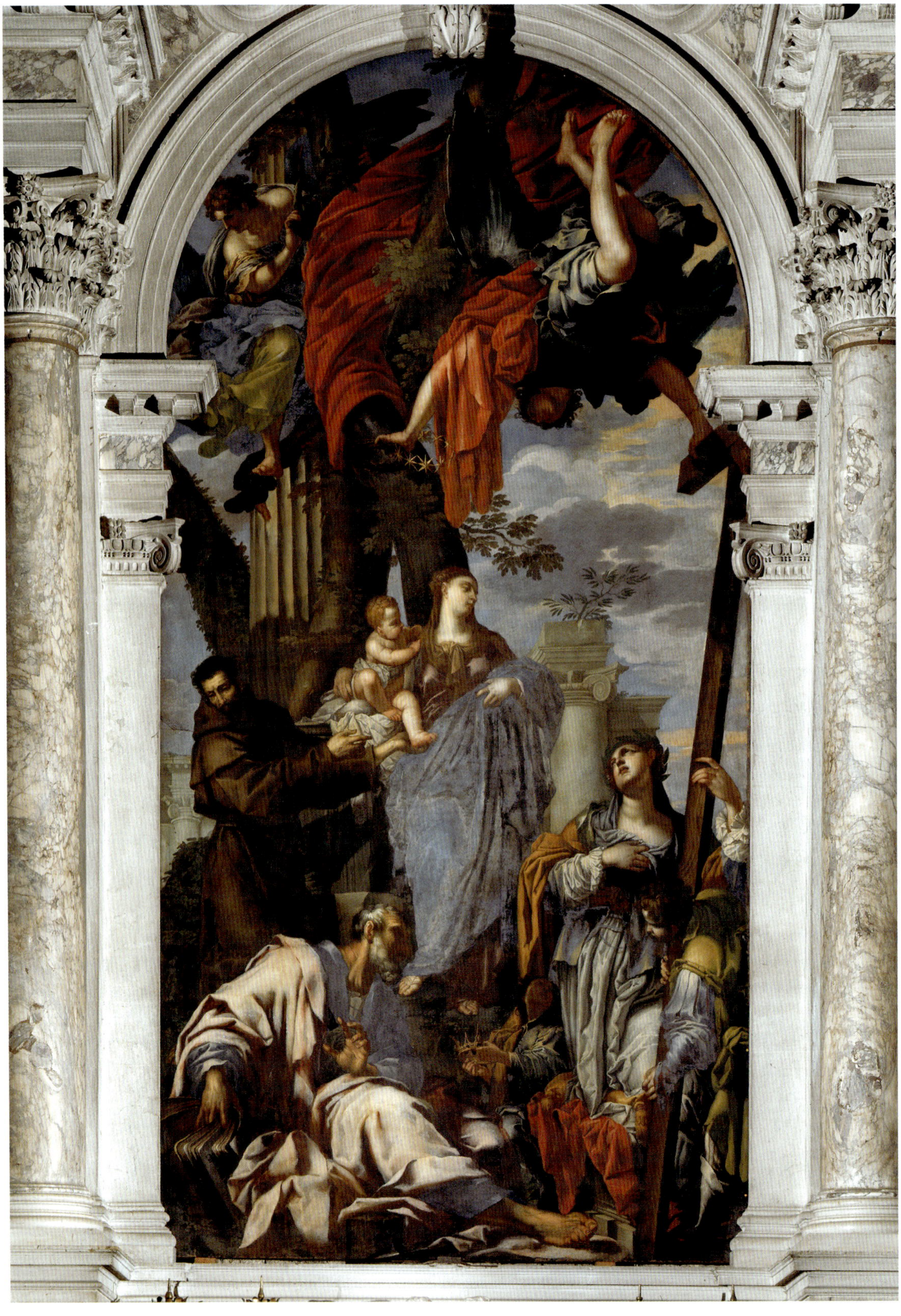

4 Francesco Ruschi, *Madonna and Child with Sts. Francis, Helen, and Matthew*, 1644–52. Oil on canvas, 508 × 256 cm. S. Pietro di Castello, Venice.

. . . The painter is more smoke than fire and wants to send his own self-portrait because there is one in your collection by Liberi and Bombelli."

Bargaining was an opportunity for self-promotion, a chance to reassure and entice the buyer. Success at bargaining probably involved forms of self-presentation and manipulation where the artist is being sold as much as the art. For those patrons who believed in Borghini's syllogism that the higher the price, the better the art, an artist's fancy dress and palatial housing must have been a guarantee of artistic quality. The art dealer Boschini held a contrary view: "Whoever wants to make a living as a painter must solicit those with money; but whoever baits the hook with gold is an idiot." What Boschini seems to mean is that a painter should not display his wealth ostentatiously—he mentions servants, expensive leather and velvet, and false honorifics—as Liberi did with his palace on the Grand Canal (Fig. 78) or as Renieri did with his house, described by Boschini as "a consistory where one sees princes from all over the world portrayed by his hand."

Painters in Venice charging the highest prices (Zanchi, Ruschi, and Ricchi) were also those paying the highest taxes and renting the most expensive houses and studios. Similar patterns can be observed in Rome (Zuccari, Cesari d'Arpino, Bernini, Cortona, Maratta, and Gaulli), Bologna (Cavedone, Reni, Guercino, Sirani, Pasinelli, and Cignani) and Naples (Ribera and Giordano). However, in those cities, unlike Venice where all but one painter rented, the wealthiest painters not only lived in the largest and most prestigious residences, but also owned their houses. Why Venice was a city of tenant painters is unclear. Lack of prosperity is not the answer since rents paid by Venetian painters were comparable to those in Rome and Bologna; rents in Florence were cheaper. When, for example, Rosa moved back to Rome from Florence, he paid double the rent for a *casuccia* ("a shabby little house," to use Spear's translation). Rather than general prosperity, it might be that there was a more uneven income distribution in Rome (where the rich were much richer).

Not all painters were so privileged as to negotiate directly with their wealthy clients. *Pittori bottegari* and other art dealers proliferated in number and wealth, creating tensions with painters and consequently close supervision and regulation by the local guild or academy. In artist biographies, art dealers were mostly mentioned as opportunists breeding on the misery and desperation of artists. Dealers changed how and where paintings were sold. More shops began to specialize in

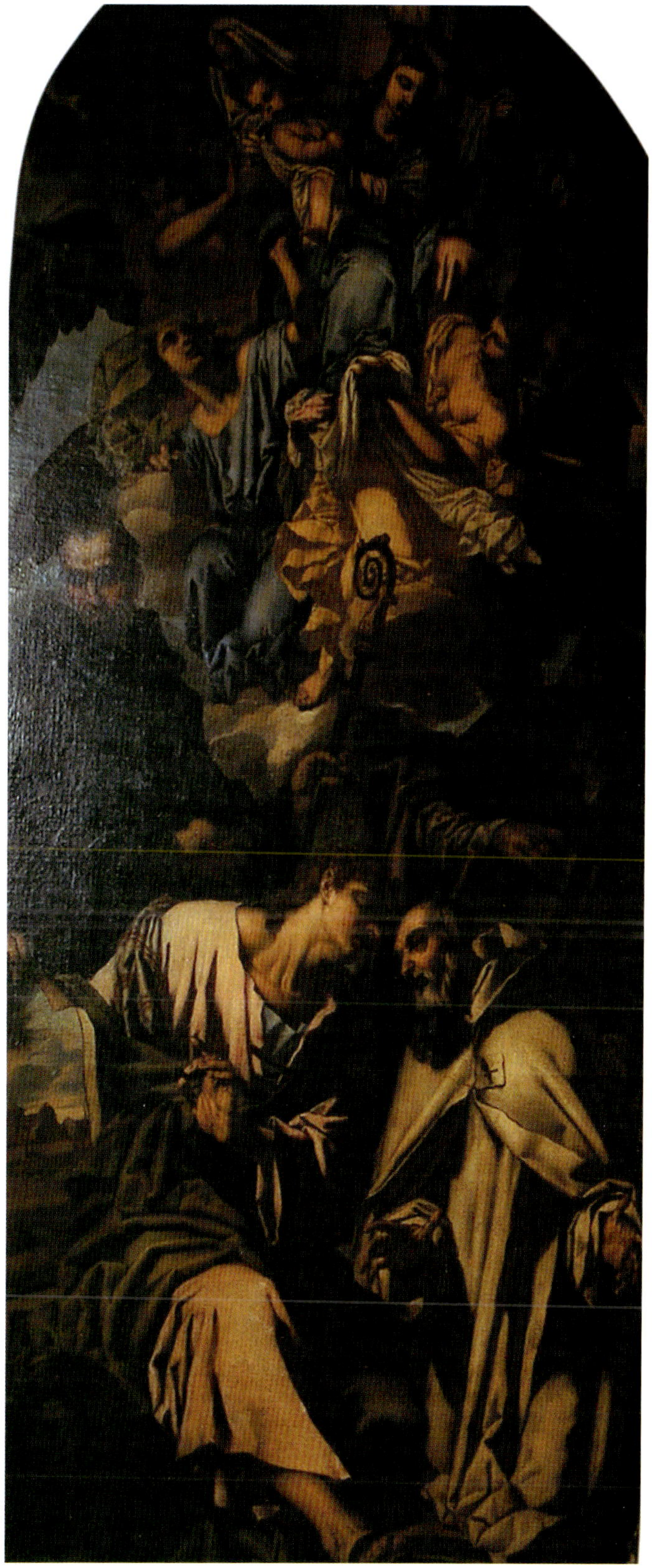

5 Francesco Ruschi, *Madonna of Loreto with Sts. Augustine, Benedict, John the Evangelist, and Romualdo*, 1661. Oil on canvas, 300 × 133 cm. S. Clemente, Venice; now Museo Diocesano.

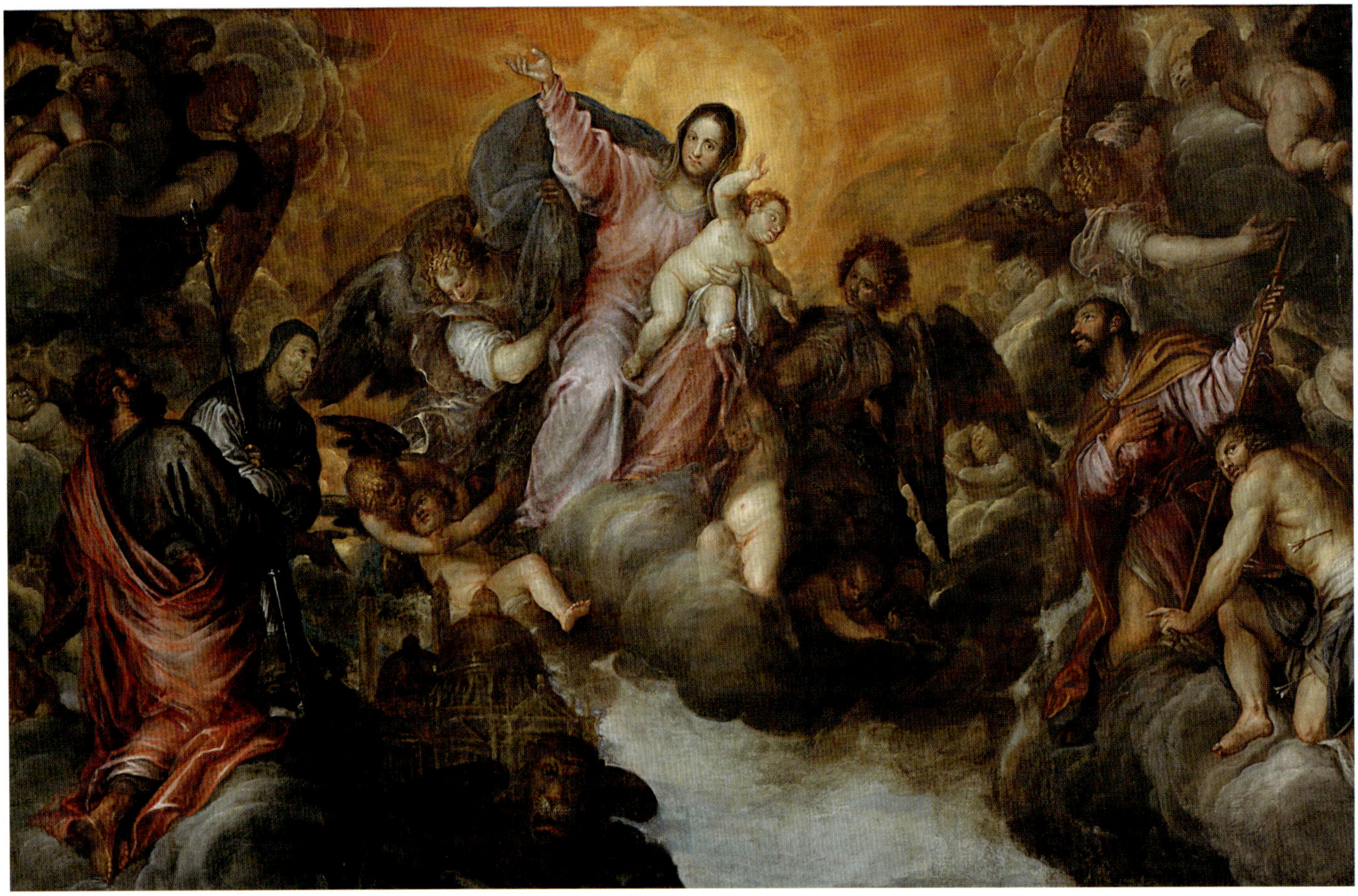

6 Bernardino Prudenti, *Madonna and Child with Sts. Mark, Roch, Sebastian, and Beato Lorenzo Giustiniani Saving Venice from the Plague*, fragment, 1631. Oil on canvas, ca. 200 × 300 cm; originally ca. 760 × 650 cm. S. Maria della Salute, Venice.

the sale of paintings; others sold paintings along with various goods and services. In response to this growing and evolving local demand, painters mass produced standardized works. The collector class also grew and diversified to include more from the professions and trades. These new consumers increased demand for low-cost paintings and helped create a market for specialists of the "lower" genres (landscape, cityscape, still life, social life, etc.) often from France, Flanders, and the Netherlands.

Low-end painters, producing works in bulk, had to rely on a fluid and surprisingly extensive network of art dealers. Sometimes they contracted themselves out to a dealer, as did Antonio Giusti and Atanasio Bimbacci to secondhand-clothes merchants in Florence. A certain Maestro Rocco ran a sweatshop in Venice where Flemish painters copied old and modern masters for sale.[87] Dealing in paintings was often a sideline to a more sustaining trade, sometimes connected to painting or other luxury trades. A part-time dealer might also be a gilder, jeweler, spicer, architect, or merchant of old clothes and general goods.[88] Sometimes it could be a fellow painter, often obscure and, in Ridolfi's words, "of little merit" such as Maestro Rocco in Venice or Anfora in Naples, who employed painters. The target consumer groups for their small landscapes, still lifes, "animalscapes" and cheap devotional images were tradesmen, craftsmen, and professionals.

Ago's study of inventories of 75 middle-class households identified an average of 23.5 paintings per house, mostly by *pittori grossi* that were priced less than three scudi.[89] Despite the modest prices and downscale clientele, art dealers could become as wealthy as those top-end painters working for the nobility. In Venice they were often the richest members of the Arte de' Depentori and Collegio de' Pittori. In seventeenth-century Genoa, Michelangelo Bertolotto earned as much selling his pupils' works as he did from his own paintings.[90] By the seventeenth century, when dealers were theoretically licensed, there were between 10 and 13 *pittori bot-*

tegari in Venice, and in Rome the number increased from 19 in 1650 to 46 in 1655 (and these are only the officially registered *pittori bottegari*).[91] In reality, there were many more dealing more casually. As the number of low-end paintings increased, and along with them the number of commercial dealers, the need for stricter legislation grew. The Accademia di S. Luca in 1670 and the Collegio de' Pittori in 1684 began sustained attempts to control and limit the sale of this "cheap merchandise."[92]

Wages, Salaries, and Prices

Giulio Mancini estimated that a "good painter" in early seventeenth-century Rome would receive 3 to 6 scudi per day. Assuming a working year of 250 days (the standard measure used by economists for laborers), this would bring annual earnings to between 750 and 1,500 scudi. Pier Dandini aspired to earn 10 scudi per day and generally succeeded in doing so.[93] Since his work was in demand, he could have earned 2,500 scudi per year—or, in other words, at the star earning power of Domenichino and Lanfranco in their most lucrative years while working in Naples: 2,000 and 3,000 scudi respectively. Antonio Triva claimed he earned 2,000 ducats annually before leaving Venice for Munich. Others probably received less: maybe 700 scudi for Claude Lorrain, 500 scudi for Caravaggio in Rome (in Naples, he averaged at least 675 scudi).

Whereas these are estimated annual incomes, data for actual annual incomes are limited to the account books by Farinati, Tinelli, Casini, Franchi, Guercino, and Alboresi. There we find huge fluctuations year by year. Farinati's lifetime average might have been 800 ducats annually, but this nominal figure disguises actual annual earnings that jumped around between 140 and 1,729 ducats. The range of annual income for Tinelli was more restricted (123 to 329 ducats). Being a popular portraitist with standard prices, Tinelli's income remained low and steady but still with a 270 percent variation from highest to lowest. Guercino's income held steadier year by year, averaging 1,500 scudi, but showed instead long-term trends, rising after he moved to Bologna and then declining as he and his art aged.[94] In contrast, two years before Guercino's death in 1666, Alboresi's net income was just 156 scudi.

Of the art centers covered in this book, salaried positions were by far more common in Florence than elsewhere. Celebrity salaries outside of Florence include 1,000 ducats for Jacopo Tintoretto (Sansaria al fondego di todeschi, 1576–94), 1,000 scudi for Francesco Cairo (working for the duke of Savoy, 1635–44), and 3,000 ducats for Bellucci (the Palatine Elector Johann Wilhelm von Pfalz, 1706).[95] In a lower rank, closer to the Medici stipends, is Bartolomeo Schedoni, who during the first decade of the seventeenth century received 300 scudi plus "wine, bread, meat, and fish conforming to the use of the [Farnese] court in Parma."[96] Giovan Nicola Rombouts from 1689 to 1692 received 240 scudi plus food, lodging, and all supplies from Marquis Giovan Vincenzo Salviati.[97]

Salaries are not the same as annual incomes. Salaried painters could supplement their stipend with individual commissions and sales (after their employment obligations were fulfilled); hence salaries represent a guaranteed minimum, not actual earnings. Presumably most painters at the Medici court, where salaries were low and stipendiaries did not always receive food, lodging, or supplies, had greater freedom than Pandolfo Reschi, who (according to Baldinucci) "had little or no time left to paint anything outside of those works he had to do for His Highness [Francesco Maria de' Medici]." Salaried painters at the Medici court were paid modestly and unequally: Jacopo Ligozzi (300 scudi per annum in 1620), Filippo Napoletano (216 scudi in 1617), Giovanni Bilivert (180 scudi in 1611), and Agostino Mitelli (although his 15 scudi per month in 1637–41 were not part of a salaried position), whether according to talent and reputation or according to the job expectations, we don't know. Colonna, who was paid "by the piece" instead of by the month, earned ten times more than his assistant Mitelli, reflecting his status as designer and figure painter. The average of 160 scudi per month that Colonna received in Florence, although generous by Medici standards, was less than the average of 200 scudi monthly he earned in 1635 for his frescoes at the Palazzo Spada in Rome.

Unlike painters working on salary, day workers were generally poorer and perceived as low status, "paid by the day just as though they were wretched peasants," wrote Armenini of those unfortunates who signed up with Arpino. If salaries correspond only loosely to annual income because they do not account for freelance work, a similar problem faces us with daily wages. They may be a more accurate measure of total earnings because no one would be paid for a day's work if the service was not rendered, and for this reason economic historians base their calculations of annual earnings on a 250-workday year. Such an assumption might be reasonable for the skilled trades, but painters and especially those struggling "dregs" (*infimi*) were probably employed more erratically. Poor Zafferino testified that "I can only find work for about eight or ten days [a month]" and suggested that this was typical for painters: "Our profession is not like others because one cannot work as much as one would like; one works when the opportunity presents itself and one works with what comes to mind."[98]

In a good month Zafferino claimed to earn 6 to 8 scudi or, if he indeed worked only eight or ten days per month, about 0.8 scudi a day. Painters paid by the day in Naples, Rome, Bologna, Modena, and Florence averaged between 0.5 to 1 scudi per day, or six times less than Mancini's hypothetical "good painter" would earn: 125 to 250 scudi annually instead of 750 to 1,500 scudi. Day workers at the Medici court as elsewhere tended to come from the poorer ranks of painters, the assistants, itinerants, and struggling youths who specialized in the "lower" genres of landscape, still life, and daily life scenes. Painters hired for copy work received about the same as a manual laborer, 2 lire per day (about 0.3 scudi) or 80 scudi a year, assuming a 250-day working year. A still life painter could receive 3 lire a day, or 120 scudi a year. An experienced assistant to Bernardino Poccetti received 4 lire or 160 scudi a year. A master (Cecco Bravo) received over 1 scudo per day, the same that Boscoli charged in 1589 and 1590 for freelance work.[99] By these standards, the obscure Neapolitan painter Domenico d'Aquino must have been happy with the contract he signed in 1623 to produce 100 paintings per month, each with one saint, at the rate of 0.5 ducats each (excluding costs), bringing his annual earnings to 600 ducats.[100]

Salaried painters (*con provvisione*) at the Medici court could receive as much as 240 to 300 scudi annually plus room and board, which is more than Boscoli and Bravo would earn if they worked a 250-day year since painters on the Medici roll received additional payments for individual works. This represents the high end of compensation. Salaries varied with time, ducal priorities, and (sometimes) fame of the artist. Under Cosimo II, they ranged from 144 to 216 scudi annually, and under Francesco I and Maria Maddalena of Austria, Cosimo II's widow, they went as high as 300 scudi. In the Netherlands, Frans van Mieris calculated his time to be worth 1 ducat per day; for Adriaen van der Werff, it was 25 guilders.[101] (Dutch painters were especially drawn to costing out their time.) A century earlier, in 1553, Lorenzo Lotto arrived at the figure of 1.5 scudi per day.[102] However, no one charged as much as Reni, who, after one of his epic gambling losses, hired himself out for 10 scudi per hour or 40 scudi per day (he only would work for four hours at this wage).[103]

Naturally, assistants could expect less, as little as 95 scudi annually plus room and/or board.[104] Antonio Guardi received even less while working for Marshal von Schulenburg in Venice, about 60 ducats per year or the same rate as the marshall's menial servants. Being inexpensive, assistants were cost effective because they enhanced production efficiency. Models, however, could be surprisingly costly. The French academy in Rome hired a model in 1673 with a salary of 400 livres, more than the professor of anatomy received and more even than the *surintendente*, La Teulière, himself.[105] The Florentine painter Filippo Furini paid his models up to 2 scudi per day, more than most painters received for their time. In Rome some models meanwhile were paid 30 baiocchi per session (0.3 scudi), much higher than the 15 scudi per month that Bernini remembers as the standard rate when he was young. Lotto paid 12 soldi (about 0.2 ducats) for a model, "for undressing a woman only to look."[106]

How do these salaries and wages compare with other trades and professions? What was the cost of living? According to the painter and biographer Passeri, writing from the 1660s to 1673, one could live "comfortably and in a dignified manner" in Rome for 300 scudi a year. The architectural painter Colonna set the price for a gentlemanly life in Florence in 1639 at 180 scudi. Stonemasons in Naples and Venice, working a 250-day year, earned about 85 ducats a year; in Rome it was closer to 100 scudi. A family of five in Rome could subsist on 90 scudi. This is consistent with Fernand Braudel's economic classification of sixteenth-century incomes defining subsistence levels at 20 scudi a year per person. Their diet would have been meager compared with a comfortable (but not wealthy) merchant who would spend 70 scudi annually on food alone. Soldiers at the Castel Sant'Angelo and the Swiss Guards earned less (no more than 40 or 50 scudi a year), but room and board were provided. The average salary at the university in Rome in 1658 was 166 scudi (comparable to the university in Padua), but like universities today your discipline determined your pay, with law faculty bringing in 650 scudi and theologians less than 65 scudi. A profession's status pegged its pay at the Medici court as well. Salaried professionals in architecture, decorative arts, and painting were paid on a hieratic scale, with engineers at the top, followed by architects, sculptors, and then (clustered around the same rate) painters, goldsmiths, and jewelers, with only miniaturists and engravers below. Painters earned on average about the same as low-level notaries. Vatican salaries for top administrators surpassed comparable positions elsewhere. The first director of the Archivio dello Stato (Fabio Orsini in 1588) received an impressive salary of 1,200 scudi, the same that the Vatican librarian would be given by mid-century. In Venice, state notaries were paid 200 ducats or more, at least after their initial promotions; in Milan the top salary was 335 scudi.[107] Poor noblemen in Venice who had to work for the state for their living received 150 to 200 ducats annually by mid-century.

In addition to the normal costs of living, painters had professional expenses that varied with the size and complexity of their work: materials (pigments, canvas, stretchers), labor (assistants, models), and miscellaneous overhead costs (rent, sometimes shipping). Pigments varied in cost. Prices of ultramarine blue, as Spear documents in the essay on Rome, could be 24 times higher than other blues and on average 160 times other colors. Ultramarine could cost more than all other material and labor costs combined, worth far more than its weight in gold. Patrons often paid for it separately to assure quality and to circumvent scamming painters, such as those satirized by Salvator Rosa. From the available but spotty evidence, it would appear that Venetians spent most lavishly on ultramarine. Of the 21 ducats, for example, that the Signoria gave Titian to cover the expense of pigments for his Trevisano votive, 95 percent went toward ultramarine (for a painting of 18 square meters).[108] For Tintoretto in 1578, it was 30 percent.[109] Other examples from Rome and Venice suggest that Tintoretto's 30 percent was not exceptional. High end expenditures on ultramarine in these cities range from 15 to 30 percent of the total price. The inclusion of ultramarine blue as an expense could dramatically affect a painter's profit margin. Antonio Carneo and Cristofano Roncalli spent 14 percent of their total payments for ultramarine.[110]

Although the cost of purchasing pigments is well documented, the cost of pigments in any given painting cannot be calculated without knowing exactly how much of each was used and how thickly they were applied. Impasto cost more than thin glazes. Frames were another major expense—they sometimes cost as much or more than the painting itself—but by the seventeenth century patrons and collectors usually purchased them separately from a frame maker.[111] Because these costs varied dramatically, and because in every instance we have crucial data missing, Spear reluctantly admits that no global conclusions about profit margins are possible.

~

Most paintings were cheap. Recent studies of seventeenth-century inventories establish an average assessed value as a bit over 1 ducat in Naples and between 1 and 5 ducats in Rome (depending on the collection).[112] Prices from prestige public commissions were much higher, but as the tables of prices in each section show, there were enormous variations even within the category of altarpieces and other chapel paintings. In most cases, the reason for any particular price is inexplicable (the exceptions tend to be prices that were set to conform with previously commissioned work). This is not to say that when prices were negotiated, painter and patron did not calculate various factors. Mancini mentions time, reputation of the painter, status of the patron, supply and demand. From contracts with painters, which presumably specify those elements that give value, we know that the number and identity of figures, the size, the materials including ultramarine, canvas and stretcher, the time of delivery, and whether the painting is autograph or studio were factored into the payment. But we cannot systematize how these and others factors were weighed, or if they even came into consideration in any given case, because pricing was aleatory (to use Ago's choice phrase in *Economia barocca*).[113] Prices can disguise private arrangements not mentioned in contracts, such as Jacopo Bassano made when he proposed "a good price between friends," or as Liberi did when he threw in a nude for "free" for the father-confessor who had commissioned an altarpiece.[114] However, just because we cannot establish how any given price was determined does not mean that we cannot draw some conclusions about the relative importance of the different factors that went into pricing. The remainder of this introduction reviews the following variables: subject, time in production, size, number of figures, medium, original and copy, age and reputation of the master, and socio-economic status of the patron and collector.

Subject

As the hierarchy of genres would suggest, history painting was the most noble and hence the most expensive of all genres, two-and-a-half times more than decorative painting at the Medici court (for frescoes). Of the lesser genres—portraits, landscapes, still lifes, and genre scenes—portraits and landscapes had the greatest variation in price, with top prices matching those of history painting. Portraits by famous history painters commanded high prices, from 100 to 150 scudi. However, when celebrity portraits are set aside along with the bottom rung of cheap portraits for 6 scudi or less, we find that portraits in early and mid-century Rome probably ranged around the average of 25 scudi that

Ottavio Leoni received. Giusto Sustermans received 25 scudi at the Medici court for three-quarter-length portraits (12 scudi for a head without hands, and 16 scudi for one or two hands). State portraits of Venetian doges also averaged 25 ducats. Tinelli, one of the most distinguished and prolific portraitists in Venice, kept an account book that shows a remarkable stability of prices, averaging about 15 ducats each. Louis Finson, probably employing a price structure while in Rome and Naples, charged between 20 and 80 scudi for his portraits, depending on "the nobility of the man."[115]

As a mature artist, Claude Lorrain could charge on average 125 to 150 scudi for his landscapes, and, if we are to believe Sandrart, that rose to 160 scudi by the end of his life, somewhat higher than Poussin received for his comparably sized history paintings. Most landscapes, however, were much cheaper. Mid-size landscapes in Naples cost 5 to 8 ducats in the early seventeenth century, doubling in price by mid-century, with exceptional peaks as high as 55 ducats. When prices of history and landscape paintings are compared, we find that collectors paid a hefty premium for iconographic edification and status-laden figures. Roscioli bought three paintings from Poussin in one year, two landscapes (*St. Matthew* and *St. John on Patmos*) for 20 scudi each and one history painting (*Continence of Scipio*) for 70 scudi.

Still lifes tended to be cheaper than landscapes. In Vicenza, those by Boriero cost about 1 ducat each.[116] In Padua, Nadal Plache was paid in the same year (1650) and by the same collector about 2 ducats each for ten floral pieces and 1.5 ducats each for eight fruit pieces but 5 ducats each for two landscapes.[117] Still lifes in Rome, as with Roman painting in general, were more expensive. A low-end average would be 6 to 8 scudi, with high-end exceptions reaching from 50 to 100 scudi. The expensive range of genre painters, notably the fashionable Bamboccianti, charged around 30 to 35 scudi. Carneo, a successful genre painter working in the Veneto, averaged 10 ducats.[118]

Production Time

A painter's productivity and hence (to some degree) his profitability depended mostly on two factors: time (the painter's speed or technical facility) and labor (the size and organization of his studio). In late seventeenth-century Rome, some patrons and collectors priced paintings according to the time in production. "They want to reckon the money by counting the days," wrote Bellori, "as in the case of other common labors." Bellori disapproved for two reasons: first, because payment by time reduced painters to the status of the laboring poor who were paid daily wages; and second, because no one could reduce painting to time since this art involved thinking as much as making. In reality, though, time was money. Paolo Piazza played on this truism with an enigmatic signature added to an altarpiece after the patron procrastinated in his payment:

P:P:P:P:P:P:P:P:P:P:P:P:P:P:P:P:P:P:

The parish priest, correctly suspecting some offence, brought Piazza to court in Castelfranco Veneto and demanded an explanation.[119] When Piazza faced the podestà, "he explained humbly and apologetically that he wrote this in such a succinct form only because time did not permit him to declare his intention more fully. The abbreviation signifies Pietro Paolo Piazza Pittor Pinse Pala Picola Per Prezzo Pocco Per Pre Pietro P . . . Piovano Però Prettende Pagamento Presto" (Piazza, painter, painted the little picture for a little price for the priest Pietro, who pretended to pay him promptly). Not only did the podestà accept this explanation, but recognizing a creative mind, he commissioned an altarpiece for the government seat, the Palazzo del Podestà.

In Bologna, Lionello Spada made an even more graphic statement to this effect when, after receiving inadequate recompense for his work in the palace of Silvio Albergati, he installed a pile of animal bones in the palace room where he had been working. These bones represented those animals he had eaten and hence how much time he had spent at work. He labelled it "Funeral of the Death Feast" (*Funerale alla morte cuccagna*). "The laws of abundance," explained Spada, harm those "who work more" but "earn less."

Painting takes time but how much time? We can gauge the relative speeds of different painters—the painterly Giordano worked faster than the polished Pre-Raphaelite Dolci, as Giordano rubbed it in when he met Dolci; or compare Reni's mass production of "Guidos" to Caravaggio's solitary, itinerant habits—but it is difficult to estimate how much time any given painting took in gestation and production. There are just too many variables and too few documents. Unlike the *giornate* of frescoes, oil paintings give no clue as to the time spent in production. Documentary evidence is scant and ambiguous. When, for example, one of Carpioni's patrons noted that "he started to sketch it on 14 July and finished it on 11 September," we do not know whether Carpioni devoted all 58 days to this one altarpiece.[120] Or do we believe Zanchi when he reassured his patron that he worked "four months continually on it . . . without doing anything else"?[121] The painting is huge (375 × 775 cm) with a crowd of figures appropriate to its subject (*Moses Striking the Rock*), but claims of devotion and exclusivity are sufficiently commonplace to become suspect (see Fig. 90 in the Venice essay). According to Tessin, Liberi "could paint a subject with four or five figures in three or four days," an observation that helped him explain how Liberi came to own a palace on the Grand Canal (Fig. 78) worth 12,000 scudi.[122] And, as we just saw, Prudenti supposedly painted a monumental altarpiece in just four days.

Technique and style affected time in production, and whereas Giordano will always be faster than Dolci, Giordano can be faster at some times and slower at others. Neither technique nor style is constant. They can vary within a painter's oeuvre, and even more pertinently they can be manipulated by the painter to maximize profits (as well as to vary the expressive and iconographic language). Pellegrini, a rich painter who was periodically strapped for cash, painted quickly by applying only one thin layer of pigment and by concealing figures in clouds.[123] Sketchy brushwork as a shorthand technique could also speed production and generate higher earnings than styles that were more attentive to details of clothing, architecture, and coiffeur, and hence slower to produce (unless it is a painterly style, like Titian's, slowly built up in layers). Tenebrism was another potentially expedient style, where large parts of the painting are ill-defined shadows or where shadows enable a painter to depict incomplete figures, suggesting more than was actually there. It is, in other words, a style designed for economy as much as expressivity.

Most famous were Giordano's "three brushes." Because of his prodigal technique, known for its speed and adaptability, "he used to say that he had three types of brushes, one of gold, one of silver, and another of copper with which he could satisfy the nobility, gentlemen, and the plebs, and that each of these classes correspond with the painting's merit proportionate to its price."[124] Karel van Mander traced the three brushes of gold, silver, and copper back to Titian, but it sounds more like Tintoretto's.[125] Other artists claimed to have three brushes tied to the patron's pocketbook. The Florentine painter Pier Dandini, according to his biographer, coined the saying that "he had brushes for every price." Of his three brushes, it was his fastest one that enabled him to reach his bold aspiration to earn 10 scudi a day, making him one of Italy's top earners during those times (which were most times) when his work was in demand. Whereas Dandini valued his fast brush, sometimes painting with both hands "like a whitewasher,"[126] the Bolognese painter Emilio Savonanzi preferred to choose his style and paint *per genio* rather than for money and resisted setting prices for his work. For those patrons who insisted on settling affairs beforehand, "he used to say that he had available for use three brushes, that is the superior, medium, and lowest, and so he left the selection of the brush to those who would choose the price."[127] This explains, his friend Ottaviano Cambi concluded, why one sees so many paintings by Savonanzi in so many different styles with different coloring and compositions.

One century later, Giordano's status amongst critics and collectors had dropped while Dolci's had risen. Quick and profitable painting like Giordano's became emblematic of the general decline of art in the seventeenth century.[128] Two causes were usually identified, and these were put into play in a dialogue between "Anton Raffael Mengs" and "Johann Joachim Winckelmann" by Niccola Passeri, a member of the Accademia Clementina in Bologna and the Accademia di Pittura in Venice.[129] "Mengs," much like Armenini two centuries earlier, thought that high prices, grandiose commissions, and indulgent patrons corrupted painters who consequently adopted sloppy techniques to maximize profits. "Winckelmann" also assigned an economic cause to contemporary artistic decline, but for him the prices were too low, so low that painters had to increase production and paint quickly "so as not to starve to death." Whatever the cause, the stylistic result was labeled in both cases as Mannerist, a style that resulted from painting too quickly.[130] Although this was meant as a critique of seventeenth-century painting, the painter who best represented this high volume but low quality practice was Giambattista Tiepolo, at least for the real Mengs. When the deliberate Mengs was suffering alongside the fiery Tiepolo in Madrid, both painting ceilings in the Royal Palace, Winckelmann consoled his friend Mengs with the epigram: "Tiepolo makes more in one day than Mengs does in one week, but they are forgotten as soon as they are seen."[131] The epigram upended Vasari's famous declaration that modern painters "can execute six paintings a year, whereas earlier artists took six years to finish one painting."[132] Unlike Winckelmann, Vasari took this to be an artistic advance of sixteenth-century over fifteenth-century painters, but such virtuosity was a questionable virtue even then, as Vasari learned for himself when he proudly announced to Annibale Caro that he completed the Sala dei Cento Giorni in 100 days, only to be brought down by Michelangelo's response that "it shows."[133] Caro's advice to Vasari was, "If you worked less quickly, you would do better."

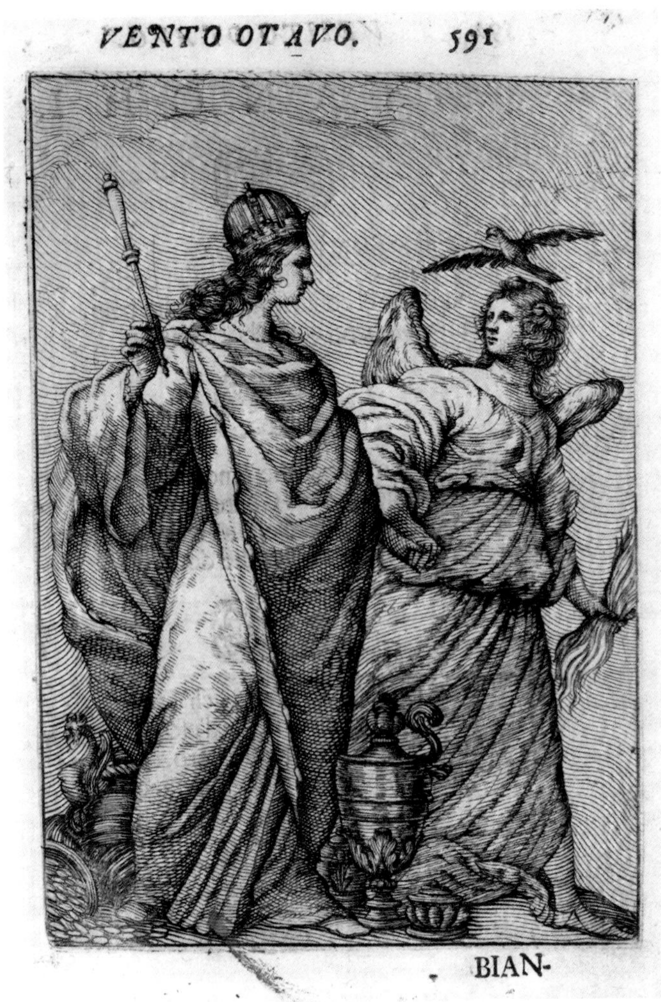

7 Marco Boschini, *Wealth and Speed*, 1660. Engraving in Marco Boschini, *La carta del navegar pitoresco* (Venice, 1660, p. 591).

As palaces and churches grew in size during the sixteenth century, eventually reaching baroque proportions, painters had to adapt by producing larger paintings. (I make this assertion without statistical proof, but until an economic mode of analysis takes root in art history, this impressionistic conclusion must suffice.) Vasari's epigram commemorates this accomplishment. Speed brought artistic benefits, but the new quicker techniques were also economically motivated. Tintoretto became synonymous with speed and profitability. "An enemy of idleness," wrote Andrea Calmo to his "brother" Tintoretto, "working to obtain profit and glory." The combination of speed and low prices (the former enabling the latter) enticed Duke Guglielmo Gonzaga of Mantua to commission two cycles from Tintoretto. "He will deliver the paintings in less time than any other painter can," the duke was reassured in 1580, "and it seems to me that they will be beautiful according to his style that is unfinished."[134] The duke had rejected other, more expensive painters before settling on Tintoretto, who undercut competing artists with his low prices and compensated for his low prices by the sheer volume of production. Boschini paired speed and riches as twin attributes of Ricchi, adding the distich to his engraving (Fig. 7): "He who is rich makes great things quickly quickly / so that wealth abounds in everything."

Slow painters must have been at a disadvantage in this market. Giambattista Piazzetta painted slowly—"his style is very finished and as a result he paints very slowly," observed Carl Tessin[135]—and despite his practice of charging high rates, he lived and died in poverty. Slow painters, however, were not always poor painters. Pietro Bellotti, "diligent painter so that a single head from his hand costs 100 scudi," knew how to open the pocketbooks of the wealthy, as Boschini put it, exchanging gold for artistic value.[136] His mid-size, single-figure painting of *Esculappio* (lost) was bought by Giovan Donato Correggio for 120 ducats, not a large sum by Roman standards but remarkable for Venice, prompting Gian Giorgio Nicolini to write an extended ekphrasis exploring every wrinkle and curl of hair that Bellotti included.[137] Liberi charged a premium if a patron wanted his "most finished style" that required the utmost "diligence in its making" (and hence the most time), 700 ducats for a mid-size, three-figure altarpiece, or nearly twice as much as comparable paintings by him.

Size

One measure of time was size. Aside from those who changed techniques and speed of execution to fit the patron's purse, painters could assume that the length of time in production would correlate approximately to the size of the painting. (They would also have to factor in the number of figures and the complexity of their composition.) Size was a convenient and common pricing standard. It was, however, one laden with prejudice. According to Armenini (*De' veri precetti della pittura*, 1587), pricing by size debased the noble art of painting and encouraged artists to be sloppy, finishing quickly by "smearing" their paint. And Bernini mocked Genoese collectors by attributing to them the quantitative mentalities of tradesmen: "The Genoese are of all the people of Italy those who have the least sensibility, which is due to the fact that they all engage in commerce, which lowers their standard of judgment and deprives them of any knowledge of other things."[138] To illustrate this, he told his cicerone in Paris, Paul Fréart de Chantelou, the story of a Genoese merchant visiting Reni at work in his studio. Having heard that the merchant was extremely intelligent, Reni asked him for an honest opinion about the work in progress. After a long pause and careful study, the merchant responded: "Since you have given me permission [to speak freely], I must tell you that I think the canvas is a little broader at the top than at the bottom." Reni burst out laughing. Baxandall, however, would have been pleased with this demonstration of the "period eye" where the specialized knowledge of merchants (measuring by sight and quantitative thinking) informed their taste in painting. For Armenini and Bernini, valuing paintings by size was either an immoral means to increase revenue or a kind of mental blinkers. It made art commercial. It reduced it to a craft and trade. Ironically it was in Florence, self-proclaimed home of the Renaissance, and not in Genoa that size became an important variable in pricing fresco decoration. This was institutionalized at the Medici court, where it was one of four payment methods (*a stima*, *con provvisione*, *a giornata*, and *a misura*), and applied mostly to palace decoration. (Church frescoes were priced more often by the unit—a chapel, a cupola, etc.)

Two exceptional cases of pricing by size—mosaics in Venice and painters' designs for mosaicists in Rome—confirm this association of craft and size. This partly explains why, in a petition regarding some incomplete payments for work in St. Peter's, Cortona disclaimed such a practice: "He has never experienced that paintings are bought and sold by the *palmo* and measurement." In reality, Cortona was paid 1 giulio per *palmo* (22.35 cm) for designing cartoons for mosaics in St. Peter's. Isolated cases in Rome, Naples, and Venice—where a "ducats to size" ratio seems to have existed for paintings by different artists for the same patron or by the same artist for different patrons—suggest that some ad hoc formula was in use even if it was not specified in the contract. Francesco Saverio Baldinucci recorded a sliding scale of prices by size for paintings by the Roman painter Filippo Lauri: 60 scudi for a painting of 1 *palmo* across, 100 scudi for one measuring 1.5 *palmi*, and 160 scudi for paintings of 4 *palmi*. While Baldinucci affirmed a correlation of price and size, the evidence itself that he presented seems to militate against the general principle. Assuming a standard proportion for canvases of 2:1, the size-to-price ratios would be an erratic 120 to 1, 89 to 1, and 20 to 1. In other words, the larger the painting, the smaller the price as calculated by size. If the larger paintings were priced at the same rate as the 1 *palmo* painting, then the prices would be 60, 135, and 960 scudi, and not 60, 100, and 160 scudi. This differential is consistent with the data presented in Table 29 in the Venice essay, which show a similar rise and fall of the "ducats per square meter" ratio.

Figures

Reni gauged the value of paintings by counting the number of figures and multiplying by a factor of 2 or 3 scudi for painters of little reputation (*pittori più bassi*) or 15 scudi for ordinary painters (*pittori ordinari*).[139] Supposedly, he himself did not charge by the figure, and since he did not mention what an extraordinary (*straordinario*) painter would receive, we can infer that he thought that payment by the figure was an inappropriate calculation for great painters like himself. In reality, Reni occasionally charged by the figure, as he did with the deputies of the Cappella del Tesoro di S. Gennaro in Naples. Charging by the figure had an ancient lineage, well known from Pliny the Elder's story of Alexander the Great paying Apelles 10 *mine* per figure for a battle scene with 100 figures. Comanini calculated this to be 150 scudi per figure or 15,000 scudi for the painting.[140] Despite this noble precedent, pricing by the figure recalled medieval guild practice and generally lost favor during the Renaissance.[141] Giuliano Serragli justified his complaint about Jacopo da Empoli's hefty 300 scudi price for a *Sacrifice of Isaac* planned for the chapel of the Sacrament in S. Marco, Florence (it was never executed) by citing a painting by Passignano with many more figures but with the same price.[142] Empoli responded with a food analogy (he loved talking about art in terms of food): "This means nothing because a single small bird is worth more than a big plate of crows." There are few seventeenth-century examples. Most famously, Guercino and his family (or at least his nephew Cesare Gennari) applied an explicit pricing formula to paintings, with a standard fee of 100 scudi per figure rising (in the case of Guercino) to as high as 190 scudi.[143] Domenichino was paid 105 ducats per figure by the deputies of the Cappella del Tesoro di S. Gennaro, less than the earlier (lapsed) agreement with Reni for 130 ducats per figure.[144] The Venetian painter Triva and the Veronese painter Balestra were paid by the figure, but only when they worked in Munich and Vienna. Giulio Rospigliosi estimated the price of paintings by Cortona, Reni, and Guercino, and set their relative economic standing, by hypothesizing a per-figure price of 100 scudi for Cortona and 150 scudi for Reni and Guercino.

Medium

Cortona disputed a belief circulating in the Vatican that paintings "in oil are valued more than those in fresco." Spear tests this claim and finds that, on balance, it is probably true.

Original or Copy, Autograph or Studio

The art market was awash with copies. Most Roman and Venetian collections had an equal proportion of originals and copies.[145] If notaries or assessors were more likely to mistake a copy for an original than the other way around, then probably more than half were copies. Since the price differential between original and copy was substantial, attribution became a matter of some considerable financial importance for collectors. A studio copy of a master's original could cost as much as half the price of the original, but generally the ratio of copy to original was closer to 1:3 or 1:4, corresponding approximately to the difference in pay between master and assistant.[146] Guercino and Reni charged between two and three times more for an original than they did for a studio production. Guercino made no distinction in price between an original by his hand and a copy of that original also by his hand.[147] Value for him, apparently, lay in its production rather than in its invention. However, Franchi and Tinelli charged twice as much for an original portrait as a copy of that original. For Titian, the differential was 4:1.

Age

Bernard Mandeville, a Dutch-born physician living in England in the early eighteenth century, updated Mancini's notes on the pricing of paintings. In addition to reputation, scarcity of the painter's work, and the master's hand (instead of an assistant's), Mandeville added the variable of age: "The Value that is set on Paintings depends . . . on the Name of the Master and the Time of his Age he drew them in."[148] And indeed, painters in demand charged higher prices as the years passed and their reputations advanced. Ludovico Carracci, Paul Bril, Poussin, Claude Lorrain, Rosa, Guercino, Farinati, and Palma Giovane are good examples that are discussed in this book, although some artists lost market value in old age. Rosa estimated that a painting sold for 100 scudi in 1652 would cost 400 scudi in 1666 were he to paint it again. What role age played in pricing can be studied by comparing payments to different painters working on the same pictorial cycle. The evidence, however, is conflicting. On the one hand, for example, the five painters of various ages decorating six chapels in S. Silvestro in Capite in Rome were all paid the same fee. On the other hand, the Collegio dei Notai of Verona hired five painters for frescoes of comparable size in the chapel and paid them on a sliding scale based mainly on age: Giambattista Canziani (age 36, 120 ducats), Alessandro Marchesini (age 37, 150 ducats), Santo Prunato (age 48, 170 ducats), and Louis Dorigny (age 46, 198 ducats). Dorigny's high payment can be explained by the fact that he was a hot property just arrived from France; unlike the older locals, he had a certain cachet and, like other foreigners, was paid at a rate higher than locals. The one inexplicable exception was Giambattista Bellotti, who at age 32 received 170 ducats, as much as the senior local painters.[149]

Painters feared the physical debilities of old age, and with good reason, since painting is a manual art dependent on control and dexterity and a visual art that relies on acute vision.[150] Without the corrective wonders of modern medicine, loss of coordination or eyesight could mean the end of one's career. Triva's salary at the court in Munich was progressively cut as he aged until he was in his 60s, too enfeebled to work and (without an income) too poor to return to Venice. He did not benefit from a pension in the way that Giovanni Bilivert, Giovanna Garzoni, and other Medici court artists did (he received 120 scudi per annum in the 1630s; she received 48 scudi in the 1660s). Physical decline, however, does not explain the loss of income experienced by Farinati and Guercino as they aged. When their annual earnings are plotted, we find a steady drop during their 60s and 70s (Table 1; for Farinati, see Table 21 in the Venice essay).

Artemisia Gentileschi and the Florentine painter Antonio Giusti lowered their prices, on average by 33 to 55 percent, when they turned 60. Amongst the contributing factors to consider for the earning power of aging painters are: (1) lower productivity, as the elderly painter thinks and moves more slowly; (2) diminishing demand as patrons exercise their prejudices about old age and turn to younger, possibly more fashionable artists; (3) an increased reliance on assistants with a consequent loss of artistic and economic value; and (4) a gradual withdrawal into voluntary retirement. Whatever the cause, the fear was pervasive even amongst the elite of Raphael pretenders, "those certain foolish painters who act like Raphaels and put on airs" who, in Rosa's words, "catching sight of old age see themselves between prison and hospital notwithstanding their vain pretenses and genius."[151]

TABLE 1 Guercino's Annual Income (in scudi), by Age

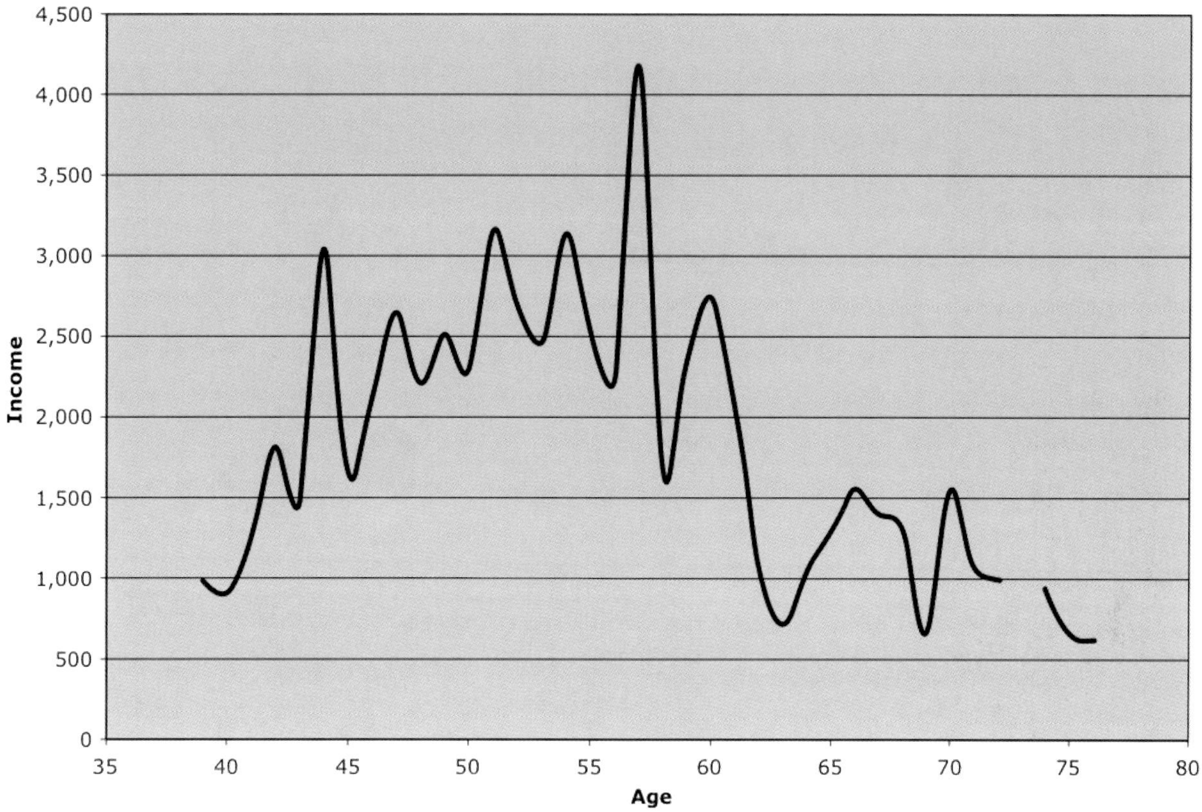

Reputation

Reni invented three classes of painters (*pittori più bassi, pittore ordinario, pittore straordinario*) in order to justify why painters charge such different prices. Reputation, by his accounting, can add five to seven times to the value of a painting (the differential between the lowly and ordinary painters). Extraordinary painters (presumably like himself) produced priceless work. The range between the three classes that Reni adumbrates, from 5 to 105 scudi, exaggerates the actual price spread for paintings of similar dimensions and figural complexity. Nowhere in our comparative price charts can a 21-fold differential be found between the cheapest and most expensive for comparable work. On the other hand, price differentials were greater than that cited by Rospigliosi: 2 : 1 between Cortona's prices and those of painters "without a big name" (*non di grosso nome*), or 3 : 1 when exceptionally expensive painters like Reni and Guercino were factored in.

Individual examples of pricing by reputation abound, and a few have already been mentioned in other contexts. A few others will be cited here.[152] When Domenico Campagnola died before starting an altarpiece and lunette for the Duomo in Padua, the patrons turned to Parrasio Michieli and raised the price from 25 to 86 ducats. The *provveditori* for the Biblioteca Marciana awarded two commissions in 1635 for paintings of equal size and with the same number of figures, both to be placed on the same ceiling. One went to the venerable, self-inscribed follower of Titian, Alessandro Varotari (Padovanino), the other to the *arriviste* painter from Genova, Bernardo Strozzi. Padovanino received 38.7 ducats, but Strozzi got only 32.3.[153]

Patron or Collector

Many painters adjusted their prices to fit the patron's purse. If the evidence collected in this book is representative, it would seem that Bolognese painters were especially inclined to do this. Franceschini did so systematically as his account book reveals, and examples from Albani, Tiarini, and Reni suggest that they, too, applied this criterion when pricing their work.

Conclusion

"Painting for profit" implies more than the exigencies of a trade and the material necessities of life. It implies that painters had a psychological motivation when money was involved, that they wanted the material and social benefits that accrued from building capital. Not all painters would admit to this, or felt comfortable with it, or even aspired to the goal of profits. Some artists like Donatello and Pontormo were indifferent; others like Zuccari and Rosa were conflicted. "Economic lives," our subtitle, also intimates that money rests on a substratum of psychology. It echoes Vasari's *Lives of the Artists* because Vasari delved first into ways that economics permeated artists' lives: how money established social status and drove art marketing, how it shaped the material conditions of living, and (most fundamentally) how it affected artistic practice, consumption, and perception. By inquiring into these areas, mostly anecdotally, Vasari opened questions that were taken up by subsequent biographers. These are our questions too. But unlike Vasari, who wrote about "the most excellent" (as his title declares), we have tried to give all painters a place in our history. Despite that noble goal, the majority of painters (as listed in censuses, guild and academy rolls, etc.) are no more than names for us. As individuals they are forgotten, though as a laboring class and as a pool of low-cost labor, they played important functions. The availability of evidence reinforces Vasari's hierarchy. The more affluent painters tend to be the most studied even today and hence provide us with the most data. The critical success of painters, their high income coming from prestigious patrons, cemented their place in history, inasmuch as early modern art histories first codified the cast that we generally accept today, whether they deserve it or not.

"Economics," as the general public understands it and to some degree as we have applied it in this book, is identified with monetary analysis where prices, rents, wages, and other monetary measures are quantified and compared. We have made a significant step forward in showing how payments vary with time and place, with patron or market, with subject or medium. Numbers bring illusions of truth, especially when aggregated into trends, and readers are advised to approach ours with due skepticism. As with any statistical analysis, monetary transactions become more reliable and subtle as the data expand. Hence this project looks forward to further research that will modify our results and methods. To that end, Richard Spear has created a searchable online database of prices that will be administered by the Getty Research Institute as a complement to its Provenance Index Database. In its start-up form it is limited to data from seventeenth-century Rome, yet it is conceived as an open-ended pilot project that can be significantly expanded as other scholars provide data from all periods of western painting.

Looking even further ahead, what benefits can economics bring to art history? What topics other than money can be analyzed quantitatively? Our book shows that size, subject, and the number of figures usually affected prices, but we do not know whether altarpieces, lateral chapel paintings, or any other pictorial format grew or shrank in size over time. On average or as a median, did they stay the same? Were they bigger or smaller in certain cities, regions, or countries? Did churches, palaces, and villas grow bigger? To date, the most advanced quantitative analyses of seventeenth-century Italian painting come from historians of collections and possessions, notably by Renata Ago, Isabella Cecchini, and Gérard Labrot. In an exemplary statistical analysis of over 1,260 Venetian inventories from 1560 to 1700, Cecchini correlated diachronically three categories of information: the size and appraised values of collections, subject genres, and socio-economic classes (patricians, citizens, artisans and shopkeepers, and workers).

Art history also needs a diachronic demographics where changes in the population of painters, their longevity, family size, and social background are plotted over a century or more. Do the numbers of painters change relative to the population as a whole? Relative to sculptors or other artists (printmakers, architects, etc.)? And how did the earning power of painters compare with those of other fine-arts professionals? Does the phenomenon of family trades decrease with the rise of academies? At different rates and times in different cities and countries? Do the number of foreigners in any given city rise or fall? And what about life expectancy? A provisional analysis that I made of 900 early modern painters surprisingly suggests that they lived longer than physicians and that seventeenth-century painters lived longer than sixteenth-century ones.

Researchers in art economics today face some inviting prospects. There are rich fields of data to cultivate, much already published in scattered discussions of individual artists, patrons, or monuments where their potential for economic analysis is left unrealized. Cultivation requires comprehensive aggregation, as we have shown for Rome, Naples, Bologna, Florence, and Venice, but there are still many cities to be studied. The potential for economic analysis that sits unrealized in the published archive of our discipline is accompanied by archival sources (city censuses, property inventories, guild and academy records, etc.) that still have not been systematically excavated. We await the results, for example, of such important current projects as those on the Accademia di San Luca (directed by Peter Lukehart) and the Roman census or *stati d'anime* (directed by Rossella Vodret). Economics is a mode of analysis that can help us think quantitatively in a discipline shadowed by quality, symbol, and other abstractions, enriching how we think about art.

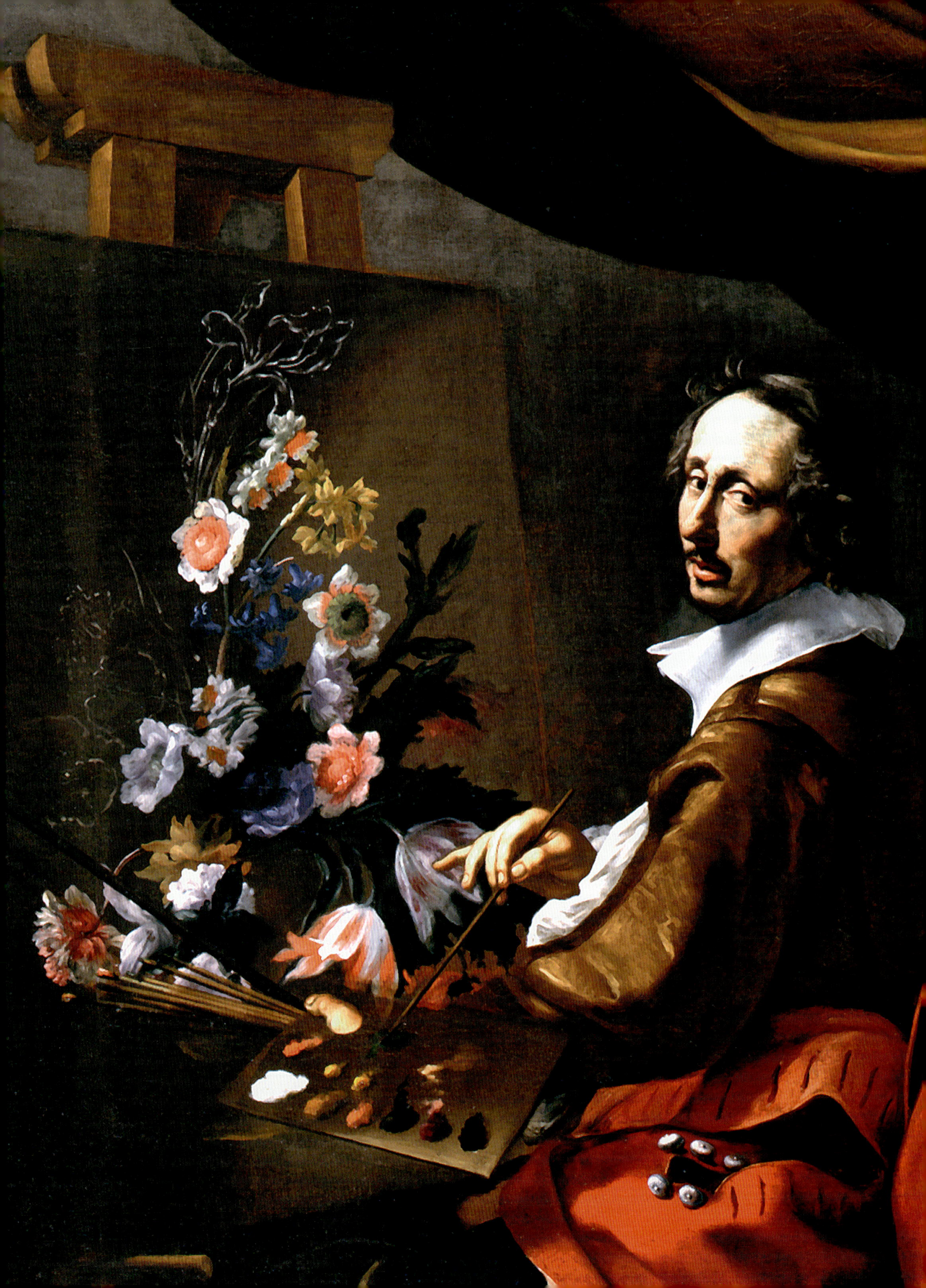

1

Rome

SETTING THE STAGE

RICHARD E. SPEAR

Economic Conditions

By the end of the sixteenth century, Rome had become an expensive and cosmopolitan center, "the most universal city in the world," thought Michel de Montaigne.[1] Yet politically and economically Rome was unusual. Despite its deep involvement in seventeenth-century European affairs of state, particularly a bitter struggle between Spain and France for political hegemony, it escaped the wars and rebellions that disrupted centers elsewhere in Italy and across the Continent. Its complex government was twofold: on the one hand, religious (the Vatican) with the bishop of Rome, the pope, in charge and, on the other hand, secular (the Campidoglio) with its own municipal authorities.[2] Renowned internationally as the papal capital and for its unparalleled historical and cultural sites, Rome neither produced nor manufactured many goods; nor, unlike the other cities discussed in this book, was it tied to maritime, textile, banking, or agricultural wealth. As a result, it was less vulnerable to the widespread economic decline that affected early seventeenth-century Italy.[3]

Rome instead was dependent on the services provided by artists and artisans, in particular jewelers and goldsmiths, as well as lawyers, notaries, bankers, booksellers, tailors, hotel keepers, and the huge bureaucracy of the Curia of the Catholic Church, not to mention many wine merchants and prostitutes.[4] Fynes Moryson, an English traveler to Italy in the 1590s, remarked that "at Venice the tribute to the State from Cortizans was thought to exceede three hundreth thousand Crownes [scudi] yearely. And the Popes holiness made no lesse gayne from this fayre trade at Rome."[5]

The composition of the city's residents was also uncommon. Nearly 60 percent were male, of which 5 percent of the population of 102,000 in 1600 were classified as "courtiers of cardinals." There were 68 bishops, 1,401 priests, 2,372 nuns, and 2,148 religious, almost another 6 percent; by mid-century these groups constituted about 7 percent of its 120,000 inhabitants.[6] Growth in Rome was more steady than elsewhere on the peninsula (see Table 32 in Renata Ago's essay). By 1700 the population reached 135,000, rising from Italy's fifth largest city in 1600 (behind Naples and Palermo in the south, Venice and Milan in the north) to third place in 1700 (only Naples and Venice remained bigger).[7]

Then there were the hordes of pilgrims, more than half a million of whom traveled to Rome during the Jubilee of 1600, five for every permanent resident.[8] They made charitable donations, spent money on goods and services, and stimulated costly public works. Another 30,000 tourists visited Rome annually, supporting an unusually large number of hotels.[9] In 1622, the city's residents and visitors could buy from 5,600 shops that employed 24,000 of its inhabitants, among which, in 1625, were 16 color or pigments merchants.[10]

Facing page: detail of Fig. 29

Sellers of pigments catered to Rome's fancy and not-so-fancy painters, who competed with one another by seeking upscale patronage in what remained an essentially client-based, demand-driven system, or by cranking out cheap landscapes and devotional images offered for a pittance on the open market (unlike in northern Europe, auctions and fairs were not an important part of the Roman art market, nor was there the equivalent of Bologna's many serious middle-class collectors). Dominating the client-based system was the court of the Church, with its wealthy Curia and extended bureaucracy. Sixtus V's expenses during his papacy (1585–90) on fountains, obelisks, streets, and the like were enormous, the Acqua Felice fountain alone costing a quarter of a million scudi, the moving of the obelisk at St. Peter's 38,000 scudi.[11] During his papacy, Paul V (1605–21) spent over 1,200,000 scudi on just four projects: St. Peter's (his expenses on the basilica exceeded the total spent during the previous 100 years), the Pauline chapel in S. Maria Maggiore, and the Vatican and Quirinal palaces, undertakings that employed countless artists and artisans. His expenditure was the equivalent of half of the total annual papal income of about 2,500,000 scudi.[12]

Other papal activities poured still more money into the economy and artists' pockets. Alexander VII's banquets for the clergy during Holy Week in 1656 cost 1,820 scudi; his three months of entertainment of Queen Christina of Sweden almost 7,000 scudi. A "festa gastronomico comico-musicale" given by Cardinal Chigi in 1668 cost 2,000 scudi.[13] No wonder that already in 1588 the economist-statistician Giovanni Bottero speculated whether Rome would "not be more like a desert than a city if the Pope held not his residence there? If he . . . spent not a great part of the revenues of the Church?"[14] No wonder, too, that in 1625 it was said, with reference to artists, that Rome is "where you go to get rich," even though many, like Taddeo Zuccaro, were greeted at its gates by hardship and servitude.[15] Others, such as Nicolò Bedino, apparently just fell into the profession: "I came to Rome with my father to live and learn some trade, and I ended up becoming a painter."[16]

Unlike in some other Italian cities—notably Florence among those discussed in this book—where one dynasty dominated politics and economic activity for generations, Rome's wealth was distributed among many families as a result of the Church's nonhereditary structure and the enormous financial rewards of clerical nepotism (a practice effectively abolished only in the eighteenth century, with considerable consequences for the arts). Rome's leading painters generally were dependent on those various families whose fortunes at one time or another were linked to the papal court.[17] Especially during the latter years of the sixteenth century and the earlier decades of the seventeenth, they benefited from an exceptionally high demand for art, thanks to a combination of available money, the need for imagery to support the intensified cult of Mary and the saints in the wake of the decrees of the Council of Trent, and many lucrative commissions to decorate new and remodeled churches, palaces, and villas in the city and its countryside.[18]

The Scudo Romano

Art in Rome usually was priced in silver scudi romani (Fig. 8). They were large coins of about 32 grams (20 percent heavier than an American silver dollar), divided into 10 giuli or paoli, 20 grossi, 100 copper baiocchi, and 500 quattrini. A testone was 30 baiocchi. The more valuable gold scudo (a doppia or doble was two of them) was occasionally specified in an artist's contract or payment. At the beginning of the century it was worth about 1.2 times the silver scudo, or 120 baiocchi; by 1700 its value had increased to about 160 baiocchi.[19] The international exchange value of the silver scudo romano remained remarkably steady throughout the century (see Table 30 in Renata Ago's essay), dipping only slightly during the final two decades.

In periods of crisis such as war, famine, and plague, seventeenth-century Italian wages and prices fluctuated from city to city, but in general they did not undergo the radical changes of the preceding century and for the purposes of this essay they can be accepted as stable in Rome.[20]

Not infrequently, full or partial payments to artists were made in goods or services purportedly equal to the amount due.[21] For instance, when Giovanni Baglione made a claim against the Santacroce family in 1604 and Cristofano Roncalli and Annibale Carracci were called in to serve as experts, Baglione was awarded 20 scudi in cash, four sacks of grain worth 10 scudi apiece, and a gold chain with six small diamonds of unspecified value.[22] The notorious diamond smuggler Fabrizio Valguarnera predictably paid in diamonds, as Giovanni Lanfranco testified in 1631. With some reluctance, Lanfranco also accepted ultramarine blue from Valguarnera at the steep equivalence of 50 scudi an ounce.[23] Salvator Rosa's *Death of Atilius Regulus* (Fig. 18) painted about 1652 was priced at 100 piastre (another name for scudi), but Rosa said that he received instead

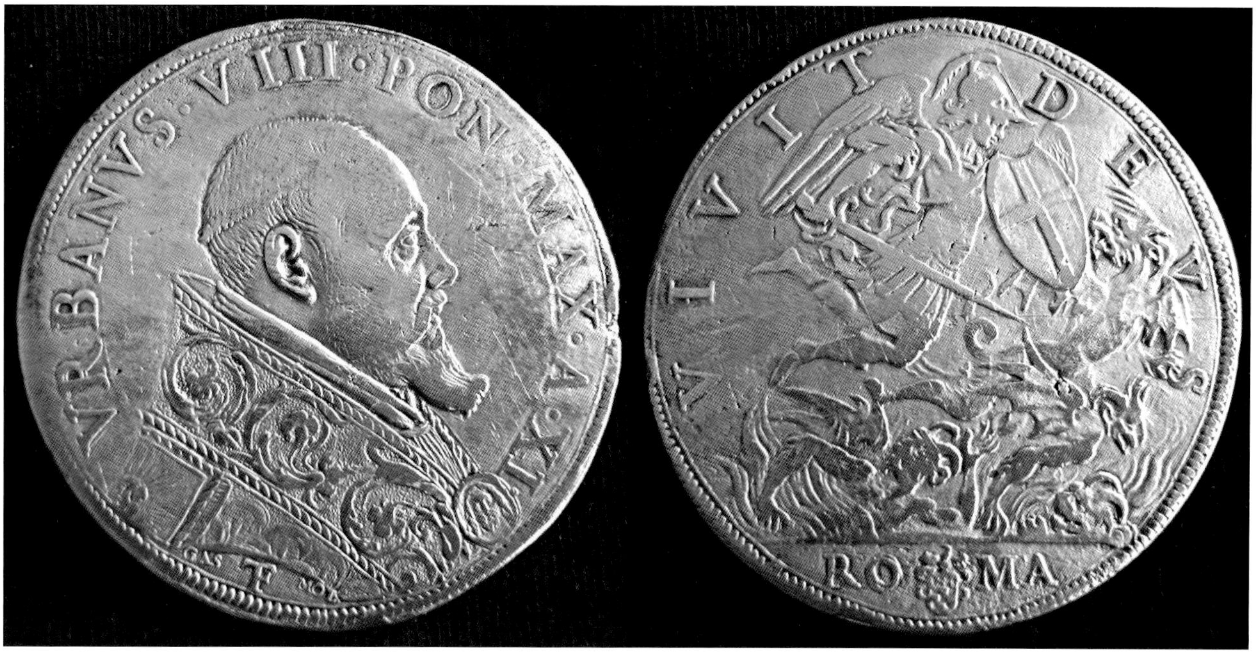

8 Roman scudo, design by Gaspare Mola, 1634 (obverse: *Urban VIII*; reverse: *St. Michael*). Silver, diameter 4.1 cm. Private collection.

"una forma di cascio parmigiano mandatami in una canestra" (a whole wheel of parmigiano sent to me in a basket).[24] For what was perhaps his last altarpiece (1639), Giuseppe Cesari d'Arpino was also paid entirely in goods worth 95.5 scudi, which included a glove box; six forks, knives, and spoons with silver handles; a length of good silk; two vases of flowers; some marzipan; and ring-shaped cakes called *ciambelle*.[25]

The practice persisted throughout the century. As "a token of his satisfaction," Pope Innocent XI gave Carlo Maratta 100 Agnus Dei, or blessed wax medallions of the Paschal Lamb, and two pairs of gloves on a silver salver for having painted a veil over the exposed breasts of the Virgin in Guido Reni's *Madonna del cucito* in the Annunciation chapel in the Quirinal palace. Maratta again was paid in goods for his *Self-Portrait* (Uffizi, Florence) requested by Cosimo III de' Medici, who "presented him with a most beautiful cabinet made in the gallery, with 72 precious jars of oil and medicaments from the distillery; moreover, he added a gold medallion with his own portrait, expressing his most gracious satisfaction and saying that just as he enjoyed having the portrait of Carlo, so it was only right that Carlo should have one of His Highness."[26] In 1677 Orazio Spada gave Luigi Scaramuccia 340 scudi in cash, nearly all of the 350 scudi he owed the painter. For the balance Spada's advisor, Padre Sebastiano Resta, suggested that the painter be given "qualche utensilj di casa," some household items, perhaps four used chairs and a table, or foods such as cheese, oil, or wine, "che non li servisse," which weren't wanted, and that Spada should just tell Scaramuccia he understood from Resta that the painter needed them.[27]

Then there is the example of Giovanni Coli and Filippo Gherardi, who in 1679 were given 13 barrels of ordinary wine by the Colonna in lieu of 26 scudi.[28] A decade earlier Francesco Cozza's payments for frescoing the vault of the library in the Palazzo Pamphilj on Piazza Navona consisted of cash, quantities of wine worth 1.5 and 2 scudi a barrel, and wheat at 6 scudi a *rubbio*, a measure close to eight bushels or about 250 liters.[29] Paintings themselves were bartered. Giulio Mancini mentioned to his brother that, not having much capital to buy paintings, he accepted them as partial payments for his medical services.[30] Far less orthodox was Agostino Tassi's substitute for wages he owed his assistants: the favors of his mistresses.[31]

Incomes

There was a huge gap between the earnings of the rich and poor painters of Rome, which wants comparison with a range of other Roman incomes, beginning with a typical wage for the lower class. A decree of March 1599 prohibited peasants working in Rome's vineyards from demanding a daily wage above 15 baiocchi until the following June and only 20 baiocchi thereafter, with the stipulations that they work without interruption from "the first hour of the day until sunset," and that half of their wages were to be paid in silver coins, half in the less desirable copper coins.[32] During 1605–7 other field workers similarly made only 15 to 22 baiocchi a day or about 50 scudi annually, less than many artists' assistants and pigment grinders earned on a daily basis.

A *muratore* or skilled mason, many of whom were employed on Rome's building projects, earned 35 baiocchi a day in 1624 (40 years later the Colonna were paying a better wage, 50 baiocchi *per giorno* to Pietro Lattani Muratore), or around 85 scudi a year (a figure comparable to that paid in Venice), though an extra 15 to 20 percent should be added onto laborers' wages for their supplemental food rations.[33] In 1613 a pair of shoes cost 50 baiocchi, over a day's worth of labor. Some tailors, soldiers at Castel Sant'Angelo, and Swiss guards also earned no more than 40 to 50 scudi a year.

Expectedly, doctors and professors were better off, and so were some cooks. One doctor aboard a papal galley was given 216 scudi a year. In 1616, when not yet papal physician but working as a prison doctor, "signor Giulio Mancini, fisico" received 9.9 scudi for three months of service, though surely that was only part of his employment at the time.[34] The average annual salary of professors at the university in Rome in 1658 was 166 scudi. Its lawyers were paid the most, 650 scudi, its theologians the least, not a tenth as much.[35] Many of the numerous cooks employed for Innocent XII's trip to Nettuno (1697) received the sizeable payment of a scudo a day, and some even a scudo and a half.[36]

Various other professionals enjoyed good incomes. Sixtus V granted Cesare Baronio a 400 scudi annual pension while working on his *Annales Ecclesiastici*.[37] Starting in 1588, Fabio Orsini, the first director (*reggente*) of the Archivio generale dello Stato, was paid the generous sum of 100 scudi a month.[38] Pompeo Targoni, papal engineer under Paul V, received the same amount, and his fame led to an outside offer in 1611 to triple his salary if he would relocate and work for the viceroy of Sicily.[39] To judge from his wages and the earnings of Domenico Fontana mentioned below, and Florentine practice too, Italian engineers commanded very high wages. In 1612 the Vatican's librarian (who at mid-century was receiving 100 scudi monthly) was appointed supervisor of the archives at Castel Sant'Angelo as well, a position worth 200 scudi a year. Giovan Battista Raimondi, described as "a man very learned in foreign languages, the first to introduce the study of Arabic into this city," had an annual papal income of 800 scudi.[40]

On the whole, the workforce of the Vatican was handsomely paid. For instance, around mid-century the general of the guards (Generale delle guardie) received 200 scudi a month, his lieutenant 80 a month plus housing; the governor of the Castel Sant'Angelo (Castellano del Castello S. Angelo) "five hundred crowns [scudi] a month entertainment [wages]," and his deputy 50 scudi a month "and as much in perquisites [*regaglie*]"; the "Cardinall Chamberlaine" (Cardinale camerlengo) between 12,000 and 14,000 annually; the vice-chancellor (Vicecancelliere) 15,000 to 16,000 annually; and the "Generall of the holy Church" (Generale di Santa Chiesa), the top military man, "in time of peace his pay is a thousand crowns a month, and in the time of War three thousand," to cite some examples from Girolamo Lunadoro's detailed *Relatione della Corte di Roma*.[41]

As antiquarian and custodian of medals for Queen Christina, the learned biographer of artists, Giovanni Pietro Bellori, was receiving 15 scudi a month in 1689, the same subsidy Christina paid her librarian.[42] His and Mancini's stipends call attention to the difficulty of gauging real incomes when stipends were for less than full-time service, not to mention the necessity of considering investment earnings, which will be discussed later. Certainly, the bell ringer of the Campidoglio, who was paid about 15 scudi a year, had other jobs in Rome.[43] That pertains to many musicians, too, who worked part-time for more than one client, receiving retainers with an obligation of availability rather than daily presence. An organist at St. Peter's testified in 1597 that for the past five years he had been earning 6 scudi a month. Girolamo Frescobaldi received the same amount, 72 scudi a year, when he was hired in 1608 as organist of the Cappella Giulia in St. Peter's, a good example of a wage that had not changed for a decade, though later Frescobaldi got a raise to 96 scudi. By the 1630s he could afford to pay 60 scudi a year for an apartment for his family and servant. The Barberini paid musicians between 3 and 15 scudi a month, while singers in the papal chapel received 25 scudi monthly, perhaps for them a full-time wage.[44]

Incomes of composers were less standardized, varying more according to a patron's wealth, expectations, and urge to please the famous. Cesare Marotta, Cardinal Montalto's principal composer of chamber music, was wooed from Naples in 1604 with unusual benefits: 100 scudi moving expenses, 25 scudi a month on top of a food allowance of 12 scudi for him and his wife, 6.6

scudi monthly for their 80-scudi-a-year apartment, 20.2 scudi every six months for firewood, and even money to buy hay for a horse. No one else in the cardinal's *famiglia*, or personnel, had such a good package, perhaps because Marotta's wife was one of Italy's most sought-after singers. Her own earnings must have increased their income substantially.

By the time Marotta died in 1630, the composer Orazio Michi was benefiting even more from Montalto's largesse. In 1622 he was given an annual pension of 300 scudi. More extraordinarily, the cardinal's testament increased it to 2,000 scudi d'oro a year. It was thought that by the end of the 1630s Michi's pension was in the range of 5,000 to 6,000 scudi, surpassing the income of the most famous painters and equaling that of some cardinals.[45]

Many of the leading cardinal patrons of art, however, were incomparably richer. Odoardo Farnese in 1593 had an income of 60,000 scudi. In 1600, Pietro Aldobrandini, from his income of 40,000 scudi, could spend 5,000 scudi on one banquet for 1,500 guests. As Soprintendente dello stato ecclesiastico, Scipione Borghese was paid 405 scudi a month, and that was just the start of what he would reap as papal nephew. In 1612, he earned 140,000 scudi and from 1605 to 1633 acquired an astonishing 6.5 million scudi.[46] Cardinal Montalto was exceptionally rich. He had an income of 100,000 scudi a year and the largest household in the Curia, numbering more than 130 people in 1612. He was generous with his money, contributing 1,000 scudi a year toward the building of S. Andrea della Valle and giving annual support to numerous scholars and creative artists, such as the Marotta and Michi.[47] Well-founded rumors had it that the annual income of the three Barberini brothers exceeded 300,000 scudi.[48]

Of course, not all cardinals were that rich, yet it was thought that for one to live in proper style in Rome during the first decade of the seventeenth century at least 8,000 scudi a year were required.[49] It was expensive even to be elevated to the position. "After the publick consistory" cardinals were expected to distribute 370 scudi d'oro in "rewards" (*mancie*) to everyone, from the participating Maestri delle cerimonie (100 scudi) down to "the Popes singing men" (30 scudi), the musicians of Castel Sant'Angelo (6 scudi), and the "Keeper of the secret Gardens" (5 scudi). Additionally, a cardinal who was present in Rome was expected to give another 500 scudi "at the least to the participant secret Chamberlaines [*camerieri segreti participanti*]." As for those who were not in Rome and received "the Hatt . . . besides the thousand duckets due for the Hatt, other three hundred duckets [is given to the Chamberlaines]. But Cardinalls which are Princes, doe give betwixt five and sixe thousand duckets."[50]

Annual incomes of nearly 100 cardinals of the period averaged over 20,000 scudi. Even relatively "poor" cardinals—Felice Peretti before becoming Pope Sixtus V and Cesare Baronio—had incomes of around 5,000 scudi a year. Antonio Barberini the Elder, while a member of the austere Capuchin order, enjoyed an annual allowance of more than 30,000 scudi. Some Roman merchants were very rich, too, earning as much as 40,000 to 50,000 scudi in a good year.[51]

Food and Other Costs of Living

Around 1600, wheat in the papal capital cost more than almost anywhere else in Europe, 4 to 5 baiocchi a kilo, about twice as much as in Naples. Its high price was a serious problem for the poor, who depended on bread and other cereals for over half of their daily calories.[52] Pasta by comparison was a luxury item, costing three times as much as ordinary bread.[53] In 1601 the price of lasagna, vermicelli, tagliolini, and macaroni was about 3 baiocchi a pound.[54] Eggs in 1600 fetched 1 baiocco a dozen. Oil that year was fixed at 22 baiocchi a *bocale* wholesale and 23 baiocchi retail, or about 2 baiocchi a liter.[55] In 1697 fine sugar cost 20 baiocchi a pound, pepper 24 baiocchi.[56]

Choice fish could be expensive: 24 baiocchi a kilo in 1615, the same price as for a pair of cocks.[57] Beef and lamb were cheaper, roughly 9 baiocchi a kilo in the mid-1620s; pork was half that price. Innards were no bargain: lamb liver cost about 15 baiocchi a kilo (testicles twice as much); sweetbreads 25 baiocchi a pair; and tripe and brains 30 and 5 baiocchi apiece, respectively.[58] While in rural areas Italian peasants rarely ate meat, in early seventeenth-century Rome average per capita consumption was 38 kilos a year.[59]

The price of ordinary wine, which after bread provided the most calories in a low-class diet, was 3 to 4 baiocchi a liter, the same as later in the century when Coli and Gherardi received those 13 barrels of wine instead of 26 scudi. Thus a liter of common wine cost 20 percent of a worker's daily wage. Per capita consumption was high, about 200 liters a year, and during Jubilee years, due to scarcity, its cost, like that of hotel rooms and bread, skyrocketed.[60]

Food prices were strictly controlled by Rome's conservators, who would "punish the sellers of Victualls, either for want of weight, or excesse of price" with fines of 25 scudi or three *tratti di corda* (punishment by lifting the victim from the arms tied behind his back)

TABLE 2 Sample Food Prices set for Rome's *pizzicaroli* (delicatessens), per 12-oz. pound, in baiocchi and quattrini

Product	1595	1600	1611	1618	1627	1635	1641	1649	1655	1666	1673	1680	1686	1689	1694	1701
Cows' milk cheese	7	7.2	8	8	8	8	8	8	8	7	8	7.5	7.5	7.5	7.5	7.5
Pecorino[63]	4.2	4	4.2	4	4.3	4.3	5	5	4.4	3.3	4.1	4	3.3	3.4	4.3	4
Ricotta	2.2	2	2.2	2.2	2.2	2.5	2.5	2	2	2.2	2.2	2	1.4	2	2.4	2.1
Butter[64]	11	12	15	15	15	15	15	15	15	14	15	15	15	15	15	15
Lard	6.2	5	6	5	6	7	6.2	6.2	6.1	5.2	5.2	5.2	4.3	5.2	5.1	6
Sausages	10	7	10	9	9	10	9.2	9.2	9.1	8.2	8.2	8.2	7.3	8.2	8.1	9
Prosciutto	6.2	5	6.2	5.4	6	7	6.2	6.2	6.1	5.2	5.2	5.2	4.3	5.2	5.1	6
Two pork tongues	5	4	6	5	4.2	4.2	4.4	5	5	5	5	4.3	3.4	4.3	4.3	5.1
Salted pork belly	10	8	10	10	9	9.3	9.2	10	9	9	9	8.3	7.4	8.3	8.3	9.1

for a first offence and *la frusta* (whipping) for a repeat violation.[61] Like the international exchange value of the scudo romano, which dipped in the 1680s but otherwise remained steady, food prices published in the frequent *bandi* (edicts) reveal unusual stability across the century (Table 2).[62]

In aristocratic households, members of the *famiglia* who were on monthly retainers customarily were given a food supplement (a *companatico* or "bread complement") of 10 baiocchi daily, enough to cover a fair portion of their provisions.[65] As a sign of his frugal living, Pope Alexander VII would not allow an expenditure of over 15 baiocchi a day on his food.[66] A 38-year-old merchant who lived comfortably spent 70 scudi in 1613, over 20 baiocchi a day.[67] Eating out naturally cost more. In the mid-1590s Fynes Moryson, while lodging at a Roman "publike Inne," spent "three giulii [30 baiocchi] on each meale."[68]

For the wealthy of Rome, food and housing, like clothing and art, were traditional signs of status. Exclusive of bread and wine, the Chigi spent about 85 scudi a month on food. Cardinal Pietro Aldobrandini's personal clothing cost 500 scudi per annum, that for his *famiglia* another 2,000.[69] The median value of a man's suit in some middle-class seventeenth-century Roman inventories was around 5 scudi, a sum similar to prices in 1627 for ready-made suits that ranged from 2.8 to 6.2 scudi, according to fabric and style.[70] In 1576–77, 34 percent of the Odescalchi family's expenditure on consumer goods was for food, 27 percent for housing, 10 percent for servants' wages, and 8 percent for clothing. Even with their high style of living, they were able to save 80 percent of their income.[71] Other Italian aristocratic households allocated roughly the same percentage of expenses for food, around 20 percent for clothing, and 12 percent for servants.[72] The cumulative expenses between 1639 and 1644 of one well-off, non-aristocratic Roman household were similar for food and clothing, 32 percent and 10.5 percent respectively, while more than 20 percent went for that most visible of status symbols, a carriage.[73] By comparison, workers spent roughly three-quarters of their income on food, leaving little for rent, household furnishings, clothing, and heat (urban prices could be double the rural prices), and hardly any discretionary income for luxuries such as art.[74]

Many Roman services and entertainment were expensive. Going to the barber could cost 35 baiocchi, a month's laundry 48 baiocchi.[75] Salvator Rosa decided that the price of attending the *commedia* at 3 giuli or the opera at 4 giuli was too much for mediocre companies and lamented that the production of a bad comic opera was 5,000 to 6,000 scudi.[76] Postal rates were substantial though stable, at a time when transportation generally was expensive. A 1-ounce letter from Bologna to Rome cost 1 baiocco, beyond Bologna twice as much. The rate increased to 4 baiocchi an ounce for heavier letters. Packages from Bologna to Rome were 8 baiocchi per 12-ounce pound. International rates were far steeper: a 1-ounce letter from Rome to Spain cost 25 baiocchi, as much as a kilo of fish or a couple of cocks, and the equivalent of laborer's daily wage.[77]

Postal service was dependent on horses, whose hire could be pricey. Moryson relates that in Italy "post-horses are to be hired in every City, and for one they commonly pay a silver crowne [scudo], that is seven Venetian lyres, for ten miles," though a "more frugall course" was to hire at only a third the price "horses of returne, so called, because they must returne home empty, if they find no passengers by chance to use them."[78]

Similarly, to ship paintings could be expensive and complicated, involving the making of weatherproof crates or metal tubes for rolled canvases, hiring porters, and paying transportation costs. In 1583, two porters received 2.3 scudi for transporting from Rome to Siena two paintings by Cristofano Roncalli measuring 3.5 × 3 meters.[79] The other expenses are not known, nor are they for sending a 350 scudi painting by Antonio Barbalonga from Rome to Catania in 1632, whose waxed crate cost 3.5 scudi.[80] Partial expenses of two Medici shipments from Rome to Florence in 1619 and 1620 are documented: 3.5 scudi for sealing with wax and tying up three crates containing six landscapes by Paul Bril, four of which were framed; and 4 scudi for a waxed crate, cord, and related packing costs for two altarpieces that measured about 4 × 2.5 meters.[81]

A detailed record of expenses incurred in shipping a group of paintings from Milan to Modena in 1635 might reflect similar charges in Rome and elsewhere in Italy. Among them (which are quoted in lire worth roughly 15 baiocchi each) were four big crates at 16 lire apiece (nearly 2.5 scudi); a thick strap and cord needed for the trip, 7.15 lire; additional cord for wrapping everything, 14 lire; a cart with a pair of bulls, two horses, and three men, at 18 lire a day, 14 days' round trip, 252 lire; a waxed canvas to cover the cart against the possibility of rain, 51 lire; two men who carried "the huge painting on their shoulders to Modena, labor and expenses," 86.5 lire; and another 86.15 lire to a servant who acted as a courier.[82] In 1627, two porters were paid 14 scudi for "having carried from Bologna to Rome on their shoulders" Reni's large *Immaculate Conception* (Metropolitan Museum of Art, New York).[83]

Rent

Like today, rent in central seventeenth-century Rome was very high, which explains why few painters owned the kind of large homes they acquired in Bologna. Housing was cheaper in Florence and Naples, too. In 1612, Tuzia, the Gentileschi's tenant and faithless chaperon of Artemisia, with her husband paid 18 scudi a year for just two rooms upstairs in the house where the Gentileschi lived in the Roman parish of S. Spirito in Sassia.[84] Three years earlier, Adam Elsheimer signed a lease for lodgings in the Campo Marzio that cost 60 scudi annually.[85] Not much later the Borghese gave Guido Reni, in addition to his monthly stipend of 9 scudi plus bread, wine, and firewood, an allowance of 50 scudi a year for rent.[86]

Those figures correspond with notarial data indicating that rent in the cheaper quarters of Rome was around 12 scudi a year, somewhat more in the via Giulia; from 25 to 30 scudi in the area of the via della Scrofa; and in the fancy zone, then as now the streets near the Trinità dei Monti—Condotti, Frattina, Babuino, the Corso—where many artists preferred to live, rents were about 35 to 40 scudi a year, peaking at 100.[87] For example, in 1613 Lanfranco, with Antonio Carracci, rented a house on the via Paolina, today's via del Babuino, for 78 scudi; in 1630 Pietro da Cortona rented a house on the vicolo Savelli not far from Piazza Navona for 60 scudi a year; and in 1649, for what he referred to his *casuccia*, ostensibly a shabby little house, "at the Trinità dei Monti, meaning the best air of Rome," Salvator Rosa was paying 80 scudi a year, nearly double what he had paid shortly earlier in Florence.[88]

Ribera's ability to rent increasingly expensive housing over a short period might reflect his quick success in Rome or perhaps just fiscal irresponsibility. Writing as an eyewitness, Mancini said that Ribera, while working for dealers on a per diem basis, led a loose life in Rome and ran up such huge debts that he had to get out of town.[89] In mid-1612 he was living in a house near the Corso that cost 21 scudi. From there he moved to another in the same area whose rent was 55 scudi, and then by late 1613 his address was the via Frattina, where he was paying 70 scudi. The lease for the first property spelled out that if Ribera "wanted to make a window in the roof to accommodate his painting he had to do so at his own expense and when he left he had to restore it to its original condition without reimbursement."[90]

Most painters, like Ribera, worked at home, as they did in all of the centers discussed in this book, and therefore they rarely had to rent separate space, unlike businessmen who wanted street-front shops or someone whose studio was as unusually productive as Guido Reni's in Bologna.[91] The printer Giuseppe De Rossi the Elder required such space and in 1633 paid 50 scudi for a corner store, twice the average yearly rent for a more modest Roman shop.[92] Similarly, those painters (*pittori bottegari*) and gilders who, like tailors, barbers, pigment sellers, cloth merchants, and secondhand dealers (*rigattieri*), handled pictures on the side from retail shops, had additional overhead.[93] According to the biographer and economist Lione Pascoli, Gaspard Dughet rented four houses in order to have easy access to nature, two in Rome and one each in Tivoli and Frascati, so his overhead was uncharacteristically high.[94]

These examples of the costs of food and rent agree with a story regarding Maratta at mid-century.[95] For nine years as a youth he lived in the home of his half-brother Bernabeo, but when they quarreled Carlo moved out. Bernabeo brought suit to recover his expenses. Before the case was dropped through Andrea Sacchi's arbitration, it had been decided that Bernabeo's compensation should be 6 scudi a month for a total of 648 scudi. If one estimates the cost of food as 10 to 15 baiocchi a day on the basis of the abovementioned *companatico* and Alexander VII's frugal budget, Maratta's food was worth around 3.75 scudi monthly, leaving 27 scudi as the credible value of his yearly lodging.

All of these incomes and prices, like the wages and fees of painters discussed below and throughout this book, should be seen in the context of Fernand Braudel's estimate that, in the Mediterranean economy of the sixteenth century, less than 20 scudi a year was a subsistence wage; between 20 and 40 a small income; and from 40 to 150 scudi quite "reasonable."[96] It has been suggested that a family of five in Rome around 1600 could get by on 90 scudi a year, another figure to bear in mind with regard to the costs of paintings and artists' earnings.[97] (It is a figure to compare with the surprising estimate Raffaella Morselli cites, that a family in Bologna could live on 90 lire a year, a fifth as much.) For those painters who prospered, and probably for many others we would call second string, Roman prices on the whole were affordable, unlike for the majority of Romans, who would have found them dauntingly steep. Among that majority were numerous painters who eked out a living on extremely paltry fees.

The Numbers and Varieties of Painters

Before taking into account the successes and failures of Roman painters in light of this economic sketch and the ways they tried to make a living, it is logical to ask, who and how many were they? Competition was keen and undoubtedly intensified as the demand for art slowed during the last third of the century when the market neared a saturation point and Rome, like Italy in general, lost its artistic hegemony.[98] The question, however, is easier to ask than to answer for Rome or any of our other cities. Data are scarce and the problems complex, from knowing who at the time considered himself to be a painter (such as the many gilders, whose work overlapped with painting), to deciding which of them should be taken into account, to estimating how many have disappeared from sight.[99] All the same, there are some good clues.

Giovanni Guerra and Cesare Nebbia, who organized and supervised the most extensive decorative commissions in Rome at the end of the sixteenth century, employed about 50 painters and gilders just at the Scala Santa, excluding their assistants and shop labor.[100] Data from the annual Easter census (*stati d'anime*) during Paul V's pontificate are partially preserved for two of the parishes where artists congregated: from 1607, 1609, 1615, and 1618–21 for S. Lorenzo in Lucina, and from 1607–13 and 1616–21 for S. Andrea delle Fratte.[101] In both areas, painters and masons (*muratori*) were the most numerous of the artists and artisans counted (a total of 231 painters and 140 masons in S. Lorenzo, 125 painters and 310 masons in S. Andrea), followed by carpenters (82 in S. Lorenzo, 64 in S. Andrea) and stonemasons (*scarpellini*) (23 in S. Lorenzo, 111 in S. Andrea). Far fewer were the sculptors (9, 29), gilders (4, 12), and *stuccatori* (4, 10) living in those parishes.

To focus on one year instead of cumulative data: the *stati d'anime* of 1619 of S. Maria del Popolo and S. Lorenzo in Lucina together recorded 116 painters among some 4,000 residents. On the basis of that count and those of the same parishes from 1604 and 1634, it has been suggested that perhaps about one or two of every 1,000 Romans was a painter, a percentage higher than estimates for Paris and roughly comparable to those for seventeenth-century Holland.[102] For a population of 125,000, this would mean 187.5 painters, however the term is defined. One list of 1634 identifies about 50 painters in Rome who belonged to the Accademia di S. Luca and more than 140 Italians and foreigners who did not.[103] Two years earlier, of the 66,000 residents in Florence, 68 were cited as "pittori." In Naples in 1640, which was three times larger than Rome, Christopher Marshall has counted only about 50 painters known by name.

In fact, in 1665 Bernini said there were 200 painters in Rome (the same number as said to be in Venice in 1682), without clarifying who in his opinion counted, though it seems unlikely that he was taking into account the many hacks.[104] "I think I know all the painters in Rome," Caravaggio testified in 1603, but then he named only a dozen and obliquely referred to the "altri."[105] At the other extreme, in 1660 Johann Theodor Sprenger observed, not as improbably at it might sound if he was lumping together all kinds of artists, that there were about a thousand painters in Rome ("Cum ego Romae eram, numerabantur ibi pictores aliquot mille").[106] A recently completed study of all of the preserved *stati d'anime* from 1600 to 1630 has collected 6,000 citations to 2,200 different "artists."[107] While comparable data from later in the century have not been gathered, the *stati d'anime* of the parish of S. Andrea delle Fratte in 1700 record 35 *muratori*, 21 painters, 21 carpenters, 5 gilders, 4 *scarpellini*, and 1 *stuccatore*.[108]

Another approach is to estimate numbers from the evidence of the nearly 140 biographies of painters in

Baglione's *Vite*, which span the period 1572–1642 and include practically all of the well-established figures. Baglione also wrote biographies of about 28 sculptors, 13 architects, 5 painter-architects, 4 sculptor-architects, and almost 20 engravers—that is, over 200 artists, not counting those he mentioned in passing. On average, 80 of those painters were active in Rome during any of the years Baglione covered, or approximately 100 different painters per decade, assuming an average lifespan of 60-plus years and a professional career of 40.[109] This number omits all of the painters' assistants, copyists, architectural decorators, and the countless lesser lights who worked on a wholly different plane by selling pictures for a few scudi or less.

Baglione also paid limited attention to the many foreign artists in Rome, notably the Flemings and French, whether they were in the city briefly or for extended periods.[110] By mid-century, the French constituted about half of all of the foreign painters working in Rome.[111] Between 1600 and 1670 there were more than 400 French artists, 78 percent of whom were painters, 14 percent sculptors, 6 percent engravers, and less than 1 percent architects. Of the total, nearly half are unknown today; among the painters, 37 percent are merely names. They and the other *oltramontani* flocked to Rome to study its monuments and tap into its thriving market, which could be done more easily than in most cities because the production of art was minimally regulated.[112]

Those foreigners and various other painters were skipped over by Baglione because, as an arch-academician, he was fundamentally interested in high-class painting by major artists on public view (nonetheless he was rebuked by Bellori for his lack of selectivity in placing Annibale Carracci among "so many incompetent painters [*nel numero di tanti imbrattatele*]").[113] And so were the other early biographers on whom we commonly rely for a general idea of Rome's community of painters. Baglione was not as candid about this as was the doctor, collector, and dealer Giulio Mancini. In his treatise on art written around 1620, Mancini relates some lively anecdotes about an unknown Capitano Gasparino, who painted several chiaroscuro façades in via Giulia. Next he mentions an equally obscure Schizzone, who also painted chiaroscuro façades that were notable only because they were executed quickly and cheaply while the crippled artist was enraged. Then in an exceptionally revealing and startlingly modern comment, Mancini admitted that he had included Gasparino and Schizzone "for fun, knowing full well that these painters have no importance and shouldn't be put forward, but consideration given only to those with reputation and fame who need to be known to scholars [*dalli studiosi*]."[114]

If one broadens Caravaggio's, Mancini's, and Baglione's points of view, far more than 80 painters were making a living in Rome. If every type is counted, surely they surpassed Bernini's estimate of 200, perhaps by two or possibly threefold. Extensive data support this assumption and paint a much broader picture of the Roman art world.[115]

The Vanished

In another Roman treatise of 1652, Giovanni Domenico Ottonelli and Pietro da Cortona defined three kinds of painters. At the pinnacle were those who "absolutely" deserved to be called excellent, earned great respect from everyone, and whose work was "esteemed, wanted, and admired." Beneath them were those of modest talent and aptitude who, easily satisfied with their work, "lived without the benefit of much fame." Lastly, there were the *infimi*, the worst of all painters with hardly any excellence [*pochissima perfettione*] who, "with no or little reputation, carry on with their work."[116]

Thanks to the pioneering research of Patrizia Cavazzini, much more is now known about the *infimi*, those she calls *pittori grossi*, who specialized in cheap, crude devotional images, portraits, and unsophisticated landscapes and still lifes, the kind of work found in the homes of bakers, boatmen, washerwomen, smiths, school teachers, and poorer merchants (that is, in the homes of collectors Mancini designated as "di stato mediocre e di stato basso"), as well as in some taverns, hospices, bathhouses, barbershops, and stores.[117] For instance, in 1602 one Giovan Giacomo di Domenico was taken in and nurtured by a cardinal's cook, to whom he turned over some 30 canvases he painted in a year. Subsequently, they were sold on the open market for a few scudi apiece.[118]

One group of Roman inventories of 75 mostly middle-class households contains on average 23.5 pictures, many of which were religious and probably made by the *pittori grossi*, whose art customarily was priced under the threshold level of three scudi.[119] For about a decade beginning in 1609, non-members of the Accademia who undertook work above that value were to get the Accademia's permission, though undoubtedly the new rule, like most others it initiated, was flaunted.[120]

Successful *pittori grossi*, for whom quantity rather than quality counted, could earn as much as 10 scudi a

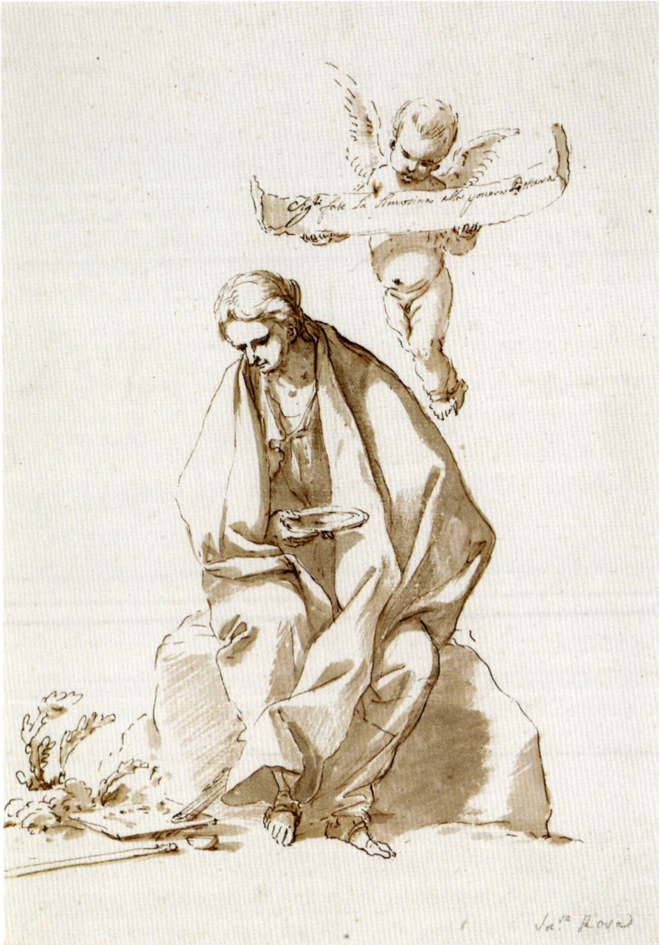

9 Salvator Rosa, *Painting as a Beggar*, ca. 1646? Pen, brown ink, and brown wash, 30.4 × 22.1 cm. Royal Library, Windsor Castle.

month, a comparatively good income in seventeenth-century Rome. However, most of them, for instance two mentioned by Philip Sohm—Giovanni Gerolamo Zafferino, who lived on "only a baiocco's worth of bread all day" or the miserable, barefoot Venetian Bartolomeo Pedon—undoubtedly would have identified with the message of Salvator Rosa's allegorical drawing of *Painting as a Beggar* (Fig. 9), "Sig^{ri} fate La Limosina alla povera Pittura" (Gentlemen, give alms to poor Painting).[121] The *pittori grossi* nonetheless posed enough of an economic threat in Rome that their activity contributed to the Accademia's efforts to thwart the open sale of art by limiting the number of retail shops. The Accademia also was opposed to artists dealing from their homes or studios in works by other artists. Both positions were based on the premise that commerce was degrading to the profession and that to exhibit art in shops was to debase it, to treat it like cheap goods, "vil merce" (similar concerns in Florence and Venice are discussed by Elena Fumagalli and Philip Sohm). Any member disregarding the prohibition was subject to a stiff 50 scudi fine.[122] Yet the practice continued throughout the century and even was sanctioned if the dozens of picture-sellers and *pittori bottegari*, painters who were allowed to run retail shops, paid the Accademia for a permit.[123]

Some collectors, including important ones, had no scruples about buying from distinctly minor painters or shopping on the open market, especially by mid-century and later when it expanded greatly. In a letter from Rome to Mantua as early as 1603, an agent of the Gonzaga reported that "this morning I was looking for paintings in shops as your lordship wanted . . . but I haven't found anything appropriate and doubt I'll find a beautiful 100-scudo picture that's worth the money. These dealers admit to not having anything of that quality."[124]

The notion of shopping for a "100-scudo picture" anticipates Mancini's observation in 1612 that "now [collectors] want rare works of quality [*cose exquisite*] and ordinary ones won't suffice . . . they need pricey works [*cose di prezzo*]."[125] Nonetheless, in 1613 Scipione Borghese gave a painter-dealer just 46 scudi for a dozen small still lifes.[126] That same year the Altemps paid 54 scudi to one Bartolomeo Cervetto pittore "for having sold 60 paintings of heads of famous men" for one of their villas.[127] At the time of his death in 1626, Simone Vai, a wealthy Florentine in Rome, owned 124 paintings worth only a few scudi apiece.[128] That bulk sales of modestly priced paintings to men of status occurred is documented not only in Scipione Borghese's purchase in 1613, but also when the dealer Mattia Capocaccia sold a group of 69 paintings to Cardinal Francesco Maidalchini in 1656 for 1,500 scudi, although in that instance Capocaccia had to take most of them back.[129]

A certain Mastro Andrea bypassed middlemen in 1592 by selling to the Jesuits 18 *Crucifixions* at 2.5 scudi apiece for their confessionals.[130] Buyers with more demanding standards wanting *santini*-like paintings turned to artists of the caliber of the Bavarian Sigismondo Laire (Siegmund Lair). Baglione relates that Laire specialized in miniature painting (Cardinal Montalto paid him 28.8 scudi in 1608 for four small paintings [*quadretti*] on lapis lazuli), often copying Rome's famous images of the Virgin, such as the Madonna del Popolo and the Madonna della Pace, and that he made a lot of coppers for the Jesuits to send off to India and Spain, from which Laire "earned a good sum of money."[131]

Laire was no *pittore grosso* and lucky in that his name survives not only in Baglione's *Vite*, as one of the dozen painters singled out by Caravaggio, and as a member of the Accademia di S. Luca and the Congregazione dei Virtuosi del Pantheon, but also in some identifiable work, unlike so many others whose lengthy roll call is a stark warning to connoisseurs seeking to match paintings with recognized painters.[132] A rare, invaluable glimpse of this lost world emerges from a census of the Campo Marzio, a central *rione* or region of Rome consisting of the parishes of S. Maria del Popolo, S. Andrea delle Fratte, and S. Lorenzo in Lucina, Rome's preferred neighborhoods for artists. Some smaller, adjacent parishes were counted in the census, too.

The Campo Marzio in 1656

A special census of Rome was taken in 1656 due to the plague, which caused a decline of nearly 20 percent in its population to 100,000, its size back in 1600.[133] Only the results for the Campo Marzio are preserved, which list 15,543 *anime* (literally souls but meaning baptized persons), 13 percent of Rome's entire population, living in 3,599 families or households. Very unusually, households were categorized economically (see Renata Ago's essay on these slippery socio-economic categories): 79, about 2 percent, were rich (*ricche*), 1,002 (28 percent) comfortable (*commode*), 2,330 (65 percent) poor (*povere*), and 188 (5 percent) miserably destitute (*miserabili*). More than 100 of the *anime* were painters—a remarkable 8.3 per thousand—about a dozen were sculptors/stonecutters (*scarpellini*), at least five were engravers, and only two were called architects. Roughly 85 percent of the artists were painters and 10 percent sculptors. Fifty-five percent of the painters were Italian, 20 percent French, and 20 percent Flemish. Nearly everyone's age and place of origin were noted. An equal number of the painters lived in households that were listed as comfortable (C.) or poor (P.). Not one belonged with the rich, only one with the *miserabili*, an unknown Fleming, Filippo Faidens, aged 32. Sculptors and stonecutters (*scarpellini*) were poor rather than comfortable by a four to one ratio.[134]

The extent of this vanished world of international painters is apparent in the many unfamiliar names and worth reciting in part: Bernardo Chulli fiammengo, about 30 years old (C.), Nicolò Roselli Lorenese, 35 (P.), Roberto dell'Hortaglia fiammengo, 54 (P.), Lamberto Fanganetti Danese, 24 (C.), Girolamo Marchi Romano, 45 (C.), Gioachimo Camera Siciliano, 40 (P.), Giovanni Vilvorti fiammengo, 50 (P.), Bartolomeo Bezini maltese, 39 (C.), Claudio Latino francese, 38 (P.), Anthes Dond fiamengo, 30 (P.), Henrico di Chach Todescho, 27 (C.), Benedetto di Rosa Siciliano, 35 (P.), Francesco Bianchetti modenese, 35 (C.), Giuseppe Asti Romano, 40 (C.), Carlo Lunet francese, 35 (P.), Guglielmo Viette francese, 76 (C.), Giovanni Baliardi Romano, 41 (P.), Agostino de Rocchi Romano, 70 (P.), Giuseppe Antonini Milanese, 76 (P.), Gioseppe Ridolfo Todesco, 26 (C.), Mauritio Lorenese, 35 (P.), Sebastiano Condia di Sardegna, 62 (P.), Pietro Gettolini Romano, 26 (C.), Giovanni Antonio Toleti Romano, 70 (C.), Francesco Castaldi Genovese, 35 (P.), Girolamo Bodonio da Piperno, 50 (C.), Giacomo de Pedibus da Fermo, 55 (P.), Alberto Cancerelli da Terni, 50 (P.), Alessio Datij da Loreto, 46 (P.), Pier Andrea Butalini Urbinato, 35 (C.), Carlo Antonio Palutani Romano, 25 (P.), Ludovico Remondi da Parigi, 36 (C), Bonensi Inglese, 30 (P.), etc.

And that is only a sample of the scores of unknowns who constituted the majority of painters in the district. It imparts a stark sense of this lost history and further draws attention to how relatively few painters in the city were native Romans. Among the small number of recognizable names were Giacinto Brandi, Giovanni Angelo Canini, Michelangelo Cerquozzi, Luigi Garzi, Giovanni Francesco Grimaldi, Filippo Lauri, Claude Lorrain, Paolo Porpora, Nicolas Poussin, and Giovanni Stanchi, all of whom were noted as living comfortably. Viviano Codazzi, Gregorio Preti, and 19-year-old Girolamo Troppa were classified as poor. Raffaello Vanni was living in the "rich" convent of S. Maria del Popolo.

It cannot be said how many of the painters in the Campo Marzio fit into Ottonelli and Cortona's second and third categories, but to judge from documented payments to a host of others, it is clear that there were many unknown painters who belonged to the second category: that is, those of modest talent and aptitude who "lived without the benefit of much fame" and yet earned a reasonable wage.

But what, for Ottonelli and Cortona, constituted fame? Did it mean working for important clients? Earning good fees? It most likely was a combination of the two, even if by those criteria we should know about Jacomo di Casselle—or was his name Castelli?—five of whose religious paintings were bought by the Vatican in the 1620s for 77 scudi. And who was Domenico Pichi, from whom the Vatican acquired five more works for the same amount in 1624? If price was an especially important marker of success, then why is Giovan Paolo Gentili/Gentile, a painter-gilder from Fano who in 1607 received 100 scudi from the Vatican for a *Crucifixion*, unknown?[135]

Baglione's Who's Who of Roman artists notwithstanding, Rome's principal families often hired outside of the mainstream. Mattei documents, for instance, record the names of Marco Antonio pittore (25 scudi in 1604 for a *Prospettiva*) and simply a "Pietro," who in 1624 was painting a *Jove* and given 10 scudi on account.[136] For Cardinal Montalto, one Marc'Antonio Magni painted a *Madonna with Sts. Cosmas and Damian* for 12 scudi (1606), plus unspecified work worth 200 to 300 scudi "per servizio della Casa nostra." Montalto paid "mastro Gismondi Pittore fiamengo" 20 scudi for four small paintings (1621) and gave Giovanni Pietro Tranquilli, another unknown painter even though he was a member of the Accademia, some 150 scudi for additional work, partially "nella stanza dove habita il Cardinale Peretti" (1604–5). The cardinal also paid Horatio Zecca/Zeccha 30 scudi for a *Christ Bearing the Cross* (1618) and another 100 scudi (1620) for a *Nativity* and two *Istoriete* for the sacristy of the Cappella Sistina in S. Maria Maggiore.[137]

Later in the century, the Chigi paid a certain Domenico Bassi 25 scudi for *Sts. Peter Martyr and Catherine of Siena with Angels* (1678). His fee was somewhat less than it appears, given that the canvas measured 6 × 10 *palmi* (134 × 223 cm) and Bassi's payment included the "expense of the primed canvas, pigments, and ultramarine."[138]

Working Per Diem

Painters of diverse rank were hired on a daily, weekly, or monthly basis, many of whom were youngsters, adult assistants, and painters from the vanished multitude. As pointed out in the Introduction and in the essay on Florence (also see Renata Ago's discussion of daily employment), per diem payments were not dignified because they put artists on the level of ordinary laborers (a view maintained by Giovanni Battista Paggi in Genoa) or even at the level of "wretched peasants."[139] Mastelletta in Bologna correspondingly balked when a merchant wanted to pay him on the basis of how many days it took for him to paint a *Madonna*.

Nonetheless, some Roman painters of considerable fame, such as Antonio Viviani, called Sordo, agreed to work that way. Having executed various public commissions in Rome (including work for Cardinal Baronio and a series of ceiling frescoes for Alessandro Sforza in the Palazzo Barberini, for which he and his team were paid 1,500 scudi), Viviani merited a short biography by Baglione, who writes that the artist "went about painting by the day, first for this one, then for others, so that he designed few of his own works."[140] Baglione does not mention Viviani's per diem earnings, but Bernardino Cesari, Cavaliere d'Arpino's younger brother and closest follower, in 1589 was paid 6 scudi for 10 days of work in the Cappella della SS. Trinità in the Gesù, the equivalent of 6 giuli per diem.[141] His famous and soon-to-be wealthy brother was paid 8 to 10 giuli a day when a young teenager.[142] A similar fee was given to Paul Bril in 1584 shortly after he settled in Rome: 14.5 giuli for two days of work, 14 giuli for two more days, and 21 giuli for three days.[143] Andrea Camassei in 1635 received 5 to 6 giuli per diem from the Barberini.[144] Another well-known painter, Gaspard Dughet, also accepted per diem wages from the Pamphilj at Valmontone, even though Pier Francesco Mola and Cozza were being paid there by the project.[145]

While all of these payments were at the upper end of the scale for daily work, Camassei's rate is surprising for an artist of his standing, though his earnings in that instance were pure profit. Other artists earned far less. Mario Trotta, who assisted Tassi and Orazio Gentileschi at the Quirinal palace, testified, "I have worked with them at Monte Cavallo this winter on a daily basis and they gave me 3 giuli a day."[146] Likewise, Mario da Pesaro, a pigment grinder, received 3 giuli a day in 1580 "per macinar colori per la cappella Paulina."[147] Nearly 40 years later (1617), "Felipo Palombo macenator di Colori" worked in the Palazzo Borghese for the exact same rate, grinding colors and readying imprimatura for Paolo Piazza.[148] Antiveduto Grammatica paid the unknown Cristoforo Orlandi only 2.5 giuli a day.[149] These rates correspond with what Michelangelo Cinganelli paid two assistants in the Casa Buonarroti in Florence: 5 giuli a day to an experienced painter and 2 giuli to the painter's young helper.[150]

Two basic economic questions pertain to this type of employment: how many days a year did painters such as Trotta and Orlandi work, and how many assistants did masters employ at 2 or 3 to 6 giuli a day?[151]

Neither question can be answered with adequate certainty, though it seems likely that assistants and many per diem painters were lucky if they worked 250 days (as noted in the Introduction, the Genoese Zafferino complained that he could find work only eight or ten days a month), and therefore earned as much as 125 to 150 scudi a year. How many hours a day they worked is a greater unknown.[152] The estimate of 250 days takes into account the inevitability of slack demand and the fact that on *feste di precetto*, Sundays and obligatory feast days when mass was compulsory, many forms of work were prohibited. Even after they were reduced in Rome in 1642, those *feste* numbered over 80, significantly reducing the work year for obedient Romans.[153] That Sundays and holidays were customarily days off for painters is suggested by a document of 1672, in which the landscape specialist Crescenzio Onofri confirmed his payments from the Colonna, whose tally of days Onofri worked (at 1.5 scudi a day) excluded "le feste e le domeniche."[154] Likewise, *muratori* and *stuccatori* hired by the Barberini in the 1630s to prepare the *salone* for Cortona's fresco (Fig. 10) were employed 23 to 25 days a month (at 4 giuli per diem, while a *muratore's* assistant was paid two-thirds as much).[155] And Carlo Ceci, who assisted Giacinto Brandi at S. Silvestro in Capite during 1682–83 (Fig. 16), was paid weekly for six days of labor.[156]

Ottonelli and Cortona address this issue and differentiate between painters and their assistants. It was suitable for the former to work on Sundays and holidays, they held, because painting is a liberal art, yet activity should be restricted to private places. Preparatory labor by *garzoni*, however, such as the grinding of colors and stretching of canvas, being menial work (*opere servili*), was not proper. This distinction they said was "common practice among painters."[157] But not always, as another affirmation of payment, probably of 1617, by an unknown Orazio Mondella indicates. He had been working under Anastasio Fontebuoni in the Palazzo Borghese for "seven continuous months, workdays as well as holidays . . . grinding colors and carrying water and doing whatever Anastasio needed."[158]

Per diem painters, like color grinders and canvas preparators, typically would have been hired as opportunities arose and therefore not been on a regular payroll, unlike some assistants retained by master painters in their shops who might be given room and board and even a wage, though at times payments were withheld until the arrangements ended.[159] A Venetian artist in Rome in 1584, Orfeo Foscari, gave an apprentice, Pietro Paolo Maderni, 18 scudi a year in addition to room and board. Similarly, Pietro Morelli in 1599 agreed to give Stefano Visconti 14 scudi plus room and board.[160] Baglione understood that Girolamo Muziano paid his two favorite assistants 6 scudi a month, which "in that time was worth a lot." That works out to 2.4 giuli daily at 25 days a month.[161]

Despite fairly consistent evidence that extra help could be had for about 3 giuli a day, sometimes with room and board, or up to 5 or 6 giuli on straight contract work—sums that correspond closely with data collected by Elena Fumagalli on Florentine wages—documentation is insufficient to estimate a master painter's annual expenditure on assistants, all the more so because patrons might have paid their wages. In 1607, the Mattei gave Lanfranco's unnamed "aiutanti" 4 giuli a day.[162] During 1610, Paolo Guidotti received 60 scudi a month for three months of labor painting a vault in the Palazzo Giustiniani at Bassano di Sutri, while his two assistants were given 20 and 10 scudi a month on top of his fee.[163] Cortona's assistants working on the ceiling in the Palazzo Barberini (Fig. 10)—Giovanni Francesco Romanelli, Giovanni Maria Bottalla, and Pietro Paolo Baldini—similarly were on the Barberini's payroll at 10 scudi a month, again the equivalent of 4 giuli a day at 25 days.[164] A mason who applied the *arriccio* to the vault also was paid 4 giuli a day.[165] Cortona's assistant in the Chiesa Nuova, "Genovese garzone del S.r Pietro," received 3 giuli a day directly from the church.[166]

On the other hand, the sculptor François Duquesnoy, undoubtedly like many painters, had to cover the cost of his assistants, which reportedly was so high during the five years he carved *St. Andrew* for St. Peter's that the 50 scudi a month he was paid (for a total of 3,000 scudi) were "not sufficient for him, given that he was maintaining men steadily for this purpose at his own expense" and taking on no other work meanwhile.[167]

Most of these examples are of relatively low-wage artists who worked in the service of major patrons and painters. Others, particularly the *pittori grossi*, were associated with picture dealers on a per diem basis, but more reputable painters, too, notably those who specialized in small canvases, might have made similar arrangements.[168] It was not uncommon in Naples, either, for painters of rank such as Cavallino to work for dealers. Pascoli records the example of Christian Reder, one of the last of the Bamboccianti in Rome (d. 1729), who turned out numerous pictures "per Mazzasette rigattiere, che lo teneva anche a giornate a lavorare" (for the secondhand dealer Mazzasette, who also hired him to work on a daily basis).[169]

Even the best-paid painter of the first half of the century, Guido Reni, purportedly made an unusual, temporary deal with a "shrewd old man" by agreeing to work for him for no less than four hours a day at the incredible rate of 10 scudi an hour, during which time Reni could produce two pictures that, Malvasia says, would be resold for 100 scudi apiece, netting the dealer a very handsome profit. In response to criticism that he was denigrating his and the artist's status, Reni made light of the affair by saying that he would have wasted those hours anyway. True or not, he was used to special financial treatment from his years in Rome, where Paul V had coaxed him back to the capital by offering him the extraordinary weekly stipend of 40 scudi plus perks.[170]

By mid-century some artists in Rome entered into "exclusive" contracts with dealers, at least for short

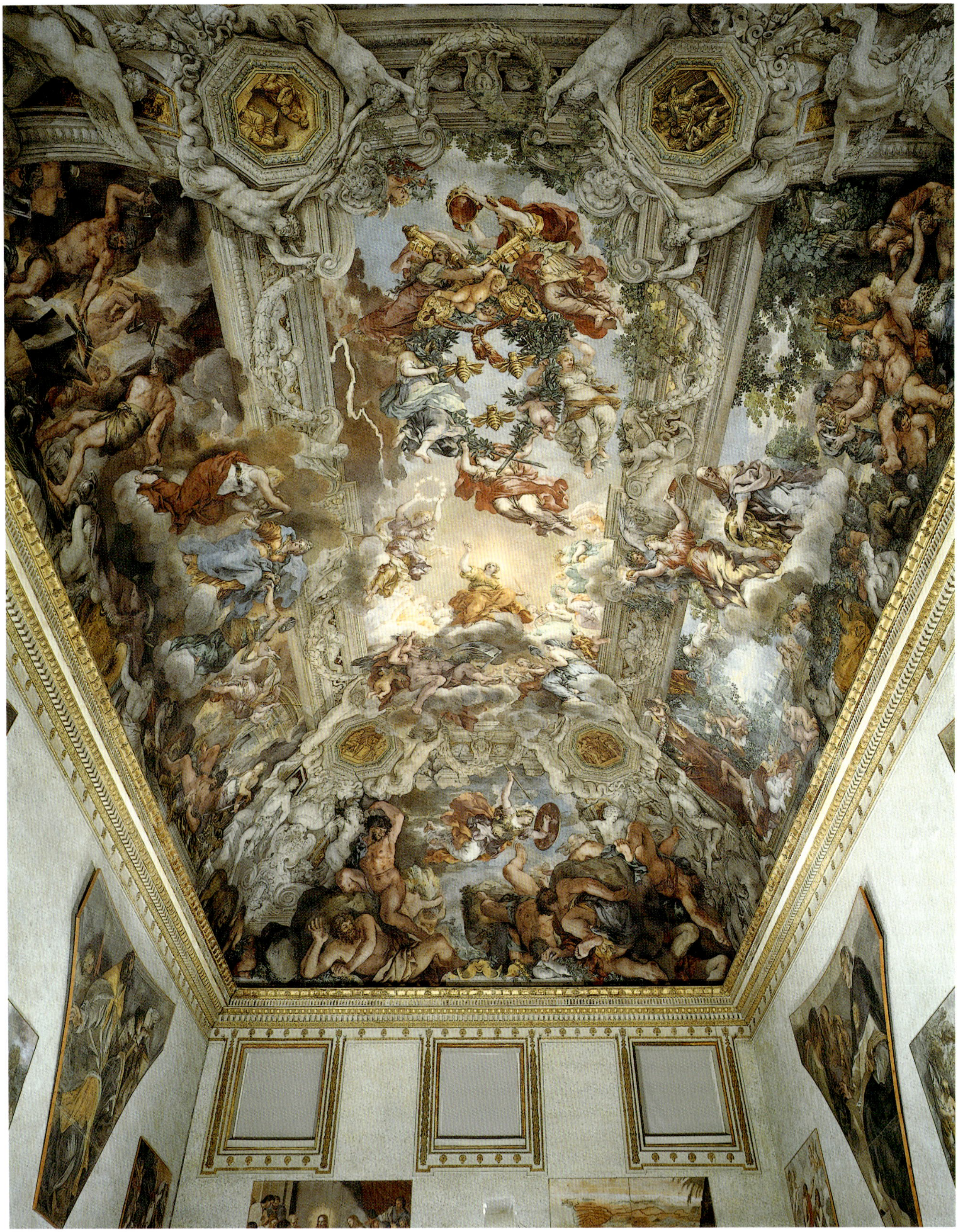

10 Pietro da Cortona, *Glorification of Urban VIII*, 1632–39. Fresco. Palazzo Barberini, Rome.

periods of time, in order to establish their financial base. They might have worked on the dealer's own premises and agreed to a certain rate of production.[171] Before Mario dei Fiori became his own agent, he had agreed to work for a picture-seller "for one continuous year . . . [and] as a man very much of his word he never that year contracted with anyone to produce so much as a sheet of paper; and when he had finished [the year], he wanted his freedom [*volle la sua libertà*] so that he could work to his greatest advantage for whomever sought him out most eagerly."[172]

Decorators and Copyists

Scores of other Roman painters, many of whom were gilders, were hired by wealthy patrons to do architectural decoration in their palaces and villas, but relatively few of their names survive beyond mention in documents. The Giovanni Pietro Tranquilli previously cited might have been one of them. An unidentified Annibale painted the Borghese family's coat of arms on Castel Sant'Angelo, for which he was paid 37.8 scudi in 1615. Pietro Contini also painted "various arms over the door of the castle" for 32 scudi, in addition to "various work" that cost the Vatican another 35 scudi in 1606–7.[173] A "Michel Angelo" worked for the Mattei at their Villa della Navicella in 1603, earning at least 25 scudi painting *grottesche*.[174] Rocco Pasquini most likely painted architectural decoration in 1615 at Cardinal Montalto's villa in Bagnaia, earning more than 175 scudi.[175] Another example specifies the kind of work those painters did. In 1616, Bernardo Polidori Pittore earned 118 scudi for a job in the Palazzo Borghese that consisted of "having painted an extraordinarily large window with grotesques, figures, arms, landscape, fictive stonework . . . for having painted another similar door . . . another painted door . . . for having painted 15 embrasures between doors, and windows . . . and also the embrasure in two rooms . . . with landscapes, figures, and grotesques."[176]

During that same year (1616) a payment to Cesare Rossetti for work in the Quirinal palace breaks down the costs of some decorative elements. Rossetti received 20 scudi for each of four corner frescoes with *putti*, 6 scudi for each of ten landscapes, 15 scudi for each of two coats of arms with *putti*, 20 scudi for each of four Virtues, 20 scudi for an architrave with garlands and small tablets (*cartellette*), 15 scudi for each of two windows with grotesques and landscapes, 24 scudi for two more windows, and 100 scudi for the large coat of arms including its gilding in the center of the vault of the Sala della Virtù where he was working.[177] The career of Giovanni Battista Magno, called Modanino, who established a reputation in Rome and Naples for his skillful ornamentation, is better documented, including collaborative work with Giacinto Brandi in the Colonna palace for which, in 1649, 60 scudi were paid for an elaborate fictive cornice and smaller sums for related decorative features, and other decorative work in 1668–69 and 1674 for Agostino Chigi, who paid Magno nearly 300 scudi.[178]

While architectural decoration was something of a specific market niche, virtually every painter of ambition in seventeenth-century Rome learned to copy, whether with pen or brush, whether from drawings, sculptures, paintings, or the live model. The central place of copying in education, production, and collecting is hard to fathom in an age that privileges originality and copyright law.[179] It is true that already by 1620 or so the cultivated writer and wealthy collector Vincenzo Giustiniani ranked three ways of copying at the bottom of his twelve categories of painting ("distinzioni, e gradi di pittori, del modo di dipingere"), yet his sophisticated taste did not stop many painters from seeking to earn or augment their incomes by copying, or the fanciest of collectors from wanting their work.[180] Nothing prevented artists from copying any painting they or their patrons pleased as long as it was accessible. Occasionally, an owner who was worried about potential damage from tracing would deny access. More rarely, a collector believed that replication of his unique picture ("unico e non copiato" Mancini called a never-copied painting) would *sverginare* it, rob it of its virginity, and thus withheld permission.[181]

Among painters of renown who were perfectly willing to copy on the side, Andrea Commodi, Pietro da Cortona's teacher, was so expert ("unico per far copie di pitture famose," said Cassiano dal Pozzo) that his copies supposedly couldn't be distinguished from originals and brought extraordinary prices.[182] Filippo Baldinucci said the same about Jacopo da Empoli's copies after Andrea del Sarto, that "non era alcuna differenza" between them and the originals, but Baldinucci's greatest praise was for the Roman painter Angelo Caroselli's ability to imitate any artist's manner and to make unrecognizable copies after painters as different as Raphael, Titian, Annibale Carracci, and Caravaggio.[183] Giulio Rospigliosi appreciated that kind of talent, in 1637 writing with pride to his brother about copies after Reni and Guercino "done with infinite diligence by someone who has no equal in copying . . . in short they put the originals to shame."[184] In those cases where both the copyist and his model were

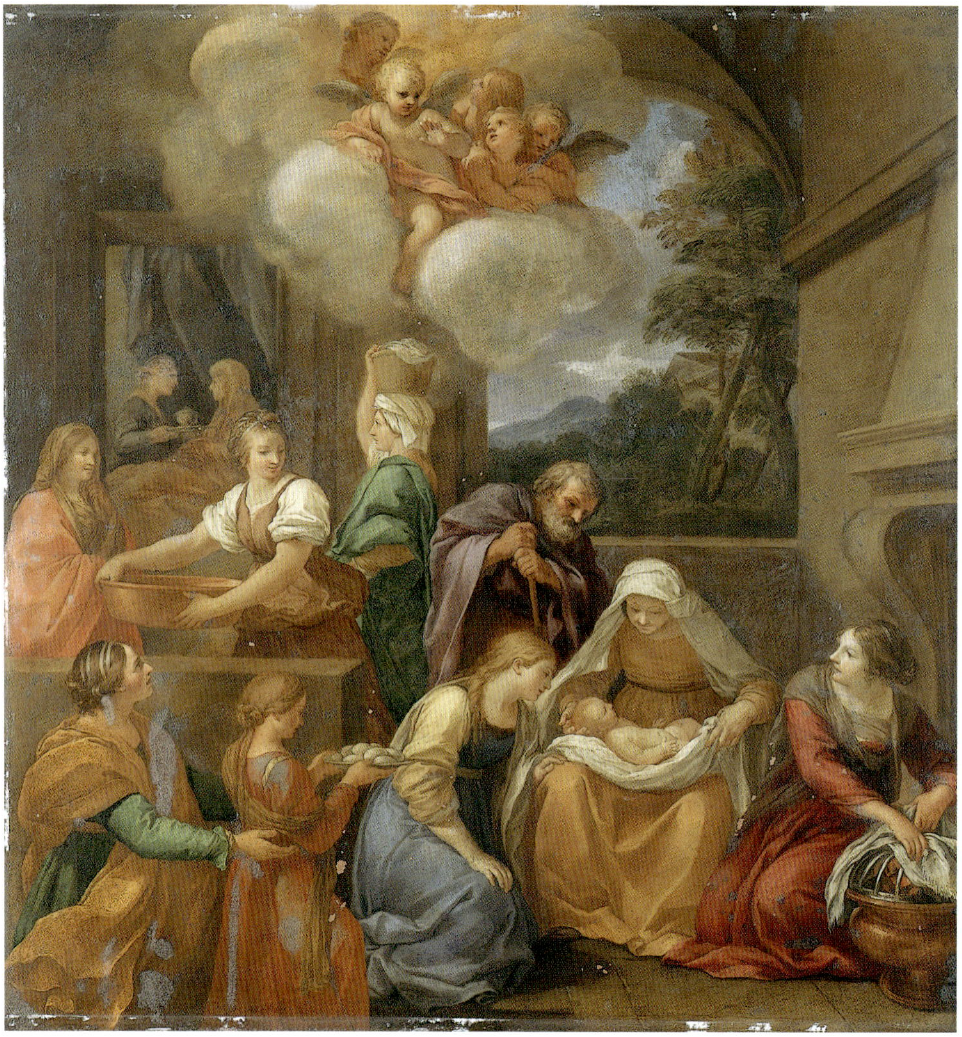

11 Ciro Ferri (after Guido Reni), *Birth of the Virgin*, 1657. Oil on copper, 57 × 54 cm. Private collection.

famous, the copy might merit a premium, as Passeri remarked with regard to a copy by Reni after Raphael: "being by the hand of Guido, [it] came to have some value, because the original is by such a great master and is copied by another of great worth."[185] Similarly, when in 1657 Ciro Ferri painted a copy-variant of Reni's fresco of the *Birth of the Virgin* in the Annunciation chapel in the Quirinal palace (Fig. 11), he received the considerable fee of 160 scudi.[186]

For the most part copies were not made to defraud, though inevitably the status of good ones became confused in the market as they changed hands. Imitations by Caroselli, or those by Pietro Vecchia and Luca Giordano, likewise could be mistaken as originals. In Venice, as Philip Sohm remarks, Sebastiano Ricci and Niccolò Cassana deliberately sold "old masters" at high prices to naive Englishmen.

More typical were the countless minor copyists such as Carlo Magnone (d. 1653). In 1642 the Barberini paid him 20 scudi for his own painting of the *Madonna and Child*, whose dimensions were greater than a *tela d'imperatore* (about 95 × 135 cm). The next year he received 10 scudi for four portraits of the French king, queen, dauphin, and Cardinal Richelieu, and another 12 scudi for an additional portrait of French royalty. Concurrently, in 1642 he earned 10 scudi for copying Sacchi's portrait of *Monsignor Clemente Merlini* (Galleria Borghese, Rome) and 22 scudi for two copies of Caravaggio's *Card Sharps* and *Fortune Teller*. Four years earlier the Barberini had paid him 20 scudi for copying Raphael's cartoon of the *Calling of St. Peter*, the most complex and possibly largest of all these copies.[187] Evidently, for Magnone it did not pay to invent his own designs.

It was characteristic of market demand that the Barberini wanted copies of both Renaissance and modern masters (in Venice, too, the scarcity and high prices of Renaissance paintings buoyed a market for copies). Although he is known by name, no copies (or original work) by Magnone have been identified, largely because there were so many copyists swelling the ranks of Rome's painters.[188] Only occasionally can documents be matched with extant copies, such as a pair of canvases (191/198 × 292/296 cm, Galleria Nazionale d'Arte Antica, Rome) by Giovanni Battista Pace, the little-known son of the still life painter Michele Pace (Michelangelo di Campidoglio), after two of Arpino's huge frescoes in the Capitoline. Pace painted them for the Chigi in 1664 for 50 scudi. At the same time (1664–65), Giuseppe Belloni was copying Romanelli's large *Bacchus and Ariadne* for the considerable fee of 170 scudi, which was increased to 175 scudi for his copy of Romanelli's *Marriage of Peleus and Thetis* in 1673 (both Galleria Nazionale d'Arte Antica, Rome), though his best known pay as a copyist was the 200 scudi he got in 1671–72 for replicating Reni's *Bacchus and Ariadne*.[189] During this time (1666) Salvator Rosa wrote sarcastically that "tutti i signori copiatori" were busy working for the French ambassador, who, not wanting to pay for originals, was having half of Rome copied "dai maggiori scarpinelli della professione" (by the biggest incompetents in the profession).[190]

The vast majority of copyists are anonymous or merely names when cited in documents. To mention a few further examples (continuing with copies after Raphael), in 1602 the duke of Mantua paid 30 scudi for each of 16 copies destined for the Spanish court by Pietro Fachetti after Raphael's designs in the Chigi chapel in S. Maria del Popolo.[191] Gian Maria Roscioli, a cleric in the Barberini circle who became Urban VII's secretary, in 1634 paid 25 scudi for a large (200 × 268 cm) anonymous copy of Raphael's *St. Peter in Prison*. Five years later he spent another 20 scudi on each of two smaller copies (145 × 145 cm) of Raphael's *School of Athens* by unspecified painters.[192] In 1630, Ascanio Pucci, another of the innumerable Roman artists who worked below Thieme-Becker's horizon, received 80 scudi from the Vatican for copying Raphael's *Attila* fresco.[193] While that large sum almost certainly means it was a big, perhaps full-size copy, Pucci's fee was substantial even when compared with rates for original work by master painters. That a copy's size was an important factor in pricing is indicated by two more Vatican payments: in 1633–34, 20 scudi apiece for easel-size copies of Raphael's tapestries by Antonio Eclisse but, again in 1634, four times as much to the equally obscure Ercole Mauritij for an altarpiece-size copy of a *St. Michael Archangel*, possibly after Guido Reni's painting for the Cappuccini. Unusually generous was the Vatican's payment of 180 scudi in 1630 to the young Giacinto Gimignani (b. 1606) for a copy of Raphael's *Battle of Ostia*.[194]

This insatiable demand for copies after Raphael, especially his frescoes in the Stanze, caused significant damage from "ladders, scaffolds, and machines, knocking and scraping the walls, or tracing the outlines of the figures using even water and varnish, which dirty the colors." At least someone who truly understood and loved Raphael's work, Carlo Maratta, was paid to restore them.[195]

Mancini himself was involved in having copies made after Caravaggio as early as 1606, including the master's *Una musica*, *Card Sharps*, and *Fortune Teller*. He wrote to his brother that those he commissioned cost 15 scudi each, a price similar to the 12 scudi Asdrubale Mattei paid in 1626 to one Giovanni di Attilio for copying Caravaggio's *Taking of Christ*.[196] In 1613 a version of the *Fortune Teller* (probably the one in the Louvre) sold for 300 scudi, or nearly 20 times what Mancini had spent not much earlier, so by those standards a copy was a bargain.

Ten to 20 scudi thus appears to have been a normal range for easel-size copies by second-tier and anonymous painters, though some copyists had to settle for less. In 1645 Carlo de Ferrari, a Milanese in Rome, commissioned the Neapolitan painter Sebastiano Coccurulli to make 15 copies "in tela d'imperatore" mostly after Raphael's frescoes in the Farnesina for only 3.5 scudi each.[197] On the basis of the price, one suspects that their quality was low, as a letter of 1684 from Angelo Doni to Francesco Maria de' Medici indirectly suggests. If Francesco Maria wanted some "giovani bravi" (talented young artists) "to copy works by Guido, Raphael, Pietro di Cortona, and the like," Doni cautioned that "one would not spend less than 10 or 12 scudi apiece."[198]

As would be expected, Francesco Maria, like Gian Maria Roscioli, expected to pay a lot less for a copy than an original, regardless of how good and faithful it might be. In 1638, Roscioli paid 60 scudi for a large original (7 × 5 *palmi*) by Andrea Camassei but the next year only a third that sum for an appreciably bigger copy (12 × 7.5 *palmi*) of Camassei's *Diana and Nymphs* (Galleria Nazionale d'Arte Antica, Rome). The same pattern pertained in 1631 when the collector-crook Valguarnera bought Poussin's *Plague of Ashdod* for 110 scudi and the same year paid Angelo Caroselli 35 scudi for copying it.[199]

The widespread practice of distributing portraits of members of the Church, aristocracy, and legendary famous men and women created a huge market for copyists, though copies of portraits, like those of landscapes, tended to be relatively cheap, mirroring the lower esteem and value of those genres in the hierarchy of painting.[200] Payments by the Chigi are characteristic: 90 scudi in 1662 to Giovanni Maria Morandi for eight portraits of various sizes of Cardinal Chigi, three of which were copies; in 1673, 10 scudi for five portrait copies by the unknown Cintio Bocchi; and in 1686, 1.8 scudi for an anonymous copy 3 *palmi* high (67 cm) of the "Ecc.ma Sig.ra D. Agnese Chigi."[201]

Further examples could be cited of payments to the endless copyists ignored by Mancini, Baglione, and the other early biographers, but the prevailing pattern of prices would not be altered, nor would the impression of a thriving market for copies that kept many Roman painters engaged.

Big Business: Pietro da Cortona

It was probably in 1667 when Pietro Berretini da Cortona (1597–1669), Rome's foremost painter, one of its chief architects, and a past *principe* of the Accademia and still a crucial figure in its affairs, felt compelled to draw up a petition to the pope in an effort to collect the remainder of his fee for work in St. Peter's. As of that date he had received only 5,200 of 7,900 scudi due for 32 cartoons he made for mosaics in the basilica. Payments had stopped in 1662, but the artist did not know if it was through "the advice of those who lack experience with this kind of work and cannot judge it, or for some other reason," he wrote, although he suspected that his fee was considered excessive and accordingly he was determined to prove otherwise.[202] His frank petition to the pope is remarkably informative about a variety of artistic and economic issues that he and his high-profile colleagues faced in Rome's competitive art world and that are central to the issues raised throughout this book.

Addressing the Most Blessed Father, he wrote:

> Pietro Berretini, humblest servant of Your Lordship, having provided the bill for the cartoons for the mosaics in the chapel of the Holy Sacrament [Fig. 12] and that of St. Sebastian in St. Peter's, for which . . . 2,700 scudi remain due . . . [considers] himself obligated to demonstrate to Your Lordship that similar cartoons have always been paid at 200 scudi each, for instance to the Cavalier Lanfranco, to Andrea Sacchi [Fig. 10, showing Lanfranco's and Sacchi's cartoons hanging on the walls left and right, and Fig. 15], and to Romanelli, his [Cortona's] student, and that the petitioner not only is satisfied with this same price, but that for those [cartoons] for the pendentives and lunettes he has on his own initiative reduced [the fee] to 150 scudi. And because Your Lordship can with more certainty of fairness make the petitioner rejoice in your favors by treating him equal to the others . . . entreats you to consider that all the altarpieces done for St. Peter's cost 1,000 scudi apiece, [even though] they are not more than a fourth [in size] of one said cupola. As for the . . . single pendentive by the Cavalier Lanfranco, it is equivalent to a portion of a cartoon of the cupola made by the petitioner; and because if one alleges that in size there is a difference of some *palmi*, the petitioner states he has never experienced that paintings are bought and sold by the *palmo* and measurement.

Undaunted by having contradicted himself on whether the size of a work should affect its value (the *palmo* in Rome was 22.35 cm), Cortona shifted focus and continued:

> It further is said that [paintings] in oil are valued more than those in fresco. As for this, one replies that the same study and labor one puts into a work in oil one puts into a fresco. Others say that the spaces between one figure and another are a weakness, [which] shows a lack of understanding of painting because sometimes those spaces are necessary for artistic reasons, as the petitioner has done, and not to save labor. Moreover, to provide a modern example regarding prices, recently 3,600 scudi were paid to the Cavalier Bernini for only two clay models of two figures for the Cathedra [Petri], whose labor it seems should not be compared with a single cupola, for which no more than 3,200 scudi is claimed; more was paid [to Cortona], 4,000 scudi, for the cupola of the Chiesa Nuova; [thus] the petitioner has made the price 800 scudi less. . . . Whence the petitioner, who does not ask for any gift, as is done by others, but only suitable payment for his labors, humbly entreats His Holiness . . .[203]

As Cortona strove to refute the possible reasons for which payments had been suspended, he sought to cover himself on all fronts. Foremost was his contention that his pricing was fair in market terms: that important painters like himself, notably Lanfranco and Sacchi, and even his own student Romanelli, were paid a certain fee for comparable work and therefore he

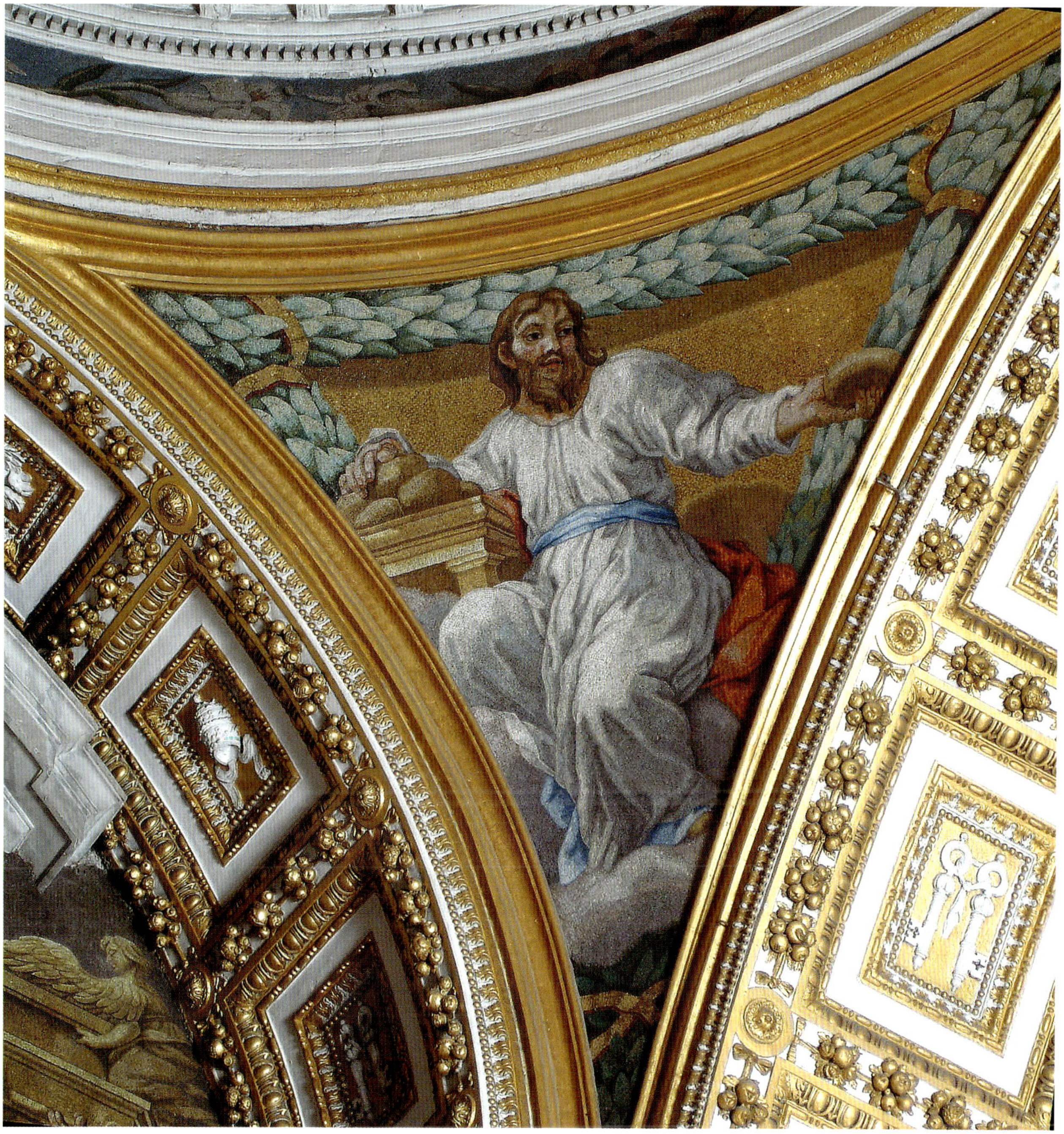

12 Pietro da Cortona (design by), *A Priest Dispensing Ceremonial Bread*, 1650s. Mosaic (executed by Orazio Manenti). Chapel of the Holy Sacrament, St. Peter's, Rome.

deserved as much; even so, he was willing "on his own initiative" to give a 25 percent discount. Cortona was correctly informed that a few decades earlier Lanfranco, Sacchi, and Romanelli had received 200 scudi for similar cartoons. He further maintained that his price was fair in terms of labor expended as determined by size. Again he was generally right in arguing that the new altarpieces in St. Peter's could (though not always did) cost 1,000 scudi, but he disregarded the fact that those exceptionally high payments were for enormous paintings and included pigment costs. For the *Death of Sapphira*, for instance, Cristofano Roncalli spent 111.5 scudi of his 800 scudi fee on ultramarine.[204]

To drive home his point about the value of labor, Cortona cited Bernini's large compensation for two clay models (paying no heed to how much of them had been executed by assistants), which he claimed did not compare to his work on just one of the two vaults he had designed.[205] Most likely he did not yet know that for the recently completed Cathedra Petri Bernini was paid 8,000 scudi (a substantial 200 scudi per month for 40 months). Instead, he compared his asking price of 3,200 scudi with the 4,000 scudi he himself had received for painting the cupola of the Chiesa Nuova, but without acknowledging that the latter project was executed in fresco from scaffolding whereas the cartoons for St. Peter's were painted more comfortably and doubtlessly more quickly in his studio.

Paying per Figure

It is ironical that Cortona was prompted to defend his artistic judgment by explaining that space between figures could be an aesthetic virtue and not a money-saving tactic. A generation earlier in the famous debates that allegedly occurred in the Accademia between Cortona's and Sacchi's supporters over what constituted good narrative composition, it was Sacchi's classicist, one might say Miesian view that less is more when it came to figural density as long as all essential personae are present, versus Cortona's Venturian rebuttal that less is a bore because epical richness is admirable.[206] It is similarly ironical that another prototypical "classical" artist, Domenichino, was accused in Naples of stuffing his designs with too many figures in order to make more money.[207] Whether or not the charge had any merit, the issue was important inasmuch as the long legacy of painting as a manual rather than a liberal art meant that pricing still could be linked to measurable labor (a cost–price relationship), and one clear way to do so was to pay by the figure.[208] Even late in the century Bellori saw a need to criticize the correlation between value and labor by condemning

> those men [who] are in a position to give remuneration for some work of painting, even if excellent and bears a famous name, [and] do not measure its merits otherwise than by the time spent, and they want to reckon the money by counting the days, as in the case of other common labors; if they knew how much it takes and how one has to rack one's brains to apply a brushstroke well to the canvas, they would not talk this way. . . . When one is to put a price on a painting by a man of worth, one's attention should not be focused on the time that he puts into it in the present; but one must recall the long exertions made over so many years.[209]

Guercino calculated his fees according to a *prix fixe*: 100 scudi per full-length figure, 50 for half-lengths, and 25 for heads.[210] While working in Naples, Domenichino was paid by the deputies of the Cappella del Tesoro di S. Gennaro on a similar basis, 105 ducats per figure, a rate significantly lower than the 130 ducats Reni had negotiated a decade earlier before he backed out of the prestigious job.[211] (Christopher Marshall points out that Reni's fee was the most expensive ever agreed in the history of Neapolitan baroque painting.) The deputies' accounting of more than 20,000 ducats' worth of Domenichino's work is a rare record of how some patrons calculated what constituted a figure when it was not obvious: a certain number of *putti* in one case, five heads of seraphs in another, an architectural and landscape background with a soldier on horseback, or four horses pulling a chariot, and so on.[212]

Although not one Roman example of this kind of contractual, meticulous counting of figures has come to my attention, painters and clients often thought in similar terms when negotiating fees, even if the exact number of figures was not a clear-cut basis for pricing. As a matter of fact, in 1637, long before drawing up his petition to the pope, Cortona was recommended by Giulio Rospigliosi to his brother Camillo in Pistoia as the best artist in Rome, yet he cautioned Camillo that Cortona charged 100 scudi for just one or two figures whereas other good painters without a big name ("ma non di grosso nome") would settle for half that amount. On the other hand, anyone could hire Reni or Guercino, but Giulio said that doing so would require more patience and the expense would be at least 150 scudi a figure.

Seven months later Giulio wrote again, now worried that, by stopping off in Bologna, Cortona might get the idea of raising his fees and "bring back here the prices of paintings prevailing in Bologna. . . . There they are without limit and Sig. Guido Reni is paid 200 scudi d'oro a figure and now he has a commission to do a painting for Crema with an agreement to pay him 2,000 scudi and a present of linens and leave it up to him to put in as many figures as he wishes."

Reni decided on four figures and three *putti* for his altarpiece in Crema.[213] His usual approach to important commissions was entirely unlike Guercino's: he relied on his celebrity status and the generosity of his patrons by waiting until they saw his finished product, hoping they would increase his compensation beyond what he

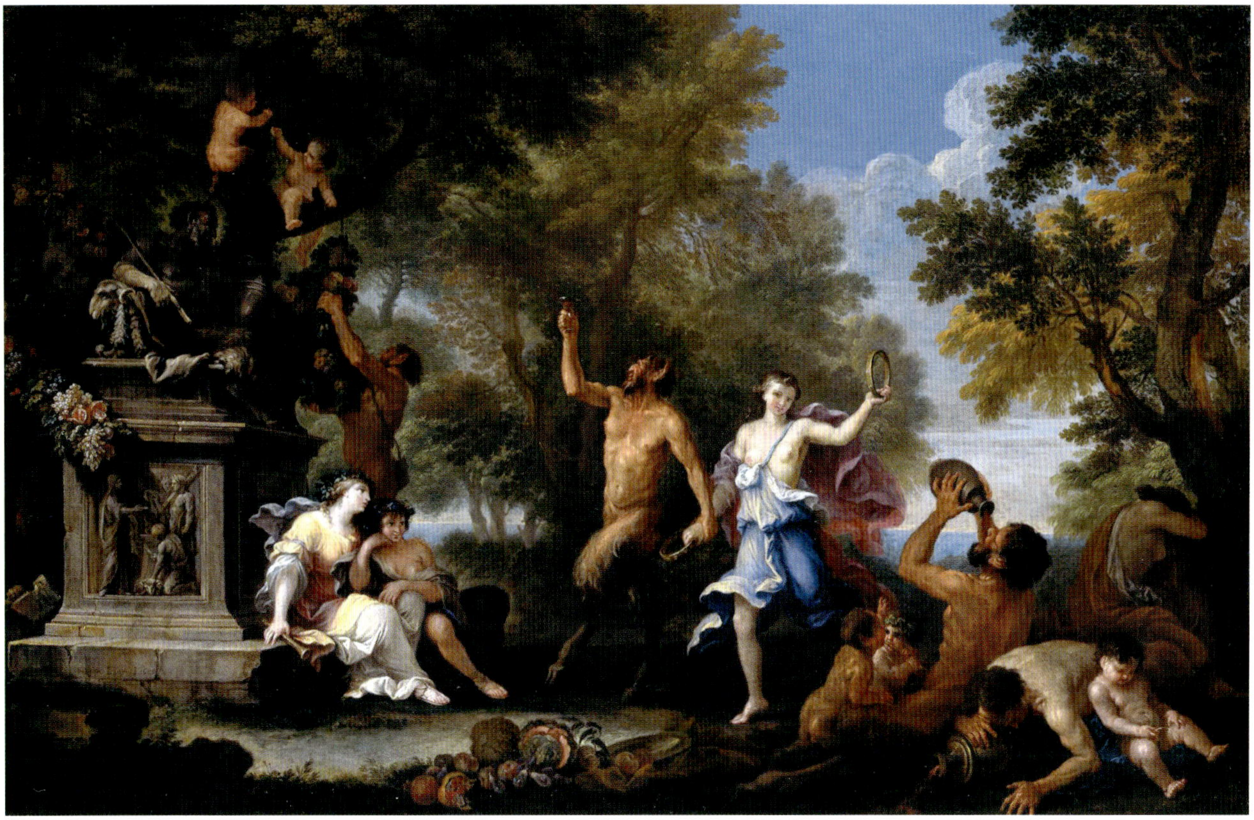

13 Filippo Lauri, *Bacchanal with Offering to Pan*, signed and dated 16?5. Oil on canvas, 43.5 × 70.5 cm. P. & D. Colnaghi & Co., Ltd., London.

would have asked. While Reni supposedly did not want to talk about prices, his tactics reveal a gambling, calculating attitude, unlike that of Guercino, or of Poussin, who "never discussed the price of his paintings" with his close patrons "but when he had completed them he would mark it on the back of the canvas, and the amount would be sent to him at home, immediately, without any subtractions."[214]

Nevertheless, even Reni could not escape thinking about value in terms of figures. In a letter of 1628 on the subject of his latest prices, which is discussed further by Raffaella Morselli, he explained that there were three kinds of painters. The lowest, the *pittori più bassi*, made full-size figures worth no more than 2 or 3 scudi apiece; figures by the *pittore ordinario* commanded 15 scudi; and the somewhat *straordinario* painter—praise to God, like Reni himself—the quality of whose art, by reaching the level of gift-giving to "signori grandi," frequently merited pricing beyond such measure.[215]

Rospigliosi's and Reni's letters make clear that the basis of pricing was flexible, and therefore how impossible it is without detailed documents to calculate and compare prices only on the basis of the number of figures or a canvas's size. In general, as Christopher Marshall points out with regard to Naples, bigger paintings cost more than smaller ones, just as more figures tended to command higher fees. The example of Roman-born Filippo Lauri, however, resists that generalization. He made a reputation—and considerable fortune, as his estate of 12,000 scudi indicates (see Table 8)—by specializing in small cabinet paintings, often with religious and mythological scenes in landscape settings (Fig. 13), and by producing still lifes as well.[216] His success in painting frescoes for the Farnese, Chigi, and Borghese families notwithstanding, Lauri "resolved to put aside grand work," wrote his biographer Francesco Saverio Baldinucci, and turned to marketing numerous small canvases. As noted in the Introduction, Baldinucci reports that, for a *quadretto* measuring just a *palmo* (22.35 cm) with two *figurine*, Lauri could easily get 60 scudi; for those measuring 1.5 *palmi*, 100 scudi; and for paintings of 4 *palmi*—like the signed one illustrated in Fig. 13—less than a meter, 160 scudi.[217] More incredible is the example of Elsheimer's small *Flight into Egypt* (31 × 41 cm, 1609, Alte Pinakothek, Munich) priced at 300 scudi.

Similarly, Carlo Dolci's small paintings (see the essay on Florence) were sold at a considerable premium due to high demand, relatively limited supply, and in his case the obvious labor expended, meaning that style or handling could be an important factor in pricing, too. Perhaps the most extreme seventeenth-century example of this is the work of Frans van Mieris, one of Leiden's *fijnschilders* or "fine painters." It is estimated that on one panel, probably the *Doctor's Visit* (J. Paul Getty Museum, Los Angeles), which measures just 44 × 33 cm, he spent 300 hours and, on an hourly basis, was paid 1,500 guilders (nearly 500 scudi), twice the price of an average Dutch house. Another of his small pictures cost 2,000 guilders, the same amount Rembrandt received for his huge *Night Watch* (originally about 440 × 500 cm, Rijksmuseum, Amsterdam). This expensive taste for painstaking technique was shared by some Italians, such as Cosimo III de' Medici, who visited van Mieris in the Netherlands in 1669 and commissioned genre scenes and self-portraits from him. Reportedly, Cosimo offered twice the asking price of the *Doctor's Visit* but still failed to acquire it. He managed to purchase the *Family Concert* (Uffizi, Florence), which measures 51.8 × 40.2 cm and cost 2,500 guilders, about 750 scudi. Clearly, a work done with great meticulousness, "gran nettezza" as Cosimo's agent described Van Mieris's style, could elevate its price dramatically.[218]

Moreover, a large canvas with empty space—or too much space between figures, as Cortona thought might have been a criticism of his cartoons—was not necessarily more valuable than a smaller, densely packed composition. For Francesco Albani, size became a matter of prestige as his reputation shifted during his later Bolognese years from that of a painter of altarpieces to a specialist in small canvases and coppers. His resentment of the shift probably had less to do with money, inasmuch as he was earning a lot by flooding the market with studio pictures, than a suspicion that his position as a serious history painter was threatened, which turns out to have been right. Rosa was similarly vexed that his small landscapes were overshadowing his larger figural paintings. He expressed surprise and sadness that a "little landscape" from his own hand was worth as much as a small painting by the celebrated "povero Albano," as he called Albani in 1652.[219] Malvasia came to the defense of small paintings by pointing out their distinguished place in the oeuvres of Brueghel, Giulio Clovio, Tassi, Cerquozzi, Jacques Courtois, and Pieter van Laer—none of whose reputations, however, rested on history painting.[220]

Quantifying by Size and Figures: Frescoes and Altarpieces

Bearing in mind Cortona's remark that "he has never experienced that paintings are bought and sold by the *palmo* and measurement" (a claim at odds with how murals often were paid for in Florence, where Cortona himself had worked), it remains tempting to tabulate data on prices and on the numbers of figures in paintings and their sizes in order to test the validity of quantifying such data and making comparisons, whether between the value of different artists, between fresco, oil painting, and mosaic, or between pricing in our five cities.[221] Unfortunately, the many variables and lack of adequate documentation compromise such efforts, as analysis of data I have gathered on Rome and the tables in our essays indicate.[222] Information on the actual techniques painters in seventeenth-century Italy used for their "frescoes" is spotty, that is to say whether it was entirely traditional *buon* fresco, a mixed technique, mainly *al secco*, etc. Throughout our book, "fresco" therefore pertains to a wide range of mural painting, generally on wet plaster.

No painter in Rome knew the ins and outs of fresco painting more thoroughly than Cortona. By the time he drafted his petition, he had worked at S. Bibiana, the Chiesa Nuova, the Palazzo Barberini (Fig. 10), the Palazzo Pitti in Florence, and the Palazzo Pamphilj in Piazza Navona. The documents on these principal projects, like those by other Roman painters of the time, provide limited evidence for answering a variety of financial questions about fresco painting, including its production cost as compared with oil painting, how often patrons or artists paid for the materials, and if fees for frescoes tended to be higher than for altarpieces, their closest equivalent in prestige. A major problem is that while contracts for altarpieces routinely specify dimensions and sometimes even the number of figures required, fresco contracts do not, nor are data on surface dimensions of frescoes often available.

Reputation, perhaps the least of quantifiable factors, could profoundly affect the financial terms of any contract or sale. When hired at S. Bibiana, Cortona was a promising painter at the beginning of his Roman career. He was paid 320 scudi for five frescoes while his much-senior Tuscan compatriot, Agostino Ciampelli, who already had worked at the Lateran and other major Roman churches, received 850 scudi for comparable decoration in the same church.[223] Such were the realities of market forces, as Mancini recognized when he wrote that one factor determining the price of a work of art is "whether an artist has acquired fame or not; many painters today, in particular Caravaggio and

Spagnoletto [Ribera], started out working well without fame and reputation."[224] As Christopher Marshall shows, Ribera's prices rose very quickly.

Baldassare Croce, in spite of having acquired fame in Rome, faced the reality of shifting fortune when the upstart Guido Reni, nearly 20 years his junior, became Paul V's favorite painter. In 1609–11, the pope paid Reni 2,000 scudi for his and his assistants' frescoes and oil altarpiece in the Annunciation chapel in the Quirinal palace, but for a similar, contemporaneous project in the Nativity chapel in the same palace (though without an altarpiece or as many minor frescoed compartments), Croce received 700 scudi.[225]

Collectors were well aware of the value of reputation, which in essence they themselves created. A classic example dates to 1608, when the Mantuan ambassador in Rome wrote back to the court about an unidentified painting by Roncalli that Rubens said was worth 400 scudi d'oro (already discounted from 500 scudi d'oro) and, the ambassador added, was by a master "considered among the top in Rome." The Duchess Eleonora replied that, while she did not intend to discuss the price, she observed that it had cost 350 scudi to acquire Caravaggio's *Death of the Virgin* (Louvre, Paris), that it was larger, and that Caravaggio was "più famoso e tenuto in maggior pregio del Pomarancio" (more famous and held in higher esteem than Roncalli). The same attitude was expressed 25 years earlier in Venice regarding Tintoretto's and Veronese's high prices: "You pay for the painter's fame."[226]

Like any artist of high ambition, Cortona would aim to defend his worth by comparing himself to esteemed and successful colleagues, picking with care examples of generous payments, given how uneven they could be. In 1670, for instance, close to the date of his petition, Ciro Ferri, his own pupil and closest disciple, was paid 6,000 scudi for frescoing the lantern and cupola of S. Agnese in Agone (that was 50 percent more than Volterrano would be paid a decade later for the most expensive, largest baroque cupola in Florence).[227] Yet the same year, the younger and less-established Filippo Gherardi was paid 1,500 scudi for frescoing with Giovanni Coli (both of whom studied with Cortona) the lantern and cupola of S. Nicola da Tolentino. Theirs was a smaller job that took 15 months to complete, but their fee, while not proportionate to Ferri's in terms of labor, arguably was proportionate in terms of fame. Another of Cortona's followers, Pietro Paolo Ubaldini, had frescoed the four pendentives in S. Nicola da Tolentino earlier (1643) for only 80 scudi.[228]

Ferri already had been hired to complete Cortona's Sala di Apollo in the Palazzo Pitti when the master stopped working for the Medici. Ferri was paid a remarkably generous 1,500 scudi for his minor share (see Elena Fumagalli's analysis of this commission). At the time of the petition, Cortona let it be known that his fee for painting a monumental altarpiece in S. Ivo alla Sapienza would be 1,000 scudi, which prompted his clients to rethink their commitment. It, too, was left unfinished when Cortona died in 1669.[229] Again Ferri was considered to complete the project, but he was turned down for asking the exorbitant sum of 900 scudi, the same price he later wanted for painting the high altar of S. Maria Maddalena de' Pazzi in Florence (Fig. 63).[230] Even so, Ferri was hired by the Fabbrica to complete Cortona's last cartoons for St. Peter's.

Perhaps because he was cast in Cortona's mold, Ferri developed a reputation as being expensive, for wanting, as pointed out in the Introduction, "to be known by others for the prices he commands." Already in 1657 his small copy after Reni (Fig. 11) cost 160 scudi. In another letter from Rome to Francesco Maria de' Medici, Angelo Doni wrote in 1685 that Ferri's canvases are rare because usually the painter works on a large scale, meaning fresco, and "those which are for sale increase in price daily"—a classic case of demand exceeding market supply. Doni continued by saying that those paintings that were available, and for which Ferri wanted at least 200 scudi each, had three figures. Then in a revealing comment that Cortona would have seconded but hesitated to tell the pope, Doni warned that "with this kind of painter of top fame one cannot haggle over prices as Your Highness knows. . . . Carlo Maratta certainly would want more and, although universally he has greater approval, those who really know *disegno* give top honor to Ferri."

Ferri could negotiate from a position of strength as a painter in both fresco and oil (and as a very successful designer of sculpture and architecture, too), as another letter from Doni confirms, in which he explained that Ferri would not part with two oil paintings for 100 doppie, the equivalent of a little more than 300 scudi. "Persisting with his initial price of 200 scudi each and assuming he'd get 350 scudi from the Marchese Pallavicino, who commissioned them to resell at a higher price, I frankly told him that the small number of figures makes me think he had inflated the price too much; it could be that, hard-pressed by something, he would make up his mind to let them go, but I don't hope for it, since these top artists protect the utmost reputation of their works."[231]

Reni was unrivalled in that regard. The cardinals at St. Peter's had to bend over backwards to get him to return to Rome in the later 1620s to paint an altarpiece in St. Peter's. They agreed to pay him more than anyone else, 1,600 scudi, twice the price of his oil altarpiece of the *Trinity* for SS. Trinità dei Pellegrini, which depicted the same subject, was very close in date, and was roughly half as big. Furthermore, they allowed him to work in fresco rather than in oil on stucco. Aware of artists' jealousies and sense of self-esteem, the cardinals agreed that "we would be well advised to arrange payment [to Reni] in such a way that the other painters will not feel encouraged to make similar claims. This is especially important because Reni will be working in fresco, and will have only half the expenses of those working in oil on stucco." After Reni abandoned the job in a huff, it was given to Cortona, who painted the altarpiece in oil on stucco and was paid the more customary sum of 1,000 scudi.[232]

Reni's fee actually is less exceptional when compared with his *Trinity* for SS. Trinità dei Pellegrini on the basis of size. For the fresco in St. Peter's, he would have earned about 53 scudi per square meter, not significantly more than the 47 scudi per square meter for the oil altarpiece. Similarly, to judge from his preparatory drawing for the abandoned fresco, the per figure rate would have been no higher at St. Peter's.

During the decades before Reni became Italy's most expensive painter, that distinction belonged to Federico Barocci, who "lived a very comfortable life of wealth" and "left a copious amount of money because he was paid whatever he wanted for his works, without argument," according to Bellori.[233] For a relatively small altarpiece of the *Institution of the Eucharist* in S. Maria sopra Minerva (1603–7), Barocci was given nearly 1,500 scudi, the equivalent of an exceptional 291 scudi per square meter. At the same time (1604) he painted a *Crucifixion* (Prado, Madrid) for 300 scudi, a fifth as much and a meager 33 scudi per meter.[234] The *Crucifixion*, however, contains only the figure of Christ, meaning its per figure rate is exceptionally high at 300 scudi, while the *Institution of the Eucharist* has a crowd equal to nine or so figures, making its per figure rate about 165 scudi, reversing the disparity between these examples. Neither comparison takes into account the fact that the figure of Christ is about 2 meters tall, whereas those in the *Institution of the Eucharist* are no more than about 1.2 meters.

The problems with such comparisons are manifest in a few further examples. Around 1590, Arpino frescoed two walls of equal size in S. Atanasio dei Greci for 75 scudi apiece.[235] While payment for them amounted to just 9.5 scudi per square meter, one scene (the *Crucifixion*) has three figures, the other (the *Coronation of the Virgin*) closer to ten, undermining the concept that the number of figures affected the price of history paintings, unless the total fee simply was being split without regard to differences in the scenes.

A few years later, Arpino was paid 200 scudi for his oil altarpiece of the *Annunciation* in the Aldobrandini chapel in S. Maria in Via and the same amount for two lateral frescoes of the *Nativity* and *Adoration of the Magi*. The altarpiece and frescoes are comparable in size, but the frescoes contain many more figures. Whether, as it would seem, the patrons considered the oil altarpiece to be of greater worth than the frescoes or possibly divided up their funds as they paid for the three scenes is unknown.[236] What is clear is that when, in 1624, a modest fee of 30 scudi was given to each of six different artists for their altarpieces in S. Crisogono (see Table 5), the *prix fixe* ignored the number of figures, even though they varied from just a little more than one to five.[237]

Because Arpino's frescoes in the Aldobrandini chapel were lateral murals, elaborate scaffolding was not needed. When it was, the cost could be significant. Just the partial expenses for the wood and carpentry of Cortona's scaffolding in the Palazzo Barberini amounted to about 400 scudi.[238] As was commonly expected of patrons, Cardinal Francesco Barberini covered its cost.

Pigments for fresco probably cost less than those for oil painting. Some of them differed because the action of lime discolors organic and artificial colors. Earth pigments, which as a category were the cheapest to buy, worked well on wet plaster, but so did the most expensive of all colors, ultramarine blue. For instance, when Domenico Passignano's work in the New Sacristy of S. Maria Maggiore was appraised in 1610 at 3,014 scudi, it included 125 scudi "for the ultramarine blue used in said project in fresco as well as in oil."[239] Its cheaper substitute, however, azurite, which commonly was used in oil painting to "stretch" ultramarine, could turn green in fresco, prompting the use of a still-cheaper blue, smalt. Some lakes that were very costly also were incompatible with fresco.[240] Two more savings in working in fresco were the expense of oil, which in seventeenth-century Rome cost about seven to eight baiocchi a pound, and varnish, which in 1614–17 ranged from nine baiocchi a pound for "Vernice Venetiana" to ten times as much for "Vernice fina da quadri."[241]

More data are required before it can be said if it definitely was cheaper to paint in fresco than oil, not only because there were so many variables in the quality and quantities of pigments used in different jobs, but also because a fresco painter might or might not have been responsible for the cost of preparing a wall, or an oil painter for buying his canvas and stretcher. I suspect, as the cardinals of St. Peter's observed, that generally fresco was the cheaper medium by measure, but even so that does not take into account the overhead of hiring more assistants for elaborate projects at 5 to 6 giuli a day.

Domenichino's reputation rests primarily on his frescoes, although his pay per meter was significantly higher for his oil altarpieces. Two masterpieces from the same period of his career are characteristic. His five frescoes of 1611/12–15 depicting the life of St. Cecilia in the Polet chapel in S. Luigi dei Francesi cover about 35 square meters. The total payment of 300 scudi works out to 8.5 scudi per square meter. His most famous painting, the *Last Communion of St. Jerome* (frontispiece) of 1612–14 (Pinacoteca Vaticana), measures nearly 11 square meters. Domenichino was paid 240 scudi for it, nearly three times the price of the Polet frescoes as gauged by surface dimensions as well as by the number of figures. For a small altarpiece of 1616, *St. Ignatius's Vision at La Storta* (Los Angeles County Museum of Art), his fee was seemingly paltry, 50 scudi. Yet its payment per meter was nearly 23 scudi, again thrice that of the Polet payment though not better on a per figure basis. The artist's top fees by either measure were for two other altarpieces, 1,200 scudi for the *Martyrdom of St. Agnes* (Pinacoteca nazionale, Bologna), 66 scudi per square meter and 80 per figure, whose high price tellingly was established by Reni, and the relatively still better fee of 800 scudi, or about 120 scudi per meter and 100 per figure, for the smaller *Conversion of St. Paul* (Cathedral, Volterra).[242]

The fee of 100 scudi for Scipione Pulzone's *Lamentation* (Metropolitan Museum of Art, New York) painted for the Gesù in 1590–91 is exceptionally high in relation to its size, the equivalent of 129 scudi a meter, but is low on a per figure basis, only 17 scudi.[243] By the latter gauge but not the former, Caravaggio consistently was better paid. For the *Calling of St. Matthew* in the Contarelli chapel, he received a measly 18 scudi a meter, about 27 scudi per figure; for the first version of *St. Matthew with the Angel*, 37.5 scudi a meter, 75 scudi per figure (a significantly higher rate than for the Contarelli lateral canvases); for the Cerasi *Crucifixion of St. Peter*, again 37.5 scudi a meter, more than 40 scudi per figure; for the *Seven Acts of Mercy* in Naples, 34 scudi a meter, roughly 45 scudi a figure; and for the *Flagellation* in Naples, 40 scudi a meter, 61.5 scudi figure, his highest per figure fee, which nonetheless pales in comparison with those mentioned that Guercino, Reni, and some other painters commanded.

Roman altarpieces by the Caravaggisti are relatively few. The highest per figure rate might have been for Vouet's lost altarpiece for St. Peter's, which cost 800 scudi, but its appearance is known only through fragmentary evidence.[244] Baglione's lost *Resurrection* for the Gesù (1601–3), which cost 1,000 scudi—much more than Caravaggio at the time had received for any painting—became the catalyst of Caravaggio's envy and scurrilous poems against the artist. To judge from its *modello* (Louvre, Paris), the artist earned about 100 scudi a figure, approximately the same rate that Spadarino earned on his altarpiece in St. Peter's.[245] Valentin's *Martyrdom of Sts. Processus and Martinian* (Fig. 14), another commission from the Fabbrica, cost 350 scudi, 50 more than Spadarino's painting, but the equivalent of only about 50 scudi per figure. A still lower rate, roughly 40 scudi a figure, pertains to Honthorst's *St. Paul Caught up in the Third Heaven* for S. Maria della Scala (S. Maria della Vittoria, Rome), which cost only about 90 scudi, but whether it qualifies as being "Caravaggesque" is debatable.[246] The same is true of Angelo Caroselli's *St. Wenceslas* (Kunsthistorisches Museum, Vienna). Equal in size to Valentin's altarpiece in St. Peter's, its fee was relatively low for a commission from the Fabbrica, just 250 scudi. Nonetheless, its per figure rate was high, about 200 scudi.[247] Payments to Orazio Gentileschi for two altarpieces are documented. For his large, densely figured *Circumcision* sent to Ancona, he received a good fee, 303 scudi, but a rate of only about 30 scudi per figure. His sizeable *Baptism* for S. Maria della Pace cost only 150 scudi, the equivalent of just 20 scudi per figure.[248]

Baglione's, Vouet's, Valentin's, and Spadarino's paintings were the most expensive Caravaggesque altarpieces in Rome (Orazio's *Circumcision* is left out of that group because it was destined for a provincial location), in part due to their large size (see Table 3). All four payments exceeded those for Caravaggio's public Roman work, which in general were 150 or 200 scudi a painting, exceptionally reaching 280 for the *Death of the Virgin* (Louvre, Paris). His altarpiece and two large lateral canvases in the Contarelli chapel together cost 550 scudi, the identical sum Vouet was offered for his large lateral canvases and frescoed pendentives and vault in the Alaleone chapel in S. Lorenzo in Lucina (1624).[249]

That public commissions in Rome were awarded to only a few of the Caravaggisti, despite their belonging to the Accademia (Bigot, Borgianni, Cavarozzi, Ducamps, Guy François, Orazio Gentileschi, Grammatica, Manfredi, Renieri, Ribera, Riminaldi, Saraceni, Spadarino, Vouet), indicates that membership in the organization was no guarantee of public advancement and financial success.[250] A case in point is Alessandro Turchi, a provincial artist who moved to Rome for his

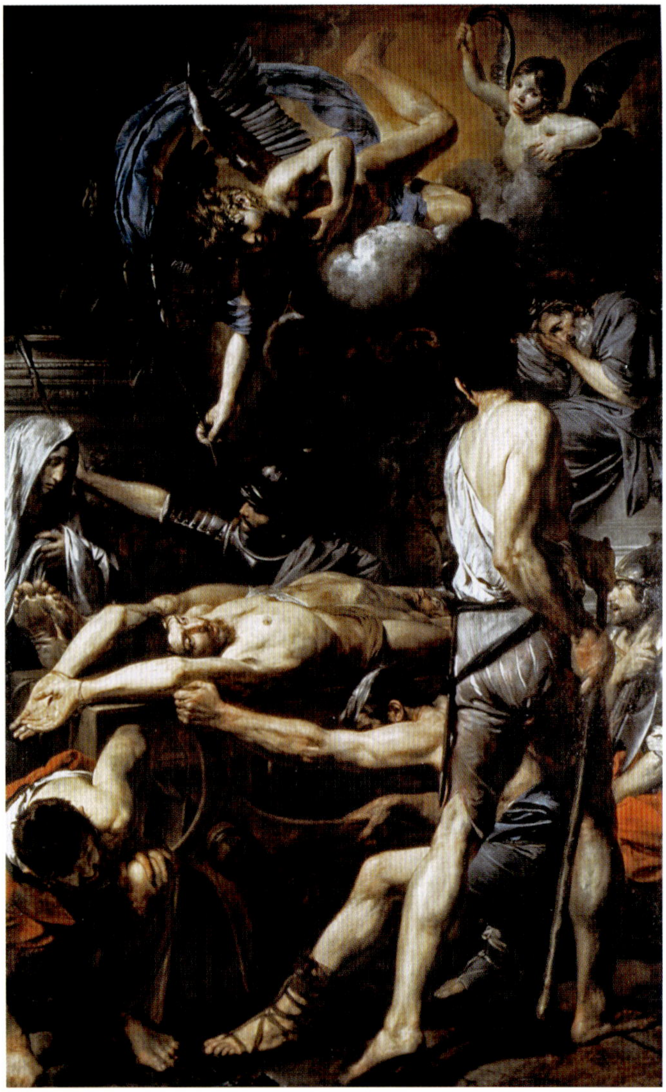

14 Valentin, *Martyrdom of Sts. Processus and Martinian*, 1629–30. Oil on canvas, 320 × 186 cm. St. Peter's, Rome.

entire career, played a big role in the life of the Accademia, became its *principe* in 1637, and yet his important commissions came mostly from Veronese, not Roman, patrons.

Many of Caravaggio's followers, especially those who adopted the "Manfredi manner," specialized in easel or gallery pictures, for which documentation is scant. Although Mancini relates that, at the time he was writing, Manfredi's art was held in "grandissima stima," citing the example of Grand Duke Cosimo II's payment of 300 to 400 scudi for some of the artist's work, individually the paintings were not particularly expensive. In 1621, the year before he died, Manfredi was paid 100 scudi by Piero Guicciardini, the grand duke's ambassador in Rome, for two paintings with three figures each, the equivalent per picture of what Guercino charged for just one half-length figure. Manfredi's fee was only moderately more than the 35 scudi that Mancini himself had paid eight years earlier for the artist's *Chastisement of Cupid* (170 × 122.5 cm, The Art Institute, Chicago), which sum included the costs of all materials and the models for Cupid and Venus. Other documented prices for Caravaggesque gallery pictures are comparably modest.[251]

In the mid-1650s, Carlo de' Medici judged that the 3,600 scudi paid to Cortona for his frescoes in the Palazzo Pamphilj "nowadays is unusually generous."[252] Cortona was accustomed to large fees for his fresco projects: for the celebrated *Glorification of Urban VIII* (Fig. 10), about 3,000 scudi plus two venal offices that yielded 7 percent, which the Barberini purchased for him for 2,210 scudi, and 6,000 scudi for the cupola, pendentives, and tribune in the Chiesa Nuova.[253] Nonetheless, by surface measure his altarpieces, like those by Domenichino—and altarpieces by artists in Florence, Bologna, and Venice—were more lucrative. One of his earliest, the *Virgin with St. Peter Damian* (1629, Toledo Museum of Art), cost 60 scudi per square meter, as did the first of his two altarpieces representing the *Martyrdom of St. Lawrence* (1637–52, SS. Michele e Gaetano, Florence, Fig. 62 in Elena Fumagalli's essay).[254] When he again painted the latter subject on a slightly smaller canvas in 1646 (S. Lorenzo in Miranda, Rome), he was paid 200 scudi, half the price of the earlier commission. He made use of a similar composition but reduced the number of figures, so while its per meter price fell from 60 to 35 scudi, its cost per figure increased from 50 to 70. None of Cortona's frescoes could compete with the rate of his 1,000 scudi *Crucifixion* for Castel Gandolfo (1666): a rewarding 250 scudi per figure and 141 scudi per square meter.[255] Obviously, not all figures, as was pointed out in Barocci's case, were equal in size in these paintings, but except for Albani's cut-rate price for his *figurine*, documents rarely make the distinction.

These examples of calculating the cost of church decoration by square meter and the number of figures are shown in Table 3 to facilitate review of the data. The prices are in scudi. When the number of full-figure equivalents cannot be determined with accuracy, as frequently is the case, the cost per figure is approximate. It should be emphasized that these examples are not systematic. They were selected only to make clear the kind of inconsistencies encountered when quantifying prices by size and figures and to contrast a few oil and fresco commissions, but not to represent any one artist's earnings or to compare prices between artists.

TABLE 3 Costs per Square Meter and per Figure of Selected Church Decoration

ARTIST AND DATE	PAINTING (oil altarpieces unless otherwise indicated)	DIMENSIONS (cm)	PRICE (scudi)	PER SQUARE METER	PER FIGURE
Pulzone, 1590–91	*Lamentation*, Metropolitan Museum, New York	114 × 68	100	129	17
Arpino, 1588/89–91	*Crucifixion*, S. Atanasio dei Greci (chapel lateral, fresco)	368 × 214	75	9.5	25
Arpino, 1588/89–91	*Coronation of the Virgin*, S. Atanasio dei Greci (chapel lateral, fresco)	368 × 214	75	9.5	7.5
Arpino, 1594–96	*Annunciation*, S. Maria in Via	257 × 166	200	47	100
Arpino, 1594–96	*Adoration of the Shepherds*, S. Maria in Via (chapel lateral, fresco)	232 × 134	100	64.5	12
Barocci, 1583–86	*Visitation*, Chiesa Nuova	285 × 187	550	104	110
Barocci, 1603–7	*Institution of the Eucharist*, S. Maria sopra Minerva	290 × 177	1,483	291	185
Barocci, 1604	*Crucifixion*, Prado, Madrid	374 × 246	300	33	300
Caravaggio, 1599–1600	*Calling of St. Matthew*, S. Luigi dei Francesi (chapel lateral)	322 × 340	200	18	27
Caravaggio, 1600–1	*Crucifixion of St. Peter*, S. Maria del Popolo (chapel lateral)	230 × 175	150	37.5	43
Caravaggio, 1602	*St. Matthew and the Angel* (destroyed)	223 × 183	150	37.5	75
Caravaggio, 1606	*Seven Acts of Mercy*, Pio Monte della Misericordia, Naples	387 × 256	340	34	45
Caravaggio, 1607	*Flagellation*, S. Domenico, Naples	286 × 213	246	40	61.5
Baglione, 1601–3	*Resurrection*, Il Gesù (lost)	ca. 780 × 450	1,000	28.5	100
Domenichino, 1611/12–15	*Life of St. Cecilia*, S. Luigi dei Francesi (lateral and vault frescoes)	ca. 35 square meters	300	8.5	10
Domenichino, 1612–14	*Last Communion of St. Jerome*, Vatican	419 × 256	240	22	30
Domenichino, 1616	*St. Ignatius's Vision*, Los Angeles County Museum	185 × 119	50	23	10
Domenichino, ca. 1619–22/25	*Martyrdom of St. Agnes*, Pinacoteca nazionale, Bologna	533 × 342	1,200	66	80
Domenichino, 1621–23	*Conversion of St. Paul*, Cathedral, Volterra	320 × 210	800	119	100
Honthorst, 1617	*St. Paul Caught Up in the Third Heaven*, S. Maria della Vittoria	400 × 250	88 or 92	9	45
Vouet, 1625–26	*The Cross, Saints, Angels; God the Father*, St. Peter's (lost)	ca. 720 × 420	800	26	
Guido Reni, 1625–26	*Trinity*, SS. Trinità dei Pellegrini	564 × 301	800	47	160
Guido Reni, 1627	*Trinity*, St. Peter's (abandoned) (fresco)	ca. 720 × 420	1,600	53	160?
Valentin, 1629–30	*Martyrdom of Sts. Processus and Martinian*, St. Peter's	320 × 186	350	58	50
Spadarino, 1629–32	*St. Valeria of Limoges*, St. Peter's	320 × 186	300	50	100
Pietro da Cortona, 1629	*Virgin with St. Peter Damian*, Toledo Museum of Art	147 × 113	100	60	40
Pietro da Cortona, 1637–52	*Martyrdom of St. Lawrence*, SS. Michele e Gaetano, Florence	320 × 210	400	60	50
Pietro da Cortona, 1646	*Martyrdom of St. Lawrence*, S. Lorenzo in Miranda	320 × 180	200	35	57
Pietro da Cortona, 1666	*Crucifixion*, Castel Gandolfo	320 × 221	1,000	141	250

Valuable as they are, documents, when incomplete, can conceal crucial stipulations. In 1598, for instance, Baglione agreed to decorate the apse of S. Maria dell'Orto in fresco for 450 scudi and to use a wide range of appropriate, beautiful colors, "particularly fine blues approximating ultramarine blue," in such a way that *secchi*, dry retouchings, which the contract noted fade quickly, were not necessary. But out of his fee, Baglione was required to pay for materials (*colle*, *calcina ben stagionata* as well as *bonissima pozzolana*) and even to come back to fix any damage at his own expense, including scaffolding as needed.[256] At the end of his career (1640) he returned to work in the same church in the Pecci chapel. For its altarpiece, two lateral paintings, and three more in the ceiling he earned just 400 scudi, and moreover had to cover the expenses of stucco work and gilding.[257] Were only the payments to him known but not the related conditions, they would appear deceptively profitable. Likewise, Barbalonga's compensation of 102 scudi for his very large altarpiece in S. Silvestro al Quirinale was even less than it seems, given that 30 scudi were for ultramarine and 2 more "for the food of my assistant."[258]

Two further examples demonstrate that documented payments when not detailed might be misleading. The expenses of a ten-month fresco project in the Palazzo Firenze in 1610 were 965 scudi, but only 450 went to the Florentine painters Cosimo Lotti and Luca Ranfi. Another 329 scudi were for unspecified materials and the *garzoni*, while the remaining 186 were spent on the "colle cioe spicconatura arricciatura et intonacatura et ponti per quanto si aspetta al Muratore."[259] Similarly, the payment of 113.31 scudi to Giovan Paolo Schor in 1662 for work in the Palazzo Chigi would be deceptive without knowing its breakdown: 44 scudi to two of his collaborators, 12 scudi to "ferdinando mio lavorante," 10 scudi for gilding, 7.31 scudi for pigments, leaving only 40 scudi for Schor and his brother.[260]

Another circumstance prompts caution when interpreting fees: a painter's attitude and generosity toward his patron. A good example is Barocci's celebrated *Il Perdono* (S. Francesco, Urbino). Bellori tells that the painter labored for seven years on it yet "contented himself" with payment of 100 scudi d'oro from the friars "because of their poverty" (they raised another 100 scudi for the artist from donations).[261] In a similar fashion, when Federico Zuccaro negotiated to paint a *Martyrdom of St. Lawrence* for the church of S. Filippo Neri in Fermo in 1604, he said it should cost 600 scudi but proposed donating half of that amount to the congregation. Inasmuch as he settled for 200 scudi, the same price that the less-famous Rubens received four years later for his *Adoration of the Shepherds* for the same patrons, the question arises if Zuccaro was charitably motivated to offer a discount to the Oratorian fathers or just maneuvering with an awareness of their budget.[262]

As for other instances of charitable pricing (the essays on Florence and Bologna provide more examples), Baglione relates that when Gaspare Celio's altarpiece for S. Carlo ai Catinari was appraised at 100 scudi, it was more than the *padri* were prepared to pay, whereupon they tried to get the artist to give 50 scudi as a donation. That happened but only at Celio's wife's urging.[263] In 1643, Gian Domenico Cerrini offered to paint a large altarpiece (330 × 190 cm) with many figures for the poor monks of S. Carlo alle Quattro Fontane "per amor et devotione verso questa Chiesa [for love and devotion to this church]," expecting only reimbursement of his expenses, food, and a gift—and very possibly the good graces of the Barberini because Cardinal Francesco was a supporter of the church. If that was his motive, then the painting belongs with what Philip Sohm discusses below as loss leaders. Even though the amount due was just 50 scudi, Cerrini was given 150, the same fee he had been paid the previous year for another altarpiece in the church.[264] A final example is Gaulli's generous acceptance of 800 scudi in lieu of the pre-established fee of 1,500 scudi for frescoing the vault of SS. Apostoli. He donated the balance as alms.[265]

Various other market-driven motivations could reduce prices, such as Reni's decision to ask for only 100 scudi for his ambitious *Massacre of the Innocents* (Pinacoteca nazionale, Bologna) in an effort to "dispel" the "adverse opinion . . . spread about maliciously [that] he was too difficult about prices."[266]

Financial arrangements for commissions could vary widely, depending not only on the money available, a client's resolve to stretch it as far as possible, and a painter's reputation, generosity, and need at the time, but also on local circumstances, such as having to pay a premium to woo an artist away from Rome for a provincial job. Domenichino was lured to Fano in 1618 with his most generous gross payment at the time, 4,000 scudi for decorating the Nolfi chapel in the cathedral.[267] When Roncalli and his three to four "gioveni," as the documents call his assistants, worked in Loreto at the end of the first decade of the century, the project cost the patron 5,600 scudi for the ceiling frescoes plus another 1,268 in expenses, including the artists' travel from Rome, 362 scudi for their food, wine, candles, a pig, and "tanto formaggio." The church additionally paid for the scaffolding and ultramarine blue.[268] As Christopher Marshall and Elena Fumagalli show in their essays below, "foreign" painters in Naples and Florence often fared much better than the locals did.

Even royalty might pay a premium to please a relocated painter. "Wishing to give proof of the particular esteem that His Majesty has for the person of Signor Poussin whom he has brought from Italy," Louis XIV, who personally provided that explanation, lavished money and comfort on the expatriate artist. Poussin reported in 1641 that he received 1,000 gold scudi in annual wages (which were in addition to generous payments for his paintings), another 1,000 gold scudi on top of the expenses for his journey from Rome ("it is true that money is very necessary in this country because everything here is extraordinarily expensive," he said), and a three-story, nobly furnished *palazzetto* in the garden of the Tuileries with nine rooms and an apartment below, stocked with a cask of aged wine.[269]

Mosaics

Another of Cortona's suspicions of why payment for his cartoons had been delayed is surprising: the notion that oil painting is more valuable than fresco work, a view Cortona rebutted by asserting that "the same study and labor one puts into a work in oil one puts into a fresco." This idea appears doubly odd—unless Cortona was thinking about profit more than prestige, which is entirely possible and is supported by the data just surveyed—given the illustrious history of fresco decoration and the fact that Cortona's cartoons were designed for neither medium but for mosaics (Fig. 12). Mancini stated with confidence that, among fresco, gouache, and oil, "there is no doubt that fresco should be preferred" as the medium requiring the greatest training and technical resolution. Oil, by contrast, "è il più facile" (is the easiest).[270]

To judge from what some patrons were willing to spend, mosaics enjoyed a higher status than either fresco or oil. In 1615, for a *quadretto* in mosaic representing only the head of San Carlo, the Medici paid Francesco Zucchi in Rome the sizeable fee of 60 scudi.[271] As Baldinucci noted in his *Vocabolario* of 1681, mosaic is "the most durable form of painting," does not fade, and remains "sempre più bella."[272] At least, that seems to have been the opinion at St. Peter's, where the Fabbrica favored a more permanent form of decoration that moreover had important associations with the early history of the Church.[273] Pascoli summarizes a lively debate over the advantages and disadvantages of replacing all of the paintings in humid St. Peter's with copies in mosaic, as did occur. One objection was that it robbed painters of their livelihood and that "with the price of just one mosaic" all of the deteriorating paintings could be replaced with "new and original works, not copies."[274]

The fees that the Vatican paid to painter-designers for original mosaics were a fraction of their real cost. Examples referred to by Cortona represent the state of affairs. During the 1630s, as Cortona reminded the pope, Lanfranco, Sacchi, and Romanelli had been paid 200 scudi for each of their colossal cartoons with a full-length saint, plus partial figures and angels, for pendentives in the chapels of the Madonna della Colonna and St. Michael. Like the few pendentive cartoons that have survived (two can be seen in Fig. 10), all probably were executed in tempera on canvas and measured about 5 × 6 m.[275]

Many of their designs were turned into mosaics by Giovanni Battista Calandra, the superintendent of mosaics at St. Peter's and a future *principe* of the Accademia. In his life of the artist, Pascoli notes that upon his death in 1644 Calandra left a sizeable legacy.[276] For executing Lanfranco's design (Fig. 15), he initially was paid 534 scudi but for having worked "con molta diligenza" was given a bonus of 222.5 scudi, bringing his total fee to 756.5 for a surface of 445 *palmi*, or 1.7 scudi per *palmo*.

Mosaics typically were paid for by measure in Rome, mirroring the way some Venetians appraised canvases and Florentines usually appraised murals in private palaces *a braccio* (by "arm's length," or about 58 cm). For Romanelli's pendentive, Calandra received slightly less, 744 scudi. Similar payments were made for Sacchi's mosaics, 697.5 scudi for the one of *St. Leo the Great*. Evidently, Calandra was responsible for materials and labor but not for the bed of stucco or its application, which the Fabbrica provided, as one of the measurements and evaluations (*misura et stima*) of the work spelled out: "manif[a] e robba sua, eccetto lo stucco et manuali datoli dalla fabrica."[277]

Mosaic was the original material of only one of the new altarpieces in St. Peter's. For his cartoon of *St. Michael*, Arpino was paid the customary fee of 200 scudi and Calandra received almost 1,800 scudi for copying it, thereby doubling the cost of the mosaic as compared with any of the oil altarpieces in the basilica. Evidently, the cardinals were prepared to spend that much on a mosaic in order to honor Urban VIII, whose patron saint was St. Michael. Their decision caught the eye of many visitors, including John Evelyn, who confessed to his diary that, amidst the "Statues, Pictures, and stately Altars, & Reliques innumerable" he saw in St. Peter's, "onely the Altar-piece of st. Michael being of Mosaique I could not passe without particular note."[278]

Long before he was elected Pope Urban VIII, Maffeo Barberini had discovered that mosaics were expensive. In 1605, he was advised by his brother Carlo about the cost of decorating the cupola of their sumptuous family chapel in S. Andrea della Valle. Carlo sent estimates for four alternatives: (1) an entirely painted cupola would cost about 600 scudi; (2) a combination of painting and stucco highlighted with gilding, 800 scudi (200 and 600 scudi respectively); (3) a cupola entirely in mosaic, 2,300 scudi (at 1.15 scudi per *palmo* and 200 scudi for the cartoons); and (4) a combination of mosaic and stucco, 2,100 scudi (500 for the stucco and gilding). The first option was chosen and the contract was given to Domenico Passignano, who was painting the rest of the chapel below. Carlo reported

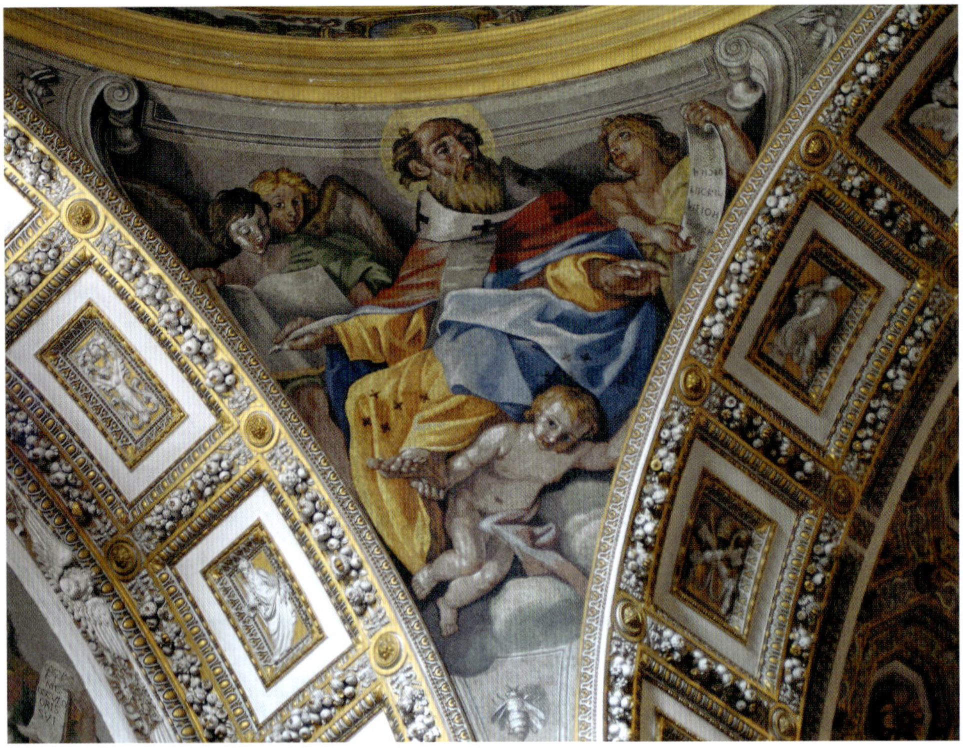

15 Giovanni Battista Calandra (after Lanfranco), *St. Cyril of Alexandra*, 1633–34. Mosaic. Chapel of the Madonna della Colonna, St. Peter's, Rome.

that Passignano, hardly an impartial judge, "praised painting the most, as being of greater excellence and less cost."[279] As this revealing document indicates, the high cost of mosaics prompted serious deliberation even by wealthy families. Predictably, mosaics were seldom commissioned privately.

Painters who designed cartoons for mosaics and other projects had relatively minor expenses and stood to net substantial profits when given a lot of work. Even when using tempera rather than chalk, their largest outlay probably was not on pigments but on paper or canvas, though neither was especially expensive. In 1635, the decade when Lanfranco and Sacchi were employed at St. Peter's, Camassei bought *carta imperiale* for three cartoons, two of which were for tapestries. He paid 4 giuli per *quinterno* of *carta imperiale* (24 or 25 sheets measuring 50 × 74 cm). Since he used three *quinterni* per cartoon, the paper for each cost 1.2 scudi. Two of the cartoons took 11 days apiece to prepare, for which the Barberini paid him at the previously mentioned rate of 5 giuli a day; the third required 15 days at 6 giuli a day, plus another 4 giuli for the eggs and glue he used in the tempera.[280] The material cost of all three cartoons therefore was about 4 scudi, less than 20 percent of Camassei's earnings of 20 scudi. Even if the painter had not been reimbursed by his patron for all of his expenses, which he was, there was a handsome profit margin in undertaking such work.

This indicates why Cortona's bill of 7,900 scudi for 32 cartoons points to huge net earnings, an issue he tactfully avoided.[281] Nor would he have wanted to bring up the series of payments to Arpino between 1603 and 1612 for his cartoons for the mosaics in the dome of St. Peter's because the fee was only 1 giulio per *palmo*. Despite a rate that sounds low, the dome's enormous surface of 72,660 *palmi* meant that Arpino was paid 7,266 scudi.[282]

Gifts

Cortona was on sure ground by closing his petition with, "Whence the petitioner, who does not ask for any gift, as is done by others, but only suitable payment for his labors . . ." He knew full well that bonuses, while far from obligatory at St. Peter's or elsewhere, were frequently given to artists in Rome as signs of appreciation, whether in cash, gold chains, or goods. At times, there could be a different motive. Pascoli relates with admiration that Giambattista Buoncuore returned a gift of some pounds of tobacco that was meant to encourage him to finish a job quickly with the response that "gifts ought to be given to men of honor only for gratitude and not for another purpose."[283]

Reportedly, Cortona himself was given an extra 200 scudi for his first *Martyrdom of St. Lawrence*.[284] The promised gift of linens to Reni and Calandra's huge 40 percent bonus for a mosaic at St. Peter's (Fig. 15) have been mentioned. For their altarpieces of *St. Peter Healing the Cripple* (1604–7) and *St. Petronilla* (1621–23), Ludovico Cigoli and Guercino received the maximum fee of 1,000 scudi, yet the Fabbrica rewarded them with gold chains worth 50 and 60 scudi more. Passignano's tip was even better: on top of the 1,000 scudi payment for his *Presentation of the Virgin in the Temple* (1627), he was given 200 scudi.[285]

In appreciation for outstanding work in Malta, Caravaggio received not just a knighthood from the grand master and a gold chain, but the less routine gift of two slaves.[286] Like gold chains, other presents were meant to bestow honor and symbolize status, such as the pair of gloves with a silver glove box costing 15.6 scudi that were given "per regalo" to Arpino in 1627 on top of his 300 scudi fee.[287]

This custom of tipping and gifting in Rome was not restricted to major commissions. For one large still life, Cardinal Flavio Chigi gave the painter Michele Pace (Michelangelo di Campidoglio) "s. 10 p. mancia," a 50 percent bonus on his 20 scudi payment.[288]

Cortona's willingness to forego any gift consequently was no small gesture. His petition apparently worked: in 1668 he was paid the outstanding balance.[289] From the time he had signed his will the previous May until his death just two years later, he was able to accrue 4,000 scudi. His estate was worth at least 100,000 scudi, which might have been surpassed only by Bernini's huge assets of 400,000 scudi.[290]

The Costs of Painting

Time

A significant factor in comparing payments—the time artists spent on particular jobs—is frustratingly elusive because the variables are many and the documentation slim. Contracts typically set a date for completion of fresco commissions and oil altarpieces alike, but deadlines were seldom met and another common contractual clause, that no other work was to be undertaken meanwhile, was also disregarded.

Especially in those cases when one knows the beginning and ending dates of a lengthy commission (Cortona worked on the *Glorification of Urban VIII* [Fig. 10] for nearly a decade, on his first *Martyrdom of St. Lawrence* [Fig. 62 in the essay on Florence] for 15 years), it is impossible to calculate the actual time devoted to a job when other projects inevitably were under way. The pace of execution—Giordano's large *St. Francis Xavier Baptizing Indians* (421 × 315 cm, Capodimonte, Naples) supposedly was done "in un giorno e mezzo e una notte" (in a day and a half and a night)—varied widely from artist to artist, though presumably painting on fresh plaster went more quickly per meter for everyone than building up layers of oil paint on canvas and waiting for glazings to dry between stages of work.[291] Mancini thought as much, writing that, while oil was the easiest painting medium, it also demanded the most patience ("voglia maggior pazienza nell'operare").[292] A notable example of profitable efficiency is Giacinto Brandi's pace in completing his huge ceiling fresco in S. Silvestro in Capite (1682–83, Fig. 16), which is about 60 meters long and yet was finished in less than a year with payment of 3,000 scudi.[293] Giordano was paid the same amount in 1685 for decorating the gallery of the Palazzo Medici-Riccardi in Florence, which he completed in five months. Pascoli opened his life of Brandi with the pointed remark, "He who wants to do too much never can do everything well."[294]

A certain sum paid to Lanfranco, Luca "fa presto" Giordano, Brandi, or Pier Dandini in Florence therefore was worth more to them than to painters with a deliberative hand such as Domenichino or Maratta—or Piazzetta in Venice, who "takes so long with his works"—not to mention someone as meticulous in his brush as Carlo Dolci, who allegedly spent six months on a portrait.[295] On one occasion when Giordano was examining Dolci's work he said to the painter, "I like everything, Carlo, but I declare that if you continue to paint this way, to invest so much time in executing your works, I think it will be a long time until you will put together the 150,000 scudi that my brush has brought me and you will certainly die of hunger."[296] Giordano could have been paraphrasing Francisco de Hollanda, who understood that the ancient painter Protogenes "was very poor, principally by reason of the great perfection he put into his work, so that he could not earn very much."[297] According to Baldinucci, Giordano had spoken in jest, but his admonition neatly links brushwork, time, and money, a theme Armenini had raised a century earlier when he concluded that *prestezza*, rapid execution, was an economic matter: the result of poor wages and consequent pressure to finish a job quickly.[298]

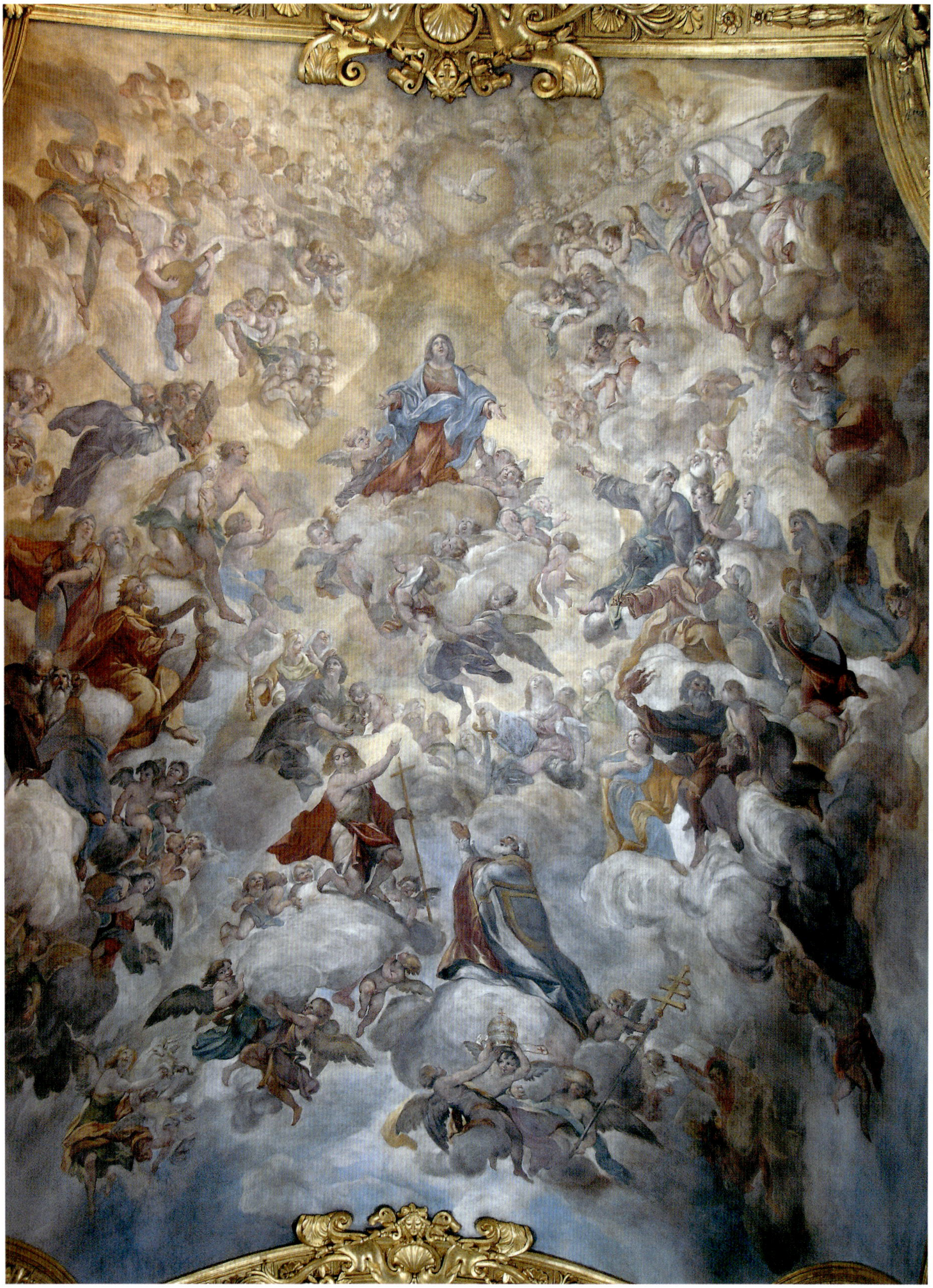

16 Giacinto Brandi, *Assumption of the Virgin*, 1682–83. Fresco. S. Silvestro in Capite, Rome.

Thus, only part of the story really was told when Cortona argued for equity by saying that he, Lanfranco, Sacchi, and Romanelli deserved to be paid the same. Evidence is slight for estimating with accuracy any of those painters' annual production, though Sacchi's undoubtedly was the smallest. Thanks to data in Guercino's *Libro dei conti*, it appears that, in peak years (1637, 1648–50), the painter turned out between 15 and 20 canvases.[299] While Maratta gained a reputation for being "dilatory and irresolute in completing his works," Bellori tried to refute the charge by asserting that "in the space of two years he made so much progress in painting that he completed twenty-two pictures in a short time, large and small."[300]

Speed of execution had another financial dimension: satisfying a buyer by delivering on time and gaining a reputation of being "available." Giulio Rospigliosi's letter of 1646 to his brother encapsulates this issue. He recommended that his brother consider hiring Andrea Camassei or some foreign painters such as Monsù Lomer (Lemaire), Monsù Mignard, Monsù Giusto (Juste de Pape) "because I expect they would provide much satisfaction and at a reasonable price. . . . Sig.r Pietro da Cortona, Monsù Pusino and il Sig.r Andrea Sacco are more famous, but I don't know if they are in Rome now and, anyway, I doubt that you could get a work from their hands for many, many years."[301] Bellori, too, was sensitive to this question, as his opening lines of Lanfranco's *vita* indicate: "A great advantage and very great profit does accrue to a person who accomplishes with ease what he undertakes, for there is someone we have seen who, by deferring works through excessive ponderation, ended by having them remain on his hands unfinished, without any reward for his extensive labors, and having allowed others to overtake him in profits and in esteem. Giovanni Lanfranco never had reason to repent of slowness."[302]

Working quickly also could avert penalties though, like contract jobs today, late fees were rarely collected. In a classic case, in 1679 Maratta was obligated to finish his *Virgin Appearing to St. Stanislas Kostka* in S. Andrea al Quirinale within a year or refund his 100 scudi advance and any further payments that had been made toward his 400 scudi fee. Despite the stipulation, he delayed and delivered the altarpiece only in 1687 without retribution.[303] Quite different was Sacchi's disastrous experience with decorating the ceiling of S. Luigi dei Francesi. Due to his slowness and declining health, and being fundamentally unsuited to organizing a team for complex fresco work, he had to give up the commission after erecting scaffolding and doing a bit of painting.[304] Ironically, his star pupil Maratta, who was expected to finish the job, himself was belittled by envious rivals as a painter of small Madonnas unfit for large commissions and as a procrastinator who "took a long time without ever reaching the end of his labors."[305] Documents cited below back up the latter claim.

Andrea Pozzo's problem was out of the ordinary. Accordingly to Pascoli, when the artist finished decorating S. Ignazio in three years (1694), he feared that the work's merits would be lessened if it became known how quickly he had painted his grand project, which amounted to some 1,000 square meters of fresco. In an effort to forestall negative criticism, Pozzo would have liked to delay the unveiling by a couple of years.[306]

One more money matter relates to speed of execution: the debates over the superiority of *colore* versus *disegno*, given that the former generally relied on swifter brushwork.[307] If buyers in general would pay more for *disegno*-based art (which is only a hypothesis since data are lacking), the knotty question is, would that have been due to the greater labor seemingly expended or to aesthetic preference, assuming that those are separable criteria? In a rare comment on the issue, Pascoli said that the opposite was true, that *colore*-based paintings sold for more due to their effortless attractiveness. *Disegno*-based work, on the other hand, "remains behind" because it is appreciated only by experts (Bellori had remarked in his lecture on the *Idea* that "the common people refer everything to the sense of sight. . . . they appreciate beautiful colors, not beautiful forms").[308] Salvator Rosa thought the same, observing that prices for Tintoretto's imperfectly drawn portraits, like those by other north Italians, were higher than prices for portraits by Santi di Tito, even though the latter's were faultless in *disegno*. "Something which I have clearly come to recognize," Baldinucci quotes Rosa as saying, "is that an excellent style of coloring is valued more than an excellent outline."[309] More data are needed to evaluate Pascoli's and Rosa's contention and to correlate the *colore–disegno* question with the reputations and prices of individual painters.

Pigments

Prices of nearly all art supplies are documented, but there is an insurmountable problem regarding the most important material, pigments, which were traded most widely in Venice. Without evidence of how many ounces of which particular colors were used in a given painting, as well as the quality of each pigment, which could drastically affect its price, it is impossible to calculate pigment expenses for individual works. Unfortunately, such data are unavailable.[310] The most expensive pigment in common use was ultramarine blue, made from lapis lazuli imported from Afghanistan, whose price in over 40 transactions from 1584 to 1688 ranged from a low of 145 baiocchi an ounce to a high of 5,000 (50 scudi), the latter the exorbitant value Lanfranco accepted in his exchange with Valguarnera.[311] Its average price in those transactions was 12.06 scudi or 1,206 baiocchi, its median 630 baiocchi. This huge variation, while greater than for other pigments in seventeenth-century Italy, underscores the need for laboratory data and records of what a painter actually paid for his pigments. In his satire *Painting*, Salvator Rosa indicates that some unscrupulous artists would try to hide their use of smalt, a cheap substitute:

> You trick both locals and the foreigners,
> pretending, when you see a simpleton,
> that dirty smalt is pure ultramarine.[312]

At the opposite end of the price scale were the widely used earth pigments, red, brown, and yellow, whose cost averaged merely 0.4, 0.3, and 0.25 baiocchi an ounce. White lead, the pigment used in largest quantities by oil painters, averaged 0.8 baiocchi an ounce.

Table 4 lists in descending order the prices of pigments bought by the Borghese during 1614–17 from a color merchant for decorating their palace in Rome.[313] An unusually rich example, it suggests that pigment costs were not significant in relation to the fees paid to prominent painters. The only exception would have been the cost of a lot of high-quality ultramarine blue, but then patrons customarily paid for it, as they did for Barbalonga's altarpiece of 1630 in S. Silvestro al Quirinale, whose *azzurro ultramarino* cost nearly half (30 scudi) as much as the artist's fee (70 scudi).[314] Conversely, when a painter's compensation was exceptionally high, such as at the Vatican, he might have been required to cover its cost. Roncalli, as mentioned, spent 111.5 scudi of his 800 scudi fee on the ultramarine in his *Death of Sapphira* in St. Peter's.

In this example, ultramarine cost only 8 scudi an ounce and therefore must have been of medium grade. Even so, only one ounce was acquired. In contrast, a lot of azurite was bought, more than 25 pounds, for use in its own right and perhaps to stretch the ultramarine. The only other expensive pigment in the list was a red lake ("lacca di grana fina"), less than two pounds of which were purchased. Brown, yellow, and red earths appear at the bottom of the list, just beneath white lead ("biacca fina di Venetia"). All of these cost less than a baiocco an ounce and were bought in large quantities: yellow earth, for example, in separate orders of 6, 7, and 10 pounds.

TABLE 4 Pigment Prices in Rome, 1614–17

PIGMENT	BAIOCCHI PER OZ.
Azzurro Altramare finissimo	800
Biadetto fino	33
Azzurro di Spagna	33
Azzurro di spagna fino	33
Azzurro di Spagna finiss[im]o	33
Lacca di grana fina	30
Azzurro di spagna mezzano	20 or 21
Verdetto fino ad olio	15
Indico fino	11.7
Corna di Cervo abrugiato macinato	10
Orpime[n]to Rosso	8.3
Orpimto roscio macinato	8.3
Giallolino di fiandra fino	5
Giallino di spagna di fiandra finisso	5
Gialdolino di fiandra finissimi	5
Gialdolino fino di francia	5
Cinabro macinato fino	5
Verderame purgato fino	5
Verderame purgato	5
Verderame	5
Lapis nero [. . .] fino	5
Curcuma pista	5
Giallo santo bello	4.2
Giallo santo fino	4.2
Spalto/Spallo fino	4.2
Lacca Verzino sottile	3
Verderame bello	2.5
Letargirio d'oro	2.5
Gesso fino	1.7
Nero di Persico	1.5
Osso di persica brugiata	1.3
Minio fino	1.2
Minio ferro da Gostantinopoli	1.2
Terra verde di Verona	1
Orpime[n]to Giallo	1
Pavonazzo di sale	1
Biacca fina di Venetia	0.8 or 0.75
Terra d'ombra fina	0.7
Terra Gialla	0.3
Terra Gialda scura fina	0.3
Terra Rossa	0.3
Terra d'Ambra di Venetia	0.3

Stretchers, Canvas, Priming

In 1608 Rubens was provided with a stretcher measuring 3 × 2 m for his 200 scudi altarpiece in Fermo. It would have cost more than 20 giuli (2 scudi) if new, but the patron enlarged one he had on hand for just 6 giuli. Other stretchers could be more expensive, whether because of the quality of the carpentry or of the wood. For Valentin's slightly bigger *Allegory of Italy* of 1627–28 (Villa Lante, Rome), the Barberini spent 8.5 scudi, which corresponds with what a carpenter was paid for comparable stretchers for altarpieces in St. Peter's by Poussin, Caroselli, Passignano, and Spadarino, among others.[315]

Normally canvas was not expensive and often it was acquired primed. In 1622, the canvas with its large, complex quadrilobed stretcher (ca. 3.5 × 2.7 m) for Arpino's *Virgin with Child and Saints* in S. Crisogono cost 14 scudi (Arpino's payment was 300 scudi).[316] Fifteen years later, the canvas and priming for Carlo Pellegrini's equally large *Martyrdom of Sts. Maurice and the Theban Legion* for St. Peter's (330 × 200 cm) cost 5.9 scudi (his fee was 400 scudi).[317] A *coloraro* who prepared some of the canvases for chapels in S. Silvestro in Capite in the mid-1690s (Fig. 21) typically charged from 8 to 10 scudi apiece for canvas and priming materials: linseed oil, white lead, red earth, carbon black, glue, pumice, and labor.[318] For five large stretchers and canvas used by Francesco Trevisani for his part of the decoration of S. Silvestro, the painter was reimbursed 50 scudi (1696).[319] The canvas alone for Maratta's very large, 1,000 scudi *Baptism of Christ* for St. Peter's (more than 5 meters high) cost 22 scudi, indicating that material costs could be substantial when a painting was exceptionally big. Indeed, the canvas and stretcher for Cortona's enormous altarpiece in S. Ivo alla Sapienza (825 × 375 cm) cost 54.3 scudi.[320]

Canvases for easel paintings understandably cost far less. For Valentin's *Samson* (136 × 103 cm, Cleveland Museum of Art), a typical *tela d'imperatore*, the Barberini gave the painter 5 scudi in 1630–31 to cover the expense of canvas (probably the stretcher, too) and pigments, plus 25 scudi for his labor.[321] Two years earlier, the Borghese spent 40 scudi on three untraced paintings of unknown size by Poussin, plus 2 scudi for the canvas, stretchers, and priming of all three.[322] Cortona's *Adoration of the Shepherds* and *Christ and the Adulteress* (Galleria Nazionale d'Arte Antica, Rome, and private collection) commissioned by Asdrubale Mattei also were painted during the 1620s for a fee of 70 scudi the pair. Measuring 146 × 227 and 132 × 226 cm, their two canvases cost 3.5 scudi.[323] But like any product, the quality and price of canvas could vary, as Salvator Rosa told Giovanni Battista Ricciardi in 1653 when he explained that "poor youths [*i poveri giovani*] try to spend as little as possible [*spender quanto meno si può*]" and therefore "it is hopeless to think that they would use a good canvas in a painting worth 3 or 4 scudi."[324]

Many other payments for canvas and priming are consistent with these numbers. When the Barberini reimbursed Camassei for the paper he bought for his cartoons, his outlay on other materials was included. For the canvas of four paintings, they gave him 4 giuli for one and 5 giuli for each of two others, and 1.8 scudi for what must have been a larger canvas, a portrait of *Taddeo Barberini's Children*.[325] In 1667, the Chigi paid "Andrea Rodati Coloraro" 16 scudi for two very large "tele imprimite" that measured 16 × 13.5 *palmi* (3.6 × 3 m) for use by Bernardino Mei. Chigi family accounts include disbursements to an aptly called "Gio. delle Tele" as well as to a "Gio. Imprimitore," who could have been the same canvas man. A "Nicolò Pietrisette Imprimitore di tele" also appears in their books. In 1662, Gio. Imprimitore received 6 scudi for "two canvases primed with oil, 15 × 11 *palmi* [3.35 × 2.5 m] to be painted in chiaroscuro." As would be expected, their cost of imperial size canvases was relatively modest: 2.1 scudi in 1692 for three *tele d'imperatore* to be used for still lifes with birds.[326]

These examples correspond by and large with what Richard Symonds entered in his notebook around 1650 under the heading "Measures & sizes of Tele da dipingere & come si vende nelle botteghe de Telari in Roma" (Measures and sizes of canvases for painting and how they are sold in stretcher shops in Rome). There the cost of the canvas for one *tela d'imperatore* cited as 4 × 6 *palmi* (ca. 90 × 134 cm) was "5 Julios" (0.5 scudi), while the canvas of a larger *tela d'imperatore*, 5 × 7 *palmi* (ca. 112 × 156 cm), which was only half again as big, cost twice as much. The canvas of a *tela da testa* 3 × 2.25 *palmi* (67 × 50 cm) cost 1.5 Julios.[327]

Of the approximately 90 scudi paid for Honthorst's *St. Paul Caught up in the Third Heaven*, four were spent on its *tela* and 6.5 on the *oltramarino*.[328] It might be noted that Honthorst, Spadarino, and Cecco del Caravaggio (Francesco Buoneri) all received substantially higher prices for their altarpieces sent to Florence in 1620 for the Guicciardini chapel in S. Felicita: 250, 200, and 200 scudi respectively. Although about the same size as *St. Paul Caught up in the Third Heaven*, Honthorst's and Cecco's canvases (Uffizi, Florence, and The Art Institute, Chicago) contain many more figures.[329]

A final example of material costs of a medium-size altarpiece (250 × 185 cm) is Giacinto Gimignani's *St.*

Thomas of Villanova Healing a Cripple (S. Maria di Galloro, Ariccia) dated 1662. The artist was paid 100 scudi, plus 10 more for "la tela telaro e colori" (canvas, stretcher, and pigments).[330]

These documents indicate that, in addition to paying for scaffolding and ultramarine blue, patrons often covered the cost of stretchers, canvas, and priming. A letter of the late 1640s by Albani's Bolognese agent Berlingero Gessi bears this out. He mentions that Albani had agreed to reduce his per figure charge from 100 to 70 testoni (from 10 to 7 scudi), a rate reflecting the small size of what the painter himself referred to as his *figurine*, and that "it is usual to pay for the stretcher, priming, and ultramarine for all painters, but negligible expense will suffice, only two or three scudi."[331]

Brushes, Paper, and Models

Most of Camassei's brushes in the mid-1630s cost a baiocco or less apiece, though two of them evidently were special: a "penello di setole grosso," a large bristle brush, cost 2.5 baiocchi, while another one similarly described cost 10 baiocchi, so presumably it was bigger and/or of higher quality.[332] Very large quantities of brushes were required for ambitious projects. In 1586, Federico Zuccaro ordered 2,880 brushes from Venice for use at the Escorial, but their cost is not recorded.[333] Prices are preserved for the 529 brushes bought in 1614–17 for use at the Palazzo Borghese. They included many ordinary bristle brushes at 1 baiocco each; small, medium, and large brushes of polecat hair (*puzzola*) set in quills at 3 baiocchi; some small bristle brushes in pine handles at 3 or 4 baiocchi and smaller ones at 2.3 baiocchi; and large white bristle brushes in lime and maple handles at 4 baiocchi.[334] Baldinucci explains that bigger brushes usually had wooden handles while little ones were set in quills from goose, swan, and other, smaller birds, according to their thickness and pliability.[335]

Prices for large quantities of paper in the same Borghese documents are higher than what Camassei spent for his cartoons 20 years later: 18 "quinterni di carta turchina p[er] fare cartone" cost 15 baiocchi per *quinterno*, as did six "quinterni di carta reale" (44.5 × 61.5 cm), six "quinterni di carta reale torchina da disegnare," four "quinterni di carta da disegnare," and six "quinterni di carta torchina p[er] diseg[na]re." More expensive were four "quinterni di carta fina da scrivere" at 20 baiocchi each. The cheapest paper was two "quinterni di carta fina" at 10 baiocchi a *quinterno*.[336]

The amount of paper used by artists varied significantly, just as did their procedures. Frescoes required cartoons but some painters made them for canvases, too. Caravaggio supposedly needed no paper, Domenichino used a minimum of ten sheets for studying just one figure in his *Last Communion of St. Jerome* (frontispiece) and for Annibale Carracci's *Hercules Bearing the Globe* in the Camerino Farnese, Bellori had seen more than 20 studies.[337] But at about a baiocco a sheet for ordinary paper for compositional and figural studies, it is hard to imagine that, for a conventional altarpiece, a painter was likely to have spent more than a scudo or so on paper for preparatory studies. Even for someone as methodical as Domenichino, the expense of paper was minor compared with his fees.[338]

Inevitably, there were other expenses in the studio, particularly when models were wanted. The Accademia offered weekly drawing sessions and made an effort to control who else hired models, but apparently it was not difficult for painters to do so privately, whether for their own benefit or that of their students and colleagues in an "accademia del nudo" or "studio del nudo."[339] Scattered documents from the Accademia suggest that it paid models 30 baiocchi a session of unspecified length. In 1628, the equivalent, 1.2 scudi a month (for four Sunday sessions), was set as the going salary.[340] That is similar to the 1.2 ducats a month Aniello Falcone and two of his associates paid a model in Naples in 1636 for two-hour sessions, three times a week, which works out to around 10 baiocchi a session.[341]

Records of private payments to models in Rome are unknown, but from certain evidence it seems likely that models, especially female ones, were expensive everywhere. Bernini commented that a good model at the time of his youth could earn 15 scudi a month, which suggests why Caravaggio, upon moving to Rome, had found them too costly to hire ("troppo dispendioso il modello").[342] In one of the letters Artemisia Gentileschi sent from Naples in 1649 to her Sicilian patron Don Antonio Ruffo, she insisted, "I want five hundred ducats for both [pictures]. . . . these are paintings with nude figures requiring very expensive female models, which is a big headache. When I find good ones, they fleece me."[343] Filippo Furini likewise had to pay dearly (nearly 2 scudi a day) for female models in Florence.[344] The question arose in the 1670s if it was worth the cost of 8 scudi a month to hire a model for the few students at the Florentine academy in Rome.[345] An even higher amount, 400 livres tournois, about 115 scudi, was being spent for a model at the French academy in Rome, more than its professor of anatomy was paid.[346] Such sums are a clear reminder of how cost effective it was to replicate, especially for someone like Orazio Gentileschi, for whose *St. Jerome* (Museo Civico, Turin, and Koelliker collection, Milan) he purportedly used a model three to four times a week for 40 days.[347]

A variety of studio props also was needed, such as an array of fabrics for history painters or appropriate objects for still life painters, but few of them cost enough to impact a painter's net earnings. Grinding stones for pigments were expensive, to judge from one in Federico Zuccaro's studio that was worth 5.6 scudi, but they lasted a long time.[348] There were incidental expenses, too, some of which were art-specific, others not. Throughout its formative years the Accademia struggled to raise money for its church, recording in 1613–14 significant pledges from some of its members that ranged from 25 to 100 scudi.[349] Special fund-raising initiatives aside, to join the Accademia apparently cost 2 scudi (it remains unclear if everyone paid up), and most members thereafter contributed only 60 baiocchi a year to the organization, while some artists who were more committed to its activities, notably Cortona, gave much more, as did Lanfranco and Bernini.[350]

Domestic servants in painters' homes were assigned a variety of tasks but hardly ever those that were handled by studio assistants. Thus, they were a luxury more than a necessity and a sign of some financial success.[351] Orazio Gentileschi's neighbor told the court at Tassi's rape trial, "so che non ha tenuto mai servitore che veramente il Gentileschi era povero huomo" (I know that he never has had a servant, that Gentileschi was truly a poor man).[352] His daughter, however, employed two servants in Rome in 1623, but they probably were a necessity for a separated, working mother. (Unlike in Bologna, women painters were uncommon in Rome.)[353] Two years later one of them went to court claiming the substantial amount of 30 scudi in back pay, though Artemisia got off with a 20 scudi settlement, the magistrate deciding that the servant had received the balance in kind.[354]

In 1649 Salvator Rosa grumbled that it was impossible to find a good servant in Rome who wasn't deceitful, uncultivated, and rude. Just the same, they expected 4 testoni (1.2 scudi) a month plus expenses (room and board), a sum "very difficult to bear for a gentleman who has no other income beyond what you [Giulio Maffei] well know."[355] Poussin, on the other hand, took pride in shunning the luxury of having a servant. When Cardinal Camillo Massimi told the painter, "I pity you that you haven't a servant" at home, Poussin replied, "And I pity your lordship more for having many of them."[356]

Though not art-specific either, eyeglasses were of particular importance to painters. The lucky ones, like Barocci, Albani, and Maratta, had good vision into old age, while others suffered.[357] Salvator Rosa complained bitterly about his failing health and in particular that "my vision has enfeebled me in a way that I can't read or paint without glasses." To have to paint "little things" caused him great despair and probably influenced the figural scale of his later work.[358] The Borghese were sympathetic to this plight of painters, purchasing from their pigments merchant six pair of glasses for Paolo Piazza at 15 baiocchi each.[359]

Other History Painters

History painters were routinely paid the highest fees and became the richest painters in Rome and Italy, yet occasionally an artist like Claude could command competitive prices for landscapes. Likewise, specialists in genre scenes such as Cerquozzi could earn a great deal of money by selling a large number of smaller pictures, as Lauri also did. Although the scope of this essay is limited to painting, it might be mentioned that Bernini's situation was unique as Rome's foremost sculptor, a leading architect, and papal favorite. (Payments for Bernini's paintings are nearly unknown.)[360] Architecture could be exceptionally profitable because very large sums of money were involved.[361] Not only were major building projects costly, but even on the construction of S. Ivo alla Sapienza, a small church, Urban VIII spent 12,000 scudi, Innocent X another 1,400 scudi, and Alexander VII 25,000 scudi more.

Some architects received annual retainers—Antonio Casone 200 scudi working for the Altemps, Domenichino 300 scudi d'oro as papal architect, all the while he remained fully active as a painter—but their main income typically was based on *misure et stime*, the measuring and evaluating of built work, on the basis of which payments were calculated and authorized. Large amounts could be earned since the *misuratore* received 2 percent of the value of what he measured (conflict of interest is no new problem in Italy). Likewise, the architect could receive 2 percent of a total *misura* up to 120,000 scudi and 1 percent above that amount.[362]

Architects also had professional knowledge that could lead to profitable real estate investments. It probably is no coincidence that the largest known seventeenth-century Roman artists' estates were Bernini's of 400,000 scudi and Cortona's of over 100,000 scudi. Domenico Fontana's possibly was comparable. Bellori relates that this architect-engineer spent his last years "living in splendor . . . for he had acquired great riches," in no small part due to the unprecedented rewards Sixtus V

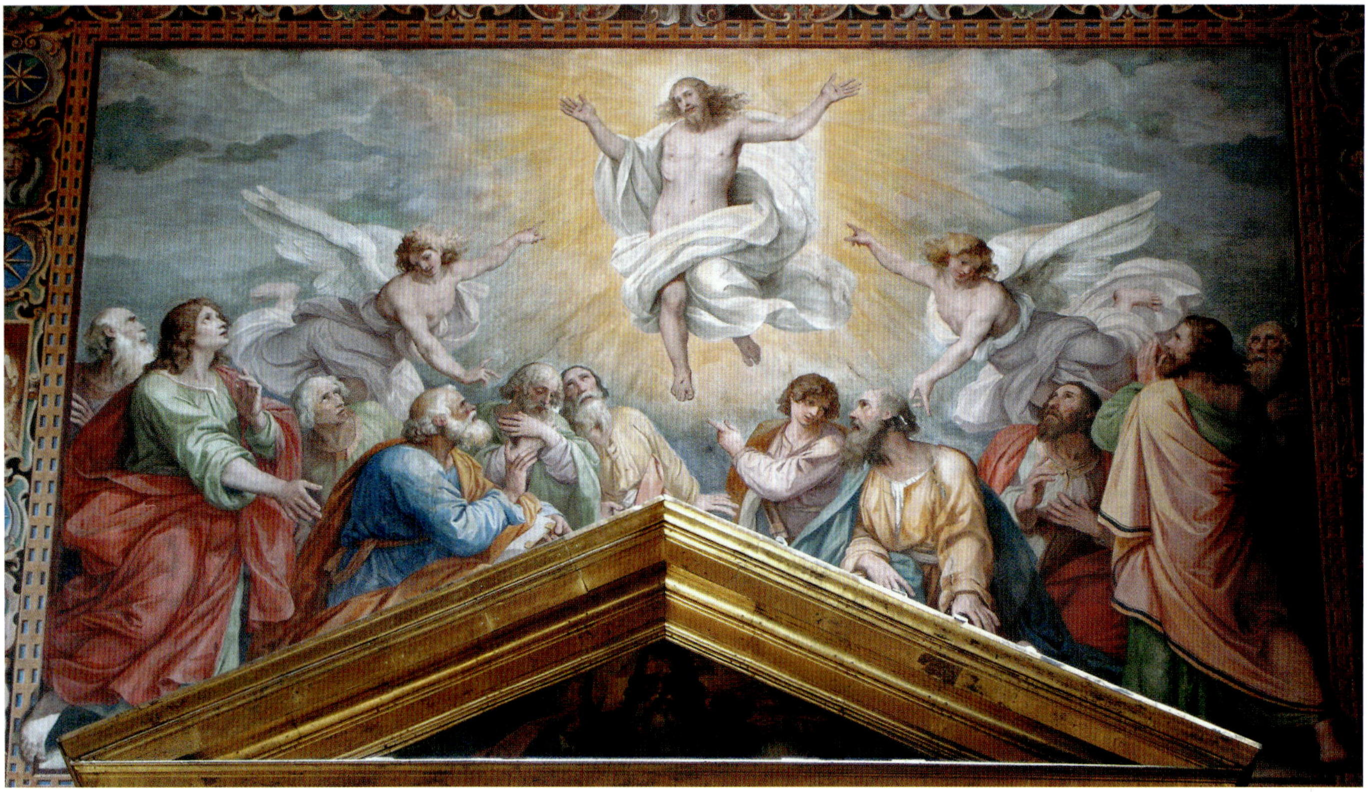

17 Giuseppe Cesari d'Arpino, *Ascension of Christ*, 1599–1600. Fresco, ca. 14 × 18.5 m. S. Giovanni in Laterano, Rome.

bestowed upon him in 1590 for moving the obelisk at St. Peter's. In addition to noble titles, he was given a pension of 2,000 scudi d'oro, 5,000 more in cash, and all of the equipment he used for the daring feat, which was estimated to be worth 20,000 scudi.[363]

Giuseppe Cesari d'Arpino

Prior to Cortona's rise to fame, the most visible history painter in Rome was Giuseppe Cesari d'Arpino (1568–1640), whose early success was largely due to his favored position with Clement VIII Aldobrandini and his family.[364] As if symbolically stepping into Barocci's shoes, the 24-year-old Arpino was awarded the commission to paint a *Coronation of the Virgin* for the Chiesa Nuova when Barocci declined the job, earning the handsome sum of 750 scudi. Three years later (1595) he undertook major fresco decoration in the Palazzo dei Conservatori for a fee of 5,000 scudi, plus lodging. His huge fresco of the *Ascension of Christ* (Fig. 17), measuring about 14 × 18.5 meters, is part of the collaborative decoration of the transept of S. Giovanni in Laterano. Herwarth Röttgen estimates that Arpino earned about 1,900 scudi on the fresco, plus another 1,000 scudi as foreman of the team, which was paid 200 scudi a week, for a total expense of 9,000 scudi.[365]

Completed in 1600, the *Ascension* elevated Arpino's status and fortune. He was knighted: no longer an artisan but a gentleman, the Cavaliere d'Arpino. The pope gave him a bonus of 100 scudi d'oro, and a gold chain and cup. Three years later he began his long involvement with making cartoons for mosaics in the dome of St. Peter's, for which he earned over 7,000 scudi. The following year, 1604, he purchased a house on the via del Corso for 3,000 scudi and hired the architect Flaminio Ponzio to turn it into a palace, which was enlarged in 1620 and perhaps even contained a theater for musical and dramatic performances. Undeniably his palace, like those of the aristocracy, was a prominent sign of its owner's status. Lest there be any doubt about its symbolic meaning to the painter, the cavaliere built a second palace in Arpino, his hometown where he no longer lived, which not only resembles an enormous triumphal arch but whose central opening is the gateway to the city.

From the perspective of 1621 back onto the formative years of the Roman baroque, Arpino was cited with

Annibale Carracci and Caravaggio as belonging to the "triumvirate of painting."[366] His fame, however (though probably not his fortune), at the time was at a critical stage as his work became ever more iconic and out of step with Roman taste. Shortly earlier he had finished an altarpiece for S. Maria della Pace that Bellori was to characterize as an "opera ridicolosa."[367] Baglione, too, regretted the direction the late work took, noting a falling off in quality in the last fresco in the Palazzo dei Conservatori and that "with advancing years [Arpino] lacked the spirit of his brush [*il valor del pennello*]."[368] Unfortunately, data are insufficient to determine if there was a parallel falling off in his prices.

Baglione, who in his autobiography contended that he was seven years younger than his real age, probably did not know that in the Easter count of 1605, assuming there was no clerical error, Arpino also lied by saying that he was only 29 instead of 38, perhaps to promote an image of the prodigy or out of vanity.[369] Inasmuch as Baglione knew Arpino personally, there should be truth in his surprising observation that the painter was unwilling to court the wealthy. That could have been a tactical, Reni-like ploy to appear hard to get or, as Röttgen speculates, the result of deep mistrust and long resentment stemming from the humiliation he suffered in 1607 by being arrested and imprisoned for illegally possessing arms, having his art collection confiscated by the Camera Apostolica, and being condemned to death—all quite possibly on trumped-up charges so that Cardinal Scipione Borghese could get 105 paintings from Arpino's collection.[370] Baglione adds that, rather than courting the wealthy (the Borghese ironically remained an important patron), the cavaliere preferred working "per gente di bassa conditione."[371]

Later in life Arpino won a few well-paid Roman commissions (in 1629–30 he received 400 scudi for each of two paintings in S. Maria di Loreto), and in 1629 he was elected *principe* of the Accademia for a third time, but he and his studio tended to be hired more by provincial clients during his final years (he died at the age of 72 in 1640). The early sources characterize him as someone spoiled by success, an embittered melancholic whose fortune and misfortunes emerged in his lifeless late style.[372]

Status Symbols

Few painters could aspire to own a real *palazzo*, let alone two as Arpino did. (In Venice only the richest of painters, Pietro Liberi, owned a seignorial palace, right on the Grand Canal (Fig. 78).) Other seventeenth-century examples are Bernini and Cortona, the closest Roman equivalents to court artists. Cortona's palace, which stood at the foot of the Capitoline until the Victor Emmanuel Monument was built, had four floors of 400 square meters each. In layout it emulated those of the aristocracy and separated the artist's working areas from its public rooms where the gentleman-artist would receive his guests. After Cortona's death, the palace was rented for 150 scudi a year to Michele Pace (Michelangelo di Campidoglio). Donatella Sparti has contrasted Cortona's and Bernini's palatial self-imaging with Poussin's in his modest *casa*, where the visitor would be greeted not by servants but by the smell of paint.[373] Gaulli, too, owned a *palazzo* where he had his studio and lived on the third floor, renting out two apartments on the lower levels.[374] Maratta's aspirations took concrete form in a country villa, an "ample dwelling" not far from Rome in Genzano where, like a Roman gentleman, he could partake in the pleasure of leisure hours without any cares ("ozio lieto senza cura alcuna").[375] Ribera, his closest Neapolitan equivalent from a financial perspective, acquired a villa with gardens, and Albani likewise spent large sums on a villa outside of Bologna.[376]

Such self-imaging could be a critical marketing strategy and should be factored in as another cost of the profession. Short of owning a palace or villa, a painter might buy a *vigna*, as Lanfranco did in 1625, evidently to expand property that his wife had been given two years earlier, and apparently not so much as a working vineyard—though *vigne* could produce income, as Pascoli says one did for Giovanni Odazzi—but as a "country" property for *otium*, for gentlemanly leisure and entertainment of guests.[377] Well before Lanfranco bought his land, a variety of artists in sixteenth-century Rome owned *vigne*, including Muziano and Giovanni de' Vecchi, just as others after him, including the sculptor Antonio Raggi, continued the practice.[378] But like other signs of status, *vigne* could become a financial burden and headache, as Mario dei Fiori's friends insisted when they talked him out of buying one, and as Albani discovered when maintaining his Bolognese properties. Although Lanfranco

> had many opportunities to work and earn a large amount of money, as one can gather from the commissions he did, he nonetheless found himself with few resources, indicating that he actually was in need rather than rich, as one might have supposed. It's quite true that his family expenses were considerable: the extravagance of his wife was beyond belief; moreover, there is to be added the continuous expenses of his *vigna*.

According to Passeri, who wrote this passage about Lanfranco's excessive luxury ("lo soverchio lusso"), the painter spent 4,000 scudi taking care of his *vigna* and had huge expenses decorating its "very comfortable" casino with his own and others' paintings (to judge from engravings of the casino, it was like a small villa). There were water displays, too, good enough to attract Cassiano dal Pozzo's attention. Lanfranco entertained generously "at an indescribable cost . . . with the result that he always found himself short of money."[379] That is no wonder, if Bellori's further information is right when he reports that Lanfranco "had maintained a splendid life with his family and an expenditure of three thousand scudi a year, in Naples where he owned a house, and in Rome where he had a vineyard at Porta S. Pancrazio, with a casino."[380]

Disguising his extravagances but not his defensive self-pity, Lanfranco wrote to Ferrante Carlo shortly after Domenichino's death in 1641:

> I haven't however borne hatred toward [Domenichino] while he was alive, and let alone now that he is dead; rather, I wished to be his friend. . . . [Domenichino] earned 18,000 ducats in eleven years; I earned 30,000 in seven and a half . . . but Domenichino didn't have the expenses I have. . . . Your Lordship could point out that there's too much difference between us; to this I reply that if Domenichino had to order one set of clothes, I have to order seven pair, etc., and this happened all the time. [Domenichino] hasn't provided dowries for daughters, as I have done; he hasn't traveled as I have, which each time, for one reason or another, has cost me at least a thousand ducats, always an excessive amount. I could say something else . . . if he had had a wife like mine, he wouldn't have been able to set aside anything for his own funeral and grave and yet at times you will hear it said that I have done nothing. I take comfort in hearing from other husbands about being abused, if not by similar creatures at least in a similar way.[381]

Lanfranco was not alone in earning a lot of money and crying poor.[382] A parallel case is Orazio Gentileschi, who in Rome and London received good fees, though not as generous as Lanfranco's.[383] In England, payments for his recorded work combined with his royal stipend equaled about 1,000 scudi annually. He evidently had a cash-flow problem, writing in 1635 that he was owed the large sum of 15,000 scudi, a third of which was to be paid in cash and the remainder in a load of grain. Even so, the artist's claim in 1629 that he was entirely out of money—rather, he said, he was more in debt ("tutto scarso di denaro, anzi di più indebitato")—is surprising. "I've never felt in a worse state than at the present; I am with debts that daily trouble me, not being used to this," was his plea the next year when trying to get money due to him. The cash-flow problem notwithstanding, Orazio, like Lanfranco, seems to have lived beyond his means, as Orazio's neighbor indicated at the rape trial of Tassi when she testified that, whenever the artist had money, he spent it lavishly.

Lanfranco's letter to Carlo draws attention to another issue: that when an artist's income, style of living, and savings are considered, the size of one's family mattered. Daughters, as Lanfranco emphasized and Artemisia Gentileschi discovered, were especially expensive. As a separated working mother, Artemisia lamented in 1649 that "this marriage [of her daughter] has broken me. . . . I need work very badly. . . . I am bankrupt [*son fallita*]."[384] (Only shortly earlier Artemisia's most wealthy rival, Ribera, was able to give his daughter a huge dowry of 5,000 ducats.) Albani's family obligations were so burdensome that the painter refocused his practice to maximize sales and income, paralleling Cerrini's sad condition in which he did not paint for glory but "to live and to help my poor relatives."[385] Domenichino's and Guercino's attitudes toward money also were affected by family responsibilities. By contrast, in England Orazio had no dependents. And that most pricey of painters, Guido Reni, was single, defending his squandering of money by asking, in Malvasia's account, "What if I do not leave a great pile of money . . . to whom will it matter? will it grieve the wife I do not have? the children? the brothers? for whom should I save and for what reason?"[386]

To own and keep a carriage was expensive and pretentious—Carlo Borromeo supposedly quipped that two things were necessary for success in Rome, love of God and a carriage—but Agostino Tassi, Giacinto Brandi and Ciro Ferri had one, as did Reni in Rome in 1627, but he sold his when his mother refused to be seen in it.[387] Noting that, rather than locking away his money, Brandi spent it to maintain a high position in society, Pascoli remarked, "as is appropriate for a painter." He similarly reported that Ludovico Gimignani "had not a small amount of money," with which he lived nobly like a gentleman ("si trattava signorilmente, e da cavaliere"). To do so required elegant clothing (often linen or silk), which painters donned as a sign of their superior status and success; in Gimignani's and Giovanni Odazzi's case, that included a wig.[388] Bellori's description of Van Dyck's attire in Rome (1622) epitomizes how dress could project image.

[Van Dyck's] manners were those of a lord rather than a commoner, and he appeared resplendent in rich attire of suits and court dress. . . . and being by nature grand and eager to become famous, therefore, in addition to his fine clothes, he adorned his head with plumes and hatbands, wore gold chains crossed on his chest, and kept a retinue of servants. And so, by imitating the pomp of Zeuxis, he drew all eyes to himself.

The expense of Van Dyck's self-fashioning, which included carriages, horses, musicians, and "sumptuous repasts . . . at a cost of 30 scudi a day," took its toll, so that "for all the riches he had acquired, Anthony van Dyck left little wealth."[389]

Salvator Rosa

Clothing was only one of the ways that Salvator Rosa (1615–73), a strong-willed painter who was also a poet, actor, and musician, projected his status. According to Baldinucci, who was well informed about the painter's stay in Florence during the1640s, Rosa managed to save only 300 of the 9,000 scudi he earned there (his Florentine stipend was modest, just 8 scudi a month plus 50 more for his annual rent) because of his huge social expenses.[390] He threw "sumptuous banquets" to entertain members of the Medici court that cost 30 or 40 scudi, and he hosted fancy dinners for his fellow members of the Accademia dei Percossi.[391]

"Tired of being far from Rome," however, Rosa returned there in 1649 "all full of pomp in ostentatious clothes with a servant in livery bearing his sword with a silver hilt."[392] Caravaggio's habit of going around the city with a sword at his side bore a more defiant message, but it was no less a self-imaging maneuver emulating aristocratic privilege. According to Bellori, Caravaggio, too, "decked himself in fine clothes and velvets," but "he never would change . . . until [they were] falling off him in rags."[393] Rosa's display of success with the Florentine nobility must have been intended for various audiences (how far removed that was from his youthful dependence on secondhand dealers "for the cost of his canvas, paints, and food"), including Bernini and Rome's literati, from whose antagonism he had escaped to Florence after imprudently offending them in his satirical comedies.[394] Seeking revenge and vindication, Pascoli writes, Rosa put "prezzi alti, ed eccessivi" (high and excessive prices) on his paintings, refusing requests to sell them, saying they were made for himself, until he finally felt vindicated and that his honor was restored.[395]

Rosa's sartorial display was intended for Rome's elite patrons, too, whose support he needed if he was to be recognized as a history painter of grand narratives with large figures rather than as a landscape specialist. "Sempre vogliono li paesi piccoli, sempre sempre li paesi piccoli"—they always want the little landscapes, always always the little landscapes—he complains in Baldinucci's *vita*, echoing a sentiment expressed in one of his own letters: "I am glad these paintings are deteriorating so that it will be forgotten that I ever painted landscapes." Even worse in his mind would have been to be associated with small pictures of low life resembling those by the Bamboccianti, whose art he caustically belittled.[396] "He didn't want ever to paint any more small pictures," Passeri said, "however great a sum of money he was offered."[397]

Rosa's troubled, paradoxical career is richly documented in the early biographies and his hundreds of letters, but even so it is impossible to draw a clear line between his egotistic behavior and marketing strategies, which overlapped and could be counterproductive when aristocratic patrons declined to meet his high demands. As targets of his poetic satires and, it was thought, his satirical painting *La Fortuna* (J. Paul Getty Museum, Los Angeles), they were reluctant to do so. Pascoli's litany of Rosa's posturings with clients, whether factual or literary inventions, rings true, such as Rosa's telling one prospective buyer that coopers and brick makers are paid by numbers and measure, not Salvator Rosa; and his rebuking a doctor for suggesting to him the idea of a painting by saying that it is no more appropriate for the doctor to do so than for Rosa to write a prescription.[398]

Rosa and Reni were equally prickly about prices and adopted some similar marketing strategies, but Rosa did not realize that he was no Reni when it came to painting figures (Baldinucci pointed out that Rosa's only altarpiece in Florence was a failure) and, as a result, that his bargaining position was far weaker.[399]

Fiercely independent, Rosa claimed on the one hand not to care about money: "it's a vile thing to work for money [*è cosa vile lo lavorare per dinari*]," Baldinucci quotes him as saying. That fits with Pascoli's understanding that "he valued his liberty more than all the honors and all the gold in the world," which might be why he declined to work as a court artist in Vienna or Stockholm. For similar reasons in Florence, Ludovico Cigoli preferred not to be tied down to the Medici. The biographers' reports correspond with Rosa's own statements that he had enough money for daily living and did not care about savings, and especially, when writing to Antonio Ruffo in 1666, his proto-Romantic position that "I don't paint to grow rich but only

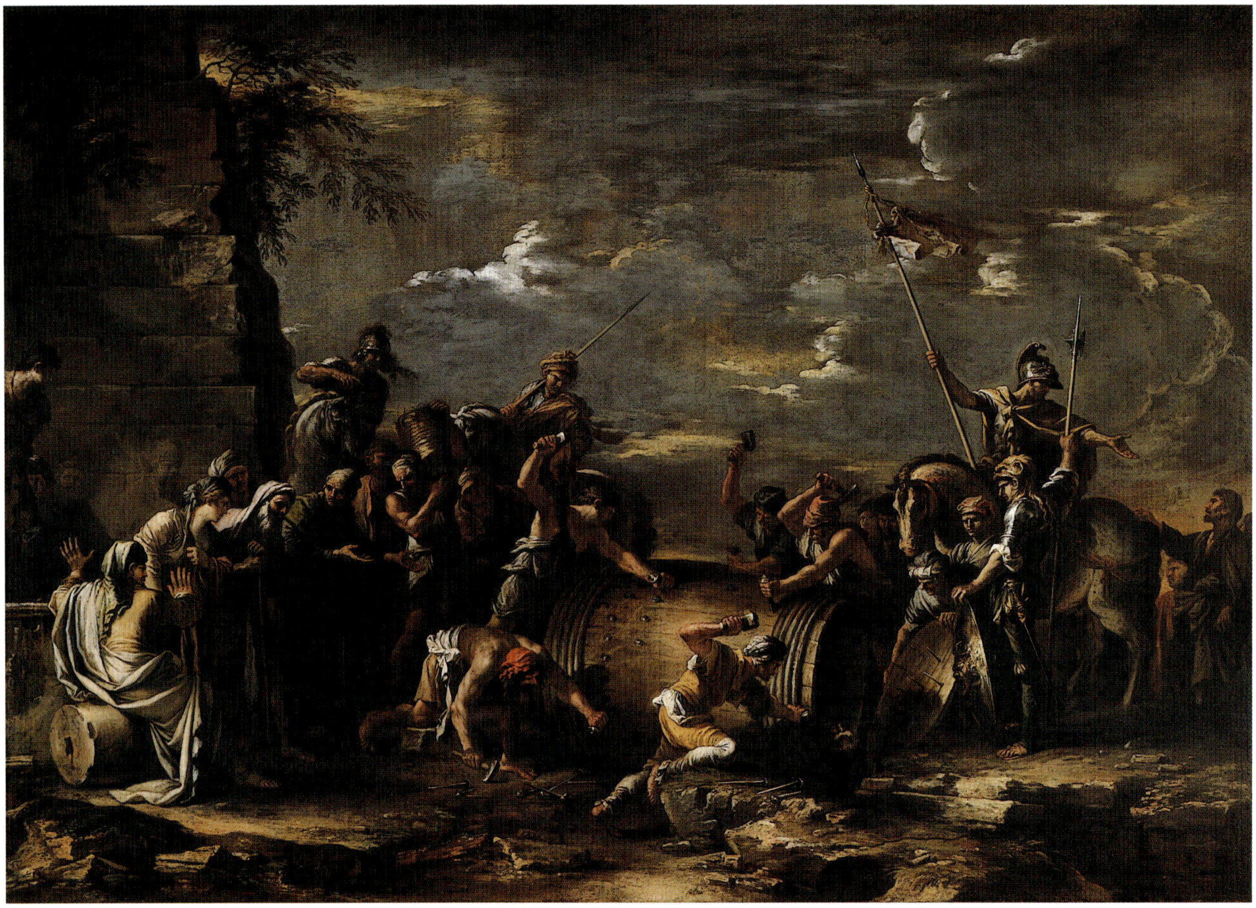

18 Salvator Rosa, *Death of Atilius Regulus*, ca. 1652. Oil on canvas, 152 × 219 cm. Virginia Museum of Fine Arts, Richmond (The Adolph D. and Wilkins C. Williams Fund).

for my own satisfaction [*non depingo per arrechire ma solamente per propria sodisfazione*]."[400] In his dialogue *Delle Ricchezze* he adopted a similar neo-Stoic stance by disdaining worldly goods.

On the other hand, perhaps at the time he admitted that he was "almost in despair because of the loss of my fortune," Rosa conceived the allegory of Painting as a beggar seated beneath a *putto* wielding a scroll inscribed, "Gentlemen, give alms to poor Painting" (Fig. 9).[401] His letters are filled with other money matters. Clearly he was pleased that his work had appreciated in value: an early *Witches*, for example, by tenfold 20 years later. He declared that he would not redo paintings for their original prices, saying in 1666 that, were he to paint the *Death of Atilius Regulus* (Fig. 18), for which he had been paid 100 scudi's worth of cheese around 1652, it would cost at least 400 scudi.[402]

But Rosa's view on the worth of his art did not necessarily coincide with the market's, as his paintings of *Democritus* and *Diogenes* (Statens Museum for Kunst, Copenhagen) graphically indicate. If Rosa is to be believed, and there is good reason to be skeptical, all of the painters in Rome said the former was worth 1,000 scudi when it was shown in the annual exhibition at the Pantheon in 1651, but he nonetheless would be glad to take 300 scudi "o ducento almeno" (or at least 200). Even at that price it did not sell. Then an offer of 250 scudi was made, but it fell through, and the painting was not sold until the next year, together with his *Diogenes* to the Venetian ambassador for 300 scudi, "which price, although not proportionate to the effort put into my paintings, however is advantageous for my purposes."[403] That same year Rosa began his enormous *Battle* in the Louvre (217 × 351 cm), which Monsignor Neri Corsini needed in a rush as a gift for young Louis XIV. "I happily seized the opportunity [despite having to work in the heat of August, he noted], whether for the excellent price [200 doble, about 600 scudi] or for the honor which could not be greater, seeing it leave Rome as a gift for a king of France."[404]

Although many of the other documented prices of his paintings vary, as a whole they are sufficiently good to account for Rosa's wealth. Representative examples include an early (1640), large (143 × 176 cm) landscape for the duke of Modena, which was paired with canvases by Herman van Swanevelt and Jacques Courtois (the duke preferred Rosa's to Swanevelt's) and cost 50 scudi.[405] Two years later he received the generous fee of 300 scudi for a much larger *Battle between Turks and Christians* (234 × 350 cm, Pitti, Florence). The same year (1642) he was paid 70 scudi for an allegory of *Fortune* for Carlo Gerini (private collection).[406] The price of a small *Battle* measuring four *palmi* (89 cm) cited in 1650 was 100 scudi. The next year Rosa's *Parable of St. Matthew* (Capodimonte, Naples) was referred to as an altarpiece worth 500 scudi, but whether he actually received that amount is unknown. For his pair of landscapes now in Glasgow (173 × 260 cm) he received 230 scudi during 1656–57.[407]

During the 1660s Antonio Ruffo bought many of Rosa's paintings, including three large landscapes for just 46 scudi; a painting about 130 cm square with figures of two satyrs and three nymphs 67 cm tall for 80 scudi; a pair of large canvases with *Pythagoras* (Staatliche Museen, Berlin, and Kimbell Art Museum, Fort Worth) exhibited in Rome in 1662 for about 400 scudi; and a half-length of the philosopher *Archytas* (private collection, Majorca) for 50 scudi.[408] In 1661 Rosa agreed to paint an altarpiece of the *Madonna del Suffragio* (285 × 185 cm) for S. Giovanni alle Case in Milan (now in the Brera) "per cento doble," about 300 scudi.[409]

Yet even during his late years Rosa could not count on getting high fees. In 1663, for instance, he exhibited a large *Catiline Conspiracy* (189 × 189 cm, Museo di Casa Martelli, Florence) that just four years later, presumably never having been sold, brought only 95 scudi at auction.[410] The previous year (1666) he had hoped to paint a grand work for Carl Emanuel II of Savoy, but at the price of 500 scudi the project collapsed.[411] In 1670, three years before his death, he received 100 scudi for a single figure of *San Torpè* (Museo d'arte, Pisa). No documents confirm what would have been his largest fee, the 1,000 scudi that Passeri improbably says Rosa was paid for his last major work, an altarpiece for S. Giovanni dei Fiorentini.[412]

Rosa's income was augmented through the sale of numerous etchings (prints could become an alternative product for the failed painter, as Passeri noted with regard to Pietro Testa), regardless of an attribute Rosa assigned to the artist in his allegorical etching *The Genius of the Artist*: "Spretor Opum" (Despiser of Wealth). He wrote that some of his largest prints sold for half a scudo apiece to dealers, who then marked them up 20 percent.[413] Rosa benefited financially from some very valuable gifts as well, such as one from the Chigi, who in 1659 paid a silversmith 106 scudi for "a bowl with a jug in silver weighing 9 pounds 3 ounces . . . to give to Salvator Rosa Painter."[414]

That Rosa actually was well-off is implied by a variety of evidence. By 1651, he had a letter of credit that allowed him to draw 200 scudi on demand, although the following year he wrote to Giulio Maffei that "I am poorer than you imagine."[415] In 1669, five years after he lamented that the Roman market was drying up, that "I could plant my brushes in the orchard" if it got any worse, and that, due to the political situation, even his modest income from investment in the wool trade had stopped and he was dependent on selling prints, Rosa wrote that "I have enough money, I turn down important commissions every day from all over Europe. . . . I have enough money to live on," at a time when his pace was as slow as a picture a year. Moreover, he was able to lend large sums to his friend and man of letters, Giovanni Battista Ricciardi. He accumulated 4,000 scudi and placed them with his most important patron and banker, Carlo de' Rossi. Invested at 6 percent, the yield of 20 scudi a month was a reasonable income in its own right. Along with material goods, he left his son 8,000 scudi in cash.[416]

Pascoli also wrote that when Rosa died he had a "grossa somma di danaro contante" (a great sum of cash) and added that Carlo de' Rossi owed the painter 6,000 scudi.[417] As the closing section of this essay suggests, an estate of about 15,000 scudi was very substantial indeed.

Other than dressing well and behaving proudly, Rosa's marketing strategies included both established and inventive tactics, perhaps none as irregular as Tassi's approach of having courtesans help him get commissions.[418] Rosa advertised, by publishing prints to widen his fame and controlling their marketing and prices; by hanging landscapes and genre scenes over his door (a youthful act, given their subject matter), which flouted the Accademia's prohibition against such crass marketing; and by displaying his work in annual art exhibitions in Rome, which at the time was an unusual practice for an important painter.[419] He even enhanced the impact of his paintings by showing them in temporary gilt "Salvator Rosa" frames, as their distinctive type of molding would become known.[420] He also depicted novel subjects, boasting that *Pindar and Pan* and *Pythagoras* had never been painted by anyone, and declaring that "since Rome has heard that I have the most unusual ideas [*io son stravagantissimo nell'invenzioni*], it is necessary to meet that expectation as much as possible."

And, like Reni, Rosa preferred not to take down payments or agree on fees in advance but instead to gamble on the generosity of his buyers. But unlike Reni, he had the crucial backup of a dealer, Carlo de' Rossi, who could decide on his prices.[421] More exceptional was Rosa's marketing ploy of signing some of his late etchings *pinxit* when no paintings stood behind them, in the hope that an inquiry about their painted models would lead to their actually being commissioned.[422]

As Jonathan Scott observed in his insightful biography, "Rosa's behaviour was so unusual that it is tempting to imagine that he was deliberately playing a role . . . in order to create a mystique about his paintings which could then be used to enhance his prices."[423]

One final letter of Rosa's deserves quoting because it provides an unusually clear view into an artist's thinking about his work. In 1666, he wrote to Ricciardi, seeking advice on whether or not he should undertake a commission to paint the vault of a prince's gallery. Having thought it over, he told his friend that, first of all, it was in a "glorious location" where there was work by the Carracci (presumably the Palazzo Farnese), which he did not have the heart to emulate even halfway; second, he had little experience, actually none, with fresco painting, never having been given the opportunity; and third, "I no longer am the youngster [*pupo*] of yesterday," so he doubted that he could keep his head upright while painting upside down. "Thus I will be awaiting your advice, reminding you that if the opportunity is taken it would be with only two purposes, the one is Glory, and the other the income."[424]

Competition

Like all of his colleagues, Rosa felt the pressure of competition, whose most terrible manifestation could be physical abuse, as Barocci discovered when his envious Roman rivals evidently poisoned him, resulting in a lifelong debilitation.[425] Domenichino experienced even worse consequences in Naples where, to the dismay of local painters, he had been awarded the city's most prestigious commission. As Passeri thought was credible, he probably succumbed to their poison, exemplifying that "interest is a wicked tyrant." Passeri was particularly hostile to competitive jealousies and their consequences, denouncing the kind of passionate favoritisms that led to blind worship of one artist and hatred of another.

He raised this issue in relation to the unveiling of Lanfranco's dome in S. Andrea della Valle, where Lanfranco and Domenichino were acrimonious rivals with partisan cohorts. He criticized those *partigiani* who, having no respect for or knowledge of the truth or understanding of reason, "call their favorite a God whose work can be bettered by no one, and their opposition a stray beast [*una bestia sparuta*], whose art hardly could be made worse."[426]

Among many examples of artistic sabotage, Bellori relates that Duquesnoy attributed the destruction of his huge stucco *modello* for *St. Andrew* in St. Peter's not to accident but rivalry, and that jealous Neapolitan artists had ashes mixed into the plaster of Domenichino's frescoes so that they would crumble.[427] Pascoli observed broad financial signs of competitive bias. "It is not always true that the fame a painter enjoyed while alive increases after his death." Instead, it might decline because, while living, artists are protected by the *grandi* and word-of-mouth support from their friends, who, with vested interests, artificially talk up an artist's worth.[428]

Artist-to-artist clashes were legendary, such as Lanfranco's with Domenichino. They fill the pages of the early *vite* with vivid accounts of physical and verbal attacks and strategies to defame. Reflecting on Lanfranco's claim that Domenichino had stolen Agostino Carracci's design for his *Last Communion of St. Jerome* (frontispiece), Bellori lamented, "I have always found through experience that when a beautiful work of art is accused of plagiarism, it is due to envious rancor at not being able to speak ill of it in any other way."[429] Baglione relates that in an effort to discredit Orazio Borgianni, Gasparo Celio told one of Borgianni's patrons that the paintings he liked "non erano originale; e per copia non erano nè meno buoni" (were not original and were not good even as copies), an incident that crushed Borgianni.[430] With similar consequences, through jealousy Maratta reportedly held back his disciple Niccolò Berrettoni ("lo teneva sempre indietro"), machinating to see that he lost a promised commission to paint the vault of S. Silvestro in Capite (Fig. 16) to the aged and exhausted Giacinto Brandi ("già vecchio, e consumato nell'arte"), which resulted in Berrettoni's decline and premature death.[431] How telling that, among the rotating positions at the Accademia, there was the *paciere*, the peacemaker.

Competition and favoritism went hand in hand, and were inevitable when Alexander VII Chigi turned over to Cortona supervision of decorating a large gallery in the Quirinal palace and entrusted him not only with its general design but with selecting, as the pope wanted, all of the best painters in Rome. The commission thus is an informative index of who was who among the history painters in Rome in 1656–57, or at least purportedly so; of their relative worth as judged by payments; and of how Cortona's list compares with history's judgment.[432]

For 20 frescoes in the gallery, more than 5,000 scudi were distributed among Lazzaro Baldi, Giovanni Angelo Canini, Carlo Cesi, Fabrizio Chiari, Bartolomeo Colombo, Guglielmo Cortese, Gaspard Dughet, Ciro Ferri, Giovanni Francesco Grimaldi, Filippo Lauri, Carlo Maratta, Jan Miel, Pier Francesco Mola, Francesco Murgia, and Giovan Paolo Schor. The documents indicate that Grimaldi and Schor were paid the most (909 and 1,040 scudi respectively), probably because in addition to their share of the narrative scenes they did a lot of decorative work that is lost. Generally, the payments to the painters were equitable, around 200 scudi for a large fresco. The obscure Francesco Murgia got as much as Maratta and Mola did, though Ferri received 385 scudi, either because he did further undocumented work or as a favorite of Cortona's.[433] The second highest fee (245 scudi) for one large fresco went to Fabrizio Chiari.

It was Passeri who recorded the pope's understanding that the best painters in Rome would collaborate on the project. He also said that the pope's wish went unfulfilled because not all of the "most celebrated painters of the time" were picked while others who were unworthy were included. Passeri did not name names, but lamented that "these are the misfortunes that occur very often when one gives the responsibility to those within the profession."[434]

It might be that Canini was given a share only through the pope's intervention rather than by Cortona's choice.[435] Other selections and omissions are more puzzling from a modern perspective. If Cesi, Chiari (Fabrizio, not Giuseppe), Colombo, and Murgia were of sufficient quality and stature to be chosen and well paid, then why were Andrea Sacchi, Francesco Cozza, Giacinto Gimignani, and Salvator Rosa passed over? (Rosa's experience with fresco was very slight, but it included collaboration with Cortona in the Palazzo Pitti.)[436] Perhaps Cortona harbored prejudice against what Rudolf Wittkower called a "Sacchi clique." The question is unanswerable, yet it draws attention to the eternal issue of how connections rather than talent can open doors.

Such were only some of the challenges that painters faced as they sought to win commissions and sell their work, as the index of the Bolognese biographer Malvasia's *Felsina pittrice* demonstrates with its numerous entries under *Concorrenza* (Competition), including that of the Carracci with other masters in order to become better known, between Caravaggio and Arpino, between Bril and Viola, between Guido and Albani, between Guido and Caravaggio, and between Guido and Domenichino, to give a few examples of artists active in Rome. *Concorrenza* is complemented in Malvasia's index with many more citations under the headings *Gelosia*, *Invidia*, *Malignità*, *Opposizioni*, *Persecuzione*, *Veleno* (poison), and *Vendetta*.

To beat the competition required successful marketing strategies. There were many more than those mentioned so far, including the well-documented plan of placing unfinished canvases around the studio in the hope that a visiting client would pay to have one completed.[437] Boasting of one's superior training could be a tactic, too, as when Lanfranco, seeking the commission to decorate the Benediction Loggia of St. Peter's with fictive stuccoes, wrote to the Fabbrica that he "could promise to paint them better than anyone else . . . being a pupil of the deceased Annibale Carracci, who was incomparable in such work."[438]

Another stratagem was gift-giving, which Rosa practiced with the expectation of a generous response.[439] Paolo Guidotti, the versatile painter, sculptor, poet, musician, mathematician, inventor, and politician, who was knighted by Paul V and honored with the right to the pope's family's name (Paolo Borghese Guidotti), regularly gave away his paintings "in dono," ready to accept expensive presents in return.[440] Yet in 1624 he, like Giovanni da San Giovanni, G. B. Mercati, Bernardino Parasole, Ippolito Provenzale, and Domenico Valeriani, received just 30 scudi from the Borghese for an oil mural (ca. 260 × 145 cm) in S. Crisogono.[441] Patrons, too, initiated gift-giving to painters as a sign of their magnanimity, perhaps with less expectation of direct reciprocity (though it could be an aspect of negotiations, as pointed out in the Introducton) than of cementing good relations with a famous artist. That probably was the motivation when Reni was in Rome in 1628 to paint his altarpiece for St. Peter's and the Barberini gave him a gold chain worth 152 scudi.[442]

Among the most common strategies for advancement was finding a major promoter while a young artist. Writing about Lanfranco's "entry" into the art world with the backing of the Sannesi family, Passeri, himself a painter who knew the situation first hand, observed how necessary that support was for any artist aiming at a "favorevole aperture" (favorable coming out). "Truth be told, to launch one's name it is critical to have the protection of a patron from the start."[443] Arpino's career was accelerated by the Aldobrandini's early patronage, Reni's by the Borghese's, Cortona's by the Sacchetti's, and Gaulli's by the Pamphilj's and Chigi's, to cite characteristic cases.

Cortona's ascent included a secondary factor, preferential treatment of *paesani*, fellow countrymen. Once again, Passeri picked up on the circumstances when he recounted that Marcello Sacchetti saw Cortona's copy of Raphael's *Galatea* (Accademia di S. Luca, Rome), liked it, asked about the artist and where he was from, and, finding out that "he was from Cortona, called him *paesano*, he himself being a Florentine." Hence he bought the painting for 60 scudi, launching Cortona's career.[444] When Rosa first arrived in Rome from Naples, he was taken in by Cardinal Francesco Maria Brancaccio, himself a Neapolitan. Corinzio Benincampo, a priest from a town close to Maratta's *patria* and who served as secretary to Taddeo Barberini, was instrumental in accelerating Maratta's early career by getting him commissions and then recommending him to the Barberini.[445]

To have a powerful patron could be extremely important for mature painters, too, yet risky, as Romanelli discovered when the Barberini fell from power and he was in danger of being identified with their disgrace. In 1646, the artist wrote to Cardinal Francesco that "it is impossible" for someone "who until now has lived under your patronage . . . and received as many favors as I have to live far from your Eminence." Consequently, as Passeri reports, Cardinal Francesco looked out for his protégé by "letting Cardinal Mazarin understand that it would give his Eminence great satisfaction if Romanelli could be given some work" in France, where the Barberini went into exile. Arrangements were made and Romanelli earned "some thousands of scudi in Paris." When he died in Viterbo, a city "where big expenses are not necessary," he left a large estate worth about 30,000 scudi.[446]

Other patrons, most notoriously Odoardo Farnese, were less caring about their artists' welfare. Annibale Carracci was put up in a little attic room, given board and 10 scudi a month while painting his masterpiece, the vault of the Galleria Farnese. Undoubtedly, he anticipated a generous payment when it was completed. But for his years of labor he received only 500 scudi d'oro, a handsome sum in its own right but so modest compared with what other important artists received for major fresco cycles that it caused Annibale's "grandissima malinconia" and professional decline.[447] By contrast, and possibly to put his adversary Odoardo to shame, Cardinal Pietro Aldobrandini presented Annibale with a gold chain worth 200 scudi for his small *Domine Quo Vadis?* (77.4 × 56.3 cm, National Gallery, London).[448]

The painter Guido Ubaldo Abbatini's stratagem for success was not through finding a patron like Cardinal Barberini but by getting himself introduced to Bernini, "the arbiter of the profession" in Passeri's words, who had control over all the coveted painting and sculpture jobs in the Vatican. But working with the artistic czar backfired when Abbatini became "enslaved" to Bernini, who betrayed his collaborator and kept him down, even belittling his achievement when Cardinal Cornaro was pleased with Abbatini's painting of the vault of his family chapel in S. Maria della Vittoria, for which Abbatini was paid about 300 scudi.[449]

It is paradoxical that Rosa, who longed for recognition, resented his success with landscapes, which exemplify another important route into the market: carving out a niche with what economists call product differentiation. Michael Montias's "innovation thesis" regarding the market in seventeenth-century Holland relies on this concept and includes two basic components: process innovation, which "reduces the cost of turning out an existing product," for example, by division of labor, replication, cheaper materials, etc., and product innovation, which "introduces a totally new commodity or changes the outward characteristics of an old one," notably new genres, such as still life and landscape painting, or distinctively new styles.[450]

Rosa's landscapes—famously typified by Horace Walpole as "precipices, mountains, torrents, wolves, rumblings"—belong to the latter category with their innovative, signature style, while his paintings of witches, like the scenes of street life by the Bamboccianti that he so despised, represent new genres in Rome, as do Mario dei Fiori's still lifes. Already in the seventeenth century an explanation of Pieter van Laer's success was that "everything new is pleasing [and] due to the newness of his *maniera* he earned a lot of money."[451] His success spawned many imitators, Passeri added, including Michelangelo Cerquozzi, in whose *vita* he remarked, "In the profession of painting one never sees anyone who has done something completely new remaining without followers."[452]

Carlo Maratta and Giovanni Battista Gaulli

After Cortona's death (1669), Carlo Maratta and Giovanni Battista Gaulli ("Baciccio") were Rome's leading history painters for the remainder of the century. Born in the Marches in 1625, Maratta entered Sacchi's Roman studio in 1637 at the age of 12. Gaulli was 14 years younger and stayed on in his native Genoa longer, settling in Rome sometime around 1657 when in his late teens. But thanks to Bernini's support, he quickly established a strong position in the Roman market and became Maratta's principal competitor. Both artists excelled in painting frescoes, altarpieces, and portraits, both designed mosaics for St. Peter's, both were elected *principe* of the Accademia, both were collectors, and both made enough money to own valuable Roman real estate. Maratta's, however, was the more diversified career, for it included many designs for architecture and sculpture and extensive conservation work.

The art of Maratta and Gaulli also epitomizes the long-standing *disegno–colore* divide, the legacy of Raphael, Domenichino, and Poussin on the one hand as opposed to that of Correggio, Lanfranco, and Bernini on the other, or, in Wöfflinian terms, "classic" versus "baroque" style. However narrow such definitions are, the economic data from Maratta's and Gaulli's lives provide another opportunity to raise the complex question of whether one style commanded higher prices and was literally more valuable than the other.

Bellori's decision to make an exception by writing about Maratta as a living artist indicates the regard with which he held the painter and links his subject to the great Michelangelo, whom Vasari celebrated while he was still alive. Maratta and Bellori also were friends. Bellori confessed that "I could not restrain my pen . . . in writing of you and praising you I do not fear the stings of envy. . . . I am impelled by the gratitude I have owed you for so many years, since you welcomed me from the time of your first studies of painting."[453]

Maratta became *principe* of the Accademia in 1664, the year Bellori delivered his influential lecture on the *Idea*, was reelected in 1700, and in 1706 was honored with the position in perpetuity. Bellori himself wrote the program for Maratta's most famous fresco, the *Triumph of Clemency* in the Palazzo Altieri (Fig. 19). Given that he knew the artist well, his information is presumably reliable.[454] "Regarding the prices of his works," he noted,

> which some have considered excessive, one may say that after Guido [Reni], Carlo has gained remuneration for painting, prompted by those who were redoubling the rewards of his labors many times over. Therefore he resolved to turn it into profit for himself, while opening the way to remuneration for others, particularly in Rome, where painters should be very grateful to him, having through his example advanced to a level of compensation that had not been the rule before.[455]

Relative to Maratta's prolific career, published documents are sparse, but those that are known support Bellori's observation that Maratta was very well paid, notwithstanding some unexceptional early fees.[456] The painter received the standard rate of 200 scudi for his contribution in the gallery of Alexander VII Chigi (1656–57). For his collaboration two years later on a series of canvases for the Chigi by Mario dei Fiori (Fig. 29 is part of the series), he was given 70 scudi, the amount paid to the other collaborators. That same year (1659) the Chigi paid him 113 scudi for a meter-square *Nativity* delivered in a frame the painter had made.[457] And thereafter, minimum prices and lifetime evaluations were 150 scudi, rising to as high as 1,500 scudi for one large oil painting.

In 1650, aged 25, Maratta began to establish an outstanding reputation through his work in more than a dozen of Rome's most prominent churches, including S. Andrea al Quirinale, S. Carlo al Corso, the Chiesa Nuova, S. Croce in Gerusalemme, Il Gesù, S. Giovanni dei Fiorentini, S. Maria del Popolo, and S. Maria in Trastevere.[458] Bellori himself had recommended Maratta for one of the first projects, the Alaleona chapel in S. Isodoro, but he lamented that in 1652, "Carlo received a very inferior reward for these labors of his." A measure of the artist's fame and worth two decades later is the *Miracle of St. Philip Benizzi* (Galleria Nazionale d'Arte Antica, Rome) painted on the occasion of Philip Benizzi's sanctification in 1671. "When [Pope Clement X Altieri] asked [Maratta] afterwards about the price that was usually paid and learned that it was 300 scudi for the picture and the decoration of the frame, it seemed little to him and he added to the general [of the Servites, who commissioned it]: 'You shall give our Carlo this money for the picture alone, the rest will be our responsibility'."[459]

The next year the Colonna paid Maratta 330 scudi for a relatively minor job of painting about 15 *puttini* on four mirrors with flowers by Mario dei Fiori and Giovanni Stanchi.[460] By then Maratta had added six canvases to Sacchi's commission for a series of Apostles (ca. 220 × 150 cm, various locations) with one life-size figure in each painting. They were appraised in the Barberini collection in 1671 at 150 scudi apiece, strikingly less than Sacchi's only completed painting, *St. Peter* (Galleria Nazionale d'Arte Antica, Rome), which was appraised at 250 scudi.[461] Other lifetime Roman appraisals of Maratta's work were higher, notably in the Carpio collection in 1682, where 11 easel paintings had an average value over 210 scudi.[462] Angelo Doni, it might be recalled, when commenting on Ciro Ferri's high prices (200 scudi a painting), observed that "with this kind of painter of top fame one cannot haggle over prices. . . . Carlo Maratta certainly would want more."

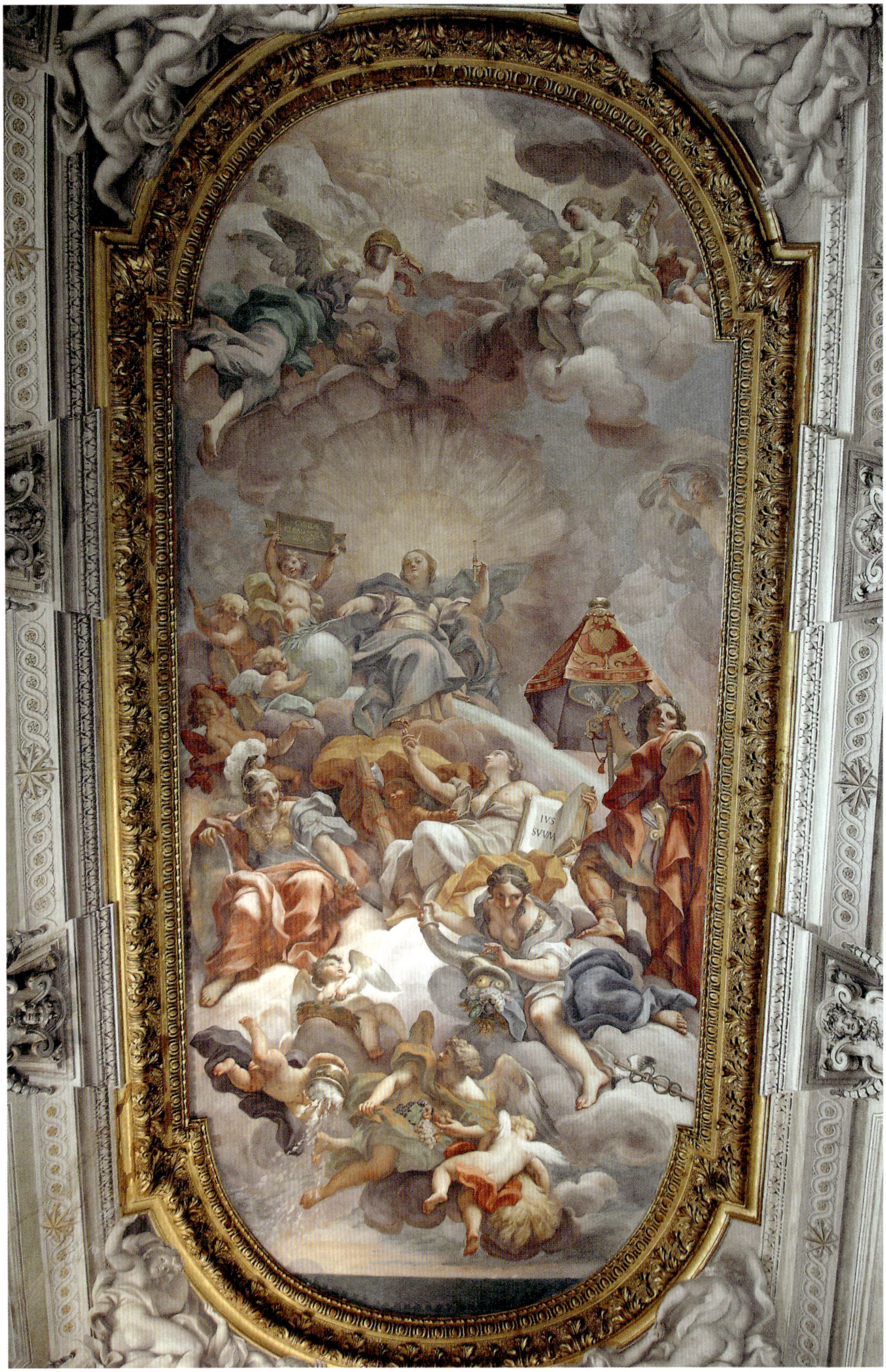

19 Carlo Maratta, *Triumph of Clemency*, 1674–77. Fresco. Palazzo Altieri, Rome.

A list of Maratta's Roman patrons includes nearly all of the city's elite: the Altieri, Barberini, Chigi, Colonna, Odescalchi, Pallavicini, Rospigliosi, Spada, as well as prominent cardinals such as Massimi and Savelli. Maratta moreover painted portraits of many of England's *milordi* and other "foreign gentlemen" (Bellori), charging 150 scudi for a full-length portrait and a proportionate amount for smaller formats.

That Maratta knew his worth, was a good businessman, and could afford to risk a loss is confirmed by an incident described by Bellori. When the artist's *Birth of the Virgin* (Bückeburg Castle, Saxony) painted for S. Maria dell'Anima was installed in the sacristy,

> there were some who objected to the price and wished to reduce it, judging it better to invest their money in a vineyard at Genzano because the wine there was good; but as Carlo persisted in the original understanding, the Congregation decide to return the picture. He took it back at once without objection and resold it . . . having achieved far better terms.[463]

While the payments cited so far were substantial, when Bellori referred to Maratta's extraordinary remuneration he might have had in mind fees such as the 3,000 livres tournois, close to 850 scudi, the painter received from Louis XIV in 1681 for *Apollo and Daphne* (205 × 229 cm, Musées Royaux des Beaux-Arts, Brussels).[464] While not all patrons were that generous (the French king additionally named the artist "Peintre du Roi"), throughout his career Maratta earned a large amount of money on his altarpieces and portraits. In 1676 the Altieri gave him 500 scudi for a modest-size painting for their family chapel in S. Maria sopra Minerva; at the end of the decade he received 400 scudi for the *Virgin Appearing to St. Stanislas Kostka* in S. Andrea al Quirinale, the picture mentioned as an example of artists' customary late completion of works despite contractual penalties for doing so.[465] In 1685, called "un Pittore così celebre" in the agreement, Maratta was commissioned to paint *St. Carlo Borromeo in Glory with Sts. Ambrose and Sebastian* for the high altar of S. Carlo al Corso. His fee was 1,000 scudi, but he covered the cost of pigments and "every other necessary material" for a painting about 9 meters high. As at S. Andrea al Quirinale, he was required to deliver within a year and—barring a "*grave malattia,* God forbid"—the church reserved the right to refuse the painting. Nonetheless, he was four years late.[466]

Three other well-documented altarpieces warrant notice. The earliest is Maratta's *Virgin and Child with Sts. Carlo Borromeo and Ignatius* for the Spada chapel in the Chiesa Nuova.[467] Commissioned in 1672 with the understanding that it would be ready for dedication of the chapel in the Jubilee year of 1675 it, too, was more than two years late. Unusually detailed and frank correspondence documents the Spada's ongoing frustration with Maratta's slowness and unreliable promises to finish, causing the patron's anguished outburst, "Dio sà quando si potrà havere [il quadro]"! (God knows when one can have the painting!)

Just as for a later project in the Chiesa Nuova, Padre Sebastiano Resta had served as advisor to the Spada. He mentioned that Domenico Canuti was interested in painting the lateral canvases in their chapel, and while he, Resta, held Canuti in high esteem, he also was impressed with the nearly completed dome by Coli and Gherardi in S. Nicola da Tolentino, so he said they should not be overlooked as viable candidates. Even though the patron remarked that if Maratta were entrusted with all three paintings "non finirebbe mai," (he would never finish), he was offered the full commission, perhaps because he had let it be known that he did not want work by others installed alongside his, as happened in S. Maria sopra Minerva where his altarpiece in the Altieri chapel is viewed beneath a fresco by Gaulli. But when Spada stipulated that the two additional canvases had to be delivered by 1675, Maratta declined, declaring it was impossible because he was too busy working on his ceiling fresco in the Palazzo Altieri (Fig. 19).

Consequently, Luigi Scaramuccia and Giovanni Bonatti were chosen, whose paintings, it was thought, would turn out well because the artists were sure to do their best to emulate Maratta's work. Each completed his canvas in less than a year and was paid 350 scudi. Maratta's fee was not much higher, 400 scudi, although the Spada surprisingly gave him a bonus of 100 scudi despite their frustration with his endless delays.

The second example is Maratta's large *Madonna del Rosario*, for which the confraternity of the Rosary in Palermo, "who kindly honored [Maratta] by waiting a number of years for its completion," paid 1,500 scudi in 1695.[468] As Bellori realized, such an exceptional fee rivaled some of Reni's. He might have added that it surpassed payments for altarpieces in St. Peter's, too.

In fact, from 1696 to 1698 Maratta himself worked for the Fabbrica di San Pietro, painting the third example, a large *Baptism of Christ* (now S. Maria degli Angeli, Rome) for the baptismal chapel. His fee was 900 scudi plus a bonus of 100 for its "qualità," not more (and in a few cases somewhat less) than the amounts paid by the Fabbrica almost a century earlier—a further example of noninflationary pricing in seventeenth-century Rome.

The lateral canvases in the baptismal chapel were painted by Maratta's assistants, Andrea Procaccini and Giuseppe Passeri, but they were not finished until 1711, two years before the master's death. Of special interest is evidence regarding the patrons' attitude toward the value of their design in distinction to their execution. Procaccini's fee was set at 700 scudi, the same as Passeri's, though Passeri was awarded 100 scudi more as a gift. Procaccini received the full payment, apparently because he was credited with both the design and execution of his painting, but Passeri was given only 400 of his 700 scudi because 300 were reserved for Maratta "per l'Inventione e Disegno del med.o Quadro" (for the invention and design of the picture).[469]

Maratta's *Triumph of Clemency* in the Palazzo Altieri (Fig. 19), the project referred to when the painter declined additional work in the Spada chapel, is a textbook example of his "classic" as opposed to Gaulli's "baroque" style (Fig. 20). It also wants comparison with Cortona's great fresco of the *Glorification of Urban VIII* in the Palazzo Barberini (Fig. 10), another huge painting honoring its papal patron in his private palace. Had Maratta finished his project (only the central fresco was executed), it might have challenged Cortona's ceiling. In the mid-1670s, the Altieri paid Maratta 1,500 scudi, but he could have earned 4,000 scudi for the complete job, paid at the rate of 100 scudi a month for two years plus a bonus of 600 scudi.[470] Forty years earlier, as previously mentioned, Cortona had received about 3,000 scudi for his fresco, plus two venal offices purchased by his patron for 2,210 scudi. While it is impossible to compare the unknown time Cortona spent with what Maratta would have needed to finish his work, the two fees (assuming Cortona's was about 5,200 scudi), when considered in relation to the dimensions of the ceilings—the *salone* of the Palazzo Barberini is a third larger than the audience chamber in the Palazzo Altieri—are uncannily alike, bringing to mind the Venetian practice of pricing large projects by size.[471]

Despite his high earnings, a papal pension of 300 scudi per annum, and an estate worth 40,000 scudi at his death, around the turn of the century Maratta decided to sell part of his vast art collection. In 1703, Clement XI matched an offer of 5,000 scudi for a group of his drawings, blocking their transfer to England in the hope, ultimately in vain, of keeping such "rare items" in Rome. Less than a decade after his death, Maratta's daughter Faustina sold the paintings she inherited from her father to Philip V for the impressive sum of 17,000 scudi.[472]

~

Like Maratta, Gaulli enjoyed patronage from the highest Roman ranks. His quick success in the city is due to Bernini's backing and prestigious work sponsored by the Pamphilj and Chigi during the 1660s. For his pendentives in S. Agnese in Agone (ca. 1666–71), commissioned when the painter was only in his late twenties, the Pamphilj gave him 1,200 scudi. Gaulli lost the bigger, 6,000 scudi contract for decorating the church's dome to the better-established Ciro Ferri. (When Ferri died leaving the dome unfinished, neither Gaulli nor Maratta would complete it.) By comparison, Domenichino, aged almost 40, was paid 2,000 scudi for his pendentives in S. Carlo ai Catinari (ca. 1628). Lanfranco was past 40 when he decorated the dome of S. Andrea della Valle (1625–28) and earned 1,600 scudi on that coveted, large project. Cortona, in his mid-fifties, was paid 6,000 scudi for his frescoes in the dome, pendentives, and tribune in the Chiesa Nuova (1651–53). Precisely when Gaulli was working in S. Agnese, a pair of less-prominent, younger painters, Coli and Gherardi, were given 1,500 scudi for frescoing the lantern and cupola of S. Nicola da Tolentino (1670).

These sums reaffirm Ferri's strong market position mid-century and also suggest that Gaulli was well on the way to receiving substantial payments for fresco work, too. His easel paintings with history subjects bought by the Chigi during the 1660s cost from 90 up to 150 scudi, the latter sum for an oval *Diana and Endymion* (ca. 220 × 180 cm, Palazzo Chigi, Rome).[473] Other Chigi payments for portraits from that decade ranged from about 20 to 50 scudi, reaching a high of 160 scudi for two portraits of Cardinal Sigismondo Chigi and Clement XI in 1670.[474] The previous year, Bernini had recommended Gaulli to the duke of Modena as a painter "di molto merito et oltre allo storiare, fa ritratti per eccelenza" (of high merit and in addition to history paintings, he excels in portraiture).[475]

Regardless of Gaulli's productivity as a portraitist, which must have augmented his income substantially (in 1670 it was reported that he made high demands [*le pretensioni*] for his portraits), few other payments are known.[476] None equals the 150 scudi level Maratta apparently charged, and none supports Pascoli's anecdote lifted from Karel van Mander's *Het Schilderboek* (1604) about "un giovani cavaliere" who, thinking a portrait by Gaulli would cost only "pochi paoli," was unwilling to pay its 100 scudi asking price. In response, the artist painted bars over the cavaliere's portrait, inscribing on it, "He is in prison for debt," thereby prompting the sitter's uncle to pay up in order to get his nephew out of jail.[477]

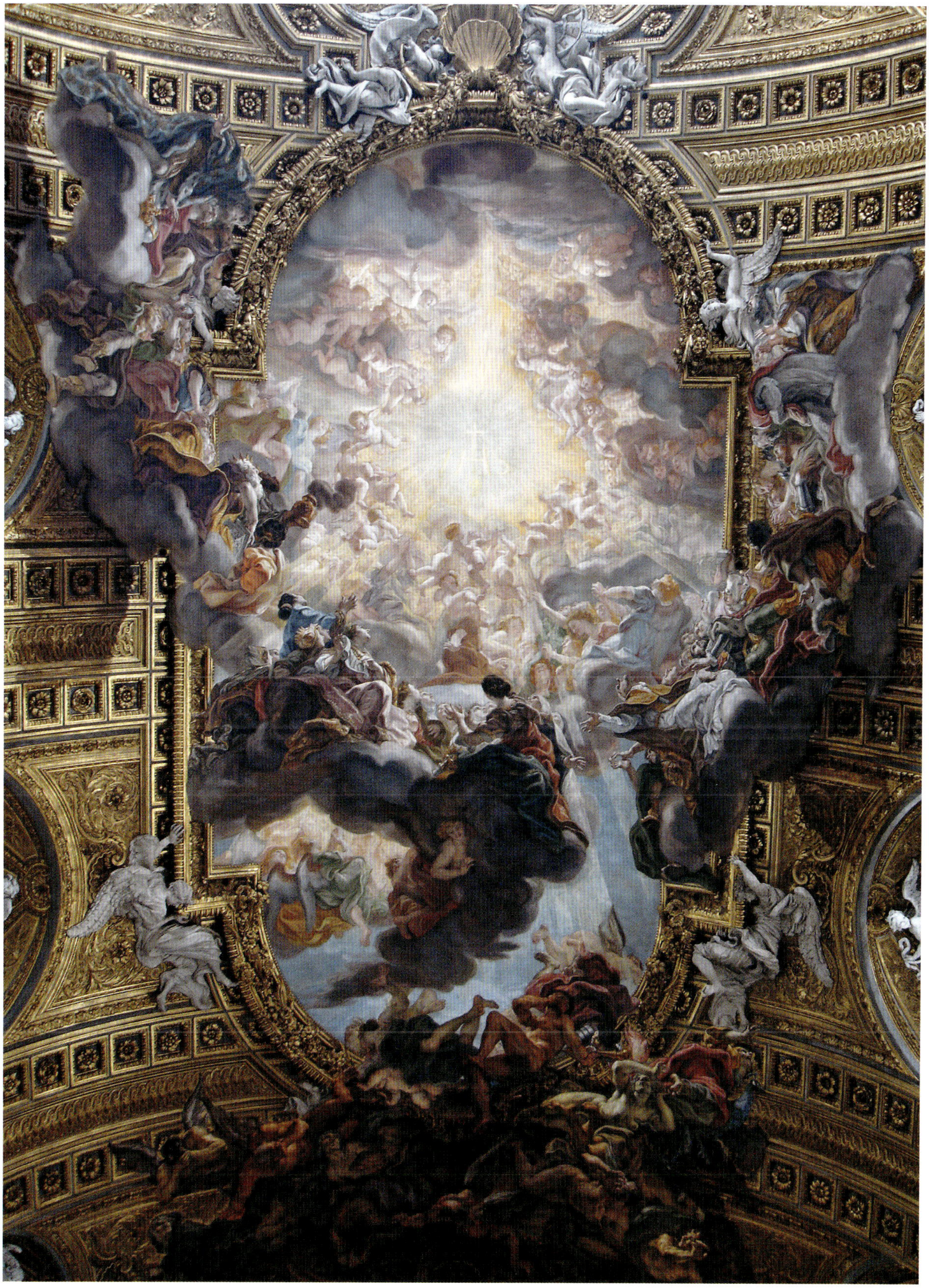

20 Giovanni Battista Gaulli, *Triumph of the Name of Jesus*, 1676–79. Fresco. Il Gesù, Rome.

The Chigi paid Gaulli 80 scudi in 1670 for painting *puttini* on a mirror and a figure of Endymion on a clock, a small sum compared with Maratta's 330 scudi payment already mentioned that the Colonna made two years later for painting *puttini* on four large mirrors.[478] In the later 1670s the two artists were commissioned to paint altarpieces of equal size in S. Andrea al Quirinale, Gaulli receiving only 100 scudi in 1676 for the *Death of St. Francis Xavier*, but Maratta 400 scudi for the *Virgin Appearing to St. Stanislas Kostka* (1679–87). Thirty years later Gaulli's remuneration from the church was no better: 200 scudi for two more paintings depicting St. Francis Xavier preaching and baptizing (1705–9).[479]

Meanwhile (1685), Gaulli had painted for the Compagnia del Gesù a *St. John the Baptist Preaching* (Musée des Beaux-Arts, Dijon), which Louis XIV's finance minister, Louvois, acquired for about a third of what Maratta had received from Louis XIV for his larger *Apollo and Daphne*.[480] Louvois was considering an invitation to Gaulli to come to Paris, but when the painting arrived he changed his mind: "le tableau de Bachiche m'a paru si mauvais que je ne suis point tenté de faire faire à cet homme la proposition de venir icy. Je n'ay de regret qu'à l'argent qu'il a cousté."[481] Given Bernini's failure in France, the response to his protégé's art is no surprise.

Gaulli's highest recorded fees for altarpieces (see Table 5) were for the *Adoration of the Shepherds* in Fermo, 400 scudi plus 10 for its *modello* in 1687, and 450 scudi in 1696 for the *Birth of the Baptist* in the Altieri chapel in S. Maria in Campitelli. Both are unusually large canvases (420 × 205 cm and 520 × 270 cm, respectively) and the *Adoration* moreover was destined for a provincial location.[482]

At least twice again Maratta and Gaulli shared space: in the Altieri chapel in S. Maria sopra Minerva and in St. Peter's.[483] In the former, Gaulli received 250 scudi (1671–72) for a fresco of the *Trinity* in a lunette above Maratta's altarpiece (1676), for which Maratta—who reportedly saw an infelicitous juxtaposition between their work—was paid 500 scudi, partly because the altarpiece was the more important commission. A similar juxtaposition would have occurred had Gaulli completed his designs for the dome and vestibule of the baptismal chapel in St. Peter's. Left unfinished when he died (1709), his drawings and a payment of 1,200 scudi were given to his heirs by the Fabbrica, which had decided not to hire anyone to complete his work. The commission was turned over to Trevisani instead.

By then Maratta had painted the baptismal chapel's altarpiece, the previously mentioned *Baptism of Christ* (1695–98). If Gaulli's oil *modello* of the *Baptism of Christ* (Musée des Beaux-Arts, Caen) was his alternative proposal, it records a commission lost to Maratta.[484] In general—and especially after the turn of the century—demand for Maratta's work was the greater, whether that should be attributed to its "classic" style or to other reasons, such as the artist's considerable social skill in attracting patrons.

Gaulli's most ambitious and lucrative project was earlier, decorating Il Gesù from 1672 until 1685 (Fig. 20). There he was chosen over three more experienced, distinguished finalists, Ferri, Brandi, and Maratta himself, thanks to Bernini's recommendation and guarantee to the father-general of the Jesuits that the outcome would be successful. Gaulli took a big risk with the commission, agreeing to paint and gild the dome, pendentives, nave, and transept vaults at his expense ("il tutto a spese sue"), gambling that, if the results were satisfactory, he would receive the enormous fee of 14,000 scudi and reimbursement for expenses. The risk paid off, and he earned an additional 3,000 scudi for frescoing the apse, plus 4,700 scudi in bonuses, totaling over 20,000 scudi.[485]

Pascoli reports that Gaulli's estate was worth 40,000 scudi, a sum that equaled Maratta's assets. Whether Pellegrino Peri, the Genoese dealer in Rome for whom the painter "worked a lot" (Pascoli), significantly enhanced Gaulli's profits is unknown, but that Gaulli was well off is clear. In 1674, before any recorded payments from the Gesù, he was able to purchase a type of annuity called a *censo* for 1,500 scudi. In 1698 he bought a house in vicolo dell'Aquila for 1,250 scudi, which by 1708 had become rental property bringing in 48 scudi annually. That year he had further income from renting two apartments for 60 and 70 scudi in the palace he owned in via del Parione where he lived and worked.[486]

~

Was Bellori right in saying that Maratta opened the way to increased prices for painting in late seventeenth-century Rome? (If so that would have differed from late seventeenth-century Naples, where prices remained stable.) But even when Bellori's view is modified by setting aside the earlier celebrities, notably Barocci, Reni, and Cortona, and the high-paid commissions from the Fabbrica di San Pietro, it is clear from the data in Table 5 that, after mid-century, only Cortona and Maratta, and Ferri for a commission in Florence (Fig. 63 in Elena Fumagalli's essay), are known to have received payments of 500 scudi or more for altarpieces.

TABLE 5 Prices of Altarpieces Painted in Rome, 1590–1700

DATE	PRICE (scudi)	DIMENSIONS (cm)	ARTIST	SUBJECT	DESTINATION
1590–91	100	114 × 68	Scipione Pulzone	*Lamentation*	Il Gesù
1592–1615	750	373 × 212	Giuseppe d'Arpino	*Coronation of the Virgin*	Chiesa Nuova
1594–96	200	257 × 166	Giuseppe d'Arpino	*Annunciation*	S. Maria in Via
1599	200	365 × 212	Annibale Carracci	*Virgin and Saints*	for Spoleto
1599–1604	800	769 × 427	Cristofano Roncalli	*Death of Sapphira*	St. Peter's
1600	200		Caravaggio	unknown	
1600–1	150	335 × 200	Cristofano Roncalli	*Assumption with Saints*	Palazzo Mattei di Giove
1601–3	1,000	ca. 780 × 450	Giovanni Baglione	*Resurrection of Christ*	Il Gesù
1602	150	223 × 183	Caravaggio	*St. Matthew and Angel*	S. Luigi dei Francesi
1602	200	273 × 177	Cristofano Roncalli	*Virgin and Saints*	S. Gregorio Magno
1602–3	800	ca. 720 × 420	Francesco Vanni	*Fall of Simon Magus*	St. Peter's
1602–7	300	277 × 185	Annibale Carracci	*Pietà with Saints*	S. Francesco a Ripa
1603	1,000	ca. 720 × 420	Domenico Passignano	*Crucifixion of St. Peter*	St. Peter's
1603–4	200?	260 × 150	Caravaggio	*Madonna di Loreto*	S. Agostino
1603–7	ca. 1,500	290 × 177	Barocci	*Institution of the Eucharist*	Chiesa Nuova
1604	ca. 200	322 × 205	Cristofano Roncalli	*Nativity*	for Naples
1604	300	315 × 235	Domenico Passignano	*Assumption*	S. Andrea della Valle
1604–5	560	ca. 720 × 420	Bernardo Castello	*St. Peter Walking on Water*	St. Peter's
1604–5	70 or 100	305 × 175	Guido Reni	*Crucifixion of St. Peter*	S. Paolo alle Tre Fontane
1604–5	300	ca. 380 × 220	Cristofano Roncalli	*Virgin Giving her Cloak to St. Simon Stock; God the Father*	S. Maria della Scala
1604–6	800	ca. 720 × 420	Giovanni Baglione	*Raising of Tabitha*	St. Peter's
1604–6	250	262 × 174	Giuseppe d'Arpino	*Virgin and Child with Saints*	SS. Trinità dei Pellegrini
1604–7	1,000+	ca. 720 × 420	Ludovico Cigoli	*St. Peter Healing*	St. Peter's
ca. 1605	280	369 × 245	Caravaggio	*Death of the Virgin*	S. Maria della Scala
1605–6	60		Guido Reni	*Assumption*	for Pinerolo
1605–7	200	274 × 155	Annibale Carracci	*Birth of the Virgin*	for Modena
1605–7	303	390 × 252	Orazio Gentileschi	*Circumcision*	for Ancona
1606	75	292 × 211	Caravaggio	*Madonna dei Palafrenieri*	St. Peter's
1607	150	300 × 241	Orazio Gentileschi	*Baptism of Christ*	S. Maria della Pace
1607	50	264 × 178	Antonio Tanari	*Sts. Pudenzia and Prassede*	S. Pudenziana
1608	100	235 × 173	Baldassare Croce	*St. Gregory Freeing Souls from Purgatory*	SS. Trinità dei Pellegrini
1608	120	280 × 175	Giovanni Baglione	*Christ Prepared for Burial*	for Naples
1609	100; 100; 100	247 × 155 (2) and 282 × 175	Giovanni Baglione	*Visitation, Nativity, Magi*	for Spoleto
1612–14	240	419 × 256	Domenichino	*Last Communion of St. Jerome*	S. Girolamo della Carità
1615	60	239 × 178	Carlo Saraceni	*St. Benno Recovering the Keys*	S. Maria dell'Anima
1616	40		"Cosimo"	*Virgin and Saints*	for Civitavecchia
1616	50	185 × 119	Domenichino	*St. Ignatius at La Storta*	Casa Professa, Il Gesù
1617	ca. 90	400 × 250	Honthorst	*St. Paul in the Third Heaven*	S. Maria della Scala
1617	60 or 90	228 × 148	Lanfranco	*Virgin with St. Lawrence*	Palazzo del Quirinale
1619–20	200	338 × 199	Cecco del Caravaggio (Buoneri)	*Resurrection of Christ*	for Florence
1620	250	338 × 198	Honthorst	*Adoration of the Shepherds*	for Florence
1620	200		Spadarino (Galli)	unknown	for Florence
1621	241	330 × 185	Antonio Tempesta	*Resurrection of Christ*	for Florence
1621–23	800	320 × 210	Domenichino	*Conversion of St. Paul*	for Volterra
1621–23	1,000	ca. 720 × 420	Guercino	*St. Petronilla*	St. Peter's
1624	30	ca. 260 × 145	G. B. Mercati	*St. Carlo Borromeo*	S. Crisogono

1624	30	ca. 260 × 145	Paolo Guidotti	*Sts. Angelo, Francis, Dominic*	S. Crisogono
1624	30	ca. 260 × 140	Paolo Guidotti	*Crucifixion*	S. Crisogono
1624	30	ca. 260 × 160	Bernardino Parasole	*St. Albert of Trapani*	S. Crisogono
1624	30	ca. 260 × 150	Ippolito Provenzale	*St. Francesca Romana*	S. Crisogono
1624	30	ca. 260 × 145	Giovanni di San Giovanni	*Three Archangels*	S. Crisogono
1624	30	ca. 260 × 150	Domenico Valeriani	*Ten Saints*	S. Crisogono
1624ff.	300	250 × 170	Guido Reni	*Virgin and Saints*	for Caprarola
1624–26	850	320 × 186	Domenico Passignano	*Doubting Thomas*	St. Peter's
1625–26	800	ca. 720 × 420	Simon Vouet	*Cross, Saints, Angels, God the Father*	St. Peter's
1625–26	800	564 × 301	Guido Reni	*Trinity*	SS. Trinità dei Pellegrini
1625–27	300	285 × 207	Andrea Sacchi	*Mass of St. Gregory*	St. Peter's
ca. 1625–27	300+	250 × 170	Giuseppe d'Arpino	*Presentation in the Temple*	Chiesa Nuova
1625–30	800 (+?)	750 × 420	Domenichino	*Martyrdom of St. Sebastian*	St. Peter's
1626–29	350	320 × 186	Agostino Ciampelli	*Sts. Simon and Jude*	St. Peter's
1626–29	200	420 × 267	Domenichino	*Virgin and Saints*	SS. Giovanni Evangelista e Petronio
1627	1,000 + 200	ca. 720 × 420	Domenico Passignano	*Presentation of the Virgin*	St. Peter's
1627	1,600	ca. 720 × 420	Guido Reni	*Trinity*	St. Peter's
1627–28	1,000	ca. 720 × 420	Lanfranco	*Navicella*	St. Peter's
1627–28	130	260 × 197	Lanfranco	*St. Silvestro Binding the Dragon*	for Caprarola
1627–28	140	255 × 167	Alessandro Turchi	*St. Anthony Preaching*	for Caprarola
1627–30	250	315 × 184	Angelo Caroselli	*St. Wenceslas*	St. Peter's
1627–32	65		Tommaso Dondini (Dovini)	*God the Father in Glory*	S. Carlo al Corso
1628–30	300	355 × 225	Lanfranco	*Immaculate Conception*	S. Maria della Concezione
1628–31	800	ca. 720 × 420	Domenichino	*Martyrdom of St. Sebastian*	St. Peter's
1628–32	1,000	ca. 720 × 420	Pietro da Cortona	*Trinity*	St. Peter's
1629	100	147 × 113	Pietro da Cortona	*Virgin with St. Peter Damian*	for Frascati
1629	300	420 × 320	Lanfranco	*Blessed Andrea Avellino*	S. Andrea della Valle
1629	400	322 × 189	Poussin	*Martyrdom of St. Erasmus*	St. Peter's
1629–30	350	320 × 186	Valentin	*Martyrdom of St. Processus and Martinian*	St. Peter's
1629–32	300	320 × 186	Spadarino	*St. Valeria of Limoges*	St. Peter's
1630	102	550 × 307	Barbalonga	*God the Father Appearing to Sts. Gaetano and Andrea Avellino*	S. Silvestro al Quirinale
1631	115	180 × 270	Barbalonga	*Coronation of the Virgin with Sts. Jerome and Bonaventure*	S. Maria della Concezione
1631	300	350 × 220	Lanfranco	*Adoration of the Shepherds*	S. Maria della Concezione
1632	350		Barbalonga	*Virgin and Angels*	for Catania
1632	50	371 × 211	Giacinto Gimignani	*Feed My Sheep*	for Palestrina
1632	150	325 × 210	Baccio Ciarpi	*Christ in Gethsemane*	S. Maria della Concezione
1633	16	ca. 340 × 180	Pietro Paolo Bonzi	*Doubting Thomas*	Pantheon
1633	150	297 × 156	Andrea Camassei	*Martyrdom of St. Sebastian*	S. Sebastiano in Campo Vaccino
1633–50	800 for 4	210 × 140 (4)	Andrea Sacchi	*Christ Carrying the Cross; St. Andrew Adoring the Cross; Martyrdom of St. Longinus; St. Helena*	St. Peter's
1634–35	125		Andrea Camassei	*Virgin and St. Bernard*	S. Caio
1634–35	85	ca. 320 × 250	Giacinto Gimignani	*Adoration of the Magi*	Collegio di Propaganda Fide
1634–35	80	ca. 265 × 180	Andrea Camassei	*Christ Calling Sts. Peter and Andrew*	Collegio di Propaganda Fide
1634–35	80	ca. 265 × 180	Carlo Pellegrini	*Conversion of St. Paul*	Collegio di Propaganda Fide

1635	150	ca. 245 × 180	Pietro da Cortona	*Deposition*	Palazzo Vaticano
1636–40	400	333 × 205	Carlo Pellegrini	*Martyrdom of St. Maurice*	St. Peter's
1637–53	400	320 × 210	Pietro da Cortona	*Martyrdom of St. Lawrence*	for Florence
1638	100	242 × 176	Pietro da Cortona	*Ecstasy of St. Alessio*	for Naples
1638	345		Giacinto Gimignani	*Christ, Virgin, Saints*	for Pistoia
1638–42	1,000	ca. 720 × 420	Romanelli	*Presentation of the Virgin*	St. Peter's
1639	ca. 100	380 × 210	Giuseppe d'Arpino	*Trinity and Saints*	S. Lucia in Selci
1639–40	100	150 × 105	Giuseppe d'Arpino	*St. Catherine of Siena*	Oratorio di S. Caterina
1642	150	330 × 190	G. D. Cerrini	*St. Ursula*	S. Carlo alle Quattro Fontane
1642	70 or 100	210 × 150	Romanelli	*Rest on the Flight into Egypt*	S. Carlo alle Quattro Fontane
1643	20		Giovanni Maria Colombo	*Virgin with Sts. Francis and Clare*	for Palestrina
1643	150	330 × 190	G. D. Cerrini	*Virgin, Child, Sts. Agnes and Catherine*	S. Carlo alle Quattro Fontane
1643	60	170 × 110	Sassoferrato	*Virgin and Saints*	S. Sabina
1644	50		Paolo Gismondi (Perugino)	*St. Sebastian Bound by Soldiers*	for Barbara (Ancona)
1644	80; 40	ca. 350 × 200; 210 × 151	Raffaello Vanni	*Birth of the Virgin*; *St. Helen*	S. Maria in Publicolis
1645	ca. 270	325 × 205	Alessandro Turchi	*Annunciation*	for Verona
1645	300	650 × 350	Romanelli	*Assumption of the Virgin*	for the abbey of St. Gall
1646	200	320 × 180	Pietro da Cortona	*Martyrdom of St. Lawrence*	S. Lorenzo in Miranda
1651	500?	200 × 120	Salvator Rosa	*Parable of St. Matthew*	unknown
1651	300	244 × 163	Andrea Sacchi	*Presentation in the Temple*	for Perugia
1651	120		Andrea Sacchi	*Immaculate Conception*	for Foligno
1657–61	400	327 × 222	Pietro da Cortona	*Immaculate Conception*	for Perugia
1659	350 for 2	350 × 267; 265 × 175	Romanelli	*Presentation of the Virgin in the Temple*; *Ecstasy of St. Teresa*	S. Maria Regina Coeli
1661–62	100	ca. 600 × 400	Lazarro Baldi	*Vision of St. John on Patmos*	S. Giovanni in Laterano
1661–64	650 for 2		Carlo Maratta	*Flight into Egypt*; *Visitation*	for Siena
1661–67	500	500 × 330	Pietro da Cortona	*Procession of St. Carlo Borromeo*	S. Carlo ai Catinari
1662	100		Gugliemo Cortese	*Vision of St. Hilarius*	S. Giovanni in Laterano
1662	32		Giuseppe Belloni	*Virgin with a Bishop and St. Venantius*	for Tivoli (?)
1662	110	250 × 185	Giacinto Gimignani	*St. Thomas of Villanova Curing a Cripple*	for Galloro
1663	110	250 × 125	Gugliemo Cortese	*St. Francis de Sales Preaching*	for Galloro
1664–65	120	300 × 198	Ludovico Gimignani	*Rest on the Flight into Egypt*	for Ariccia
1664–65	120	300 × 180	Giacinto Gimignani	*Death of St. Anthony Abbot*	for Ariccia
1665	120	300 × 200	Alessandro Mattia da Farnese	*St. Rocco*	for Ariccia
1665	160	295 × 196	Bernardino Mei	*St. Agustine Meditating on the Trinity*	for Ariccia
1665	120	294 × 197	Emilio Taruffi	*St. Francis de Sales Crushing Heresies*	for Ariccia
1665	200	296 × 198	Raffaello Vanni	*Death of St. Thomas of Villanova*	for Ariccia
1665–66	120; 120	ca. 300 × 190 each	Giacinto Gimignani	*Martyrdom of St. Lucia*; *St. Carlo Borromeo*	for Lucignano della Chiana
1665–67	100		Lazzaro Baldi	*Mission of the Apostles*	Collegio di Propaganda Fide
1665–71	500	325 × 222	Carlo Maratta	*Immaculate Conception with Saints*	for Siena
1666	1,000	320 × 221	Pietro da Cortona	*Crucifixion*	for Castel Gandolfo
1669	1,000?	ca. 340 × 195	Salvator Rosa	*Martyrdom of Sts. Cosmos and Damian*	S. Giovanni dei Fiorentini

1669	400		Giacinto Brandi	*Annunciation*	S. Maria Annunziata
1670	100	164 × 108	Salvator Rosa	*St. Torpè*	for Pisa
1671–75	105	242 × 133	Gaulli	*Virgin, Child, St. Anne*	S. Francesco a Ripa
1672–77	500	380 × 200	Carlo Maratta	*Virgin and Child with Sts. Carlo Borromeo and Ignatius*	Chiesa Nuova
1673	300	500 × 300	Guillaume Cortese	*Assumption*	for Monteporzio Catone
1676	100 (+?)	280 × 180	Gaulli	*Death of St. Francis Xavier*	S. Andrea al Quirinale
1676	500	ca. 300 × 200	Carlo Maratta	*Virgin, St. Peter, Saints*	S. Maria sopra Minerva
1676	200	360 × 220	Pietro Lucatelli (with Ciro Ferri)	*Assumption*	for Siena
1677	200	396 × 232	Giovanni Maria Morandi	*Annunciation*	for Siena
1678	25	223 × 134	Domenico Bassi	*Saints and Angels*	for Perugia
1679–87	400	280 × 180	Carlo Maratta	*Virgin and St. Stanislas Kostka*	S. Andrea al Quirinale
1680	300	403 × 241	Ciro Ferri	*St. Augustine Appearing to St. Teresa*	for Siena
1682–84	900	470 × 275 (enlarged)	Ciro Ferri	*Virgin Giving a Golden Chain to S. Maria Maddalena de' Pazzi*	for Florence
1684	75	220 × 200	Francesco Trevisani	*Trinity with Sts. Bernard and Catherine of Siena*	for Siena
1685–87	75	401 × 263	Francesco Trevisani	*Martyrdom of the Santi Quattro Coronati*	for Siena
1685–90	1,000	ca. 935 × 500	Carlo Maratta	*St. Carlo Borromeo in Glory*	S. Carlo al Corso
1686	130	370 × 200	Lazzaro Baldi	*Annunciation*	S. Marcello al Corso
1687	60	350 × 220	Francesco Trevisani	*St. Anthony Preaching to the Fish*	for Siena
1687	400	420 × 205	Gaulli	*Adoration of the Shepherds*	for Fermo
1688–89	100	397 × 266	Francesco Trevisani	*Christ with Sts. James and Philip*	for Siena
1691	60		Francesco Trevisani	*Virgin Presenting Jesus to Blessed Felice da Cantalice*	for Siena
1693–96	450	520 × 270	Gaulli	*Birth of the Baptist*	S. Maria in Campitelli
1695	1,500		Carlo Maratta	*Madonna del Rosario*	for Palermo
1695–98	1,000	550 × 400	Carlo Maratta	*Baptism of Christ*	St. Peter's
1695–1711	700; 800	550 × 320 each	Carlo Maratta and studio	*St. Peter Baptizing; Baptism of Saints*	St. Peter's

The extent to which Bellori's claim might pertain to other commissions is difficult to determine, though being a student of Maratta's undoubtedly was advantageous. At the time when the master was commissioned to fresco the audience chamber in the Palazzo Altieri (Fig. 19), two of Maratta's students, Fabrizio Chiari and Niccolò Berrettoni, were among the other artists hired to decorate the palace, along with two teams consisting of Francesco Cozza, Giovanni Andrea Carloni, and Paolo Brozzi, and Domenico Canuti and a *quadraturista*. For their four smaller but elaborate ceiling frescoes, which took less than a year to complete, the Altieri paid Chiari 450 scudi, Berrettoni 475 scudi, and the two teams 670 and 500 scudi respectively.[487]

Fees for other fresco projects of the 1670s and 1680s varied widely. At the low end of ecclesiastical commissions, during 1678–79 a group of painters—Paolo Albertoni, Carlo Ascenzi, Giovan Battista Benaschi, Giovan Battista Boncore, Fabrizio Chiari, Ludovico Gimignani, Pio Paolini, Francesco Rosa, and Girolamo Troppa—were given equal payments of only 100 scudi regardless of their standing (Ascenzi, for instance, is virtually unknown) for their ceiling frescoes over the side aisles of S. Carlo al Corso. In 1681, Luigi Garzi received 200 scudi for his larger *Glory of Angels* behind the main altar.[488]

At the high end, Brandi earned 3,000 scudi for just a year's labor painting the *Assumption of the Virgin* on the ceiling of S. Silvestro in Capite (1682–83, Fig. 16).

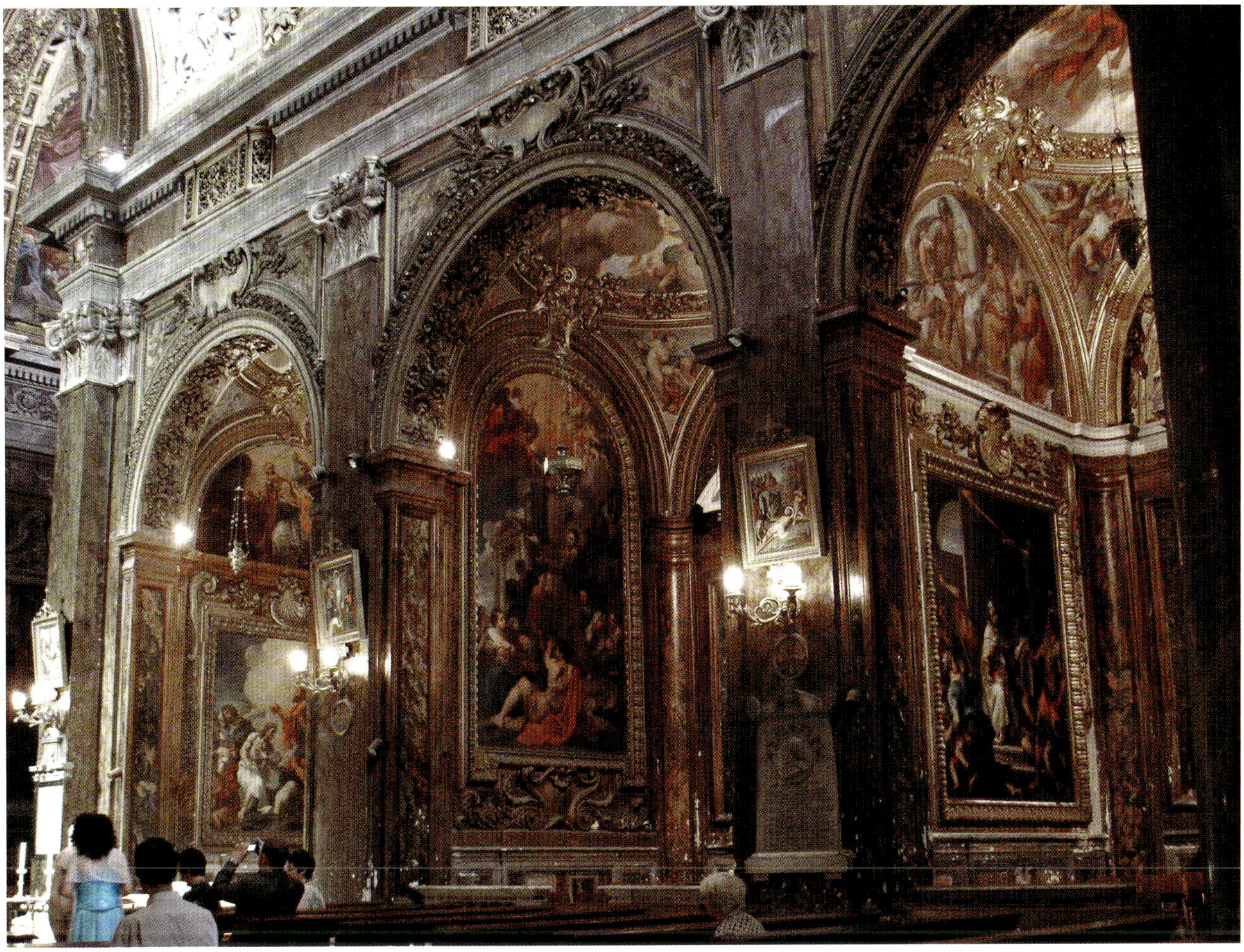

21 Chapels decorated 1695–96. Right aisle, S. Silvestro in Capite, Rome.

The frescoes by Ludovico Gimignani in the apse and transepts of the same church (1688–90) cost 1,500 scudi.[489] Earlier (1677–79), at the time the ceilings of the side aisles were being decorated, Brandi frescoed the vault of the nave in S. Carlo al Corso for 1,200 scudi. His contracts for it and the cupola (1671) are unusually explicit in laying out the church's obligation to pay Brandi for "everything he needs [*ogni cosa concernente al bisogno*]," including erecting and taking down scaffolding, suitable ladders for accessing it, a *muratore* to assist in readying the surfaces, ultramarine blue, and two rooms placed at the painter's disposal.[490]

Canuti's impressive ceiling in SS. Domenico e Sisto (1674–75), with elaborate *quadratura* by Enrico Haffner, cost the church 780 scudi, not much considering its size and complexity.[491] Similarly, one of the most ambitious secular frescoes of the time, Cozza's *Apotheosis of Casa Pamphilj* (1667–73) in the Palazzo Pamphilj on Piazza Navona, together with the artist's fresco in the entrance hall, cost just 535 scudi, again a small amount in light of the artist's lengthy labor and densely figured composition.[492]

Still other, later data preclude simple conclusions about pricing in relation to an artist's fame and the amount and kind of work required. During 1695–96, a group of Rome's leading painters decorated six chapels in S. Silvestro in Capite (Fig. 21). Probably because they were too busy or too expensive, Maratta and Gaulli did not participate in the project. Giuseppe Chiari, Luigi Garzi, Giuseppe Ghezzi, Ludovico Gimignani, and Francesco Trevisani did. Despite the significant differences in their ages and fame (Garzi and Ghezzi were roughly 10 years older than Gimignani and 20 years older than Trevisani, who was undertaking his first major Roman commission), and regardless of the amount of fresco and oil painting required—each chapel entailed painting a vault, lunettes, four pendentives, an altarpiece and/or two large lateral canvases, the

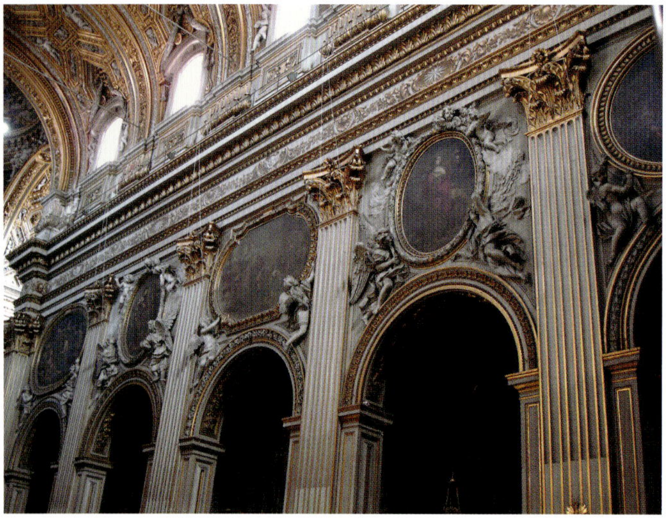

22 Nave decorated 1698–1700. Right side, Chiesa Nuova, Rome.

kind visible in Fig. 21—every painter received a flat fee of 400 scudi.[493] Only shortly later (1698–1700), Giuseppe Chiari was paid 800 scudi, plus a bonus of 150, for his ceiling fresco of the *Apotheosis of Marcantonio II Colonna* in the Colonna palace.[494]

Undoubtedly, funds at S. Silvestro were limited, yet a 400 scudi fee per artist for so much labor, like many of the other payments just cited, challenges the view that Maratta's success had a substantial effect on prices in Rome. Nor do payments of 1698–1700 for 15 large canvases for the nave and transepts of the Chiesa Nuova modify this doubt. Even though Maratta and Giovanni Maria Morandi were given first choice of the biblical subjects, and in deference to their age the series was to be done in oil on canvas rather than from scaffolding in fresco, neither artist eventually participated (Maratta once more explained that he was too busy). After much uncertainty and the advice of Padre Resta, the commission was divided up among five of Rome's leading painters, Lazzaro Baldi, Giuseppe Ghezzi, Giuseppe Passeri, Domenico Prodi, and Daniel Seiter. They were paid only 150 scudi for each of 11 very large canvases (all more than 4 meters wide) and 100 scudi for four somewhat smaller ovals (Fig. 22).[495]

Padre Resta had previously advised the Spada on choosing artists for their family chapel in the Chiesa Nuova. On that occasion they had asked him for a list of candidates to consider. Resta's reply of 1672 is precious evidence of a sophisticated connoisseur's ranking of Italian painters, some of whom he classified as old or young.[496] In Resta's view, the first-class painters active in Rome were Giovanni Bonatti, Brandi, Guillaume Cortese, Ferri, Maratta, and Morandi. Others working elsewhere in Italy were Scaramuccia, Volterrano, Pietro Vecchia, Pietro Liberi "et altri di Venetia," and Domenico Piola from Genoa. Although first class, Federico Bianchi, Antonio Busca, Ercole Procaccini "et altri di Milano" could not be recommended by Resta "because they do not have styles similar [*stili analogici*] to the taste of modern Rome," which he explained meant the style of the Carracci and their school in Bologna and Rome. Other painters in Resta's top category were Carlo Cignani, Agostino Mitelli (who actually had died in 1660), and Mattia Preti.

His second rank was subdivided between *pittori vecchi* and *giovani*. The old ones were Baldi (then just 48), Cerrini (66), Fabrizio Chiari (about 57), and Cozza (67). The young painters were Paolo Albertoni (?), Coli (36), Gherardi (29), Gaulli (32), Ludovico Gimignani (29), Francesco Rosa (34), and Girolamo Troppa (42). Two more were named as being second class: Canuti and Emilio Taruffi.

The list is erratic, unavoidably affected by Resta's taste, his perception that Caraccesque painting was Rome's preferred style (his list nevertheless includes both *disegno* and *colore* practioners), and his spotty memory (some of the names were listed as an afterthought). Nonetheless, it is a remarkably reliable guide to Rome's best painters around 1670 as perceived today. As with Cortona's selection of the leading painters to work in the gallery of Alexander VII in 1656–57, there are omissions, such as Benaschi, Bernardino Mei, and Giuseppe Ghezzi in Rome, and Andrea Celesti, Giordano, Livio Mehus, and Antonio Zanchi elsewhere, to name only a few examples of artists who surely belonged in the second category at least. Inasmuch as the role of advisors such as Resta could be critical when commissions were awarded, one wonders if and how painters might have tried to influence their recommendations.

Explicitly correlating quality with price, Resta added a warning that the fees expected by the first-class painters in his list were high. Moreover, even some of the younger, second-tier painters were so audacious that they were asking "prices equal to the first."

Regardless of what Resta called "prezzi alti," doubt persists that there was a significant increase in prices toward the end of the century, as a survey of nearly 160 prices of altarpieces painted in Rome from 1590 to 1700 indicates (Table 5). Although further data from the less well-studied later decades could modify this suspicion, it is important to recognize that during those years fewer new churches were being built or remodeled, thereby decreasing commissions for altarpieces.[497]

These prices can be compared with Elena Fumagalli's estimate that earlier seventeenth-century altarpieces by painters of rank in Florence typically cost from 100 to 200 scudi, which is similar to Christopher Marshall's estimate for Naples.

The average price in Table 5 is about 350 scudi; the mean is 200 scudi. The prices should be evaluated with care. Some dimensions are rough approximations while others are unknown. Due to the erratic availability of data, the number of figures in paintings and the responsibility for material costs are not specified.[498]

It should be kept in mind that while all of the public and private commissions just mentioned were being awarded, countless painters in Rome continued to try to make a living by producing landscapes, still lifes, and other modestly priced pictures. Those artists would not have recognized Bellori's rosy view of the market. A good example is Philipp Peter Roos, known as Rosa da Tivoli, who worked for Gaulli's one-time dealer, Pellegrino Peri. Peri's inventory lists more than 70 pictures by Rosa, who was nicknamed "Mercury" for his rapid pace of production. Even so, with a large family and poor financial skills, he needed a large loan from Peri, who eventually confiscated some of Rosa's household goods when the artist defaulted.[499]

The Genres

A hierarchy of subject matter or genres was not codified until later in the seventeenth century with publication of André Félibien's preface to the *Conférences de l'Académie royale . . . 1667* (1668), in which he ranked "all sorts of manners [toutes sortes de manieres] of representing natural objects [les corps que sont dans la nature]" and the "different artists [Ouvriers] who apply themselves to different subjects."[500] Nonetheless, it had long been understood among theoreticians, artists, and collectors that the most dignified ("les plus nobles") and worthy subjects ("les grands sujets") depicted man and his actions rather than landscape or, yet lower down the ladder, lifeless, inanimate objects ("he who does landscapes perfectly is above another who only does fruit, flowers, or shells"). Nearly a half-century earlier, Mancini had paid attention to these distinctions, to what he called the "spetie della pittura nate della differenza delle cose imitate" (categories of painting arising from the differences in the objects copied), advising his readers that "the painter is all the more perfect in relation to the degree he works with his fantasy and invention."[501]

Portraiture

To portray man simply as an individual, however, was to *ritrarre*, to reproduce, to copy, unlike history painting, which required imaginative interpretation of edifying subject matter and often the invention, and development, of multi-figural designs.[502] Therefore, history painting, which involved figures in motion, was more demanding of both creative talent and time; and hence "a painter who only does portraits has not yet reached that high perfection of art and cannot claim the honor the most learned [*sçavans*] receive."[503] As Vincenzo Giustiniani said, who put portraiture fourth from the bottom among his twelve "methods" of painting, just above three ways of copying, what really matters in portraiture is the fashioning of heads "so that they are good likenesses."[504]

It consequently is consistent that portraiture was paid less than history painting even if Baglione thought that, for his portraits, Caravaggio "was paid more than others got for history paintings," a claim Bellori refuted by noting that Caravaggio "made three portraits a day for a grosso [0.05 scudi] apiece."[505] There is no evidence to support either assertion. History painters, whose fame rested on their talent to represent figures, seldom declined portrait commissions, just as they often agreed to paint landscapes as a supplement to their incomes or to keep their patrons happy. And as would be anticipated in any competitive market, some painters embraced the opportunity to capitalize on the demand for portraits and thus made it their specialty, foregoing the likelihood of attaining great fame or fortune.

The scope of the demand might be indicated by data from five sample inventories of some of the city's largest, representative collections from the beginning to the end of the century (Table 6): 19 percent of the paintings in the Aldobrandini collection in 1603 were portraits; 15 percent of the Giustiniani collection in 1638; 37 percent of Antonio Barberini's collection in 1671; 19 percent of Camillo Massimi's collection in 1677; and 19 percent of the Colonna palace collection in 1689. In four out of five cases, portraiture as a category was second only to history painting, albeit usually by a significantly large margin.[506]

Of these collections, only Antonio Barberini's was appraised. On average, its portraits were half as valuable (39 scudi) as the history paintings (87 scudi) and roughly comparable to the landscapes (36 scudi).

An indication of the immeasurable demand for portraits emerges in two other inventories. One was drawn up in 1616 when the goods of an obscure painter-gilder, Nicolao Ventura, were sequestered. Of the 767 paintings

TABLE 6 Percentages by Subject Categories of Paintings in Five Roman Collections

INVENTORY	HISTORY	PORTRAIT	LANDSCAPE	GENRE	STILL LIFE
Aldobrandini, 1603	72	19	4	5	>1
Giustiniani, 1638	74	15	7	2	>1
Antonio Barberini, 1671	42	37	14	1	2
Camillo Massimi, 1677	48	19	24	4	>1
Colonna, 1689	49	19	16	>1	>1

described, 338 were portraits of popes, cardinals, saints, princes, poets, and others, and 324 were called portraits of heads. The inventory of Mario dei Fiori (d. 1673), the still life specialist who also operated as a dealer, lists over 500 portraits.[507] One more example is Cardinal del Monte's collection, which contained 277 portraits of "popes, emperors, cardinals, dukes, and other famous men with some women."[508]

The results of one study of 54 middle-class Roman inventories that on average contained 23.5 paintings roughly correspond with the percentages in Table 6 as regards history and landscape subjects. Fewer portraits were found in these middle-class households, where ancestors would not have been put on display as status symbols.[509] Still lifes were more numerous, while genre scenes were surprisingly rare. From a total of 2,040 paintings, 1,671 can be identified by subject categories: 59 percent of those were history paintings, 18 percent portraits, 11 percent landscapes, less than 1 percent genre scenes, and 9 percent still lifes.[510]

Scipione Pulzone's career as described by Baglione represents the pull that grand subject matter could have on a painter. Despite having completed portraits of the most illustrious sitters, including the pope, cardinals, and the grand duke of Florence, Pulzone was not willing to sacrifice fame and fortune by remaining a portraitist. Instead, he aspired to join the ranks of "the other excellent painters [*de gli altri eccellenti Pittori*]" and resolved "to paint histories and altarpieces [*fare delle istorie, e tavole d'altare*]."[511]

It cannot be said if fame or fortune was the stronger force drawing him, though the latter is more measurable despite the scarcity of documented portrait payments. Many prices for history paintings have been cited throughout this essay, including equivalent per-figure rates that, for the most esteemed painters, were 100 scudi and more. Predictably, the highest fees for portraits were earned by those same famous history painters, who could receive comparable per figure compensation. It has been mentioned, for example, that Maratta was paid 150 scudi for a full-length portrait and a proportionate amount for smaller formats. "It was, however, difficult for him to devote himself to them," Bellori relates, "as he was hindered by his other occupations, and he excused himself from them, even though he was stimulated by the prices and the liberality of those gentlemen who sought after him."[512]

Although in his life of Gaulli Pascoli gave the account of the naive *cavaliere* who was shocked to discover that the painter expected 100 scudi for a portrait, the Chigi documents tell a different story. In 1667, Gaulli received 45 scudi for two lost portraits of unspecified size of Alexander VII and Cardinal Chigi; in 1669, 100 scudi for a *Madonna* and a "ritratto grande" of Clement IX, another 50 scudi for a portrait with three cardinals, and 21 scudi for seven copies of portraits of "li Sig.ri Rospigliosi"; and, in 1671, 36 scudi for six portraits, one of which was a "tela grande."[513]

The most prominent portraitist in early seventeenth-century Rome was Ottavio Leoni, who today is chiefly remembered for his portrait drawings. Relatively few prices of his oil paintings are documented.[514] In 1608, Cardinal Montalto paid him a total of 75 scudi for three portraits of the cardinal himself.[515] That amount was similar to Montalto's payment the next year to one Francesco Carli of 30 scudi apiece for seven portraits, plus 18 scudi for the expense of bringing them from Florence to Rome.[516] To judge from some of many Altemps payments to Leoni, Montalto's cost of 25 scudi per portrait was rather typical: in 1610, they paid him only 6 scudi for a portrait of "S.ra Dona Annamaria," although the same year another 30 scudi for "un quadro grande di Dona Maria," and 35 scudi in 1612 for a portrait of Cardinal Altemps, which presumably was also large. Five years later Leoni received 150 scudi for "sei quadri di homini illustri di nostra casa," 25 scudi for a portrait of another illustrious Altemps, again 25 scudi for a portrait of a member of the household, and, in 1617–18, 50 scudi for two more portraits of family members and 40 for an undoubtedly larger canvas with "li sei figlioli del signor Duca patrone" (the six children of the duke).[517] During 1618, Leoni also painted a cycle depicting the life of S. Aniceto in a private chapel in the Palazzo Altemps, receiving at least 250 scudi for his oil murals.[518] He was paid more for his portraits by Paolo Giordano Orsini, though most likely for larger canvases: 60 and 40 scudi in 1623–24 for likenesses of Giordano and his wife. By the measure of another payment in 1624, Leoni's prices were relatively high: Giordano paid Giovanni Campagna just 32 scudi for 16 "quadri diverse teste di casa Orsini," that is, for a series of family portrait heads.[519]

The history painter Antonio Barbalonga, a student of Domenichino who in 1631 had earned 115 scudi for an altarpiece, was paid 100 scudi in 1633 for four portraits of Urban VIII and Cardinal Antonio Barberini, or again 25 scudi each.[520] Another painting of a comparable value reflects portraiture's inherent lower cost relative to history painting, given that in this example the same artist, the same patron, approximately the same date, and even comparable designs are involved. In 1630–31, the Barberini paid Valentin 25 scudi plus 5 scudi for the materials for his painting of a seated Samson measuring 136 × 103 cm (Cleveland Museum of Art). Two years earlier they had paid him only 20 scudi for a life-size portrait of Cardinal Francesco Barberini seated at a table with a crucifix that was about 223 × 134 cm, or twice as large.[521]

Often prices were considerably lower. Passignano received only 12 scudi d'oro (roughly 15 scudi) in 1603 for two untraced portraits of Clement VIII and Cardinal Aldobrandini.[522] During 1609, shortly after completing six frescoes in the Vatican for 400 scudi and while working at S. Gregorio Magno for a comparable fee, Reni painted a portrait for even less money: just 8.5 scudi for the recently discovered, bust-length portrait of Cardinal Giacomo Sannesi (Fig. 23). The same year Reni paid out merely 3 scudi to an unnamed person to paint two portraits of Cardinal Michelangelo Tonti.[523]

Yet a large size did not always mean a high price (for a scale of portrait fees pegged to specific sizes, see Elena Fumagalli's discussion of Giusto Sustermans's practice in Florence). In 1631, Giovanni Ferri Senese, an established artist with an usually wide repertoire (portraits, religious figures, battles, animals, genre scenes, *vedute*), earned just 10 scudi apiece for his portraits of Urban VIII seated in a chair and of Cardinal Barberini, the latter "un retratto grande."[524]

One of the most successful portraitists in late seventeenth-century Rome was the Fleming Ferdinand Voet. His smallest portraits could cost as little as 1.6 to

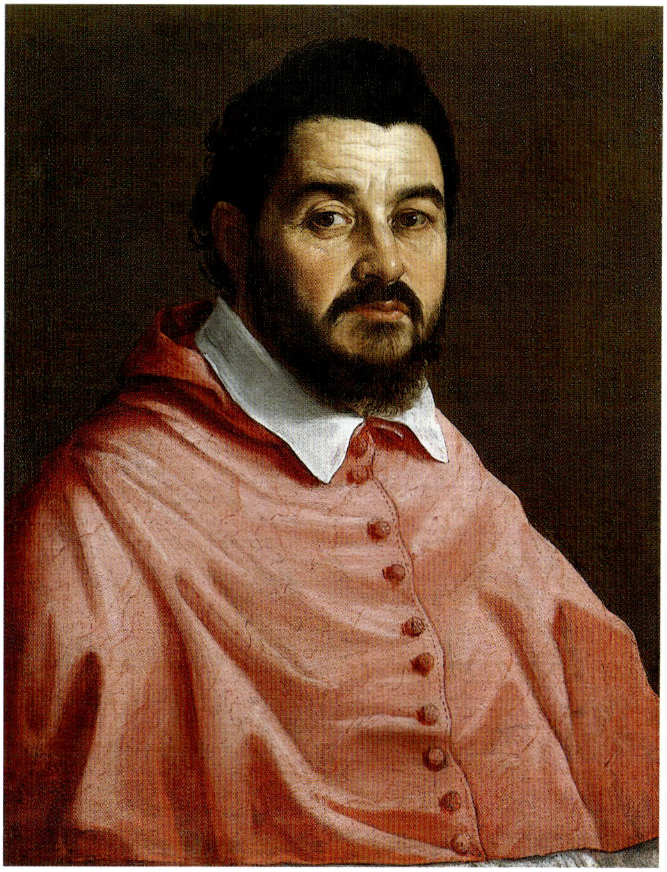

23 Guido Reni, *Cardinal Giacomo Sannesi*, 1609. Oil on canvas, 65 × 50 cm. Private collection.

3 scudi and his bigger ones around 15 to 20 scudi, although in 1670 he received the extraordinary sum of 180 scudi for a portrait of Queen Christina.[525] As with Gaulli, the Chigi's payments to him were generally modest: 60 scudi in 1672 for "diversi ritratti in tela alti p[al]mi 3"; 12 scudi in 1674 for a "ritrattino"; and 24 scudi in 1679 for a portrait of *Cardinal Chigi* that was a *tela d'imperatore*. For portraits by Pietro Paolo Vegli, Alessandro Mattia da Farnese, and Giuseppe Nasini, the Chigi family typically paid just 2 or 3 scudi.[526]

Other scattered payments and early inventory appraisals support the impression formed from these prices that, with few exceptions, portraits commanded modest fees when compared with history paintings, and that for a portraitist to have high earnings he had to be very productive. (Documents indicate that Tiberio Tinelli in Venice painted about 15 to 20 portraits a year.)[527] For Leoni, to gross 1,000 scudi annually would have meant selling a 25 scudi portrait every nine days. Prudently, he diversified his subject matter instead.

Baglione's short life of the late sixteenth-century portraitist Antonio de' Monti sums up the high demand yet limited rewards that were typical of portraiture. He wrote that Antonio could "superbly transcribe [*ritrarre*] from nature," whereupon "everyone wanted the portrait of the pope [Gregory XIII] by Antonio de' Monti." Accordingly, Antonio "acquired a good reputation and earned a 'reasonable' sum of money [*Acquistò egli per ciò, buon nome, & anche guadagno di ragionevol somma di danari*]."[528]

Genre

Portraiture might not have been a path to fortune but it was entirely respectable, unlike a new variety of genre scenes that in the eyes of some artists and critics, including Rosa, Sacchi, Albani, Testa, Bellori, Passeri, and Camillo Massimi, was monstrous.[529] On one level the fierce opposition was theoretical, that its imagery not only failed to transcend nature (which includes man and his activities), but deliberately chose to represent nature at its worst and lacked decorum. On another level the opposition was defensively economic because genre scenes by the Bamboccianti were selling well, as Rosa protested in his satire, *Painting*: "Such paintings are so very highly prized / you see them in the princes' galleries / resplendent in the finest gilded frames." Unspoken is the message that important collectors should have more elevated taste and that their scudi should go to the more worthy, and increasingly frustrated, painters.[530]

Passeri put it succinctly when he noted that low-life paintings by the Bamboccianti were being bought by "quante persone, e di nascita non ordinaria . . . e comprano anche a prezzo non piccolo" (a lot of people, not just of common birth, and not even at low prices). While Table 6 in the previous section indicates that genre painting constituted a minor portion of some of Rome's great collections, it should be noted that percentages for it and other new genres (landscape and still life) are skewed because the collections contained many paintings from the Renaissance, when those genres did not yet exist.

Passeri's attack on pictures with "soggetti bassi" that are "vili, privi di nobilità" (lowly subjects, vile, wanting in nobility), which do little more than entertain the ignorant public, was juxtaposed with his defense of Reni's extraordinary prices of as much as 400 or 500 scudi a figure. Those high prices, however, were set not for personal gain, he argued, but to promote the glory of painting, which more than any profession deserved to be honored and recognized.[531] His equation of money with respect could not be clearer.

Italian genre painting did not begin when Pieter van Laer, called Bamboccio, arrived in Rome around 1625, though it was his sort of small pictures, and those by his Northern followers such as Jan Miel and Roman-born Michelangelo Cerquozzi, that raised hackles. Four scenes of vendors of meat, fish, poultry, and vegetables by Bartolomeo Passerotti (various locations), for instance, were acquired by the Mattei considerably earlier (1603) for 100 scudi. That was not much money for four large canvases but, like Annibale Carracci's similar *Butcher's Shop* (Christ Church, Oxford), their ambitious size, likely allegorical content, and roots in the work of Pieter Aertsen, Joachim Beuckelaer, and Vincenzo Campi readily distinguish them from the new wave of small-scale low-life painting that swept Rome and found a lucrative market niche.[532]

As with portraits and landscapes, original prices of genre paintings are meagerly documented, in part because they often are just cited as *paesi* in inventories. There is sufficient evidence nonetheless, especially when compared with appraisals from early inventories, to form a picture that mirrors Pliny's remark about Peiraïkos, whom Bellori likened to van Laer as an "imitator of the worst." That ancient painter, Pliny wrote, depicted "barbers' shops, cobblers' stalls, asses, eatables and similar subjects." He "could give consummate pleasure, selling [his paintings] for more than other artists received for their large pictures."[533]

The best evidence of the value of bambocciate emerges from the work of van Laer. Two of his paintings owned by Swanevelt were stolen in 1635 and ended up in the hands of the dealer Niccolò Simonelli and then in the lap of the criminal tribunal.[534] Testimony indicated that "whoever would want to have paintings by Bamboccio similar to those stolen from Swanevelt would need to pay at least 30 to 35 scudi."[535] That estimate fits perfectly with a Barberini payment to van Laer of 30 scudi for one of his paintings bought through Bernini in 1634. It represented a night scene with a Gypsy, figures, and animals and measured about 67 × 56 cm.[536] A year earlier, Gian Maria Roscioli paid 18 scudi for a much smaller, framed picture by van Laer (about 30 × 25 cm) with "diversi animali."[537]

Like van Laer, who "due to the newness of his *maniera* earned a lot of money" (Passeri), Cerquozzi was highly successful as his follower. Passeri knew him personally and reports that initially the painter was satisfied to set modest prices in order to allure collectors to his van Laer-like pictures with small figures of rustic peasants and animals (Fig. 24). From numerous payments Cerquozzi earned a lot of money ("un assai di guadagno"), all the while yearning to be different. When finally he

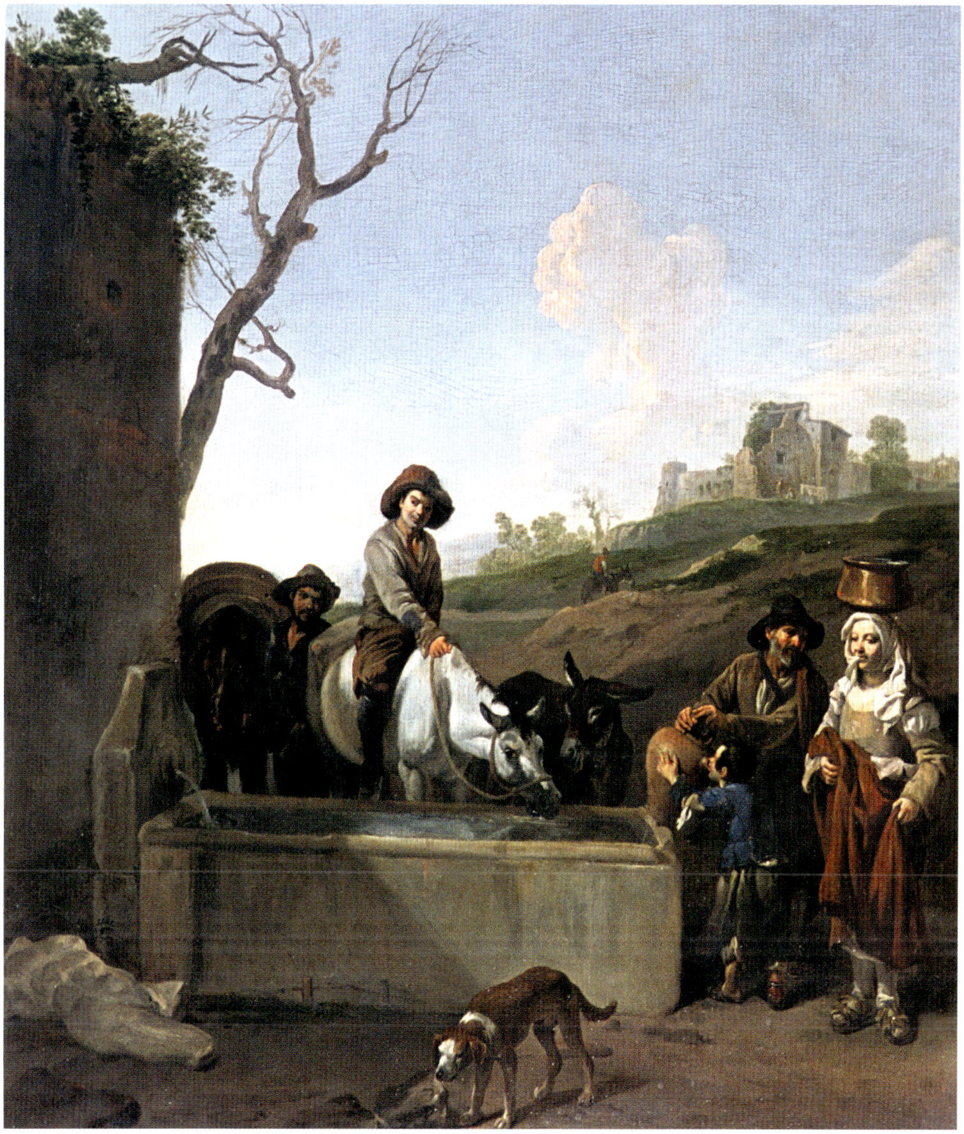

24 Michelangelo Cerquozzi, *Watering Trough*, ca. 1640–45? Oil on copper, 49.5 × 43.5 cm. Galleria Nazionale d'Arte Antica, Rome.

was well off with hundreds of scudi, he did not know what to do with his windfall and began losing sleep over it. Increasingly paranoid, he hid his money inside a plaster cast and beneath his house. At night he even went by foot to Tivoli to bury 500 scudi among the ruins. Peace came only when he was convinced to invest his money in *monti*, the kind of relatively secure bonds that many painters bought. Later in life Cerquozzi raised his prices and lived in good style, but generally he was so tightfisted that the expression arose, "sei più cotica di Michel'Angelo" (you are more miserly than Cerquozzi).[538]

Of particular interest is Passeri's knowledge that the money and property Cerquozzi left to his nephew (the artist owned a house as well as various gold and silver objects) yielded 25 scudi a month, "che possono servire di comodo trattenimento ad ogni stato onorevole."[539] That is, in Passeri's Rome of 1660, with an income of 300 scudi a year one could live "comfortably and in a dignified manner," a sum to be measured against the fees and income of artists cited throughout this study.[540]

Cerquozzi's success was due not only to his ability to tap into van Laer's market but to paint still lifes and acquire a separate reputation as a painter of battles, so much so that he became known as Michelangelo delle Battaglie. In 1649, the Sicilian collector Antonio Ruffo paid 80 scudi for a *Battle* by him that measured about 103 × 155 cm.[541] Cerquozzi catered to Spanish clients in Rome and even wore Spanish garb, yet he was perfectly willing to work for their opposition. His most famous collaborative project was with Viviano Codazzi on the *Revolt of Masaniello* for Bernardino Spada (Galleria Spada, Rome), who belonged to the Francophile faction in Rome and in 1648 paid 40 scudi for it. As Laura Laureati remarked, Cerquozzi's acceptance of Spada's commission suggests that he "made no pretense of loyalty to one political faction or another and was concerned only with procuring commissions and satisfying his clients," an observation that pertains to artists more widely.[542]

Jan Miel arrived in Rome in the early 1630s and was also successful as a painter of bambocciate, becoming sufficiently known and respected that around 1650 he could turn to painting large religious works for churches. Baldinucci characterized his individual talent for representing "merry groups of idlers, urchins, rogues, and other such types" with appropriate physiognomies, gestures, clothing, etc., adding that his works entered "all the cabinets of the most noblemen of Rome, Florence, and elsewhere." As a result, his earnings were very great. In 1658, he settled in Turin, where he was presented with a diamond-studded Cross.[543]

Even more than Cerquozzi, Miel found collaborative opportunities by painting figures for Codazzi, Dughet, Salucci, and Angeluccio, though no documents record what he was paid for that kind of work. Passeri attributed Miel's success in Rome to van Laer's departure ca. 1637 (his style, he thought, was "totale imitazione" of van Laer's), and to his ability as the son of a merchant to negotiate well, including sales by barter, exchange, and other *cabale profittevoli*, profitable intrigues.[544]

There can be little doubt, in light of the hostility the Bamboccianti aroused and the early biographers' consistent accounts, that van Laer, Cerquozzi, and Miel had good incomes even if, on average, their small genre scenes were priced well under 50 scudi and close in range to the portrait prices mentioned in the previous section. Nevertheless, 25 to 30 scudi for a small painting was substantial.

Like the data regarding landscape and still life pictures discussed below, prices of genre painting should not be taken as the measure of an artist's market value. Rather, market value ought to be assessed by multiplying prices by output, but unfortunately the rates of production are rarely known. Similarly, if the total economic value of the different genres were to be calculated and compared, it would be necessary to take into account the very large number of painters who produced portraits, genre pictures, landscapes, etc., many of whom belong to the "vanished."

Genre painting was mostly in the hands of the scores of Flemish and Dutch artists in Rome who belonged to the society of foreigners called the Schildersbent or Bentvueghels, the majority of whom came from the Low Countries but others from Germany, England, Scandinavia, Austria, and elsewhere. In the early 1630s, the Bent challenged the Accademia's authority to tax its members—previously, donations were voluntary but in 1633 a contribution became compulsory, 36 baiocchi for Italians, 42 for foreigners—and it won its case.[545] Some 30 artists belonged to the Bent when it was organized a decade earlier. During the century of its existence (ca. 1620–1720) there were nearly 500 members, whose numbers peaked during the third quarter of the century. Because the Bent opposed academic procedures, its majority were not history painters. Looking back from an eighteenth-century perspective, it was observed that many of the Bent's members were poor and employed by greedy dealers, for whom they worked "either by day wages or by piece."[546]

Cerquozzi's fame as a battle painter notwithstanding, the real specialist in the field was Jacques Courtois (Giacomo Cortese), confusingly known, like his brother Guillaume (Guglielmo), as Borgognone. Battle paintings, even when generic rather than historic—that is, when not representing a specific event—were thought to be more elevated than low-class genre scenes. Frequently they were larger, they required more figures, and accordingly they tended to command higher prices. To cite good examples, in 1617, Cardinal Montalto paid Antonio Tempesta 80 scudi for a *Battle* on copper a meter long and then another 100 scudi in 1621 for two small *Battles* again on copper.[547] Rosa's high fee of 300 scudi in 1642 for his large *Battle between Turks and Christians* has been cited. A decade later Monsignor Corsini paid Rosa even more for his equally large *Battle* (217 × 351 cm) to present, as previously mentioned, to the king of France. While proud of the latter commission and its good price (about 600 scudi), Rosa still denigrated the subject category: "I think you know how repugnant I find this sort of painting," he wrote to Ricciardi, who wanted a battle scene about 115 × 200 cm for a friend, "even though it is my home ground for beating any painter who wants to attack me. . . . for your sake, I won't make [your friend] spend more than 300 scudi. And you can add that, if the request hadn't come from you, I would not have done it at any price." But not quite. "He should know that I've more or less vowed not to paint this sort of picture unless I'm paid the price of a Raphael or a Titian."[548]

At the beginning of his career, according to Baldinucci, Cortese (b. 1621) was given monthly stipends of 12 and 25 scudi. In 1649, two large *Battles* measuring 100 × 300 cm (Gerini collection, Florence) cost 90 scudi. Around 1657, the artist received 30 doppie, more than 90 scudi, for an unspecified *Battle*.[549] In 1664 and 1665, the Chigi bought two of his *Battles*, one measuring 4 × 3 *palmi* (about 90 × 67 cm) for 40 scudi, the other, measuring 4 *palmi*, for 50 scudi. Those fees are marginally lower than the 60 scudi they paid Aniello Falcone in 1663 for a *Battle*.[550] In a letter to Claude's patron J. F. von Waldstein dated 1668, it was mentioned that Cortese expected 24 doppie (close to 75 scudi) for his paintings.[551]

Meanwhile, Cortese had entered the Jesuit novitiate in 1657. Baldinucci, who talked with the artist and personally bought some of his *Battles* "a gran costo," tells that Cortese put aside the sizeable sum of 1,000 doppie upon taking the habit.[552] At first he worked as an artist for the church but then resumed painting battles for his clients. Ruffo was one of them, whose inventory includes a painting 6 × 4 *palmi* (134 × 89 cm), "con figuretti bambocci, che vi sono molti soldati, mano del Burgugnone che si fe' gesuita, quadro di molta stima e preggio" (little Bamboccianti figures with many soldiers among them, hand of Borgognone, who is a Jesuit, a painting of high esteem and value), worth 40 Sicilian onze, about 95 scudi.[553]

Northerners continued to paint genre scenes throughout the century. Theodor Helmbreker worked in Rome from the 1650s until his death ca. 1696; he was highly successful in continuing the van Laer–Cerquozzi tradition and painting some religious works for private and public commissions. In a letter of 1685 to Grand Duke Cosimo III regarding bambocciate, Helmbreker is mentioned as being "absolutely the best in that sort of painting [*assolutamente il primo in tal sorta di pittura*]; but to give him what he asks, that is, 10 doppie [more than 30 scudi] for a canvas of 4 *palmi* [about 90 cm] . . . one struggles for years to pry it out of his hands."[554]

Christian Reder, too, one of the very last of the Bamboccianti, whom Pascoli mentioned as working on a daily basis for a secondhand dealer, could be expensive. Pascoli records that when he died in 1729, among his works were two large paintings measuring 7 × 5 *palmi* (156 × 112 cm) representing an *Encampment* and an *Ambush*. They had not sold, he understood, because Reder went too far by expecting the exaggerated price of 200 scudi.[555]

Landscape

Landscape painting was a step down the ladder from figural work, as Giustiniani made clear in ranking it seventh among twelve types of painting, the top four of which were all assigned to figural modes.[556] For traditionalists who linked price with labor, its value could be difficult to judge, since its number of figures did not seem to matter, as Claude's colorful quip, that he sold his landscapes and gave away his figures, indicates.[557] Moreover, leaving aside mural decoration, there was relatively less variation in the size of landscapes than in history painting or portraiture, and normally landscape did not depend on mimetic accuracy. As a result, its value, more than any of the other genres, relied heavily on the viewer's subjective judgment.

While the bulk of landscapes sold to the Roman public were cheap, those by its leading specialists, Paul Bril, Nicolas Poussin, Gaspard Dughet, Claude Lorrain, and a few other *oltramontani* were not.[558] Payments to their Italian contemporaries are less well documented because, relative to the many Northerners active in Rome, few Italians of note made their living as landscape specialists.[559]

Not one payment for any of Domenichino's easel landscapes is recorded, though there are a few for his colleague and sometime collaborator, Giovanni Battista Viola, dating from 1607 to 1615 and ranging from 15 to 25 scudi, mostly for canvases of unknown size.[560] Similarly, many payments to Agostino Tassi are preserved for his major projects, but for his easel pictures there are just a few documented prices: the substantial fee of 130 scudi in 1619 for a pair of large landscapes (about 194 × 135 cm) bought by the grand duke of Tuscany; a series of payments for paintings and drawings for the Barberini in 1633, including the astonishing sums of 300 and 350 scudi for two canvases commemorating Taddeo's recent activities; and 75 scudi in 1639 again from the Barberini for three large and four small paintings.[561]

There are no lifetime payments for Elsheimer's landscapes. The year after the artist's death, however, Rubens wrote in 1611, "in my opinion [Elsheimer] had no equal in small figures, in landscapes, and in many other subjects. . . . I pray that God will forgive Signor Adam his sin of sloth, by which he has deprived the world of the most beautiful of things, caused himself much misery, and finally, I believe, reduced himself to despair; whereas with his own hands he could have built up a great fortune and made himself respected by all the world." Rubens would have liked "to have that picture on copper" of the *Flight into Egypt* (Alte Pinakothek, Mun-

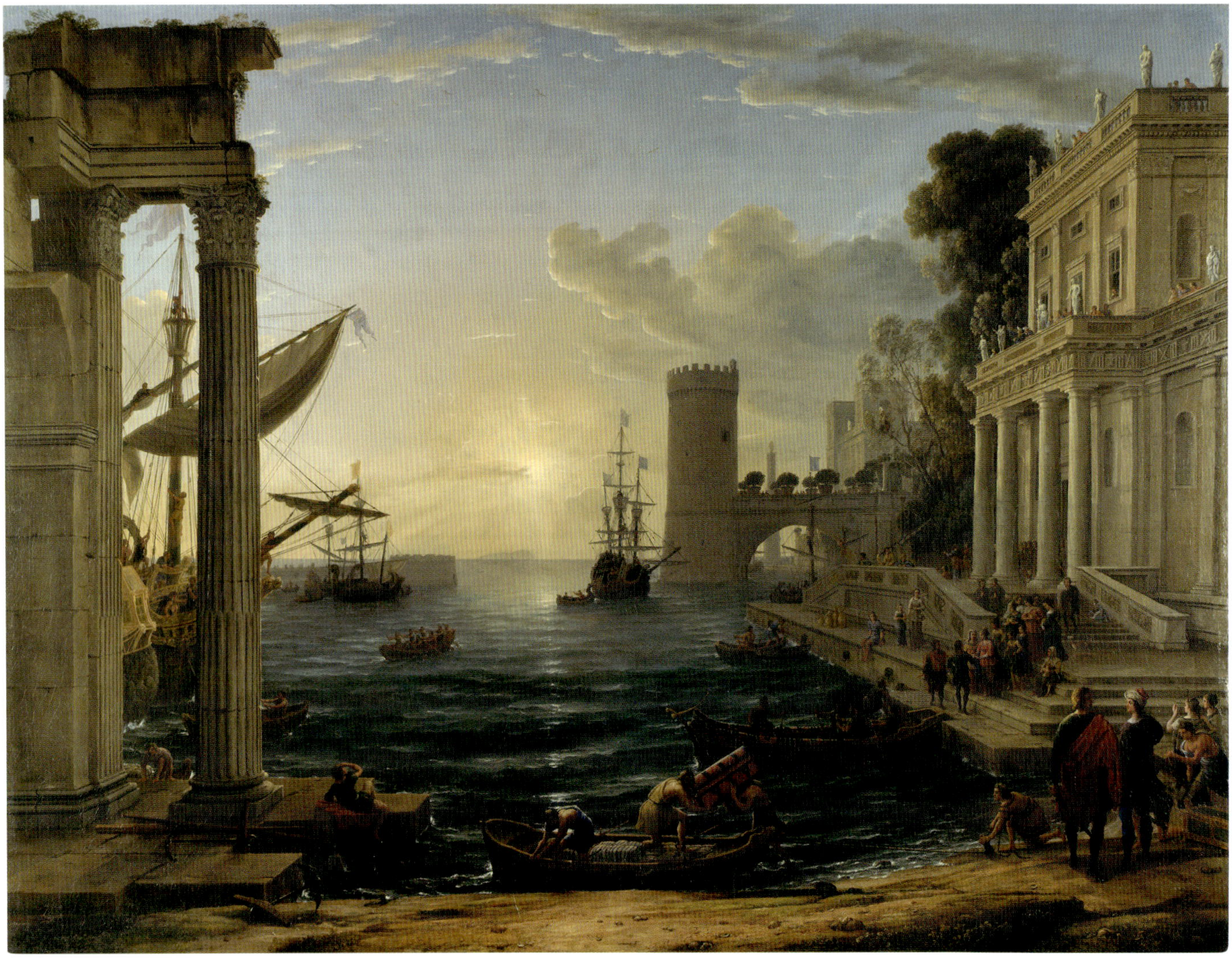

25 Claude Lorrain, *Seaport with the Embarkation of the Queen of Sheba*, 1648. Oil on canvas, 148 × 194 cm. National Gallery, London.

ich), "but I fear that the high price of 300 crowns [scudi] may prevent it."

That extraordinary sum for a painting measuring only 31 × 41 cm undoubtedly was due to its dazzling technique and market rarity, as another set of early documents indicates. Negotiations had begun in 1612 to buy Elsheimer's masterpiece, a small, seven-panel private altar with stories of the True Cross in landscape settings (Städelsches Kunstinstitut, Frankfurt). Tassi advised the grand duke of Tuscany to buy the work, which he had seen in the home of a Spaniard in Rome. Although Cigoli thought it was not good enough for the grand duke's collection, negotiations continued. Seven years later, the grand duke was informed that the Spaniard was in financial trouble and willing to accept less than the 3,000 scudi he had hoped to get. By the end of the year, the deal was closed for the much reduced but still considerable price of 800 scudi.[562]

Recorded payments to Rome's most famous landscape specialist, Claude Lorrain (Fig. 25), are few, but luckily they span 35 years of his long career.[563] To the data in Table 7 might be added Antonio Ruffo's acquisitions by 1663 and 1667 of two more landscapes, one measuring about 52 × 54 cm, the other about 64 × 90 cm, for 60 and 80 scudi, though it is undocumented if the purchases were from Claude himself or a second party.[564]

Meager as these records are in relation to Claude's large oeuvre, they show a steady increase in payments. Following two unusually high sums in 1639 and 1647–48 (the landscape illustrated in Fig. 25 was one of the two paid for in 1647–48), Claude's prices reached a

TABLE 7 Documented Payments to Claude Lorrain

DATE	PRICE (scudi)	SIZE (cm)	BUYER and *LIBER VERITATIS* NUMBER
1634	43 for two	ca. 95 × 135	Roscioli (unidentified)
1639	155	102 × 133	Carlo de' Medici (L.V. 28)
1639	40	99 × 129?	Angelo Giori (L.V. 43?)
1639	35		Paolo Giordano Orsini (L.V. 33)
1646	100 (+?) for two	150 × 200	Pamphilj (L.V. 113, 119)
1647–48	450 for two	152 × 201; 148 × 194	Duke of Bouillon (L.V. 113, 114 [Fig. 25])
1654	307+ for three	147 × 248 143 × 251; 34 × 42	Cardelli (L.V. 129, 134, 132)
1655	225 for two	100 × 137	Alexander VII (L.V. 136–37)
1663	150+	116 × 158	Halmale/de Wael (L.V. 160)
1664–65	250 for two	87 × 153, 91 × 155	Colonna (L.V. 162, 167)
1668–69	300 for two	107 × 140	Waldstein (L.V. 173–74)

minimum of 100 scudi by the 1650s and 125 to 150 scudi by the next decade. Sandrart, in fact, reported that Claude's mature works sold for 100 scudi d'oro (the equivalent of about 160 scudi), and even more.

Marcel Röthlisberger estimated that Claude painted about 250 pictures during his lifetime, Marie-Nicole Boisclair increased the figure to 300.[565] Assuming an average selling price of 125 scudi for 275 works, which might be generous because many of the early and smaller paintings commanded less, one arrives at about 35,000 scudi as Claude's lifetime earnings for 50 years of work. That is an average annual gross income of about 700 scudi from the paintings, exclusive of sales of prints or drawings and investment income, such as from the painter's many bank bonds.[566]

Those were good earnings, particularly for someone who was not a history painter but a specialist in one of the lowest genres. In addition to his bank savings of over 5,000 scudi, Claude's household inventory documents valuable goods, such as diamond rings, silverware, and linens, some of which surely were gifts from his many lofty patrons. Baldinucci understood that his estate was worth 10,000 scudi.[567] In contrast, Bellori said that Poussin, who like Claude essentially painted easel pictures for private patrons (except while in Paris, where he had an unusually high income), accumulated 15,000 scudi during his lifetime. But it is impossible to know if Poussin, who lived frugally, just managed his money better. Bellori observed that 15,000 scudi "seemed little in view of [Poussin's] frugality and the many works he had executed."[568]

Whatever the explanation, both artists enjoyed a privileged economic status in Rome, albeit their earnings did not approach those of their peers who could earn huge fees by painting altarpieces and frescoes. For landscape painters, even mural decoration could be poorly paid, bringing to mind Pliny's account of the landscape specialist Studius. Producing "a delightful effect," Studius's mural work was available "at a very small cost."[569]

Gaspard Dughet's murals illustrate this point. From the time of his frescoes at S. Martino ai Monti in the later 1640s, for which he was paid only about 10 scudi for the larger frescoes and as little as 3 scudi for the smaller ones, to his later projects for the Borghese and Colonna, it appears that he earned relatively less doing mural paintings than easel pictures. Evidently, some patrons associated high fees for murals with history subjects and literally downgraded the worth of landscape decoration. Mancini implied as much when he noted not only the rarity of public landscape commissions but the secondary status of those that existed. Moreover, he observed that when such projects were collaborative, they were attributed to the painters who did the figures, not the landscapes.

It might be that Dughet was willing to take on mural commissions to establish or maintain good relationships with important patrons, as probably was the case with Domenichino, who was paid relatively little, 200 scudi, for his large fresco landscape cycle at the Aldobrandini villa in Frascati.[570] Much later in the century (1672), the landscape specialist Crescenzio Onofri was paid just 1.5

scudi a day for decorating the Colonna's palace, a rate that in all probability was less remunerative than his arrangements 15 years later in Florence, where he received the relatively generous monthly stipend of 15.5 scudi from Ferdinand de' Medici, plus payment for work.[571]

Dughet was prolific and successful, in some ways more so than Claude, if Boisclair is right in estimating his output at 400 paintings over 40 years, and if Baldinucci is right in saying that Dughet's estate was worth 25,000 scudi, two-and-a-half times Claude's and almost double Poussin's. When a client refused to pay Dughet 300 scudi, which Dughet understood Rosa had been paid for its intended pendant, the artist held his ground and sold it to another admirer for that price. Yet other figures suggest that, on average, Dughet was paid no more than around 100 scudi per picture, less than Claude but significantly more than van Laer and his followers received for their bambocciate—and twice as much as Domenico Gargiulo, Naples's foremost landscape painter, commanded. In a letter of 1665 to Antonio Ruffo, Abraham Brueghel indicated that a Claude would cost twice as much as a Dughet of comparable size.

Still, in a typical year Dughet earned as much as Claude because he worked more quickly and his output was greater. According to Dughet's brother, the painter could complete a large canvas in a day.[572] Exaggerated or not, it acknowledges Dughet's facility, especially when compared with Claude's production in the 1650s and later when, partly due to gout, he finished as few as three or four canvases a year. Claude, however, was lucky to be reliant on many foreign clients and thus less affected by swings in the local market, which Rosa experienced. In 1664 Rosa lamented that "it's been a year since commissions have been given, even by a dog," and that he had on hand unsold pictures worth a thousand scudi.[573]

Dughet's penchant to work rapidly, like Lanfranco's to paint large fresco cycles quickly, might have had economic incentives: to maximize income and boost a market image of a painter who would meet his deadlines. Claude, on the other hand, could prosper with a limited output because his prices had risen to 125–150 scudi, which equaled and often surpassed the fees that a number of history painters, including Poussin, received for easel pictures and even for some altarpieces (see Table 5). That remarkable accomplishment is probably what Baldinucci had in mind when he wrote that Claude's "pictures have been sold at prices almost no longer heard of for their kind."[574]

Only Paul Bril as a landscape painter might have approached that status previously.[575] Though a favorite of Sixtus V and Rome's elite collectors, in 1601 his fees were still moderate: for five big paintings of their estates that were to be executed on single pieces of canvas and mounted on stretchers at the painter's expense, the Mattei promised to pay 30 scudi each plus Bril's travel expenses on horseback to view and draw perspectives. In 1607, Cardinal Montalto paid Bril 50 scudi for two landscapes for his villa, the same fee he paid Viola for two landscapes that year. But by 1610, one of Bril's paintings was said to have cost an unprecedented 200 scudi d'oro, about 240 scudi. In 1621, the year after Bril became the first Northerner and first landscape artist to be elected *principe* of the Accademia, Ferdinand Gonzaga was cautioned that his paintings were "non sol care, ma carissime" (not just expensive, but very expensive), and that each of 24 large landscapes for his Villa La Favorita would cost about 100 scudi apiece, a sum that corresponds exactly with Baglione's report that Bril "did not want to paint if he wasn't paid a hundred scudi for each of his landscapes."[576]

Despite Bril's prominent reputation as a muralist, it seems that for him, too, easel paintings were more lucrative (that might be why toward the end of his career he produced more and more cabinet pictures), although some of his fresco projects probably paid well. For his and his collaborators' pergola and landscape lunettes of 1611–12 in the Borghese's Loggia della Pergola (now Palazzo Pallavicini Rospigliosi), in which Reni painted ten pair of *putti*, Bril received 700 scudi. Unfortunately, it is not known what Reni was paid for his contribution to the project or if his fee might have come out of the 700 scudi. A couple of years later, Bril again shared a Borghese commission with Reni and Antonio Tempesta. His four frescoes of the *Four Seasons* in the Casino dell'Aurora (Palazzo Pallavicini Rospigliosi) cost just 60 scudi, unsurprisingly far less than either the 200 or so scudi Reni received for his celebrated *Aurora* or the same sum Tempesta was paid for two long figural friezes, though neither of those payments, especially for Reni's complex fresco, was particularly generous.[577]

Two other *oltramontani*, Jan Both and Herman van Swanevelt, shared a prestigious foreign commission with Claude, Dughet, Poussin, and others: the decoration of Philip IV's Buen Retiro with landscapes. In 1636, just about the time of the Spanish project, Both was paid only 7 and 8 scudi by Roscioli for a pair of small coppers. Two years later Roscioli bought a *quadro da testa*, a canvas about 65 × 50 cm, by Both for 9 scudi, and then the next year two *tele d'imperatore* landscapes for 20 scudi apiece. It was a benefit to Both's net earnings that he followed Roman practice, which was common elsewhere in Italy, of selling his works unframed. For Both's *tele d'imperatore*, for example, Roscioli paid almost 2.5 scudi for a pair of frames and 7 scudi more to gild them, adding 25 percent to their cost. Comparatively, that was not so expensive. For framing a copy of an Arpino for which he had paid only 12 scudi, Roscioli spent 14 scudi, more than its purchase price. While gilding was quite expensive—for a large frame it might cost 125 scudi—a lot of money was spent on precious frames, too, such as one in silver for an unfinished Romanelli that Giuseppe Belloni completed in 1663. Though measuring only about 78 × 67 cm, it cost 75 scudi.[578]

Swanevelt's fees were roughly similar to Both's. In 1641, the Barberini paid 40 scudi for two very large landscapes by him. In Antonio Barberini's inventory of 1671, in which Claude's *St. George* (Wadsworth Atheneum, Hartford) was appraised at 150 scudi, big canvases by Swanevelt were appraised at only a quarter as much. It is hard to know to what extent market conditions prompted Swanevelt's move to Paris in the 1640s, or to what degree his departure could have depressed the value of his work in Rome. In any case he reportedly was successful in France. An Englishman in Paris in 1647 lamented his high prices, remarking that a "paese di Monsr. Herman, which cost 25 crouwnes [scudi], was sold here [in Paris] for 25 pistolls," the equivalent of about 75 scudi. Yet, at his death in 1655, Swanevelt's estate was worth 4,200 scudi, less than half of Claude's, and paintings in his posthumous inventory were given low appraisals, from about 10 to 20 scudi. Due to their worth as capital assets for future printing, the plates for his landscape etchings were given equivalent appraisals of roughly 13 scudi apiece.[579]

Thus, it is not surprising that Roscioli, too, paid less for landscapes by Swanevelt than by Claude or Both: in 1633, only 35 scudi for three canvases by him whereas seven years later he bought Poussin's landscapes with *St. Matthew* (Staatliche Museen, Berlin) and *St. John on Patmos* (Fig. 26) for 40 scudi the pair, about the same price he paid for big landscapes by Claude and Both.[580]

The earliest cited payment to Poussin was for his battle scenes of the mid-1620s, only 7 scudi apiece. The first indication of a landscape price appears in a letter by Cassiano dal Pozzo dated 1630. Cassiano mentions unspecified works by Poussin available at 15 to 20 scudi each, which he thought were preferable to those by either Filippo Napoletano or Bril, indicating that he had landscapes in mind. In fact, 20 scudi was the price Roscioli paid ten years later for each of his landscapes by Poussin.

Although the cost of Poussin's history pictures rose quickly, they rarely reached the 200 scudi range. The average of all of the two dozen or so known payments to Poussin is around 125 scudi, which drops to nearly 110 scudi per easel picture when the exceptional payment of 400 scudi for his altarpiece of *St. Erasmus* for St. Peter's is put aside.[581] That figure is very similar to Claude's average price.

The Roscioli documents are especially revealing. The same year that Roscioli spent only 20 scudi apiece for the landscapes with *St. Matthew* and *St. John on Patmos* (Fig. 26), he paid Poussin 70 scudi, three-and-a-half times as much, for the *Continence of Scipio* (Fig. 27), which is only slightly larger.[582] It is hard to escape the conclusion that here is exceptional evidence that, all things being equal—same patron, same artist, same date, similar dimensions—a landscape painting was considerably cheaper to acquire than a figural work.

The logical follow-up economic question is, were landscapes cheaper to produce? Given that prices of canvas, priming, and stretchers were basically the same for all easel paintings, the main comparative measure for material costs is pigments. Were those used in predominantly green, brown, and blue paintings, say in Poussin's *Landscape with a Man Washing his Feet at a Fountain* (National Gallery, London), less costly than the brightly colored pigments needed for a scene such as Poussin's *Rape of the Sabine Women* (Fig. 28)? The evidence is regrettably scant, given that one needs to determine not only which pigments landscape and history painters regularly used, but the quantity of each pigment, and its quality and cost, which varied significantly.

Some conjectures can be offered on the basis of educated guesswork and scattered laboratory analyses carried out by the National Gallery, London.[583] The most expensive pigment Poussin presumably used in the *Rape of the Sabine Women* is ultramarine for the bright blue robes. To judge from its richness, it probably was of high quality, certainly superior to ultramarine ashes, the low-grade, pale, last extraction from lapis lazuli. In 1646, the Pamphilj paid Grimaldi only 21.4 scudi for 5.5 ounces of ultramarine and "other expenses," indicating that it must have been low quality.[584] Artists knew how to stretch ultramarine, as Rosa remarked and Poussin might have done in the *Sabines* by layering it over cheaper azurite or smalt. In any case, because the paint of the *Sabines* is thinly applied, it is hard to imagine that even an ounce of ultramarine was needed.

The second most costly pigment that Poussin and his contemporaries commonly used was red lake, in the *Sabines* to enrich the vermilion robe of the old woman kneeling in the center. The finest red lakes, however,

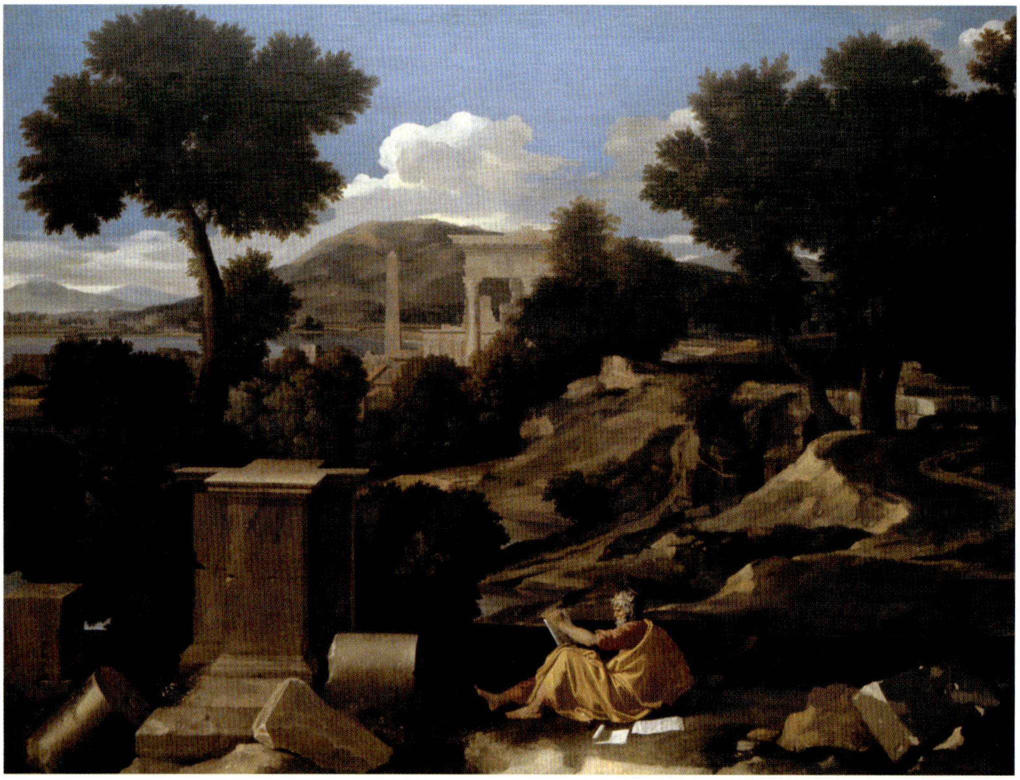

26 Nicolas Poussin, *Landscape with St. John on Patmos*, 1640. Oil on canvas, 102 × 136 cm. The Art Institute, Chicago.

27 Nicolas Poussin, *Continence of Scipio*, 1640. Oil on canvas, 114 × 163 cm. Pushkin Museum, Moscow.

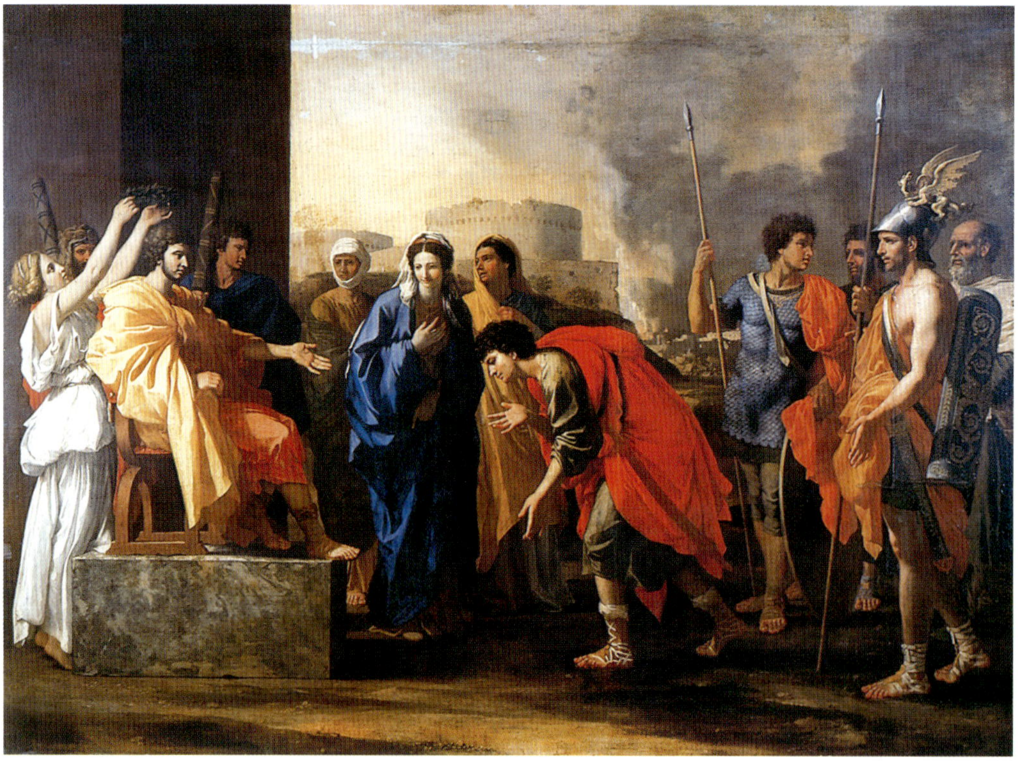

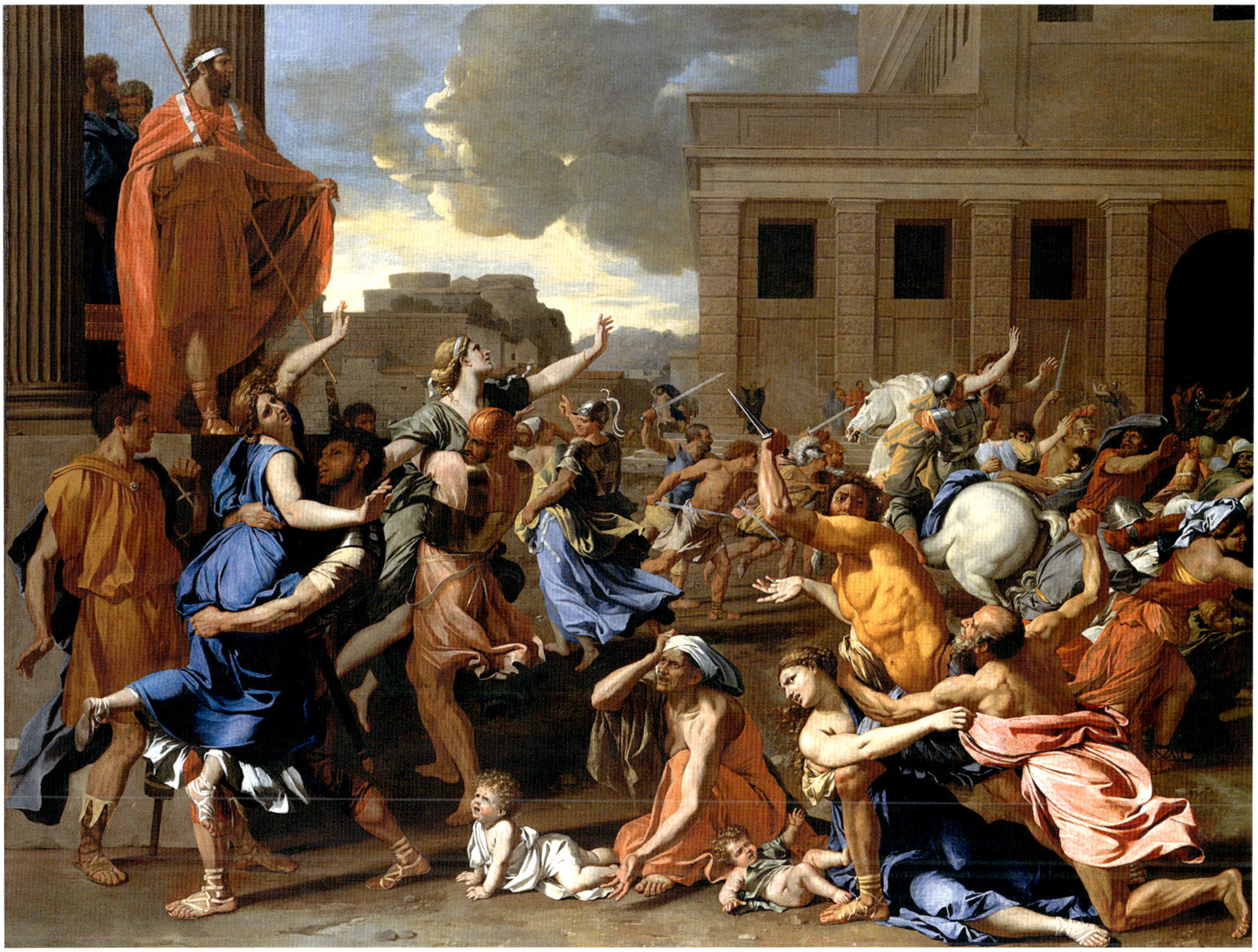

28 Nicolas Poussin, *Rape of the Sabine Women*, 1633–34. Oil on canvas, 155 × 210 cm. Metropolitan Museum of Art, New York.

cost no more than 3 to 5 scudi an ounce. Rarely, fine azurite could cost as much.

Poussin again used ultramarine in the sky of the *Landscape with a Man Washing his Feet at a Fountain*. Claude similarly used ultramarine in the sky of his *Landscape with Cephalus and Procris* (National Gallery, London), and in the foliage at the left of the painting, mixed with yellows, greens, and white. The color of the foliage of the main tree was achieved by mixing ultramarine with green earth and some yellow and smalt. The gray-green color of the middle distance is made mostly of ultramarine with a little yellow and white.

The sky of Claude's *Seaport with the Embarkation of the Queen of Sheba* (Fig. 25)—one of a pair of paintings that cost about 450 scudi (Table 7)—contains ultramarine and maybe some smalt. The sea, too, has ultramarine, as does the tree at the right. Claude used a very small amount of high-quality ultramarine for the intense blue stockings of the turbaned man standing in the foreground at the far right, and ultramarine and red lake for his purple tunic, that is, the two most expensive pigments. For his *Seaport with the Villa Medici* (Uffizi, Florence), which in 1639 cost 155 scudi (Table 7), Claude asked for and presumably received an advance of 30 scudi for "l'azzurro oltramarino."[585] Although it is unknown if he really spent that much money on the blue pigment, the document suggests that presumably it was not an unreasonable request for one of his marines.

None of the three green pigments generally available to seventeenth-century painters were entirely satisfactory, whether because they were insufficiently saturated or were unstable. Hence Claude, Dughet, Poussin, Rosa, and their colleagues frequently made their greens by mixing blue, often ultramarine, with one or more yellows, typically a lake and yellow ochre, and a black and green earth.[586]

Pending more laboratory evidence, this data provisionally suggest that landscapes might not have been significantly cheaper to paint than figural scenes since they often contained expensive pigments. Nonetheless, the hierarchy of artistic genres had serious financial consequences for landscape painting as a whole, which is clearly indicated by data from Roman inventories. At the beginning of the century, when landscape had a small share of the upscale market, the Aldobrandini collection in 1603 consisted of only 4 percent landscapes (Table 6). Thirty-five years later, 7 percent of the Giustiniani collection included landscapes.[587] The pace increased as the century progressed, with landscapes reaching 24 percent of Camillo Massimi's collection in 1677, which included nine paintings attributed to Dughet and five by Claude.[588]

Though it is slippery to compare inventories of Dutch private collections with those of Rome's grand collections (especially because landscapes, like still lifes, often were displayed in Roman country residencies and did not appear in inventories), it might be noted that, by mid-century, landscapes were the most common subject in Dutch households and they also constituted the largest subject category at the Orphan Chamber auctions in seventeenth-century Amsterdam. Yet even in the Netherlands, the most valuable works were history paintings, whose price level could be almost double that of landscapes.[589] Similarly, the greatest value given to any landscapes in Antonio Barberini's collection in 1671, 150 scudi alike for Claude's *St. George*, Poussin's *Landscape with St. Matthew*, and an unidentified Rosa, was much less than the values given to some history paintings of the period, such as 900 scudi for a Sacchi, 500 each for a Lanfranco and an Albani, and 450 for a Cortona.[590]

Scores of landscapes in princely collections were of modest value because so many landscape specialists worked at the low end of the market, not infrequently filling bulk orders, such as the 38 large canvases the bishop of Gaeta ordered in 1605 from the Flemish painter-dealer Karel Oldrago, which were to be delivered in six months. Oldrago was to paint four of them himself for 16 scudi apiece and design all of the others, for another 5 scudi each, which then were executed by Baldassare Lauri, who received from 8 to 10 scudi per canvas. On average, those 38 paintings cost about 14 scudi.[591] In 1621, Baldassare Lauri was paid 1.5 scudi a day to paint another 83 landscapes, large and small, in just five months, which meant a significantly lower average cost of less than 2.5 scudi.[592] And then there were ten huge gouache landscapes appraised at 5 scudi each, and many unattributed, unidentifiable landscapes serving as overdoors and overwindows in Antonio Barberini's collection that were given values as low as 2 or 3 scudi apiece.[593] Even someone of Crescenzio Onofrio's standing was paid only 15 scudi by the Colonna in 1671 for painting ten "paesini diversi" in their palace, three on a door, seven at a window.[594]

Many other landscape painters, despite lofty patronage, have entirely vanished. A particularly good example is the mysterious Giovanni Francione, by whom Francesco Barberini owned 38 landscapes, two of which were medium in size and cost 6 and 10 scudi. Even a "Compagno di Francione" is cited in the Barberini documents. Paolo Giordano Orsini's brother Ferdinando paid 30 scudi for an oval landscape on copper to one "Cornelio pittore," who possibly was the Dutchman Cornelis van Poelenburgh. If so, that sizeable fee for a small picture represents the premium that a finely wrought work might bring, but also the competition that local artists faced from the many Northern landscape painters active in Rome.[595]

Still Life

"The fifth method is to know how to portray flowers and other tiny objects. . . . Caravaggio said that to make a fine painting of flowers was as much work for him as to make one of figures."[596] For those artists and critics who scorned genre painting, however, there was nothing redeeming about still life painting. From their idealist perspective, Albani and Testa derided it as doubly damnable: it lacked human (or as they saw it, any) life and was rote transcription without invention.[597]

The inclination to lionize Caravaggio's role in the origins of Italian still life painting overlooks the fact that even he, the arch-naturalist who supposedly equated it with figural work, gave up still life painting as soon as more prestigious and lucrative commissions came along. If Cecco del Caravaggio (Francesco Buoneri), the Pensionante del Saraceni, Pietro Paolini, or any of the other Caravaggisti painted independent still lifes, those pictures constituted a minor part of their oeuvres. This pertains to Cerquozzi as well, whose bambocciate and battle scenes far outnumber his still lifes. In a similar way, most of the other early Italian still life painters in Rome, unlike their Flemish counterparts, were not exclusive in their practice. Tommaso ("Mao") Salini painted history subjects and portraits, and Pietro Paolo Bonzi ("Gobbo dei frutti" or "dei Carracci") painted landscapes—and one altarpiece, for which he was paid only 16 scudi—although Agostino Verrocchi and Giovanni Battista Crescenzi seem to have been more committed to the genre.[598] Thus far, few still lifes can be securely attributed to any of those pioneers (an exception is Bonzi's documented swags with fruits and flowers of 1622 in the vault of the gallery of the Palazzo Mattei di Giove, painted in collaboration with Cortona), despite the listing of 115 paintings of flowers and fruits in Salini's studio at the time of his death in 1625.[599]

Rarer still are documented payments to these painters. In 1619, Salini was given 90 scudi for 12 "quadri diversi di fiori" for the Borghese's Villa Mondragone (a decade earlier he had been paid 85 scudi for a double-sided processional banner).[600] The following year he sold a dozen more still lifes to Cosimo II de' Medici, who spent 100 scudi on a gold chain to give the artist as the "value of 12 paintings of flowers and fruits." Although Bonzi "devoted himself to painting fruits from life" and "in that genre could not be surpassed" (Baglione), he is mentioned only twice in payments for easel pictures: in 1633 as "Lonzi," when he was given 60 scudi for six "quadri di frutti e fiori" for the Vatican; and in 1636, the year he died, when Roscioli paid 30 scudi for five small "quatri da testa" by "Gobbo," two of which had flowers, two had fruit, and one a pair of pheasants.[601]

Among other sporadic payments from early in the century is one to Tommaso Campana in 1619 for supplying decoration, like Salini, for the Villa Mondragone. He was paid 60 scudi for "diversi quadri" of animals and fish.[602] The same year, the obscure Antonio Tanari received 45 scudi for a large painting of fish for the Medici. Two years earlier they paid him 30 scudi for two paintings of fruit; the same year they paid 43 scudi to one Baldassar Baderni, "pittore all'Arco di Portogallo," for two paintings of fruit, flowers, fish, and birds.[603] An earlier payment to Tanari (1609) of 205 scudi for two still lifes with fruit for Cardinal Montalto's villa is so out of line with these other early fees (typically in the 10 scudi range) that it must have been for work of exceptional size or complexity.[604] Tanari's trajectory was the opposite of Jan Miel's. Instead of moving up the ladder to the rank of history painter, Tanari had started with a commission for an altarpiece in S. Pudenziana in 1607, albeit for a fee of only 50 scudi.[605] Given its routine design, it is hardly surprising that no other figural work from his hand is known.

Roman still life painting came into full maturity with the careers of Mario Nuzzi (Mario dei Fiori), Salini's nephew and presumed student; Michele Pace (Michelangelo di Campidoglio); and the three Stanchi brothers.[606] Of these, Mario's career is especially interesting from a financial perspective, despite the scarcity of documented payments to him. Most of those that exist were made by the Chigi "on account" (sums such as 20, 30, 60, and 80 scudi) during 1658–59 for "paintings done and to be done" by Mario, without further specifications.[607]

In 1659, the Chigi paid him 100 scudi as final settlement (*saldo*) "and entire payment" for five canvases designated as 6 × 9 *palmi* (134 × 201 cm). They actually measure 195 × 265 cm, a good example of the rough approximations often found in early measurements, and consist of a set of the *Four Seasons* and a portrait of *Mario dei Fiori Painting a Vase of Flowers* (Fig. 29), with Mario's portrait by Giovanni Maria Morandi (all Palazzo Chigi, Ariccia).[608] Mario painted the flowers in the *Seasons* while the figures are by four of Rome's leading artists: Carlo Maratta, Giacinto Brandi, Filippo Lauri, and Bernardino Mei. The *giustificazione* (financial justification) notes that Lauri received 60 scudi for *Spring*, that the other collaborators on the *Seasons* were paid by Cardinal Flavio Chigi, and that Mario paid Morandi an unknown sum for his portrait. The five frames cost an additional 50 scudi.[609]

Maratta and Brandi and probably Mei were paid 70 scudi apiece for their allegorical figures of the seasons and *putti*, bringing the total cost of the figural work to 270 scudi, as compared with 100 scudi for the flowers and portrait. Hence Mario's fee of 20 scudi per painting (less whatever he paid Morandi) was roughly twice the going rate for (often smaller) still lifes a half-century earlier.[610] Only five years later (1664), the Chigi paid him 200 scudi for painting flowers on four mirrors (at the time a new decorative fashion in Rome), measuring 5 × 3 *palmi* (112 × 67 cm) each.[611] By then, Mario already had painted larger mirrors (248 × 166 cm) for the Colonna in collaboration with Maratta.

Pascoli narrates a colorful story about Mario as a young painter who discovered that dealers were profiting enormously as his prices escalated to a level "ch' era maggiore che non credeva" (that was greater than he could believe). Hence he decided to cash in on the insatiable demand by opening his own studio in the heart of Rome "presso strada delle carrozze" (near the via delle Carrozze), that is, on what in his day was, and remains, the via Mario dei Fiori. Tracking Mario's financial success in a *vita* focused on money, Pascoli reports that Mario's friends dissuaded him, even though he had put aside sufficient funds, from buying a *vigna*, which had ruined other wealthy artists and could become nothing but a big headache, and also from

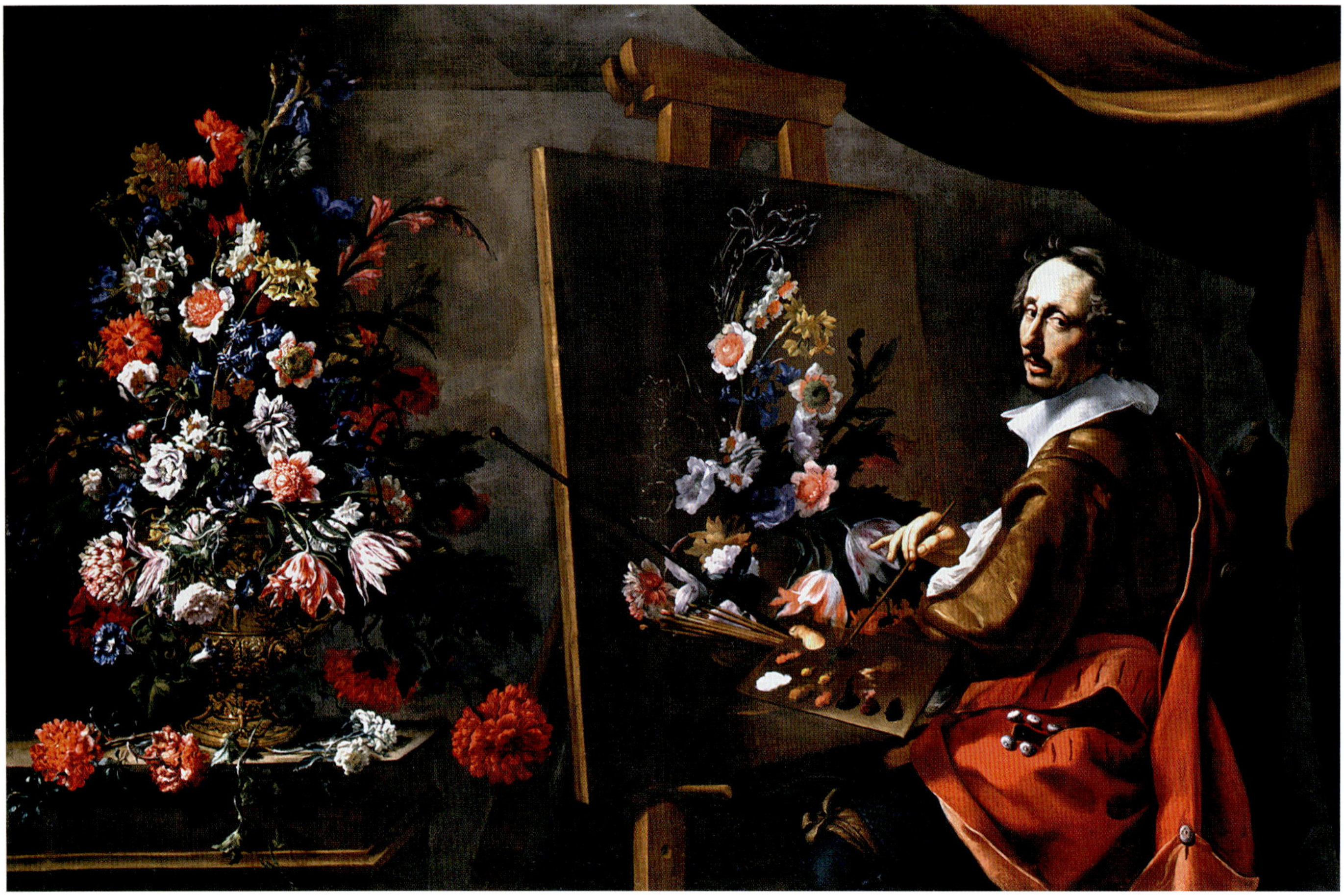

29 Mario dei Fiori and Giovanni Maria Morandi, *Mario dei Fiori Painting a Vase of Flowers*, 1659. Oil on canvas, 195 × 265 cm. Palazzo Chigi, Ariccia.

building a second house, his backup plan to keep his capital from remaining idle. They advised him to invest his savings instead in various financial instruments such as *luoghi di monti*, *censi*, and *uffizi vacabili*.[612]

There is solid evidence that Mario was resolved to take control of the sale of his art and supplement his income as a dealer. In 1655, the Accademia, to which he belonged as well as to the Congregazione dei Virtuosi del Pantheon, voted to issue him a *patente*, a license, in response to his application to be allowed "to keep open in Rome a shop to resell paintings" as a "Pittore Bottegaro." His would be one of four to six such shops allowed by the Accademia's regulations from early in the century.[613] His postmortem inventory contained nearly 800 paintings, the majority of which were not by him and presumably were commercial stock.[614] Data are too scanty for calculating an average selling price of his own work, though four inventory appraisals drawn up during his lifetime (1671) support an estimate of 20–25 scudi for his medium-size still lifes.[615]

Documented prices for still lifes by Giovanni, Niccolò, and Angelo Stanchi, who collaborated with some of Rome's major painters, including Maratta, Ferri, Dughet, Luigi Garzi, and Filippo Lauri, and whose work was purchased by Rome's elite collectors (the Barberini, Borghese, Chigi, Colonna, and Pamphilj, among others), were marginally higher. These include 50 scudi in 1638 for a garland with the Barberini arms; 32 scudi the next year from Roscioli for a canvas measuring about 145 × 190 cm with flowers surrounding *putti* painted by Camassei, who, as the figure collaborator, was paid a higher fee, 47 scudi (the canvas cost another 1.9 scudi); and the same year (1639), 15 scudi again from Roscioli for two smaller paintings of flowers and fruit, 90 × 67 cm. Other payments to the Stanchi were made in 1660: 40 scudi for each of four large still lifes (156 × 112 cm) by Giovanni for the Chigi, and 50 scudi apiece for a pair of *tele d'imperatore* for the Colonna. In 1672, Niccolò, who three years earlier had been earning a scudo a day working for the Colonna, was paid 150 scudi for his ceiling of "verdura e fiori" in the Colonna palace.[616]

Unsurprisingly, in such a labor-intensive genre, size mattered a lot when it came to establishing value. In 1675 and 1677 respectively, the Chigi paid Niccolò only 15 scudi for three small framed paintings ("quadretti di mezza testa") and 35 scudi for five others, four of which were *tele da testa* (ca. 65 × 50 cm), the fifth a *tela d'imperatore* (95 × 135 cm). The Chigi also paid Abraham Brueghel 20 scudi in 1674 for two *tele da testa* of flowers. In a remarkable admission to Antonio Ruffo three years earlier, Brueghel granted that the "value [of Mario's work] is greater than mine," but he asked Ruffo to bear in mind that taste for his own paintings will endure for many years and that "as of now their full capital is not evident [*non mostrino presentemente tutto il loro capitale*]."[617]

Two further Chigi payments to Niccolò Stanchi confirm that small still life paintings by leading specialists could be remarkably cheap: 18 scudi in 1680 for six flower paintings designated as *quadretti* of 1.5 *palmi* (34 cm), and a smaller payment that unites the lowliest of the genres: only 2 scudi in 1683 for Niccolò's vase of flowers designated as a *quadretto* and commissioned as a cover for "un quadro di bambocciate."[618]

These artists were very popular, as Angelo Doni implied when writing to Francesco Maria de' Medici in 1684. "Among the many painters who do flower still lifes," he reported from Rome, "there are at least six who are well qualified and for the most part are students of the leaders, Mario, Stanchi, and Brueghel, and their prices are modest; they expect 3 or 4 scudi for a *quadro da testa* or 4 *palmi* [90 cm]."[619] Doni did not name whom he had in mind, whether Italians or some of the foreign still life artists.[620] Nor did Salvator Rosa name names or specify sums when he wrote to Ricciardi in 1662 that in his opinion prices of the best flower painters in Rome were out of sight.[621]

As Table 6 above indicates, still lifes constituted the smallest category of paintings in five aristocratic Roman collections, even though they were more popular in some middle-class households. That there was a huge quantity of them (and genre paintings, too) worth just a few scudi apiece on the Roman market at the end of the century is documented in the inventory (1699) of the dealer Pellegrino Peri's stock, which consisted of a staggering 2,491 pictures.[622]

Among all categories of painting, still life's mimetic underpinning and naturalistic appearance generally lowered its market value despite its increased labor cost, making it the least cost effective genre in Rome except, perhaps, for its most admired specialists. In Naples, on the other hand, where the genre flourished, it appears to have been valued more highly.[623]

Still lifes with animals, if they should be designated as still lifes (let alone as *nature morte*), were potentially of higher status when depicting live models (as Félibien clearly put it, "He who paints live animals is more praiseworthy than those who represent only dead things without movement").[624] One of Rome's still life painters was a leading specialist in portraying animals, Michele Pace, called Michelangelo di Campidoglio, who worked for the Chigi and Colonna but otherwise is poorly documented.[625] His earliest recorded fee from the Chigi is dated 1658, when he received 20 scudi for a large painting (ca. 112 × 156 cm) identified as that depicting a Moor with two hunting dogs (Palazzo Chigi, Rome). The same amount was paid the next year for an even larger *Woman with Animals* (ca. 112 × 200 cm) as well as for an *Egyptian Goat* with other animals, of the same dimensions. In 1660, Pace was given 20 scudi plus a tip of 10 scudi for a painting of two figures with fish, about 134 × 200 cm. Three more Chigi payments to him, always for very large canvases, were 20 scudi apiece.[626] His work for the Colonna differs by depicting flowers and fruit. Two of his paintings acquired by them in 1661 were identified simply as *Frutti*, one a large canvas (156 × 200 cm) costing 36 scudi, the other much smaller (67 cm) at half the price.[627]

The Neapolitan artist Paolo Porpora worked in Rome during the third quarter of the century and also benefited from the Chigi's taste for still lifes. Twice in 1661 they bought what apparently was a pair of pendant canvases, each measuring 112 × 156 cm and each costing 40 scudi. One depicted sea turtles, marine vegetation, and rocks, and the other "various animals." The artist signed the verification of payment as "Paoluccio Napolitano Pittore de Fiori, et animali."[628]

When Porpora died in Rome in 1673, Michele Pace probably was already dead. Mario dei Fiori also died in 1673, which was the year that Giovanni and Angelo Stanchi are last noted in records. Niccolò Stanchi remained active at least until 1690, by which time a Dutchman, Karel van Vogelaer, who would become known as Carlo dei Fiori, and two Germans, Frans Werner van Tamm and Christian Berentz, were in Rome collaborating with Rome's foremost painters, including Maratta, and enjoying high aristocratic patronage.

Berentz specialized in a Northern style of still life painting based on dazzling displays of foods and crystal vessels. His principal patron was Marquis Niccolò Maria Pallavicini, in whose palace he lived awhile and who, in 1696, acquired a large canvas (250 × 175 cm, Capodimonte, Naples) filled with flowers, fruits, and crystal objects, and two figures by Maratta. The high fee of 400 scudi presumably was due to Maratta's collaboration, but Pascoli writes that for very complex still lifes Berentz would ask as much as 500 scudi and a fifth that sum for small ones, refusing to lower his prices by even a scudo when clients bickered. Berentz, however, was careless about money, saving nothing for his old age. Debts and rent became such a burden that he needed financial assistance during his last years, when he lived alone in the hospice of San Michele.[629] His inadequate planning brings to mind Ridolfi's comments on Antonio Aliense's failure to plan for his old age, and Bellori's remarks on Sacchi's financial imprudence. Sacchi's estate

> was not very opulent, given his large expenses and how little he worked at the end of his life, for he perceived too late how detrimental it was to him . . . that he neglected the reward for his labors and did not ask for just payments, considering that the years of his early youth were spent in sweat and discomfort without any gain whatever, and what is worse yet, without his having provided adequately for illness and for old age.[630]

The Bottom Line

Pascoli prefaced his life of Berentz by posing the question: why does Italy have more outstanding artists than do countries north of the Alps? His answer, not surprisingly from an economist, was economic: the cost of education. In the North, he says, potential artists are discouraged from entering the profession because they have to pay to study: in England, a pound (about 4 scudi) a month; in Holland, 100 guilders a year (about 30 scudi), which is what Sandrart says Rembrandt and Honthorst charged their students; in Germany, about the same; and in France, 24 scudi.[631] "This does not happen in our country, where with the slightest knowledge [*ogni piccola cognizione*], one goes to study in any school and in any academy without paying even a penny. And this advantageous and generous benefit is what keeps turning out many artists of great quality, which is surpassed nowhere else in Europe."[632]

Albeit exaggerated and naive (what Pascoli meant by "qualunque scuola, ed in qualunque accademia" is unclear), his explanation most likely has some merit, even if it fails to explain why artists pursue their profession in the first place. That complex issue was addressed around 1390 by Cennino Cennini, who recognized an "impulse" and "natural enthusiasm" for the profession, which was more laudable, he felt, than taking up painting "because of poverty and domestic need, for profit."[633] Ottonelli and Cortona listed five motivations for becoming an artist: (1) financial gain, which the authors similarly thought is not a sufficient reason; (2) zeal for participating in a public, civic life of virtue through instruction; (3) the urge to express inner feelings; (4) a yearning to win honor; and (5) most important and common, natural inclination and talent, which one feels in oneself from childhood ("la naturale inclinatione, & il genio, che un soggetto sente in se stesso in fino da' primi anni").[634] For Bellori, the true artist is motivated by "that innate pleasure [*quell piacere innato*] that acts from within us and makes us operate"; the artist consecrates his love entirely to his work and, as Domenichino purportedly put it, "paints only for himself and for art [*dipingeva solo a se stesso ed all'arte*]."[635]

Gross Incomes

Of all the early biographers of seventeenth-century painters in Rome, Mancini and Pascoli paid the most attention to "financial gain," the first of Ottonelli's and Cortona's reasons for becoming an artist, with Mancini uniquely trying to explain what factors determine the price of a painting. He nonetheless had to admit that, despite his efforts to clarify market mechanisms, "painting cannot have an intrinsic fixed price," as this study and the rest of our book indicate.

Any price for a painting, he realized, depends on too many variables, including not just the quality of the artist, the relative excellence of a particular work, the artist's investment of time in learning his trade (which later Bellori would emphasize) and in making the object under consideration (hence its size and number of figures counted, as did its materials), but also the status of the seller and purchaser, which makes a big difference. Mancini further observed that the price of a painting is affected by its age, rarity, and condition, as well as by a dealer's expenses. It fluctuates according to a painter's reputation, which might lag behind his youthful achievement, as happened with Caravaggio and Ribera. Undoubtedly, a wealthy prince might pay more for a painting than would a collector of middling status. Hence the buyer, not the artist, ultimately determines a work's worth. "For all these reasons, it doesn't seem that one can give a definite price to paintings."[636]

Mancini made no effort to assign relative weight to these various factors that establish a work's value. As someone involved in the market, however, he might have added the appeal of making a lucrative investment, which could increase demand and raise prices, as Boschini would argue happens. Bellori sensed this when he remarked that "commissions came to Guido [Reni] in droves. . . . many works were . . . sought after for gain, due to the example of those that have doubled the profit on them many times over."[637]

Mancini also left out of his analysis the effect of subject matter, and, more significantly, he made no distinction among the genres when writing that a good painter could earn 3 to 6 scudi a day, though in all probability was referring to figural painters.[638] Multiplying his average daily rate of 4.5 scudi by 250 days yields an annual income of 1,125 scudi, 10 to 20 times what a mason in Rome earned and a lot more than many other incomes mentioned in the first part of this essay. Indeed, it is well in line with my estimates of the incomes of a number of history painters.

Guercino had not yet begun to keep his detailed account book when he was in Rome in 1621–23, but it provides an exceptionally good record of a major painter's income while working in Cento and Bologna. It ranged from a minimum gross annual income of around 1,000 scudi to a high of 4,000 (p. 29, Table 1)—which was still only half of the estimated minimum income a cardinal needed—averaging about 1,500 scudi. Guercino, however, spent as much as 50 percent of his earnings on running an unusually complex family studio.[639]

Domenichino's average income during 1616–25 in Rome, Bologna, and Fano might have been about the same, 1,500 scudi, though Bellori understood that the "the cause of [Domenichino's] departure from Rome was the meagerness of his fortune; for the work at Sant'Andrea [della Valle], in addition to having been reduced, [he] did not receive the remuneration that was proper. . . . His other work at San Carlo [ai Catinari] was so poorly rewarded that he did not bother to proceed with the cupola." But in fact for his pendentives and choir frescoes at S. Andrea della Valle, Domenichino was paid nearly 3,500 scudi, and for the pendentives at S. Carlo ai Catinari, 2,000 scudi at 200 per figure, a substantial rate. Later in Naples he made close to 2,000 scudi a year, "an accumulation of riches sufficient to establish and maintain him in magnificent estate over the course of many years' employment," Bellori thought. The documents, however, do not show that there was such a radical difference between the artist's Roman and Neapolitan incomes.[640]

Lanfranco earned considerably more in Naples, 30,000 ducats over the course of seven-and-a-half years or 3,000 scudi per annum, mostly from fresco cycles and 9,000 scudi from Spanish royal commissions.[641] Known payments for Orazio Gentileschi's Roman work were substantial if not exceptional, but they are too few to compare with his earnings in London, which were close to 1,000 scudi annually for his recorded work.[642] Only a very crude estimate can be made for Caravaggio's income during his mature Roman years, ca. 1600–6, when the majority of documented payments were made.[643] They total about 2,120 scudi for 14 paintings, an average of 150 scudi. During that period, Caravaggio painted at least 20 works of sufficient importance that they were mentioned in the sources. Were 150 scudi the average fee for them all, which is wholly hypothetical, his annual income from only the documented commissions would have averaged at least 500 scudi. Bellori nonetheless understood that when the painter fled Rome in 1606 he was *senza denari*, without money.[644] During the following two years in Naples he earned 1,350 scudi from five commissions, nearly doubling the average Roman price to 270 scudi.

Annibale Carracci's Roman prices are too poorly documented to allow valid comparison with Caravaggio's, especially because Odoardo Farnese's stingy compensation for Annibale's years of working in the Galleria Farnese (10 scudi a month plus 500 scudi d'oro) broke his spirit and diminished his production, Bellori's approving claim that Annibale had a "fine philosophical attitude in despising money [*dispregio de' denari*]" notwithstanding.[645] Annibale's highest recorded fee in Rome was 2,000 scudi for decorating the Herrera chapel in S. Giacomo degli Spagnoli with 19 frescoes executed mainly by his studio (with regard to Table 3, that is 26 scudi per square meter and only 35 scudi per figure). About half of the scudi went to Albani.[646]

While the payment is unknown for Annibale's altarpiece in the Cerasi chapel in S. Maria del Popolo, where Caravaggio received 150 scudi apiece for the lateral canvases, there is evidence from another commission involving both painters. Rich documentation from 1605–7 tracks Cesare d'Este's remarkable patience but failed efforts to get work from them for a chapel in Modena. Annibale's large altarpiece, the *Birth of the Virgin* (279 × 159 cm, Louvre, Paris), commissioned for 200 scudi, was eventually refused due to continuous delays caused partly by the painter's illness. Concurrently, Caravaggio was to provide a smaller, lateral painting of one of the Mysteries of the Virgin with Joachim and Anne for 50 to 60 scudi. Caravaggio complained that its (unknown) size was too small for him and that other painters would be more suited to that kind of work, yet he accepted the commission with a demand for down payments. In the end, due to his brawls and eventual flight from Rome, and despite his assurance that it would be done in a month (an important clue to how quickly he might complete a picture), Caravaggio probably never even started the work nor did he return the 32 scudi he took from the duke as an advance. In one of the many letters written by the duke's agent in Rome, who had been pressing both artists to deliver, the agent related that upon running into Caravaggio, "s'arrosisci quando mi vede" (he blushed upon seeing me).[647]

The Modena commission overlapped with Annibale's work on another altarpiece, a *Pietà with Sts. Francis and Mary Magdalene* (Louvre, Paris) that probably was commissioned by Odoardo Farnese and is equal in size (277 × 185 cm) to the Modena altarpiece. Its compensation was a necklace worth 300 scudi, more than Caravaggio was paid for any of his Roman altarpieces.[648]

How many other painters earned 1,000 scudi or more a year? Clearly not the majority, especially if minor figures, copyists, and the vanished are counted. But even among the successful elite, say Baglione's 140 painters, the evidence is too thin to make a credible estimate.

Additional Income

Painters supplemented their incomes in a variety of ways. The most common was to invest in *monti*, long-term bonds, whose shares were called *luoghi*, which in their more popular, redeemable, and inheritable form (*monti non-vacabili*) paid about 5 percent per annum; less frequently money was placed in *censi*, the kind of annuity Gaulli purchased. Cortona owned many *luoghi*, although their combined yield at the time of his death was only 4 percent.[649] As liquid instruments they could be easily sold or left as bequests, whether to relatives or, as occurred with Girolamo Rainaldi, Jan Miel, and Giovanna Garzoni, to the Accademia.[650] Generally, they were safe investments, more so than the unfortunate Giovanni Ghisolfi's. His friend Salvator Rosa lamented that Ghisolfi, who had saved up 600 scudi "giulio by giulio" for "some important need," lost everything when his Milanese bank collapsed.[651]

Successful painters, like Gaulli, might have owned rental property as well. Federico Zuccaro supplemented his substantial income by letting a "casa grande" for 100 scudi a year, a "casa piccola" for 36, "due granari" (two barns) for 37, an "altro granaro più piccolo" for 22, and "una stanziola sotto detti granari" (a small room beneath the barns) for 8 giuli a month, totaling more than 200 scudi per annum of extra income.[652] That ownership of *monti* and real estate was almost routine for painters of standing is implied by Pascoli's remark regarding Antonio Gherardi. He "left little capital to his heirs. . . . he owned a small house in Rieti . . . in Rome he didn't have real estate or *luoghi di monti*."[653]

Other routes to secondary income were closely linked to the painter's profession, such as designing tapestries and other household furnishings, whose values could far exceed those of paintings.[654] Teaching would have been a natural path were it not, as Pascoli observed, that in Italy students were not accustomed to paying their mentors.[655] Some painters of high reputation nonetheless charged. Reni, for instance, set a hefty fee of a doppia a month, taking the position that he should be compensated if a grammar school teacher was paid and, moreover, that his fee would discourage the rabble.[656] In Florence, too, some pupils paid.

Dealing was common, especially as the Roman market became more open by mid-century, and painters increasingly wanted to sell directly from their studios.[657] Beginning in 1635, anyone of any profession in Rome who openly sold paintings was subject to a tax of 10 scudi a year. In 1650, 19 painters paid for the right, in principle to sell only their own work; by 1655, the year in which Mario dei Fiori applied for his *patente* to deal more broadly, the number had increased to 46. That same year 28 art dealers paid the tax, but undoubtedly many more ignored it. Throughout the century the Accademia had trouble collecting the tax, even though it was significantly reduced under Clement VIII.[658] There is no information on how much money Mario dei Fiori and others earned by dealing, or if Maratta's large collection, which was filled with copies after other artists along with his own work, was lucrative commercial stock.[659]

Nor does one know what finder's fees painters were given by collectors, or if gaining their indebtedness was perhaps adequate compensation. In a rare documented example that probably is atypical given the artist's rogue nature, Agostino Tassi kept half of the 100 scudi price of a painting he sold to a courtier of Cardinal Maurizio di Savoia.[660] Perhaps more usual, at least for big transactions, was the 1 percent commission paid in 1685 to Jacques Brunet for arranging the 3,000 scudi sale of Poussin's *Rape of the Sabine Women* and *Triumph of Flora* in the Omodei collection to Louis XIV (both Louvre, Paris).[661]

Appraising was an artist's area of expertise, too, but starting in 1595 the Accademia attempted to control all formal appraisals, whether verbal or written, of painting, miniatures, stucco work, gilding, and "whatever else belonged to the painter's trade," by appointing 12 official *estimatori*, six painters and six *artigiani*. They were allowed to keep only one-third of the 2 percent appraisal fee, the balance going to the Accademia. Unlike in Venice, where painters could appraise independently, a stiff fine was imposed on anyone who did so on his own.[662]

As with the *misura et stima* of architecture, conflicts of interest were built into the process because the *estimatori* were evaluating their colleagues' work and they themselves could benefit twice: immediately from the percentage and in the long run from higher market prices. In 1606, Arpino and Antiveduto Grammatica were asked to appraise five new altarpieces in the *navi piccole* of St. Peter's. In every case, their generous appraisals were lowered, from 1,300 scudi for paintings by Passignano and Baglione to 1,000 and 800 scudi, respectively; from 1,000 to 800 scudi for Roncalli's and Francesco Vanni's work; and from 700 to 560 scudi for Bernardo Castello's altarpiece. A more blatant example is the inventory of Costanzo Patrizi's collection, which was appraised by Arpino in 1624. Not surprisingly, the highest values were given to his and his brother's own paintings.[663] As Count Teodoro Sangiorgio put it with regard to the pricing of Tintoretto's work, "every profession supports its own."[664]

From painter to painter expertise varied, yet it was widely agreed that painters were the best judges of art. Pascoli remarked on Francesco Cozza's particularly broad knowledge of old and modern masters and that both buyers and sellers deferred to his opinions.[665] The most recognized painter-appraiser mid-century was Antonio della Cornia, who in 1635 was recommended to the duke of Savoy as "expert in the various styles of painting [*diversità delle maniere de' pittori*] . . . matchless in Rome for judging the best paintings [*per dar giuditio de quadri migliori*]."[666] He served as one of the Accademia's *estimatori* and was celebrated as an expert copyist. After working for Rome's top aristocracy, he died rich and famous in 1654 despite his modest creative talent.

Restoring paintings was another way to earn extra money. Mancini prudently recommended that, while in principle cleaning is advisable, it should be undertaken only by experts who are familiar with dirty paintings ("ma però da huomini intelligenti che conoschino la sordidezza della pittura"); otherwise it would be better to leave them alone.[667] Painters were entrusted with both simple and complex projects. In 1617, Anastasio Fontebuoni was paid 19 scudi for retouching a frieze in the Palazzo Borghese.[668] Antonio della Cornia, "pittore famosissimo," was hired in 1653 to touch up Salviati's work in the Chigi chapel in S. Maria del Popolo.[669] One G. B. Manelli Pittore received 12 scudi from the Chigi in 1683 "for having cleaned 15 paintings, large and small covered with mildew that are at the garden." That year the Chigi spent 3 scudi relining a canvas by Lanfranco, a job entrusted to a pigments merchant. The same sum was allocated for another relining in 1689, when 34 paintings were cleaned for 4 giuli apiece, a big *Fall of the Giants* for 1.2 scudi, and a *Battle* for the same amount, relining included.[670] Giuseppe Ghezzi became such a favorite of Queen Christina that she "entrusted no one but him to clean the paintings in her valuable gallery."[671]

Occasionally, artists were hired to conserve their own work. An especially complex job was Passignano's restoration in 1624 of his badly damaged *Crucifixion of St. Peter* in St. Peter's. Painted on slate, it had been washed many times during the previous 20 years, resulting in cracking and paint loss. For his work he was paid 60 scudi, the same fee that was given to Baglione four years later for "retouching all" of his *St. Peter Raising Tabitha* in St. Peter's.[672]

Frescoes also required care. During 1647–50, Magno (Modanino) worked on some in the Vatican, mostly doing retouchings but also extensive repainting and consolidation work, though his bill of 103 scudi was reduced to 64.[673] Even a painter of Maratta's standing, or in Venice Sebastiano Ricci's, worked as a restorer, notably on Raphael's frescoes in the Farnesina and Vatican. He was appointed *officium custodis picturarum*, keeper of all of the paintings in the Vatican, including the Sistine Chapel, and released from any penalties that might result from litigation over his work. He also restored the frescoes in the Galleria Farnese, a fresco by his teacher Sacchi, and an ancient fresco in the Barberini collection, in addition to altarpieces by Lotto, Barocci, and Annibale Carracci.[674]

Another way painters could turn a profit was by collecting and in due course selling. Together with his father Giacinto, Ludovico Gimignani formed what Pascoli called "una buona raccolta" (a good collection) of old and modern paintings, drawings, and prints, which he often sold "to great advantage."[675] Less usual was the commercial venture of Giovanni Guerra, who with Cesare Nebbia supervised many of the major decorative projects in late sixteenth-century Rome. Ever the entrepreneur, Guerra, with Gaspare Bianchi, owned a pigments shop that profited from selling supplies to his *équipe* of painters.[676] Other less ambitious activities were undertaken by minor artists, such as Antonio pittore alla Minerva, who in 1608 was paid 22 scudi by Cardinal Montalto "for having gilded a large frame with a painting by Raphael," or Pietro Riera pittore, who in 1613 similarly was paid 41 scudi for gilding a number of frames for the Altemps.[677]

Pascoli's profile of Giovanni Odazzi, a student of Ciro Ferri, exemplifies the painter who diversified. Because he was prolific, well paid, and the recipient of many generous gifts, he could buy *luoghi di monti* worth thousands of scudi. He also owned a profitable *vigna*, invested in valuable pieces of silver, and restored old and modern masters.[678]

Painters' Estates

Painters' wealth can be judged not only from their annual incomes, which are rarely known with certainty, but from the size of their estates. The evidence is sporadic and when available imperfect, usually coming from biographers rather than formal appraisals, although the biographers might have had access to reliable information. Neither annual nor cumulative earnings, however, can be extrapolated from the size of an estate because the ability to save money varied so greatly from one painter to another. Moreover, assets could have come from sources other than an artist's work, such as inherited property or a dowry (Raffaella Morselli discusses dowries in Bologna and Renata Ago their broader socio-economic importance). These uncertainties aside, the values of estates reported in the early sources present a picture of many wealthy artists, particularly among the history painters.

Accumulation of even a few thousand scudi indicates substantial surplus capital at a time when 1,000 scudi would pay the average salary of a Roman professor for seven years, or a skilled mason's salary or rent in the city's most expensive quarters for a dozen years. Passeri, as mentioned, considered an income of 300 scudi a year sufficient to live "comfortably and in a dignified manner." All of the estates mentioned so far were very substantial, from Bernini's and Cortona's enormous assets of 400,000 and 100,000 scudi, to Romanelli's (30,000), Dughet's (25,000), Poussin's (15,000), Rosa's (15,000), Claude's (10,000), and Swanevelt's (4,200).

According to Passeri, who personally knew Domenichino and his family, the painter left his daughter 20,000 scudi.[679] That equals the total sum the deputies paid him during the last decade of his life for decorating the Cappella del Tesoro di S. Gennaro, and 13 times his estimated minimum annual income for the period 1616–25. If, on average, Domenichino earned 1,500 to 2,000 scudi a year for 30 years as a mature artist (1611–41), he would have had to save more than a third of his gross income to build up an estate of 20,000 scudi. That might have been possible if, as seems likely, he led a frugal life and benefited from many perks such as free housing while working outside of Rome. Otherwise he managed to acquire substantially more money than the documents reveal, whether from his art or other sources.

Pascoli's interest in the value of painter's estates was unique among the early biographers, probably because of his training as an economist. His information is richest on artists who died while he was researching his *vite*. He reports that Mattia Preti was so generous, refusing payments and gifts and donating 100,000 scudi to charity, that he left only 5,000 scudi and a house whose rental income was 44 scudi. Pascoli's notion of "only" was not limited to 5,000 scudi. He thought that when Daniel Seiter died with an estate of about 10,000 scudi, he "left little."[680] Such terminology is revealing because in Rome those were large sums of capital, indicating that Pascoli's expectations, which were formed through an extensive knowledge of painters' lives, were high.[681] Pascoli names a dozen painters and sculptors whose estates were worth 10,000 scudi or more, of whom seven, and the three richest, were painters (Table 8).

For other artists Pascoli provides no specific figures but he thought they left little ("poco lasciò"), such as the sculptors Domenico Guidi and Melchiorre Caffà,

TABLE 8 Painters' and Sculptors' Estates said by Pascoli to be Worth at Least 10,000 scudi

PAINTERS	VALUE	SCULPTORS	VALUE
Romanelli, G. F.	<50,000	Monnot, Pierre Étienne	<30,000
Maratta, Carlo	<40,000	Ferrata, Ercole	12,000–15,000
Gaulli, G. B.	<40,000	Raggi, Antonio	12,000
Ferri, Ciro	<30,000	Rusconi, Camillo	12,000
Chiari, Giuseppe	20,000	Mazzuoli, Giuseppe	8,000–10,000
Lauri, Filippo	12,000		
Seiter, Daniel	10,000		

the latter not because he was unsuccessful but because he spent generously on himself and his friends and cut a fine figure.[682] Giovanni Francesco Grimaldi, too, earned "gran denaro" through "generoso pagamento," but Pascoli did not know the size of his estate. Nor did he know the value of other estates, including that of Benedetto Luti, who, regardless of his fame and status, left his six children only modest capital ("mediocre capitale"). The biographer gives no figures for Canini, whose brother likewise inherited "mediocre capitale," or for Gian Domenico Cerrini, who "always spent lavishly to maintain himself as a gentleman." As for Giovanni Battista Benaschi, he "did not leave much capital, even though he had earned a lot." And so on, making one suspect that, on the whole, the painters who made it into Pascoli's *vite* were well-to-do and that their estates, or at least their incomes, should not be called modest.[683]

Finally, there is the timeless if unanswerable question: does the push of poverty produce better art? Mancini posed the problem by asking if it is better for a painter to be "comfortable and rich or poor and needy [*che sia commodo et ricco o ver povero et bisognioso*] for his glory and for him to be of use to the world." He decided it is preferable to be comfortable and rich because quality, which is linked to good pay and adequate time, is more important than quantity, a consequence of need.[684]

Luigi Scaramuccia, author, painter, printmaker, art agent, and appraiser, also raised his voice on this issue. In *Le finezze de' pennelli italiani* (1674), he argued that the wealthy young painter rarely, if ever, would study ceaselessly and sweat sufficiently to excel in his difficult profession. His view mirrors Barocci's, who "used to remind the young that comforts are an impediment to anyone who wants to get ahead."[685] On the other hand, Scaramuccia held that if a young painter's needs were too acute, his studies would suffer and the progress of his *bell'ingegno* derailed. For this reason he proposed a compromise: that, for the sake of art, the painter should have *mediocre fortuna*, a little wealth.[686] Such speculations aside, most painters undoubtedly would have identified with Baglione, who in 1629 testified that although he had not appraised his personal goods, he felt, "I am not as rich as I would like to be."[687]

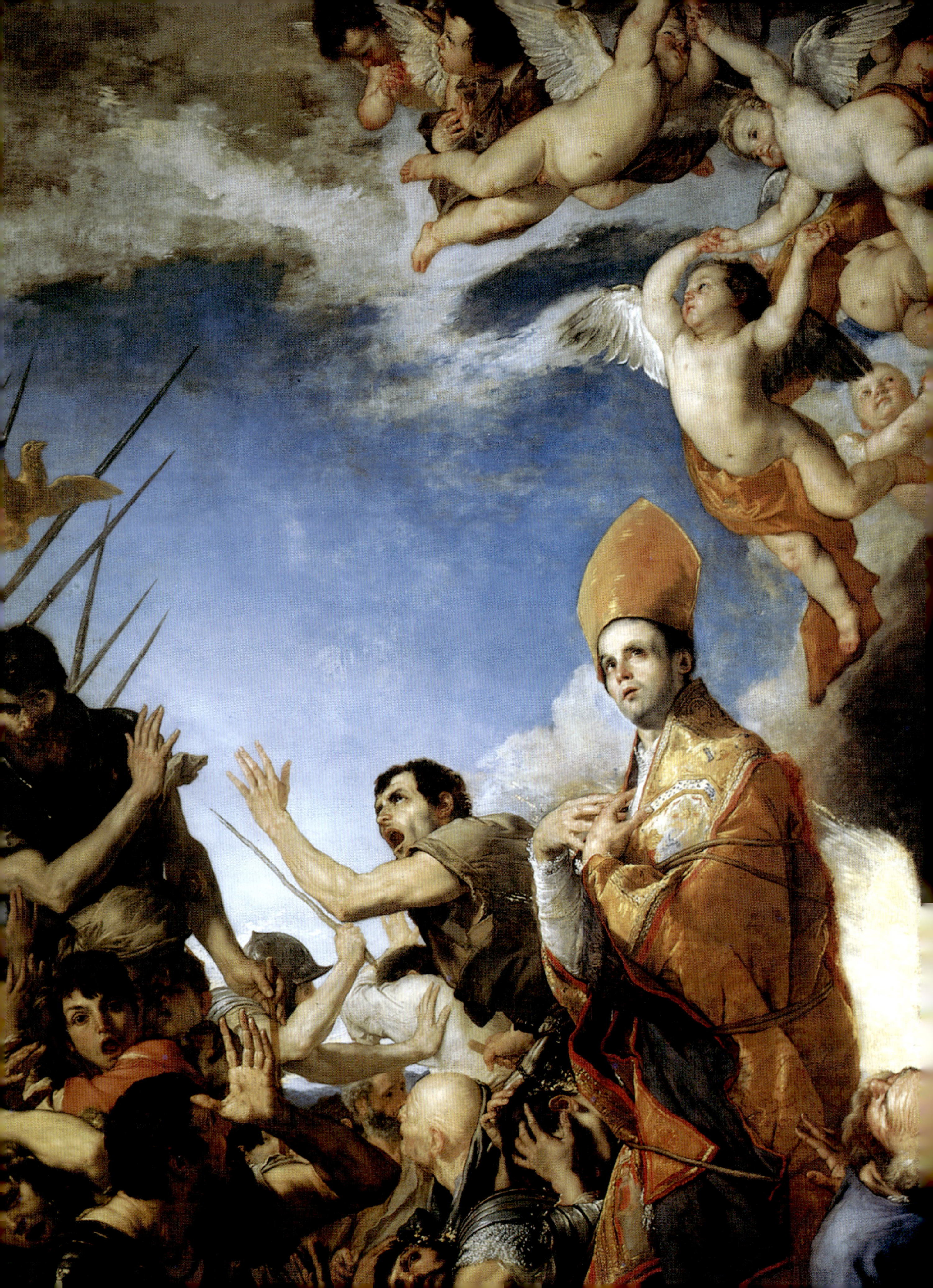

2

Naples

CHRISTOPHER R. MARSHALL

Introduction: The Industry of Neapolitan Baroque Painting, from Small Fry to Big Fish

September 1644, and a painter lies dying, "vulneratum" or wounded as expressed in the dry notarial Latin of the day, most probably as a result of a brawl somewhere in the narrow, crowded, and in this instance also violent back streets of Naples. His wife stands grieving while his best friend compiles a list of his belongings (in an unusually unrefined dialect for an inventory document, one of many indicators of the relatively modest material circumstances of their situation).[1] Certainly this was most unfortunate for this poor soul, but lucky for us, as it transpires, since it resulted in an unusually detailed snapshot of a fully operational Neapolitan baroque workshop—as opposed to the typically sorted-out state of painters' studios as recorded in legacies and inventories at the end of their careers.

He was not rich by any means, this otherwise totally unknown painter named Onofrio de Anfora, but he was certainly industrious. One senses the paint still drying on many of the 200 canvases listed in the inventory: an unfinished head of St. Nicholas, "diversi tele picole di diverse mesure sbozati et senza sbozare" (various small canvases of varying dimensions some roughed out and others still to begin), and three portraits, one finished, the other two only just started. Evidently Anfora made his living producing for the most part cheap standardized devotional subjects that he could turn out quickly and according to a semi-industrial rate of efficiency: a head of St. Januarius (the patron saint of Naples) or "due vercenelle una madonella" (two small virgins and a small Madonna). This common reliance on offsetting relative cheapness against maximized serial efficiency (there was no premium on original compositions at this sector of the market) was also true of his larger canvases. Many were lined up like merchandise on a store rack: two paintings of *St. Nicholas* measuring just over 2 meters, two of *St. Agatha* measuring half as much, and so on.

All of this aids our understanding of the standard stock in trade of painters working at the lower reaches of the Neapolitan art market—painters who are not recorded in the standard histories and who remain, for the most part, frustratingly obscure today. It shows, for example, that most of Anfora's paintings were left unframed in his workshop (150 out of 200), even those completed. This would have naturally made business sense since it would have allowed Anfora to fit a frame from his separately maintained stock, presumably on the spot, if the buyer so desired (thereby allowing him to introduce a certain price differential into the sale, which would have been useful, one suspects, given that the differently graded frames were in many instances just as valuable as the modestly priced paintings themselves).[2] Yet what is perhaps even more revealing—and what

Facing page: detail of Fig. 41

challenges more thoroughly our commonly mistaken notions about the nature of an artist's production at the time—is how much of Anfora's workshop stock was not by his own hand.

This modest painter included in his workshop stock no fewer than 30 pictures that were certainly not by him. These are described as "vecchio" (old) or, in one case, "antico" (antique—very old—presumably therefore marginally more valuable than the others). Their subjects ranged from further instances of the kinds of simple devotional works in which Anfora specialized—"Una madonella con cornice vechia" (a small framed Madonna, old)—to more complex biblical narratives—an *Adoration of the Magi*, two paintings of *Tobias and the Angel*—and on to examples of more recently developed genres that Anfora would almost certainly not have practiced himself: "Doi battagliole di dui palme con doi quatri di frutti et una montagnia di somma di dui palme e mezzo e uno S. genaro et una madona picola uno quatro di fiori di tre palmi scarzo vechi" (two small battles measuring ca. 53 centimeters, with two paintings of fruit and a high mountain measuring ca. 66 centimeters, and a St. Januarius and a small Madonna, a painting of flowers measuring ca. 75 centimeters, [all of them] old). Evidently, then, Anfora sought to maximize his sales by diversifying his output, bringing in old paintings in other styles and formats and thereby acting, in his own modest way, as a secondary dealer on the side.

But he didn't just trade in old work. A separate section appended to the end of the list itemizes 50 paintings (a quarter of his stock, in other words) that Anfora had purchased with money loaned to him by his wife's aunt—and that thus now constituted a debt that needed to be liquidated before any proceeds could accrue to his widow from future sales. None of this group of paintings is described as "vecchio," so they were all produced relatively recently and thus represented further potential primary market sales, and a high proportion were framed (24 out of 50, as opposed to 30 out of 150 for those in the other, main list). This suggests that they represented the pick of the works not painted by Anfora himself, the choicest "new old masters" in other words, that Anfora had presumably brought together for sale in his workshop over the course of his regular movements buying—and no doubt also bartering and trading in his own work wherever possible—from other Neapolitan workshops.

He may have been operating at a modest level of the market, then, but Anfora nonetheless had the wherewithal to advance his business by generating enough extra capital to diversify his output and buy more stock. If one assumes, for the sake of argument, that these paintings averaged 2 ducats each in value (the standard currency in Naples and a common price for cheap work, as presently to be explained), this would mean that they would have earned for Anfora a potential 100 ducats (or more) worth of extra sales—a not inconsiderable increase to his trade, since it would have been worth as much as two or even three years of rent on his workshop. Relatively humble he may have been, yet Anfora's inventory vividly documents the enterprising and business oriented acumen that all successful painters needed to maintain, no matter what their position in the overstocked art world of seventeenth-century Naples.

Anfora was not, in any event, at the bottom of the heap. Even this supposedly small fry artist had yet smaller fish working under him. In fact, no fewer than 14 of the paintings listed in his inventory (most of them bought with the loaned money) were by the only artist whose name is actually spelled out in the lists of work. All that is known about this artist, Pietro Pesce (who also had a work, still unfinished, in Anfora's workshop), is that he was an almost equally obscure follower in the 1650s and 1660s of the leading landscape painter of the day, Domenico Gargiulo.[3] In the 1640s, Anfora probably paid Pesce on a daily basis at the common per diem rate of around a ducat or a little less. So, the inventory also brings Pesce momentarily out of the shadows as a yet more struggling junior artist drawing on Anfora's relatively better-established business resources to receive the initial support of workspace and materials that he needed to get his career off the ground. Clearly, Anfora operated well below the lofty heights of Jusepe de Ribera, with his huge earnings and substantial levels of workshop assistance. Yet even he had a diversified business strategy that involved him in employing more junior painters to paint for him, at least on occasion.

Raising the Curtain: Demographics, Population, Construction, and Artistic Migration

This kind of entrepreneurial thinking was necessary if one wanted to maintain a foothold or even, God willing, get ahead in baroque Naples. In truth, all manner of opportunities were potentially available in the southern Mediterranean port city, although artists needed to remember that Naples operated according to an entirely different dynamic from Rome, Venice, or any of the other baroque centers discussed here. Naples was, in the first instance, a Spanish viceregal dominion, as it had been since 1506. It was the principal center of the entire Spanish Kingdom of Naples, a sprawling, vast, and ultimately unmanageable realm stretching half the length of Italy from close to Rome in the mountains of Abruzzo Ultra all the way down to Naples, Salerno, Messina, Palermo, and onwards to the tip of Sicily. As the military, administrative, mercantile, and urban centerpiece to this vast imperial domain, Naples's population growth had accordingly long since outstripped any of the other cities in the Italian peninsula.

A veritable flood of migration from the provinces to Naples was encouraged in great part by the viceregal decision to exempt the city itself from direct taxes, while at the same time imposing a heavy and systematic tax burden on the outlying regions as a means of financing the ongoing Spanish wars. By the early seventeenth century, then, the countryside was becoming more and more depopulated while Naples itself had swollen to a teeming population approaching 300,000—three times that of Rome, for example, and also a third larger again than Venice, its only Italian near rival. Incredibly, it seems that this unregulated population explosion was not to be curtailed, at least not in the long run, by a series of cataclysmic disasters that befell the city during the opening decades of the century. First, an eruption of Mount Vesuvius in 1631 threatened to bury the city and its surrounds in the same way that an eruption had entombed Pompeii and Herculaneum centuries earlier.[4] This was followed by a full-scale popular uprising in 1647–48 that caused untold destruction and almost unseated both the Spanish administration and the Neapolitan aristocracy more generally.[5] Finally, a terrible plague swept through the city in 1656 killing up to a third or even perhaps half of its 400,000–450,000 inhabitants.[6] The aftereffects of the plague in particular—famine and economic uncertainty—lingered for years, and yet the population of the city still climbed once again to the half-million mark by the end of the century.

In the early seventeenth century, Naples was in the middle of a boom period as huge new building works were being undertaken across the city in the private and public sectors alike. In the first instance, the city's status as the engine of baroque popular devotional culture—"la fedelissima," or the most faithful city, as it termed itself—was continuously fed by the growing population as well as by its status as the most fertile center for the renewed energies of the Counter-Reformation. As a result, dozens of churches, convents, monasteries, and hospices were either substantially renovated or built anew during the period by such recently arrived orders as the Jesuits, Theatines, Oratorians, or by previously established orders like the Carthusians, who completely rebuilt and extended their ancient charterhouse overlooking the bay of Naples.[7] At the same time the building of new palaces in Naples was proceeding at a feverish rate, the result of the increased emphasis on building up Naples as an urban center more generally, as well as of a recent, astute viceregal strategy of defusing the potential for sedition from among the kingdom's leadership bases in the growing middle classes and the local aristocracy.[8] The viceroys achieved this by creating an enhanced court culture and requiring aristocrats to spend part of every year resident in Naples. Another and yet more canny and lucrative strategy was to ensure the ongoing collaboration of the aristocracy and rising middle classes in their administrative regimes through the policy of selling off public revenues in both direct and indirect taxes and lands, the latter of which resulted in the alienation of many towns and properties previously in the royal domain (while also resulting in the potential for many nouveau riche families to acquire aristocratic bearings either by intermarriage with older families and/or through the wholesale acquisition of land and titles).[9]

As a result of all this, and as far as the possibilities for painting were concerned, early seventeenth-century Naples offered an exceedingly rich platform for ambitious painters. The strongest proof of this lies in the disproportionately large numbers of foreign painters seeking to work there. Caravaggio began this veritable flood of talent when he found an immediately enthusiastic reception for his work among the local Neapolitan patrons after his flight from Rome in mid-1606. In the subsequent decades his example was followed by scores of Romans, many of them Caravaggesque painters, seeking to profit from the continued interest among Neapolitan patrons in this style long after Caravaggio's influence had waned decisively in other cities. Ribera, for example, ended up expressing the quintessence of Neapolitan baroque naturalism, but he too was an immigrant, arriving in Naples in 1616 in his mid-twenties following periods spent first in his native Valencia and then in Bologna and Rome. Others drawn to Naples included Giuseppe Cesari d'Arpino (working on frescoes for the Carthusians of S. Martino 1588–91 and again 1595–97), Domenichino (active in Naples Cathedral from 1631 until his death in 1641), Lanfranco (working 1634–46, first for the Neapolitan Jesuits, and then for the Theatines and Carthusians as well as for the cathedral itself), Artemisia Gentileschi (whose Spanish Hapsburg contacts encouraged her to relocate to Naples in 1629, where she was to stay until her death in the mid-1650s),[10] and Mattia Preti (who left his native Calabria for greener pastures first in Rome but then in Naples for an extraordinarily productive decade around the time of the plague of 1656).

Scores of less high profile painters—but no less interesting for that—also made the trek down to Naples during this period. François de Nomé and Didier Barra helped launch an interest in ruin painting and architectural *vedute*, respectively, following relocations from their native Metz and then Rome at the beginning of the century. The same is true of the *quadratura* painter, Viviano Codazzi, originally from Bergamo but active in Naples for more than a decade in the mid-1630s, before the disturbances of the revolt of Masaniello in 1647 caused his hasty exit for Rome. Charles Mellin left for Rome at the same time after spending six years in Naples. Johann Heinrich Schönfeld, a highly original and influential *petit-maître* hailing from southern Germany, spent 15 productive years in Naples from the mid-1630s onwards. The Spanish status of viceregal Naples also meant that it attracted more than its fair share of Spanish painters. Juan Do hailed from Ribera's home region in Valencia, but then spent the rest of his life in Naples from the mid-1620s onwards. The list could go on—and would, in any event, be greatly increased if one were to add the scores of painters lured to Naples to try their luck after initial years spent in the outlying provinces: the region of Apulia, for example, drew from its boundaries both the brothers Cesare and Francesco Fracanzano as well as Francesco Guarino, who probably arrived a little later than they did, at the end of the 1620s. Even Guido Reni tried his hand at Neapolitan residence, at least, that is to say, until the vengeful and resentful local painters found his presence there too provoking and in 1622 conspired to intimidate and coerce him to leave as soon as possible and return to Rome.

Attitudes to Painting in Baroque Naples

But it was not all milk and honey in this vast arena of possibilities for work. The Hispanic influence on Neapolitan aristocratic culture was one ever-present factor that tended to keep prices down and recognition for work relatively modest. As the well-known case of Velázquez in Madrid would soon demonstrate, Spanish patrons may well have greatly appreciated the qualities of painting, yet their understanding of the corresponding social status of painters themselves and the underlying intellectual significance and value attached to painting as a liberal art was much less developed than elsewhere in Italy, particularly in Rome. Added to this was the relative novelty at the beginning of the century of the entire phenomenon of art collecting and connoisseurship. It needs to be stressed that Naples did not have a widespread tradition of exalted sixteenth-century patronage, such as would sow the seeds for the efflorescence of ecclesiastical and aristocratic art collecting during the Roman baroque. At the beginning of the seventeenth century, collecting by the professional classes in Naples had only just commenced, and the aristocracy had only recently moved en bloc to the city and, thence, to consider building and enriching their palaces. The oft-quoted statements of Jusepe Martínez bear repeating in this context. In 1625 this Aragonese painter and theoretician visited Naples where he was shown around the churches and private collections of the day by none other than Ribera himself. He was not overly impressed by what he saw, however, and he concluded, probably reasonably accurately, that "since I had come from Rome, everything seemed small to me, as in this city people are more concerned with military matters and horsemanship than with the art of painting."[11]

The situation was changing, nonetheless, and there were also exceptions, some quite notable, such as was evident in the growing culture of literary academies that occasionally connected also with like-minded painters such as Massimo Stanzione, among others.[12] At the same time, Naples also did not lack a small, elite group of stars, namely Jusepe de Ribera, Stanzione, and Battistello Caracciolo, who were able to leverage influential aristocratic backing in order to gain prestigious knighthoods during the 1620s and 1630s (although most of the knighthoods were conferred, tellingly, via papal, and thus Roman, intercession rather than from Naples or Spain directly).[13] In general, though, Neapolitan painters were essentially considered to be artisans, and painting was contracted as such and paid for accordingly. The idea that an artist could, by contrast, insist on the innate dignity of his calling and refuse to put a simple, finite price on his work in line with other artists—to indulge in the inflationary gift-giving strategies, in other words, of an artist like Guido Reni—was unheard of in Naples. There were no Neapolitan treatises on art theory to back up such thinking, no literary equivalents to Vasari, Baglione, Baldinucci, et al. to model the ideal of painters as noble practitioners (at least not until Bernardo de' Dominici in the eighteenth century), and, perhaps most importantly, there was no Neapolitan painters' academy to insist on the status of painting as a liberal art until well into the eighteenth century.

The cumulative effect of all of this was enough to discourage an intellectually minded, independent, and status conscious artist like Salvator Rosa. After an early promising career in Naples, Rosa nonetheless felt the need to leave the city as soon as he could in the late 1630s for what must have seemed more conducive settings in Rome and Florence. There Rosa sought to emulate—in his own characteristically idiosyncratic and not entirely successful way—the path of Poussin as a deeply intellectual and intrinsically noble painter of complex history paintings.

Neapolitan Currency: Economic Background and Foreign Exchange

Another factor mitigating the Neapolitans' ability to increase their prices on the basis of the supposed innate nobility of painting was the underlying social and financial uncertainties that remained a constant strain on business throughout the seventeenth century. The basic monetary unit in Naples was the ducat, a silver coin, equivalent in value to the subdivided currencies of 5 tari, 10 carlini, and 100 grana. The ducat held strong at the end of the sixteenth century and stood, at that stage at least, at a favorable exchange rate of 1 to 1 with the Roman scudo.[14] This was not to last, however, and the constant ebbing of finances and resources away from the kingdom (in 1638 the combined total of tax revenues flowing out of the kingdom and into the Spanish royal coffers was a staggering 5,808,838 ducats),[15] coupled with the ongoing Neapolitan situation of hardship and social unrest, soon took their toll on the economic well-being of the city and the strength of the Neapolitan currency, as Table 30 in Renata Ago's essay so clearly documents.

In 1611, the Royal Mint responded by precipitating a free fall in the value of the ducat when it literally devalued the silver carlino by progressively taking out the proportion of silver used to mint each coin. As a result, the ducat and its related currencies were progressively devalued in the nine years that followed. The year of 1620 represented the nadir of what was, in effect, a process of cumulative recession, whereby the ducat plunged in value to less than 0.6 of the Roman scudo.[16] The Neapolitan economic theorist, Gian Donato Turbolo, accordingly lamented that this had a disastrous effect on foreign trade, meaning that Neapolitan goods could now only be sold abroad at "prezzi vilissimi."[17] What could have been an economic advantage for the important Neapolitan painters—their art becoming available at bargain prices abroad—did not materialize because, until Luca Giordano's rise to international fame, the demand for their work (in distinction to cheap serial imagery) simply was not there.

This economic crisis had many ramifications, not least of which was that it encouraged a number of painters to leave Naples, if they could, for potentially more favorable markets abroad. Some notable foreigners resident in the city chose to conclude their affairs and make their way back to their homelands in the North. Dirck Hendricksz (better known via his Italianate name of Teodoro d'Errico) left Naples for Amsterdam sometime in 1610 after a long and highly successful career specializing in the prestigious *soffitti cassetonati*, or elaborately gilded and decorated wooden coffered ceilings, that had proven so popular among the great Counter-Reformation church renovation projects during the last years of the sixteenth century.[18] He was followed shortly thereafter by Louis Finson, an early Neapolitan associate of Caravaggio and sometime dealer in his work, who left Naples in late 1612 to return to Amsterdam, following periods spent initially in Spain and France, where he attempted to sell Caravaggio's Neapolitan-period *Madonna of the Rosary* (Kunsthistorisches Museum, Vienna), prior to his death in 1617.[19]

Some key local artists also tried their luck outside the kingdom during this period. Caracciolo travelled frequently between Naples and Rome during the years 1614 and 1617 (where he even enrolled in the Accademia di S. Luca) and then again from 1618 through to the early 1620s, when he was active at the court of Grand Duke Cosimo III de' Medici in Florence as well in Genoa.[20] Stanzione also spent a few years in Rome seeking work, first in 1617–18 and then again in the later 1620s.[21]

Yet both these artists ultimately returned to Naples, and it is not difficult to understand why. The dominant traditions of Caravaggism followed by a wave of second-generation Bolognese "classicism" were readily importable to Naples, as the tremendous success of Caravaggio's and Lanfranco's stays in the city attest. Yet the opposite was not the case. Throughout the first half of the seventeenth century, Neapolitan art represented a highly localized, regional specialization that attracted very little demand among collectors beyond its borders. A few exceptional artists did manage to buck this trend (most notably Ribera among his Spanish compatriots). Yet these exceptions remained just that. Aniello Falcone, for example (Fig. 30), specialized from the 1630s onwards in producing Neapolitan Caravaggesque adaptations of the contemporary genre battle scenes being developed in the North by artists such as Esaias van de

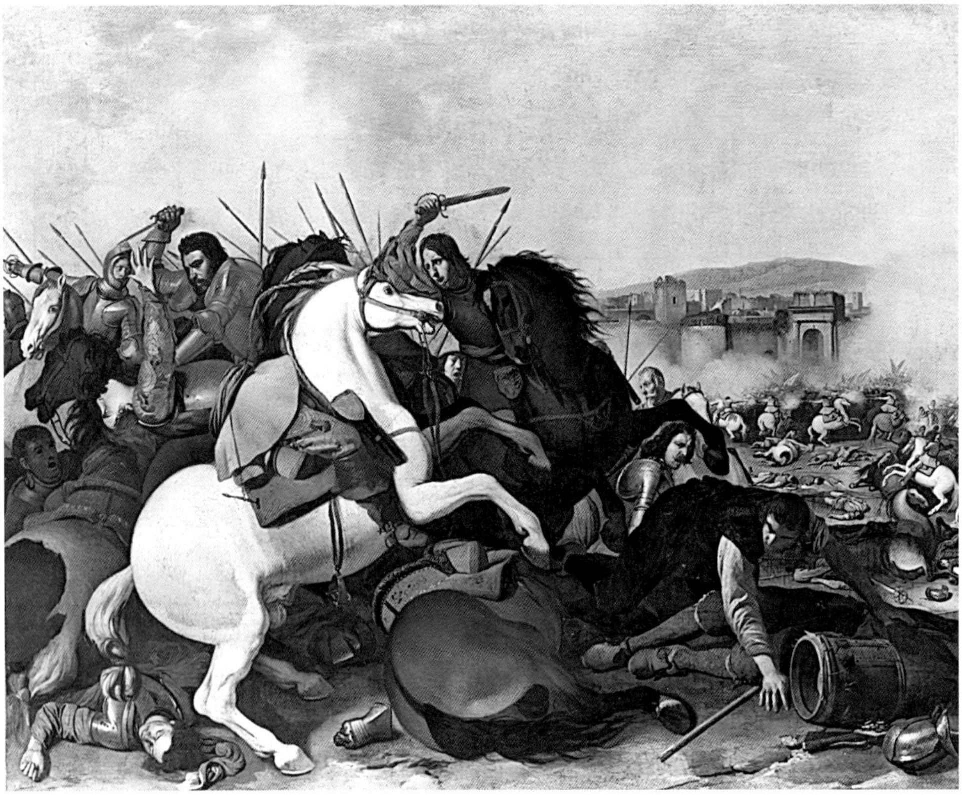

30 Aniello Falcone, *Battle Scene*, 1640s. Oil on canvas, 84 × 104 cm. Bayerische Staatsgemäldesammlungen, Munich.

Velde among others. This novel subcategory of painting was highly influential among Falcone's followers (as discussed below in the case of Andrea de Leone). Falcone also managed to attract the attention of a number of leading collectors as far afield as Spain, France, and Belgium, as well as in central and northern Italy. Yet the fact that Falcone's international reputation was considered so noteworthy as to warrant mention in the dedicatory inscription placed on the artist's tombstone, following his death from the plague in 1656, underscores the extent to which foreign collecting of Neapolitan art remained limited, at best.[22] Outside interest in Neapolitan art would not occur until the unprecedented global success achieved by Luca Giordano from the 1660s onwards.

Unlike the many foreign painters immigrating to Naples, the vast majority of Neapolitan painters thus had no choice but to remain at home and make the best of the situation. In the years after 1620 the ducat remained relatively stable, even strengthening somewhat in the 1630s, though it fell once again during the last decades of the century.[23] Within its own frame of reference in the Kingdom of Naples itself, the ducat's buying power continued to compare reasonably well with the scudo, as demonstrated below in relation to a comparison of Roman and Neapolitan salaries and cost of living indices. Yet the damage had been done, and the native currency stood thereafter as permanently devalued in comparison with stronger foreign currencies—and with the solid Roman scudo in particular.

Public Commissions and the Impact of Foreign Labor

It was against this background of recent economic devaluation that Guido Reni insisted in 1620, as part of the package that would induce him to leave Rome for Naples, on receiving 130 ducats per figure for his work at the Cappella del Tesoro di S. Gennaro in Naples Cathedral.[24] Although the deputies presiding over this, the most prestigious public commission of the day, accepted his price, the fee stood at a full 20–25 ducats over and above what any other highly ranked painter would have been able to receive as a per figure rate for any of the other major public commissions of the period (see Table 9 below). It accordingly remained an otherwise anomalous high water mark of the most expensive fee ever agreed in the history of Neapolitan baroque painting. This nonetheless attracted, predictably enough, an unprecedented degree of enmity from among the local Neapolitan painters, who saw to it that Reni never even began his work or received payment from the deputies of the Tesoro.

The story of Reni's aborted attempt to undertake the Cappella del Tesoro commission in 1620–21 has come to assume semi-legendary status.[25] The circumstances surrounding the commission were, in fact, already compromised prior to Reni's arrival in Naples, since his appearance on the scene had followed an earlier, equally unsuccessful attempt in 1616–18 to award the commission to Arpino. Arpino had only proceeded as far as receiving his 600 ducat down payment before departing for Rome, never to return. De' Dominici believed that Arpino had left as a result of an attack on his life by the local competitors, as led by the leading Neapolitan fresco painter Belisario Corenzio. The real reason for Arpino's reneging on the contract, however, seems to have been a surfeit of commissions in progress requiring his attention back in Rome.[26] Corenzio and his associates, on the other hand, certainly did physically intimidate Reni and his assistants in 1622, a fact that emerged under confession following an investigation and the judicial torture of one of the perpetrators of the attack, a stuccoist associate of Corenzio's named Domenico Capuano.[27] Reni never returned to Naples, and the commission remained in abeyance until Domenichino was finally induced down to Naples by

TABLE 9 Costs per Square Meter and per Figure of Neapolitan Church Commissions

ARTIST AND DATE	PAINTING (oil altarpieces unless otherwise indicated)	DIMENSIONS (cm)	PRICE (ducats)	PER SQUARE METER	PER FIGURE
Caravaggio, 1606–7	*Seven Acts of Mercy*, Pio Monte della Misericordia	390 × 260	400	40	50
Santafede, 1612	*Resurrection of Tabitha*, Pio Monte della Misericordia	306 × 205	100	25	12.5
Caracciolo, 1615	*Liberation of St. Peter*, Pio Monte della Misericordia	310 × 207	100	16	25
Caracciolo, 1617	*Earthly Trinity*, Pietà dei Turchini	340 × 230	150	21	21
Caracciolo, 1622	*Washing of the Feet*, choir lateral, S. Martino	393 × 390	333	22	47.5
Caracciolo, 1631	*Assumption*, S. Martino	244 × 170	251	62	36
Finoglio, 1626	*Circumcision*, S. Martino	255 × 170	100	16	14.25
Domenichino, 1631–41	*Scenes from the Life of St. Januarius*, Cappella del Tesoro, Naples Cathedral	various (total fee for many frescoes and altarpieces)	22,500		
Domenichino, 1640	*Martyrdom of St. Januarius*, Cappella del Tesoro, Naples Cathedral	355 × 220	1,575 (part of previously cited total fee)	196	105
Lanfranco, 1634–40	*Christ Blessing*, cupola, *Four Evangelists*, pendentives, frescoes, Gesù Nuovo	various	10,000		
Lanfranco, 1637–39	*Ascension, Apostles, Angels, Crucifixion*, nave and choir frescoes, S. Martino	various	7,500		
Lanfranco, 1638–46	Choir and nave frescoes, and 5 oil paintings each 403 × 208/210, 1 oil painting 404 × 307, SS. Apostoli	various	10,000		
Lanfranco, 1643	*Paradise*, cupola fresco, Cappella del Tesoro, Naples Cathedral	various	7,000		
Lanfranco, 1646	Vault frescoes, Casa Professa, Gesù Nuovo	various	500		
Pacecco de Rosa, 1636	*St. Nicholas*, S. Martino	255 × 164	80	20	40
Ribera, 1637	*Pietà*, S. Martino	264 × 170	400	72	66.5
Ribera, 1647	*St. Januarius Escaping from the Furnace*, Cappella del Tesoro, Naples Cathedral	320 × 200	1,400	215	100

Ribera, 1651	*Last Communion of the Apostles*, choir lateral, S. Martino	400 × 400	900 or 1,000	56	100
Stanzione, 1638	*Pietà*, overdoor, S. Martino	240 × 320	300	50	50
Stanzione, 1639	*Last Supper*, choir lateral, S. Martino	393 × 393	1,000	66	100
Stanzione, 1639–40	*Scenes from the Life of the Virgin*, choir ceiling frescoes, Gesù Nuovo	various	1,400		
Stanzione, 1642–44	*Scenes from the Lives of Sts. Peter and Paul*, nave frescoes, S. Paolo Maggiore	various	3,000		
Stanzione, 1649	*Visitation*, Gesù Nuovo	338 × 205	250 (less cost of ultramarine)	35	35.5
Domenico Gargiulo, 1641	*Last Supper*, S. Maria della Sapienza	306 × 202	120	20	24
Beltrano, 1646	*Madonna of Purgatory*, Chiesa delle Anime del Purgatorio, Nola	395 × 263	80	8	
Beltrano, 1649	*St. Jerome and the Angel*, S. Agostino degli Scalzi	210 × 171	50	14	16.5
Charles Mellin, 1646	*Immaculate Conception*, S. Maria Donnaregina	352 × 230	170	21	24.25
Vaccaro, 1652	*St. Hugh Supervising the Construction of Lincoln Abbey*, lateral, S. Martino	205 × 305	200	33	28.5
Vaccaro, 1660	*Intercession of the Madonna for the Souls of Purgatory*, S. Maria del Pianto	350 × 250	100	11	11
Mattia Preti, 1653	*St. Nicholas of Bari*, S. Domenico Soriano	217 × 157	50	14	25
Mattia Preti, 1657–60	*Crucifixion with Franciscan Saints; Madonna and Child Adored by Clares*, S. Lorenzo Maggiore	350 × 200	400 (200 each)	28	22.25
Mattia Preti, 1657–59	*Scenes From the Life of St. Celestine and of St. Catherine of Alexandria*, nave and transept, S. Pietro a Maiella	10 large canvases: 5 in the nave, 5 in the transept; diameter 360 (2 canvases); 145 × 400 (2); 370 × 370 (1); diameter 370 (2); 300 × 150 (2); 450 × 500 (1)	1,100: 550 for the nave paintings, 550 for the transept paintings (110 ducats average per painting)		
Giordano, 1661	*Crucifixion Adored by Patron Saints of Naples*, S. Maria del Pianto	400 × 315	100	8	25
Giordano, 1675	*Martyrdom of St. Placido*, S. Giustina, Padua	373 × 185	200	28	25
Giordano, 1684	*Christ Falls the First Time* and *Christ Nailed to the Cross,* lateral altarpieces, S. Maria Regina Coeli	152 × 204; 152 × 206	200 (100 each)	33	16.5

the Tesoro's deputies in 1631. He too was menaced, and at the time of his death aged 60 in 1641, with the commission still unfinished, his widow accused the Neapolitans of foul play, believing, whether rightly or wrongly, that certain individuals had conspired to poison his food.[28]

The attempts of the deputies to secure the services of no fewer than three non-Neapolitan painters for the most prestigious local commission have been interpreted as indicating an ingrained prejudice against the accomplishments of native talent.[29] In truth, however, the controversies surrounding the Cappella del Tesoro commission are not so much a reflection of any innate Neapolitan bias against local painters as illustrative of a lack of a strong native tradition of Neapolitan fresco painting prior to the 1630s. This was evident as far back as the 1580s and 1590s when the Carthusians of the Certosa di S. Martino had selected Arpino, in this instance successfully, to work on two sets of frescoes in the choir of their church (1588–91), followed by the completion of his work for the choir and a new set of frescoes for the sacristy (1595–97).[30] Arpino had received the sum of 800 ducats for the first half of his work on the choir alone. Belisario Corenzio, who went on to enjoy considerable success as the leading local frescoist in the decades thereafter, had probably, in fact, been trained in fresco while assisting Arpino on this venture.[31]

The stories of Corenzio strong-arming his rivals over the years are legendary. Already in the later seventeenth century, Carlo Celano recorded the accusation that Corenzio murdered his former pupil, Loise Rodriguez, over a disputed contract, a charge repeated in the eighteenth century and still not discredited in the recent literature.[32] Be this as it may, the lack of a strong local school of fresco painting was furthered by the Neapolitan taste toward the end of the sixteenth century for commissioning elaborate gilt wooden ceilings filled with inset paintings for the churches of the period.[33] As a consequence, fresco painting never became as firmly entrenched in Naples as it had in Rome. The subsequent ascendency of Caravaggio and his school in the second and third decades of the seventeenth century compounded this tendency, as artists like Ribera and his workshop all undertook productive careers working entirely in oil on canvas, as Caravaggio had also done earlier at no particular cost, it seemed, to his career.

That the Neapolitans could nonetheless coexist with foreign fresco specialists resident in the city was confirmed shortly after Domenichino's entry into Naples. In 1634 Lanfranco was also encouraged to move to Naples where he soon took on a feverishly productive series of major works. These included frescoing the cupola and pendentives of the Gesù Nuovo (1634–40, the cupola subsequently destroyed in an earthquake of 1688), the nave ceiling and end lunette of the choir of the Certosa di S. Martino (1637–39), the choir and chapel of the Sacrament of Pozzuoli Cathedral (1636–46, both destroyed), a particularly extensive series of frescoes in the nave and choir of the Theatine church of SS. Apostoli (1638–46), and even the cupola of the Cappella del Tesoro following the death of his old rival Domenichino in 1641 (Fig. 31).[34]

The importance of foreign connections for Lanfranco's Neapolitan work needs to be borne in mind when considering the artist's hectic activity during these years. The Gesù Nuovo contract, for example, had been awarded to Lanfranco not through the agency of the Neapolitans, but rather through the intercession of the general of the Jesuit Order back in Rome. Similarly, the Roman Carthusians had already hired Lanfranco for important commissions some 15 years prior to his work in Naples,[35] and the same applies to Lanfranco's work at the Theatine church of SS. Apostoli, which followed directly on from Lanfranco's frescoing of the cupola of the order's Roman mother church of S. Andrea della Valle during the 1620s. Finally, Lanfranco's career in Naples was also strongly promoted by the Barberini-affiliated archbishop of Naples, Cardinal Ascanio Filomarino, and above all by the Spanish viceroy himself, the count of Monterrey, who had previously collected Lanfranco's work during his earlier stay in Rome as Spanish ambassador to the Holy See.

With such high-ranking foreign backing, then, it is no surprise to find that Lanfranco was amply compensated for his frescoes once he settled in Naples. He received 10,000 ducats for the Gesù Nuovo frescoes,[36] 7,500 ducats for the S. Martino frescoes,[37] 7,000 ducats for the cupola of the Cappella del Tesoro,[38] and 10,000 ducats for his work at SS. Apostoli (which included five very large oil paintings for the choir of the church, for which he was paid 1,500 ducats, or 300 ducats each).[39] (On the other hand, and perhaps predictably enough given the large sums involved, there was still considerable disagreement surrounding these payments, and Lanfranco ended up quarrelling with the Jesuits, Carthusians, and the Theatines about his final fees.)[40] There is no question, however, but that Lanfranco remained one of the highest paid, and also most intensely busy, artists in Naples during the 1630s and 1640s. From these major works alone—and not counting the other commissions for which there is no documentation, such as for Pozzuoli Cathedral—Lanfranco netted 34,500 ducats over a 12-year period, or an average of 2,875 ducats per year.

Nonetheless, and in marked contrast to Domenichino and Reni before him, Lanfranco seems not to have received any particular harassment from the locals during all of this highly profitable activity, which he undoubtedly would have reported back in one of his many voluble letters to his Roman protector, Ferrante Carlo, if it had been the case. What accounts for this exception? One possibility is that, once the initial outrage at the Cappella del Tesoro commission had played itself out through the antagonism of the older generation of local artists—as led by Corenzio (who was 65 in 1622)—and had then had time to abate in the years that followed, the Neapolitans had faced reality and accommodated themselves to the presence of this second foreign fresco specialist in their midst. Lanfranco was not, in any event, a direct competitor to the vast majority of Neapolitan artists. He remained fully committed to a small circuit of high-profile, mainly foreign-sponsored, fresco commissions that did not impinge on Neapolitan patronage more broadly.

His work did not, for example, impinge in any significant way on Ribera since Ribera never practiced

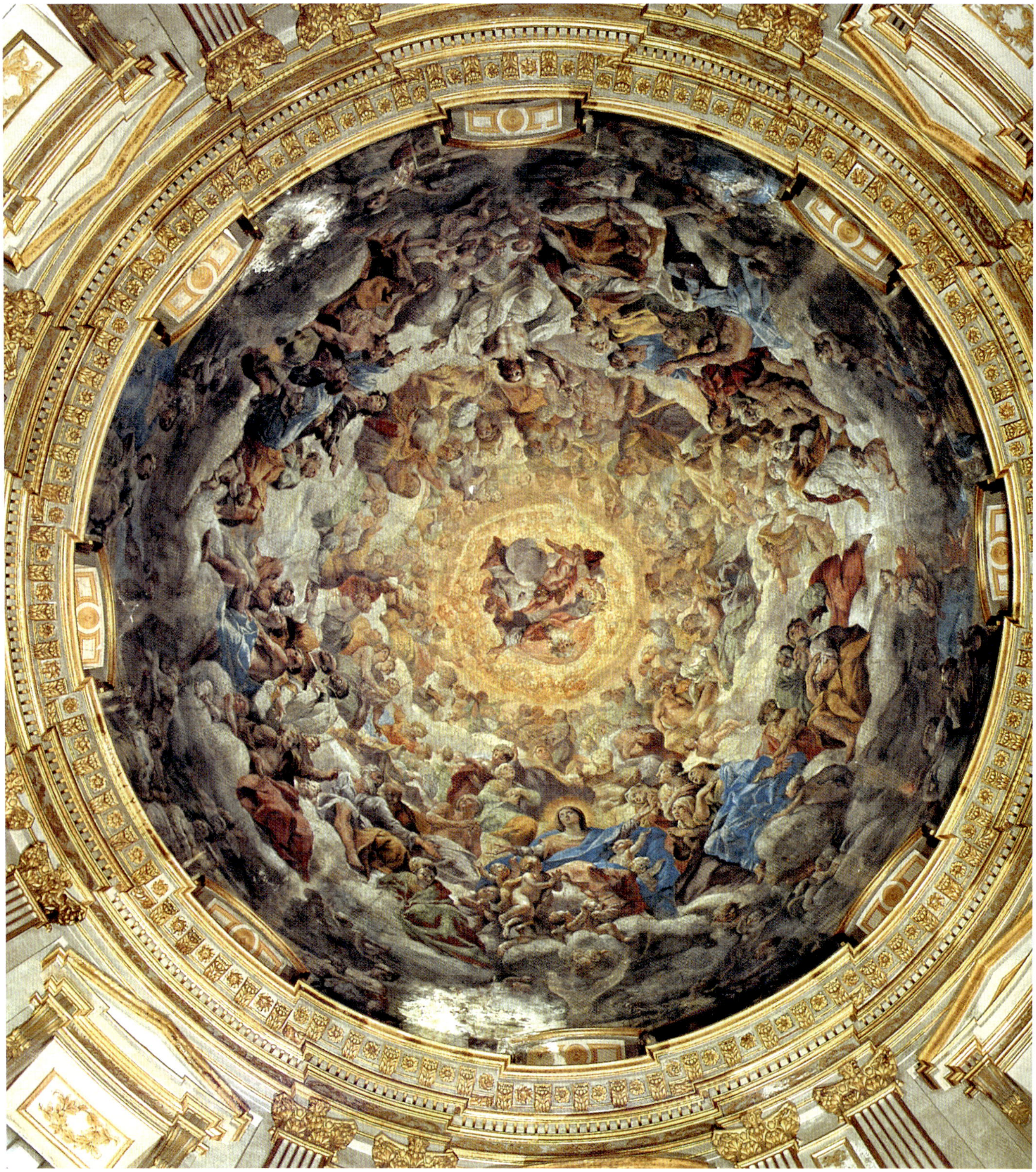

31 Giovanni Lanfranco, *Paradise*, 1643. Fresco. Cappella del Tesoro di S. Gennaro, Naples Cathedral.

fresco to begin with. Similarly, the next rising star of Neapolitan fresco painting, Massimo Stanzione, who began to win major fresco contracts from the early 1630s onwards, had a much larger workshop than Lanfranco and was active in a broader sweep of commissions, including numerous altarpieces. There were one or two inevitable moments of overlap and competition: Stanzione, for example, secured the contract for the Gesù Nuovo choir frescoes after Lanfranco had initially been led to believe that the job had been earmarked for him.[41] But there was work enough for the both of them. While Lanfranco was fully engaged with pre-existing projects, Stanzione was well situated to pick up the contracts that Lanfranco was unable to take on. It would be more accurate, therefore, to conclude that Stanzione profited from Lanfranco's presence since it helped stimulate the market for fresco painting, a situation from which Stanzione was perfectly positioned to benefit in the years that followed.

Cost of Living, Salaries, and Dowries

Naples was marginally cheaper to live in than Rome, but not greatly so, at least in terms of the cost of goods and the buying power of the ducat within Naples itself prior to its devaluation on the foreign exchange. Wheat cost around 3.5 carlini per kilo (or 0.35 of a ducat), making it only a little cheaper than the 4 or 5 baiocchi per kilo needed to buy wheat in Rome.[42] One contemporary report estimated that an individual living at a subsistence level needed 6 *tomoli* of wheat to live on per year (or 240 kilos converting to around 650 grams of bread a day), thus costing each person around 8.5 ducats per year.[43] Wine, on the other hand, was cheaper still. It cost just under 3 grana per litre (or 0.03 of a ducat) and thus again was only a little cheaper than in Rome.[44] Fish varied in price: high-quality types could cost up to 29 grana (0.29 of a ducat) per *rotolo* (the *rotolo* being equivalent to just under a kilo).[45] Cheaper and more plentiful varieties like sardines, on the other hand, cost only 18 grana per *rotolo*. Beef was cheaper still: 8–12 grana per *rotolo* (0.08–0.12 of a ducat), for example, although veal would have been prohibitively expensive for most Neapolitans at 25–30 grani per *rotolo* (that is to say, nearly a third of a ducat). Again, all of these prices compare reasonably well with the previously cited costs of commodities in Rome.

Rent would have been one of the largest expenses for the majority of Neapolitan painters. The trades in Naples were all highly localized, and since the beginning of the century painters were particularly found in a tightly interlocking neighborhood centered upon the Piazza della Carità in the heart of the city. This area was optimally situated for trade since it stood between the seats of government, the court and the Spanish residents who represented the state. There the local painters lived and worked in a concentrated commercial district interspersed with the workshops of their colleagues in the related trades of gilding, sculpting, carving, and secondhand dealing. To purchase a workshop in this area constituted a long-term financial investment that would have been well beyond the means of most painters. In 1619 the going price for a workshop in the area was 1,610 ducats.[46] Instead, painters would more commonly pay rent on their workshops (which were, in any event, generally owned by one of the local churches, convents, or aristocratic families).[47] The challenge of paying the rent—normally around 30 to 40 ducats per year—should not be underestimated, particularly for painters positioned at the lower reaches of the market. It is one of the main reasons why so many elected to begin their careers by starting more modestly instead, either by renting out single rooms or by banding together in partnerships to share the costs involved in maintaining workshops.[48] Alternatively, as was the case for an artist like Pietro Pesce cited at the beginning of the discussion, many painters started out more simply still by painting for day rates in workshops belonging to better-established independent masters.

Almost every painter of the period—in common with the other artisans in the area as well—chose to keep costs down by combining his business and residential occupancy and lived either at the back of the workshop or in a small suite of generally four rooms placed directly above. This made sense financially. Only the grandest painters were ever in a position to be able to live separately from their place of work. One of the few exceptions was, predictably enough, Ribera, who in 1619 elected to purchase outright, for the considerable sum of 1,900 ducats, a house and garden for his extended family in the strada di S. Spirito in the centre of the artists' quarter.[49] In 1641, in an even greater proclamation of his considerable financial and social attainments, he purchased—for the even higher asking price of 3,100 ducats—a small villa with adjoining garden on the outskirts of Naples in the much sought-after area of the Borgo di Chiaia. To help recoup his costs he initially chose to rent this property out for 100 ducats per year—more than double the price of the annual rent payable on a painter's workshop and living quarters in the city itself.[50] His neighbor in the Borgo di Chiaia was none other than Massimo Stanzione, his chief competitor for the position of leading painter of baroque Naples.[51] Such princely living—particularly welcome during those long, hot summer months—was completely beyond the means of the rest of the Neapolitan painters who were compelled instead to sweat it out, cheek by jowl, in the city below.

How hard was it to earn enough money to be able to have enough to eat, pay the rent, keep one's family, and live reasonably comfortably in baroque Naples? The answer naturally depends on the social and financial expectations of the individual in question, but it is true to say that for those Neapolitan painters who were either lucky or talented enough to reach a comparably high level of public recognition, their earnings could be quite satisfactory. As will be discussed, the 200 ducats or thereabouts that Ribera, Stanzione, and a handful of other painters were able to command for each of their major oil paintings compared very favorably with many annual salaries of the day.

To give some examples, at the end of the sixteenth century the maestro of the viceregal chapel received a salary of just 73 ducats per year, while the viceregal soprano received 60 and the organist received 36 ducats. In 1645 a captain of the guard received lower rates still at 40 ducats,[52] while a priest could expect even less, just 20 ducats as the annual fee paid to one of the confessors at the convent of S. Severo Maggiore in 1620.[53] As the last salary underscores, though, many of these wages were really only stipends rather than what we would understand as wages today. Their recipients would have been expected to supplement their stipends from other sources of support, such as would have been provided by a priest's community and archdiocese.

Actual salaries could, in any event, be either much higher or considerably lower. In 1649, for example, the standard weekly wage at the Certosa di S. Martino for six days' work as a *piperniero*, or stonemason, was 2 ducats—an annual wage of 82.5 ducats for a nominal 250-day year—almost exactly comparable prior to devaluation to the 85 scudi a year paid to Roman masons.[54] At the other end of the spectrum, though, the annual stipends paid to holders of high-ranking public offices could be astronomically high by comparison. The president of the Camera Reale, for example, was paid 6,000 ducats per year for his post, while the *reggente della Vicaria* (regent of the viceregal court) received 2,400 and a mere councillor received 1,400.[55]

The huge disparity of social and economic scale between even the highest ranked Neapolitan painters and their ecclesiastic and aristocratic patrons thus needs to be borne in mind when assessing the relative prosperity attained by at least some of these artists. A further way of illustrating this is through the example of painters' dowries. Dowries were extremely important for heads of households because they represented one of their biggest costs and were seen by artists, as by aristocrats, as a public declaration of financial security. In 1616, for example, the painter Giovan Bernardino Azzolino had attained a certain degree of financial success that enabled him to provide his daughter, Caterina, and her fiancé, Jusepe de Ribera, with a respectable dowry of 600 ducats. This sum reflected both Azzolino's financial position and his shrewd recognition of the future status of his son-in-law: Ribera already was a meteorically rising star who would soon become the kingpin of the Neapolitan art world.[56] By comparison, Belisario Corenzio was only able to apportion half as much to his daughter when she came to marry in 1641, a sum which was more in keeping with the customary amounts committed by reasonably successful artisans at that level.[57]

Azzolino's faith in Ribera's future prospects certainly paid off. This was demonstrated, among other respects, by Ribera's ability three years after the marriage to purchase outright a family house for the considerable sum of 1,900 ducats, as has been mentioned. Twenty-eight years later, the cycle then repeated itself a generation down the family line when the time came for Jusepe and Caterina de Ribera's own daughter to marry. This fortunate child received a huge dowry worth no less than 5,000 ducats.[58] This sum surpassed the highest financial aspirations of all the other artists of the period, with the single possible exception of Stanzione. Even it pales into insignificance, however, by comparison with the 20,000 ducat dowry brought by Vittoria Albrici to her marriage in 1617 to Francesco Antonio Francone, prince of Pietracupa.[59]

The Price of Painting

When studying the available data for prices for Neapolitan paintings across the course of the seventeenth century one is struck, in the first instance, by their relative stability and lack of fluctuation. Paintings are not dissimilar in this respect to the stability encountered in the prices for wine, oil, and other commodities of the day. There is, in fact, only one really significant moment of inflation in the cost of paintings for the whole of the seventeenth century. At the beginning of the century, it was still common for prestigious chapel altarpieces to be commissioned for a total price

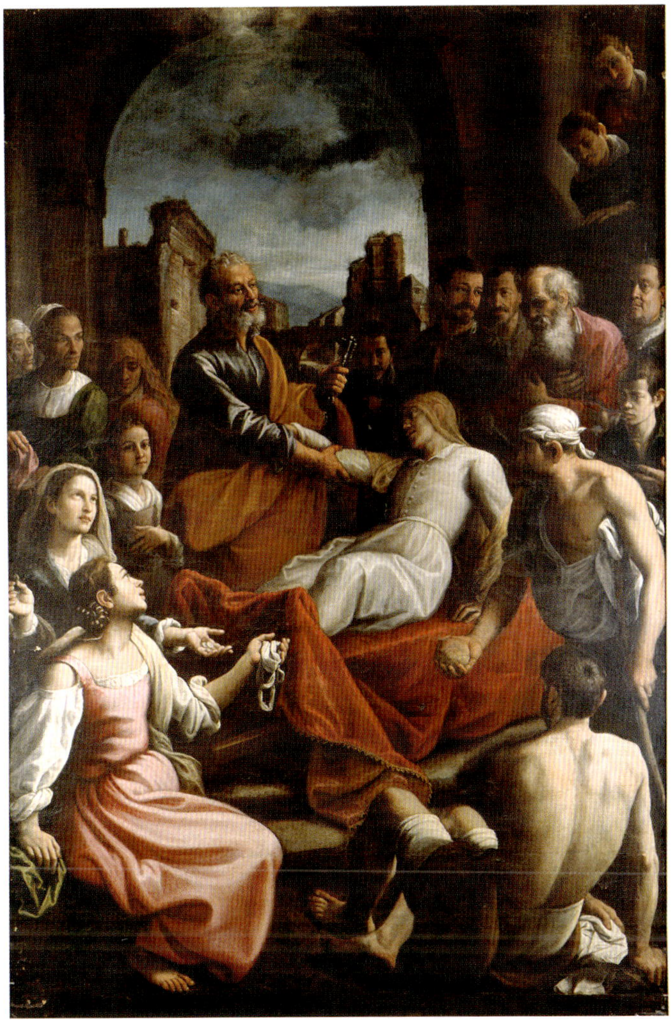

32 Fabrizio Santafede, *Resurrection of Tabitha*, 1612. Oil on canvas, 306 × 205 cm. Pio Monte della Misericordia, Naples.

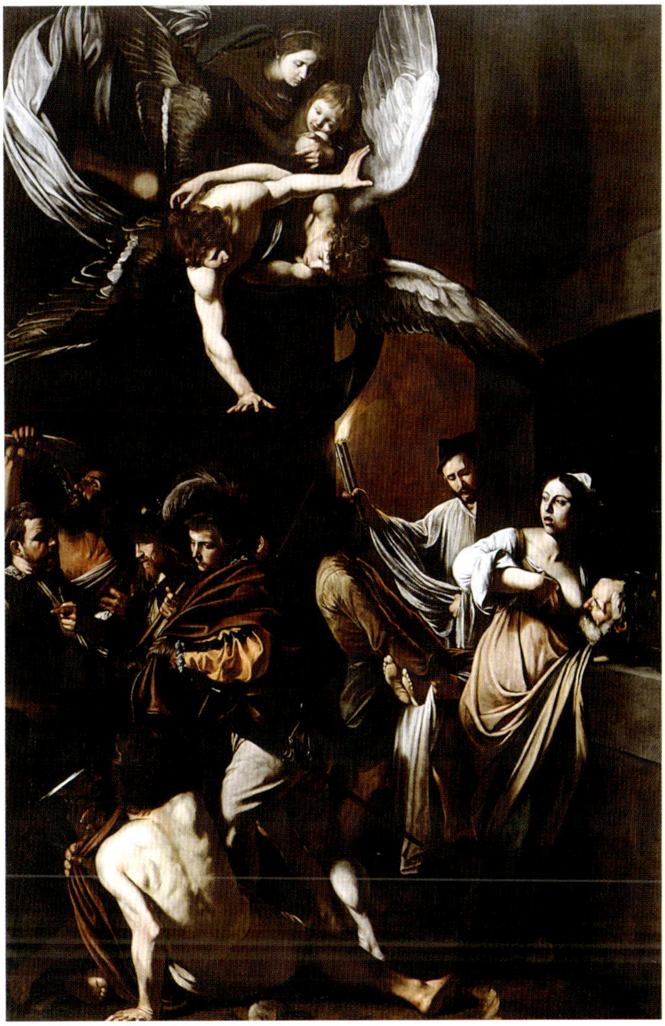

33 Caravaggio, *Seven Acts of Mercy*, 1606–7. Oil on canvas, 390 × 260 cm. Pio Monte della Misericordia, Naples.

of 100 ducats (see Table 9). This is how much the aristocratic donors for three of the seven altarpieces in the church of the Pio Monte della Misericordia decided in 1608 to pay for paintings by Fabrizio Santafede (Fig. 32), Caracciolo, and Carlo Sellitto (although Sellitto died before completing his altarpiece).[60] All three of these leading artists agreed to the same amounts for other altarpieces painted during the same period.[61]

In 1606, by contrast, Caravaggio was offered 400 ducats for his major altarpiece in the same church (Fig. 33).[62] Caravaggio was, of course, exceptionally famous, and his *Seven Acts of Mercy* was also exceptionally large. Yet Caravaggio's presence in Naples created an extraordinary stimulus to Neapolitan taste. It was the single most influential factor leading to a greatly increased appreciation of the importance of painting on the part of patrons and painters alike. Caravaggio's Neapolitan legacy stimulated the creation of the Neapolitan baroque style, the power of which encouraged patrons to leave aside their previously popular late Mannerist altarpieces painted on wood with elaborately carved and gilded frames in favor of the new manner of dramatically rendered, tenebrist compositions painted on canvas. This change in taste, combined with a renewed interest in art collecting and in commissions in both the private and public sectors, helped to strengthen and consolidate the prices paid for paintings.

A price correction in the cost of Neapolitan paintings in the 1620s grew out of the previously noted broader economic pressures that were an ever-present feature of the period. Prices for wheat and oil climbed rapidly during 1621–22, following an economic slump during the previous years. Their prices subsequently stabilised thereafter as the ducat slowly regained its value

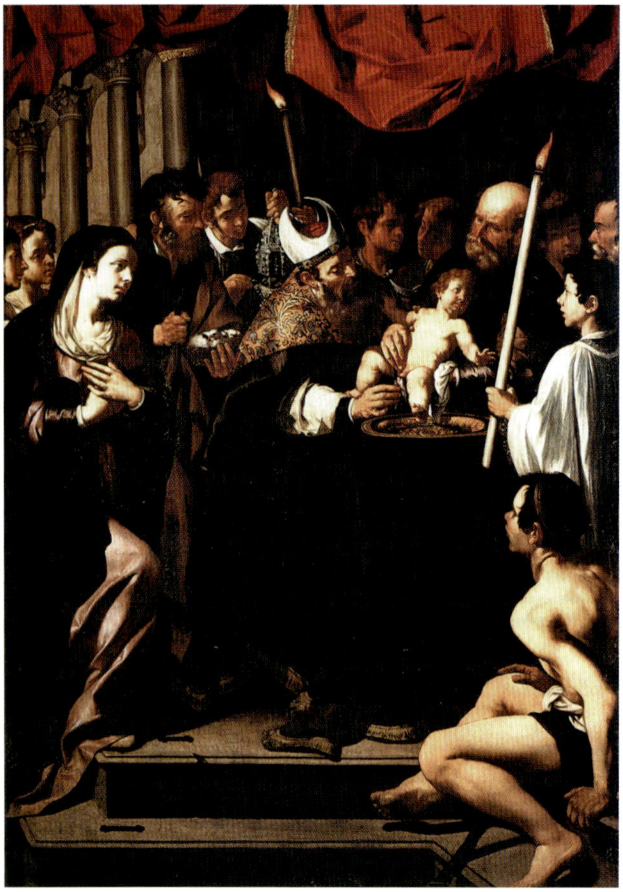

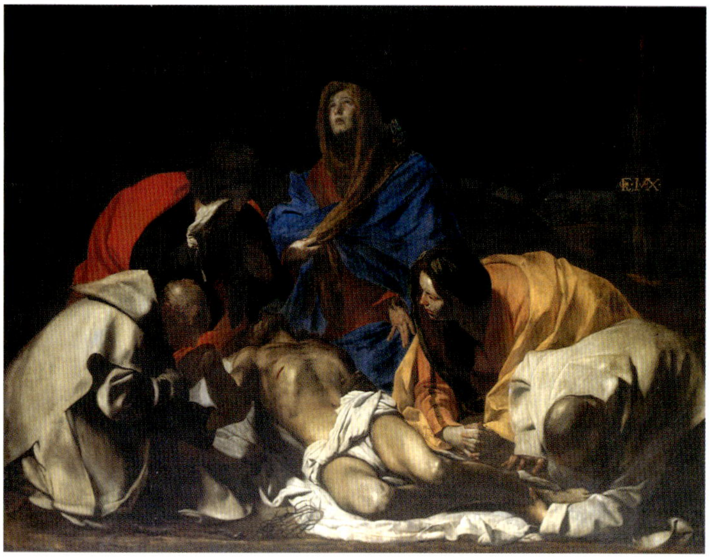

34 (left) Paolo Finoglio, *The Circumcision*, 1626. Oil on canvas, 255 × 170 cm. Certosa di S. Martino, Naples.

35 (above) Massimo Stanzione, *Pietà*, 1638. Oil on canvas, 240 × 320 cm. Certosa di S. Martino, Naples.

relative to pre-1611 exchange rates.[63] In effect, and as a result of this coming together of the combined factors of taste and economics, the 1620s and 1630s constituted the key moment when prices for Neapolitan painting shifted from a belated continuation of sixteenth-century price structures toward relatively more generous prices that were comparable to those commanded for similar work in other cities.

This can be readily demonstrated from the scores of payments for altarpieces over the course of the seventeenth century as tabulated above (Table 9). In the 1620s it was still reasonably common for well-known painters to receive 100 ducat commissions for altarpieces: this was the amount paid to Paolo Finoglio, for example, for an altarpiece at the Certosa di S. Martino in 1626 (Fig. 34).[64] From the 1630s onwards, however, this became less and less the case. Altarpieces commissioned at the Certosa di S. Martino testify to this change. Accordingly, 251 ducats were paid in 1631 for Caracciolo's *Assumption of the Virgin*, 300 ducats in 1638 for Stanzione's *Pietà* (Fig. 35, technically an overdoor placed in the nave, although this wouldn't have affected the price), 400 ducats for Ribera's painting of the same subject in 1637 (Fig. 36), and 200 ducats for Andrea Vaccaro's altarpiece of *St. Hugh* in 1652.[65]

All four of these paintings compare reasonably well in their size and number of figures. Caracciolo's *Assumption* contains the equivalent of around seven figures and measures 244 × 170 cm, Stanzione's *Pietà* contains six and measures 240 × 320 cm, and Vaccaro's contains the equivalent of around seven figures while measuring 205 × 305 cm. Only Ribera's picture was more expensive in relation to its size and number of figures: containing the equivalent of just under six figures and measuring 264 × 170 cm, it cost 400 ducats. Conversely, Finoglio's *Circumcision* of 1626 seems a bargain at just 100 ducats for a painting measuring 255 × 170 cm and containing the equivalent of six figures.

Altarpieces constitute a particularly useful standard for assessing price trends across time since, unlike frescoes, they are reasonably standardized in their dimensions (being generally 2–2.5 meters high by 1.75–2 meters wide) and their usual number of figures (generally the equivalent of between four to six figures and only rarely exceeding eight). Unlike the more varied nature of fresco production, they are thus more com-

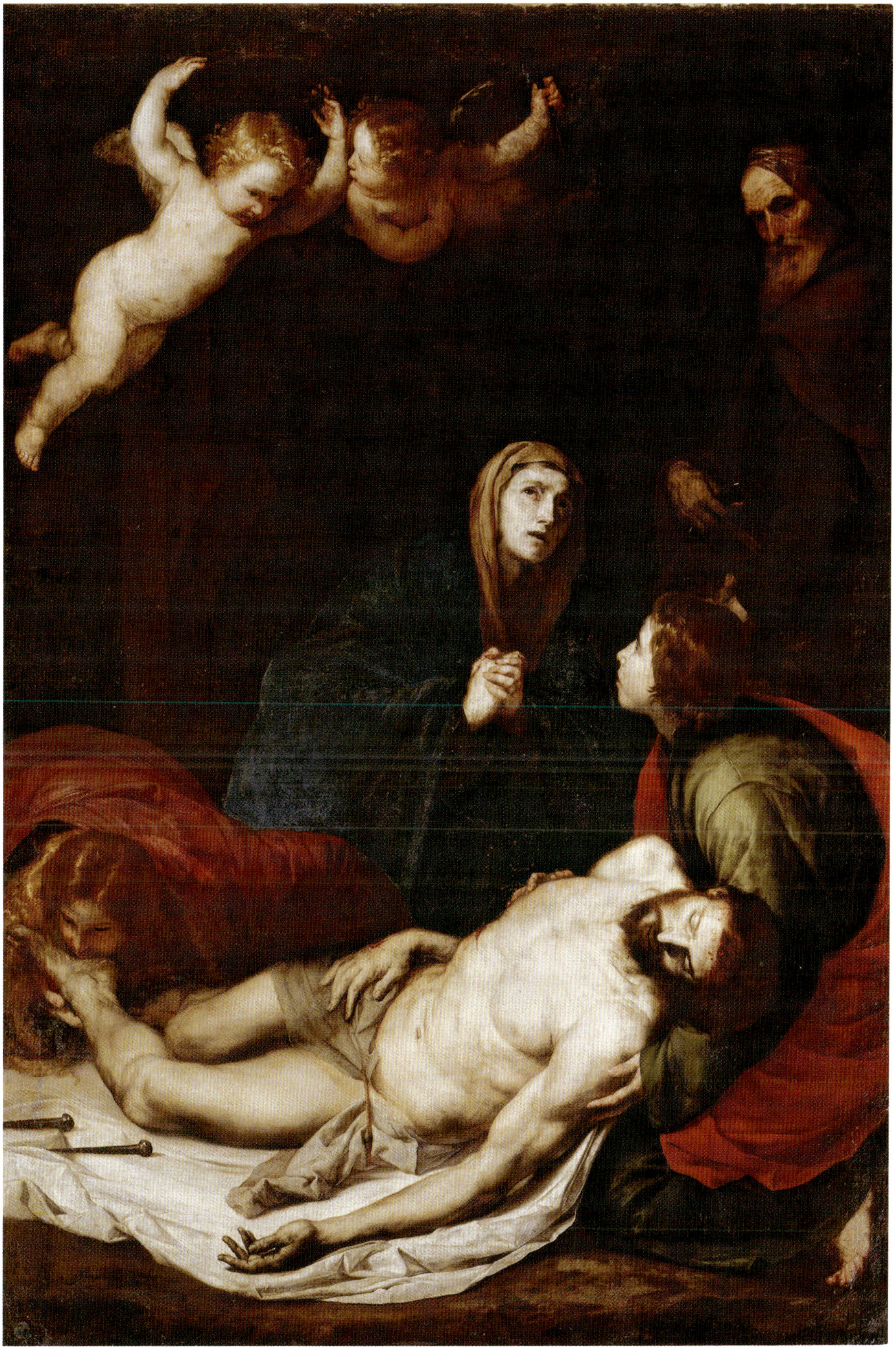

36 Jusepe de Ribera, *Pietà*, 1637. Oil on canvas, 264 × 170 cm. Certosa di S. Martino, Naples.

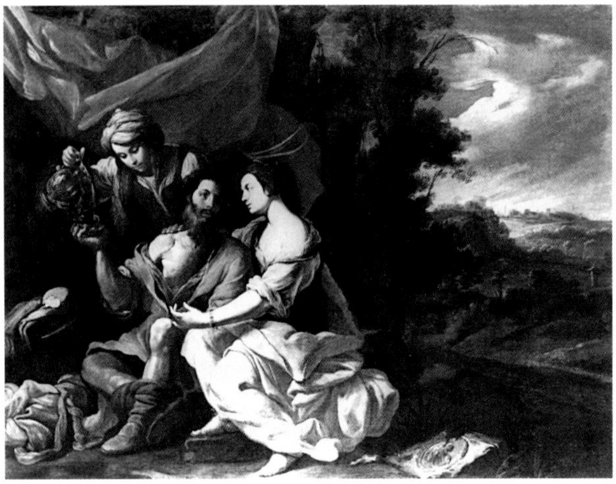

37 Agostino Beltrano, *Lot and his Daughters*, ca. 1640s. Oil on canvas, 74 × 99 cm. Molinari Pradelli collection, Marano di Castenaso.

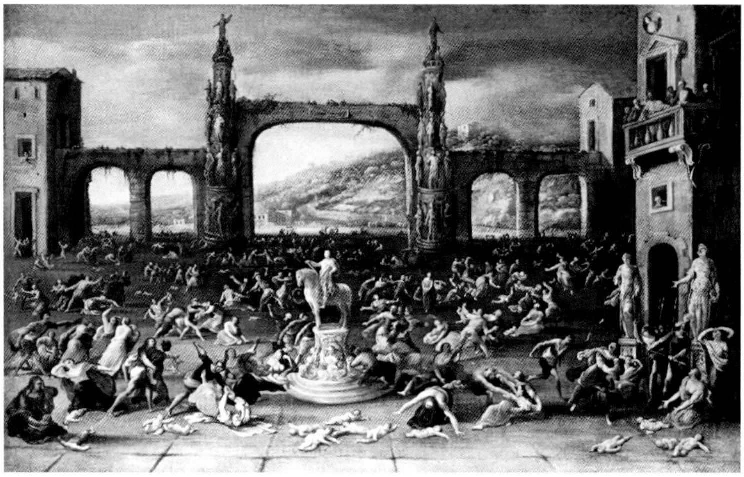

38 Scipione Compagno, *Massacre of the Innocents*, signed and dated 1642. Oil on canvas, 65.5 × 104 cm. Galleria Nazionale d'Arte Antica di Palazzo Corsini, Rome.

parable in terms of time and materials spent in their productions. The same is also true, at a lower end of the scale, of landscapes, since from an early date they were also produced according to relatively standardized dimensions.[66] The early landscape specialists, for the most part Northerners resident in Naples during the first three decades of the century, commonly received between 5 and 8 ducats for each of their medium-size paintings. Luise Cruis, for example, received 8 and 7 ducats for separately commissioned paintings in 1594 and 1595, while in 1612 he was paid 60 ducats for 12 paintings of "Eremitaggi." (These would have constituted a series of hermit saints set amid expansive landscapes similar to the kinds of paintings and prints popularised by Jan Brueghel during this period.[67]) In like manner, Jacopo Coppola was paid 8 ducats in 1610 for "uno quadro di paesi," while Ferrante Maccario was paid the same amount in 1616 for a landscape by Lanfranco Massa (Massa being the Neapolitan agent for the Genoese collector, Marcantonio Doria, who was also a significant patron of Ribera, Azzolino, and Caracciolo during the same period).[68]

The landscape specialists of the next generation, by contrast, could expect to receive at least double this amount for comparable works. In 1656 the previously mentioned view painter, Didier Barra, received 80 ducats for two views, one of the port of Naples, the other of Venice.[69] Sometime in the 1640s Don Antonio Ruffo of Messina paid Agostino Beltrano 20 ducats for a painting of a "paese con l'historia di Jacob figure picciole" (landscape with the story of Jacob [with] small figures).[70] An example of this kind of picture—albeit with figures that are somewhat larger than would have been the case in Ruffo's canvas—is illustrated in Fig. 37. In 1641 and 1650 Scipione Compagno was rather better paid when he received 50 ducats apiece for two separately commissioned paintings that would have corresponded to his customary compositions of expansive landscapes filled with small, sketchy figures (Fig. 38).[71] The leading landscape painter of the day, Domenico Gargiulo, occasionally commanded yet higher prices: he was paid 110 ducats in 1659, for example, for two paintings measuring around 132 × 185 cm (Fig. 39).[72]

Putting the prices of altarpieces together with landscapes, then, it is possible to discern a clear, across the board price rise over the course of the 1620s and 1630s. This must have encouraged the significant influx in the ranks of young apprentices working their way through the lower echelons of the Neapolitan workshops during that period. A particularly high number of painters emerged from the mid-1630s onwards at the dawning of a boom period termed the Golden Age of Neapolitan painting. And yet this growth in both prices and painters was, at the same time, a double-edged sword. One of its effects was to add to the strain of competition, as Ribera's and Stanzione's success, in particular, led to their generating unusually large workshops whose junior members would subsequently go on to compete among themselves and with others for a not infinitely expanding number of contracts. Moreover, it should be kept in mind that meanwhile prices were not rising. Thus, at the end of the seventeenth century, it is not uncommon to find a painter of the calibre of

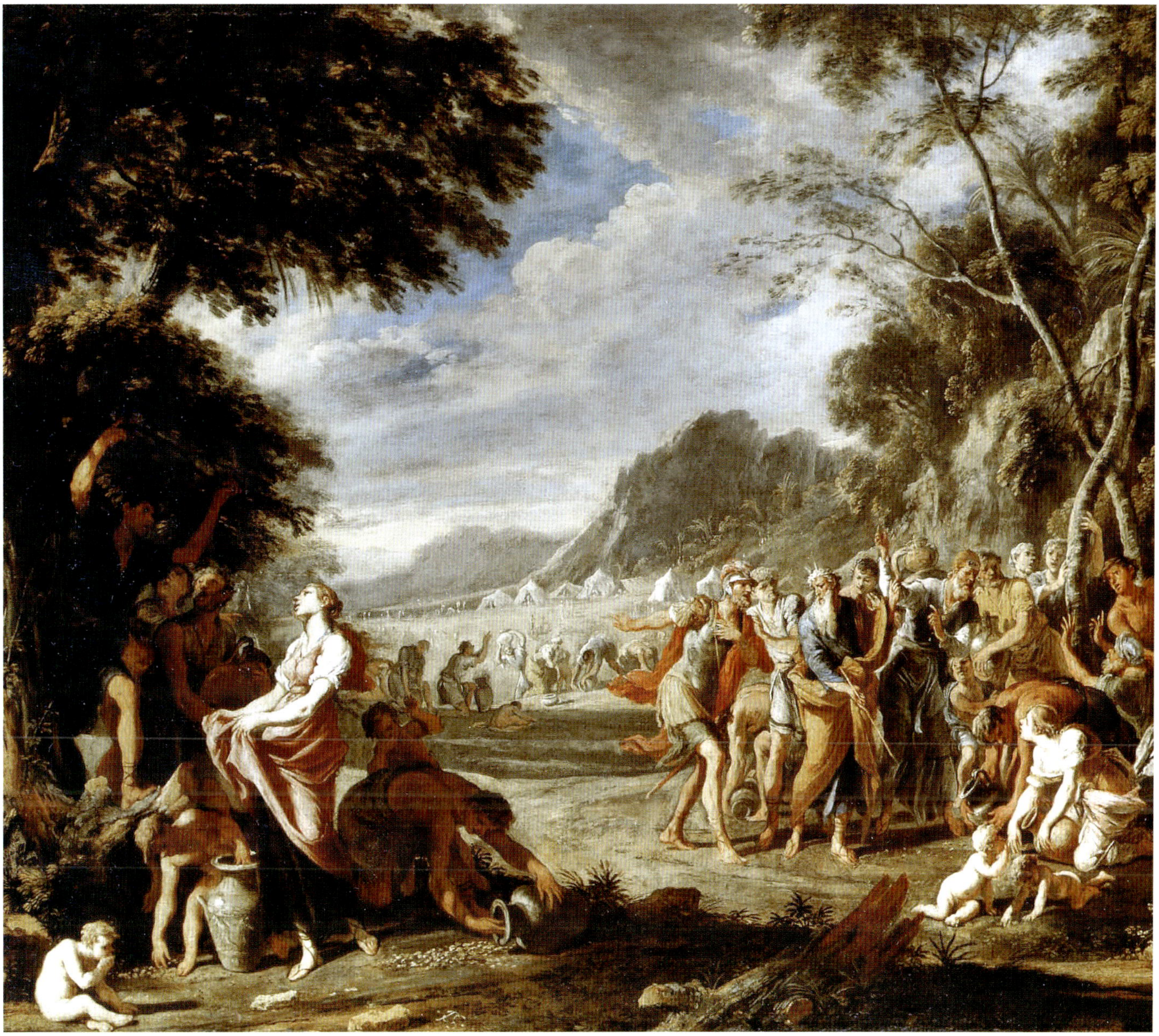

39 Domenico Gargiulo, *Gathering of the Manna*, ca. 1650s. Oil on canvas, 104 × 125 cm. Private collection.

Giordano himself—at that stage not only the city's leading artist but also the first Neapolitan with a truly international reputation—accepting 200 ducats, or sometimes even less, for an altarpiece.[73]

A further consequence of price stability after the 1630s is that artists did not receive higher prices as they entered the later stages of their careers, which would have been the more usual development, as discussed by Philip Sohm in the Introduction. The previously mentioned Gargiulo (b. ca. 1609–10), who received as much as 55 ducats apiece for two paintings in 1659, was unable to raise his prices soon thereafter. His fees from the end of his career are accordingly not any higher than those of several decades earlier; in fact, we find him accepting only 30 ducats in 1670 for a privately commissioned painting measuring 105 × 132 cm.[74] While certainly more than reasonable according to the standards of the day, this amount is still small compared with the leading Roman landscape painters. In the previous pages, Richard Spear has noted Claude's ability during the later stages of his career to increase his prices up to an average of 125 to 150 scudi per painting. This

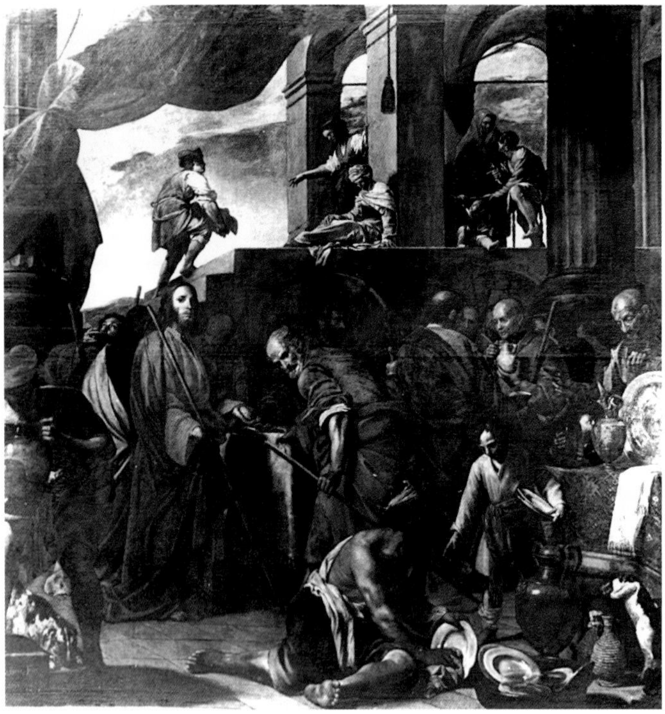

40 Massimo Stanzione, *Last Supper*, 1639. Oil on canvas, 393 × 393 cm. Certosa di S. Martino, Naples.

comparison may not be entirely fair to Gargiulo given that Claude was, unlike him, internationally renowned and also a slower and more meticulous painter. Still, the slightly less famous and at the same time equally rapid-fire Dughet was also able to raise his prices to 100 scudi per picture in his later years, an average that is much higher than Gargiulo was able to achieve for his otherwise comparable landscape paintings.

This levelling out of the earning power of Neapolitan artists during the most successful middle to later periods of their careers can be demonstrated in the cases of both Ribera and Stanzione, who by far were the two most successful painters of the day. Stanzione started out modestly, receiving just 13 ducats in 1616 for a privately commissioned altarpiece measuring 185 × 132 cm, and then 80 ducats—rather better but still not spectacular pay—for an altarpiece for the archbishop of Salerno in 1620.[75] In 1630, however, he received the biggest break of his career when he was awarded the commission for the decoration of an entire chapel in the Certosa di S. Martino.[76] The success of this work launched him on the wider stage, enabling him to take on scores of assistants and to sign contract after contract for major public fresco commissions and altarpieces—to become the inheritor, in fact, of Lanfranco's mantle as chief frescoist for the city. These included choir frescoes for the Jesuits of the Gesù Nuovo (1639–40), a vast series of frescoes in the nave of the Theatine church of S. Paolo Maggiore (1642–44), and an extensive series of frescoes for the recently canonized St. James of the Marches in the Franciscan church of S. Maria la Nova (1646–47).

The agreed amounts for these huge contracts made him the best paid local painter of the time: 2,000 ducats was his fee for the chapel of St. Bruno at the Certosa di S. Martino, 1,400 ducats for his work at the Gesù Nuovo, and 3,000 ducats were spent on the frescoes of the cupola of S. Paolo Maggiore alone.[77] Concurrently, and unlike Lanfranco, Stanzione was able to diversify his operations and to secure contracts for many of the most expensive altarpieces of the period: 1,000 ducats in 1639 for one of the choir paintings in S. Martino (Fig. 40), 1,600 ducats in 1642 for two altarpieces in the Chiesa dell'Annunziata, and 500 ducats for one of the altarpieces left unfinished by Domenichino at the Cappella del Tesoro at Naples Cathedral.

These were extremely high prices by Neapolitan standards. Yet, they were also correspondingly huge, complex, and immensely demanding works situated at the uppermost limits of Neapolitan patronage that would have required major resourcing on Stanzione's part in terms of time, materials, and workshop management. This was as true of the altarpieces as it was of the frescoes. Although now lost, the altarpieces at the Chiesa dell'Annunziata were enormous in size: reputedly 14.5 *palmi* or just under 4 meters in width.[78] Stanzione's 1,000 ducat painting for the choir of the Certosa di S. Martino was also huge: just under 4 by 4 meters. If we counterbalance these one-of-a-kind deluxe contracts with the prices paid for Stanzione's more workaday commissions during these boom years, we find that, for all his undoubted success, his prices nonetheless remained steady and were not subject to any major inflation as a result of his growing preeminence on the local scene. In 1643, for example, Stanzione painted an altarpiece measuring around 164 × 119 cm for the modest price of 100 ducats, while the last altarpiece of his career, the *Visitation* at the Gesù Nuovo, was commissioned in 1649 for 250 ducats for a work that was a little larger than usual (338 × 205 cm) and for which the painter was also required to pay for the ultramarine.[79]

The same plateauing of prices is evident for Ribera. He also began his Neapolitan career receiving relatively modest payments: 15 ducats for a single half-length in 1616 and 10 ducats for a head in 1620.[80] At the same time, though (and unlike Stanzione, who had to wait 15 years before finding comparable success), his prices rose very quickly—thanks in great part to the more immediate interest in his work among the leading collectors of the day. Already, in 1618, he received 100 ducats for a *Martyrdom of St. Bartholomew* commissioned for a Florentine collector and, in 1623, 150 ducats for a *Pietà* commissioned for Marcantonio Doria in Genoa.[81] When he came into his own from the later 1620s onwards, his prices were consistently among the highest of the period (although, as has been noted, since he was only proficient in oil on canvas, he never partook of the major fresco cycles monopolized by Stanzione and his workshop). He was able, in this manner, to command the sums of 500 ducats for a privately commissioned series of 12 philosophers in 1636, 400 ducats for a *Pietà* for the Certosa di S. Martino of 1637, 530 ducats in 1646 for an altarpiece for the Palazzo Reale, 1,000 ducats (or thereabouts) for another of the choir paintings in the Certosa di S. Martino (a problematic work that was not completed until 1651), and the huge fee of 1,400 ducats in 1647 for the main altarpiece of the Cappella del Tesoro in Naples Cathedral (Fig. 41).[82]

These were uncommon amounts to be sure, and yet they were equally extraordinary contracts. They were either unusually extensive (the philosophers, numbering 12 canvases or 41.6 ducats each), exceptionally large (the Certosa di S. Martino choir painting, measuring 400 × 400 cm), or extremely prestigious (the altarpieces at the Palazzo Reale and the Cappella del Tesoro). If we accordingly counterbalance these high-water marks with the sums received for Ribera's more ordinary commissions, we find that he too was not able to increase his prices significantly during the latter stages of his career. In 1645–46, for example, he was paid 200 ducats for a painting of *Apollo and Marsyas*,[83] and in 1649–50 Don Antonio Ruffo of Messina paid him 270 ducats for a *Pietà* measuring around 260 cm.[84]

This lack of price inflation for the costs of prestigious private and public Neapolitan paintings is also evident during the second half of the seventeenth century. During the 1650s, for instance, Mattia Preti found great success for his innovative combination of the bedrock traditions of Caravaggesque naturalism with the rhetoric of the high baroque. In 1657–59, he received a contract for the entire ceiling of the church of S. Pietro a Maiella (comprising ten large canvases set into the nave and transept), as well as two major altarpieces for S. Lorenzo Maggiore. Yet the prices for these works were not especially high in comparison with the earlier examples cited. He was paid a total of 1,100 ducats for the S. Pietro a Maiella canvases, a quite low average of 110 ducats per painting since they were for large works that measured as much as 4 meters across. He also received 200 ducats each for the S. Lorenzo altarpieces, even though they too were unusually large at 350 × 200 cm and contained the equivalent of seven figures each.

The difficult social and economic circumstances of the period must have impacted on these relatively low prices, since the contracts were undertaken in the direct aftermath of the devastating plague of Naples of 1656, which had killed up to a half of the population of the city. Contemporaneously, Andrea Vaccaro and Giordano were surely also reducing their fees significantly out of a sense of devotion when they undertook to complete two very large and prestigious altarpieces commissioned on behalf of the viceroy. These were painted for the votive church of S. Maria del Pianto, constructed in the years immediately following the plague, on the site of a mass grave reserved for its victims on a hill to the north of the city. They did their work for the exceptionally low price of 100 ducats each.[85]

Yet these relatively low prices remained constant for the rest of the century. Giordano, for example, accepted no more than 200 ducats for large altarpieces commissioned in 1675 and 1684. Although immensely successful across scores of high-profile commissions both within Naples and abroad, Giordano was, in fact, never a tremendously expensive artist. His pathway to an even greater level of financial success than that enjoyed by Ribera and Stanzione in the 1630s and 1640s was the exact opposite route of that favored by the inflationary marketing strategies of an artist like Guido Reni. Instead of raising his prices, Giordano increased his productivity to unprecedented levels, thanks in great part to the efforts of the most highly productive and efficient workshop of the period. His studio became legendary in its own day for its prodigious levels of productivity, as is indicated by the master's own nickname of "Luca fa presto."

The accuracy of his sobriquet is borne out by the enormity of Giordano's oeuvre. Ferrari and Scavizzi's catalogue raisonné of 1992 lists no fewer than 1,000 extant autograph paintings, to which scores more were added in an addendum volume a decade later.[86] That number contrasts starkly with the 300 prime autograph canvases listed for Ribera or the 230 extant autograph paintings recorded for Stanzione (in his case, however, one must take into account substantial fresco work). An even greater gap exists with the known output of Artemisia Gentileschi—just 58 paintings—whose gender precluded the winning of many public commissions or the running of a traditional workshop.[87] Her family responsibilities undoubtedly took a toll on what other-

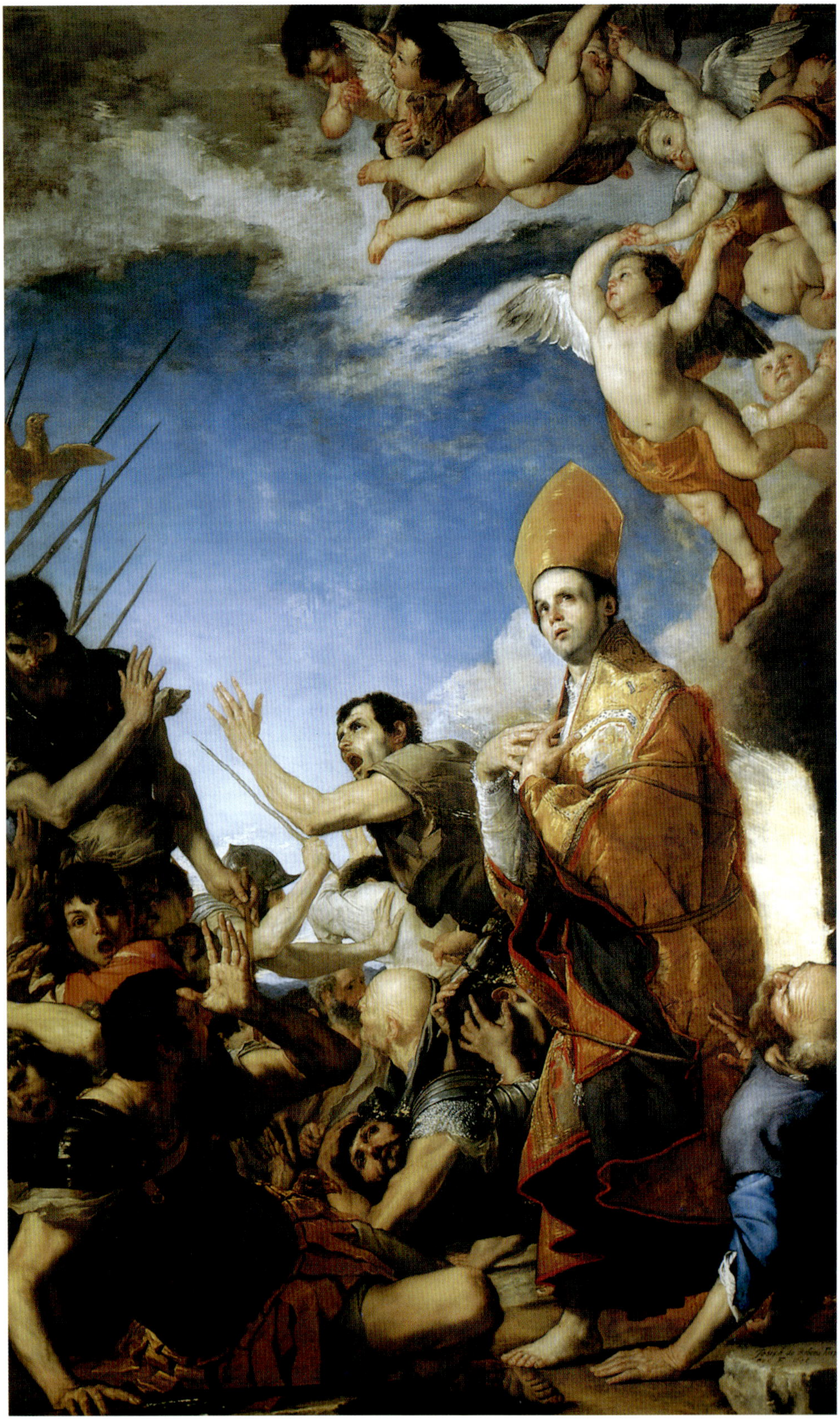

41 Jusepe de Ribera, *St. Januarius Escaping from the Furnace*, 1647. Oil on copper, 320 × 200 cm. Cappella del Tesoro di S. Gennaro, Naples Cathedral.

wise might appear to have been more than adequate time to produce a lot more work.

Giordano, then, did deserve to be called "fa presto." It is also clear from the documents that if he could not use scarcity as an argument to justify high prices, he was more than able to compensate for that loss through the sheer volume of his workshop's productivity and by varying his pricing according to the different types of painting he was working on, often many at once. For example, while receiving 200 ducats for the major altarpieces previously mentioned, he could charge between 60 and 100 ducats for medium-size, privately commissioned history paintings.[88] Moreover, his productivity and earnings were increased through his readiness to work with other independent specialists. In 1669, for instance, Giuseppe Recco was commissioned by the Marchese di Noja to produce two large still life paintings, one of fruit, the other of fish, with central figures by Giordano. They were priced at 100 ducats each, with Giordano receiving an unspecified share for his collaboration.[89]

Giordano's flexibility was one of the fundamental keys to his success. (Unfortunately, we have inadequate data to pin down examples of what the artist meant when he said that he worked with three kinds of brushes, as discussed by Philip Sohm in the Introduction.) Throughout his long and prodigiously active career, Giordano was able to maintain his patrons' interest in his work through a highly diversified base of production allied with an often equally inventive series of audacious marketing strategies. It seemed he could paint anything, from frescoes to altarpieces to mythologies and so on, all executed in a dazzling array of styles, from Riberesque to Rubensesque and all points in between. He also worked in many of the newer genres never contemplated by the masters of the previous generation. These included decorated cabinets with inset paintings, paintings on glass, and genre and still life imagery treated on a scale normally reserved for major mythological and religious canvases (Fig. 42). Rather than attempting the inflated pricing strategies of a Guido Reni—strategies that were not, in any event, appropriate to the different understanding of painting and the economic situation that prevailed in Naples—Giordano concentrated throughout his career on working in an ever-increasing abundance of variations and evolutions of style and categories of painting.[90] In this he was following a peculiarly adaptive and Neapolitan path to economic success.

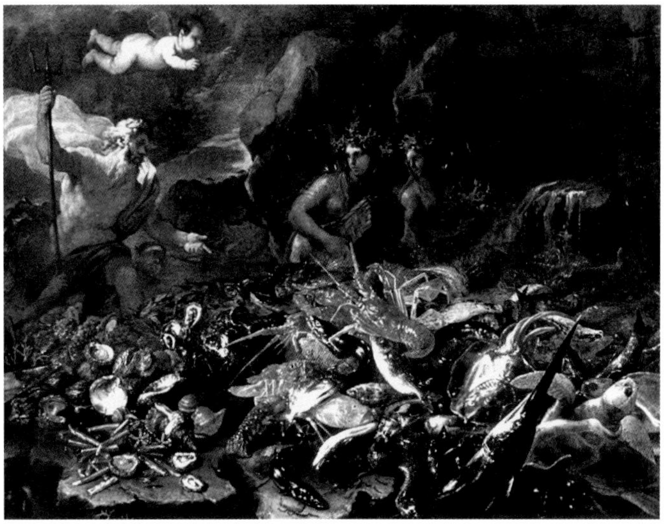

42 Luca Giordano and Giuseppe Recco, *Riches of the Sea with Neptune and Two Sea Nymphs*, ca. 1683–84. Oil on canvas, 234.5 × 296 cm. Art Gallery of South Australia, Adelaide.

Price Limits and the Power of the Patron

All of this information points to another important moderating factor that impacted on payments. We have seen that prices for painting in Naples remained reasonably stable and standardized throughout the century, save for their inflation in the 1620s and 1630s. It has also been shown that the latter increase was as much the result of broader economic factors as of an evolution in taste. This suggests that the standardization of prices for painting in seventeenth-century Naples—the lack of wide variation within categories and the absence of any artist attempting successfully to raise prices over time—means that the ultimate arbiters of prices in seventeenth-century Naples were not so much the painters as the patrons themselves, which Mancini already had implied was the situation in Rome. In effect, and to return to the issue of the understanding of painting in Naples as being fundamentally artisanal, pictures were evidently viewed as standardized goods, whose price structures could be fixed accordingly. When a collector set out to acquire work, he knew, as a result, reasonably clearly in advance what he would need to pay: 10 ducats or less for low-end work, 20–30 ducats for pictures by moderately ranked painters—particularly landscapes and the like—and up to around 200 ducats for work by the leading painters of the day (unless he was commissioning frescoes or deluxe altarpieces/gallery paintings, in which case he needed to be prepared to go higher).

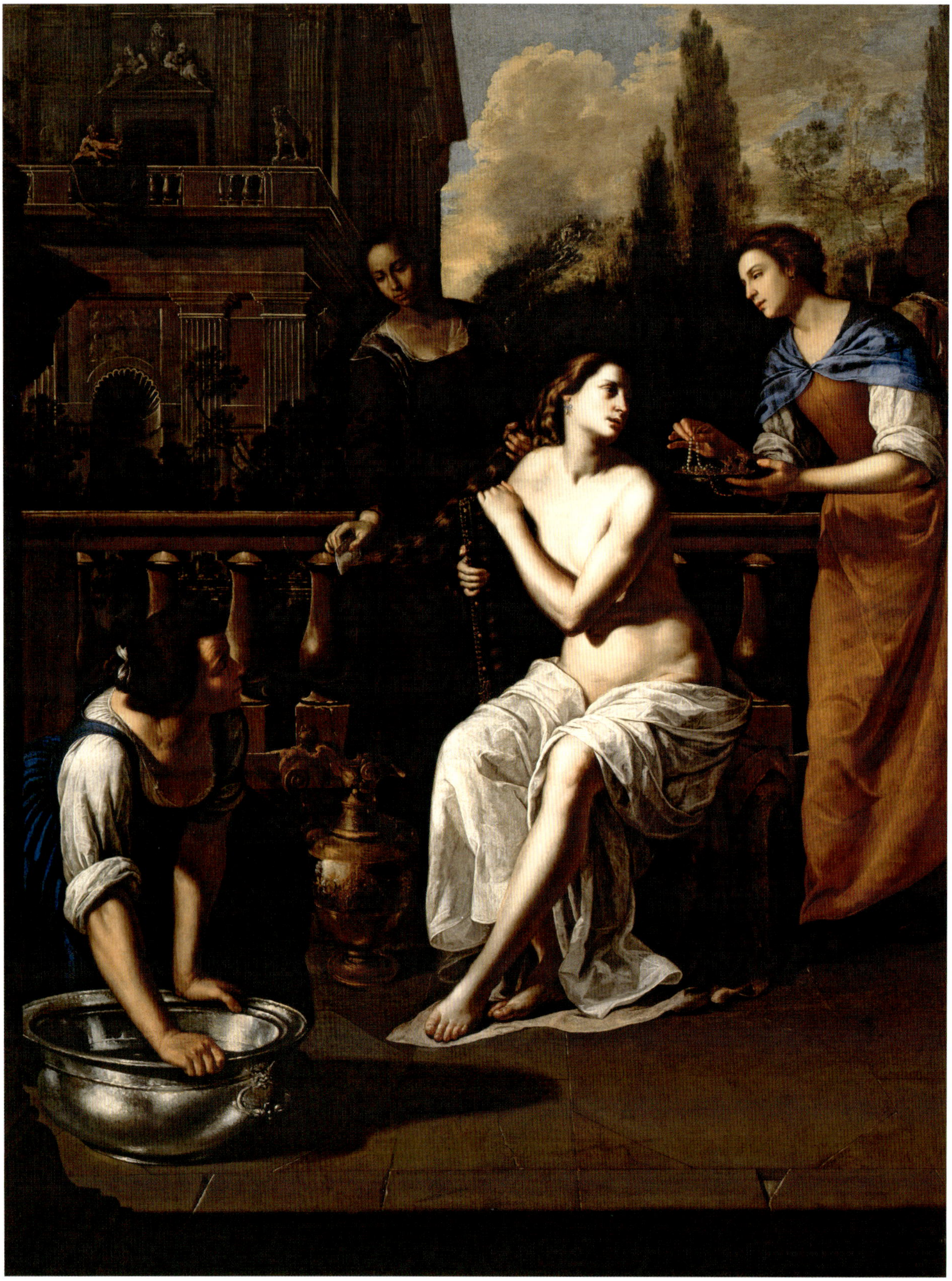

43 Artemisia Gentileschi, *David and Bathsheba*, ca. 1636–38. Oil on canvas, 265.4 × 209.5 cm. Columbus Museum of Art, Columbus (Schumacher Fund).

This unspoken "glass ceiling" effect for the uppermost limits of what a patron might expect to pay within each category appears particularly to have come into play in the field of expensive privately commissioned gallery paintings. Those of an unusually demanding size and number of figures occasionally commanded a rate closer to 300 than the more standard 200 ducats. Ruffo's 270 ducat *Pietà* by Ribera (1649–50) has been noted. Ruffo also paid Stanzione during the same period 300 ducats for a large *Judgment of Paris* measuring ca. 211 × 263 cm, the same amount received by the artist for a *Persephone* in 1636.[91] Likewise, Andrea Vaccaro was paid 280 ducats for a *Meeting of David and Abigail* in 1643, which must also have been unusually large and complex.[92] These are atypical amounts and counterbalanced by the more common, standard fee of 200 ducats per large gallery painting all of the major painters of the day received, irrespective of dimensions and the number of figures. That is what Artemisia Gentileschi agreed in 1636 as the price per canvas for three large paintings of *Bathsheba* (Fig. 43), *Lucretia*, and *Susanna*, precisely the same amount agreed for Ribera's previously cited *Apollo and Marsyas* of 1645 as well as for a large painting of *Diana and Actaeon* painted in 1636 by Niccolò de Simone (a pupil of Stanzione who seems nevertheless to have been quite lucky to receive such a high sum at that date).[93]

This fee of 200 ducats for large gallery paintings, only occasionally rising to 300 ducats and no more, does not compare favorably with the top prices attained by the leading painters of Rome and Bologna for comparable work during the same period. Guercino, for example, while working in his native Cento, received 400 scudi from Cardinal Spada for his *Death of Dido* of 1631, 600 scudi for his *Christ Expelling the Money Lenders* of 1634, and 508 scudi for his *Meeting of David and Abigail* of 1637.[94] The well-known dealer and diamond thief Fabrizio Valguarnera was compelled to pay 200 scudi in 1630 for only a workshop copy of Pietro da Cortona's *Rape of the Sabines*,[95] and Reni's high rates go without saying: 400 scudi, for example, for his *Immaculate Conception* painted for the Spanish ambassador in 1627.[96]

Guercino has been characterised as something of an artisanal tortoise, maintaining an old-fashioned reliance on a per figure pricing structure, as contrasting with the inflationary pricing strategies employed by Reni, the more modern hare.[97] This may well be true in relation to Reni and other high-ranking painters active in Rome and Bologna, but as far as Naples was concerned it was anything but a cheap and old-fashioned way of doing business. In 1649, the notoriously stingy Don Antonio Ruffo of Messina tried to beat Guercino down on his price for a painting. Guercino nonetheless stuck to his guns and explained in a now famous passage that, since Ruffo was proposing a sum beneath his customary fee of 100 scudi per figure, then he would accordingly provide him with "poco più di mezza figura" (a little more than half a figure).[98] In the end, Ruffo relented and paid Guercino the full 100 for a single figure.

The Neapolitans, on the other hand, had no such unambiguous yardsticks of pricing to draw on in the face of recalcitrant patrons. Stanzione was dismayed to find Ruffo haggling over his fee at the very moment that his *Judgment of Paris* was nearing completion. He complained that "if this had been made for any other person it would not have left my house for less than 500 ducats, since it is a profane history using naked women and made with great care and intelligence . . . but since I value your patronage more than all of the profits of the world, I will be content with 300 ducats."[99] As previously noted, Stanzione's claim to have normally received 500 ducats for a work of this kind is doubtful, to say the least. Yet his complaints concerning the exceptional costs involved in its production ring true enough. As he correctly underscores, he would have had to find female nude models for one thing, not a common procedure in baroque Naples and presumably therefore payable at a premium given that the otherwise strong sense of Neapolitan decorum among patrons meant that works of this kind are only rarely encountered.[100]

Artemisia Gentileschi experienced similar difficulties with Ruffo. She was at work during the same period on two unusually large and complex mythologies, each measuring ca. 204 × 259 cm, depicting *Galatea* and *Diana and Actaeon*. Ruffo typically haggled over fees but was met with a barrage of counterarguments. Perhaps the most revealing was Gentileschi's comment of 13 November 1649: "I must caution Your Most Illustrious Lordship that when I ask a price, I don't follow the custom in Naples, where they ask thirty and then give it for four. I am Roman, and therefore I shall act always in the Roman manner."[101] She also tried the Guercino tack of angling for a high per figure standardized fee: "Everywhere else I have been I was paid one hundred scudi per figure. And this was in Florence, as well as Venice and Rome, and even in Naples when there was more money."[102]

Gentileschi's comments are of interest in attesting once again to the financial difficulties experienced in Naples following the revolt of Masaniello of 1647–48. They also provide further evidence of the gambit of negotiating claims made by baroque painters when pushed by miserly patrons. In point of fact, Gentileschi would have been lucky to receive 100 ducats (or scudi since she seems to have referred to the two currencies interchangeably) per figure for any of her previous commissions. Her upper limit per painting seems to have been 200 ducats, and this for a series of three paintings that included a composition with four figures. She herself in any event directly undermined the veracity of this claim when she wrote to Ruffo two years later offering him pictures of *Perseus and Andromeda* and *Joseph and Potiphar's Wife* for the significantly reduced fee of 90 scudi each.[103] It seems, then, that like Stanzione—or any other painter pushed to the limit by a patron attempting to change the terms of the agreement halfway through a commission—she was quite prepared to bend the truth a little in order to introduce a negotiating ploy that might help her to maintain her previously agreed price.

Like Stanzione also, Gentileschi complained about the cost of models: "When I receive the bill of exchange for 50 ducats I will finish the painting, because the expenses are intolerable, because out of the fifty women who undress themselves, there is scarcely one good one. And in this painting I cannot use just one model because there are eight figures, and one must paint various kinds of beauty."[104] In the end, though, all of these arguments were to no avail. Gentileschi was over a barrel, and she knew it. She ultimately let the *Galatea* go for 160 ducats and the *Diana and Actaeon* for 230. At just under 200 ducats per picture, this was certainly far beneath Guercino's way of doing business (particularly given that the *Diana and Actaeon* contained no fewer than eight figures and animals as well). But Gentileschi must have taken comfort in the fact that it was still a very high sum as far as Naples was concerned and not too much less than Stanzione's and Ribera's prices for comparable work.

Conclusion: Swimming Upstream or Mid-level Specialization and the Small Fry Once More

The dynamism of the Neapolitan art world was generated by the collective efforts of much more than just these relatively comfortable, upper echelon painters (although it should be recalled, in passing, that even their success was not enough to insulate them from the risk of end-of-career financial woes).[105] It is worthwhile returning, then, and by way of conclusion, to the lower ranked artists who, like their more affluent colleagues, had to cope with the demanding costs of housing, food, clothing, and material overheads. They had to find the means of paying 30 to 40 ducats a year for rent of a workshop in addition to all of the other expenses previously mentioned, on top of 8.5 ducats or more per year for bread alone. To this must be added the often not insignificant costs (at least at the lower levels of the market) of materials. The previously encountered landscape painter, Domenico Gargiulo, was reimbursed between 1.5 and 5 ducats for the canvases used for his easel paintings executed for the Certosa di S. Martino.[106] How, then, did these more modestly ranked painters offset their costs and turn at least some kind of profit on their work?

It was never easy, even when these artists won commissions for altarpieces or other potentially lucrative work because their fees typically were far below those given to Ribera and his high-profile colleagues. Painters such as Gargiulo, Beltrano, and other former pupils of Ribera and Stanzione, like some associates of Aniello Falcone, all worked sporadically on public commissions, which they realized could help maintain their public profile and boost their reputation, but at the same time they prudently developed specializations in small paintings, even though their prices were pitifully meager compared with what their former masters were being paid.

Andrea de Leone (1610–1685) provides a revealing example of this situation. He developed a highly productive career from the later 1630s onwards painting first medium-size mythologies in the manner of Poussin, but then above all else by specializing in the crowded battle scenes filled with small sketchy figures that remain closely dependent on the template developed by Aniello Falcone a decade earlier (Fig. 44).[107] His battle scenes are generally modest in size. A signed example in the Louvre measures 103 × 130 cm, while another at the Museo di Capodimonte is 78 × 123 cm.[108] They would accordingly have been much quicker and easier to produce than altarpieces and other monumental church commissions by Stanzione and his colleagues.

At the same time, Leone was also versed in fresco and monumental figure painting. He had been trained by the leading frescoist of the generation prior to Stanzione, Belisario Corenzio, and this skill enabled him to switch over from his smaller cabinet paintings into the field of church commissions from time to time.[109] Nonetheless, the much lower prices he received relative to Stanzione and his colleagues probably discouraged him from specializing in these more ambitious projects. In 1677 Leone received 520 ducats for frescoing the Galeota chapel in the cathedral.[110] This occurred

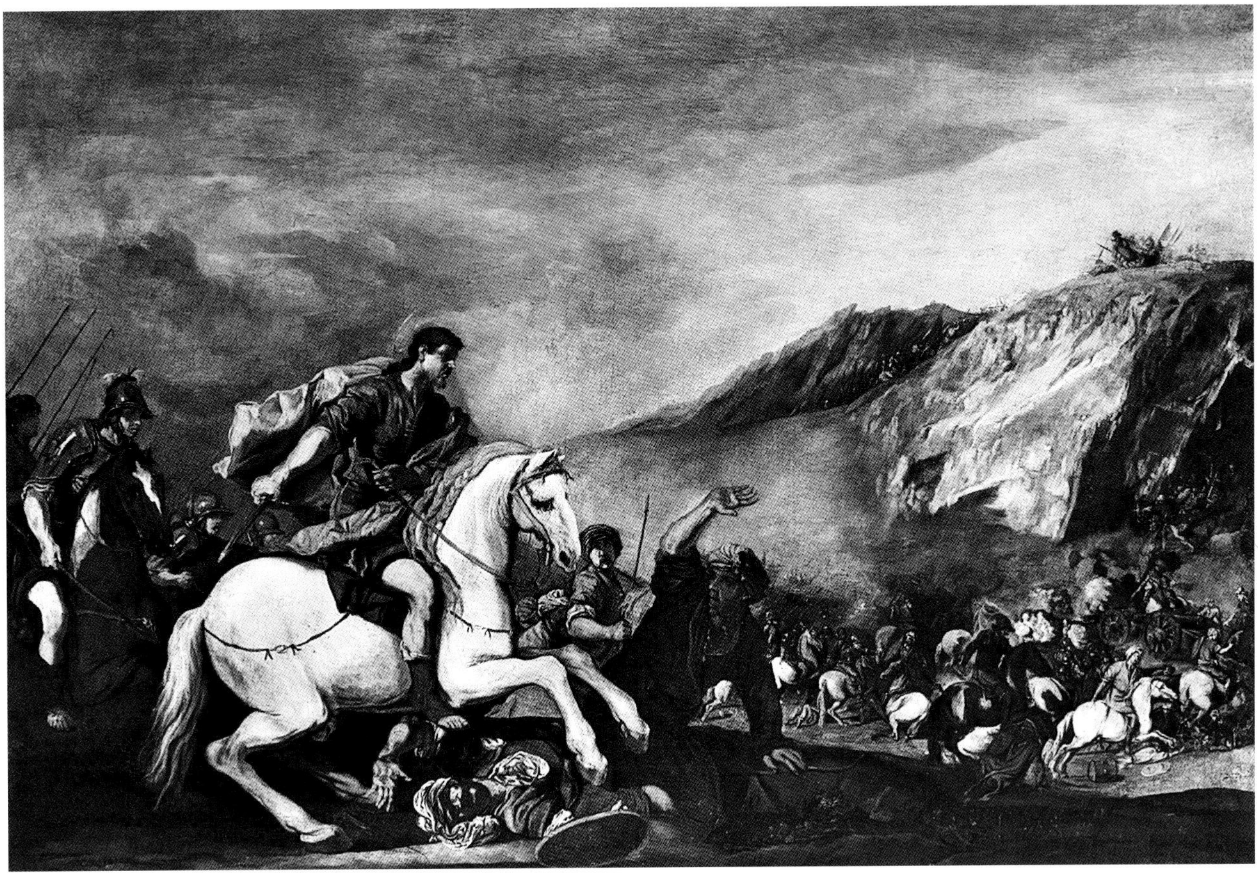

44 Andrea de Leone, *St. James at the Battle of Clavijo*, ca. 1640s. Oil on canvas, 87 × 126 cm. Private collection.

late in his life and must have been seen by him as something of a milestone: the chapel was in a prestigious location in the cathedral, and its patron was one of the highest ranking civil administrators of the period, as well as a noteworthy collector of Preti and other leading contemporary artists.[111] Yet 520 ducats for an entire chapel was a triflingly low price when compared with Stanzione's earnings. Stanzione received 2,000 ducats for his chapel in the Certosa di S. Martino, it will be recalled, and even when the likely fee he received for three altarpieces in the chapel is deducted, a sum remains that is at least double what Leone was paid for a comparable amount of work. Compounding the situation, Leone received very low prices for his *quadretti*. Galeota paid him just 12 ducats in 1679 "per due quadretti tonni," or two small paintings in tondo format, that were presumably examples of Leone's small-scale battle pieces.[112]

A similar disparity between prices for large and small works can be seen in the case of altarpieces by Stanzione's former workshop assistants. Like Leone, Agostino Beltrano specialized in smaller paintings depicting biblical or mythological subjects set amid expansive landscapes and populated with small-scale figures. His works were priced comparably to Leone's. In the 1640s, as already mentioned, Don Antonio Ruffo acquired a small landscape with the story of Jacob with small figures by Beltrano, together with a battle painting by Leone, for 20 ducats each.[113] Beltrano's training under Stanzione also enabled him to compete for bigger church commissions from time to time. In 1649, however, he was paid only 50 ducats by the monks of S. Agostino degli Scalzi for a large altarpiece of *St. Jerome and the Angel* (Fig. 45).[114] Then in his mid-forties, Beltrano had spent much of the previous decade assisting Stanzione on many of his most significant commissions. Although still working in the master's orbit, Beltrano had begun to branch out on his own. *St. Jerome and the Angel* represents this ambition. Undertaken in tandem with a modest contract for work in fresco,[115] in all probability it appeared more profitable than work for private collectors, such as the 20 ducats Ruffo paid for one of his landscapes with small figures. But the *St. Jerome* is four times the size of such land-

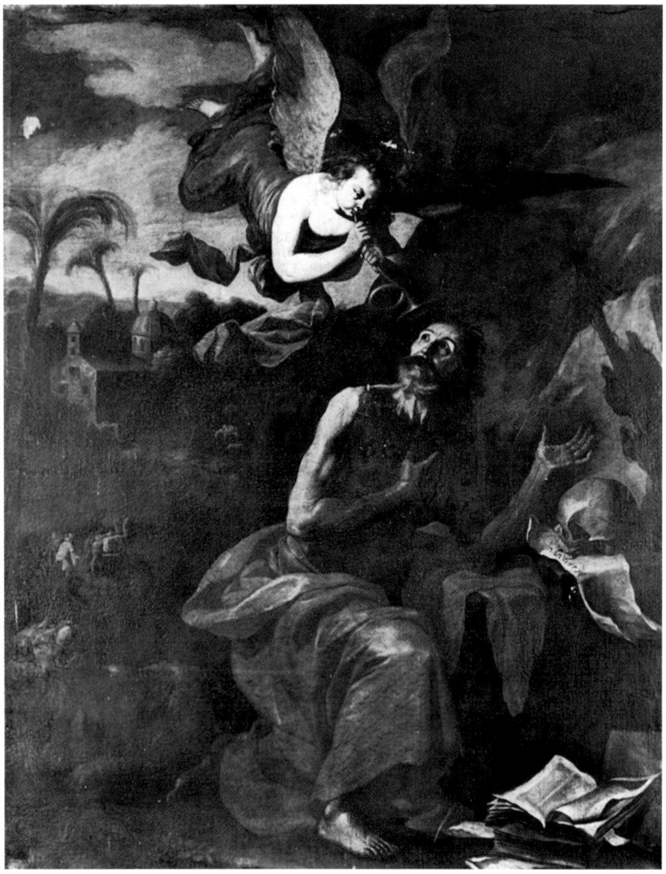

45 Agostino Beltrano, *St. Jerome and the Angel*, 1649. Oil on canvas, 210 × 171 cm. S. Agostino degli Scalzi, Naples.

scapes and includes two meticulously rendered life-size figures that almost certainly would have required life drawing. Thus Beltrano must have worked much harder to earn, in effect, only a bit more than double his usual price.

The design of Beltrano's altarpiece was dependent not only on Stanzione's work, but more specifically on a famous composition of Ribera's painted in 1626 (Fig. 46). Although the complete documentation for it is lost, a payment for its expenses is known, indicating that Ribera was paid 40 ducats to cover just the cost of its pigments.[116] It can also be established that a frame for a comparable altarpiece by Beltrano would have cost as much as 38 ducats.[117] Hence the monks' choice of Beltrano was a highly cost-effective strategy. They received a close variant on a famous composition by a reasonably well-known painter for a quarter (or even less) of what it would have cost them had they acquired the work from Ribera himself. The finished result probably cost not much more than its frame.

For painters ranked lower than Beltrano, even 50 ducats for an altarpiece must have seemed enviably high. In 1637, Antonio Giordano—father of the subsequently immensely successful Luca Giordano—received just 7.5 ducats for five paintings of *St. Nicholas*: an average of just 1.5 ducats per picture.[118] This kind of payment represents the ongoing specialization in Naples of cheap, serially produced devotional images that were noted hanging in Onofrio de Anfora's workshop at the beginning of our discussion. Antonio Giordano accordingly belonged to the *pittori più bassi* as categorized by Reni and discussed in the essays on Rome and Bologna. He was at the bottom of the heap, that is to say, along with the previously cited examples of Onofrio de Anfora, Pietro Pesce, and others of their kind. Ribera and his most successful colleagues, by extension, would rank with Reni himself—those *pittori straordinari*, as Reni called them—right at the top, despite their relatively lower earnings. Gargiulo, Beltrano, and the other pupils of Ribera and Stanzione, on the other hand, could all be placed in the second tier: with the *pittori ordinari*, as Reni correctly albeit somewhat uncharitably characterised their position relative to the others.

And yet it needs to be remembered that in Naples the distinctions between these ranks of artist were more fluid than this abstractly stratified characterization suggests. For one thing, it was certainly possible for *pittori più bassi* to work in a manner that brought them in other respects closer to the ranks (and pay scales) of the *pittori ordinari*. Antonio Giordano spent much of his career active in the workshop of Ribera, where he was said to have specialized in half-length pictures of *St. Anthony* and other saints which, following retouches by the master, were sold as originals by Ribera himself.[119] These workshop products would have cost prospective buyers much more than 1.5 ducats each if they really were sold as the work of Ribera. At the same time, Giordano the elder developed an interesting specialization that suggests he was an artist with more potential and individuality than only an anonymous workshop assistant or an obscure anonymous painter toiling away at the bottom of the artistic ladder.

In 1630 his name crops up in one of the most interesting texts written on Neapolitan art and culture prior to De' Dominici in the eighteenth century, Giulio Cesare Capaccio's *Il Forastiero* of 1630. The reference occurs in the context of a discussion of the most important private collection of the day: that of Gaspard Roomer, an extremely wealthy Flemish merchant and highly influential patron and collector of work by Falcone, Luca Giordano, Rubens, and scores of others. Capaccio's detailed description of Roomer's collection lists paintings by Stanzione, Ribera, Van Dyck, Saraceni,

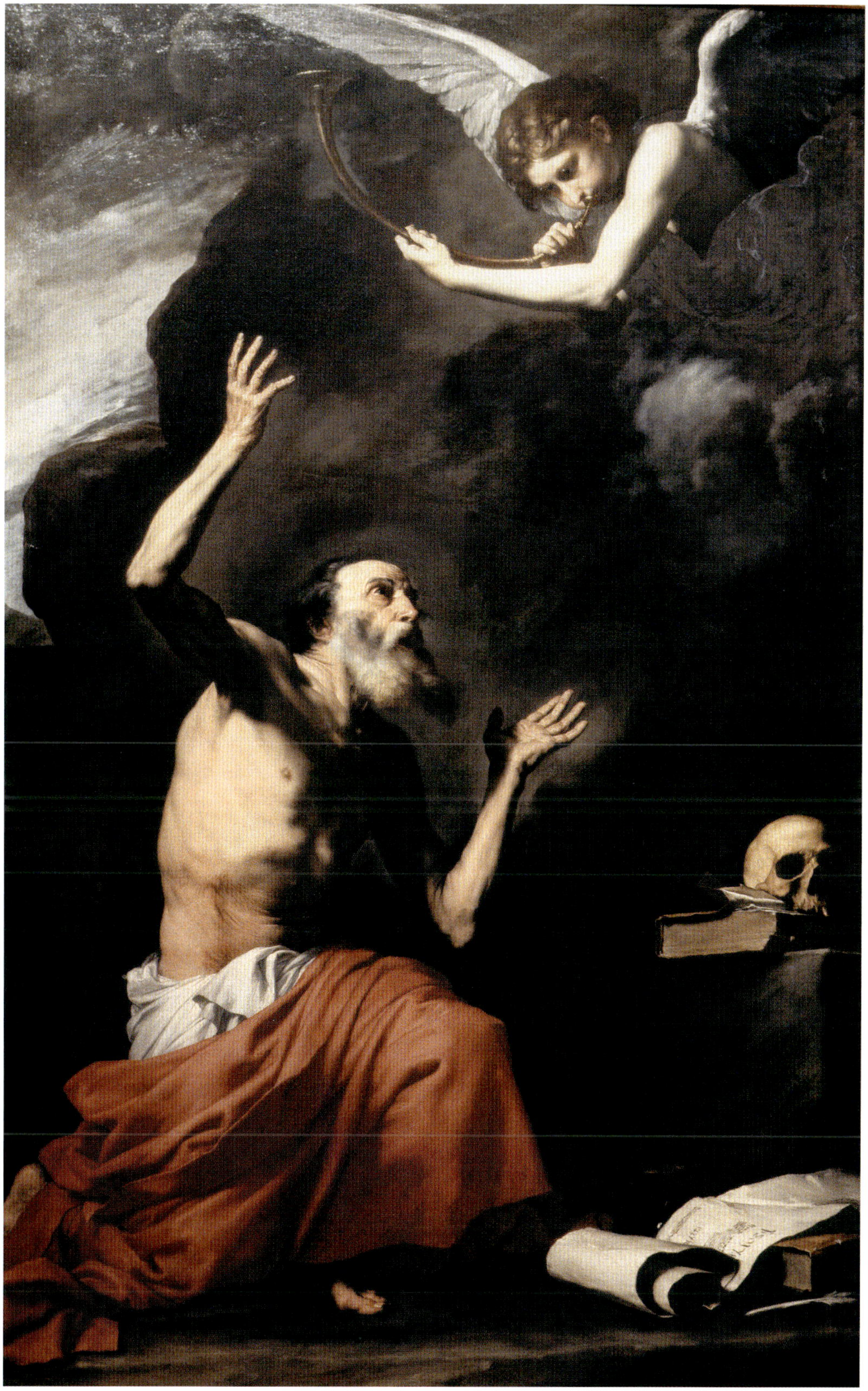

46 Jusepe de Ribera, *St. Jerome and the Angel*, 1626. Oil on canvas, 262 × 164 cm. Museo e Gallerie Nazionali di Capodimonte, Naples.

Brueghel, Bril, etc. Yet among this noteworthy list mention is made of battle pieces by not only Falcone but Antonio Giordano.[120] The contemporary battle piece—or battle scene without a hero as characterised by Fritz Saxl in his classic account—represented a highly innovative, new subcategory of genre painting at the time. In the later 1630s and 1640s, Falcone's name would become synonymous with this specialization in a manner that brought him considerable distinction and even a certain degree of international renown, as noted.[121] That Giordano the elder was painting (presumably) similar work at this early date suggests that he might merit more fame than just as Luca's father.

To consider this issue from the opposite perspective, it is equally true to say that the distance separating the *pittori ordinari* from the *pittori più bassi* was often not so great as might be assumed. The previously cited prices of 30, 20, or even occasionally 10 ducats for work by Leone, Beltrano, Gargiulo, and the other landscape specialists of the 1630s to 1650s were for reasonably large paintings. Smaller formats, by contrast, could be considerably cheaper. A particularly clear illustration of this comes from an unusually detailed and carefully compiled inventory drawn up by Domenico Gargiulo in 1659 for the heirs of one of his longest standing and most important aristocratic patrons.[122]

Gargiulo's evaluations are highly revealing. He was careful to appraise his larger canvases at prices comparable to those cited above. Yet at the same time he evidently saw nothing demeaning in assigning much lower valuations to his smaller paintings: 10 and 8 ducats respectively, for example, for landscapes with *David and Goliath* and *Lot and his Daughters* measuring around 53 × 66 cm, which moreover included their frames. Works by Ribera's pupils were also evaluated at similarly low prices. For example, two of Hendrick van Somer's paintings, which otherwise are documented by a sole altarpiece commission of 1641, were appraised at just 8 ducats each for half-length compositions of *St. Joseph* and *St. Bartholomew*, again including the frames, and measured around 79 × 105 cm.[123] With values as modest as these, it is no wonder that so many second-tier artists worked hard at supplementing their earnings throughout their careers by turning their hands to a range of related jobs, such as restoration, appraising, and particularly art dealing, which most Neapolitan painters developed as a sideline as a matter of course.[124]

Such flexibility no doubt helped keep the wolf from the door during those off months—which may have been more common than we might otherwise imagine—when the earnings were not coming in at a steady rate of, say, 20 ducats a month. One needed always to be resourceful in seventeenth-century Naples, a fact that is underscored in a particularly revealing anecdote in De' Dominici's lives of the Neapolitan baroque painters. The story appears in the account of the careers of Cesare and Francesco Fracanzano, two brothers cited at the beginning of this discussion as emigrants from Apulia to Naples in the 1620s. De' Dominici's narrative begins with a philosophical meditation on the rarity of success. He states that he does not know whether it is because of the high number of painters or simply ill fortune that reduces certain painters to a miserable working existence. Only a few reach the ultimate success of a Raphael or a Titian. Cesare and Francesco Fracanzano failed in their ambitions. Although highly distinguished painters, they ultimately disgraced themselves in response to the pressures brought about by economic hardship.[125]

De' Dominici comments frequently on the financial difficulties experienced by Cesare and Francesco. The two painters could not find work after leaving Ribera's studio (a move that seems to have occurred sometime in the early to mid-1630s). They were accordingly forced by need to paint devotional paintings for some of their painter acquaintances for little money (a practice that would have found them working for day rates in the workshops of one or other of their better established colleagues, as for example was previously noted in the case of Pesce working for Anfora).[126] A small number of commissions subsequently improved their prospects marginally, but still not sufficiently to alleviate their difficulties. The situation worsened for Cesare when he married and had to provide for a large family. He and Francesco now found themselves in desperate straits:

> they were without commissions to such an extent that they were forced to paint half-figures for secondhand dealers, and sometimes not even finding anyone ready to buy their work, they were forced to hawk them through the city selling them at a low price in order to buy their daily food. So, coming then into an unfortunate and miserable existence they were induced once again to paint for the shopkeepers those heads of St. Anastasius which they place at the head of children's cradles in order to keep them from illness. This misery was such that it somewhat diminished both the goodness and the reputation of their works, since for the sake of speed they painted them heedlessly, and without study. . .[127]

In stressing the "miserable" nature of the downward slide of the Fracanzanos' later careers, De' Dominici was clearly making a point about the difficulty of the profession, so much so that one strongly suspects him of exaggerating the truth in order to emphasise the moral of his story.[128] Still, his account vividly evokes the cut and thrust of the economic reality underlying the Neapolitan art world, and it rings true on a fundamental level with many of the examples discussed here. Painters like Gargiulo, Beltrano, Leone, the Fracanzanos, and many more whose names could be cited in this context were not so far removed, in many respects, from the struggles of the *pittori più bassi*. And even the exceptional success stories of Ribera and his ilk were at one and the same time also not so comfortably insulated from the pressures of economic concerns. All of these artists are linked together, moreover, in their admirably pragmatic and resourceful responses to the ongoing challenge of how best to develop their careers in a manner that continued to bring them success, no matter how they defined that much sought after but elusive quality. It was a struggle, to be sure. Yet looking back on the body of work they collectively produced, one is struck by the extent to which their labor represents an extraordinarily dynamic achievement of creativity, flexibility and resilience, no matter how we choose to define those most fundamental yet equally elusive terms of artistic success.

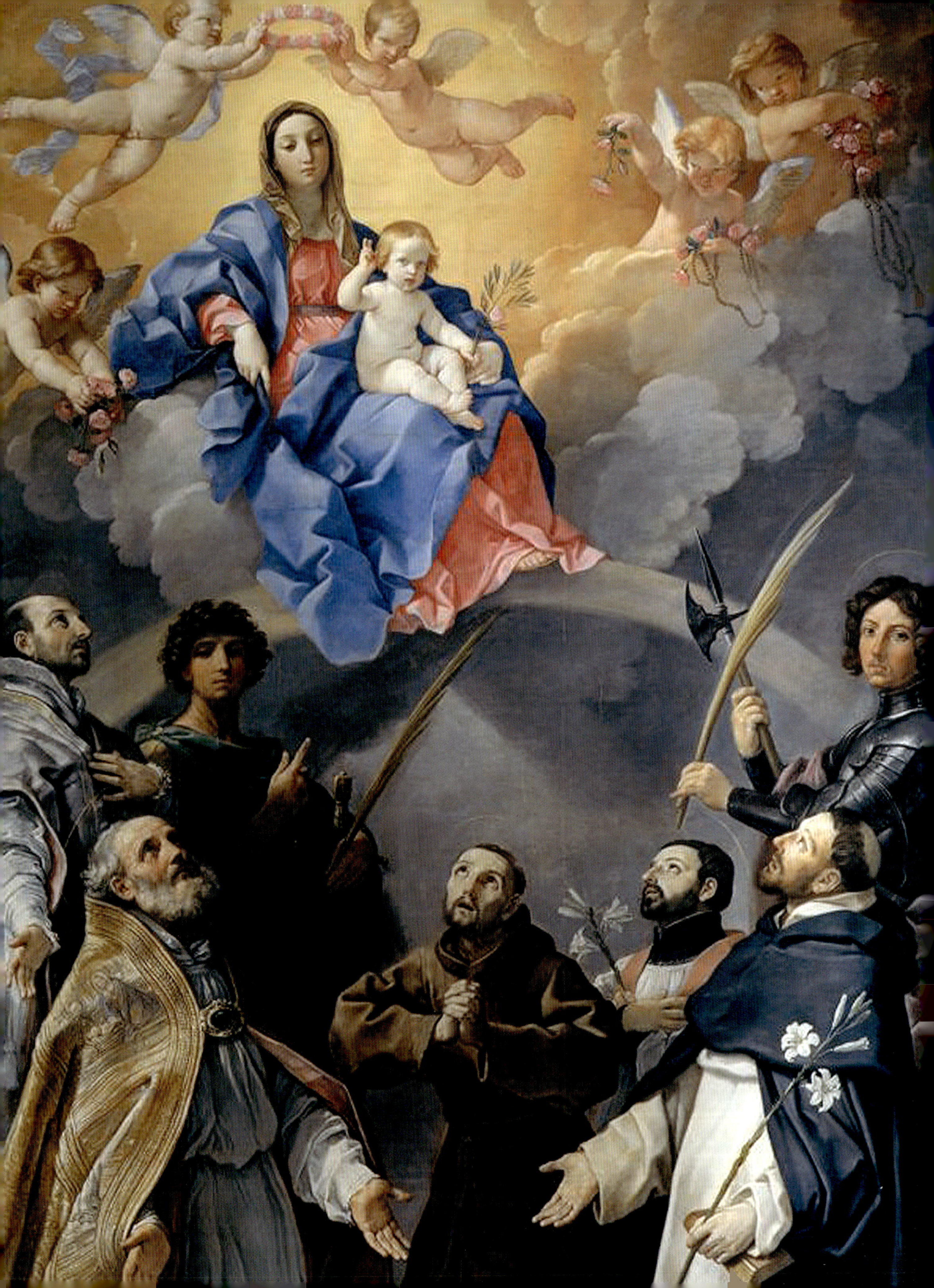

3

Bologna

RAFFAELLA MORSELLI

Social Background of the Bolognese Community

Around 1600, Bologna was the second city of the Papal States. With a population of nearly 70,000 inhabitants, including residents and *forastieri* (that is, everyone from everywhere else) it was more populous than any other non-capital European city, except for Lyon. One-third of the population earned a living in the production of both crêpe and ordinary silk veils (a safeguard against changing fashions) and other luxury textiles such as organzines and drapes (including brocade, damask, and velvet).[1] This industrial specialization stemmed from the fact that, as early as the sixteenth century, Bologna had developed a highly advanced hydraulic system. Four hundred sluices, the highest concentration in Europe, collected water from canals such as the Navile (a tributary of the Reno River) and delivered it throughout the city, powering the water wheels of various factories. "Bolognese windmills" (a hydraulic wheel and mechanical spooler used for silk production), fulling stocks (used to thicken wools and make felt), paper mills, grain windmills, and water-powered saws fueled Bologna's economic fortunes. Its vertically tiered economy—handling in one locale various processes from gathering to dyeing to spinning and weaving—and its technologically advanced factories employed thousands of specialized workers and created an economic base that helped support the masses of farmers who periodically poured into the city to sell their products. Finished veils and semifinished organzines from Bologna invaded markets both near and far: from Venice to the Levant, from France to Germany.[2] The sector was led by the 50 or 60 merchants who belonged to a powerful organization, the Arte della Seta or guild of silk merchants.

Famines and economic recessions cut into Bologna's workforce, first in 1590–91, when a famine reduced the population to 59,000; and then again, between 1619 and 1624 after the population had recovered to a level of about 67,000, a series of bad investments and Sixtus V's decision to levy a tax of 40 bolognini per pound of exported organzine (which was abolished in 1617) laid the way to a further dip, this time to 62,000. This diversion of capital compounded the effects of a general European economic crisis in 1619–20. The disastrous plague of 1630 worsened matters by leaving the city with barely more than 46,000 inhabitants, while at the same time tearing apart its industrial base. In the autumn of 1630 the plague gradually subsided, and little by little Bologna returned to its normal life. Still, it left a sense of dismay and loneliness among the survivors that was inevitable in the wake of such a catastrophe.

The image of the city crossed by funeral carriages transporting the plague-stricken cadavers remained etched in everybody's eyes and was immortalized in the

Facing page: detail of Fig. 47

votive banner that the Senate entrusted to Guido Reni (Fig. 47). First displayed to the public on 27 December 1630 in the church of S. Domenico, it depicts Bologna's patron saints as they entreat the Virgin to release the city from this scourge. Along the bottom register, one sees a funerary scene of a gloomy Bologna with covered wagons carrying the dead to the communal graves outside the city walls. It was by no coincidence that the pictorial description of this state of affairs would have been given to Reni. As the standard-bearer of artistic rebirth, he was cherished by the Cardinal Legate Bernardino Spada, by the city's senators and nobles, by men of letters and doctors, by bankers and grand merchants, and by the bourgeois and the masses who through "the astonishment of that hand, reached an even more ardent level of devotion."[3] One thing ties together the plague, the city's government, and its hopes for economic rebirth: silk, which Reni used as a pictorial support for the votive banner of S. Domenico. Scholars who discuss the unusual choice of silk instead of canvas tend to focus on its stylistic implications:[4] the white lead required for the priming, the brightening of the palette, the new direction of the artist's career. The fact that silk had been used previously for banners because of its light weight has been noted, too.[5]

Still, one must also remember what silk signified for the city: the survival of half the population that made its living in the silk industry. Carlo Cesare Malvasia described the reasons for the choice of silk solely in terms of the material's incorruptibility. He does, however, add a significant detail when read in this context: Reni deliberately ordered "some pure and strong silk rags."[6] They must have been extraordinarily expensive, to judge from Malvasia's implication that the silk alone for Reni's *Fable of Latona* for the king of Spain, left unfinished at the artist's death, cost 40 scudi, or some 200 lire.[7] Saints and Senate, the urban economy, and "the Apelles of our times" were all at center stage in praying to the Virgin Mary, and their prayer was borne by silk. Rather than remaining just a stylistic or functional feature, the silk support acted as a powerful support in reaffirming Bolognese identity.

Society reorganized from the ashes of the plague. New social players emerged: the noble family who acceded to the Senate and went on to occupy one of the seats in the Ufficio dei Riformatori e del Senato,[8] the merchant who sought to widen his commercial horizons, the artisan who managed to rebuild his workshop. Merchants and bankers began to acquire real social importance. Thanks to commerce and business, an array of Bolognese families, many of modest origins, were successful in accumulating vast fortunes during the seventeenth century. After spending an appropriate time settling into their new roles—in other words, after having abandoned business and taken up a noble lifestyle for at least a generation—many were co-opted into the senatorial class, where they replaced extinguished noble lines or families in financial ruin. Although wealth alone was not sufficient, it was nonetheless a prerequisite for joining the ruling class. Merchants rather than scholars constituted the primary pool for recruitment. From the fateful day of Guido Reni's plague banner, the economy slowly resumed its normal pace and accelerated dramatically over the course of the next 50 years, permitting the Bolognese to return their attention to intellectual pursuits.

The period from 1630 to 1680, embracing close to three generations of artists, merchants, and collectors, saw the development of the most visible aspects of the city's artistic economy. At its beginning Reni was entering the final phase of his life, and his most important pupils and followers were becoming independent masters. Meanwhile, following Reni's death in 1642, Guercino moved to Bologna and confirmed hierarchies in pricing. As buyers of art became collectors, a new market regulating purchases took hold. The Compagnia dei Pittori began to employ professional appraisers; dealers and speculators prospered. Malvasia recorded these changes in his monumental lives of Bolognese painters, *Felsina pittrice*, which he published in 1678. During this period, paintings became a sound economic investment, which changed their status and the rules underlying their distribution.

Artists, of course, were the cornerstone of this market. Although varied in their social and qualitative pedigree, all were tied to the market's laws of supply and demand, to the services it offered, and to the formulation of its prices.[9] But how many artists were working in seventeenth-century Bologna? If it is ever possible to answer this question given the absence of the Compagnia dei Pittori's archives, it is by collating seventeenth-century sources (above all Antonio Masini and Malvasia) in order to make an estimate.[10] When the painters first mentioned by Masini in his *Bologna perlustrata* of 1650 are added to those from the 1690 revision, and then to those found only in Malvasia, one reaches a number of about 300 spread across the whole century. To this count should be added those artists who are not mentioned by the sources such as Reni's many pupils, who were said to total almost 150, but more realistically numbered about 50.[11]

This fairly rough tally includes both male and female painters who worked in oil and fresco, those who were basically decorators, and those who, more rarely, were

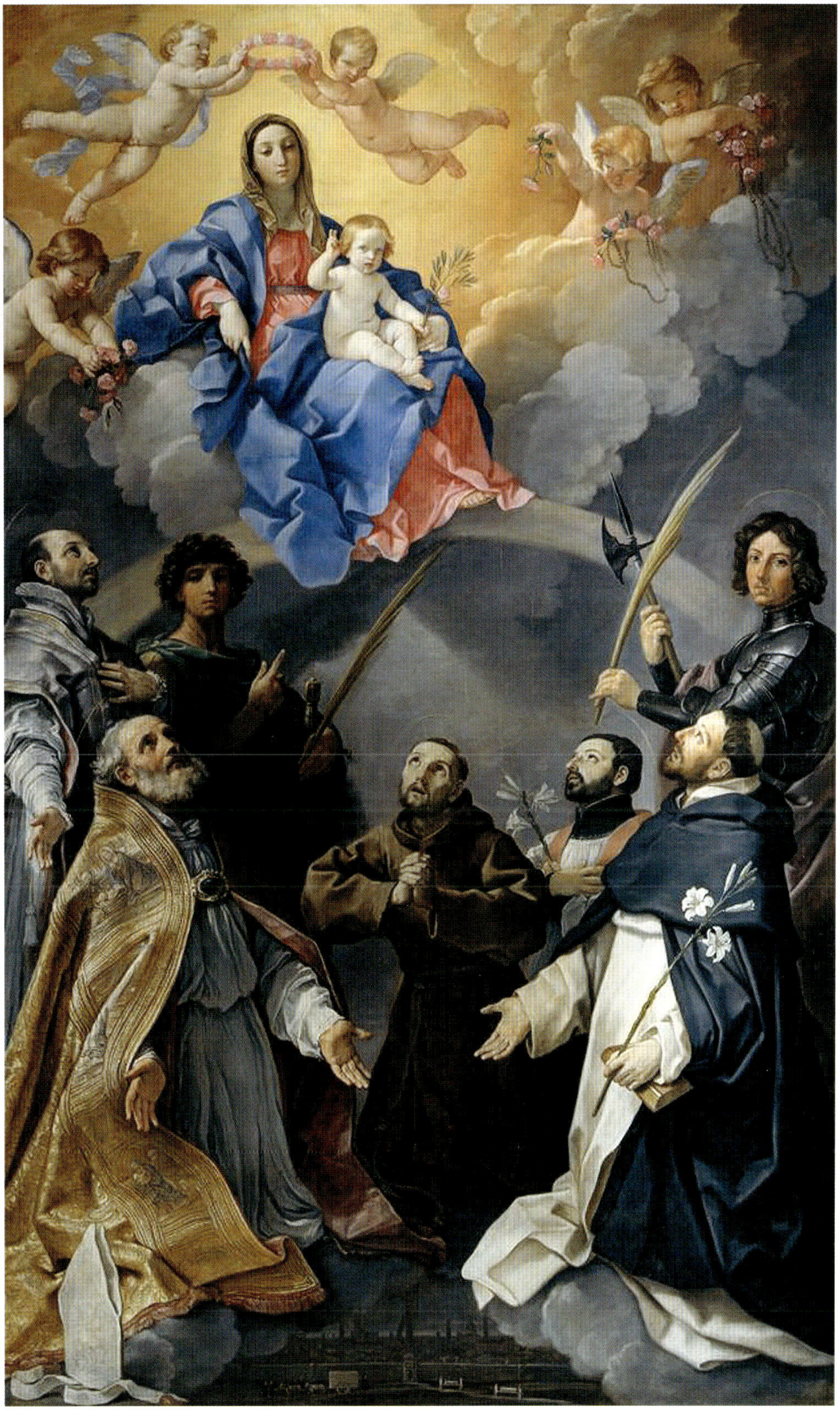

47 Guido Reni, *Madonna del Rosario* ("*Pala della peste*"), 1630. Oil on silk, 382 × 242 cm. Pinacoteca nazionale di Bologna.

sculptors. Only some are known today; many are not. While these numbers might be too imprecise for economic historians, at least they indicate how prevalent artists had become in the merchants' city. That is, one can estimate statistically that, over the course of the seventeenth century there were some 140 painters at any time who worked, had buyers, and earned enough to support themselves and their families.[12] They were therefore fully integrated into the economy of their region, giving art dealers and merchants a chance to prosper and to expand their market beyond the city limits. Their prosperity rested on the economic vitality of those inclined to buy art.

Lay people and clergy, contending for local glory, decorated their new palaces with friezes and frescoes and bought gallery paintings for display, while others ordered new altarpieces for their family chapels. In 1604, one could find 50 confraternities and 21 other charitable institutions in the city that, in addition to individual parishes, offered new opportunities to whomever appeared on the scene and thereby contributed to the dynamism of the Bolognese art market.[13]

There were various social typologies of the consumer of art, but the feature that most distinguished seventeenth-century Bologna from other Italian cities was the great influence wielded by bourgeois clients and buyers: self-employed professionals, artisans, wholesale traders, and prestige businessmen. The factors that led to such strong demand among the middle class can be found in the city's political structure, in the weakness of the pontifical legate, and, above all, in the organization of the local economy. Bologna was a crossroads of commercial exchange, favored by textile production. The artistic products created by local craftsmen were marketed, traded, and resold alongside pieces of silk cloth. In addition Bolognese artists were producing paintings of the highest quality which held pride of place also on the international market.

An examination of almost a thousand legal inventories cataloguing estates of varying importance and size (but containing at least ten paintings) reveals that all social classes, starting with the lower middle class, were acquiring works of art on the Bolognese market.[14] Examining these lists is like going through a primer of the city's trades and professions: accountants, actors, architects, musicians, notaries, pharmacists, soldiers, university professors, and—among the artisans and tradesmen—barbers, blacksmiths, booksellers, butchers, cobblers, confectioners, dyers, embroiderers, fishmongers, goldsmiths, grocers, haberdashers, hatters, farriers, innkeepers, ironmongers, makers of cups and carriages, masons, merchants selling grain, silk, cloth, tobacco, and spirits, painters, pharmacists, potters, sculptors, tailors, and tanners. It is not surprising, therefore, that there were such a great number of craftsmen in the city, as well as a similarly large group of service workers, including tradesmen who had shops "ad usum vendendi picturas et Sanctos" selling devotional images and copies of Reni's work, in particular, to the many foreigners who came to the city's silk cocoon market at the Pavaglione.[15]

Cost of Living

Before analyzing artists' expenditures and revenues, it is necessary to determine how much it cost to live in seventeenth-century Bologna and if, therefore, being a painter instead of another professional made good economic sense, as it did for Girolamo Curti, called Dentone, one of the most noteworthy Bolognese *quadraturisti*, who began working as a poor silk weaver but then rose to become a painter.[16] Knowing the rules and nature of the urban market allows us to understand the relationships between public power, guilds, and consumers. First of all, it might be useful to set up some kind of foreign exchange kiosk, which will allow the conversion of other currencies into the lire used in Bologna. One lira was made up of 20 soldi or 20 bolognini; 1 soldo equalled 12 denari; 1 scudo was worth 4 to 5 lire (hereafter, scudi usually will be cited in lire at this exchange rate); 1 ducatone was worth 5 to 8 lire; 1 doppia equalled 12 lire; 1 doblone, which was tied to the price of gold, was 16 to 20 lire; and 1 zecchino was worth 11 to 12 lire.[17] The right to print currency was a significant acknowledgment of Bologna's sovereignty within the Papal States; at the same time, it was a profitable enterprise and ensured the stability of the city's monetary policy. Bologna proudly expressed its independence by minting a coin that displayed the city's coat of arms on one side and the insignia of the Papal States on the other.

The Bolognese Senate had to govern alongside the pope's legate, who was appointed every three years and, in theory, had the power to intervene in every aspect of governance. In practice, however, few papal legates in the seventeenth century chose to act on this authority and instead preferred to enjoy the honors and pleasures of one of the richest and most highly prized legations. The legate was, therefore, mainly a figurative transitory position, which left the Senate with a great amount of room for maneuvering. Indeed, unpopular legates like Benedetto Giustiniani (1606–11) were removed (one year before the end of his second mandate, in Giustiniani's case) in order to avoid the anger of the Bolognese people.[18]

If the administrative value of the legate lapsed during the sixteenth and seventeenth centuries, the impact of the Papal States on Bologna's financial sector did not.[19] The main sources of income (about three-quarters of the legation's revenue) came from a series of indirect taxes, tariffs, and excise duties.[20] The primary excise duties were applied to the production and sale of foodstuffs and to trade, the lifeblood of Bolognese society: grain, the slaughter of animals and sale of meat, the sale of fresh and salted fish, the production of sweets and biscuits, the toll to enter the city, the buying and selling of rags, the making of silk in the Piazza del Pavaglione, the use of public space by craftsmen, and the monopoly of salt. Two important duties escaped the Camera Apostolica authority: customs, for which the Gabella Grossa was responsible, and the tax on wine. Duties and tariffs on the Pavaglione and the silk industry were increased seven times between 1530 and 1651. Three increases hit the *moline*, the duty on the making and selling of bread, between 1506 and 1600, the same number that was imposed on the *rettaglio*, the duty on slaughtering animals.

It should be no surprise, therefore, that paintings followed this inflationary trend since the prices of paintings were tied to the costs of primary goods and to the taxes on craftsmen. Some comparative examples of the prices of large altarpieces should prove instructive (for further examples, see Table 10). In 1568, Orazio Samacchini collected about 200 lire for the *Crucifixion with the Virgin, St. John the Baptist, and Ulisse Gozzadini* (S. Maria dei Servi, Bologna).[21] Bartolomeo Passerotti received 240 lire for his altarpiece of 1583 painted for the Gabella Grossa chapel (Pinacoteca nazionale di Bologna). Four years later, Ludovico Carracci was paid 200 lire for the *Conversion of St. Paul* for S. Francesco

TABLE 10 Costs per Square Meter and per Figure of Bolognese Altarpieces

ARTIST AND DATE	PAINTING (original location in Bologna, unless otherwise indicated)	DIMENSIONS (cm)	PRICE (lire)	PER SQUARE METER	PER FIGURE
Bartolomeo Passerotti, 1583	*Presentation of the Virgin in the Temple*, Palazzo della Gabella	390 × 198	240	31	27
Ludovico Carracci, 1587	*Conversion of St. Paul*, S. Francesco	279 × 171	200	42	44
Ludovico Carracci, 1594	*Vision of St. Hyacinth*, S. Domenico	375 × 223	250	30	55
Ludovico Carracci, 1595–96	*Transfiguration*, S. Pietro Martire	438 × 268	600	51	100
Guido Reni, 1599–1600	*Assumption of the Virgin*, parish church of Pieve di Cento	400 × 280	462	41	46
Giacomo Cavedone, 1600	*St. Stephen in Glory*, S. Stefano, Sassuolo	219 × 148	85	26	57
Denis Calvaert, 1601	*Paradise*, S. Maria dei Servi	560 × 300	700	42	32
Ludovico Carracci, 1608	*Ascension of Christ*, S. Cristina	412 × 268	645	58	117
Ludovico Carracci, 1614	*St. Martin Sharing his Cloak*, Cathedral, Piacenza	420 × 210	386	44	129
Alessandro Tiarini, 1614–15	*St. Domenic Reviving a Newborn*, S. Domenico	600 × 340	600	29	50
Guido Reni, 1614–16	*Pietà dei Mendicanti*, S. Maria dei Mendicanti	704 × 341	3,600+	151	360
Giacomo Cavedone, 1616	*St. Francis Receiving the Stigmata*, S. Maria dei Poveri, Crevalcore (Bologna)	170 × 140	70	29	70
Guido Reni, 1617	*Assumption of the Virgin*, S. Ambrogio, Genoa	442 × 287	5,000	394	280
Domenichino, 1619–22/25	*Martyrdom of St. Agnese*, S. Agnese	533 × 342	6,000	329	545
Guercino, 1620	*Investiture of St. William*, S. Gregorio	345 × 231	600	75	100
Domenichino 1621–25	*Madonna of the Rosary*, S. Giovanni in Monte	498 × 289	2,000	135	143
Guido Reni, 1622–23	*Crucifixion with Sts. Julius and Catherine*, S. Maria Corteorlandini, Lucca	217 × 172	660	177	220
Guercino, 1625	*Crucifixion*, Madonna della Ghiara, Reggio Emilia	440 × 245	4,000	371	889
Alessandro Tiarini, 1628	*Invention of the Rosary*, S. Domenico, Cremona	500 × 635	3,600	113	257
Alessandro Tiarini, 1629–30	*Ecstasy of St. Francis*, Madonna della Ghiara, Reggio Emilia	314 × 198	1,040	167	231
Alessandro Tiarini, 1629–39	*Holy Family with Sts. Anthony, Genesius, and Luigi Gonzaga*, S. Prospero	325 × 224	1,040	143	189
Guido Reni, 1631–42	*Assumption of the Virgin*, S. Maria degli Angeli, Spilamberto	290 × 204	2,500	422	500

Francesco Albani, 1632	*Annunciation*, S. Bartolomeo di Porta Ravegnana	365 × 295	800	453	160
Francesco Albani, 1634–35	*Madonna and Child with Angels and Sts. Roch and Sebastian*, Collegiata, S. Giovanni in Persiceto	314 × 225	1,600	226	320
Guido Reni, 1637	*Assumption of the Virgin*, Chiesa degli Oratoriani, Perugia	240 × 160	400	104	130
Simone Cantarini, 1637	*St. Stephen Martyr*, S. Stefano, Bazzano	265 × 185	250	51	167
Simone Cantarini, 1637	*Transfiguration*, Forte Urbano, Castelfranco Emilia	310 × 200	500	81	91
Francesco Albani, 1639–41	*St. Andrew Adoring the Cross of his Martyrdom*, S. Maria dei Servi	400 × 200	1,000	125	200
Guido Reni, 1640–42	*Adoration of the Shepherds*, Certosa di S. Martino, Naples	485 × 330	15,000	937	1100
Alessandro Tiarini, 1640–44	*Madonna della Ghiara Adored by Sts. Francis Xavier and Ignatius Loyola*, S. Giorgio, Reggio Emilia	345 × 210	1,120	155	149
Elisabetta Sirani, 1657	*Baptism of Christ*, S. Girolamo della Certosa	400 × 500	1,000	50	71
Carlo Cignani, 1661	*Madonna and Child with Sts. John the Baptist, Theresa, and Carlo Borromeo*, S. Lucia	385 × 229	1,000	113	222
Benedetto and Cesare Gennari, 1667–68	*S. Leopardo before the Cross*, Cathedral, Osimo	415 × 257	750	70	167
Benedetto Gennari, 1696–97	*Martyrdom of St. Bartholomew*, S. Bartolomeo, Rovigo	380 × 266	2,400	237	533

(Fig. 51). However, by 1601 Denis Calvaert earned some 700 lire for his altarpiece of *Paradise* in S. Maria dei Servi, and in 1608 Ludovico received 645 lire for the *Ascension of Christ* (S. Cristina, Bologna). Eight years later, Guido Reni's fee for his exceptionally large *Pietà dei Mendicanti* (Fig. 48) was an astonishing 3,600 lire.

In examining the tax increases that weighed on the local economy throughout the century, the extraordinary expenses of the city's participation in the Papal States' military campaigns, including the transport and billeting of troops, must not be overlooked. The conquest of Ferrara alone cost the Bolognese treasury 450,000 lire, while providing room and board for the Papal States' troops in Bolognese territory used up no less than 200,000 lire between 1646 and 1649.[22]

In order to provide some terms of comparison with basic consumer goods, it is worth noting that a slice of cheese cost 0.5 lire, while a kilogram of bread *da staffa* cost 0.1 lire on average, a stable price regulated by the Calmiero perpetuo del fornaio.[23] With 0.33 lire one could purchase a kilo of meat and with 8 lire a *corba*, or approximately 74 liters, of wine.[24] Or, by quite different yardsticks, a well-made walnut chair cost 12 lire and bail for a murder defendant reached 2,500 lire. A small dowry was worth 100 lire and a good one 800, to which another 200 lire would be added in furnishings and other incidentals.[25] Women confined to the convent of St. Paul paid a monthly fee that varied from 3 to 16 lire. At the end of their service as spinners, the poor girls at the Barracano who embroidered and weaved veils received a dowry from the textiles entrepreneur who had employed them amounting to 1,000 lire.[26] A silk weaver earned just 5 bolognini a day, though a family reportedly could live modestly on only 90 lire per year.[27] Marchioness Virgilia Malvezzi Ruini's farm in the town of nearby Gesso was estimated to be worth 3,250 lire in 1644 and provided 140 lire in income, therefore enough to get by on.

Guercino, on the other hand, at the height of his career earned between 5,000 and 20,000 lire annually. When he acquired his home in via Sant'Alò, which comprised two floors and at least ten rooms including a living room and atelier, he spent 4,250 scudi, more than 20,000 lire. At the opposite end of the scale Giuliano Dinarelli, a pupil and copyist of Reni, was allotted 1 scudo per month and provided with meals. Meager as that was, Dinarelli counted on the possibility of career advancement this gave him. Meanwhile, Reni was giving 8 scudi per month to his errand boys, in addition to the tips they might collect for their deliveries.[28] This rate, which equals an annual salary of 96 scudi or about 500 lire, is very close to the 4 giuli often paid to painters' assistants in Rome at the time.

The Politics of Artists' Prices

In a place as active and busy as seventeenth-century Bologna, it is not surprising that after a period of economic growth there emerged a widespread awareness (even a theoretical awareness, as Olivier Bonfait has often noted) of art's economic value and, consequently, the expression of a politics of the price of art.[29] A city so closely tied to trade could not help but be affected by the emergence of new markets and new wealth, especially when some stars of European painting were living in Bologna and prepared to supply the demand. And so the hierarchization of profits originating in artistic production became the Senate's business, too. In 1616, upon delivery of his altarpiece for S. Maria dei Mendicanti to the Bolognese Senate (now Pinacoteca nazionale di Bologna), Reni saw his fee increased by 500 lire; he was also given a prize "to motivate him and the other Bolognese painters to advance magnificently and become excellent."[30]

The Senate's profound interest in the renewed and economically revived art industry was a sign that the progress of the arts was highly prized in cultured Bolognese society. The increase in the price of paintings was a phenomenon that bore witness to the feverish demand for art, the capacity of artists to meet the demand, and the diversification of the market, which evidently found the ability to satisfy different types of buyers. Evidence of this trend is provided by the range of "prices" in Malvasia's *Felsina pittrice*: "low and attractive prices" (*prezzi bassi ed amorevoli*), which entice buyers, especially when they are convinced of having found a good investment for the future; "high prices" (*prezzi grandi*), which were initiated by Ludovico Carracci and Guido Reni; and "painters' prices" (*prezzo de' pittori o alle loro pitture*), which would determine the value of paintings in Bologna during the seventeenth century.[31] These pricing strategies arose from the changing status of painters and the increasing autonomy of the artistic profession. The idea of "selling by reputation" (*vendere per riputazione*) became a sort of slogan for Bolognese painters at the start of the seventeenth century and was powerfully exemplified by the Carracci.[32]

In a letter written in 1628, and discussed previously by Richard Spear, Reni established three categories of painters: that of the inferior artists (*pittori più bassi*), who could not obtain more than 2 or 3 scudi for large, life-size figures; that of the ordinary painter (*pittore ordinario*), who could, at most, ask the buyer for 15 scudi per figure; and that of the "somewhat extraordinary painter" (*pittore un poco straordinario*), who, like himself, could name his own price based entirely on the success and quality of his work and not on size or number of figures.[33] "It is customary in Bologna today" to price by talent. No longer adequate to have values set by the market or by dealers and middlemen interested solely in making a quick profit, it was necessary to define new criteria and to reappraise the artist's social status: "Painters today," wrote Reni in the same letter, "have started to study seriously. . . . Paintings must be well made and approved by those in a position to recognize good art." Paintings were therefore tentatively channeled into (admittedly fragile) categories that further increased the gap between works that were produced to sell quickly and others that began to acquire significant value as masterpieces.

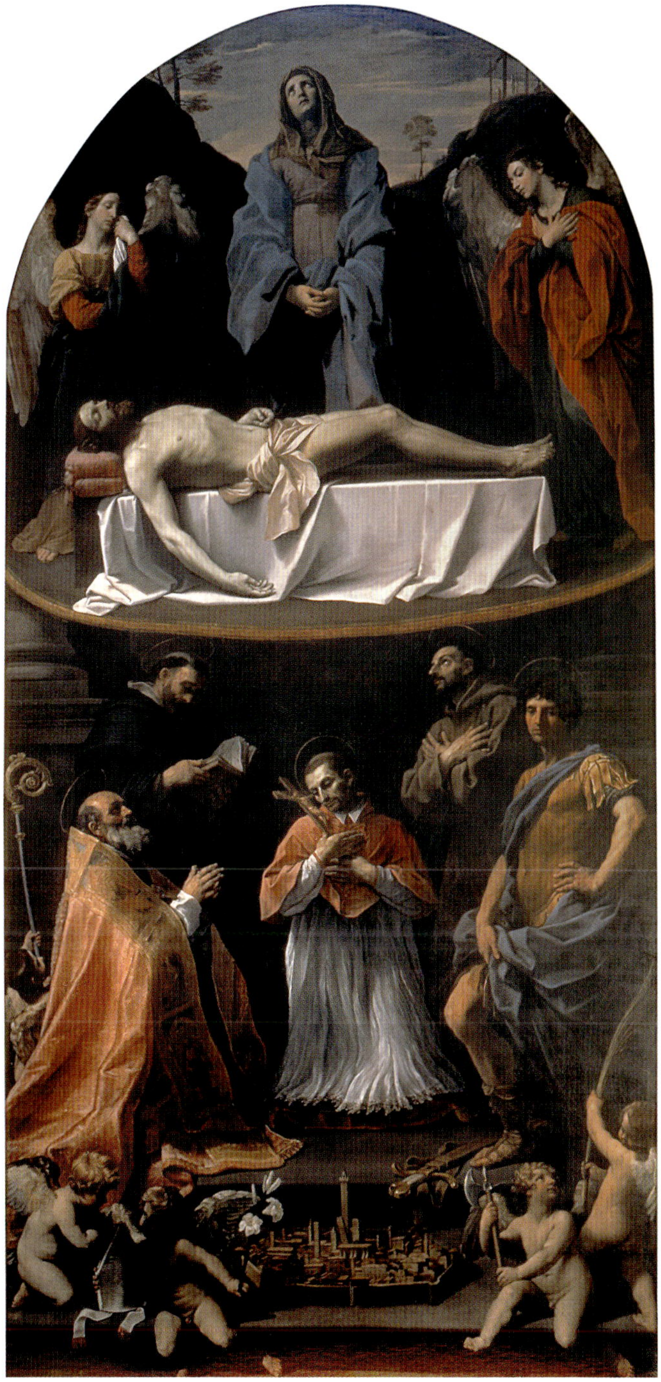

48 Guido Reni, *Pietà dei Mendicanti*, 1616. Oil on canvas, 704 × 341 cm. Pinacoteca nazionale di Bologna.

And the distinction became ever sharper. Even the statutes of the Compagnia dei Pittori were no longer sufficient, although they had guaranteed painters an unprecedented independence ever since 1598, when Ludovico Carracci convened the new council of 30 *assunti* (the members of the Compagnia who formed the council), and laid out a new set of regulations (which were approved by the Bolognese Senate and implemented in 1600).[34] It was precisely here that the foundations were laid for a new vision of the artistic profession. Painters were to enjoy pre-eminence over the cotton and wool merchants because the Compagnia dei Pittori was "in a state of prosperity and fame today, and one hopes for more in the future so that they will surpass every other guild with their noble and valorous profession."[35] Unlike anywhere else in Italy at the time, the guild's membership was open to professions other than painters. "Sculptors, architects, stuccoists, fortification engineers, makers of playing cards, gilders, goldbeaters, embroiderers, and vendors of drawings, paintings and prints, fans and masks" were admitted as *ubbidienti* (younger members with restricted privileges) without access to its directorial positions. Artists and merchants coexisted equally within this guild, with the aim of ensuring a self-reinforcing cycle of production and sales.

Following the example of Ludovico Carracci at the end of the Cinquecento, Reni set in motion a process of modernization and integration into the city's art economy that thereafter became unstoppable. Reni was very proud of it. Among his many statements, it is enough to take just the one where he is forced to respond to the silly question, as recorded by Malvasia:

> who was the more worthy, he or Guercino of Cento. "I am, Fathers," he quickly and boldly replied, "and I could tell you the reasons in terms of art but you would not understand them. Therefore these three simple reasons will do. First, because my pictures sell better than his. I, in fact, taught him how to be paid well. Secondly, because he fishes out my ideas and tries to work the way I do. I never followed his way of doing things. On the contrary I've always kept my distance from him. Finally, because all the other artists follow my style and not his.[36]

Reni, in other words, had opened up a new road to the painting market, while Guercino had done nothing more than to establish more precise accounting rules. When it came to imitation and the flocks of Reni's imitators, Guercino was certainly in no position to compete, closed as he was in the sheltered world of his family and relatives, who, moreover, used the same pricing system as Guercino. Cesare Gennari, for instance, charged 25 scudi for a head. According to Malvasia, Guercino

> did not want to do wrong to the common and public appraisal that he had made of these prices: to which, having [been] asked about the price, he responded that he himself would not evaluate his own works but would follow the common practice and the price given to them by others.[37]

Upon Reni's death in 1642, a new price adjustment occurred. Bellori noted the role Reni had played in the revaluation of the artist's commercial status: "Regarding prices one can say that he remunerated painting, not only in Bologna and Lombardy but even in all of Italy where prices were depreciated and buyers expected the lowest prices."[38]

The restructuring of Bologna's industry and commerce included new groups of middlemen. In the art world these included appraisers and dealers. Across the century the painters' guild listed 46 expert appraisers who specialized in painting and nothing else. In many cases, the painters themselves evaluated the works of their (often contemporary) colleagues, testifying to the system's evolution and anticipating what was to happen a few decades later.[39] Between the second and third decades the professional role of the expert gradually acquired public recognition as distinct from the painter. It started as a simple, lowly trade and blossomed into an entrepreneurial category regulated by laws and statutes. Moreover, this evolution followed the laws of Bologna's art market during the golden century. Experts were good at recognizing the hands of individual painters and their different styles as they changed over time. Copies were valued with the quality of the copyist in mind.

The simple *zavaglio*, a rag merchant who also was a general expert, would earn a minimum of 6 denari per lira of appraised value of works priced between 25 and 100 lire, or about 2.5 percent.[40] Those experts could earn a maximum of 50 lire for estates worth more than 10,000 lire, or only 0.5 percent. In the latter case, though, they would quantify goods not as individual objects but in bulk.[41] It would seem incongruous that a *zavaglio* could earn more on minor items and less on valuable property, but an autograph note by appraisers adds the factor of time and labor involved when liquidating assets: real property, for instance, is very different to assess than a painter's back room, where items have to be dealt with one by one. After the plague, there was a growing need for professionals who knew how to evaluate assets not just in terms of the volume of objects involved, but based on their individual quality. This saw the emergence of specialized experts—silversmiths, jewelers, booksellers, and obviously painters—who were recognized by the related companies and had the right to evaluate and demand appropriate compensation. Those specializing in paintings and drawings, for instance, belonged to the artists' guild: established painters, such as Albani, Canuti, Cignani, Giovan Battista Bolognini, Gian Gioseffo Dal Sole, Agostino Mitelli, Giuseppe Rolli, and Giovanni Maria Viani, all practiced this profession.

Already in the third decade of the century, experts could be categorized either as generalists or as specialists in individual areas. Generalists typically would have been unable to identify the author of a painting, unless the heir already knew the name from family tradition or because of a direct acquisition of the work. Specialized consultants were hired to deal with more valuable estates or where the presence of exceptional works in a smaller estate demanded a more careful evaluation. A professional painter, registered in Bologna as a public *zavaglio*, was usually employed in the appraisal of large picture galleries. Even in this case, however, the precise attribution of the entire collection was not guaranteed. Carlo Cignani and Lorenzo Pasinelli, for instance, two widely recognized painters who often worked as consultants for Bolognese inventories, identified only those paintings that met certain criteria. They could be originals or copies, but were required to be Bolognese; they could be by known artists or workshop pieces, but had to be the work of either the appraisers' own masters or the artists of their generation. Furthermore, they left purely decorative paintings to the generalists and excluded canvases painted outside the city walls, which were labelled generically as being by a "foreign hand" (*mano forestiera*).[42]

Perspectives of Investigation

Recent scholarship on the economics of Bolognese painting has focused primarily on Guercino and Reni, the artists who represent opposing attitudes toward the marketing of art in seventeenth-century Bologna. These two stars are important because they provided a fundamental thrust to the politics of pricing, but they should not be taken as norms. It is preferable to understand them more as potent *exempla* for the ranks of their students, followers, and imitators than as evidence of daily practice. For the economic status of painters below the heroic level of Reni and Guercino, one must rely on contracts, notarial deeds that establish the purchase and sale of land lots and houses, and loans and investments in city banks. From these one can begin to reconstruct their social status. These data should be interpolated with information provided by Malvasia, including his notes that were not used in the printed version of the *Felsina pittrice*. Indeed, Malvasia used thousands of documents, of different types, that were made available to him by the Compagnia dei Pittori, by the artists themselves, and by their friends, allowing him to read and study personal documents and books of private accounts.[43] On the whole, this information greatly enriches our image of that remarkable artistic environment in which painters worked: a sort of cultural autarchy, unique in seventeenth-century Italy.

The Artist's Career

Social Status

What was the culture and education of Bolognese artists in the seventeenth century? By 1600 it was already clear that taking up the painter's profession, even at a low rung on Reni's ladder, would ensure a much more profitable livelihood than any other artisan's trade, as will be shown later. As a result, whenever someone demonstrated the slightest talent in art, there was a strong financial incentive to enter the profession.[44] At the end of their chosen path, some achieved significant social recognition and were able to buy houses and land, rent out workshops, save money, and provide dowries for their daughters. In other cases artists were led to ruin by their own hands, the result of their temperament, bad habits, or unsound investments.

Painters became and remained poor in a variety of ways. Lionello Spada exemplifies the poor aspirant who had to work hard just to survive, one of many who "in order to eat decided to paint."[45] He began his career grinding colors for Cesare Baglione, before moving on to coloring fresco backgrounds and spending hours on scaffolding together with Girolamo Curti, until finally he progressed to the more amenable business of oil painting. As he was very poor, he would ring the church bells at S. Martino Maggiore in order to take advantage of their meal, after which he would devote himself to painting. He also worked as a model in order to pay his dues to the Compagnia dei Pittori. After a Caravaggesque interlude, he moved to Reggio Emilia, and after having married a woman of high social standing, he opened a workshop and school, but fell into disgrace after his patron Cesare d'Este died and Spada's pay was terminated. His life ended badly, worsened by his haughty character, which left its mark on his late style.[46]

Giovanni Paderna, a fresco painter of less humble origins, lacked the talent of Spada, but he also lacked the self-destructive behavior that limited Spada's financial success.[47] His decision to become a painter was economically motivated. He devoted his life to art after having started to work as a bookkeeper in Marcantonio and Giulio Cesare Felini's workshop, where he saw first hand that a painter's career might ensure a steady income. He dedicated himself entirely to painting, later working under Agostino Mitelli and Angelo Michele Colonna, the best Bolognese *quadratura* painters, before returning to his first teacher, Jacopo Borboni, with whom he formed a partnership. He remained an assistant or partner through most of his career, unable to support himself and his family comfortably through independent work.

The case of the indigent Giacomo Cavedone is a more complex and nuanced story of money and status. He came from a humble background. His father had to turn to the commune of Sassuolo (his hometown near Modena) in 1591 for financial support of Giacomo's training:

> Magnificent Gentlemen, as Master Pellegrino the Painter wishes that his son Giacomo learn the art of painting, in which he is already capable of success when it is taught to him by a skilful man, yet on the other hand given how poor he finds himself, being unable to provide him with the necessary living items outside of Sassuolo without the help of others, humbly he appeals to your Lordships and, together his aforementioned son, entreats them that as fathers of his fatherland they might want to assist him with sufficient help and keep him in Bologna for two or three years to learn said art there.[48]

The commune responded to his request by providing Giacomo with 1 scudo per month for three years so that he would be able to study at the famous school of the Carracci.[49] His social background, however, predestined him to a life in which he would never be called "sir" (*signore*), regardless of the esteem he commanded and the economic success he obtained. Despite his intellectual aspirations in drafting books on painters, techniques, and paintings in Bologna, despite his membership to the Accademia dei Baldi, and despite his access to the highest artistic circles of Passerotti and the Carracci, Cavedone never escaped a reputation as master craftsman.[50] Reni always called him "master" (*mastro*) and never "sir" (*signore*), the title he honored the Carracci and Albani with.[51] Money never bought him a *cursus honorum*. Guercino also came from an underprivileged social background and could study painting only with charitable aid. Had it not been for the prelate Antonio Mirandola, who believed in Guercino's talent and later became one of his most important clients, Guercino would not have been able to reach the social status he later achieved.[52]

Guido Reni came from somewhere in the middle. His father, Daniele Reni, worked for the Signoria of Bologna as a salaried musician. His mother, Ginevra Pozzi, received a dowry of 400 lire, a respectable amount that pointed to her reasonably prosperous roots. Guido had inherited a stake in a house from his grandmother, Orinzia Trevisi Pucci, which in 1642 he would leave in turn to his aged nephew.[53] His godparents from baptism—two Bolognese notables, Bartolomeo Marescotti and Caterina Dell'Armi—signify Daniele Reni's aspiration to an elevated cultural and social network of academies and senatorial palaces.[54] Such an intellectual class would deeply influence the artist's later ambition of comfortably inhabiting the same world as his buyers (men of letters, high prelates, crowned heads, and popes).

If a good number of Bolognese stars came from the region's poor, many others boasted a more privileged background. Francesco Gessi, for example, inherited 13,000 lire from his father, which he deposited in the city bank. Invested at 5 percent, this would have been enough to live on (though it would have meant a rather frugal life), but instead Gessi decided to earn his living as a painter and use his inheritance as a safety net.[55] Perhaps the arrogance he displayed towards Reni at certain moments of his career came from this economic confidence. Other financially independent painters included Lorenzo Garbieri, who received from his family two old houses in via Cartoleria, some bank credits, and two parcels of land, which allowed him to live at ease and to devote his unfettered attention to his work.[56] The same thing happened to Giovanni Battista Fulcini, a painter who was stylistically but not economically inferior to Garbieri and who spent 250 lire just to obtain a papal brief.[57] The father of Francesco Albani was a rich silk merchant, and his mother came from the noble Torri family. Giovanni Andrea Sirani's family ran a successful apothecary in Bologna, which ensured the family's economic well-being and brought them into daily contact with artists.

Family wealth played an important role in the artist's career, but so too did cultural education, which deeply influenced the artist's relationship with his clients. To understand such a divide, it is enough to compare two accounting receipts among the many that are available for interpretation: the first was written by Giacomo Cavedone in 1619, the second by Cesare Gennari in 1665. In 1619, Cavedone already had a public role in Bologna: he replaced no less an artist than Ludovico Carracci as steward of the painters' guild, although he certainly was not of Carracci's cultural level. Indeed, he struggled to write correctly, as one can deduce from his receipt for an *Ecce Homo* for the Oratorio della Morte, Reggio Emilia (now private collection), issued by the Confraternita della Buona Morte.[58] A lack of punctuation and poor sentence structure, along with grammar and spelling mistakes, are among the distinguishing features of the receipt: "O auto linstoria," for instance, appears instead of "Ho avuto l'istoria." In contrast, when Cesare Gennari wrote to Alfonso Gonzaga di Novellara regarding his painting of the *Death of Adonis* (formerly Gemäldegalerie, Dresden), we find an exemplary epistolary style despite an occasional spelling error.[59] Guercino and his collaborators also demonstrated a perfect command of written language, reflecting a high level of education. This ensured them privileged access to precious objects, books, sources, and high quality goods.[60] Reni's position was somewhere in between. Although he was an extremely talented speaker (and a favorite of Bolognese intellectuals), Malvasia found him to be uncomfortable with writing and proved his point by listing all of Reni's spelling mistakes in his notes for the *Felsina pittrice*.[61] But perhaps the artist used two different systems: one for everyday needs, like filling in his notes, and a more controlled and sophisticated one for letters.[62]

At any level, the artistic profession provided real opportunities for economic success; it is not surprising, therefore, to find such a large number of professional artists working in the city. According to Malvasia, Raimondo Cometti, an otherwise unknown Bolognese painter, after years of working hard and living frugally, eventually was able to buy a house and several bank bonds.[63] Cavedone, on the other hand, who had achieved sufficient financial success to purchase a large house in the Mirasole di Mezzo district, was forced to sell it in 1633 following the loss of his whole family during the plague and the debts he had amassed to pay for treatment of his wife and son.[64] Albani provides an even more glaring example. In the latter part of his life and his career, having been saddled with a 70,000 lire debt by his brother and financial manager Domenico, the artist was forced to work quickly and with the help of his workshop, to the detriment of the quality of his art. Cavedone and Albani suffered financially because of life's misfortunes. Others, whose steady income could have ensured a comfortable life, did the damage to themselves. Such was the case with Mastelletta, a psychologically disturbed painter who voluntarily ostracized himself from society in the second half of his life, even though earlier he sagaciously filled orders quickly and for a good price.

Real Estate, Land, Rent, and Other Property of the Artist

Unlike in the other cities in this study, painters in Bologna did not live in particular areas of town. Rather, each went where luck and money allowed. Typically a painter's house—its size, location, and furnishings—was tied to his income. It tended to be a single house with two floors and at least six rooms, and was only rarely contiguous to the artist's studio. In order to have a look around the artist's house, it is worth starting with the two masters, Reni and Guercino. Reni lived in via delle Pescherie, in the heart of Bologna's market district and in the parish of S. Andrea delle Scuole, although in 1622 he claimed to live in the parish of S. Andrea del Mercato, the home to many workshops, "for the reason that the market of foods was the beating heart of the city's economic life."[65] Malvasia wrote that "what pleased [Reni] most was to have a great many rooms with work going on in many of them at the same time," and yet he disliked pomp and grandeur during his Bolognese period.[66] His residence was open to his pupils, friends, and patrons—but its decoration was spartan.

As for Guercino, the exact details of his house are known. He bought a grand residence in 1644, two years after Reni's death, large enough to house all his relatives from the Gennari family along with his studio. Located in via S. Alò (via del Carbone today) in the parish of S. Niccolò degli Albari, it was decorated with princely pomp and was suitable to host even the most noble patrons. As Bonfait calculated, Guercino became very well off, so much so that he also could operate a pawnshop in Cento, which Malvasia specifically linked with his fame and prosperity ("fu così stimato, ed accarezzato").[67]

Some Bolognese painters before Reni and Guercino also owned their own property and lived there in comfort. In 1572, the little-known Tommaso Romani bought the house of the Cavaliere Michele Volta in the S. Mamolo district of the city, in the parish of S. Giacomo dei Carbonesi;[68] a few months earlier, Romani had also purchased a farm called la Casetta, "the little house," in the town of Stiatico.[69] In 1578 Domenico Tibaldi, both a painter and an architect, bought a house located in the parish of S. Andrea delle Scuole from one Carlo Berò for the price of 2,000 lire; it bordered another of his residences that was described as "grande."[70] In 1583 Denis Calvaert, the most noteworthy Flemish painter living in Bologna, paid 2,900 lire for a house located in the street of Mascarella.[71]

At the start of the new century, property prices in both the city and countryside increased relative to the cost of living and basic goods. Nonetheless, artists were earning more and, therefore, buying up more real estate. Obscure and famous painters alike appear as contracting parties for the sales of property ranging from tiny houses to small estates and from hemmed-in gardens to important palaces. The explanation for these purchases comes down to family factors, inheritances, advantageous marriages, and family size: in short, the wealth the artist had accumulated over his career. And so we find some painters who started out extremely poor and then rose up in society until they were able to acquire sizeable properties, while others began their careers in a good financial position but lost their wealth because of misfortune or lifestyle; still others earned huge amounts only to spend it all on sumptuary goods.

Residences of Bolognese painters are sometimes reliable indicators of their economic status. Girolamo Curti, a fresco painter known for his sobriety in life, was convinced that he was among the luckiest people in the world, since he rose from the ranks of silk-working, where he earned only 5 bolognini per day. Indeed, he managed to buy two houses, the first in via Pietralata, as well as a neighboring house located in via S. Felice.[72] According to Malvasia, it was a small purchase: he likely paid 5,000 lire for the first property, with a debt of 1,000 lire owed to Angelo Michele Colonna. Upon his death, the house was worth 7,000 lire.[73] The oil and fresco painter Matteo Borboni, on the other hand, lived in a large house of his own in the parish of S. Mamolo.[74] He led a privileged life, at least judging from the magnificence of his house and the canny success of being elected 19 times to a top managerial office (*massaro*) in the painters' guild.

Prospero Fontana owned two houses at the end of his life, his residence near S. Cristina and a second one in via Galliera, which he left to his wife along with an annuity of 350 lire. His daughter Lavinia, also a painter, inherited most of his estate.[75] Bartolomeo Passerotti's two-story house and studio in the parish of S. Michele del Mercato was handsomely furnished.[76] Carlo Cignani acquired two apartments through redemption, both located in via Sant'Isaia, in the same parish where the artist already resided.[77] He obtained a count's title and thereafter lived like a noble, although the documents about him reveal that he also acted as a silk dealer and ran a paper mill.[78]

Residences, however, did not always reflect a painter's fame. Eustachio Canuti, a painter who managed to conduct a successful business without being noticed by Malvasia or other contemporary Bolognese sources, lived just outside the city, at the Meloncello near Porta Saragozza in a large and pretentiously furnished two-story house.[79]

Where painters resided and what they owned at the end of their lives (when their estates were most often appraised) may not coincide with their economic fortunes during the preceding decades. Cavedone purchased a house in via Mirasole Grande in 1614, was forced to sell it in 1621, only to buy it back in 1624 before selling it again, once and for all, in 1633 (he had to wait until 1644 for the final payment).[80] Giovanni Andrea Sirani lived on via San Felice in a once sumptuously furnished house that became barer during his last four years, when illness led him to sell many of his possessions.[81] Pier Francesco Cittadini, on the other hand, was a prolific painter who managed to acquire only a modest house in the parish of S. Procolo with simple furnishings.[82] When he wanted to purchase a parcel of land valued at 3,100 lire, he could only muster a meager deposit of 100 lire, not enough to secure the purchase.[83] Even the more successful Francesco Gessi lived in a small home with a kitchen and foyer on the ground level and three rooms on the upper floor that he shared with his apprentices.[84]

Pasinelli's properties set an entirely different standard than any of the previous painters. His real estate holdings, according to an inventory of 1707 (seven years after his death), included a small palace with three apartments in the S. Maria Maggiore parish (richly furnished and valued at 6,000 lire), a garden purchased from the friars of S. Martino, a general store, and two parcels of land (both with manor houses) located outside the Porta Saragozza.[85] In total, taking into account all of his furniture, real estate, credits, and debits, his estate reached the considerable sum of 43,854 lire.[86] Managing an estate that size could be distracting, but Pasinelli resolved this potential problem by delegating responsibility to his brother-in-law Giovan Battista Moretti.

Alessandro Tiarini, on the other hand, had a more complex portfolio to manage and chose to do so himself.[87] According to the legal notices of four Bolognese notaries, no other local painter had drawn up so many sale and purchase deeds, rental agreements including agricultural property, real estate exchanges, and dowry repayments.[88] Tiarini's involvement in such endless financial transactions weakens Malvasia's claim that he "loved the work more than the pay."[89] He leveraged his wealth into a higher social status. He lived with a number of servants in his home in via Mirasole; he always dressed in silk clothing; but above all, he held important positions like *massaro* and then *sindaco* of the painters' guild, the Compagnia dei Pittori, and was also a professor at Ghisilieri's Accademia del Disegno. The dowry for his daughter Dorotea, when she was married to Francesco Carboni, a student and collaborator of Tiarini's, included 3,000 lire and a house in via Broccaindosso.[90] When she was widowed in 1636, Dorotea married a merchant with great economic potential, who sold the house and invested the proceeds.[91] Like the best Bolognese families, Tiarini even acquired a chapel dedicated to the Blessed Virgin.[92] Apparently only one other artist, Angelo Michele Colonna, had a private chapel (in S. Bartolomeo at Porta Ravegnana), although he had obtained it as part of his payment for painting the frescoes of the church's vault in 1666.[93]

Francesco Albani was by far the richest painter in Bologna. The documents collected by Malvasia and augmented by Giovanni Pietro Zanotti tell a dismal story of how Albani was swindled by his brother and relatives and forced to sell some of his properties to support his family of 11 children. Albani's financial affairs had started well. He received a dowry of 20,000 lire and two houses in Rome from his first wife.[94] After her death, he married Doralice Fioravanti, who brought him a handsome dowry of 10,000 lire. He then decided to return his inheritance from both his father and mother (Malvasia says it was substantial), which he gave to his brother Domenico since his own earnings were more than sufficient. Domenico wanted more. He convinced Francesco to return to Bologna from Rome and to remit to him all his profits and interest. Worse still, he persuaded Francesco to let him act as his financial administrator so that Francesco could devote himself entirely to painting. Unlike Pasinelli, who prospered while his brother-in-law managed his estate, Albani's choice of his brother initiated his financial downfall. Albani himself contributed to it by pursuing two expensive passions: books (he had an immense library) and a property called Della Querzola, which he fancied to be another Tivoli or Frascati but was actually a monetary sinkhole.[95] He also owned a farm called Medola, which he was forced to sell for 20,000 lire to help pay off a 70,000 lire debt after his brother had squandered his earnings. In a letter written to the painter Girolamo Bonini in 1654, Albani calculated his debts and expressed his wish to live long enough to pay everyone back. He didn't.

Most of the painters' properties discussed here were commodious by contemporary standards. The documents sometimes indicate the presence of a workshop (*bottega*), school (*scuola*), or academy (*accademia*), suggesting that studio and residence existed in the same building. Not all painters were able to live this way. Matteo Borboni worked outside his home in a one-room space near the Scuole Pie.[96] Cavedone also worked in a room (*stanza*), located in via di S. Pietro, which previously belonged to Ludovico Carracci.[97] Malvasia writes that Lorenzo Garbieri exhibited his paintings in his own home, located in via Cartoleria; starting in 1620, however, he rented a house with a workshop to be used for painting in via S. Mamolo, according to a rental contract with the father of the church of S. Maria de' Galluzzi (located near the house).[98]

Pasinelli had a school in via Imperiale (called dei Mulini), while Tiarini ran an academy for study of the nude within the space of his own large house. Schools and academies were different. Painting took place in both, but the terminology of *scuola* and *accademia* suggests the former served as training workshops for paying students whereas the latter could be a more informal mix of apprentices, amateurs, and young professionals. *Botteghe*, on the other hand, were workshops that also served as salesrooms. As for the housing of the painters' guild, at least after its separation in 1572 from the guild of the sheath makers, sword makers, and saddlers, it used the proceeds (9,000 lire) from the sale of a house in the parish of Sts. Fabiano and Sebastiano to buy the so-called Drapers' Room (stanza dei Drappieri) located in the via Cimarie for its meetings. Four years later, the guild purchased an apothecary's workshop called the Pigna Vecchia, near S. Giovanni de' Carbonesi.[99]

It might be noted that things were different in Modena, a nearby city but one with a different government. In 1637, Ludovico Lana, the city's leading painter, asked to be given some rooms in the Palazzo della Comunità to be used as an academy and private studio. The commune granted his request and even absorbed the cost of 500 Modenese lire to restructure, restore, and decorate the rooms.[100]

Professional Accreditation and Types of Earnings

When the painters' guild was established in 1572, its financial management had not yet been codified.[101] The judicial process was carefully controlled to resolve disputes between painter and patron. Appraisers had to be approved by the guild and had to pay registration fees of 40 lire for non-residents and 20 for residents.[102] All of the 46 known recognized experts are mentioned by Masini as amongst the city's leading painters, which indicates the importance given by the Compagnia to quality control and product protection. Taxes and fees, payment for instruction, and sales practices in the *botteghe* were haphazardly regulated, if at all, leaving master painters complete autonomy. Consider, for example, the idiosyncratic practices of charging (or not charging) students at schools and academies. When Reni entered the Carracci academy at age 20, he paid no fee and received no other form of payment. He was, however, required to sketch and prepare canvases for the Carracci. Prizes (*premi*), not earnings (*guadagni*), were the currency of their academy, suggesting a fluid relationship between work, education, and pay.[103] The financial conditions of apprenticeship depended on the individual master. Albani helped his collaborators by giving them a few gold scudi.[104] As an established master, Reni often charged his students high fees, especially later in his life as his debts mounted, but for other, more advanced students who served as assistants, he was more generous. Francesco Gessi and Giuliano Dinarelli received monthly stipends, the latter's being 1 scudo plus meals (or 5 lire, about 17 times what a silk weaver would have earned).[105]

Wages paid by master painters were unregulated but followed certain ad hoc guidelines. Fees for work away from home were usually higher. Masters could also expect better pay abroad, although not always. Cavedone, who received 20 scudi per month from Reni in Rome, saw his pay rise by 50 percent when he accompanied Reni to Loreto.[106] Tiarini and his collaborator Luca Ferrari, on the other hand, received a meager 234 lire for 39 days' work in nearby Modena, or about 6 lire a day.[107] Giacomo Alboresi received a monthly salary of 50 ducatoni, about 400 lire, from Angelo Morosini for his frescoes in Padua.[108] Benedetto Gennari, on the other hand, fared much better with the king of England in 1684, earning a grand salary of 2,000 scudi per year (10,000 lire), in addition to payments for individual works, room and board, and miscellaneous gifts. He was paid 800 scudi (4,000 lire) for a portrait of the queen.[109] Gennari accepted what Guercino had obstinately refused ever to do: move away from Bologna. Guercino refused even the king of France, who had offered him a stipend of 1,000 ducatoni a year (8,000 lire), plus another 1,000 ducatoni for travel, lodging in a princely residence, and payments for each finished painting. Even this generous offer was not enough. Why leave home when, according to Bonfait's estimates, Guercino, at the height of his career in Bologna, was able to earn up to 20,000 lire a year?[110]

The earning power of different masters is difficult to reconstruct because the types of paintings and pricing policies were so various. Albani, for instance, painted small images on copper of the miraculous *Madonna della Ghiara*, reportedly two each night, and sold them to the citizens of Reggio for just 12 lire each.[111] Reni contracted himself out for 40 scudi per day to paint for four hours, a celestial wage that still allowed his employer, the father of Giovan Battista Manzini, to make a profit in selling each small painting for 80 scudi.[112] Producing a minimum of two paintings every four hours, Mastelletta, a distracted man, took offense when the value of his paintings was calculated as a function of time. When a merchant offered half the asking price of 40 lire for a lovely *Madonna* on the grounds that it had taken Mastelletta only four days to complete it and hence could rest easy knowing that he had earned 5 lire per day, the painter responded by cutting the canvas with a knife and saying that if he could earn so much in so little time, then he could also afford to carve up the fruit of his labor.[113]

The differences between payments and the quality of work are also the result of infinite gradations and subject to such variables as the status of the patron, studio assistance, the subject, the number of figures, and the work's dimensions.[114] Special prices were often arranged on an ad hoc basis as a modified form of gifting. Reni charged the Leoni for only two of the figures in a lost altarpiece of the *Madonna and Child with Saints* for S. Tommaso di Strada Maggiore, in effect giving them the upper part of the painting as a gift, in recognition of a favor they previously had done for him. The Leoni still had to pay Reni the exorbitant price of 1,200 lire. Similarly, when Reni painted his famous *Crucifixion* (Pinacoteca nazionale di Bologna) for the church of the Cappuccini, he donated half the sum to the friars, of whom he was a particularly devoted follower, and made the merchant Boselli pay the other 300 scudi.[115] Earlier, in 1602, Ludovico Carracci gave to the confraternity of S. Rocco an enormous votive banner (tempera and pastel on paper) that was executed by his student Baldassarre Aloisi (called Galanino). Ludovico requested a small compensation from the confraternity, to which he then donated the work.[116] He also painted a *Sacrifice of Isaac* in 1607 for his friend Angelo Michele Risi; insisting that he should not be paid, he received gifts worth 60 lire. He exchanged a *Martha and the Magdalene* "con tre figure" (with three figures) for nine cases constructed of high-quality wood and a set of white majolica plates and glasses with his coat of arms.[117] Tiarini painted a *St. Anthony Abbot* (destroyed during the Second World War), as well as seven chiaroscuro banners, as a gesture of gratitude for the hospitality and medical care he received in 1625 from the Servite monks in Scandiano (Reggio Emilia). An expense sheet from the hospital indicates that, in return, Tiarini was given four handkerchiefs worth 24 lire.[118]

Other exceptional cases that affected painters' incomes include payments for an idea or a preparatory sketch. In 1601 Bartolomeo Cesi received various payments for drawings for the *Mysteries of the Rosary* (S. Domenico, Bologna).[119] For a large drawing of the *Madonna and Child* with a crown of roses framing her, Cesi was paid 6 lire; for an angel of similar size and style, he received 3 lire; and for a drawing combining the two, he received 9 lire. The last was used as a promotional aid, exhibited in S. Domenico to encourage alms for the chapel's decoration. Cesi then made a cartoon, more detailed and probably larger judging from the higher price of 20 lire, that was sent as a model to an embroiderer. Flaminio Ruffini, the patron of Tiarini's *Madonna della Ghiara with Sts. Francesco Saverio and Ignatius Loyola* (S. Giorgio, Reggio Emilia), gave to a certain Francesco "some copper to make a small model or painted drawing" as an iconographic guide for Tiarini. Francesco received only 1 lira and 8 soldi for his model.[120]

A much more complex analysis needs to be made regarding copies. How much was paid for them when done on commission, and was there any pattern to the payments? On occasion copies were made at the time of the original, perhaps to record a work that was leaving Bologna for good. That apparently was the case with Reni's *Christ Bearing the Cross.* The original of ca. 1620 (National Gallery, Valletta, Malta) was copied by early 1621 as a tabernacle cover for the church of S. Salvatore in Bologna (now Musée des Augustins, Toulouse). The fathers of the church paid Reni 50 lire for a reduced copy. He in turn relied on Giacomo Castellini for assistance, who received the modest sum of 20 lire, suggesting a sort of financial partnership with the master, who retouched the copy.[121] Another situation involves famous artists being asked to copy a painting or banner that was of special significance to a community. A banner that was painted by Bertoia in 1590 for the city of Parma was then copied in 1625 by Tiarini, who received 150 lire for his work.[122] Yet another pattern involves copies that were mandated in contracts as an integral part of the original commission. In 1632, for instance, Duke Francesco I d'Este invited Guercino to Modena to paint portraits of himself and his wife Maria Farnese, along with copies of the portraits.[123] Guercino was paid 630 scudi for both originals and two sets of copies, which was toward the high end of his normal prices for original full-length portraits (150 to 200 scudi) and studio copies (50 to 75 scudi). Guercino's policy of discounting copies is consistent with Roman and Venetian practices.[124]

The Invisible Domestic Economy of Women Painters

More women painters per capita worked in seventeenth-century Bologna than anywhere else in Italy: Lavinia Fontana, Elisabetta, Barbara, and Anna Maria Sirani, Ginevra Cantofoli, Lucrezia Bianchi, Anna Maria Panzacchi, Caterina Mongardi, Angela Teresa Muratori, Teresa Maria Coriolani, Maria Oriana Galli Bibiena, Maria Lucrezia Scarfaglia, and others who are not as widely mentioned in the sources.[125] Both indomitable and lucky, they were esteemed throughout Europe, invited to the top courts in Italy, and collected internationally. Cultured and refined women, they started schools and salons, they produced paintings for local and international markets, and yet they were economically invisible. Public documentation that would allow us to compare their earnings, investments, and revenues barely exists because women were not allowed to sign public documents in the seventeenth century. Those contracts that do exist are listed under the names of their guardians. Signatures by women were not considered valid and required the cosignatory of their legal guardians for the document to be legitimate.[126] It is not coincidental that, unlike male painters, Lavinia Fontana and Elisabetta Sirani signed more than 70 percent of their works, as if to reaffirm their role as artists which might otherwise be denied them. Because contracts and purchases were not notarized, these transactions were mostly made by personal arrangement and private correspondence.

Lavinia Fontana was the daughter of a prosperous and respected painter. Her marriage contract, which included a rich dowry, was signed in 1577 by her father Prospero and her future husband and manager, Giovan Paolo Zappi.[127] She worked for the dukes of Mantua and Urbino, for the Spanish royal family, and for Cardinal Bernerio in Rome, for whom she painted the altarpiece of *St. Hyacinth* (S. Sabina, Rome) in the Jubilee year of 1600. Starting in 1604 she was in Rome as a guest of Cardinal d'Este. The contract for the *Stoning of St. Stephen* (S. Paolo fuori le Mura, Rome) was both drafted and signed in her absence, with her husband and Cardinal Bernerio, her protector, signing on her behalf in 1603.[128] It states that Fontana would be paid the same price as her male colleagues, although the total amount of the payment is never mentioned. This equity underlines the dignity and high quality of her work without, however, upsetting the legal prerogatives of male painters. But the conditions set forth in the contract were atypical and prejudicial. The painting's value would be established only after its completion. If it was deemed to be as good as or better than

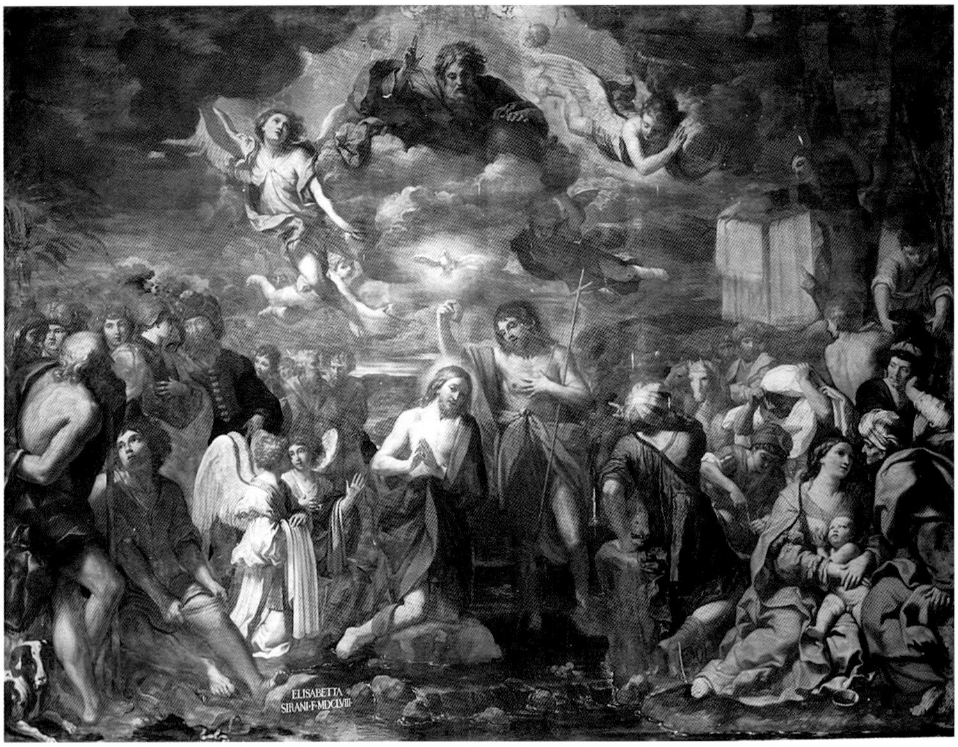

49 Elisabetta Sirani, *Baptism of Christ*, 1657. Oil on canvas, 400 × 500 cm. S. Girolamo della Certosa, Bologna.

paintings by men, she would be paid with a few courtesies (*cortesie*) but not with money. However, if it were to be deemed inferior, she would have to refund an unspecified amount of money that she had received earlier, presumably as a deposit. The delivery of materials and the payment would take place "in the way and the manner which is customary with other painters." It seems, therefore, that while Lavinia's talent as a painter was recognized, her professionalism was not, to the point that Zappi had to guarantee his wife's work. Her career and earnings were managed entirely by her husband, who in his will of 1607 appointed Lavinia the sole heir of his estate.

Elisabetta Sirani's case presents a greater range and variation. Her identity inevitably was tied to that of her family, in part because, as an unmarried woman, her father, the successful painter Giovanni Andrea, held all of her rights. Although she gradually became emancipated—she even opened an academy entirely for women—she stayed cloistered at home throughout her short life. In 1657, when just 19 years old, she was commissioned to paint a *Baptism of Christ* (Fig. 49) and was paid 1,000 lire in the next year, the equivalent of what her male colleagues would have received for such a huge (20 square meters) and complexly figured painting.[129] Despite receiving market value for her labor, seventeenth-century sources chose to represent her as a "virtuous woman" who did not care about money. Indeed, Malvasia described the "most modest prices" that she was given by Europe's crowned heads and chose to emphasize instead the precious gifts she received, which were put on display in her father's house in the via Urbana.[130]

Sirani kept a register of the paintings she made between 1655 and 1665. Unfortunately, this diary-memo makes no reference to prices or payments, but only lists the gifts that she received in recognition of her impeccable reputation. Her receipts were managed by Giovanni Andrea, as Malvasia underlines: "The rewards given for these [paintings] went to the father, who then used them for the common good of the house . . . saving in an armoire all the silver, gold, jewels, and the like, which were given as gifts."[131] Sirani lists about 195 paintings executed in ten years. Not included were those works she deemed not "noteworthy," whether artistically or socially.[132] When the paintings cited are added to those not on her list, Sirani's total oeuvre comes to about 300, an extremely productive average of 30 works per year. Guercino, by way of contrast, completed only 111 paintings during the same period,

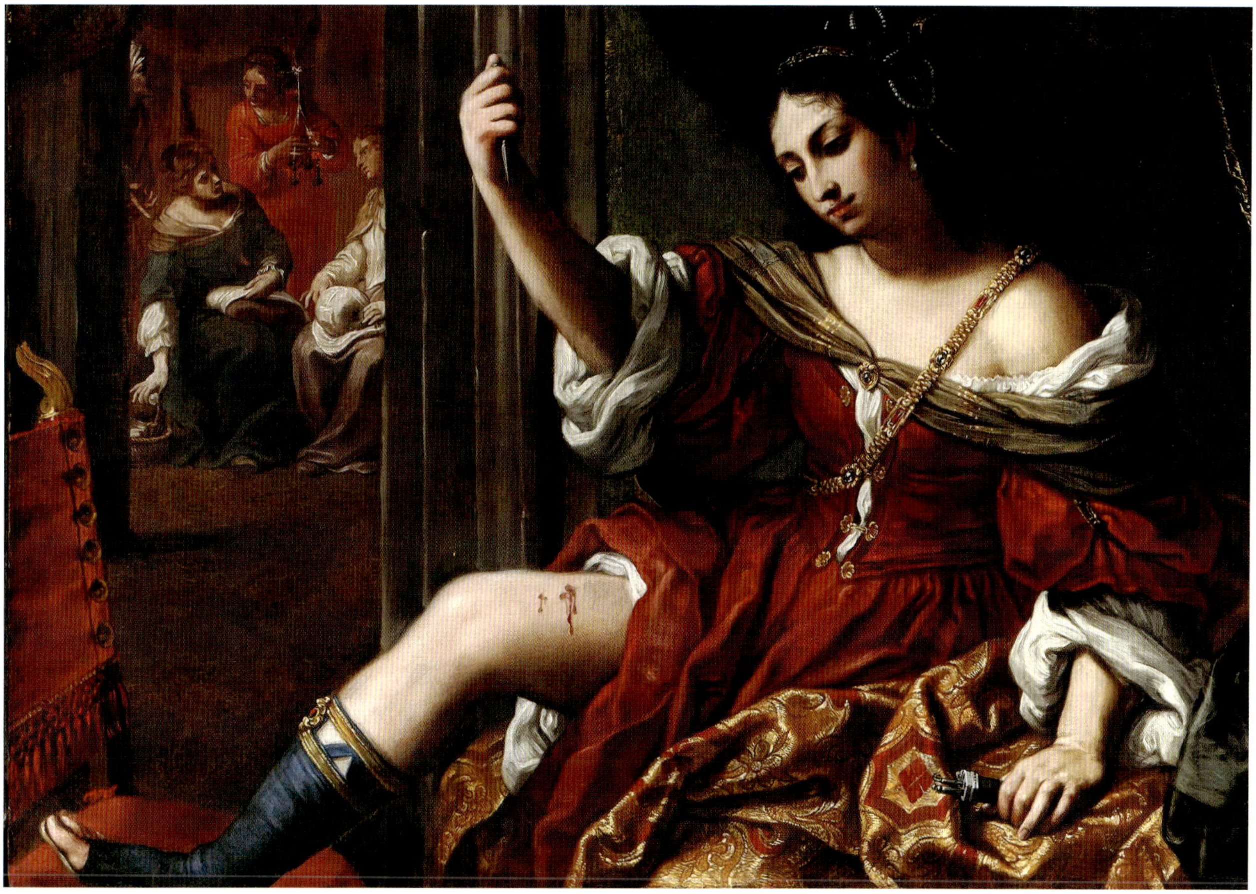

50 Elisabetta Sirani, *Portia*, 1664. Oil on canvas, 101 × 138 cm. Private collection.

though many were large altarpieces. Sirani's reluctance to list payments and prices does not mean that they could not be translated into a monetary value, whether or not she received payment in cash or as gifts.

The problem is finding a method to establish those values in order to compare them with payments received by men. One way is to compare early appraised values of her paintings with works by other painters (assuming comparable dimensions and numbers of figures), such as Guercino. It should be stressed, however, that inventories typically represent posthumous opinions, not original prices. One case where the conditions of comparability are nearly met (same collector, same appraiser, same inventory, though unsure dimensions) involves Simone Tassi, a silk merchant and art dealer. Tassi's inventory was compiled by Filippo Brizio, a painter and licensed appraiser, just six years after Elisabetta's death and five years after Guercino's.

Tassi bought three paintings from Sirani between 1660 and 1664.[133] Her *Portia* (Fig. 50) was valued at 500 lire, compared with the *St. Jerome* by Guercino (location unknown), which was valued at only 120 lire.[134] This might suggest that at the time Sirani's reputation rivaled and even surpassed that of the aged Guercino, but the size of his lost canvas is unrecorded; presumably it included at least a half-length figure. Sirani's dazzling work depicts an extremely ornate, full-length figure in the foreground and, through a doorway, several young women working on a lace pillow and turning on a light, so it well might have been a more ambitious composition than Guercino's.

Therefore Guercino's *Venus and Cupid* (90 × 127 cm, private collection) might make a better comparison, since it was painted about at the same time as the *Portia* and is similar in complexity and size (*Portia* measures 101 × 138 cm).[135] Guercino received 325 lire for it in 1664, compared with the 500 lire valuation of Sirani's *Portia*. The appraisal of Guercino's work, however, was carried out in 1671, seven years after the original payment, which compounds the difficulty of comparing the value of Sirani's work and that by her male colleagues.

The financial loss to the Sirani family upon the early death of Elisabetta is poignantly described in a letter of 1665 by Count Andrea de' Buoi to Giovan Carlo de' Medici.[136] Although then sickly, Giovanni Andrea Sirani was forced to start painting again. When the family estate was inventoried only one year after Elisabetta's death, the library, a few musical instruments, some furniture, painter's tools, and plaster casts remained, but Giovanni Andrea's collection and all of Elisabetta's paintings were gone.[137]

Contracts and Payments

Notarized contracts were the preferred form of agreement for public commissions. For private buyers, however, more casual agreements predominated. Receipt of delivery and payment might be recorded but rarely the original terms of agreement. For this reason, contracts remain our best source for sales information. A few examples will be cited. One of the more formal and well-defined contracts was drawn up in 1601 between Denis Calvaert and Marc'Antonio Seccadenari for an altarpiece depicting *Paradise* for the church of S. Maria dei Servi.[138] Witnessed by the painter Cesare Aretusi and the bricklayer Pietro de Mai, it specified the measurements, the iconography and composition (established by a small model by Calvaert), and the time frame for completion (two-and-a-half years). Confirmation of Calvaert's completion of the work and any disputes about the adherence to the terms of the contract would be adjudicated by a commission of experts. The payment in three installments and the presence of a penalty clause were economic incentives for compliance and were commonly used, as, for example, in a 1583 contract between Passerotti and the Gabella Grossa, the city's customs agency.[139] In both contracts, penalties were set at twice the price of the altarpiece. In addition to the economic clauses regarding penalties and withheld payments, a judicial review further encouraged compliance. Calvaert agreed to submit his finished work to a panel of experts, as did Ludovico Carracci for a *Conversion of Saint Paul* (Fig. 51) to be placed in the Zambeccari chapel in S. Francesco.[140] Other than the usual stipulations of deadline, size, subject, and payments towards expenses, the Carracci–Zambeccari contract included a rare clause concerning the visual qualities of the altarpiece: if, after its installation, the lighting conditions in the chapel required some retouching and revarnishing, then Ludovico would have to do so.

Contractual terms reflect a patron's confidence in the painter's honesty and reliability. Between 1618 and 1623, Tiarini signed several contracts with the members of the Madonna della Ghiara in Reggio Emilia. With each completed work, the board gained confidence in the painter and the contract conditions became less and less specific. In the board's words, Tiarini went from being a painter of "singular excellence" to a "most excellent painter" (*pittore eccelentissimo*). The one fixed condition concerned the painting's autograph status, namely that Tiarini and only Tiarini would do the work (that it be *di sua mano*).[141] This condition of authenticity appeared often in later Bolognese contracts. In 1680, Francesco Orsi, a trustee for the sanctuary of the Madonna del Fuoco in Forlì Cathedral, required of Carlo Cignani that "this work be of his own hand and creation, so that it will be known as truly of his own hand and work; and for his companion and assistant, in order to create and perfect said work, and in the painting of it, he cannot and must not take anyone other than Signor Felice his son."[142] In other words, the only exception to this rule would have Cignani's son doing some of the work, and not the group of helpers whom the painter usually brought along.

Deposits, another recurring contractual condition, were frequently given to established painters, who often were inundated with work, as a financial (and hence moral) claim on the artist's time in the future. The strategy did not always work. The overextended Reni received two deposits of 600 lire and 100 zecchini in 1631 and 1632 for an altarpiece of the *Assumption of the Virgin* (Alte Pinakothek, Munich). The commissioning confraternity of S. Maria degli Angeli in Spilamberto had to wait ten years for its completion. The length of delay is not so odd as the fact that, when the work was finished in 1642, Reni claimed that he never received the advance payments that had been deposited for him years earlier.[143] The confraternity capitulated. "Today we have paid him 500 ducatoni all at once," they noted in 1642, adding that "to the deliverer of the letter, we gave a gratuity of 4.2 lire."[144] Reni had to return many advances because he defaulted on his obligations. He was so famous and in such demand that he could flaunt the imperatives implied by deposits and penalties. After his death, his cousin offered either to return unfinished paintings to their buyers or to reimburse them; predictably, given the artist's fame, most chose the first option.[145]

A colorful borderline case, for all of its many implications for Reni and the city, was the commission of a large altarpiece representing the *Triumph of Job* (Notre Dame, Paris) to be placed in S. Maria dei Mendicanti in a chapel dedicated to St. Job and belonging to the guild of silk merchants.[146] The church of the Mendi-

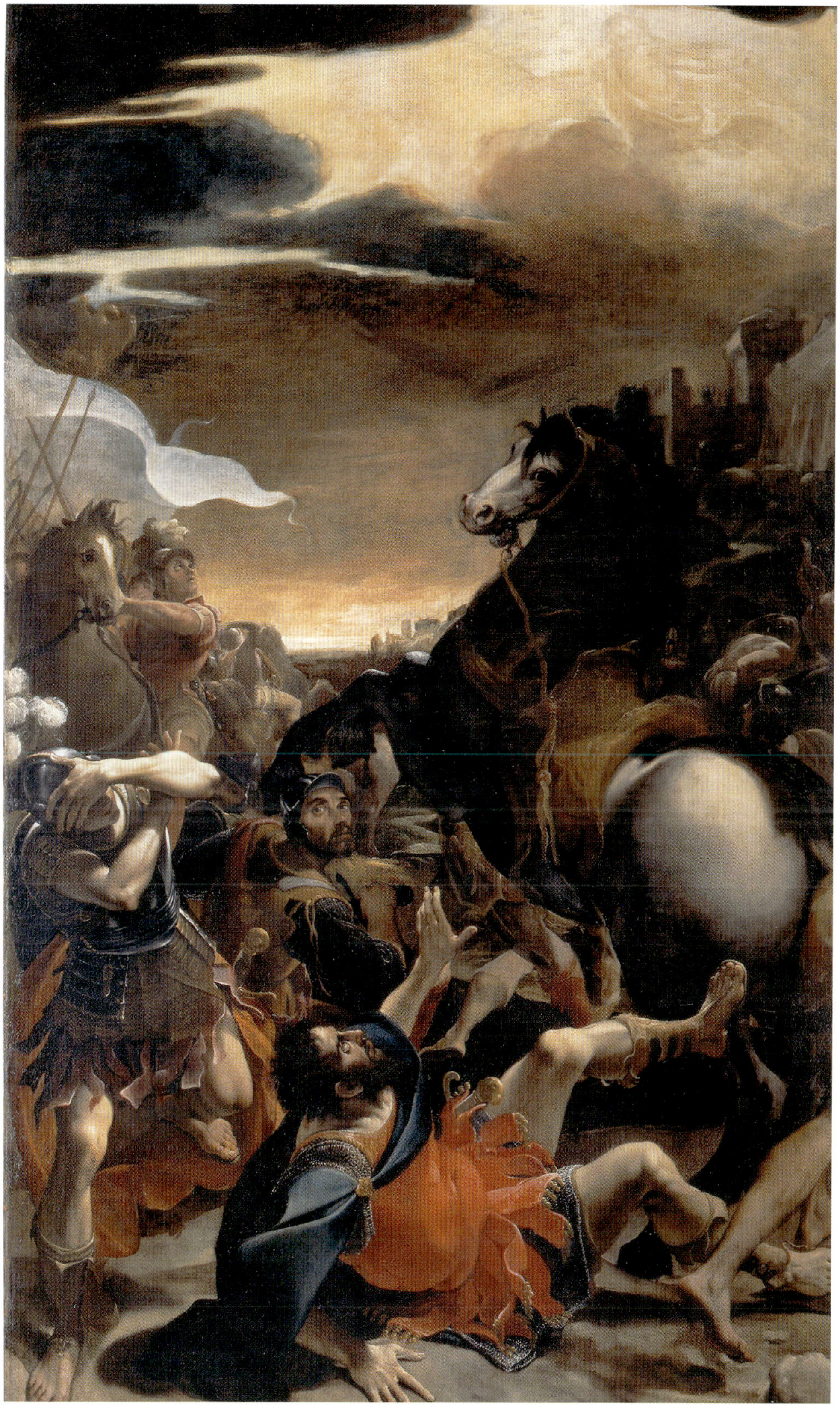

51 Ludovico Carracci, *Conversion of St. Paul*, 1587. Oil on canvas, 279 × 171 cm. Pinacoteca nazionale di Bologna.

canti represented the city's trades: each one acquired and decorated an individual chapel, commissioning Bologna's most fashionable painters. It was a type of contest between the most representative professions to demonstrate their religious devotion and their economic weight. As we have seen, in 1616 Reni already had delivered to the Bolognese Senate a monumental *Pietà* for the church (Fig. 48). Six years later, this richest of the guilds aimed to acquire even greater visibility in the church, and so they, too, naturally turned to "the greatest man in painting alive today in Europe . . . the Painter of Paradise."[147] When in 1622 the silk merchants commissioned their altarpiece from Reni, they had already spent 13,190 lire on the coat of arms carved in hard sandstone above the entrance, the two lateral columns brought from Parma, the polychromatic altar, and the other paintings. The contract is accompanied in the archives by a novelistic *Ricordo dell'accordo* made up of 35 pages that cover all the steps, interventions, speeches, decisions, and words exchanged in this 14-year affair. Never content with the payment he received, Reni kept raising his bid, starting with 3,000 lire, reaching 7,500 lire, and finalized at a record 9,500 lire.[148] Besides negotiating his contract, Reni breached it so seriously that alternatives were sought and Guercino and Domenichino contacted. In the end, the confraternity's chancellors accepted Reni's actions and demands, including a reduction in the number of figures from 25 to 18.[149] The deal closed with hostility.

The practice of gifting was central to the negotiations between painters and buyers. In Bologna, Ludovico Carracci, Reni, Guercino, Elisabetta Sirani, Carlo Cignani, and even the minor Giacomo Alboresi benefited from it. The gifts were extremely diverse: from medals offered by the community to gem-studded crosses, sets of silverware, pieces of extremely expensive cloth, majolica, and prized foodstuffs. Gifts went above and beyond the contractual relationship and spoke to the privileged relationship between the parties, the painter's honor, and the patron's munificence. As Guido Guerzoni noted, the social status of the artwork and the moral standing of its author were at stake.[150]

Pricing Pictures

How were paintings priced? Size, number of figures, and materials all played a role. These variables had less effect on still lifes, portraits, and landscapes, which were priced more by genre. Little is known about how smaller background figures might have influenced the cost of a painting. Prices also varied according to the painter's reputation, as Reni famously observed in 1628: a mediocre painter should ask for no more than 10 to 15 lire for each large figure; an "ordinary" painter, 45 to 50 lire; and an extraordinary one allows the buyer to determine the price. Painters could try to designate themselves as ordinary or extraordinary (who would choose to be mediocre?), but in the end it was the various art communities (dealers, collectors, patrons, other painters, and critics) that decided. Reni, in other words, described a market-driven pricing system. A related factor was the place of a painting within an artist's career. It is obvious that a young painter struggling to establish his reputation would not dare to make excessive demands regarding payment, but instead would be as concerned, if not more so, with winning the commission and carving out a niche in the market. A less obvious but more important factor involved the painting's function, whether it was intended for private or public use. Paintings on canvas for private residences were, amongst other things, a financial investment that could accrue value with time and add to a family's wealth. Public works, notably altarpieces, had social and religious functions, whether they were privately commissioned for a family chapel, commissioned by religious orders, or donated by benefactors to the congregation. (There were also public commissions, like Reni's banner for the plague ordered by the Bolognese Senate that filled official and celebratory roles, but they were quite rare.)

Another pricing variable arose from domestic and foreign markets. The lowest paid painters were those whose clientele were strictly local and whose prices were established solely within the context of the domestic market. More famous painters commanded higher prices at home because their reputations had been validated regionally, nationally, or internationally, and as a result their local prices could be leveraged using the higher prices from foreign commissions as their comparative scale. Not all painters exploited their national or international reputations. It seems that Tiarini and Albani chose not to benefit economically, while Reni certainly did.

With so many variables at play, and with no set hierarchy of factors or standard protocols of pricing, it is best to approach the problem of pricing through individual examples (see further data in Table 10 above). In 1594 Ludovico Carracci painted a large (375 × 223 cm) altarpiece of the *Vision of St. Hyacinth* for S. Domenico (Louvre, Paris). He was paid 250 lire, a high price that certainly was not typical at the time, even for a painting in an important church by a painter, such as Ludovico, at the peak of his fame.[151] The *Vision of St.*

Hyacinth became a standard for pricing that Ludovico himself quickly surpassed. In 1596 he received 600 lire for a larger altarpiece (438 × 286 cm) of the *Transfiguration* for S. Pietro Martire (Fig. 52).[152] Monsignor Dionigi Ratta, a high-ranking Bolognese prelate who intended to place the work in the main altar of the church, started negotiating with Ludovico in 1593, concluding in 1596. Ratta was determined to have Ludovico as the painter, despite the delays and high price, and despite a competing offer from the aged Prospero Fontana to paint it for a lower fee and in just three months.

These were the years, 1595 to 1600, when Reni appeared on the scene and entered into competition with Ludovico over the value of their works. In 1595 Reni painted a small *God the Father* (49.5 × 53 cm, private collection) intended as part of an altarpiece in S. Petronio. As a young painter needing publicity, Reni accepted just 16 lire.[153] Four years later, he executed the *Assumption of the Virgin* for the parish church of Pieve di Cento (*in situ*), a large altarpiece (400 × 280 cm) with about ten life-size figures, for which he received a payment of 462 lire.[154] The much higher price reflects not only its greater size and figural complexity, but also Reni's rising fame in Bologna and its provinces. Three years later while in Rome, Reni received an advance of 218 lire toward a total of 478 lire for a mural in S. Michele in Bosco, Bologna, of *St. Benedict Receiving Gifts from Farmers* (known through a replacement copy *in situ* by Giovanni Maria Viani).[155]

For Reni, Rome had opened the doors to a market that was superior to Bologna's, and so, from then on, he held his prices in line with Roman standards. The prices he charged in Rome were higher than those he could have expected in Bologna, although when he returned to his native city he tried to maintain their level. He succeeded in doing so with the *Pietà dei Mendicanti* (Fig. 48). Executed in 1616 for the Bolognese Senate, it was one of the most expensive works in seventeenth-century Bologna. As mentioned, Reni was paid 3,600 lire, plus a gold chain worth 200 lire and, in a public ceremony, was awarded a medal depicting the city of Bologna on one side and the words *Senatus bononiensis* on the other. Admittedly, the *Pietà* was unusually large (704 × 341 cm) and has some ten life-size figures, but the recompense of 3,800 lire was even larger.[156]

Compare his fee with that given to Cavedone, who in 1614 received 500 lire for three vault frescoes in the Arrigoni chapel in S. Paolo Maggiore: a *Circumcision*, *Jesus with the Doctors in the Temple*, and *Flight into Egypt*, each 200 × 250 cm, plus two oil paintings of the *Adoration of the Shepherds* (Fig. 53) and *Adoration of the Magi* (Fig. 54), each 237 × 138 cm. Cavedone's payment of 500 lire represents fair market pricing of large chapel decorations at the time.[157] Ten years later (1625) Cavedone's paintings for the Fabbretti chapel in the same church brought him 600 lire, which were similar in size but fewer in number.[158] During the intervening decade Cavedone did no work that would have enhanced his reputation, and the later paintings were no better in quality (and some say were much worse) than the earlier ones, and yet their price was higher.[159]

A far more complex story emerges when the ups and downs of Tiarini's prices during this period are examined. Tiarini received 600 lire for an imposing *St. Domenic Reviving a Newborn* painted during 1614–15 (Fig. 55).[160] Six hundred lire for a large work (600 × 340 cm) with about a dozen figures was a rather modest amount, though within market standards, and Tiarini might have assumed that having a painting in one of Bologna's most important churches would be a sound career investment. He was only partly right. In 1616 he received 480 lire for both *Esther before Ahasuerus* and *Judith and Holofernes* (S. Maria di Canepanova, Pavia), each with three or four figures and each 250 × 200 cm.[161] But in 1627 he received only 250 lire for *Abigail Receiving the Gifts of David* with seven figures and measuring 419 × 115 cm (S. Maria di Campagna, Piacenza).[162] The breakout work came in 1629 in Reggio Emilia (Madonna della Ghiara) where he received 1,040 lire for an *Ecstasy of St. Francis*.[163] It contains the equivalent of only five or six life-size figures on a canvas of relatively moderate dimensions (314 × 198 cm). A year earlier, in 1626, he had delivered an enormous canvas (500 × 635 cm) depicting the *Invention of the Rosary* (Museo Civico, Cremona). It was a prestige work, commissioned by the confraternity of the Rosary and assigned to Tiarini by the governor of Cremona. Possibly its quick completion, in only 40 days, was motivated by the substantial payment of 3,600 lire. Even for a large painting filled with about 14 figures, Tiarini's price was exceptional.[164] Only Guercino earned as much at this time: 4,000 lire for a large *Crucifixion* (440 × 245 cm, also for the Madonna della Ghiara), although five years earlier (1620) he was paid just 600 lire for the *Investiture of St. William* (345 × 231 cm) for S. Gregorio in Bologna.

From these examples it would appear that paintings executed outside Bologna tended to be valued more highly than those for the domestic market. Yet Domenichino's case tells a different story. In 1619 Pietro de' Carli commissioned him to paint an enormous *Martyrdom of St. Agnese* (533 × 342 cm) for S. Agnese (Pinacoteca nazionale di Bologna) with about 11 full-length

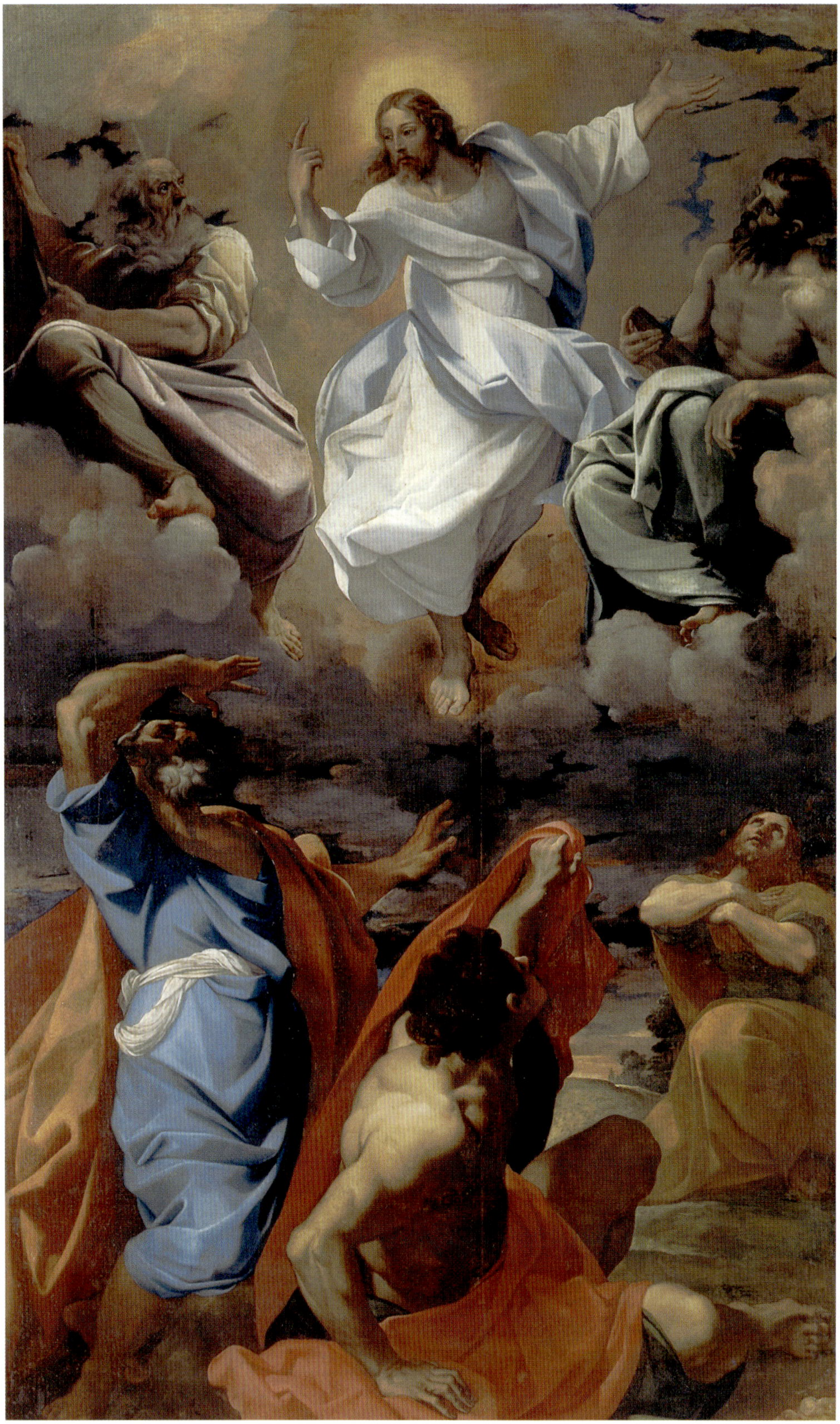

52 Ludovico Carracci, *Transfiguration*, 1595–96. Oil on canvas, 438 × 286 cm. Pinacoteca nazionale di Bologna.

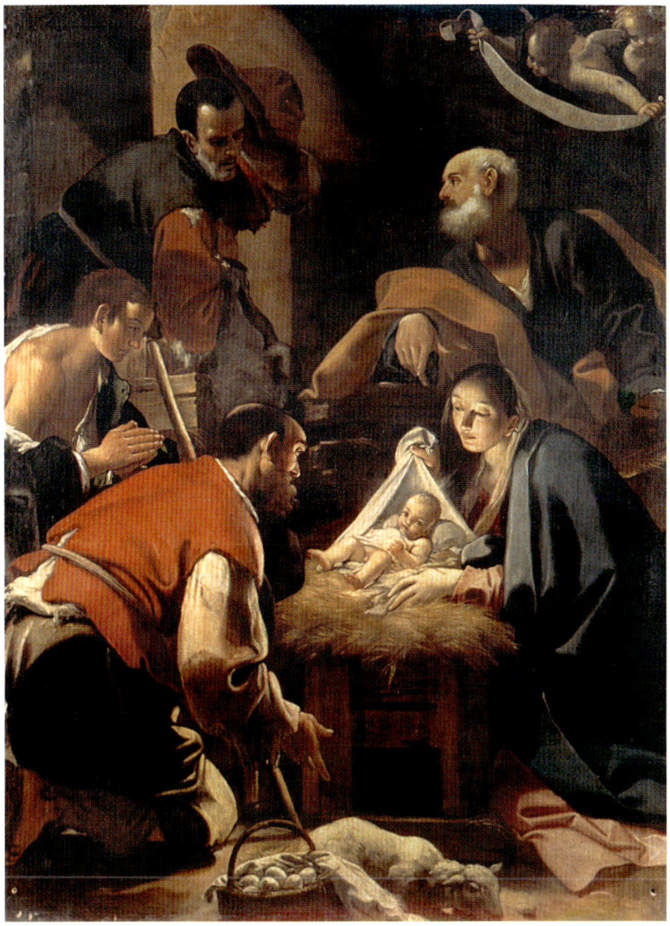

53 Giacomo Cavedone, *Adoration of the Shepherds*, 1614. Oil on canvas, 237 × 183 cm. S. Paolo Maggiore, Bologna.

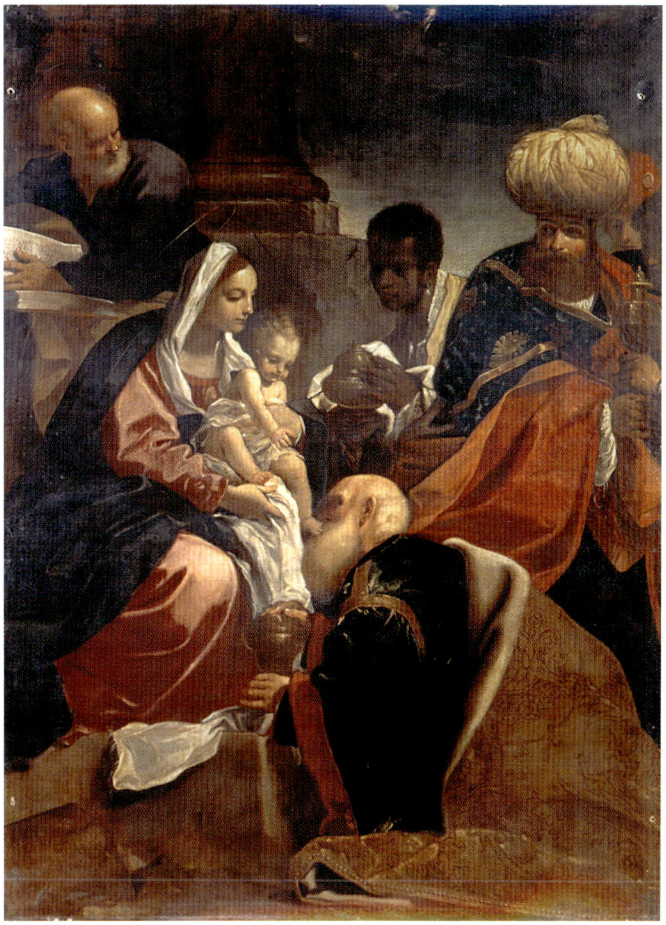

54 Giacomo Cavedone, *Adoration of the Magi*, 1614. Oil on canvas, 237 × 183 cm. S. Paolo Maggiore, Bologna.

figures, and paid Domenichino the astronomical sum of 1,200 scudi (6,000 lire).[165] Nonetheless, Domenichino's *Madonna of the Rosary* for S. Giovanni in Monte (Pinacoteca nazionale di Bologna), a painting of the same period with similar features—498 × 289 cm and a few more figures—cost much less: 2,000 lire.[166]

Like so many artists, Albani set different prices for different patrons. He charged Maurizio di Savoia, the brother of Duke Vittorio Amedeo I, 1,000 lire for each of the famous four elements: *Fire*, *Air*, *Water*, and *Earth* (each 180 cm diameter, Galleria Sabauda, Turin).[167] A few years later, Albani executed a monumental *Annunciation* for the Fioravanti chapel in S. Bartolomeo di Porta Ravegnana (Fig. 56) that was so widely admired it was nicknamed "dal bell'angelo" (the Annunciation of the beautiful angel). He was paid 800 lire for a painting with just two life-size figures (albeit with a crowd of smaller ones).[168] Between 1639 and 1641 the Gozzadini family paid Albani 1,000 lire for the *St. Andrew Adoring the Cross of his Martyrdom* (Fig. 57).[169]

After the 1630s, prices of well-established painters remained more or less stable until late in the century. They rose slightly with the fashionable Carlo Cignani, who, as early as 1661, earned 1,000 lire for a *Madonna and Child with Sts. John the Baptist, Theresa, and Carlo Borromeo* for S. Lucia (Fig. 58). Ten years later, the electress of Bavaria, Adelaide Enrichetta of Savoy, commissioned from Cignani a *Holy Family with King David* (Theatinerkirche, Munich). It was larger and had more figures than the S. Lucia altarpiece, but not enough to explain the fourfold price differential (4,000 lire). The higher price probably reflected the patron's lofty status.[170]

Table 10 includes representative altarpieces painted in Bologna and for nearby communities, with reference to their original locations when known. Prices are in lire; payments made in other currencies have been converted into lire for consistency.

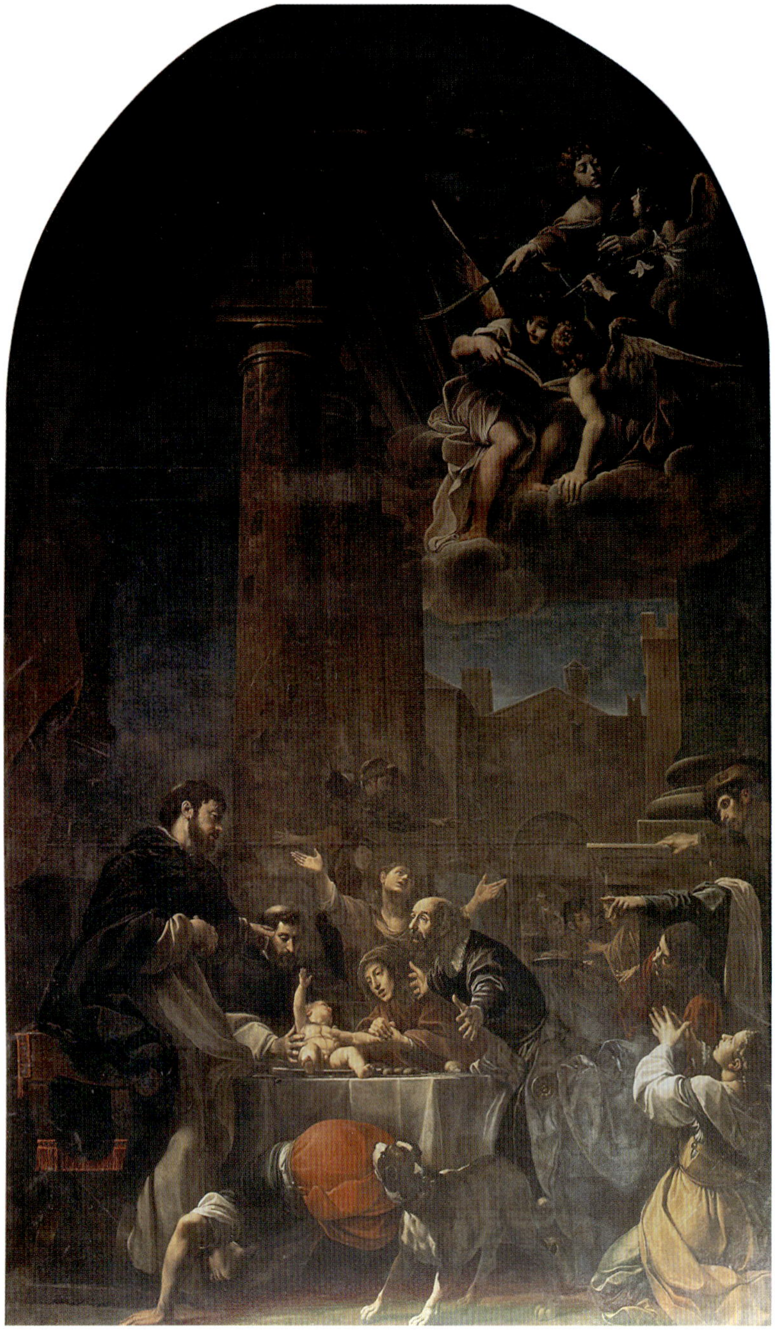

55 Alessandro Tiarini, *St. Domenic Reviving a Newborn*, 1614–15. Oil on canvas, 600 × 340 cm. S. Domenico, Bologna.

Frescoes

Lionello Spada was certainly right when he declared that the "laws of plenty" harmed those "who worked the most and earned the least."[171] He was referring to a dispute about his payment for frescoes in the palace of Silvio Albergati in via Saragozza, Bologna.[172] After repeated objections Denis Calvaert and Bartolomeo Cesi were called in as expert appraisers.[173] Spada was known as a bully and meddler, and might even have put himself in a difficult position. He had not wanted to establish a price before starting his work despite Albergati's wishes. While on the job, he expected to be given an unlimited supply of food, outstayed his

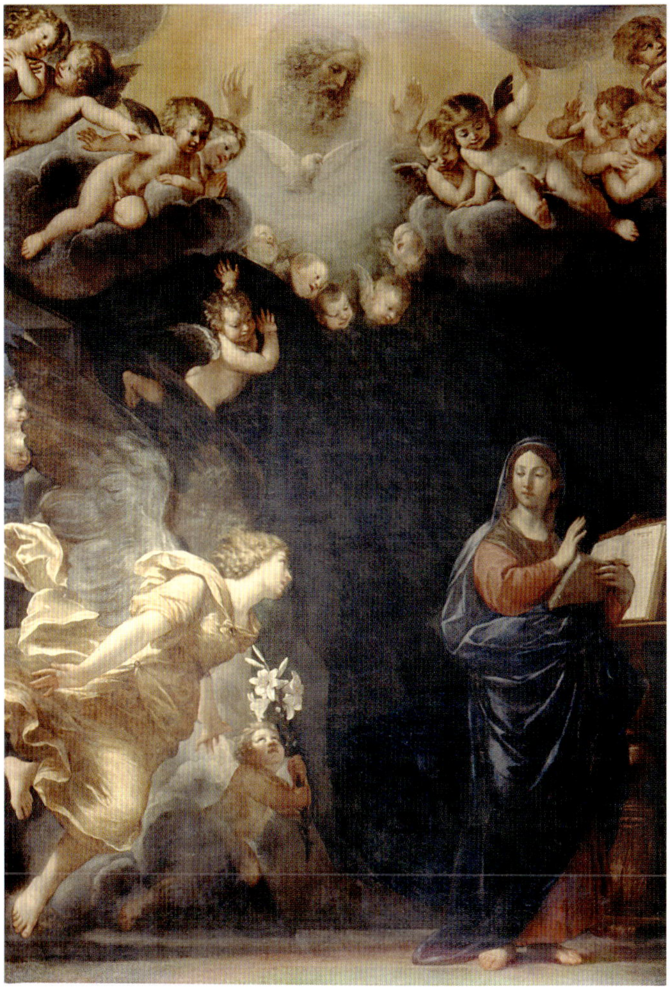

56 Francesco Albani, *Annunciation*, 1632. Oil on canvas, 365 × 295 cm. S. Bartolomeo di Porta Ravegnana, Bologna.

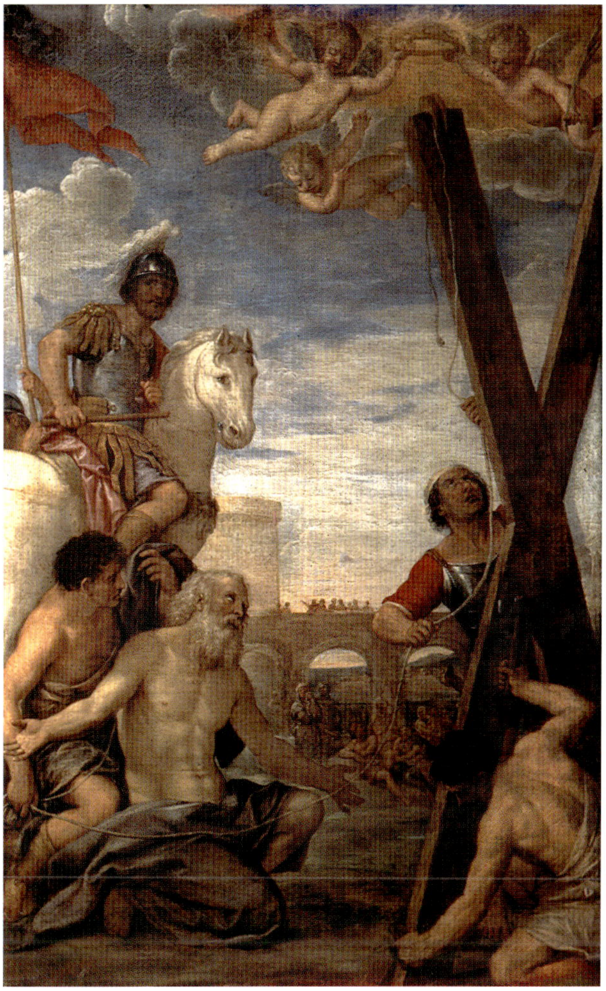

57 Francesco Albani, *St. Andrew Adoring the Cross of his Martyrdom*, 1639–41. Oil on canvas, 400 × 200 cm. S. Maria dei Servi, Bologna.

welcome, and Malvasia reported that he constructed a pyramid of bones in the center of the room from the animals he had eaten during his stay! As if that were not enough, over the pyramid he placed a sign reading *Funerale alla morte cuccagna* (Funeral of the Death Feast). His bizarre behavior contravened a fundamental principle of professional conduct, not to mention basic hygiene, treating Albergati's palace as his own and as if he were a Reni, when he was nothing of the sort.

Frescoes in Bologna were less profitable than oils on canvas. Unlike in Rome and Naples, early in the seventeenth century they were relatively rare. Despite such famous exceptions as the cycles by the Carracci in the Palazzo Fava and Palazzo Magnani and the multi-authored cycle in S. Michele in Bosco, most frescoes at the time were simple decorative friezes, inserts, or isolated figures, such as over fireplaces. Later in the century, however, the pleasing techniques of skyscapes and scenographic architecture helped make frescoes more popular in Bologna and predictably led to the rise of specialists. Prices for frescoes likewise rose with their increased popularity. The highest fee paid to a Bolognese painter working in Emilia was 1,900 ducatoni (15,200 lire) for Guercino's cupola in the Piacenza Duomo, a whopping sum for a commission already one-quarter finished by Morazzone and with relatively few figures. It took Guercino one-and-a half years (May 1626 to November 1627), although he probably painted some canvases during that time as well.[174]

Another high return for a fresco commission was the 10,400 lire earned by Tiarini for decorating the Madonna della Ghiara in Reggio Emilia from 1619 to 1623, an impressive sum but one that required the artist

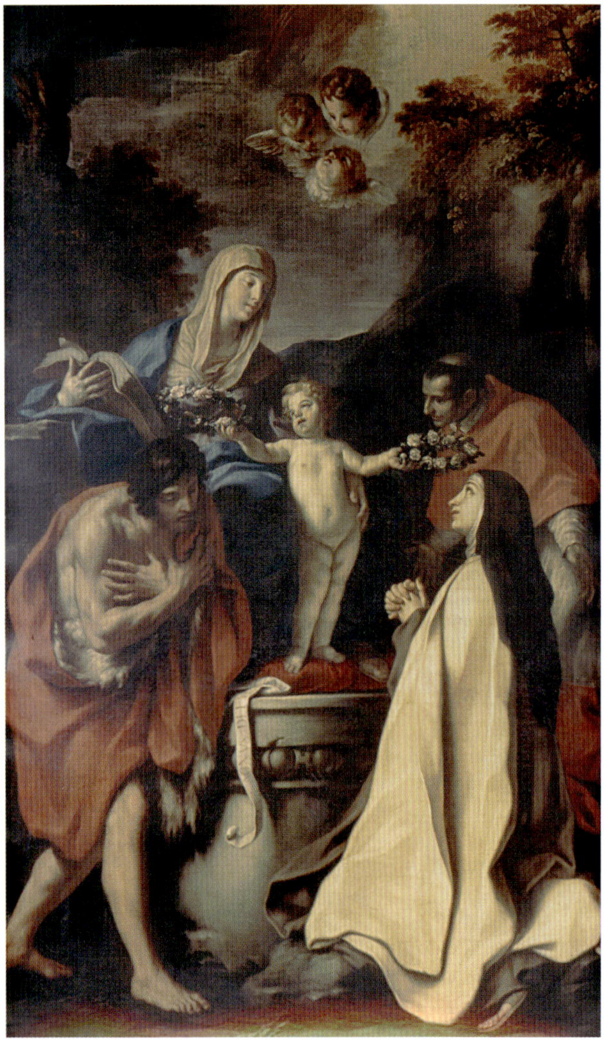

58 Carlo Cignani, *Madonna and Child with Sts. John the Baptist, Theresa, and Carlo Borromeo*, 1661. Oil on canvas, 385 × 229 cm. Pinacoteca nazionale di Bologna.

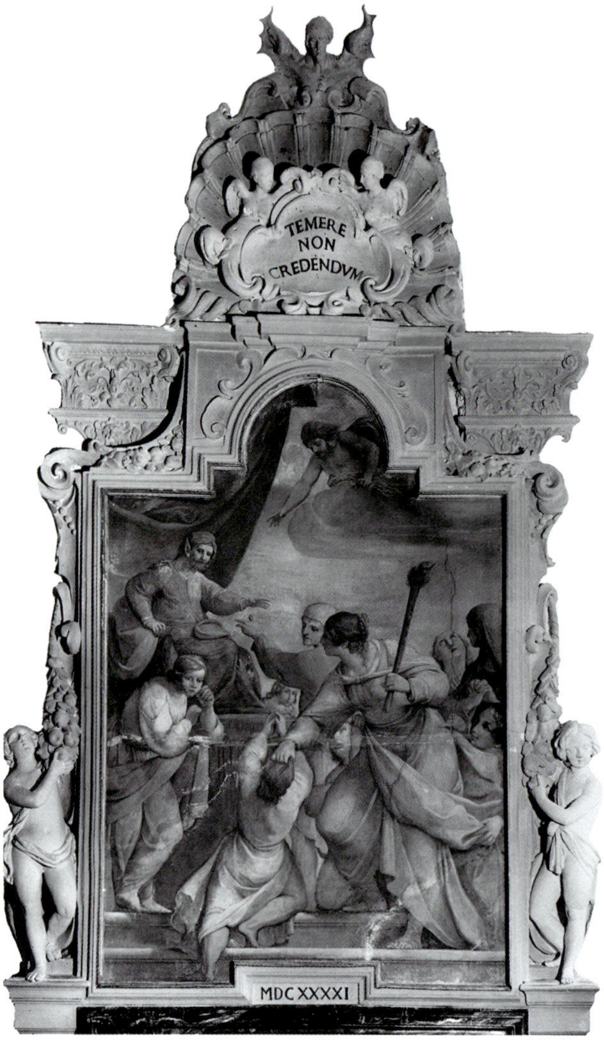

59 Alessandro Tiarini, *Calumny of Apelles*, 1640. Fresco. Convent of S. Procolo, Bologna.

to pay for "the best colors possible." Tiarini earned 1,312 lire and 3,150 lire for two other fresco cycles in Parma for the Farnese.[175] However problematic it may be to compare these prices, it is clear that Bolognese fresco painters never achieved the earning power of Lanfranco and Domenichino in Naples. The sums paid to Tiarini in 1630 and in 1640 for the *Nativity of the Virgin* in S. Maria dei Servi and the *Calumny of Apelles* in the convent of S. Procolo (Fig. 59) were of decidedly lesser value: 250 and 160 lire respectively.[176] From the late sixteenth century on, fresco decoration had a relatively stable price that was contingent on the number of figures, which surprisingly was unaffected by the price variations over time for oil paintings and the forces of the market, exchange, trade, and collecting.

Quadratura frescoes, however, had a different pricing structure than figure painting. For a confirmation of these claims, and a revealing spreadsheet of the costs and benefits of fresco painting, we turn to the account book kept by the *quadratura* painter Giacomo Alboresi, who made meticulous notes on every commission.[177] Because both his payments and time spent are always mentioned, we are in a unique position to gauge the relation of time to cost. Working with Canuti, Alboresi took just ten weeks to decorate a room in the Palazzo Fantetti, for which he received 500 lire. During the next two weeks, he worked on other commissions earning 100 lire. Although that work differed in type and complexity, the pay scale of 50 lire per week remained the same. His profits, however, would vary since normally he was expected to pay for colors, lime, and scaffolding. These could total about 30 to 40 percent of the contract's value.[178] For the entire year of 1664, Alboresi earned a total of 964 lire after expenses. This amount clearly is not comparable to earnings by Guercino, Reni, Albani, or Tiarini, but for a simple fresco painter it meant a good living. In contrast, Colonna signed a contract in 1665 to fresco the vault of S. Bartolomeo, with Alboresi's help, for some 5,500 lire, with an end date of 14 December 1666.[179]

Conclusion

When standing back from this survey, the problems that beset such a study come into focus: notably the diversity of issues involved and the inconsistency of available data. Those disparities, which are inevitable in the state of current research, are especially apparent when one considers the scarcity of contracts and payments, and our ability to understand the complexities of the motivations behind them. Nonetheless, a plausible picture emerges, which is unimaginable only on the basis of traditional catalogues of artists and their work or on isolated documents. It reveals the extraordinary vitality of the painters' profession in Bologna and the ability of painters to survive in impressive numbers, both within and outside the Compagnia dei Pittori and private academies. If it might be objected that the two bright stars of Bolognese painting, Reni and Guercino, have unduly cast their shadows over this study, it is on the basis of their politics of pricing that one can measure the successes and failures of other painters and their market support. For Reni, Guercino, and all of the others, it is crucial to bear in mind the influential role of social origins, education, and status in Bologna, and their potential effects on patrons' relations with painters.

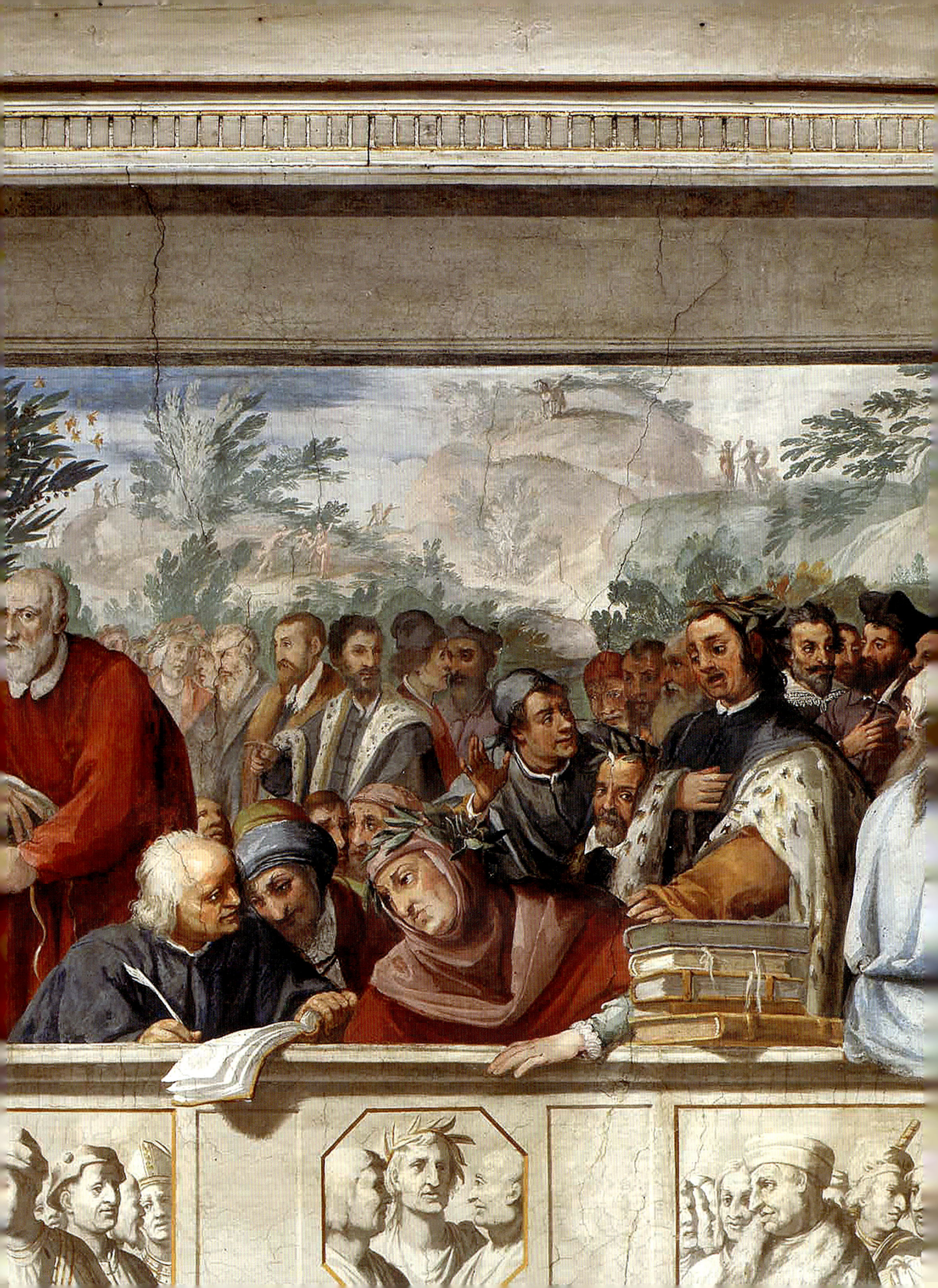

4

Florence

ELENA FUMAGALLI

The Painter's Life

The Medici court was central to the political, social, and economic life of seventeenth-century Florence and must therefore be considered in relation to the city's artistic life. A mature court apparatus began evolving under the reign of Ferdinand I (1587–1609) and was consolidated under Cosimo II (1609–21), Ferdinand II (1628–70), and Cosimo III (1670–1723).[1] Recently, historians have shown how the court functioned as an "'economic institution' because it represented a concentration of the ruling class, because it formed the focal point for a wide variety of products, services, and financial flows, because it established models for behavior and consumption, and because it managed clientels, public and private businesses, information, and decisions."[2]

Apart from this aspect of the Medici court as an economic institution, which needs further study, the city's economy was still based on its traditional strengths: the wool and silk industries, which provided employment for about 30 percent of the city's 70,000 inhabitants. Yet the local economy was in decline both in the agricultural sector and in commerce and industry, which had been weakened above all by the loss of several different markets; particularly tough crises hit Florence in 1619–22 and 1629–30, with recovery coming only at the end of the century.[3] The currency in use was the silver scudo (or piastra or ducato), which equalled 7 lire; 1 lira equalled 20 soldi; 1 soldo was worth 12 denari.

How Many Painters Were There?

Calculating the number of painters in seventeenth-century Florence is difficult. Not all painters belonged to the Accademia del Disegno—even fewer in the second half of the century, at a time when Florentine nobles increasingly requested to join—and, as a result, the institution's documents are only partially useful in calculating how many of the city's residents made a living from painting.[4]

Some interesting proposals can be made on the basis of the *Descritione del numero delle case e delle persone della città di Firenze fatta l'anno MDCXXXII distinta a quartieri*, a census that provides both places of residence and the composition of each family unit, including servants.[5] The indication of a person's job beside his name is very frequent, if not always complete, and this sets an initial limitation on statistics concerning painters. Furthermore, while the census includes Florence's four *quartieri* (S. Spirito, S. Croce, S. Maria Novella, S. Giovanni), it excludes the city's outlying areas. It is important to note that this census was taken after the plague that raged through Tuscany in the early 1630s. In total, the population included 66,056 people, 29,837 male and 36,219 female (of these, 916 were clerics and 4,001 were nuns). Seventy-four painters are recorded: 68 with the title of *pittore* and 6 as *dipintore*. The latter term probably referred to a category of artisans, people who only painted everyday items like furniture. For some painters,

Facing page: detail of Fig. 60

only the first name was given (as was the case with all the *dipintori*), and although it was sometimes accompanied by the patronymic, it is nearly impossible to identify them. Thanks to primary sources and archival documents, others are more or less known to us.

If having servants was a sign of economic standing, the 1632 census contains some surprises since even painters who are practically unknown today enjoyed this privilege. Single women servants were recorded as living in the houses of Giovanni Bilivert, Giovambattista di Galeazzo Ghidoni, Matteo Confortini, Michelangelo Cinganelli, Francesco Furini, Carlo Dolci, Cesare Landini, Jacopo Vignali, Matteo Rosselli, Domenico Casini, "Stefano pittore," Francesco Curradi, Bartolomeo Salvestrini, "Francesco pittore," and Francesco Ligozzi; two women were with Nicodemo d'Agnolo Ferrucci, Benedetto Veli, Andrea Commodi, and Gio. Coccapani; and one man and two women served in Giusto Sustermans's house. Of the 68 painters in the 1632 census, half belonged to the Accademia del Disegno.[6] Only three were not Italian: "Marchionne Focalar Tedesco," "Gio Fiammingo" (perhaps Jan Fyt), and the previously mentioned Giusto Sustermans.[7]

Expenses

Although archival research yields significant information on the earnings of painters, as discussed in the following sections, their expenses can be reconstructed only in a fragmentary manner. The Accademia del Disegno's records and artists' biographies are often revealing, not only about the financial status of well-known painters but also of the second rank and even the unknown: that is, groups different from those usually studied by art historians.[8] Information provided by printed sources and archival documents makes it possible to sketch a preliminary portrait of the material conditions within which painters lived and worked.

A fixed and unavoidable expense involved the renting of a workshop and house, which were sometimes, though not always, one and the same. In 1620, for example, the brothers Domenico and Valore Casini, both portraitists, were working in via della Scala, where they rented space from Marquis Jacopo di Lorenzo Salviati. They paid 30 scudi per year for it, a sizeable amount when compared with similar cases.[9] Jacopo Chiavistelli kept a workshop in some of Gherardo Frescobaldi's rooms "just after the Santa Trinita bridge" ("sceso il ponte Santa Trinita") in the 1650s and 1660s; he paid 7 scudi every six months, or 14 scudi annually, not even half of what the Casini brothers spent.[10] There are numerous documents regarding the rent paid by Cecco Bravo, about 7 lire (1 scudo) per month; often he settled his debts owed to his landlords with paintings.[11] Although it is difficult to assess these sums without descriptions of the properties in question, it is certain that rent affected the painter's monthly budget. A passage from Baldinucci's life of Fabrizio Boschi confirms this: "A great man, who highly valued [Boschi's] *virtù*," paid a visit to Boschi in his studio and inquired about the rent for his workshop and home. Since the (unrecorded) amount seemed excessive to him, he advised the artist to save by producing a few more paintings.[12]

The cost of materials was, at least in part, usually covered by the patron (and almost always for the ultramarine blue, the most expensive pigment), yet for lack of information it is not possible to determine how much the painter typically paid. Except for an account of colors provided to Luca Giordano in 1685 while he was working for Marquis Francesco Riccardi, prices of pigments in seicento Florence have not been precisely established.[13]

Then there was the cost of models, about which there is detailed information in Baldinucci's life of Furini. The painter reportedly spent a great amount to obtain female models (whom he paid from 10 to 14 lire per day, or up to 2 scudi, quite a considerable amount). Indeed, this sometimes cost the painter more than "a head with bust, for which he was normally paid ten doble [approximately 27 scudi]."[14] Baldinucci's account of the high cost of using models is confirmed indirectly in a letter written in 1645 by Furini while he was working in Rome for Duke Jacopo di Lorenzo Salviati. In it, the painter complained about the lack of female models in Rome, "despite the fact that I have spent what in Florence would have allowed me to complete ten of these paintings."[15]

Other fixed expenses included the monthly salary for the artist's assistants.[16] The particular family circumstances of each painter, however, must be considered case by case, since some, but not all, of them were the head of a large family with a wife, children, and a variety of relatives.

Painters, Dealers, Merchants

It seems to have been the prerogative of second-tier painters, who could not rely on direct commissions, to sell their work on the open market. The subject of the art market is noticeably absent from Baldinucci's *Notizie* because he was writing about well-known artists. The only significant exception occurs in the life of Furini, where the artist's youthful years in Rome with Giovanni Mannozzi (called Giovanni da San Giovanni) are described. Baldinucci recounts how Furini tied to "sell something made by Giovanni to art dealers, but this rarely succeeded, and for only a little money" (Baldinucci then tells a story about the sale of a *storietta* by Mannozzi for 10 giuli, "a price only slightly greater than that of a bare canvas").[17]

The later biographies by Francesco Saverio Baldinucci (Filippo's son) and Giovan Camillo Sagrestani more often mention the sale of paintings on the market, and do not fail to emphasize how painting for *rigattieri* (secondhand dealers) was the sign of a second-rate artist. This type of judgment was used for a clearly derogatory purpose in the polemic between Pier Dandini and Antonio Franchi about the latter's disappointing portrayal in the *Abcedario pittorico* by Pellegrino Orlandi (1704), whom Dandini had provided with information about Florentine painters. Among the negative assessments of Dandini collected by Franchi in revenge, one came from the Lucca-born architect Domenico Martinelli, who pointedly claimed that Dandini could only paint for *rigattieri*.[18]

Toward the end of his career as a decorator, Antonio Giusti became a habitué of *rigattieri*. Having fallen on hard times,

> he once again began doing oil paintings, mostly of landscapes and animals of all types . . . to the point that, having amassed no small amount of money, he had the urge . . . not to satisfy his creditors, but rather, having left the painter's profession, to deal in paintings and to make decorations [nastri a opera] of all types. And therefore he had various foreign and relatively unknown painters produce paintings, which he then sold by the dozen to secondhand dealers and shopkeepers, at prices which at times were so low that he even took a loss and instead was satisfied with what he earned from his own [works]—these too were painted fast and without care.[19]

In other words, as he aged, Giusti became "more a trader than a painter," and employed other artists like the landscapist Jona Ostilio, a certain Vittor ("an excellent painter of animals"), and Pandolfo Reschi, all of whom were specialists in genre painting.[20]

Understandably it was this last category of painters who, according to the biographers' accounts, mainly sold their works through middlemen on the art market. In this context, the obscure Antonio Bracciolini becomes interesting. If we are to believe Francesco Saverio Baldinucci, Bracciolini devoted himself to painting battle scenes, "believing that he could thereby improve his [financial] situation since at that time there was no painter in Florence who worked in these."[21] Early eighteenth-century biographers also provide a thorough portrait of Bracciolini and record his work for dealers. Baldinucci mentions Guido Bellini, "a secondhand dealer, great friend of his and hoarder of ordinary paintings" ("rigattiere suo grand'amico e grande incettatore di quadri volgari"), while Sagrestani names Domenico Tronci.[22]

Painters sometimes worked for the art market at the end of their careers, like Giusti and Atanasio Bimbacci, another fairly prominent decorator who, at the end of his working life, "moved into a little room on the piazza S. Pulinari, working for secondhand dealers."[23] This happened early in some artists' careers as well, according to Francesco Saverio Baldinucci's account of the young Bartolomeo Bimbi. Bimbi was asked by "a most civil citizen with excellent taste in painting and a merchant of paintings more than any other thing, called Bettin Francesco Seminati" to copy works by Carlo Dolci "to send them to many places over there, beyond the mountains, for a great price, due to the reputation that they deservedly had in those regions."[24]

To judge from a contemporary witness, so too did Pandolfo Reschi. Newly arrived in Florence, "not knowing where to take shelter, he went to an inn called della Rosa in the via de' Calzaioli, where he made some small paintings that he sold, with the innkeeper's assistance, to the dealer Troni in piazza d'Orto S. Michele." Troni exhibited them in his workshop, where they were noticed by Antonio Giusti, who tracked down Reschi and invited him to come live with him. Reschi appears to have stayed for about seven years, evidently working for Giusti most of the time.[25]

The Accademia del Disegno's documents shed light on certain workshops in seicento Florence that sold paintings because, if the relationship between a painter and a *rigattiere* degenerated, the legal proceedings were heard by its tribunal. In 1692, for instance, the painter Giuliano di Andrea Penci cited "Santi Cavallini dealer at the Duomo" for having paid him only 17 scudi for five canvases that, according to the artist, were actually worth more than 30. Penci was supposed to be paid "half in goods and half in cash," but Cavallini only gave him "a used quilt, a pair of bad, used sheets, a bad and torn dressing gown, and a painting with an old-style frame" that, altogether, were worth 4 scudi at most.[26]

Besides selling through dealers, artists could access markets outside the city by participating in trade fairs or collaborating with others to export their work. Giovanni Maria Casini, who was the father of the portraitists Domenico and Valore, accumulated a sizeable fortune over his life and ultimately left his sons with personal property and real estate.[27] In 1598, he went to the Pisa fair with eight canvases by Andrea Boscoli (no doubt in addition to his own works). He sold two of them, paid Boscoli, and returned the others to him.[28] In 1602 and 1603, Casini appears to have been a partner—along with Zanobi Serzelli and later also Curzio Cerrini—in selling 150 of his own paintings (for the most part of animals and fruits) on the Palermo market and 60 in Seville. In Spain 48 paintings were sold for 2,000 reals (roughly 150 scudi), prompting a lawsuit on behalf of Giovanni Maria that, although it dragged on after his death, asserted his claim (as well as his partners') to one-third of the revenue.[29]

Only in rare cases is there evidence of painters buying and selling other artists' work. Filippo Baldinucci discusses the practice in reference to Passignano, who was "hired to appraise highly valued paintings and other similar things."[30] Francesco Saverio Baldinucci notes that Pier Dandini returned from a trip to northern Italy with canvases "that were sold for a high price," while during a trip to the Marche the unknown Santi Rinaldi, a painter of landscapes and battles and a student of Francesco Furini, "had the good luck to see, in public and private places, various paintings by Titian, Barocci, Carracci, and other famous painters. From this experience, he had the idea to take note of the paintings and their prices, with the names of their owners, and proposed them to His Majesty, the Most Christian King Louis XIV of France, who had already felt the desire to decorate and enrich the marvelous villa of Fontainebleau" (but once he arrived in Paris, the project did not succeed).[31]

Earning "by day, or by appraisal, or on salary"

"On Salary"

Given the central role of the grand ducal court in Florentine life, it is clear why painters might aspire to gain employment there. On 3 September 1588, Ferdinand I named Emilio de' Cavalieri, a Roman nobleman loyal to the duke, superintendent of all the artists working for the Galleria dei Lavori of the Uffizi, where *pietre dure* (semi-precious stones) were manufactured for the Medici—the origin of the present Opificio delle Pietre Dure.[32] The document of appointment categorizes artists according to the way they were paid, "by day, or by appraisal, or on salary."[33] These three categories provide a general summary of the artists' main earning categories and, at least in part, correspond to their social standing.

Payment "by day" was the lowest level, since it placed the artist on the same footing as socially inferior trades like bricklayers and farmhands.[34] Payment "by appraisal," whereby earnings were derived from payments for individual works, was the most common. The total sum was not always determined in advance and often was only finalized after the work's completion; this could lead to arguments between artist and patron, which were sometimes brought to the tribunal of the Accademia del Disegno.

To be "on salary," usually a monthly stipend, was undoubtedly less common, even though there are numerous references to it in documents and literary sources. Based on an agreement, the artist committed to work exclusively for his employer (with the exception of special dispensations); in exchange, the artist received a fixed monthly salary and, from time to time, an additional payment for the works that he completed. Normally the salary or *provvisione* did not include room and board, which were provided separately, but perhaps the term at times referred more generally to the total amount of money required to support oneself for a month. Certainly, the *provvisione* held symbolic (not just economic) value, since it was a sign of the patron's respect for the painter.[35] Indeed, if one compares the total monthly salary with the payment for an individual work, the latter amount will always appear to be higher than the former. Nevertheless, the advantage of a fixed monthly income should not be underestimated; nor should the other privileges enjoyed by the patron's "family" when installments and payments for paintings could often be irregular and delayed.

Warren Kirkendale's studies of musicians in the service of the Medici have clarified the methodological problems involved in conducting documentary research on "the court establishment," particularly as regards the relationship between artists and the grand ducal court.[36] Among the salaried artists at the Medici court, there were few painters: the preferred relationship with them was defined as *a stima* (on appraisal) and was based on the payment for an individual work. Furthermore, the majority of salaried artists came from other cities. Evidently, the *provvisione* was the best way to keep them in Florence. Between the end of the sixteenth and the first two decades of the seventeenth centuries, salaried painters at the grand ducal court appear to have been affiliated with the Galleria dei Lavori, but this practice declined during the seventeenth century.

Some artists might have considered salaried employment at court to be too limiting. Such seems to have been the case with Ludovico Cigoli, according to the biography written by his nephew Giovan Battista Cardi. Ferdinand I is recorded as having made several offers for "*provvisione* and rooms in the Galleria," which the artist always refused out of a love of freedom and in order to follow his personal interests.[37] A similar account, from later on, concerns Cosimo Ulivelli. According to an anonymous biographer, after Cosimo III had bestowed a favor on the artist, he gave him "a room in the Royal Gallery to have him ready for every occasion. But, as [Ulivelli] was preoccupied by his desire to find a wife, . . . he failed to frequent the gallery and, deaf and mute to Capponi's invitations [Ferrante Capponi, member of the grand ducal court], and after various warnings from him, his key [to the gallery] was taken away from him along with the prince's esteem."[38]

From an examination of the rolls of the Medici court from the grand duchies of Ferdinand I to Cosimo III, one can conclude that the monthly salary of an artist was on average higher than that of other salaried members of the court. However, among the artists, the painter's salary was not the highest. The top salary went to the engineer. Next, more or less in order, came the architect, sculptor, cutter of semi-precious stones, and goldsmith; the painter appears to have been at about the same level as these last two, while the miniaturist and engraver were paid less. This ranking of salary levels remained in place throughout the century, and underscored the precise hierarchy of the various specializations.

The artist's salary not only encumbered the state treasury (Depositeria generale); it also came from other sources like the Guardaroba, the office responsible for managing the collection of art objects and other items belonging to the court,[39] or the prince's Camera, his most intimate circle.[40] One could receive a salary without being on the grand ducal payroll, just as one could be included—and thereby benefit from its many privileges—without being paid a monthly salary. For example, this was the case with Cristofano Allori, who was enrolled in 1611 and in February 1616 obtained an enormous loan worth 2,000 scudi in order to pay off his debts; the money was to be returned within three years and, instead of interest, would be "paid off with brushstrokes."[41] In 1620, when the artist was very ill and close to death, he begged the grand duke to cancel his debt by acquiring all the paintings he had started for him, the grand duchess, and the Guardaroba, with the suggestion that they be completed by his student Zanobi Rosi.[42] Among the painters in Cosimo II's rolls who "did not receive a salary but enjoyed privileges," we also find Jacopo Ligozzi (who was reintegrated only in the last months of Cosimo's reign), Giovanni da San Giovanni, Jacopo Chimenti da Empoli, Filippo Furini, and Cosimo Lotti.[43]

Between the end of the sixteenth and the first decades of the seventeenth centuries, the salaried painters at the grand ducal court belonged essentially to the group of those who were employed by the Galleria dei Lavori. The Veronese painter Jacopo Ligozzi was a noteworthy example. He arrived in Florence in 1577 at Francesco I's behest and received a monthly salary of 25 scudi until at least 1591. This was a sizeable amount, given that the only other artist to receive the same salary at the time was the sculptor Giambologna, while Bartolomeo Ammannati and Bernardo Buontalenti received only 20 and 10 scudi respectively.[44] As long as Francesco I was alive, Ligozzi was provided with lodging for himself and his family, as well as a servant, and a workshop at the Casino di San Marco. However, when Ferdinand I succeeded Francesco in 1587, the painter had to move his studio to the Uffizi and lost his lodgings. He rented a house in via Larga, but as early as January 1589 he petitioned the grand duke to cover the additional expense.[45]

As of 1593, Ligozzi was no longer included in the list of salaried members of the Medici court and no longer had a studio at the Uffizi. From a letter of his dated 1603 to Grand Duchess Christina of Lorraine, we learn that his sudden change of employment conditions was precipitated by his employment outside the court, which had been reported by the Medici's Guardaroba. Ligozzi continued to work occasionally for the Medici—he was still included in the grand ducal rolls but without receiving a salary—until 1620, when he wrote to Cosimo II in order to obtain a *provvisione* once again.[46] From August of that year he received 15 scudi until his death in 1627.[47]

The reduction in Ligozzi's salary from its level during the reigns of Francesco I and Ferdinand I is related to a broader change at court. In particular, it was the result of a drastic reassessment of the gallery's expenses announced in December 1620 in a letter written by Christina of Lorraine to the Guardaroba Maggiore Vincenzo Giugni, in which she asked him, on behalf of Cosimo II, to reduce expenses "starting the following February 1."[48] Cosimo II died just then, in February 1621. This date coincided with the distancing of many artists whom Ferdinand I's successor had maintained on a court salary and sometimes in a familial relationship.[49] Among those affected were Jacques Callot, who in 1614 had board and then 8 scudi per month, and the painter Filippo Napoletano, who came to the court in 1617 and was paid 18 scudi per month.[50]

Furthermore, starting in 1611 Cosimo II granted a 15 scudi monthly salary and a studio to Giovanni Bilivert, and in 1615 (according to Baldinucci, but in reality probably later) he sent Francesco Bianchi Buonavita to study in Rome with a *provvisione* of 12 scudi.[51] These were two further cases of artists affiliated with the Galleria dei Lavori. The generous treatment given to these last two painters must be read in light of their fathers' respective roles. Jacques Bilivelt (better known as Bilivert) was *provveditore*, and Matteo Nigetti proposed that Bilivert's son Giovanni work as his assistant, "especially for finding the patterns [*macchie*] in semi-precious stones and making drawings of figures and landscapes for inlays."[52] The father of Francesco Bianchi Buonavita, Giovanni, also worked in the Manifattura granducale, "as an engineer and director of operations involving *pietre dure*"; upon Francesco's return from Rome, Arch Duchess Maria Maddalena of Austria made sure he found a home and workspace, and had him paint on stone.[53]

During Cosimo II's years, painters' *provvisioni* thus varied from 12 to 18 scudi. These are rather high figures when compared with the salaries of other court workers, and put painters (like most artists) on a medium-to-high footing with respect to other groups of *provvisionati*.

With the proviso that there is still no systematic study of the economic issues concerning the grand ducal court, I have taken as my criteria for comparison the rolls of the years 1611–12, 1615–16, and 1618, and the lists of salary recipients from 1622–23 and 1623–24.[54] From this research, it appears that the monthly salary of painters during Cosimo II's time was similar to that of the majority of "gentiluomini di camera" (court gentlemen), who were paid 16 scudi per month; "segretari minori" (minor secretaries), whose monthly pay ran from 10 to 20 scudi per month; and the most well-paid musicians (for this much larger group, salaries show greater variation, ranging from a minimum of 4 to a maximum of 16 scudi).

As mentioned previously, other artists were generally paid a little more than painters. Under Cosimo II, Giulio Parigi, an engineer, received 30 scudi per month; the sculptor Pietro Tacca 25 scudi; Matteo Nigetti, an architect, and Cristofano Gaffurri, "intagliatore di gioie" (gems carver), 20 scudi; the jeweler Iona Falchi and the stucco worker-architect-decorator Costantino de' Servi 18 scudi; and the drawing teacher Remigio Cantagallina 15 scudi.[55]

In 1623, the Flemish painter Giusto Sustermans, who arrived in Florence in the fall of 1620 and was the Medicis' portraitist for around 60 years, was documented in the roll of Maria Maddalena of Austria, the widow of Cosimo II and regent for her son Ferdinand, as receiving 6 scudi worth of provisions.[56] In a few years his salary ballooned: from a letter written by Maria Maddalena in 1627 and recorded by Baldinucci, one learns that he was receiving 25 scudi "as well as room and board in our palace," and also payments for each work "whenever it may be commissioned by us."[57] His first protector's generosity was not extended by Grand Duke Ferdinand II, who, upon his mother's death in 1631, cut Sustermans's monthly salary to 20 scudi.[58] Much later, in 1649 during a time of economic difficulty, Ferdinand II suspended over 60 salaries: 17 servants (*camerieri*), 1 groom (*scudiero*), 3 secretaries, 3 chaplains, and 40 other miscellaneous employees lost their income, including Sustermans, who was not immune despite his international fame.[59]

In June 1670, immediately after Cosimo III took power, Sustermans asked for confirmation of his monthly 5 scudi for board—a sum he was evidently already receiving—probably to maintain his privileges as a courtier rather than for economic reasons.[60] He had become the owner of numerous properties, an indication of his comfortable economic standing ("in sum, he lives in extraordinary grandeur, more like a knight than an artist").[61] Nevertheless, over the years he also experienced hard times, such as when he had to ask the court for a 340 scudi loan in February 1660, which was cancelled in 1669 when he completed two large portraits of Cosimo III and his spouse Marguerite-Louise d'Orléans.[62] We know that paintings were considered to be a form of currency: in 1669, Sustermans also agreed to paint the portraits of three young Medici princes in exchange for a tax exemption on farmland he had recently purchased.[63]

In August 1654, Sustermans signed a very interesting agreement with the grand ducal Guardaroba concerning the prices of portraits he was to paint for the court: 12 scudi for a bust portrait without hands; 16 scudi for a portrait 1.25 *braccia* high, with one or two hands; 25 scudi for a three-quarter-length portrait; one-half of these amounts for copies retouched by the master; and, finally, for full-length portraits, his fee would be agreed upon for each work. The adoption of fixed prices was easier in the case of portraiture, with its standard formats. This is confirmed also by the account books of Domenico and Valore Casini, who were active in the first decades of the Seicento, and of Antonio Franchi, who became Florence's main portrait painter after the death of the Flemish master.[64]

The miniaturist Giovanna Garzoni appears on the grand ducal salary roll between June 1642 and 1651.[65] While she was in Paris in 1640, she told Ferdinando de' Bardi, the Medici ambassador, about her desire to work for the Medici, conveying "that she demonstrated that she would be content with any honorable form of remuneration."[66] For around nine years (in December 1651 she was documented again as being in Rome) she received 12 scudi per month, in addition to individual fees for her works. There is no doubt that she must have become wealthier during her Florentine years, as demonstrated by the investments she made in *luoghi*, or bonds, of the Monte di Pietà and the Monte del Sale, and then laboriously tried to redeem them after her final move to Rome.[67] Nevertheless, despite the financial benefits of her Florentine sojourn, later correspondence between Garzoni and members of the Medici dynasty (she continued to work for the Florentine court) is characterized by a plaintive tone and constant requests for money (increasingly necessary because of her infirmities?).[68] In 1658 (and perhaps before) she received a pension of 3 scudi per month from Cardinal Carlo de' Medici and 2 scudi from his nephew Giovan Carlo. After the latter's death, for a year (1664) the miniaturist received a 4 scudi per month pension from Ferdinand II; and in 1665, to secure what the late cardinal had given her, she turned to Prince Leopoldo.[69]

As with the painter Gian Domenico Cerrini, distance did not interrupt relations between Garzoni and the Medici dynasty.[70] This sort of salary-pension (it is defined both ways in the archival documents) that Garzoni received almost until her death in 1670 can be traced to the court's habit of turning salaries into pensions for their servants who were older and therefore no longer working.[71]

Garzoni's case was not unique in demonstrating how a painter could maintain a salaried relationship with more than one representative of the Medici family. Indeed, it is necessary to distinguish between the grand duke's court and those of the dynasty's other members. In 1619, the 19-year-old Stefano della Bella, a draftsman, engraver, and painter, wrote to Lorenzo de' Medici, Cosimo II's brother, asking "to be placed on the roll with a salary in order to live decently."[72] He successfully ensured that his salary (which, according to Baldinucci, totaled 6 scudi) was paid even during his stay in Rome in the 1630s "to learn how to paint."[73] After Lorenzo's death in 1648 and Stefano's return from Paris, he became a member of Ferdinand II's family. His name appears in the register of their salaried members for 1656–57.[74] He was given 8 scudi per month and at the same time benefited from a studio in the Galleria dei Lavori.[75]

As already noted, from 1611 to 1621 Bilivert received a salary from Cosimo II to work in the Galleria dei Lavori. Because of an illness in the last ten years of his life, between 1634 and 1637 he received 10 scudi per month from Cardinal Carlo de' Medici which, according to a widespread practice, was supposed to be repaid to the cardinal in paintings.[76] In the 1640s, the Sienese engraver and quasi-painter ("mezzo pittore") Giuliano Periccioli traveled back and forth between Siena and Rome to work for Ferdinand II on a series of maritime maps that were intended to illustrate the second edition of Robert Dudley's *Arcano del mare*. Although he was given a salary of 16 scudi per month by the grand duke (he was paid by the grand ducal Depositeria of Siena), Prince Mattias also reimbursed his travel expenses in 1645 and 1646.[77] Upon his return to Siena in 1647, Giuliano wrote to Ferdinand II's brothers in order to recommend his own brother and collaborator Girolamo for several vacant salaried positions, and in 1648 he entreated the grand duke to lend him the huge sum of 250 scudi to pay off his debts.[78] Similarly, when the newly elected Cardinal Giovan Carlo de' Medici went to Rome in 1645, Sustermans was added to his roll with a "very noble salary" of 10 scudi per month, despite already receiving a salary from the grand duke.[79]

Many painters—primarily those of a middling reputation but with some exceptions—were enrolled as their patron's "aiutanti di camera" (gentlemen of the chamber) and normally were paid less than salaried artists at the grand ducal court.[80] From 1631 to 1648 Vincenzo Mannozzi held this position with Lorenzo de' Medici for a monthly salary of 8 scudi.[81] According to Baldinucci, Livio Mehus was "aiutante di camera" of Cosimo III for a certain period, and continued to receive the benefits associated with the position, including his 8 scudi monthly salary, even when he was no longer on the roll after the grand duke's marriage to Marguerite-Louise d'Orléans in 1661.[82] Giovanni Montini, a little-known but refined student of Jacopo Vignali, was recorded as an "aiutante di camera" on Carlo de' Medici's roll at the time of the cardinal's death in 1666.[83] Cecco Bravo must have had a similar arrangement when he moved to Innsbruck in 1660, to the court of Archduke Ferdinand Charles and Anna de' Medici, and began to receive 8 scudi per month.[84]

Reschi's position in 1686 as an "honored chamber helper" ("aiutante di camera d'onore") to the new Cardinal Francesco Maria de' Medici in Rome carried a 6 scudi monthly salary.[85] According to another contemporary witness, Reschi remained one of Francesco Maria's *provvisionati* until his death; in the 1690s, Francesco Maria even paid the rent for his house.[86] A different example is provided by the Sienese painter Giuseppe Nicola Nasini (1657–1736), who was still young when he secured the patronage of Cosimo III, who gave him a salary at the grand ducal academy in Rome from 1681 to 1685, and later in Venice. When he returned to Florence in September 1689 to work on an important commission for the grand duke, Nasini was referred to as his "aiutante di camera d'onore" and received a yearly salary of 300 scudi.[87] That was an inordinate sum for the job, but more comprehensible if it is taken together with the position of architect of the Galleria dei Lavori, which Nasini received in 1690.[88]

Including painters in the ranks of their "aiutanti di camera" seems to have been a widespread practice among the nobility. For about a 20-year period starting in 1624, Felice Ficherelli served Alberto de' Bardi, and later his brother Piero, as *cameriere* (manservant). As we know from the testament of Alberto, who died in 1632, and from other unpublished documents, the painter received room, board, and 25 scudi per year in exchange for giving the family one painting per year.[89] Confirming Baldinucci's account, we find that Reschi, before becoming part of the Medici circle, was Pier Antonio Gerini's "aiutante di camera," which provided him with room, board, and a monthly salary of 8 scudi.[90] The same was true for Mehus, who worked in Pistoia for a member of the Forteguerri family, who later introduced him to the Medici.[91]

In other cases, the painter would receive a salary without being included in a roll. One example from the Medici dynasty is the relationship between Prince Giovan Carlo de' Medici, the brother of Ferdinand II, and Salvator Rosa. It is still uncertain whether the young Neapolitan painter wanted to leave Rome at the end of 1640 because of certain quarrels or whether he found the offers made to him by Fabrizio Piermattei, the Medici agent in Rome, to be particularly appealing.[92] In either case, Rosa moved to Florence for over eight years. From the autumn of 1640 until January of 1648, he received 8 scudi per month from Giovan Carlo's Camera, the equivalent of the salary of an "aiutante di camera," even though Rosa appears never to have held such a position.[93] Furthermore, according to his *possessioni* (the prince's expense account), Giovan Carlo also paid the rent for Rosa's house at the Croce al Trebbio (50 scudi per year), where the painter ran his Accademia dei Percossi.[94] In some cases, Giovan Carlo also paid for Rosa's pigments.[95] One more example might be cited from the end of the century. The Roman landscape painter Crescenzio Onofri was living in Florence and working for Grand Prince Ferdinand, who paid him a monthly salary of 15.5 scudi.[96]

The salaried relationship linking painters to members of the Medici dynasty can be found with other families, too, which is recorded more by literary sources than in documents. Baldinucci writes that between the 1610s and 1620s, Cosimo Lotti received a monthly salary of 5 scudi from his friend Giovan Battista Strozzi.[97] According to the biography written by his student Domenico Peruzzi, Furini found himself in financial difficulty after he returned from Rome at the end of 1622, with five mouths to feed. Galileo Galilei suggested that Furini work for him for 10 scudi per month, with separate arrangements for the payment of each work, but it is uncertain whether the offer was accepted.[98]

Five scudi was the monthly salary Roberto Strozzi gave 18-year-old Antonio Franchi in 1656, under the condition that he would paint only for the Strozzi family.[99] Later, Franchi worked for Cardinal Girolamo Buonvisi and in 1679 he lived in Zanobi Martini's house "with a dobla [roughly 2.7 scudi] per month and no more."[100] The relationship between Ottavio Vannini and the Del Rosso family must have been similar to Franchi's with the Strozzi: the Del Rosso owned many of his works "since he was very close to this house, from which he always received notable support."[101]

Being a *provvisionato* was not necessarily advantageous for the artist, since it could limit earnings. Francesco Saverio Baldinucci describes how this was the case with Reschi, an artist to whom "little or no time remained . . . to work for anyone besides His Highness [Francesco Maria de' Medici]. . . . And so he began to earn so little that sometimes, since he lacked the courage to appeal to his patron's generosity, he had to ask his most faithful friends for some help in meeting his expenses."[102]

There were other types of salaries that were different from those examined thus far. Some were essentially scholarships. It was not unusual for a painter at the beginning of his career to receive a monthly salary to work in a important artist's studio or to study away from his hometown. The case of Domenico Tempesti (1654/55–1737) was typical. When he showed promise in art as a young man, Tempesti first was sent to the workshop of Baldassarre Franceschini (Volterrano), and was paid a monthly salary of 7 scudi by Cosimo III. With his expenses covered, he then went to Paris (1676–79) to study engraving with Robert Nanteuil. When he returned to Florence, the artist was assigned a room in the grand ducal gallery until he exchanged his etching utensils for pastels.[103] That was an unprofitable career move according to Tempesti's correspondence with the grand ducal secretary Apollonio Bassetti at the start of 1690.[104]

Cosimo III provided other artists with "scholarships" to complete their studies in Rome. From 1673 to 1676, both Atanasio Bimbacci[105] and Antonio Domenico Gabbiani received 3 scudi per month,[106] along with room and board, to study at the Medici academy in Palazzo Madama, which had been founded by the duke himself. Likewise, the student of Gabbiani, Tommaso Redi, was in Rome from 1689 to 1700 "with 5 scudi per month, in addition to room and board."[107]

Baldinucci's account of the young Mario Balassi reveals another relationship between master and pupil. At 18, Balassi moved from Matteo Rosselli's workshop to that of Domenico Cresti (Passignano), where he was paid the sizeable sum of 10 scudi per month to put the master's drawings on canvas and sketch them ("bozzarla").[108] Evidently, this example refers to an artist whose career was already well under way, and who filled an important role within a workshop. Francesco Leoncini provides a similar case, helping Bernardino Poccetti "in his work as a painter" and receiving a monthly salary of 8 scudi.[109]

To learn the trade, however, students could pay the master, as evidenced by Antonio Franchi's detailed recollection from late 1690: "Nicolao Corsetti came to my house in Florence at midnight with his son Giovanni Maria and departed two days later, leaving his son to study painting with me, with the agreement that he would pay me for part of the expenses of said boy, or 6 cratie [a silver coin of the lowest quality, worth one-twelfth of a lira] per day."[110]

"By Day"

A widely documented type of payment that appears to have been more common than the *provvisione* (salary) was *a giornata*, or by the day. It corresponded to an occasional collaboration, limited in time, that could be given to painters making their debut on the market, or to more mature, autonomous artists willing to work under certain conditions. Payments "by the day" varied according to the different tasks performed in the workshops by painters, and were not necessarily limited to painting. For example, in 1645 Furini sent a letter to Duke Salviati by way of Bartolomeo di Matteo Pogni, his day laborer (*giornante*), whose job involved collecting money and negotiating the painter's proposals with the purchaser.[111] Some students of Poccetti's, who were testifying at a trial following their master's death (1612), described how, although they worked independently from him, they occasionally helped him "by the day." Antonio da Rovezzano received compensation of 4 lire per day.[112]

Francesco Saverio Baldinucci records that before Bartolomeo Bimbi became an independent painter, he worked for others and never earned more than half a tollero (3 lire) per day.[113] In 1689, Carlo Berti was paid 2 lire per day to work for Antonio Franchi and copy his paintings; to keep count, he wrote the number of working days on the back of the canvases.[114]

Sometimes artists were forced by economic necessity to work by the day. When in 1687 Andrea Scacciati found himself in a tight situation because he could not obtain money owed to him, he received a 2 scudi loan from Antonio Franchi and, shortly afterwards, worked a *giornatella*, a short day, for him painting "some fruit and an olive branch" for 6 lire (almost 1 scudo).[115]

Daily payment was adopted for mural painting, too. Painters' daily pay varied according to their qualifications and their commitments. A good example is the decoration of the Casa Buonarroti, commissioned by Michelangelo Buonarroti the Younger (1568–1647), an important man of letters and patron of the arts who wanted to celebrate his great-uncle and family.[116] Among those who took part in the extensive work, which lasted from 1615 to 1637, Michelangelo Cinganelli, an active fresco painter and the heir of his master Poccetti's decorative tradition, employed various low-profile helpers who worked by the day. In order to paint part of the ceiling of the Chamber of Night and Day, one of his students, a certain Paolo Antonio, received 3.5 lire per day, while his young helper, Luca, earned 1.5 lire per day.[117]

The much higher daily rate (1 scudo and 1 lira, excluding colors) that Cecco Bravo received for painting the Casa Buonarroti studio in July 1636 had a different implication (Fig. 60).[118] Perhaps the painter and patron were unable to agree on how the work should be carried out and therefore decided on an arrangement for their mutual benefit: one that ensured the painter would be fairly compensated, yet left open the option for the patron to find another artist if he were unsatisfied. In fact, Cecco was to be fired after a few days.

The variety of payment at the Casa Buonarroti suggests that Michelangelo the Younger negotiated an individual agreement with each artist. An unknown Lorenzo worked decorating the studio for a few days after Cecco Bravo's departure (Matteo Rosselli put the value of his work at 2 scudi); then Leonardo Ferroni did some piecework; and finally Rosselli and his student Domenico Pugliani earned 20 and 50 scudi respectively for the walls they painted.[119]

Jacopo Vignali's payment was still different. In 1621 he had asked that partial payment for his work in the so-called Chamber of the Angels be made in goods, specifically with a "soma" (about 70 liters) of oil with a market value of 7 scudi, 1 lira.[120] The oil was worth

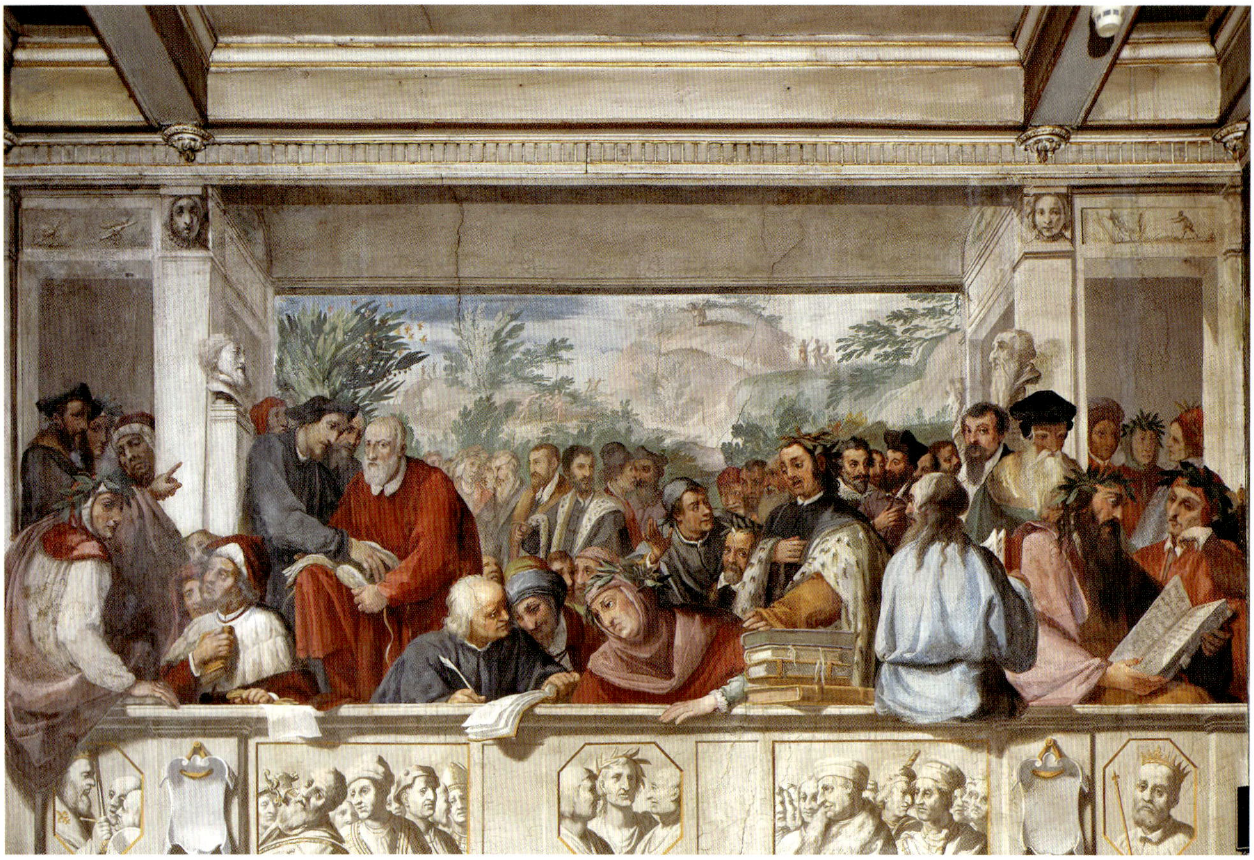

60 Cecco Bravo, *Illustrious Tuscans: Poets and Authors*, 1636. Fresco. Studio of the Casa Buonarroti, Florence.

more than the *Jacob's Dream* painted a few months earlier by Vignali in a ground-floor room, for which he was paid 6 scudi.[121] In 1628, in the final bill for other work completed in the same building, Vignali again would ask to be paid in kind.[122] At the time this system was common in many trades,[123] and in some cases was even used by the grand ducal court to pay salaries.[124]

The daily earnings of painters discussed thus far were all much greater than those of other trades. According to the biography of Furini written by his student Peruzzi, in the 1620s Furini's uncle earned barely more than 1 lira per day from his wool workshop.[125] The production of *pannilana* (cloth of wool), which had been central to the Florentine economy, collapsed in the first 20 years of the century.[126] During this same period, as mentioned, the daily wage of an unskilled laborer, at around 1 lira, was not much different.[127]

Daily payments to some artists, however, could be substantial, particularly when driven by ambition. In the biography of Pier Dandini written in the eighteenth century by Giovanni Targioni Tozzetti, which was based on original sources, Tozzetti writes that it was extremely well known (*a cosa notissima*) that, at a certain point in his career, Dandini wanted to earn 10 scudi per day and that he worked toward this goal by making speed of execution his modus operandi. This earned him the reputation of having "brushes for all prices."[128] Such evidence prompts reflection on the relationship between style and earnings, especially if Dandini really never turned down a commission and instead devoted more or less time to the work depending on the payment.

"By Appraisal"

The report concerning Dandini's "brushes for all prices" raises one of the central questions about painters' earnings: who determined the price of a painting or a fresco? Clearly, the answer cannot be unambiguous. First, it is necessary to distinguish between an artist working for a patron with whom there was a direct relationship and someone producing works for an "anonymous" market, which obviously followed different rules. The first case requires consideration of some factors appropriately defined as "contingent and intangible" that had a substantial effect on payments and, therefore, on painters' earnings: factors such as "patriotism," "piety," and the different relationships that existed between artists and patrons.[129]

The same artist might be paid different amounts for providing the same service or a very similar product. Indeed, in each circumstance a work might be created differently: the painter's time in planning and execution would change, as would the deadline for completion. Such circumstances could also influence a painter's style.

An example, regarding the large number of lunettes in Florentine cloisters, is provided below (see pages 197–98). What is clear is that the painters who received the highest remuneration were those whose lunette was funded by an aristocratic patron rather than by a monastic order. This does not mean that a painter would avoid poorly paid projects since extending his client base always remained a priority.

Literary and documentary sources concerning the appraisal of paintings point in two directions: on the one hand, they reveal the tendency of certain artists to keep their prices low, while on the other they prove that the patron's role was fairly decisive, in part because painters worked more frequently than presumed without having established the price beforehand, though one wonders if this was also a common practice among other types of workers at the time.

Baldinucci records several related anecdotes. One concerns Poccetti, who, when asked to appraise the paintings for the stage set up in S. Maria del Fiore to celebrate Cosimo II's marriage to Maria Maddalena of Austria in 1608, replied that he "asked for a very low price for his own works, while he estimated twice as much for those by others, because he valued money little and also, he said, because his expertise with the brush enabled him to make them for this price, unlike the other painters. . . . However, he wanted this small sum to be paid promptly."[130] Giovanni da San Giovanni also did not like to charge a "set price" for his works;[131] in Francesco Saverio Baldinucci's *Lives*, Bartolomeo Bimbi and Tommaso Redi are described as quoting prices that were too low compared with other artists' rates.[132]

Carlo Dolci, on the other hand, commanded very high prices for both small and medium-size paintings, including sales outside of Florence. On the Venetian market, for example, his works did not sell for less than 100 scudi; he even received 200 and 300 scudi respectively for two different versions of the *Christ Child with a Flower Garland* (Thyssen Bornemisza Museum, Madrid, and Kunsthistorisches Museum, Vienna), and another 300 scudi from Marquis Pier Francesco Rinuccini for a "figure as lovely as nature itself of St. John the Evangelist seeing the mysterious vision of the woman clothed in the sun, crushing the dragon."[133]

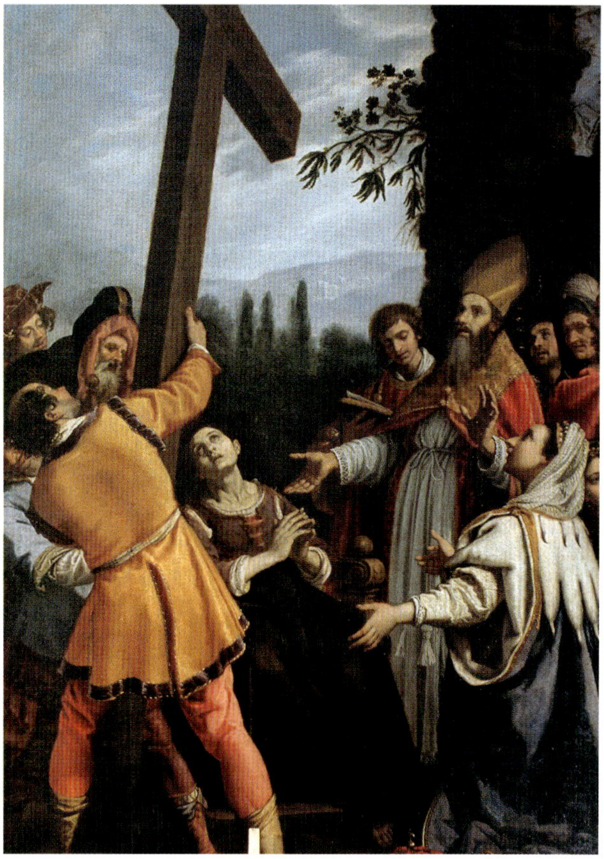

61 Giovanni Bilivert, *Discovery of the True Cross*, 1621. Oil on canvas, 341 × 224 cm. S. Croce, Florence.

As for the role of the patron in determining the price of a work, there are various kinds of testimonials, which differ according to the relationship between the artist and the recipient. Baldinucci mentions that Gregorio Pagani painted an altarpiece for the parish church of Sciano for his friend, the poet Giovanni Berti (*Madonna and Saints*, 1592, Hermitage Museum, St. Petersburg), and may have already sent it when Berti was asked the price. When the painter supposedly quoted an extremely modest amount, Berti told him as much and increased the final payment, adding other goods.[134]

Generosity was a virtue involved in friendship, but was also characteristic of those in power. It is understandable, therefore, that some well-known artists from outside Tuscany who were invited by Ferdinand II to paint in the Palazzo Pitti moved to the grand ducal

TABLE 11 Costs per Square Meter and per Figure of Florentine Altarpieces*

ARTIST AND DATE	PAINTING (oil altarpieces in Florence unless otherwise indicated)	DIMENSIONS (cm)	PRICE (scudi)	PER SQUARE METER	PER FIGURE
Aurelio Lomi, 1608	*St. Sebastian Before the Tyrant*, SS. Annunziata	280 × 205	200	36	20
G. B. Paggi, 1608	*Flagellation of St. Sebastian*, SS. Annunziata	289 × 205	200	34	40
Matteo Rosselli, 1612	*The Immaculate Conception*, SS. Annunziata (now Polo Museale Fiorentino, depositi)	450 × 262	120		
Giovanni Bilivert, 1621	*Discovery of the True Cross*, S. Croce (Fig. 61)	341 × 224	150	20	30
Passignano, 1621	*Almsgiving of St. Lawrence*, S. Croce	341 × 224	150	20	30
Matteo Rosselli, 1621	*Christ, Virgin, St. Francis*, S. Croce	341 × 224	150	20	30
Matteo Rosselli, 1624	*Coronation of the Virgin*, S. Maria di Candeli (lost)		125		
Cecco Bravo, 1625	*St. Nicholas of Bari Freeing Three Unjustly Condemned Youths*, S. Simone	originally ca. 272 × 170	ca. 44	10	11
Matteo Rosselli, 1626	*St. Paul Discharged*, Cathedral, Volterra	320 × 220	200	29	33
Fabrizio Boschi, 1630–31	*Vision of St. Bernard of Clairvaux*, S. Maria Maddalena de' Pazzi	228 × 214	200	41	33
Pietro da Cortona, 1637–52	*Martyrdom of St. Lawrence*, SS. Michele e Gaetano	320 × 210	400 (+200?)	60	50
Lorenzo Lippi, 1642	*Martyrdom of St. James Major*; *Assumption of the Virgin* (lunette)	375 × 243; 100 × 243	100	9	12
Mario Balassi, 1642–43	*Assumption of the Virgin*, SS. Michele e Gaetanoi (lost)		200		
Jacopo Vignali, 1649	*Martyrdom of St. Lucy*, SS. Annunziata		180		60
Ciro Ferri, 1682–84	*The Virgin Presenting a Golden Chain to S. Maria Maddalena de' Pazzi*, S. Maria Maddalena de' Pazzi	470 × 275 (enlarged)	900	70	129
Luca Giordano, 1685	*Mystical Marriage of S. Maria Maddalena de' Pazzi*, S. Maria Maddalena de' Pazzi	360 × 160	300	52	60

* The costs per figure and per square meter were not major market issues for altarpieces in Florence. The data are included only for comparison with data from the other cities.

capital without knowing in advance how much they would earn. Instead, they relied on the generosity of their patron (see pages 189–95). A similar dynamic was at work in Antonio Franchi's relationships with his clients. Originally from Lucca but a resident of Florence, he often noted in his *Giornale della pittura* (1683–1709) that, with the order for a portrait, "agreements [on price] have not been made."[135] Only after a work was delivered would he decide whether or not to complain about the payment, as can be observed, case by case, in his *Giornale*. Franchi had a clear idea about the value of each painting and described it in writing. If he accepted a lower than average price, he would always explain his decision with reference to a particular circumstance, which usually involved pleasing the patron with an eye on future profit. It might have been relatively easy to set standard fees for portraits, but it is questionable, given all of the variations, if other types of painting could be as readily categorized by price.

Currently I am conducting research as systematically as possible on the prices of altarpieces painted in Florence during the seventeenth century. As a category, altarpieces generally have homogeneous characteristics (although within certain limitations their sizes vary), which allows us to draw conclusions from a set of quantitative data. According to the examination conducted thus far, mainly from the first half of the century, it appears that the price for an altarpiece executed by a moderately famous painter ranged from 100 to 200 scudi (Table 11).

There were also exceptional cases in which the painter's fee was higher than average. According to Baldinucci, Jacopo da Empoli received 416 scudi for his altarpiece depicting *St. Ivo, Protector of Widows and Orphans* (1616, 291 × 215 cm, Galleria Palatina, Florence) commissioned by the Magistratura dei Pupilli.[136] In the spring of 1637, Francesco Franceschi and Pietro da Cortona similarly agreed on 400 scudi as payment for a large altarpiece of the *Martyrdom of St. Lawrence*

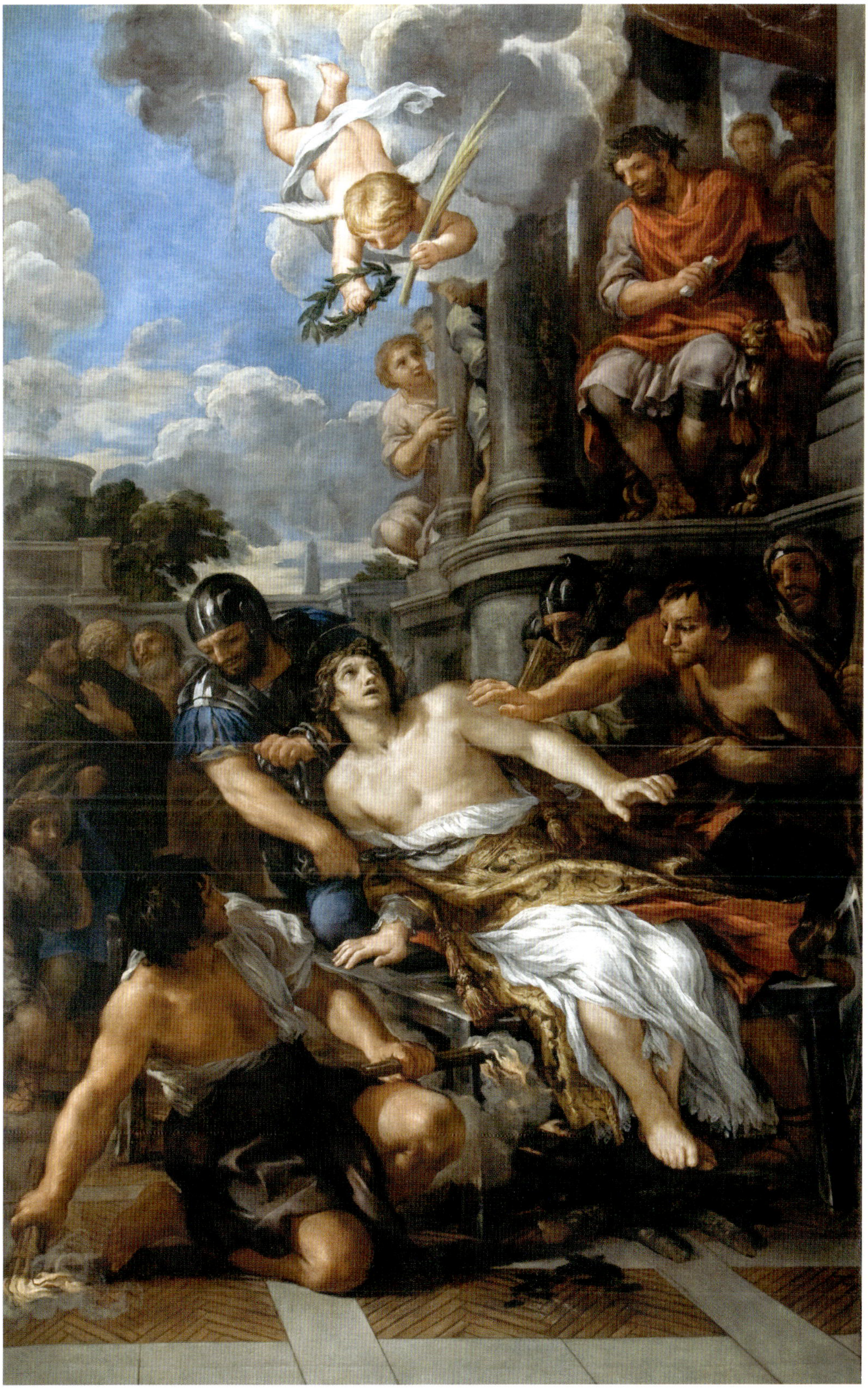

62 Pietro da Cortona, *Martyrdom of St. Lawrence*, 1637–52. Oil on canvas, 320 × 210 cm. SS. Michele e Gaetano, Florence.

(Fig. 62) for the Franceschi chapel in the church of SS. Michele e Gaetano to be completed within 18 months—an example of how the Tuscan painter, who was living in Rome at the time, commanded much higher prices than his Florentine colleagues. According to Francesco Saverio Baldinucci (and confirmed in part by documentary reports), Cortona "started it in Florence, but perhaps weighed down by his other work he abandoned it. . . . This delay lasted for about 12 years when, finally, after a raise of 200 scudi, he finished the work. When received in Florence, it gave such satisfaction both to the patron and to the whole city that no one regretted this increase in price."[137]

Another exceptional case, where the unusually large size (465 × 265 cm) certainly played a role, involved the altarpiece of *St. Louis Invites the Poor to Supper*, commissioned from Simone Pignoni by Luigi Guicciardini for his family's altar in S. Felicita (*in situ*). Giovan Camillo Sagrestani emphasized that the painting was completed "at the time when Giordano was here in Florence," indicating 1682. When there was disagreement between Pignoni and the patron over payment, "Giordano said he wanted to purchase it for 100 doppie [approximately 275 scudi] and make a copy of it for the church. But, having heard this, they easily agreed to give him what he asked" and paid Pignoni 400 scudi, plus another 30 doppie.[138]

A final payment example that falls outside the norm concerns the decoration of the apsidal chapel of S. Maria Maddalena de' Pazzi, where Cosimo III took a leading role in the church's refurbishment. The main altarpiece was assigned to Ciro Ferri (Fig. 63), who, with Paolo Falconieri acting as his intermediary, asked for 900 scudi in the summer of 1682. This was his going rate for similar works, but "with the knowledge that Luca Giordano already had one of the lateral paintings, and since the nuns knew they could get a much better price from him [Giordano], he wondered whether the nuns would take the commission from him and give it to Giordano with the excuse of not being able to spend too much."[139] In fact, a short while later, Giordano agreed to paint both lateral paintings for 300 scudi (Figs. 64 and 65).[140] From documents dated just slightly later, at least two reasons emerge that explain why the Neapolitan painter kept his price so low. Presumably, the more important was Volterrano's competition for one of the two lateral paintings. In fact, Giordano offered to do the second one for free, effectively painting two for the price of one. Second, Giordano's personal devotion to the Magdalene perhaps was a factor.[141]

Ferri took more than two years until he finally delivered his work in August 1684. He was paid by Cosimo III because the nuns had held that his work would be too expensive for them. Giordano, on the other hand, took only a few weeks in 1685 to complete his paintings, which indicates how, for these two artists, speed was an important factor in pricing their works. Clearly, Giordano understood that speed of execution was a key to economic success, as the passage from Baldinucci's biography of Dolci, quoted in the Introduction and the essay on Rome, makes so evident. There, Dolci's "incomparable diligence" and the Neapolitan's "wonderful speed" are placed at opposite poles on a scale of earnings.

Non-Florentines

Moving to Florence

Compared with a city like Rome, the artistic and cultural world of seicento Florence has long been considered to have been closed and inaccessible to foreigners, a view that undoubtedly is exaggerated. Throughout the century there was no lack of artists from other cities who stayed there for more or less extended periods. Their presence in the capital of the grand duchy was due to different factors and led to a variety of economic results. Artemisia Gentileschi, for example, left Rome after Agostino Tassi's trial for rape, arrived in Florence in 1613 with her husband Pierantonio Stiattesi (whom she had married in late 1612), and stayed there until 1621.[142] Gentileschi's case was a peculiar one. As Keith Christiansen has argued, "it is in Florence that Artemisia's status as an independent artist really begins, and it is for this reason that her transformation during those crucial years, 1613–20, merits close study."[143] This assertion also pertains to her economic status. Many complaints were lodged by her creditors to the tribunal of the Accademia del Disegno between 1614 and 1619.[144] Furthermore, numerous documents from the archive of Michelangelo Buonarroti the Younger, who had a close personal relationship with the painter, describe her financial difficulties.[145]

In Florence Artemisia outfitted a studio for the first time, according to Elizabeth Cropper's interpretation of a carpenter's bill for domestic and professional items between September 1614 and April 1615.[146] Although the artist commanded the esteem of Cosimo II and his wife Maria Maddalena, as evidenced by the works she left in Florence, Artemisia does not appear to have enjoyed special favors from the Medici family during her first Florentine years. It has been presumed that her enrollment in the Accademia del Disegno—which did not immediately follow her arrival in Florence but only

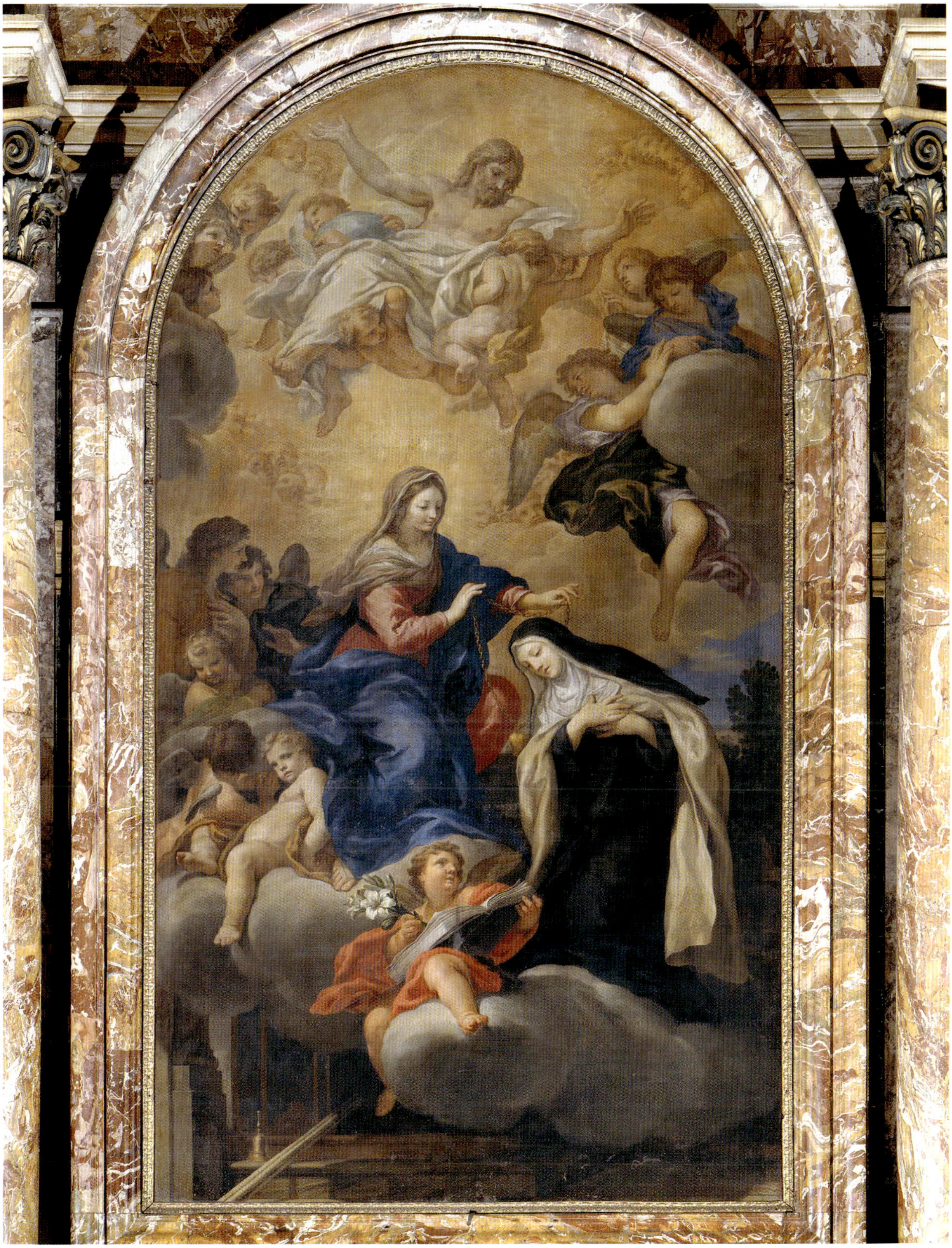

63 Ciro Ferri, *The Virgin Presenting a Golden Chain to S. Maria Maddalena de' Pazzi*, 1682–84. Oil on canvas, 470 × 275 cm (enlarged). S. Maria Maddalena de' Pazzi, Florence.

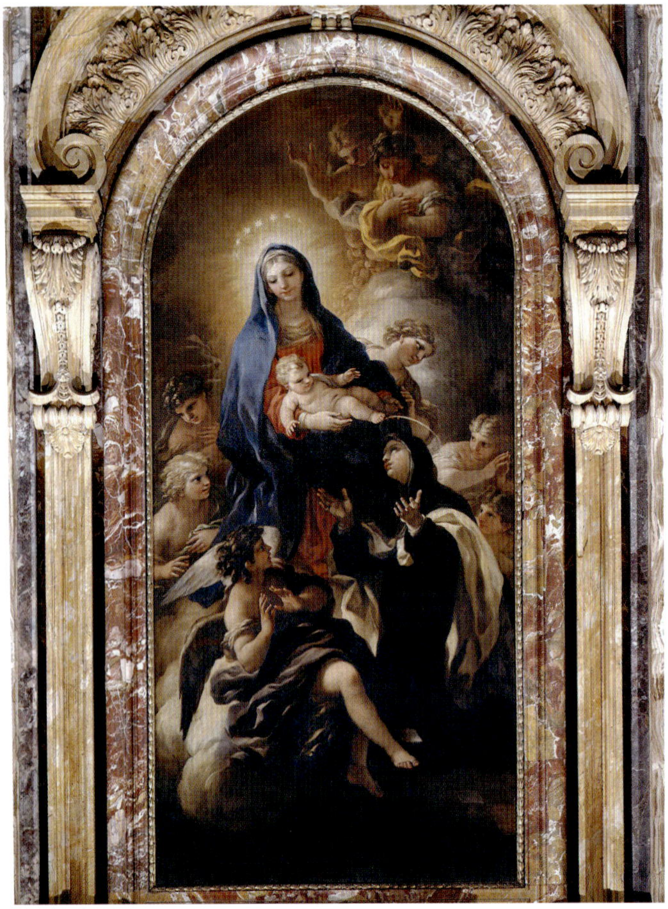

64 Luca Giordano, *The Virgin Offering the Child to S. Maria Maddalena de' Pazzi*, 1685. Oil on canvas, 360 × 160 cm. S. Maria Maddalena de' Pazzi, Florence.

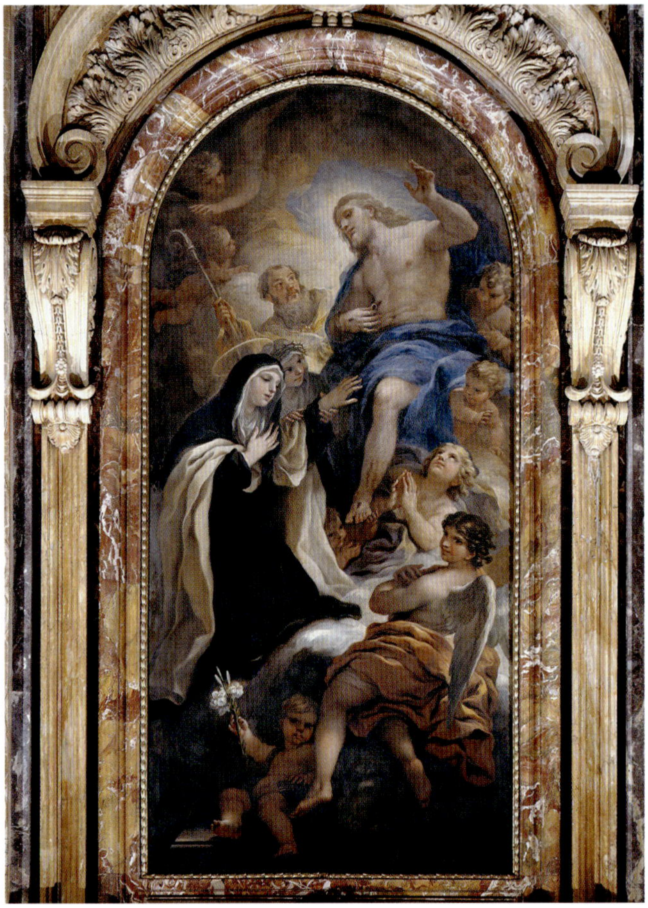

65 Luca Giordano, *Mystical Marriage of S. Maria Maddalena de' Pazzi*, 1685. Oil on canvas, 360 × 160 cm. S. Maria Maddalena de' Pazzi, Florence.

occurred on 19 July 1616—might have been the result of Cosimo II trying to protect Artemisia from her many creditors.[147] In June 1619 she turned to Cosimo II because of her husband's debts, for which she was now held responsible, whereas previously she had relied on the kindness of Buonarroti, who gave her small advances whenever she asked.[148] Between 1615 and 1616, Artemisia was apparently paid more than the other painters who provided works for the ceiling of the Casa Buonarroti's gallery.[149]

Even so, evidence regarding Artemisia's Florentine sojourn is fragmentary (there is no information about how much any of her easel paintings cost). Undoubtedly, her four pregnancies in five years (between September 1613 and October 1618) led to economic hardship for the family, albeit that only one daughter survived to the end of Artemisia's Florentine period.[150] Nor are there details regarding where she worked (probably at home) or with whom. Several unpublished accounts dated to January 1619 show that one Simone Carducci had given her a 10 scudi advance for a *Virgin* that he "wanted by her own hand, and not by those who work for her," an indication that perhaps Artemisia already had assistants early in her career.[151]

If Orazio Gentileschi's daughter sought shelter in Florence to distance herself from the repercussions of the rape trial, the Perugian painter Gian Domenico Cerrini arrived there between 1656 and 1657 to escape the constant criticism of his decoration of the cupola of S. Maria della Vittoria in Rome.[152] In a letter from about ten years later from Rome to Prince Leopoldo de' Medici in mid-1666, the artist lamented his economic difficulties: "In Florence I took a wife for nothing and I had nothing and extremely poor relatives, so that it was necessary to make many paintings to live and endure the necessary expenses while I did the lunette in Santo Spirito. If I did not have my beloved signor Tomasso, I would have starved to death. At that time I did not paint for glory, I painted to live and to help my poor relatives."[153] Cerrini emphasized the help given to him by Tommaso Fantacci, the Medici's Maestro di dispensa (Master of the Larder), who supposedly introduced him to the members of the grand ducal family.[154] For them he executed a number of paintings, although relative to the many mentioned in Medici inventories, few are known in payments (some were painted in the years after Cerrini's Florentine sojourn).[155] To judge from two 100 scudi gifts from Prince Mattias in 1658 (for *più quadri fatti*) and Ferdinand II in 1659, the Medici were not particularly generous with Cerrini.[156] On the other hand, in 1661 the grand duke paid him 170 scudi for a *Moses*, which was more in line with prices of the time for a painting of that size (225 × 182 cm, Polo Museale Fiorentino, Florence, depositi).[157]

In Cerrini's letter of 1666 to Leopoldo de' Medici, the painter defined himself as an "enrolled servant of the most serene grand duke [Ferdinand II]" (*arolato servitore del serenissimo gran duca*), a status that was to be renewed by Cosimo III in 1670.[158] When, as of 1663, Cerrini was in Rome, his staying on the grand ducal payroll meant retaining "protection from a distance" and a working relationship from which he could gain economic advantages.

In other cases, artists who wanted to change their residence would make an explicit request to do so or they accepted offers to move to the grand ducal capital. In February 1640, Giovanna Garzoni sent news from Paris to the Medici court that she ardently wanted to return to Italy, "unable to become used to French customs," and she wondered "if your Majesty were inclined to have me come to Florence."[159] She arrived there in 1642 and for the following nine years received a salary from Ferdinand II.

A small notebook entitled *Debtors, Creditors, and Memoirs* (Accademia di S. Luca, Rome) begun in December 1646 sheds light on the amounts the Medici paid Garzoni for her miniatures. The most generous seem to be those given by the grand dukes: 100 scudi from Ferdinand II for a floral wreath with two *amorini* (small cupids) at the center and a head of St. John the Baptist; a gold chain, also worth 100 scudi, for a "life-sized hare"; another 70 scudi chain from Prince Leopoldo for a head of Catherine of Savoy and a large flower vase; and 4 doppie (11.5 scudi) from Cardinal Giovan Carlo for a porcelain vase with flowers, in the shape of a hexagon.[160] In 1649, in order to collect for her works painted for Lorenzo de' Medici, Garzoni had to turn to Ferdinand II, who paid her 100 scudi.[161] While it is difficult to understand the criteria on which the miniaturist's pay was calculated (probably both subject and size mattered), she undoubtedly grew wealthier during her Florentine years, as noted above.

According to his biographers, Rosa likewise put together a sizeable fortune in Florence (1640–48). Baldinucci reports that he earned the considerable sum of 9,000 scudi while there but that he took only 300 back to Rome, having spent the rest on the academy he founded in the grand ducal capital.[162]

Invited Artists

A variety of foreign painters worked in Florence on important decorative projects. Ferdinand II invited several to participate in the decoration of the Palazzo Pitti: Pietro Berrettini, a native of Cortona who was then living in Rome (1641–47); Angelo Michele Colonna from Bologna (1637–41); and Cortona's Roman student Ciro Ferri, who completed his master's unfinished work in Florence (1659–61, 1663–65). In the 1680s, two of the most prominent Florentine noble families—the Corsini and the Riccardi—hired Luca Giordano to paint the cupola of the Corsini family chapel in the church of the Carmine (1682) and the gallery of the Riccardi palace in via Larga, acquired from the Medici a few years earlier (1685).

According to a long-standing tradition, foreign artists were guaranteed reimbursement of their travel expenses and room and board in addition to the payment for their work.[163] Scaffolding was covered by the patron, and sometimes the materials were, too, at least in part. To judge from my own documentary research, it appears that painters did not make preliminary agreements with the grand duke but that they did so with other Florentine families (Angelo Michele Colonna with the Niccolini, Luca Giordano with the Corsini and the Riccardi).

When Cortona, Colonna, and Ferri were hired by Ferdinand II to paint in the Palazzo Pitti, their fees were not established in advance. Evidently, working for Ferdinand II was a guarantee in itself and difficult to refuse. Such must have been the case with Giovanni da San Giovanni, the first artist to work on the renovation of the Medici palace. He was from San Giovanni Valdarno and therefore a subject of the grand duke, but he had long been active in Rome and elsewhere. In May 1635 he wrote through an intermediary to the head of Cardinal Guido Bentivoglio's household to request that his goods be sent to him, "because His Most Serene Highness [Ferdinand II] had me in his palace to paint the grand salone."[164] Meanwhile he had received 100 scudi to cover the cost of the colors and gold needed to start the work in the Palazzo Pitti.[165] By December 1636, when he died, Giovanni had completed the ceiling, the architectural framework on the walls, the wall opposite the windows, and two lunettes on the western side (later destroyed and repainted by Cecco Bravo). For his work he received 2,000 scudi as well as board.[166] In a letter written to the Maestro di Casa of Cardinal Bentivoglio, he noted that "[the grand duke] feeds me in the morning and sends me many different foods and recently he came to the scaffolding to see me and asked me how I was being treated . . . and he continued to ask me what the kitchen and larder were giving me."[167]

Giovanni da San Giovanni's pay and working conditions resembled those of Colonna and Cortona more than of the Florentines Cecco Bravo, Vannini, and Furini, who were hired to complete the decoration of the *salone* after Giovanni da San Giovanni's death. This underlines the esteem in which he was held, almost as if he were a foreigner. On the basis of his letter of May 1635 cited above, it seems that he still had a close relationship with Cardinal Bentivoglio and that his recruitment by the grand duke occurred without advance notice.[168]

The impression that painters hired by Ferdinand II to work in the Palazzo Pitti did not know in advance how much they would earn is substantiated in an anonymous biography of the Florentine *quadratura* painter Jacopo Chiavistelli. There, in a section on Angelo Michele Colonna, it is said that when Colonna was invited to Florence in 1637 he requested Agostino Mitelli's assistance, whereupon Mitelli asked Colonna how much he would earn. Colonna replied that "in Florence it did not seem right to write to whomever had received from the grand duke the task of dealing with him, and with princes of this rank, it is not appropriate to negotiate in advance; that whatever treatment he received, so too would Mitelli." But Mitelli insisted on establishing his pay in advance and demanded 15 scudi a month.[169] That proved to be very little when compared with the 6,000 scudi that the grand duke gave Colonna. Colonna was paid that sum for the decoration of the ceilings and walls of three large rooms of the Palazzo Pitti's ground-floor apartment executed between the end of November 1637 and August 1641. (However, for nine of those months Colonna did not work on this project.)[170]

The final sum must have been established while work was in progress, perhaps at the time of the first large payment of 2,700 scudi (6 July 1638), of which 700 ducati (scudi) were given "as an advance for work already completed and 2,000 ducati as an advance on work still to be done."[171] This covered six months' work and probably referred to the execution of the *quadratura* on the ceiling of the first room adjacent to the *salone*, and perhaps a little more, considering that the decoration of this space was completed in 1639, the date inscribed on the wall.[172] After a second payment of 2,000 scudi in June 1640, the painter requested the balance of 1,000 scudi in March 1641, which was paid to him in two installments.[173] The total amount was substantial, but considering that Colonna worked at the Pitti palace for 36 months (or maybe a little less), he earned around 160 scudi per month, from which his assistants' pay must be subtracted. If this amount was about ten times what the painter agreed to give his assistant Mitelli, it was less than the 200 scudi monthly (gross) that he earned in 1635 for his decoration of the main *sala* of the Palazzo Spada in Rome.[174]

Unpublished correspondence between Colonna and Marquis Filippo Niccolini, Maestro di Camera of Prince (and later Cardinal) Giovan Carlo de' Medici, another important patron of the artist, sheds light on the ill treatment Colonna received at court. In January 1639 the painter wrote to Niccolini because Biagio Marmi, Guardaroba of Palazzo Pitti, had forced him to move out of his apartment into a less desirable ground-floor room together with his young assistant (Mitelli?).[175] Colonna lamented that he was being persecuted by Marmi and expressed his "desire to receive cash instead of board and even leave the court." He continued: "I have been in various other courts and was treated well. This one [the Medici court] has the reputation of treating [its guests] extremely well and better than others, but to me the opposite seems to be true, or perhaps it is just my ill fortune [Son stato in diverse altre corte e son stato ben tratato. Questa [h]a voce di trattar benissimo meglio di tutte, a me pare vada al contrario, o che sia mia mala fortuna]." In another letter of early February, Niccolini assured the painter that he would intervene personally to improve Colonna's situation, with regard to both his room and board ("sì d'abitatione come di vit[t]o"). For the former, the artist was given monthly rent for his house, while for the latter Colonna wrote that the Sotto Maestro di Casa was going to pay him 15 scudi a month, "which is insufficient . . . to live like a gentleman, in other words at an appropriate level for me [che non sono a bastanza . . . a viver da galant'huomo over da par mio]." Lamenting that life was more expensive in Florence than in Rome, Colonna complained that the grand ducal officials had not welcomed his request to have his board paid in cash, and therefore had lowered the amount considerably, as evidenced by the daily list of food provided to the artist: "eight loaves, four chickens (or a capon and two pullets), meat, liver, soup, fruit, cheese, two flasks of good wine, worth 1 pound each, and candles."[176]

Despite Colonna's complaints about the treatment he received at the Medici court, the success of his decorations in the Palazzo Pitti opened the doors to a two-decade-long relationship with Florence. Colonna worked there many times until 1663. Between 1641 and 1658, for instance, he painted for Giovan Carlo de' Medici on numerous occasions. Documents confirm that again he had trust in his patron's generosity, or else turned to Marquis Filippo Niccolini to mediate on his behalf. In 1641 Niccolini wrote to Giovan Carlo: "[Colonna] asked me for the money for his work in the *casino* [in via della Scala, Giovan Carlo's residence], and yet I could never extract an amount from his mouth since he always left the price up to me. I paid him 200 scudi; he showed himself to be satisfied, having relied freely on my discretion. Still, he gave word that the work will be appraised at 300 scudi, and although they are Bolognese, they are more clever and more shrewd than the Florentines."[177] Later, in 1658, the fee of 800 scudi (including colors and gold) for painting the loggia and the "façade near the door" appears to "have been agreed upon with the signori Marquis Niccolini, Marquis Guidoni and Ferdinando Tacca."[178]

With regard to Colonna's many jobs for Niccolini until the 1660s, it seems that there were preliminary agreements. This is confirmed in the documents of payment sent to the painter, both in the summer of 1657, for the decoration of the *sala* and the loggia of the family palace in via dei Servi (365 scudi for three months' work, excluding room and board), and in 1663 for the gallery (800 scudi for about five months' work).[179] In the latter instance, Colonna used Giacomo Alboresi as his assistant, whom he compensated with "62.5 ducatoni" without covering his expenses, which was slightly less than what he had given Mitelli almost 30 years earlier.[180]

It appears that Pietro da Cortona also painted the Planetary Rooms (Sale dei Pianeti) in the Palazzo Pitti without an advance agreement with Grand Duke Ferdinand II. In a letter of August 1641, the superintendent of the Medici Fabbriche, Andrea Arrighetti, summed up the commitments involved in the work on the first room, namely the conditions under which the three stucco workers had come from Rome and the other monthly payments necessary for the undertaking (a mason, a manual laborer, and materials), "without taking into further account for the time being that which must be given to Cortona in the end."[181]

In his fundamental study of Cortona's frescoes in the Palazzo Pitti, Malcolm Campbell concluded from this passage, "It would appear that the remuneration of the painter was already fixed, but not to be bestowed until the completion of at least the first room, if not the entire project."[182] I think the letter instead indicates that the grand duke still did not know how much he was going to pay the painter. Another letter seems to confirm this. Written by Arrighetti in May 1642, it sums up the costs of the work on the first room, "without that which Your Highness will give to Cortona."[183] Furthermore, another letter written by the Medici ambassador in Rome, Gabriello Riccardi, to the grand ducal secretary, Giovan Battista Gondi, in April 1654 contains a suggestive statement by the painter concerning the agreements he had made for the principal decorative undertakings up to that date: "Lady Olimpia [Pamphilj] recently called him and asked him what he should receive for having painted the gallery [of Palazzo Pamphilj], and he replied that he had not asked for anything from the grand duke or from the Barberini, and he would do the same with the pope [Innocent X]."[184]

Cortona worked on the Planetary Rooms from August 1641 to October 1647, although he, too (like Colonna), was not there uninterruptedly (he spent almost all of 1643 in Rome). Among his biographers, André Félibien (who, after having passed through Florence, was in Rome from May 1647 to August 1649) wrote in his *Entretiens* that Cortona received 10,000 scudi from Ferdinand II, a statement later repeated by Pascoli.[185] Francesco Saverio Baldinucci, on the other hand, made explicit reference to some courtiers who were hostile to the painter and accordingly delayed and cut his payment in order to drive him out of Florence.[186] Hostility in local circles to a foreign artist is something of a leitmotif of the biographical genre, but in some cases, like that of Colonna, it seems to be more than just a literary invention and therefore should be considered a plausible explanation of certain facts.

An unpublished register of Ferdinand II's extraordinary expenses reveals that, during his Florentine years, Cortona received only some advances (500 scudi in July 1644 and 1,500 scudi in two parts in 1645) for a total of 2,000 scudi—a modest amount compared with Colonna's pay, which is explainable perhaps by his slow progress at the outset and/or delayed payments due to the hostility of some of the Medici ministers.[187] Certainly, Cortona did not have a close relationship with the court. Although he had been guaranteed lodging at Palazzo Pitti as well as full board (of which he took advantage), at least at the beginning of his stay in Florence he decided to live with his friend Michelangelo

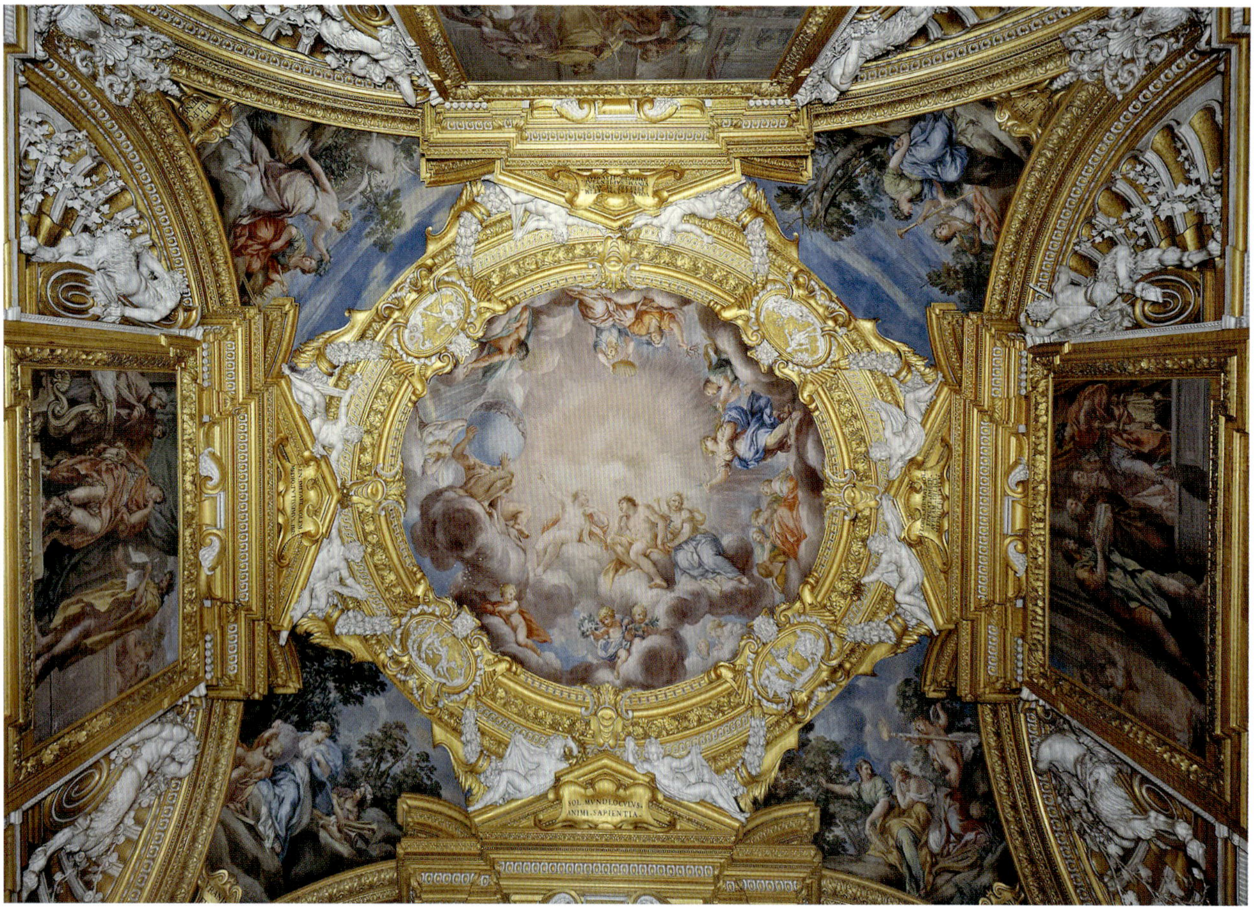

66 Pietro da Cortona and Ciro Ferri, *Apollo Pointing out Hercules to the Prince*, 1644–47 and 1659–61. Fresco. Room of Apollo, Palazzo Pitti, Florence.

Buonarroti the Younger, probably to enjoy greater freedom.[188] There is no evidence that, despite the latter's complaints in mid-1641 that putting Cortona up was inconvenient, the artist moved elsewhere.[189] Having been absent during 1643, he left Florence again in 1647 to work in S. Maria della Vallicella and the Palazzo Pamphilj in Rome. Meanwhile he maintained good relations with the Medici, yet he never returned to Florence to complete the Planetary Rooms and get his final payment.

By 1659, when the negotiations for the marriage of Prince Cosimo III were already well under way, the decoration of the Planetary Rooms in the Palazzo Pitti could no longer remain incomplete.[190] It has not been recognized that this was the reason behind a decisive turn of events in a saga that had dragged on for too many years. Because of Cortona's age and precarious health, it was decided by mutual agreement between the various parties that the decoration would be completed by his closest collaborator, Ciro Ferri, based on the master's cartoons.[191] As customary, the Medici ambassador paid a visit to Ferri in order to invite him to Florence. In correspondence of 1659, there is reference to just one room and to the possibility that Cortona would return to Florence to put the final touches on the work.[192] Another letter, of August 1659, seems to confirm that the marriage of the future Cosimo III provided the motivation for a "final agreement." In it, the grand ducal secretary invited the Medici ambassador in Rome, Carlo Rinuccini, to expedite "those drawings by Pietro da Cortona, so that his young pupil [Ferri] can come here as soon as possible and finish the work in one of the grand duke's antechambers because, given that we cannot wait 100 years to hold a marriage in this most serene house, it would be incongruous for the most noble apartment of this palace to be a room full of scaffolding on such an occasion."[193]

Ferri, who had arrived in Florence at the start of November 1659, "was invited to dismount within the

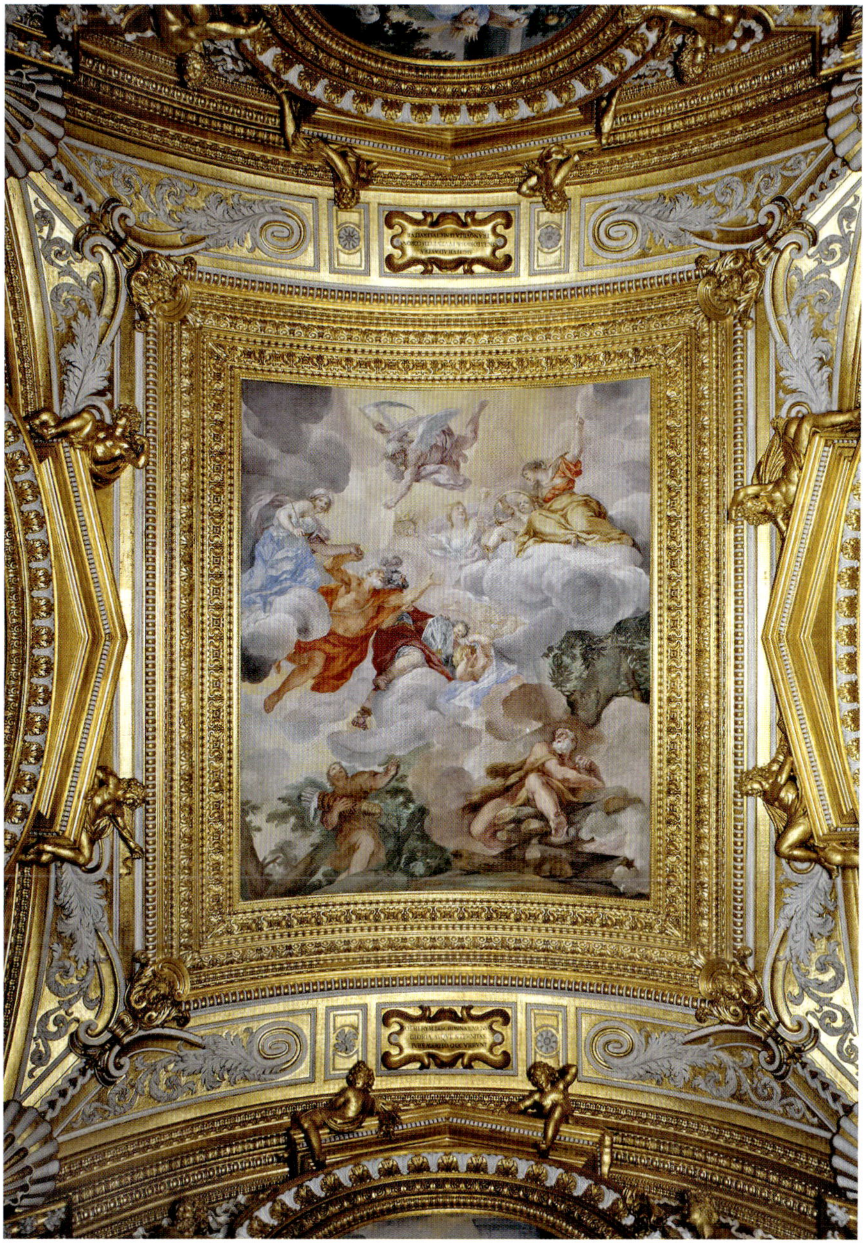

67 Ciro Ferri, *The Prince Crowned by Fame and Eternity*. 1663–65. Fresco. Room of Saturn, Palazzo Pitti, Florence.

precincts of the palace itself, where lodging and refreshments were prepared for him."[194] Unlike Colonna and Mitelli and his master Cortona, Ferri always took advantage of the court's hospitality. For him, too, the fee for his work seems to have been defined verbally and only at the end, as underscored by a letter from Andrea Arrighetti of February 1661, when the painter had just finished the ceiling of the Room of Apollo (Fig. 66): "The same was expressed to him [Ferri] by me personally. I have remained in agreement with him that he would be paid 1,500 scudi for said work."[195] Ferri had worked 15 months and was therefore earning a monthly salary of 100 scudi; his board came to 45 scudi a month and he had an assistant.[196] Ferri earned about a third less than Colonna, but his board merited three times as much (considering that prices at the time were relatively stable, that might help explain Colonna's grievances in 1639). When Ferri returned to Florence in June 1663 to paint the Room of Saturn (Fig. 67), he lived "as usual" next to the Palazzo Pitti larder; this time

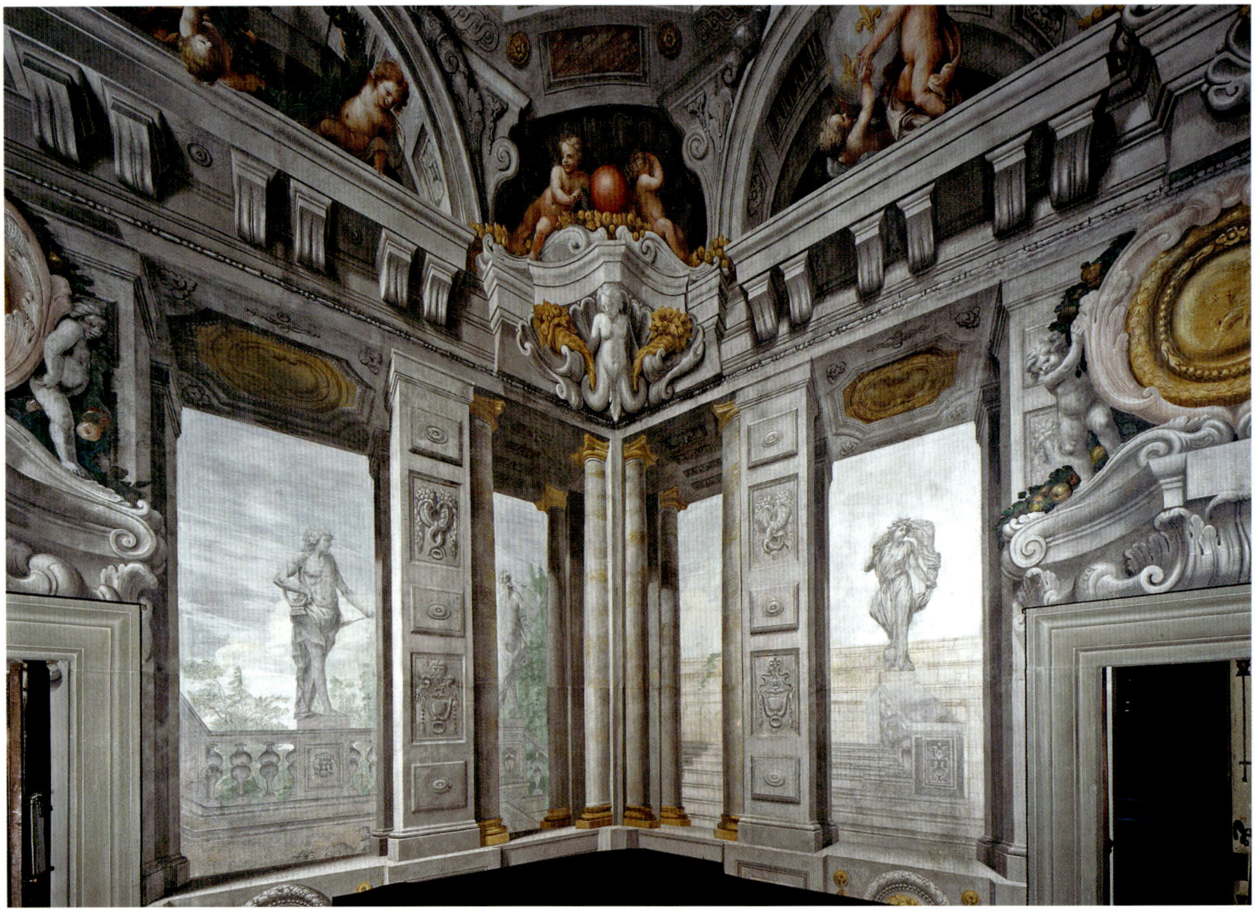

68 Jacopo Chiavistelli and collaborators, fictive architecture, 1661. Fresco. Palazzo Pitti, Florence.

he was accompanied by his wife, daughter, and brother-in-law.[197] Apparently without ever receiving an advance, he worked on the cartoons and decoration for over two years, until his work was "unveiled" on 6 August 1665, the second anniversary of the birth of Prince Ferdinand, Cosimo III's first born son.[198] The Depositeria paid Ferri a little more than 1,122 scudi, but only on the following 9 October when the painter was already working in Bergamo.[199] Possibly the Medici hoped to hire him again and withheld full compensation in order to make him return to Florence.

That Ferri did not set prices in advance for work for the grand duke is confirmed by his own words, transcribed in 1682 by his protector, Paolo Falconieri: "[Ferri] did not name a price with the grand duke, his patron, . . . he had never done this, nor did he want to do it now."[200] As with Colonna, working at Palazzo Pitti gave Ferri a lasting relationship with Florence and in particular with the grand ducal family, which later proved to be very generous towards him.[201]

In a pioneering analysis of the decoration in the Palazzo Pitti, Malcolm Campbell underlined the value of comparing the different types of remuneration that artists received during the 1630s and 1640s.[202] He argued that Florentine salaried painters working at the Palazzo Pitti between 1638 and 1642—Bravo, Vannini, and Furini—were paid more frequently but nonetheless received in total less money than foreign painters.[203] This disparity continued in later years. In February 1661 Ferri had received 1,500 scudi for completing the Room of Apollo, on which he had worked for two years. A few months later, Jacopo Chiavistelli and his partner Andrea Ciseri received 2,700 scudi for their *quadratura* frescoes on the vaults and walls of the "*salone* with the eight rooms" in the future Grand Duke Cosimo III's apartment on the ground floor of Palazzo Pitti (Fig. 68).[204] The size of their painted surfaces was unparalleled, and so was the speed of execution: they completed their work in just a few months. Moreover, except for a few details, Chiavistelli painted primarily

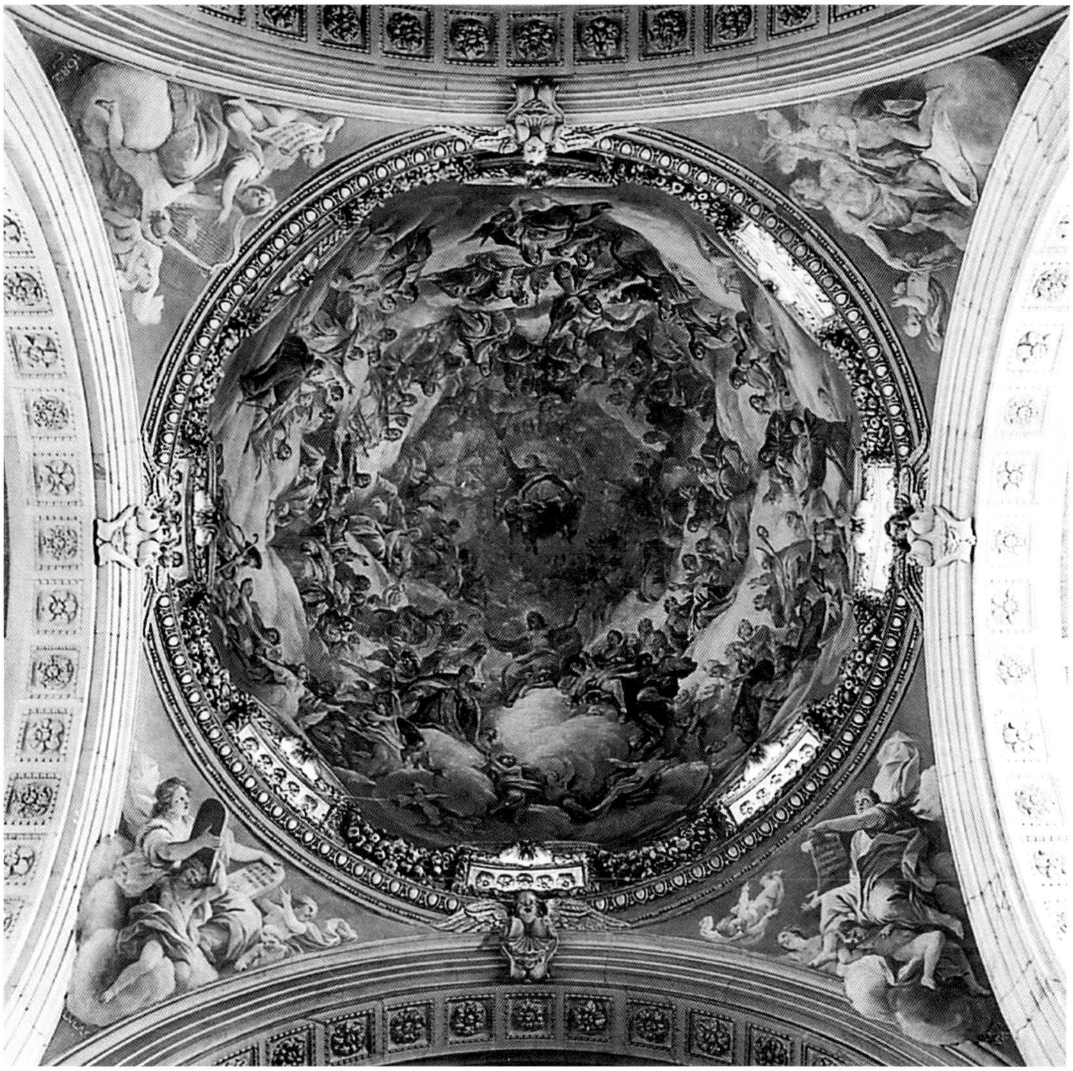

69 Luca Giordano, *S. Andrea Corsini in Glory*, 1682. Fresco. S. Maria del Carmine, Florence.

in monochrome and therefore contributed a less demanding and a less costly work than the frescoes executed by Ferri.

Like Cortona, Giordano was lodged not with his Florentine patrons but instead with his friend Andrea Del Rosso, whom he paid for his hospitality with paintings.[205] Accounts confirm that Giordano signed precise agreements with the Corsini and Riccardi families before coming to Florence or, at any rate, before starting his work for them. A letter from Baron Carlo del Nero to Prince Lorenzo Onofrio Colonna in March 1682 reveals that Marquis Bartolomeo Corsini had offered Giordano 2,000 scudi (in addition to all his expenses for a total of 2,766 scudi, according to the Corsini account books) to decorate the cupola of the family chapel in the church of the Carmine, which Luca "fa presto" completed in less than nine months (Fig. 69).[206]

Prior to the Corsini chapel, the highest sum paid for decoration of a cupola in a private chapel had gone to Volterrano, who had received 1,400 scudi for his *Coronation of the Virgin* and *Sibyls* in the pendentives in the Niccolini chapel in S. Croce. Volterrano's work, however, had dragged on from the autumn 1653 to April 1661.[207]

In September 1682, Giordano agreed with Marquis Francesco Riccardi to paint the gallery of his palace for 1,000 doppie (about 2,850 scudi). He fulfilled the agreement in just five months, between April and August 1685, and was paid immediately thereafter.[208] A recently discovered letter written by Andrea Del Rosso to Marquis Filippo di Bartolomeo Corsini on 13 August

1682 describes the arrangement between Giordano and Riccardi as if it were a true contract, and it confirms that Corsini and Del Rosso were its guarantors.[209] The patron agreed to cover the masonry expenses to prepare the vault, and to pay for the scaffolding and ultramarine blue; the painter was required to provide the other colors and to give Riccardi the *macchie* of the decoration without charge—an important condition given the increasing demand among collectors for Giordano's sketches. Finally, if Riccardi was pleased with the results, he was to give the artist a gift that was commensurate with his satisfaction.

Giordano was given preferential treatment in comparison with other painters working in the Palazzo Riccardi, including Chiavistelli.[210] In January 1692, Marquis Riccardi was taken to court by the painters Giuseppe and Tommaso Nasini regarding their two ceilings depicting the *Fall of the Giants* and *Mount Parnassus*.[211] According to their depositions, they had worked for Riccardi without a prior agreement and had not received advances during their work, and hence were asking to be paid.[212] The ceilings were appraised by Annibale Niccolai and Atanasio Bimbacci at 100 scudi each, which Riccardi paid in 1698, despite the strong protests by the Nasini, who contested the appraisal as being too low and requested that new experts be consulted.

As these examples indicate, Florentine patrons' agreements with local or foreign painters were based on different criteria, with the size of a commission and perhaps the time required to complete it being contributing factors. There is no doubt that Giordano's speed, which depended on the artist's technical expertise—the Riccardi gallery was executed *a calce* (or mezzo-fresco, i.e., on partially dry plaster) and *a secco*—made him the foreign artist who became the richest during his Florentine sojourn.

Mural Painting

Earning "By Size"

There were two principal methods of paying for mural decoration: by the day or by size (*a misura*). The first has been referred to, although it should be emphasized that rarely is it possible to verify how many days in a month or a year an artist worked on any given project. The second method is well documented, yet the difficulty of calculating a painter's earnings stems from other unknown factors, such as the duration of a job, the size of the surface decorated, and who covered the material expenses.

Payments, which often took into account whether work was executed by a master or student, were based on appraisals either "by *braccio*" (literally, an "arm's length") with reference to the measurement of the painted surface, or "by room" (*a stanza*), or "by lunette" (*a lunetta*).[213] In Florentine church cloisters and the ground floors of private palaces, lunettes at the top of walls were especially common.

In August 1619, the consuls of the Accademia del Disegno hired Matteo Rosselli, Filippo Tarchiani, and Jacopo Ligozzi to appraise the frescoes in Gianfranco Grazzini's villa in Castello, near Florence, painted by Pietro Salvestrini, a student of Poccetti's and a specialist in ornamental painting. The appraisers established precise criteria for the valuation and specified that the expenses for colors and food were Salvestrini's responsibility. The history painting was valued at 49 soldi (a little more than 2 lire) per square *braccio* and the grotesques at 19 soldi (slightly less than 1 lira). Other paintings were valued as a lump sum ("three items, all three to be paid 8 scudi"), while compensation for more modest work, such as a family coat of arms on stools, was left to the patron's discretion.[214] Evidently, in addition to size, the hierarchy of genres discussed by Richard Spear mattered.

A contract signed in March 1679 between Giovanni Garzia Mannozzi, the son of Giovanni da San Giovanni, and the Tempi family for decoration of their palace specifies that the painter would receive 14 crazie (1 lira and 2 soldi) per square *braccio* "of every painting of friezes, overdoors, and others," and 16 crazie for "other paintings in the galleria, alcove, or salotto." Evidently, the first rate pertained to ornamental motifs and the second to history painting.[215] The same criteria reappear in a list of work by Jacopo Chiavistelli, the most prolific Florentine fresco painter of the second half of the century, in the Palazzo Riccardi. Drawn up in October 1689, it distinguished between different levels of compensation by *braccio* based on the type of painting: from 1 lira, 13 soldi, 4 denari for the decoration of the chapel's *ricetto* (anteroom) to 13 soldi, 4 denari for the wainscot at the base of the walls.[216]

A noteworthy case involved several Bolognese painters whom Grand Prince Ferdinand hosted in 1685 in his villa at Pratolino while they were painting a room there. An agreement made with Vincenzo Ranuzzi, Ferdinand's *cameriere segreto*, gave them lodging at the villa and "20 lire per working day when they were working only on friezes and 23 lire, 10 soldi per day when they were working on figures."[217]

The variables in payments *a misura* are striking. For instance, Bartolomeo Neri, a specialist in architectural details and ornament, was given a sizeable amount (4.3 lire per *braccio*) for decorating the vault of the ground-floor gallery of the Palazzo Corsini in the early 1650s. Yet in 1653, Chiavistelli and Andrea Ciseri were working in the same palace for 2 lire per *braccio*.[218] Neri, however, was senior and Chiavistelli's teacher, whereas his student was just starting out on his own.

Sagrestani's and Baldinucci's accounts regarding Antonio Giusti seem more exceptional. After serving an apprenticeship with Mario Balassi, Giusti began to work independently on "architecture and friezes with flowers and animals" and "he made himself so desirable . . . that he was paid at the rate of one piastra [scudo] per *braccio*, and earned up to 20 piastre per day." Later, according to Baldinucci, as the painter grew older and the value of his works diminished, this price fell by a third.[219] Sagrestani repeats the information and adds that Giusti's fame reflected a well-paid phase of fresco painting in Florence, though more data are needed to establish if it was in higher demand during the second half of the century. The sizeable fortunes amassed by two of the most active decorators of the period, Chiavistelli and Cosimo Ulivelli, provide support for Sagrestani's observation. According to their biographers, they accumulated the impressive sums of 40,000 and 30,000 scudi respectively.[220]

At times artists were compensated for their murals simply "by room" (*a stanza*). For example, for his extensive work in the Palazzo Salviati (now Gerini) in via Ricasoli, executed at the end of the sixteenth century, Poccetti and his collaborators were paid *a stanza*: 40 scudi to the master, 30 scudi to his assistants. Advances were made weekly, following the common practice for paying masons and laborers.[221] It seems that payments "by room" typically referred to the decoration of ceilings with a *storia* in the center and grotesque motifs surrounding it, as well as lunettes below. If this kind of payment reflects a generally low level of compensation for Florentine murals, it should be borne in mind that Baldinucci and other sources report that Poccetti demanded little.[222]

Lunettes and Ceilings

Starting in the last two decades of the sixteenth century, Florence witnessed an impressive revival in painted lunette cycles, both in religious and secular architecture. In the footsteps of a tradition that traced its origins to the fifteenth-century cycles in the Chiostro Verde of S. Maria Novella and the Chiostro degli Aranci in the Badia, the late sixteenth-century post-Tridentine demand for religious painting with a clear didactic aim prompted the city's principal monastic orders to promote a specific type of decoration in their cloisters: extended pictorial cycles depicting the history of their founders or of the order itself.[223] The cycles were often financed by noble families who in some way were related to the convents or had family chapels and burials in the churches.

Ligozzi (1600–5), Giovanni da San Giovanni (ca. 1616–19), Filippo Tarchiani, Galeazzo Ghidoni (162?), and Nicodemo Ferrucci worked on the *Stories of the Life of St. Francis* in the cloister of Ognissanti. One of Ligozzi's lunettes, the *Meeting in San Giovanni Laterano*, fetched 50 scudi, which was much more than the norm.[224] The decoration of the large cloister at SS. Annunziata, begun around 1604, dragged on for several decades, too, and was financed by members of the principal Florentine families. Poccetti, Ventura Salimbeni, Donato Mascagni, and Rosselli took part in the work.[225] Baldinucci reports that Poccetti received 25 scudi from Archbishop Alessandro Marzi Medici for having painted the lunette of the *Blessed Amideo Amidei Resurrects a Drowned Youth*. He noted that this was a *prezzo ordinario*, an "ordinary price," which Poccetti demanded for the other lunettes as well.[226] Poccetti, he adds, painted it in 18 days, "working only six hours per day."[227] For another lunette executed in 1605 in the same cloister for the Carlini family, Poccetti received 30 scudi, including the cost of colors.[228] Apparently, he paid his assistants very little. According to a Servite friar's account, one of them, Antonio da Rovezzano, received just 2 scudi from his master for executing a lunette depicting the *Seven Founders of the Order who Decide to Retire from the World*.[229]

These and other examples confirm Baldinucci's claim about Poccetti's willingness to work for low fees. In contrast, Ventura Salimbeni, who was less esteemed and received the same 25 scudi payment for each of his four lunettes in the Annunziata, decided after painting the first one that he wanted twice that amount.[230]

Painters earned much less when they worked directly for a monastic order. At the start of the century (1600–1), the Camaldolesi of S. Maria degli Angeli hired Donato Mascagni, Poccetti, and Bernardino Monaldi to decorate their cloister and paid them only about 6 scudi per lunette.[231] A generation later in 1633, Giovanni da San Giovanni, Nicodemo Ferrucci, and Jacopo Confortini, under the commission of individual Vallombrosan fathers, painted lunettes in the refectory at the convent of S. Trinita: "Each was paid 14 scudi per lunette counting the spandrels above the capitals."[232] And to cite an example from the end of the century,

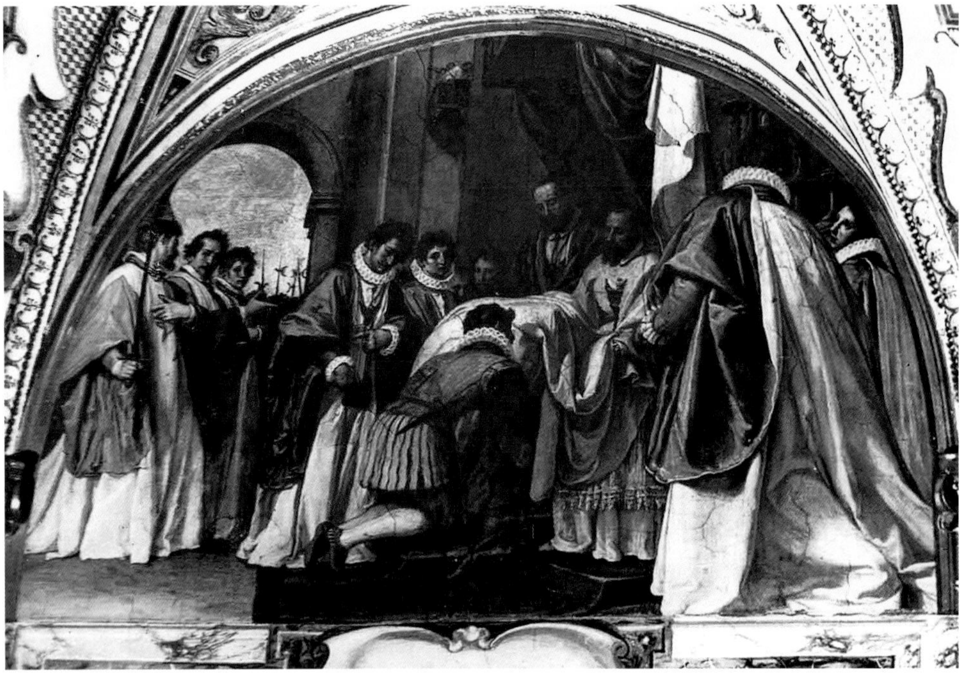

70 Ottavio Vannini, *Investiture of Francesco I into the Order of S. Stefano*, 1622–23. Fresco. Room of Francesco I, Casino di S. Marco, Florence.

in 1692 the friars of the convent of S. Marco paid Pier Dandini 34 scudi "from what was left over in the Spezieria" for having painted the final two lunettes of the first cloister, whose decoration had begun way back in the 1610s.[233]

Despite the low fees, perhaps painters accepted this type of work out of necessity and with the hope of later obtaining more highly paid commissions. Moreover, the religious devotion of each artist, which is repeatedly mentioned in Baldinucci's *Vite*, might have been a factor as well. Passignano's strong devotion to S. Giovanni Gualberto, to cite a good example, led him to work for the Vallombrosan Order almost for free, accepting just 45 scudi for his paintings in the chapel with the relics of the founder of S. Trinita (1594). The convent's Ricordanze explicitly state that his work was "painted almost entirely out of his own devotion [dipinte quasi per sua devozione]."[234] A similar case involves Pier Dandini, who between 1688 and 1689, after having painted the cupola and three lunettes of the chapel of St. Bernard in the church of S. Frediano in Cestello, "also wanted to do the altarpiece of the said chapel and was content with a simple gift of 30 scudi for his kindness."[235]

Lunettes in private palaces earned no more than those in privately funded cloisters. Cardinal Carlo de' Medici commissioned Vannini (Fig. 70), Rosselli, Boschi, Anastasio Fontebuoni, Filippo Tarchiani, and Michelangelo Cinganelli to paint a series of lunettes for his Florentine residence, the Casino di S. Marco (1621–24). Six scudi were paid for the smaller ones by Boschi, 15 to 18 scudi for the larger ones by the assistants of Rosselli, Cinganelli, and Vannini, and 18 to 26 scudi for those painted by the masters themselves.[236] For their lunettes in the "loggetta della Stufa" in the Palazzo Pitti, painted before 1627, Rosselli and Vannini similarly were paid about 20 scudi.[237]

The fees paid for lunettes and for ceilings with history paintings in the Casino di S. Marco were not very different. In fact, Vannini's vault painting was valued at 24 scudi, less than the 26 scudi for his lunettes. In Fontebuoni's case, his vault was valued at 30 scudi, and the surrounding grotesques at the sizeable sum of 5 lire per square *braccio*.[238]

Ceiling painting, however, had its dangers: "Fresco painting from scaffolding, under the vaults with lime mortar, is not only immense and extraordinary effort but also causes illness; as the record shows, almost all the painters who worked on such large-scale works were ill for a long time."[239] Nonetheless, a moderately successful Florentine painter would generally have earned less for painting a ceiling than for an altarpiece, as the records of the Palazzo Corsini's *fabbrica* from the 1690s suggest. For the ceiling with *Virtue Tempted by*

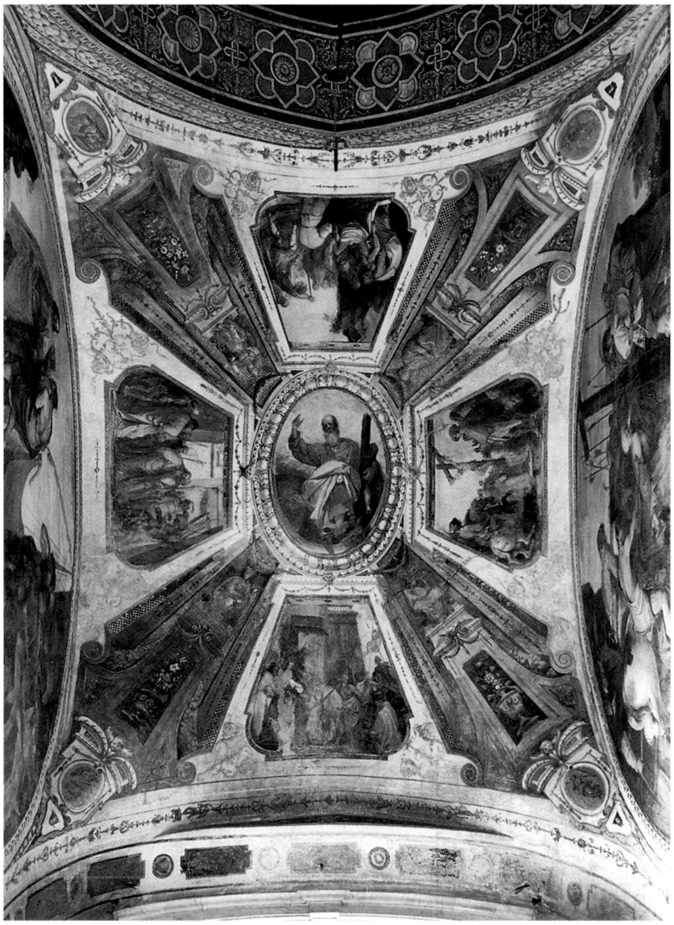

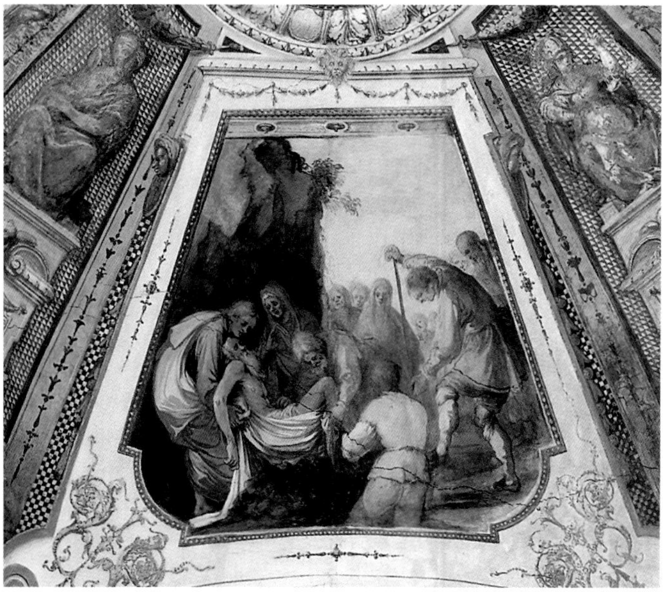

71 (left) Giovanni da San Giovanni, *Scenes from the Life of St. Andrew*, 1621. Fresco. Calderini chapel, S. Croce, Florence.

72 (above) Giovanni da San Giovanni, detail of Fig. 71.

Vice and Protected by Jupiter, Minerva, and Mercury, Cosimo Ulivelli received only 50 scudi in 1692; in 1696, 10 more were paid to Pier Dandini for his ceiling; and the same year Atanasio Bimbacci received 70 scudi for his two *sfondi*: that is, for his paintings in the center of two ceilings.[240]

At the end of the century, Gabbiani was earning more for ceilings of various sizes: 100 scudi for *Jupiter on Olympus* (1691, Villa Medici, Poggio a Caiano); 400 scudi for the mezzanine galleries in the Palazzo Pitti (1692–93); 400 scudi for the *Apotheosis of Cosimo il Vecchio* completed in 1698 at Poggio a Caiano; and 300 scudi in 1700 for a ceiling with the *Allegory of Valor and Eternity* painted for the Corsini.[241]

Chapels and Cupolas

Painters in Florence often received an inclusive sum for a chapel's decoration, including costs for the altarpiece, vault, lunettes, and lateral paintings. This makes it impossible to identify the value of each part, although it is important to remember that fresco murals were normally priced more modestly than oil altarpieces. Such cumulative payments exist, for example, for the Theatine church of SS. Michele e Gaetano, whose side chapels of the transept and nave were decorated between the 1620s and 1640s. In 1631, Rosselli painted the altarpiece (*The Nativity*), a lateral canvas (*The Visitation*), the vault and two lunettes of the Bonsi chapel; in 1632 he received a total of 350 scudi for all of his work.[242] Also in that year Vignali painted the vault, two lunettes, and a lateral canvas in the chapel on the opposite side of the transept, for which he was paid 150 scudi.[243] Between 1642 and 1643 Lorenzo Lippi was paid the same amount for decorating the vault and three lunettes in the Ardinghelli chapel.[244] And for the same amount of work, Angelo Michele Colonna received 200 scudi from Francesco Franceschi in 1643.[245]

Following a sixteenth-century practice with deep roots in Florentine tradition, the vaults of these chapels painted by Florentine artists were divided into five sections, with a central episode and four lateral images,

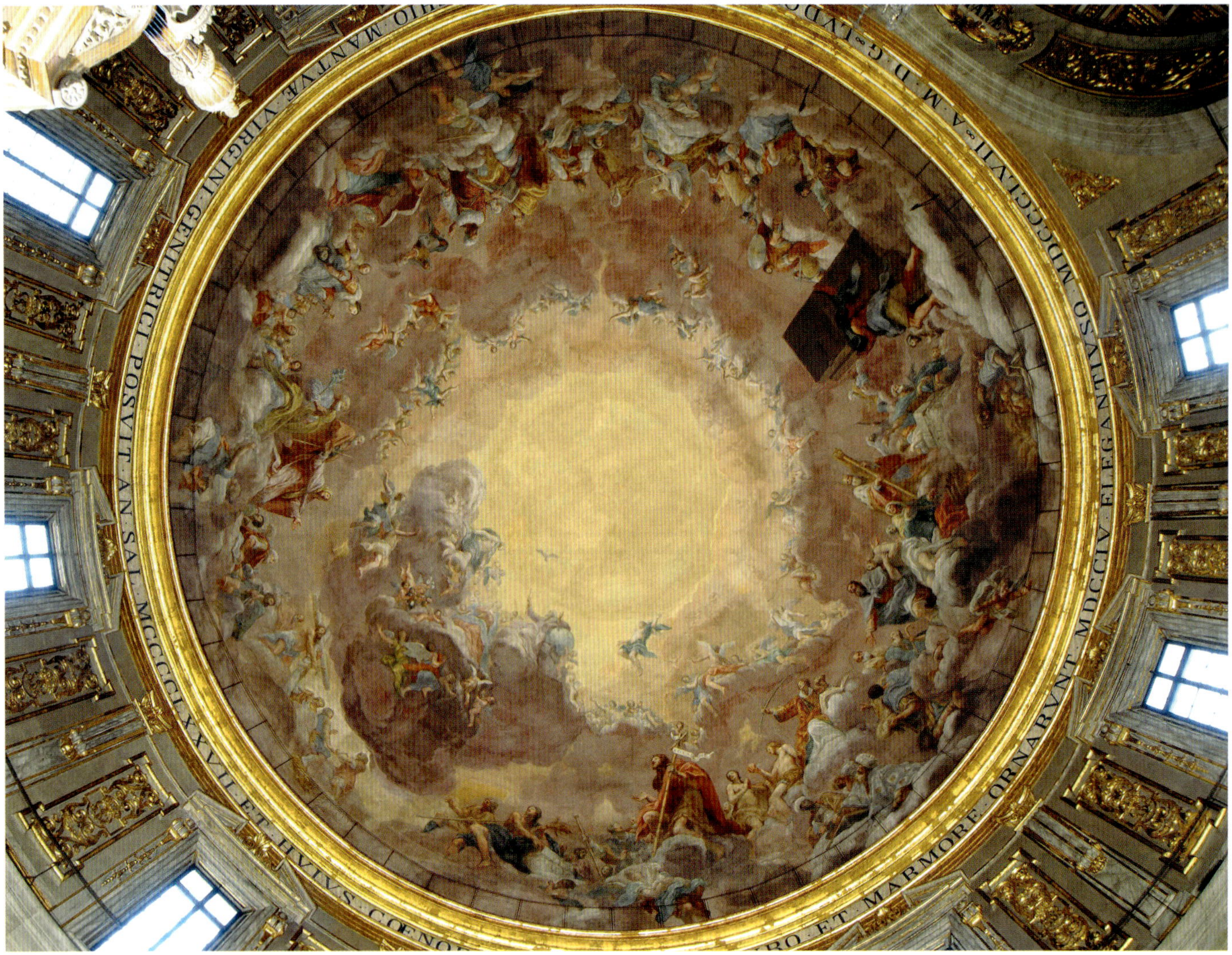

73 Baldassarre Franceschini (called Volterrano), *Assumption of the Virgin*, 1680–83. Fresco. SS. Annunziata, Florence.

some of which were entirely ornamental. Documents for the mural decoration of the Calderini chapel in S. Croce (Figs. 71 and 72) provide a useful breakdown and point of comparison. A receipt signed by Giovanni da San Giovanni in 1621 indicates that the 470 scudi total payment was divided thus: the parts with figures were valued at 235 scudi, or 95 scudi for the center of the cupola, which contained four stories at 20 scudi per story and a figure in a central oval at 15 scudi, and 140 scudi for the two lateral lunettes; 35 scudi for several ornamental passages; and 200 scudi for the gilded ornaments in the cupola ("lo spartimento della volta tutto messo a oro con quattro figurine d'oro, vasi architetture e fogliami").[246] The high appraisal of the latter part reflected the costly materials used to decorate the cupola.

At the end of the century the chapels of the Cistercian church of S. Frediano in Cestello were renovated. An artist was assigned to each by the sponsoring abbots. Pier Dandini received 400 scudi in 1688–89 to paint the cupola, pendentives, and three lunettes in the chapel of St. Bernard; immediately afterwards he painted the altarpiece of *St. Bernard of Clairvaux Prays for the Souls in Purgatory*, for which he received only a "gift" of 30 scudi.[247] In 1694, Alessandro Gherardini was paid 700 scudi for the decoration of the entire chapel dedicated to the Nativity of the Virgin, including its altarpiece.[248] The less well-known Giovan Camillo Ciabilli received the same amount for the chapel of Sant'Anastasio.[249] Further evidence indicates that arrangements between the abbots and painters varied greatly. In early 1695, Antonio Franchi agreed with Abbot Ferdinando Buonmannelli to decorate the chapel of St. John the Baptist for half of what had been given to Gherardini the previous year: 350 scudi for the cupola, three lunettes, and altarpiece. The painter requested a "small wooden cupola for preparatory study," prepared canvas, and blue pigment. The altarpiece was delivered in October, and Franchi received 200 scudi for it. He then began the wall decorations, but nudged on by his protector Lorenzo Aldimari, in 1699 he asked that his fee be increased on the grounds that he had worked more than foreseen. In 1706 he was awarded an additional 100 Roman scudi.[250]

Compared with Giovanni da San Giovanni's payment in 1621 for the Calderini cupola in S. Croce (95 scudi plus 35 for ornamental passages), Volterrano's fee in 1650 for painting the small cupola and pendentives of the Colloredo chapel at the Annunziata was far better. Initially he was paid 200 scudi, but the sum was doubled following an appraisal by Vignali and Vincenzo Dandini, who judged the painter's initial request to have been "modest."[251] Moreover, Volterrano, who had been ill a long time before starting work, asked the Servites at the Annunziata "to be given a room in this convent just as the same convent provided him with food," a request that was granted.[252]

During the second half of the century, a large number of cupolas were decorated in private chapels, apses, and transepts. Surviving contracts indicate that scaffolding and masonry were generally at the patron's expense, and that payments to painters were based on reports describing the "work's progress."

In 1665 Livio Mehus signed a contract with the fathers of S. Maria della Pace whereby he agreed to paint the *Glory of St. Bernard* in the cupola of their church and four *Cardinal Virtues* in the pendentives for 300 scudi, given by the Marquis Filippo Niccolini. The agreement stipulated that he would be paid in ten monthly installments or in another manner of his choice, provided that "he was working." For the materials he was to receive an additional 5 doppie (13 scudi) for the "colors, paper, or similar things." He was also offered food during the day and the evening as well if he could not return home and had to spend the night at the convent. The friars who signed the agreement concluded with great flexibility that "we will do the little that we can, and when he wants to eat meat he will advise us a day in advance, so that we can satisfy his request, as all the fathers will do their best so that he may be as contented as possible."[253] Although Mehus's cupola is lost, the church's assembly room exists, its small size suggesting that the artist's work, for which he was paid between November 1666 and February 1667, was relatively modest.

Volterrano's cupola of the tribune of the Annunziata (1680–83) was much more demanding, as was Gabbiani's in S. Frediano in Cestello (1698–1718). The former project (Fig. 73), funded with a 6,000 scudi inheritance from Prior Donato dell'Antella, required two sets of scaffolding, one in 1677 at a cost of 300 scudi, the other in 1678 for 360 more. Volterrano and the Servites agreed that the painter would receive 3,800 scudi and, if there was any money left over, another 200, or 4,000 scudi in all, payable in six-monthly installments.[254] The convent's Ricordanze specify that the work was started on 19 September 1680 and that "the painter did not work continuously, but took the summer months off and other times too and sometimes was indisposed; thus it appears that he completed this work in about two years."[255] It was the most highly paid and biggest cupola in seventeenth-century Florence. Volterrano painted it alone, having fired his assistant Ulivelli after two-and-a-half months. Perhaps due to the cupola's size, Volterrano's contract did not specify a deadline for its completion.

The agreement signed by Gabbiani with the Cistercian Abbot Ferdinando Maria Romanelli in 1698, on the other hand, set a limit of five years for the artist to finish the decoration of the cupola and pendentives of the church of Cestello, for which he was to be paid 2,250 scudi (Fig. 74).[256] Just as Volterrano had been initially proposed by Mattias de' Medici to paint the tribune of the Annunziata—"advice" which the Operai of the Servite church acted on about 20 years later—the Cistercian documents likewise make no mystery of the fact that Gabbiani was touted for the Cestello work by Grand Prince Ferdinand. The terms of the agreement were even more specific than those cited previously. The sum promised to the artist already included "that discretionary part which is usually referred to as the gift given at the work's completion [quella parte di convenienza che suole usarsi con nome di regalo finita l'opera]." A series of payments were clearly stipulated: "100 Italian doble upon the writing of the contract," another 150 in July 1699, and 100 each July thereafter until the total amount had been paid, "supposing, however, that each year he should paint and work according to the measure of payments [supposto però che anno per anno dipingesse e operasse a misura de' pagamenti]." As usual, the friars would pay for the scaffolding and masonry expenses. On his part, Gabbiani agreed to paint according to the instructions provided concerning the subject matter, as well as "to pay for the ultramarine blues, varnishes, cartoons, and similar things." In 1710 the cupola was almost finished, even though the painter, who had received a little more than

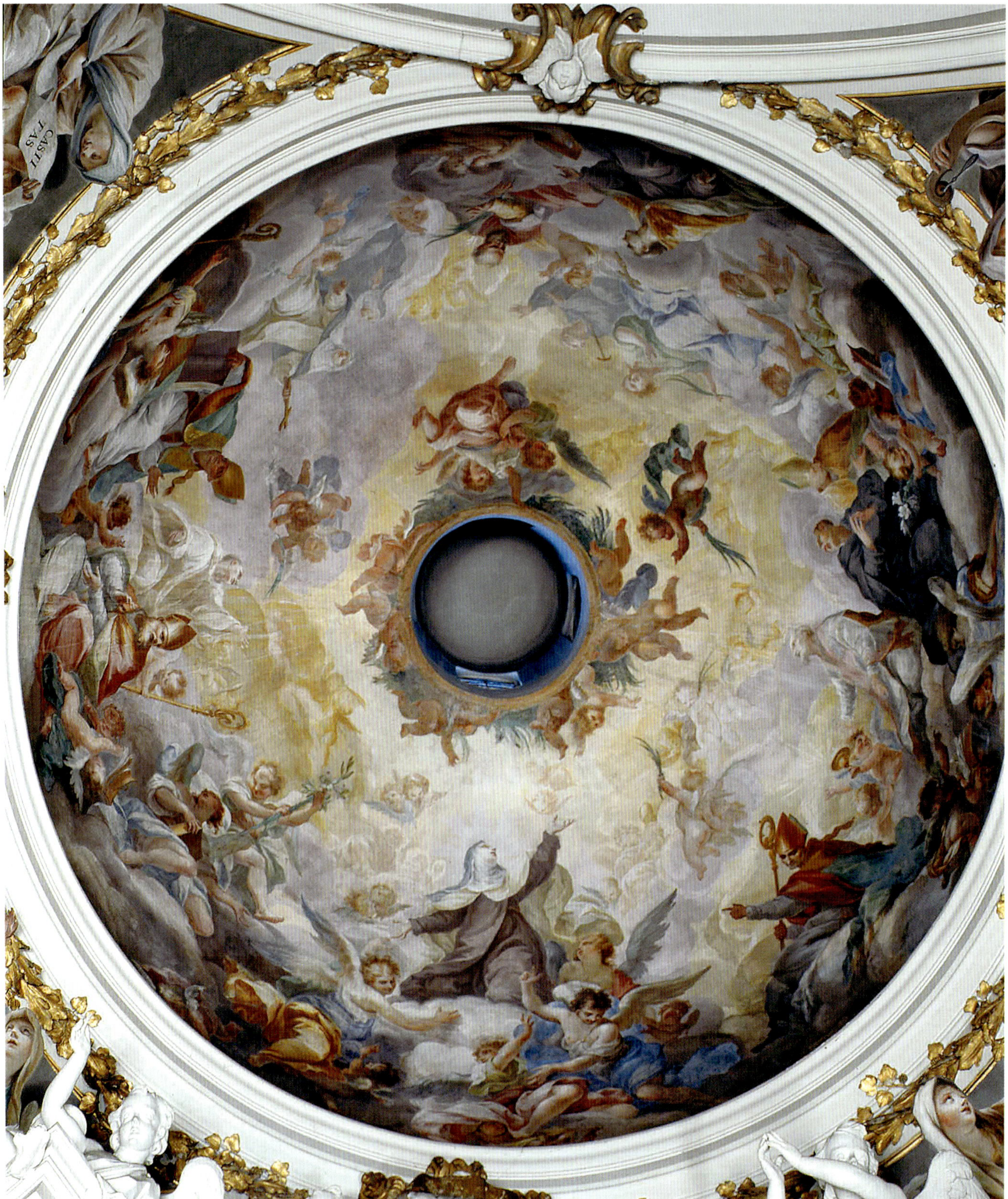

74 Anton Domenico Gabbiani, *Assumption of the Magdalene*, 1698–1718. Fresco. S. Frediano in Cestello.

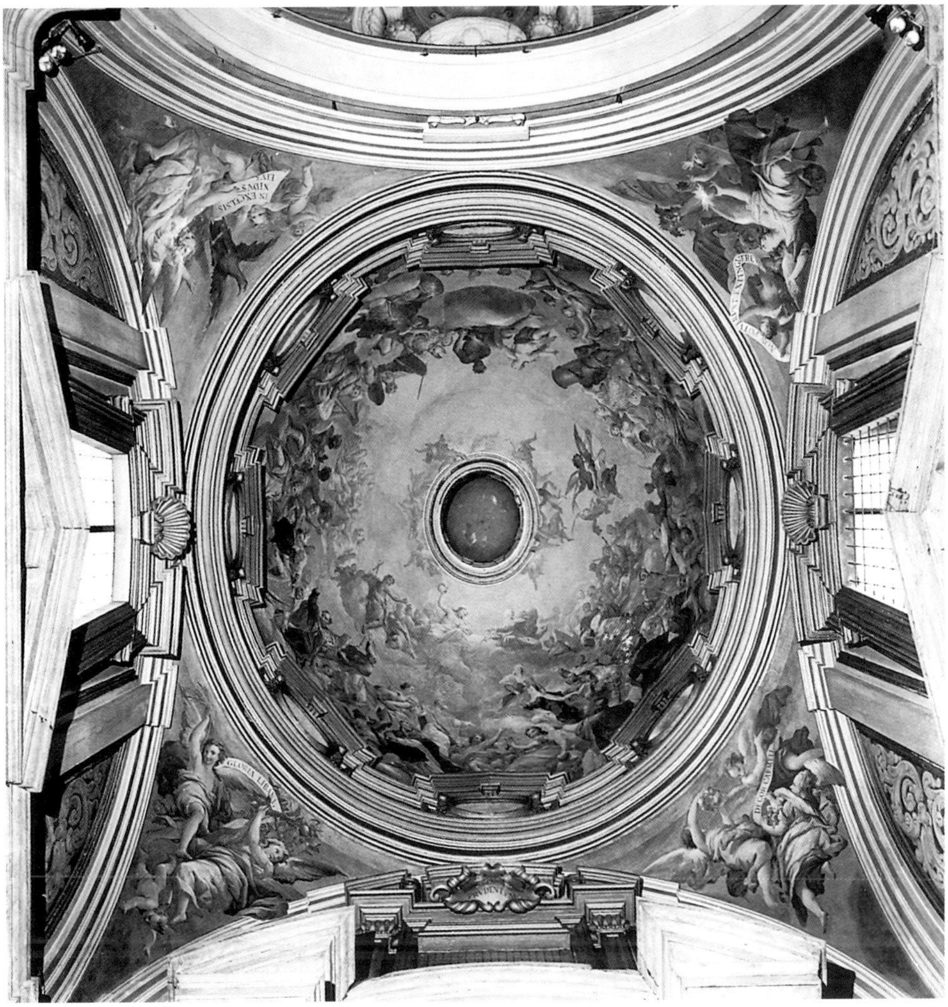

75 Pier Dandini, *S. Maria Maddalena de' Pazzi in Glory*, 1700–1. Fresco. S. Maria Maddalena de' Pazzi, Florence.

1,500 scudi, only finalized the *accomodamenti* ("final touches") in 1718. The pendentives, however, were still not painted, and meanwhile a rift had emerged between Gabbiani and the friars. They accused him of being interested "not in painting the said cupola, but in his own business in various places," all the while they had to pay half a scudo per day for the masons and laborers he had requested. And to make matters worse, their church was filled up with scaffolding. Not surprisingly, Gabbiani's requests to be paid the full amount were unsuccessful.

On a more positive note, it is said by the diarist Settimanni that for decorating the cupola of the apsidal chapel of S. Maria Maddalena de' Pazzi (Fig. 75), commissioned by Cosimo III, Pier Dandini executed the work "without any other reward but that which he hoped for from God through the mediation of that saint."[257]

In sum, the documentation examined in this essay suggests that, much more often than suspected, painters in Florence worked without having negotiated their compensation in advance. Second, in comparison with local painters, foreigners at the Medici court evidently enjoyed privileged economic conditions. Finally, with regard to mural painting, methods of payment differed. Not surprisingly, earnings were determined by the extent of a painter's actual participation in a project. Some were paid by the day, others by the job, with a clear distinction betweeen figurative and decorative work. Yet, as in the case of lunettes, the size and number of figures were not necessarily correlated to the compensation a painter received.

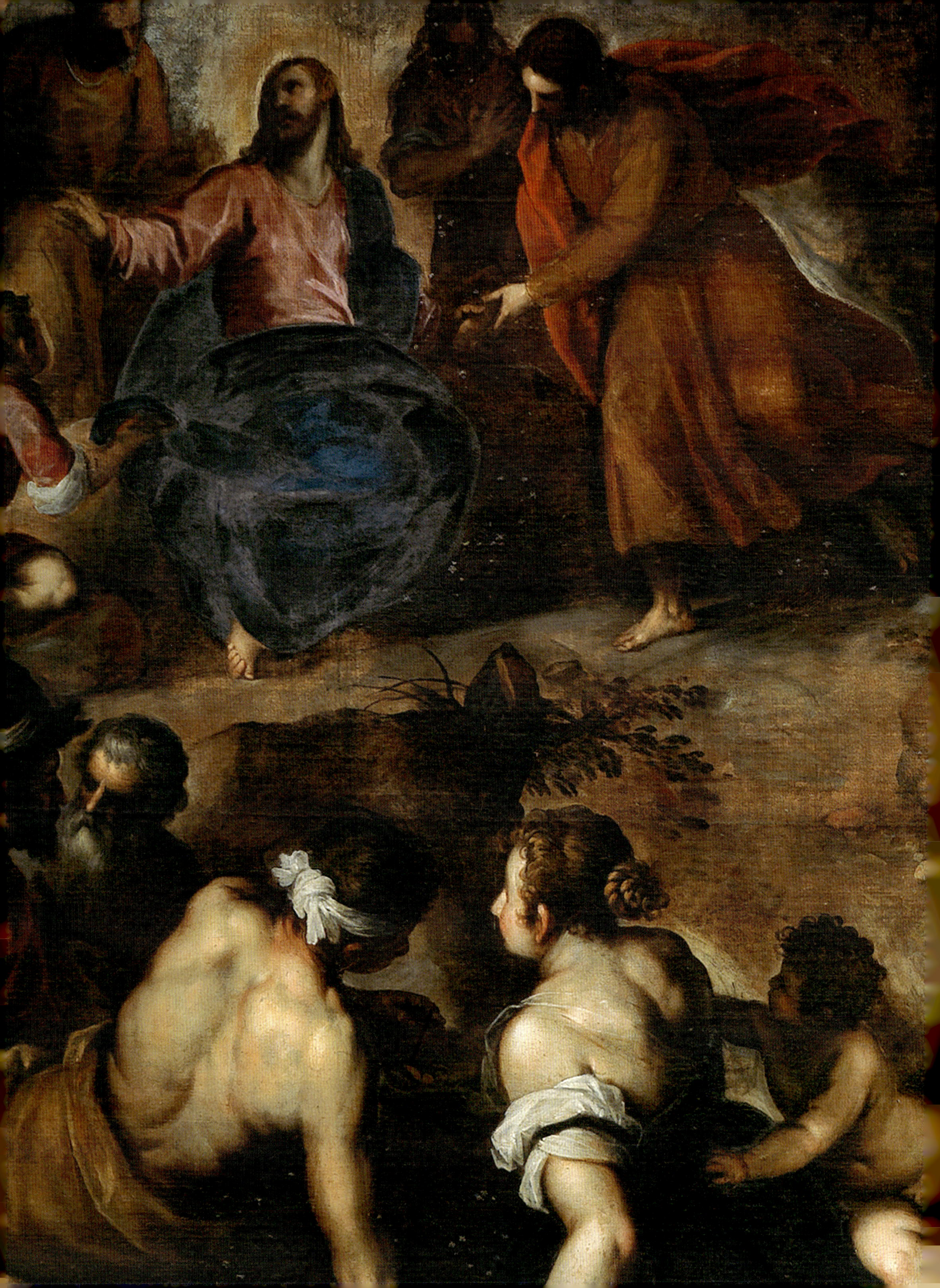

5

Venice

PHILIP SOHM

Introduction: Demographics and Currencies

Venice was Italy's second most populous city in the seventeenth century, about twice as large as Florence and Bologna and surpassed only by Naples. Like most other Italian cities, with Rome as a notable exception, Venice's population experienced precipitous drops due to various plagues (especially those of 1576 and 1630–31) and resilient recoveries (see Table 12).

Survival rates from the plague of 1630–31 show the nobility enjoying the privileges of power. Justly proud of its status as Europe's oldest republic—specificially, a constitutional oligarchy—Venice's stability derived from its intricate council and committee structure that helped the conservative nobility to resist sudden changes. Table 12 also shows, unexpectedly, that the elite group of citizens (*cittadini*) survived the plague at an even higher rate than the nobility. Venetians could be enrolled as citizens if they met criteria regarding their trade or profession and their residency in Venice (15 years for *cittadini ordinarii* and at least two generations for *cittadini originarii*). In addition, *cittadini originarii* must possess "honorable status," meaning that neither they nor their fathers could have exercised a "manual" or "mechanical" trade. Although disenfranchised, citizens often became wealthy and influential through commerce and as top-level bureaucrats. In 1603, when Giovanni Nicolò Doglioni updated Francesco Sansovino's survey of Venice, he divided the remaining population between artisans (*artigiani*) at 78 percent, household servants and stewards (*servitori* and *massare*) at 7 percent, and clergy at 3 percent.[1]

The currency of account in Venice was the lira and its subunits (20 soldi to the lira and 12 denari to the soldo).[2] The ducat as a currency of account was worth 6 lire and 4 soldi. While debts and credits were often calculated in lire, cash payments were made in ducats which were divided into 24 grossi, with each grosso further subdivided into 32 piccoli. As the republic's pre-eminent coin, the silver ducat (Fig. 76) remained fairly constant in weight (depending on the value of silver) with some dramatic corrections, one tied to the plague of 1630–31 when the ducat was reduced in weight from 26.26 grams in 1621 to 20.1 in 1635. The less frequently used silver scudo weighed (and hence was valued) the same as the ducat. The silver zecchino remained a constant 45.5 grams and hence changed in value against the ducat from 1.6 in 1608 to 2.0 in 1621 and 2.4 in 1635. The gold ducat and the gold doppia, double the ducat's value as its name suggests, were rarely used in payments to painters. Venetian territories usually used the ducat but also maintained local curriences. The Veronese and Vicentine trono was worth about a quarter of a silver ducat.

Facing page: detail of Fig. 86

Rhetoric of Decline: Perceptions and Reality

> The reasons why we have so few excellent painters are not hard to plumb since there is really little profit to be made. The way that the few monopolize the available work, redistributing some of it to assistants, is worth considering because if this practice were jettisoned by [this elite] and by the shops as well that profit (possibly in excess) from the work of others, then the sum total available to painters in general would be larger. It is clear that the art of painting is in decline if today everything other than painting is used to decorate palaces. The Venetian school has always been held in esteem, but today all civilized nations have their own style that they love, and except for the few great gentlemen and experts, they do not go searching for other good paintings. . . . [When collectors look for paintings] they buy them by the dozen, sold in bunches in the shops and bought from poor starving painters at the lowest price. . . . There are few excellent painters today, and if they want to make a living, they usually travel abroad (Francesco Tron, President, Milizia da Mar, 1757).[3]

How did the glorious tradition of Venetian painters arrive at such a dismal state? In his dire report on the shape of art in 1757, Francesco Tron repeated an economic explanation that the newly founded Collegio de' Pittori first formulated in 1679: foreign competition and a drain abroad of native painters, rich and greedy painters who did not want to share the wealth, and poor painters who were commercially exploited by dealers. During this period the Milizia da Mar was the magistracy responsible for the collection of taxes from the Collegio. Like many other taxpayers, Venetian painters wanted to pay lower taxes, and to achieve this goal they needed to convince the Milizia da Mar that their business was suffering. The Milizia da Mar, on the other hand, wanted to maximize tax revenues, and yet it accepted the painters' economic diagnosis of artistic decline, presumably because it had some merit. Dislocation, depredation, and exploitation form the socioeconomic nexus that painters used to explain artistic decline. Economic justice and financial reward foster artistic vitality; their absence engenders decay.

Tron wrote within an established Venetian tradition that took the seventeenth century as the heart of a dark age wedged between two golden ages. Chronologies of this dark age differed from periodizations of Roman and Neapolitan art, and hence Venice requires a different temporal frame from other essays in this book. In Rome, where the arrival of Annibale Carracci in 1595 and the public debut of Caravaggio as a history painter in 1600 coincided with the new century, it is reasonable to think of art history in calendric terms. For Naples, too, modern (i.e., seventeenth-century) art can be dated to Caravaggio's transformative visit in 1606. Venice, however, was exceptional in this regard as in so many others. By the 1730s Venetians generally agreed that art first entered a new dark age with the death of Titian in 1576, and only emerged from its decline around 1730 with the resurgent splendor of Tiepolo. The historiography of Venetian artistic decline started around the time of Tintoretto's death, possibly in 1589 when Giambattista Leoni anticipated the death of Venetian painting. Titian and Veronese were dead, and Tintoretto at age 71 would presumably soon follow: "And, may they forgive me, and may all the others forgive me, but it seems to me that the refinement and the lofty technique could be dead with these worthy men."[4]

If Leoni sounded wistful or regretful, Federico Zuccaro wrote with vindictive scorn when he opened his poem *Lamento della pittura sul l'onde venete* (Mantua,

TABLE 12 Population of Venice, 1576–1696[5]

YEAR	GENERAL POPULATION	NOBILITY	CITIZENS	COMMONERS	CLERGY	FOREIGNERS
1576	170,000 (est.)					
1578	120,000 (est.)					
1581	134,871					
1586	148,097	6,439 (4.3%)	7,692 (5.2%)	126,535 (85.4%)	4,182 (2.8%)	3,249 (2.2%)
1607	188,970	6,322 (3.3%)	14,471 (7.7%)	151,153 (79.9%)	5,810 (3.1%)	11,214 (5.9%)
1624	141,625	5,546 (3.9%)	10,575 (7.46%)	125,504 (88.6%)		
1633	102,307	4,297 (4.2%)	9,790 (9.6%)	88,156 (86.2%)		
1642	120,307	4,457 (3.7%)	9,358 (7.8%)	97,249 (80.8%)	4,756 (3.9%)	4,487 (3.7%)
1670	132,000 (est.)					
1696	138,067					

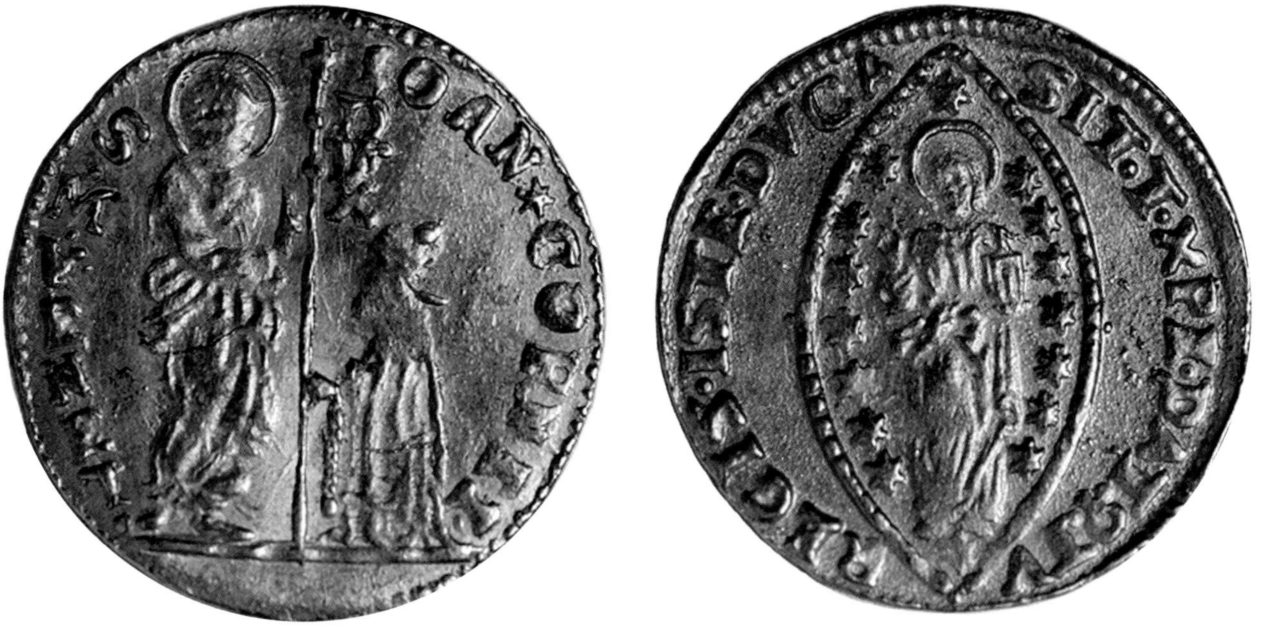

76 Venetian ducat, 1631–46. Princeton University, Numismatic Collection.

1605) with the appalled author meeting a shabby "Painting," dressed in rags. What happened to you and your glorious tradition, he asks "Painting," who responds by blaming Tintoretto and his sketchy style.[6] Zuccaro made the tattered and stained clothes of "Painting" to signify her poverty and the painterly style that created it. Artistic and financial degradation coexist within this allegorical figure as cause and effect, identified with each other linguistically where *macchia* signifies the physical stains of poor dirty clothing, the moral blemish of professional dereliction, and the cause of it all, Tintoretto's sketched style. As Giulio Cesare Gigli noted ten years later, Zuccaro was hardly a neutral observer but instead one filled with "an inflated envy . . . and malice" that came from losing twice to Tintoretto in competitions: once at the Scuola di San Rocco because of Tintoretto's sneaky gift, and later at the Palazzo Ducale when the Signoria chose Tintoretto's *modello* for the monumental *Paradise*.[7] Marco Boschini blamed Zuccaro's "pestilent poison" on a disappointed foreigner's bias.[8]

What is peculiar about the status of seventeenth-century Venetian painting, as viewed by contemporaries, is how Zuccaro's image of Venetian "Painting" reduced to ragged penury became the way that Venetian painters looked at themselves. In 1679 the painters submitted to the Senate the following depressing statement about current affairs in the art world:

> The profession of painting, noble in origin and miraculous in effects, always flourished in this serene and happy land. In dignified times, painting maintained a position of high esteem, envied by other countries and admired by posterity, but these first expert artists were struck over the head by a contagious plague and hence languished and declined for a while and became involved with the abuses of the age, involving certain vulgar and low-class trades. Today we find painting incumbered in the same tombs either because it is neglected or because of the poverty of our masters.[9]

This collective representation of themselves drew on themes then in general circulation, including a nostalgia for better times, the burden of living in the shadow of a glorious tradition, and the sense of decay and impoverishment.[10] The "contagious plague," a common metaphor of cultural decline, is here given an unusual twist by associating it with the plague of 1631 that was thought to initiate an economic depression. The intersection of demographics and economics as an explanation for artistic decline was launched into art historiography by Anton Maria Zanetti (1771) and Luigi Lanzi (1789):

> After these years, especially [the plague years of] 1630 and 1631 when so many painters died, the relics of the good Venetian school were being lost [to export], and most of the paintings in the mid-seventeenth

century took on a different character. Signor Zanetti points out that around this time some foreign painters established themselves in this city and subsequently the realm of painting was in their hands.[11]

"Decadence" (*decadenza*) and "rebirth" (*risorgere*) remained for Venetian artists the frustrating gap between the present and the past. In 1724 the Collegio found art to be flourishing elsewhere but not in Venice. Germans and other foreigners came to study in Rome, Naples, Florence, and Bologna, but in Venice (the Collegio claimed) painting is "humiliated and almost expired":

> Many people practice the profession today but of these only a few make a good living; the others who want to do so are always moving from place to place, either forever or from time to time. They go with their happy brushes to toil in foreign lands, abandoning their homeland where they are debtors. Other painters, and these are the majority in the Collegio, debase themselves to commerce and produce work of little merit. They find it difficult to live and even to pay their dues, which are going up all the time because the best [and hence richest] painters are no longer here in Venice contributing fees.[12]

The Collegio gave two economic explanations for artistic decline. The first closely followed the standard explanation amongst modern economic historians for Venice's economic "crisis" in the seventeenth century, where Venetian trade in wool, silk, and spices lost out to foreign competitors as new trade routes opened up and as new means of production were developed. The loss of economic opportunity in Venice, goes the second explanation, encouraged the best painters to leave and work elsewhere, thus impoverishing those left behind. Scarcity of money led painters into commerce, thus debasing art even further. Art and commerce embraced and dragged each other down. Venice was thus trapped in an artistic-economic devolution where supply and demand acted as a natural selection process in reverse, removing the best from the city and leaving behind the mediocre who then could not sustain, much less carry forward, the noble tradition of Venetian painting.

How accurate were the Venetian painters and the cultural elite when they identified an artistic decline and ascribed it to market factors? Did art history really shadow economic history? On the one hand, the Collegio commentaries fit too well into a culture of complaint to be taken as impartial analyses. Paolo Pino, for example, complained that painters were less well paid now (1548) than in the past.[13] No evidence exists to suggest this is true, even though for a struggling painter like Pino it must have seemed to be true. Later painters made no mention of deflation, but it is implicit in the repeated references to poverty and their struggle for subsistence. From the patron's point of view, prices seemed to be escalating. In 1580 the Maggior Consiglio tried to halt the rising prices of portraits (the state generally paid for portraits of the various procurators):

> In the Procuracy di Citra, where previously they used to spend 5 ducats on the Procurators' commissions, and then at the most 10 ducats for each one, as can be seen from the account books, 70 ducats were then spent on them. Now one discovers that this expenditure has increased so much that up until 1578, on 14 admissions of 14 Procurators, 696 ducats 9 grossi 18 piccoli have been spent, and besides this a goodly sum of the Procurators' money has been spent on pictures and portraits of the Procurators. Whence, in order to prevent this kind of expenditure from increasing each year, which brings the said Procuracy into disrepute, it is ordered that, since the [procuracies] cannot spend more than 15 ducats on each Procurator's admission . . .[14]

By their account, portrait prices first doubled and then quintupled before rising sevenfold. While it is true that a state portrait could cost as much as 70 ducats, their claim that portraits "previously" cost 5 ducats seems as unlikely as their mandated maximum of 15 ducats proved to be untenable. Tintoretto's payment in 1560 of 25 ducats for the official portrait of *Doge Girolamo Priuli* (Accademia, Venice), the same rate that Titian was given over 30 years earlier, suggests that the Signoria indulged in some rhetorical inflation.[15] Like Pino, the Maggior Consiglio viewed prices through a prism of self-interest.

Of the two claims, Pino's and the Maggior Consiglio's, the latter is more accurate, at least in 1580 following three decades of price stability. Average prices during this period (1550–80) were remarkably consistent, fluctuating between 10 and 12 ducats per square meter (Table 13). (For reasons that will be explained later, size is the most reliable denominator of value.)

Looking at the seventeenth and early eighteenth centuries, a surprising pattern can be observed where long periods of stability are punctuated by sudden increases, raising prices to new and ever higher plateaux. From 1580 to 1660, prices held at a steady average between 15 and 16 ducats with a dip only during the plague decade of the 1630s.[16] After prices rose temporarily to 18 ducats per square meter in the 1640s, a rise of 20 percent, they returned to 15 in the 1650s. In the 1660s, however, prices jumped by 66 percent and, besides the

TABLE 13 Average Prices (ducats per square meter) of Big Oil Paintings in Churches and Public Buildings, by Decade, 1550–1750 (data compiled from Appendix 1)

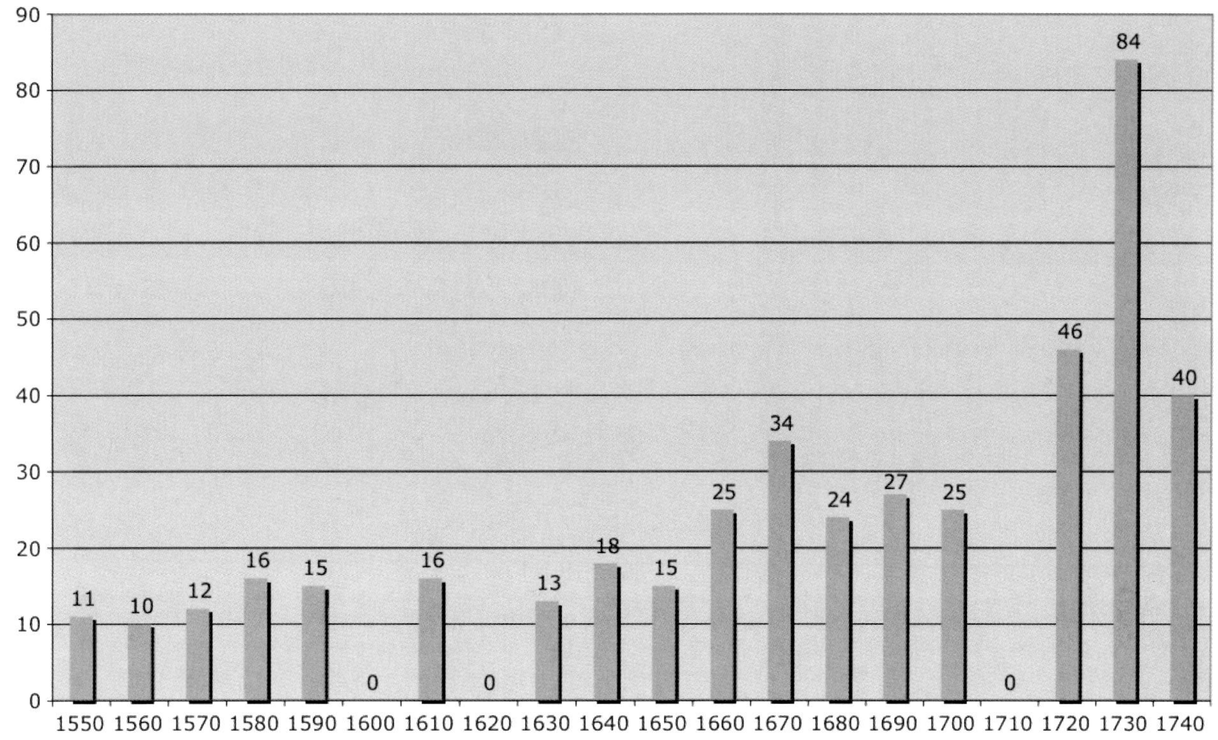

NB. The decades of 1600, 1620, and 1710 have insufficient data; minimum sample = 5.

anomalous 1670s, remained in the range of 24 to 27 ducats per square meter for half a century until they doubled and more.

Before any significance can be attached to this pattern of punctuated stability, the question of inflation in general must be addressed. Were prices in paintings simply matching trends in wages and goods? Most economic historians have concluded that wages and goods were relatively stable in seventeenth-century Venice, leaving aside the plague years of 1630–31 and their immediate aftermath, which are often identified as a tipping point for the Venetian economy. The data that they have collected are, however, too incomplete to make a detailed comparison with prices of paintings. Table 14, showing the price of bread from 1624 to 1646, bears out their conclusion while also demonstrating how much prices of a basic commodity can fluctuate, even year to year.

The price of olive oil also rose and fell on a yearly basis, but the variations did not follow those of bread because the issues of production, distribution, and taxation differed. Table 15, comparing the price of wheat and the wages of manual labor, shows a predictable correlation in the rise and fall of wheat prices and workers' wages from 1556 to 1741, trending upward until 1630 and then dropping by 25 percent (wages) and 100 percent (wheat) until 1670 before rising again more slowly.

TABLE 14 Price of a Bushel (24.4 liters) of Bread in Venice, in lire (decimalized)[17]

1624	19.19	1636	23.86
1625	20.24	1637	17.54
1626	22	1638	13.68
1627	23.6	1639	12.16
1628	31.26	1640	12
1629	32.83	1641	15.95
1630	30.27	1642	19.31
1631	28.96	1643	19.57
1632	22.61	1644	18.48
1633	14.42	1645	15.04
1634	13.5	1646	21.07
1635	24.4		

TABLE 15 Wheat and Wages in Venice, 1556–1741[18]

YEARS	WHEAT IN LIRE PER STARO (35.2 liters) PLUS % CHANGE		DAILY WAGE IN SOLDI PLUS % CHANGE	
1556–60	5.0		19.3	
1586–90	7.4	+50%	27.08	+50%
1626–30	11.1	+50%	44.85	+60%
1671–73	5.8	−100%	35.41	−25%
1710–14	8.0	+50%	44.11	+25%
1737–41	8.1	+1%	37.92	−10%

Table 16 lists wages in various important sectors: construction, glass manufacturing, arsenal work, and baking.

Painting prices also inflated at about the same rate between 1550 and 1580, but afterwards showed none of the inflation or deflation of wheat and wages between 1580 and 1710. After 1710 wages and prices of wheat and paintings rose, but with paintings spiking at a much higher level.

Since only one of these three moments of inflation correlates to inflation of other goods and services, another explanation must be sought for painters. The most likely involves high earners entering the market. The first increase of about a third in the 1580s occurred as the aging masters (Titian, Tintoretto, Veronese, and Bassano) were being replaced by their emulating epigones. Palma Giovane, especially, demanded and received higher prices starting in the early 1580s and set a new standard that was eventually matched by other painters. The second increase of about two-thirds occurred in the 1660s as young Venetian stars such as Pietro Liberi and Antonio Zanchi began to achieve international fame and dominance of the local market. The even larger jump of 85 percent in the 1720s (and possibly starting in the previous decade) was exceeded in the 1730s by a stunning one of 121 percent. These increases correlate to a phasing in of a new self-proclaimed renaissance, led by Sebastiano Ricci, Giovanni Antonio Pellegrini, Giambattista Piazzetta, and Giambattista Tiepolo.

Art and Commerce

The four major books on painters and painting written by Venetians in the seventeenth century were dedicated to art collectors or art dealers: G. C. Gigli's *La pittura trionfante* (Venice, 1615) to Daniel Nys, Carlo Ridolfi's *Maraviglie dell'arte* (Venice, 1648) to Jan and Gerard Reynst, Marco Boschini's *La carta del navegar pitoresco* (Venice, 1660) to Leopold Wilhelm of Augsburg; Boschini's *Le ricche minere della pittura veneziana* (Venice, 1674) was dedicated to the Collegio that oversaw painters and art dealers.[20] More than just a convergence of art and commerce, it shows a dependence of art history and art criticism on commerce. It also suggests how eco-

TABLE 16 Daily Wages (in soldi) with Percentage Change[19]

	1581–90	1611–20	1621–30	1631–40	1651–60	1661–70	1671–80	1711–20
Master, building	42.47	61.76 +50%	67.66 −10%			88.68	60.78 −30%	
Laborer, building	27.08	41.63 +54%	44.85 +8%			47.14	37.26 −20%	44.11 +18%
Master, glass				60	107.63 +75%	117.59 +10%	104.58 −10%	
Laborer, glass				57.75	54.92 −5%	42.82 −20%	42.75 0%	
Foreman, Arsenal	42				80			
Master, Arsenal	29				44			
Baker			26.66	29.33 +10%	29.33 0%	29.33 0%	29.33 0%	29.3 0%

nomic values could be entwined with the aesthetic and critical responses to art. This was not a uniquely Venetian phenomenon. Luigi Scaramuccia, painter and author of *Le finezze della pittura* (Cesena, 1674), and Agostino da Sant'Agostino, author of *L'immortalità e gloria del pennello ovvero descrizione delle pitture di Milano* (Milan, 1671), were active as art agents and valuers, and could have written their books on painting and art history as a means to establish their credentials.[21]

Boschini's *Carta* best illustrates the tensions and attractions between art and money. Boschini was inscribed in the Collegio as a painter, miniaturist, and printmaker, but most of his income came from the art trade: restoring, appraising, and selling old master and modern Venetian paintings.[22] He also engaged in the sale of artificial pearls and ornamental glassware. His earliest engraved work was a currency conversion table, *Tariffa del cambio degli scudi forestieri* (1635), an uncanny prefiguration of his later interests in commerce and foreigners.[23] The *Carta* is, amongst other things, a self-advertisement for Boschini as art dealer and advisor and a self-interested promotion of sixteenth- and seventeenth-century Venetian painting, primping the masters to help inflate their prices. His promotional enthusiasms where nearly every painter is a genius, every painting a masterpiece, helped entice and buoy the collectors' acquisitive appetites. Because he acted as an art dealer, touting or selling paintings to the Este, Gonzaga, Hapsburgs, and Leopoldo de' Medici at a time when Venice's artistic patrimony was being quickly sold, the *Carta* has been dismissed as "nothing more than a grandiose sales catalogue."[24] This accusation, however unfair it might be especially in light of Boschini's own condemnation of the art exporting business as "theft," does call our attention to the intersection of commerce and criticism in the *Carta*, one that would have been more blatantly exposed had he finished his book on private collections.[25]

The *Carta* opens with a noble collector "Eccelente," and his art advisor "Compare," a thinly veiled surrogate for Boschini, preparing themselves for an art tour of Venice by gondola. Boschini himself did this "almost by profession," according to Baldi, who noted in 1677 how Boschini "guides people to see these paintings."[26] Boschini's self-designation as Compare signified in current parlance more than its conventional meaning as "colleague," but was specifically applied by the nobility to artists who served them in building their art collections.[27] Eccelente's first question to Compare concerns news from the Rialto: who is buying what in the art world? To the questions, "What piques their curiosity? What are foreigners asking about, searching for and buying?" Compare responds that "everyone wants to make their own art collection; everyone hires their own pilot, their own expert; and if you listen, everyone is talking about painting."[28] This may or may not be true, although recent studies suggest that the number and size of collections rose dramatically in the sixteenth century and continued to do so into the seventeenth century.[29] In a remarkable survey of over 1,000 inventories, Isabella Cecchini documented how quickly the size of painting collections rose between 1560–62 and 1610–15.[30] Where patricians previously owned an average of 3.4 paintings, by the second decade this figure rose to 13.1. Citizens (*cittadini*) owned on average the same number of paintings as the nobility in the 1560s. That figure rose by 1610–15, to an average of 10.9. Artisans and shopkeepers went from 2.3 to 4.7. In part, this can be explained by an accumulation of paintings over various generations especially amongst the nobility, but considering the four-fold increase in the size of noble collections, it also suggests an increasing demand. Large collections became more numerous as well. Those with 16 to 30 paintings constituted only 1 percent of all inventories in the 1560s, rising to 3 to 4 percent in the 1610s.

In another survey by Cecchini of 260 inventories dating between 1640 and 1700, we see that paintings comprised 23 percent of the total value of household possessions owned by the nobility; for the new nobility, it came to 28 percent; and for merchants and the professions, paintings averaged 19 percent of the total value of all goods.[31] With substantial sums being invested in art, Boschini's advice that you cannot collect art (new or historical) without an expert painter's advice was intended to create a demand for his services. Beware of frauds, Boschini continued, because "there are an infinite number of art dealers who run here and there like inexhaustible bloodhounds searching for their prey."[32] The nobleman Alessandro Savorgnan fell into the hands of one such fraudulent *compare*, as he called his art advisor Niccolò Bambini, who led him to believe that his collection of about 1,000 paintings had doubled in value since he purchased them.[33]

Above all, Boschini wanted to convince his readers that art was a sound investment: "Oh what a beautiful investment this will be, better than trade with the Levant."[34] Painters, Boschini thought, should exploit the opportunities that came with rich collectors:

> Oh poor Venetian painters who had such great judgment in painting but knew nothing about this great fortune [*ventura*, hence with a sense of future speculation], a great fortune [*fortuna*] for foreigners who come to this city with thousands in gold and who

now multiply it tenfold. More than painting itself, this is a pretty trade.[35]

In the *Ricche minere* Boschini asked collectors and painters to remember that Tintoretto sold his monumental paintings at Madonna dell'Orto for a measly 50 ducats each, but that "today" they would be worth 50,000 ducats.[36] Although the first figure of 50 ducats is accurate, he exaggerated their current value to show that art futures are worth speculating on and that the Tintorettos of today will be worth a fortune in the future. In other words, he hoped to do two things: to increase values of contemporary painting by increasing demand, and to encourage painters to market their works at the highest prices possible. "He who has his paintings," Boschini wrote of the now forgotten and worthless Filippo Zaniberti, "has zecchini for sure."[37] Visiting Venice in 1664, Monconys commented on the inflation of prices: "Veronese was paid only 100 pistoles for the *Wedding at Cana* compared to the fathers of S. Benedetto, who want to sell it for at least 3,000."[38]

Boschini was generating demand for the moderns as surrogate ancients just as the Signoria was admitting new families to the nobility in an attempt to offset expenses for the War of Candia. Wanting to legitimate their status, the new patriciate started collecting art. The Correggio brothers bought in bulk, sometimes in the Piazza di San Marco, and amassed a collection of 600 paintings with an average unit value of 20 ducats.[39] The Widman were more selective, concentrating on sixteenth-century Venetian painting.[40] Quintiliano Rezzonico, who also wanted to build up the family collection of Venetian old masters and was helping Livio Odescalchi do the same in Rome, complained of the high costs: "Proposals for paintings by Titian, Veronese, Tintoretto, Palma Vecchio, and other famous ancients come in all the time, but since they only talk about thousands of scudi, I do not propose them to you."[41] Wanting to emulate the older families, they sought cinquecento masters, but scarcity and high prices sent many to seek copies, pastiches, old master homages, and other contemporary paintings. As an art dealer, Boschini hoped to capitalize on this new demand by arguing that contemporary painting was really just a continuation of the golden age and that whatever they might buy now will soon be worth much more later.

It was a bargain by comparison with the old masters. When Pittoni, Piazzetta, and Trevisani appraised Marshal von Schulenburg's collection, they divided it between "illustrious ancients" (mostly sixteenth century) and "illustrious moderns" (mostly seventeenth century), and added up the number of paintings and total value of each category, respectively 78 paintings worth 30,200 ducats and 205 paintings worth 19,375, as if to juxtapose their relative values (with the ancients worth on average 400 percent more per painting than the moderns).[42] Appraisals of other collections show an even greater price differential. Boschini understood this to be a collecting opportunity that his friends and colleagues in the art community could benefit from. Collections devoted exclusively to contemporary painting began to appear. Stefano Conti decided to collect only contemporaries because of "his fear of being swindled with old paintings and being seen drinking copies instead of originals."[43] He commissioned 76 Venetian paintings (out of a collection of 94) after visiting several painters in their studios. Algarotti curated a gallery of contemporary painting for Augustus III.[44]

~

Boschini despised shops selling paintings as both sweatshops and places of trade, representing the low end of his competition. In this respect he was voicing the sentiment of painters in general:

> One finds modern frauds who produce paintings in workshops as if they were little bunches of ribbons reckoning on enriching themselves. They display, with commercial malice, these rare little works in little boxes, and claim: these beautiful works come from far away; this is fine painting and subtle work. . . . Oh poor Painting, so diminished in the hands of shopkeepers, workers, Jews, plebians.[45]

The merchandising of art worried Boschini because it signified a loss of social status for artists, penned together with the lowest of social, economic, and religious classes. How art was sold and by whom also diminished the economic value of paintings and hence the earning power of legitimate artists who had to compete with hacks. The brand of "art" was under seige.

As one of the last Italian art centers to phase out guilds and institute in their place a state-approved academy, Venetians had a longer time to debate the question about art and commerce. Was art a craft or liberal art? As late as 1620, the Signoria had to prod the Arte dei Depentori on this one. The Arte had been electing *gastaldi* (the guild heads) who could neither read nor write. Should they continue to do so, the Signoria warned, a fine of 10 ducats would be levied.[46] A related question—did sales and trade demean art and make artists members of a craft instead of a liberal art?—was addressed in 1596 when the Arte sued two painters who refused to join the guild, one from a noble

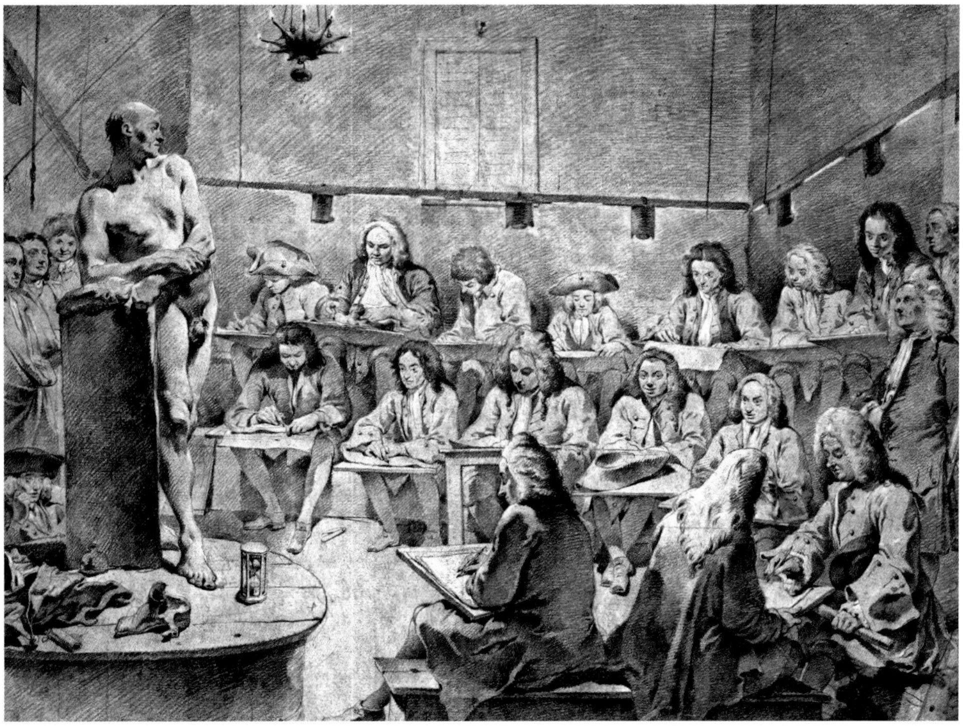

77 Giambattista Tiepolo, *Life Drawing* ("*Scuola del nudo*"), ca. 1718. Black and white chalk, 41 × 54 cm. Private collection, London.

family (Giovanni Contarini) and another from the *cittadini originarii* (Pietro Malombra). In their defense they did not claim exemption by deploying the commonplace argument that painting is a liberal art and therefore should not be subject to guild strictures. Instead, they defended themselves by affirming themselves as "civil persons" who painted for delight and not financial gain. The Arte rebutted their claims by producing records of payment. Contarini and Malombra replied that "if anyone wanted one of his paintings, he would be presented with it without a demand for payment following the nobility of his soul." The Giustizia Vecchia found against the defendants, and they were made to pay all legal costs. Contarini joined the Arte in the following year, but Malombra resisted for 20 more. Within the Arte, as early as 1619, some painters wanted to liberate themselves from the practice of shopkeepers hiring painters outside of the guild to produce goods for sale in their shops. This, claimed the Arte, dishonored the profession by producing "sad things."[47] Although their claim can be seen as self-serving—to boost the membership and hence fees collected—it also indicates an underlying anxiety that quality declines when art is driven solely by profit.

The concern that money corrupts reappeared with Boschini and became a focal issue in the 1680s. When in 1679 painters in the Arte started their campaign to separate and institute a Collegio, they explained that their profession had "languished and declined for a while and become involved with the abuses of the age involving certain vulgar and low-class trades." One result was poverty by virtue of association with the low-class trades ("alcuni triviali e minutissime arti").[48] The proposed Collegio was more of a reorganized Arte than a liberal arts Accademia with faculty and curriculum.[49] Many informal art academies existed at the time, run by individual painters in their houses as meeting places for discussion and life studies, including Liberi, Zanchi, Giambattista Rossi, Pietro Vecchia, Agostino Litterini, Antonio Molinari, Ludovico David, and Gregorio Lazzarini.[50] No Italian city other than Bologna (perhaps) has so many on record, and at least two foreigners travelling in Italy found the life study academies in Venice noteworthy. Maximilian Misson describes two such academies in 1688: "Venice is perhaps the city in Europe where young painters can best study nature. There are two academies where there are always choice nudes, one for each sex. . . . Anyone can enter."[51] Misson described the room as a "theater" probably because of its tiered design similar to the life drawing class illustrated by Tiepolo ca. 1718 (Fig. 77).[52] A bit earlier Philip Skippon observed with some prurient interest that the "naked man or woman" was "expos'd in a publick room."[53] The popularity of modeling studios may be a function of Venetian interests in naturalism, as Misson intimates, but equally the absence of a state-sponsored academy must have also contributed to the demand. Only in 1724 did the Venetian Senate establish a formal Accademia and then only after they realized how far art had declined and how backward the republic had become compared with other major cities.

In 1680 the Giustizia Vecchia approved "the separation of the Arte dei Depentori who are of the liberal arts from those others in the mechanical arts."[54] Those "others" include "gilders (*doratori*), decorative and house painters (*dipintori*), painters of musical instruments (*cimbanari*), stationers (*cartolari*), miniaturists (*miniatori*), leather painters (*coridori*), painters of wax fruit, and still life painters (*naranzeri*, *fruttarioli*)." Painters (*pittori*) earned far more per capita than those other craftsmen, judging at least from their tax returns, and so there might have been a financial incentive in separating. Still, they enjoyed a status and political power within the Arte disproportionate to their numbers or aggregate taxes. For example, the top ten vote earners in the 1637 election for the Arte's board (*banca*) included seven painters, one gilder, one leather painter (the largest constituency), and one house painter.[55] The probability that the painters were motivated more by status than money is suggested by the terms of separation set by the Milizia da Mar, the procuracy also responsible for galley recruitment: being "civil persons and not mechanical or manual," painters would no longer be subject to mandatory service in the galleys; instead, their aggregate taxes would be raised from 120 to 300 ducats per annum.[56]

A new Collegio de' Pittori was formally instituted in 1682. One year later, the prior of the new college appealed to the Milizia da Mar to reduce their tax burden because "us poor painters," rhetorically including himself despite the fact that he was then Venice's best paid painter, are financially oppressed by the shops (*botteghe*) that sell paintings at the lowest possible price. He called them pirates (*passavolanti*).[57]

Socio-economic Status

As the Arte and Collegio documents reveal, painters in Venice were preoccupied with status, both social status (craft painters vs. art painters) and economic status (rich painters concentrating wealth and creating poor painters). In the first election of officers for the newly founded Collegio, earning power translated directly to high office. Those running for prior, the top office, were Liberi and Zanchi.[58] Economically equal, judging from their taxes in the top bracket, Liberi won by an overwhelming vote of 21 to 7 probably because the Collegio decided one day earlier to hold its meetings in Liberi's palatial house on the Grand Canal (Fig. 78). In the subsequent election for two *consiglieri* (the Collegio's second most prestigious post), Zanchi and Carl Loth won against contenders paying a fraction of their taxes.[59]

Demographics and Income Distribution

In 1640 the Arte dei Depentori listed 74 painters, as we understand the term in this study: that is, excluding gilders, textile designers, leather workers, playing card makers, sign painters, and miniaturists.[60] Membership lists of guilds are notoriously unreliable, since painters like other craftsmen avoided inscription. In this case, however, the Arte's figure of 74 is reasonably close to the censuses of 1633 and 1642 made by the Provveditori alla Sanità in the wake of the 1630–31 plague.[61] Because the Provveditori adopted the terminology of the Arte, we can distinguish between painters (in our sense of the word) and the craft painters, and were it not for the missing documents from two *sestieri*, we could arrive at a precise population figure. Nevertheless, by extrapolating the number of painters living in these missing *sestieri* from their population as a whole (a figure recorded by Martinioni), it is reasonable to say that 80 painters were living in 1633, rising (like the city's population in general) to 92 in 1642.

After the painters left the Arte to form the Collegio de' Pittori in 1682, they complained to the Senate that of the 200 painters then working in Venice only 32 were inscribed and paying dues.[62] Two years later, possibly as the result of a campaign to force painters to join, the figure rose to 59, rising further to 99 in 1690, and to 120 in 1712, before dropping to 112 in 1726.[63] The Collegio de' Pittori only slightly inflated the population of painters when it claimed it to be 200 in 1682; four years later 180 painters paid taxes.[64] On the other hand, the numbers of registered painters, even at their highest levels of 100 or more, inevitably underestimate the true population, since many painters (especially foreigners) avoided inscription. Nevertheless, the numbers still speak of a community far larger than the one we know from history books. Assuming that the rate of avoidance was the same in 1640 as in 1690, then the population of painters increased by 34 percent, much

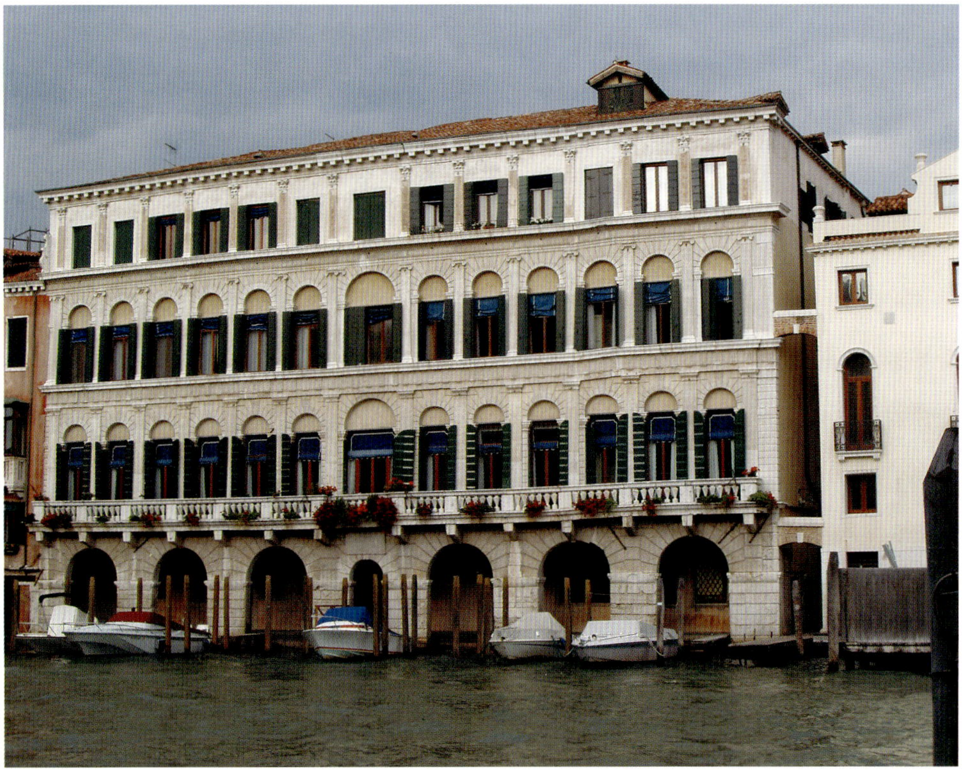

78 Palazzo Moro-Lin, Venice (designed by Sebastiano Mazzoni for Pietro Liberi, ca. 1670).

faster than the expansion rate of 15 percent for the general population: 120,000 in 1642 to 138,000 in 1696. The most notable change in the population of painters came between 1712 (72) and 1730 (53), a drop of about 27 percent, when Venice was haemorrhaging artists to foreign lands.

Most names on the Arte and Collegio lists are just that, only names. The forgotten painters churned out cheap stuff for tradesmen and craftsmen, or worked as specialists for known masters (often painting landscape and drapery). Even some of the painters deemed to be noteworthy by Boschini in 1660 (he included 46 in the chapter devoted to living painters) and by Martinioni in 1663 (41) remain merely names.[65] If we were to take Boschini's and Martinioni's lists literally, then between 24 and 27 percent of all painters were women. While Boschini and Martinioni might have distorted these proportions in order to show how many daughters of famous painters followed in their fathers' footsteps, or to show the strength of family dynasties in Venice, it is true nevertheless that many of the forgotten painters were women.[66]

~

The starving artist is a stereotype based on unhappy realities. Francesco Buduin, a painter without a known oeuvre, lived in "a house for the shameful poor," an official residential designation used by notaries.[67] Boschini in his youth, when he was trying (unsuccessfully) to establish himself as a painter, lived in a house so "ruined" that he had no "place to paint . . . calmly."[68] Late in life he was described as a "poor man."[69] The preceding sections show how impoverished artists reached a crisis point in the mid- and late seventeenth century and finally caught the attention of the Signoria, who understood that poverty and the consequent flight of artistic talent threatened the republic's international reputation. In 1682 the Collegio declared to the Milizia da Mar that there was an elite of "five or six principal painters" who practically monopolized "the business of this profession" in Venice, leaving most others "of poor fortune." Names were not given, but the elite at that time probably included the top taxpayers (in descending order): Liberi, Zanchi, Loth, Sebastiano Bombelli, Federico Cervelli, and Andrea Celesti (a list, it should be noted, that closely follows critical opinion then and now). Zanchi as prior of the Collegio blamed unscrupulous shopkeepers for the low prices that forced painters into poverty. The Collegio's tax records of 1684 to 1686 show three art dealers earning (or declaring earnings) more than any painter other than Liberi, Zanchi, and Loth, stuffing their pockets at the expense of painters too poor even to pay taxes.[70] This lopsided income distribution persisted into the eighteenth century (and remains a chronic irritant in the art scene even today). In 1717 art shopkeepers earned on average over twice as much as painters (paying 28 lire in taxes compared to 11 lire, the average tax of painters).[71] Even when the 30 percent top earners amongst painters are compared with the dealers, they still lose out (28 lire against 21 lire). Tron, as noted earlier, called painting "a lucrative profession" but only for the few, with everyone else being constrained to emigrate if they wanted to earn a good living.

"Poverty is a killer," wrote Paolo Pino in 1548.[72] He knew about it first hand, and it can still be sensed in a few passages where he adopts an aggrieved tone: "No one will pay for a painting unless you go begging for money from one end to another." He warns painters against their two main enemies: *povertà* and greed. Not much changed in the following century. Even critically acclaimed and financially successful painters like Pietro Bellotti and Antonio Triva could die in penury. When Giovanni Segala lived downstairs from the wealthy and knighted painter Celesti, he enjoyed a good standard of living but died indebted 20 years later.[73] Bartolomeo Pedon, "reduced to working for shopkeepers," walked around barefoot with only a tattered cloak and sword to cover his naked body, although in his case it could have been his drinking, smoking, and debauchery that contributed to this abject state.[74] Poor painters could be the victims of circumstance, such as Triva's misguided departure from Venice, or a dissipated lifestyle like Pedon's. Others faced *povertà* because of their adherence to a meticulous pictorial style, as in the cases of Bellotti and Piazzetta. Abstinent and studious, Piazzetta "worked more for glory than for profit" and consequently "reduced himself in old age to such poverty and anxiety that he hastened the end of his days," dying in the anguished knowledge that he left his family penniless.[75] He refused to paint faster to earn more money; he insisted that all painting be done by his own hand; he refused to leave his beloved Venice to take up lucrative offers from foreign patrons.

Poverty and loss of income hovered everywhere in Carlo Ridolfi's biographies of Venetian painters, born (most likely) from his bitterness as an income earner.[76] Talented painters like Andrea Schiavone were rewarded with penury. Honest painters like Domenico Brusasorci were so averse to fraud that they squandered their talent to avoid poverty. Ridolfi even managed to project his own failure to earn money onto the wealthy Titian, claiming that Titian "lived in Venice in reduced circumstances."[77] His sympathy for the hard-working poor ended with the complaining Antonio Aliense, who painted himself carrying on his back his wife, her nurse, her uncle, and her son from a previous marriage. Showing it to his friends, he would explain, "This is the burden I'll bear until I die."[78] Ridolfi intervened in this self-assessment and blamed Aliense, not his family, for the situation. He lived luxuriously and spent imprudently, "paying little heed to the years [i.e. old age] which bring difficulties and worries."

~

TABLE 17 Taxes (in lire) Paid by Top Income Earners (top 20 percent) in the Collegio de' Pittori, 1639–44, Arranged by Income[79]

	1639	1640	1641	1642	1643	1644
Padovanino	16.0	9.0	18.0	9.0	9.0	25.0
Renieri	16.0	4.5	9.0		2.7	
Heintz	12.0	11.8	15.6			
d'Anna	12.0	9.0	4.5	14.4	14.2	
Sadeler	10.0	6.0	15.0	5.4	5.4	7.2
Ridolfi	8.0	4.8			9.6	
Forabosco	6.0	3.6	3.6			16.0
Vecchia	6.0	4.8	9.6	9.6	9.6	9.6
Morello		18.0			9.6	11.0
Paulini		6.0	14.4			12.0
Brunello		4.8		4.8	4.8	9.8
Triva				4.0	6.0	7.0
Pietra				6.0	6.0	7.0

TABLE 18 Taxes (in lire) Paid by Top Income Earners (top 30 percent) in the Collegio de' Pittori, 1684–86, Arranged by Income[80]

	YEAR OF BIRTH	AVERAGE TAX 1685–86	1684	1685	1686
Liberi	1605	87		50	124
Bombelli	1635	78		50	105.4
Zanchi	1631	78	74.3	50	105
Loth	1632	78		50	105.4
Arno[81]	1628	69		32	105.4
Tamagnin	1655	68	49.6	32	105.3
Caffi	?	65		25	105.4
Cervelli	1625	55		30	80.6
Mainardi	?	53		32	74.4
Celesti	1637	52		25	80
Braù	?	51	74.3	22	80.6
Stom	1600	42	37.2	22	62
Fumiani	1645	41		32	49.6
Dorigny	1654	31	40	18	43.3
Lambranzi	1632	31	31		31
Lazzarini	1655	31		18	43.4
Bambini	1651	28	31	19	37.2
Cassana	1659	25	37.2	13	37.2
Molinari	1665	23		22	24.8
Diamantini	1621	22	31	13	31
Bellucci	1654	16		12.5	18.6
Pellegrini	1624	15	20	10	20
Manaigo	1666	15	20	10	20
Brentana	1656	14		9.5	18.6
Molinari	1633	11	31	10.5	12.4
Pittoni	1654	9		6.5	12.4
Venier	1644		37.2		27.9

The most secure means to measure relative economic standing is provided by the occasional tax records from the Arte dei Depentori before 1682 and the Collegio de' Pittori thereafter. Each taxed their members according to their declared yearly income (the *insensibile*) and by a flat rate (the *taglione*). The resulting data, given in Tables 17 and 18, are revealing despite their limitations, the most serious being the absence of a formula that would allow us to correlate taxes paid to professional income earned. Also, as with any tax collection system, its reliability depended on the honesty of both parties, guild member and tax collector. Farinati was one such honest painter.[82] Between 1584 and 1595 his taxes rose at the same rate of 25 percent as his income. Whatever cheating existed—and some was inevitable, especially amongst painters, who proved themselves to be the artful dodgers amongst the Venetian trades—it may be fair to assume that the results balanced out and the relative standing of painters would be maintained (unless some were more successful cheaters and managed to do so consistently over several years).[83]

The disparity of income between top and bottom earners is striking, even in the top quartile where it can be by a factor of three. Between 1639 and 1644, 74 master painters were recorded as paying taxes through the Arte. Those in the top 20 percent income bracket included, as expected, Padovanino (Alessandro Varotari), Renieri, Heintz, Ridolfi, Forabosco, and Vecchia. Four of these 13 elite earners were art dealers (d'Anna, Paulini, Morello, and Pietra, who also worked as a copyist and restorer). Those in the bottom 80 percent are virtually or completely unknown. Little here is new. In the sixteenth century, enormous price differences existed even amongst famous painters. One glaring example is the portrait prices earned by Jacopo Bassano, at an average of 3 ducats, and by Titian, starting at a mandated low of 25 ducats for ducal portraits (because he also received 100 ducats per annum as holder of the *sansaria*) and rising to hundreds of ducats.

After a 40-year gap, the tax records reappeared between 1684 and 1686, when the Milizia da Mar levied an annual tax of about 272 ducats, based on a per capita tax of 23.4 lire for the 72 master painters. The Collegio then redistributed the taxes, based on an unspecified flat rate, so that those painters who earned more, paid more. As Table 18 shows, income distribution was lopsided enough to have painters even in the top quartile paying taxes below the per capita rate.

Those prosperous individuals who were paying twice the per capita rate (or more) included the critically acclaimed Bombelli, Celesti, and Cervelli, along with three art dealers (Arno, Caffi, and Tamagnin). All but two (the portraitists Bombelli and Cassana) were history painters. The top earners—Liberi, Bombelli, Zanchi, and Loth—earned over three times the per capita rate, with Liberi in one year topping it by a factor of five. The economic stars during this period tended to be older painters: Liberi at 80 years and older, Cervelli at 60, Loth at 54, Zanchi at 53, Bombelli at 50, and Celesti at 48. The top 13 painters were all 40 years old or over. It was not exclusively an economic gerontocracy. Molinari (20), Cassana (26), Brentana (29), Lazzarini (30), Dorigny (31), and Bambini (34) earned just over the per capita rate. Bellucci (31) and Pittoni (31) earned less, and in the latter case much less, than the per capita rate while still remaining in the top 30 percent of earners. Table 18 also shows how much incomes varied year by year, a phenomenon also found in Tiberio Tinelli's account book (Table 20).

When tax records re-emerged in 1717 (see Table 19), we find Zanchi's economic status (then age 86) somewhat in decline, ranking sixth highest (tied with Angelo Trevisani) of the 84 painters listed. He was surpassed in earnings by 235 percent by the new stars, Nicolo Bambini and Sebastiano Ricci. As with the taxes paid during the 1680s, the 1717 record proves a reliable reflection and predictor of artistic success, as judged by the critics.[85] The young Tiepolo, then only 21 years old, was tied for fifteenth place. Ranking above him, although not by much (about 25 percent higher earnings), were the more established painters Giambattista Pittoni, Piazzetta, and Gerolamo Brusaferro, still considered today to be Venice's premiere painters. High income, however, did not always translate into critical success. The now-forgotten painter Agostino Litterini earned more than Zanchi; Zanchi the Younger (who never emerged from the shadow of his father) and the equally obscure Cristoforo Tasca, Francesco Duramano, Nicolò Rossi, Valentin Picini, Piero Uberti, and Ferdinando Fochi earned as much as or more than Tiepolo.

TABLE 19 Taxes (in lire) Paid by Top Income Earners (top 30 percent) in the Collegio de' Pittori, 1717[84]

PAINTER	TAX
Bambini, Ricci	59
Litterini, Stom	27
Trevisani, Zanchi	25
Marchesini	24
Fochi	22
Carlevarijs, Zenobio	21
Piazzetta, Pittoni, Brusaferro	19
Uberti	17
Visentini, Zanchi the Younger, Tasca, Duramano, Tiepolo, Steur, Rossi, Picini	15
Mariotti	14
Migliori	13
Spagnol, Cavanis	12

~

Financial insecurity led some painters to enhance their incomes, although not substantially, by making copies and restoring old masters, and by consulting and collecting agent fees. Because copies sold for far less than originals—Tinelli's markdown rate ranged between 55 and 68 percent, while Titian's markdown rate was 75 percent—this was not a lucrative business.[86] Antonio Guardi accepted a meager monthly stipend, really servant's wages, from Marshal von Schulenburg to produce mostly copies of old and modern masters.[87] Rosalba Carriera employed an inebriate Flemish painter to launder, paint landscapes and still lifes, and make copies. Talentless painters (*di poco spirito*), she thought, made the best copies.[88] There were exceptions. Successful painters (including Fumiani, Zanchi, and Ricci) made prestige copies of more famous cinquecento old masters and sold them for 9 to 16 ducats per square meter, less than their own originals cost and far less than the price that the original model would have cost on the art market.[89] Oddly, and this tells us something about price inflation in the art world, the copyist could be paid more than the creator of the original. In 1671 Zanchi received 1,000 ducats for his copy of Veronese's *Feast at Cana*, whereas almost a century earlier Veronese received only 324 ducats for the original.[90] Copies that were intended to pass as expensive originals, unlike those just mentioned that were commissioned as copies, could bring in much more (although those cases, by their very nature, are difficult to document). Crime pays, unless like Giambattista Volpato you were caught and brought to trial.[91] Ricci and Niccolò Cassana sold "old masters" at high prices to the less savvy English. Cassana, who lacked originality and had a talent only for mimickery, would have been "a poor man" if it were not for this practice.[92] Another talentless Venetian, Rocco da San Sebastiano "pittore di poco pregio," devised an exploitative system of mass production, hiring Flemish artists who lived and worked in his house making copies of paintings by "good masters" and selling the results at considerable profit.[93] It even helped Rocco develop "a good and masterly style" of his own.

Restoration, like copying, enabled painters to make or enhance their income modestly, and in at least one case the same painter, Michiel Pietra, practiced both restoration and copying so successfully that the Collegio listed him in the top 10 percent of earners.[94] Others, like the obscure Lelio Bonetti, subsisted on small fees (4 ducats to clean and repaint nine small panels, and he had to supply the paint).[95] Even the famous Ricci received a pittance for major and complicated work: 9 ducats in 1695 for a now lost altarpiece for the Compagnia di San Giovanni dei Fiorentini in Bologna, a job that caused him "anxiety."[96] Other restoration contracts to established painters were more generous and, as with copies, reflect price inflation over time.[97] Rossi, one of Venice's first professional restorers, held the office of state conservator, a position that brought a 130 ducat salary plus fees for individual jobs (100, 110, 130, 150, 160, and 230 ducats, plus expenses).[98] He was also the highest bidder in 1684, against Zanchi and Loth, for a contract to restore Tintoretto's *Paradise* and the *Venetian Ambassadors Meet Federico Barbarossa in Pavia* (Palazzo Ducale). The cost of restoration could be more than half as much as the cost of a new painting. When in 1631 two ceiling paintings by Veronese and Schiavone in the Libreria di San Marco needed restoration, Filippo Esegreneo submitted an estimate of 10 ducats each and the procurators accepted; however, when he increased it to 16 ducats each, the procurators decided to commission new replacements by Padovanino and Bernardo Strozzi for 25 and 30 ducats respectively.[99]

The last important supplementary source of professional income for painters came from valuation and agent fees. "One who is a painter knows this business of old paintings well," noted Paolo del Sera, who was himself trained as a painter (although he, like Boschini, earned his living as an art agent).[100] Most prominent appraisers were practicing painters (Boschini, Heintz, Agostino Lama, Renieri, Francesco Rosa, Vecchia, and Zanchi) and one was a sculptor (Clemente Molli). Their fees for an appraisal varied, presumably depending on the size of the collection and distinction of the appraiser, between 4 and 7 ducats to a record figure of 300 ducats.[101] Art dealers—that is, those who acted as intermediaries between collectors—could earn even more, generally between 5 and 10 percent of the sale by one account but much higher in particular cases, sometimes even exceeding the prices of their own work.[102] Tiepolo received 124 ducats for helping Algarotti buy two paintings by Borgognone for Augustus III.[103] In another instance, Tiepolo was paid 41 ducats to appraise some stucco work in the Cappella del Santissimo (Santo, Padua), 7 ducats more than he was paid a few months later by the patron to produce a *modello* for the chapel vault.[104]

Annual Incomes

Annual incomes, notoriously difficult to establish for Italian painters, are important because they enable us to compare the economic status of painters relative to each other and to other trades and professions. Prices of individual paintings can help, but there are too many complicating factors (time in production, size, number of figures, etc.) to estimate annual earnings. Painters' estates are also a flawed measure of their financial success. Liberi and Bellotti, for example, managed to spend their considerable earnings faster than they could paint and left negligible estates at their deaths.[105] Loth claimed to paint only when he wanted: "a man who must take up the brush only when the moon is good and he wants to work"; he did not charge top prices, yet managed to gather the largest estate of any painter in seventeenth-century Venice.[106] Luckily in Venice, account books, tax records, and a few serendipitous letters to prospective patrons abroad give a more complete picture than elsewhere.

As a provisional step toward understanding economic status, estates give us a snapshot of temporal changes and geographic differences. Sixteenth-century Venice, for example, did not foster the super-rich as did Rome. Even the most successful lived modestly, avoided expensive habits, and left their families comfortable but hardly rich (Veronese) or borderline impoverished (Tintoretto); Jacopo Bassano left a successful practice to his sons but few capital investments. Titian, as always, was exceptional.[107] The dead rich artist became more common in seventeenth-century Venice, but few accumulated estates as large as 10,000 scudi: in Venice there was only one recorded example (Loth at 32,000 ducats) compared with 21 in Rome, far fewer than the ratio of artists in these two cities: about 1:3, depending on the source. (One painter, Nicola Grassi, nearly made the cut with an estate of 9,000 ducats.)[108] In Venice, an artist who owned a seignorial palace like those of Zuccaro, Arpino, Bernini, and others, was thought to be living beyond the means that any artist should have.[109] Liberi's palace on the Grand Canal (see Fig. 78), designed for him by the painter Sebastiano Mazzoni, left his son Marco so encumbered with debts as to practically nullify his estate. Rich painters became more common in eighteenth-century Venice. Ricci bought 200 *campi* (plots of land) near Mirano for 7,050 ducats.[110] Tiepolo lived "like a rich gentleman" as did Giovanni Antonio Pellegrini, both with sufficient liquidity to lend or gift large sums to various churches, both benefiting from rich foreign patrons and lucrative fresco projects.[111]

The Sansaria al fondego di Todeschi was an annual state stipend for the state painter whose symbolic capital was usually greater than the income itself. It required little work and initially brought Titian 100 ducats when he successfully campaigned to replace Giovanni Bellini.[112] By the time Tintoretto inherited the position in 1574, it paid a substantial 1,000 ducats per annum.[113] (For the last 17 years of his life, he was the only Venetian to hold two salaried positions, the second being the 100 ducats from the Scuola di San Rocco as artistic advisor.) Early in the seventeenth century, after most of the pictorial decoration of the Palazzo Ducale was complete, the Signoria discontinued this tidy sinecure. When they established a new curatorship of public painting charged with conservation and restoration, the salary was set at a modest 130 ducats per annum plus payments for each restoration ranging from 50 to 230 ducats.[114] The position of "Pittor Ducale," held by Pietro Vecchia between 1640 and 1672, was unpaid since it involved only occasional oversight of cartoons for the basilica mosaics.[115] The "Master of Mosaics," on the other hand, received an annual salary of 140 ducats.[116]

These salaries compare favorably with other government salaries, and when the painters' earnings from individual commissions are factored in, it becomes clear just how well paid they were amongst the professional class.[117] A sergeant leading a company of 150 infantry men earned about 140 ducats, more than grammar school teachers (80 ducats) and not much less than humanities teachers at more advanced levels (150 ducats). Government officials—notaries, secretaries, or lawyers but also sinecure positions for poor noblemen—did not earn much more than teachers or masters of skilled trades. Starting salaries for chancellory notaries and secretaries were less (100 ducats), although with promotions they would generally rise to an average of 200 ducats per annum.[118] Poor noblemen with official functions earned about the same as humanities teachers (120 to 160 ducats) in the late sixteenth century, rising to 150 to 200 ducats by the mid-seventeenth century.[119] But these were paper salaries. Some positions, especially those involved in tax collection, included a percentage of revenues handled. A customs notary for the Datio del Vin declared his income in 1672 at 530 ducats, or nearly triple his paper salary.[120] Most, however, were not positioned to augment their pay so lavishly.

If seventeenth-century Venetian painters wanted the security of a guaranteed income, they had to leave the republic, or at least many painters thought so according to the Collegio records. Many did leave and became part of the talent drain that so concerned the Signoria. In 1609 Sante Peranda entered into the service of the prince of Mirandola for an annual pension of 300 ducats, plus housing, expenses, and payments per painting.[121] In 1706, the Palatine Elector Johann Wilhelm von Pfalz offered Bellucci an annual salary of 3,000 talers (roughly at parity with the ducat).[122] Bellucci accepted but did not remain long. Carl Gustav Tessin, talent scout for the king of Sweden, thought that Tiepolo would make the perfect court artist because of his speed and neo-Veronesian style.[123] He feared, however, that the king could not afford him. His initial estimate that it would take 1,500 gold ducats to tempt Tiepolo away was three times the amount that the king was willing to pay and 500 ducats less than Tiepolo's final demand. "Poor Tiepoletto" wouldn't touch it, wrote Tessin, because he claimed to earn at least 1,000 ducats annually in Venice. Tiepolo called his salary demand an "ultimatum"; Tessin called it an "impudence."

Emigration did not always bring financial security, despite the impression that the Collegio gave to the Milizia da Mar. Triva left Venice in 1669 for Munich, a decision that he later regretted, claiming that he had earned 2,000 ducats each year in Venice.[124] Initially in Munich his situation improved. For his salary of 484 ducats (plus wine, beer, and bread), he was obliged to paint ten figures and could choose to paint more at the rate of 48 ducats per figure (32 for a half-figure). When Triva voiced his regrets, at age 68, his salary had been reduced at first to 320 ducats and then eliminated altogether. With a paralyzed hand, Triva was destitute, longing to return home but unable to afford the journey. Bellotti also met an unhappy economic fate when he left Venice. He had been earning a conspicuous 50 doppie per figure, a sum worthy of gossip, when in 1670 he went to work for the duke of Ucedo, governor of Milan, for a monthly stipend of 100 scudi and 12 lavish plates of food.[125] A decade later he accepted a salaried position with Duke Ferdinando Carlo Gonzaga for just 20 scudi per month, and four years after that he retired to Gargnano, impoverished and possibly dependent on his brother.

Venice is blessed with an unusual range of painters' account books that allow annual incomes to be precisely calculated. Jacopo and Giambattista Bassano earned an average of 1,080 lire (about 174 ducats) annually between 1541 and 1543 (the years with the most complete entries).[126] Not all of this was profit—the Bassano charged the costs for wood, carpentry, and gilding separately—but with some reduction for expenses, this left them with earnings close to a master stonemason. Masters of the skilled trades, such as stonemasons, could earn 120 ducats per year, assuming they worked 250 days per year at the average daily wage of just over 3 lire.[127]

Tiberio Tinelli (1586–1638), knighted portraitist of the literary elite, kept an account book between 1618 and 1633 that shows production in bulk, usually between 15 and 20 portraits a year, without a commensurate accumulation of high earnings (Table 20).

In his best years, his annual earnings hovered around a respectable 300 ducats. Evidently, even a distinguished portraitist such as Tinelli could earn in one good year what a history painter would earn with one altarpiece. Ridolfi, who knew first hand the difficulties of earning a decent living as a portraitist, commented on the disparity between Tinelli's critical and economic fortunes:

> Although he never stopped painting continually, he never earned any other than meager recompense for his industrious work. He had at least the relief amongst his misfortunes to see himself favored by a king and honored by many gentlemen who often honored his work with their protection, a currency of the kind of metal that you cannot spend.[129]

TABLE 20 Annual Income of Tiberio Tinelli[128]

YEAR	ANNUAL INCOME IN DUCATS (lire)	AVERAGE PRICE OF PORTRAITS IN DUCATS (lire)
1619	132 (954)	7 (51)
1620	269 (1,022)	(no portraits)
1621	130 (519)	21 (86)
1622	252 (1,058)	18 (75)
1623	no data	no data
1624	123 (920)	7 (43)
1625	198 (1,486)	6.7 (50)
1626	202 (1,517)	11.5 (86)
1627	283 (2,121)	20 (149)
1628	213 (1,703)	16 (128)
1629	329 (2,631)	14 (110)
1630	220 (1,762)	18 (146)
1631	209 (1,674)	11 (89)
1632	293 (2,341)	22 (178)
1633	283 (2,261)	20 (163)

Table 20 also indicates how annual income could rise as an artist becomes established, the years of lowest earnings in Tinelli's case coming before his late 30s.

Paolo Farinati (1524–1606), a busy but undistinguished painter charging below average prices, left an extensive record of earnings spanning 33 years from 1573 to 1606. Tables 21 and 22 shows just how erratic

TABLE 21 Annual Income of Paolo Farinati[130]

YEAR	ANNUAL INCOME IN LIRE (incomplete data)	ESTIMATED ANNUAL INCOME IN LIRE (extrapolated)	AVERAGE PRICE PER PAINTING IN LIRE
1573	131	662	131
1574	286	817	143
1575		531	
1576	218	749	55
1577	190	721	48
1578	186	717	93
1579	999	999	250
1580	151	682	50
1581	418	418	139
1582	570	570	114
1583	680	680	227
1584	914	914	183
1585	451	451	150
1586	319	319	80
1587	534	534	134
1588	949	1,480	190
1589	579	1,100	145
1590	629	1,160	157
1591	726	1,257	182
1592	327	858	109
1593	620	620	155
1594	175	175	88
1595	1,149	1,149	230
1596	1,202	1,202	400
1597	1,058	1,589	353
1598	1,729	1,729	432
1599	728	1,259	243
1600	397	397	198
1601	140	140	70
1602	270	270	90
1603	331	331	331
1604	503	503	251
1605	184	184	184
1606	267	267	

TABLE 22 Estimated Annual Income of Paolo Farinati in lire, Graphed by Age (based on Table 21)

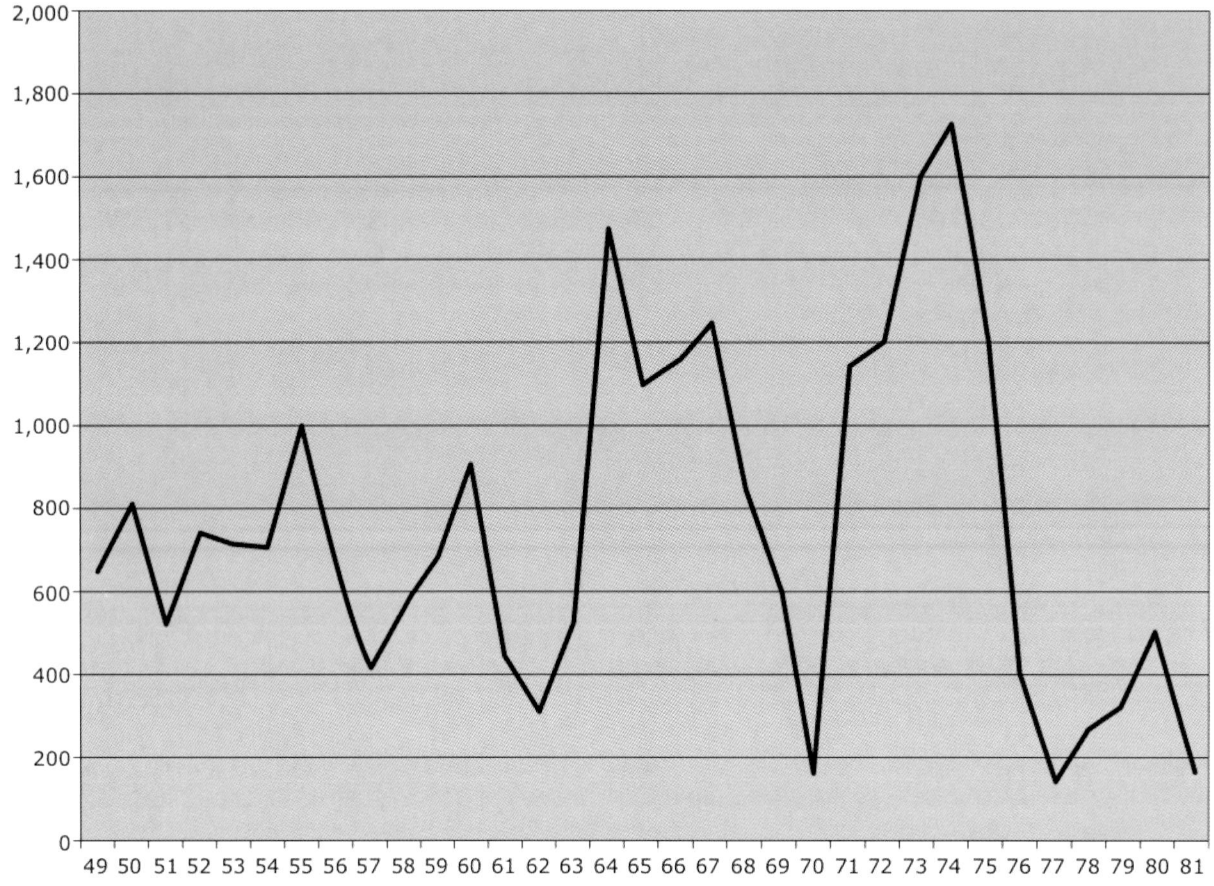

an established artist's earnings could be, jumping by as much as 650 percent from one year to another.

In half of the years recorded, his annual income rose or fell by over 100 percent, with seven years seeing a change of 300 percent or more. Farinati's accounts thus support the claim by Zanchi to the Milizia da Mar about "the instability of this profession" and "the inconstancy of our profession." Farinati did achieve some consistency of earnings during five peak years (1595–9) and during the slump that started in 1600 and ended in 1606 with his death. The latter follows an established pattern of poor earnings in old age. (Farinati was 77 in 1601.) From Rosalba Carriera's diaries, we also see her annual production and income declining steadily after she turned 50. Her income between 1725 and 1728 was, for each successive year, 968, 924, 814, and 638 scudi as a result of declining production (44, 42, 37, and 29 paintings in each of these years).[131]

In his bad years, and there were many (about a third of the recorded 35 years), Farinati earned a marginal income of 20 to 70 ducats. Unskilled laborers earned about 54 ducats per year. This was more than Loth calculated for his brother, who had dissipated his wealth and could not be entrusted with more than a daily allowance of 2 lire.[132] (Loth hoped his brother could make it on a per diem of 2 lire, but he anticipated that 3 lire would be needed.) Those not on family welfare but relying on Venice's charitable institutions received much less. During the 1690s the Arte dei Calegheri redefined its subsistence support for members who could no longer work.[133] In 1691, no one could live on the guaranteed 50 ducats per year, and even when it was raised five years later to 70 ducats per year, it was only a temporary measure until they settled on 81 ducats per year. Living expenses for a noble monk, with free lodging, amounted to 60 ducats per annum.

Bassano, Tinelli, and Farinati were mid-income painters. Others earned with one painting more than they did in one year. Consider the average price of paintings by the elite (see Tables 27 and 28): Palma

TABLE 23 Annual Rents Paid by Painters, 1650–1700 (see Appendix 2 for lists of painters and their rents)

SOCIO-ECONOMIC CRITERIA OF RENTS IN SEVENTEENTH-CENTURY VENICE	POOR: 30 ducats and under	COMFORTABLE: 31–50 ducats	RICH: 51–100 ducats	WEALTHY: 101 ducats and over
Painters (total of 39)	23%	36%	33%	8%

TABLE 24 Annual Rents Paid by Painters, 1700–50 (see Appendix 2 for lists of painters and their rents)

SOCIO-ECONOMIC CRITERIA OF RENTS IN SEVENTEENTH-CENTURY VENICE	POOR: 30 ducats and under	COMFORTABLE: 31–50 ducats	RICH: 51–100 ducats	WEALTHY: 101 ducats and over
Painters (total of 18)	5%	33%	45%	17%
Rents of general population in parish of S. Fosca, 1740	Under 50 ducats: 66%		12%	10%
Rents of general population in parish of SS. Apostoli, 1740	Under 50 ducats: 73%		19%	5%

Giovane (214 ducats), Francesco Ruschi (297), Liberi (332), Zanchi (355), Ricci (322), Balestra (244), and Pittoni (387). By comparison, the average price of paintings by Tinelli was 56 ducats, and by Farinati it was 35. Low end painters, usually genre or landscape specialists, earned even less: Carneo (6 ducats) and Guardi (4 ducats).[134] The gap between poor and rich, and the uncertainty of regular employment, resemble the income inequality and working conditions of Venice's courtesans more than its master craftsmen, teachers, or bureaucrats. (The only craftsmen who could compete with a successful painter were mirror makers: up to 900 ducats per annum.)[135] The cheapest courtesans, about 125 of the 210 whose prices were published in 1566, could earn between 250 to 500 scudi a year, assuming they had just one client per day for the same 250 days as our hypothetical stonemason.[136] Courtesans in the top income bracket (13 of the 210 listed) charged 10 to 20 scudi, thus enabling them to earn as much as 2,500 to 5,000 scudi per year (assuming their popularity matched their prices). A few exclusive courtesans charged 25 to 30 scudi. Those were the official rates listed with the government, but they could become even richer with big spenders like Giovan Battista Ottoboni, who blew 3,000 ducats on a single courtesan.[137] Another get-rich-quick job with a limited lifetime tenure was corpse bearer during the plague years (1576 and 1631), who could earn up to 440 ducats in one year (20 ducats a month plus 200 ducats as a bonus for completing their annual contract), should they survive.[138]

Residences

The Decime sopra le X Savi gathered episodic but comprehensive census records listing the location of the resident's dwelling or workplace and the amount of rent paid and to whom. From a provisional survey of this material, three trends can be observed. First, painters' homes served as their studios, the phenomenon of studios as separate workplaces occurring later. Second, painters were relatively prosperous judging by their rents (see Tables 23 and 24).

Beltrami proposed four economic categories (poor, comfortable, rich, and wealthy) for seventeenth-century Venetian tenants. By this standard, 41 percent of painters were rich or wealthy during the second half of the century, rising to 62 percent for the first half of the eighteenth century. What is surprising, however, is how few painters were poor, just one-quarter. This becomes especially clear when the general distribution rates of rents in two parishes (SS. Apostoli and S. Fosca) are compared with the painters then resident in the

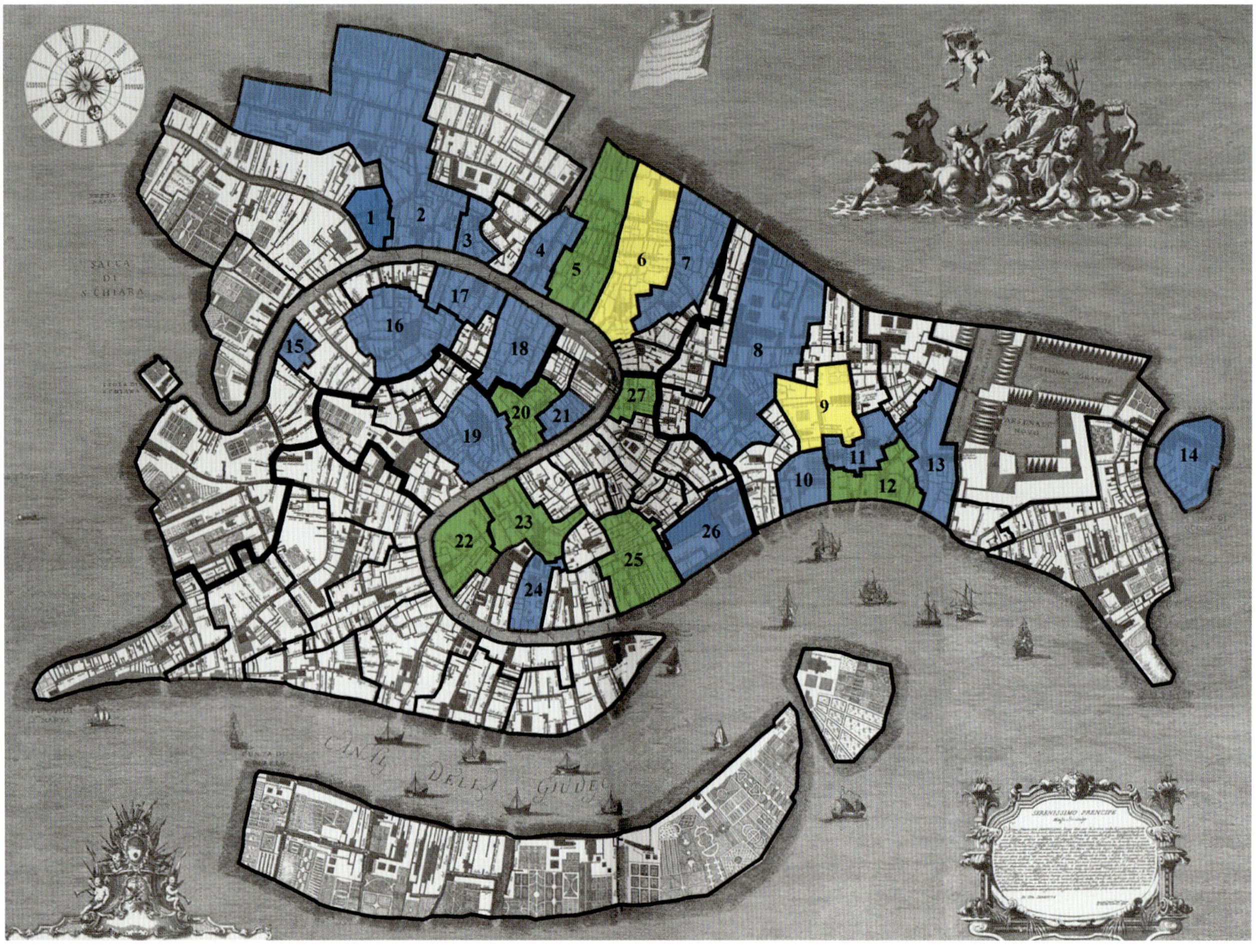

79 Painters' residences, 1633 (data from Venice, A.S.V., Provveditori alla Sanità, Anagrafi, b. 568–71). Color key indicates number of painters per parish: 0 = White, 1–2 = Blue, 3–4 = Green, 5+ = Yellow

parishes. Whereas between two-thirds and three-quarters of the general population was living in poverty, only 5 percent of the painters were. The census data also show a rising prosperity for a few lucky individuals: Ludovico David, from a rent of 40 ducats in 1661 to 120 ducats in 1679; Giambattista Pittoni, from 48 ducats in 1712 to 90 ducats in 1740; and Giovanni Antonio Pellegrini, from 90 ducats in 1712 to 174 in 1740. That rents are a reliable indicator of an artist's financial success (or failure) will be shown at the end of this essay, where the various economic indicators of different painters are compared.

And third, while many lived scattered about the city, seeming to conform to the current view that Venice (unlike Rome and Florence) had no painters' neighborhood,[139] a closer look shows a tendency to congregate in a few parishes (Figs. 79 and 80). When in 1633 the Provveditori alla Sanità made their census account after the plague of 1630–31, the 58 painters then resident in Venice were living in just over half the city's parishes, about the same ratio observed later in the century.[140] (The *sestiere* of Dorsoduro is not documented and hence is not included in this count.) The distribution is more imbalanced than this statistic sounds. About 40 percent of the painters lived in just five of the recorded 60 parishes, and the top eight parishes contained 55 percent of all painters. Of the 61 painters documented between 1650 and 1711, about half lived in seven parishes, and about one-quarter lived in two parishes: S. Pantalon and SS. Apostoli. The distribution patterns in 1633 shifted somewhat during the later seventeenth century, with the area between S. Maria della Formosa and S. Giovanni in Bragora losing some of its density. Most areas, however, that were favored by painters in 1633, notably those around SS. Apostoli and S. Samuele, retained their appeal throughout the century. (The concentration in S. Pantalon cannot be accurately gauged before mid-century.)

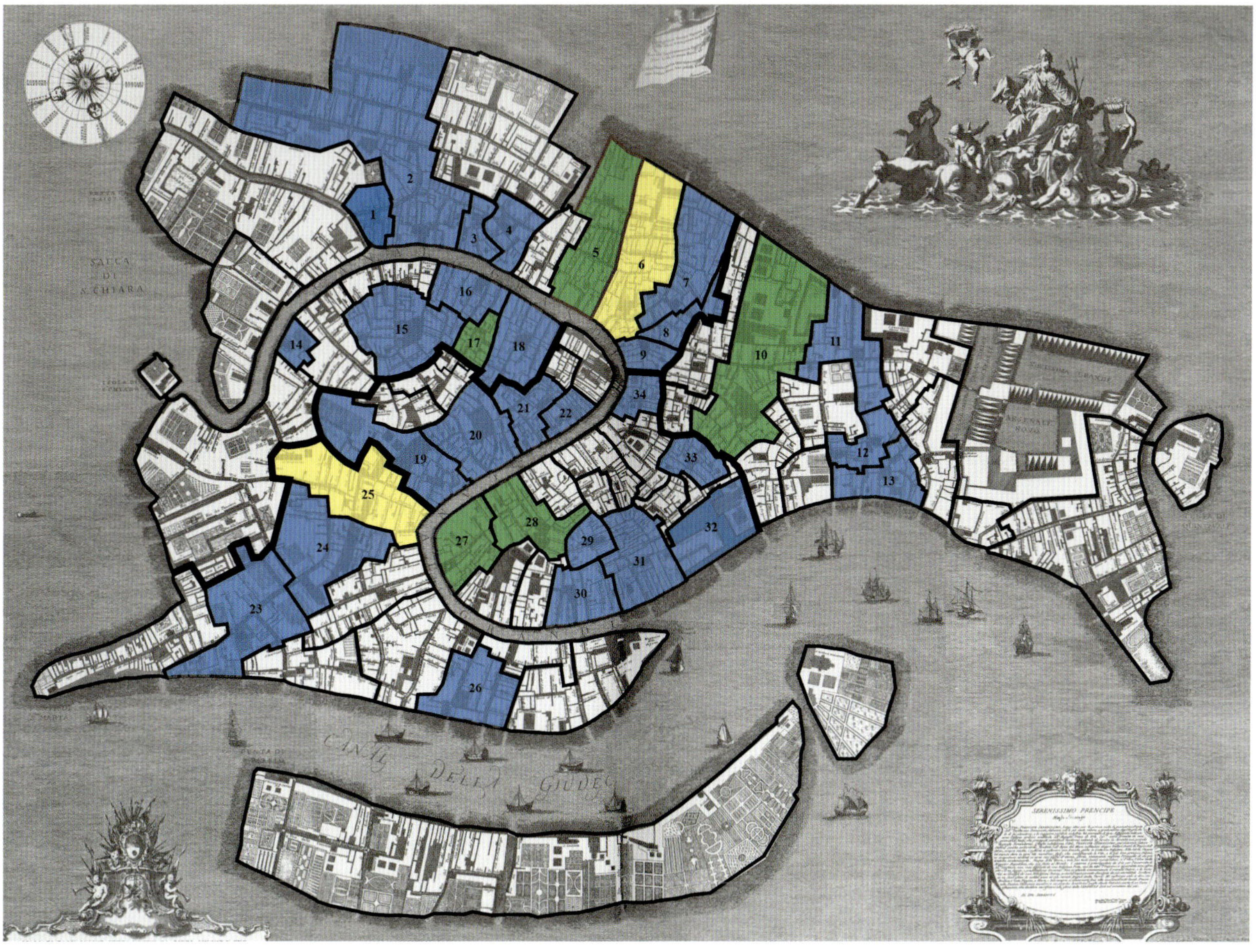

80 Painters' residences, 1650–1711 (data from Appendix 3). Color key indicates number of painters per parish: 0 = White, 1–2 = Blue, 3–4 = Green, 5+ = Yellow

Between 1650 and 1711, painters moved out of the traditionally poorest parishes, often those with a concentration of Balkan immigrants (S. Martino and S. Pietro di Castello). Other poor Balkan quarters like S. Antonin, S. Giovanni in Bragora, and S. Marina dropped from nine painters in 1633 to just two between 1650 and 1711 and none thereafter. These areas also housed a large proportion of carpentry shops, bronze foundries, and other industries related to the nearby Arsenal. The parishes of the two S. Simeones (S. Simeone Grande and Piccolo), which formed the center for the wool industry, also drew few painters, as did the area around the Castelletto, a fortified residence for prostitutes near S. Matteo di Rialto (only one painter in 1633, one between 1650 and 1711, and none thereafter). In contrast, and with a certain inevitability, the dye industry (centered at SS. Apostoli and S. Giovanni Crisostomo) and the adjacent silk industry (at S. Canzian and S. Maria Nova) were magnets for painters. SS. Apostoli and S. Giovanni Crisostomo were also home to many Germans, drawn by proximity to the Fondaco dei Tedeschi, and it is in those parishes that foreign painters (and not just Germans) settled in mid-century.

Figure 81 shows how painters had redistributed themselves between 1724 and 1745. Whereas SS. Apostoli and vicinity had been home to 26 percent of the city's painters, by 1724–45 the population had dropped to 18 percent. The S. Pantalon community was relatively stable, unless one includes the concentration across the Grand Canal at S. Samuele, when we find a dramatic halving (from 18 percent to 9 percent of the total population of painters). During this period we also see a modest increase of painters around the Piazza di S. Marco and along the commercial zone extending to the Rialto, probably in response to the consolidation late in the seventeenth century of shops run by licensed *bottegheri* selling (or reselling) paintings.[141] The number of *bottegheri* sanctioned by the republic was consistently

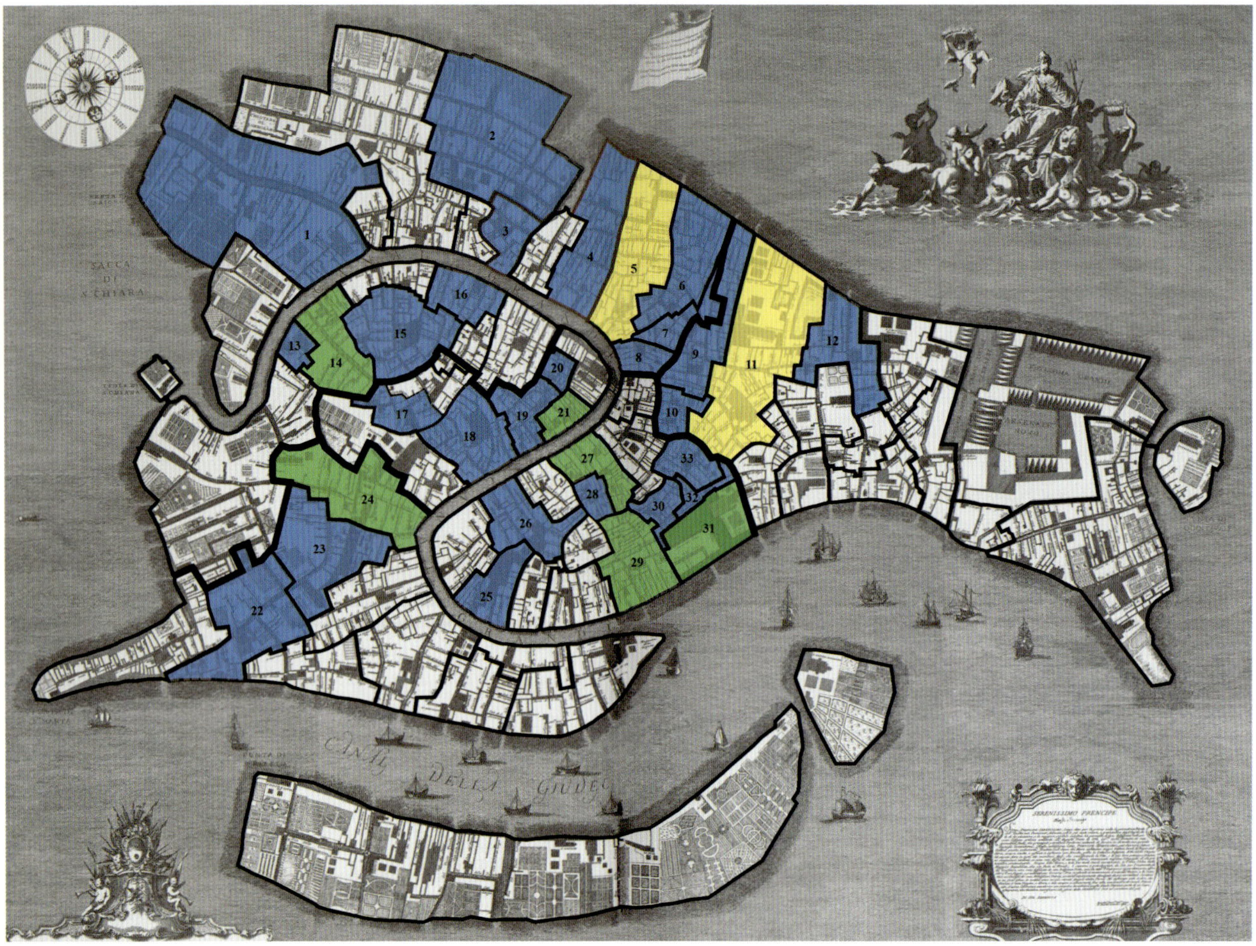

81 Painters' residences, 1724–45 (data from Appendix 3). Color key indicates number of painters per parish: 0 = White, 1–2 = Blue, 3–4 = Green, 5+ = Yellow

modest, ranging between 10 and 13 in the years 1690 to 1730, or one-third the number recorded in Rome in 1675.[142]

Social Status

This is a fluid category. Any economic status, whether it is measured by aggregate wealth, type or quality of possessions, earning power, etc., confers a degree of social status. In Venice, there were four social classes: nobility, *cittadini originarii*, *cittadini ordinarii*, and everyone else. Several painters were knighted by European nobility (Celesti, Liberi, Tinelli, Giuseppe Dimantini, and Giacomo Morati, whoever he was), but the honor was purely nominal without conferring the rights and responsibilities of the Venetian nobility. Despite the fact that several painters received such honors along with a commensurate income, a perception persisted that a career choice in painting was not a good one. Nadal Melchiori, who lived in Venice from 1686 to 1701 before returning to Bassano del Grappa, confirmed the Collegio's self-assessment. He began to make biographical notes about painters in 1721. Some were preceded, as in Vasari's *Vite*, with general statements about the state of the arts:

> We have arrived at such a delicate age that many today explain it as a weakness of the soul if a civil and comfortable person were to practice any profession, however worthy, as if, in their way of understanding, no one enters the arts except those of obscure blood or poverty, being thus constrained to enter such employment: an opinion truly false and blameworthy.[143]

Testing out Melchiori's account of the socio-economic status of artists, or at least his perception of public opinion, against the data reveals an underlying truth, less extreme than he would have us believe but still tending in the right direction. As the status of the arts rose in Venice during the sixteenth century, and as the market value of the great masters shot up in the seventeenth, the humble family background of artists remained relatively stable. (This is assuming that the available evidence, much of it biographical, is skewed toward the more dignified professions if for no other reason than proof of the arts' nobility.) Three painters—Giovanni Contarini, Andrea Visentini, and Angelo Trevisani—belonged to the nobility by rights of birth. Dario and Alessandro Varotari (Padovanino) came from the Paduan nobility, and Claudio Ridolfi and Dario Dal Pozzo from the Veronese nobility. Not many more were *cittadini originarii*, a small group of families (less than 2 percent) with two minimum qualifications: at least two generations resident in Venice and a father who did not engage in a "manual" trade. Although the precise number is difficult to determine, they include Pietro Malombra (whose father was a chancellor), Pietro Damini, and Giovanni Antonio Zonca. Many more painters were *cittadini ordinarii*, a class that required birth in Venice and 15 years of productive residence.

Painting as a family business was common throughout Italy in the fifteenth century, but more than other artistic centers, Venice and its dominions maintained artistic dynasties that started in the early sixteenth century and thrived into the seventeenth. The most famous of these—Vecellio, da Ponte, Caliari, Robusti, Negri—are known by their superstars: Titian, Jacopo Bassano, Tintoretto, Palma Vecchio, and Palma Giovane. But there were other equally hardy though less distinguished painter families with three or more generations spanning the sixteenth and seventeenth centuries: Farinati, Ligozzi, and Brusasorzi. Other painters whose fathers were also painters include Padovanino, Girolamo Maganza, Leonardo Corona, Peranda, Francesco Maffei, Michelangelo Aliprandi, Molinari, Cassana, Giovanni Battista Zannoni, Antonio Canal (Canaletto), and Bernardo Bellotto. In most cases, father–son relations were both commercial and artistic (sons were usually followers of their fathers without developing an independent style). Besides in-house training and an established network of patrons, "sons of painters" also benefited economically when they matriculated at the Collegio de' Pittori, where they paid one-third the fees of painters coming from families outside the profession.[144]

Of those painters whose paternal profession is known, about half (26 of 50) followed their fathers.[145] The other family backgrounds are too various to allow generalization. They are listed here in an approximate social hierarchy:

Marcantonio Bassetti	lawyer
Claudio Ridolfi	lawyer
Giuseppe Alberti	notary
Francesco Ruschi	physician
Antonio Aliense	naval commander
Maffeo Verona	law clerk
Giovanni Francesco Carota	spice merchant
Antonio Balestra	merchant
Simone Brentana	wool merchant
Alessandro Marchesini	architect
Giovanni Battista Rossi	sculptor
Antonio Calza	jeweler
Alessandro Turchi	sword maker
Tiberio Tinelli	weaver
Giovanni Segala	tailor
Pasquale Ottino	ceramicist
Francesco Montemezzano	carpenter
Girolamo Brusaferro	boatsman or gondolier
Gregorio Lazzarini	barber
Antonio Marieschi	butcher
Pietro Ricchi	weaver
Antonio Zanchi	baker
Giovanni Battista Volpato	baker
Martino Cignaroli	baker

I cannot say whether the presence of four Jewish painters two successful ones (Pietro Liberi and Francesco Ruschi) and two unknowns (Grazia ebrea and Mariana ebrea)—was typical of Italy or a consequence of the republic's liberal policies (liberal only by comparison with other harsher states).[146]

Children of rich artists who did not follow their fathers' profession showed an upward mobility at least in their marriages and the impressive size of the dowries given to their daughters: Titian 2,400 ducats, Palma Giovane 2,000 ducats, Benedetto Caliari 2,000 ducats, Marieschi 1,640 ducats, Biagio Falcieri 1,100 ducats, Molinari 1,000 ducats, and Giambattista Langetti 1,000 ducats.[147] Most painters, however, scraped together much smaller dowries that corresponded to those given by craftsmen and fishermen: Parrasio Michieli 100 ducats, Giovanni Pietro Meloni 120 ducats, Camillo Mantovano 180 ducats. Painters or their children often married into families of other painters or those related professions in their neighborhood. One of Cassana's daughters married a surgeon working in a local barber shop; a second married a local printer. Niccolò Renieri's daughters married two painters, Daniel van den Dijck and Pietro Vecchia.[148] The children of Clorinda Renieri and Pietro Vecchia married a lawyer and an expert in mathematics. Cassana was godfather to the painter Giulia Lama.[149] For his marriage

Niccolò Bambini had the local printer and bookseller Francesco Brigna confirm his good character because Bambini (like Vecchia, Renieri, van den Dijck, and many other painters) was living in SS. Apostoli, close by Brigna's shop in S. Giovanni Crisostomo.[150]

Because gifting was a commercial transaction masquerading as a social exchange, it will be introduced here. "It is better to give them away," wrote Antonio Lupis to the painter Angelo Valle, "than to sell them thus humiliating the profession and prejudicing the work."[151] Gifting relied on a belief, where both buyer and seller are complicit, that selling paintings was not mercantile but an exchange between equals, where payment was never discussed but only assumed to be forthcoming based on the generosity and social standing of the patron. Art and the artist are thus cleansed of demeaning associations with the lucre of trade and hence the taint of commodification and craft. The artist is not a craftsman or businessman but a purveyor of beauty and ideas. Art transcends economic value. It is priceless, as Pliny the Elder concluded regarding Zeuxis' gifting practice.

The practice and ideology of gifting originated in ancient Greece, but it did not become popular until the mid-sixteenth century, notably with Michelangelo, Titian, and Tintoretto. Whereas Michelangelo's gifting was ideologically and economically pure, Titian's inveterate greed and lavish recompense from Europe's nobility proved an irresistible symbiosis. He possibly learned how to manipulate patrons through gifting from Gentile Bellini at the Scuola di S. Marco. In 1527, Titian sent two paintings as gifts to Federico Gonzaga, and in 1537 when the nuns of S. Maria degli Angeli refused to pay the (then) exorbitant price of 500 ducats for an *Annunciation* (now lost), he sent it to Empress Isabella and received in return from Emperor Charles V a gift of 2,000 scudi. He subsequently amassed the first fortune in Venice's art community. Tintoretto's gifting, however, was more of a shrewd business practice, what is called today a "loss leader." The seller gives something free or at below cost price trusting that the buyer will be hooked for full-price purchases in the future. According to Ridolfi, Tintoretto donated the monumental *Last Judgment* and *Worship of the Golden Calf* to the church of Madonna dell'Orto, asking only for material costs (100 ducats). His gifts were often accompanied by other forms of persuasion. In 1574 he wrote to the Council of Ten expressing his sincere regret that he had been unable to shed his own blood at the Battle of Lepanto; in compensation he proposed to paint "a portrait of the triumphant battle" and give it to the state. In return he hoped the council would award him with the next available *sansaria*, anticipating that the nonagenarian Titian would die soon.[152]

A more specifically targeted gift in 1564 by Tintoretto to the Scuola di S. Rocco leveraged a free *Apotheosis of St. Roch* into a multi-decade monopoly decorating the then-empty boardroom, chapter hall and lower meeting hall. Because the *scuole grandi* were charitable confraternities, painters' gifts fell readily into the spirit of their mission. Gentile Bellini's gift to the Scuola di S. Marco and Girolamo Dente's to the Scuola della Carità were probably sincere expressions of piety.[153] Tintoretto's motives were less pure or, starting with Vasari and continuing into the seventeenth century, they were deemed to be mercenary. Not only did Tintoretto offer it as a loss leader, but he circumvented the competition instituted by the Scuola. Veronese, Tintoretto, Zuccaro, and Giuseppe Salviati were invited to submit drawings for this ceiling painting. Tintoretto ignored the prescribed procedure, secreted a finished painting onto the ceiling on the night before adjudication, and won the commission and a lifetime's worth of future employment. So famous did this episode become that when in 1668 Luca Giordano secretly placed an *Assumption of the Virgin* (Fig. 82) on the Salute altar that had been left vacant for four years by the dilatory Baldassare Franceschini, called Volterrano, and offered it to the church at a discounted rate (one-third of his price), the jealous Florentine agent Sera called it "a Tintoretto turn" because it was an unsolicited offering at a discounted price (200 ducats compared with the 720 ducats that Volterrano would have received).[154]

Oddly Titian and Tintoretto, as pioneers of mercantile gifting, did not engender a local tradition in the seventeenth century except as a pretense to avoid paying taxes to the Arte, as we saw in the case of Contarini and Malombra. So much of Venetian seicento painting is an emulation, homage, or pastiche of cinquecento masters, but the practice of gifting practically disappeared or, if it survived, it did so with less frequency than in Bologna or Rome.[155]

Supply and Demand

Prices rise when demand rises, or so the Genoese painter Paolo Gerolamo Piola testified in court when the judges turned to the question of why paintings increase in value over time.[156] Scarcities of Van Dycks led to high prices and, in response, to local painters making copies for those who could not afford or discern originals. Much the same happened in Venice where a limited pool of Venetian old masters and an

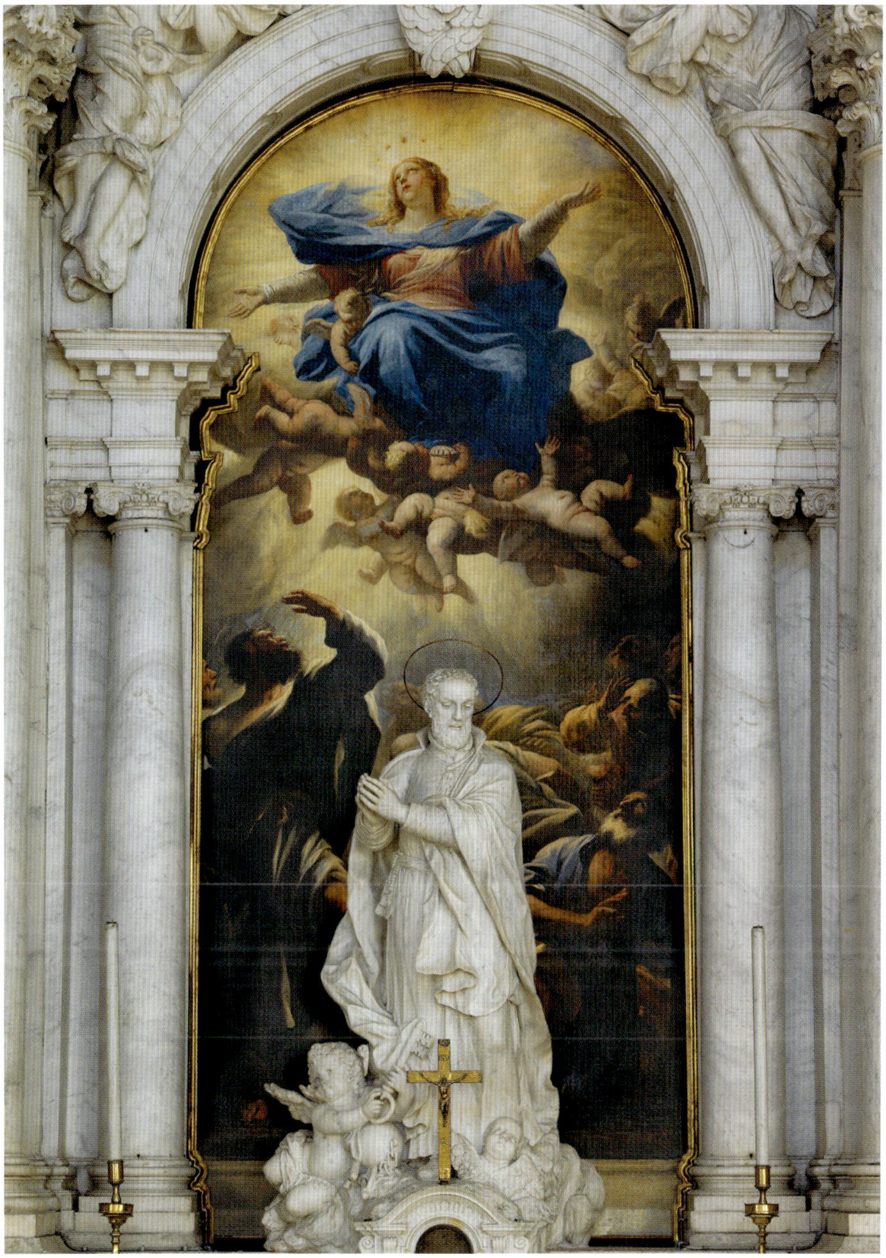

82 Luca Giordano, *Assumption of the Virgin*, 1668. Oil on canvas, 520 × 260 cm. S. Maria della Salute, Venice.

expanding market for them led to an inflationary trend in prices for contemporary painting. Rich painters knew how to play the market. In 1602 Alessandro Turchi wrote grudgingly from Verona about Palma Giovane's success in Venice. Being "one of the best in this art" and hence much in demand, Palma capitulated to his baser instincts for profit ("l'avidità del guadagno") and raised his prices.[157] Table 25 does not bear out his claim, at least when the measure of ducats per square meter is applied.

Some local painters—Turchi mentioned Farinati and Brusasorzi—were Palma's artistic equals, but being less in demand even though they painted for Venetian patrons, they produced cheaper work more quickly. The documentary evidence concerning Palma's rising prices is more equivocal than Turchi would have us believe, although they do trend upward over time. Turchi was on more solid ground when he asserted a price differential between painters in Verona and Venice; as Table 26 shows, prices in Venice were on average 83 percent

TABLE 25 Prices of Paintings by Palma Giovane (compiled from data in Appendix 1)

Year	Price in ducats	Ducats per square meter	Ducats per figure
1583	220	52	20
1584	138	10	9
1586	47	5	8
1589	553	26	33
1589	160	26	6
1592	75	8	4
1593	390	23	17
1595	180	14	45
1598	130	48	65
1599	53	14	9
1608	300	73	100
1609	300	11	150
1610	100	20	25
1611	100	20	14
1612	231	10	21
1613	400	15	14
1617	252	27	18
1618	176	21	15
1618	550	20	55

higher than in Verona (75 percent higher when prices are calculated by size). However, as Ridolfi noted ironically, Palma's ambition and tireless habits resulted in a diminished demand for his paintings and consequently in lower prices toward the end of his life.[158]

The effects of demand on an artist's prices can be observed even more clearly in the case of Canaletto. Early in his career he was charging 76 ducats per painting, but ten years later, after his discovery by the English whose demand exceeded his capacity to supply, his prices rocketed to 400 ducats and beyond. "The fellow is whimsical and varying his prices every day," complained Owen McSwiney, probably mistaking market adjustments for whimsy.[159] "He's so much follow'd," wrote Consul John Smith in 1730, "and all are so ready to pay him his own price for his work." Predictably such a heated market produced cut-rate imitators. Bernardo Bellotto was one of the best. Instead of 400 ducats or more, he charged just 110 ducats in 1741 for similarly sized cityscapes of Venice, and in one case a year earlier he supplied four paintings to a favored collector for 9 scudi.[160] Francesco Algarotti, who received the 110 ducat view on consignment from Zanetti, liked what he saw and asked his brother Bonomo who this painter was and how much he really charged, suspecting that Zanetti had inflated the price for Algarotti's royal clientele. Algarotti was then in Berlin and recognized Bellotto as "a painter who closely imitates the style of Canaletto, makes the water much better than him but doesn't have his finish." Zanetti also sent a Bellotto to Henry Howard, hoping that the view of Venice would remind the earl of Carlisle of him. Even more he hoped that his English friends would be charmed and decide to order more views at "an honest price" of 60 ducats. Zanetti reassured the earl that Bellotto was as good as Canaletto, "who now you pay for the name and fame only."[161]

Posthumous Profit

"It is not always true that the fame a painter enjoyed while alive increases after his death."[162] In presenting this observation by Lione Pascoli, Richard Spear has given reasons why this might be so, noting how social networks support painters' prices. Still, Pascoli's phrase "it is not always true" suggests expectations to the contrary. Seicento sources confirm this. "No one is more praised than when they're dead," wrote Lupis to the Neapolitan painter Angelo Valle hoping to console him for failed expectations in life.[163] "While Lotto was alive," Lupis continued, "he did not become famous, but now he is celebrated as a Bergamesque Apelles." "When he was alive," Federigo Capponi wrote of Paul Brill in 1626, "he asked 200 scudi for [a nocturne], but now they are demanding 300 scudi."[164] The painter Georg Christoph Martini, writing in Lucca shortly after Cassana's death in 1718, explained that Cassana's animal paintings were selling "at very high prices because this artist [is] recently deceased in Venice."[165] Sera, writing from Venice in 1656, reassured Leopold de' Medici that the purchase of paintings by Strozzi would be a sound investment: "It is certain that the paintings by this man will appreciate greatly with time just as they have increased in price since his death" (12 years earlier).[166]

Boschini, one of Sera's friends, fanned the fires of speculation while at the same time disavowing the belief that the value of art lies with money:

> Because I am a true friend of Painting, I will not do as certain others do today who paint only for the financial return and hope to make great profit with time, so that as soon as they have a painting, they say: "Oh what a beautiful production! What a worthy invention! Certainly (if I dare to express my opinion) it will be worth a fortune when he dies."

Boschini may mock the motives of those who paint and collect, but he does not deny the truth that prices were rising and would rise further after a painter dies: "What a beautiful thing this is! If one paid a thousand zecchini to a worthy painter in life, then after his death (oh, how amazing!) there is no limit to it becoming priceless."[167] Indeed, Boschini pounds away at this theme hoping to convince collectors to buy from contemporary Venetian painters: "Oh what a beautiful investment this is! . . . One can well say that one day these paintings will be worth their weight in gold and diamonds. . . . Our Venetian painters today will be held, after their death, in such high esteem that everyone will run after them like people do today after Veroneses and Titians."[168]

Collectors responded to this reasoning: if art is a commodity and an investment, then speculations on art futures are only natural. Quintiliano Rezzonico thought that Giordano's paintings were overpriced and would age badly by darkening and losing color and therefore would be less critically acclaimed, and yet, despite all this, he remained convinced that the prices would rise after his death, then 25 years away.[169] He cited Monsù Cosino as evidence. In life Rezzonico's friends were uninterested in buying Cosino's work, but now, after his death, "they run around begging with gold in their hand. His sketches, even if badly sketched, go for 37 scudi." Rezzonico made exceptions. If Livio Odescalchi wanted a cheap genre painting by Rosso Genovese, Rezzonico advised him to wait until after the artist died.[170]

We do not know what painters thought about death as a marketing opportunity, but Ridolfi probably voiced a majority view amongst those struggling for success, in other words painters who felt the same bitterness as he did about his failed career:

> One sees a series of paintings by Jacopo Bassano in the church of S. Maria Maggiore which could be resold today for a 1,000 scudi. With his labor, this worthy painter gave to many people material for their enrichment. And it is also true that amongst the many excellent professions, worthy painters have met this unhappy fate of not benefiting in life from the sweat of their labors, as if they were enemies of the gods who use this merciless fact that the world abhors the *virtù* of gallant men in life in order to enrich them after death with praise that costs nothing.[171]

Emigration and Immigration

The history of seventeenth-century Venetian painters cannot be understood without reference to emigration and immigration. Even the simple terminology "Venetian painters" is problematic since so many foreigners made Venice their home, and many more who stayed for shorter periods left their imprints on the city. Venice became in the seventeenth century, much more than in its golden age, a cosmopolitan artistic center of international exchange, known as a place with many foreign painters, a free and open society where they could enjoy Venice's famed *libertà*. Whereas foreigners saw and exploited Venice's freedom and commercial internationalism, Venetian painters attributed their slipping economic standing to immigrant painters. The Collegio, as outlined in the first section, maintained a pessimistic (if sometimes inconsistent) view of emigration and immigration for nearly a century. Of the painters listed and discussed by Martinioni as working in Venice in 1663, about half were foreigners; and if women painters are removed (he mentioned them more as curiosities than as productive painters), then foreigners outnumbered Venetians by two to one. In his chapter on living painters, Boschini first discussed 18 painters born in Venice or the Veneto, then quickly skipped over the 11 women, and concluded with 17 foreign painters.[172] Numbers aside, the fact that Boschini and Martinioni listed and discussed living foreign painters separately is itself an act that speaks of an awareness of immigration as a distinctive aspect of Venetian artistic culture.

Collectors and dealers confirmed the high standing of foreigners. According to Rezzonico, writing from Venice in 1680, "there is no painter of value here today" (except for Loth who was Venetian only by adoption).[173] Six months later he repeated himself: "Here in Venice there are now no worthy painters" (again making exceptions for Loth and another foreigner, Giacinto Brandi).[174] Sera wrote to Cardinal Carlo de' Medici that the three best painters working in Venice in 1662 were Volterrano, Bellotti, and Ricchi, painters whom he believed (incorrectly) to be from Florence, Lucca, and Siena.[175] Sera's bias, favoring foreign over native painters, persisted in the National Gallery exhibition *Venetian Seventeenth Century Painting* (London, 1979), where over half of the paintings on display were made by painters born and trained outside of Venice and whose reputation rests substantially on work done elsewhere in Italy.

By 1713 the Collegio de' Pittori reported to the Milizia da Mar that "the Collegio is composed mostly of foreigners."[176] This rise in foreign expertise was experienced in other areas. Thirty-one of the 65 students who matriculated from the Università degli stampatori e librai between 1641 and 1660 were foreigners.[177] Patents awarded by the Senate to foreigners rose from 32 (or about 7 percent of the total between 1550 and 1600) to 48 (or about 14 percent of the total between 1600 and 1650) and held steady at this rate for the rest of the century.[178] As the Venetian wool and silk industries lost market share during the seventeenth century, the number of patents awarded to foreigners rose from none in the sixteenth century to 4 (40 percent of all patents on wool technologies) between 1600 and 1650 to 13 (30 percent) between 1650 and 1700.

The reasons for immigration to Venice must have been as varied as the painters who came. Incentives included freedom, economic opportunity, a thriving foreign community, and a painterly tradition of colorism that many found sympathetic to their own work. Strozzi turned to Venice because its legendary freedom must have looked pretty good from his windowless prison cell in Genoa. Speaking through his guarantor for an immigration request, Strozzi claimed Venice "as mother and communal father for those who do not want to work badly . . . . This most serene city [is] refuge for the oppressed and asylum of liberty."[179] Strozzi probably meant personal freedom, but he appealed to the republic's pride in its independence from foreign political domination and to the Venetian painters' pride in their indigenous painterly style, the *libertà* of the brush that Boschini equated with Venetian personal freedom.[180]

Other painters without such compelling reasons as Strozzi emigrated to Venice because, like him, they found in Venice the source (or at least, a receptive audience) for their painterly styles, a place where their colorism could earn them some money. Giordano went to Venice because "he always loved the beautiful paintings of Venice more than others."[181] The immigrants Langetti, Fetti, Strozzi, and Mazzoni also painted in a freer, more coloristic style. According to Boschini, every foreigner then painting in Venice, at least those worthy of mention, studied and admired the Venetian style.[182] On the other hand, a Tuscan painter such as Volterrano failed despite a prestigious inaugural commission for the Salute.

Immigration was further stimulated by Venetian collectors who valued contemporary Bolognese, Florentine, and Roman painting more than their local painters. When Renieri and Vecchia appraised the Widman collection in 1659, for example, they gave contemporary Venetian paintings an average value of 55 ducats, compared with the 180 ducat average for foreigners.[183] (This statement, like any other about "Venetian" painters or paintings, is semantically ambiguous since in this case only 5 of the 15 so-called "Venetian" painters collected by the Widman were actually born in Venice or the Veneto.)[184] When prices differed for identical commissions (same patron, same date, same size, etc.), it was inevitably the foreigner who received more.[185]

Giordano and presumably other foreigners profited from Venice in another way than as the fertile and appreciative home of painterly colorism. Boschini accused Giordano of emigrating for profit because it brought a unique marketing opportunity: "Painters often enjoy complaining to each other about those who come to Venice for profit and introduce many copies of their work presenting them as if they were originals."[186] Giordano, always an aggressive marketeer, was also accused of this deceptive practice by an anonymous seventeenth-century biographer.[187]

Fewer economic opportunities for wealth acquisition might have been available in Venice than in Rome, but there were market niches waiting to filled. Pietro Tempesta (né Pieter Mulier) wrote in 1687 how Venice "is truly a city to be enjoyed because there is always something new to see and is always full of foreigners."[188] Collectors welcomed him "because there are many figure painters here but hardly any painters of landscapes, marine scenes, and animals." As Tempesta noted, foreigners felt at home in Venice because there were so many other foreigners, often living in close proximity to each other (as described above).

Despite Strozzi's expectation and Tempesta's experience, other immigrants faced a hostility toward foreign competitors. Dürer suffered from the secrecy and jealousy of Venetian painters, and a century later Friulian painters claimed that foreign painters were stealing business from them.[189] The Venetian Arte encouraged foreigners to join after six months' residence in the city. In 1652 foreign masters paid four ducats annually for membership, nearly double the fee for Venetians. In 1664 matriculation costs for masters entering the Arte rose to 25 ducats for foreigners compared to the five ducats paid by Venetians.[190] The mood became more protectionist, according to the Arte, because of "the prejudices that most of our profession have about those coming to this city from foreign states and being allowed to work here with notable adverse effects on the Arte and its members who find it difficult to compete."[191] Four years earlier the Arte intervened with the Council of Ten to stop the Bolognese painter Domenico Ginassi from continuing his work for the Scuola del Santissimo Sacramento in the church of S. Antonin.[192] However, by 1724, when the Collegio (the body that replaced the Arte) was lobbying for an Accademia, the mood had changed. Now the painters wanted to attract foreigners to the city, especially young painters who might otherwise go to the academies in Florence,

Bologna, or Rome, "in order to help revive the liberal arts of painting, sculpture, and architecture."[193] The Accademia in Verona was proud of its 17 foreign students, naming different competitors (in Madrid, St. Petersburg, and Parma), and decided to boost enrollment by making fees equal for residents and foreigners alike.[194]

Emigration coexisted with immigration, further destabilizing the sense of a native school. In 1683 Zanchi, then prior of the Collegio, testified to the Milizia da Mar: "Something causes the instability of this profession where painters come and go and are poor and cannot get paid."[195] By 1713, it was not only Venetians emigrating for economic reasons but foreign residents as well. The Collegio de' Pittori identified three reasons for its financial problems. "The first reason is that the Collegio is composed mostly of foreign members who, not being able to earn a living in Venice, are abandoning the republic. . . . These artists are transients, not citizens as this fact demonstrates. The second reason is that Venetian painters are not finding work at home commensurate with their ability and hence are taking up employment abroad, as Bellucci, Ricci, Cassana, Pellegrini, and others native to the Serenissima have done. These are amongst our most famous painters and they are leaving to abandon their country and continue their work abroad."[196] The third reason involves painters not paying taxes either because they have already left Venice (Brusaferro is cited here) or because they are at the point of leaving Venice owing to a lack of commissions (Balestra and Cassana are cited).

Ten years later Angiolo de Coster identified three types of painter: "the *virtuosi* who attend to their studio in order to gain glory and honor for their country" and "those who wander about, going now here now there looking for somewhere to subsist."[197] (He forgot to mention the third type, possibly expats like himself.) Those who travelled to "subsist" are now overshadowed by the critically and financially successful who travelled for profit. Three of Verona's top earners, Turchi, Ottino, and Bassetti, left for Rome before 1630, coincidentally escaping the plague that killed so many of their colleagues.[198] Painters must have thought of Rome not just as the city of antiquities and Raphael, but as the city of high prices where their income could be doubled. In negotiating the price for an altarpiece by Cerano in Milan, Fra Atansio told the patron, Francesco Gambara, that Cerano would probably accept 250 scudi, but that if he were to go to Rome at that time (in 1625) he could be paid twice that amount. Rome, he noted, is "where you go to get rich."[199] Genoa also attracted foreigners with higher pay. Ricci earned 80 genovine per week (plus room and board) working there, more than he earned in Venice and more than the Genoese painter Antonio Maria Casoni earned at the same time from the same patron (1 scudo per day). For the second half of the century, Germany, France, and England beckoned successful Venetians (Bellotti, Triva, Bellucci, Pellegrini, Ricci) more often than did Rome or Genoa.

The motives for emigration invariably included money, except for an idealist or two like Pietro Rotari, who "went painting around not for the money, but for his pleasure and fame he went to cities where this art was valued more than in Verona."[200] Titian was easily tempted by fame and money when he was invited to stay in Augsburg by Charles V. "He returned to Venice," commented Ridolfi, "after being kept in Germany for the space of five years bringing with him 11,000 scudi worth of gift." The homebody Tintoretto could benefit only indirectly, lacking the will to travel and consequently the contacts with patrons who could have made him rich. Nevertheless, he managed some remunerative foreign commissions, typically bringing in his high fees, the highest (400 ducats) being for an *Adoration of Shepherds* (Fig. 83) for Philip II in 1583, even though he apparently left most of the painting to his son Domenico.

Marketing Strategies

Immigration can thus be seen as a market response by painters to fulfill a demand in supply. Some painters adopted marketing strategies of marginal legality or unusual inventiveness in order to generate a greater demand for their product. Tintoretto in his youth, like many other painters in Venice, exhibited his works along the Merceria and at the Rialto, a practice of accepted illegality. The purpose was not just to sell the paintings—only the poorest *pittori di minor fortuna* would rely on this means for their living—but to advertise the painter with the hopes of gaining more lucrative commissions.[201] The regulation of public sale of art, first recorded in 1436, set out the terms of sale: "No person, neither Venetian nor foreign, should dare to sell any painting in Venice except painters who belong to the Arte . . . and then it is legal to sell them in the shops (*botteghe*) but in no other place in the city except during the Festa della Sensa." This restriction of commerce was widely ignored, judging from the repeated issue of new edicts banning public sales, and evidently deteriorated in the seventeenth century when the regulation had to be renewed and strengthened: "No painter can sell paintings of any kind as one sees in recent bad prac-

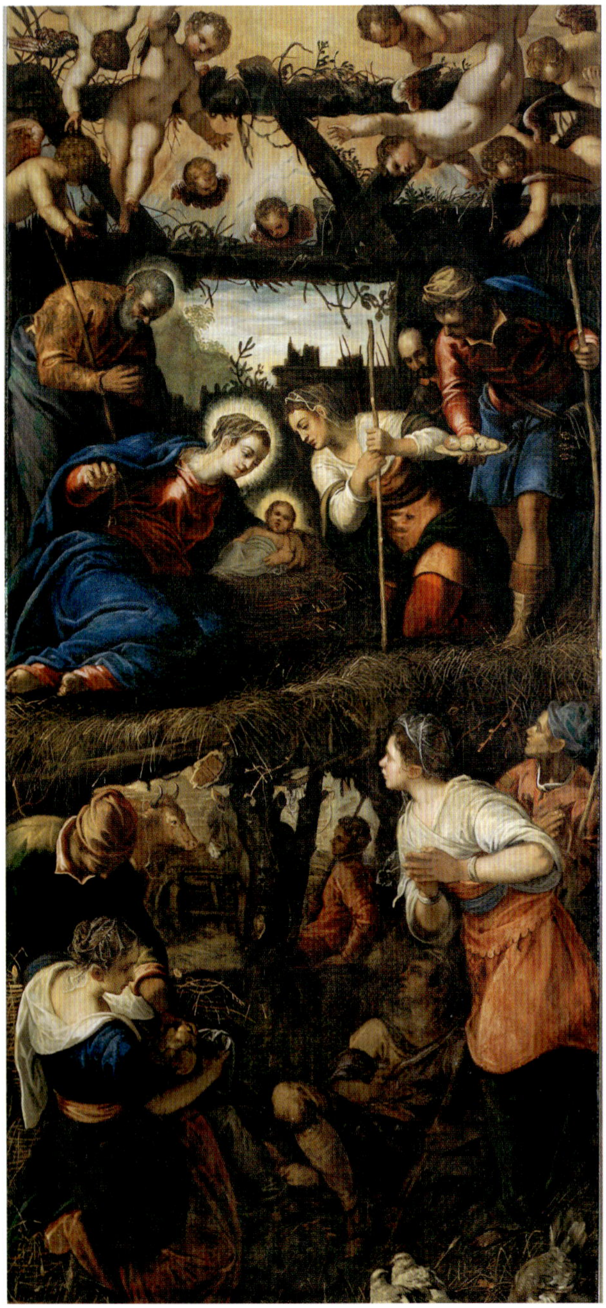

83 Jacopo and Domenico Tintoretto, *Adoration of Shepherds*, 1583. Oil on canvas, 432 × 186 cm. Real Monasterio de San Lorenzo, Escorial.

tice; selling paintings in the *piazze* and *campi* and in any other place without exception will incur confiscation of the paintings and a fine of 10 ducats for each infraction."[202]

A marketing device that was apparently not used elsewhere in Italy was the lottery. Lotteries for cash prizes and goods were occasionally held in sixteenth-century Venice, possibly inspiring Lotto to enact his name by organizing a lottery of 30 intarsia cartoons and 16 paintings.[203] The second known lottery was held in 1666 by Renieri, who brought the idea to Venice from the Netherlands, where art lotteries were sometimes held.[204] Some 6,062 tickets were sold for just over 2 ducats each for 76 paintings with an appraised value of about 18,000 ducats. For those purchasing tickets, this would seem like a great opportunity: 2 ducats for a painting of an average value of 237 ducats. For Renieri, however, it would seem to be a losing proposition: 12,400 ducats in ticket sales for a collection worth 18,000, especially after the republic took its 5 percent commission. The only explanation is that Renieri knew appraised values were generally inflated over actual sale prices. (Presumably Renieri was prohibited from making the appraisal himself since this was a state-sanctioned auction approved by the Provveditori di Comune.) A physician of Greek origin hoped to exploit the interest that Renieri's lottery had generated. He decided his painting colleciton was worth 60,000 ducats, but according to Paolo del Sera it was "all junk, that is copies and faked antique things." When the official appraisal by two painters came in at 1,500 ducats, the lottery was cancelled, much to the city's amusement.

Location

One reason to study art economies in the Veneto instead of just Venice, besides the fact that there existed a free exchange of art and artists within the Venetian Republic, is to test out the standard assumption that prices are higher in cities where demand is higher than in towns. Anecdotal evidence can be easily adduced to prove this point, but having sufficient data allows us to provide a statistically significant conclusion. Table 26 ranks locales from the most to the least remunerative.

TABLE 26 Prices of Paintings by Location (compiled from data in Appendix 1)

LOCATION	AVERAGE PRICE IN DUCATS	AVERAGE PRICE IN DUCATS PER SQUARE METER
Bergamo	360	66
Brescia	295	34
Treviso	249	12
Venice	218	21
Padova	178	35
Vicenza	148	21
Udine	140	15
Veneto towns	126	17
Verona	119	12

Bergamo places first because the *deputati* of S. Maria Maggiore were both wealthy and ambitious. They hired top artists from Venice and elsewhere and paid top prices to do so, in one case five times the rate they had been paying local artists for similar work.[205] Without their willingness to bankroll their ambition, Bergamo would have sunk into provincial mediocrity, at least by economic standards. The middling position of Venice is more difficult to explain, given the expectations that the concentration of wealth, political power, and artistic heritage would translate into higher prices and greater opportunities for painters. These data support the painters' claims to the Signoria that their profession was languishing financially (discussed on pp. 206–10 above) and that cheap foreign painters were driving down prices. The bottom ranking of Verona confirms Scipione Maffei's account in 1732 of seventeenth-century Verona as a cultural backwater. He gave no particular reason for this, but one possible cause might be the plague of 1630 that hit Verona harder than any other Veneto city. In the following section, using Tables 27 and 28, it will be shown how higher prices outside of Venice were often a factor of prestige commissions given to Venetian painters.

Another aspect of location that had economic implications involves the hierarchy of spaces with churches. The cheapest paintings were placed on ceilings (13 ducats per square meter), closest to heaven but visually marginal, followed by wall paintings (18 ducats per square meter), on average 38 percent more than ceiling paintings. Meter-for-meter, however, altarpieces brought in the highest prices at over twice as much as ceiling paintings (27 ducats per square meter).

Setting Prices

Taste and Style

"Every house has its painter," lamented the struggling painter Paolo Pino, "if one puts on sale a painting by Titian, they will say that it's a mediocre thing and ten quattrini or worse will be offered."[206] Artistic value, an expression of personal taste even when it is presented as part of an objective hierarchy (Raphael is better than Perugino and hence more valuable), affected monetary value in profound ways, especially in the world of collecting old masters. Prices that painters charged corresponded to intrinsic variables such as the costs of production; they also responded to artistic quality, an artist's reputation and style, and other intangible factors. "You pay for the painter's fame," Bernardino Garbelli told a collector in 1583 in order to explain the high prices of paintings by Tintoretto and Veronese.[207] The presence of these subjective criteria as influential variables that helped set market value is readily recognizable; however, their precise effects cannot be so easily measured.

The Widman, Sagredo, Schulenburg, and Bonamin collections were valued by two or more painters, each

TABLE 27 Average Prices for History Painting: Painters in Venice (data compiled from Appendix 1)

ARTIST	SAMPLE SIZE; DATES	AVERAGE PRICE, IN DUCATS	AVERAGE PRICE, DUCATS PER SQUARE METER	AVERAGE PRICE, DUCATS PER FIGURE
Bassano	9; 1551–88	46	14	8
Tintoretto	16; 1551–93	73	7	6
Veronese	6; 1555–82	172	10	15
Palma Giovane	19; 1583–1628	214	21	33
Padovanino	6; 1626–35	137	29	39
Ruschi	3; 1641–61	297	43	58
Ricchi	3; 1646–71	131	14	21
Bellotti	4; 1658–81	411		
Liberi	7; 1659–80	332	33	49
Zanchi	15; 1668–1712	355	34	38
Fumiani	3; 1679–1706	97	32	10
Ricci	14; 1682–1733	322	46	47
Piazzetta	5; 1718–43	230	128	163
Pittoni	8; 1733–46	387	79	51
Tiepolo	7; 1733–44	523	29	67

TABLE 28 Average Prices for History Painting: Painters in Padua, Vicenza, Verona, and Brescia (data compiled from Appendix 1)

ARTIST	SAMPLE SIZE; DATES	AVERAGE PRICE, IN DUCATS	AVERAGE PRICE, DUCATS PER SQUARE METER	AVERAGE PRICE, DUCATS PER FIGURE
Farinati	22; 1576–1602	53	11	10
Tinelli	54; 1618–33	56		
Carneo	4; 1667–77	4	7	2
Maffei	6; 1644–57	120	10	21
Carpioni	2; 1669–72	65	11	12
Celesti	9; 1680–1706	145	8	13
Balestra	5; 1706–36	244	52	47

with a different estimate for the various paintings. Sometimes the assigned monetary value differed by as much as 450 percent. Tomas Francesco Ergo and Pieter de Coster thought the paintings owned by the estate of Lucrezia Bonamin were worth 4,170 ducats. Lucrezia's sons disagreed, and commissioned another team (Nicolò Allegri and Lelio Bonetti) who came back with a total of 18,373 ducats.[208] More often the differences were closer to 50 percent. In the Widman inventory of 1659 drawn up by Renieri and Vecchia, Renieri gave a painting by Ricchi, his friend and stylistic soulmate, a value of 40 ducats; Vecchia thought it was worth only 25 ducats.[209] Happy and prosperous Tiepolo valued the Sagredo collection at 32,394 ducats, while the poor and strugglinng Piazzetta came up with a figure of 23,746.[210] Looking at their valuations of individual paintings, greater differences of taste and value emerge. Some are almost predictable. Tiepolo, the "new Veronese," gave Veronese's *Annunciation* (Thyssen Collection, Madrid) one of the highest prices in the collection: 380 ducats. Piazzetta came in with a stingy 80 ducats. A Rembrandt also impressed Tiepolo, who priced it at 350 ducats, but the normally restrained Piazzetta topped that with 500 ducats (Algarotti linked Piazzetta and Rembrandt as latter-day Caravaggios).[211] The two second most valuable paintings in Piazzetta's opinion were his own *Angelo Custode* (Los Angeles County Museum of Art) and a *Philosopher* by Salvator Rosa, tied at 400 ducats. More unexpectedly, Tiepolo valued two of Bassano's nocturnal paintings more than Piazzetta did, even though Piazzetta perpetuated a form of seventeenth-century tenebrism into the mid-eighteenth century (300 vs. 100 ducats, 100 vs. 40 ducats): unexpected at least until one reads the appreciative letter by Tiepolo regarding Bassano's use of white in shadows.

Comparative prices based on the artist's reputation and the demand for his work are evident in commissions from different painters by the same patron at the same time for comparable work (in size and complexity). Aggregate averages show both convergences in the prices of contemporaries as well as marked divergences even when Carneo, a genre specialist, is factored out (Tables 27 and 28).

Why did average prices vary? Clearly, artistic quality, as we judge these artists today, was not a dominant factor. Was Veronese really twice as good as Tintoretto? Was Zanchi five times better than his muse Tintoretto? When size is factored in, then the differences shrink, another reason to argue for size as a strong variable. Chronology must also be a factor (see Table 13). Liberi and Zanchi, equally renowned and working at the same time, received closely comparable prices, measured either by size or by absolute sums.

When average prices varied greatly amongst contemporaries, quality and reputation need not be the primary cause. Paintings by Ricchi, for example, were a bargain; whether measured by size or number of figures, he charged on average one-third less than Bellotti. A difference of this magnitude might signal a higher critical reputation, and textually a tenuous argument could be made to this end, but a stronger determinate must be the economic effects of Bellotti's obsessively detailed style (Fig. 84). Yes, his hyper-realism did inspire a rare literary genre—the book in praise of a single painting (Gian Giorgio Nicolini, *Le ombre del pennello glorioso del molt'illustre signore Pietro Bellotti, eccellentissimo pittore*, Venice, 1659)—but it also cost him considerable time to produce. Having to paint more slowly, he could produce fewer works than the comparatively speedy and sketchy Ricchi, who often abbreviated with shadows and thinly painted surfaces (Fig. 85). As a result, Bellotti's paintings were rarer commodities. Limited supply might have increased demand; it certainly raised prices.

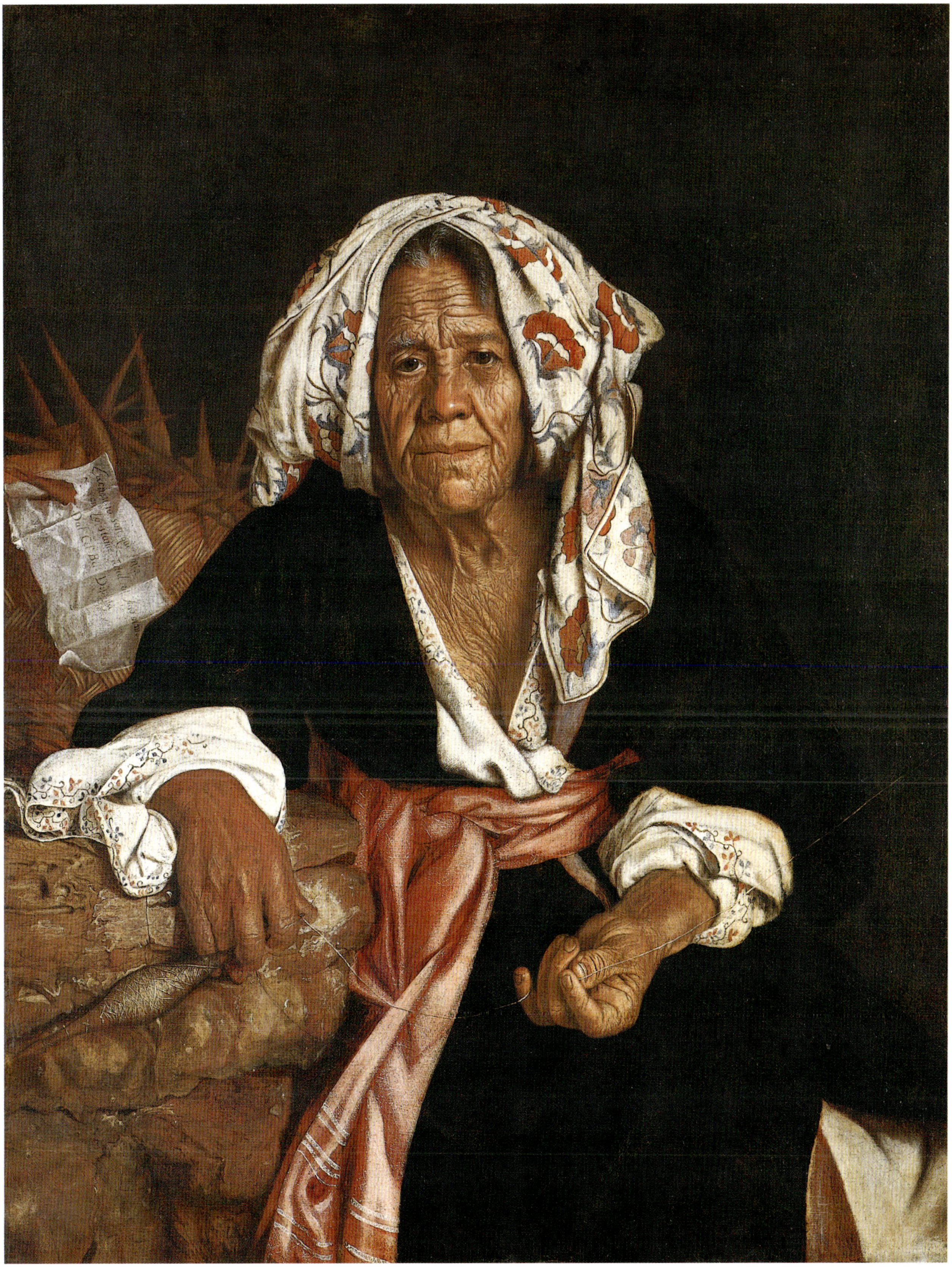

84 Pietro Bellotti, *Fate Lachesis*, 1654. Oil on canvas, 95 × 81 cm. Staatsgalerie, Stuttgart.

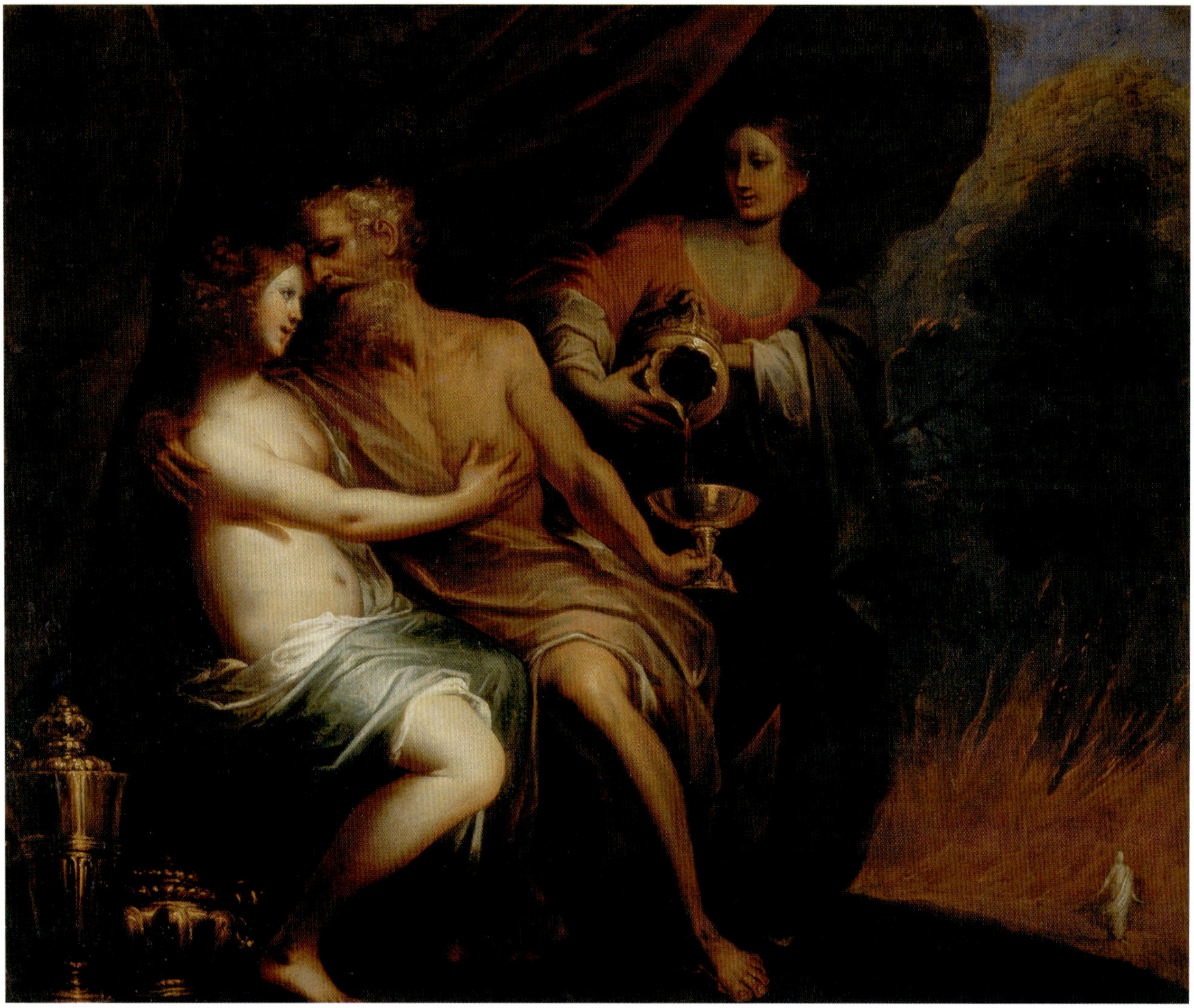

85 Pietro Ricchi, *Lot and his Daughters.* Oil on canvas, 97 × 118 cm. Museo del Settecento Veneziano, Ca' Rezzonico, Venice.

This is not to say that reputation did not influence price. The differences noted in Tables 27 and 28, at least those of price by size (where size helps stabilize other variables), could be even greater when celebrated painters are compared with struggling stringers. Examples exist where different painters producing comparable work (in size and complexity) for the same patron at the same time were paid differently. In 1613 the fathers of S. Maria dei Carmini commissioned two large lateral paintings for their presbytery, a *Multiplication of the Loaves and Fishes* (Fig. 86) by Palma Giovane and a *Gathering of the Manna* (Fig. 87) by the unsuccessful and virtually unknown Marco Vicentino. Both paintings were the same size (25.8 square meters) and with comparable numbers of figures (about 28), and yet Palma received 400 ducats and Vicentino only 140. The price of celebrity was about threefold.[212]

Artistic value and hence economic value are often taken to be subjective, much as Pino did in his complaint, but the judicial system held another view. When disagreements arose between painter and patron regarding price after a contract was signed and the painting was completed, the matter could then be referred to a judicial review.[213] Usually two painters were assigned to evaluate the disputed work and to determine a fair price.[214] Besides the Venetian examples that I have cited in the Introduction, only one more will be mentioned here: the testimony in 1618 by Antonio Aliense to the Provveditori al Sal regarding paintings by Domenico Bruni for the Palazzo Ducale (now lost).[215] There were two parts to his mandate: were the paintings "worthy of the chamber," and did Bruni follow the terms of his contract? Aliense answered the first by arguing that Bruni not only followed the initial instructions but exceeded

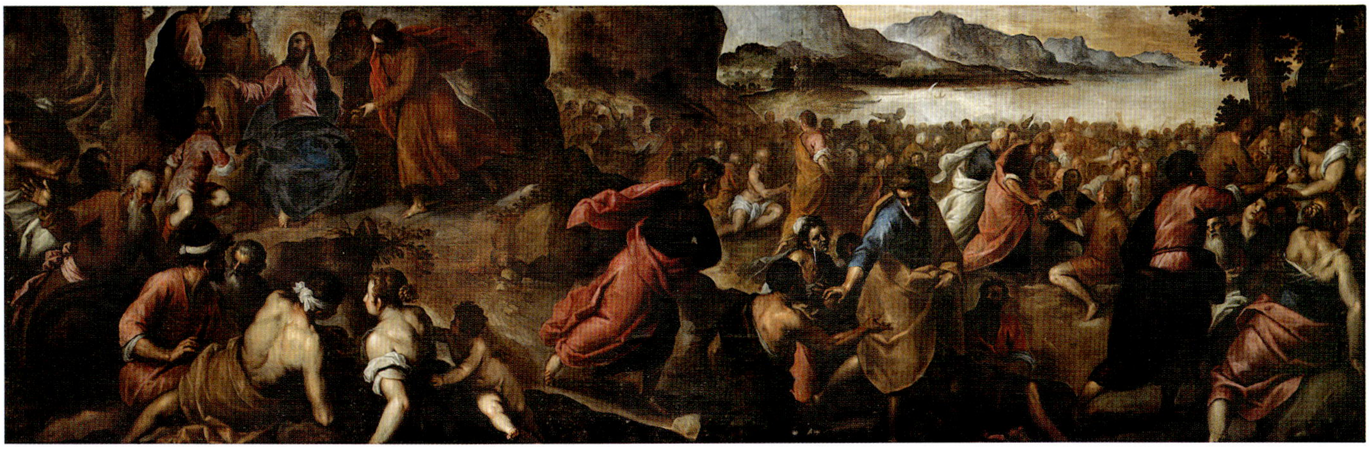

86 Palma Giovane, *Multiplication of the Loaves and Fishes*, 1613. Oil on canvas, 300 × 860 cm. S. Maria dei Carmini, Venice.

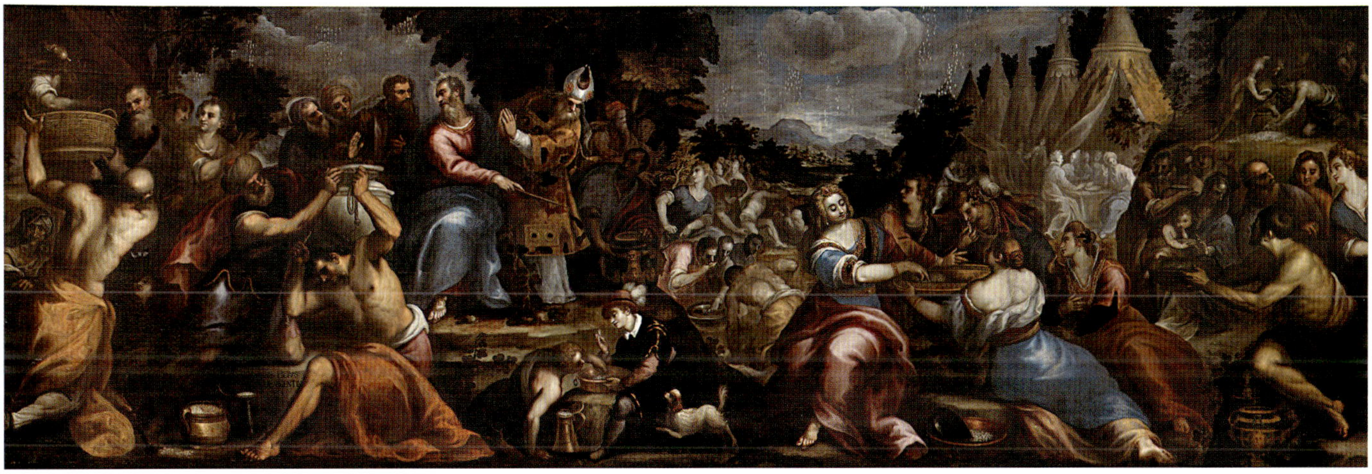

87 Marco Vicentino, *Gathering of the Manna*, 1613. Oil on canvas, 300 × 860 cm. S. Maria dei Carmini, Venice.

them by including details not found in the submitted sketch and by applying his knowledge of perspective to adjust scale and sightlines appropriate to the site:

> I find that the works are more correct than the sketch . . . first of all because the groups of flowers would have been too large and out of proportion if they had been made according to the sketch because they are at a height much closer to our field of vision.

He went on to note that the architecture is more complicated, more sophisticated in perspective, and adjusted to suit the site and viewing conditions. Aliense concluded that these and other improvements added 100 ducats (33 percent) to its value:

> There are also gilded arabesques and flower vases on pedestals and other things that show greater effort and augment the work's beauty. Consequently, it seems in my mind that all the aforementioned constructions are worth 100 ducats more than they would have been worth if the work had followed the preliminary design. And, as the above work is presented, I estimate that it cannot be worth less than 400 ducats.

The premise that an objective correlation existed between price and artistic quality might be partly a judicial convenience. It was also assumed by others to be true. "I advise you not to try and save 30 or 40 ducats because then in the end you'll have a messy and dirty thing," advised Giacomo Romanello to a prospective patron regarding an altarpiece by Zanchi.[216] He was comparing Zanchi and Liberi, who were equals in economic terms but not in his subjective world of artistic taste.

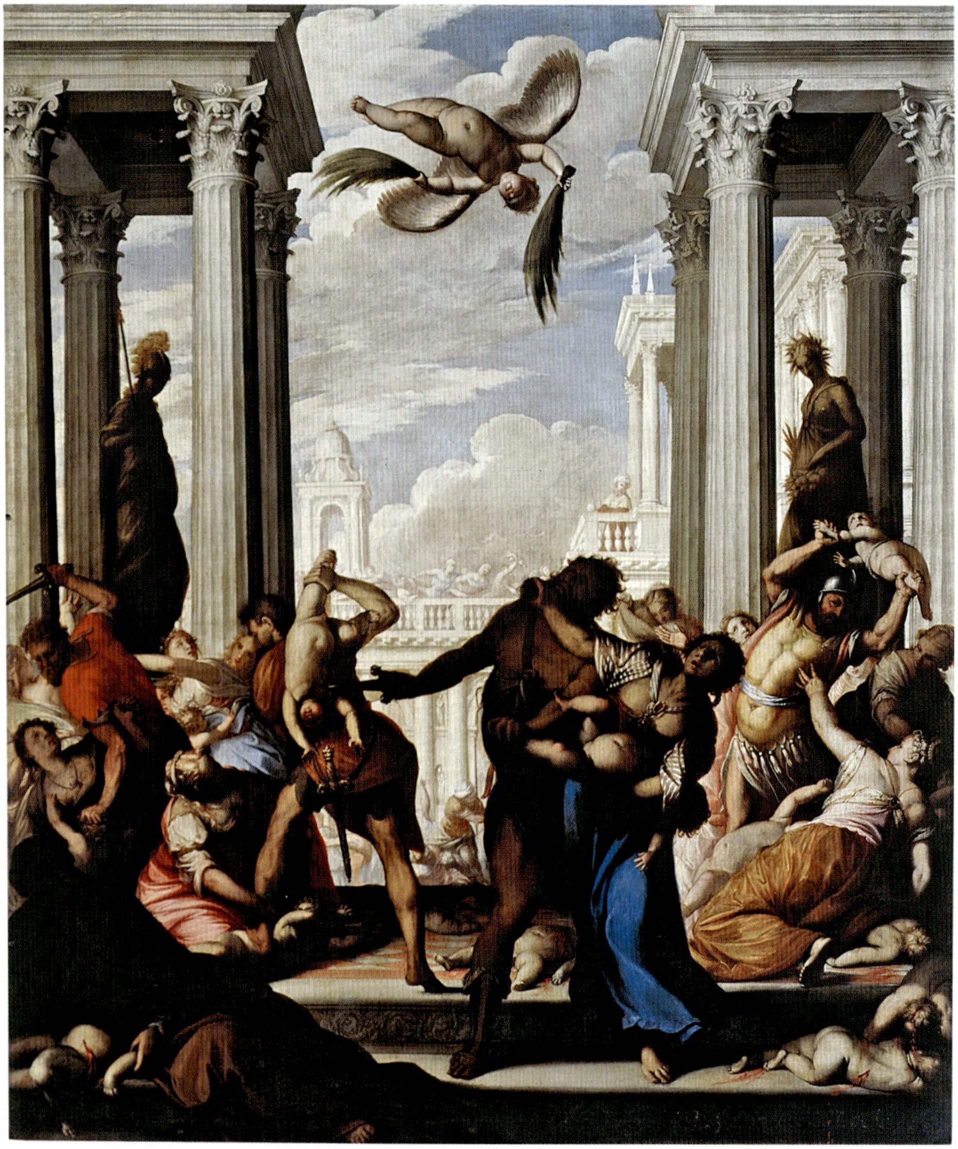

88 Massimo da Verona, *Massacre of the Innocents*, 1657. Oil on canvas, 375 × 350 cm. S. Maria Maggiore, Bergamo.

Size and Figures

Size matters, not so much for its effect on material costs but for its effect on time in production. Between 1644 and 1656, Maffei priced his work at the same rate of 8 ducats per square meter regardless of the painting's size or number of figures.[217] So too did Liberi. He painted or agreed to paint two altarpieces in S. Caterina (Vicenza), *St. Anthony with Angels* and the *Mystical Marriage of St. Catherine*, in 1671 and 1672 for 100 and 270 ducats respectively. Despite the variance in size (4.1 and 10.9 square meters), and despite the obvious difference in quality (the *St. Anthony* seems to be a studio production), he was paid at about the same rate of 24 and 25 ducats per square meter.[218] Similarly, the *deputati* of the Treviso Duomo paid Celesti and Zanchi at the same rate of 7 ducats per square meter for paintings in the presbytery that were 12.3, 14.3, and 31 square meters and included between 10 and 25 figures.[219] In 1701 the Scuola dei Fabbri e dei Ferrai paid Molinari and Francesco Pittoni at nearly the same rate (39 and 40.6 ducats per square meter) regardless of the number of figures or compositional complexity of their paintings (Molinari's was a *sacra conversazione* with eight figures; Pittoni's was simply two angels).[220] And for a large-scale decoration in the Palazzo Caldogna in 1676, Carpioni charged at the

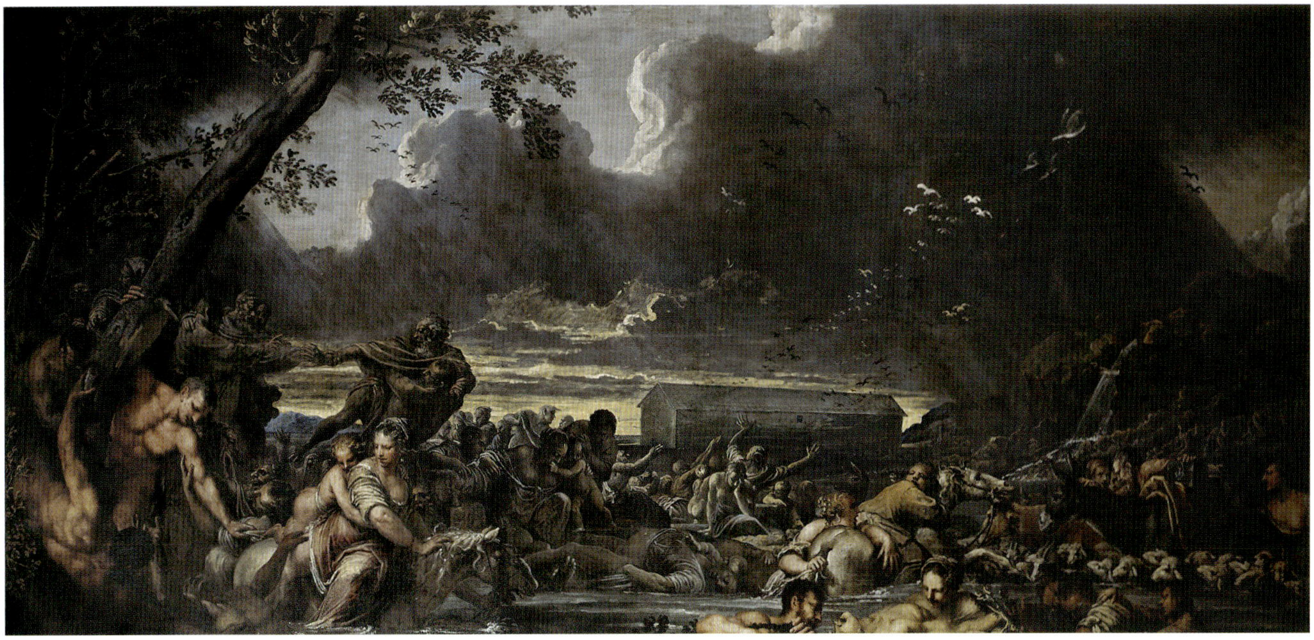

89 Pietro Liberi, *The Flood*, 1660. Oil on canvas, 375 × 775 cm. S. Maria Maggiore, Bergamo.

same bargain rate of 3 ducats per square meter regardless of the number of figures or the size (which ranged from 4.6 to 17.6 square meters).[221] When size and figures varied but the square-meter value remained constant, it can be reasonably certain that size mattered.

Whereas we do not know whether it was Carpioni or Caldogna who set the pricing formula by size, in the case of Pietro Liberi and Massimo da Verona at S. Maria Maggiore in Bergamo, it was clearly the patron. In 1657 Massimo da Verona received 221 ducats for his 13.1 square meter *Massacre of the Innocents* (Fig. 88).

Three years later Liberi received 500 ducats for *The Flood*, over twice the size at 29 square meters (Fig. 89).[222] Despite the disparity of size and despite the fact that the *Massacre* has about 18 figures and the more expensive *Flood* has only 10, the rate remained the same for both painters: 17 ducats per square meter. That rate, however, changed over time. When in 1668 Zanchi painted *Moses Striking the Rock* (Fig. 90) for part of the same cycle at S. Maria Maggiore, he received 825 ducats or nearly two-thirds more than Liberi for his *Flood* even though both paintings were identical in size. (Zanchi did offer more figures, but the contract only mentioned size.)

Zanchi's prices generally matched Liberi's (see Table 27), and both were shrewd bargainers (see the Introduction). The determining variable seems to be chronological. Eight years is not a long time, but it was precisely during those years that the *deputati* of S. Maria Maggiore were raising their prices ever higher in order to entice foreign celebrity painters (including, later, Giordano and Ferri). Venetians learned from Liberi's experience that more could be earned in Bergamo than Venice. In 1659, one year before painting *The Flood*, Liberi received 400 ducats (100 less than in Bergamo) from the Signoria for the *Victory of the Dardanelli* (Fig. 91). Both paintings had similar numbers of figures (about ten, even though they seem more crowded than that), but the *Victory of the Dardanelli* was about 85 percent larger. Measured by size, he earned more than twice as much in Bergamo than Venice. The lesson that Zanchi could have learned when it was his turn to negotiate a contract with S. Maria Maggiore was that he could expect more than his average rate.

However complicated all of this might seem, the picture becomes murkier still when all of the data about size and price are compiled and presented as aggregate averages (Table 29).

Looking at the column of average prices up to 10 square meters, prices rise continually and almost consistently with size. The unexpected jump in average price between paintings under 1 square meter and paintings between 1 and 2 square meters can be explained by the number of small cheap genre paintings. Above 10 square meters, the numbers become erratic, dropping by a third or more for sizes between 10 and 25 square meters. Here, mysteriously, it appears that painters were paid less for larger paintings than for smaller ones. Prices begin to rise again for paintings

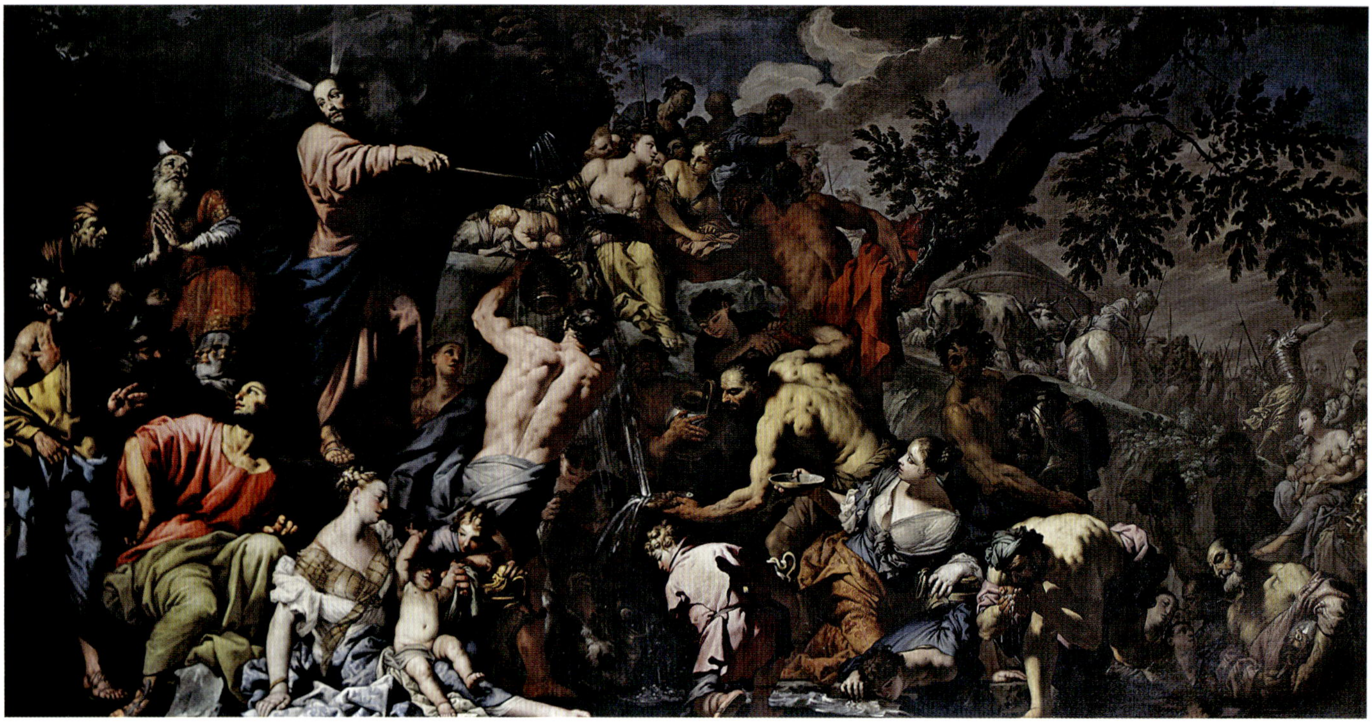

90 Antonio Zanchi, *Moses Striking the Rock*, 1668. Oil on canvas, 375 × 775 cm. S. Maria Maggiore, Bergamo.

larger than 25 square meters, but they are still disproportionately cheap when considered on a ducats per square meter basis. The column of prices per square meter confirms that large paintings (over 10 square meters) were cheaper not just in absolute terms but even on the basis of cost per square meter and remained relatively cheap as they increased in size. The cluster of prices between 21 and 27 ducats per square meter for mid-size painting between 3 and 6 square meters, cheaper than smaller and larger paintings, cannot be easily explained. One thing is clear, though: Venetian painters did not command the high prices (as measured by size) of the Romans, where paintings costing 30 to 290 scudi per square meter were not uncommon.

A painter's reputation could affect prices, especially when the famous are compared with the obscure, but often price differentials mean less than they appear when painters of comparable status are considered, as I argued in the preceeding section. How variables such as a painter's reputation or technique influenced style will probably remain mysterious, except in such extreme cases as Bellotti and Ricchi. Complicating the issue even further is size. I will argue here that a painter's reputation may be a weaker determinate than the size of the painting. This is clearly seen to be the case when Algarotti made the price calculations for a contemporary Venetian gallery that he was buying for Augustus III. The history painters whose assigned subjects required several figures of about two feet high (68 cm) would be paid 102 gold ducats each for a painting of 2.25 square meters. The landscape painters, whose figures would be smaller and fewer, would be paid 51 gold ducats for each painting of 1.21 square meters. In other words, history painters were paid at the same rate as landscape painters. Neither the number nor the kind of figures nor the hierarchy of genres affected the price. Even in this culturally sophisticated circle, only size mattered, with one exception. As a friend and admirer of Piazzetta, "the most elaborate and studied painter of all, extremely slow and very difficult to control," Algarotti decided that he should be paid (secretly) twice as much as the others: "Since this painter takes so long with his works and is paid accordingly, he must absolutely have 200 sequins for this work."[223]

Art historians today may resist the notion of a size-dependent price because it conjures up the bias of art as craft where the craftsman is paid pro rata by piecework or by day. Giovan Battista Armenini, in his lament of 1587 on the general decline of painting, accused some painters of paying their assistants by the day, "as if they were abject peasants," and there are "even those who pay by the breadth of the hand."[224] In a parody of

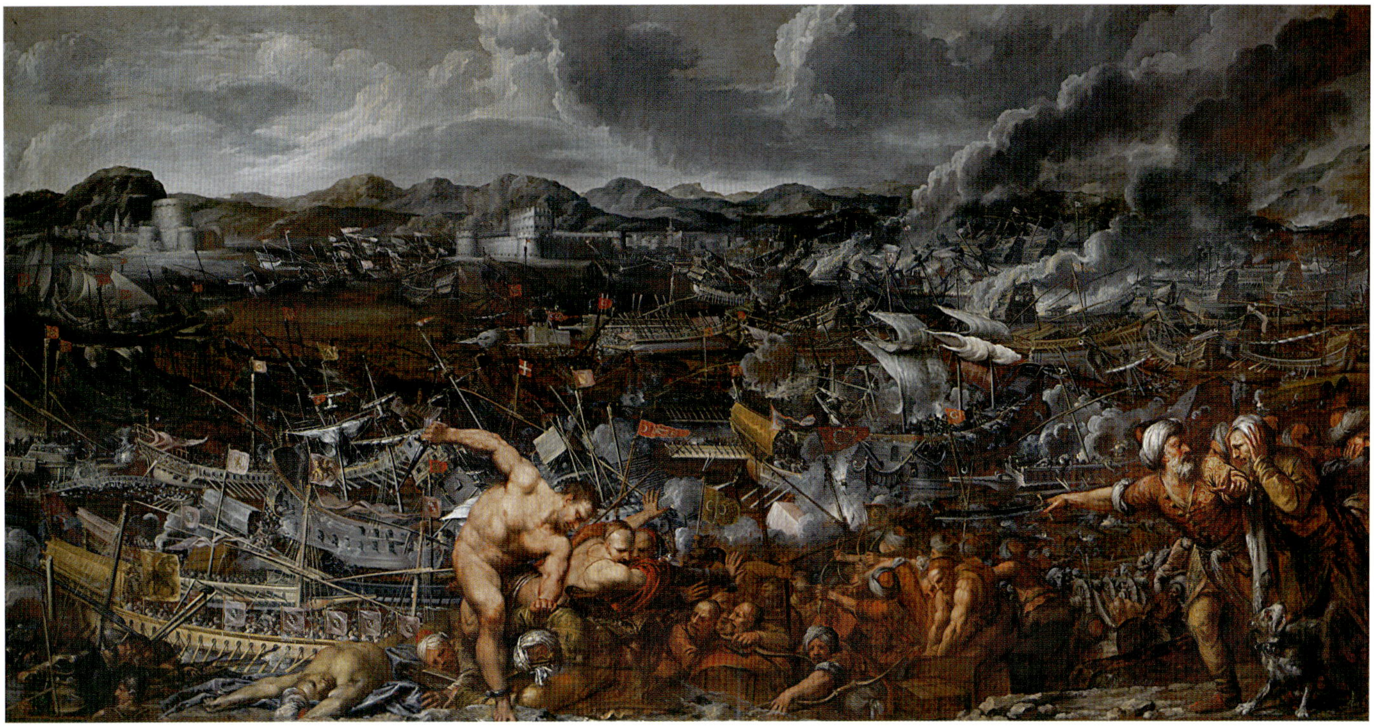

91 Pietro Liberi, *Victory of the Dardanelli*, 1659. Oil on canvas, 520 × 1,005 cm. Palazzo Ducale, Venice.

craft valuations by size, Karel van Mander tells the story of Emperor Maximilian I paying Lucas van Leyden as many ducats as it would take to cover the surface of a *Last Judgment*.[225] The negotiations between the Arte and the Signoria illustrate just how persistent craft pricing practices were in Venice, despite Renaissance humanist theorizing. Painters could leverage size into money when they negotiated with patrons who believed that the bigger the painting, the more expensive it should be, as if paintings were like silk. Francesco Solimena convinced the church of S. Rocco in Venice that his asking price of 500 scudi for each of two altarpieces was a bargain because the king of Sardinia gave him 1,000 ducats for a painting that was over twice as large.[226] Duke Gugliemo Gonzaga decided that Tintoretto should be paid only 58 scudi per painting for the Duchesi series instead of the 100 scudi per painting he had received for the Marchesi series, even though both paintings involved compositionally complex battle scenes. The price differential (a 42 percent reduction) corresponds closely to the size differential (39 percent reduction) with one series costing 12 ducats per square meter, the second 11 ducats.[227]

~

Painters outside of Venice, most famously Guercino and sometimes even Guido Reni, set their prices by the number of figures depicted. This practice can be traced back through Mancini to Apelles, but it was rare in Venice, possibly because it was considered foreign—something, for example, that Triva did after he left

TABLE 29 Prices of Paintings by Size (compiled from data in Appendix 1)

SIZE (square meters)	AVERAGE PRICE (ducats)	DUCATS PER SQUARE METER: AVERAGE FOR ALL PAINTERS
0–1	16	27
1–2	74	49
2–3	87	35
3–4	100	21
4–5	120	27
5–6	142	26
6–7	230	35
7–10	287	34
10–14	190	16
15–19	165	9
20–24	180	8
25–29	413	15
30+	393	8

Venice to paint in Munich, or that Balestra did when painting for the Elector Lothar Franz von Schönborn[228]—or perhaps no painter in Venice then had the stature that allowed this kind of standardized practice. Of the 300 or so contracts and many more letters, diaries, etc. that have been gathered for this study, only three (all from the first half of the sixteenth century) give a specific figure price. First in 1503, when Lotto and Pennacchi appraised the St. Erasmus altarpiece by Vincenzo dai Destri, they concluded that each of the three full-length figures was worth 8 ducats.[229] Second in 1540, when Bassano was called upon to add one figure to a fresco, he charged a measly 2 lire and 8 soldi.[230] And the third in 1549, when Lotto notes in his account book that he would receive 1 scudo per figure for a banner in Ancona.[231] Other documents make reference to the number of figures but only in the most general terms. Bernardino Garbelli, writing to Barbara Maggi Gambara from Venice in 1583, put the issue in pithy if vague terms: "Multiplying the figures will multiply the cost."[232] Zanchi explained to his Vicentine contact in 1672 that "the altarpiece is more difficult and involves more figures," thus justifying a higher price that came with a change of subject (see the Introduction for further discussion). Or, as the Bolognese painter Domenico Canuti wrote in 1672 to Camillo Galvani in Venice: "As for the price, I cannot accept less than 400 scudi since [the altarpiece] will be large and have an abundant number of figures."[233]

What might be concluded from the Venetian tendency to price paintings by size rather than the number of figures? It could be taken to confirm an opinion that Venetian painters considered painting much more than just a figural problem. What constitutes the surface or adheres to it—color and brushwork—are just as important. If the surface is important to the conception and appreciation of art, as Boschini argued, then a painting with more surface could be seen as more valuable. Similarly, the privileging of the figure for pricing by Mancini, Guercino, and others seems a natural extension of *disegno*-based aesthetics that was more foreign to Venice than Rome and Bologna.

The only case in Venice where a standard per-figure rate existed involved the cartoons that painters prepared for the Basilica di S. Marco mosaicists.[234] These cartoons involved little other than figures, their outlines and inner contours, and hence the procurators settled on prices set by the number of figures drawn and made the terms clear: two half-figures equalled one figure; seven heads equaled one figure. Mosaicists, on the other hand, were paid by the foot (about 2.3 ducats). Although standardized, the rate changed with time and exceptional circumstances. The rate dropped from a high of 6 or 7 ducats per figure between 1580 and 1610 to a low of 3 ducats in 1610. Painters resisted the procurators' attempt to lower the rate in 1610 and thereby contain the costs. Exceptions were quickly made. Palma Giovane managed to receive the old rate of 7 ducats per figure in 1612, but the new standard rate of 5 ducats per figure was set in the same year by Maffeo da Verona, who (lacking Palma's distinguished reputation) argued for a 2 ducat raise (i.e. from 3 to 5 per figure) on the basis of the "quality" of his work, much better than the "badly composed . . . older work" found in the basilica, and because his design was not just "a simple drawing." (The Maestro de Musaico had his annual salary increased at the same time.) In 1628 Girolamo Pilotti received the same rate as Maffeo da Verona: 62 figures at 5 ducats per figure, with two figures thrown in for free.[235]

Like any commonplace, Venetian exceptionalism needs occasional review and revision. This was recently done at a conference on "Venice Reconsidered", where in some lively discussions exceptionalism was reaffirmed (a partial record is found in the published essays). The case of Venetian painters pricing by size is partly sustained by such exceptionalist beliefs. Other instances of exceptionalism are more tangible. The Venetian climate treated frescoes badly, and consequently few frescoes were produced. What were the economic consequences for painters? Most obviously, with fewer large-scale commissions, painters reaped smaller profits from large studio productions. A small consolation was a repository of oil paintings from the golden age ready to be certified for export, faked, and pastiched. Because Venetian art had a different historiography from other cities, one whose mythic golden age of Titian, Veronese, and Tintoretto helped catalyze a lively old masters market, painters who were appraisers, dealers, and agents profited. These modest opportunities, however, paled in comparison with the absence of fresco commissions. Living in the cosmopolitan emporium that was Venice, a city without a court and full of foreigners competing with new genres and new styles, successful Venetian painters had to be especially entrepreneurial. The absence of an official academy was another distinctly Venetian condition. What stood in its place, the Arte and later the Collegio, were essentially guilds. It is difficult to be precise about the economic consequences. Unintended collateral effects of a guild might include the retention of a guild and trade mentality that encouraged a greater equality of wage and income than the actual free market system would normally produce. This could help explain why Venice lacked the price volatility of other Italian centers, at least before the 1670s.

Appendices

Appendix 1 Big Oil Paintings in Churches and Public Buildings: Venice and the Veneto, 1550–1750

NB. Arranged chronologically. When more than one painting is listed, this means that the paintings are the same size and painted for the same location. The price and size per square meter refer to only one painting; the other painting(s) are the same size, same price. Prices have been rounded to the nearest whole figure; sizes have been rounded to the nearest decimal.

A Price in ducats
B Size in square meters
C Ducats per square meter
D Number of figures
E Ducats per figure

DATE	A	B	ARTIST	TYPE	C	D	E	PAINTING AND LOCATION
1551	8	1.0	Bassano	altar	8	7	1	*Descent of the Holy Spirit* (S. Giacomo, Lusiana)
1551	270	9.0	Ponchino	altar	30	10	27	*Christ in Limbo* (S. Liberale, Castelfranco)
1551	50	30.6	Tintoretto	organ	1	22	2	*Vision of St. Peter; Beheading of St. Paul; Presentation of the Virgin* (Madonna dell'Orto, Venice)
1552	5	1.0	Bassano	wall	5	3	2	*Mystic Marriage of St. Catherine* (Wadsworth Atheneum, Hartford, CT)
1552	5	3.8	Tintoretto	organ	1	4	1	*Mark and John, Luke and Matthew* (S. Maria Zobenigo, Venice)
1552	10	7.7	Tintoretto	organ	1	10	1	*Conversion of St. Paul* (S. Maria Zobenigo, Venice)
1555	171	18.3	Titian	wall	9	10	17	*Votive for Doge Marcantonio Trevisan* (Palazzo Ducale, Venice; lost)
1555	351	14.4	Veronese	altar	24	9	39	*Transfiguration* (Duomo, Montagnana)
1555	50	17.9	Veronese	ceiling	3	5	10	*Vasthi Repudiated; Esther Crowned by the Assyrians; Triumph of Mordecai* (S. Sebastiano, Venice)
1556	60	4.2	Franco	ceiling	14	4	15	*Diana and Acteon* (Biblioteca Marciana, Venice)
1556	60	4.2	Licinio	ceiling	14	2	30	*Allegory of Vigil and Sacrifice* (Biblioteca Marciana, Venice)
1556	60	4.2	Salviati	ceiling	14	3	20	*Athena between Fortuna and Virtue* (Biblioteca Marciana, Venice)
1556	60	4.2	Schiavone	ceiling	14	4	15	*Triumph of the Captains* (Biblioteca Marciana, Venice)
1556	60	4.2	Veronese	ceiling	14	4	15	*Music* (Biblioteca Marciana, Venice)
1560	50	84.8	Tintoretto	wall	1	59	1	*Last Judgment* (Madonna dell'Orto, Venice)
1560	50	84.8	Tintoretto	wall	1	33	2	*Adoration of the Golden Calf* (Madonna dell'Orto, Venice)
1562	118	4.7	Bassano	altar	25	5	24	*Crucifixion with Virgin and Sts. Mary Magdalen; John the Evangelist; and Jerome* (Museo Civico, Treviso)
1562	324	66.2	Veronese	wall	5	51	6	*Wedding at Cana* (S. Giorgio Maggiore, Venice; now Louvre, Paris)
1563	15	4.0	Tintoretto	altar	4			*Madonna and Child with Saints* (S. Benedetto, Venice; now Galleria Estense, Modena)
1563	225	14.1	Michieli	wall	16	8	28	*Votive for Doge Lorenzo Priuli* (Palazzo Ducale, Venice; lost)
1563	78	17.6	Campagnola	wall	4	7	11	*Podestà Marino Cavalli Presented by St. Mark to Christ with Sts. Prosdocimo, Giustina, Anthony, and Daniel* (Palazzo del Podestà, Padua)
1563	15	3.3	Tintoretto	altar	5	7	2	*Madonna and Child with Sts.* (S. Benedetto, Venice; now Galleria Estense, Modena)
1564	400	42.3	Titian	ceiling	9	6	67	*Allegory of Brescia; Vulcan with Cyclops; Allegory of Ceres and Bacchus* (Palazzo Comunale, Brescia; lost but engraved)

1565	35	1.8	Michieli	wall	19	2	17	*St. Prosdocime and St. Justine, St. Anthony and St. Daniel* (Duomo, Padova)
1565	250	65.6	Tintoretto	wall	4	50	5	*Crucifixion* (Scuola di S. Rocco, Venice)
1567	68	17.8	Tintoretto	wall	4	24	3	*St. Roch in Prison Comforted by Angel*; *St. Roch Healing with the Animals* (S. Rocco, Venice)
1568	50	3.6	Bassano	altar	14	8	6	*Adoration of the Shepherds with Sts Victor and Corona* (S. Giuseppe, Bassano del Grappa; now Museo Civico).
1568	80	10.9	Tintoretto	wall	7	8	10	*Transportation of Body of St. Mark* (Scuola di S. Marco, Venice; now Accademia)
1572	97	41.1	Veronese	wall	2	19	5	*Supper of St. Gregory the Great* (Santuario del Monte Berico, Vicenza)
1573	61	4.4	Vecellio, C.	altar	14	10	6	*Altarpiece of the Rosary* (S. Maria Assunta, Lentiai)
1575	150	12.6	Veronese (& Benedetto)	altar	12	10	15	*Martyrdom of S. Giustina* (S. Giustina, Padua)
1575	40	3.0	Veronese, studio	altar	13	5	8	*Beheading of Baptist* (Chiesa Parrocchiale, Dossena [Bergamo])
1576	18	5.4	Farinati	altar	3	2	9	*St. Stephen and an Angel with Palm in Air* (S. Stefano, Garda)
1576	7	0.7	Farinati	gonfalone	10	8	1	*Madonna in Glory with Confraternity Members*; *St. John the Evangelist* (S. Giovanni in Foro, Verona)
1577	405	26.3	Moroni	wall	15	49	8	*Last Judgment* (S. Pancrazio, Gorlago)
1578	57	19.3	Bassano, F.	wall	3	9	6	*Battle of Cadore*; *Battle of Casalmaggiore*; *Battle of Maclodio*; *Battle of Polesella* (Palazzo Ducale, Venice)
1578	50	2.3	Tintoretto	ceiling	22	4	12	*Three Graces*; *Vulcan and the Cyclops*; *Wedding of Bacchus and Ariadne*, *Pallas, and Mars with Concord and Peace* (Palazzo Ducale, Venice)
1578	129	11.0	Tintoretto	wall	12	15	9	*Giovanni and Francesco Gonzaga named Marchese by Emperor Sigismondo* (Palazzo Ducale, Mantua)
1578	44	3.7	Varotari, D.	altar	12	7	6	*Birth of the Virgin* (S. Maria di Praglia, Padua)
1579	75	6.8	Tintoretto	wall	11	15	5	*Federico II enters Milan* (Palazzo Ducale, Mantua)
1580	33	2.0	Bassano	altar	16	6	6	*Virgin in Glory with Sts Agatha and Apollonia* (S. Giuseppe, Bassano del Grappa; now Museo Civico)
1580	6	1.9	Farinati	gonfalone	3	6	1	*Christ carrying the Cross*; *Lamentation with St. John the Evangelist and the Magdalen* (Chiesa parrocchiale, Lonato; lost)
1580	17	1.6	Veronese, studio	altar	11	4	4	*Madonna and Child Crowned by Angels* (S. Giovanni in Xenodochio, Cividale)
1581	7	0.6	Farinati	wall?	12	2	3	*Annunciation*; *Magdalen* (lost)
1581	28	4.3	Farinati	altar?	7	3	9	*Sts. Jacob Apostle, Sebastian, and Fabian* (S. Giovanni Battista, Lonato)
1582	64	6.3	Farinati	altar	10	4	16	*Madonna and Child with St. Emilio and Donor* (S. Maria ed Emiliano, Padengo)
1582	32	2.4	Farinati	altar	13	10	3	*Resurrection* (Chiesa di Calcinato, Brescia; lost)
1582	50	6.7	Veronese	altar	7	8	6	*Adoration of the Shepherds with St. Jerome* (S. Giuseppe, Venice)
1582	1,000	25.2	Zuccaro	wall	40	22	45	*Submission of Federico Barbarossa* (Palazzo Ducale, Venice)
1583	220	4.2	Palma Giovane	altar	52	11	20	*Assumption* (S. Giuliano, Venice)
1583	400	6.0	Tintoretto, D.	altar	67	13	31	*Nativity* (Escorial)
1584	78	11.5	Brusasorci	wall	7	12	6	*Finding of Moses* (Museo di Castelvecchio, Verona)
1584	20	3.3	Farinati	gonfalone	6	1	20	*St. Nicholas* (Confraternità dei Mugnai, Verona)
1584	138	13.6	Palma Giovane	wall	10	15	9	*Christ in Glory Blessing Doge Renier Zen* (Oratorio dei Crociferi), Venice
1584	20	4.5	Tintoretto	altar	4	6	3	*Adoration of the Cross* (S. Marcuola, Venice)
1585	100	5.6	Vecellio, C.	altar	18	6	17	*Madonna and Child in Glory with Sts. Fabiano and Sebastian and the Podestà Loredan* (Duomo, Belluno)

1586	30	6.4	Farinati	altar	5	4	7	*Madonna and Child with Sts. John the Baptist and Donato* (lost)
1586	47	9.7	Palma Giovane	wall	5	6	8	*Pasquale Cicogna Helps at Mass*; *Pasquale Cicogna Receives Announcement of his Election as Doge*; *Pasquale Cicogna Visits Oratorio of the Crociferi* (S. Maria dei Crociferi, Venice)
1588	80	4.8	Bassano, J. and L.	altar	16	5	16	*Nativity* (S. Giorgio Maggiore, Venice)
1588	51	6.3	Farinati	altar	8	4	13	*Madonna and Child with Sts. Francis and Nicholas* (S. Nicolò, Verona)
1588	9	1.6	Maganza	wall	6	1	9	*St. Vincent* (Palazzo del Comune, Vicenza; now in Museo Civico)
1589	553	21.6	Palma Giovane	ceiling	26	17	33	*Fall of Manna*; *Elija Fed by Angel*; *David Receives Bread from Abimelec* (S. Maria dei Crociferi, Venice)
1589	160	6.2	Palma Giovane	ceiling	26	26	6	*Assumption* (Oratorio dei Crocifieri, Venice)
1590	39	4.8	Farinati	altar	8	5	8	*Madonna in Glory with Saints* (Museo di Castelvecchio, Verona)
1591	49	26.4	Farinati	altar	2	2	24	*Madonna and Child with Holy Spirit* (S. Stefano, Verona)
1592	70	8.8	Cavagna	altar	8	14	5	*Assumption* (S. Maria Maggiore, Bergamo)
1592	19	0.5	Farinati	wall	38	8	2	*Lamentation with Nicodemus and other Figures* (Chiesa dei Cappuccini, Verona)
1592	75	9.6	Palma Giovane	wall	8	17	4	*Brazen Serpent*; *San Cleto*; *Sant'Elena* (S. Maria dei Crociferi, Venice)
1592	90	21.7	Tintoretto	wall	4	20	5	*Last Supper*; *Gathering of Manna* (S. Giorgio Maggiore, Venice)
1593	70	13.0	Cavagna	wall	5	9	8	*Nativity* (S. Maria Maggiore, Bergamo)
1593	42	5.0	Cavagna	wall	8	4	10	*Esther before Ahasuerus*; *Judith and Holofernes* (S. Maria Maggiore, Bergamo)
1593	390	23.0	Palma Giovane	wall	23	23	17	*Death of St. Anthony*; *Entombment of St. Anthony*; *Miracles of S. Sabba*; *Assumption of S. Sabba* (S. Antonin, Venice)
1593	28	4.7	Farinati	altar	6	8	4	*Christ in Heaven with Sts. Per, Diego, Bernardino, and Anthony Abbot* (now Palazzo Nievo, Vicenza)
1593	70	4.8	Tintoretto	altar	15	9	8	*Deposition* (S. Giorgio Maggiore, Venice)
1593	150	8.0	Tintoretto, studio	altar	19			*Mystical Marriage of St. Catherine* (S. Caterina, Vicenza)
1593	150	8.3	Tintoretto, D.	altar	18	10	15	*Coronation of the Virgin with Sts. Benedict, Gregory, and other Benedictine Saints and Patrons* (S. Giorgio Maggiore, Venice)
1595	8	0.4	Farinati	wall	20	4	2	*Madonna and Child with Sts. Augustine and Monica* (Princeton University Art Museum)
1595	85	2.3	Farinati	altar	37	4	21	*Madonna and Child with Sts. Francis and Anthony of Padua* (Chiesa parrocchiale, Trevenzolo; lost)
1595	180	12.7	Palma Giovane	wall	14	4	45	*Madonna and Child with Sts. Hermagoras and Mark* (Palazzo della Comunità, Udine; now Museo Civico)
1597	19	0.8	Farinati	wall	24	10	2	*Miracles of St. Hyacinth* (S. Giovanni Battista, Piacenza)
1597	34	3.5	Farinati	altar	10	2	17	*Baptism* (S. Marcuola, Venice)
1598	46	6.2	Farinati	wall	7	5	9	*Martyrdom of St. Fabian*; *St. Benedict Abbot Revives a Child* (S. Sisto, Piacenza)
1598	130	2.7	Palma Giovane	altar	48	2	65	*Stigmatization of St. Francis* (S. Nicolo dei Frari, Venice; now Accademia)
1599	53	3.8	Palma Giovane	altar	14	6	9	*Crucifixion*; *Baptism* (S. Maria Assunta, Lentiai [Belluno])
1600	62	7.2	Farinati	altar	9	6	10	*Madonna and Child in Glory with Sts. Francis and Anthony of Padua* (Chiesa, Roncho; now Castelvecchio, Verona)
1600	400	58.5	Farinati	wall	7	26	15	*Miracle of Bread and Fishes* (S. Giorgio in Braida, Verona)
1602	59	16.2	Farinati	altar	4	6	10	*Mystical Marriage of St. Catherine with Donor Giovanni Francesco Trivela* (S. Caterina di Siena, Verona)

1608	300	4.1	Palma Giovane	altar	73	3	100	*Madonna and Child with St. Hyacinth* (S. Domenico, Reggio Emilia)
1609	300	27.1	Palma Giovane	altar	11	2	150	*Annunciation* (Duomo, Sàlo)
1610	30	5.6	Maffeo Verona	altar	5	5	6	*Presentation of the Virgin* (Zitelle, Udine)
1611	100	5.1	Palma Giovane	altar	20	7	14	*Visitation* (Chiesa del Paradiso, Modena; now Galleria Estense)
1612	231	22.1	Palma Giovane	altar	10	11	21	*Christ in Glory with Sts. Mark, Peter, and Paul* (Scuola di S. Marco, Venice)
1613	400	25.8	Palma Giovane	wall	15	29	14	*Multiplication of Loaves and Fishes* (S. Maria dei Carmine, Venice)
1613	140	25.8	Marco Vicentino	wall	5	27	5	*Gathering of Manna* (S. Maria dei Carmini, Venice)
1617	252	9.3	Palma Giovane	altar	27	14	18	*Emperor Heraclitus Carrying the Cross* (Duomo, Urbino)
1618	176	8.3	Palma Giovane	altar	21	12	15	*St. Benedict Receives Children Mauro and Placido in the Church* (S. Giustina, Padua)
1618	550	27.6	Palma Giovane	wall	20	10	55	*Fifteen Mysteries of the Rosary* (S. Nicolò, Treviso; lost)
1624	31	4.2	Palma Giovane, studio	altar	7	7	4	*Coronation of the Virgin* (S. Maria Assunta, Ciano del Montello [Treviso])
1626	70	5.75	Padovanino	altar	12	4	17	*Madonna and Child with Justice and St. Mark* (Palazzo Pubblico, Pordenone; now Museo Civico)
1631	350	49.4	Prudenti	altar	7	20	17	*Madonna and Child with Sts. Mark, Roch, Sebastian, and Beato Lorenzo Giustiniani Saving Venice from the Plague* (S. Maria della Salute, Venice)
1634	39	4.2	Padovanino	ceiling	9	5	8	*The Nile, Atlas, Astronomy, and Geometry* (Biblioteca Marciana, Venice)
1635	300	18.0	Padovanino	ceiling	17	5	60	*Parable of the Wise and Foolish Virgins* (Chiesa degli Incurabili, Venice; now Accademia)
1635	61	2.9	Renieri	wall	21	8	8	*Last Supper* (S. Giovanni Battista, Dossena)
1635	32	4.2	Strozzi	ceiling	8	4	8	*Sculpture* (Biblioteca Marciana, Venice)
1644	130	15.6	Maffei	wall	8	11	12	*Glorification of Podestà Gaspare Zane* (Palazzo del Podestà, Vicenza; now Museo Civico)
1644	540	13.0	Ruschi	altar	42	7	77	*Madonna and Child with Sts. Francis, Helen, and Matthew* (S. Pietro di Castello, Venice)
1644	296	6.7	Turchi	altar	44	5	59	*Annunciation with Sts. Joseph and John the Baptist with Beato Giovanni Marinoni* (S. Nicolò, Verona)
1646	54	6.3	Ricchi	altar	9	6	9	*Deposition* (parish church, Ghedi)
1648	45	4.8	Triva	wall	9	10	10	*Moses Saved from the Water* (S. Maria di Campagna, Piacenza)
1649	100	10.7	Maffei	wall	9	10	10	*Glorification of Alvise Foscarini Inquisitore del Monte di Pietà* (Palazzo del Monte di Pietà, Vicenza; now Museo Civico)
1649	130	15.1	Maffei	wall	9	7	19	*Glorification of Podestà Girolamo Priuli* (Palazzo del Podestà, Vicenza; now Museo Civico)
1652	129	5.4	Ricchi	altar	24	4	32	*St. Anthony of Padua with Christ Child* (S. Antonio, Cles [Trent])
1655	130	14.2	Maffei	wall	9	8	16	*Glorification of Podestà Alvise Foscarini* (Palazzo del Podestà, Vicenza; now Museo Civico)
1656	130	14.0	Maffei	wall	9	7	19	*Glorification of Podestà Tommaso Pisani* (Palazzo del Podestà, Vicenza; now Museo Civico)
1657	102	4.9	Maffei	altar	21	2	51	*Visitation* (Oratorio dei Proti, Vicenza)
1657	221	13.0	Massimo da Verona	altar	17	18	12	*Massacre of Innocents* (S. Maria Maggiore, Bergamo)
1659	400	52.0	Liberi	wall	8	9	44	*Victory of the Dardanelli* (Palazzo Ducale, Venice)
1660	200	14.0	Heintz	wall	14			*Last Judgment* (San Antonin, Venice)
1660	500	29.0	Liberi	wall	17	10	50	*The Flood* (S. Maria Maggiore, Bergamo)
1661	150	3.9	Ruschi	altar	40	5	30	*Madonna with Sts. Anthony, Augustine, and John the Baptist* (S. Antonin, Venice)

1661	200	4.0	Ruschi	altar	50	6	33	*Madonna di Loreto with Sts. Augustine, Benedict, John the Evangelist, and Romualdo* (S. Clemente, Venice; now Museo Diocesano)
1663	150	13.5	Vecchia	wall	11	17	9	*Offering of Noah* (S. Antonin, Venice)
1665	107	5.0	Triva	altar	21	4	27	*Rest on the Flight into Egypt* (S. Cristina, Turin)
1668	825	29.0	Zanchi	wall	28	19	43	*Moses Striking the Rock* (S. Maria Maggiore, Bergamo)
1668	430	13.5	Giordano	altar	32	10	43	*Assumption of the Virgin* (S. Maria della Salute, Venice)
1669	70	5.5	Carpioni	altar	13	6	12	*Madonna and Child with Four Saints* (for S. Caterina, Vicenza, but never completed)
1669	150	14.2	Giordano	wall	11	20	8	*Rape of Sabines* (Ca' Giogalli, Venice)
1669	130	9.0	Zanchi	altar	14	7	19	*Holy Trinity with Saints* (S. Nicolò, Treviso)
1669	300	5.5	Zanchi	altar	55	4	75	*Madonna and Child with Sts. Anthony of Padua, Nicholas of Bari, Gaetano, and Francis of Sales* (S. Caterina, Vicenza)
1671	100	4.1	Liberi, studio	altar	24	4	25	*St. Anthony with Gloria of Angels* (S. Faustino e Giovita, Vicenza; lost)
1671	210	25.0	Ricchi	wall	8	10	21	*Struggle of Jacob and the Angel*; *Jael and Sisera* (S. Giustina, Padua; lost)
1671	1,000	66.3	Zanchi	wall	15	51	20	Copy of Veronese's *Wedding at Cana*
1671	160	4.7	Zanchi	altar	34	8	20	*Birth of the Virgin* (Santuario della Natività di Maria, Sombreno)
1672	60	5.9	Carpioni	altar	10	5	12	*Vision of St. Benedict* (S. Caterina, Vicenza)
1672	270	10.9	Liberi	altar	25	13	21	*Mystical Marriage of St. Catherine* (S. Caterina, Vicenza)
1672	550	4.3	Zanchi	altar	128	4	138	*Holy Trinity with Sts. Benedict and Scolastica* (S. Faustino e Giovita, Vicenza)
1674	900	53.9	Zanchi	ceiling	17	35	26	*Last Judgment* (Scuola di S. Fantin, Venice)
1676	700	7.3	Liberi	altar	96	5	140	*Ecstasy of St. Geltrude Receiving the Stigmata* (S. Giustina, Padua)
1679	60	15.0	Fumiani	ceiling	4	12	5	*Pentecost* (S. Filippo e Giacomo, Vicenza)
1679	94	7.4	Zanchi	wall	13	6	16	*Marriage at Cana* (Duomo, Capodistria)
1680	90	19.0	Celesti	wall	5	10	9	*Invention of the Cross* (Duomo, Vicenza; now Seminario Vescovile)
1680	210	5.8	Liberi	wall	36	5	42	*Sacrifice of Noah* (Duomo, Vicenza)
1680	67	11.8	Zanchi	wall	6	4	17	*Victory of Constantine*; *Submersion of Pharoah's Army in Red Sea*; *Annunciation* (Duomo, Vicenza)
1682	24	5.8	Ricci	wall	4	5	5	*Beheading of the Baptist* (Oratorio di S. Giovanni de' Fiorentini, Bologna; lost)
1685	200		Bellucci	wall				*Drowning of Pharoah's Army in Red Sea* (S. Spirito, Venice)
1688	25	1.9	Celesti	wall	13	4	6	*Adoration of the Magi* (Duomo, Salò)
1688	25	6.3	Celesti	altar	4	8	3	*Madonna in Glory with Sts. Stephen and Joseph* (Duomo, Salò; now S. Bernardino)
1690	233	15.0	Zanchi	ceiling	16	26	9	*Birth of the Virgin*; *Coronation*; *Assumption* (S. Maria Zobenigo, Venice)
1691	726	5.75	Loth	altar	126	4	181	Copy of Veronese's *Wedding at Cana*
1692	226	25.2	Celesti	wall	9	16	14	*Virgin with St. John the Baptist Appealing to Christ to Free Lonato from the Plague* (Palazzo Comunale, Lonato)
1692	75	2.2	Lazzarini	wall	34	4	19	*Rest on the Flight into Egypt* (for Conti collection; now Neue Palais, Bildergalerie, Potsdam)
1692	75	2.2	Lazzarini	wall	34	3	25	*Angelica and Medoro* (for Conti collection, now Neue Palais, Bildergalerie, Potsdam)
1694	60	4.5	Beverensi	altar	13	4	15	*Virgin Mary with Sts. Filippo Neri and Francesco di Sales* (S. Filippo e Giacomo, Vicenza).
1695	29	0.5	Molinari	altar	58	2	15	*St. Anthony with Infant Christ* (Scuola di S. Rocco, Venice)
1696	230	31.0	Celesti	wall	7	24	10	*Last Judgment* (Sacristia Canoniacale, Treviso)

1696	100	14.3	Celesti	altar	7	4	25	*Fall of Simon Magus* (Duomo, Treviso; lost)
1696	87	12.3	Zanchi	wall	7	9	10	*Martyrdom of Sts. Teonisto, Tabra, and Tabrata; Baptism of the Count of Treviso; Transfiguration* (Duomo, Treviso)
1697	198	20.6	Dorigny	wall	10	2	99	*Annunciation* (Palazzo del Comune, Cappella dei Notai, Verona; now Museo di Castelvecchio)
1699	170	20.6	Bellotti, G. B.	wall	7	7	24	*Adoration of the Magi* (Palazzo del Comune, Cappella dei Notai, Verona; now Museo di Castelvecchio)
1699	150	20.6	Marchesini	wall	7	7	21	*Adoration of Shepherds* (Palazzo del Comune, Cappella dei Notai, Verona; now Museo di Castelvecchio)
1700	150	5.9	Ricci	altar	25	3	50	*Vision of S. Lorenzo Giustiniani* (S. Croce della Giudecca, Venice; lost)
1700	120	20.6	Canziani	wall	6	3	40	*Sacrifice of Isaac* (Palazzo del Comune, Cappella dei Notai, Verona; now Museo di Castelvecchio)
1700	112	5.6	Celesti	wall	20	6	19	Ten New Testament scenes (S. Pietro e Paolo, Toscolano Maderno)
1700	170	20.6	Prunato	wall	8	9	19	*Presentation in the Temple* (Palazzo del Comune, Cappella dei Notai, Verona; now Museo di Castelvecchio)
1700	60	4.9	Zanchi	altar	12	2	30	*Sts. Martin and Rose* (S. Martino, Conegliano)
1701	180	4.4	Molinari	altar	40	10	18	*Virgin and Child with Sts. Joseph, John the Baptist, Peter, Carlo Borromeo, Liberale, and Eligio* (S. Moise, Venice)
1701	44	1.1	Pittoni, F.	wall	39	1	44	*Two Angels* (S. Moise, Venice)
1703	258	42.7	Celesti	altar	6	14	18	*Martyrdom of St. Lawrence* (S. Lorenzo, Verolanuova)
1705	120	2.8	Fumiani	wall	43	8	15	*Sacrifice of the Daughters of Jefte* (for Conti collection)
1705	89	5.0?	Perini	altar	18			*Invention of the Cross* (S. Croce delle Zitelle, Verona)
1706	100	2.2	Balestra	wall	45	4	25	*Adoration of the Shepherds* (for Conti collection; now Neue Palais, Bildergalerie, Potsdam)
1706	120	2.8	Balestra	wall	43	2	60	*Juno and Argus* (for Conti collection, now private collection, Verona)
1706	238	50.0	Celesti	wall	5	14	17	*Birth of the Virgin; Assumption* (S. Lorenzo, Verolanuova)
1706	110	2.2	Fumiani	wall	50	11	10	*Presentation in the Temple; Dispute in the Temple* (for Conti collection, now Northampton Art Gallery)
1706	100	22.0	Zanchi	wall	5			Six New Testament scenes (Ognisanti, Treviso)
1707	75	1.85	Lazzarini	wall	40	4	19	*Moses Striking the Rock; Rebecca at the Well; St. Cecilia Performing* (for Conti collection; location unknown)
1709	335	10.9	Ricci	altar	31	5	67	*Immaculate Conception with Sts. Anne, Joachim, and Anthony of Padua* (S. Maria delle Grazie, Bergamo; now Istituto Missionario del Paradiso)
1711	110	1.9	Ricci	wall	58	4	27	*Allegory of Fame* (Palazzo Ducale, Venice)
1712	276	5.2	Zanchi	wall	53	4	69	*Moses Receiving Tablets of the Law* (Palazzo Pretorio, Montagnana [Padua])
1718	240	8.7	Piazzetta	wall	28	2	120	*Guardian Angel* (Scuola dell'Angelo Custode, Venice)
1720	300	9.2	Ricci	altar	33	3	100	*Guardian Angel* (Scuola dell'Angelo Custode, Venice)
1724	81	1.9	Ricci	wall	43	5	16	*Abraham Driving out Hagar; Solomon Worshipping the Idols* (Castello di Rivoli, Turin; now Galleria Sabauda)
1725	424	11.1	Ricci	altar	39	7	61	*Madonna in Glory with Archangel Gabriel and Sts. Eusebius, Sebastian, and Roch* (Venearia Reale, Turin; now Università degli Studi)
1725	675	10.7	Ricci	wall	63	21	32	*Moses Striking the Rock; Susanna before Daniel* (Castello di Rivoli, Turin; now Galleria Sabauda)
1725	58	2.4	Grone	altar	24	4	14	*Madonna and Child with Sts. Joseph and Anthony* (S. Spirito, Borgo Padovano in Cittadella)
1727	300	3.9	Ricci	altar	77	5	60	*St. Maurus Healing a Sick Child; St. Maurus Rescuing Brother Placid from Drowning* (S. Paolo, S. Paolo d'Argon [Brescia])
1727	151	6.7	Ricci	wall	23	4	38	*David Reproved by Nathan* (Castello di Rivoli, Turin; now Palazzo Reale)

1729	251	4.3	Balestra	altar	58	6	42	*St. Gregory the Great Receives Christ Dressed as a Pilgrim; St. Gregory the Great Displaying Bloodied Corporale* (S. Paolo, S. Paolo d'Argon [Brescia])
1729	512	9.1?	Ricci	altar	56	11	47	*Martyrdom of St. Maurice and the Theban Legion; St. Louis of France Exhibiting the Crown of Thorns* (Basilica della Superga, Turin)
1730	350	10.3	Ricci	altar	34	9	39	*Last Communion; Martyrdom of St. Lucy* (S. Lucia, Parma)
1730	500	7.0	Ricci	altar	71	9	56	*Pope Gregory the Great Interceding for Souls in Purgatory* (S. Alessandro della Croce, Bergamo)
1733	207	2.7	Pittoni, G. B.	wall	77	10	21	*Sacrifice of the Daughters of Jefte* (Palazzo Reale, Turin)
1733	94	1.2	Pittoni, G. B.	wall	78	6	16	*Sacrifice of Iphigenia* (for Maresciallo von Schulenburg; now J. Paul Getty Museum, Los Angeles)
1733	600	6.7	Ricci	altar	90	11	55	*St. Francis of Paola Reviving a Child; St. Helen Finding True Cross* (S. Rocco, Venice)
1733	600	6.7	Trevisani	altar	90	14	43	*Miracle of St. Anthony* (S. Rocco, Venice)
1733	57	2.2	Tiepolo	altar	26	1	57	*St. Francis of Sales* (S. Maria Maddalena dei Filippini, Udine; now Museo Civico)
1734	270	9.8	Pittoni, G. B.	altar	28	9	30	*Institution of the Order of the Sisters of the Visitation* (S. Maria della Visitazione, Milan)
1734	216	5.9	Tiepolo	altar	37	5	43	*Martyrdom of St. Agatha* (Basilica del Santo, Padua)
1735	270	4.6	Pellegrini, G. B.	altar	59	10	27	*Martyrdom of St. Catherine* (Basilica del Santo, Padua)
1735	194	4.6	Pittoni, G. B.	altar	42	12	16	*Martyrdom of St. Bartholomew* (Presidenza della Veneranda Arca del Santo, Padua)
1736	425	6.6	Balestra	altar	64	8	53	*Virgin Appears to St. Francis of Sales* (S. Maria della Pace, Brescia)
1736	324	6.5	Balestra	altar	50	6	54	*The Virgin and St. Francis* (S. Maria della Pace, Brescia)
1737	1,613	8.6	Pittoni, G. B.	wall	188	8	201	*Alexander the Great Enters Babylon* (Patrimonio Nacional, Madrid)
1737	64	5.2	Tiepolo	altar	12	2	32	*Sts. Hermagoras and Fortunatus* (Duomo, Udine); *Guardian Angel* (S. Maria Maddalena dei Filippini, Udine; now Museo Civico)
1738	71	5.1	Tiepolo	altar	14	2	35	*Christ on the Cross with God the Father* (Duomo, Udine)
1740	2,306	58.1	Tiepolo	ceiling	40	30	77	*Assumption of the Virgin* and other subjects (Scuola di S. Maria dei Carmini, Venice)
1743	270	12.1	Pittoni, G. B.	wall	22	6	45	*Martyrdom of S. Esteria* (Duomo, Bergamo)
1743	270	15.0	Tiepolo	altar	18	5	54	*Martyrdom of St. John, Bishop of Bergamo* (Duomo, Bergamo)
1743	41	0.7	Piazzetta	altar	59	1	41	*St. Dominic* (Gesuati, Venice)
1744	680	11.8	Tiepolo	ceiling	58	4	170	*Allegory of Fortitude and Wisdom* (Palazzo Barbarigo, Venice; now Palazzo Rezzonico)
1746	270	5.9	Pittoni, G. B.	altar	46	5	54	*Madonna and Child with Sts. Joseph, Margaret of Cortona, and Anthony of Padua* (S. Alessandro della Croce, Bergamo)

Appendix 2 Rents, 1650–1750

1 ANNUAL RENT (IN DUCATS), 1650–1700

160	Antonio Zanchi
131	Pietro Liberi (1651)
120	Ludovico David (1679)
100	Pietro Liberi (1661)
90	Niccolò Renieri, Antonio Lech, Antonio Dana, Francesco Diana
85	Nadalina pittora
70	Francesco Triva, Giuseppe Heintz, Antonio pittore
60	Pietro Ricchi, Pietro Vecchia, Giacomo Petrelli
54	Andrea Celesti
50	G. B. Langetti, Francesco Castiago, Carlo Romano, Clemente Molli
47	Nicolo pittore
44	Ludovico David (1661), Giacomo Cobouret, Faustino pittore
35	Zulian pittore, Zuanne pittore, Lorenzo Gianori
32	Giovanni Favo, Romio pittore, Andrea pittore todesco
30	Sebastiano Mazzoni
24	Giovanni Segala, Giacomo Groppo, Anonymous Flemish
16	Domenico Rubinato, Francesco Pera
13	Francesco Brazazi, Iseppe pittore

2 ANNUAL RENT (IN DUCATS), 1700–1750

The parishes of S. Fosca and SS. Apostoli were chosen because they were favored by painters. Not included in the figures are owner occupancy rates: S. Fosca: 12 percent; SS. Apostoli: 16 percent.

174	G. A. Pellegrini (1740)
170	G. B. Tiepolo
110	Giovanni Fontana
100	Francesco Zuccarelli
90	G. B. Pittoni (1740), G. A. Pellegrini (1712)
80	Nicolo Grassi
70	Francesco Fontebasso
60	G. B. Piazzetta, G. B. Crosato
55	Antonio Canal
50	Girolamo Brusaferro
48	G. B. Pittoni (1712)
44	Pietro Longhi
40	Louis Dorigny
36	Francesco Albotto, Francesco Fontana
16	Francesco Sismonini

Appendix 3 Residences by Parish

1 PAINTERS' RESIDENCES, 1650–1711 (SEE FIG. 80)

Cannaregio		
1	S. Leonardo	Iseppo pittore
2	S. Marcuola	Marco Boschini
		Antonio Meneghini
3	Maddalena	Giacomo Cobouret
4	S. Fosca	Francesco Castiago
		Francesco Caldei
5	S. Sofia	Giovanni Battista Langetti
		Abram Rammundo di Bordeos
		Andrea todesco pittore
		Francesco Mantovano
		Francesco Triva
6	SS. Apostoli	Zulian pittore
		Sebastiano Mazzoni
		Nadalina pittora
		Antonio pittore
		Michiel Pietra
		Pietro Vecchia
		Niccolò Bambini
		Agostino Litterini
7	S. Canzian	Pietro Vecchia
8	S. Maria Nova	Giovanni Segala
		Andrea Celesti
9	S. Giovanni Crisostomo	Guido Cagnacci
Castello		
10	S. Maria Formosa	Flemish painter
		Niccolò Cassana
		Nicola Grassi
		Antonio Molinari
11	S. Giustina	Antonio Dana
12	S. Antonin	Zuanne pittore
13	S. Giovanni in Bragora	Francesco Diana
Santa Croce		
14	S. Simone Picolo	Julian Borghini pittore (son of Raffael Borghini), living in calle longa
15	S. Giacomo dell'Orio	G. B. Pittoni
16	S. Stae	Daniel van den Dijk
		Pietro Ricchi
17	S. Maria Mater Domini	Francesco Pera
		Giovanni Molinari (corte del Figher)
		G. A. Pellegrini
18	S. Cassiano	Niccolò Renieri
San Polo		
19	S. Tomà	Zuanne Favo
20	S. Polo	Iseppo Ens (Heintz)
		Francesco Caurioli scultore
21	S. Aponal	Willem Drost
22	S. Silvestro	Francesco Pera
		Carl Loth
Dorsoduro		
23	Angelo Raffaele	Luca Carlevarijs
24	S. Margherita	Giacomo Petrelli
25	S. Pantalon	Pietro Ricchi
		Francesco Triva

		Padovanino
		Francesco Brazazi
		Lodovico David
		Daniel Hertz
26	S. Agnese	Lorenzo Gianori

San Marco

27	S. Samuele	Pietro Liberi
		Romio pittore
		Girolamo Brusaferro
		Clemente Molli
28	S. Angelo	Domenico Rubinato
		Carlo Romano pittore
		Sebastiano Ricci, 1681–1717
		Piero Pivato
		Carl Loth
29	S. Fantin	Faustino pittore
30	S. Maria del Giglio	Giacomo Groppo
31	S. Moise	Sebastiano Ricci, 1717–34 (in Procuratie Vecchie)
		Antonio Lech
32	S. Marco (piazza)	Pietro Liberi
		Antonio Zanchi
33	San Zulian	Niccolò Cassana
34	S. Bartolomeo	Nicolo pittore

2 PAINTERS' RESIDENCES, 1724–45 (SEE FIG. 81)

Cannaregio

1	S. Geremia	Francesco Polazzo
		Mattio Bortoloni
2	S. Marcilian	Silvestro Manaigo
		Michiel Marieschi
3	S. Fosca	G. B. Bettoni
4	S. Sofia	Giorgio Matteo Steur
5	SS. Apostoli (Birri)	Angelo Trevisani
		Antonio Visentini
		Antonio Bolis
		Agostino Litterini
		Giovanni Pietro Zampieri
6	S. Canzian	Francesco Musletti
		Liberal Beltrame
7	S. Maria Nova	Gioseppe Cortesi
8	S. Giovanni Crisostomo	Francesco Giusti
		Romualdo Mauro

Castello

9	S. Marina	Bernardo Bellotto
10	S. Lio	G. B. Piazzetta
		Paolo Gasperini
11	S. Maria Formosa	Pietro Gradicis
		Canaletto
		Bortolo Nasari
		Francesco Griffini
		Nicola Grassi
12	S. Giustina	G. B. Tiepolo

Santa Croce

13	S. Simon Piccolo	Niccolò Bambini
14	S. Simon Grande	Monsu Germano
		Pietro Roselli
		Francesco Pittoni
15	S. Giacomo dell'Orio	G. B. Pittoni
		Girolamo Brusaferro
16	S. Stae	Fabricio Marcoleoni

San Polo

17	S. Stin	Domenico Bertan
		Gerolamo Scalabrin
18	S. Polo	Ferdinando Focchi
		Giacomo Concolo
19	S. Aponal	Valentin Piccini
20	S. Mattio	G. B. Mariotti
21	S. Silvestro	Antonio Rebolo
		Alessandro Marchesini
		G. B. Augusti

Dorsoduro

22	S. Sebastiano	Anzolo Rubi
23	S. Margherita (S. Maria dei Carmini)	Gioseppe Zanchi
		Luca Carlevarijs
24	S. Pantalon	Antonio Canal
		Gregorio Lazzarini
		Pietro Longhi

San Polo

25	S. Stefano	G. A. Pellegrini
26	Sant'Anzolo	Cristoforo Tasca
27	S. Luca	Domenico Fontana
		Michiel Marieschi
		Francesco Albotto
		Lorenzo Torelli
28	S. Paterniano	Bartolomeo Pedon
29	S. Moise	Domenico Valeriani
		Pietro Uberti
		G. B. Arcangeli
30	S. Geminiano	Giovanni de Domenico Fontana
31	S. Marco (piazza)	Gasparo Diziani
		Sebastiano and Marco Ricci
32	S. Basso	Domenico Coronato
33	S. Zulian	Michiel Marieschi
		Francesco Sismonini
	(PISCINA)	Francesco Zuccarelli

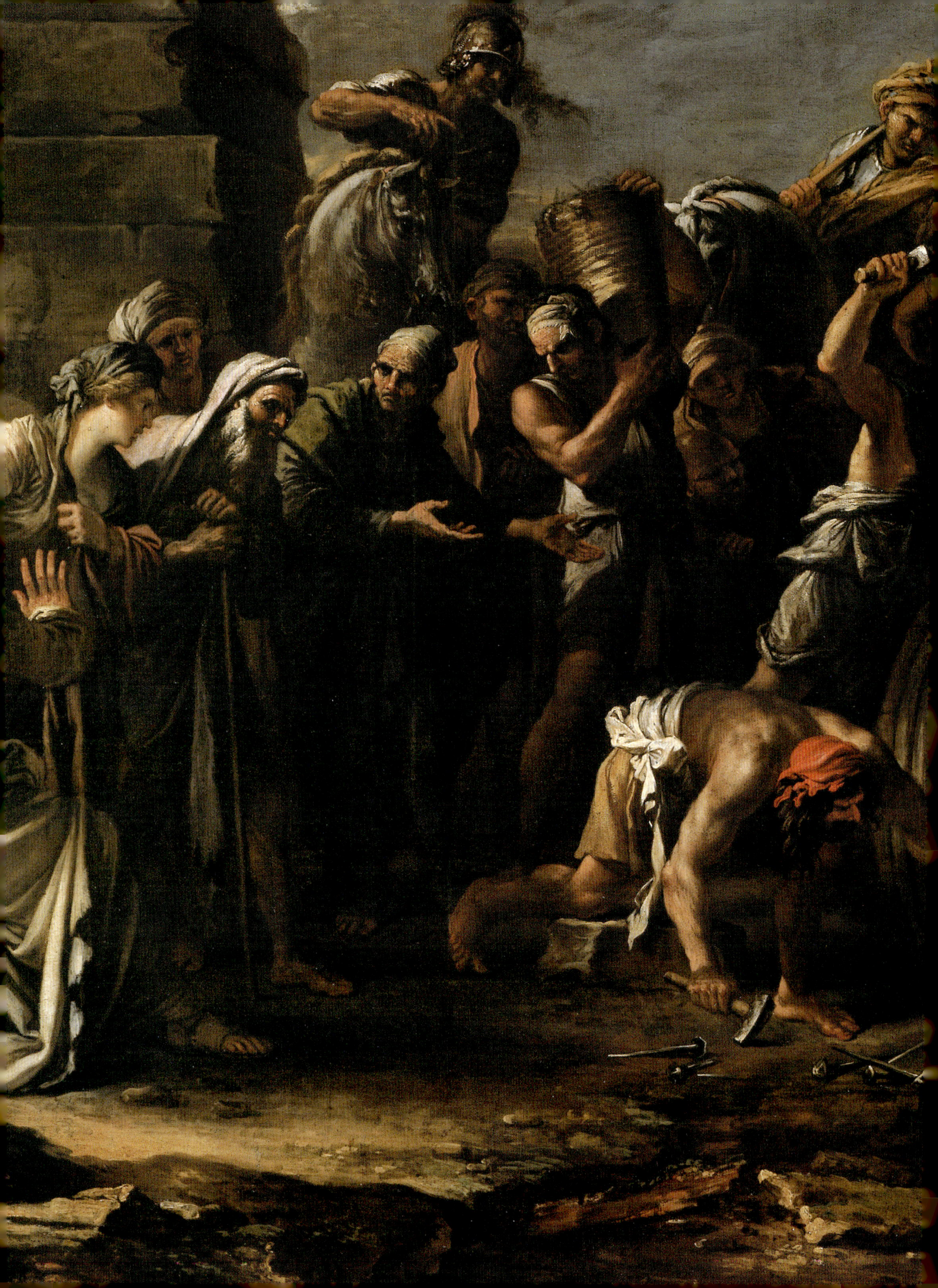

6

Five Industrious Cities

RENATA AGO

The Economic Circumstances of the Five Cities

What were the economic and working conditions in seventeenth-century Rome, Naples, Bologna, Florence, and Venice? Had the flow of wealth coming from industry and trade during the Renaissance really dried up, as has long been claimed? Had the "betrayal of the bourgeoisie," the oligarchic closing of city governments, and the re-feudalization of the countryside really prevented opportunities for social climbing, thereby consigning Italian society to a long phase of cultural and economic stagnation? Although not as catastrophic as some would have it, the indicators made available to us by economic historians for central and northern Italy do indeed reveal the seventeenth century as a period of slow growth or economic stagnation, characterized by a reduction in the profit margins of capital. This did not translate necessarily into a deterioration of living conditions.

The expression "crisis of the seventeenth century" has long been part of historians' language. The economic circumstances, however, do not exactly fit their chronological division. The first signs of difficulty became apparent in the 1570s; signs of recovery already began to appear after 1660.[1] In making this conclusion, economic historians rely on the relationship between population and resources. We know—they say—that the Cinquecento was characterized by a constant increase in the number of "mouths to feed" and that this had important consequences for the distribution of income. Because of growing numbers in the labor force, real wages decreased and settled at levels of mere subsistence. At the same time, the increasing demand for agricultural products had made land ever more valuable. As land rents started to rise and with wages reaching the floor where further decreases were no longer possible, profit margins declined toward the end of the century. This led to a situation where returns on investment contracted and, consequently, traditional investments became less advantageous. All of this was reflected in interest rates. In the middle of the sixteenth century, they began to fall thanks also to developments in financial services that put more money into circulation.[2]

During the late sixteenth and early seventeenth centuries, earlier demographic increases leveled off, owing to an increase in mortality rates and, as the age of marriage rose, to a decrease in fertility rates. The plague of 1630–31 in central and northern Italy, the typhus epidemics of 1648–49, and yet another plague in 1656–57, this time in central and southern Italy, led to a further, sharp population decline.[3] The resulting pressure on resources and prices, which had done nothing but increase in the previous century, now underwent a decisive adjustment. With a typically Malthusian dynamic,

Facing page: detail of Fig. 18

the demographic tragedies wrought by the plague and typhus brought the relationship between population and resources back into equilibrium, and restored the productivity levels of labor. Faced with a decrease in demand, the prices of agricultural products returned to slightly less than late sixteenth-century levels, while wages, above all in cities, began to regain their purchasing power.[4] As the cost of living decreased in the second half of the century, income inequalities, which had been extremely high at the end of the sixteenth century, returned to lower levels.[5] There was less wealth, but at least it was distributed slightly more equally.

A population reduced by 10 to 20 percent naturally generated less demand for foodstuffs, and this affected price levels in general. In the 15 years following the 1630–31 plague, moreover, a series of good harvests contributed further to keep grain prices down and to push land rents lower. And if the famines of the late 1640s caused by typhus and poor harvests created a new, brusque upsurge in prices, this was not sufficient to bring land rents back to the high levels of the first decades of the century. Investing in grain production therefore became less and less profitable, to the point that in the last decades of the Seicento the Annone (the bureau that regulated grain provisions) had to intervene in order to prop up prices. Where soil conditions and sufficient capital allowed, landowners reacted by investing in more profitable crops like grapes, olives, citrus fruits, cotton, and, near larger population centers, other vegetables and fruits. Elsewhere, less productive but still arable lands were abandoned to pasture.

As was generally the case with epidemics of infectious diseases, cities—with their higher concentrations of fleas, ticks, and human beings—were hit harder than the countryside. Over the course of the seventeenth century, Venice lost 0.7 percent of its population, Florence 0.3 percent, and Naples 0.4 percent; Bologna remained at late cinquecento levels; and only Rome increased by 3.2 percent.[6] As Paolo Malanima explains, "It would be natural to think that central and northern Italy had become a 'backwards and depressed area' by around 1660–80. If we look more carefully, however, it is not like this."[7] Indeed, along with grain prices the cost of living also decreased, particularly in cities. Furthermore, and from our perspective this is the most important point, all of this modified the levels of income. Land rents remained low, suffering from the effects of a lower demand for land and grains; earnings rose, on the other hand, in both the countryside and the cities.

Profits inevitably stagnated and were further undermined by competition from English and Dutch merchants who began in 1573 dispatching their ships to the Mediterranean. The crises of the early seventeenth century further reduced rental incomes and, as prices began to collapse, holders of capital began to disinvest from traditional grain production. More profitable investments were sought. They were to be found in various sectors: in the types of specialized farming described above; in an industrial reorganization based on silk rather than on wool; in the widespread employment of women who were cheaper than men; and finally in a restructured financial sector.

In the course of the sixteenth century, the system of accruing capital and its investment and redistribution by banks and other financial services had changed substantially, giving small investors in particular new opportunities. States, suffering from insufficient fiscal revenues, developed more efficient and widespread methods of collecting taxes and managing public funds. Between the fifteenth and sixteenth centuries, Venice, Genoa, Milan, Florence, and Rome all created new organizations, generally called *monti*, with new systems of consolidating and organizing public debt. The *monti* traded shares (*luoghi* and *titoli*) that were normally negotiable and could therefore be ceded to third parties: heirs, creditors, and so forth. The relative abundance of shares, in which painters often invested, and the parallel reduction in the profit margins of agriculture, commerce, and manufacturing led to a progressive drop in interest rates, which in Rome, for instance, fell from 7–10 percent at the end of the sixteenth century to 3–4 percent a century later.[8] Private banks soon became involved in managing these new financial resources, both through an intermediary role in the purchase and sale of *monti* shares, and more directly through investments in riskier financial speculation like currency trading.[9] The credit system of *ancien régime* societies, however, was not limited to public debt bonds and to currency exchanges. Cities developed thick networks of credit relationships between private citizens, based essentially on the *censo*, a perpetual annuity derived from rents or mortgaged real estate. Variable interest rates reflected the more personal relationship between debtor and creditor, changing according to their status and negotiating power.

An analysis of the economic conditions in our five cities must include trends in the housing market. The example of Venice demonstrates how much the financial sector contributed to the income of the proprietary classes. Despite a prolonged lull in demographic and urban expansion and in property sales, the gross revenue from construction—that is, the relationship between purchase price and its value in terms of rent—grew from 3 percent in the first decades of the century to 10 percent in the second half. Concurrently, agricultural returns fell from 5–8 percent to 3–4 percent, public bond returns from 5 percent to 2–3 percent, and interest rates in private credit from 6 percent to 4–5 percent.[10] Conspicuous consumption aside, investment in urban real estate turned out to be the most profitable way to use one's money. Presumably, the housing market would have been more lively if much of the urban fabric had not already been so developed during the sixteenth century. Because of its site with such limited land availability, perpetual leases in Venice became rare as did other concessions for long-term use in exchange for new construction and renovations.[11]

Rome's situation was completely different. The vast ring of the Aurelian walls contained enormous, still empty spaces, and a large part of land suitable for building belonged to churches, monasteries, and charitable institutions. Unlike in Venice, emphyteutic contracts continued to be used at least until the start of the seventeenth century, and indeed third-generation or even perpetual concessions facilitated the development of the Campo Marzio district.[12] Thus, in the course of the seventeenth century, the property of confraternities, hospitals, and other *luoghi pii* grew significantly both in numerical terms and in their profitability as rents on houses and workshops increased, at least until 1680.[13] The confraternity of the Trinità dei Pellegrini calculated in 1680 the value of its numerous apartments at a rent-capitalization rate of 4 percent.[14] In late seventeenth-century Rome, construction investments were undoubtedly more advantageous than those in agriculture and equal, if not slightly more attractive, to other financial investments.[15]

Finally, it is difficult to say how much the tax burden of the Italian states influenced income distribution. The available data suggest that, on the whole, the burden of taxation was limited, especially in the capital cities that enjoyed privileges exempting them from some taxes, duties, and other *gabelle*.[16] In the course of the seventeenth century, moreover, they remained stable or increased only slightly. Furthermore, because of the organizational commitment it would have required, direct taxation was little developed and likely had an impact somewhere around 5 percent of per capita income.[17] As a result, the fiscal coffers were filled mostly through indirect collection in the form of duties, monopoly rights, and taxes on urban market exchanges.[18] Despite this usually low fiscal pressure, exceptional events could push taxation up, affecting the wealth of individuals at certain times and places. In Venice, for instance, the financial requirements tied to the War of Candia (1645–69) led to an increase in direct taxation, which in turn translated into an increase in the amount of property seized from insolvent debtors, a practice whose victims were mainly the owners of small lodgings and workshops.[19]

Cost of Living

In order to evaluate the effective economic conditions in which seventeenth-century painters worked, indices are needed that allow comparisons between the different cities. Most important for comparative purposes are exchange rates and the relative weighting of living costs. But with the present state of research, only the first of the two can be securely addressed. There are a sufficient number of reliable sets of data concerning the values of currencies. Table 30 shows the general depreciation of commonly used currencies compared with the scudo d'oro di marca, the currency of account. The purchasing power of the Roman scudo d'oro remained stable throughout the century, unlike currencies in the other cities that trended steadily downward. By 1650, for example, the Venetian ducat had depreciated by one-third against the Roman scudo.

Exchange rates tell only part of the story and can be misleading if considered in isolation. Currencies of account were not those used for most commercial transactions. Small unit coinages (Table 31) like Roman baiocchi were more subject to inflation than was the relatively stable scudo d'oro; as a consequence, in 1595 the scudo d'oro was worth 122 baiocchi, in 1630 it had risen to 133 baiocchi, and by 1650 its equivalent was 150 baiocchi.[20] An analogous development took place in Florence, where between 1600 and 1680 the scudo d'oro increased from a little more than 10 to more than 13 lire, or from 203 to 266 soldi;[21] and in Bologna, where the scudo d'oro went from 100 bolognini in 1600 to 150 in 1650, a level that it maintained more or less until the end of the century.[22] In Venice, on the other hand, the ducat was pegged at 124 soldi for this whole period, although the ducat underwent a strong devaluation against the scudo d'oro, which was worth about 212 soldi in 1599 but rose sharply to 430 in 1650 before the scudo d'oro started to fluctuate between 320 and 400 soldi until the end of the century.[23]

International money markets, however, were phenomena that did not have a direct and automatic effect on family budgets, and to compare the successes and failures of the various trades practiced in different cities, it is more important to be able to determine the variations in living costs over time and place. This task is

TABLE 30 Purchasing Power of the Local Exchange Currencies* Compared to the scudo d'oro di marca at the Trade Fairs of Bisenzone[24]

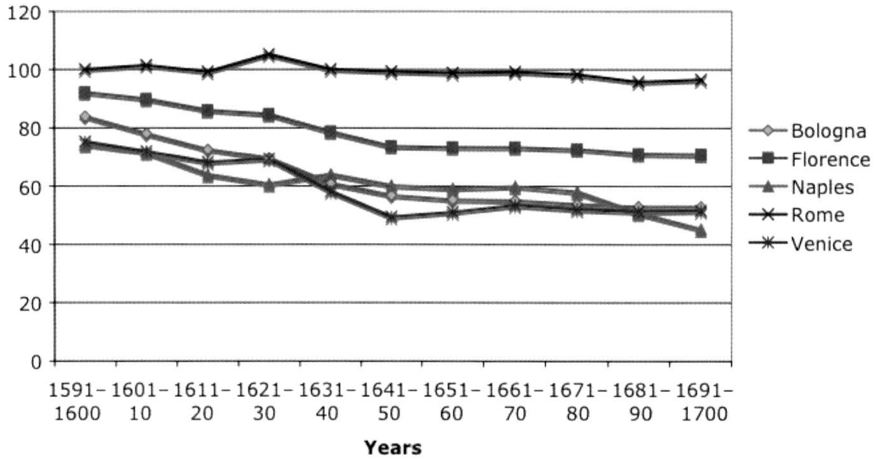

*Bologna's scudo di cambio, Florence's scudo d'oro di stampa, Naples's ducato d'argento, Rome's scudo d'oro di stampa, and Venice's ducato corrente.[25]

TABLE 31 Purchasing Power of 100 units of Small Coinage (bolognini, soldi, baiocchi) Compared to the Official Currency of Exchange*

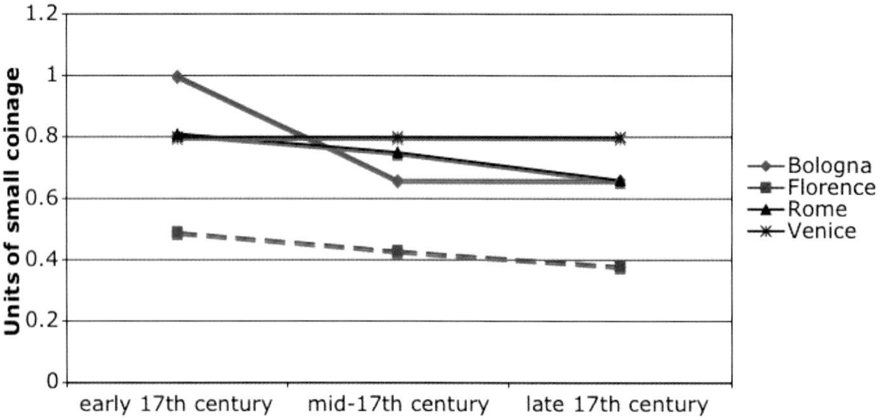

*The Bolognese lira was worth 20 bolognini; the Florentine and Venetian lira was worth 20 soldi; and the Roman giulio was worth 10 baiocchi. See the note to Table 30 for the different official currencies of exchange.

made complicated by how little we know about family incomes and expenditures. On the income side, difficulties arise because few existing sources are homogeneous and complete. The best available data refer to the wages of construction workers, because the large architectural projects kept the most complete archives. Unfortunately, with the exception of Florence, the data are very fragmentary. Still, provisional conclusions are possible. At a median wage early in the century, a master mason in Florence could buy between 7 and 8 kilos of bread with his daily earnings, about the same as his counterparts in Naples and Venice, while a Roman was better off and could buy more than 10. This relative advantage lasted only until the 1630s, when a Roman mason could buy 12 kilos of bread, a Venetian mason 13 kilos, and a Neapolitan mason somewhat more. In

Florence, however, the purchasing power of wages remained lower, almost always staying below 10 kilos.[26]

In evaluating differences in the cost of living between cities, one must also rely on other indicators, starting with contemporary assessments. In Venice, poverty subsidies were worth 50 ducats per year, but due to protests over the amount's insufficiency, they were raised to 81 at the end of the century; in any case, the painter Carl Loth held that his brother could not have lived on less than 176 ducats per year, all the while hoping that he would have been satisfied with 120.[27] In Rome, a "comfortable" merchant declared that he spent 70 scudi per year on food alone; considering that food accounted for about 50 percent of income, we arrive at a total of 140 scudi per year, an amount that is consistent with other accounts and estimates.[28] If in Venice workers spent a little more on costs of living, wages were probably somewhat higher.[29] Taking into account the different values of the local currencies, the cost of living would appear to be similar in Rome and Venice. As soon as one climbs the social ladder, however, needs—and, with them, expenses—increased: in Rome, subsidies for the wards of the nobility were around 350–400 scudi per year, and in Venice, with an annual income of 300 ducats, Tinelli was not considered to be well paid.[30]

Comparison can also be made between the charitable dowries offered by confraternities and other *luoghi pii* and by public institutions. In Bologna, throughout the seventeenth century, 60 percent of the dowries granted by the Monte del Matrimonio (the Marriage Bank) fluctuated between 100 to 500 lire, while another 8–9 percent varied from 500 to 1,000 lire, with an overall average of around 320 lire, or a little less than 43 scudi.[31] During the same period, dowries from the Casa del Soccorso maintained similar levels.[32] In Rome, the dowries paid by the confraternity of the SS. Annunziata fluctuated between 25 and 75 scudi.[33] And in Florence, most dowry benefits recorded in the testaments of the charitable amounted to 50 scudi.[34] As we can see, the nominal values of the dowries assigned by charities were more or less equivalent in Bologna, Florence, and Rome.

Social Stratification: The Middle Classes

Returning to our initial question about the working conditions and living standards in these five cities, we might also ask whether they were populated simply by a small wealthy core and a great indigent mass, as certain entrenched clichés about Rome and Naples would have us believe. Or were there middle classes made up of prosperous merchants and artisans, members of the liberal professions like doctors and lawyers, and by people who held low-ranking public offices? Which social group did humanists, poets, painters, sculptors, architects, and musicians belong to?

If a general argument about economic circumstances is still possible, any sort of synthesis concerning the social stratifications in our five cities is more complicated. Although they were all capital cities, they belonged to state structures that varied widely in terms of size, economic activity, and political institutions. Venice was a republic while Florence was a principality; Rome was under the temporal and spiritual authority of the pope, as was Bologna at one step removed; and Naples was part of the Spanish empire. Their early modern histories also differed greatly: Venice and Florence had been—and, to some extent, remained—among the richest cities in Europe, at the center of the most advanced economic systems; Bologna, in addition to being another industrial city like Venice and Florence, was home to the oldest European university; Rome was the seat of the Catholic Church and, as such, was open to the entire Catholic world; Naples had been at the center of long-standing dynastic disputes among foreign sovereigns and had long been the most populous city in Italy and one of the most populous in Europe. Within certain limitations, one can attempt a comparative analysis.

As one can see from Table 32, the populations and demographic rates of change differed for each city. Naples was by far the largest, and Venice and Rome were double, or almost double, Florence and Bologna. Despite this, the population's distribution by income levels presented some common characteristics. According to a census undertaken at the end of the seventeenth century, there were about 21,000 noble families in all of Italy, representing about 1.5 percent of the population. They were concentrated in the cities, where nobles were proportionally more numerous.[35] A census undertaken in Rome after the plague of 1656 categorizes families as the rich (*ricche*), comfortable (*commode*), poor (*povere*), and destitute (*miserabili*). At the two extremes, the rich made up 2–3 percent of the population and the destitute 5–6 percent. The poor were the overwhelming majority with 64–65 percent, more than double the 27–28 percent who were categorized as comfortable.[36] Yet income levels did not necessarily match social status. Nobles, for example, could be poor, as demonstrated by the many institutions set up to help the "ashamed poor," or those poor people who, for status reasons, needed to hide their conditions at all costs. Great financiers could be more

TABLE 32 The Populations of the Five Cities at the Start of the Seventeenth Century, after the Plagues of 1630 and 1656, and at the Start of the Eighteenth Century

	EARLY SEVENTEENTH CENTURY	AFTER THE PLAGUE	EARLY EIGHTEENTH CENTURY
Naples	267,973 (1606)	150,000 (1658)	215,608 (1707)[37]
Venice	141,625 (1624)	102,243 (1633)	137,867 (1696)[38]
Rome	102,760 (1603–7)	99,029 (1657)	134,785 (1698–99)[39]
Florence	76,000 (1622)	56,000 (1660)	74,678 (1730)[40]
Bologna	67,000 (1617)	46,000 (1631)	67,000 (1700)[41]

wealthy than many noblemen, even if they did not boast a noble title.

In order to understand the social structure of our five cities, we must concentrate on the two middle sections of the population: those of the comfortable and the poor, who together made up more than 90 percent of the total population. Poor, in the culture of the time, meant something fairly different from its meaning today. Poverty was based less on a pre-established level of income than on a perception of one's living conditions. It depended on various noneconomic factors, linked to age, gender, the degree of family or work-related independence, and the network of a person's social relations. Those who felt poor were people who lived entirely off their work and did not own real estate, or they might have possessions but insufficient liquid equity to ensure a standard of living appropriate to their social status. Almost all women felt poor if they did not have a man to rely on. Poverty was thus a relative condition, measured against the wealth of other members of the same social group. Some cardinals, for example, were defined as being poor and therefore were given suitable benefits by the Church. On the other hand, in the absence of unemployment subsidies or pensions, anybody who lost his job would become destitute and therefore would be forced to turn to one of the many charitable institutions that, by no coincidence, had spread in Italian cities during the sixteenth and seventeenth centuries.[42] The comfortable, by contrast, were those who could count on an unearned income, usually from an urban or rural property, sufficient for their needs. However, the boundaries between these two groups were not all that rigid and often were crossed, whether upwards or downwards.

The poor included all those laborers who lived off their wages—the spinners and weavers who were so numerous in Venice, Bologna, Florence, and Naples—but also many master artisans who had opened a workshop because of an inheritance, dowry, or some other windfall.[43] Large numbers of servants, porters, street vendors, and unskilled laborers in all five cities would normally be considered to be poor as well. Members of the liberal professions, especially those at the start of their careers, might also be classified as poor, including doctors, young clerks working for lawyers or notaries, and low-level employees in state bureaucracies. Lacking other sources of income besides what they earned in their jobs, they found themselves in a highly precarious position. A good part of their income was absorbed by food expenses, as we will see shortly, and a bad harvest that led to increases in the price of grain and bread could affect their standard of living, not just in the price of goods but also in their income as demand for their goods and services dropped. Thus, from poverty they could fall into destitution. The same applies to painters, whose works were subject to an elastic demand, responsive to the availability of expendable incomes.

Guilds and confraternities dedicated to helping those rendered destitute by economic crises intervened with special alms, low-interest loans, foundling hospitals for newborns and small children, institutes that specialized in the care of young and teenage girls, and full-fledged general hospitals for all groups of the poor, including adults.[44] Many painters appeared in this category of the poor, and qualified for these charities.[45] Such, for instance, was someone like Onofrio de Anfora, whom Christopher Marshall describes as working for a daily wage similar to that of a manual laborer, combining artistic production with other trades.[46] Even painters honored by biographers could also live in poverty, like Bartolomeo Pedon, who walked around Venice with torn clothes and no shoes, or like Tintoretto, who was forced to turn to public welfare toward the end of his successful career.[47]

Urban social hierarchies based on a combination of profession, status, and property are nearly impossible to reconstruct given the data available. Contemporary accounts are often compromised by biases and clichés. For example, Montesquieu declared in 1729 that there were at least 50,000 lawyers and other members of the legal profession in Naples, while Giuseppe Maria Galanti estimated the number to be 6,314 at the end of the eighteenth century.[48] Even if we succeeded in collecting reliable data on the number of members belonging to each trade or profession, one would still have to connect them with income. For now a highly approximate discussion must suffice.

Montesquieu's exaggerations aside, Italian cities with large law courts were full of lawyers. Not only could they earn a good income, but they also enjoyed the highest level of social prestige available to non-nobles. Tomaso Garzoni, in his *Piazza universale di tutte le professioni del mondo* (1585), described their situation in this way: "Jurists are noble because of the marks offered to them by the doctorate, that is the doctoral cap . . . the finger ring . . . the gold decoration . . . the manly robe, signs that they want to live quietly as peaceful men"; and a little later he continued: "It is necessary, to save his honesty and reputation, that a lawyer dresses honorably, according to his status."[49] In effect, becoming a lawyer was a secure path to social advancement, and the honorary titles reserved for lawyers were just below those bestowed on nobles. It is probable, therefore, that they were mainly included amongst the comfortable. But lawyers were also a heterogeneous group, and if some were called upon to discuss important cases and to consult on prominent issues, others had to be satisfied with more modest work and pay. The situation for medical doctors was more complex. Traditionally, debate about the liberal arts juxtaposed the nobility of medicine to that of law, and usually decided in favor of lawyers, even though some doctors enjoyed a solid professional reputation and a prestigious clientele and even managed on occasion to enter the patriciate.[50] Strongly intertwined with the liberal professions were those in charge of a public office, from the judges of minor courts to the officers of governmental bodies that were not reserved to the nobility.

The socio-economic status of merchants resists generalization because it was the largest and most varied group. At the top were the great families specializing in international finance and luxury goods. Managers of tax collection from customs and excise duties, and even of state treasuries and mints, often came from this group. As financiers, using capital gained in trade and commerce, they invested heavily in the *monti* and landed estates, thus emulating (and sometimes entering) the ranks of the nobility. Their wealth made their sons and daughters coveted marriage partners, and was yet another way a merchant family could acquire an estate or obtain the sovereign's investiture for it.[51]

Not many merchants could afford these activities and gain access to socio-political elites by means of fungible capital. Most owned smaller businesses and could at best be included amongst the comfortable. Gaining a noble title, at least in just one generation, would be an unrealistic ambition, but many were at the top of the working classes and master artisans with whom they shared control over manufacturing. In Venice, Bologna, and Florence, where trade guilds were central to the commercial and political lives of their city, merchants preserved important vestiges of their old power, in terms of both prestige and wealth. Even if they were formally excluded from government charges, they still managed to influence political decisions concerning trade through their various associations and guilds.

The artisans' milieu was more homogeneous and egalitarian, even though this group included both master artisans who owned a workshop and employed several workers as well as poor day laborers who struggled to put lunch and dinner together. Those at the top of the most powerful guilds, like the Arte della Seta in Bologna, stood above their laboring dependents.

Finally, we must add to the various socio-professional groups discussed here the social microcosm employed by the nobility. The higher ranking employees, who could often boast the title of "gentleman," included the secretaries, agents, *maestri di camera* or chamber masters (who ran the ceremonial aspect of their master's life), *maestri di casa* or masters of the house (who, on the other hand, took care of the household management, supplies, and furnishings), librarians, curators of artistic collections and gardens, and so forth. This skilled household staff was important, not because of its numbers (in fact, quite small) but because its members served as a link to other social groups, thus acting as intermediaries between their rich and noble *signori* and the throng of merchants and craftsmen who lived off their employers' conspicuous consumption. Moreover, many of these household offices required a high level of education and culture, which in turn translated into reputation and prestige, and therefore represented good opportunities for social promotion.

The middle classes with some purchasing power, therefore, were not totally absent from our five cities, and the cultural level of many of them further favored the spread of a taste for novelty. It was this group, as well as the much smaller number of noble families and ecclesiastical agencies, that gave rise to the demand for artistic goods, and it was often this same milieu that produced the connoisseurs who acted as intermediaries between the world of great patrons and the artists themselves.

Among those who belonged to the middle classes we must finally include moderately successful painters, such as the Bolognese Girolamo Curti, who could legitimately claim that being a painter was real progress compared with being a silk weaver.[52] Many painters belonged to this upwardly mobile group. The Roman census of 1656 shows that they made up exactly half of those who declared themselves to be artists.[53] Like those in public positions or members of the liberal professions, they possessed a certain culture and could claim, and actually enjoyed, social respectability. For professional reasons, many of them were in contact with noble circles, and this led them to identify themselves with and emulate the values of the elite. Whenever possible, their professional earnings were strengthened with investments, joining or following the lead of their noble masters. For example, Giovanni Battista Gaulli purchased a property in 1674 that promised an income of about 60 scudi per year, and by 1708 he earned at least 178 scudi from the rent of his three apartments.[54] Their standard of living often followed that of their social superiors, which encouraged them to act like gentlemen, as Ludovico Carracci did in wearing a lynx coat —and being trailed by a retinue of students.[55]

Painters, like other trade and laboring journeymen, sought work where they could find it, seeking open and profitable markets and contributing to a remarkable geographic mobility. Merchants also sought new markets, as did intellectuals and artists of all kinds, attracted by the opportunities to be engaged by more generous or more powerful protectors and to benefit from a more favorable milieu for their science or their art. Even nobles were mobile. Thanks to the Curia, which attracted prelates from all the large cities in Italy, Rome was the center for aristocrats of diverse origins who entered into multistate alliances and relations of kinship.[56] Ideas, tastes, fashions, and lifestyles thus had the opportunity to mix together and to spread beyond the geographic and political barriers that divided the peninsula's many small states, contributing to the formation of the "Italian" style that was readily identified as such by foreign travelers and intellectuals.

Professional Associations

Members of the trades and professions that we have encountered thus far all belonged, respectively, to either a guild or college. Lawyers, doctors, and notaries had their own college (*collegio*) with prescribed rules for the admission to and practice of their profession. Privileges of identification were defined, such as the right to wear a robe decorated with fur or a gold belt or a cap. Stiff sanctions against those without required qualifications making unauthorized claims to the profession protected members against possible undue competition from those belonging to less noble professions (such as surgeons in the case of doctors, or solicitors in the case of lawyers).[57] Often, however, the rules of admission to a college insisted on an honorable birth rather than on professional qualifications and only accepted those who could demonstrate patrician origins. Entry into a college thus became a question of prestige and, as such, attracted members of the nobility who saw it as a means to declare and publicly display their social status.[58] In general, they had no intention to work in the profession, leaving its actual practice to less noble surrogates. Qualifying university degrees were not difficult to obtain. In most cases, regular attendance of university courses was not mandatory. Private lessons, offered by professors for a fee, were often sufficient. What was said of the Collegio dei medici of Naples—that it "confers the doctorate to whomever pays, with an exam that was a mere formality"—could be said of many other professional colleges in Naples and elsewhere.[59]

From the mid-sixteenth to the early eighteenth centuries, the professional colleges tried to expand their jurisdiction, often at the expense of other corporate bodies, whether a guild, college, or confraternity. To protect their jurisdiction, each profession defined its own prerogatives with ever greater meticulousness. These groups claimed legal authority not only over their members, but more generally over anyone who practiced the profession, and sought to punish any transgressors. Their activism was only partly effective. Theirs was a losing battle where much of the profession ended up escaping their control.[60]

A similar dynamic of market instability and attempted expansionism characterized the activities of the guilds during this same period. Trade associations between the sixteenth and seventeenth centuries endured times of great turbulence, marked by ruptures, the birth of new organizations, separations between the associations of masters and associations of workers, and, everywhere, by an extremely long series of judicial controversies aimed at redefining the borders between one association and another and at redrawing the map of privileges, monopolies, and exclusions. In almost all the cities, merchants and tradesmen sought successfully to obtain an autonomous statute that protected them from lesser interlopers, as when tailors took secondhand dealers to court, since the latter tended to invade their area of business, or when shoemakers (*calzolai*) tried to limit the cobblers (*ciabattini*).[61] The guilds, like the professional associations, also had to defend themselves against those who practiced their trade without being a member of any guild, either because they enjoyed special privileges granted to them by a sovereign—as often happened with soldiers—or because they pretended to do nonprofessional work for friends or neighbors, as women generally did.[62]

This centrifugal process challenged an increasingly frustrated desire of the established and historically privileged guilds and colleges to limit and regulate who could engage in activities over which they claimed a monopoly. In some cases, this even led to the formation of new places of worship, separate and reserved for members only.[63] These same centrifugal forces of professional fragmentation were countered by confraternities and other devotional associations that accepted members from across the social spectrum. In doing so, they reopened those channels of communication between different social and professional strata that the process of professional fragmentation tended to close. In this way, the competition and conflict shifted from the socio-professional level to the plane of devotional social relations. Confraternities were also characterized by fiery rivalries, manifested during religious festivals and processions when each one tried to secure the position with greatest visibility and prestige. By helping to unknot and retie the threads of social and professional relations, confraternities created new possibilities for individuals to engage with those from different social and professional classes.

Analogous trends led to the formation and development of the various academies of painting in Florence, Rome, Bologna, and Venice.[64] Painters wanted to distance themselves from the old trade guilds—which were too closely associated with artisans—and hence they tried to reinforce the promotion of painting as a liberal art and of painters as gentlemen by aiming to improve the cultural education of the young and to keep their distance from mechanical and commercial activities. In this case, too, being part of an academy became an issue of prestige, to the extent that members of the nobility sought to become affiliates.[65] However, as in the other trades and professions, many painters remained outside their association in order to escape their taxes and jurisdictional control. Only in Naples, which at the start of the century still lacked important collectors, did painters take longer to attract the public's attention, and consequently an academy was not founded until much later.[66]

Urban Classes, Economic Conditions, and Patrimony

Most heads of families, unless they were members of the nobility or the destitute (those who "only owned the clothes on their backs," as they were defined at the time), generally had to rely on three types of resources: the estate inherited from their fathers; their wives' dowries; and income from their trades or professions, along with additional earnings from the children who were still subject to their paternal authority. The principles of Roman law that served as the foundation of most legal regulations in early modern Italy established that the rights and responsibilities of the *pater familias* could only be acquired with the death of one's own father. Until then, even if he had his own children, and even though he worked and was economically independent, a man remained a dependent of his own father and therefore was proscribed from certain activities. In particular, he could not take on debts or sign contracts, which always had to be co-signed by his father. His own earnings in theory had to enter the family's estate run by his father. In order to free himself from this situation of dependence and acquire the full rights of an adult man, there was no other way than emancipation, which was a formal act to be completed in the presence of a notary. Acts of emancipation, however, were infrequent.

The problems of dependency were resolved in other ways: either simply by ignoring the law or by relying on mortality rates and short average lifespans to remedy the situation. Studies of rural communities have shown that, in general, men waited to marry and have a family until their father was dead and the family estate divided among his heirs.[67] We are less well informed about cities, but it is likely that, here too, generational change coincided with the transfer of the estate. In any case, the testaments of fathers were full of advice on their sons' future, and only rarely contained instructions for already married sons.[68] The dominion of a *pater familias* over his sons, daughters, and wife meant that income was a function not so much of the individual as of the family.

As Raffaella Morselli has shown, family origins were important for artists, too. Francesco Gessi and Lorenzo Garbieri enjoyed paternal inheritances that were considerable.[69] As for Francesco Albani, his social origin must have been quite high, as Malvasia says, given that he managed to obtain a very large dowry from his first wife consisting of two houses in Rome and 20,000 lire (about 4,000 scudi) in cash.[70] Many painters inherited their father's profession along with his material goods and patronal contacts, thus giving rise to family dynasties, a phenomenon that was especially common in Venice.[71] Others came from professional families of comfortable means and therefore benefited from influential family connections, as did Guido Reni. And finally patrons could become surrogate fathers, as with Guercino, who could study and make a name for himself thanks only to the protection of his first patron.

Besides the inheritance from one's father, a wife's dowry represented the financial base on which almost all new families were built. And certainly no girl, from any milieu, married without a dowry. Confraternities, trade guilds, and other institutions to help the poor all had developed systems to collect funds for the dowries of their members' daughters. Female institutions charged with the education of deprived girls and adolescents made their wards do some sort of work—most often spinning, weaving, or sewing—and capitalize on their small earnings to give them a dowry when they married. These dowries, surely not very large but at least guaranteed in cash (rather than goods or property), made the girls from these institutions highly desirable brides for young artisans who, thanks to this small capital, could open a workshop. Furthermore, the future wife knew a trade and therefore could also contribute to the family earnings with her own work.[72]

Other dowries included personal property in the form of clothes, linen, jewelry, furniture, and kitchen furnishings, whose value was assessed and declared in the nuptial contracts. These functional goods could be used at pawn banks (*monti dei pegni*) where goods that were surrendered to secure a loan usually consisted of female objects like clothes, linens, and jewelry.[73] Goods could also be rented to a neighbor who lacked the most basic domestic goods and would therefore pay a small fee to use them. The nicer clothes, for instance those purchased for the wedding, could even be sold.[74] Artisans' wives worked too, sometimes in their husband's workshops, sometimes for another artisan, sewing, spinning, weaving, or embroidering either at home or elsewhere, or washing and ironing clothes, starching collars and cuffs, and so forth. Some cooked for the workshop. From these and other activities, an industrious wife could significantly supplement her husband's income, as recent studies have demonstrated.[75] Certain industrial sectors regularly employed women, who were paid less, improved productivity, and hence were in great demand by employers. Various stages of silk production in Bologna and Florence and the handling of glass pearls in Venice were typically female jobs.[76]

At a higher rung on the social ladder, dowries that could be cashed in might include precious clothes, jewels, real properties, and, above all, credit instruments. They could therefore provide important injections of liquidity to a husband's business or, alternatively, be left in their original credit form, thus ensuring a regular and secure income. The information collected in this book on the dowries of painters' wives and daughters is consistent with these practices. Successful artists pursued respectability through the marriage of their children, too, and therefore gave their daughters similar dowries to those of rich artisans. For her marriage with Francesco Carboni, Tiarini gave his daughter a house in Bologna and 3,000 Bolognese lire (equal to about 400 scudi) in cash.[77] Other painters also approached the level of rich merchants or members of the minor nobility. The daughters of Palma Giovane and Benedetto Caliari received 2,000 Venetian ducats, and Jusepe de Ribera's daughter no less than 5,000 Neapolitan ducats.[78]

Another important source of income for a hardworking *pater familias*—in other words, one who did not just live off his land rent and other investments—was the earnings of his trade or profession. These varied greatly, however. Some could rely on the capitalization of their wage as an apprentice and begin their work with a small sum added to their wife's dowry. But not everybody was in this situation, because the wage could be requisitioned by one's father or because, simply, no wage had been paid, and instead it was the apprentice's family who paid the master who taught him his trade.[79] The same thing happened to many young men who were preparing to learn the art of painting, as the essays collected here show. Pascoli expected that teaching should be free everywhere in Italy, but in practice conditions were subject to great variation.[80] The recompense of adult men also varied greatly, even within the same trade and with the same qualifications, to the point that the best-paid worker could earn up to a third more than the least paid.[81] In 1625, for example, a Roman stationer explained to a judge who was questioning him on the wage of his assistants that in his first year of employment he had received about 16 scudi, while for the next year the same employer had given him 24.[82] A study of Venetian glassmakers' daily wages shows an even greater range of figures: with the same qualifications, the most highly paid employees earned about twice as much as the lowest paid.[83] To this we must add that some wages were partly paid in food or food and lodging, while others were not: in 1624, another Roman artisan recounted, for example, that paper workers were paid between 2.5 and 4 giuli per day, depending on the provision of food or lodging, and various other accounts confirm his assertions.[84] On the other hand, a meal at an inn would have cost around 1 giulio, which was precisely the difference between one pay level and the other.[85] Finally, daily wages were subject to seasonal variations, generally higher in summer than in winter: "In the summer, men making string were given 3 giuli plus expenses and slept at their own home, and in winter they were paid 35 baiocchi without expenses or 25 with."[86]

An important factor in determining the level of pay was the length of employment: day laborers earned proportionally more than those who were paid a monthly or even annual wage for the same work.[87] The daily equivalent of a Venetian mason, calculated on a monthly or even annual basis, could be half as much as a worker hired by the day.[88] The higher daily pay of temporary workers compensated them for the greater risk of being unemployed. From the employers' view, it enabled them to find additional manpower at particularly busy times. Even monthly wages were not necessarily tied to stable work relationships, but might also arise from seasonal employment. Leather tanning, for instance, was essentially summer work and a master hired workers only in those months. "In our *arte* [the production of parchment]," a Roman contemporary declared, "we do not work from September until Easter . . . to the point that if the master wants to stay at the workshop on his own, he doesn't need to have workers or apprentices."[89] The same was true for construction. In Murano, where the glassmakers' ovens were turned off in August and September, the statutes of the guild required contracts of employment to be no longer than one working season.[90]

The length of employment and the presence (or lack) of payment in goods were not the only variables that influenced wages. Other determining factors included the length of a worker's apprenticeship, his experience, his technical expertise, and the degree of specialization achieved. Venetian master glassmakers, for instance, were paid more or less depending on whether they specialized in glassblowing, in the production of glass sheets for mirrors and windows, or in the production of less valuable handmade articles.[91] The availability of skilled labor also influenced pay. The employees of a Roman tanner said that they deserved five or six scudi per month, rather than the usual three or four, "because there are no people in his trade"; and a particularly able Venetian master glassmaker was hired under very advantageous terms after several masters had tried to win him over.[92] Naturally, the same applied to those occupations, like painting, which gave personal ability a market distinction.

In other cases, geographic origin could determine a different level of earnings. In Venice, citizens and residents had more privileges than foreigners; in Rome, where the most highly qualified workers came from outside the city, the opposite occurred. Moreover, every trade had its own rules governing the movement from one professional level to another, and every guild statute defined different functions based on age, expertise acquired, and the relationship with the guild itself. Although different positions should in theory correspond to these different qualifications, in reality this was not always the case. Earnings of workers and masters overlapped, and moving from one task to another did not always correspond to a change in pay.[93] In any case, professional careers and earnings of artisans were anything but linear: salaries could increase or decrease from time to time, according to the individual job or market conditions and labor competition in general. For painters, the same thing occurred. Paolo Farinati's account clearly documents this extreme from one year to another.[94]

A comparison between the salary levels of different trades introduces another variable even more profoundly influential than supply and demand mechanisms. Within the least specialized trades, differences in pay were limited. In Venice, for example, the daily wages of workers employed in the glassworks, in the Arsenale shipyards, and in construction all fluctuated within the same range, from 30 to 50 soldi.[95] In Rome, the earnings of tanners, stationers, and paper workers (between 3 and 4 giuli per day) were higher than the wages paid by the church of S. Giacomo degli Spagnoli to masons working on the construction of its houses (about 2.5 giuli per day); however, we do not know if the latter were given food as well, which would have added 1 giulio a day, and therefore would have brought construction wages to the same level as the trades tied to leather tanning. With greater specialization within a trade, the differences between pay levels also grew more marked. If in Rome master masons received around 4 giuli per day, about the same amount as the most expert tanners, in Venice a master glassmaker earned significantly more than a master mason (on average 100 soldi rather than 75), and master carpenters in the Arsenale shipyards received even higher wages (150 soldi on average).[96]

If we move from master artisans to the public offices and the liberal professions, any appearance of standardization based on market rules disappears. Individual agreements took on greater importance to the point that theology professors at the Sapienza earned about one-tenth of law professors in the same *studium*.[97]

Writing about a "labor market" under these conditions is, therefore, misleading. Every trade had its own regulations that affected pay, and its most authoritative members were often asked to bear witness about them. Impersonal market factors, like the conditions of labor demand and supply, influenced wages as well, but pay also depended on the professional qualification of the worker as defined by the trade norms more than by the market.[98] Differences in pay could also be affected by the social and legal standing of the contracting parties. For example, the treatise *De salario seu operariorum mercede* by the Roman jurist Lanfranco Zacchia recognized that, in order to be fair, a salary had to be commensurate not only with the worker's professional skills but also with his "quality"—in a social sense—asserting that individual agreements should still be respected even if they had fallen short of these moral rules. Zacchia echoed actual practice, having collected and summarized decisions from the principal courts.[99]

An even greater range can be found with painters' earnings where value adhered not just to the producer and product but to the social network where the transactions took place. Indeed, as all the essays in this book show, it is practically impossible to identify a single criterion by which to evaluate paintings. The expectation that prices should correspond to a painting's dimensions, the time spent, or the number of figures depicted was for the most part accepted by painters of a lower rank and often was disdainfully rejected by more established artists. Beginning with Giulio Mancini, those in the art business were aware that it was impossible to establish objective criteria for prices; painters and theorists advocated competent experts, who alone could fairly set the price for paintings.[100] None of this diverged from the positions held by most theologians and jurists on the criteria for the establishment of prices. On the contrary, neo-scholastic philosophers invoked the principle of desirability of a good as the only legitimate measure of its value, and, as noted, the lawfulness of private negotiation was also upheld for disputes over pay.

Home Economics of the *Pater Familias*

Contemporary literature on *oeconomica* tells us that the first duty of the *pater familias* was to preserve what he had received from his ancestors and, if possible, to increase it in turn, in order to pass it on to his descendants.[101] To this end, he had to balance earnings with expenses, trying to "be more seller than buyer," as Alberti advised.[102] Family resources were, therefore, divided judiciously between consumption and investment. To ensure that expenses did not exhaust available resources was a difficult achievement for those who lived entirely off their own work. Indeed, the structure of family expenses was heavily conditioned by its income level. Reliable research for the poorest classes is lacking because, in general, the poor did not leave account books. It has been estimated, however, that in "quiet" years with stable agricultural prices, about 80 percent of a poor family's income was spent on the purchase of foodstuffs, consisting mostly of bread, while the remaining 20 percent had to cover rent, clothing, occasional heating, and other domestic expenses.[103] Faced with these data, the concept of the "cyclical poor" loses its abstractness and become laden with meaning: it was enough for the price of grain or other essential agricultural products to increase, following a bad crop, a war, or some other factor, for a family to be unable to purchase sufficient food. Consequently, families were forced to seek public or private welfare. During famines, city streets filled with beggars, and charitable institutions had to increase their aid.

Further up the social hierarchy, the data become more plentiful and reconstruction less hypothetical. In the middle of the seventeenth century, a notary from Verona apportioned his expenses as shown in Table 33.

Even a notary prosperous enough to afford precious objects and works of art, to keep at least one servant, and to spend something on his children's education, still allotted almost half of his expenses for food. And it is likely that many of those "comfortable" painters discussed in this book followed the same pattern of consumption, as the *post mortem* inventories cited by Raffaella Morselli suggest.[104]

TABLE 33 Percentage Distribution of the Notary Folognino's Domestic Expenses[105]

TYPE OF EXPENSE	PERCENT
Food	47
Clothing	19
Housing	11
Servants' salaries	1
Health and medicine	2
Entertainment	6
Precious objects and works of art	2.5
Taxes	1
Alms	0.5
Various	10
Total	100

A few years earlier, a wealthy Roman widow recorded her distribution of expenses where food represented only 30 percent of her cost of living (Table 34).[106]

It is not difficult to imagine that this was the model for the most successful painters, those who lived like nobility and whose inventories included lavish furnishings and rare and precious objects.[107]

Naturally, the type of food varied with income, and while the poor consumed almost entirely bread, the well-off and the rich could also afford meat, cheese, oil and butter, vegetables, and even sugar.[108] The expenses for clothing and, above all, for home furnishings were concentrated in specific periods of one's life, and for the remainder were limited to repairs, additions, or replacements. Thus marriage, or the time when one started an independent family life, was an occasion for exceptional expenses that required special funds. Dowries, with their trousseaux of clothes, linens, furniture, and various accessories, precisely met this need.

Literature on the *pater familias* advised, as mentioned, not to acquire debts and to be more "sellers than buyers," but in a hierarchical society, especially one whose social imperatives of noble liberality demanded considerable cash outlays, wealthier families could struggle to keep up appearances. It was often consumption and social status rather than income that determined expenses.

In order to increase income, many heads of families practiced more than one profession so that the earnings from one would make up for periods of inactivity in the other or, more simply, to raise earnings. Among artisans, such practices were completely normal, as many accounts demonstrate: "There are parchment makers who do other jobs like tanning leather," a Roman explained.[109] Various master artisans ran more than one workshop, even for unrelated trades, as evidenced by the many cases of barbers, tailors, or apothecaries who also sold paintings and other art objects, or the master masons who, in addition to building houses, also took care of their furnishing and rental.[110] Many maintained ties to the agricultural sector, one that required considerable manpower, and employed farmhands for their vegetable gardens and vineyards within the city walls and for other miscellaneous jobs.[111]

As one climbed the social hierarchy, opportunities for diversification did not diminish but, on the contrary, seemed to increase. Agents for large families, for example, often managed their own businesses, and in the world of barristers, notaries, holders of minor offices, doctors, surgeons, and so forth, most performed more than one job. Diversification could also occur

TABLE 34 Percentage Distribution of the Widow Pellegrina's Domestic Expenses[112]

TYPE OF EXPENSE	PERCENT
Food	31.72
Clothing	10.64
Housing	2.13
Apothecary	0.51
Carriage	20.67
Funeral	1.52
Alms	2.08
Other expenses*	30.73
Total	100.00

*Including servants' wages.

within family strategies: daughters would marry men from the same trade as their fathers, while sons would be trained for a different job. Or, on the contrary, daughters could be "married out" while their brothers inherited their fathers' workshops.[113] Sons of prosperous parents might enter an ecclesiastical career or a profession such as medicine or law. Among painters, above all in Venice, it was customary to do the same thing, by initiating at least one son into the father's profession.[114]

Artists also diversified their activities to enhance their income, as one can see from these essays. Those who could offer their services as expert appraisers, a well-paid job in Rome, Venice, and Bologna (less so in Florence), gained extra income that brought with it considerable social cachet. Others served as restorers when the opportunity arose; some bought paintings and then resold them; others made copies of famous works. Some hired painters poorer than themselves and sold their work at a profit. And it was also not rare for these different activities to be practiced all at once by the same person.[115]

Monies for a standard of living commensurate with one's social status could also be attained through shrewd investments, especially in credit, agriculture, and construction. Individual credit, in addition to legal ownership of shares in the *monti*, was a favored form of investment, as evidenced by notaries' registers in various cities. Because an annuity might have a relatively low capital value, and with interest rates remaining high until the end of the seventeenth century, it was one of the most important sources of additional earnings for any family with even the smallest liquid reserves.[116] Besides private credit, the industrious classes commonly invested in agricultural land, especially in areas just outside of cities. Renting a vegetable garden or a vineyard located within the city walls or immediately outside allowed them not only to produce for their own consumption, but also to sell vegetables, fruit, and even flowers to city greengrocers or to perfumers and could thereby prove to be a profitable undertaking, especially at a time when the purchasing power of wages was improving.[117] Indeed, one can find many rental contracts for vineyards among notaries' papers.[118] Another investment opportunity was to be found in construction, whether one managed to buy a house, obtain one with a perpetual lease, or just rent one in order to sublet a part of it.

House ownership was distributed unequally in our five cities: 95 percent of Venetians were renters, as was the case in Milan and Turin.[119] In Florence, the percentage of owners was noticeably higher, up to 20 percent. We lack specific figures for Rome, but judging from the frequency of property sales and rentals it would seem that the situation was closer to Florence than to Venice. Some families took in lodgers, charging them for housing and eventually food. Some apprenticeship contracts—particularly those that provided the greatest protection for the apprentice's living conditions—stipulated that the boy's father pay a monthly sum for his son's training and living expenses. This model was also repeated at higher levels of society. Those in the liberal professions, including university professors, could earn more from their students directly, whom they often kept as boarders, than from the salaries that they received from the *studium*.[120]

A way to protect oneself from unpredictable economic circumstances was to diversify the sources of earnings by investing in or working outside of one's own trade or profession. This pertained especially to those, like painters, who relied on income in a relatively uncertain profession. This at least is what is suggested by the fact that contemporary biographies of artists often discussed good and bad investments, how shrewd and far-sighted or reckless and prodigal their subject was. Pascoli's life of Giovanni Odazzi, quoted by Richard Spear, is an excellent example of this, as are his reflections on Mario dei Fiori's investments, or Malvasia's comments on Guercino's nonartistic pursuits.[121]

In an uncertain economy, such as that of the *ancien régime*, those who worked for a living developed a whole range of stratagems, including labor diversification and micro-investments.[122] Recent research shows that forms of credit were essential instruments of survival in the economic and social system. Indeed, credit enabled the economy to overcome the liquidity crises that regularly afflicted all social classes. Hiring contracts for apprentices, assistants, and masters at the Murano glassworks, for instance, often gave an advance on pay, with the amount contingent on the workers' contractual strength.[123] And several Roman master artisans declared that they gave their poorest workers an advance for food.[124]

Another fundamental form of credit was made up of deferred payments, which more or less all vendors gave to their most "respectable" clients. The long lists of credit attached to workshop inventories, even for small sums, demonstrate how widespread this practice was. Being able to postpone payment allowed people to wait until pay day or the completion of a job, and hence allowed them to maintain their standard of living without too many dips or brusque interruptions.

One final and extremely important source of credit came from the pawn banks (*monti di pegni*) found everywhere in Italian cities starting in the fifteenth century. In this case, clothes, jewelry, and domestic items could temporarily be converted into money in order to overcome times of crisis—paying an overdue debt, for instance—and, once again, to continue daily life without disruptive bumps. This system was based on a person's respectability and on the fact that he had the bare minimum of resources necessary to access credit: he had to be recognized as solvent by the vendors to whom he resorted, and (obviously) he had to have domestic items to pawn. There was therefore a close correlation between owning things and having access to various forms of credit, and this once again brings to light the contributions of wives to the family economy.[125]

Granting payment deferrals and accepting an advance instead was often essential in retaining important patrons. Many painters, especially the superstars like Pietro da Cortona, knew this from personal experience.[126] On the other hand, those who "wanted to be paid promptly" also had to be ready to accept a "very low price," as Baldinucci recounts in his life of Bernardino Poccetti.[127] Various artists also found that their work could be leveraged into a source of credit, thus allowing them to receive loans, often quite large ones, in exchange for a commitment to repay them in paintings.[128]

The economic calculations of a seventeenth-century *pater familias* were not limited to just income and expenses. The social chains of reciprocity must also be taken into account, those that tied individuals not just to their extended family but also to their neighbors, colleagues, members of their religious association, and so forth. Indeed, sometimes social imperatives conflicted with rational economic calculations. Thus, it happened that the *pater familias* might have to provide free assistance to unemployed relatives or sick employees, or he might have to contribute to the collection of alms for the widows and orphans of his own guild or college. It also happened that, in the name of friendship or family ties, he would have to work for free. This "gift economy" of generalized reciprocity expected everyone to contribute to the general welfare without immediate monetary recompense, knowing instead that support from others in times of need would be available. The system did not always function so elegantly. We find workers lodging court cases concerning recompense for their salary that, in the name of friendship, had been temporarily given up. Charitable institutions were perfectly aware of the intersections between the practices of gifting and those of commercial exchange, and were often forced to intervene when a party refused to provide a relative with the expected aid and tried instead to unload the burden on public institutions.[129]

The same ambiguity between the gift economy and commercial exchange occurred with various forms of payment. Landowners paid for goods and services in agricultural products—grain, oil, coal, wood, and others—rather than with money. Payment in kind involved all types of suppliers, from shoemakers to silversmiths and painters, as these pages show.[130] Workers might be partially paid in goods, an offering or *donativo*, as was the case with the Murano glassworks.[131] Nevertheless, this type of compensation did not escape the logic of commercial exchange. The value of these goods or "gifts" was precisely calculated in monetary terms and entered as a business expense.[132]

The gift economy was an especially important feature of the relationship between many painters and their patrons. Because a gift was supposedly freely given, it differed from monetary payment in that it conferred a higher degree of honor on its recipient. Painters gave their works for "free" but always with the expectation of recompense. Guido Reni was perfectly aware of how these things worked, as was Salvator Rosa, who received Parmesan cheese in exchange for his *Death of Atilius Regulus* (Fig. 18 in the essay on Rome).[133] As with payment deferrals, gifts could also translate into credit, requiring the beneficiary to give other commissions to the artist who had honored him thus.[134] If many forms of gifts were covertly or openly opportunistic, there were others that were sincere and instead attempted to return to the community some of the honors and riches that had been bestowed on the painter. The mutual gifting between Barocci and the friars of S. Francesco in Urbino, or that between Zuccaro and the church of S. Filippo Neri in Fermo, should be interpreted as a means for a wealthy painter to share his riches in socially and religiously beneficent ways.[135]

Urban Resources

With their higher concentration of nobles and wealthy merchants, cities were clearly the most active markets of the time, especially where luxury goods and services were concerned. It was there that one would encounter demand for the most elaborate handmade articles and exotic or rare goods. Court societies, which included those analyzed here, fostered competitive behavior when it came to sumptuary expenses.

Various economic factors during the seventeenth century affected the noble estates, including how agricultural land rents were assessed and collected and who benefited from that income. As the nobility grew in number and as state bureaucracies expanded, those who claimed to be part of the elite increased. Competition for public resources meant that the great seventeenth-century families grew less wealthy than their ancestors a century earlier.[136] As their wealth was rescaled, the index of distributive inequality decreased, as we have seen, and the purchasing power of salaried employees increased. The loss of economic power of the very rich was therefore compensated with a new distribution of wealth, which affected a greater number of social strata. More individuals could acquire luxury goods, thus increasing demand and stimulating production. In effect, the inventories that have been collected and analyzed show a growth in the quantity and variety of domestic goods, even for people of modest means.

Whether luxury consumption could exert a dynamic role for the economy in general was a subject of some controversy. The mercantilist outlook of many governments tended to condemn conspicuous consumption, blaming it for the ruin of families and even sovereign states because it drained gold and silver currencies from their coffers to those of countries producing luxury goods. In this group we find eastern countries (from Turkey and Egypt to India and China) that continued to absorb a considerable part of the wealth produced in Europe and (even) America. During the seventeenth century, many Italian cities became tributaries to the production and commercial initiatives of northern Europe.[137] Rome, which did not have a tradition of manufacturing, imported manufactured goods and workers from other Italian states and from countries beyond the Alps. The sumptuary laws that were passed on several occasions in Rome, Florence, Bologna, and Venice attempted to prevent their subjects' excess consumerism by limiting the display of gold, pearls, embroidered trimmings, and other precious materials or symbolic goods.[138] This did not discourage consumers, and especially female consumers, as the moralists complained. Merchants and artisans were, however, of the opposite opinion and disapproved of the politics of austerity, which occasionally was adopted by a few of the more ascetic and rigorist popes.[139]

What is a luxury product? Anthropologists and sociologists question the distinction between necessary and superfluous goods by asserting that all consumption is "necessary" depending on the social imperatives of the group involved.[140] In the seventeenth century, a noble who did not live *more nobilium* would have compromised his noble status and threatened his title, just as a citizen of good reputation needed to respect the rules of social conduct and appearance if he wanted his status to be recognized.[141] A lawyer marked his station with his robe and hat, as we have seen; merchants and master artisans also dressed to distinguish themselves from their employees. Books such as Cesare Vecellio's *The Ancient and Modern Customs of All Parts of the World* (*Gli habiti antichi e moderni di tutte le parti del mondo*) of 1590 contain illustrations depicting the differences in clothing not only between cities and between nations but also between social classes and professions. They show how social identities were tied to their outward appearance. The structure and furnishing of a house, the number and quality of the servants employed, the possessions of public display such as carriages and horses were all, to some degree, codified by the social class to which one belonged, or aspired to belong.

Luxury items, therefore, were distinguished from ordinary objects not by some intrinsic quality or monetary value, but by a hierarchy of social uses and conventions.[142] At any rate, this was the conviction of those—whether as theologians or as jurists—who wrote about "fair prices."[143] Luxury items were those objects given symbolic value by those in a community who had the power and status to establish rules in this area.[144] In this way, luxury was clearly differentiated by social class, and since luxury for farmers was not the same thing as for merchants, so too luxury for the literati was not the same as for nobles.

Objects take their value from, and in turn give value to, other objects. Household goods, for instance, enhance each other in defining a domestic interior. Painters who represented interiors knew this well as they constructed settings according to the interrelationships among the objects portrayed. Something similar happens with the relationship between people and their possessions, where possessions define an objectified image of the owner. Thus, to give an impression of "mediocre" luxury, available to the "comfortable" (*comodi*) classes and in some cases even to the poor, it was important to possess not just a single luxury item, but rather a group of household furnishings that together conveyed an image of luxury without excessive costs. Some books, together with a few paintings, some natural curiosities, a few pieces of silverware, possibly some porcelain, a fan, or snuffbox would be enough to create an impression of wealth for someone who could not afford a master painting or an illuminated manuscript. The owners of such domestic spaces acquired a different social physiognomy when surrounded by such objects. With their merchants boasting international trade links, and with their artisans providing objects for every pocketbook and every social image, our five cities were able to satisfy the demands of every group locally and abroad.

That demand was, however, too weak to create an impersonal and self-regulated market, and being able to rely on a network of social relations was essential both for those who wanted to sell their goods or services and for those who wanted to buy them. A particularly precious asset was the web of urban social institutions that put one group in contact with others, sometimes from different socio-economic milieus, enabling relationships between people who would have otherwise remained foreign and distant. From this point of view, many confraternities turned out to be extremely important. At the Roman confraternity of S. Maria dell'Orto, for instance, foreign artisans and merchants (foreigners and out-of-towners were in the majority here) belonging to different guilds and living in various neighborhoods had an opportunity of forging acquaintances and friendships. Several members of the local nobility also belonged to the confraternity of S. Maria dell'Orto. This network of relationships could enable someone to find a suitable spouse for his son or daughter, or to find new work or a new business partner or a new employee, or to secure a loan, or to find a house or a vineyard to lease or rent.[145]

The hospital of S. Maria Nuova in Florence acted in more or less the same way: the houses and workshops that it owned were almost all rented out to people with ties to the hospital, whether they were employees, suppliers, or even creditors. The hospital could thus exchange the rents of its houses with the goods and services provided by their inhabitants.[146] As for Venice, weavers were eager to rent houses belonging to foreign ambassadors because they were often located near an area of intense commercial activity and were exempt from taxation; from their viewpoint, ambassadors thereby benefited from higher rents.[147]

Work, credit, and rent were, as we have said, fundamental components of the *pater familias'* economic calculations. An agency enabling him to extend his social network and, consequently, to increase his opportunities to access one or more of these crucial resources constituted an important advantage. But working for a powerful person, or renting from him (or her), or supplying his/her house with goods and provisions further facilitated things by offering access to the sort of protection that every good patron had to be willing to provide his clients, which included, for example, the possibility of finding refuge in his house when threatened by the police, or finding support during a conflict with a competitor, or having an authoritative recommendation before entering into contact with a new client, and so forth.[148] As the countless examples contained in this book show, this was of vital importance for those who lived off commissions, like painters.

Prestige and Social Climbing

How did painters in the seventeenth century respond to these socio-economic opportunities and obstacles? What level of wealth and social rank could they aspire to? Annual income is difficult to document even when there are payments for individual works or projects. For painters who were salaried by wealthy patrons, the problem does not seem to arise. Yet, even in those cases there remained a certain amount of uncertainty, because it is difficult to say if the artist really worked full-time for his patron. For those who were paid by the day, the problem of extrapolating annual income from daily wages is not easily overcome, because it requires sweeping assumptions regarding the number of days that a painter worked in any given year. We know from early eighteenth-century polemics that the number of religious holidays, when in theory work was forbidden, was very high and, furthermore, varied from place to place. The greater difficulty, however, concerns a realistic estimation of the number of days when the artist could find employment. According to Cipolla, it would have been difficult for a day laborer to find work on more than 200 days a year, and it is likely that many painters who were paid daily wages—the most precarious and lowly of payment methods—shared a life of underemployment with many of their laboring contemporaries. Like day laborers, day painters probably cobbled together different kinds of jobs in order to survive. In spite of this, by connecting data on an artist's prices and rate of production, the contributions to this book demonstrate how one can reasonably extrapolate monthly or even annual incomes. These hypothetical incomes, however, would not include related professional activities, family labor, or investment income. Usually this information is only partially available, if at all.

Aggregate incomes are not sufficient to establish a family's wealth or social status. Parts of an estate, especially the residence, its furnishings, and luxury goods, did not generate income, but were crucial both for a family's social standing and for the potential for social ascent in the future. For most families, the passage from living off earned income to living off investment income—that is, being a *rentier*—did not occur in just one generation. Many noble families started as merchants or financiers who eventually accumulated large fortunes and invested in high status careers or marriages for their children and grandchildren so that they could eventually buy prestigious public or ecclesiastic positions, acquire citizenship, and sometimes even qualify for and purchase noble status.[149]

Again, inquiries are frustrated by inadequate information. We know that some of the great seventeenth century painters succeeded in accumulating large estates. Artists working in Rome were by far the richest: at his death, Pietro da Cortona left behind an estate worth more than 100,000 scudi, while Loth, who seems to have been by far the richest painter working in Venice, accumulated just 32,000 ducats.[150] All the other estates of known value were worth much less: in Rome, Romanelli's totaled around 50,000 scudi, Maratta's and Gaulli's 40,000, and those of Dughet, Poussin, Rosa, and Claude were substantially less, between 10,000 and 25,000 scudi. In Venice, other than Loth, only Nicola Grassi, with 9,000 ducats, approached those amounts. These are not negligible sums, especially since they belonged to a single individual, not a whole family, and in this sense they were comparable to personal estates acquired by high-ranking clergymen. Cardinal Fabrizio Spada, for example, left an inheritance of "just" 92,251 scudi; and Cardinal Camillo Cybo, who came from a family of ruling princes, expected still more. He remarked that he could live well on an annual income of 7,000 to 8,000 scudi, in theory the equivalent of 150,000 scudi in capital, but that large sum always remained elusive.[151]

Dowries are a useful measure of a family's wealth and status, both of the bride's and groom's. Two sisters might receive different dowries if, for example, one was destined for a hypergamic marriage and the other was not. In the absence of anything better, however, even a unique unit like a dowry can be a useful measure of comparison. Here then we find that Cortona's entire estate of 100,000 scudi was equal to the dowry of one of the richest Roman heiresses, Princess Olimpia Giustiniani, who married Maffeo Barberini in 1653, while Claude's 10,000 scudi estate was decidedly more than the 8,000 scudi that the Mellini family (who belonged to a mid-ranking noble family) offered to the young Marquis Lante.[152] Merchants' daughters received much less, with 2,000 to 3,000 scudi considered to be a relatively high amount. The dowries of Neapolitan painters were markedly less, and none was nearly as high as what Ribera exceptionally managed to give to his daughter.[153]

Another way of understanding a painter's social status is through expenses, consumption, and standard of living rather than accumulated capital. Consumption was tied to the demands of a given social milieu more than any financial imperative. Of those painters who could afford a noble lifestyle, Cortona lived in a four-story palace with the same suite configuration of antechambers as noble residences; Maratta spent much time like an aristocrat, living "in happy idleness" in his villa in Genzano, and Ribera and Albani also had expensive suburban villas. Guercino's residence in Bologna was furnished with pomp worthy of a prince.[154] Albani owned an immense library in Bologna.[155] Lanfranco bought a vineyard with a casino outside of Porta S. Pancrazio and decorated it with statues, fountains, and plays of water, thus gaining the admiration of Cassiano dal Pozzo.[156] Tiarini acquired a private chapel in the church of S. Procolo, Bologna.[157] Some, like Reni or Brandi, also had a carriage—the highest mark of distinction—and "acted like a nobleman or a knight" by carrying a sword or, better yet, having a page carry it for him, and by preparing sumptuous banquets for the gentlemen of the court.[158] Van Dyck spent at least 30 scudi a day during his stay in Rome to keep a horse and carriage, and to host banquets with musical accompaniment. He also left a lasting impression by going around the city in court dress with a plumed hat and two gold chains, and by keeping a formation of servants around in baronial style.[159]

Other painters, even if they could afford it, were happy with more moderate lifestyles. In Rome, Poussin lived modestly without servants, while in Bologna Gessi shared with his apprentices a small residence of five rooms on two floors.[160] For most artists, nevertheless, this more modest lifestyle was not the result of a choice: their earnings were simply not enough to provide better.

The ostentation of wealthy artists cannot be reduced to mere emulation of aristocratic behavior or, at least, was not limited to that. It can be traced back to the social imperatives from which ostentatious living derived. In the case of seventeenth-century Italy, this context involved a debate over "true nobility." Those who had already attained, usually through inheritance, positions of social and political superiority argued that the closed ranks of nobility were historically justified, citing the value of bloodlines and the inherited nature of aristocratic characteristics. Others argued, not without self-interest on their part, that authentic nobility was a personal virtue proven by demonstrated merits rather than by an accident of birth.[161] True nobility, they argued, came from recognized achievements and prestige earned by their "excellence" in artistic, scholarly, or other fields. If earned in this way, they should be entitled to express their standing in a material fashion. Pascoli even asserted that painters had the *duty* to live nobly in order to manifest the nobility of their art publicly.[162] Men of letters took up analogous positions. In his biography of Giambattista Marino, the Venetian nobleman and founder of the Accademia degli Incogniti, Giovan Francesco Loredano, theorized it in this way: "an exemplary, satisfied glorification of a poet who takes his revenge on the world and becomes great, with all the requisite and brilliant excess of great men."[163]

Because personal "virtue" was tied to an artist's or poet's individual qualities, it was difficult to transfer the resulting social distinction to one's heirs. None of our painters managed to consolidate his position sufficiently to establish a noble lineage for his children or grandchildren.[164] Even Bernini did not succeed at this task, despite being the richest and most acclaimed of all. Yet, as Baldinucci explains, his burial took place "with the pomp suitable to the man's merit and to the opportunities and love of his sons," making a clear reference to Bernini's 400,000 scudi estate.[165]

A few decades earlier, in 1631, Paolo Spada, a collector of papal taxes who had recently immigrated from Romagna, also left an estate of 300,000 to 400,000 scudi. His strategy regarding his children's careers had been more or less the same as Bernini's: two sons took up ecclesiastical careers—one eventually become a cardinal—and the other two married with the expectation that they would perpetuate the family line. The real jump in status came with the second generation when, thanks to the cardinal, a grandson of Paolo Spada managed to marry the heiress of a noble Roman family, whose modest dowry included the invaluable title of *marchese* and the right of investiture over Castel Viscardo.[166]

Bernini's children followed more or less the same path. His firstborn daughter Angelica married a count, and several of her sisters became nuns. His firstborn son Pietro Filippo became a canon at S. Maria Maggiore and entered into the prelature, but his career stalled at the mid-level ranks. Finally, Paolo Valentino, heir to the family name, married into the noble Maccarani family without, however, gaining an inheritable title. Even with testamentary bonds, the creation of a trust, and an admonishment to his children that they should continue to live together and not divide the estate, the second generation Bernini did not managed to capitalize on their sizeable inheritance by acquiring a *signoria* or a cardinal's hat and obtaining a noble title. Gian Lorenzo's death returned them to obscurity.[167]

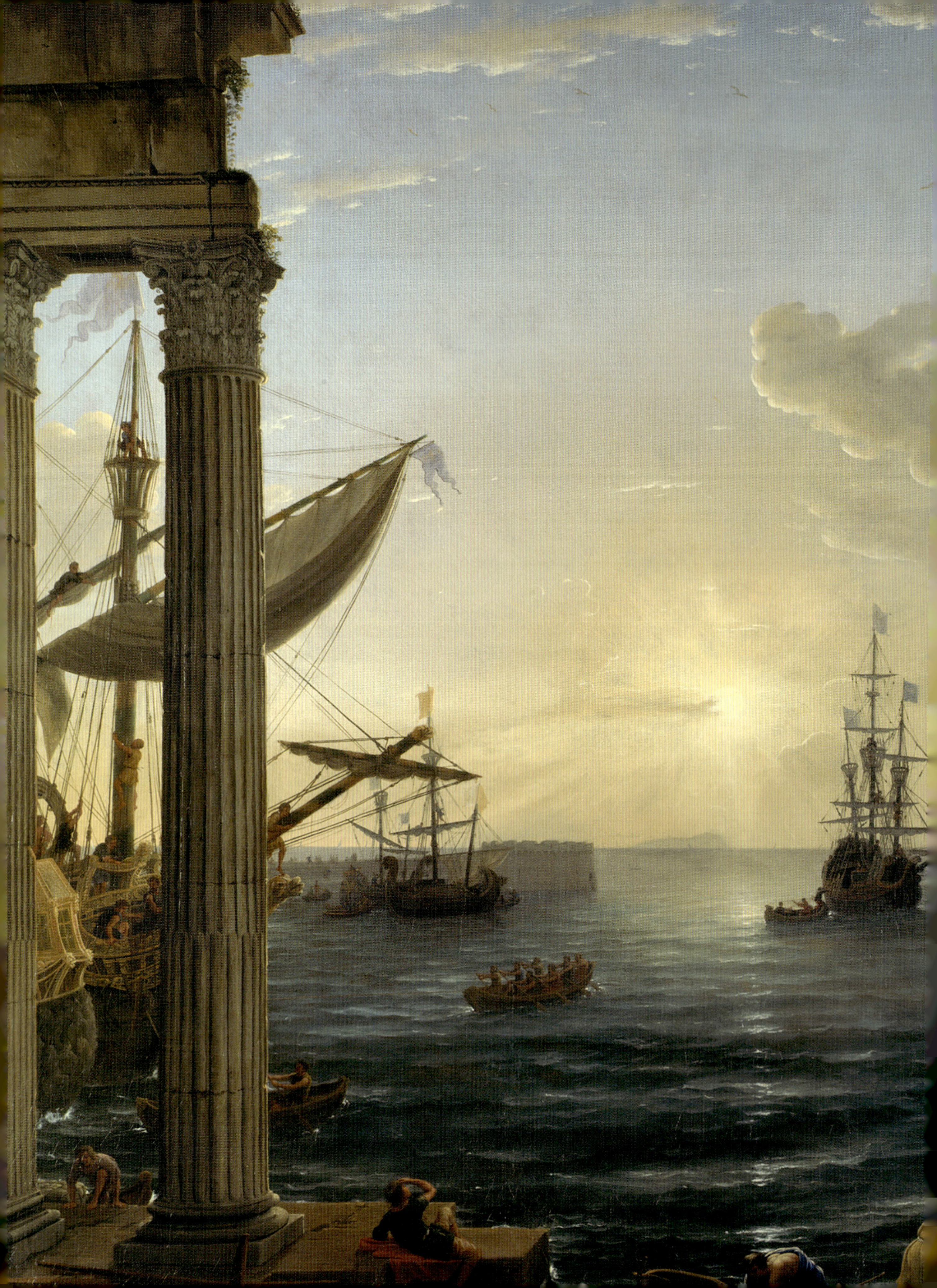

7

The Painting Industry in Early Modern Italy

RICHARD A. GOLDTHWAITE

Why should an economic historian take any interest at all in painting as an economic activity? Painters were a miniscule part of the workforce, rarely approaching as much as 1.5 per 1,000 inhabitants—about 0.5 percent of all adult males—in any city in the seventeenth century, even in Rome, and most of them earned no more than skilled craftsmen.[1] For all the fame many of them enjoyed, then and now, and for all the presence their work still has in Italian cities and in the world's museums, their production counted for hardly anything in the total gross national product of Italy at the time. It is not surprising, therefore, that no economic historian has written about Italian painters or paintings during the period of the industry's maximum splendor, extending from the Renaissance to the baroque. Art historians could presumably profit from the study of how much money patrons spent for painting, how the art market functioned, how much painting cost, and how much painters earned—all those subjects addressed in the essays in this book—for the economic circumstances in which painters worked can have considerable importance for the understanding of their mode of production and even the nature of their art. Art historians, however, have not shown much interest in the subject, except for those who study Florentine painting (although even they hardly go much further than the early sixteenth century) and a few others who recently have undertaken research on seventeenth-century Rome, notably Richard Spear (whose work has culminated in this collection of studies) and several younger scholars studying dealers. Economic historians, in any event, would presumably find research into these matters a waste of time, of purely antiquarian interest, for, in the end, what importance would generalizations about such a remote corner of the marketplace have for understanding anything relevant to the overall performance of the economy?

Divers Perspectives and Misdirected Initiatives

The hypothesis that painting was of no importance as an economic activity in baroque Italy, presented here by fiat at the outset of this essay can be rendered more persuasive by putting it into perspective. One approach is to take a comparative point of view, looking at another place where, in fact, the subject has been well studied: the Low Countries. The art markets at Bruges in the fifteenth century, at Antwerp in the sixteenth century, and in Holland generally in the seventeenth century have been exhaustively studied not only by art historians but also by historians, economic historians, and even economists. In the seventeenth century these industries included artists of the rank of Rubens, Rembrandt, and Vermeer, and the market for quality products extended more widely throughout the population

Facing page: detail of Fig. 25

than in Italy. Production, prices, and earnings of the Dutch industry in particular have been subjected to refined economic analysis. Jan de Vries and Ad van der Woude, in their recent survey of the Dutch economy in its golden age, have no hesitation in categorizing painting as "a true industry" that underwent both product and process innovation in the full sense of those terms of analysis. Yet these scholars—both of whom have, in fact, written about painting elsewhere—dedicate no more than one page to the subject in a book that is over 700 pages long, and no one painter is ever named.[2] They mention the industry only because they had to take stock of the considerable scholarly work done on it, and this material served their purposes because they could use the results of that research to support some of their generalizations about the "first modern economy"; but otherwise they would never have remarked the subject. Taken on its own and put into the context of the overall economy, painting was of no importance whatsoever.

We come to the same conclusion about painting in Italy if the subject is put into a perspective taken from a comparison with another art form: architecture. Architecture is by far the most expensive kind of art; yet notwithstanding its extraordinary development in Renaissance and baroque Italy, the resources that were poured into building activity contributed hardly anything to the general course of the economy, even at the local level. In quattrocento Florence the owner of a new, or rebuilt, palace paid out anywhere between 2,500 and 5,000 florins in construction costs, an amount close to the 3,000-or-so florins that a wool firm paid out annually for wages in the local labor market. Considering that the number of new and rebuilt palaces reached about 100 in the course of the fifteenth century, and that wool shops numbered well over 100 at any one time, it takes no calculating skills to conclude that palace-building contributed little to the flow of money into the local marketplace. The 30,000 florins the Strozzi paid out over a 15-year period at the end of the century to build what was the city's most expensive palace of the century, the largest by far and faced on three sides by stone, had no more impact on the flow of money into the local market than did a single wool shop. What the cathedral works spent annually at the beginning of the century to construct Brunelleschi's famed cupola had no greater an impact on the economy. The entire cost of erecting the cathedral over almost one-and-a-half centuries, in fact, probably did not exceed by far the value of the patrimony that the city's wealthiest citizen reported in his 1427 tax declaration of assets (*catasto*), which amounted to less than 2 percent of the entire wealth of the city as reported in that document.

A stronger case for the impact of resources poured into prestige architecture can be made for baroque Rome, another moment famed for its boom in architecture. The 1,200,000 scudi Paul V spent for four of the largest projects over his 16-year pontificate (1605–21), consuming about 3 percent of the papacy's total income, are equivalent, in wages, to an annual input into the economy of about 1,500 man-years of unskilled labor out of a population of around 20,000–25,000 households, enough to have a perceptible impact on the local economy. Very little of the money paid out for construction costs, however, ended up in the hands of people who, by any stretch of the imagination, can be labeled as artists. In any event, the cost of painting, even for the most extensive fresco cycles cited in this volume, pales to insignificance in comparison with these construction costs.

If our perspective on painting is broadened beyond this comparison of it with the most expensive of the arts—architecture—to take in instead all the visual arts together, we can finally bring a certain historiographical tradition to bear on our view of the subject, for this wider context has caught the attention of historians. And how could it not, since the visual arts and luxury crafts are so prominent in the life and culture of Italy from the fifteenth to the seventeenth centuries and still so highly visible today in the artistic patrimony generated during those centuries? One current in this historiographical tradition, however, associates the flourishing of the arts with economic decline. It goes back to the oft-cited notion (subsequently bloated into a "thesis") of Roberto Lopez about "hard times and investment in culture" (1953): the arts prospered in the Renaissance because they were an alternative outlet for wealth once the economy faltered and reinvestment of earnings discouraged. Within the economic sphere this idea received a kind of theoretical formulation by the economist John Hicks in his *Theory of Economic History* (1969): the point at which economic expansion is arrested may, in fact, be "a wonderful moment," releasing not only resources but also redirecting intellectual vigor from business to culture, as happened in fifth-century Athens and Renaissance Italy.

The economic historian Ruggiero Romano, staying within the sphere of the Italian economy of the early modern period, took the argument one step further by reformulating the investment-consumption link as consumption-versus-investment, and concluded that the expenditures for the arts, by deflecting resources from investment to wasteful consumption, put "a brake" on the economy and hence is a major explanation for the economic decline of Italy.[3] The logic linking this formula to the so-called Lopez thesis brings us full circle: economic decline released resources for the arts, and the use of those resources for the arts assured the further decline of the economy. Social historians have put their own spin on this thesis by bringing one of their favorite dynamics into play: the transformation of entrepreneurs into *rentiers*, of capitalists into aristocrats, and "the return to the land," thereby providing an appropriate social context for the emergence of "patronage," a concept so dear to art historians. The basic economic assumption, however, is that the arts, however much may have been spent for them, are a wasteful use of resources because artistic production does not generate further economic activity.

So we return to our original proposition, now reinforced by historiographical tradition and a certain economic logic: why study the economics of the arts in general, let alone any one of them, such as, for instance, painting? The prospect of linking economics and art, however, has recently taken on considerable glamour of its own, apart from any larger issues about the state of the Italian economy. What has caught historians' attention is the art market. Over the last dozen years or so, there have been many international conferences on the subject, organized by both art historians and historians, some resulting in the publication of their proceedings. This interest in the art market has taken two directions. On the one hand, art historians, ever anxious to put the subject they study in a wider context, have concentrated on economic aspects of the artist's life: workshop, production, prices, earnings. The focus has been mostly on Renaissance Florence, since there is a long bibliography to build on and extensive archival resources to be exploited; but the studies in this volume represent the first serious effort to extend research of this kind beyond Florence and beyond the fifteenth century. On the other hand, some art historians have widened the view of the art market, casting their net to take in all "art." They thereby extend the discussion well beyond the traditional "fine arts"—painting, sculpture, architecture—to include all kinds of luxury objects; and since luxury itself lacks definition, they soon find themselves embracing all arts and crafts and even material culture in general. This trajectory from art to the arts to the arts-and-crafts to material culture, now marking a major trend in Italian historical studies, has drawn attention almost exclusively to the demand side of "the art market," to the culture of consumption, and to consumerism.

Economic historians, too, have been much aroused by the wide-ranging explorations into "the art market," one of the clearest manifestations of this being the organization of a week-long international conference on the subject sponsored in 2001 by the Istituto Datini at Prato, the pre-eminent organization dedicated to the economic history of Europe from the late Middle Ages to the eighteenth century. The economic historians who have taken this path, however, have for the most part lost the orienting direction of their specific discipline. In following their colleagues to the demand side, they find themselves in realms of human behavior where the tools of economic analysis have been little honed, and they slide into social and cultural history. They treat the buyer of these products under the rubric of "patron," a loaded term that removes him or her from the normal operations of the market. Attempts have been made to subject "patronage" to economic analysis by assessing art for its value as symbolic capital, but this takes the discussion out of the realm of economics strictly speaking and into that of sociology and culture.[4]

In addition to this methodological problem, the very object of these studies on the demand side of the art market remains elusive, for no one has isolated a common quality of the divers objects categorized as "art" and subjected that to economic analysis. Economist do this in their analysis of the contemporary art market, but they usually define their subject as institutions that explicitly identify themselves as having something to do with art—art schools, art fairs, government art programs, art museums, art galleries, auction houses, foundations, etc.—a criterion that does not work for the earlier period inasmuch as the Italian word *arte* did not distinguish between what we call art and ordinary skills. Economists can study the prices for "art" that emerge from the activities of these institutions, especially, of course, auction houses and galleries; but they rarely look at the supply side of the market to study the production of "art" objects, where they would have to confront the diversity of those objects. In any event, the current interests of economists in the art market, as well as their recent exploration into behavior economics, which does in fact take the discipline to the demand side, have not yet spilled over into the discipline of economic history, certainly not that corner of the discipline dedicated to the study of Italy from the fourteenth to the seventeenth centuries, when the place, more than any other, was the European center for the production of painting, sculpture, and architecture.

Nevertheless, once the path was opened that proceeded from "the art market" to material culture and on to new consumer behavior—whether one wants to tag this as "consumerism" or not—economic historians might be expected to follow along, taking up those aspects of the subject that most cry out for economic analysis: producers, production, and the market. The question remains, however—to return to the opening query—why should they focus on such a miniscule part of the scene as painting? Nothing in this brief historiographical overview suggests that there is a missed opportunity in the failure to explore the subject—except, of course, the lack of any empirical study to put a bit of substance on the proposition, if for no other reason than to substantiate it. That is what this essay proposes to do, albeit to a somewhat different end.

Growth and Development of the Industry

Panel painting first emerges as a distinct identifiable artisan activity, significant for the quality if not the quantity of output, in several Italian cities during the fourteenth and fifteenth centuries; and subsequently, down through the seventeenth century, the production of painting underwent a most remarkable—indeed unique—transformation: demand shot up, painters introduced new techniques in response to this demand, the market where their products were traded became considerably more articulated in its structure and functioned more efficiently, the producer and his product gained considerable cultural status, and the client, too, gained status through the possession of these products. So for the economic historian the question arises, how did all this play out in the marketplace? That is, did these developments lead to improved productivity? Did they impinge on prices, and, if so, was it to the benefit of both the buyer and the seller? And, finally, what does all this tell us about the economy in general?

Thanks to the studies collected in this volume, which concentrate on the seventeenth century, we now have a much clearer view of the impressive growth and development this industry had undergone by that time. To measure the change in the industry (and throughout we shall use this term from the economist's jargon to simplify the language in discussing the overall productive, profit-making enterprise of painters), the polarities will be, on the one hand, fifteenth-century Florence and, on the other, the composite view of the seventeenth century that emerges from these studies of five cities—Rome, Naples, Bologna, Florence, and Venice. The industry in fifteenth-century Florence is exceptionally well documented and has been extensively studied; hence, we have a solid historiographical base for making comparisons through time. The pitting of Florence for the earlier period against the five cities for the later period offers in itself an index to the growth of the industry, for in the fifteenth century no other city, not even Venice, had such a vigorous market for painting and a local industry to sustain it, whereas in the seventeenth century the Florentine industry lagged far behind that of each of the four other cities (and Genoa, one of the most vigorous markets for painting at the time, could be added to this list).

Demand

FUNCTIONAL, DEMOGRAPHIC, AND ECONOMIC COMPONENTS

Growth of the Italian industry resulted from increased demand for more pictures in both religious and domestic spaces. The proliferation of private chapels entailed the furnishing of them with the complete liturgical apparatus, including an altarpiece and perhaps frescoes. This private demand, in fact, went hand in hand with an increase in the construction of new churches to accommodate both the late medieval reform movements that split off from some of the traditional orders and the creation of the new orders that arose out of the Counter-Reformation movement. Moreover, pictures came to serve a new function in the private home as devotional and decorative (and even collectible) objects. This demand for them grew with the radical transformation of the home of the rich from a place subdivided into a few sparsely furnished multifunctional spaces to one broken up into a much more articulated complex of rooms with specific functions—for dining, for sleeping, for entertaining, for praying—each with its appropriate furnishings, including pictures not to mention also what Vincenzo Scamozzi called, in 1616, "quell genere di fabriche che si dicono Gallerie" for the exclusive display of pictures and other works of art.

A contributing dynamic to consumption of this kind arose from the growth of population in urban markets and at the same time from an increase in disposable wealth, both phenomena of extraordinary dimensions. The initial demand for painting among the general population in the second half of the fourteenth century was, in fact, a function, at least in part, of the redistribution of wealth at the time of the Black Death and the subsequent recovery of the population, even though many cities, like Florence, were not to reach pre-plague levels until the nineteenth century. From the mid-fifteenth to the early seventeenth centuries the population of Florence increased by 50 percent, that of Venice by somewhat more, in Bologna it doubled, in Rome it tripled (not counting the enormous influx of pilgrims and tourists, whose presence probably increased the population by one-quarter at any one time), and in Naples—the fastest growing city in Europe—the population grew by almost nine times. The latter two cites were capitals of newly consolidated states, Naples becoming the residence of the territorial nobility and Rome attracting rich families from all over Italy who aspired to a place in the papal establishment. Population growth of these dimensions had a major impact on the consumer market. Although deadly plague hit all these cities early in the seventeenth century, the population rebounded almost immediately (in contrast to the situation after the Black Death) to reach a level at the end of the century where it had been at the beginning—in Rome it reached a level more than one-third higher. In fact, the momentary redistribution of wealth resulting from the plague was in itself a major stimulus to renewed demand.

If there were more people in the marketplace, there was also more wealth circulating among them, for demographic change was complemented by ever greater capital accumulation, notwithstanding Italy's receding position in a European economy then undergoing rapid globalization. Greater disposable wealth manifested itself in the lower cost of money, that is a falling interest rate. Given the structure of Italian society, a disproportionate share of this wealth ended up in the hands of the rich, who became much richer in the course of the fifteenth and sixteenth centuries. For their palace completed at the beginning of the sixteenth century, the heirs of Filippo Strozzi paid out 30,000 florins, whereas 75 years earlier, in the 1427 *catasto*, only five men had a net taxable wealth higher than that figure. A few years later, in 1528, the Venetian ambassador estimated that there were 50 Florentines worth over 50,000 florins; and toward the end of the century the Riccardi, not yet at the height of their fortune, had an income alone of almost 25,000 scudi. By this time, the richest merchants in Rome and Milan were earning twice this amount. It has been estimated that the elite in Genoa, the most important international banking center in Italy at the time, saw their estates grow by four times from the mid-sixteenth century through the first quarter of the seventeenth century, and that in 1624 560 of the city's nobles had an average taxable wealth of 50,000 scudi. A few merchants in contemporary Venice could pay the fee of 60,000 ducats to be admitted to the nobility. By the seventeenth century, the richest Italians had estates with values that went into seven figures, a level of wealth unimaginable two centuries earlier by even the most prosperous merchant bankers.[5]

Inasmuch as the increased demand for luxury goods and services by these richer people resulted in a redistribution of some of this wealth into the hands of artisans who supplied the market with these things, some highly qualified artisans—including some painters—were able to improve their earnings over other workers. What we might call a middling class emerged, however small it was, that reinforced the demand of the rich for services and better quality goods. The clearest evidence that more people in the middling classes had greater disposable income is the appearance of deposit institutions, such as the Monti di Pietà, welfare organizations, and public banks, for these institutions owed their existence to the service they provided as outlets for the savings of people of modest means, a new function in the credit market that private banks were not prepared to perform.[6] These same people also entered the consumer market. A tax census made in Florence in 1552 reveals that 42 percent of households had at least one servant. And they also bought more durable goods, including pictures. In a letter to Benedetto Varchi, Vasari observed that there was not a shoemaker's house in Florence without a Flemish painting. In Venice the number of households with 10 pictures increased four times in the second half of the sixteenth century, 1,000 households sampled in seventeenth-century Bologna had 10 or more pictures, and 75 middle-class households sampled in contemporary Rome had an average of 23.5 pictures. Two centuries earlier in Florence it would be difficult to find even a wealthy household with as many as 10 pictures. The trickling down of the increased private wealth in the hands of the rich clearly stimulated consumption beyond their ranks, although this multiplier effect of consumer spending did not reach the "revolutionary" stage where it arrived in eighteenth-century England.

CULTURAL COMPONENTS

Paintings are just one index of increased consumer spending, and hardly the most important. Yet two new dynamics came into play on the demand side in the market for pictures that no other artisan industry enjoyed and that therefore merit singling out for closer observation: the mounting prestige of art and the collecting of art objects, especially pictures—both obviously interrelated cultural phenomena, the latter being, in part, one measure of the impact of the former on the market.

The emergence of the cultural prestige of art and the artist is one of the most notable phenomena that define "the Renaissance." The development has been well studied: it goes back to the extraordinary fame Giotto enjoyed even in his own time, the subsequent diffusion of his fame through all ranks of Florentine society, and its enlargement to incorporate the painters and sculptors who followed him. This tradition of praise of its artists came to be a defining quality of the city; and by the sixteenth century its strength was such that Cosimo I, the first duke (and later grand duke) of Tuscany, sought to manipulate the notion of Florence as a city of art, especially exploiting the myth of the patronage of his Medici ancestors in the previous century, as a historical justification for the establishment of the family now as ruler of the city. That a new prince could utilize such a myth to a political end marks how much cultural status art and artists had gained by this time also outside of Florence, for Cosimo directed this propaganda in part to the community of rulers into which he had gained entrance. And in the seventeenth century the Medici continued to define their identity through the collecting and patronage of art. This cultural phenomenon reached canonical form in the *Lives* of Vasari; he presents that history as the story of the progress of painting, sculpture, and architecture culminating in his own time, thereby taking the first step toward separating out what have become the fine arts from ordinary crafts. The very word *progresso* was used by Vincenzo Borghini in a letter of 1563 in which he sought to convince Cosimo I of the great benefit the newly formed Accademia del Disegno would bring to the city, to the state, and "even to the entire world."[7]

Thus, painting and the painter assumed a distinct cultural identity with a historical dimension that raised both above other artisan categories. The notion of the "old master" emerged with the growing posthumous fame of some sixteenth-century artists: Raphael, Andrea del Sarto, Correggio, Titian, and a few others (Mantegna being the only painter from the preceding century). Within just a few years after the death of some of these artists, princes were forcibly seizing their more famous pictures from the religious institutions for which they were originally executed, but in the course of the century the ever-growing demand for the work of these deceased artists gave rise to a secondary market with its more systematic mechanisms for the spoliation of the country's churches.

The major manifestation of the status of painting on the demand side of the art market is the appearance of the picture collection, a phenomenon hardly limited to princely circles. In Florence the Botti had 120 paintings and engravings in 1588; Jacopo Corsi owned 70 pictures at the time of his death in 1602, and the number more than doubled by the time of his brother Bardo's death in 1625. The heirs of Bernardo Vecchietti found 92 paintings on the walls of his famous villa "Il riposo"; the Riccardi had 159 pictures in 1612; and the 1626 inventory of Piero Guicciardini lists 230 paintings. Giovan Carlo Doria in Genoa had 431 pictures in 1617 and 691 in 1621. In Venice the merchant Bartolomeo Dafin had 114 pictures on his death in 1650; the collection of the merchant Francesco Bergonzi had over 100 pictures when it was inventoried (after his death) in 1670, and by 1704 Bergonzi's son Giorgio had increased the collection to 300 pictures.[8] It is not always easy to distinguish a collection from the totality of all the pictures that one might find in a household. Beginning in the sixteenth century, however, some people began assembling pictures according to specific criteria—Niccolò Gaddi in Florence collected drawings, Duke Vincenzo I Gonzaga portraits of famous women, Cardinal Leopoldo de' Medici artists' self-portraits—and not just as decorative objects to be scattered about the house; these pictures might be displayed in a room or gallery set apart just for that purpose. A collection thus became a vehicle for the personal expression of the taste of its owner, and in Rome collectors often put their pictures on display in public exhibitions.

The consciousness with which a collector assembled his collection might surface not just in the opening of a gallery but also in his concern that it be properly inventoried. In his testament the Genoese Gio Vincenzo Imperiale mentioned an inventory that he himself had drawn up in 1648; and in 1694, on the death of another Genoese, Gio Francesco Brignole Sale, his heirs found an inventory of his pictures, along with their value, that he also had made in his own hand. Some collectors made testamentary provisions for the eventual disposition of their collections as a particular kind of property that should be kept together after their death. The Venetian Gabriele Vendramin (d. 1552) requested that his collection not be sold unless there was urgent need, and then not for 15 years after his death; and in his testament of 1664 another Venetian, Cristoforo Orsetti, asked for an inventory of his pictures and requested that they be sold only as a whole. The Genoese banker Ottavio Costa (d. 1639) stipulated in his testament that his collection in Rome (and he specifically refers to works of Caravaggio and Guido Reni) was to be sent to his native town, Albenga, to remain there in perpetuity as the property of his family, never to be alienated.[9]

The growing interest in collecting pictures also manifested itself in the book Giulio Mancini wrote ca. 1620 to instruct the collector on matters of connoisseurship, attribution, identification of forgeries, and display of pictures (although it was not published until the twentieth century). Collecting also aroused concern about conservation and restoration of pictures. In Naples the painter-dealer Giacomo de Castro (d. ca. 1687) gained something of a reputation as a restorer of old paintings and had an official position to this effect in a local church.[10] This new consciousness resulted in the appointment both at the Vatican and at the doge's palace in Venice of a salaried official to oversee the care of pictures.

Buying and selling in this market raised the prospect that a painter's work might be more valuable after his death and led to the possibility that a collection—in other words, art—represented a conscious investment. Already in the middle of the sixteenth century, the aforementioned Venetian Gabriele Vendramin, on dictating his last will and testament, recognized the potential monetary value of his collection. Anticipating criticism from his heirs that he had spent too much for his pictures, he admits that they had cost hundreds of ducats, as can be seen from his account books; but then he adds that since they could be sold for much more than he had paid out, his heirs, far from being deprived of even a ducat as a result of his acquisitions, could actually realize a profit from them.[11] In the charged atmosphere created by the hurried efforts of a few English nobles to put together a collection, the duke of Buckingham's agent in Italy advised his employer that the value of his pictures would rise threefold by the time of his death, and he mused over the pleasure it would give the duke to live for another century so he could scoff at those who were criticizing him for spending money for these things.[12] In his essay Philip Sohm shows how this theme was played in Venice, where, on the one hand, Marco Boschini used it to convince collectors to buy contemporary paintings and where, on the other hand, Carlo Ridolfi commiserated with living artists who earn little knowing that prices of their work might well rise after their death. The consequent possibility of speculation is another dimension in the growth of this secondary market for pictures.

The demand for pictures extended beyond the confines of local markets to take in much of Italy, and the increasing international traffic in these goods heightened awareness also of what might be called the national cultural patrimony. Today we know how added cultural value can reach the point where a picture is assessed as an inalienable cultural property of a state and thereby removed altogether from the reach of collectors in the international market. This happened for the first time in Florence, a city famed for its old masters already in the sixteenth century. There legislation in 1602 outlawed the export of the work of 18 painters, including some non-Florentines (and the legislation laid down procedures for allowing artists themselves, through their academy, to add others to the list). In 1616 the Florentine agent of the Gonzaga in Mantua reported that since this export restriction blocking foreigners from buying pictures reduced competition, it would be easier to find pictures for sale (although he does not say whether he thought it possible to circumvent the export restrictions).[13] No other legislation like this appeared in Europe until the eighteenth century, but elsewhere in seventeenth-century Italy a rising consciousness of art as part of the local patrimony occasionally led to calls for protection from foreign buyers. In Mantua in the late 1620s, public criticism arose in reaction to the foreigners who were buying large chunks of the Gonzaga collections, and the chief merchant arranging the sales was well aware of it. In Venice a generation later, Marco Boschini, in the first *vento* of his *La carta del navegar pitoresco*, lamented the excessive sale of works of art of his city to foreigners; and concern for protecting the city's patrimony gave rise to sporadic, albeit limited and ineffective, legislation. In 1703 Clement XI attempted to block the transfer of a group of Maratta's drawings to England by offering 5,000 scudi for them in the hope, ultimately in vain, of keeping such "rare items" in Rome.[14]

In short, in the seventeenth century the demand side of the market for painting was very different from what it had been two centuries earlier. The demand for art in the domestic setting had risen exponentially, and the collecting of pictures gave a particular impetus to this demand and brought into existence a new, secondary market that widened to include pictures by some deceased painters. Moreover, once aroused, the collecting instinct tends to generate its own internal forces, of the kind economists would recognize at work in the contemporary market, that further augment demand: the desire, informed by greater knowledge, continually to redefine and to complete the collection ("rational dependence"), the use of the collection as a manifestation of status ("signaling"), and the competitive instinct directed against other collectors. In this way, through a "demonstration effect," the collection becomes part of a new consumption model.

Through this new model the cultural status gained by these products and their producers impinged on the demand for goods that now brought a certain prestige also to their owners. This "discovery of painting," a notable cultural phenomenon in Renaissance Italy (which perhaps has its first manifestation in the pretentious intellectual satisfaction Petrarch took in the Giotto he owned), is surely worth considering also for its social implications in the way it has recently been studied for eighteenth-century England.[15] Modern painting, in short, took its place alongside the older tradition of collecting classical antiquities, a development that no other artisan industry experienced, at least not to the same extent. The discovery of modern painting, however, unlike the discovery of ancient art, involved also the producers. We thus find ourselves moving into a market in which a particular producer enjoyed not only increased demand for his products but a considerable enhancement of his cultural status. And the question that should naturally attract the economic historian is how this cultural status impinged on the producer's economic status, a problem that in and of itself merits attention for what it might tell us about market behavior in general, quite apart from how we evaluate the presence of that particular activity in the overall performance of the economy. Here is a missed opportunity in the economic historiography of Italy outlined at the opening of this essay. In the following discussion the painting industry will be subjected to economic inspection to see how it responded to this new demand for its products. It will focus on improved production techniques, on infrastructural refinement of the market, and on the consequent economic benefits for the producer, now also fortified with a new cultural status.

Production

Already in the second half of the fourteenth century testaments document the demand for relatively inexpensive devotional pictures, and art historians have noted how painters responded to an expanding market for their products. Painters began working more on their own and less in collaboration on the kind of large prestigious projects that characterize the first chapter in the history of Italian painting, the early Trecento. As a result workshops increased in number, they were smaller in size, and they appeared outside the large centers—for instance, at Borgo Sansepolcro, a town with a population of only about 4,000, where local painters were sufficiently active executing major tabernacles, altarpieces, murals, and other miscellaneous work to create a working environment that could nourish the early formation of Piero della Francesca. On the one hand, as H. W. van Os has argued, this changed situation in workshops favored innovation, with the result that their products reveal greater diversity if also less sophistication in the overall pluralism of styles that emerged.[16] On the other hand, lesser painters resorted to the mechanical and uniform execution of figures in order to cut costs. In the course of the fifteenth century, painters continued to improve the efficiency with which they produced paintings by introducing new techniques and reorganizing the production process. By the end of the century, Cennino Cennini's treatise on painting written at the beginning of the century was already out of date. Continuing along this path in response to ever-increasing demand, the industry underwent a virtual revolution over the next two centuries. A self-perpetuating and constantly renewed tradition of skills emerged that in itself generated further demand for the products of the industry.

NEW TECHNOLOGY

The major technical innovations came in the fifteenth century with the shift from the use of tempera and gold leaf on wood to oil first on wood and then on canvas. The former method was time-consuming and costly since the wood surface required considerable preparation before being painted. Moreover, the wood structure of an altarpiece itself was often an essential part of the finished artistic product, consisting of elaborately carved and decorative woodwork that usually cost more than the painting and restricted the painter's work by determining the form of the areas to be painted.[17] The practice of gilding the background of paintings required the application of gold leaf and then the decoration of it by punching, incising, or applying *pastiglia*—a time-consuming and expensive process that could constitute as much as 30 to 40 percent of the total cost of the finished product. With the use of oil paints on canvas, gilding was abandoned, and major altar pictures began to be produced independent of a pre-existing frame. This new practice thus reduced both time and costs in those stages of the production processes that were ancillary to the actual painting. Whereas for a fifteenth-century painter such as Neri di Bicci materials and work preparatory to actual painting constituted at least 50 percent of costs, the total expenses for materials incurred by a painter working in seventeenth-century Rome, including the canvas, its stretcher, and oils (excepting only ultramarine blue), amounted to only a few scudi, or around 5 percent of the price an accomplished painter might receive for a finished easel painting.

The new medium, as compared with tempera, also allowed the painter to work with greater autonomy, independent of other specialist artisans, and therefore more rapidly; and at the same time it gave him considerable flexibility in how he painted. This flexibility, in turn, infinitely enlarged his stylistic options, including the way he handled the very materials he worked with, that is the oils. Seicento painters like Guido Reni and Luca Giordano developed the *pittoresco* style, which put into relief the physical nature of the paint itself and the sheer beauty of the brushstroke with which it is worked. Philip Sohm has called this performative mode of brushwork a "shorthand to make cheap paintings quickly," and raises the question that puzzled critics at the time whether this "visible rapidity" represented financial expediency or an aesthetic criterion.[18]

If, thanks to these technological innovations, painters were able to work more quickly, another innovation, drawing on paper, facilitated the preparatory process leading up to the actual painting. Florentine painters, in the vanguard of those taking up drawing on paper, had the advantage of working in the immediate market area of what was perhaps the most important center for the production of paper in Italy after Fabriano—at Colle Valdelsa, where the industry took root at the end of the thirteenth century, and also, somewhat later, at Pescia and Prato. The practice of drawing on paper offered the painter nothing less than what Carmen Bambach has called "the revolutionary design technology of the Quattrocento."[19] Painters increased the efficiency with which they worked out problems regarding the representation of details and the organization of the picture space preliminary to painting; and in allowing them to work out their ideas more easily and with greater spontaneity, drawing increased their efficiency in creativity. Moreover, a drawing could become an important instrument in the negotiations for a commission: it served the painter in communicating his ideas to the client preliminary to actual production, and for the client it opened up the possibility of greater input into the nature of the final product.

In facilitating the copying and studying of ideas from other painters, the practice became, in effect, an ongoing educational process that enlarged the painter's personal pictorial vocabulary and stimulated his creative imagination. Artists built up collections of books of drawings for use in their shop. Since these also circulated among themselves, they were an important medium for the diffusion of artistic ideas and knowledge of the profession. In this way a producer could also use drawings to advertise his production. Drawings themselves, in fact, became products that could be marketed as art objects in their own right, and the expanded market for this kind of work that followed on the development of printing brought a new industry into existence within the artisan sector of the economy. Dürer was one of the first prominent artists to recognize the market potential of woodcuts and engravings that could be sold widely in multiple copies, each carrying his famous logo as an advertisement and guarantee.[20]

At the industry-wide level these technical innovations revolutionized production. They facilitated both preparatory work and the manufacturing process, with the result that the producer was able to improve his productive capacity. Being able to work out ideas by drawing on paper and then to realize them by painting with oils on canvas, the painter, more than any other artisan producer such as the goldsmith and sculptor in wood or stone, was able to reduce—even minimize, with respect to all other crafts—the material barriers that lay between his creative ideas as artist and the physical expression of those ideas in a finished product. In this sense, painting became easier, both less costly and physically less demanding.

The results of these developments over the period covered in this survey are clear. First of all, the general level of the technical ability of painters throughout the profession steadily improved—as anyone can see for himself by walking through the local museum in many Italian cities, such as, for instance, Turin or Ferrara, taking in the local painting galleries in chronological order from the fourteenth to the seventeenth centuries. Second, the stylistic variety within any one line of products increased almost infinitely—or at least to the coefficient equivalent to the number of painters. Style freed the producer from craft traditions, differentiated one from another, and defined a specific niche in the market for each. Moreover, the proliferation of styles in the course of the fifteenth, sixteenth, and seventeenth centuries offered the producer the possibility of experimenting and manipulating taste to his own advantage.

Productivity, with respect to the time it took a painter to produce a painting, surfaces again and again as a criterion used by contemporaries for judging what was happening in the industry during these years. Early in the sixteenth century Sebastiano del Piombo (according to Vasari), when rebuked for how slowly he painted, responded with despair that new painters were arriving on the scene in Rome who could do in two months what took him two years to do. In his life of Perugino, Vasari himself observed that the art of painting had reached such a level of perfection by the time he was writing, in the middle of the sixteenth century, that the painter who knew how to draw and use colors could paint six pictures in one year whereas it took his teachers six years to do just one painting. One could play the economist's game with these "statistics": if for Sebastiano del Piombo efficiency had increased 12 times—that is 2 instead of 24 months to produce one picture—for Vasari it had increased 36 times—2 instead of 72 months. For the economist this is an increase in productivity of between 1,100 and 3,500 percent in half a century! With all allowance for the wild inflation of these "statistics" by the rhetoric both these painters used, they nevertheless were observing a real change in the painter's productivity.

It often happens that adjustment to technical innovation calls into question cultural values, and certainly what happened in painting generated a clash of opinion about whether change in the industry was a good or a bad thing with respect to the criteria used to evaluate the finished product. Vasari boasted about what he saw as progress—a concept that, with respect to artistic expression, he regarded as the principal dynamic in the history of painting and that, with respect to productivity, the economist considers a major criterion for economic growth. On the other hand, Giovan Battista Armenini (1530–1609), who also reported del Piombo's despair at this shift in the industry, was repulsed by this new situation, not inspired as Vasari was; and he rationalized his early renouncement of the profession by his distaste for what he considered the consequent decline in painting. The issue gave rise to much of the mythology in the history of painting that emerged in the Renaissance. When Vasari boasted about having frescoed the *sala* in the palace of the Cancelleria in Rome in 100 days, Michelangelo famously retorted, "It shows!" Tintoretto's use of his materials in a sketchy style that very much lessened the time it took to finish a painting aroused the criticism from some of his contemporaries that he worked too fast, too impatiently, and too carelessly. Luca Giordano was called "fa presto" Giordano—do-it-in-a-hurry Giordano—so great was his rate of production. It was reported that on a visit to Carlo Dolci's shop Giordano upbraided his colleague for painting so slowly, claiming that Dolci would never accumulate the wealth he had and that instead would probably die of hunger.

ORGANIZATIONAL INNOVATIONS

Besides technical innovations in the production process, painters also improved the organization of work within their shops. In the fourteenth century the industry was largely organized around the corporate structure of the guild: painters had their own shops, but they operated them as guild masters who made contractual arrangements with apprentices according to the traditions and regulations of the larger collective group to which they belonged. This changed in the course of the Renaissance. Employers began to draw on the open market for their workforce, and the cash nexus came to dominate the labor contract. Hence, there was greater fluidity within the ranks of employees. Already in the fifteenth century Neri di Bicci, who had one of the largest shops in Florence, was using paid assistants, and there was considerable turnover in their ranks. Armenini, looking back to his youth as a painter working in Rome in the early sixteenth century, attributed much of what he considered the decline of painting to the practice of treating shop assistants more as hired workers than as apprentices.[21] In the next century many painters organized the work in their shops in this way, as employers who resorted to the market both for students and for day laborers. Guilds still existed, but in some places painters organized an academy, a professional organization that sought to protect the status of their members through behavioral norms rather than to interfere in the internal operations of the shop.

Some scholars think that this kind of arrangement facilitated the circulation of artistic ideas, inasmuch as a youth could move from one shop to another, thereby learning from more than one master. The painter, in any event, worked with the greater flexibility made possible by the rules of the marketplace, no longer tied to the corporate regulations typical of the medieval guild; as a result, the shop functioned more efficiently. Shop organization varied according to the needs of particular artists. If some painters depended on paid labor, others, like Reni in Bologna, also took in paying students. Guercino ran his shop in provincial Cento and later in Bologna as a family business, employing relatives and showing little interest in teaching. In Bologna the Carracci created a strong corporate sense among the workers in their shop, or "academy," subordinating their emerging individual stylistic propensities to a strong and specific unity of purpose.[22]

Within the shop painters also streamlined the production process. Using paper to make a cartoon, they developed a technique for reproduction of pictures: this involved drawing a copy on paper, punching holes along its outline and then tracing the picture on the surface to be painted. In this way the shop of the so-called Pseudo Pier Francesco, at Florence in the second half of the fifteenth century, reproduced an impressive number of images of Fra Filippo Lippi and Pesellino; no fewer than 160 paintings have been identified that derive from 64 cartoons.[23] Using copying techniques, a painter, like Ghirlandaio and Botticelli, could build up a repertoire of decorative motifs—for example, landscapes, architecture, floral decoration—that he could use to vary reproductions of standardized images. By thus varying a standard product, the producer strengthened his position in the expanding market for devotional pictures.

In some larger shops the reproduction process became the specialization of painters who worked in something approximating a production line. The employer made a sketch of the essential image, employees did the details such as birds, animals, landscapes, and drapery or in other ways made variant copies of the employer's prototype, and in the final stage the employer put on the finishing touches. Titian organized his shop around such "a production-line basis."[24] Pier Francesco Mola, in seventeenth-century Rome, had his employees reproduce his ideas in copies and variants to which he added the finishing touches and sold as his own work.[25] Guido Reni used his students to produce pictures in which his own hand was imitated and minimized, making it difficult to identify their variants and copies from the master's. The inventory of his shop on his death lists a large number of pictures that were either copies or unfinished.[26] This process often creates problems about how to attribute the final product. The economic importance of this kind of collaborative division of labor consists in the possibility of specialization for the worker and in the enlargement of the range of products for the shop.

Between technical and organizational innovation, painters at the high end of the market very much increased their output. Tintoretto may have produced as many as 10 to 12 pictures annually. Guercino in his peak years produced between 15 and 20 pictures annually, some of them variant copies that he sold at the same price as the originals. The record, however, must surely go to Veronese, whose output, between over 700 surviving autograph and workshop pictures and about as many documented pictures that do not survive—and not counting those that have gone undocumented—amounted to over 1,400 pictures in 40 years, or about one every ten days.[27] The inventory made of Reni's house on his death in 1642 lists over 100 pictures plus a large number of unfinished canvases, and Pietro da Cortona's residence at Rome where he had his shop has been called a "factory-palace" (*palazzo-fabbrica*), so large was the quantity of the artist's production.[28]

NEW PRODUCTS

Although painters who claimed status might have preferred to work on commission, much of the growth of the industry that began in the later fourteenth century consisted in production for direct sale in the marketplace. For example, Neri di Bicci, besides producing major altarpieces on commission, sold paintings directly out of his shop to the public. He produced many small inexpensive tabernacles, about a third of the buyers being artisans; and in several instances the buyer seems to have been a shopkeeper who bought Neri's products for resale.[29] In addition, about a fifth of his production went to merchants for export. In the early fifteenth century the merchant of Prato, Francesco di Marco Datini, bought pictures and other devotional objects in the Florentine market for resale in Avignon, and later in the century customs records in Rome document the importation of such things in that city. Lorenzo Lotto sent paintings to acquaintances in other cities—a gilder in Venice, a mercer in Loreto, a jeweler who was going to Messina—to be sold, and in 1550 he organized a raffle of 46 paintings in Ancona (which, however, was not successful).

By the seventeenth century the industry had added many new products to its output, many of them produced by specialized painters, namely small pictures of religious and mythological stories, battle scenes, landscapes, animals, still lifes, and devotional images. Annual production levels of some of these painters at the low end of the market may have reached as high as the 100 to 150 pictures Michael Montias estimated as the potential output of contemporary Dutch painters in the seventeenth century, but the Italian industry has not yet been studied with this problem in mind. These new products were sought by collectors and by clients, many from the lower economic classes, who wanted something other than the kinds of large history and religious pictures that Italian painters had traditionally been producing. As a result of this widening of the range of subject matter and of specialization, an entire division of the industry came into existence that produced these kinds of pictures. Shops of established painters sold these things as a sideline, and many well-known painters—for example, Annibale Carracci in Bologna, Caravaggio in Rome, and Ribera in Naples—began their careers in this line of work, painting still lifes, copies of portraits, and other such pictures. Some shops specialized in these cheaper products. This new market in Italy attracted Flemish painters, who (unlike Italians) had a tradition of doing products of this kind; and it also gave rise in the 1620s to a new school of painters in Italy, called the Bamboccianti, who (perhaps out of a critical rebellion to the excesses of baroque culture) did pictures representing people of the lower classes in scenes of everyday life. That some major seventeenth-century painters, like Poussin and Claude Lorrain, made a career rarely producing an altarpiece is another mark of how much the industry had changed.

Another new product on the market was the copy, the production of which was much facilitated by the use of paper for tracing.[30] Painters also began making copies of more famous paintings: the copy of an old master, of a portrait, and even, beginning in the later sixteenth century, of a contemporary picture. Alessandro Allori in Florence, for example, was making copies of pictures by Andrea del Sarto and Raphael within a generation after their deaths. By the seventeenth century the market for copies was booming, and some painters specialized in this kind of product. Something of the market for copies is reflected in a report the Gonzaga agent in Florence made in 1602.[31] The agent had no problem finding Florentine artists to make copies of old masters and portraits, and prices varied. He reported that one painter there could make 100 portraits in only two months at a cost of only 3 to 5 scudi, and another had recently sent as many as 200 in one shipment to Spain. Lodovico Buti was prepared to make copies of portraits of 12 saints in six months at 25 scudi each but was bargained down to about 17 scudi each, whereas another painter, Jacopo Ligozzi, would have asked 50 scudi (originals would have cost 300 to 500 scudi each, according to the agent). In one instance, the agent bought a picture by Andrea del Sarto and paid to have a copy made for the owner; in another, he did not get the copies he wanted because the painter sold them to someone else. Finally, as mentioned earlier, painters made copies of their own paintings—another sign of the rising status of their profession. At one point, to meet certain economic problems, Albani reorganized his shop to make replicas of his own paintings; and Mola's shop employed assistants to turn out copies of his own work as well as that of others.[32] The demand for copies gave rise to another new product, the forgery, raising a problem to which people became increasingly sensitive in the course of the seventeenth century.[33]

One representative of this new entrepreneurial spirit among painters was Bernardo Strozzi in Genoa, all the more significant since he belonged to a religious order. His large workshop employing many youths specialized in making copies, or near-copies and variants, and pictures in series within a limited range of subject matter. One of the witnesses in the famous case brought against Strozzi in 1625–26 because of his commercial activities testified that he had a contract with the painter to sell pictures that included 36 emperors on horseback, six copies of a St. Jerome, five of an *Ecce Homo*, and two of a *Pietà*.[34]

To what extent the widening of the range of products and the expansion of a line of less costly products represented growth of the industry with respect to the number of producers and the level of output is impossible to say for lack of any precise data; but, as stated at the outset of this essay, in no place in seventeenth-century Italy, not even in Rome, did painters constitute a significant part of the working population. However, developments in the production process of the painter, both technical and organizational, stimulated by this expansion of the market led to what can be categorized under the economist's rubrics of product differentiation, product innovation, and process innovation, presumably indicators of greater productivity. In the historiography of Dutch art, development of this kind has been incorporated into what is known as the Montias innovation thesis, which takes its name not from an art or economic historian but from an economist—the late Michael Montias—whose archival research and economic analysis enlarged our understanding of how Vermeer and other Dutch painters worked as entrepreneurs. Yet the painting industry was presumably the only industry in Holland that reached this level of development, it being the sole reference listed under the entries for "process innovation" and "product innovation" in the index to the aforementioned book on "the first modern economy" by de Vries and van der Woude. Which is all the more reason to regret the lack of any study of the Italian industry along these lines for any period in the long history of painting in Italy.[35]

Transformation of the Market

The link between demand and producer is the market, and it, too, came to function more efficiently. In the fifteenth century the market was organized around the commission nexus, dependent on initiatives taken by a client to contract with a painter for a painting; and only a small part of industrial production, almost entirely relatively inexpensive devotional pictures, was directed to sale by the producer on the open market. In the course of the sixteenth century, the market began to look a little like what it has since become: a specific art market had come into existence in which painters aggressively promoted themselves and their profession, intermediaries bought and sold pictures, shops displayed pictures for sale, painters could show their wares in exhibits and at fairs, private collections functioned as incipient museums displaying pictures to a wider public, and some international merchants, working for Europe's great collectors, added paintings to the stock of commercial goods they traded in.

Self-Promotion

In the traditional art historical view of things, the relation between painter and client falls under the category of "patronage," and the literature on the subject tends to treat the relation as a cultural phenomenon, an extra-market arrangement that is removed from the normal dynamics of supply and demand. Yet, notwithstanding production on commission and the consequent dependence of the industry on the initiative of the buyer-patron, the client entered the market when he searched for a painter, and in that market the painter operated in some way or other in order to make himself known to potential buyers. The two met in the market to contract for the production of a specific product. The cultural baggage that both brought to the bargain, of course, impinged on their behavior; and it is hardly surprising that as the status of both art and artist grew, the painter became more assertive in his approach to the client.

The growing self-consciousness of painters as a distinct class of craftsmen is one of the great themes in the history of Renaissance Italy. They came to have a strong sense of the history of their profession, and they could read in Vasari's *Lives* about the progress their craft had undergone from Giotto down to their own times, first manifest in Florence but by Vasari's time widely apparent throughout Italy. They saw some of their immediate forebears raised to the status of old masters whose pictures were sought by collectors, some were able to sell their own work to these same collectors, and some saw demand arise for copies of their own work. They undoubtedly knew a colleague or two whose work for a rich and powerful client had been rewarded with a conspicuous token of respect, such as a gold chain or an honorary knighthood. They were aware of a growing literature on their craft, including tracts on art, collective biographies, and the other relevant publications that appeared increasingly from the sixteenth century onwards, most written by one of their own but also some written by men outside their ranks who enjoyed cultural and intellectual status in society at large; and they experienced the emergence of a debate about the relative merits of painting as compared with sculpture and architecture. Their own intellectual efforts were modest at best and none were learned by the standards of their time, but here was an artisan—the painter—who in the course of two centuries succeeded in separating himself out from other artisans on the basis of cultural claims.

Painters brought this rising cultural status into play in their efforts to sell themselves and their products in the market. Collectively, they promoted their image as a distinct class of artisan, one with certain cultural pretensions. In several of the major cities—Florence, Bologna, Venice, Rome—they sought to disassociate themselves from traditional guild society by setting up an "academy" in imitation of what intellectuals and people of the upper class with cultural interests were doing. The academy served as a kind of professional organization that offered them a modest educational program and sought to regulate their behavior in the market according to criteria consonant with the prestige its members claimed. The Accademia di S. Luca in Rome operated on the principle that the artist best maintained his status by working with clients personally and that he degraded himself and his profession if he sought to sell his products across the counter.

Not surprisingly, a hierarchical distinction arose between those painters of quality who produced traditional history paintings and those who mass produced portraits and popular genre scenes—between the "giants" of the profession and the "pygmies" who Andrea Sacchi thought were threatening the status of the profession. In 1590 the Genoese painter Giovanni Battista Paggi, in an effort to disassociate himself from the guild, took legal action against the guild's efforts to require membership, arguing that he worked on commission and not out of a shop. Salvator Rosa failed to make himself known in Rome when he first went there from Naples and worked on the open market, selling small pictures to shopkeepers who then resold them. So he returned to Naples and tried another tack. This time he sent a picture to a well-placed acquaintance in Rome, Niccolò Simonelli, who had an important post in the household of a cardinal, in the hope that Simonelli would promote the picture. Simonelli put it on display at the Pantheon on the occasion of a special exhibition mostly of loaned paintings of prominent painters, and he attached to it a label in which he praised Rosa as the Demosthenes of modern painting. Given Simonelli's reputation, this advertisement had the effect of spreading Rosa's fame in Rome, thereby assuring him a different reception on his return.[36]

In this kind of social and cultural environment the painter promoted his business not so much through the normal channels of the marketplace as through the cultivation of personal relations in the hope of gaining a commission. The painter's marketing problem in finding commissions, therefore, was to cultivate a special relation with potential clients by attempting to enter into their world. The emergence of a distinct culture of painting throughout the society beyond the ranks of painters, complete with a growing literature on the subject, facilitated the opening of opportunities for painters to make the appropriate accommodations to people who had a higher economic and social status than they had.

Armenini dedicates much of his treatise to how an artist should deal with his patron: he should conduct himself in accordance with the norms of the client's social status, he should have some knowledge of literature so he can discuss things with his patron, he should always uphold the dignity of his craft and seek to educate the client about it, and he should make sure that his work reflects the culture of his client.[37] Painters might thereby gain access to the social and intellectual circles of their clients, and the personal bonds between them generated a network through which they could perform market functions such as dealing, promotion, consulting, and appraising. This mode of operations seems to have been particularly prominent in Bologna, a relatively small city not dominated by a court, where through such personal networks within the ruling class the interest of painters found a civic outlet in the public promotion of painters and their work.[38] One device painters used to circumvent normal market procedures was the game of gift exchange so characteristic a feature of social relations in this period. Titian sent noncommissioned pictures to Philip II assuming that a countergift in the form of payments would be forthcoming. Guido Reni, going one step further in playing this game, famously refused to talk about the price of a commissioned painting in the certainty that the client, on receiving the finished product, would reward him handsomely. This behavior has been called a marketing technique to arouse demand and therefore raise the price of his work. But by putting the emphasis more exclusively on cultural evaluation, social behavior of this kind—what Elizabeth Honig has recently called "the Honor System"[39]—can also be seen as a rejection of the market and an attempt to create an alternative to it as a site for the determination of value.

To promote themselves as producers targeting specific clients, self-imaging through such external manifestations as clothes, residence, and social manners became a notable marketing strategy of those painters who sought high status. Eccentricity of behavior also became an observed characteristic of artists in the sixteenth century, especially inspired by the model of Michelangelo; and the figure of the modern artist emerges full blown in Rosa, who would do about anything to attract public attention, from painting unusual subjects to presenting himself as an eccentric genius.

Ultimately what counted, however, was the product a painter sought to sell, and his style became the essential instrument by which he could put the stamp of his own individuality on his products. In this sense, style was a technique, like any other, that could be used to introduce innovation in the production process in order to make the finished product more marketable. Already in the later fourteenth century, painters were clearly breaking away from strict craft traditions to explore their own ways of "probing, exploring, canvassing alternatives," and with this "novel emphasis on invention and originality began the elevation of the artist's status."[40] Historians of Renaissance art, looking afresh at their subject in response to the current interest in the art market, have begun to suspect that the increasing insistence of artists on individual style served as a kind of self-advertising, whether it be Pollaiuolo's adaptation of the new techniques of Northern painting, or Neri di Bicci's effort to bring his retardataire style up to date by introducing fashionable stock motifs such as perspective and classical architecture into the picture space, or Bachiacca's imitation of other artists to construct an original pastiche of styles.

The growing self-consciousness of style, accelerated by the technical innovations of the fifteenth century that simplified the process of production, reached the point where a painter could make his mark by displaying his bravura in the brushstroke itself. It has even been suggested that the emergence of a strong sense of personal style on the part of Venetian painters, along with a growing sense of connoisseurship on the part of clients, precluded the need for the former to sign their pictures.[41] The more forcible assertion of individual style generated a self-consciousness among painters as unique producers. Individualization of style is product differentiation with a vengeance. Today we are only too familiar with how important the frequency of change in style, or fashion, is as a stimulus to consumption, and in a certain sense this dynamic of continual renewal found its first major manifestation in the market for painting in the Renaissance. Style could also be manipulated by any one painter in order to adjust his products to different price levels, as Giordano claimed to do with his "three brushes," one in gold, one in silver, and one in copper.

Vasari understood how all this played itself out in the marketplace. The figure of the painter presented by

Vasari, himself a painter, is convinced of his cultural status and driven by the desire for recognition. Thus, as he concluded (in his life of Raphael), "to live in a state of natural harmony and agreement . . . is completely alien to our character as painters." "Competition of our artists [he observes in his life of Pordenone] is certainly a nutrient that maintains them." Competition as another dynamic that increasingly drove the producer created a new atmosphere in the marketplace, sharpening the painter's sense of the market and conditioning his behavior in it. Vasari's consciousness of the market he himself dealt in is manifest in his record book—the oldest of its kind to survive—that was nothing more than a list of the products he sold out of his workshop with the basic information: subject, date, client, price. Vasari punctuated his lives of artists with comments about their involvement in the market and about their competitive instinct. In his life of Perugino, he asks why was it that "in Florence, more than elsewhere, men perfected all skills and especially painting?" His answer: Florentine "artisans" are driven, beyond their critical spirit, by "the need to be industrious . . . and to know how to make a living." In his life of Franciabigio, he explains the painter's competition with Andrea del Sarto in strictly economic terms: that is, his desire to better the economic status of his family. In Venice Titian was prepared to accept lower prices if the commission gave him greater public exposure; and Tintoretto, trying to undercut Titian, followed what has been called a "client-oriented" and "market-driven" policy, directed to get more business by asking prices lower than what might have been expected.[42]

Competition by producers obsessed with self-fashioning in order to sell their products could lead to open rivalry. The Renaissance has been called "an inherently rivalrous age," extending from the rivalry between Ghiberti and Brunelleschi at the cathedral of Florence in the early fifteenth century to that a century later between Sebastiano del Piombo and Raphael at Agostino Chigi's villa in Rome and between Titian, Tintoretto, and Veronese in Venice, where "cut throat," "acrimonious," and "heated" competition, "deceitful" and "self-promotional tactics," "one-upmanship," and "grandstanding" were the order of the day.[43] It has been noted how, in the seventeenth century, some painters "manipulated and traumatized their competitors" even to the point of engaging in the infamous personal campaigns of defamation that could lead to violence and court suits.

Competition is a key concept Vasari used to explain the behavior of the painter, and he may in fact have been the first author writing in Italian who used this term. In any event, we have here a new mentality, inasmuch as the concept of "competition," with reference to behavior of an economic operator, had never emerged previously with such clarity, not even in the business world of the great entrepreneurs who had been driving the proto-capitalist economy of Italy since the twelfth century.[44] In this perspective the outpouring of artistic imagination that we call the Renaissance took place in an economic culture pervaded by the entrepreneurial spirit and fed by the cultural values conferred by society on artisan bravura. If, on the one hand, this economic culture generated the maximum development of human capital, on the other hand it ended by commodifying those very artistic qualities that today we appreciate as spiritual values detached from the material world.

Infrastructure

In the seventeenth century the industry was producing all those new kinds of products at the lower end of the market already noted: namely, devotional pieces, copies, portraits of historical figures, genre scenes, and other small decorative paintings. Some painters enlarged the stock of their own paintings by buying pictures from other painters. And the plundering of churches began. In Florence Giovanni Navese, pupil of Vasari, rummaged through churches to buy pictures for Piero d'Agnolo Guicciardini, including, in 1603, a *Pietà* by Andrea del Sarto purchased illegally from the Servite friars at SS. Annunziata.[45] The Neapolitan artist-dealer Giacomo de Castro (d. 1687), on commission from the viceroy, surveyed the major paintings in Neapolitan churches that might be purchased for shipment to Spain. Demand increased to the point where intermediaries, some themselves painters and some from outside the profession, moved into the market to profit from the situation. Shopkeepers of all sorts such as secondhand dealers, barbers, and tailors sold paintings in their shops as a sideline, and ambulant picture sellers hawked their wares on the street, like the one illustrated in a well-known print made after a Carracci drawing.[46]

Out of this activity a specific market began to take shape as a well-defined structure that attracted investment and stimulated enterprise. In Naples the merchant Anielo Mele, who dealt in painting on the side, operated much like the modern dealer in that he specialized only in paintings for clients at the upper end of the market. Some dealers went further to build links to supply through what we might call a vertically integrated structure, contracting with painters for the exclusive right to buy their work or directly employing painters to work on their premises. The Neapolitan merchant Carlo della Torre speculated in the market by commissioning paintings from Giordano, which he paid for in advance, with the intention of selling them after completion.[47] In Rome Domenico Castiglione, who operated a shop in the last quarter of the seventeenth century, employed young painters to make mostly copies and kept on hand a large inventory of pictures for sale.[48] A contemporary of his, Pellegrino Peri, specialized in genre paintings, apparently dealing in nothing else. He employed artists to work for him to keep up his stock, he sold their products at the low end of the market but also supplied major collectors, sometimes he sold picture in blocks and sometimes he rented them out; on his death he had an inventory of 2,491 paintings.[49] Some Venetian painters were themselves dealers, contracting for products from other painters and putting them to work in their own shops.

Shops at the very lowest end of the market could also be well stocked. The Neapolitan painter Onofrio de Anfora, dredged up from complete obscurity by Christopher Marshall, had some 200 paintings of devotional subjects on hand when an inventory of his shop was made while he was dying in 1644. At least 80 were not by him, 50 having been purchased from other painters and 30 being described as old or very old; some were finished and some not; they were in all sizes, some framed and some not (and he had a supply of frames around, presumably to be fitted on a picture at a client's request); and none was probably worth more than several ducats. At Rome, the largest market in Italy, the stock in a shop could amount to hundreds of paintings: Nicolao Ventura, another completely unknown painter, had 767 paintings on hand when his possessions were confiscated in 1616, and almost 800 were listed in the inventory made on the death of Mario de' Fiori in 1673.[50] One Venetian dealer possessed 551 paintings.

A few dealers became relatively wealthy, and there were complaints that dealers exploited poor artists. As early as 1619 the Accademia in Rome attempted to limit the number of shops selling pictures, in effect licensing dealers; and in 1684 the Collegio de' Pittori in Venice also sought to regulate this traffic by taxing dealers. It remains an open question to what extent some of these dealers created value by obtaining higher prices for the paintings they dealt in.[51] And no one has yet looked at this emerging figure of the art dealer as an intermediary of taste who in an expanding market determined buyer preference and directed industrial output accordingly. They built up their stock by buying and commissioning paintings and by organizing production, but how did they define the market they were appealing to, what were their strategies to educate the public and promote sales, and what were their pricing strategies—in short, all those aspects of the contemporary markets in Holland studied by Michael Montias and in Antwerp studied by Neil De Marchi and Hans J. Van Miegroet (whose articles are cited throughout this survey)?

Lotteries and auctions were two promotional devices used in seventeenth-century Holland and, toward the end of the century, in London, but they seem to have been no more than very occasional events in the Italian art market.[52] In London, where, in the absence of a local industry of any importance, the market grew up around the sale of imported products, the auction became a regular event, taking on a formal structure organized around rules and the shared expertise of specialized dealers; and it was there, in the eighteenth century, where the figure of the auctioneer assumed his modern guise in the art market as a professional full-time dealer.

Although the more pretentious painters had a prejudice against direct sale of their products on the open market, some were nonetheless tempted to take initiatives other than self-advertising to get their work to a wider public. They kept pictures on display in their studios to show to prospective buyers, some unfinished to be completed according to the client's specification. They could also advertise themselves through prints. Already in early sixteenth-century Rome Raphael recognized the importance of prints for the diffusion of knowledge of his work, and in Venice Titian earned some income from copyrights on prints of his pictures. In 1562 the printer Giorgio Marescotti appealed to Cosimo I in Florence for special permission to sell prints after mass on feast days, including some that were after works by various painters. Public exhibitions were another outlet for the sale of their pictures, but much direct sale through this institution may have been a last resort for the more pretentious painters. In the fifteenth century pictures were to be found for sale on certain fair days, but by the seventeenth century painters themselves, sometimes through their academy, organized major exhibitions to make themselves known through the exclusive display of pictures in public places. Exhibitions were most common on the seventeenth-century Roman scene, where there were several in the course of the year, including the one at the Pantheon mentioned above where Rosa made his debut in the city. Rosa used all these techniques: he kept unfinished pictures in his shop hoping clients would pay to have them finished, he advertised as yet unfinished paintings through prints, and he displayed pictures in public notwithstanding the prohibition of the Accademia.

Internationalization

A notable development in this increased traffic in paintings, along with the greater articulation of the market, was its expansion beyond the confines of local markets—what might be called the internationalization of the market. From Giotto onward some painters traveled abroad to work on commissions, and over the following centuries painters from out of town were forever showing up in many Italian cities. In the fifteenth century Florentine painters were the most prominent travelers: many had commissions in Rome, Uccello and Andrea del Castagno went to Venice, and Benozzo Gozzoli worked much of the time in the provincial markets of Tuscany and Umbria. In the next century Lorenzo Lotto spent most of his career traveling to the provincial cities of the Veneto and the Marche. The expansion of the market for paintings in Rome and Naples, both growing capital cities, and in Genoa, the financial center of Italy, attracted painters from all over Italy. Far from stimulating local producers, the demand in these three cities, none with a strong local school of painters, was almost entirely satisfied by immigrants.[53] Even Florence in the seventeenth century, for all of the fame of its tradition in the history of painting, attracted many painters from abroad, including Ligozzi, Rosa, Giordano and, from beyond Italy, Bilivert and Sustermans. By this time, painters were circulating widely throughout the peninsula, and some went farther afield, leaving Italy for the courts north of the Alps.

If some painters traveled abroad in response to demand, a few were able to attract demand from abroad without having to leave the local market. Examples of such occasional commissions from abroad abound from the fourteenth century onward, but eventually a few producers emerge who were able to attract much work from abroad. Titian cultivated princes to get commissions from them, but—except for two visits to Augsburg and one to Rome, each for less than a year—he managed to stay at home in Venice, carefully avoiding being drawn into direct court service abroad. By the end of the sixteenth century, some painters had sufficient prestige that they could work in provincial centers far away from the major urban markets where the demand for their products arose. While Jacopo Bassano's son Francesco, responding to the growing demand for the family's products, opened a shop in Venice, Jacopo himself remained in the small provincial town of the family's origin working on the many commissions that arrived from Venice and elsewhere. The market came to him, so to speak, as it did also for Guercino, who returned to his hometown of Cento, for Barocci, who remained in Urbino, and for Reni, who, once having established his fame, left Rome, the largest art market in Italy, and returned to Bologna. As much as 40 percent of Guercino's commissions came from places beyond the Emilia-Romagna area where he resided.[54]

Another aspect of internationalization was the opening of the Italian market to both imports and, eventually, immigration of non-Italian painters. One-third of Lorenzo de' Medici's collection of 142 paintings at the time of his death in 1492 was Flemish, and these products also found buyers at the low end of the market among shoemakers in Florence, as already observed. The importation of Flemish paintings into Venice also grew in the course of the sixteenth century.[55] The Flemish industry was ahead of Italy's in producing the kind of products—namely, landscapes, still lifes, and genre scenes of various kinds—for which there was a growing demand in Italian markets from the fifteenth through to the seventeenth centuries.

Virtually nothing is known about this traffic, however. Art historians have focused on the reciprocal stylistic conditioning of these two painterly cultures, but economic aspects of this enlargement of the Italian market to foreign products have gone completely unstudied. What role did dealers play in mediating tastes between these two cultures? To what extent were they "signalers of taste"? What was their "practice of selecting and sanitizing certain Netherlandish elements in known products" to meet market demand? And what was the pricing policy? These are all problems that De Marchi and Van Miegroet have explored in relation to the importation of Netherlandish art into the Parisian market in the second half of the seventeenth century.[56]

By the seventeenth century foreign producers themselves, especially the Flemish, were moving into the principal Italian markets for their products. They had a notable presence both as dealers and as painters in Genoa, which had direct business relations with Antwerp.[57] In the collection of Giovanni Agostino Balbi (d. 1621), for example, 63 of the 154 paintings were Flemish. Perhaps half of the painters in Venice were foreign born. But it was above all in Rome that the industry had a large constituency of painters from across the Alps. Besides the attraction of the market in this cosmopolitan capital, the many foreigners among papal officials and courtiers brought painters from their homeland, and many others came to study the city's famed ancient monuments or to do their apprenticeship there. In a 1656 census of one area within the city (see the essay on Rome), 45 percent of the painters residing there were non-Italian, and it has been estimated that about half of foreign painters in the city were French.

More than anything else, growth of demand in the secondary market generated by collectors internationalized the traffic in pictures, and the market mechanism that emerged to make contact between buyers and sellers in different cities was the figure of the agent. Isabella d'Este in Mantua sent agents abroad to find pictures by specific artists; and Francis I, seeking pictures along with sculpture and antiquities in Florence, found a major agent in Battista della Palla, who commissioned works and tried to pry others away from their owners in order to satisfy his client. A century later, agents of one kind or another were prominent figures in the art market.

Some of the best documented worked for the Gonzaga dukes in Mantua, scouring Italy for pictures of all kinds to build up the famous ducal collection. The agent of Vincenzo I (1587–1612) on the lookout for works by old masters in Florence and Lucca tracked down rumors of pictures that might be bought, sought opinions about the authenticity of the ones he saw, bargained with their owners to bring the price down, and offered to supply copies in order to conclude a sale. One agent sizing up the market in Florence reported that prospects were good for finding pictures for sale because money was scarce, landowners were cash-hungry, and export restrictions reduced competition among foreign buyers. Another agent placed portraits of saints in a church and had them blessed so that they could be exported as religious objects, which were exempt from customs charges. In 1605 Vincenzo, finding that he had only one Perugino in his collection, had an agent search the province of Perugia to find another. His successor Ferdinand (1612–26) sent out agents on missions to buy pictures in bulk, and one of these returned from Bologna with 143 paintings from a collection there.[58]

A big spurt of demand in the international market came at the beginning of the seventeenth century when a few enormously rich men in northern Europe went in for collecting Italian as well as Flemish pictures in a major way.[59] Most prominent among the first generation of these foreigners were several English nobles in the circle of the first two Stuart kings—the earls of Somerset, Salisbury, and Arundel, the marquis of Hamilton, and the duke of Buckingham—and then the king himself, Charles I. These men amassed large collections of pictures, numbering in the hundreds—there were 1,500 in the king's collection—in only several years, sometimes buying them by the lot from Italian collectors. Buckingham (who paid £10,000 sterling—about 40,000 scudi—for Rubens's personal collection of paintings and sculpture) bought around 400 Italian pictures in four to five years; Arundel bought most of his collection of 600 pictures in only three years. The Civil War that broke out in 1642 put a stop to the buying spree of these English collectors, and in the ensuing political turmoil their collections were disbursed, with the result that many pictures went back on the market.

Meanwhile, buyers from other countries moved into the market. The king of Spain, having already inherited the large collection of Philip II, was a major buyer of Charles I's collection when it went on the block; and a 1686 inventory of the Spanish royal collection lists 77 Titians alone in the royal residence at Madrid. The duke of Lerma, Philip III's principal minister, had a collection that at one time reached 2,747 pictures.[60] In France, Marie de' Medici bought some Italian pictures in the 1620s, but the first major collector was Richelieu, although his collection of 272 pictures was much smaller than those built up by the English. Mazarin, however, owned over 500 pictures on his death in 1661; and his contemporary, the Parisian banker Everhard Jabach (ca. 1618–1695), who also dealt in pictures, built up what has been called one of the most important collections of Italian paintings and drawings in Europe.[61]

Most of these early foreign collectors bought sight unseen, delegating the selection and acquisition to resident ambassadors or personal agents who traveled around Italy looking for pictures. Notable foreign collectors who themselves showed up in the Italian market toward the end of the century include the earl of Exeter, who bought or commissioned a total of almost 400 pictures in the cities he visited on his grand tour in the 1680s, and Marquis Gaspar de Guzmán (d. 1687), who built up much of his collection of some 3,000 paintings while Spanish ambassador in Rome and then viceroy in Naples. By this time the art market in Italy was thoroughly internationalized: painters were moving about to different urban markets, commissions were being directed to painters outside local markets, and agents of collectors were circulating throughout the peninsula looking for purchases.

Dealers moved into this international market alongside the personal agents of foreign collectors. Gerrit Uylenburgh, who along with his father had an active business as a painter and dealer in Holland, went to Italy on a buying trip in 1663; and the most expensive pictures in the inventory of his stock made after his death in 1674 were Italian.[62] The Flemish painter Niccolò Régnier established himself as a dealer in Venice, an important market for foreign collectors, buying pictures for resale and serving buyers as a consultant. He was prepared to provide the work—even forgeries—of any painter of all the major Italian schools, not just Venetian. Just before he died he put his entire collection up for sale through a lottery.[63]

International merchants, too, took an interest in this market. Already at the very beginning of the seventeenth century, the Genoese companies of Gavotti & Pozzobonelli and Herrera & Costa were doing some trading in pictures, mostly for the Spanish market.[64] Some of the agents of the great English collectors were merchants in Livorno and Venice, the two most important Italian port cities. The Florentine merchant Paolo del Sera, active in Venice from 1632 to 1672, was himself an amateur painter and collector and served as agent for Cardinal Leopoldo de' Medici. Another merchant in Venice, the Fleming Daniel Nys (d. 1647), arranged sales to collectors such as Arundel, Marie de' Medici, and Richelieu. On the death of Ferdinand, duke of Mantua, in 1626, Nys, knowing that the duke's successor, his brother Vincenzo II, was not interested in art, immediately set his eyes on the Gonzaga collections with the prospect of buying pictures for resale to foreign collectors, especially the English king. He was prepared to pay between 40,000 and 50,000 scudi for this venture, but in the end he fell on bad times because the king failed to pay for things that had been sent off to him, and problems with creditors forced Nys to sell his stock.[65]

In the 1620s another Flemish merchant, Antoine Goetkindt, who sold Flemish pictures in Paris, sent a Flemish painter to Italy to copy and buy Italian pictures. Another supplier of the market in Paris was the French merchant-banking firm of Lumague-Mascranni in Rome. Active in the 1630s and 1640s, it seems to have developed a distinct sideline buying art in Rome for resale in France to, among others, the court.[66] Other international merchant bankers from outside Italy who have been documented as showing up in the Italian art market include the Germans Hainoffer and Gerhard, the Fleming Lucas van Uffel, whose collection went up for auction in Amsterdam after his death in 1638, and the Dutchman Jan Reynst (d. 1646), whose collection also in Amsterdam included almost 200 Italian pictures.

Limits to Expansion

To sum up: the market for painting in the seventeenth century was a very different place from what it had been two centuries earlier. On the demand side, the public was better informed about painting. Private collections were accessible within limits, exhibitions were occasional events, publications regarding the market included books about art and artists, and the consciousness of the history of painting was informed by the scholarly approach of writers such as Baldinucci in Florence and Malvasia in Bologna. A lively secondary market had grown up: the public could find pictures on sale at various shops around town and at occasional exhibitions; dealers bought pictures and employed painters to produce pictures that they then sold; agents of collectors and speculators circulated through the market looking for specific products; and the presence of products, producers, and agents from out of town, and from beyond Italy, gave a cosmopolitan atmosphere to the proceedings. In this market emerged the figure of the painter-consultant who could make attributions and authenticate "old master" paintings, even taking on something of a professional guise with its recognition by the Accademia di S. Luca in Rome. Producers had the flexibility to shift production through a range of products directed to different price levels; they could become dealers; and they could supplement their income in this market by doing copies, making prints, restoring pictures, and serving buyers as appraisers, authenticators, consultants, and agents. In short, the variety of channels that had opened up to facilitate the sale of products by making them more readily available and better known to potential buyers constituted a more articulated market structure.

The market, moreover, was relatively free, resistant to the controls that producers' associations tried to impose, whether they were guilds acting in the spirit of medieval corporatism or the modern academy attempting to affirm the dignity of a profession under threat from expansion at the low end of the market. In Venice, for instance, the guild continued to legislate against the display of pictures outside of the painter's shop, but by the time of Tintoretto painters were doing it; and in Rome the Accademia attempted to license shops that sold pictures and to impose fees on all formal appraisals but in the end failed to regulate these activities.

This market, no longer dominated by the traditional personal nexus of the commission, was now driven in large part by an anonymous demand. And even though the more prestigious painters preferred, if they could, to avoid the open market in favor of the personal commission from a buyer of high social status, some of these got their start working in the market, gradually building up a reputation that allowed them to shift to the commission nexus. In this sense, the expansion of the open market, far from replacing older arrangements, facilitated the producer's effort to arrive at the privileged position where he could attract commissions.

Moreover, the internationalization of the market, with the influx of foreign painters and paintings on the one hand and the opening of outlets to clients abroad on the other, enriched the culture in which the painter worked. It has been claimed that the first truly cosmopolitan art market was to be found in seventeenth-century Rome, where a diversified demand was satisfied by a differentiated industry and where there was a multiplicity of artistic expression and a strong sense of professional dignity. In short, the painting industry consisted of an international community; and freedom of access to it, the circulation of diverse artistic traditions within it, the increase in the variety of products and specialization, and a quasi-professional status improved the painter's potential for defining and perfecting his particular talent, thereby enlarging his potential as a creative artist. In other words, these developments facilitated the fostering and growth of human capital. From the fifteenth to the seventeenth centuries, the industry and the market it served had undergone an extraordinary transformation.

Nonetheless, the market had its limits. At the low end the major limitation in the development of this Italian industry was its failure to orient its production in a major way to a market area that extended much beyond the different cities where it was located, let alone to markets outside of Italy. In this respect, contrast with the industry in the Low Countries is instructive. Already in fifteenth-century Bruges, which was a great international emporium that attracted merchants from the Continental hinterland, from the Hanseatic cities in the Baltic, and from England and Italy, painters engaged in serial production on a large scale and sold their products at the city's frequent international fairs. The shift of this northern European emporium from Bruges to Antwerp in the next century further enlarged marketing opportunities for painters, Antwerp being a far larger center of international commerce and finance. Moreover, painters there worked relatively free from the kind of guild regulatory system that characterized the Bruges industry. In 1540 they established themselves in permanent quarters for the year-round sale of pictures at the Antwerp Bourse, and at one point, in 1565, these sales areas came under the management of a single entrepreneur. Much of this production was export-led. Some local Antwerp merchants commissioned products, financed their export, and, in some instances, handled sales abroad, achieving a degree of vertical integration unknown in Italy.[67]

In Spain already in the third quarter of the sixteenth century, Flemish merchants dominated the market for paintings in the rapidly growing city of Madrid; and by the beginning of the next century they were major importers of paintings from their homeland to Seville, whence the market opened up to the American colonies.[68] In 1611 fifteen Antwerp dealers had stalls at fairs in Paris, notwithstanding opposition to their presence by authorities intent on protecting the interest of local painters; and through to the second half of the century Flemish paintings dominated imports to Paris, although a few efforts were made (such as those mentioned above) to obtain pictures also in Italy.[69] When in the following century exporters pushed also into the new markets opening up in Germany, they promoted Dutch and Flemish pictures much to the disadvantage of Italian products.[70] The importation of Flemish pictures into Italy was probably no less impressive than for these other places, but there is yet no study of the commercial system through which this was done. In addition to the export trade from the Low Countries, there were all those painters who themselves went abroad, especially to Paris, to England, and to Italy; and in Italy, as already observed, they show up in impressive numbers, especially in Genoa, Venice, and Rome.

The market in Italy never reached this level of development: the industry's production for export outside of Italy was negligible, as was the emigration of producers (notwithstanding the prestige of the relatively few who were attracted to northern European courts). Whereas major international merchants from Antwerp and Holland, like Renieri, Ulyenburgh, Nys, and Goetkindt, took initiatives in Italy to buy pictures, we know of no Italians—perhaps only for lack of research on the subject—who operated in the art market abroad in a major way, either buying the work of foreign producers or selling that of Italians. Significantly, only one Italian merchant is recorded as having appeared in the booming Paris market in the second half of the seventeenth century. Moreover, the Italian industry did not challenge these Northerners and their products in its own market area.

Prices, Profits, and Productivity

Prices

The growth and development of this particular industry and the greater structural articulation of market activity meant that by the seventeenth century more variables were coming into play in the determination of prices. At the low end of the market were the small genre scenes and other standardized pictures often produced in series. Most of them probably cost no more than a few scudi each—this at a time when an unskilled worker in the construction industry who managed to work full-time might be able to earn around 35 scudi in a year, the most skilled construction worker twice that, and highly skilled artisans perhaps twice as much again. Such relatively cheap decorative objects constituted the bulk of most collections.

At the high end of the market were the works of the "old masters." Their prices, as today, fluctuated according to the particular circumstances surrounding the sale. The few non-Italians who entered the market paid the top prices; they had enormous resources and were in a hurry to put together their collections. In 1621 Buckingham's agent paid 950 ducats for a Titian; and ten years later Hamilton's agent paid about 600 ducats for each of two Raphaels, 1,200 ducats for a Titian, and 1,800 ducats for a Giorgione.[71] Some old master paintings, however, fetched much higher prices when they were resold abroad. In 1627 the Flemish merchant Nys, who bought pictures from the Gonzaga of Mantua with an eye on their resale in England, was prepared to pay 4,000 scudi for a Madonna by Raphael, 2,000 scudi for one by Andrea del Sarto, and 2,000 scudi for two pictures by Correggio.[72] At the auction of the pictures of Charles I in 1649, Philip IV paid from 800 to 2,400 scudi for pictures by Titian and the enormous sum of 10,000 ducats (£2,000 sterling) for a Raphael, perhaps the highest price on record for the period, although none of the other pictures fetched more than several hundred pounds sterling. Only when Richelieu entered the competition in a follow-up sale did prices rise to an even higher level: £4,300 sterling for a Correggio and £4,900 sterling for a Titian.[73] Undoubtedly, the royal provenance of these pictures explains their extraordinarily high prices. In Italy the 7,000 ducats Giovan Filippo Spinola paid in 1650 for Veronese's *Supper in the House of Simon* (Galleria Sabauda, Turin), which included the cost of having a replacement copy made, was perhaps the highest price paid by an Italian collector.[74] Other pictures by Veronese went for prices ranging from 1,000 to 6,000 ducats.[75]

The dynamic behind this relatively sudden surge in the prices of old masters in the early seventeenth century may have been a matter of the fashion of the moment. The invasion of the market by English collectors came to an end with the fall of the monarchy. Very few Italians were prepared to pay more than 1,000 scudi for a Raphael, Andrea del Sarto, Correggio, or Titian, the high end of the market for contemporary painting; and most of the work of these old masters sold for much less.[76] Duke Vincenzo I Gonzaga haggled to bring the price of a Madonna by Andrea del Sarto down from 1,300 to 1,000 scudi, but was able to buy another picture by Andrea del Sarto and one by Raphael for only 200 scudi.[77] However, we know little about the rhythm of collecting in Italy, notwithstanding the current interest of art historians in *collezionismo*. There is a point at which a collection began to grow at a slower pace or ceased to grow altogether; and furthermore, as a result of the decrease in the velocity of the circulation of wealth among the rich in Italian society at the time, the ranks of collectors probably saw little renewal. One contemporary observer, Salvatore Castiglione, commenting on the situation in Genoa in 1661 after the sale of the notable Imperiale collection and the death of two other prominent collectors, thought that with the disappearance of this first generation of Genoese collectors, "who took pleasure in, and could spend for, pictures of quality," the end of an era had come.[78] In any event, at a time when the very rich had estates worth over a million ducats, "old master" prices were still very contained: with some notable exceptions, they fall into a range not much different from that for leading contemporary painters.[79] It is only toward the end of the seventeenth century when foreigners began to flow into Italy on the grand tour that the market for old masters took off.

It is the high end of the market for pictures by prestigious contemporary painters, however, that interests us here. This category includes those traditional products—altarpieces, history scenes, and major portraits—that the industry had been turning out since the fifteenth century, and one ought to be able to put together a price series. For what happened to the prices of these products over the long run constitutes one criterion for judging the effect of the growth and development of the industry on its overall performance in the marketplace. Although no one has yet put together a comprehensive price series for these kinds of pictures, we now have enough data at our disposal to detect the trend over the period being considered here, going from the fifteenth to the seventeenth centuries, the terminal point in the industrial and market development that is the subject of this survey. There is much data about prices for the fifteenth century scattered through the art historical literature, and the studies in this volume complement this material by providing an extraordinary quantity of data for the seventeenth century. These studies, in fact, constitute a model that could be used to pursue more systematic research into prices going back over the preceding centuries.[80]

For at least three reasons one would expect that the changes that had taken place in the industry by the seventeenth century would have resulted in considerably greater price variation. First, the notable improvement in techniques and workshop organization presumably allowed the painter to work more efficiently and with greater flexibility, the result being more leeway in setting his prices. Second, the keener competition among painters should have manifested itself in price rivalry, of the kind exemplified by Titian and Tintoretto in Venice. Finally, one consequence of the cultural prestige that both art and the artist had gained was the emergence of a hierarchy of painters ranked according to reputation, and this too should have been reflected in prices. Guido Reni exemplifies most strikingly how an artist could exploit his fame to get the highest prices. In addition to these dynamics within the industry, the emergence of connoisseurship on the demand side of the market should also have impinged on prices, for it sensitized demand to such values as attribution, authenticity, rarity, physical condition, and even previous ownership. Variation in prices was, in any event, a notable characteristic of the art market in the seventeenth century. At the time, experts called in to assess the value of collections could come up with wildly different estimates. In the 1617 inventory of pictures in the collection of Giovan Carlo Doria, 16 pictures were assessed at 100 scudi or more; the highest, a work by Paggi, was 500 scudi. But only four years later the Paggi picture was assessed at 1,000 scudi, still the highest, and 49 others at 100 scudi or more.[81] In the 1672 inventory of the pictures Cardinal Antonio Barberini left in bequests, only 30 out of the over 400 pictures were assessed at more than 200 scudi and only 6 above 500 scudi, the highest 3 being 1,000 scudi (a Leonardo, a Raphael, and a Correggio); but in the assessment made in 1686 of 30 pictures belonging to Prince Urbano Barberini, no fewer than 12 fell into a range of 1,200 to 7,000 scudi (the latter for a Poussin and a Parmigianino).[82] And the authors of this volume, whose charge was to say what they could about the subject, have produced arrays of prices that almost defy analysis.

And these authors also point to the extreme difficulty, if not impossibility, of establishing how prices of pictures were determined. These products were, by their very definition as works of art, unique. The measurable variables by which they can be objectively differentiated today—size and number of figures—have some correlation to prices in general, and specific painters—most famously Guercino—based their prices on such calculations. Also important were technique, subject matter, reputation of the painter, his sales pitch, the buyer's generosity, the specific circumstances of a commission, and the location of the market, all of which were erratic variables. Two other factors that might have gone into the price of a seventeenth-century picture—both indicators of how much the market had evolved by that time—were the dealer's expenses and investment appeal, but these, too, are imponderables (and unstudied) and most likely of slight importance.

If, on looking over the mass of data that we now have at our disposal, we are struck above all by the extraordinary variability of prices in the market for painting, closer inspection reveals that, at least at the top end of the market, prices generally rose over the course of the sixteenth century by a factor of between two and three, somewhat more than the price of the basic basket of consumables. Prices of most altarpieces in Italy during the period generally considered the Renaissance, from the fifteenth through to the early sixteenth centuries, hovered around 100 florins; some cost as much as 200 florins, but very few paintings anywhere in Italy cost more than 200 florins. The price level rose somewhat in the sixteenth century. Allori, working in Florence at mid-century, received around 200 florins for his altarpieces, and this was the estimate for the large paintings to go in the 30 new altars projected in Cosimo I's scheme for the modernization of Santa Croce and S. Maria Novella. In Venice the large paintings produced for the doge's palace and the scuole grandi cost from 100 to 300 scudi. By the next century prices for comparable paintings throughout Italy were at this level or somewhat higher. In Florence the price of an altarpiece by a better known painter ranged between 100 and 200 scudi. In Naples the standard price for major works by the best painters was closer to the 200–300 scudi level; in Venice most major pictures cost from 300 to 350 scudi. Sohm estimates that in Venice the price per square meter for large paintings, of the kind that served on altars and in other public places, rose from about 10–12 ducats in the middle of the sixteenth century to about 24–27 ducats toward the end of the seventeenth century, an increase of around 150 percent at the most. The price of many products of the painting industry, however, did not rise by this much.

It is probably safe to conclude, on the basis of the data in this volume, that, in general, altarpieces and major history paintings by leading artists in the seventeenth century ranged in price between 200 and 400 scudi. Portraits and landscapes by the best painters—Van Dyck in Genoa and Claude in Rome, for instance—cost less, about 100 to 150 scudi and even below. Many altarpieces fell into a range of 50 to 150 scudi, and most items by living artists in collections for which we have assessments were appraised at much less. Pictures costing as much as 400 scudi, however, are not difficult to find. Among the pictures for which price data are recorded in these essays, 43 cost from 500 to 1,000 scudi (15 of which were the enormous altarpieces commissioned for St. Peter's), only 19 cost more than 1,000 scudi, and 9 of these more than 1,600 scudi (the highest price recorded for the market in Rome, arguably the most active of all). Four of these latter were pictures by Reni, and he seems to have been the only painter whose prices often reached a level as high as 1,000 scudi.

These exceptions apart, it would seem that the general price level of major paintings by leading painters from the fifteenth to the seventeenth centuries rose by only somewhat more than the inflation index of about 100 percent that obtained for the cost of an ordinary basket of consumables, an index considered so high that it gave rise to the concept of "the price revolution" (although the annual increase would have been hardly perceptible). This index, however, synthesizes the prices of those basic consumables that are considered to be close to meeting the minimum needs for survival, and it has been used primarily in conjunction with the study of wages at the low end of the market to establish the course of the real value—the purchasing power—of those wages over the period of "the revolution." On both counts such studies are of limited use in evaluating what happened in the industry being studied here. On the one hand, goods such as paintings obviously did not figure in the basic basket of consumables at the bottom of the market; and on the other hand, the wages of many artisans rose at a much higher rate than did those of workers used in these price studies (for the most part, workers in the construction industry).[83] Moreover, we lack data both for the prices of durable goods beyond the range of those in the basket of basic necessities and for the earnings of workers of middling status.

It is in this light, and not just against the indices of the price revolution, that we must judge the performance of the painting industry. And, in any event, as observed at the outset of this essay, the rich who became much richer and those at the middling economic level who very much improved their circumstances enjoyed an increase in their capacity for consumption that much outpaced the rise in the general price level. Since the rise of the price for paintings at the high end of the market only slightly exceeded the rise of that general price level, those people who were better off saw a decline in the price for paintings relative to their increased ability to spend. In fact, for many of the people of the class that traditionally bought paintings, these products became bargains. At the end of the fifteenth century, one of the wealthiest men in Florence, Filippo Strozzi, who left an estate worth about 100,000 florins, could well afford to pay the 200 florins that the most expensive altarpiece would have cost him; but for the wealthiest people in seventeenth-century Italy, who were worth more than a million scudi, a picture by Reni that cost 1,000 scudi was a bargain, not to mention the much lower prices of the work of almost all other prestigious painters. From the buyer's side of the market, the performance of the industry was decidedly positive.

Indeed, this is exactly what one might expect, given that the growth and development of the industry over the preceding century, as it has been described here, resulted in more efficient production, so that the prices of its products, relative to the rise of private wealth, were contained and even brought down. By increasing his output over a given time without a significant rise in his costs, the painter improved his productivity, ending up earning more without having to raise the prices of his products. Other factors may also have come into play to contain prices for these products. Prices may have been subject to a certain stickiness: that is, the traditional notion of what was the standard price for a product served as a brake on a rise in prices. The force such a traditional notion had in the marketplace has been cited as an explanation for the stickiness of workers' wages throughout Europe in the early modern period that resulted in a lag of wages behind the rising price of basic consumables. Moreover, the highly competitive nature of painters may also have served to keep prices within a limited range, since very few of them could, like Reni, dare to demand a price that was completely outside that range. And, finally, there is the basic demand–supply mechanism always at work in the marketplace: demand, as much as it had increased, may have been more than met by an increase in supply resulting from growth of the industry and increased efficiency in production. All of these factors—increased productivity, stickiness of the traditional notions of price, competition, equilibrium of demand and supply—constitute the economic logic that could explain the containment, even reduction, of the relative price of paintings over the fifteenth, sixteenth, and seventeenth centuries. None of these factors, however, has been studied for any product, let alone paintings.

Earnings

Further evidence of improved productivity in the industry would be a rise in painters' profits resulting not from higher prices for their products but from increased output. Unfortunately, it is impossible to document how much, on the average, painters earned in a year. In fifteenth-century Florence probably no painter had an annual income that exceeded by much that of any other highly skilled craftsman, and certainly none earned anything like the 100 florins Brunelleschi received as salary as head mason at the cathedral works. The figures we have for some painters two centuries later would indicate that these men were earning very much more. We are told that Lanfranco earned 3,000 ducats a year and Domenichino somewhat less while they were in Naples, that Guercino earned from 1,000 to 4,000 scudi at the height of his career, that many history painters earned around 1,000 scudi a year, that any number of other painters earned over several hundred scudi a year, and that even a middling painter in Rome might have earned as much as 120 scudi—all figures that (factoring in the inflation index) put them well above the income level of painters in fifteenth-century Florence.

There are serious problems in interpreting all these figures, however. They are, first of all, presumably figures for gross, not net, income. Although figures have been assembled to give us a precise idea of a painter's expenses—the cost of his materials, the rent of his studio, the wages of his assistants, even the fees for models—we have no cost analysis of the internal operation of any one artist's workshop. In other words, we know virtually nothing about the attendant costs to higher production levels. Another problem in understanding these figures is the volatility of a painter's income depending on the particular circumstances of his situation at any one time, including his reputation at the moment and aging, hence reduced capacity to work. For the moment, therefore, the figures we have for the income of the top earners in the seventeenth century are suggestive at best. Nevertheless, the very size of these figures indicates that some painters were earning much more than what the best painters earned two centuries earlier.

Some, in fact, earned enough to leave estates that were significantly larger than that of any earlier Renaissance painter. Neri di Bicci, the wealthiest painter that can be documented in fifteenth-century Florence, declared real estate worth 690 florins in his 1480 tax report, enough to put him solidly in the middling class of artisans. A generation later, Raphael and then Michelangelo accumulated impressive patrimonies, but both stood out much above the crowd of painters because they enjoyed the official patronage of the pope, including a salaried office in the papal bureaucracy. The documentation of later sixteenth-century painters leaves the impression that painters did not reach a much higher economic level than that of Neri di Bicci a century earlier. Jacopo Bassano left little property; Allori in Florence and Tintoretto in Venice left estates comparable to that of Neri; it does not seem that Titian, for all the touting of the high fees he presumably commanded and his several handsome pensions, left much more of an estate; and Veronese is considered to have been comfortable but by no means wealthy.[84] Vasari in Florence and Giulio Romano did very much better, but this was largely thanks to their work as architects with an official position in a princely court.

In the seventeenth century the mass of painters had only modest success, probably no better than the average artisan or shopkeeper. A 1656 survey of the distribution of wealth of one area of Rome reveals that while no painters were wealthy, there were about as many who were comfortably off as were poor. There were some painters, however, who were better off than painters had ever been before, leaving estates very much larger than anything that earlier painters, such as Neri di Bicci, could have imagined as possible. In Florence Jacopo Chiavistelli was able to save 40,000 scudi and Cosimo Ulivelli 30,000 scudi; in Venice Loth left an estate of 32,000 ducats, although it was the only estate of a painter worth more than 10,000 ducats; in Rome Maratta and Gaulli left estates worth about 40,000 scudi; and some 20 painters, including Poussin and Claude, left estates worth 10,000 scudi or more. Ribera in Naples was able to buy a house for 1,900 ducats and a villa for 3,100 ducats and to provide his daughter with a dowry of 5,000 ducats. However, some of the highest earners for one reason or another did not accumulate much of an estate to leave to heirs: for instance, Reni, who had no heirs to think about, lived somewhat extravagantly and gambled heavily, and Federico Zuccari, who was paid handsomely by the various princes for whom he worked, left an estate heavily burdened with debt, largely as a result of his ambitious project for building a palace in Rome—a project, however, that could only have been conceived by one with means far beyond that of any fifteenth-century painter.

In a society where dowries ranged from 15,000 to 20,000 florins in Florence and reached as high as 100,000 scudi in Rome, no painter ever entered the ranks of the rich. Nor did any painter do as well as some prominent foreigners in the courts of the great European kingdoms. Velázquez in Spain, for instance, enjoyed stipends and allowances worth over 1,500 ducats a year, free housing, and a high price (500 ducats, later raised to 700 ducats) for each painting he did for the king; and in France both Le Brun and Mignard left estates worth approximately 600,000 livres (roughly equivalent in purchasing power to 85,000 scudi in Italy).[85]

If some seventeenth-century painters earned much more than what painters had earned in the past, it was because they worked more efficiently, not because relative prices for their products had risen. And it is to be kept in mind that painters relied on market arrangements of one kind or another, be it a commission or an across-the-counter sale. Unlike architects and sculptors such as Michelangelo and Bernini, both of whom accumulated considerable wealth, painters, with rare exception, could not gain posts in a princely bureaucracy or at a court, and they could not count on generous subsidies from a patron for long-term employment. Dependence on the market, containment of prices, and higher earnings point to greater productivity.

Culture in the Marketplace

In the course of the fourteenth to the seventeenth centuries the market for paintings underwent a transformation as perhaps no other. It was penetrated by new cultural values affirming the status of producer and product, it enjoyed a vigorous demand, it had developed a complex structure of intermediary agencies, and it was supplied by an industry that had undergone considerable growth and development. The improvement in the performance of the industry manifested itself both in relatively lower prices for buyers (who also got the added value of greater cultural prestige) and higher earnings for at least some producers (which complemented their higher cultural status). In fact, the cultural qualification added parenthetically to the above conclusion about the performance of the industry suggests a curious market phenomenon: the resistance of prices to added cultural value. The considerable enhancement of the prestige enjoyed by painters and their products seems to have had less of an effect as a countervailing force working against the functioning of the market according to the classic demand–supply mechanism than one might have expected. Prestige had a limited impact both on the demand side in that buyers' needs and taste did not pull prices up and on the supply side in that producers were not successful in pushing prices very far up. It is only in the retrospective view we have today, conditioned by the prestige the industry has gained in the meantime, that the Italian industry appears much ahead in a cultural if not an economic sense.

On the demand side, the telling factor was the lack of responsiveness of the price of paintings to an enormous increase in private wealth, what the economist would call the inelasticity of the price of paintings. For all the cultural prestige of painting and for all the consequent refinement of demand by connoisseurship and the conditioning of supply by the uniqueness and rarity of products, demand did not pull prices up much beyond their traditional level. Prices for painting, it seems, were negatively correlated to that of other luxury goods, such as jewelry, plate, and clothing, and, as in Holland, seem to have fallen into line with household furnishings. For instance, in 1694 the paintings in the famous Brignole collection in Genoa were evaluated at 20,000 scudi, but this collection constituted only 13 percent of the total value of the household goods divided a few years later, which did not include jewelry and clothing, both of which, by contrast, would have represented relatively extravagant expenditures. As mentioned by Philip Sohm, a sample of Venetian inventories spanning the second half of the seventeenth century reveals that paintings constituted 23 percent of the total value of household possessions, which, however, probably did not include jewelry and clothing. For the moment, however, we have no studies of the preferences that determined how the wealthy as consumers allocated their greater resources for the acquisition of durable goods in the marketplace.[86]

With expenditures for paintings at a relatively low level, no one had a significant amount of capital tied up in a collection. For all their much touted patronage, the rich in baroque Italy spent an insignificant part of their wealth on art in general, let alone paintings. In a recent analysis of the expenditures on art by Bartolomeo III Arese (1610–1674), one of the most prominent men on the Milanese scene in the seventeenth century, Andrea Spiriti concludes that over the last 33 years of his life Arese spent no more than 7.5 percent of his income on "art," which included considerable expenditure on building, complete with gardens and furnishings, and of this not more than 1 percent went for easel painting. And in Rome only 1.5 percent of the expenditures of the rich and powerful Borghese over 29 years went for the acquisition of painting and sculpture together.[87] In fact, in the price lists collected in this volume, almost all of the 62 pictures that cost more than 500 scudi were for ecclesiastical, not domestic, settings.

We do not yet know much about the market value of collections, however, despite the vigorous study of collecting and collections that marks one of the most recent trends in art historical research. No one, it seems, was buying pictures as an investment, even though many people were aware of the rising prices of the pictures of some painters, particularly of the emerging old masters, as we have seen. Obviously, in the long run the monetary value of a collection could rise considerably, especially when in the eighteenth century foreigners invaded Italy on the grand tour looking for works of art, but this phenomenon could hardly have entered into the calculations of collectors a century earlier. Bernard Mandeville, writing about the secondary art market in northern Europe at the beginning of the eighteenth century, thought that an essential element in the pricing of art was the social rank of the owner, but it remains to be seen how much the collecting of painting in Italy pulled prices up by endowing these objects with the social prestige of their owners.[88]

Paintings, whether by old masters or by living artists at the top of the market, enjoyed nothing like the prestige of classical art. The impetus for collecting antiquities, well under way in the fifteenth century, far outpaced the collecting of paintings, and government measures to protect ancient objects from exportation goes back to that century and has a continuing tradition. The inflated market value of antiquities relative to that for contemporary painting and sculpture, a ratio that reached as high as ten to one, is reflected in the valuations of the famous Medici inventory of 1492, drawn up on the death of Lorenzo il Magnifico. In the sixteenth century the traffic in antiquities reached the point where a few dealers joined together in formal partnerships and conducted their business through networks that extended throughout Italy and beyond the Alps, a degree of organization unknown among dealers in paintings notwithstanding the internationalization of the market.[89]

On the supply side, what in the final analysis may have mattered most in the market for painting was ideology, for in the marketplace the prestige that the painter and his products had gained was up against certain insuperable countervailing forces. Any ambition that painters may have had to improve their social status was doomed to failure, notwithstanding their cultural pretensions and their efforts to refine their lifestyle. They did not have the cultural credentials, since few could claim authority for erudition and learning, whatever their familiarity with classical and literary texts. And they did not have the social credentials, since they worked with their hands, a criterion of status (excluding even those engaged in retail trade) that had gained rapid ground in the sixteenth century among capitalist elites of the major Italian cities. As Renata Ago observes, not one painter succeeded in entering the nobility or consolidating his status so that his heirs could. Some were knighted and a few received titles, but this amounted to no more than a gesture in the gift economy of the time and did not lead to social advancement, although it might also have carried a material award, such as a gold chain. Clients' gestures toward a painter, in fact, seldom went beyond the occasional reward. They were not patrons in any real sense of that term: they did not provide continual ongoing financial support, and few took a painter into their homes as dependents or into their circle of intimate associates. Unlike architects and musicians, painters could rarely find a lucrative and prestigious position in the bureaucracy—and hence the court and household—of a ruling prince.[90]

Painters, of course, did not have the economic resources to move themselves or their children into the upper class, and the sensitivity to their economic status manifest in their writings leads one to wonder how much their expectations had been aroused by their cultural pretensions. They considered their economic status fairly low and were resentful of this. Their writings reveal a full range of concerns arising from a preoccupation with wealth: a fear of poverty, anxiety about money, the notion of the starving artist, the sense of being exploited by dealers, resentment of the success of a few artists at the top, and suspicion of a link between quality and price and between success and greed. Given their cultural pretensions, some were driven to rationalize their frustration by maintaining—in complete ignorance, as we have seen—that things had been better in the past and that they were living in the shadow of a glorious tradition. But if such a notion left them with a sense of decline, they could rationalize their way out of this frame of mind by speculating about whether it is not better that an artist be poor and whether in fact money corrupts. Bellori went so far as to assert the extreme conceit: that painters really produce their products for the love of their art—for art's sake, not for money. In any event, most of the odds and ends of contemporary comments on these economic aspects of the artist's life in the seventeenth century come from the writings of artists themselves, and one wonders to what extent their agitation about these matters derived from a preoccupation with false expectations that precluded a realistic assessment of the market in which they operated.

The very prestige that painters only too eagerly sought seems to have carried with it values that prejudiced painters themselves against the market. Their academies in both Venice and Rome explicitly expressed distaste for the commercial side of the painter's activity. The academy in Rome tried to limit the number of retail shops, to block members from dealing in the works of others, to forbid the exhibition of work in their shops, and in other ways to prevent any activity that debased the profession by treating its products like cheap goods. Thus, the more pretentious painters adapted the antimarket values of their patrons; they disassociated themselves from demeaning trade and sought to establish relations with their upper-class clients outside the marketplace and in the economic realm of the commission nexus and of the gift. Reni, of course, is the primary exhibit here: he went all the way in embracing the nexus of a gift culture to the exclusion of that of normal market exchange—and he consistently got more for his pictures than any other Italian painter.

Honig regards this "antimarket discourse of valuation" by artists during the sixteenth and seventeenth centuries as being directed "to shore up an alternative mode of value-making . . . threatened by the market." But how "correctly" she thinks these writers perceived the threat is precisely the problem that cries for attention, at least in the Italian, as distinct from the Flemish–Dutch, case.[91] For in the final analysis the cultural pretensions of painters found too little resonance on the demand side of the market to make much difference. They could not change the set of values their clients attached to material goods, and they could not modify the negative notions their clients had about market activity, manual labor, and social status. For all the growth and development of the industry, in so many ways more impressive for this industry than for any other, market forces were not strong enough to induce these producers to compromise their adherence to traditional social values. They were creatures of their age, and in fact one wonders how much of the concern that generated the literature in which they sought to establish their cultural credentials was primarily directed to crossing the ideological barrier that defined their society. And on intellectual grounds, for all the pretensions of a few of them to define what it was they were doing—and for all the effort made today to justify their case—they could not gain full respectability. As Edward Gibbon wrote in his journal later in the eighteenth century, "Poetry descends from the sky, painting rises from the earth . . . the painter, unlike the poet, does not find his origins in the depth of his soul." In his classic study of art in seventeenth-century Rome, Francis Haskell noted the "general decline in the status of the artist which had set in after the High Renaissance and had never been totally reversed. . . . Art was no longer self-sufficient . . . [and the artist] lost some of his mystique."[92] The fact that painters in the Low Countries did not labor under such cultural pretensions may be part of the explanation of why the market was so much more dynamic there than in Italy, and yet it is not a little ironic that out of this market emerged at least one painter, Rubens, whose solid cultural credentials far outclassed those of any Italian painter.

In conclusion, the economic historian, in trying to understand why prices of contemporary art remained so low notwithstanding its much augmented cultural value as well as the greater disposable wealth of the rich, finds himself straying into a path that perhaps otherwise he would never have entered studying any other industry—a path leading him toward confrontation with a peculiar feature of the preindustrial economy, what Renata Ago has called the baroque economy: the role of culture in the operations of the marketplace. Although this industry—to go back to the opening observations of this essay—contributed scarcely anything to gross national product and the traffic in its products constituted an insignificant corner of the marketplace, its impressive growth and development have characteristics that are central to the problems that inspire the study of economic history in general. For the industry operated in a market still permeated with cultural values of a premodern economy. Here, in fact, is one of the most difficult—and most fascinating—challenges that economic historians must always confront: evaluating the role in the marketplace of cultural values different from our own, including those values that economic historians, following today's economists, only too readily assume explain past economic behavior. Cultural and economic values as they come into play in the marketplace, however, are not mutually exclusive. Recently Michael Hutter and David Throsby have pointed the way for the exploration of their interrelation in the process of evaluation and called for a multidisciplinary approach to study of the subject.[93] And there cannot be many fields that offer richer materials for such an investigation than the history of the painting industry in Renaissance and early modern Italy.

Notes

Preface

1 Bologna as part of the Papal States politically is an exception, but its artistic importance we felt required inclusion. We had planned on including Genoa, but the documentary data available are insufficient.

2 We decided not to merge our tables because of the subjective nature of each author's decision of what constitutes a "figure."

3 While various specialized studies have replaced Martini's rare book (which is now available on the website of the Biblioteca Nazionale Braidense: www.braidense.it), none is equal to it in its broad sweep. For Italian seventeenth-century exchange rates, a valuable complement to Martini is Guercino's *Libro dei conti. . .* (Ghelfi, 1997). For further discussion of monetary questions see the Introduction and Renata Ago's essay, especially Tables 30 and 31.

4 See note 222 in the essay on Rome.

Introduction

1 The years in parentheses indicate when the account books were kept. Farinati, 1968; Strina, 2000; Ghelfi, 1997; Miller, 1991 and 2001; Heikamp, 1963; and Goldenberg Stoppato and Mannini, 1997. Franchi's *Giornale di entrate e uscite* remains unpublished but was consulted by Fumagalli for this book. Alboresi's account books have been consulted by Feinblatt (1979) and others but never published; Morselli refers in her chapter to the originals in the Archiginnasio, Bologna. Sixteenth-century account books available for comparison include those by Lorenzo Lotto (Lotto, 1969); Giulio Romano (Ferrari, 1992); Giovanni da Udine (Cargnelutti, 1987); Francesco and Jacopo Bassano (Muraro, 1992); and Alessandro Allori (Supino, 1908). Sculptors' account books include those by Annibale Caccavello (Filangieri di Candida, 1896) and Alessandro Vittoria (Predelli, 1908). For the account book of the Milanese painter Flaminio Pasqualini, see Berra, 2008.

2 Goldthwaite, 2003, p. 426.

3 Cavazzini, 2004a, and Ago, 2006.

4 Rosa, 1995, p. 108 ("Satira sulla pittura," III.424ff.).

5 Hollanda, 1998, p. 107.

6 Hollanda, 1998, p. 79.

7 Borghini, 1998, pp. 105–6.

8 Spear, 1997, on Reni's gambling.

9 Lupis, 1675, p. 15 (letter to the Neapolitan painter Angelo Valle).

10 Bottari and Ticozzi, 1822, IV, p. 63 (letter of 1665 from David Brembati in Bergamo to Mario De Tassis in Brescia): "Questo è il migliore che si trovi di presente in Lombardia, venuto apposta da Roma per abbellire suddetta Chiesa [S. Maria Maggiore]; ma dubito che la spesa le parrà troppo grande perché in S. Maria per 16 quadri sono convenuti darli 4,300 Ducatoni. Il pittore [Ciro Ferri] veramente è delli primi d'oggidì che si trovi in Italia ed egli si conosce per tale, e vorrebbe anco esser conosciuto dagli altri per il prezzo che ne pretende."

11 Tessin the Younger, 2002, p. 117.

12 Borean, 2000, p. 183 (inventory of the Correggio collection, 1663).

13 Navarro, 2005, p. 87.

14 Vasari, 1966–87, III, p. 595.

15 Summerscale, 2000, p. 174.

16 Vasari, 1966–87, IV, p. 12, translation by Bull, in Vasari, 1965, p. 254.

17 Waldman, 2006, pp. 69–70 (Vasari's bleak assessment of Raffaellino's final years is confirmed by payments for his last works that were lower than payments for his earlier works and lower

than industry standards, equivalent to those paid to young and unknown painters); Vasari, 1966–87, IV, p. 119.

18 Malvasia, 1841, II, p. 181.

19 Ridolfi [1648], 1965, II, p. 117; see also Ridolfi on Schiavone (I, p. 258).

20 Comanducci, 1999, p. 162, on Neri di Bicci.

21 Comanini, 2001, p. 109.

22 Mancini, 1956–57, I, p. 242.

23 Ridolfi [1648], 1965, I, p. 171.

24 Hollanda, 1998, p. 133.

25 On Michelangelo's clothes, see Barolsky, 1991, pp. 26–29.

26 Vasari, 1966–87, VI, p. 112.

27 Michelangelo, letter to Niccolò Martelli, January 1542. For a poignant juxtaposition of his real and perceived wealth, see Hatfield, 2002.

28 Rosa, 1995, p. 105 ("Satira sulla pittura," III.307ff.).

29 Lupis, 1685, p. 68.

30 Summerscale, 2000, pp. 224–25.

31 Hollanda, 1998, p. 107: "And what shall I say of the fortunate Venetian Sebastiano who, albeit the times were not favourable, received from the Pope the Uffizio del Piombo, with the honour and profit that such a post entails, although the lazy man painted but two pictures in Rome."

32 According to Bellori ([1672] 1976, pp. 182–83), Barocci used to tell young painters that "le commodità sono d'impedimento a chi desidera venire avanti, e che il piacere d'imparare condisce ogni disagio e fatica."

33 Magalotti, 1991, p. 68.

34 Rosa, 1995, p. 105 ("Satira sulla pittura," III.307ff.). Bellori, writing in the margins of his copy of Baglione's *Vite* close to the time Rosa composed his "Satire on painting": "vendere la sua mercanzia è stato la ruina di molti belli ingegni, che l'hanno seguitato, avendo corrotto, et fatto cadere affatto la Pittura" (quoted by Röttgen, 2002, pp. 210–11). They might have been thinking of the famous concluding section (XLIV) from *On the sublime* by "Longinus," or just as likely (considering their interests in stoicism) they had in mind Seneca's cultural critique of materialism, as had Junius in 1637 (II.ix.7; in edition cited: II, p. 166): "Of luxury, sayth *Seneca* the Rhetorician, 'There is nothing so deadly to the wit of man as luxurie.' [Seneca, I. Praef. 7] Of Avarice, sayth *Epictetus*, 'The desire of riches maketh men base minded.' [*Epicteti disserationes*, IV.4.1]."

35 Armenini, 1988, bk. I, ch. 1. For a discussion of Armenini on the profession of painters, see Williams, 1995 and 2007.

36 Pigozzi, 1999, pp. 116–17 (from the preface of *Essemplario della nobile arte del dissegno*, 1612).

37 Lomazzo, 1993 p. 24.

38 Comanini, 2001, p. 109 (conclusion); Borghini, 1584, 98.

39 Sohm, 2007, pp. 131–48. Junius, 1991, I, pp. 165–66, quoting Petronius Arbiter, *Satyricon*, 88.

40 Vasari, 1966–87, V, p. 561.

41 Hochmann, 1988, p. 71: "Questa tasa più a Giorgio che a Taddeo si conviene emendare e maligno a dir questo anzi con molta carita cristiana si dilevata accetare e sovenire molti giovani forestieri per il cui tratenimento e degno di molta laude e non di biasimo come indegniamente gli da questo maledico."

42 Gronau, 1936, p. 226 (no. CCCXLVI, letter from Grazioso Graziosi, writing from Rome, to Francesco Maria II della Rovere, 1593): "Il Federico Zuccaro . . . si è imbarcato in un suo capriccio poetico, il quale sarà facilmente la rovina de suoi figlioli, essendosi posto à Fabbricare un Palazzotto senza un proposito al mondo, in un sito stravagantissimo che in pittura potrebbe riuscire una bella cosa, et gli assorbisce facilmente quanto fin qui ha fatto di capitale, oltre l'haverlo disviato quasi in tutto dalla sua professione, perche adesso non lavora se non qualche cosa in casa sua solo per necessita de denari." In another letter written two years later, Graziosi commented that Zuccaro "ricerverà sempre per prezzo eccessivo ogni piccola cortesia. . . . Io sapendo per prova in mille cose, che queste cortesie riescano più costose, che i cari prezzi, mi sono ingegnato piu che ho potuto, di tirarlo fuora, ma per adesso non è stato possible."

43 For Graziosi, see Gronau, 1936, p. 226; and Zuccaro, 1608, p. 4.

44 Gronau, 1936, p. 226 (no. CCCXLVI; letter from Graziosi to della Rovere, 1593).

45 Rosa, 2003, pp. 342–43, no. 321 (1 April 1666).

46 Rosa, 2003, p. 344, no. 323 (29 May 1666). Ten years ealier when Rosa experienced another five-month hiatus (p. 225, no. 201, 9 September 1656), it was for psychological reasons, fears of the plague: "Sono 5 mesi che non ho tocchi pennelli, parlandosi in questi tempi d'ogni altra cosa che di pittura, e quello che prima di queste turbolenze valeva dieci adesso va uno, né si trova chi lo voglio."

47 Lukehart, 1993, pp. 37–58.

48 For their excellent review of art exports, see De Marchi and Matthew, 2007, pp. 252–59. See also the important work by Miguel Falomir, 2006.

49 Boselli, 1971, p. 76.

50 For the population of painters in Verona, see Fanfani, 1959, p. 95; for Brescia, see Tedoldi, 2003, p. 67; for Milan, see Guerzoni, 2006, p. 45; for Genova, see Sivori Porro, 1989, pp. 359–60.

51 For Zafferino, see Lukehart, 2007, p. 111, n. 38. For Federico's series of biographical drawings, see Brooks, 2007, pp. 6–45.

52 Malvasia, 1841, I, p. 327; trans. Summerscale, 2000, p. 248.

53 Bellori [1672], 1976, p. 531.

54 Seravalli, 1696, p. 403.

55 For colorists being paid more than *disegno*-based painters, see Sohm, 1991, p. 61, and Spear below.

56 Schnapper, 2004, pp. 277–80, 216.

57 Serres, in a paper delivered at the College Art Association's annual meetings, Boston, 2005.

58 Bonfait, 2000 and 2002b; Marshall, 2003; and Spear and Morselli herein.

59 Schnapper, 2004, pp. 206–7.

60 Saccardo, 1981, p. 68.

61 Schnapper, 2004, pp. 201–11.

62 O'Malley, 2003, pp. 167–68.

63 Ghelfi, 1997, pp. 32–33.

64 Peri [1639], 1682, p. 26, discussed by Cecchini, 2003, pp. 123–24.

65 Baracchi and Giovanardi, 1998, pp. 134–35 (letters to Francesco d'Este from Scalabrini, his ambassador in Venice, 24 September and 15 October 1639).

66 On gifting in the seventeenth century, see Spear, 1994 and 1997; Warwick, 2000, pp. 55–75; and Guerzoni, 2006, pp. 260–64.

67 The studies by Lukehart are fundamental to these questions and to the socio-economic conditions of artists in Genoa: 1987, pp. 209–14, and 1993, pp. 37–58.

68 Paggi to his brother Girolamo, 1591 (Bottari and Ticozzi, 1822, VI, no. 17, pp. 71–72).

69 Bottari and Ticozzi, 1822, III, nos. 178 and 179, pp. 361–69 (letters of 1691–2 from David in Rome to the Regents of S. Maria Maggiore in Bergamo).

70 Marshall, 2005, and Spear, 2005.

71 The letters are published in Saccardo, 1981, pp. 40–46, 60–70.

72 Spear, 1994, p. 597. Regarding Guercino's *St. Philip Neri in Ecstasy* (S. Maria di Galliera, Bologna), with its empty top half leaving St. Philip Neri and two angels to rattle around below, Spear draws the important conclusion that "caution is needed, therefore, when discussing the 'simplicity' and 'austerity' of some of Guercino's late compositions, or his penchant for half-length figures, lest aesthetic judgment be confused with economic policy."

73 Damerini, 1969, p. 77.

74 Baracchi and Giovanardi, 1998, p. 134 (letter from Scalabrini to Francesco I d'Este, 4 August 1640).

75 Marshall, 2005, p. 6, and Spear, 2005, p. 157.

76 Ridolfi [1648], 1965, II, p. 204.

77 Tintoretto, 1578 (Syre, 2000, pp. 239–42); Prudenti, 1638 (Bratti, 1915, pp. 471–72); Cavagna, 1592 (Coppa and Rossi, 1987, p. 156); and Cervelli, 1677 (Haskell, 1963, p. 219).

78 In addition to the examples cited below, see the dispute between Gerolamo Forabosco and his patron in 1646 where the experts were "all painters," Bortolo Scaligero, Pietro Vecchia, and Domenico Bruni.

79 Giovan Paolo Cavagna suggested that the design (*disegno*) of his fresco should be judged against the four paintings by Francesco Bassano in the same chapel (without consideration of its *colorito* since Bassano had painted in oil and his was in fresco). When in 1700 Simone Brentana and Biagio Falcieri reviewed a painting by Santo Prunato, they were asked to consider "the art, merit, and craft" of the painting in relation to its size. Writing in the same year, Averoldo noted Brentana as one of the best connoisseurs of art. In 1638 Sante Peranda and Tiberio Tinelli considered the "diligence" that Bernardino Prudenti used for his altarpiece in the Salute to arrive at the hefty price of 600 ducats. An altarpiece by Sisto Badalochio may not be equal to one by Michelangelo, Raphael, or Correggio, concluded the Modenese painter Camillo Gavasseti in 1613, but it still was deemed "good and beautiful" and hence worth 55 scudi. In 1661 the *deputati* of S. Maria Maggiore in Bergamo complained about the quality (*qualità*) of Pietro Liberi's *Flood*. Liberi went to Bergamo to make some changes and satisfied the *deputati*, who voted eight to four in favor of Liberi. One year later for the following commission of a *Last Judgment*, the *deputati* were unhappy that some figures had their heads missing, a not unexpected state of affairs considering the subject. This time Liberi resisted, and Francesco Cairo and Pietro Vecchia were appointed as adjudicators. The results of their judgment are lost.

80 Syre, 2000, p. 239.

81 Magagnato, 1966.

82 Guzzo, 1995, p. 200.

83 In only one case known to me did an artist object: when the *deputati* at S. Maria Maggiore in Bergamo decided to review a painting by Ciro Ferri, the artist was sufficiently threatened to withdraw the painting and close his account for 13 others.

84 Hopkins (2000, pp. 213–14) accepts the unlikely story of a four-day production.

85 Bratti, 1915, p. 473.

86 Hochmann, 1992b, p. 88, and Marshall, 2004, pp. 45–46.

87 Ridolfi [1648], 1965, II, p. 101.

88 Fumagalli below; Matthew, 2006, pp. 322–24; Migliorini and Assini, 2000, p. 20; and Coen, 2004, p. 422.

89 Ago, 2002, pp. 383–86.

90 Migliorini and Assini, 2000, p. 20.

91 Cecchini, 2006, pp. 127–28.

92 Lorizzo, 2003b, pp. 325–27; for Venice, see Sohm below.

93 Bellesi, 1992, pp. 141–44.

94 For studies of Guercino's accounts, see Bonfait, 1990; Spear, 1994, p. 598; Ghelfi, 1997; and Spear, 2003, p. 313. For a graph of his income, see below in this Introduction.

95 Colombo, 1983, p. 221 (Cairo).

96 Negro and Roio, 2000, pp. 41–42, 44–46.

97 Pinchera, 2002, pp. 643–44.

98 Lukehart, 2007, p. 111, n. 38.

99 Heikamp, 1963, p. 184.

100 Marshall, 2006.

101 Bok, 1998, pp. 105–6.

102 Muraro, 1984, p. 151.

103 Spear, 1994, p. 601.

104 In addition to the examples cited in the Rome and Bologna essays, Jacopo da Empoli paid his assistants 3 lire and 10 soldi per day, or about 140 scudi per year; no mention is made of room and board: Pisani et al., 2004, p. 237.

105 Coquery, 2002, p. 153, and Gady, 2002, p. 165.

106 Lotto, 1969, p. 98 (September 1547).

107 For Milan, see Chabod, 1985, pp. 281–450.

108 Lorenzi, 1868, pp. 284–85, doc. 608 (19 August 1554).

109 Hochmann, 1992a, pp. 44, 50.

110 For Carneo, see Goi, 1995. For Roncalli, see Spear below.

111 For costs of frames in the sixteenth century, see Matthew, 2006, pp. 316–17.

112 Labrot, 2002, p. 272, and Ago, 2002, pp. 382, 400. See also the important work in this area by Cecchini, 2000; Borean, 1999 and 2000; Morselli, 1999 and 2002; and Cavazzini, 2004a.

113 Ago, 1998.

114 Matthew, 2006, p. 320 (Bassano).

115 Bodart, 2007, p. 28. In a letter from Nicolas-Claude Fabri de Peiresc of May 1613: Finson "ne travaille qu'à force d'argent, et ne prend pas moings de vingt escus pour un portraict, en ayant faict de la hauteur de l'homme de prix de 50 ou 8(0) escus."

116 Saccardo, 1981, p. 3.

117 Mancini, 2001, p. 43.

118 From the account books by Lodovico Caiselli, Carneo's primary patron (see Goi, 1995). When history painters turned to genre, they could receive much more: Forabosco in 1671 (116 ducats); Bellotti in 1681 (226 ducats); and Piazzetta in the early 1740s (300 ducats).

119 Melchiori, 1964, pp. 75, 179–80.

120 Saccardo, 1981, p. 96.

121 Zampetti, 1988, pp. 403–5.

122 Tessin the Younger, 2002, p. 375.

123 Knox, 1995, p. 165.

124 De' Dominici, 1742–45, I, p. 433.

125 Van Mander, 1994–99, IV, p. 197 (life of Dirck Barentsen).

126 Bellesi, 1992, p. 141.

127 Malvasia, 1841, I, p. 230 (Ottaviano Cambi, letter of 23 July 1666).

128 For seventeenth-century views, see Sohm, 1991.

129 Passeri, 1795, pp. 100–10, 120.

130 For seicento Manieristi, see Sohm, 2007, pp. 131–66.

131 Winckelmann, 1763, p. 27.

132 Vasari, 1966–87, IV, p. 10, translation by Bull, in Vasari, 1965, p. 253.

133 Caro, 1574, I, pp. 271–73; Caro, 1957–61, II, pp. 62–64 (letter addressed to Vasari, dated 10 May 1548).

134 Syre, 2000, p. 242.

135 Bettagno and Magrini, 2002, pp. 81–82.

136 Martinioni, in Sansovino, 1663, p. 23 (in catalogue appended at end of book).

137 Borean, 2000, p. 181. For a discussion of the commission and Nicolini's pamphlet, see Anelli, 1996.

138 Chantelou, 1985, p. 189.

139 Ciammitti, 2000, pp. 194–203; Spear, 2003, p. 316; and Morselli herein.

140 Comanini, 2001, p. 109. Hollanda, 2003, p. 156, claims that 1 *mina* was worth 10 *cruzados*.

141 For fifteenth- and sixteenth-century examples, see Matthew, 2006, p. 312. For an argument against Renaissance practices of pricing by figure, see O'Malley, 2003.

142 Marabottini, 1988, p. 18, quoting from Zaballi's *Vita* of Jacopo da Empoli (Biblioteca Nazionale Centrale di Firenze, Ms. Magliabechiano, II.III.110, fols. 150–54).

143 Bonfait, 1990, pp. 71–94; Spear, 1994, pp. 592–602; and Spear, 2003, pp. 310–20.

144 Spear, 1982, I, pp. 286–87, 334–36, and Spear below.

145 Cecchini, 2000, p. 214, and Ago, 2006, pp. 140, 146.

146 Originals and copies in the Netherlands were priced at "approximated fixed ratios," usually 3 : 1 or 4 : 1, according to De Marchi and Van Miegroet, 1994, p. 453; and De Marchi and Van Miegroet, 1996b, pp. 27–70.

147 Spear, 1994, p. 596.

148 Bernard Mandeville, *The Fable of the Bees*, 1705, as updated edition of 1728, *The Grumbling Hive*, quoted by De Marchi and Van Miegroet, 1994, pp. 454–55.

149 For the commission, see Magagnato (1966), who, however, does not discuss the relation of age and price.

150 Sohm, 2007, pp. 61–82.

151 Rosa, 1995, p. 108.

152 When the *sindaci* of S. Martino in Alzano were given prices by three painters that were beyond their budget—80 scudi by Cignaroli for an altarpiece, and 25 scudi each by Zuccarelli and Polazzo for two smaller side panels—they had to decline (see Pinetti, 1921, pp. 22–25). Then Zuccarelli, wanting to help a young compatriot, turned their attention to Francesco Capella, who proposed a price of 20 scudi for the altarpiece and 7.5 scudi for each panel.

153 Ruggeri, 1993, p. 104.

1 *Rome*

1 Montaigne, 2003, pp. 1,141–79 on Rome (p. 1,173 for the quotation). Portions of the introductory material of this essay appeared in Spear, 2003.

2 For an overview of Rome's political structure and inevitable conflicts of power, see Nussdorfer, 1997.

3 Sella, 1997, pp. 19–49 (especially pp. 35–41), and Malanima, 1998 and 2002, pp. 182–205, on Italy's industrial decline.

4 For a detailed description of the Vatican's enormous personnel, see Lunadoro, 1654, and Delumeau, 1957–59, pp. 416–32, on Rome's prostitutes, who states that a regular prostitute charged anywhere from 1 to 4 scudi while a deluxe one was paid up to 12 scudi, but without clarification of what those distinctions meant. The most thorough study of Rome's prostitutes is Storey, 2008 (pp. 65 and 115 on their numbers, pp. 116–25 on their categories, and pp. 167–71 on their earnings).

5 Moryson, 1903, p. 411, and Philip Sohm's essay below on the high earnings of Venetian courtesans.

6 See Sonnino, 1997, pp. 62–66, on this abnormal male–female ratio as being not entirely attributable to Rome's religious character.

7 Cerasoli, 1891, for year-by-year census data (Jews, who numbered 4,500 in 1668, were not included in the annual count); Sonnino, 1997, whose figures are cited here. For a richly documented study of the Roman Jews' involvement in the commerce of art, see Masetti Zannini, 1974a.

8 Romani, 1948, as well as Delumeau, 1957–59, *passim*.

9 Delumeau, 1957–59, pp. 142, 186–87, reporting that in 1615 Rome had 360 hotels (Ago, 1998, p. 8, gives the conflicting number of 120 hotels in the 1620s, along with 652 *osterie*). The owner of the most famous hotel, the Orso, became so rich that he could leave his daughter a dowry of 30,000 scudi (Delumeau, 1957–59, p. 142).

10 Ago, 1998, p. 8.

11 See the data from Domenico Fontana's account book of 1585–89 in Bertolotti, 1881a, I, pp. 75–76.

12 Dandelet, 2008, p. 47; Delumeau, 1957–59, p. 765; and Hammond, 1994, p. 4.

13 Montagu, 1989, p. 218, n. 68. For detailed expenses of Innocent XII's trip from Rome to Nettuno in 1697, including cooks, food, tableware, table decoration, etc., see Di Schino and Lucciclienti, 2001.

14 As cited by Nussdorfer, 1992, pp. 27–28. Determining the budget of the Vatican is notoriously difficult; for the seventeenth century, see, among various studies, Lutz, 1973, with further references on pp. 32–34, nn. 1–6.

15 For the remark of 1625, see the Introduction above; for the drawing of *Taddeo at the Entrance to Rome Greeted by Toil, Servitude, and Hardship*, see Brooks, 2007, pp. 28–29, cat. 4.

16 Testimony of 1619; see Cavazzini, 2008c, p. 50.

17 See Reinhard, 1991, and Reinhardt, 1998. In his richly documented thesis, Ferraro, 1994, counts some 500 titled and untitled noble Roman families, 20–25 percent of whose mature males entered ecclesiastical careers (pp. 49–75, 142). See also the Introduction and essays in Burke and Bury, 2008.

18 The principal analysis of wealth and demand for art in Renaissance Italy is Goldthwaite, 1993. See Delumeau, 1957–59, pp. 258–61, 275–76, 358, regarding Rome's new and newly remodeled buildings.

19 Stumpo, 1985, pp. 24–29, and for extensive documentation on the weights and values of coins and precious metals, Archivio Segreto Vaticano [hereafter ASV], Arm. IV–V, t. 66 *passim*. From around 1610 until the end of the century, silver was gradually devalued in Europe following a long period when the nominal prices of gold and silver rose at fairly steady, similar rates. See Braudel and Spooner, 1967, pp. 378–86. For overviews of the Italian economy from the late Middle Ages to Unification, see Malanima, 2002 (appendix 3 on prices) and 2003. Malanima focuses on the Italian

economy in the seventeenth century (1998, p. 198, n. 85, regarding the difficulty of constructing a price index for all of Italy).

20 Vigo, 1974; Malanima's writings as cited in the previous note; and Piola Caselli, 1999, pp. 393–94, for an overview of prices and salaries.

21 On payments in kind, see Ago, 1998, pp. 198ff., and Ago, 2006, pp. 3–15. Welch, 2005, pp. 81–89, discusses the uncertainties of values of bartered goods as well as payments in cash during the late Renaissance.

22 O'Neil, 2002, pp. 171–72, 316–19.

23 Spear, 2003, p. 319, n. 75, and Spear, in press.

24 Rosa, 2003, p. 357, no. 335 (1666). If the wheel was the size of modern ones, around 35 to 40 kilos, its value could not have been close to 100 scudi. In 1601 and 1697, parmigiano in Rome cost 14 and 12 baiocchi per 12-oz. pound (ASV, Arm. IV–V, t. 71, p. 15, and Di Schino and Lucciclienti, 2001, p. 57).

25 Röttgen, 2002, p. 187.

26 Bellori, 2005, pp. 417–18, regarding Reni, adding that Maratta was "in a quandary," not wanting to alter the fresco of the Virgin, so he retouched it with "colors of pastel powders ground with gum Arabic" that could be removed with a sponge; and p. 428 for the *Self-Portrait*.

27 Pampalone, 1993, p. 73, n. 4.

28 Gozzano, 2004, p. 143, and Strunck, 2007, p. 526, doc. 1679,00,00.

29 Montalto, 1956, pp. 44, 52.

30 Maccherini, 1997, p. 71. For other examples of paintings being bartered, see Cavazzini, 2008c, pp. 127–28.

31 Cavazzini, 1997, pp. 408–10.

32 *Regesti di bandi* . . . , 1920, I, p. 135, no. 864.

33 See Strunck, 2007, pp. 503–4, docs. 1665,04,10b and 1668,00,00c, for payments to Lottani; Vigo, 1974, p. 390, regarding supplemental rations; and Ago, 1998, pp. 8–9, for a lower estimate that specialized workers earned about 3 scudi a month.

34 Orbaan, 1920, p. 317.

35 Mancini, 1956–57, I, pp. 141, 250; Stumpo, 1985, pp. 39–40; and data kindly shared with me by Joseph Connors based on his unpublished research on architects' earnings.

36 Di Schino and Lucciclienti, 2001, pp. 49–50, with daily rates for the "aiutanti" (40 to 80 baiocchi) and the "garzoni" (30 to 50 baiocchi).

37 Pastor, 1938–61, XXII, pp. 190–91. In 1601 a copy of the book cost Cardinal Montalto 2.8 scudi (Archivio Storico Capitolino, Rome [hereafter ASC], Archivio Cardelli, Appendice Savelli, vol. 33, Registro di mandati del Cardinal Montalto, 1601–1602, unpublished information kindly provided by Belinda Granata).

38 *Regesti di bandi* . . . , 1920, I, p. 95, no. 581.

39 Orbaan, 1920, pp. 78, 80, 193, 259 (with further *avvisi* concerning his salary).

40 Orbaan, 1920, pp. 285, 287.

41 Lunadoro, 1654, pp. 1–40, 78–79 *passim* for data on the Vatican and "all the officers belonging unto it, with the value of their offices, as they are sold by the Pope." The first edition appeared in 1635 and was subsequently revised. The job titles in Italian are cited from the edition of 1660.

42 Montanari, 2002, p. 105.

43 Orbaan, 1920, p. 339.

44 Bertolotti, 1884, p. 53; Hammond, 1994, pp. 3, 8; Hill, 1997, I, p. xx. Cosimo Cortelli, "cantore nella cappella pontifica," was paid 16.5 scudi "per il presente mese" on 19 November 1613 (Orbaan, 1920, p. 314); if that sum was for 18 or 19 days, he too was receiving 25 scudi a month.

45 Hill, 1997, I, pp. 24–35, on Marotta and Michi.

46 For these and other related incomes, see Delumeau, 1957–59, pp. 441, 455–56, 461–63; Hammond, 1994, pp. 3–8; Wright, 2000, p. 77; and Ferraro, 1994, pp. 246–68, with charts of the annual incomes of some of Rome's noble families. For analysis of data regarding huge papal donations to family members, see Ferraro, 1994, pp. 1,063–108. See also Reinhard, 1974 and 1991, pp. 335–36; Reinhardt, 1998, p. 89; and Völkel, 1993.

47 Hill, 1997, I, pp. 2–4, and Granata, 2008–9, pp. 14–16, 23–35, on Montalto's wealth and his *famiglia*, with many examples of their salaries and benefits.

48 Pastor, 1938–61, XXVIII, pp. 47–48.

49 Wright, 2000, p. 77.

50 Lunadoro, 1654, pp. 123–24. There are slight variations in the figures in different editions.

51 Ferraro, 1994, pp. 255, 1,113, and Delumeau, 1957–59, p. 464, on Roman merchants.

52 For discussion of the cost of wheat, see Braudel and Spooner, 1967, pp. 392–96, and their methodological overview of interpreting the history of prices, pp. 374–486; Sarti, 2002, pp. 177–78, on bread consumption; Reinhardt, 1997, on Rome's bread supply; and ASV, Arm. IV–V, t. 63, which contains extensive documentation. The price of a loaf of bread was maintained at 1 baiocco but its weight varied, triggering public alarm when lowered (see Gigli, 1958, *passim*).

53 ASV, Arm. IV–V, t. 71, pp. 171 (173), 178 (180), and Revel, 1979, p. 39.

54 By mid-century the price had declined to 2 baiocchi. See the *Bandi contra vermicellari*, ASV, Arm. IV–V, t. 63, pp. 171 (173), 178 (180).

55 *Regesti di bandi* . . . , 1920, I, p. 140, no. 894.

56 Exotic spices, such as cinnamon, cloves, and saffron, were much more expensive. See Di Schino and Lucciclienti, 2001, p. 59.

57 Many of the following prices are cited by Petrocchi, 1970, pp. 176–79, taken from archival data of the congregation of Sant'Onofrio (the Roman *libbra* he cites equaled 0.339 kg). In 1697, salt cod also cost about 24 baiocchi a kilo (preserved tuna half again as much), in which year a pair of young cocks or a pair of hens cost 30 baiocchi, a pair of doves 15 baiocchi, and a pair of pigeons 12.5 baiocchi (Di Schino and Lucciclienti, 2001, pp. 57, 62).

58 Di Schino and Lucciclienti, 2001, pp. 54–55 (1697).

59 On meat supply and consumption, see Nussdorfer, 1992, pp. 29, 31; Revel, 1979, pp. 42–44; Sarti, 2002, p. 177; and Piola Caselli, 1999, p. 402, for a chart of annual consumption of some foods ca. 1700.

60 Romani, 1948, p. 221, and Delumeau, 1957–59, pp. 177ff., on Jubilee year prices. On the types, quantities, and consumption of wine in Rome, see Revel, 1979, pp. 45–46, and Sarti, 2002, pp. 184–86, on wine and beer. Inasmuch as 13 barrels of wine contained about 750 liters, a liter was worth 3.5 baiocchi.

61 Lunadoro, 1654, p. 66, and ASV, Arm. IV–V, t. 71 *passim*.

62 ASV, Arm. IV–V, t. 71 *passim*. With slight variations in spelling, the foods in Table 2 are cited as casio vaccino & di riviera, pecorino, ricotta, butiro, lardo, salciciotti, presciutto, lengue di porco, and summata (I am indebted to June di Schino for iden-

tifying summata as salted pork belly). However, as mentioned above (note 52), while the price of a loaf of bread was constant its weight fluctuated. As noted in a recent summary of the *bandi* (Palumbo, 2005), they are a rich, untapped source of information.

63 Prices were about 1 baiocco higher for aged pecorino.

64 Prices increased about 2 baiocchi from the feast of St. Michael (29 September) through Carnival.

65 Hill, 1997, I, p. 22.

66 Pastor, 1938–61, XXXI, p. 327.

67 Ago, 1998, p. 86.

68 Moryson, 1907, I, p. 301 (and II, p. 114, for a similar cost per Italian meal).

69 Montagu, 1989, p. 218, n. 70, and Pastor, 1938–61, XXIII, p. 525.

70 Cipolla, 1967, pp. 23–24, and Vigo, 1974, pp. 381–82. See Ago, 2006, pp. 59–85, on furniture in middle-class Roman apartments (for median values of beds, chairs, and tables, about 5, 2.5, and 3 scudi respectively, p. 69, Table 7); p. 90, Table 2b, for an example from 1667 of the value (more than 35 scudi) of the utensils in a well-furnished kitchen of a Roman goldsmith; and p. 97, Tables 9–10, and p. 116, Table 13, on clothing values. For discussion of the complex task of computing real wages on the basis of historical prices and wages (with additional references), see de Vries, 1993, especially pp. 89–98, although without reference to Italy.

71 Cipolla, 1967, pp. 28–29. Their fame as patrons notwithstanding, only 1.5 percent of the Borghese's expenditure was on paintings and sculpture (Goldthwaite, 1993, pp. 29–30).

72 Visceglia, 1991, pp. 212–15, and p. 221, Table 1, for expenses on specific categories of food.

73 Ago, 2006, p. 50, Table 2.

74 Malanima, 1998, p. 31; see Renata Ago's essay for the example of a Veronese notary whose expenses included 2.5 percent for precious objects and art.

75 Hill, 1997, I, p. xix, with more prices of commodities, though his equivalents in 1996 U.S. dollars should be approached with caution.

76 Rosa, 2003, p. 136, no. 121 (1652) and p. 384, no. 365 (1669).

77 Delumeau, 1957–59, pp. 67–68, and ASV, Arm. IV–V, t. 70, pp. 42–146.

78 Moryson, 1907, III, pp. 472–73.

79 Chiappini di Sorio, 1983, p. 24.

80 Danesi Squarzina, 2003, *Documenti*, pp. 106–7.

81 Corti, 1989, p. 135, no. 18 (Bril's paintings) and p. 132, no. 56 (see below regarding these Caravaggesque altarpieces for the Guicciardini chapel in S. Felicita).

82 Campori, 1870, pp. 138–40, no. XIII.

83 Lavin, 1975, p. 30, docs. 255–56.

84 Garrard, 1989, p. 419.

85 Andrews, 1972, p. 599. Late in 1580, Montaigne rented lodgings in the Campo Marzio opposite S. Lucia della Tinta for 20 scudi a month, in which he was "well accommodated with three handsome bedrooms, dining room, larder, stable, and kitchen," plus a "cook and fire for the kitchen" (Montaigne, 2003, pp. 1,141–42).

86 Malvasia, 1841, II, p. 14 (Bellori, 1976, p. 499, says the monthly stipend was 15 scudi).

87 Bassani and Bellini, 1993, p. 75, n. 14. For overviews of where artists lived in the city, see Bousquet, 1980, pp. 96–97; Sparti, 1997, pp. 25–29; and for much higher rental rates of palaces, partial or entire, see Ferraro, 1994, pp. 418–26, and ch. 9 regarding purchase and rental prices of Roman real estate, from merchants' shops to palaces.

88 The notarial document recording Lanfranco's rent is unpublished (information courtesy of Erich Schleier). For Cortona's rent, see Sparti, 1997, p. 30, n. 31; for Rosa's rent, see Rosa, 2003, pp. 21–22, no. 26, as well as p. 23, no. 27 and p. 39, no. 41; and Elena Fumagalli's essay below for Rosa's and other Florentine rents.

89 Mancini, 1956–57, I, pp. 249–51.

90 Danesi Squarzina, 2006, pp. 244–46, for the documents on Ribera's residences.

91 See Cavazzini, 2008b, p. 74, regarding the tendency of painters in seicento Rome to decare that they worked "in casa mia."

92 Consagra, 1992, pp. 146–48.

93 Lorizzo, 2003b; Cavazzini, 2004a, pp. 363–64; and Cavazzini, 2008c, pp. 19–24, on the overlapping activities of painters, gilders, and dealers.

94 Pascoli, 1965, I, p. 59.

95 Bellori, 1976, p. 579.

96 Braudel, 1975, I, p. 458. See also Malanima, 1998, p. 29.

97 Romani, 1948, p. 139, n. 184, citing the estimate by A. Fanfani, which appears low relative to other estimates of the average annual cost of bread and wine per adult (about 17 scudi).

98 Haskell, 1963, pp. 161–66, Johns, 2000, and Bowron, 2000; see also Sohm, 2007, pp. 146–47, regarding Italy's artistic decline ca. 1700 and France's supremacy.

99 Cavazzini, 2008c, pp. 18–26, for discussion of the loose definition of a painter.

100 Bevilacqua, 1993, p. 38, who estimates that Guerra and Nebbia employed about 100 workers altogether.

101 Amadio, 2005, and Zicarelli, 2005, with further breakdowns of the artisans by profession and nationality, and for bibliography on the *stati d'anime*.

102 Bonfait, 2003, pp. 68–69, with further discussion of the economic impact of the Roman artistic community. On the *stati d'anime*, see the discussion in Bousquet, 1980, pp. 91–94.

103 Piacentini, 1939.

104 Chantelou, 1985, p. 248; for Venice, see Philip Sohm's essay below.

105 Friedlaender, 1955, p. 276.

106 As quoted in Bousquet, 1980, p. 94.

107 Rossella Vodret kindly provided these figures prior to publication of the study she directed, which is scheduled to appear in 2010 (Rome: L'Erma di Bretschneider).

108 Pampalone, 2004.

109 The lifespan of 103 of Baglione's painters averaged 59.98 years. The average lifespan of 60 painters discussed by Pascoli was 64.5 years. For further evidence that many seventeenth-century Italian painters lived long lives, see Sohm, 2007, p. 15. It should be borne in mind regarding these data that while life expectancy at birth in seventeenth-century Italy was only about 25 years, infant mortality was high (200 to 300 per thousand, accounting for 25–30 percent of all deaths). See Malanima, 2002, pp. 52–68.

110 Schnapper, 2004, p. 149. Early in the century, the French who arrived with a royal pension received 450 livres tournois annually, or about 150 scudi.

111 Bousquet, 1980, on which the following remarks are based. See also Lanfranconi, 2002, and Cipriani, 2002.

112 Cavazzini, 2008c, p. 19, regarding Rome's weak efforts to regulate artists.

113 Bellori's marginal note in Baglione, 1642, p. 106, in the facsimile edition, 1935.

114 Mancini, 1956–57, I, pp. 212–14.

115 In addition to the examples provided here and below, see Bertolotti's numerous publications for scores of unknown artists, and Bousquet, 1980, p. 95 *passim*, regarding the large number of French artists in Rome, many of whom remain unidentified (in 1636, for example, 38 French artists were living in three central parishes; in 1650, 45; in 1666, 38). Masetti Zannini, 1974b, likewise documents a large number of unknown artists active in late sixteenth-century Rome.

116 Ottonelli and Cortona, 1973, p. 232. Sparti, 1997, pp. 91–93, argues that Cortona's role in the treatise was minor.

117 Cavazzini, 2004a, especially pp. 353–57 *passim*, on the rise of collecting in Rome after ca. 1570, particularly in middle-class homes; Cavazzini, 2008c, pp. 4–5, 26–31, 96–99 *passim*; Ago, 2002 and 2006, pp. 148–49; and Mancini, 1956–57, I, p. 141.

118 Cavazzini, 2008c, pp. 83–84. Guerzoni, 2006, pp. 47–54, also calls attention to the bottom end of the market for paintings and especially to their low value as compared with many luxury objects.

119 Ago, 2002, pp. 383–86. For examples of paintings worth less than a scudo, see Cavazzini, 2008c, p. 96.

120 Cavazzini, 2008c, p. 45.

121 Zafferino's average earnings were about six to eight scudi a month (Lukehart, 2007, p. 108).

122 Missirini, 1823, pp. 70, 83 (in 1607 the fine was reduced to 10 scudi); and Lorizzo, 2003b, p. 325.

123 Cavazzini, 2008c, pp. 43–48, on the Accademia and its lower-status affiliate, the Compagnia, to which *pittori bottegari* would belong; and Lorizzo, 2003b. See also Salvagni, 2008, on the Accademia's early years.

124 Furlotti, 2003b, p. 266, n. 25.

125 Maccherini, 2005, p. 396.

126 Cavazzini, 2004a, p. 363.

127 Spezzaferro, 2002, p. 47.

128 Cavazzini, 2008c, p. 86.

129 Lorizzo, 2006, pp. 348–49.

130 Bailey, 2003a, p. 223.

131 Baglione, 1642, p. 353, and Granata, 2003, p. 49.

132 Cavazzini, 2008c, pp. 38–41.

133 For the census, see Narducci, 1870; Bodart, 1967, with a fuller transcription of portions of the document; and Storey, 2008, pp. 180–87, with particular reference to prostitution. See also Bousquet, 1980, p. 50, n. 10; and, for population data, Cerasoli, 1891, and Sonnino, 1997. For the more devastating effect of the plague in Naples, see Christopher Marshall's essay below.

134 Numbers are approximate because the census was not always consistent in the information provided nor can its classifications by profession be certain (e.g., the engraver Dominique Barrière is listed as a painter). Moreover, the economic classification by household precludes knowing if someone at a particular address might have been better or worse off than the head of the house.

135 Pollak, 1928–31, I, p. 391, nos. 1419–20, 1422, and Orbaan, 1920, p. 299, no. 61. See Cavazzini, 2008c, pp. 148–49, and p. 158, doc. 3, on the hundred or so cheap paintings in Gentili's estate (1626).

136 Cappelletti and Testa, 1994, p. 140, no. 39, and p. 150, no. 39. With regard to "Pietro" and similar names and the problem of identifying them, see the discussion in Masetti Zannini, 1974b, pp. xi–xvi; and also Cavazzini, 2008c, pp. 14–18, on identification of artists with the same names and variations in spelling.

137 Granata, 2003, pp. 48, 50, 51, 53, 55.

138 Golzio, 1939, p. 293, no. 571.

139 Williams, 2007, p. 96, discusses Armenini's view (1586) that a surfeit of young artists led to low, per diem payments to them ("in our time this shabby and disgraceful practice has flourished") and, as a result, the exploitation of artists by other artists.

140 Baglione, 1642, p. 104. For the Sforza payment to "Antonio Viviani e Compagni," see Hibbard, 1971, p. 223.

141 Zuccari, 1984, p. 32.

142 Röttgen, 2002, p. 5.

143 Bertolotti, 1880, p. 57.

144 Lavin, 1970, pp. 192–93 (seven years earlier, Camassei had received 25 scudi "per havere lavorto un mese in dipingere nella Galleria" in the Villa Sacchetti at Castel Fusano [Merz, 1991, pp. 175, 318]). In 1595 a Paolo venetiano was paid for working in Asdrubale Mattei's Palatine villa "p. sette giornate che ha lavorato al giardino, e colori, sc.ti 3 e cinquanta" (i.e., 5 giuli per diem including the cost of pigments); a Rinaldo pittore worked on the same project the same year for a giulio a day more; and in 1612 Michelangelo Vestri testified at the rape trial of Agostino Tassi, "la professione mia è di pittore . . . et quando io vado a giornata mi guadagno cinque giulii il giorno" (I am a painter by profession . . . and when I work by the day I earn 5 giuli). See Cappelletti and Testa, 1994, p. 148, nos. 13, 15, and Cavazzini, 2001, p. 442.

145 *Francesco Cozza* . . . , 2007, p. 283, doc. 3 (there is a discrepancy, however, between Dughet's payment, the number of days worked, and the stated rate).

146 Cavazzini, 2001, p. 434.

147 Bertolotti, 1881b, p. 23.

148 Fumagalli, 1994, p. 98, n. 51. Another color grinder, Claudio francese, worked under Arpino and then Tassi at the Villa Lante in Bagnaia, earning 6 scudi a month in 1615. The census of 1656 of the Campo Marzio lists just one "Macinatore de colori" and one "Imprimitore di colore," the former living in Girolamo Troppa's "poor" household, the latter in one that was "comfortable" (Bodart, 1967, pp. 502, 519).

149 Corradini, 1996, p. 74. Baldassare Croce in 1613 paid Aloisio Zanzani, "pittore che me ne seruei in casa dell'Ill.mo Cardinale Montalto," 3.5 giuli "al giorno" (Bertolotti, 1885, p. 154). During 1682–83, Carlo Ceci earned 4 giuli a day assisting Brandi in S. Silvestro in Capite (Fig. 16), another example of stable wages across the century (Lavin, 1957, pp. 47–48, docs. 4–13).

150 See Elena Fumagalli's essay.

151 This rate accords with those paid to Mario Balassi, Francesco Leoncini, and Carlo Berti in Florence (the equivalent of 3 to 4 giuli per diem), cited by Elena Fumagalli.

152 An exception is the documented case of Bernardino Pocetti working six hours a day for 18 days on frescoes in Florence (see Elena Fumagalli's essay). In Bologna, Reni reportedly paid his assistants 96 scudi a year, but they received extra money for work completed.

153 Gigli, 1958, p. 224, lists the *feste di precetto* and notes that their reduction allowed *artigiani* to work without the threat of police harassment. See also Welch, 2005, pp. 111–14, regarding work on Sundays and holidays.

154 Gozzano, 2004, p. 145, and Strunck, 2007, p. 510, doc. 1672,04,28.

155 Verdi, 1983, pp. 95–98.
156 Lavin, 1957, pp. 47–48, docs. 4–13.
157 Ottonelli and Cortona, 1973, pp. 261–63.
158 Fumagalli, 1994, p. 98, n. 55.
159 Cavazzini, 2008c, pp. 49–64, for discussion of apprenticeships, including examples in which students paid their masters.
160 Masetti Zannini, 1974b, pp. xxix–xxx.
161 Baglione, 1642, p. 52.
162 Schleier, 2002, p. 422.
163 Faldi, 1957, p. 295, doc. V.
164 Scott, 1991, p. 212.
165 Scott, 1993, p. 332, n. 29.
166 Sparti, 1997, p. 130, docs. 11c, 11f.
167 Bellori, 2005, p. 230.
168 See Cavazzini, 2008c, pp. 137–38, 150–51, for examples of painters, some of stature, who worked awhile for dealers.
169 Pascoli, 1965, II, p. 356. For a depressing example of a failed painter (Antonio Giusti) who turned to marketing pictures through *rigattieri* in Florence, see Elena Fumagalli's essay.
170 Malvasia, 1841, II, pp. 34 and 19 respectively. In addition to Raffaella Morselli's discussion of Reni's finances in this volume, see Spear, 1997.
171 Lorizzo, 2006, pp. 353–54, for discussion of three such examples (Castiglione, Gaulli, and Vanvitelli).
172 Pascoli, 1965, II, p. 60 (translation based on Lorizzo, 2006, p. 354, n. 47).
173 Orbaan, 1920, p. 300, no. 165, and p. 316, no. 50. Elena Fumagalli informs me that two Annibales worked for the Borghese during this period: Annibale Durante and Annibale Corradini. See Cavazzini, 2008c, pp. 20–24, on gilders who did decorative painting.
174 Cappelletti and Testa, 1994, p. 141, nos. 53, 59. Cavazzini, 2008c, p. 18, on the confusing frequency of this name.
175 Granata, 2003, p. 53.
176 Fumagalli, 1994, p. 49, and p. 97, nn. 46, 47.
177 Briganti, Laureati, and Trezzani, 1993, pp. 136–41, no. 11, and p. 312, doc. 7.
178 On Magno, see Fumagalli, 2007a, and, for his work for the Colonna, Strunck, 2007, p. 490, doc. 1649,00,00?; for his work for the Chigi, see Petrucci, 1992, p. 122, nos. 23–25, 31. Another, very detailed breakdown of the value of decorative work is a list of Giovanni Maria Mariani's painting in the Colonna palace dated 1668 (Strunck, 2007, p. 505, doc. 1668,07,31).
179 Spear, 2004b, and for further discussion of the copying of prints, which could be prohibited through "privileges," see Bury, 2005.
180 Enggass and Brown, 1970, pp. 16–20.
181 Maccherini, 1997, p. 83. The atypical attitude that there might be a premium in the uniquely existing object arises again in an undated draft of the will of Pellegrino Peri, the Genoese dealer active in Rome at the end of the century cited below with regard to Gaulli and Rosa da Tivoli. Peri ordered his executors to give one of his legatees a still life by Andrea Bonani from his large stock of Bonani's work and, more specifically, a canvas "che non hò fatto mai Copiare" (that I never had copied), implying its greater worth (Lorizzo, 2003a, p. 162, n. 22).
182 Anselmi, 2004, p. 356, and Baglione, 1642, p. 334.
183 Baldinucci, 1845–47, III, pp. 10–11, 743–45.
184 Negro, 1999, pp. 28, 30, 68, 195.
185 Passeri, 1934, p. 36.
186 Borsi, 1974, p. 261, 28 August 1657; Sestieri, 1994, I, p. 72; Lo Bianco, 1997, pp. 416–17; and Merz, 2005, p. 469, n. 23 (recently with Whitfield Fine Art, London). Thirteen years later (1670), for a slightly smaller copper (52 × 39 cm) of the *Adoration of the Shepherds* (Denis Mahon collection, London), Ferri again was well paid, 100 scudi (Merz, 2005, p. 236).
187 Lavin, 1975, p. 496.
188 There is no evidence to support the suggestion that he painted the copy of Caravaggio's *Lute Player* with Wildenstein and Company.
189 Golzio, 1939, p. 285, no. 805, for Pace's paintings; for Belloni's copies for Cardinal Francesco Barberini, see Merz, 2005, p. 467, nn. 18–19.
190 Rosa, 2003, p. 354, no. 332 (1666).
191 Furlotti, 2003a, p. 378, no. 501.
192 Corradini, 1979, p. 193, no. 9, and p. 194, no. 67.
193 Pollak, 1928–31, I, p. 393, no. 1437.
194 Pollak, 1928–31, I, pp. 395–96, nos. 1453–55 (Eclisse); I, p. 393, no. 1439 (Mauritij); I, p. 393, no. 1436; and Merz, 2005, p. 117 (Gimignani).
195 Bellori, 1976, p. 617.
196 Maccherini, 1997, pp. 71–92, and Cappelletti and Testa, 1994, p. 150, no. 45.
197 Ago, 2002, p. 383.
198 Gualandi, 1844–56, III, pp. 229–30, no. 423. For further examples of many inexpensive copies by artists in Romanelli's circle, see Merz, 2005, pp. 186–91.
199 Corradini, 1979, p. 194, nos. 49, 69 (Roscioli), and *Roma 1630 . . .*, 1995, pp. 162–71, 229 (Valguarnera).
200 Ago, 2006, pp. 149–51, regarding the demand for portraits, and the recent corpus of Roman portraiture, Petrucci, 2008, with discussion of the problem of replicas, I, pp. 113–19. See Cavazzini, 2004b, regarding copies of landscapes.
201 Golzio, 1939, p. 285, no. 4499; p. 292, no. 904; p. 297, no. 748.
202 DiFrederico, 1983, p. 61.
203 Sparti, 1997, pp. 132–33, doc. 17a, and Lo Bianco, 1997, p. 36 and n. 107.
204 Kirwin, 1972, p. 536.
205 The numerous recorded payments for the Cathedra Petri include many to Bernini's assistants for the "modelli," though none corresponds with the sum of 3,600 scudi (Battaglia, 1943).
206 Missirini, 1823, pp. 111–13. Sparti, 1997, pp. 91–93, doubts that such debates really occurred.
207 Spear, 1982, I, pp. 69, 289.
208 O'Malley, 2005, concludes that pricing of Renaissance altarpieces, which depended foremost on the quality of materials and craftsmanship, cannot in general be correlated with the number of figures.
209 Bellori, 2005, p. 356.
210 Spear, 1994.
211 Spear, 1982, I, p. 286–87. See Table 30 in Renata Ago's essay for a table of exchange; values fluctuated widely in Naples.
212 Spear, 1982, I, pp. 334–36.
213 Negro, 1999, pp. 27–28, and p. 67, nn. 47, 49, for the Rospigliosi correspondence. The altarpiece for Crema representing *St. Mark in Prison* is large, 390 × 227 cm, and was left unfinished at Reni's death (Spear, 1997, pp. 314–15).
214 Bellori, 2005, p. 325.

215 Ciammitti, 2000 (I do not believe her reading of *ordinario* is supported by contemporary usage).

216 *Colnaghi . . .*, 2008, p. 46, no. 12, for the Lauri. On his little-known activity as a still life painter, see Bocchi and Bocchi, 2005, pp. 499–506.

217 Riccio, 1959, p. 13.

218 Buvelot, 2005.

219 Rosa, 2003, p. 153, no. 137.

220 Malvasia, 1841, II, p. 173.

221 See especially Philip Sohm's essay below on Venetian pricing by size and figures. The admirable study by Schnapper, 2004, is compromised by relying too narrowly on dimensions as the gauge of value. His approach was from the perspective of the collector and secondary market, however, rather than the artist, the focus of this book. The most ambitious attempt using regression analysis to quantify prices and value of art of this period is Gérin-Jean, 2001, but his method and results raise many unresolved problems. It might be noted that an inventory drawn up in 1659 of the stock of the Roman dealer Francesco Saluzzi divided paintings into groups according to more than a dozen categories of size (Lorizzo, 2006, p. 357, n. 57).

222 I have tabulated nearly 1,000 prices of paintings in seventeenth-century Rome, including a small number of inventory evaluations and resale prices from an artist's lifetime. By mid-2010 the data will be accessible through an online database administered by the Getty Research Institute (for a summary of the project, see Spear, 2010).

223 Briganti, 1962, pp. 167–70, cat. 12.

224 Mancini, 1956–57, I, p. 139.

225 Briganti, Laureati, and Trezzani, 1993, pp. 30–47, no. 2, and pp. 50–51, no. 5.

226 Chiappini di Sorio, 1983, p. 30, for Eleonora's response, and the essay below on Venice for Bernardino Garbelli's remark of 1583.

227 For Volterrano's work in the Annunziata, see Elena Fumagalli's essay below.

228 Zandri, 1987, p. 102, n. 2 (lantern and cupola), and p. 101, n. 1 (pendentives).

229 Sparti, 1997, pp. 60–61.

230 Fig. 63 in Elena Fumagalli's essay below.

231 Gualandi, 1844–56, III, pp. 240–42, letter 430, and p. 242, letter 431, both of 1685.

232 Rice, 1997, pp. 163, 205–13, cat. 6.

233 Bellori, 2005, pp. 169–70.

234 Spear, 2003, p. 313.

235 Röttgen, 2002, pp. 240–41, cats. 20–21.

236 Abromson, 1976, p. 336, nos. 42–43, and Röttgen, 2002, pp. 282–83, cat. 52.

237 Antinori, 2005, p. 98.

238 Scott, 1993, for a rare study of scaffolding of the period. The cost of 435 chestnut planks in 1632, e.g., is unrecorded (40 oak planks cost 6 scudi). John Scott, who kindly provided the transparency used for Fig. 10, confirmed for me which expenses are recorded and that the total cost is unknown. See Elena Fumagalli's essay for examples of the costs of scaffolding (300 and 360 scudi) in Florence in 1677–78.

239 Corbò, 1968, p. 325 (Passignano was given a bonus of 100 scudi "in recognition of the hard work and diligence").

240 On the techniques of fresco painting and its pigments in seventeenth-century Rome, see Richard Symonds's text based on Canini's practice, and Mary Beal's discussion, in Beal, 1980, pp. 167–68.

241 Multiple purchases of varnish in 1628–29 for work at the Villa Sacchetti, Castel Fusano, cost 20 baiocchi a pound (Merz, 1991, pp. 317–20). For pigment costs, including some for oil and varnish, see Spear, in press.

242 Spear, 1982, I, pp. 178–84, cat. 42; pp. 175–78, cat. 41 (prior to discovery that he was paid 240 rather than 50 scudi); p.117, cat. 117 (and Denunzio, 2000, pp. 374–76, for the payment); pp. 216–17, cat. 63; and pp. 230–32, cat. 79.

243 Bailey, 2003a, p. 210, for the payment.

244 Rice, 1997, pp. 216–21, cat. 8.

245 Rice, 1997, pp. 246–49, cat. 15.

246 Megna, 2003, pp. 89–90, 100.

247 Rice, 1997, pp. 238–41, cat. 12.

248 Christiansen and Mann, 2001, pp. 64–67, cat. 7, and pp. 77–79, cat. 11. On Orazio's earnings more broadly, see Spear, 2005, to which should be added the 90 scudi he received for lost fresco work in the apse of S. Nicola in Carcere (Bissell, 1981, pp. 216–17, cat. L-18, and Abromson, 1976, p. 355), and the 400 scudi payment for his work in S. Giovanni dei Fiorentini (Germond, 1993).

249 Thuillier, 1990, pp. 212–14.

250 Lemoine, 2003, pp. 51–53.

251 Mancini, 1956–57, I, p. 251; Maccherini, 1999; and Corti, 1989, p. 132, no. 58, regarding Manfredi. Payments for other easel or gallery paintings by the Caravaggisti active in Rome are scarce. The Barberini paid Valentin 15 scudi in 1627 for his *David*, 20 scudi in 1628 for his portrait of *Cardinal Francesco Barberini*, and 25 scudi in 1630–31 for his *Samson* referred to below; they paid him considerably more, 100 scudi, for his lost *Beheading of the Baptist*, which, however, was much larger than an easel picture (see Lavin, 1975, pp. 42–43, docs. 341–43). Perhaps that fee led Valentin to ask for 100 scudi from Fabrizio Valguarnera (1631) for a painting of a Gypsy and soldiers (possibly the one in Toronto measuring 190 × 265 cm [Mojana, 1989, p. 178, cat. 64]), but Valentin settled for 80 scudi. Cardinal Filomarino paid 15 scudi (1627) and 10 scudi (1632) respectively for a *St. Jerome* and a portrait of the cardinal's brother by Valentin (Lorizzo, 2001, pp. 405, 410, 411). Spadarino's portrait of *Gregory XV* also cost 10 scudi in 1621 (Benocci, 2006, p. 15). A few payments for easel paintings by Antiveduto Grammatica are known: 25 scudi for a *Christ Among the Doctors* acquired in 1616 by a dealer (Cavazzini, 2004a, pp. 365–66); 50 scudi apiece in 1611 for his *Europa* and *Judith*; and 70 scudi in 1621 for a *Madonna* and a *St. Sebastian*, all bought by Cardinal Montalto (Cavazzini, 2001, pp. 291–92, n. 19, and ASC, Archivio Cardelli, Appendice Savelli, vol. 54, Registri di mandati del Cardinal Montalto, 1619–21, the latter reference kindly provided by Belinda Granata; see also Granata, 2006, pp. 110–11, n. 39, on payments to Grammatica). In 1609, the Mattei paid 40 scudi for a pair of paintings by Saraceni (Cappelletti and Testa, 1994, p. 124, no. 24, and p. 142, no. 3). In 1618 Vouet received only 6 scudi from Paolo Giordano Orsini for an unidentified *quadretto* on copper (Benocci, 2006, p. 14); in 1623 and 1627 respectively, Cardinal Filomarino spent 250 scudi for 15 paintings of the Apostles, Christ, Mary, and St. John by Vouet, and another 120 scudi for Vouet's 12 paintings of *Angels* (Lorizzo, 2001, pp. 404–5, 411).

252 Sparti, 1997, p. 134, doc. 20.

253 Scott, 1991, pp. 212–15, and Sparti, 1997, pp. 130–31, doc. 11a (due

to love for St. Philip Neri and the congregation, Cortona apparently accepted 5,350 scudi instead).

254 Cortona expected to be paid more for the latter commission (400 scudi) than his Florentine colleagues would have expected; see Elena Fumagalli's essay below.

255 Lo Bianco, 1997, cat. nos. 34, 53, 52, and *Regesto*, p. 488. I am indebted to Francesco Petrucci for measuring the *Crucifixion* in Castel Gandolfo for me.

256 O'Neil, 2002, pp. 314–15, doc. 2.

257 O'Neil, 2002, pp. 323–24, doc. 33.

258 Bell, 1988.

259 Gualandi, 1844–56, I, pp. 302–3, no. 129.

260 Golzio, 1939, p. 70, no. 4314.

261 Bellori, 2005, p. 163.

262 Spear, 2003, p. 311.

263 Baglione, 1642, pp. 379–80.

264 Mancini, 2005, p. 124, no. 8; p. 130, no. 11; and p. 273, docs. 7–8.

265 Pantanella, 1999, p. 337.

266 Bellori, 2005, p. 356.

267 Spear, 1982, I, pp. 201–10, cat. 56.

268 Posner, 1963.

269 Bellori, 2005, pp. 317–18, 320.

270 Mancini, 1956–57, I, p. 22, and Spear, 1997, pp. 31–32.

271 Corti, 1989, p. 137, no. 9.

272 Baldinucci, 1681, p. 102.

273 DiFrederico, 1983, on the mosaics of St. Peter's in general, and pp. 5–6 regarding their associative value.

274 Pascoli, 1965, II, pp. 26–27.

275 Four cartoons for mosaic pendentives in St. Peter's are in the Galleria Nazionale d'Arte Antica, Rome: inv. nos. 2234, Lanfranco, *St. Bonaventure* (5.1 × 6 m); 2235, Sacchi, *St. Leo the Great* (4.4 × 5.75 m.); 2236, Sacchi, *St. Thomas Aquinas with Sts. Peter and Paul* (5.1 × 6 m); and 2233, Carlo Pellegrini, *St. Bernard* (4.4 × 5.75 m), who also was paid 200 scudi (Pollak, 1928–31, II, p. 579, nos. 2,334–37).

276 Pascoli, 1965, II, p. 33. For a recent, richly documented study of Calandra's career, see Cifani and Monetti, 2006.

277 Pollak, 1928–31, II, pp. 550–52 (Lanfranco), 580–81 (Romanelli), 575–77 (Sacchi).

278 Rice, 1997, pp. 249–52, cat. 16.

279 Schütze, 2007, pp. 58–69, 266–67 (doc. III).

280 Lavin, 1970, pp. 192–93.

281 See below regarding the cost of canvas, which could have been as much as 30 scudi for a very large cartoon; even so, that would have left considerable profit in a 200 scudi fee.

282 Pollak, 1915, pp. 76–77, no. 39.

283 Pascoli, 1965, II, p. 283.

284 Lo Bianco, 1997, p. 366, cat. 53, citing Baldinucci.

285 Abromson, 1976, pp. 347–48, nos. 91–102, and Rice, 1997, pp. 175–82, cat. 1, and pp. 197–204, cat. 5(a).

286 Bellori, 1976, p. 226.

287 Röttgen, 2002, p. 448, cat. 221.

288 Golzio, 1939, p. 281, no. 3396.

289 Lo Bianco, 1997, *Regesto*, p. 488.

290 Sparti, 1997, p. 143, and Sparti, 1993, p. 343.

291 The story of Giordano rapidly painting the huge altarpiece appears in De' Dominici, 1742–45, III, pp. 416–17.

292 Mancini, 1956–57, I, p. 22.

293 Lavin, 1957, p. 44.

294 Pascoli, 1965, I, p. 129.

295 On Dandini and Piazzetta, see the essays on Florence and Venice, and the Introduction regarding Dolci.

296 Baldinucci, 1845–47, V, p. 358, and the Introduction above regarding Dolci's demise from shame and remorse.

297 Hollanda, 1928, p. 103 (Dialogue 4.8).

298 Williams, 2007, p. 97, on Armenini's text.

299 Ghelfi, 1997.

300 Bellori, 2005, p. 415.

301 Negro, 1999, p. 30, and pp. 68–69, n. 59.

302 Bellori, 2005, p. 281.

303 Mezzetti, 1955, pp. 352–53, doc. 1.

304 Sutherland Harris, 1977, pp. 100–1, no. 81. Bellori, 2005, p. 386, writes that "despite the fact that [the patron, Cardinal Antonio Barberini,] prodded him continuously, [Sacchi] put it off so much from one season to the next that in the end, confined to bed by his illness, he left that lord nothing but the desire for the work"; Passeri, 1934, p. 301, relates that Cardinal Antonio was disappointed with "sua tardanza."

305 Bellori, 2005, p. 404.

306 Martinetti, 1967, p. 30 (with reference to Pascoli, 1965, II, p. 258).

307 Sohm, 1991.

308 Pascoli, 1965, II, pp. 317–18 (*colore* "dà subito nell'occhio, ed è da ognun conosciuto, laddove il disegno resta addietro, ed è da' soli maestri osservato"); and Bellori, 2005, p. 61.

309 Sohm, 1991, pp. 60–61.

310 Pigment identification usually is prompted by localized problems or research goals; analysis of all pigments in a painting is not only expensive but traditionally given low priority. Moreover, identification of pigments often remains uncertain.

311 See Spear, in press, for these and some 400 other payments for pigments. The cheapest price of ultramarine I have tabulated, 30 baiocchi an ounce, is so low for the real pigment that I suspect it might have pertained to ultramarine ashes instead.

312 Scott, 1995, p. 87.

313 ASV, Archivio Borghese, vols. 7927 and 7928. On the use of these pigments by Paolo Piazza, see Fumagalli, 2002.

314 Bell, 1988.

315 Spear, 2003, p. 314.

316 Röttgen, 2002, p. 431, cat. 195.

317 Rice, 1997, pp. 213–16, cat. 7.

318 Lavin, 1957, p. 49, doc. 31.

319 DiFederico, 1971, p. 67, doc. 19.

320 For Maratta's canvas, see DiFederico, 1968, p. 196, doc. 3 (specified as 18 *palmi*); and for Cortona's altarpiece, Sparti, 1997, p. 60. These and similar prices argue against identificaton (Colantuono, 2008) of a modestly sized painting of *Latona* (143 × 115 cm, private collection, Atlanta) with an unfinished late work by Reni for Philip IV that Malvasia, 1841, II, p. 42, said was so enormous ("un immense telone") that its canvas cost 40 scudi (x-ray evidence of the painting, which stylistically is unconvincing as a late Reni, precludes that it ever could have been immense). Also see Raffaella Morselli's opinion below on Reni's lost *Latona* (it is not clear from his text, however, that Malvasia meant that the huge painting was on silk rather than on canvas).

321 Lavin, 1975, p. 43, doc. 345.

322 Amadio, 1998, p. 145.

323 Cappeletti and Testa, 1994, p. 149, no. 28, and Lo Bianco, 1997, pp. 309–11, cats. 19, 20.

324 Rosa, 2003, p. 178, no. 159.
325 Lavin, 1970, p. 192.
326 Golzio, 1939, p. 72, no. 2956; p. 291, no. 1498; p. 284, no. 4301; and p. 300, no. 1070.
327 Beal, 1980, p. 293.
328 Megna, 2003, pp. 90, 100.
329 Corti, 1989, pp. 111, 131–32, nos. 52–54, 56. Spadarino's altarpiece for Florence is unknown.
330 Golzio, 1939, p. 416 (f. 659).
331 Gualandi, 1844–56, II, pp. 170–92, letters 218–28.
332 Lavin, 1970, p. 193. Two presumably quite large brushes used in the Villa Sacchetti at Castel Fusano "da imbiancare" cost 50 baiocchi in 1628 (Merz, 1991, p. 315).
333 Galán and Cuesta, 1997, pp. 173–75.
334 ASV, Archivio Borghese, vol. 7927, fols. 42s, 67v, and vol. 7928 (unpaginated).
335 Baldinucci, 1681, p. 120.
336 ASV, Archivio Borghese, vol. 7927, fols. 20d, 42s, 67v, and vol. 7928 (unpaginated).
337 Bellori, 1976, p. 92.
338 As with other materials, the price of paper varied according to its quality and size. My estimate of about a baiocco a sheet derives from the purchases in 1633 of five reams of 500 sheets, each for 26.3 scudi, and in 1657 of a ream of high-quality paper for 1.8 scudi and a ream of high-quality French paper for 1 scudo (see Consagra, 1988, p. lxxxvii and especially p. xcvi, n. 6). For an overview of Renaissance paper, see Landau and Parshall, 1994, pp. 15–21 ("the mere cost of paper . . . was not a significant percent of the cost of [Dürer's *Melancolia I*]").
339 See the discussion in Cavazzini, 2008c, pp. 72–80.
340 I am grateful to Ann Sutherland Harris for generously sharing with me notes she made in the Accademia's archives.
341 In Naples, the model, Paolo Savione, was contracted to work for about three months (Archivio di Stato di Napoli, Notai del Seicento, Notaio Francesco de Martino, scheda 174 protocollo 14, 1636, fol. 22r–v; reference provided by Christopher Marshall).
342 Chantelou, 1985, p. 35, and Bellori, 1976, p. 213.
343 Spear, 2003, p. 314, and Christopher Marshall below on Artemisia's remarks on models.
344 See Elena Fumagalli's essay below.
345 Spear, 2003, p. 314.
346 Coquery, 2002, p. 153.
347 Spear, 2003, pp. 314–15, and Spear, 2005, pp. 154–56.
348 Archivio di Stato di Roma, Archivio dell'Archiconfraternità dell'Annunziata, 1609, vol. 38, fol. 74v.
349 Gallo, 1998, p. 315.
350 Missirini, 1823, p. 95. Hence the membership fee was significantly lower than the cost of joining the Compagnia dei Pittori in Bologna or the Venetian Arte (see Raffaella Morselli's and Philip Sohm's essays). For a detailed example of one painter's participation in the Accademia's activities (Francesco Cozza), see Pampalone, 2008, pp. 92–98. In her "Appendice documentaria," Salvagni, 2008, frequently mistranscribes contributions that painters made to the Accademia as in scudi rather than in baiocchi, thereby making their modest donations appear to be a hundredfold larger than they were.
351 Spear, 2003, pp. 311–12. Less than half of the families in Florence in 1551 had any servants at all; 23 percent had just one servant; 18 percent had two to five, and 5 percent had over five. For examples of many Florentine painters who had servants, see Elena Fumagalli's essay.
352 Cavazzini, 2001, p. 442, fol. 111.
353 See the remarks in Cavazzini, 2008c, pp. 41–43.
354 Christiansen and Mann, 2001, p. xvii.
355 Rosa, 2003, p. 23, no. 27.
356 As reported by Bellori, 2005, p. 325.
357 Bellori, 1976, p. 199, on Barocci, and for an astute discussion of artists' fading eyesight, Sohm, 2007, pp. 76–81.
358 Rosa, 2003, pp. 325–26, no. 305 (1664); p. 332, no. 310 (1665); and pp. 333–34, no. 311 (1665).
359 ASV, Archivio Borghese, vol. 7928 (unpaginated).
360 An exception is the modest payment of 9 scudi in 1624 for his painting on copper of *Sts. Peter and Paul* (Pollak, 1928–31, I, p. 391, no. 1423).
361 I am indebted to Joseph Connors for most of this information on architects, which is drawn from his unpublished lecture, "Finance and Design in Four Religious Structures: A Comparative Study" (2004), and a file of data on financing architecture that he generously shared with me.
362 Schiavo [ca. 1964], p. 68, cites a document of 1679 stating that the Altieri's architect, G. A. de' Rossi, was to be paid according to this schedule.
363 Bellori, 2005, pp. 147, 150.
364 See Röttgen, 2002, from which much of the following data are taken.
365 Röttgen, 2002, p. 326.
366 Röttgen, 2002, p. 170, in a letter from Ottavio Rossi to the painter Pietro Marone.
367 In a marginal note in Baglione's *Vite* (Röttgen, 2002, pp. 400–1, cat. 160).
368 Baglione, 1642, pp. 372–74.
369 Röttgen, 2002, p. 125.
370 Röttgen, 2002, pp. 129–33, on this extraordinary affair and see the analysis in Granata, 2008–9, pp. 41–49.
371 Baglione, 1642, p. 374.
372 Röttgen, 2002, pp. 200–2, and Sohm, 2007, pp. 157–60.
373 Sparti, 1997, pp. 31–42.
374 Pantanella, 1999, p. 337 (23 August 1708), and discussion of Gaulli below.
375 Bellori, 1976, p. 642.
376 See Christopher Marshall's and Raffaella Morselli's essays.
377 Schleier, 2002, pp. 46, 426, and for a recent, detailed analysis of Lanfranco's *vigna* and casino, see Schleier, 2007.
378 Masetti Zannini, 1974b, p. xxxvi, on sixteenth-century artists; Pascoli, 1965, II, p. 392 (Odazzi), and I, p. 251 (Raggi).
379 Passeri, 1934, p. 154, and Anselmi, 2004, p. 361, for Cassiano's remark (1626). For engravings and the remains of Lanfranco's casino, as well as traces of its decoration, see Schleier, 2007; Gatta and Serafinelli, 2007; and Banchini, 2007.
380 Bellori, 2005, p. 288.
381 Spear, 2002, p. 128, with further remarks on the possible stylistic implications of Lanfranco's financial situation.
382 In 1629, however, Lanfranco admitted that he was "nè ricco nè povero ma ho tanto che mi basta et le mie robbe consistono in robbe mobili e stabili" (Cavazzini, 2008b, p. 89).
383 Spear, 2005, on Orazio's and Artemisia's finances.
384 Spear, 2005, p. 150, with further discussion of her economic situation; see also Marshall, 2005 and his essay in this volume, as

well as Philip Sohm's essay on the size of dowries some Venetian artists gave their daughters.

385 See Elena Fumagalli's essay for his letter of 1666.

386 Spear, 1994, p. 601.

387 Cavazzini, 2002, p. 404; Haskell, 1963, p. 18; and Spear, 1997, p. 44.

388 Pascoli, 1965, I, p.132; II, pp. 306–7; and II, p. 398. See also Spear, 1997, pp. 23–24, on artists' clothing and Renata Ago's essay below on clothing as sign.

389 Bellori, 2005, pp. 216–20. For an excellent discussion of Van Dyck's (later) lavish entertaining in the context of socialibity centered on artists, see Bauer and Bauer, 2008.

390 On Rosa's stay in Florence, see especially Fumagalli, 2007b, pp. 38–75.

391 On the Accademia, see Fumagalli, 2007b, pp. 62–66, and Bauer and Bauer, 2008, with regard to artists entertaining one another.

392 Baldinucci, 1845–47, V, p. 454; Scott, 1995, pp. 55–59, on the Accademia dei Percossi and Antonio Malatesta's poem, "To Salvadore for a Dinner"; and Passeri, 1934, pp. 390–91, on Rosa's return to Rome.

393 Bellori, 2005, p. 185.

394 Passeri, 1934, p. 386, recounts Rosa's early reliance on *bottegari rivenditori*. See also Scott, 1995, pp. 5–6, and pp. 21–22 regarding Bernini, as well as Fumagalli's discusson of Rosa's move to Florence, 2007b, pp. 39–40.

395 Pascoli, 1965, I, pp. 70–71.

396 Baldinucci, 1845–47, V, p. 485, and Rosa, 2003, pp. 355–56, no. 334 (1666) regarding his landscapes. Haskell, 1963, pp. 22–23, 126–28, 142–45 *passim*, and Scott, 1995, offer many perceptive comments on Rosa's personality, artistic views, and marketing strategies.

397 Passeri, 1934, p. 396.

398 Pascoli, 1965, I, p. 84.

399 Baldinucci, 1845–47, V, p. 460; Passeri, 1934, p. 396, analyzes the weaknesses of Rosa's large figures (poor drawing, unnatural coloring, displeasing *arie di teste*, stiff fabrics, etc.). Fumagalli, 2007b, p. 75, points out that the altarpiece is not from Rosa's Florentine period but the early 1660s.

400 Baldinucci, 1845–47, V, 499; Pascoli, 1965, I, p. 87; and Rosa, 2003, p. 391, no. 373 (1669), and pp. 342–43, no. 321 (1666).

401 Rosa, 2003, pp. 12–13, no. 13 (1646), and Mahoney, 1977, I, p. 291, no. 24.5. Mahoney speculates that, rather than being a commentary on painters' fees, the drawing represents Rosa's low opinion of contemporary painting. For discussion of the image in a broader context of related allegories, including Elsheimer's drawing of the poor artist, see Thielemann, 2008. For a second allegory of "poor painting" by Rosa, see Alsteens et al., 2009, pp. 68–69, no. 32.

402 Rosa, 2003, pp. 356–57, no. 335 (1666).

403 Rosa, 2003, p. 98, no. 92 (1651); p. 108, no. 100 (1651); p. 112, no. 102 (1651); and p. 153, no. 137 (1652).

404 Rosa, 2003, pp. 161–62, no. 144 (1652), and p. 167, no. 150 (1652).

405 Scott, 1995, pp. 23–25.

406 Fumagalli, 2007d, pp. 40, 154, cat. 7, and p. 70 (*Fortune*).

407 Fumagalli, 2007b, pp. 74–75.

408 Rosa, 2003, p. 45, no. 46 (1650), and p. 110, no. 101 (1651); and De Gennaro, 2003, p. 85, no. 382; p. 92, no. 419; p. 93, no. 425; p. 97, no. 443.

409 Rosa, 2003, p. 274, no. 252 (1661).

410 Lisa Goldenberg Stoppato in Fumagalli, 2007d, p. 200, cat. 29.

411 Salerno, 1963, p. 99.

412 Passeri, 1934, pp. 394–95; for his minor and exceptional work in fresco in the Palazzo Pitti, see Scott, 1995, p. 35.

413 Passeri, 1934, p. 184 (Testa), and Rosa, 2003, p. 293, no. 271 (1662).

414 Golzio, 1939, p. 279, no. 2044.

415 Scott, 1995, p. 95, and Rosa, 2003, p. 158, no. 140.

416 Rosa, 2003, pp. 319–20, no. 300 (1664); p. 388, no. 369 (1669); pp. 391–92, no. 373 (1669); p. 278, no. 254, an offer to loan Ricciardi 1,000 scudi in 1661; p. 349, no. 328 (1666); and Passeri, 1934, p. 399.

417 Pascoli, 1965, I, p. 81.

418 Cavazzini, 2008c, p. 129.

419 Scott, 1995, p. 19, regarding the paintings that Baldinucci, 1845–47, V, p. 441, relates served as signs.

420 Scott, 1995, p. 134.

421 Rosa, 2003, p. 349, no. 328 (1666); p. 294, no. 272 (1662); p. 108, no. 100 (1651); and Baldinucci, 1845–47, V, pp. 483–84.

422 Rosa, 2003, p. 316, no. 296 (1663).

423 Scott, 1995, p. 136.

424 Rosa, 2003, pp. 350–51, no. 329 (1666).

425 Bellori, 1976, pp. 184, 199.

426 Passeri, 1934, pp. 65, 150.

427 Bellori, 1976, pp. 292, 356.

428 Pascoli, 1965, I, p. 51, and Philip Sohm's discussion below of posthumous reputation and prices.

429 Bellori, 2005, p. 385.

430 Baglione, 1642, p. 141.

431 Pascoli, 1965, I, pp. 185–88.

432 The fundamental study of the gallery and its documents is Wibiral, 1960. For a recent summary with updated literature, see Briganti, Laureati, and Trezzani, 1993, pp. 191–207, no. 20.

433 Bellori, 1976, p. 584, writes that Maratta's and Mola's frescoes were judged the best and given a "premio di cento scudi" each, which is not mentioned in the documents.

434 Passeri, 1934, p. 369. For discussion of some patron-initiated "competitions" between artists in the early seventeenth century, see Brown, 2001a.

435 Sparti, 1997, p. 64, n. 22.

436 On the confusing documentation of Rosa's four frescoes in the Palazzo Pitti, for which the painter might have received 175 scudi, see Fumagalli, 2007b, p. 49.

437 See Bauer, 1987, for documented examples, and Cavazzini, 2008b, pp. 78–81, with regard to the common practice of painters selling from their studios, not infrequently with the help of "intermediaries" (Cavazzini, 2008c, pp. 129–31).

438 Schleier, 2002, p. 69, n. 27.

439 Pascoli, 1965, I, pp. 71–72, for examples of Rosa's exchanges. The literature on gift giving in early modern Europe is large; see Findlen, 1994, p. 348, n. 6, for references, and Philip Sohm's essay below.

440 Baglione, 1642, pp. 303–4; Faldi, 1957, pp. 286–87; and Haskell, 1963, p. 14.

441 Antinori, 2005.

442 Lavin, 1975, p. 30, doc. 259.

443 Passeri, 1934, p. 141.

444 Passeri, 1934, pp. 374–75.

445 Bellori, 1976, pp. 575–78.

446 Pollak, 1913, p. 50, no. 2, for Romanelli's letter, and Passeri, 1934, pp. 310–11, 313. See Merz, 2005, pp. 169–85, for the most thorough summary of Romanellli's career.

447 Malvasia, 1841, I, p. 405 (publishing G. B. Bonconti's letter of 1599); Baglione, 1642, p. 108; Zapperi, 1999, p. 91; and Bellori, 1976, p. 78, for an explanation that a Spanish courtier influenced the inadequate final payment by pointing out to Odoardo his cumulative expenses on Annibale's wages and food. Bellori (p. 360) quotes Domenichino as saying that Odoardo's parsimony placed Annibale among the *disgraziati*.

448 Zapperi, 1999, pp. 93–94.

449 Passeri, 1934, pp. 235–40, and Barcham, 2001, p. 361.

450 Montias, 1990, for his early discussion of these concepts.

451 Passeri, 1934, pp. 73, 286.

452 Passeri, 1934, p. 285.

453 Bellori, 2005, p. 396 (and p. 37, n. 137, regarding the completion of Maratta's *vita* after Bellori's death).

454 For instance, Bellori, 2005, p. 401, writes that Maratta "had thirty Spanish doubloons given him as recompense" by Alexander VII for a *Nativity*. The Chigi archives indeed record the payment in 1659 as 113 scudi, the equivalent amount.

455 Bellori, 2005, p. 426.

456 Stella Rudolph has published only a small portion of her research on Maratta but declined to contribute to this essay.

457 Golzio, 1939, p. 280, no. 2046.

458 Bellori, 2005, pp. 400–1.

459 Bellori, 2005, pp. 400–1, 406.

460 Safarik, 1981, pp. 86–87, nos. 109–12; Gozzano, 2004, p. 240; and Strunck, 2007, p. 511, doc. 1672,06,08.

461 Spear, 1972, pp. 65–67, no. 33, for the series, and Lavin, 1975, pp. 317–18, IV.Inv.71, nos. 312, 320, 325.

462 Burke and Cherry, 1997, I, pp. 729ff., and II, p. 1,133.

463 Bellori, 2005, p. 415; Maratta "resold it to Count Lippi . . . having achieved far better terms than the first time."

464 Mezzetti, 1955, pp. 319–20, no. 18.

465 Schiavo [ca. 1964], pp. 199–200, and Mezzetti, 1955, pp. 352–53, docs. 1, 2.

466 Drago and Salerno, 1967, pp. 80–81, n. 45. Bellori, 2005, p. 419, writes that the altarpiece is "39 palmi high."

467 See Pampalone, 1993, for a detailed analysis of construction and decoration of the Spada chapel, on which this information draws.

468 Bellori, 2005, pp. 433–34.

469 DiFederico, 1968.

470 Schiavo [ca. 1964], pp. 95–99.

471 See Philip Sohm's essay below.

472 Pascoli, 1965, I, p. 141, records the pension; see Bershad, 1985, for Maratta's and his wife's property and his daughter's sale to the king of Spain; and see Westin and Westin, 1975, pp. 9–10, regarding Maratta's drawings and the aborted sale of 1703.

473 Enggass, 1964, pp. 156–57, 181, doc. 42.

474 Golzio, 1939, p. 289, nos. 3249, 118, and Pantanella, 1999, pp. 332 (15 January 1667) and 333 (31 July 1670); see also the discussion below in the section on portraiture.

475 Pantanella, 1999, p. 333 (15 March 1669).

476 Pantanella, 1999, p. 333 (13 September 1670).

477 Pascoli, 1965, I, p. 208. An analogous story was later recounted by Bernardo de' Dominici, for which see Marshall, 2006, pp. 363–64.

478 Golzio, 1939, p. 290, no. 599.

479 Enggass, 1964, pp. 141, 179, docs. 30–31.

480 Gady, 2002, p. 168.

481 "Baciccio's painting seems to me to be so bad that I'm not tempted the least to see to it that this man is invited here. I only regret the money it has cost." See Pantanella, 1999, pp. 335–36 (23 July 1685).

482 Pantanella, 1999, p. 336 (12 May 1687 and 10 August 1696).

483 For the Altieri chapel, see Schiavo [ca. 1964], p. 199, and for their projects in St. Peter's, DiFederico, 1983, pp. 68–70 (Maratta) and 71 (Gaulli).

484 *De Saint-Pierre de Rome à Aix-en-Provence*, 2005, p. 25.

485 Haskell, 1963, pp. 80–81, for a summary of the complex project; Enggass, 1964, pp. 31, 135–40, and 176–79, docs. 12–27; and Pantanella, 1999, *passim* (p. 335, 2 January 1680, indicates an actual payment of 12,000 rather than 14,000 scudi).

486 Pantanella, 1999, pp. 334 (25 September 1674), 336 (27 September 1698), and 337 (23 August 1708).

487 Schiavo [ca. 1964], p. 73 *passim* (Chiari might have received 615 scudi). See *Francesco Cozza . . .*, 2007, p. 284, doc. 9, for some different, generally higher figures.

488 Drago and Salerno, 1967, pp. 102–15. Known payments to Ascenzi and Boncore were 50 scudi "a conto" but presumably matched the others of 100 scudi; Albertoni's payment, too, must have been that amount rather than "1,000" scudi as transcribed.

489 Lavin, 1957, p. 44, and Gaynor and Toesca, 1963, pp. 81, 93.

490 Drago and Salerno, 1967, pp. 64, 76–77, n. 28, and pp. 78–79, n. 34.

491 Feinblatt, 1952, p. 46.

492 Montalto, 1956, p. 52, and *Francesco Cozza . . .*, 2007, p. 284, doc. 6.

493 Gimignani, however, who exceptionally was assigned two chapels, was paid only 200 scudi for the one dedicated to the Immaculate Conception, which required no lateral canvases. For the documentation, see DiFederico, 1971. Compare the situation at S. Silvestro with the contemporaneous decoration of chapels in S. Frediano in Cestello (discussed in Elena Fumagalli's essay), where entire chapels were also assigned to individual artists but payments from private sponsors varied.

494 Strunck, 2007, p. 545, doc. 1699,00,00d, and p. 557, doc. 1700,11,15.

495 Dunn, 1982, for discussion and documentation of this complicated project.

496 This remarkable document is transcribed in Pampalone, 1993, pp. 54–55, n. 2.

497 To generalize from data in Blunt, 1982, new construction and remodeling during the first half of the century as compared with the second half yields a ratio of about 2:1. Moreover, many late sixteenth-century churches were being decorated in the early decades of the seventeenth century, and most of Rome's larger churches, which required more altarpieces, were completed before 1650.

498 Bibliographic references cannot be accommodated in this essay; they and information regarding numbers of figures, etc., when known are in the database referred to in note 222 above.

499 Lorizzo, 2006, pp. 355–56.

500 Félibien, 1668, Preface (unpaginated).

501 Mancini, 1956–57, I, pp. 113, 13.

502 The exceptional portraitist, however, might operate with "wise imitation" (*Imitatio sapiens*), as the inscription in Bellori's allegorical engraving for Van Dyck suggests. Even so, Bellori spoke of portrait painters as being those "who cherish no Idea and are at the mercy of ugliness of the face or body, being unable to

correct the deformities of nature without taking away the likeness, else the portrait would be more beautiful and less like," and he lamented that Van Dyck worked without a "perfect idea" (*perfetta idea*) (Bellori, 2005, pp. 215, 60, 220, respectively).

503 Félibien, 1668, Preface (unpaginated).

504 Enggass and Brown, 1970, p. 17.

505 Baglione, 1642, pp. 139 and 136 (Bellori's marginal note in his copy of Baglione's *Vite*). On Caravaggio as a portraitist, see Varriano, 2006, pp. 87–98.

506 Percentages are rounded to the closest whole numbers and are based on data in Eskridge, 1979; Beaven, 2003; and Gozzano, 2004, p. 106. Due to many ambiguous subject classifications, the percentages inevitably are imprecise and total less than 100 percent, yet on the whole they should provide a fair picture of the composition of the five collections. It should be stressed, however, that inventory appraisals usually included frames and were not the same as prices paid to artists, especially when drawn up years later. The collections contained many paintings that were not seventeenth-century Roman and moreover reflected the interests of particular, often aristocratic collectors, not the Roman market as a whole.

507 Bauer, 1987, p. 95, with further data and discussion of portraiture. On Ventura, see Cavazzini, 2008c, *passim*.

508 Cavazzini, 2008c, p. 120.

509 But see Cavazzini, 2008c, pp. 100–6, for some examples of portraits of owners of middle-class Roman households.

510 See the table in Ago, 2002, p. 386, including a breakdown by male and female owers. My calculations exclude from her data the categories of architecture, miscellaneous subjects, and those of a compound nature (history and architecture, portrait and landscape). Her research draws on 76 inventories, of which 22 contained no paintings.

511 Baglione, 1642, p. 53.

512 Bellori, 2005, p. 411.

513 Golzio, 1939, p. 289, no. 3249; p. 289, no. 118; and p. 291, no. 1411. It seems unlikely, as proposed in *L'Ariccia del Bernini*, 1998, pp. 140–42, no. 37, that a portrait in the Palazzo Chigi, Ariccia, measuring only 71 × 59 cm, was the one designated in 1669 as a "ritratto grande."

514 See Robbin, 2000, for his (unpriced) death inventory (Robbin misinterprets the word *testa* as meaning a portrait of a head whereas it is a measurement, *tela da testa*), and Sani, 2005.

515 Granata, 2003, p. 49.

516 Granata, 2003, p. 50.

517 Scoppola, 1987, pp. 300–1, and Spezzaferro, 2002, pp. 45–46, 48–49.

518 Scoppola, 1987, pp. 300–1.

519 Benocci, 2006, pp. 19, 21.

520 Currò, 1958, pp. 57–58.

521 Lavin, 1975, p. 42, doc. 343.

522 D'Onofrio, 1967, p. 62, n. 30.

523 See Pepper, 1971, p. 315, no. 5, and p. 316, no. 48 ("Canle" Tonti undoubtedly should read "Car.le") for the documentation in Reni's account book. For the portrait of Cardinal Sannesi (Fig. 23), see Sickel, 2006; a "ritratto del Sig. Card. Tonti . . . del Guidoreni" was inventoried in the Maccarani collection in Rome in 1667 (Di Macco, 1994, p. 208).

524 Cappelletti and Testa, 1994, p. 150, nos. 41–42.

525 For Voet's prices, see the documentary appendix in Petrucci, 2005, pp. 315–30.

526 Golzio, 1939, p. 292, nos. 139, 1665, and p. 294, no. 1401 (the latter payment of 1679 has tentatively been identified with a portrait of Flavio Chigi in a private collection; see *L'Ariccia del Bernini*, 1998, pp. 138–40, no. 36). For payments to Vegli, Mattia da Farnese, and Nasini, see Petrucci, 1992.

527 See Philip Sohm's essay below.

528 Baglione, 1642, p. 56.

529 For Massimi's unpublished letter to Bellori, see Montanari in Bellori, 2005, p. 24.

530 Haskell, 1963, pp. 140–41; Piereth, 1997, pp. 78–117; and Spezzaferro, 1998, for discussion of the collecting of Bamboccianti art (see Piereth, pp. 118–22, on its prices, though without new data; she concludes that the price of a typical bambocciata ca. 1650 was about 10 scudi); and Scott, 1995, pp. 86–90, on the satire *Painting*.

531 Passeri, 1934, p. 96, and Roworth, 1978, pp. 111–16, on Rosa's, Passeri's, and others' attacks on the Bamboccianti.

532 Cappelletti and Testa, 1994, pp. 114–17, nos. 15–18.

533 Pliny the Elder, 1982, xxxv.112; Bellori, 1976, p. 16.

534 Capitelli, 2004, pp. 376–77, and especially p. 396, n. 9, for the complexities of the case.

535 Bertolotti, 1880, pp. 132–35, who first published the documents.

536 Lavin, 1975, p. 3, doc. 18.

537 Corradini, 1979, p. 193, no. 4.

538 Passeri, 1934, pp. 286–88.

539 Passeri, 1934, p. 290. Pascoli, 1965, I, p. 36, writes that Cerquozzi left 1,050 scudi in two bank accounts, but at the average rate of about 5 percent that would not yield 300 scudi a year; indeed, Cerquozzi's testament and inventory mention larger sums (Briganti, Laureati, and Trezzani, 1983, pp. 378–81). Baldinucci, 1845–47, VII, p. 111, cites the figure of 8,000 scudi.

540 Angelo Michele Colonna, claiming in 1639 that life in Florence was more expensive than in Rome, further held that an income of 180 scudi a year was not adequate to live like a gentleman there (see Elena Fumagalli's essay on Colonna's Florentine career).

541 De Gennaro, 2003, p. 71, no. 324.

542 Briganti, Laureati, and Trezzati, 1983, pp. 134–35, and Haskell, 1963, pp. 136–40 (p. 146, n. 28, for Spada's payment), on Cerquozzi's patronage.

543 Baldinucci, 1845–47, V, pp. 112–14.

544 Passeri, 1934, pp. 220–21.

545 Lanfranconi, 2002, p. 213.

546 Verberne, 2001.

547 Granata, 2003, pp. 53, 55.

548 Rosa, 2003, p. 162, no. 144 (1652), as trans. in Scott, 1995, p. 100.

549 Baldinucci, 1845–47, V, pp. 208–11, and VII, p. 122; Di Dedda, 2008, p. 39; and Pascoli, 1965, I, pp. 114–15.

550 Golzio, 1939, p. 286, no. 876 (acquired to accompany a *Battle* by Falcone); p. 288, no. 1467; and p. 285, no. 189.

551 Morper, 1961, p. 213.

552 Baldinucci, 1845–47, V, p. 207, and VII, p. 122.

553 De Gennaro, 2003, p. 89, no. 408.

554 Briganti, Laureati, and Trezzani, 1983, pp. 341–43.

555 Pascoli, 1965, II, pp. 356–57.

556 Enggass and Brown, 1970, p. 18.

557 Claude's remark is reported by Baldinucci, in Röthlisberger, 1961, I, p. 56.

558 See Cavazzini, 2008c, pp. 94–95, 109–11, for discussion of land-

scapes in middle-class households, and Spear, 2004a, for an earlier version of this analysis of landscape painting.

559 G. B. Viola, Filippo Napoletano, and Crescenzio Onofri are the notable exceptions. Evidence is insufficient regarding Giovanni Francesco Grimaldi and Salvator Rosa for judging how much they earned selling landscapes compared with their fewer but well-paid figural works. On Grimaldi, see notes 575 and 683 below.

560 Granata, 2003, pp. 39–40, 48, 50, 53 (paintings for Cardinal Montalto, two of which were frescoes at 25 scudi each, and two of which almost certainly are the canvases in the Patrizi collection measuring 39 × 50.5 cm, for which see Pedrocchi, 2000, pp. 328–29, no. 177); Della Pergola, 1955–59, I, p. 49; and Brugnoli, 1957, p. 277, doc. VII, for payment of 45 scudi to Viola for a month and a half's work at Bassano di Sutri.

561 Corti, 1989, p. 143, no. 46; Cavazzini, 1998, p. 226; Cavazzini, 2008a, pp. 82–83; and Lavin, 1975, p. 41, doc. 329.

562 Andrews, 1977, pp. 154–55, cat. 26, and p. 50, doc. 14; and pp. 146–47, cat. 16; for the payment, see Corti, 1989, p. 144, no. 52. See, too, Cavazzini, 2008c, p. 130. For discussion of Elsheimer's poverty, see Spear, 2003, pp. 314, 317.

563 Prices for Claude's paintings are cited in Röthlisberger, 1961, I, p. 57, n. 16; Morper, 1961, pp. 203–17; Garms, 1972, p. 86, no. 368; Corradini, 1979, p. 193, no. 18; Fumagalli, 1991, p. 577, n. 49; Wine, 2001, pp. 70–71, 78; Spear, 2004a; Beneš, 2005; and Gozzano, 2007. Table 7 does not include partial payments if the full price is unknown.

564 De Gennaro, 2003, p. 93, no. 421, and p. 96, no. 437 (perhaps L.V. 123 and 165); and Röthlisberger, 1961, I, p. 303, on Ruffo's acquisitions of paintings by Claude.

565 Röthlisberger, 1961, I, p. 13, with a breakdown of his rate of production per decade; and Boisclair, 1986, p. 163.

566 In her analysis of Claude's bank account, Gozzano, 2005, p. 288, suggests annual earnings of 300 scudi instead, which I think is much too low in light of all of the other evidence.

567 Gozzano, 2007, for a detailed study of Claude's bank accounts; Colombier, 1960, p. 53; and Baldinucci, in Röthlisberger, 1961, I, p. 62.

568 Bellori, 2005, p. 324.

569 Pliny the Elder, 1982, xxxv.116.

570 Boisclair, 1986, for payments to Dughet; Mancini, 1956–57, I, p. 261; and Spear, 1982, I, pp. 18–19, with a list of payments to Domenichino for frescoes and altarpieces.

571 Gozzano, 2004, p. 145; for Onofri's Florentine stipend and terms of employment, see Elena Fumagalli's essay below.

572 Boisclair, 1986, pp. 163, 304, 25, 104, 161, respectively.

573 Rosa, 2003, p. 319, no. 300.

574 Baldinucci, in Röthlisberger, 1961, I, p. 57.

575 Pascoli, 1965, I, pp. 46–49, writes that Grimaldi, too (who also did figural work, was an active designer of theatrical sets, and a prolific printmaker), made a lot of money (*gran danaro*) thanks to the "generoso pagamento" he received, that he was called to Paris with a "grosso stipendio," and that his paintings, already expensive while the artist was alive, "crebbero fuor di misura doppo morte, e carissime sono anche presentemente." Yet some very large landscapes (13 × 4 *palmi*) by him cost only 50 scudi, easel-size *tele d'imperatore* 36 scudi, and small ones (*tele da testa*) just 15 scudi. On the other hand, for figural decoration in the Duomo of Tivoli and the Alexander VII Gallery of the Quirinal palace discussed above, Grimaldi was paid 600 and 909 scudi respectively (Matteucci and Ariuli, 2002, pp. 289–91). See also note 683 below.

576 Bril's prices are summarized in Ruby, 1999, pp. 36–38, and Cappelletti, 2005–6, pp. 318–27 (most of the documented payments, however, are in the 35–50 scudi range, including late small landscapes); for Montalto's payments to Bril and Viola, see Granata, 2003, p. 297.

577 Hendriks, 2003, pp. 27, 64–67; Negro, 1996, pp. 25 and 35, n. 47 (the payment of 700 scudi to Bril was for "tutte le pitture da lui fatte in quadri, muri, loggia et altro"); and Angela Negro's essay on the Loggia della Pergola, in Hendriks, 2003, pp. 87–100. The documented payments to Reni and Tempesta likewise included some unspecified work.

578 For Roscioli, see Corradini, 1979, pp. 193–94, nos. 31, 32, 61, 73, 10, respectively; for the gilding of frames of Giuseppe Belloni's copies after Romanelli and Reni, see Merz, 2005, p. 467, nn. 18–19; and for the silver frame around the Romanelli–Belloni, see Merz, 2005, p. 205 (Belloni was paid 35 scudi for finishing Romanelli's *St. Teresa* and for a copy of the *Mystical Marriage of St. Catherine*, both on copper).

579 Lavin, 1975, pp. 306–7, nos. 286, 289, 292–94, 296, 301, 305; and, on Swanevelt's career in France, Szanto, 2003a, pp. 199–205.

580 Corradini, 1979, p. 193, no. 6, and p. 194, no. 81.

581 For documented payments to Poussin, see Rosenberg and Prat, 1994, and Amadio, 1998, pp. 144–53, as well as Lorizzo, 2001, p. 405. For Cassiano's letter, see Rinehart, 1961, pp. 43–44, and 57, letter 10.

582 Corradini, 1979, p. 194, no. 80.

583 For the former I am indebted to Dorothy Mahon at the Metropolitan Museum of Art, New York, and Barbara Berrie and Sarah Fisher at the National Gallery of Art, Washington, D.C.; for the latter to Jo Kirby of the National Gallery, London.

584 Garms, 1972, p. 204, no. 996.

585 Fumagalli, 1991, p. 577, n. 49.

586 Kirby and Saunders, 1998, pp. 155–59. See, too, the rich contribution by Kirby, 2000.

587 Eskridge, 1979, p. 231, n. 71; p. 235, n. 134; pp. 126, 155–56.

588 Beaven, 2003, p. 23.

589 Vries, 1991, p. 266 *passim*; Montias, 2002, pp. 87–92; and Montias's masterful book, 1996.

590 Lavin, 1975, IV.inv.71, pp. 296–303, nos. 223, 245, 231, 161, 248, 105, 112, respectively.

591 See Cavazzini, 2008b, pp. 81–82, for documentation of the commission.

592 Cavazzini, 2008c, pp. 37, 95.

593 Lavin, 1975, IV.inv.71, pp. 315–22, nos. 474, 589, 594, 613, 634, for examples of some low-value landscapes hanging over doors and windows; and no. 587 for the ten anonymous gouaches (they were appraised along with four others by Grimaldi, which were worth four times as much). *Vedute* painting was primarily an eighteenth-century genre and thus falls beyond the scope of this essay, yet it should be mentioned because it developed in Rome during the final decades of the century, notably through the practice of Gaspar van Wittel (Vanvitelli), who, with other *vedutisti*, opened a lucrative market niche directed at the swelling numbers of grand tour travelers. Paintings of architecture in early seventeenth-century Rome were cheaper than landscapes (Cavazzini, 2008c, p. 136).

594 Strunck, 2007, p. 509, doc. 1671,11,12.

595 Lavin, 1975, pp. 485–86, for Francione and his "Compagno," and

Benocci, 2006, p. 30, for "Cornelio." Northern artists in Italy often were called just by their first names, especially if a surname was as foreign as Poelenburgh; it is possible nonetheless that another Cornelio was the artist.

596 Enggass and Brown, 1970, p. 17.

597 Cropper, 1984, pp. 104–9. Giustiniani placed the painting of grotesques higher (eighth) than still life painting because it was "very difficult," requiring the "study of ancient paintings . . . erudite knowledge of antiquity" and, mostly tellingly, *invenzione* (Enggass and Brown, 1970, p. 18). Prospero Orsi ("Prosperino delle grottesche") specialized in this genre and was paid 30 scudi by the Mattei in 1614 for "un quadro di diversi uccelli"; other Mattei payments to him were for unidentified or religious work (Cappelletti and Testa, 1994, pp. 144, no. 22, and 332).

598 For Bonzi's altarpiece in the Pantheon, see Lo Bianco, 1987, p. 93.

599 Laureati, 2001, for a good summary of the status of the problem, and Cavazzini, 2008c, pp. 107–9, on still lifes in early seventeenth-century Roman collections. See Bocchi and Bocchi, 2005, pp. 21–42, on Verrocchi and pp. 43–65 for Laura Laureati's essay on Cerquozzi as a still life painter, and Whitfield, 2007, for an effort to assign a group of still lifes to Prospero Orsi at the beginning of the development of the genre.

600 Vannugli, 2006, pp. 68, 70–71, for the payment of 1608 for the lost *stendardo*.

601 For Salini, see Della Pergola, 1955–59, II, p. 220, doc. 77; Ehrlich, 2002, pp. 279–80, doc. 7; Corti, 1989, p. 145, no. 55; and Cavazzini, 2008c, pp. 32–34, on his repetitive production. For Bonzi, see Baglione, 1642, p. 343; Pollak, 1928–31, I, pp. 391–92, no. 1424; and Corradini, 1979, p. 193, no. 33.

602 Della Pergola, 1955–59, II, p. 220, doc. 77; Ehrlich, 2002, pp. 279–80, doc. 7.

603 Corti, 1989, pp. 134, nos. 7, 12, and 144, no. 50; and on Tanari, Fumagalli, 1995, p. 71, and Gregori, 2006.

604 Granata, 2003, p. 50; for two still lifes by Tanari acquired by the Medici in 1617, see Fumagalli, 1995, p. 71.

605 Della Volpe, 2005.

606 Among the many publications on Italian still life painting, see Salerno, 1984; Porzio, 1989; Gregori and Prinz von Hohenzollern, 2002; Bocchi and Bocchi, 2004; and especially Bocchi and Bocchi, 2005.

607 For a recent discussion of Mario's oeuvre, see Bocchi and Bocchi, 2005, pp. 67–142.

608 *L'arte per i papi . . .* , 1990, I, pp. 85–89, no. 27.

609 Golzio, 1939, p. 280, no. 2076, for the 100 scudi payment to Mario (and p. 278, nos. 436, 558, 559, 741, 941, and p. 279, nos. 1032, 2020, for the payments *a buon conto*). Golzio's 1939 publication of the *giustificazione*, p. 280, misleadingly suggests that Mario paid Morandi 50 scudi; Golzio's reproduction of the document (1965, p. 5), however, reveals that the amount is unspecified whereas the 50 scudi were for the frames.

610 Golzio, 1939, p. 278, no. 901 (Maratta), and p. 280, no. 2077 (Brandi). Mei's fee was part of a lump sum payment of 225 scudi for it and two other paintings (p. 281, no. 3245).

611 Golzio, 1939, p. 286, no. 874 (the four mirrors cost 86 scudi), with additional payments to Mario for three frames, for gilding them, and for three *pietre di paragone o negro antico*. See Rudolph, 1979, for discussion of mirror decoration.

612 Pascoli, 1965, II, pp. 57–64 (and Marshall, 2006, pp. 363–64, on Pascoli's account of Mario's early career). See Ferraro, 1994, pp. 329–93, on these and other common forms of investment in Rome.

613 Lorizzo, 2003b, p. 326, with further discussion of this practice and its problems for the Accademia.

614 Bauer, 1987, p. 95.

615 Lavin, 1975, p. 310, nos. 366 (20 scudi), 376 (20 scudi), 379 (25 scudi), and p. 311, no. 398 (25 scudi), all about 55 cm high and framed.

616 Lavin, 1975, p. 41, doc. 326a; Corradini, 1979, p. 194, nos. 75, 76; Golzio, 1939, pp. 280, no. 2114, and p. 281, nos. 3379, 3385; Gozzano, 2004, pp. 221, 231; and Strunck, 2007, pp. 506, doc. 1668,08,02, and 511, doc. 1672,09,23b. For a review of the known documents on the Stanchi, see Laura Laureati in Porzio, 1989, II, pp. 770–71; Ravelli, 2005; and Maria Silvia Proni's essay in Bocchi and Bocchi, 2005, pp. 245–328, to which should be added Strunck, 2007.

617 Golzio, 1939, p. 200, no. 1855; p. 293, no. 3456; and p. 292, no. 1647; and Porzio, 1989, II, p. 759.

618 Golzio, 1939, p. 294, no. 1981, and p. 295, no. 1260.

619 Gualandi, 1844–56, III, p. 225, no. 420.

620 See Bocchi and Bocchi, 2004, on the foreign painters.

621 Rosa, 2003, p. 284, no. 261.

622 Lorizzo, 2003a, and 2006, pp. 352–56. Giuseppe Ghezzi did the appraisal; the average price of Peri's pictures was just 7.35 scudi.

623 As suggested by Christopher Marshall on the basis of payments to Luca Forte and Giuseppe Recco in the 100 to 200 ducats range.

624 Félibien, 1668, Preface (unpaginated).

625 Bocchi and Bocchi, 2005, pp. 399–446 (essay by Ludovica Trezzani).

626 Faldi, 1966, p. 145, for the painting with a Moor, as well as four paintings of 1665 in the Palazzo Chigi at Ariccia depicting greyhounds with views of Chigi properties in the background (see also *L'arte per i papi . . .* , 1990, II, p. 81). For the payments, Golzio, 1939, p. 246, nos. f.94–f.95; p. 278, no. 670; p. 279, nos. 2022 and 2043; p. 280, no. 2080; p. 281, no. 3396; p. 283, no. 3717; and p. 287, no. 1139.

627 Gozzano, 2004, pp. 212, 231, 232.

628 Golzio, 1939, p. 283, nos. 3720, 3854.

629 Pascoli, 1965, II, pp. 361–67.

630 For Ridolfi's comments, see the essay on Venice below, and Bellori, 2005, p. 387, regarding Sacchi.

631 Sandrart, 1925, pp. 173, 203.

632 Pascoli, 1965, II, pp. 358–59. See Cavazzini, 2004b, p. 133, and 2008c, pp. 56–64, for examples of Italian students who were charged for their lessons, but often as live-in apprentices.

633 Cennini, 1954, pp. 2–3.

634 Ottonelli and Cortona, 1973, pp. 17–20.

635 Bellori, 2005, p. 34.

636 Mancini, 1956–57, I, pp. 9–10, 139–41, and Furlotti, 2003b, for analysis of Mancini's criteria and the Gonzaga's collecting. See, too, Vincenzio Borghini's discussion of prices and value of art in the context of the *paragone* between sculpture and painting. Borghini insists that neither the material cost nor the expenditure of time of production matter, but that a work of art is to be judged by "l'ingegno" it displays (Barocchi, 1971, I, pp. 630–35). Guerzoni, 2006, pp. 233–34, 257, remarks on this text and the broader complexities of analyzing prices (pp. 231ff.).

637 Bellori, 2005, p. 363. For Boschini's views, see Philip Sohm's essay.
638 Mancini, 1956–57, I, pp. 141, 250.
639 Spear, 2003, p. 313.
640 Bellori, 2005, pp. 259–60, and also pp. 266–67 regarding Domenichino's pricing of private pictures.
641 Spear, 2003, pp. 313–14, and Bellori, 1976, p. 394. See Christopher Marshall's data on Lanfranco's Neapolitan earnings in the following essay.
642 Spear, 2005.
643 That the pattern of rejection of some of Caravaggio's altarpieces "resembles a ploy to gain notoriety, raise his prices, and, astutely, get two sales for a single commission" (McTighe, 2006, p. 586) seems improbable and in any case lacks supporting economic evidence.
644 Bellori, 1976, p. 225.
645 Bellori, 1976, pp. 81–82.
646 Bellori and Malvasia give somewhat different accounts of Annibale's and Albani's generosity in insisting that the other deserved most of the fee (Bellori, 2005, pp. 94 and 112, n. 127).
647 Marcolini, 1998.
648 Malvasia, 1841, I, p. 325, and Loire, 1996, pp. 133–38, for discussion of the complex issues regarding the date and destination of Annibale's altarpiece.
649 Spear, 2003, p. 319, n. 61, with further references regarding *monti*; for Cortona's investments in them, see Sparti, 1997, pp. 140–44.
650 From unpublished documents in the Accademia's archives made available to me by Ann Sutherland Harris.
651 Rosa, 2003, pp. 243–44, no. 222 (1659).
652 Zuccaro, 1655, fol. 75v.
653 Pascoli, 1965, II, p. 293.
654 Guerzoni, 2006, pp. 47–58 *passim*.
655 But for discussion of student-apprentices who paid, see Cavazzini, 2008c, pp. 49–64.
656 Spear, 1997, p. 225.
657 See Cavazzini, 2008c, pp. 130–34, on Agostino Tassi's dealing, and pp. 147–48.
658 Missirini, 1823, pp. 96, 128–29; and Lorizzo, 2006, pp. 344–45 and graph 11 for further data from the Accademia's archive.
659 Bershad, 1985.
660 Cavazzini, 2008c, pp. 130–31.
661 Gady, 2002, p. 168.
662 On Venice, see Philip Sohm's essay below; Missirini, 1823, p. 68; and Gallo, 1998, pp. 313, 315, for an example of an appraisal payment to the Accademia (2.4 scudi in 1604 by Orazio Gentileschi for appraisal of his work for the Ubertini), and Cappelletti, 2005–6, p. 321, for a similar sum (2 scudi) paid by Paul Bril the same year for appraisal of his work in the Palazzo Cesarini. The fine for unauthorized appraising was set at 10 scudi for any appraisal up to 100 scudi and 10 percent of the appraised value above 100 scudi. See Cavazzini, 2008c, pp. 126–27, for further discussion of painters as appraisers.
663 Pedrocchi, 2000, pp. 40–41, 387–89.
664 Riedl, 1998, p. 194, doc. 28 (and Chappell and Kirwin, 1974, on the commission in St. Peter's); the sixth painting in the series, by Cigoli, was not yet finished at the time of the appraisal. See the Introduction regarding Count Sangiorgio's quip.
665 Pascoli, 1965, II, pp. 73–74.
666 Di Macco, 1994, p. 210, with rich documentation on the artist's career.
667 Mancini, 1956–57, I, p. 145.
668 Fumagalli, 1994, p. 49 and 98, n. 53.
669 Di Macco, 1994, p. 212.
670 Golzio, 1939, pp. 201, no. 1656; 296, no. 1383 (perhaps the painting now in Bologna: Schleier, 2002, pp. 304–5, no. 95); and pp. 298–99, no. 986.
671 Pascoli, 1965, II, pp. 204, 207.
672 Pollak, 1928–31, II, pp. 293–94, 571–73.
673 Bertolotti, 1882, pp. 85–86.
674 Manuela Mena, in her entry (Maratti, Carlo) in the Grove *Dictionary of Art*, links Maratta's undertaking of restoration work to the "political and economic factors [at the end of the century that] caused official and aristocratic patronage to decline." See Montanari in Bellori, 2005, p. 13, and Bellori's text on Sacchi and Maratta, pp. 383–84, 410, 431–32; and Rudolf, 1979, p. 13, on Maratta's restoration of the ancient fresco fragment.
675 Pascoli, 1965, II, pp. 302–3.
676 Masetti Zannini, 1974b, pp. 12–13, and Bevilacqua, 1993, p. 39.
677 ASC, Archivio Cardelli, Appendice Savelli, vol. 35, Registro di mandati del Cardinal Montalto, 1607–1611, an unpublished document kindly provided by Belinda Granata; and Spezzaferro, 2002, p. 46.
678 Pascoli, 1965, II, pp. 392, 398.
679 Passeri, 1934, p. 65.
680 Pascoli, 1965, II, pp. 112 and 330.
681 See the essays by Elena Fumagalli regarding Cosimo Ulivelli's and Jacopo Chiavistelli's savings of 30,000 and 40,000 scudi in Florence, where those were very substantial sums, and by Philip Sohm regarding Venice, where few artists' estates were as large as 10,000 scudi (the biggest was Carl Loth's of 32,000 ducats, which were close in value to scudi).
682 Pascoli, 1965, I, pp. 246, 255, 258.
683 Pascoli, 1965, I, p. 233; II, p. 125; II, p. 234; and I, p. 46. An exceptionally detailed document of 1673 should be mentioned that breaks down the value of different components of Grimaldi's ceiling and frieze in the Colonna palace, including four landscapes at 80 scudi, six *Virtues* at 48 scudi, four medallions with surrounding gold and chiaroscuro ornamentation at 20 scudi, etc. See Strunck, 2007, p. 512, doc. 1673,01,25, for Grimaldi's request totaling 690 scudi, which was reduced to 480.
684 Mancini, 1956–57, I, 242. For further discussion of this issue, see Philip Sohm's Introduction.
685 Bellori, 2005, p. 160.
686 Scaramuccia, 1965, p. 192.
687 Cavazzini, 2008b, p. 90: "io non sono tanto ricco quanto vorrei essere."

2 *Naples*

1 Labrot, 1992, pp. 69–71, Inv. 7.
2 The published Getty inventories omit references to drawings, frames, and other related items. In the Anfora inventory these omitted references include "dieci tunni indagliati grandi [item 14a] . . . tre dozzini di tonni picoli di ligniamo [item 16a] . . . uno tunno piccolo indagliato e dorato [item 19a]."
3 For Pesce, see De' Dominici, 1742–45, III, p. 211, and Sestieri and Daprà, 1994, pp. 47–49.

4 For the eruption of Mount Vesuvius of 1631 see the discussion and references cited in Causa, 1956.
5 For the revolt of Masaniello, see the discussion and references cited in Marshall, 1998.
6 For the plague of 1656, see De Renzi, 1867; Galasso, 1982, pp. 46–47; and Strazzullo, 1957, pp. 7–16.
7 De Maio, 1983.
8 The classic account remains Labrot, 1979, as further amplified and updated in Labrot, 1993.
9 Astarita, 1992, pp. 217–23; Calabria, 1991, pp. 39–47; Villari, 1993, pp. 98–109.
10 Marshall, 2005, citing previous literature.
11 Martínez, ca. 1675, cited by Pérez Sánchez and Spinosa, 1978, pp. 9–10.
12 Schütze, 1992 (who also discusses Cesare Fracanzano's association with the Neapolitan literati), and Schütze, 2001, *passim*.
13 For Stanzione's knighthoods, see Schütze and Willette, 1992, pp. 45–52. For Ribera's see Chenault, 1976, *passim*, and for Caracciolo's see Stoughton, 1973, p. 5.
14 Calabria, 1991, p. xv and *passim* more generally for this issue.
15 Calabria, 1991, p. 134.
16 Turbolo, 1629, p. 14; Faraglia, 1878, pp. 206–7.
17 Turbolo, 1629, p. 28.
18 Vargas, 1988, pp. 136–38.
19 For a recent account of Finson's Neapolitan career, see Papi, 2001.
20 Causa, 2000, pp. 351–57.
21 Schütze and Willette, 1992, pp. 41–57.
22 For the now lost inscription on Falcone's tomb, see Saxl, 1939–40, p. 78, n. 2. For international interest in Falcone's work, see Marshall, 2006, pp. 371–72.
23 The rate of exchange between the ducat and scudo apparently fluctuated more radically than indicated in Table 30 in Renata Ago's essay (based on Da Silva), at times reaching about 0.8:1. See Guerra, 1844, p. 168; Spear, 1982, I, p. 299, n. 2; and Pacelli, 1984b, p. 94, n. 29: "duc. 60 valuta di scudi 45 di moneta romana."
24 Spear, 1982, I, p. 286.
25 The fullest account remains Strazzullo, 1978, and see Spear, 1982, for an account of the commission with particular reference to Domenichino's work there 1631–41.
26 De' Dominici, 1742–45, III, p. 263; for discussion see Strazzullo, 1978, pp. 49–50, and Röttgen, 2002, pp. 170–71 and 496–97, cat. A.
27 For the documentation, see Nappi, 2002, p. 94, doc. 5.
28 Spear, 1982, I, pp. 20–21, 71, 299–302.
29 Haskell, 1982, p. 61.
30 Röttgen, 2002, pp. 22–30, 59–62, and pp. 242–45, 290–92, 297–303, cats. 22, 30, 62, 64.
31 Leone de Castris, 1991, pp. 186–89, 193–98.
32 Celano [1692], 1974, IV, p. 1, 255. For discussion, see Strazzullo, 1985, p. 139.
33 Vargas, 1988.
34 See Schleier, 2002, pp. 46–52, with previous bibliography.
35 For discussion, see Schütze, 1993.
36 Schleier, 2002, p. 47.
37 Faraglia, 1885, pp. 456–58.
38 Schleier, 2002, p. 50.
39 Schleier, 2002, p. 50. For the canvas paintings produced for the choir see pp. 314–17, cats. 99–103.
40 Schleier, 2002, pp. 46–52, 314, 382. For Lanfranco's dispute with the Carthusians, see further Bernini, 1982, p. 98.
41 Schleier, 2002, p. 47.
42 The price fluctuated at certain periods, particularly during the revolt of Masaniello in 1647–48. See Faraglia, 1878, p. 174. The price cited here is arrived at by dividing by 40 the prices paid for a *tomolo* of wheat (40 kilo in weight).
43 Calabria, 1991, n. 47, p. 17.
44 Faraglia, 1878, pp. 255–56, provides cumulative prices from 1550 to 1649.
45 This and the following information concerning food prices is taken from Faraglia, 1878, pp. 264–65.
46 Prota Giurleo, 1952, p. 29.
47 Borrelli, 1988, pp. 38–39; Stoughton, 1978, p. 210.
48 For the practice of renting out single rooms, see Amabile, 1890, p. 20; for partnership rentals, see Delfino, 1984, pp. 159–60, doc. 27, which also constitutes an unusually detailed rental agreement.
49 Nappi, 1990.
50 For Ribera's "casa palaziata," see Prota Giurleo, 1953, p. 101. Prota Giurleo transcribed part of the purchase agreement only, minus the price, and subsequent researchers have not been able to trace his original notarial source (Finaldi in Pérez Sánchez and Spinosa, 1992, p. 246). However, the sum of 3,100 ducats can be determined from another more recently published document which cites the annual 1 percent tax rate of 31 ducats that Ribera was required to pay on the property (Nappi, 1990, p. 183, doc. 46). For Ribera charging 100 ducats rent on this property, see Nappi, 1990, p. 183, doc. 44.
51 For Stanzione's house, see Prota Giurleo, 1955, pp. 24–25, and Schütze and Willette, 1992, pp. 150–51, n. 160.
52 Faraglia, 1878, pp. 210–11.
53 Carderi, 1971, p. 22.
54 For weekly wages for *pipernieri*, see Archivio di Stato di Napoli, monasteri soppressi, vol. 2143, fols. 57r–v, 93r.
55 Faraglia, 1878, p. 288. The Camera Reale was the highest court in the Kingdom of Naples with responsibility for the realm's financial as well as legislative administration.
56 Delfino, 1987, republished in full in Pérez Sánchez and Spinosa, 1992, pp. 232–34.
57 For Corenzio's daughter's dowry, see D'Addosio, 1912–13, p. 53. For a comparable dowry of this level, see Nappi, 1998, p. 176, doc. 139.
58 The marriage contract between Margarita Ribera and Giovanni Sersale was published for the first time in Pérez Sánchez and Spinosa, 1992, pp. 247–48.
59 Caracciolo, 1959, p. 32.
60 Whitfield and Martineau, 1982, p. 116.
61 Examples include a 1598 commission to Fabrizio Santafede for an altarpiece in the church of Aversa outside Naples (Prota Giurleo, 1952, p. 16), a 1613 commission to Carlo Sellitto for an altarpiece in the church of the Cappucini (Bologna and Causa, 1977, p. 134, doc. 36), and a 1608 commission to Battistello Caracciolo for altarpieces (now destroyed) in the Chiesa del Monteoliveto (Causa, 2000, p. 351).
62 For Caravaggio at the Pio Monte della Misericordia, see Bologna in Cassini and Sapio, 2005, pp. 106–7, cat. 4, with previous bibliography.
63 For the sharp rise in the cost of wheat and oil during 1621–22, see the "tavola grafica dei prezzi del grano e dell'olio dal 1550 al 1625" in Faraglia, 1878, pp. 428–29.

64 Faraglia, 1892, pp. 658–59.

65 For documentation of Caracciolo's *Assumption*, see Stoughton, 1973, p. 145 and cat. 57, and Causa, 2000, pp. 356–57. For Stanzione's *Pietà*, see Schütze and Willette, 1992, p. 209, cat. A46. For Ribera's *Pietà*, see Faraglia, 1892, p. 670. For Vaccaro's *St. Hugh*, see Faraglia, 1892, p. 661.

66 For the standardization of the dimensions of landscape paintings, along with other types of cabinet painting, see Marshall, 2000, p. 20 and p. 32, n. 40.

67 D'Addosio, 1912–13, p. 54.

68 For the documentation for Jacopo Coppola, see Nappi, 1983a, p. 43. For Maccario, see Delfino, 1984, p. 158.

69 Nappi, 1992, p. 27.

70 Ruffo, 1916, p. 30.

71 The *Massacre of the Innocents* (Fig. 38) is characteristic of Compagno's work. For the 1641 commission, see D'Addosio, 1912–13, p. 46. For the 1650 commission, see Strazzullo, 1955, p. 21, doc. 45.

72 Nappi, 1992, p. 74. Though slightly smaller than the two paintings of 1659, the *Gathering of the Manna* (Fig. 39) represents well Gargiulo's work of the period.

73 For documentation of the 200 ducat price agreed in 1684 for an altarpiece by Giordano at the church of S. Maria Regina Coeli, see Nappi, 1991, p. 178.

74 Nappi, 1983b, p. 75.

75 Schütze and Willette, 1992, pp. 264–65, cats. D23 and D24.

76 Schütze and Willette, 1992, pp. 196–97, cat. A24; Schütze, 1993, *passim*.

77 Schütze and Willette, 1992, pp. 225–27, cat. A73.

78 For the probable size of these lost paintings, see Schütze and Willette, 1992, pp. 265–66, cat. D34.

79 Schütze and Willette, 1992, p. 244, cat. A108.

80 Delfino, 1986, p. 114.

81 Nappi, 1990, p. 181; Delfino, 1984, p. 160.

82 For the *Twelve Philosophers*, see Nappi, 1983b, p. 78. For the *Pietà*, see Faraglia, 1892, p. 670. For the Palazzo Reale *Immaculate Conception* (destroyed during World War II), see Nappi, 1983a, pp. 48–49. For Ribera's *St. Januarius Escaping the Fiery Furnace* in the Cappella del Tesoro of Naples Cathedral, see Faraglia, 1885, pp. 449–50. The price for Ribera's *Communion of the Apostles* was subsequently disputed by his heirs, and a number of varying (and contradictory) summaries of payments were drawn up by the Carthusians to resolve the issue, followed by an extra payment as final settlement. Its cost is described as being either 900, 985, or 1,300 ducats, for which see Faraglia, 1892, pp. 670–78.

83 For documentation for the *Apollo and Marsyas,* see Nappi, 1983b, p. 78, and Nappi, 1990, p. 184.

84 Ruffo, 1916, p. 46, n. 1.

85 The fullest account of the circumstances surrounding the commission remains Wethey, 1967.

86 Ferrari and Scavizzi, 1992 and 2003.

87 Spinosa, 2003; Schütze and Willette, 1992; and Bissell, 1999.

88 See, e.g., the 60 ducats paid to Giordano in 1675 for a painting of *Samson and Delilah* measuring around 158 × 132 cm (Novelli Radice, 1982–83, p. 183). Other relevant documents are found in Nappi, 1991 (e.g., 200 ducats paid to Giordano by Vincenzo Samuelli on 8 July 1672 for two unspecified paintings: p. 173).

89 Nappi, 1991, p. 174.

90 For Giordano's marketing strategies and associations with entrepreneurial dealing, see Marshall, 2003 and 2006.

91 For the *Judgment of Paris,* see Ruffo, 1916, p. 54, and Schütze and Willette, 1992, pp. 262–63, cat. D15. For the *Persephone,* see Nappi, 1983b, p. 78.

92 Nappi, 1983b, p. 80.

93 For Gentileschi's 1636 commission, see Nappi, 1983b, p. 76, and Marshall, 2005, pp. 15–16, for discussion. For Simone's *Diana and Actaeon*, see D'Addosio, 1912–13, p. 505.

94 Costello, 1950, pp. 249–50, nn. 3–4.

95 Costello, 1950, pp. 243–46, 264.

96 Costello, 1950, p. 247, and Spear, 1997, pp. 18, 140–41, for discussion.

97 Spear, 1994, *passim.*

98 Ruffo, 1916, p. 97. For discussion, see Haskell, 1980, p. 209, and Spear, 1994, p. 597.

99 Ruffo, 1916, p. 55.

100 For discussion, see Marshall, 2005, pp. 10–11.

101 Ruffo, 1916, p. 52, as translated in Garrard, 1989, pp. 398–99.

102 Garrard, 1989, p. 390.

103 For further discussions of Gentileschi's pricing strategies with reference to these and other documentary references, see Spear, 2005, and Marshall, 2005, pp. 16–21.

104 Ruffo, 1916, pp. 46–48, as translated in Garrard, 1989, p. 393.

105 For Gentileschi's reduced earnings at the end of her career, see Marshall, 2005, pp. 18–24. For Ribera's late financial difficulties, see the begging letters written by him to the prior of the Certosa di S. Martino in 1651 (Pérez Sánchez and Spinosa, 1992, p. 251).

106 Faraglia, 1892, p. 667.

107 For Leone's career and early association with Aniello Falcone, see particularly Blunt, 1939–40; Novelli Radice, 1976; and Brejon de Lavergnée, 1984.

108 Bréjon de Lavergnée in Causa et al., 1984, I, p. 241 cat. 2.54; Bréjon de Lavergnée, 1984, pp. 664, 679, cat. 28, fig. 643.

109 For Leone's training in fresco and workshop assistance to Corenzio, see De' Dominici, 1742–45, III, pp. 80, 144; Pacelli, 1984a, p. 163.

110 Rizzo, 1984, p. 314.

111 For Giacomo Capece Galeota, Duke of Regina (1617–80), see A. Musi in *Dizionario biografico degli italiani*, XVIII, 1975, pp. 434–35. For his importance as a patron and collector, see Labrot and Ruotolo, 1980, p. 32. For his patronage of Preti, see Nappi, 1980, pp. 65–66, doc. 158.

112 Rizzo, 1984, p. 314.

113 Ruffo, 1916, pp. 30, 32.

114 D'Addosio, 1912–13, p. 608.

115 D'Addosio, 1912–13, p. 608.

116 Nappi, 1988, pp. 129–52 and p. 138 for the Ribera.

117 Rizzo, 1987, p. 153, doc. 2, 1647 payment for the frame of Beltrano's *Madonna and Souls in Purgatory* in Nola.

118 Nappi, 1983b, p. 76.

119 De' Dominici, 1742–45, III, pp. 72–75.

120 Capaccio, 1630, pp. 863–65. The best discussion remains Vaes, 1925, pp. 188–95.

121 Saxl, 1939–40.

122 Labrot, 1992, pp. 113–15, Inv. 19. This inventory lists works belonging to Gargiulo's earliest and most important patron. Its dating, evident care of compilation, and frequent correspondence with primary documentation of prices cited throughout this essay

make it particularly useful as an indicator of primary market prices. In this it differs from most other inventories that were either drawn up much later than the time in which their artworks were assembled or else whose notional and often inflated valuations need to be treated with discretion or even suspicion. It is accordingly the only inventory used in this manner in this study.

123 For van Somer's 1641 altarpiece at S. Maria della Sapienza, see D'Addosio, 1912–13, p. 510. For the recent literature on van Somer, see Spinosa, 1995, pp. 223–30, and Bologna, 1996, pp. 12–17.

124 Marshall, 2000.

125 De' Dominici, 1742–45, III, p. 82; "Così appunto accadde a Cesare, e Francesco Fracanzano fratelli, molto virtuosi in pittura, ma disgraziati a segno, che stentavano a satollarsi di pane: come nella seguente narrazione farem palese."

126 De' Dominici, 1742–45, III, p. 82.

127 De' Dominici, 1742–45, III, p. 85.

128 An attempt to separate fact from fiction within De' Dominici's account on the basis of what little is known about the Fracanzanos' careers has been made recently by De Vito (2004).

3 *Bologna*

1 Guenzi and Poni, 1987, and Poni, 1990.

2 This state of economic hegemony reached a crisis point at the end of the seventeenth century when large mechanical spinning wheels were introduced in Piedmont, Lombardy, and the Veneto.

3 Faleoni, 1649, pp. 691–92. On the plague pallium, see the record in Mazza, 1988, pp. 136–38, and Emanuela Fiori's entry in Bentini et al., 2008, pp. 69–74, cat. 35.

4 Pepper, 1979.

5 For precedents, see Spear, 1997, p. 389, n. 87.

6 Malvasia, 1841, II, p. 42.

7 Colantuono, 2008, pp. 201-16, identified this painting as one now in Atlanta, Mark Freeland Collection, which is a fragment of an unfinished painting. It is on canvas, and in my opinion is probably a version of a work that has since disappeared.

8 Between 1465 and 1660, 87 families occupied positions in the Senate and the Ufficio dei Riformatori, since these were inherited, lifelong positions.

9 Guerzoni, 2006, pp. 20–30.

10 Masini, 1666 and 1690, in the edition with the list of painters printed by Arfelli, 1957, in particular pp. 204–34.

11 Pellicciari, 1988, pp. 119–41; Pirondini, 1992, pp. 11–16.

12 This estimate is derived by dividing the number of painters (350) by the years in question (100) times the years of an average working career (40).

13 Zarri, 1989, pp. 161–200.

14 Morselli, 1997. In particular, see the introductory essay, "Società, pittori e mercato dell'arte nella Bologna di Carlo Cesare Malvasia," pp. XIII–XXXVI.

15 An example is provided by the workshop of Enrico Kaiel, known as Henry the Fleming. See Morselli, 1992a, pp. 275–76.

16 Malvasia, 1841, II, p. 112: "Sgridato più volte dagli amici, e dalle camerate di tanta bassezza d'animo, e viltà: che volete che più chieda, rispondeva: un par mio, un povero filatogliero, che non si guadagnava più che cinque bolognini il giorno? vi par'egli poco sia giunto a valutare la sua giornata un testone, e mezzo scudo?"

17 Salvioni, 1961, pp. 516–18. Hereafter, all costs, payments, and revenues will be noted in Bolognese lire to facilitate comparison.

18 Baldi, 1961, pp. 175–79.

19 Piro, 1976, pp. 117–82.

20 Carboni, 1995.

21 Roversi, 1967, pp. 15–263.

22 Carboni, 1995, p. 77, n. 29.

23 That is, bread sold retail, unlike bread that was simply cooked by the baker (*da massaria*) or bread produced with the customer's own grain (*da impastaria*). See Guenzi, 1978, pp. 391–97, and Guenzi, 1981, pp. 153–87. It should be remembered that the area surrounding Bologna produced a substantial quantity of hemp and silk for trade, but not enough food to feed the city's population. The government collected information about the internal harvest and that in the bordering areas. It set an official price that was intended to discourage the import of foreign grain and to protect farm revenues.

24 On this issue, see Fanti, 1980, p. 124.

25 Ferrante, 1983.

26 According to Luisa Ciammitti's research, Angela Brindani, for example, became Suor Rosa in the convent of S. Benedetto in 1699 and received a dowry worth 1,600 lire from Paris Boschi, the owner of the veil factory. See Ciammitti, 1979, p. 762.

27 These figures are taken from the documents published by Niccoli, 2000.

28 Malvasia, 1841, II, pp. 24, 33.

29 Bonfait, 2002b, pp. 837–47 with preceding bibliography.

30 Gualandi, 1840–45, I, p. 187.

31 Malvasia, 1841, I, p. 34, and II, pp. 42, 271, for examples of this theme; and Bonfait, 2002b, pp. 838–39.

32 Malvasia, 1841, I, pp. 174–75.

33 Letter published and analyzed by Ciammitti, 2000, pp. 194–203. In 1627, Reni charged the count of Oñate 200 scudi per figure for the *Immaculate Conception* (Metropolitan Museum of Art, New York), according to a letter the artist wrote to Antonio Galeazzo Gibbia. For the painting of the Virgin with two angels, Reni charged a total price of 400 scudi. See Malvasia, 1841, II, p. 27.

34 Unfortunately, the painters' guild documents are lost. They are partially known through the words of Malvasia, who, in many parts of his *Felsina pittrice*, asserts that he has the crates containing the guild's documents in his possession; he used them widely throughout his work. For the transaction between the guild of the Bombasari and the painters' guild, see Gualandi, 1840–45, III, pp. 164–65; Malaguzzi Valeri, 1897, pp. 309–14; and, for the statutes of the painters' guild, Bodmer, 1939, and Cammarota, 1984, pp. 293–326. For the surviving lists of those affiliated with the guild, see Feigenbaum, 1999, pp. 353–77.

35 Gualandi, 1840–45, III, p. 164.

36 Malvasia, 1841, II, p. 49; translated from Malvasia, 1980, p. 118.

37 Malvasia, 1841, II, p. 271.

38 Bellori [1672], 1976, p. 531.

39 Morselli, 1997, "Periti." The list comes from the consultation of 968 legal inventories preserved in the Archivio Notarile of the Archivio di Stato in Bologna.

40 For the definition of the guild of the *zavagli*, with its rules and regulations, see Gheza Fabbri, 1980, pp. 163–80, and, for the documentation, Biblioteca comunale dell'Archiginnasio di Bologna,

Fondo Speciale, Arte dei Drappieri e Strazzaroli, cartone VII fascicolo VII, sottofascicolo 4, unnumbered loose page within a note of expenses dated 1678.

41 Information about the intermediate appraisals is lacking, and therefore it would be methodologically incorrect to calculate a percentage on a statistical basis.

42 Morselli, 1998a.

43 On the reliability of Malvasia's use of source material, see Dempsey, 1990, and Summerscale, 2000, p. 38 with previous bibliography.

44 Guerzoni, 2006, found the opposite situation when examining Este material in Modena.

45 Malvasia, 1841, II, p. 73.

46 For his biography and a register of documents, see Monducci, 2002.

47 Malvasia, 1982, p. 162.

48 Tiraboschi, 1786, p. 360.

49 The reply from the commune of Sassuolo was on 11 August 1591. See Cionini, 1902, pp. 364–65.

50 Malvasia, 1841, II, p. 146; Tiraboschi, 1786, p. 360. See the register in Negro and Roio, 1996.

51 Malvasia, 1982, p. 46.

52 Malvasia, 1841, II, p. 280.

53 Spike, 1988, p. 43.

54 Cavalli, 1955, p. 35.

55 Malvasia, 1841, II, p. 247.

56 Malvasia, 1841, II, p. 215.

57 Malvasia, 1841, II, p. 217. Malvasia cites the figure of 50 scudi, which were worth 5 Bolognese lire each.

58 Giles, 1986, II, pp. 367–68.

59 Bagni, 1986, p. 344. The painting had a pendant, the *Birth of Adonis*, which was transferred to Dresden and also destroyed during the Second World War.

60 Malvasia, 1841, II, p. 272, wrote that Cesare Gennari "Guadagnò tesori con le sue fatiche; li spese generosamente, e la maggior parte in sollievo degli altri. Acquistò col danaro una gran casa, e nobile in Bologna. Acquistò luoghi in campagna; mobiliò il tutto alla nobile. Lasciò in casa addobbi, pitture, e argenti, gioie, danari, e crediti. Eresse capelle, altari, li fornì di tutti gli arredi necessarii, le perpetuò con legati pii, visse onoratamente con gran prudenza, con gran timor di Dio . . . "

61 Marzocchi, 1980, p. 46: "he wrote incorrectly: he wrote 'ca' and 'co' with an 'h' . . . he wrote *telle* with two ls, he wrote *messatta* with two ts, he wrote *pottere* with two ts, *capara* with one r, he wrote *abbacho*." It is clear that Malvasia is referring to what he himself could check for accuracy: in other words, the painter's account books that Sirani left him.

62 Malvasia seems to be working on account books when he analyzes spelling errors, while the 1628 letter mentioned previously seems to be more controlled and knowledgeable. Perhaps somebody reread and corrected what Reni wrote, but even in that case the gap between the two styles of writing is quite notable.

63 Malvasia, 1841, II, p. 118.

64 See also the following section on real estate.

65 Gualandi, 1840–45, I, p. 118.

66 Malvasia, 1841, II, p. 44 (as translated in Malvasia, 1980, p. 109). For the legal inventory drawn up at Reni's death in 1642, see Spike, 1988; for the exploration of Reni's house see Morselli, 2007.

67 Malvasia, 1841, II, p. 260. On the issue of prices charged by Guercino, see Bonfait, 1990 and 2002b, and Spear, 1994.

68 Gualandi, 1840–45, III, p. 154.

69 Gualandi, 1840–45, III, p. 154.

70 Gualandi, 1840–45, III, p. 157.

71 Gualandi, 1840–45, III, p. 158.

72 Malvasia, 1982, p. 60.

73 Malvasia, 1841, II, p. 111.

74 Morselli, 1998a, p. 114.

75 Gualandi, 1840–45, III, p. 181.

76 Gualandi, 1840–45, III, p. 179.

77 16 March 1681, Forlì, Archivio Reggiani, Archivio Cignani, folder n1, file I.

78 Buscaroli Fabbri, 1989.

79 Morselli, 1998a, p. 133.

80 Cicatelli, 1930–31, pp. 417, 429, n. 4; Archivio di Stato di Bologna (hereafter abbreviated ASBo), notaio Bernardino Andrioli, in Roli, 1953–54, pp. 63–65; Malvasia, 1982, pp. 39, 46.

81 Morselli, 1998a, pp. 413–15. The total value of his estate came to 1,972 lire.

82 Morselli, 1998a, p. 168.

83 ASBo, notaio Barilli Gian Luigi, 5.9.10. The land was located partly in Zola Predosa and partly in S. Lorenzo in Collina.

84 Morselli, 1998a, pp. 233–34. Gessi's home and studio were located in via della Rosa in S. Barbaziano parish.

85 ASBo, notaio Vanotti Carlo 5.7.8. For the inventory of 1707, see Morselli, 1998a, p. 374.

86 Morselli, 1998a, p. 374.

87 The inventory complied after his death in 1668 contains only a few things in his residence, located in the parish of S. Procolo (see Morselli, 1998a, p. 422). Since he had been suffering from a long-standing infirmity, he probably had already bequeathed everything to his daughter Dorotea and sons Francesco and Alessandro.

88 Tiarini and his son-in-law would rent two farms to each other (one in Ozzano, the other in Castelguelfo) with the aim of securing further profit from cultivating the land. ASBo, notaio Martino Diolaiti, b. 5, 1653–60; Morselli, 1996, p. 203; ASBo, notaio Montecalvi Orazio, 5.10.11: "Essendo che dall'anno 1644 del mese di novembre la signora Antonia Ravagli Fiegni concesse ad affitto un luogo posto nel comune di Ozzano al signor Alesandro Tiarini per tempo e termine di anni nove et per la presente il signor Alessandro Tiarini fa instantia di renuntiare a detto luogo; detta signora Antonia per compiacere al detto si contenta di assolverlo dall'obbligatione di detta locatione con le conditioni infrascritte, cioé: che il detto signor Alessandro lasci alla detta signora Antonia li denari che sborsò al principio di detta locatione, che sono la somma di lire 300; e più il detto signor Alessandro gli paghi al presente alla celebratione della scritura da farsi per la presente absolutione lire 60; e più gli facci buoni la pretensione che haveva per il presente anno della tempesta il medesimo signor Alessandro con la sudetta Antonia; e più gli rinontia il credito che ha il signor Alessandro con li contadini che al presente stanno sul detto luogo, che è la somma di lire 46 e detto credito sarà autenticato." ASBo, notaio Diolaiti Martino, 6.7.8: "Con la presente dichiarano i signori Alessandro Tiarini e Pietro Facini haver fatto tutti li conti degli affitti della possessione di Castel Guelfo condotta dall'istesso Facini, come per instrumento rogato agli anni passati, et havendo visto li denari pagati al sudetto Tiarini per conto di

detti affitti e si è trovato che il detto Facini per tutto l'anno 1652 resta debitore al sudetto Tiarini di lire 2700 e soldi 16 per conto e saldo fatto tra di loro concordemente dichiarando inoltre che il sudetto signor Facini nonostante d'havere a continuare detta locatione ancor due anni di presente ha rinuntiato e rinuntia a sudetta locatione consignando al sudetto signor Tiarini la medesima possessione seminata di corbe trenta formento, corbe quattro fava, corbe quattro spelta, corbe una marzola."

89 Malvasia, 1841, II, p. 138.

90 ASBo, notaio Francesco Bosi, 5, 57; Monducci, 2000, p. 358, doc. 95.

91 ASBo, notaio Pompeo Cignani, 5, prot. P, c. 30; Monducci, 2000, p. 358, doc. 96.

92 Fanti, 1963, p. 169. Guercino, too, had acquired a private chapel for himself and his family, but in Cento at the church of the Rosary.

93 This is a clause in the contract between the Theatine fathers of S. Bartolomeo and Angelo Michele Colonna. See ASBo, notaio Alessandro Andrei, 6.10.11 (22 March 1665).

94 Gualandi, 1840–45, III, pp. 101–7.

95 Malvasia, 1841, II, pp. 152–55, 181–82, 191. When Della Querzola was sold by his two daughters, Anna and Ginevra, who had inherited it, it was purchased by Odoardo Pepoli for 60,000 lire.

96 Morselli, 1998a, p. 115.

97 Biblioteca comunale dell'Archiginnasio, Bologna, Ms. B 16, XVII cent, c. 205r.

98 Malvasia, 1982, p. 102, and Gualandi, 1840–45, III, p. 166, for the contract.

99 Gualandi, 1840–45, III, pp. 154, 155, 157.

100 See Silingardi, 2003, pp. 150–52. One Bolognese lira was worth 1.5 Modenese lira.

101 The ASBo holds documents from the sixteenth to eighteenth centuries in 50 folders ordered according to individual art guilds, within which there is a folder dedicated to painters. This section can be found in the collection entitled "Assunteria di arti" (1666–1797, also with documents from the sixteenth century), in the series of "Notizie sopra le arti." This is what survives today, although Malvasia had access to all the registers and complete documentation. In many parts of the *Felsina pittrice*, he demonstrates a good knowledge of these documents. See Feigenbaum, 1999.

102 The draftsman and engraver Oliviero Gatti joined the painters' guild in 1626 with a payment of just 20 lire rather than the usual 40, in recognition of his long stay in Bologna. Scipione Bagnacavallo also joined in the same year; he also paid 20 lire. See Malvasia, 1982, p. 111.

103 Malvasia, 1841, II, p. 7.

104 Malvasia, 1841, II, p. 179.

105 Meanwhile, he gave errand boys a salary of 8 scudi per month, or 40 lire. They would also receive gifts and tips. Malvasia, 1841, II, p. 24.

106 Malvasia, 1841, II, p. 146. See also Pepper, 1971.

107 Monducci, 2000, p. 354, doc. 71.

108 Malvasia, 1982, pp. 21–24; Roli, 1977.

109 Arfelli, 1957, pp. 210–11.

110 Bonfait, 1990 and 2002b. On the yearly totals of Guercino's earnings, see Spear, 1994, p. 598.

111 Malvasia, 1841, II, p. 151.

112 Malvasia, 1841, II, p. 34. Manzini had published *Il trionfo del pennello: Raccolta d'alcune composizioni nate a gloria d'un Ratto di Elena di Guido*, Bologna. See Ciammitti, 2000, p. 203, n. 71, for identification of the so-called "sagace vecchio" (Malvasia) as the father of Giovan Battista Manzini.

113 Malvasia, 1841, II, pp. 127–29.

114 See the Introduction to this volume.

115 Pepper, 1984, pp. 234–35, no. 55.

116 Brogi, 2001, p. 184. In turn, it was placed in the altar of the main chapel, where it remained until the end of the eighteenth century (Pinacoteca nazionale di Bologna). See also Ciammitti, 2001, and Anna Stanzani's catalogue entry in Bentini et al., 2006, pp. 255–58, cat. 173.

117 Malaguzzi Valeri, 1918, pp. 29–48.

118 Monducci, 2000, p. 353, doc. 65.

119 Redigonda, 1960, pp. 201–3.

120 Monducci, 2000, p. 351, doc. 55.

121 Pepper, 1984, p. 238, no. 65, copy 1.

122 Chiusa, 1985.

123 Natale, 1979, nos. 10–11. One set of the copies and both of the originals are lost. The second set of copies has been identified by Denis Mahon in the Musée d'Art et Historie of Geneva. See also Bagni, 1986, pp. 267–70, 279–80, and Martinelli Braglia, 1998.

124 See the essays by Spear and Sohm in this volume.

125 There is an abundant bibliography on the topic of women painters in Bologna. For the latest contribution on Elisabetta Sirani and her circle with bibliographic references, see Graziani, 2004, pp. 119–35. On Ginevra Cantofoli, see the recent volume by Pulini, 2006, and on female self-portraiture in early modern Bologna, see Bohn, 2004a.

126 Bohn, 2004b, pp. 107–17.

127 Graziani, 1994, p. 212.

128 Galli, 1940, pp. 118–22, doc. no. 10, transcribed by Cantaro, 1989, pp. 208–9.

129 Crespi, 1772, p. 21, and Modesti, 2004, p. 172.

130 Malvasia, 1841, II, p. 295.

131 Malvasia, 1841, II, p. 400.

132 Malvasia, 1841, II, p. 401.

133 Oretti, *Descrizione delle pitture . . .* , in Modesti, 2003, p. 386, n. 79: *Portia* (Fig. 50), *Head of the Virgin*, and a *Saint Anthony and Infant Jesus* painted in 1662 for the Tassi family altar in the church of S. Leonardo in Bologna (now in the Pinacoteca nazionale, Bologna), which was exhibited at the celebration of the Sacrament under the Palazzo Gessi arcade.

134 Morselli, 1998a, pp. 416–21, n. 74. According to Malvasia, but not with the painter's accounts book, the *St. Jerome* was painted for Cardinal Savelli in 1650. Still, the merchant Tassi might have been involved in the acquisition of this painting.

135 For Guercino's picture, see Brogi, 1994, pp. 61–64.

136 Quoted by Modesti, 2003, pp. 380, 384.

137 Morselli, 1998a, pp. 413–15, n. 73; Modesti, 2004, p. 135, n. 209.

138 Gualandi, 1840–45, I, pp. 3–8.

139 Gualandi, 1840–45, I, pp. 95–98.

140 Gualandi, 1840–45, II, pp. 132–33.

141 Artioli and Monducci, 1970, p. 177, doc. XXXIV, and p. 182, doc. XLIX. I will not enter into the complex debate concerning *di sua mano* and the originality of Reni's works. For more on this subject, see Morselli, 1992b, and Spear, 2002, pp. 79–98. For the interesting discussion about paintings *di sua mano*, the literature is rich: see Spear, 1997, pp. 253–75 for Guido Reni; O'Malley,

1998, pp. 155–78, for contracts from the Quattrocento and Cinquecento; and Sohm, 2001, pp. 153–59.

142 Emiliani, 1979, pp. 32–33.

143 According to Pepper, 1984, p. 284, no. 183, the dates should be moved up to 1638–39 on the basis of a statement by the father-prior who ordered him to go to Bologna to take the altar "which Mr. Guido Reni had made a long time ago" ("che già tanto tempo fa aveva fatta il Sig. Guido Reni"). In these years, however, Reni's deliveries were greatly delayed and he urgently needed money. It was unlikely that he kept a 500 ducatoni canvas ready. The phrase "had made" (aveva fatta) should be read as "was commissioned" rather than "finished".

144 Soli, 1930, p. 32.

145 On Reni's changing financial fortunes, see Spear, 1997, and Morselli, 2007.

146 Malvasia, 1841, II, p. 37, describes it as a time-consuming work, perhaps because it "was made from spite rather than for glory." Based on a misinterpretation of the documents, critics dated the commission to 1601, until Spear's revisions in 1989, pp. 367–72, and, later, Spear, 1997, p. 346, n. 87, which date it correctly. The church of S. Maria dei Mendicanti was connected to the Opera pia dei Mendicanti and was supported by the Bolognese Senate, the Tribunes of the People (Tribuni della Plebe—four in total, one for each area of Bologna, they practiced artisanal and commercial trades together with art guild members), and the Vice Pontifical Legate. The first brick was laid on 1 June 1601 by Archbishop Alfonso Paleotti. In 1603, the main chapel was consecrated; in 1608, so was the entire church. The project was entrusted to the architect Floriano Ambrosini, who divided the church into five chapels per side, as well as the main altar. Starting from the right, the chapels belonged to the Monticelli family, the Mattoliani, and the guilds of the salt merchants, ironmongers, and spice merchants. On the left side, after the presbytery, were the chapels of the goldsmiths, carpenters, silk merchants, the Zamboni family, and the Lini family. See Guidicini, 1869, V, pp. 217–19; Masini, 1666, pp. 135, 252; Malvasia [1686], 1732, pp. 81–84; and Raule, 1829.

147 *Ricordo dell'accordo fatto con il Signor Guido Reni*, published by Gualandi, 1840–45, I, pp. 126–27.

148 The total paid to Reni was 9,500 lire but the painter wanted more: 1,000 lire per figure.

149 The calculation of the number of figures in the painting was dutifully recorded by the guild and included "six whole figures, eight half-figures and, from a distance, another four half-figures, in addition to two animals, for a total of 20."

150 Guerzoni, 2006, p. 259.

151 Brogi, 2001, pp. 169–70.

152 Brogi, 2001, p. 174.

153 *Guido Reni*, 1988, p. 195.

154 Pepper, 1969, pp. 482–83, and *Guido Reni*, 1988, p. 196.

155 Emiliani in *Guido Reni*, 1988, p. 26.

156 Gualandi, 1840–45, I, pp. 187–88. If we include the four small *putti* sitting on the first stone step, the figures total 13.

157 Negro and Roio, 1996, pp. 113–16, nos. 38–42.

158 Roli, 1953–54, pp. 126–27; Negro and Roio, 1996, pp. 145–49, nos. 91–96. The paintings were the *Birth of the Baptist* (205 × 192 cm), the *Baptism of Christ* (300 × 200 cm), the *Carrying of the Body of the Baptist* (205 × 192 cm), as well as three other canvases depicting the *Preaching of the Baptist* (250 × 200 cm), a *Glory of Angels* (180 cm diameter), and the *Beheading of the Baptist* (250 × 200 cm), which were painted by Francesco Camullo, perhaps based on drawings by Cavedone.

159 Negro and Roio, 1996, pp. 122–24, no. 52.

160 Venturino Alce, 1958, pp. 395–99. After the first installment of 200 lire on 26 November 1614, other payments followed: on 16 March of the following year, Tiarini received a small advance of 16 lire in order to buy ultramarine blue, then another 200 lire in April, and the same as a final payment on 5 June 1615 (for a total of 600 lire).

161 Ghelfi in Benati, 2001, pp. 48–49, nos. 70–71.

162 Benati, 2001, p. 109, no. 176.

163 Ghelfi in Benati, 2001, pp. 102–3, no. 172.

164 Benati, 2001, pp. 97–98.

165 Spear, 1982, pp. 216–17, no. 63; see also Gian Piero Cammarota's catalogue entry in Bentini et al., 2008, pp. 247–50, cat. 131.

166 Spear, 1982, pp. 214–16, no. 62; see also Gian Piero Cammarota's catalogue entry in Bentini et al., 2008, pp. 236–41, cat. 129.

167 Puglisi, 1999, pp. 144–45.

168 Puglisi, 1999, p. 155.

169 Puglisi, 1999, p. 177.

170 Buscaroli Fabbri, 1989, pp. 105–14.

171 Lionello Spada in Malvasia's *vita*, 1841, II, p. 81.

172 For the history of the palace (now Bersani Galletti, located in via Saragozza 26–28), see Roversi, 1974, p. 280.

173 Cesi was at home in Palazzo Albergati, having painted the ceiling of honor in the palace's *piano nobile* "with beautiful figurines, ornate decorations and little *putti* and a beautiful frieze with 15 stories and, to divide one from the other two, he completed the work with chiaroscuro," according to what Marcello Oretti wrote at the end of the eighteenth century (*Descrizione delle pitture . . .*, part I, p. 119).

174 Bagni, 1983.

175 Ghidiglia Quintavalle, 1966, p. 44.

176 Monducci, 2000, pp. 340–41, doc. 12; and Fanti, 1963, p. 246.

177 Malvasia, 1982, pp. 21–24.

178 Accounts book of Giacomo Alboresi, Ms. B 16, Biblioteca comunale dell'Archiginnasio, Bologna; see also Feinblatt, 1979, pp. 618–30.

179 ASBo, notaio Alessandro Andrei 6.10.11. The ceiling was uncovered on 6 August 1667, and the date is on a plaque in the third chapel on the left, which belonged to Colonna and was frescoed by him. See Roli, 1977, p. 245.

4 *Florence*

1 Bertelli, 2002, pp. 11–46; Fantoni, 2002; and Bertelli and Pasta, 2003. Throughout this essay, dates are cited in accordance with the conventional calendar and not the Florentine calendar, in which the new year began on 25 March.

2 Fantoni, 2002, p. 110.

3 Malanima, 1982, 1993, and 2001, pp. 66–70.

4 There is a lack of quantitative investigations of this topic.

5 Biblioteca Nazionale Centrale di Firenze (hereafter BNCF), Pal. E.B. 15.2.

6 These calculations are based on Zangheri, 2000.

7 Fyt's Florentine sojourn is generally tied to specific documentary evidence from 1636–37. Therefore, 1632 seems too early for a reference to him, especially since Fyt was in Paris during 1633–34.

8 For Rome in the first decades of the Seicento, see Cavazzini, 2008c.

9 Biblioteca Moreniana di Firenze (hereafter BMF), Ms. Bigazzi 74, fol. 51r.

10 Archivio di Stato di Firenze (hereafter ASF), Accademia del Disegno (hereafter AD) 70/83, unpaginated. An interesting example of a rental contract can be found therein, no. 40: Filippo Bargiacchi rented "two ground-floor rooms of his house in via de Martelli" to the "mettidoro" (gilder) Vincenzo Frusoni for the price of 12 scudi per year, payable in bimonthly installments.

11 Matteoli, 1990, pp. 124–25. For an accurate summary, see Barsanti and Contini, 1999, pp. 130ff.

12 Baldinucci, Filippo (hereafter simply Baldinucci, in distinction to Francesco Saverio Baldinucci), 1845–47, III, pp. 651–52: "Veramente ell'è gran pigione; ma voglio insegnarvi io il modo d'abitar bene, siccome voi ora abitate, e pagar manco. Fate due, o tre quadri di più l'anno, siccome potete anche farne molti di vantaggio a quel ch'io dico, e pagherete meno."

13 BNCF, Nuove Acquisizioni (hereafter NA) 641, I/2, fol. 90.

14 Baldinucci, 1845–47, IV, p. 642.

15 Corti, 1971, p. 21. Salviati became duke of Giuliano in 1627.

16 See pages 180–81 below.

17 Baldinucci, 1845–47, IV, p. 229.

18 See Nannelli, 1977, p. 328, n. 13.

19 Baldinucci, F. S., 1975, p. 180.

20 Sagrestani, 1971, pp. 191, 198, and Epe, 1990, pp. 219–20.

21 Baldinucci, F. S., 1975, p. 254.

22 Baldinucci, F. S., 1975, pp. 254–59; Sagrestani, 1971, p. 202.

23 Sagrestani, 1971, pp. 205–6.

24 Baldinucci, F. S., 1975, pp. 240–41.

25 Bonazzini, "Bisdosso ovvero Diario (1672–1705)," fols. 208–09, in Barbolani di Montauto, 1996, pp. 165–66. Troni perhaps was the Tronci mentioned by Giovan Camillo Sagrestani. A Filippo Tronci *rigattiere* appears in the list of 1661–62 gift-givers at Cosimo III's marriage (ASF, Miscellanea medicea [hereafter MM] 725, fol. 338).

26 ASF, AD 72, fol. 634ff.

27 On G. M. Casini, see Goldenberg Stoppato, 2004b, pp. 166–67, 196, n. 13.

28 Heikamp, 1963, pp. 195–96.

29 ASF, AD 65, unpaginated.

30 Baldinucci, 1845–47, III, pp. 448–49: "chiamato a stimare quadri d'alto pregio, ed altre cose somiglianti."

31 Baldinucci, F. S., 1975, pp. 272, 197, respectively.

32 Giusti, 1988.

33 "A giornata, o a stima, o con provisione" (ASF, Mediceo del Principato [hereafter MP] 62, fol. 226; see Kirkendale, 1993, p. 34).

34 According to Parenti, 1939, as summarized in his appendix 1, the median daily wage of a laborer in the first 20 years of the Seicento was slightly more than 1 lira, while a farmworker's pay ranged from 12 to 15 soldi per day.

35 Fantoni and Goldenberg Stoppato, 2003, p. 37.

36 Kirkendale, 1993.

37 Cardi [before 1629], in Baldinucci, 1974–75, VII, p. 51. See also Baldinucci, 1845–75, III, p. 257.

38 Manni, 1772, unpaginated.

39 During Cosimo II's reign, this was true for Jacques Callot (see below) and probably for Filippo Napoletano, but there is no broader research specifically on this topic.

40 This was the case for the salary that Salvator Rosa received from Giovan Carlo de' Medici, as noted below. For the meaning of "Camera," see Chauvineau, 2003.

41 Kirkendale, 1993, p. 634, no. 317, and Pizzorusso, 1982, pp. 106–7.

42 Pizzorusso, 1982, pp. 116–18.

43 ASF, Guardaroba medicea (hereafter GM) 309, fols. 38r–v, 39r. For Giovanni da San Giovanni, see also Mannini, 1986, III, p. 101.

44 Conigliello, 1990a, p. 22, 36, n. 10.

45 Conigliello, 1990a, p. 23.

46 Conigliello, 1990a, p. 22, and p. 36, n. 10; ASF, GM 332/3, fol. 250. See Conigliello, 1992, p. 218 *passim*, for a detailed account of Ligozzi's turbulent personal finances.

47 ASF, Depositeria Generale Parte Antica (hereafter DGPA) 395, fol. 41 (September 1622–August 1623); DGPA 396, fol. 11 (September 1624–August 1625); DGPA 1522, fol. 27 (1625–26).

48 ASF, GM 332/3, fol. 251, Christina of Lorraine to Vincenzo Giugni, 27 December 1620.

49 The source material also alludes to this; see Baldinucci in his lives of Jacques Callot (1845–47, IV, pp. 380–81) and Giovanni Bilivert (IV, p. 305), here in light of information given to Baldinucci by his student Orazio Fidani (Baldinucci, 1974–75, VII, p. 69).

50 Callot had "le spese sole in tinello per un anno" (*tinello* was the table where courtiers ate together). See also Ternois, 1962, p. 217, and Kirkendale, 1993, p. 635. On Callot's salary, see Ternois, 1962, p. 218. See for October 1615 to August 1616, ASF, GM 336, fols. 11v, 15r, 17r, 20r, 23v, 27v, 31v, 34r, 37r, 40v, 41v. In GM 309, fol. 38v (undated: 1617?), Callot is recorded among the family members included in the roll but without "provvisione." Regarding Filippo Napoletano, see ASF, GM 309, fol. 12r, 1617, and also Targioni Tozzetti, [1780], 1967, III, p. 17: "Questo Filippo da Liagno Pittore, con scudi 18 al Mese, lo trovo descritto nel Ruolo della Corte di Toscana dal 1 settembre 1620 per tutto Agosto 1621."

51 For Bilivert: Contini, 1985, pp. 183–84, app. doc. 45 and Contini, 1986, III, pp. 34–35. See also ASF, GM 309, fol. 12r. For Buonavita: Baldinucci, 1845–47, IV, pp. 312–13. For a chronology of his stay in Rome, see Contini, 1989, pp. 76–77.

52 Baldinucci, 1845–47, IV, p. 305.

53 Baldinucci, 1845–47, IV, pp. 312, 313.

54 With regard to economic issues at court, see the pioneering work of Fantoni, 2002. For the earlier years, see, respectively, ASF, DGPA 1520 and 1521; MM 30/19, fols. 1–5. And for the 1620s, ASF, DGPA 395; DGPA 396.

55 For a summary, see Kirkendale, 1993, p. 625, no. 258. In Ferdinand I's roll, Costantino de' Servi "fa di stucco" (stucco worker) was listed with a monthly salary of 12 scudi (ASF, DGPA 389, fol. 11). From December 1607 his salary was increased to 18 scudi, and he was placed in the "classe de' diversi" (a miscellaneous category covering different fields): ASF, DGPA 389, no. 769. In 1612, while he was in Wales, his salary was paid to his wife: ASF, DGPA 389, no. 1149 (see also ASF, DGPA 1520, fol. 12). For Cantagallina, see ASF, DGPA 395–96, and Kirkendale, 1993.

56 ASF, MM 18/2, fol. 71. See Fantoni and Goldenberg Stoppato, 2003, p. 36; Goldenberg Stoppato, 2004a, p. 72.

57 Goldenberg Stoppato, 2004a, p. 72. See Baldinucci, 1845–47, IV, pp. 487–88: "con le stanze e il piatto del nostro palazzo, e col pagamento ancora di tutte l'opere che di mano in mano se gli commettano da questa casa."

58 ASF, DGPA 1524, fol. 122l. Kirkendale, 1993, p. 637.

59 ASF, MP 1840, fol. 72v. Fantoni and Goldenberg Stoppato, 2003, p. 37, n. 37, without a citation of the numbering of this document.

60 Fantoni and Goldenberg Stoppato, 2003, p. 37, who nonetheless seem to refer to the 5 scudi as a salary rather than just board (in any case, it is a modest sum).

61 See Fantoni and Goldenberg Stoppato, 2003, pp. 37–40, and p. 41, n. 61 ("insomma sta con una grandezza straordinaria, più da cavaliere che da artista," ASF, MP 5215, fol. 106, Paolo del Bufalo to Carlo de' Medici, Florence, 17 March 1638).

62 ASF, MP 1843, fol. 16v (12 February 1669).

63 ASF, GM 669bis, fols. 702–3 (12 September 1669).

64 Fantoni and Goldenberg Stoppato, 2003, p. 38; Fumagalli, forthcoming.

65 ASF, DGPA 1528, fol. 179l; DGPA 389bis, fol. 56r–l (1647–48).

66 "Mostrando di contentarsi di ogni onorevole intrattenimento" (Fumagalli, 2000, p. 11).

67 ASF, MP 5325, fol. 79, Giovanna Garzoni to Giovan Carlo de' Medici, 18 August 1657 (kindly pointed out to me by Silvia Mascalchi). Orlandi, 1719, p. 206: "dimorò lungo tempo in Firenze, dove acquistò ricchezze, e molti luoghi di Monte". See also Pascoli, 1992, p. 899.

68 Part of this correspondence is published in Casale, 1991, pp. 208–12.

69 See ASF, MP 5357, fol. 306, Giovanna Garzoni to Giovan Carlo de' Medici, 30 November 1658 (kindly pointed out to me by Silvia Mascalchi); ASF, DGPA 692, no. 134; and ASF, Carteggio d'artista (hereafter CA) IX/12, fol. 193, Giovanna Garzoni to Leopold de' Medici, 4 July 1665.

70 For Cerrini see below.

71 Kirkendale, 1993, pp. 38–39.

72 "Di essere messo a ruolo con provisione per poter tirare avanti" (Borea, 1975, p. 27). See also Borea, Petrioli Tofani, and Langedijk, 1977, p. 37.

73 Baldinucci, 1845–47, IV, p. 606, and ASF, MP 5168, Registro di rescritti e ordini, 1629–45, fol. 39r, 17 March 1635 (heretofore mistaken as 1634).

74 ASF, DGPA 1531, fol. 115r–l.

75 ASF, GM 509, fol. 45r (see Romei, 1997, pp. 39–40, n. 32). After describing the contents of the "workshop of Stefano della Bella engraver of prints," he adds that two other artists moved there on the orders of Marquis Cerbone del Monte.

76 "To relieve my house" ("per sollevare la Casa mia"), which had six "mouths" in 1632; see Contini, 1985, p. 192, doc. 81, and pp. 193–95, docs. 86–90.

77 The payment of his salary during 1646–48 is recorded in ASF, DGPA 673, no. 392 (1646); ASF, DGPA 674, no. 449 (1647) and no. 454 (1648); and MM 264/20, fol. 8 (1647).

78 Crinò, 1987, pp. 150–53, in particular docs. 73–75, 87. On the relationship between the painter and the Medici, see also Mirto, 1999.

79 Baldinucci, 1845–47, IV, p. 498. ASF, MP 5358, fol. 770r.

80 On the role of the "aiutante di camera," see Chauvineau, 2003, pp. 85–86. Previous studies of the court have not focused on painters working in this role.

81 ASF, MM264/20, fol. 10. See also Mascalchi, 1986, III, pp. 111–12.

82 Baldinucci, 1845–47, V, p. 534.

83 ASF, MP 5380. Montini was working for Carlo de' Medici at least from 1647 (see Oliveti, 2001–2, p. 142). It should be pointed out that the following artists appear in Cardinal Carlo's roll, without further details about their salaries (if they were paid at all): Orazio Fidani (1631–32), Virginio Zaballi (1632), the unknown Piero Corradi (1631), Romolo Panfi (1660) and, a few months before Carlo's death, Volterrano (February 1666). See ASF, MP 5278, "Ruolo dell'Illustrissimo et Reverendissimo Signor Cardinale Medici," "Nota del Ruolo che di nuovo ha cominciato . . . ," and "Quaderno delle grazie," 1654–66, fols. 444r, 375r.

84 See Anna de' Medici's letter to Leopoldo from 17 November 1660 in Masetti, 1962a, pp. 145–46.

85 Baldinucci, F. S., 1975, p. 221; Barbolani di Montauto, 1996, p. 12.

86 Bonazzini, "Bisdosso ovvero Diario (1672–1705)," fol. 210, in Barbolani di Montauto, 1996, pp. 166, 174–75, for the monthly rent of 2 scudi. Two other painters appear in Francesco Maria de' Medici's roll: the Bolognese Antonio Ugolini, his "aiutante di camera," for the modest amount of 2 scudi per month (1696–1706: ASF, Congregazione di carità di san Giovanni Battista, IV series, 240, fol. 16) and Pier Dandini (Bellesi, 1992, p. 164, but his economic standing is unknown). According to Francesco Saverio Baldinucci (1975, p. 180) the painter-decorator-merchant Antonio Giusti was one of Francesco Maria de' Medici's relatives.

87 Moücke, 1752–62, IV, p. 37; Nasini, 1872, p. 37.

88 ASF, MP 1533, fol. 1647, Giovan Camillo Cateni to Apollonio Bassetti, 20 March 1690. Pier Maria Baldi followed the same path ("aiutante di camera" to architect of the Galleria). A painter at first, until his death in 1686 he helped Nasini's career (on which see Visonà, 1990, pp. 11–12, and pp. 14–15, n. 26).

89 Benassai, 2002, p. 35 and oral communication. See also Baldinucci, 1845–47, IV, p. 564: "spesato nella casa degli eredi per tutto il tempo che egli avesse durato a vivere, e questo, non con altro aggravio, che di fare a' medesimi ogni anno un quadro a propria elezione."

90 Baldinucci, F. S., 1975, pp. 220, 222.

91 Baldinucci, 1845–47, V, pp. 528–29.

92 Passeri, who would later confuse Giovan Carlo with Mattias, cites quarrels as the reason (1995, p. 390), but there is no confirmation of his explanation. Alternatively, see the undated letter, probably of 1640, sent from Rome by the poet Antonio Abati, part of Brancaccio's circle, to his friend Diego Gera, in Cesareo, 1892, II, pp. 149–55, in particular pp. 152–55.

93 For the period from February 1644 to January 1648, see ASF, DGPA 1604, and also but with incomplete information, Scott, 1995, p. 238, n. 16.

94 ASF, Scrittoio delle Regie Possessioni (hereafter SRP) 4268, fols. 55r (1642), 69r (1645), 119r (1648).

95 ASF, SRP 4268, fol. 53v, 2 October 1641: 24 scudi, 2 lire, 8 soldi "per un conto di più colori dati al Rosa pittore per più semestri."

96 For 1697–98, see Strocchi, 1978, p. 431.

97 Baldinucci, 1845–47, V, p. 8.

98 Barsanti, 1974b, pp. 85–86.

99 Nannelli, 1977, p. 323, n. 6.

100 Baldinucci, 1974–75, VI, p. 404.

101 "Per esser egli stato molto familiare di questa casa, dalla quale ricevé sempre notabili aiuti" (Bocchi and Cinelli, 1677, p. 168).

102 "Poco o punto di tempo restava . . . di operare per altri fuori che per Sua Altezza. . . . E perciò incominciò a scarseggiare tanto di guadagno che talvolta, non avendo tant'animo di ricorrere alla

generosità del suo padrone, occorrevagli chiedere a' suoi più fedeli amici qualche sussidio per supplire alle spese" (Baldinucci, F. S., 1975, p. 225).

103 See Santi, 1980, I, p. 475; Corsini, 1918, pp. 151–52; and Spinelli, 1991. For the workshop in the Galleria dei Lavori see ASF, GM 509, fol. 67v.

104 ASF, MP 1533, fols. 1,521v (28 January 1690) and 1,577v (23 February 1690).

105 For Bimbacci, see Pascoli, 1981, p. 381 ("[Leopoldo de' Medici] mi fecie avere dal Serenissimo G. Duca Ferdinando tre scudi il mese acciò studiassi la Pittura . . . morì S. G. Duca Ferdinando, e successe il suo Figlio Cosimo terzo, e mi raffermò detto sussidio, e volse mandarmi a studio a Roma") and p. 388, nn. 5–6; see also Rossi, 1875, p. 98.

106 For Gabbiani, see Visonà, 1990, pp. 11, 14, n. 22. Previously Gabbiani had obtained 4 scudi from Ferdinand II (Zangheri, 2000, p. XVI).

107 Baldinucci, F. S., 1975, p. 391.

108 Baldinucci, 1845–47, IV, p. 587. It is plausible that this information came from a "little book" in which Rosselli recorded his income and expenses, as mentioned by Baldinucci (p. 155), who certainly consulted it.

109 ASF, AD 64, fol. 267r. In fol. 216 2 scudi per week is mentioned.

110 Biblioteca degli Uffizi (hereafter BUF), Ms. 354/2, unpaginated, 15 December 1690.

111 Corti, 1971, p. 19.

112 ASF, AD 64, fol. 319r. See Vasetti, 1996, pp. 70, 82, and p. 92, nn. 8–9.

113 Baldinucci, F. S., 1975, p. 241.

114 BUF, Ms. 354/2, 30 April and 20 May 1689.

115 BUF, Ms. 354/2, 28 September and 6 November 1687.

116 For the documents, see Procacci, 1965, and Vliegenthart, 1976.

117 Procacci, 1965, p. 35, n. 49.

118 Buonarroti notes that "a lire 8 il dì a mie spese di colori e palchi e pennelli né mestica e gesso e altre cose siffatte" (Procacci, 1965, p. 17).

119 Procacci, 1965, pp. 18, and pp. 37–38, nn. 76–79.

120 Procacci, 1965, p. 14.

121 Procacci, 1965, p. 14.

122 Procacci, 1965, pp. 35–36, n. 52.

123 Malanima, 1982, pp. 160ff.

124 Fantoni, 1994, pp. 34–35.

125 Barsanti, 1974b, p. 84.

126 Malanima, 2001, p. 67, fig. 12.

127 Malanima, 2001, p. 67, but see also Parenti, 1939, appendix 1.

128 Targioni Tozzetti (mid-eighteenth century), in Bellesi, 1992, p. 141.

129 O'Malley, 2005, p. 116.

130 Baldinucci, 1845–47, III, pp. 146–47.

131 Baldinucci, 1845–47, IV, p. 220.

132 Baldinucci, F. S., 1975, pp. 250, 398.

133 Baldinucci, 1845–47, V, pp. 344–47, 351. For the *Christ Child*, see *Il Seicento Fiorentino*, I, p. 452, cat. 1.254, and Borean, 2000, p. 131. The second painting is lost.

134 Baldinucci, 1845–47, III, p. 41.

135 "Non si son fatti patti" (BUF, mss. 354/2 and 354/7).

136 Baldinucci, 1845–47, III, p. 12.

137 Baldinucci, F. S., 1975, p. 103; Chini, 1984, pp. 152, 323, doc. 58B; and Leoncini, 1990, pp. 25, 28.

138 Sagrestani, 1971, p. 192, and Fiorelli Malesci, 1986, p. 186. According to Moücke (1752–62, III, p. 90), Giordano supposedly offered as much as 1,000 scudi for the painting.

139 "Sapendo che Luca Giordano aveva avuto uno de quadri laterali dubitava che le monache, che possono sperare molto miglior prezzo da lui, vogliono, con la scusa di non poter spendere tanto, levarglielo e darlo a Giordano" (ASF, MP 3948, Paolo Falconieri to Apollonio Bassetti, Rome, 25 July 1682 [Goldberg, 1983, p. 381, n. 150]).

140 ASF, MP 3948, Apollonio Bassetti to Paolo Falconieri, 15 September 1682 (Goldberg 1983, p. 384, n. 161). See also Fumagalli, 2007, pp. 88–92.

141 Pacini, 1997, pp. 158–59, docs. 41, 43, 44.

142 On 21 September 1613 her first son, Giovan Battista, was born. For the painter's Florentine years, see Garrard, 1989, pp. 34–53; Papi, in Contini and Papi, 1991, pp. 43ff.; Cropper, 1993; Bissell, 1999, pp. 139–44, 157–62; and Contini, in Christiansen and Mann, 2001, pp. 313–19.

143 Christiansen, 2004, p. 114.

144 Documents brought to light in part by Del Bravo, 1967, p. 82, n. 11. See ASF, AD 64, fols. 422r–v, 439r–v, 651r, 680r, 683–85, 724r, and ASF, AD 65, unpaginated.

145 For a summary of the various interpretations on this topic, see Bissell, 1999, pp. 158–59.

146 ASF, AD 65, unpaginated, and Cropper, 1993, p. 760.

147 ASF, AD 65, unpaginated, and Cropper, 1993, p. 760.

148 See, with regard to her debts, ASF, AD 64, fol. 724r (and Del Bravo, 1967, p. 82, n. 11).

149 Artemisia received 34 rather than the 10 scudi given to the other painters (Procacci, 1965, pp. 12–13, and Vliegenthart, 1976, pp. 170–73), but perhaps that sum was not only for her *Inclination*, since in the register of payments she is said to be in debt to Buonarroti. Cropper, 1993, p. 760 and n. 5, casts doubt on the claim that Artemisa was paid three times as much as her colleagues and suggests a different interpretation of the payments.

150 Cropper, 1993, underlines that every son was baptized in a different parish, probably a sign of continuous changes of residence.

151 ASF, AD 64, fol. 683r, 7 January 1619, and also fols. 684r, 685r. In June 1616 there is a record of an assistant ("Lorenzo suo garzone") collecting a payment from Buonarroti (Vliegenthart, 1976, p. 173).

152 See Mancini, 2005.

153 ASF, CA IX/16, fol. 140r (Borea, 1978, p. 22, and Mancini, 2005, p. 279).

154 On this circumstance, see Navarro, 2005.

155 For Cerrini's Florentine activity, see Borea, 1978, and now Mancini, 2005.

156 Respectively, ASF, ASF, MP 5487, fol. 16r, 27 January 1658 (Borea, 1978, p. 19), and ASF, DGPA 814, fol. 46v, 9 April 1659.

157 Borea, 1978, pp. 18–19, and Mancini, 2005, p. 198, n. 43.

158 Borea, 1978, p. 22; Mancini, 2005, p. 279; and ASF, MP 1843, fol. 62r.

159 Fumagalli, 2000.

160 Cipriani, 1976, pp. 244–45, and Casale, 1991, pp. 216–17.

161 ASF, MP 1840, fol. 73r, 8 November 1649.

162 Baldinucci, 1845–47, V, p. 454.

163 Warnke, 1991, pp. 201ff.

164 Banti, 1977, p. 93.

165 Giglioli, 1949, p. 195.

166 See ASF, DGPA 1048, no. 1207, September–October 1641,

"Ristretto della spesa fatta in dipingere lo stanzone a terreno nell'appartamento del Serenissimo Gran Duca." Of the 2,000 scudi the painter received, 500 were paid in four installments between May and December 1635 (Giglioli, 1949, p. 195), while the rest was paid the following year: in ASF, MM 40/3, c. 9, for 1636, he was paid 1,786 scudi (the 286 scudi extra must have been for his board).

167 Banti, 1977, pp. 93–94.

168 The letter of 19 May 1635 begins as follows: "Molto Illustre e molto Reverendo, scrivo al maestro di casa del Eminentissimo Signor Cardinale Bentivoglio, nostro padrone, acciò che voi siate mezzo a farmi inviar le mie robe, perché Sua Altezza Serenissima [Ferdinand II] mi ha fermato in palazzo suo a dipingere il gran salone" (Banti, 1977, p. 93).

169 Leoncini, 1984, p. 321.

170 The detailed order of payments to Colonna, which amounted to 6,000 scudi, is in ASF, DGPA 1048, no. 1207. From July to October 1638 and from June to October 1639 there is no record of payment to the craftsmen who were preparing the walls for the painters. For the payments, see Matteucci and Raggi, 1994, pp. 276–78; Fumagalli, 2007c.

171 ASF, DGPA 800, fol. 82v.

172 See Raggi in Matteucci and Raggi, 1994, p. 277.

173 ASF, DGPA 1046, no. 223.

174 Neppi, 1975, pp. 269–70.

175 Colonna's letters to Niccolini were generously made available to me by Riccardo Spinelli, who mentioned them briefly in Spinelli, 2004, p. 53.

176 A final account for the work shows that for the artist's *parte* (board), nearly 1,180 scudi were spent from 21 November 1637 through August 1641, in addition to 178 scudi to rent the house; see ASF, DGPA 1048, no. 1207, and also Campbell, 1966, p. 136, n. 34 (ASF, FM 140/127).

177 "[Colonna] mi ha domandato il denaro del lavoro fatto al casino, né mai ho potuto cavarli di bocca la sua pretensione, rimettendo sempre in me il prezzo. Gl'ho pagato scudi 200, egli ha mostrato d'essere rimasto soddisfatto, essendosi rimesso liberamente. Ma tuttavia ha dato un motto che sarà l'opera stimata 300 scudi, e se bene sono bolognesi sono destri et accorti ne loro interessi più che non sono i fiorentini" (ASF, MP 5308, fols. 166–67). It is difficult to determine which work the document refers to; in my opinion, the amount seems too small for the decoration of the *sala*, as suggested by Matteucci and Raggi, 1997, p. 399, n. 10. See also ASF, P 4262, fol. 28v: "A spese del Giardino di via della Scala scudi 2200 buoni a Angiol Michele Colonna pittore per le apposte pitture fatte in detto luogo e prezzate d'accordo con il marchese Niccolini" (Matteucci and Raggi, 1997, p. 399, n. 13).

178 ASF, P 4263, fol. 8.

179 Spinelli, 1998, p. 40, nn. 64 and 72 ("E a dì 13 detto [luglio 1663] scudi cento moneta di lire sette per scudo pagati a buon conto a Angelo Michele Colonna, per dipingere tutta la mia galleria di Firenze, restati d'accordo per prezzo di scudi ottocento").

180 Feinblatt, 1979, p. 629.

181 Campbell, 1977, pp. 187, 230, doc. 16: "senza fare per adesso altro conto di quello che in fine si sia per havere a dare al medessimo Cortona."

182 Campbell, 1977, p. 187.

183 Campbell, 1977, p. 192, and p. 239, doc. 65: "senza quello che V. A. darà al Cortona."

184 ASF, MP 3381, unpaginated, 20 April 1654 (see Fumagalli, 1997, p. 79, doc. 13).

185 Félibien, 1725, VI, pp. 170–71, and Pascoli, 1992, p. 51: "avendo compite certe pitture, che erano più avanzate dell'altre, [Pietro] dimandò licenza al Granduca di poter trasferirsi per breve tempo a Roma, che gli fu conceduta; e quantunque gli facesse dare diecimila scudi per i lavori perfezionati, arrivato che vi fu, non pensò più al ritorno."

186 Baldinucci, F. S., 1975, p. 105.

187 ASF, MM30/4. According to the documents found by Campbell, 1977, pp. 246–47, docs. 104–5, the amount was for 1,500 scudi, of which 500 were given in 1644 and the remaining 1,000 in 1645. The chronology of Cortona's rooms remains unsure. See Campbell, 1977, pp. 185–222, and more recently Tordella, 2003.

188 Campbell, 1977, p. 231, doc. 22, regarding his lodging.

189 Campbell, 1977, pp. 231–32, doc. 22.

190 Acton, 1987, pp. 39–40ff.

191 For Ferri's arrival in Florence, see Fumagalli, 1997, pp. 49–53.

192 ASF, MP 3537, 8 and 14 July and 1 August 1659.

193 ASF, MP 3537: "quei disegni di Pietro da Cortona, acciò il suo giovane possa venir qua quanto prima a finire il lavoro in una delle anticamere del Granduca, perché non havendo a tardarsi cent'anni l'occasione d'haversi a far nozze in questa Serenissima Casa, sarebbe incongruenza che in quella congiontura non s'havesse a vedere nell'appartamento più nobile di questo palazzo una stanza piena di palchi."

194 "Fu condotto a smontare adirittura a palazzo, dove per lui erano preparate stanze et reficiamenti" (ASF, MP MP 3537, 3 November 1659, letter from the grand ducal secretary to Carlo Rinuccini).

195 Campbell, 1977, p. 252, doc. 118. The same letter specifies that, until then, Ferri had received two payments of 200 scudi each, which have not been found.

196 Campbell, 1977, p. 252, doc. 119.

197 Campbell, 1977, p. 253, doc. 123.

198 Campbell, 1977, p. 254, doc. 125.

199 ASF, DGPA 818, fol. 72r.

200 Goldberg, 1983, p. 381, n. 150, and ASF, MP 3948, 25 July 1682: "non faceva prezzo col Gran Duca ch'era suo Padrone, . . . non l'aveva mai fatto, né voleva farlo adesso."

201 See, for example, the account of the decoration of the apsidal chapel in S. Maria Maddalena de' Pazzi above.

202 Campbell, 1966.

203 Campbell, 1966, p. 137.

204 Leoncini, 1984, p. 327, n. 135 (23 November 1661).

205 Andrea Del Rosso to Apollonio Bassetti, 7 February 1682: "ho un quadro di nuovo di suo, che me lo dona . . . che per segno di gratitudine per l'alloggio e cagione che la mia casa patisce di danno tanti migliara di scudi" (Sparti, 2003, p. 171).

206 Gozzano, 2004, p. 257, for the letter to Colonna. For the payments ("per resto, e saldo delle sue fatighe . . . nel dipingere la cupola della mia cappella de Sant'Andrea Corsini nella Chiesa del Carmine . . . , che in tutto fa l'intiero prezzo, e final pagamento secondo l'accordato"), see Lankheit, 1957, p. 59, doc. XII (7 September 1683) and the unpublished documents in the Corsini archive, Room II, Giornale n. 1678, co. 133, ca. 99, cc. 53r (7 March 1682) and 78r (5 January 1683). Payment to Giordano was sent to Naples (with regard to the Bank of Naples, see Delfino, 1999, p. 139).

207 Spinelli, 1990 and 1993, pp. 136ff.
208 See ASF, MP 3948, Apollonio Bassetti to Paolo Falconieri, 15 September 1682 (Goldberg, 1983, p. 384, n. 161), and more generally on the topic, Sparti, 2003.
209 Fumagalli, 2007b, pp. 100, 105.
210 BNCF, NA 641, I, ins. 2, fols. 49–50.
211 ASF, AD 72, fols. 1–11. See also Nasini, 1872, pp. 41–42, and Büttner, 1990, p. 164.
212 ASF, AD 72, fol. 6: "li signori comparenti [i Nasini] hanno inteso di servirlo [il Riccardi] non per interesse mecanico, ma solo per ricevere dalla di lui cortesia e munificenza quello si fusse compiaciuto darli, non avendo nel tempo della fatta opera mai ricevuto né domandato cosa alcuna."
213 The Florentine *braccio* was equivalent to 58.3 cm. At times measurements were made by the *braccio quadro*.
214 ASF, AD 64, 30 August 1619, transcribed in Faini, 1965–66, pp. 309–10.
215 ASF, AD 72, fol. 514.
216 BNCF, NA 641, I, ins. 2, fols. 49–50.
217 ASF, DGPA 433, fol. 63r, 17 August 1685 (Strocchi, 1978, p. 433): "e di giorno lavorativo gli si dessi lire 20 quando lavoravano di soli fregi e a giorni che lavoravano figure lire 23.10." The document continues, "[h]anno fatto di giorni di fregi numero 36 giorni, di figure numero 30."
218 Guicciardini Corsi Salviati, 1989, p. 120, docs. 5 (1650–53) and 8 (1653).
219 Baldinucci, F. S., 1975, pp. 179–80: "architetture e fregi con fiori e animali" . . . "si rese talmente desiderato . . . che le pitture a fresco erangli pagate a ragione d'una piastra il braccio, trovandosi a guadagnare fino a venti piastre il giorno." Sagrestani (1971, p. 191) mentions 18 crazie per *braccio*. On Giusti, see Mazzetti di Pietralata, 2001.
220 Leoncini, 1984, p. 345, and Manni, 1772, unpaginated.
221 Vasetti, 1996.
222 In 1585 for the decoration of the entire room, vault, and walls of the Palazzo Capponi, Poccetti received 390 scudi (*Palazzo Capponi*, 2001, p. 152).
223 Bailey, 2003b, p. 23.
224 Conigliello, 1990b, p. 32, and p. 37, n. 9 (ASF, Carte Riccardi 645, fol. 283r–l). See also Conigliello, 1992, p. 210, under 26 October 1605.
225 Poccetti painted 14 lunettes, Salimbeni and Rosselli 4 each, and Mascagni 2. See Vasetti, 1994, p. 27, and pp. 38–39, nn. 101, 103, and Bailey, 2003b.
226 Baldinucci, 1845–47, III, p. 145: "che per poco che fosse, era però a lui un gran guadagno, come quegli che in nessuna mai altro tempo non impiegò, che un'intera settimana." Poccetti's demand is confirmed in the Ricordanze of the convent of the Annunziata, which specify that, for the *Death of the Blessed Uguccione and Sostegno* paid for by Alessandro di Camillo Strozzi in 1610, "(come l'altre) arrivò alla somma di scudi 25." See Bailey, 2003b, p. 31, n. 46 and appendix (the author, however, errs in interpreting some payments, confusing scudi and lire).
227 Vasetti, 1994, p. 27.
228 Giglioli, 1910.
229 ASF, AD 64, fol. 320r.
230 Bailey, 2003b, p. 31.
231 *Il chiostro camaldolese* . . . , 1998, pp. 158–60. In 1600 Mascagni was paid 224 lire (32 scudi) for 6 lunettes; in 1601 Poccetti and Monaldi were paid respectively 210 lire (32 scudi) and 196 lire (28 scudi) for 5 lunettes. Monaldi also received a separate payment of 14 lire (2 scudi) for a lunette.
232 Giglioli, 1949, p. 192, and Leoncini, 1987.
233 Palagi, 1873, p. 15, n. 3. On the cloister, see Proto Pisani, 1990, pp. 341–42.
234 Cassarino, 1987, pp. 355–56.
235 This is noted in the monastery's Ricordi (ASR, Compagnie Religiose soppresse da Pietro Leopoldo [hereafter CRSPL], 425, no. 80, fol. 89r).
236 Masetti, 1962b, pp. 104–9.
237 Rosselli received about 20 scudi per lunette, Vannini 45 scudi for two lunettes (see Facchinetti Bottai, 1979, pp. 88–89, nn. 8, 10).
238 Masetti, 1962b, p. 105, who reads scudi rather than lire in the payments per square *braccio*.
239 Masetti, 1962b, p. 106. Unfortunately, the documents on the decoration of the Casino di S. Marco, which Masetti partially transcribed, have been impossible to locate for more than 20 years.
240 Guicciardini Corsi Salviati, 1989, p. 122, doc. 17, p. 124, doc. 36, and p. 126, doc. 42.
241 Chiarini, 1976, p. 337, and p. 343, nn. 23, 36.
242 Chini, 1984, p. 316, doc. 50b.
243 Paid to his heir in 1652: see Chini, 1984, p. 318, doc. 51F.
244 Chini, 1984, pp. 140–42, 325–26.
245 Chini, 1984, p. 323.
246 Poggi, 1910, pp. 39–40.
247 ASR, CRSPL, 425, no. 80, fol. 89r; CRSPL, 426, n. 84, c. 83d, 16 April 1688 (the documents on the chapels of St. Bernard and the Nativity of the Virgin are mentioned in Spinelli, 1989, p. 118, n. 26). See Bellesi, 1990.
248 ASR, CRSPL, 426, no. 84, fol. 108l.
249 ASR, CRSPL 427, no. 91, fols. 116–19 (December 1704–June 1706).
250 For the documents, see BUF, Ms. 354/7, fols. 19v–21r, 35v, 37v–38v, and also ASF, CRSPL, 425, no. 80, fols. 94l–95l.
251 Fabbri, 1990, pp. 91–92. See also Falciai Prunai and Orefice, 1981, p. 51.
252 Fabbri, 1990, p. 91.
253 ASR, CRSPL 761, unpaginated, partially transcribed in Härth-Ragaller, 1976, p. 290. Receipts for payments, with Mehus's signature, are on the back of the contract signed with the friars.
254 ASF, CRSGF 119, no. 55, fols. 192r–194r (mentioned in Fabbri, 1996, p. 47).
255 ASF, CRSGF 119, no. 55, fol. 231r–v, but on fol. 230v it is specified that work was not actually completed until July 1683.
256 ASF, CRSPL, 415, no. 59. See Conti, Niccolucci Cortini, and Vadalà Linari, 1997, pp. 112 17; Spinelli, 2003, pp. 106–19.
257 "Senz'altra mercede, che quella che sperava dal Signore Iddio per intercessione di detta Santa." See Pacini, 2005, pp. 171–75, 208, doc. 51 (14 August 1701). Payments are unknown for the project. That Dandini actually painted the cupola without compensation is indicated by Antonio Franchi, who thought that Dandini did so in order to obtain a sinecure or an ecclesiastical pension ("un offizio o pensione") for one of his sons (BUF, Ms. 354/4).

5 *Venice*

1 Sansovino, 1603, pp. 194–208.
2 Papadopoli Aldobrandini (1893–1919) is still the standard refer-

ence for Venetian coins and currencies. For an excellent review of seventeenth-century Venetian and Veneto curriences, see Mozzato and Mueller (2000).

3 Del Negro, 1998, pp. 83–91; Montecuccoli degli Erri, 1999, pp. 20–21.

4 Leoni, 1593, pp. 27–29 (letter to the Venetian painter Montemezano explaining why he should come to Rome); reprinted in Bottari and Ticozzi, 1822, V, p. 53.

5 Table based on Beltrami, 1954; Favero, 1991; Zannini, 1993a, Table II.3; and Pezzolo, 2003, p. 151.

6 Zuccaro, 1605, pp. 119, 127.

7 Gigli [1615], 1996, p. 55.

8 Boschini [1660], 1966, p. 389: "Zucaro forestier rosega in gola."

9 Bassi, 1941, pp. 127–28.

10 In a letter of 1681 to Andrea Celesti, Giovanni Muti described their time as "questi anni di fango" (Mucchi and Della Croce, 1954, p. 63). Girolamo Albrizzi, in the preface to *Teatro della crudeltà* (Venice, 1696) dedicated to Zanchi, applauded the painter for defending art "nell'infelicità de' nostri tempi." Gian Francesco Loredano and Pietro Michiel (1680, p. 7) expressed a sense of loss at the inexplicable absence of great masters: "Ma, che si può fare? Son morti quei pittori, che con gli scherzi de' pennelli rubbavano l'eternità alla gloria." See also Lupis (1680, pp. 352–53) on the degraded state of Venetian painting.

11 Lanzi [1789], 1968–70, II, pp. 129–30.

12 Bassi, 1941, pp. 133–37.

13 Pino [1548], 1960, I, p. 108.

14 Chambers and Pullan, 2001, p. 409 (Decree of the Great Council, 11 September 1580; previously unpublished).

15 Lorenzi, 1868, p. 307, doc. 656, 23 December 1560.

16 The higher than average prices in the 1640s can be accounted for by the presence of the high-priced Ruschi. One exception to price inflation that helps to prove the validity of an argument for price stability: in 1610 the Signoria dropped the official per figure price paid to painters for their designs of mosaics in the Basilica di S. Marco, but within two years painters had effectively reversed this policy, forcing prices back to their original level (Cecchetti, 1886, p. 46).

17 Mattozzi et al., 1983, pp. 271–303.

18 For wheat prices and wages, see Zannini, 1999, pp. 473–502.

19 This table was compiled from the following sources: Rapp, 1986, p. 168; Pullan, 1964b, pp. 414–16, 424–26; Georgelin, 1978, p. 185; Trivellato, 1999, pp. 245–73; Zannini, 1999, p. 495; Davis, 1991, p. 59.

20 For collections and collectors in seventeenth-century Venice, see the impressive essays in Borean and Mason, 2007, including an extensive biographical appendix of 46 collectors and agents. The book must now be considered the definitive and most comprehensive survey of this subject. In addition, for Boschini and Leopold Wilhelm, see Fletcher, 1979, pp. 416–24; Merling, 1992; and Loh, 2006, pp. 247–48. For Gigli and Nys, see Agosti and Ginzburg, 1996, and Morselli, 1999. For Ridolfi and the Reynst brothers, see Logan, 1979, and Loh, 2006, p. 248.

21 For Sant'Agostino and Scaramuccia as art valuers, see Morandotti, 2001, p. 169.

22 Martinioni in Sansovino, 1663, II; Fletcher, 1979; Merling, 1992; Cecchini, 2000.

23 Loh, 2006, pp. 244–45.

24 Fletcher, 1979, pp. 416–24. Martinioni ("Quinto catalogo," p. 22, in Sansovino, 1663) describes Boschini as "così pratico e intendente della Pittura, e di conoscer le maniere de pittori, che i Prencipi, & altri Personaggi di stima fano Capo con esso, sì per accrescer le lor Galarie, sì anco per formarne."

25 Martinioni (in Sansovino, 1663, II, "Primo catalogo," p. 8) assumed it would be "la Seconda Parte della Carta del Navegar." For his condemnation of art exporting, see Boschini [1660], 1966, pp. 22–24. Boschini dedicated the *Minere* (1664) to the doge and the Collegio because he hoped this "index" would help the republic to "maggiormente invigilare alla di loro [le pitture] custodia." L. Olivato (1974) discusses the renewed activity of the Provveditori al Sal in the late seventeenth century in preserving the city's paintings. Pitacco (2007b) and De Fuccia (2007) give us an excellent idea of the extent of the problem from the point of view of foreign collectors.

26 Alfonsi, 2002, p. 274 (letter from P. M. Baldi to A. Bassetti, 14 August 1677).

27 Von Ludwig, 1911, p. 92 (testament of Philipp Esengren, 19 May 1631), and Radassao, 1998, p. 151 (testament of Alessandro Savorgnan, 22 July 1699), where Savorgnan called Niccolò Bambini, who was going to help him sell his collection of paintings, "mio compare."

28 Boschini [1660], 1966, pp. 21–22.

29 Jestaz, 2001, pp. 185–201. For the influx and influence of foreign collectors in Venice, a continuing topic for Boschini (who dedicated the *Carta* to one of them), see Pitacco, 2007b.

30 Cecchini, 2008, pp. 173–76, 184–86.

31 Cecchini, 2000, pp. 31–79.

32 Boschini [1660], 1966, p. 22.

33 Radassao, 1998, p. 151 (Savorgnan testament of 22 July 1699). For Savorgnan, see Pitacco, 2007a, p. 316.

34 Boschini [1660], 1966, p. 616. For art as an investment in Venice, see Cecchini, 2007, pp. 146–51.

35 Boschini [1660], 1966, pp. 22–23.

36 Marco Boschini, *Le ricche minere della pittura veneziana*, Venice, 1674; edition cited: Boschini [1674], 1966, p. 747.

37 Boschini [1660], 1966, p. 502.

38 Monconys, 1666, II, p. 414.

39 Borean, 2000, pp. 89–133.

40 Magani, 1989, pp. 34–38.

41 Pizzo, 2000, p. 55.

42 Binion, 1990, pp. 269–70.

43 Martini, 1969, p. 237; quoted by Betti, 2003, p. 115. Georg Christoph Martini was a painter living in Lucca from 1727 to 1745.

44 Boschini ([1660] 1966, pp. 599–600) discussed the spatial integrity of a contemporary collection, separate from the hanging of old masters: the old masters should be hung in a large room, furnished with crimson and gold velvet, facing the Grand Canal, whereas the moderns, being less valuable, could go into a smaller antechamber decorated with green velvet. See also Cecchini, 2000, p. 23.

45 Boschini [1660], 1966, p. 177.

46 Vio, 2004, p. 370.

47 Bassi, 1941, p. 193.

48 For further discussion of this complaint, see Shaw, 2006, pp. 112 and 116–17.

49 For an excellent discussion of the transition from guild to college, see Shaw, 2006.

50 For an excellent review of life studies in Venetian academies, see Whistler, 2004, pp. 370–96. For Rossi's academy, see Radassao, 1998, p. 132. For Zanchi's academy, see Safarik, 1978, p. 84 (quoting a letter of October 1662 from Filippo Leoncello to Jan Czernini, the imperial ambassador to Venice). For David's academy, see Ivanoff, 1957, pp. 248–53; Sohm, 2002, pp. 739–40; and Fossaluzza, 2004. The Accademia de' Filaleti that met in the house of either Giovanni or Battista Nani was, in Boschini's words, "una Accademia universale" that covered the arts and sciences including life drawing for painters and dilettantes as well as drawing from gesso casts: Boschini [1674], 1966, p. 744. There has been some confusion about the location and activities of the Filaleti; for the most complete coverage, see Merling, 1992, pp. 161–70. For Vecchia's academy, see Bordignon Favero, 1984–85, pp. 115–33, and Pancheri, 2001, pp. 111–16. For Litterini's academy, see Bordignon Favero, 1994, p. 152, and Leopardi, 1977. For Liberi's academy, see Boschini [1660], 1966, p. 534, and Ruggeri, 1996, pp. 44–49.

51 Misson's letter, published in *Nouveau voyage en Italie*, is quoted by Whistler, 2004, p. 395.

52 Morassi, 1971, pp. 43–50.

53 Whistler, 2004, p. 395, quotes from Philip Skippon's *An Account of a Journey made thro' Part of the Low Countries, Germany, Italy, and France* describing his visits to Venice between October 1663 and March 1665.

54 Bassi, 1941, p. 128; Bassi, 1975, p. 127 (in Collegio appeal to Senate, December 1682).

55 Venice, Archivio di Stato, Giustizia Vecchia, Capitoli, b. 204, filza 236.

56 Favaro, 1975, p. 91.

57 Favaro, 1975, p. 219. For the expansion of shops selling paintings during the late seventeenth century and continuing into the eighteenth century, see Binion, 1970, pp. 92–101; Cecchini, 2000, pp. 162–84; Montecuccoli degli Erri, 1998 and 1999, pp. 17–21.

58 Venice, Biblioteca Correr, Ms. Cl. IV, 123 (Mariegola del Colleggio de SS.vi Pittori), 13 January 1683, c. 10–11: Liberi (21 yes, 1 no); Zanchi (7 yes, 16 no).

59 Venice, Biblioteca Correr, Ms. Cl. IV, 123 (Mariegola del Colleggio de SS.vi Pittori), 13 January 1683, c. 10–11. For the two offices of *consiglieri*: Zanchi (22 yes, 1 no), Celesti (15 yes, 9 no), Loth (15 yes, 9 no), Frezzato (6 yes, 17 no). Loth, who paid twice the amount of tax as Celesti, won the runoff: Loth (16 yes, 8 no), Celesti (12 yes, 11 no). Frezzato, the clear loser, paid less than a quarter of what Celesti paid in tax.

60 Favaro, 1975, pp. 163–75. For the numbers of painters in the sixteenth century, see De Marchi and Matthew, 2007, pp. 266–68.

61 Venice, Archivio di Stato, Provveditori alla Sanità, Anagrafi, b. 568–71.

62 Cecchini, 2000, p. 158.

63 For Arte and Collegio registrations, see Binion, 1970, pp. 99–101, and Favaro, 1975, pp. 137–228. For Collegio enrolments in 1757, see Montecuccoli degli Erri, 1999, pp. 20–21.

64 Favaro, 1975, pp. 205–11.

65 Sansovino, 1663, II (supplement by Martinioni: "Quinto catalogo," pp. 21–23). Boschini [1660], 1966, pp. 525–606 (Venetians: pp. 525–62; women: pp. 563–66; foreigners: pp. 566–606).

66 For women painters in Venice, see Magani, 1996.

67 Venice, Archivio di Stato, Cancelleria inferiore, Notai diversi, Inventari, 2 June 1607; cited by Palumbo Fossati, 2007, p. 17.

68 According to Boschini himself, in an appeal submitted to his landlord, the Scuola di San Rocco; quoted by Maschio, 1976, p. 121.

69 Letter from P. M. Baldi to Bassetti, 14 August 1677, quoted in Alfonsi, 2002, p. 274.

70 Favaro, 1975, pp. 195–214. Recently some excellent studies on art dealing in Venice have been published by Matthew, 2003; Shaw, 2006; Mason, 2007, pp. 110–11; and especially Cecchini, 2000, 2002, 2006, and 2007. Although dealers could earn more than painters, the Collegio restricted their voting rights and the right to hold office.

71 Montecuccoli degli Erri, 1999, pp. 19–20; compare the tax rates of the top 20 percent of painters in my Table 17 below with the taxes of the ten dealers listed in 1712: 13 lire, 13, 14, 18, 18, 31, 31, 42, 51, 51.

72 Pino [1548], 1960, I, p. 119.

73 Vielli, 1998, pp. 176–79.

74 Orlandi, 1753, p. 91; Temanza, 1963, p. 37.

75 For letters from Piazzetta concerning his poverty, see Ravà, 1921, p. 56; Pinetti, 1921, pp. 19–21; and Sartori, 1976, p. 196.

76 For Ridolfi on the decline and sociology of art, see Sohm, 2002, pp. 725–56.

77 For Schiavone, see Ridolfi [1648], 1965, I, p. 258; for Brusasorci, see Ridolfi [1648], 1965, II, p. 117; for Titian, see Ridolfi [1648], 1965, I, pp. 162–63.

78 Ridolfi [1648], 1965, II, p. 219.

79 Data compiled from Favaro, 1975, pp. 161–94.

80 Data compiled from Favaro, 1975, pp. 195–214.

81 The painter-dealer Arno owned 551 paintings with an average value of 2 ducats (total value of 1,102 ducats).

82 For Farinati's taxes in 1584 (8 soldi) and in 1595 (10 soldi), see Farinati, 1968, p. xv. For Farinati's income for these years, see Table 21.

83 For evidence of avoiding taxes by noncompliance, see Cecchini, 2000, p. 165.

84 Data compiled from Montecuccoli degli Erri, 1999, pp. 19–20.

85 Da Canal, 1809 and 1810; Zanetti, 1733; Maffei, 1731. For a discussion of Venetian art literature in the 1730s, see Sohm, 1991, pp. 197–239, and Sohm, 1995, pp. 51–66.

86 From a 200 scudi original of the *Martyrdom of St. Lawrence*, Titian offered to have a copy made for 50 scudi: García-Frías Cecha, 2003, pp. 17–20. From Tinelli's account book (Strina, 2000), the following average prices (in ducats) of copies can be established along with how much less they cost than original portraits in that year: 1622: 7.6, 41 percent; 1625: 4, 38 percent; 1626: 4, 32 percent; 1628: 6, 37 percent; 1629: 5.6, 40 percent; 1630: 6, 34 percent; 1633: 8.7, 45 percent.

87 Binion, 1990, pp. 103–13.

88 Sani, 1985, II, p. 796 (letter from Pietro Petroni Caldana [in Pirano] to unknown recipient in Venice, 17 August 1702).

89 For Fumiani, see Fossaluzza, 1988, p. 117 (regarding his copy [1692–93] of Veronese's *Wedding at Cana*, formerly in Treviso, Convento di San Teonisto, refectory). For Ricci, see Daniels, 1976, p. 89 (regarding his copy of Raphael's Stanza dell'Incendio fresco, *Coronation of Charlemagne*, taken over from Charles Desforêts in 1693). Desforêts had wanted 800 scudi but Ricci accepted 400 scudi. For Zanchi, see the following note.

90 Zampetti, 1988, p. 404.

91 Bordignon Favero, 1978–79, pp. 129–93.

92 Vertue, 1936, p. 82 (entry from 1711).

93 Ridolfi [1648], 1965, II, p. 101.

94 Favaro, 1975, pp. 162, 165, 175, 184, 186, 190–91. For Pietra, see Cecchini, 2007.

95 Olivari, 1987, p. 103.

96 Scarpa, 2006, p. 351.

97 Palma Giovane in 1589 at 1.6 ducats/square meter: Mason Rinaldi, 1984, p. 71. Esengren in 1631 at 4.0 ducats/square meter (this price was deemed to be too high and the contract was nullified): Zorzi, 1987, pp. 220, 478. Giambattista Rossi in 1684 at 3.1 ducats/square meter: Olivato, 1974, p. 20. Ricci was paid 184 ducats in 1721 to restore Veronese's *Andrea Contarini Returns from Chioggia* (Palazzo Ducale, Sala del Maggior Consiglio): Moretti, 1978, p. 113, and Scarpa, 2006, p. 68. Santo Piatti in 1737 at 6.1 ducats/square meter: Rossi, 1985, p. 202. Giambattista Pittoni in 1738 at 15 ducats/square meter: Zava Boccazzi, 1979, p. 106.

98 Olivato, 1974, pp. 20–26, 99–101.

99 Zorzi, 1987, pp. 220, 478.

100 Cecchini, 2007, pp. 149–51. For a discussion of art appraisals, see Alfonsi, 2002, and Cecchini, 2007, pp. 151–52.

101 For Giovanni Massari's fee of 4 ducats, see Morello, 1999, p. 178. For Agostino Lama's fee of 12 ducats, see the 1699 inventory of the painting collection of Andrea and Federigo Cornaro: Biblioteca Correr, Ms. P.D. 2216/II, fol. 93v. For Boschini's fee of 300 ducats (for his inventory in 1679 of Alvise Pisani's collection), see Gottardo, 2002, p. 263. Despite such high fees, Boschini referred to himself in 1677 as a "poor man."

102 For 5 percent, see Fletcher, 1979, p. 418. In 1743 Tiepolo received goods worth 17 ducats for his assistance in purchasing Holbein's *Madonna*, in Ca' Delfino (Morassi, 1962, p. 233). For 10 percent, see Radassao, 1998, p. 151 (Alessandro Savorgnan offered Niccolò Bambini 10 percent of the sales for his collection in 1699).

103 Morassi, 1962, p. 233.

104 Sartori, 1976, pp. 228–29.

105 Kunert, 1931, p. 547; Anelli, 1996, pp. 84–85.

106 For Loth's working habits, see Pizzo, 2000, letters 11, 29 and 36. For Loth's estate, see Ewald, 1965, pp. 43–51.

107 For Veronese, see Ridolfi [1648], 1965, I, p. 348, and Pignatti, 1976, pp. 258–60. For Tintoretto's appeal to the Senate in 1577 for special consideration, "non havendo entrate, ne industria alcuna, salvo questo poco di mio esercitio," see Lorenzi, 1868, p. 391, doc. 801, and Borean, 2007a, p. 434. His plea of poverty, "povertà mia con il carico di moglie, et figlioli n. otto," was not an exaggeration according to Mason, 2008, p. 117. For Titian, see Puppi, 2004.

108 Moretti, 1984, p. 18.

109 Lanzi, 1968–70, II, p. 132: "Fu anche buon architetto, e il cav. Liberi si valse del suo [Mazzoni] disegno per fabbricare in Venezia quel suo bel palazzo che sembra eccedere la fortuna d'un pittore."

110 Scarpa, 2006, p. 66.

111 For Tiepolo as a "rich gentleman," see Alessandro Longhi, 1762, unpaginated. Tiepolo lent 6,000 ducats to the Board of Works of the Pietà in 1757: Molmenti, 1909, p. 41. Tiepolo earned 1,900 ducats for the Gesuati fresco ceiling (1737–39) and 3,000 ducats for the Scalzi ceiling (1745). Dorigny received 3,165 ducats for his frescoes in the Udine Duomo (1709–14).

112 For a history of the Sansaria and Titian, see Wethey, 1975, pp. 227–28.

113 Pallucchini and Rossi, 1982, p. 127.

114 Olivato, 1974, pp. 15–16, 97–98.

115 Cecchini, 2000, p. 116.

116 Cecchetti, 1886, doc. 384 (28 November 1612).

117 Pullan, 1971, pp. 406–7; Pezzolo, 2003, p. 107.

118 Zannini, 1993a, pp. 139–41.

119 Pullan, 1964a, pp. 120–22; Pullan, 1971, pp. 406–7; Marcato, 2002, pp. 95–136.

120 Zannini, 1993a, pp. 219–22.

121 Campori, 1855, p. 352.

122 Zava Boccazzi, 1990, p. 115 (letters of 6 March and 29 May 1706).

123 The correspondence between Tessin and Harleman regarding Tiepolo has been collected and edited by Bettagno and Magrini, 2002, pp. 81–87.

124 For the following on Triva, see Longo, 1984, pp. 87–96; Longo, 1987, pp. 188–99.

125 For his payment for a single figure, see Martinioni, in Sansovino 1663, II, p. 23 (catalogue supplement). For his work in Milan and Mantua, see Anelli, 1996, pp. 84–85.

126 Muraro, 1992, pp. 14–18.

127 Pullan, 1971, p. 179; Pezzolo, 2003, p. 107.

128 Based on uncompiled data in Strina, 2000.

129 Ridolfi [1648], 1965, II, p. 287.

130 Based on uncompiled data in Farinati, 1968.

131 Data gathered from Sani, 1985.

132 Ewald, 1965, pp. 43–47.

133 Vianello, 1993, pp. 39–46.

134 For Carneo and Guardi, see below. For the Donà brothers' purchase of two animal scenes by a "Domenico pittor" for 37 lire (about 3 ducats each), see Borean, 2007b.

135 Trivellato, 2000, pp. 52–53, 57.

136 Anon, 1566, unpaginated.

137 Barcham, 2001, p. 87.

138 Preto, 1978, p. 41.

139 Palumbo Fossati, 2007, pp. 14–16.

140 Venice, Archivio di Stato, Provveditori alla Sanità, Anagrafi, b. 568–71.

141 For the establishment of a commercial art quarter around the Piazza di S. Marco, see Cecchini, 2000, pp. 162–84.

142 Cecchini, 2006, pp. 127–28.

143 Melchiori, 1964, p. 78.

144 Venice, Biblioteca Correr, Ms. Cl. IV, 123 (Mariegola del Collegio de SS.vi Pittori), 29 August 1682, c.20. The "figliuoli de' pittori" paid 5 ducats compared with other "Terrieri" (painters from Venice and the Veneto), who paid 15 ducats. Foreigners paid only 10 ducats. This rebate tries to correct a tendency of foreigners to avoid inscription into the Collegio; at the same time the Collegio extended the grace period for foreigners to register from three days to six months (c.21).

145 For sources of parents' professions, see Ridolfi [1648], 1965, II, pp. 101, 207, 264; Melchiori, 1964, pp. 78, 126; Gualdo, 1972, pp. 44, 64, 70–71, 78–80, 85; Brenzoni, 1972, pp. 9, 28, 31, 33, 48, 68, 73, 76–81, 87, 112, 138, 179, 191, 207, 246, 252, 285, 295, 298; Rossi, 1991, p. 12; Banzato and Fantelli, 1993, p. 11; Bordignon Favero, 1994, p. 355; Dal Poggetto, 1996, p. 9; Pietropolli, 2002, p. 123.

146 For Grazia and Mariana, see Boschini [1660], 1966, p. 566.

147 For Molinari, see Moretti, 1979, p. 59; for Langetti, see Mantovanelli, 1990, p. 95; for Marieschi, see Montecuccoli degli Erri and Pedrocco, 1999, p. 58. For all others, including those with lower dowries, see Hochmann, 1992a, pp. 41–43.

148 Lemoine, 1997, pp. 54–63.

149 Zava Boccazzi, 1978–79, p. 615.

150 Nacamulli, 1987, pp. 184–88.

151 Lupis, 1675, pp. 15–16.
152 For Tintoretto's gifting and other marketing strategies, see Hill, 1993, pp. 107–20.
153 Rosand, 1982, p. 237, doc. 24. In 1557 Girolamo Dente proposed to the Scuola della Carità that he receive no payment beyond expenses for the large painting (345 × 600 cm), probably the *Annunciation* (on deposit in Mason Vicentino): "ma solo che la Scola li faccia far il quadro, e gli faccia dar li colori, per il che suppliranno ducati dieci perché quanto all'opera non riceva cosa alcuna."
154 For Sera's description of Giordano's play, see Fileti Mazza, 1987, pp. 439–42.
155 In 1672 Giulio Carpioni reduced his price for an altarpiece from 80 to 60 ducats out of respect for the patron Giamberlanno. And in 1690 Zanchi declared that the ceiling painting of a *Gloria* (S. Maria Zobenigo, Venice), when finished, would be worth 700 ducats but as an act of charity (and rights to burial) he would accept 234 ducats. And finally Gregorio Lazzarini wrote to the collector Stefano Conti in 1705 that he would not set a price for his painting as long as he could be reassured that it would not be less that the others (Bellucci and Marchesini) doing similar work "since they would mock me, not you." None of these examples, and they are the only ones I found, qualify as gifting since conditions are always attached.
156 Migliorini and Assini, 2000, p. 68.
157 Boselli, 1971, pp. 43–44.
158 Ridolfi [1648], 1965, II, pp. 203–4.
159 Constable, 1976, I, pp. 14–15.
160 Kowalczyk, 1995, pp. 73–75.
161 Kowalczyk, 1995, p. 74.
162 Pascoli, 1992, p. 119.
163 Lupis, 1675, pp. 15–16.
164 Barocchi and Bertelà, 2005, I, p. 41.
165 Martini, 1969, p. 237; quoted by Betti, 2003, p. 115: "Di Cassana è una serie di animali dipinti con non comune tenerezza, e acquistati a caro prezzo, perché questo artista, recentemente deceduto a Venezia, si faceva spesso pagare 200 talleri anche i quadri di modeste proporzioni."
166 Filetti Mazza, 1987, p. 11.
167 Boschini [1660], 1966, pp. 519–20.
168 Boschini [1660], 1966, pp. 616–17.
169 Pizzo, 2000, letters 11 and 29.
170 Pizzo, 2002, doc. no. 4, p. 125.
171 Ridolfi [1648], 1965, I, pp. 398–99.
172 For Martinioni's and Boschini's living painters, see note 65.
173 Pizzo, 2000, p. 63.
174 Pizzo, 2000, p. 73. Note also Girolamo Albrizzi, writing in 1696 on the "infelicità de' nostri tempi" which proves to be "un Tormento della Virtù" for artists like Antonio Zanchi "pittore celeberrimo," to whom Albrizzi dedicated *Il teatro della crudeltà*.
175 Barocchi and Bertelà, 2005, I, p. 157.
176 Favaro, 1975, p. 221.
177 Ulivioni, 1977, pp. 98–99.
178 Berveglieri, 1995.
179 Barzazi, 1981–82, pp. 45–63. For Micanzio, see Barzazi, 1986.
180 Boschini [1660], 1966, p. 98: "In conclusion the Venetian style carries with it the same freedom that everyone enjoys who lives in this city." For Algarotti's use of artistic and political *libertà*, see Algarotti [1763], 1961, p. 22.
181 Ferrari, 1966, p. 129 (in an anonymous seventeenth-century life of Giordano).
182 Boschini [1660], 1966, p. 567.
183 Magani, 1989, pp. 34–38.
184 Renieri and Vecchi did not specify what distinguished "Venetians" from "foreigners." For the higher valuation of foreigners working outside of Venice, see the appraisal in 1681 of the Dolfin collection by Litterini. It shows prices between 250 and 300 ducats each for the Bolognese painters, many times higher than the prices of Liberi, Vecchia, and Langetti, which hovered in the 30 to 70 range (Borean, 1999).
185 For altarpieces of identical size and number of figures commissioned at the same time for the church of S. Rocco, Ricci received 600 ducats and Solimena 860 ducats (Rossi, 1976–77, pp. 444–45). For a similar situation in Bergamo, where Ciro Ferri was paid more than local painters, see Haskell, 1963, pp. 218–19.
186 Boschini [1660], 1966, p. 26.
187 Ferrari, 1966, p. 94.
188 Cecchini, 2000, pp. 159–60. According to Boschini ([1660] 1966, pp. 256–58), foreign painters of landscapes and still lifes clustered around the Rialto.
189 Panofsky, 1964, p. 109, and Romano, 1899, pp. 2–3.
190 Favaro, 1975, pp. 62–64; Cecchini, 2000, p. 159; Vio, 2004, p. 371.
191 Cecchini, 2000, p. 159.
192 Vio, 2004, p. 122.
193 Bassi, 1941, pp. 138–39.
194 Marchini, 1976, p. 253.
195 Favaro, 1975, p. 219.
196 Favaro, 1975, p. 221.
197 Favaro, 1975, p. 225.
198 Borelli, 2002, p. 204.
199 Boselli, 1971, p. 76.
200 Guzzo, 1990–91, p. 270.
201 Ridolfi [1648], 1965, I, pp. 248, 252–3, and II, p. 15. See Hill, 1993, pp. 107–20.
202 Translations by Cecchini, 2003, pp. 391–92.
203 For Lotto's lottery and other practices of this most versatile of marketeers, see Matthew, 2003.
204 Savini Branca, 1965, pp. 93–107; Fantelli, 1974, p. 87; Cecchini, 2000, pp. 200–1, and 2007, pp. 146–48. For a failed art auction of paintings owned by Giorgio Bergonzi held in 1712 after his death by the confraternity of the Poveri Vergognosi at S. Martino and by his heirs, see Borean, 2002b, pp. 97–108.
205 Noris, 1987, pp. 144–45.
206 Pino [1548], 1960, I, p. 119.
207 Boselli, 1971, p. 25.
208 Borean and Cecchini, 2002, p. 197. For the disparity of valuations by different experts in the sixteenth century, see Mason, 2007, pp. 111–12.
209 Magani, 1989, pp. 34–36. For an excellent collection of previously unpublished valuations of collections by painters, see Benussi, 2007.
210 Mazza, 2003, pp. 126–68.
211 Algarotti [1763], 1969, p. 422.
212 Mason Rinaldi, 1974, pp. 251–54.
213 Tintoretto, 1578 (Syre, 2000, pp. 239–42); Prudenti, 1638 (Bratti, 1915, pp. 471–72); Cavagna, 1592 (Coppa and Rossi, 1987, p. 156); Cervelli, 1677 (Haskell, 1963, p. 219).
214 Peranda and Tinelli reviewed an altarpiece by Prudenti in 1638. In the dispute between Forabosco and his patron in 1646, the experts were "all painters," Bortolo Scaligero, Vecchia, and Domenico Bruni. Mazzoni and Stroifi were appointed in 1652

to set the price of an altarpiece by Ruschi (San Pietro in Castello, Venice). Cairo and Vecchia adjudicated between Liberi and the *deputati* of S. Maria Maggiore (Bergamo) in 1662. Brentana and Falcieri reviewed a painting by Prunato in 1700.

215 Makrykostas, 1993, pp. 176–81.
216 Saccardo, 1981, p. 63. For further discussion, see the Introduction to this volume.
217 See, for example, Battista Franco, Giulio Licinio, Giuseppe Salviati, Schiavone, and Veronese in 1556: Von Ludwig, 1911, p. 144; Paolucci, 1981, pp. 287–99.
218 Saccardo, 1981, pp. 40–48; Zampetti, 1988, p. 405.
219 Mucchi and Della Croce, 1954, pp. 101–2; Zampetti, 1988, pp. 403, 413.
220 Vio, 2004, p. 505; Craievich, 2005, p. 156.
221 Morello, 1999, pp. 162–78.
222 Pinetti, 1916, pp. 122–25.
223 Bettagno and Magrini, 2002, pp. 106–7 (letter to Count Brühl, 9 August 1743).
224 Armenini, 1988, p. 26.
225 Van Mander, 1994–99, IV, p. 86.
226 Rossi, 1976–77, pp. 439–44.
227 For Tintoretto in Mantua, see Syre, 2000. In 1610 Francesco Gambara was told that 20 or 25 ducats would buy a small painting of two *palmi* in height (Boselli, 1971, p. 129): "Per risposta di quello che mi commanda per quelle inviatemi per il Signor Giulio Cesare, le dico che hò parlato al Pittore, qual poco si sa ressolvere del prezzo per non haver cose fatte, pure dice che con 20 overo 25 scudi veronesi da 6 lire venetiane, la servirà con ogni diligenza d'un quadretto d'altezza de doi palmi incirca, et di longhezza proportionata sopra il quale fara cose spirituali se cosi lei vorrà o altro à suo gusto."
228 Longo, 1984, pp. 87–96; Longo, 1987, pp. 188–99; Baccheschi and Ghio, 1989, p. 97.
229 Humfrey, 1993, p. 152.
230 Muraro, 1992, p. 15.
231 Matthew (2006, p. 311) also notes that Lotto set appraised prices of paintings based on the number of figures.
232 Boselli, 1971, p. 25.
233 Saccardo, 1981, p. 68.
234 Cecchetti, 1886, docs. 384ff.; Mason Rinaldi, 1984, p. 70.
235 Scarpa, 1993, pp. 49–56.

6 *Five Industrious Cities*

1 Malanima, 1998, pp. 136–37, and 2002, pp. 544–45.
2 De Luca, 1996.
3 Demographers calculate that northern Italy lost 20 percent of its population between 1600 and 1650: see Del Panta et al., 1996, p. 79; see also Malanima, 1998, p. 146.
4 Vigo, 1974.
5 For the index that measures the rate of inequality in income distribution, see Malanima, 2002, p. 270.
6 Del Panta et al., 1996, p. 82.
7 Malanima, 1998, pp. 145–46.
8 Piola Caselli, 1988 and 1990.
9 De Luca, 1996.
10 Chauvard, 2005, pp. 233–39.
11 Chauvard, 2005, pp. 85–95.
12 Fregna, 1990, pp. 75–76, 130–31.
13 Fregna, 1990, pp. 69–70, 77–78.
14 Fregna, 1990, pp. 77–78.
15 The process seems to be analogous in Bologna and Florence (see Fregna, 1990, p. 182, and Benfante, 2003).
16 Cipolla, 1974. The Neapolitan revolt of 1647 was triggered by the attempt to violate such privileges; see Villari, 1967, and Benigno, 1999.
17 Malanima, 1998, p. 5.
18 Malanima, 2002, pp. 304–6.
19 Chauvard, 2005, in particular ch. 3.
20 Stumpo, 1985, p. 28.
21 Stumpo, 1985, p. 25.
22 Da Silva, 1969, I, pp. 330–31.
23 Da Silva, 1969, I, pp. 359–61.
24 My graph is based on the data presented in Da Silva, 1969, I, pp. 320–3, using the average of the lowest and highest figures for each decade.
25 Da Silva, 1969, I, p. 291.
26 Vigo, 1974; Reinhardt, 1991; Martinat, 2004; Mattozzi et al., 1983; see the Venice essay.
27 See the Venice essay.
28 See the Rome essay, and Ago, 1998, p. 86.
29 See, for example, the salaries of glassmakers and master carpenters in Trivellato, 2000.
30 I would like to thank Simona Feci for having provided this information about the pupils Mattei (in the 1620s) and Ginnasi (in the 1660s). For Tinelli, see the Venice essay.
31 Carboni, 1999.
32 Ferrante, 1983.
33 D'Amelia, 1988.
34 Fubini Leuzzi, 1999.
35 Spagnoletti, 1988.
36 Beltrami, 1954, p. 227; Pullan, 1978, pp. 988–89; Petraccone, 1978a and 1978b; and Malanima, 2002, pp. 266–67.
37 Petraccone, 1974.
38 Beltrami, 1954, and Pezzolo, 2003, p. 151.
39 Sonnino, 1997, p. 56.
40 Del Panta, 1974, pp. 14–16, and Boutier and Paoli, 2005, pp. 332–33.
41 Bellettini, 1961.
42 Pullan, 1978; Geremek, 1986; and Gutton, 1974.
43 See Romano, 1970, and Ragosta Portioli, 1999.
44 Pullan, 1978.
45 According to the Roman census of 1656, exactly half of the painters living in the Campo Marzio district were defined as poor (see the Rome essay). In Venice, however, it seems that far fewer were poor: no more than 5 percent, at least to judge by the rent they could afford (see the Venice essay).
46 See the Naples essay.
47 See the Venice essay.
48 Rao, 2005, p. 41.
49 Garzoni, 1996, pp. 182, 241.
50 On the relationship between the liberal professions and the nobility, see Doria and Savelli, 1990.
51 In the Kingdom of Naples, previously free communities were sold as fiefs in exchange for money, and Genoese bankers were among the first to purchase them. In the Papal States, there were no new infeudations, but many estates nonetheless changed hands. See Ago, 1994.
52 See the Bologna essay.

53 See the Rome essay.
54 See the Rome essay. On the primacy of land rent in *ancien régime* culture, see Grenier, 1996.
55 See the Introduction.
56 Ago, 1990, and Signorotto and Visceglia, 1998.
57 See Betri and Pastore, 1997. In this way, the association managed to purge both these tensions and the forms of competition that also existed internally, among more or less powerful and fortunate members.
58 Doria and Savelli, 1990.
59 G. M. Galanti as cited in Marin, 2005, p. 128, and Gentilcore, 1997.
60 Gentilcore, 1997.
61 Groppi, 2002, and Poni, 1989.
62 Groppi, 2002.
63 For example, where workers were unable to form a new trade guild, they founded a confraternity; see Martini, 1965.
64 In Bologna and Venice, painters' associations took on the names respectively of *compagnia* and *collegio* rather than *accademia*: see the Bologna and Venice essays.
65 The Florentine case was particularly glaring: in the later part of the century, nobles increasingly applied to join the Accademia (see the Florence essay).
66 See the Naples essay.
67 Delille, 1977, and Ago, 1990.
68 Ago, 1997, and Bellavitis, 2008.
69 See the Bologna essay.
70 See the Bologna essay.
71 See the Venice essay.
72 Groppi, 1996b.
73 Ferrières, 2004.
74 Allerston, 2000.
75 De Vries, 1993.
76 Groppi, 1996b, and Bellavitis, 2006.
77 See the Bologna essay.
78 See the Venice and Naples essays. As one can see from Table 30, the value of the three currencies was more or less equal, despite being well below that of the Roman scudo.
79 Ago, 1998, pp. 182–84.
80 See the Rome essay.
81 Vigo, 1974, p. 391.
82 Archivio di Stato di Roma (hereafter ASR), Tribunale civile del Senatore (TCS), b.2083, c.399, 20 October 1625.
83 Trivellato, 2000, p. 55.
84 ASR, TCS, b.2083, c.122v, 29 February 1624; ASR, TCS, b.2083, c.115v, 31 January 1624.
85 ASR, TCS, b.2083, c.604, 15 October 1626.
86 ASR, TCS, b.2083, c.115v, 31 January 1624.
87 ASR, TCS, b.2083, c.399, 20 October 1625.
88 Trivellato, 2000, p. 76.
89 ASR, TCS, b.2083, c.958, 20 September 1628.
90 Trivellato, 2000, p. 291.
91 Trivellato, 2000, pp. 57–58.
92 For the tanner's employees, see ASR, TCS, b.2083, c.122v and c.132, 29 February 1624; for the glassmaker, Trivellato, 2000, pp. 52–53.
93 Trivellato, 2000, pp. 57, 61.
94 See the Venice essay.
95 Trivellato, 2000, p. 75.
96 Piñeiro, 1996, p. 143, regarding the Roman wages.
97 See the Rome essay.
98 Ago, 1998, and Trivellato, 2000.
99 Zacchia, 1658 and 1659; Trivellato, 2000, p. 81.
100 Ago, 1998.
101 Frigo, 1985.
102 Alberti, 1994, p. 218.
103 Cipolla, 1974, p. 48. It emerges from Roman inventories that in many cases there were neither fireplaces nor braziers and that candles and oil lamps were similarly rare: Ago, 2006.
104 See the Bologna essay.
105 Tagliaferri, 1968.
106 Ago, 2006, p. 50; Mira, 1940; Cipolla, 1974; Malanima, 1977; and Visceglia, 1991.
107 See the Bologna essay.
108 Visceglia, 1991, p. 221.
109 ASR, TCS, b.2083, c.958, 20 September 1628.
110 Ago, 2006, and Coen, 2004.
111 Ramella, 1984.
112 Ago, 2006, p. 50.
113 Cerutti, 1992, and Canepari, 2007.
114 See the Venice essay.
115 See the Rome, Venice, Bologna, and Naples essays.
116 In Rome, for example, one could acquire *censi* (a form of annuity) worth 25 scudi, equal to the sum that pious organizations usually assigned to a dowry.
117 Canepari, 2007, and Ago, 1998.
118 Ago et al., 1998.
119 Chauvard, 2005; D'Amico, 1994; and Curto, 1995.
120 Biagioli, 2006, with evidence regarding Galilei.
121 See the Rome and Bologna essays.
122 Tebbutt, 1984.
123 Trivellato, 2000, p. 63.
124 ASR, TCS, b.2083, c.604, 15 October 1626, and c.749, 8 July 1627.
125 McCants, 2007. For Rome, see Travaglini, 1990 and 1992.
126 See the Rome essay.
127 See the Florence essay.
128 See the case of Cristofano Allori cited by Elena Fumagalli.
129 Groppi, 1996a.
130 Ago, 2006.
131 Trivellato, 2000.
132 See Betri and Pastore, 1997, and Marin, 2005.
133 See the Rome essay
134 The relationship between Tintoretto and the Scuola di S. Rocco was typical in this sense (see the Venice essay), while Cerrini's offer to paint an altarpiece for the church of S. Carlo alle Quattro Fontane for free seems to have followed the same logic (see the Rome essay).
135 See the Rome essay.
136 Visceglia, 1995.
137 Malanima, 1998.
138 Muzzarelli, 2002.
139 Fragnito, 1993.
140 Douglas and Isherwood, 1980.
141 Laws on *dérogeance* were very severe at times and withdrew noble status from those who practiced the mechanical arts or fell short of the noble lifestyle in another way (see Labatut, 1978).
142 Grenier, 1996.
143 Schumpeter, 1954; Clavero, 1991; Todeschini, 2002; and Ago, 1998.
144 Douglas and Isherwood, 1980.
145 Canepari, 2007.

146 Benfante, 2003.
147 Della Valentina, 2003.
148 Local chronicles like the *Avvisi di Roma* are full of such episodes; see Ago, 1998.
149 Ago, 1990. Examples include the Borghese, Barberini, and Pamphilj in Rome, and the Ottoboni in Venice. See Menniti Ippolito, 1996.
150 See the Venice essay.
151 Ago, 1990a, p. 135.
152 Ago, 1990a, p. 165.
153 See the Naples essay.
154 See the Rome, Naples, and Bologna essays.
155 See the Bologna essay.
156 See the Rome essay.
157 See the Bologna essay.
158 See the Rome essay.
159 See the Rome essay.
160 See the Rome and Bologna essays.
161 Donati, 1988.
162 See the Rome essay.
163 Varese, 1980, p. 244.
164 For some examples of "bourgeois" careers crowned by ennobling, see Tucci, 1990; for Florence, see Angiolini, 1990.
165 Karsten, 2007, p. 150.
166 Fosi and Visceglia, 1998, pp. 211–13.
167 For this information on Bernini, see Fagiolo dell'Arco, 2001.

7 *The Painting Industry in Early Modern Italy*

1 Neil De Marchi and Hans J. Van Miegroet have estimated the number of painters per 1,000 at different times in selected cities as follows: 0.8 at Florence in 1470; 1.4–2.8 at Bruges in 1470–88; 1.3–2.4 at Antwerp in the sixteenth century; 0.8–1.9 at Haarlem in the first half of the seventeenth century; 0.9–1.0 at Amsterdam in the seventeenth century; 0.9–1.0 at Paris in the seventeenth century; and about 1.5 at Rome in the seventeenth century. See De Marchi and Van Miegroet, 2006a, pp. 114–16. They stress, however, that outside the estimates for the Low Countries no great weight can be put on these numbers.
2 De Vries and van der Woude, 1997, pp. 342–43.
3 Lopez, 1953; Hicks, 1969, pp. 58–59; Romano, 1974, p. 1,865.
4 For example, Roche, 1986.
5 Goldthwaite, 1993, pp. 54–62.
6 Goldthwaite, 2009, pp. 468–76.
7 Letter published in Vasari, 1923, p. 716.
8 The city best studied for collecting is Venice: see Borean and Mason, 2007.
9 Assini, 2004, p. 150 (Imperiale); Restagno, 2004, pp. 425, 430 (Costa); Tagliaferro, 1995, pp. 298–305 (Brignole Sale); Lauber, 2002, pp. 58–59 (Vendramin); Borean, 2002a, p. 8 (Orsetti). Inventories of paintings were inserted into testaments of Giovan Battista Balbi (d. 1657) and Francesco Maria Balbi (1704): Grendi, 1997, p. 122; and in the testaments of various members of the Durazzo family from 1634 to 1698 bequests of individual pictures are made to specific persons: Puncuh, 1984, pp. 212–13. On the emergence of a sense of a collection as a particular kind of property, see Findlen, 2004 (her concern, however, is with collections of scientific interest not of art objects).
10 Marshall, 2000, pp. 20–23.
11 Lauber, 2002, p. 47.
12 Portier, 1996, p. 57.
13 Luzio, 1913, pp. 267–68.
14 A review of legislation protecting the artistic patrimony of Italian states (the earliest regarding almost exclusively classical antiquities) can be found in Guerzoni, 2006, pp. 265–96. For Venice, see Olivato, 1974, pp. 47–52.
15 Pears, 1988.
16 Van Os, 1985; this theme has recently been elaborated by Steinhoff, 2007.
17 Gardner von Teuffel, 1983, pp. 323–30.
18 Sohm, 1991, pp. 4–9. On the adaptation and diffusion of Flemish oil techniques in Florence and the new possibilities it offered, see Nuttall, 2004, ch. 10; see also Wright, 2003, pp. 229, and Rohlmann, 2003.
19 Bambach, 1999, p. 186 (her book has much material about drawing as a technical innovation).
20 The expansion of the market for prints is summarized by Brewer, 2002.
21 Williams, 1995.
22 Feigenbaum, 1993, p. 70.
23 Holmes, 2004.
24 Hope, 1980, pp. 157–58.
25 Spezzaferro, 2004, p. 331.
26 Spear, 1997, p. 242.
27 Huber, 2005, pp. 28–29.
28 Spike, 1988 (Reni), and Sparti, 1997 (Pietro da Cortona).
29 Kubersky-Piredda, 2003, p. 117; other evidence of this market is documented by Procacci, 1960, pp. 12, 39ff.
30 Bauer, 1986.
31 Luzio, 1913, pp. 320ff.
32 Spear, 1997, p. 21, and Spezzaferro, 1989.
33 Spear, 1997, pp. 269–71.
34 Assini, 1995, and Galazzi, 1995. On Strozzi's entrepreneurial activities outside his shop, see also Alfonso, 1981.
35 De Marchi and Matthew, 2007, is the first study that addresses the problem of a comparison of the art markets in Italy and the Low Countries.
36 Capitelli, 2004, pp. 383–84.
37 Williams, 1995, pp. 527–29.
38 Modesti, 2003.
39 Honig, 2008.
40 Maginnis, 1997, p. 196.
41 Matthew, 1998, p. 641.
42 Hope, 1980, pp. 77–84 (Titian), and Nichols, 1999, pp. 101–10 (Tintoretto).
43 Goffen, 2002, p. 4, and Ilchman, 2009.
44 On this issue, see Goldthwaite, 2009, pp. 390–92, 588–89.
45 Lydecker, 1987, pp. 239–41.
46 Lorizzo, 2003b, adds much rich detail to the brief description of this secondary market in the classic study of Haskell, 1963, ch. 5. See also Cavazzini, 2004a; and Pickrel, 1984, pp. 311–12. For Venice, see Cecchini, 2005; on Naples, Marshall, 2000. The print representing the ambulant seller of pictures is reproduced on the title page of *The Art Market in Italy 15th–17th Centuries*, 2003.
47 See two articles by Marshall, 2000 and 2006.
48 Pickrel, 1984.
49 De Marchi and Van Miegroet, 2006a, pp. 102–3 (citing references to articles by Loredana Lorizzo).
50 Bauer, 1987, p. 95.

51 See the comment of De Marchi and Van Miegroet, 2006b, p. 381.
52 De Marchi, 1995.
53 Boccardo, 2001, p. 143.
54 Bonfait, 1990, p. 80.
55 On the Venetian market for Flemish art, see Aikema, 2003, and Cecchini, 2005, p. 168, n. 25.
56 De Marchi, Van Miegroet, and Raiff, 1998.
57 Goldthwaite, 2004, p. 17.
58 Luzio, 1913, pp. 261–72.
59 Brown, 1995, surveys these collectors, although he has hardly anything to say about the market in Italy.
60 Elliott, 2002, pp. 553, 555.
61 Lammertse and van der Veen, 2006, pp. 258, 270–74.
62 Lammertse and van der Veen, 2006, pp. 72, 239–42.
63 Savini Branca, 1965, pp. 50–59.
64 Terzaghi, 2007.
65 Morselli, 2000, p. 151.
66 Szanto, 2003b.
67 See De Marchi and Matthew, 2007.
68 Falomir, 2006, pp. 144–49.
69 De Marchi and Van Miegroet, 2006a, pp. 90–91, and Szanto, 2002, pp. 175, 177.
70 North, 2006, pp. 290, 296–97.
71 Portier, 1996, pp. 55–57.
72 Morselli, 2000, pp. 154–55.
73 Brown and Elliott, 2002, pp. 59–68.
74 Leoncini, 1997, p. 125.
75 Cecchini, 2003.
76 See the price series collected by Gérin-Jean, 1998.
77 Piccinelli, 2000, p. 21 and doc. 392.
78 Boccardo, 2001, p. 140.
79 Note the prices in Gérin-Jean, 1998, and in Portier, 1996.
80 Prices for the fifteenth century have been collected by O'Malley, 2005, pp. 133–34, and by Kubersky-Piredda, 2005, pp. 425–576.
81 Farina, 2002, pp. 192–205.
82 Lavin, 1975, pp. 336–52, 421–22.
83 On this point, see Goldthwaite, 2009, pp. 570–71, 574–75.
84 Goldthwaite, 2009, pp. 581–82 (Allori); Nichols, 1999, p. 101 (Tintoretto); and Puppi, 2004, p. 82 (Titian).
85 Elliott, 2002, pp. 555, 559; Schnapper, 2004, pp. 264–83.
86 See the comments of De Marchi and Van Miegroet, 2006b, pp. 66, 85.
87 Spiriti, 2004, p. 412, and Goldthwaite, 1993, p. 93.
88 Cited by De Marchi and Van Miegroet, 1994, p. 454.
89 Fortini Brown, 2007.
90 For painters at the Medici court in the seventeenth century, see Fumagalli, 2007c.
91 Honig, 2008, p. 90.
92 Haskell, 1963, p. 16.
93 Hutter and Throsby, 2008.

Bibliography

Abromson, Morton: *Painting in Rome during the Papacy of Clement VIII (1592–1605): A Documented Study* (Ph.D. diss., Columbia University, 1976), Ann Arbor: U.M.I., 1976.

Acidini Luchinat, Cristina: *Taddeo e Federico Zuccari fratelli pittori del Cinquecento*, Milan: Jandi Sapi, 1999.

Acidini Luchinat, Cristina, Luciano Bellosi, Miklos Boskovits, Pier Paolo Donati, and Bruno Santi (eds.): *Scritti per l'Istituto Germanico di Storia dell'Arte di Firenze: Settanta studiosi italiani*, Florence: Le Lettere, 1997.

Acton, Harold: *The Last Medici*, London: Methuen, 1932 (revised edition, 1958, Italian edition, *Gli ultimi Medici*, Turin: Einaudi, 1987).

Ago, Renata: *Carriere e clientele nella Roma barocca*, Rome: Laterza, 1990a.

Ago, Renata: "Endogamia ed esogamia nel Lazio," in *La popolazione delle campagne italiane in età moderna*, Bologna: CLUEB, 1990b, pp. 329–41.

Ago, Renata: *La feudalità in età moderna*, Rome: Laterza, 1994.

Ago, Renata: "Norme e regole: I ceti urbani davanti al notaio," in *Disuguaglianze: Stratificazione e mobilità sociale nelle popolazioni italiane (dal sec. XIV agli inizi del secolo XX)*, vol. 2, Bologna: CLUEB, 1997, pp. 540–41.

Ago, Renata: *Economia barocca: Mercato e istituzioni nella Roma del Seicento*, Rome: Donzelli, 1998.

Ago, Renata: "Collezioni di quadri e collezioni di libri a Roma tra XVI e XVIII secolo," *Quaderni storici*, XXXVII, 2002, pp. 379–403.

Ago, Renata: *Il Gusto delle cose: Una storia degli oggetti nella Roma del Seicento*, Rome: Donzelli, 2006.

Ago, Renata, Alessandra Camerano, Marina D'Amelia, and Emanuela Parisi: "I trenta notai capitolini: Schedatura dei protocolli del 1645," in *Popolazione e società a Roma dal medioevo all'età contemporanea*, ed. E. Sonnino, Rome: Il Calamo, 1998.

Agosti, Barbara and Silvia Ginzburg: "Introduction," in Giulio Cesare Gigli, *La pittura trionfante*, ed. Barbara Agosti and Silvia Ginzburg, Porretta Terme: I quaderni del Battello ebbro, 1996.

Agosti, Giovanni (ed.): *Per Andrea Celesti a Toscolano*, Brescia: Grafo, 1991.

Aikema, Bernard: "Tesori ponentini per la Serenissima: Il commercio d'arte fiamminga a Venezia e nel Veneto fra Quattro e Cinquecento," in *Tra committenza e collezionismo: Studi sul mercato dell'arte nell'Italia settentrionale durante l'età moderna*, ed. Enrico Maria dal Pozzolo and Leonida Tedoldi, Vicenza: Terra ferma, 2003, pp. 35–48.

Aikema, Bernard and Dulcia Meijers: *Nel regno dei poveri: Arte e storia dei grandi ospedali veneziani in età moderna, 1474–1797*, Venice: Arsenale, 1989.

Aikema, Bernard, Rosella Lauber, and Max Seidel (eds.): *Il collezionismo a Venezia e nel Veneto ai tempi della Serenissima*, Venice: Marsilio, 2005.

Alberti, Leon Battista: *I libri della famiglia*, ed. R. Romano and A. Tenenti, Turin: Einaudi, 1994.

Alfonsi, Maria Stella: "Cosimo III de' Medici e Venezia: I primi anni di regno," in *Figure di collezionisti a Venezia tra Cinque e Seicento*, ed. Linda Borean and Stefania Mason, Udine: Forum, 2002, pp. 265–301.

Alfonso, Luigi: "Liguri illustri: Bernardo Strozzi," *La Berio*, XXI, 1981, pp. 12–37.

Algarotti, Francesco: *Saggio sopra l'Accademia di Francia che è in Roma*, Livorno: Marco Coltellini, 1763 (critical edition, ed. Giovanni da Pozzo, Bari: G. Laterza, 1961).

Algarotti, Francesco: *Saggio sopra la pittura*, Livorno, 1763 (critical edition, F. Algarotti and S. Bettinelli, *Opere*, ed. E. Bonora, Milan and Naples, 1969).

Allen, Robert: "The Great Divergence in European Wages and Prices from the Middle Ages to the First World War," *Explorations in Economic History*, XXXVIII, 2001, pp. 411–47.

Allerston, Patricia: "Clothing and Early Modern Venetian Society," *Continuity and Change*, XV, 2000, pp. 367–90.

Alpers, Svetlana: *Rembrandt's Enterprise: The Studio and the Market*, Chicago: University of Chicago Press, 1988.

Alsteens, Stijn et al. (eds.): *Raphael to Renoir: Drawings from the Collec-*

tion of Jean Bonna (exh. cat., Metropolitan Museum of Art, New York), New Haven and London: Yale University Press, 2009.

Amabile, Luigi: *Due artisti ed uno scienziato Gian Bologna, Jacomo Swanenburgh e Marco Aurelio Severino nel Sto. Officio Napoletano*, Naples: Real Università, 1890.

Amadio, Sonia: "Per una prima ricognizione di dipinti di Nicolas Poussin: Regesto di documenti di collezioni romane tra Seicento e primo Settecento," in *Nicolas Poussin: I primi anni romani* (exh. cat., Palazzo delle Esposizioni, Rome, 1998–99), Milan: Electa, 1998, pp. 144–53.

Amadio, Sonia: "Demografia artistica: Ricerche negli stati delle anime, 1: Artisti famosi e nomi senza opere nella parrocchia dei Sant'Andrea delle Fratte," in *Arte e immagine del papato Borghese (1605–1621)*, ed. Bruno Toscano, San Casciano Val di Pesa: Libro Co. Italia, 2005, pp. 17–31.

Andretta, Stefano: *La repubblica inquieta: Venezia nel Seicento tra Italia ed Europa*, Rome: Carocci, 2000.

Andrews, Keith: "The Elsheimer Inventory and Other Documents," *The Burlington Magazine*, CXIV, 1972, pp. 594–600.

Andrews, Keith: *Adam Elsheimer: Paintings-Drawings-Prints*, New York: Phaidon and Rizzoli, 1977.

Anelli, Luciano: *Pietro Bellotti 1625–1700*, Brescia: La Valsabbina, 1996.

Angelozzi, Giancarlo: "Nobili, mercanti, dottori, cavalieri, artigiani: Stratificazione sociale e ideologia a Bologna nei secoli XVII e XVIII," in *Storia illustrata di Bologna II*, ed. W. Tega, Milan: 1989, pp. 41–60.

Angiolini, F.: "Accumulazione della ricchezza e affermazione sociale nella Toscana medicea," in Guarducci, 1990, pp. 611–32.

Anon., *Questo si è il catalogo de tutte le principal et più honorate cortigiane di Venetia, il nome loro et il nome delle loro pieze, et le stantie ove loro abitano, et di più ancor si narra la contrata ove sono le loro stantie, et etiam il numero de li dinari che hanno da pagar quelli gentilhomeni che desiderano entrar nella sua gratia*, Venice: Hieronimo Calepin, 1566.

Anselmi, Alessandra: *Il diario del viaggio in Spagna del Cardinale Francesco Barberini scritto da Cassiano dal Pozzo*, Madrid: Doce Calles, 2004.

Antinori, Aloisio: "I dipinti murali degli altari di San Crisogono per Scipione Borghese: Giovanni Battista Mercati, Bernardino Parasole, Ippolito Provenzale," in *Arte e immagine del papato Borghese (1605–1621)*, ed. Bruno Toscano, San Casciano Val di Pesa: Libro Co. Italia, 2005, pp. 91–105.

Arese, Franco: "Una quadreria milanese della fine del Seicento," *Arte Lombarda*, XII, 1967, pp. 127–42.

Arfelli, Adriana: "'Bologna perlustrata' di A. P. Masini e l''aggiunta' del 1690," *L'Archiginnasio*, LII, 1957, pp. 187–237.

L'Ariccia del Bernini (exh. cat., Palazzo Chigi, Ariccia), Rome: De Luca, 1998.

Armenini, Giovan Battista: *De' veri precetti della pittura*, Ravenna: Francesco Tebaldini, 1587 (critical edition, ed. Marina Gorreri, Turin: G. Einaudi, 1988).

L'arte per i papi e per i principi nella campagna romana: Grande pittura del '600 e del '700 (exh. cat., Palazzo Venezia, Rome), Rome: Quasar, 1990.

Artioli, Nerio and Elio Monducci: *Gli affreschi della Ghiara in Reggio Emilia*, Milan: Cinisello Balsamo: Arti Grafiche Amilcare Pizzi, 1970.

Aspetti e cause della decadenza economica veneziana nel secolo XVII: Atti del Convegno 21 giugno–2 luglio 1957, Venezia, Isola di San Giorgio Maggiore, Venice and Rome: Istituto per la collaborazione culturale, 1961.

Assini, Alfonso: "Gli atti del processo del 1625: Un nuovo documento," in *Bernardo Strozzi: Genova 1581/82–Venezia 1644* (exh. cat., Palazzo Ducale, Genoa), ed. Ezia Gavazza, Giovanna Nepi Sciré, and Giovanna Rotondi Terminiello, Milan: Electa, 1995, pp. 365–72.

Assini, Alfonso: "Le fonti d'archivio per la storia del collezionismo," in *L'Età di Rubens: Dimore, committenti e collezionisti genovesi* (exh. cat., Palazzo Ducale, Palazzo Rosso, and Palazzo Spinola, Genoa), ed. Piero Boccardo, Milan: Skira, 2004, pp. 147–57.

Astarita, Tommaso: *The Continuity of Feudal Power: The Caracciolo di Brienza in Spanish Naples*, Cambridge: Cambridge University Press, 1992.

Baccheschi, Edi and Lilli Ghio: *Antonio Balestra*, Bergamo: Poligrafiche Bolis, 1989.

Baglione, Giovanni: *Le vite de' pittori, scultori et architetti dal Pontificato di Gregorio XIII del 1572 in fino a' tempi di Papa Urbano Ottavo nel 1642*, Rome: 1642 (facsimile, ed. Valerio Mariani, Rome: Calzone, 1935).

Bagni, Prisco: *Guercino a Piacenza: Gli affreschi della cupola della cattedrale*, Bologna: Nuova Alfa, 1983.

Bagni, Prisco: *Benedetto Gennari e la bottega del Guercino*, Bologna: Nuova Alfa, 1986.

Bailey, Gauvin Alexander: *Between Renaissance and Baroque: Jesuit Art in Rome, 1565–1610*, Toronto: University of Toronto Press, 2003a.

Bailey, Gauvin Alexander: "Catholic Reform and Bernardino Poccetti's Chiostro dei Morti at the Church of SS Annunziata in Florence," *Apollo*, CLVIII, September 2003b, pp. 23–31.

Baldi, Camillo: "Descritione della città, territorio, qualità, costumi e forma del Governo e del popolo di Bologna, Bologna 1605, manoscritto," in M. Fanti, "Le classi sociali e il governo di Bologna all'inizio del XVII secolo in un'opera inedita di Camillo Baldi," *Strenna storica bolognese*, XI, 1961, pp. 133–79.

Baldinucci, Filippo: *Vocabolario toscano dell'arte del disegno*, Florence: Santi Franchi, 1681.

Baldinucci, Filippo: *Notizie de' professori del disegno da Cimabue in qua*, Florence: Santi Franchi, 1681–1728 (ed. Francesco Ranalli, Florence: Battelli, 1845–47; reprint, ed. Paola Barocchi, Florence: SPES, 1974–75).

Baldinucci, Francesco Saverio: *Vite di artisti dei secoli XVII–XVIII: Prima edizione integrale del Codice Palatino 565*, ed. Anna Matteoli, Rome: De Luca, 1975.

Baldissin Molin, G: "Le 'Postille' di Bartolomeo Campagnola alle 'Vite' di Bartolomeo Dal Pozzo," *Bollettino del Museo Civico di Padova*, LXXXI, 1992, pp. 147–74.

Bambach, Carmen: *Drawing and Painting in the Italian Renaissance Workshop: Theory and Practice, 1300–1600*, Cambridge: Cambridge University Press, 1999.

Banchi pubblici, banchi privati e monti di pietà nell'Europa pre-industriale: Atti del Convegno, Genova, 1–6 ottobre 1990, Genoa: Società ligure di storia patria, 1990.

Banchini, Roberto: "Il Casino di Giovanni Lanfranco 'ne' Monti di Bravetta': Il contesto e l'architettura, prime valutazioni," *Bollettino d'arte*, XCII, no. 140, 2007, pp. 149–58.

Banti, Anna: *Giovanni da San Giovanni pittore della contraddizione*, Florence: Sansoni, 1977.

Banzato, Davide and Pier Luigi Fantelli (eds.): *Pietro Damini 1592–1631* (exh. cat., Palazzo della Ragione, Padua), Milan: Electa, 1993.

Baracchi Giovanardi, Orianna: "Arte alla corte di Francesco I," *Atti e memorie: Deputazione di storia patria per le antiche provincie modenesi*, XX, 1998, pp. 120–53.

Barbolani di Montauto, Novella: *Pandolfo Reschi*, Florence: Edifir, 1996.

Barbone Pugliese, Nuccia: "A proposito di una 'Salita al Calvario' di Domenico Tintoretto in Puglia," *Arte veneta*, XLVIII, 1996, pp. 97–105.

Barcham, William L.: *Grand in Design: The Life and Career of Federico Cornaro, Prince of the Church, Patriarch of Venice and Patron of the Arts*, Venice: Istituto Veneto di Scienze, Lettere ed Arti, 2001.

Barea Toscan, Francesca: "Pietro Donà committente d'artisti nel Castello di Montegalda," *Arte veneta*, LIII, 1998, pp. 168–76.

Barocchi, Paola (ed.): *Trattati d'arte del Cinquecento fra manierismo e controriforma*, Bari: G. Laterza, 1960.

Barocchi, Paola (ed.): *Scritti d'arte del Cinquecento*, Milan and Naples: Riccardo Ricciardi, 1971.

Barocchi, Paola (ed.): *Pittura e scultura nel Cinquecento: Benedetto Varchi, Vincenzio Borghini*, Livorno: Sillabe, 1998.

Barocchi, Paola and Giovanna Gaeta Bertelà (eds.): *Il Cardinale Carlo Maria Maddalena, Don Lorenzo, Ferdinando II, Vittoria della Rovere 1621–1666*, Florence: SPES, 2005.

Barolsky, Paul: *Why Mona Lisa Smiles and Other Tales by Vasari*, University Park, PA: Pennsylvania State University Press, 1991.

Barsanti, Anna: "Una vita inedita di Francesco Furini," *Paragone*, XXV, no. 289, 1974a, pp. 67–87.

Barsanti, Anna: "Vita di Francesco Furini," *Paragone*, XXV, no. 291, 1974b, pp. 79–99.

Barsanti, Anna and Roberto Contini (eds.): *Cecco Bravo pittore senza regola, Firenze 1601–Innsbruck 1661* (exh. cat., Casa Buonarroti, Florence), Milan: Electa, 1999.

Barzazi, Antonella: "Documenti sulla protezione accordata dalla Serenissima Signoria a Bernardo Strozzi: Il contributo di Fra Fulgenzio Micanzio," *Atti dell'Istituto Veneto di Scienze, Lettere ed Arti*, CXL, 1981–82, pp. 45–63.

Barzazi, Antonella: *I consulti di Fulgenzio Micanzio: Inventari e regestri*, Pisa: Giardini, 1986.

Bassani, Riccardo and Fiora Bellini: "La casa, le 'robbe', lo studio del Caravaggio a Roma: Due documenti inediti del 1603 e del 1605," *Prospettiva*, no. 71, 1993, pp. 68–76.

Bassi, Elena: *La Regia Accademia di Belle Arti di Venezia*, Florence: Le Monnier, 1941.

Battaglia, Roberto: *La cattedra berniniana di San Pietro*, Rome: Reale Istituto di Studi Romani, 1943.

Bauer, Linda Freeman: "A Letter by Barocci and the Tracing of Finished Paintings," *The Burlington Magazine*, CXXVIII, 1986, pp. 355–57.

Bauer, Linda Freeman: "Oil Sketches, Unfinished Paintings, and the Inventories of Artists' Estates," in *Light on the Eternal City: Observations and Discoveries in the Art and Architecture of Rome*, ed. Hellmut Hager and Susan C. Scott Munshower (Papers in Art History from The Pennsylvania State University, II), University Park, PA: Pennsylvania State University Press, 1987, pp. 93–107.

Bauer, Linda and George Bauer: "Van Dyck's Club," *Zeitschrift für Kunstgeschichte*, LXXI, 2008, pp. 259–71.

Beal, Mary: *A Study of Richard Symonds: His Italian Notebooks and their Relevance to Seventeenth Century Painting Techniques* (Ph.D. diss., Courtauld Institute of Art, 1978), Ann Arbor: U.M.I., 1980.

Beaven, Lisa: "Cardinal Camillo Massimi (1620–1677) as a Collector of Landscape Paintings: The Evidence of the 1677 Inventory," *Journal of the History of Collections*, XV, 2003, pp. 19–29.

Bell, Janis C.: "The Date of Antonino Barbalonga's God the Father Appearing to Saints Gaetano and Andrea Avellino," *Source*, VII, 1988, no. 2, pp. 17–19.

Bellavitis, Anna: "In fabbrica e in casa: Il lavoro femminile nelle 'conterie' a Venezia," in *Perle e impiraperle: Un lavoro di donne a Venezia tra '800 e '900*, Venice: Arsenale, 1990, pp. 9–21.

Bellavitis, Anna: "Le travail des femmes dans les contrats de la Giustizia Vecchia, à Venise, au XVIe siècle," in *La famille, les femmes, le quotidien: Textes offerts à Christiane Klapisch-Zuber*, ed. I. Chabot, J. Hayez, and D. Lett, Paris: Publications de la Sorbonne, 2006, pp. 181–95.

Bellavitis, Anna: *Famille, genre et transmission à Venise au XVIe siècle*, Rome: École française de Rome, 2008.

Bellesi, Sandro: "Cappella di San Bernardo di Chiaravalle in San Frediano in Cestello," in *Cappelle barocche a Firenze*, ed. Mina Gregori, Cinisello Balsamo: Silvana Editoriale, 1990, pp. 199–220.

Bellesi, Sandro: "Una vita inedita di Pier Dandini," *Rivista d'arte*, XLIII, 1992, pp. 89–188.

Bellettini, Athos: *La popolazione di Bologna dal secolo XV all'unificazione italiana*, Bologna: Zanichelli, 1961.

Bellori, Giovan Pietro: *Le vite de' pittori, scultori et architetti moderni*, Rome: Mascardi, 1672 (critical edition, ed. Evelina Borea, Turin: Einaudi, 1976).

Bellori, Giovan Pietro: *The Lives of the Modern Painters, Sculptors and Architects*, trans. Alice Sedgwick Wohl, notes Hellmut Wohl, introduction Tomasso Montanari, Cambridge: Cambridge University Press, 2005.

Beloch, G.: "La popolazione di Venezia nei secoli XVI e XVII," *Nuovo Archivio Veneto*, II, 1902, pp. 5–49.

Beltrami, Daniele: *Storia della popolazione di Venezia dalla fine del secolo XVI alla caduta della repubblica*, Padua: CEDAM, 1954.

Beltrami, Daniele: *Forze di lavoro e proprietà fondiarie nelle campagne venete dei secoli 17 e 18: La penetrazione economica dei veneziani in terraferma*, Venice: Istituto per la collaborazione culturale, 1966.

Benassai, Silvia: "Il collezionismo dei Bardi: Nuove acquisizioni per Felice Ficherelli," *Paragone*, LIII, no. 627, 2002, pp. 33–51.

Benati, Daniele: *Alessandro Tiarini: L'opera pittorica completa e i disegni*, Milan: Federico Motta, 2001.

Benati, Daniele and Lucia Peruzzi: *L'amorevole maniera: Ludovico Lana e la pittura emiliana del primo Seicento*, Cinisello Balsamo: Silvana, 2003.

Benati, Daniele and Marco Bona Castellotti (eds.): *Guido Cagnacci* (exh. cat., Museo della Città, Rimini), Milan: Electa, 1993.

Beneš, Mirka: "Claude Lorrain's Pendant Landscapes of 1646–50 for Camillo Pamphilj, Nephew of Pope Innocent X: Classicism, Architecture, and Gardens as Contexts for the Artist's Roman Patronage," *Storia dell'arte*, no. 112, 2005, pp. 37–60.

Benfante, Filippo: "Le proprietà urbane dell'ospedale di Santa Maria Nuova (Firenze XVI–XVIII secolo)," *Quaderni storici*, XXXVIII, 2003, pp. 325–44.

Benigno, Francesco: *Specchi della rivoluzione: Conflitto e identità politica nell'Europa moderna*, Rome: Donzelli, 1999.

Benocci, Carla: *Paolo Giordano II Orsini nei ritratti di Bernini, Boselli, Leoni e Kornmann*, Rome: De Luca, 2006.

Bentini, Jadranka et al. (eds.): *Pinacoteca nazionale di Bologna: Catalogo generale, 2: Da Raffaello ai Carracci*, Venice: Marsilio, 2006.

Bentini, Jadranka et al. (eds.): *Pinacoteca nazionale di Bologna: Catalogo generale, 3: Guido Reni e il Seicento*, Venice: Marsilio, 2008.

Benussi, Paola: "Appendice documentaria," in *Il collezionismo d'arte a Venezia: Il Seicento*, ed. Linda Borean and Stefania Mason, Venice: Marsilio, 2007, pp. 335–83.

Bernini, Giovanni-Pietro: *Giovanni Lanfranco (1582–1647)*, Parma: Centro Studi della Val Baganza and Associazione "Communità di Terenzo," 1982.

Berra, Giacomo: "La collezione d'arte del canonico e pittore Flaminio Pasqualini nella Milano del seicento," *Paragone*, LIX, no. 695, 2008, pp. 67–110.

Bershad, David L.: "The Newly Discovered Testament and Inventories of Carlo Maratti and his Wife Francesca," *Antologia di Belle Arti*, 1985, no. 25–26, pp. 65–84.

Bertelli, Sergio: "Palazzo Pitti dai Medici ai Savoia," in *La Corte di Toscana dai Medici ai Lorena* (Atti delle giornate di studio, Archivio di Stato e Palazzo Pitti, 15–16 dicembre 1997), ed. Anna Bellinazzi and Alessandra Contini, Rome: Ministero per i beni e le attività culturali, Direzione Generale per gli Archivi, 2002, pp. 11–109.

Bertelli, Sergio and Renato Pasta (eds.): *Vivere a Pitti: Una reggia dai Medici ai Savoia*, Florence: Olschki, 2003.

Bertolotti, Antonio: *Artisti belgi ed olandesi a Roma nei secoli XVI e XVII*, Florence: Gazzetta d'Italia, 1880.

Bertolotti, Antonio: *Artisti lombardi a Roma nei secoli XV, XVI e XVII*, Milan: Hoepli, 1881a.

Bertolotti, Antonio: *Artisti urbinati in Roma prima del secolo XVIII*, Urbino: Righi, 1881b (reprint, Bologna: Forni, 1974).

Bertolotti, Antonio: *Artisti modenesi, parmensi e della Lunigiana in Roma nei secoli XV, XVI e XVII*, Modena: Vincenzi, 1882 (reprint, Bologna: Forni, 1977).

Bertolotti, Antonio: *Artisti veneti in Roma nei secoli XV, XVI e XVII*, Venice: A spese della Società, 1884.

Bertolotti, Antonio: *Artisti bolognesi, ferraresi ed alcuni altri del già stato pontificio in Roma nei secoli XV, XVI e XVII*, Bologna: Zanichelli, 1885.

Bertrand, Pascal-François (ed.): *Nicolas Tournier et la peinture caravagesque en Italie, en France et en Espagne*, Toulouse: Framespa-CNRS France méridionale et Espagne, 2003.

Berveglieri, Roberto: *Inventori stranieri a Venezia (1474–1788): Importazione di tecnologia e circolazione di tenici artigiani inventori: Repertorio*, Venice: Istituto Veneto di Scienze, Lettere ed Arti, 1995.

Betri, Maria Luisa and Alessandro Pastore, "Introduzione," in *Avvocati, medici, ingegneri: Alle origini delle professioni moderne*, ed. M. L. Betri and A. Pastore, Bologna: CLUEB, 1997, pp. 3–15.

Bettagno, Alessandro and Marina Magrini (eds.): *Lettere artistiche del Settecento veneziano*, Vicenza: Neri Pozza, 2002.

Betti, Paola: "Nuovi ritrovamenti per la Galleria Conti di Lucca," *Arte veneta*, LX, 2003, pp. 112–29.

Bevilacqua, Mario: "L'organizzazione dei cantieri pittorici sistini: Note sul rapporto tra botteghe e committenza," in *Roma di Sisto V*, ed. Maria Luisa Madonna, Rome: De Luca, 1993, pp. 35–46.

Biadego, Giuseppe: *Di Giambettino Cignaroli pittore veronese: Notizie e documenti*, Venice: R. Deputazione Veneta di Storia Patria, 1890.

Biagioli, Mario: *Galileo's Instruments of Credit: Telescopes, Images, Secrecy*, Chicago: University of Chicago Press, 2006.

Bianconi, Lorenzo and Thomas Walker: "Production, Consumption and Political Function of Seventeenth-Century Opera," *Early Music History*, IV, 1984, pp. 209–96.

Biasutti, Gugliemo: *I Libri 'De scossi, e spesi' del Cardinale Daniele Delfino ultimo Patriarca di Aquileia*, Udine: Agraf, 1957.

Bikker, Jonathan: "Drost's End and Loth's Beginnings in Venice," *The Burlington Magazine*, CXLIV, 2002, pp. 147–56.

Bikker, Jonathan: *Willem Drost (1633–1659): A Rembrandt Pupil in Amsterdam and Venice*, New Haven and London: Yale University Press, 2005.

Binion, Alice: "The 'Collegio dei Pittori' in Venice," *L'Arte*, III, no. 11–12, 1970, pp. 92–101.

Binion, Alice: *La galleria scomparsa del maresciallo von der Schulenburg: Un mecenate nella Venezia del Settecento*, Milan: Electa, 1990.

Binotto Soragni, Margaret: "I dipinti della chiesa dei Santi Filippo e Giacomo di Vicenza," *Saggi e memorie di storia dell'arte*, XII, 1980, pp. 79–109.

Binotto Soragni, Margaret: "Committenza, artisti, botteghe a Vicenza nei secoli XVII–XIX: Problemi interpretativi di un itinerario archivistico," *Arte veneta*, XXXVII, 1983, pp. 261–71.

Bissell, R. Ward: *Orazio Gentileschi and the Poetic Tradition in Caravaggesque Painting*, University Park, PA: Pennsylvania State University Press, 1981.

Bissell, R. Ward: *Artemisia Gentileschi and the Authority of Art*, University Park, PA: Pennsylvania State University Press, 1999.

Blunt, Anthony: "A Poussin–Castiglione Problem: Classicism and the Picturesque in 17th Century Rome," *Journal of the Warburg and Courtauld Institutes*, III, 1939–40, pp. 142–47.

Blunt, Anthony: *Guide to Baroque Rome*, New York: Harper and Row, 1982.

Boccardo, Piero: "Il collezionismo della classe dirigente genovese nel Seicento," in *Geografia del collezionismo: Italia e Francia tra il XVI e il XVIII secolo*, ed. Olivier Bonfait et al., Rome: École Française de Rome, 2001, pp. 129–43.

Boccardo, Piero (ed.): *L'Età di Rubens: Dimore, committenti e collezionisti genovesi* (exh. cat., Palazzo Ducale, Palazzo Rosso, and Palazzo Spinola, Genoa), Milan: Skira, 2004.

Boccazzi Mazza, Barbara: "Da Vincenzo da Canal a Francesco Algarotti: Itinerario Critico," *Studi Veneziani*, L, 2005, pp. 157–69.

Bocchi, Francesco and Giovanni Cinelli: *Le bellezze della città di Firenze*, Florence: Gio. Gugliantini, 1677.

Bocchi, Gianluca and Ulisse Bocchi (eds.): *Pittori di natura morta a Roma: Artisti stranieri 1630–1750 / Still Life Painters in Rome: Foreign Artists 1630–1750*, Viadana: Arti Grafiche Castello, 2004.

Bocchi, Gianluca and Ulisse Bocchi (eds.): *Pittori di natura morta a Roma: Artisti italiani 1630–1750 / Still Life Painters in Rome: Italian Artists 1630–1750*, Viadana: Arti Grafiche Castello, 2005.

Bodart, Didier: "'La descrizione del Rione di Campo Marzio di Roma': Artistes à Rome durant la peste de 1656," *Bulletin de l'Institut historique belge de Rome*, XXXVIII, 1967, pp. 475–531.

Bodart, Didier: "Louis Finson (Bruges, 1585–Amsterdam, 1617) et Naples," *Les Cahiers d'Histoire de l'Art*, no. 5, 2007, pp. 26–35.

Bodmer, Heinrich: *Ludovico Carracci*, Burg bei Magdeburg: A. Hopfer, 1939.

Bohn, Babette: "Female Self-Portraiture in Early Modern Bologna," *Renaissance Studies*, XVIII, 2004a, pp. 239–86.

Bohn, Babette: "Il fenomeno della firma: Elisabetta Sirani e le firme dei pittori a Bologna," in *Elisabetta Sirani: Pittrice eroina, 1638–1665* (exh. cat., Museo Civico Archeologico, Bologna), ed. Jadranka Bentini and Vera Fortunati, Bologna: Compositori, 2004b, pp. 107–17.

Boisclair, Marie-Nicole: *Gaspard Dughet*, Paris: Arthéna, 1986.

Bok, Marten Jan: "Pricing the Unpriced: How Dutch Seventeenth-Century Painters Determined the Selling Price of their Work," in North and Ormrod, 1998, pp. 103–11.

Bologna, Ferdinando: "Per Giovanni Ricca: Con qualche aggiunta a Enrico Fiammingo, al Monrealese e a Gian Giacomo Manecchia," in *Ricerche sul '600 napoletano, 1994–1995: Scritti in memoria di Raffaello Causa*, Naples: Electa, 1996, pp. 9–37.

Bologna, Ferdinando and Raffaello Causa (eds.): *Mostra didattica di Carlo Sellitto, primo caravaggesco napoletano* (exh. cat., Museo di Capodimonte, Naples), Naples: Museo di Capodimonte, 1977.

Bonfait, Olivier: "Il pubblico del Guercino: Ricerche sul mercato dell'arte nel XVII secolo a Bologna," *Storia dell'arte*, no. 68, 1990, pp. 71–94.

Bonfait, Olivier: "Le livre de comptes, la mémoire et le monument: La carrière des artistes à Bologne durant l'époque moderne," *Annales: Economies, sociétés, civilisations*, VI, 1993, pp. 1,497–518.

Bonfait, Olivier: *Les tableaux et les pinceaux: La naissance de l'école bolonaise (1680–1780)*, Rome: École française de Rome, 2000.

Bonfait, Olivier et al. (eds.): *Geografia del collezionismo: Italia e Francia tra il XVI e il XVIII secolo*, Rome: École Française de Rome, 2001.

Bonfait, Olivier (ed.): *L'Idéal classique: Les échanges artistiques entre Rome et Paris au temps de Bellori (1640–1700)*, Paris: Somogy, 2002a.

Bonfait Olivier: "Le prix de la peinture à Bologne aux XVII et XVIII siècles," in *Economia e Arte secc. XIII–XVIII: Atti della Trentatreesima Settimana di Studi, 30 aprile–4 maggio 2001*, ed. Simonetta Cavaciocchi, Florence: Le Monnier, 2002b, pp. 837–47.

Bonfait, Olivier: " 'Molti franzesi e fiammenghi che vanno e vengono non li si puol dar regola': Mobilité géographique, mode d'habitat et innovation artistique dans la Rome de Nicolas Tournier," in *Nicolas Tournier et la peinture caravagesque en Italie, en France et en Espagne*, ed. Pascal-François Bertrand and Stéphanie Trouvé, Toulouse: CNRS, 2003, pp. 65–75.

Bonfiglio Dosio, Giorgetta: "Un episodio di commercio di quadri a Venezia nella seconda metà del Seicento," in *Scritti in onore di Gaetano Panazza*, Brescia: Ateneo di Brescia, 1994, pp. 285–88.

Bordignon Favero, Elia: "Il processo per furto e falso contro G. B. Volpato pittore del '600," *Atti e Memorie dell'Accademia Patavina di Scienze, Lettere ed Arti*, XCI, 1978–79, pp. 129–93.

Bordignon Favero, Elia: "La bottega di Pietro Vecchia a Venezia," *Atti e Memorie dell'Accademia Patavina di Scienze, Lettere ed Arti*, XCVII, 1984–85, pp. 115–33.

Bordignon Favero, Elia: "L'attività tarda di Jacopo Bassano: Un documento inedito," *Arte veneta*, XLIV, 1993, pp. 66–68.

Bordignon Favero, Elia: *Giovanni Battista Volpato: Critico e pittore*, Treviso: De Longhi, 1994.

Borea, Evelina: "Dipinti alla Petraia per don Lorenzo de' Medici: Stefano della Bella, Vincenzo Mannozzi, il Volterrano, i Dandini e altri," *Prospettiva*, no. 2, 1975, pp. 24–39.

Borea, Evelina: "Gian Domenico Cerrini: Opere e documenti," *Prospettiva*, no. 12, 1978, pp. 4–25.

Borea, Evelina, Anna Maria Petrioli Tofani, and Karla Langedijk (eds.): *La quadreria di Don Lorenzo de' Medici* (exh. cat., Villa Medicea, Poggio a Caiano) Florence: Centro Di, 1977.

Borean, Linda: "Appunti per una storia del collezionismo a Venezia nel Seicento: La pinacoteca di Lorenzo Dolfin," *Studi Veneziani*, XXXVIII, 1999, pp. 259–91.

Borean, Linda: *La quadreria di Agostino e Giovan Donato Correggio nel collezionismo veneziano del Seicento*, Udine: Forum, 2000.

Borean, Linda: "Prefazione," in *Figure di collezionisti a Venezia tra Cinque e Seicento*, ed. Linda Borean and Stefania Mason, Udine: Forum, 2002a, pp. 7–10.

Borean, Linda: "Nel '700 una doppia lotteria polverizza una collezione: e un Raffaello è a New York," *VENEZIALTROVE*, I, 2002b, pp. 97–115.

Borean, Linda: "Mercanti collezionisti a Venezia nel Seicento," *Schifanoia*, XXIV–XXV, 2003, pp. 187–203.

Borean, Linda: "Documentation," in *Tintoretto* (exh. cat., National Gallery, London), ed. M. Falomir, Rome: Holberton, 2007a, pp. 417–50.

Borean, Linda: "Il collezionismo e la fortuna dei generi," in *Il collezionismo d'arte a Venezia: Il Seicento*, ed. Linda Borean and Stefania Mason, Venice: Marsilio, 2007b, pp. 63–83.

Borean, Linda and Isabella Cecchini: "Microstorie d'affari e di quadri: I Lumaga tra Venezia e Napoli," in *Il collezionismo d'arte a Venezia: Il Seicento*, ed. Linda Borean and Stefania Mason, Venice: Marsilio, 2007, pp. 159–232.

Borean, Linda and Stefania Mason (eds.): *Figure di collezionisti a Venezia tra Cinque e Seicento*, Udine: Forum, 2002.

Borean, Linda and Stefania Mason (eds.): *Il collezionismo d'arte a Venezia: Il Seicento*, Venice: Marsilio, 2007.

Borelli, Giorgio: "Tra Seicento e Settecento," in *Storia di Verona: Caratteri, aspetti, momenti*, Vicenza: N. Pozza, 2002, pp. 195–225.

Borenius, Tancred: *The Picture Gallery of Andrea Vendramin*, London: Medici Society, 1923.

Borghini, Gabriele: "Giacinto Brandi: Un documento ed alcuni dipinti inediti," *Commentari*, XXIII, 1972, pp. 385–93.

Borghini, Raffaello: *Il Riposo*, Florence: Giorgio Marescotti, 1584.

Borghini, Vincenzo: "Selva di notizie," in *Pittura e scultura nel Cinquecento: Benedetto Varchi, Vincenzio Borghini*, ed. Paola Barocchi, Livorno: Sillabe, 1998.

Borrelli, Gennaro: "La borghesia napoletana della seconda metà del Seicento e la sua influenza sull'evoluzione del gusto da barocco a rococò: Parte terza," in *Ricerche sul '600 napoletano*, Milan: L&T, 1988, pp. 7–50.

Borroni Salvadori, Fabia: "Committenti scontenti, artisti litigiosi nella Firenze del Settecento," *Mitteilungen des Kunsthistorischen Institutes in Florenz*, XXIX, 1985, pp. 129–58.

Borsi, Franco et al.: *Palazzo del Quirinale*, Rome: Editalia, 1974.

Boschini, Marco: *La carta del navegar pitoresco: Ed. critica con la "Breve Instruzione" premessa alle "Ricche Minere della pittura veneziana"* (critical edition, ed. Anna Pallucchini, Venice and Rome: Istituto per la collaborazione culturale, 1966; *Carta* first published 1660, *Ricche Minere* first published 1674).

Boselli, Camillo: *Nuove fonti per la storia dell'arte: L'Archivio dei Conti Gambara presso la Civica Biblioteca Queriniana di Brescia, I: Il Carteggio* (Coll. Memorie. Istituto Veneto di Scienze, Lettere ed Arti, XXXV, fasc. 1), Venice: Istituto Veneto di Scienze, Lettere ed Arti, 1971.

Bottacin, Francesca: "Tra pittura e poesia: Tiberio Tinelli e l'Accademia degli Incogniti," *Studi Veneziani*, XLI, 2001, pp. 247–58.

Bottari, Giovanni Gaetano and Stefano Ticozzi: *Raccolta di lettere sulla pittura, scultura ed architettura*, Milan: G. Silvestri, 1822.

Botteri Ottaviani, Marina (ed.): *Pietro Ricchi 1606–1675* (exh. cat., Museo Civico, Riva del Garda), Milan: Skira, 1996.

Bousquet, Jacques: *Recherches sur le séjour des peintres français à Rome au XVIIème siècle*, Montpellier: A.L.P.H.A., 1980.

Boutier, Jean and Maria Pia Paoli: "Letterati cittadini e principi filosofi: I milieux intellettuali fiorentini tra Cinque e Settecento," in *Naples, Rome, Florence: Une histoire comparée des milieux intellectuels italiens (XVIIe–XVIIIe siècles)*, ed. Jean Boutier, Brigitte Marin, and Antonella Romano, Rome: École Française de Rome, 2005, pp. 331–403.

Boutier, Jean, Brigitte Marin, and Antonella Romano (eds.): *Naples, Rome, Florence: Une histoire comparée des milieux intellectuels italiens (XVIIe–XVIIIe siècles)*, Rome: École Française de Rome, 2005.

Bowron, Edgar Peters: "Painters and Painting in Settecento Rome," in *Art in Rome in the Eighteenth Century* (exh. cat., Philadelphia Museum of Art), ed. Edgar Peters Bowron and Joseph J. Rishel, Philadelphia: Philadelphia Museum of Art, 2000, pp. 295–303.

Bowron, Edgar Peters and Joseph J. Rishel (eds.): *Art in Rome in the Eighteenth Century* (exh. cat., Philadelphia Museum of Art), Philadelphia: Philadelphia Museum of Art, 2000.

Bratti, Ricciotti: "Notizie d'arte e di artisti," *Archivio Veneto*, XXX, 1915, pp. 435–85.

Braudel, Fernand: *The Mediterranean and the Mediterranean World in the Age of Philip II*, trans. Siân Reynolds, New York: Harper and Row, 1975.

Braudel, Fernand and Frank Spooner: "Prices in Europe from 1450 to 1750," in *The Cambridge Economic History of Europe, Vol. IV: The Economy of Expanding Europe in the Sixteenth and Seventeenth Centuries*, ed. E. E. Rich and C. H. Wilson, Cambridge: Cambridge University Press, 1967, pp. 374–486.

Bréjon de Lavergnée, Arnauld: "Nouvelles toiles d'Andrea di Lione: Essai de catalogue," in *Scritti di storia dell'arte in onore di Federico Zeri*, ed. Mauro Natale, Milan: Electa, 1984, II, pp. 656–80.

Brenzoni, Raffaello: *Dizionario di artisti veneti: Pittori, scultori, architetti, etc. dal XIII al XVIII secolo*, Florence: Olschki, 1972.

Brewer, John: "Positioning the Market: Art, Goods and Commodities in Early Modern Europe," in *Economia e Arte secc. XIII–XVIII: Atti della Trentatreesima Settimana di Studi, 30 aprile–4 maggio 2001*, ed. Simonetta Cavaciocchi, Florence: Le Monnier, 2002, pp. 139–48.

Briganti, Giuliano: *Pietro da Cortona*, Florence: Sansoni, 1962.

Briganti, Giuliano, Laura Laureati, and Ludovica Trezzani: *The Bamboccianti*, trans. Robert Erich Wolf, Rome: Ugo Bozzi, 1983.

Briganti, Giuliano, Laura Laureati, and Ludovica Trezzani: *Pittura antica: La decorazione murale* (Il patrimonio artistico del Quirinale), Milan: Electa, 1993.

Brogi, Alessandro: "Un Guercino delgi anni estremi," *Paragone*, XLV, no. 527, 1994, pp. 61–64.

Brogi, Alessandro: *Ludovico Carracci*, Ozzano Emilia: Tipoarte, 2001.

Brooks, Julian: *Taddeo and Federico Zuccaro: Artist-Brothers in Renaissance Rome* (exh. cat., The J. Paul Getty Museum, with essays by P. M. Lukehart, C. Strunck, and R. Williams), Los Angeles: The J. Paul Getty Museum, 2007.

Brown, Beverly Louise: "The Black Wings of Envy: Competition, Rivalry and Paragone," in *The Genius of Rome* (exh. cat., Royal Academy of Arts, London, and Palazzo Venezia, Rome), ed. Beverly Louise Brown, London: Royal Academy of Arts, 2001a, pp. 250–73.

Brown, Beverly Louise (ed.): *The Genius of Rome* (exh. cat., Royal Academy of Arts, London, and Palazzo Venezia, Rome), London: Royal Academy of Arts, 2001b.

Brown, Jonathan: *Kings and Connoisseurs: Collecting Art in Seventeenth-Century Europe*, New Haven and London: Yale University Press, 1995.

Brown, Jonathan and John Elliott (eds.): *The Sale of the Century: Artistic Relations between Spain and Great Britain, 1604–1625*, New Haven and London: Yale University Press, 2002.

Brown, Judith: "Prosperity or Hard Times in Renaissance Italy?" *Renaissance Quarterly*, XLII, 1989, pp. 761–80.

Brugnoli, Maria Vittoria: "Gli affreschi dell'Albani e del Domenichino nel Palazzo di Bassano di Sutri," *Bollettino d'Arte*, XLII, 1957, pp. 266–77.

Burke, Jill and Michael Bury (eds.): *Art and Identity in Early Modern Rome*, Aldershot: Ashgate, 2008.

Burke, Marcus B. and Peter Cherry: *Collections of Paintings in Madrid, 1601–1755* (Documents for the History of Collecting, The Provenance Index of the Getty Information Institute), Los Angeles: The J. Paul Getty Trust, 1997.

Bury, Michael: "Infringing Privileges and Copying in Rome, c. 1600," *Print Quarterly*, XXII, 2005, pp. 133–38.

Buscaroli Fabbri, Beatrice: "Carlo Cignani a Monaco, nuovi documenti," *Paragone*, XL, no. 475, 1989, pp. 105–14.

Buscaroli Fabbri, Beatrice: *Carlo Cignani: Affreschi, dipinti, disegni*, Padua: Nuova Alfa, 1991.

Büttner, Frank: "'All'usanza moderna ridotta': Gli interventi dei Riccardi," in *Il Palazzo Medici Riccardi di Firenze*, ed. Giovanni Cherubini and Giovanni Fanelli, Florence: Giunti, 1990, pp. 150–68.

Buvelot, Quentin: "Frans Van Mieris' Reputation," in *Frans Van Mieris 1635–1681* (exh. cat., Royal Picture Gallery Mauritshuis, The Hague, and National Gallery of Art, Washington, D.C.), Zwolle: Waanders, 2005, pp. 12–26.

Calabria, Antonio: *The Cost of Empire: The Finances of the Kingdom of Naples in the Time of Spanish Rule* (Cambridge Studies in Early Modern History), Cambridge: Cambridge University Press, 1991.

Cammarota, Gian Piero: "I Carracci e le Accademie," in *Bologna 1584: Gli esordi dei Carracci e gli affreschi di Palazzo Fava* (exh. cat., Pinacoteca nazionale, Bologna), Bologna: Nuova Alfa, 1984, pp. 293–326.

Campbell, Malcolm: "Medici Patronage and the Baroque: A Reappraisal," *The Art Bulletin*, XLVIII, 1966, pp. 133–46.

Campbell, Malcolm: *Pietro da Cortona at the Pitti Palace: A Study of the Planetary Rooms and Related Projects*, Princeton: Princeton University Press, 1977.

Campori, Giuseppe: *Gli artisti italiani e stranieri negli stati estensi: Catalogo storico, corredato di documenti inediti*, Modena: R. D. Camera, 1855.

Campori, Giuseppe: *Raccolta di cataloghi ed inventarii inediti*, Modena: Vincenzi, 1870.

Canepari, E.: *Stare in "compagnia": Strategie di inurbamento e forme associative nella Roma del Seicento*, Soveria Mannelli: Rubbettino, 2007.

Caniato, Giovanni and Michela Dal Borgo: *Le arti edili a Venezia*, Rome: Edilstampa, 1990.

Cantaro, Maria Teresa: *Lavinia Fontana bolognese "pittora singolare" 1552–1614*, Milan: Jandi Sapi, 1989.

Capaccio, Giulio Cesare: *Il Forastiero, dialogi di Giulio Cesare Capaccio*, Naples: Giovan Domenico Roncagliolo, 1630 (revised edition, 1634).

Capitelli, Giovanna: "'Connoisseurship' al lavoro: La carriera di Niccolò Simonelli (1611–1671)," *Quaderni storici*, XXXIX, 2004, pp. 375–401.

Cappelletti, Francesca (ed.): *Decorazione e collezionismo a Roma nel Seicento: Vicende di artisti, committenti, mercanti*, Rome: Gangemi, 2003.

Cappelletti, Francesca: *Paul Bril*, Rome: Ugo Bozzi, 2005–6.

Cappelletti, Francesca and Laura Testa: *Il trattenimento di virtuosi: Le collezioni secentesche di quadri nei Palazzi Mattei di Roma*, Rome: Argos, 1994.

Caprara, Vittorio: "Una lettera inedita di Sebastiano Ricci," *Arte veneta*, XLII, 1988, pp. 162–63.

Caracciolo, Ambrogino: "Alcuni notizie sulla famiglia Francone e l'arredamento di una casa patrizia napoletana al principio del sec. XVIII," in *Studi in onore di Riccardo Filangieri*, vol. 3, Naples: L'Arte Tipografica, 1959, pp. 29–50.

Carboni, Mauro: *Il debito della città: Mercato del credito, fisco e società a Bologna fra Cinque e Seicento*, Bologna: Il Mulino, 1995.

Carboni, Mauro: *Le doti della "povertà": Famiglia, risparmio, previdenza: Il Monte del Matrimonio di Bologna (1583–1796)*, Bologna: Il Mulino, 1999.

Carderi, Benedetto: *S. Severo Maggiore in Napoli una chiesa da salvare: Note storiche ed archivistiche*, Teramo: Cattedra Cateriniana, 1971.

Cardi, Giovan Battista: "Vita di Lodovico Cigoli, [ante 1629]," in Filippo Baldinucci, *Notizie de' professori del disegno da Cimabue in qua*, ed. Francesco Ranalli, Florence: Battelli 1845–47 (reprint, ed. Paola Barocchi, Florence: SPES, 1974–75), vol. 7, pp. 40–64.

Cargnelutti, Liliana (ed.): *Giovanni da Udine: I libri dei conti*, Udine: Casamassima, 1987.

Caro, Annibale: *De le lettere familiari*, Venice: Manutio, 1574.

Caro, Annibale: *Lettere familiari*, ed. Aulo Greco, Florence: Le Monnier, 1957–61.

Casale, Gerardo: *Giovanna Garzoni: Insigne miniatrice 1600–1670* (with an essay by Paola Lanzara), Milan and Rome: Jandi Sapi, 1991.

Cassani, Silvia and Maria Sapio (eds.): *Caravaggio: The Final Years* (exh. cat., National Gallery, London), Naples: Electa, 2005.

Cassarino, Enrica: "Domenico Passignano e la Cappella delle Reliquie di S. Giovanni Gualberto," in Marchini and Micheletti, 1987, pp. 184–91, 355–56.

Causa, Raffaello: *L'eruzione del Vesuvio nel 1631, un dipinto di Micco Spadaro ed un poemetto di G. B. Bergazzano*, Naples: L'Arte Tipografica, 1956.

Causa, Raffaello et al. (eds.): *Civiltà del Seicento a Napoli* (exh. cat., Museo di Capodimonte and Museo Diego Aragona Pignatelli Cortes, Naples), Naples: Electa, 1984.

Causa, Stefano: *Battistello Caracciolo: L'opera completa*, Naples: Electa, 2000.

Cavaciocchi, Simonetta (ed.): *Economia e Arte secc. XIII–XVIII: Atti della Trentatreesima Settimana di Studi, 30 aprile–4 maggio 2001*, Florence: Le Monnier, 2002.

Cavalli, Gian Carlo: *Guido Reni*, Florence: Vallecchi, 1955.

Cavazzini, Patrizia: "Agostino Tassi and the Organization of his Workshop: Filippo Franchini, Angelo Caroselli, Claude Lorrain and the Others," *Storia dell'arte*, no. 91, 1997, pp. 401–31.

Cavazzini, Patrizia: *Palazzo Lancellotti ai Coronari*, Rome: Istituto Poligrafico e Zecca dello Stato, 1998.

Cavazzini, Patrizia: "Artemisia in Her Father's House," and "Appendix I: Documents Relating to the Trial of Agostino Tassi," in *Orazio and Artemisia Gentileschi* (exh. cat., Palazzo Venezia, Rome, Metropolitan Museum of Art, New York, and St. Louis Art Museum, St. Louis), ed. Keith Christiansen and Judith Mann, New York: Metropolitan Museum of Art and New Haven and London: Yale University Press, 2001, pp. 283–95, 432–44.

Cavazzini, Patrizia: "Towards a Chronology of Agostino Tassi," *The Burlington Magazine*, CXLIV, 2002, pp. 396–408.

Cavazzini, Patrizia: "La diffusione della pittura nella Roma di primo Seicento: Collezionisti ordinari e mercanti," *Quaderni storici*, XXXIX, 2004a, pp. 353–74.

Cavazzini, Patrizia: "Claude's Apprenticeship in Rome: The Market for Copies and the Invention of the Liber Veritatis," *Konsthistorisk Tidskrift*, LXXIII, 2004b, pp. 133–46.

Cavazzini, Patrizia (ed.): *Agostino Tassi (1578–1644): Un paesaggista tra immaginario e realtà* (exh. cat., Palazzo Venezia, Rome), Rome: Iride, 2008a.

Cavazzini, Patrizia: "Oltre la committenza: Commerci d'arte a Roma nel primo Seicento," *Paragone*, LIX, no. 82, 2008b, pp. 72–92.

Cavazzini, Patrizia: *Painting as Business in Early Seventeenth-Century Rome*, University Park, PA: Pennsylvania State University Press, 2008c.

Cecchetti, B. (ed.): *Documenti per servire alla Storia dell'Augusta Ducale Basilica di San Marco*, Venice: Ferdinando Ongania, 1886.

Cecchini, Isabella: *Quadri e commercio a Venezia durante il Seicento: Uno studio sul mercato dell'arte*, Venice: Marsilio, 2000.

Cecchini, Isabella: "Per un'analisi del mercato artistico a Venezia nel Settecento," in *Officina Veneziana: Maestri e Botteghe nella Venezia del Settecento* (exh. cat., Centro culturale Sant'Agostino, Crema), ed. Fabrizio Magani and Filippo Pedrocco, Milan: Skira, 2002, pp. 69–80.

Cecchini, Isabella: "'Fatte varie, et diverse esperienze per essitar esse Pitture': Prezzo e valori di stima: Breve analisi di un campione seicentesco a Venezia," in *Tra committenza e collezionismo: Studi sul mercato dell'arte nell'Italia settentrionale durante l'età moderna*, ed. Enrico Maria dal Pozzolo and Leonida Tedoldi, Vicenza: Terra ferma, 2003, pp. 123–36.

Cecchini, Isabella: "Il cantiere di Palazzo Ducale dopo l'incendio del 1574," *Storia di Venezia Rivista*, II, 2004, pp. 39–59.

Cecchini, Isabella: "Al servizio dei collezionisti: La professionalizzazione nel commercio di dipinti a Venezia in età moderna e il ruolo delle botteghe," in *Il collezionismo a Venezia e nel Veneto ai tempi della Serenissima*, ed. Bernard Aikema, Rosella Lauber, and Max Seidel, Venice: Marsilio, 2005, pp. 151–72.

Cecchini, Isabella: "Troublesome Business: Dealing in Venice, 1600–1750," in *Mapping Markets for Paintings in Europe, 1450–1750*, ed. Neil De Marchi and Hans J. Van Miegroet, Turnhout: Brepols, 2006, pp. 125–34.

Cecchini, Isabella: "I modi della circolazione dei dipinti," in *Il collezionismo d'arte a Venezia: Il Seicento*, ed. Linda Borean and Stefania Mason, Venice: Marsilio, 2007, pp. 141–66.

Cecchini, Isabella: "Collezionismo e mondo materiale," in *Il collezionismo d'arte a Venezia: Dalle origini al Cinquecento*, ed. Michel Hochmann, Rosella Lauber, and Stefania Mason, Venice: Marsilio, 2008, pp. 165–92.

Celano, Carlo: *Notizie del bello, dell'antico e del curioso della città di Napoli divise dall'autore in dieci giornate per guida e comodo dei viaggiatori*, Naples: G. Raillard, 1692 (reprint, ed. Atanasio Mozzillo et al., and reprint from the edition of 1856–60, ed. Giovan Battista Chiarini, Naples: Edizioni Scientifiche Italiane, 1974).

Cennini, Cennino: *The Craftsman's Handbook*, trans. Daniel V. Thompson, Jr., New York: Dover, 1954.

Cerasoli, F.: "Censimento della populazione di Roma dall'anno 1600 al 1739," *Studi e documenti di storia e diritto*, XII, 1891, pp. 169–99.

Cerutti, Simona: *Mestieri e privilegi: Nascita delle corporazioni a Torino, secoli XVII–XVIII*, Turin: Einaudi, 1992.

Cesareo, Giovanni Alfredo: *Poesie e lettere edite e inedite di Salvator Rosa*, Naples: R. Accademia di Archeologia, Lettere e Belle Arti, 1892.

Cevese, R.: "Altari del Sei e Settecento a Vicenza e nel suo territorio," in *Onus istud a Domino: Il Magistero Pastorale di Arnaldo Onisto vescovo di Vicenza: Studi di Storia e di Arte vicentina in onore del suo giubileo sacerdotale*, ed. T. Motterle, Vicenza: S. Giuseppe-G. Rumor, 1984, pp. 381–421.

Chabod, Federico: *Carlo V e il suo impero*, Turin: Einaudi, 1985.

Chambers, David and Brian Pullan (eds.): *Venice: A Documentary History, 1450–1630*, Toronto: University of Toronto Press, 2001.

Chantelou, Paul Fréart de: *Diary of the Cavaliere Bernini's Visit to France*, trans. M. Corbett, ed. Anthony Blunt and George Bauer, Princeton: Princeton University Press, 1985.

Chappell, Miles L. and W. Chandler Kirwin: "A Petrine Triumph: The Decoration of the Navi Piccole in San Pietro under Clement VIII," *Storia dell'arte*, no. 21, 1974, pp. 119–70.

Chauvard, Jean-François: "La formation du prix des maisons dans la Venise du XVIIe siècle," *Histoire & Mesure*, XIV, 1999, pp. 331–68.

Chauvard, Jean-François: *La circulation des biens à Venise: Stratégies patrimoniales et marché immobilier (1600–1750)*, Rome: École Française de Rome, 2005.

Chauvineau, Helène: "Nella camera del granduca (1590–1666)," in *Vivere a Pitti: Una reggia dai Medici ai Savoia*, ed. Sergio Bertelli and Renato Pasta, Florence: Olschki, 2003, pp. 69–108.

Chenault, Jeanne: "Jusepe de Ribera and the Order of Christ: New Documents," *The Burlington Magazine*, CXVIII, 1976, pp. 305–7.

Chiappini di Sorio, Ileana: "Documenti inediti per la pittura veneta del Seicento e Settecento," *Bollettino dei musei civici veneziani*, XII, no. 1–2, 1967, pp. 30–46.

Chiappini di Sorio, Ileana: "Cristoforo Roncalli detto il Pomarancio,"

in *I Pittori bergamaschi dal XIII al XIX secolo: Il Seicento, I*, Bergamo: Poligrafiche Bolis, 1983, pp. 1–201.
Chiarini, Marco: "Antonio Domenico Gabbiani e i Medici," in *Kunst des Barock in der Toskana: Studien zur Kunst unter der letzen Medici*, Munich: Bruckmann, 1976, pp. 333–43.
Chini, Ezio: *La chiesa e il convento dei Santi Michele e Gaetano a Firenze*, Florence: Giunti, 1984.
Il chiostro camaldolese di Santa Maria degli Angeli a Firenze: Restauro e restituzione del ciclo di affreschi (Quaderni dell'Ufficio Restauri della Soprintendenza per i Beni Artistici e Storici di Firenze, Pistoia e Prato, 4), Florence: Centro Di, 1998.
Chiusa, Maria Cristina: "Un gonfalone comunale commesso a Tiarini," *Aurea Parma*, LXIX, 1985, pp. 39–41.
Christiansen, Keith: "Becoming Artemisia: Afterthoughts on the Gentileschi Exhibition," *Metropolitan Museum Journal*, XXXIX, 2004, pp. 101–26.
Christiansen, Keith and Judith Mann (eds.): *Orazio and Artemisia Gentileschi* (exh. cat., Palazzo Venezia, Rome, Metropolitan Museum of Art, New York, and St. Louis Art Museum, St Louis), New York: Metropolitan Museum of Art and New Haven and London: Yale University Press, 2001.
Ciammitti, Luisa: "Conservatori femminili a Bologna e organizzazione del lavoro," *Quaderni storici*, XIV, 1979, pp. 760–64.
Ciammitti Luisa: "'Questo si costuma ora in Bologna': Una lettera di Guido Reni, aprile 1628," *Prospettiva*, no. 98–99, 2000, pp. 194–203.
Ciammitti, Luisa: "*Vago e Forte*: Ludovico e Galanino per lo stendardo di San Rocco: Un processo a Bologna nel 1636," in *Vago e Forte: Ludovico e Galanino per lo stendardo di San Rocco: Un processo a Bologna del 1636* (exh. cat., Pinacoteca nazionale, Bologna), Bologna: Compositori, 2001, pp. 11–32.
Cicatelli Amelia: "Di alcune opere di Giacomo Cavedoni," *Bollettino d'arte*, XXIV, 1930–31, pp. 417–30.
Cifani, Arabella and Franco Monetti: *Giovanni Battista Calandra (1586–1644)*, Turin: Allemandi, 2006.
Cionini, Natale: *Teatro ed arti in Sassuolo*, Modena: 1902.
Cipolla, Carlo M.: *Money, Prices, and Civilization in the Mediterranean World*, New York: Gordian, 1967.
Cipolla, Carlo M.: *Storia economica dell'Europa pre-industriale*, Bologna: Il Mulino, 1974.
Cipriani, Angela: "Giovanna Garzoni, miniatrice," *Ricerche di storia dell'arte*, no. 1–2, 1976, pp. 241–54.
Cipriani, Angela: "Presenze francesi all'Accademia di San Luca: 1664–1675," in *L'Idéal classique: Les échanges artistiques entre Rome et Paris au temps de Bellori (1640–1700)*, ed. Olivier Bonfait, Paris: Somogy, 2002, pp. 223–28.
Ciriacono, S.: "Mass Consumption Goods and Luxury Goods: The Deindustrialization of the Republic of Venice (16th–18th Centuries)," in *The Rise and Decline of Urban Industries in Italy and in the Low Countries (Late Middle Ages–Early Modern Times)*, ed. Herman van der Wee, Leuven: Leuven University Press, 1988, pp. 41–61.
Ciracono, S.: "The Venetian Economy and its Place in the World Economy of the 17th and 18th Centuries: A Comparison with the Low Countries," in *The Early Modern World-System in Geographical Perspective*, ed. H. G. Notz, Stuttgart: Franz Steiner, 1993, pp. 120–35.
Clavero, Bartolomé: *Antidora: Antropologia catolica de la economia moderna*, Milan: Giuffrè, 1991.
Coen, Paolo: "Vendere e affittare quadri: Giuseppe Sardi, capomastro muratore e mercante d'arte (Roma, XVIII sec.)," *Quaderni storici*, XXXIX, 2004, pp. 421–48.
Colantuono, Anthony: "Guido Reni's Latona for King Philip IV: An Unfinished Masterpiece: Lost, Forgotten, Rediscovered and Restored," *Artibus et Historiae*, no. 58, 2008, pp. 201–16.
Colnaghi: Old Master Paintings, 2008, London: Colnaghi, 2008.
Colombier, Pierre du: "Poussin et Claude Lorrain," in *Nicolas Poussin* (CNRS Colloques Internationaux, Paris, 1958), vol. 1, Paris: Centre National de la Recherche Scientifique, 1960, pp. 47–56.
Colombo, Silvano: "Registro," in *Francesco Cairo 1607–1665* (exh. cat., Museo Civico, Varese), Varese: Lativa, 1983, pp. 221–27.
Colucci, Isabella: "Il salotto e le collezioni della Marchesa Boccapaduli," *Quaderni storici*, XXXIX, 2004, pp. 449–93.
Comanducci, Rita Maria: "'Buona artista della sua arte': Il concetto di 'Artista' e la pratica di lavoro nella bottega quattrocentesca," in *Arti Fiorentine: La grande storia dell'Artigianato, Vol. II: Il Quattrocento*, ed. F. Franceschi and G. Fossi, Florence: Giunti, 1999, pp. 149–65.
Comanini, Gregorio: *The Figino or On the Purpose of Painting: Art Theory in the Late Renaissance*, trans. and ed. Ann Doyle-Anderson and Giancarlo Maiorini, Toronto: University of Toronto Press, 2001.
Conigliello, Lucilla: "Alcune note su Jacopo Ligozzi e sui dipinti del 1594," *Paragone*, XLI, no. 485, 1990a, pp. 21–42.
Conigliello, Lucilla: "L'intervento di Jacopo Ligozzi e il completamento del ciclo," in *Il chiostro di Ognissanti a Firenze: Restauro e restituzione degli affreschi del ciclo francescano*, Florence: Centro Di, 1990b, pp. 31–37.
Conigliello, Lucilla: *Jacopo Ligozzi: Le vedute del Sacro Monte della Verna, i dipinti di Poppi e Bibbiena* (exh. cat., Poppi Castle, Poppi), Poppi: Biblioteca Comunale Rilliana, 1992.
Consagra, Francesca: "The Marketing of Pietro Testa's 'Poetic Inventions'," in *Pietro Testa 1612–1650: Prints and Drawings*, ed. Elizabeth Cropper, Philadelphia: Philadelphia Museum of Art, 1988, pp. lxxxvii–civ.
Consagra, Francesca: *The De Rossi Family Print Publishing Shop: A Study in the History of the Print Industry in Seventeenth-Century Rome* (Ph.D. diss., The Johns Hopkins University, 1992), Ann Arbor: U.M.I., 1992.
Constable, William George: *Canaletto: Giovanni Antonio Canal 1697–1768*, 2nd edition, rev. J. G. Links, Oxford: Clarendon Press, 1976.
Conti, Luigi, Marta Niccolucci Cortini, and Maria Vadalà Linari: *San Frediano: Un culto, un popolo, una chiesa*, Florence: Polistampa, 1997.
Contini, Roberto: *Bilivert: Saggio di ricostruzione*, Florence: Sansoni, 1985.
Contini, Roberto: "Giovanni Bilivert," in *Il Seicento fiorentino: arte a Firenze da Ferdinando I a Cosimo III* (exh. cat., Palazzo Strozzi, Florence), vol. 3, Florence: Cantini, 1986, pp. 34–36.
Contini, Roberto: "Francesco Bianchi Buonavita, 'primo giovane' del Bilivert," *Annali della Fondazione di Studi di Storia dell'arte Roberto Longhi*, II, 1989, pp. 71–100.
Contini, Roberto and Gianni Papi (eds.): *Artemisia* (exh. cat., Casa Buonarroti, Florence), Rome: De Luca, 1991.
Coppa, Simonetta and Francesco Rossi (eds.): *Il Seicento a Bergamo* (exh. cat., Palazzo della Ragione, Bergamo), Cariplo: Cassa di Risparmio delle Provincie Lombarde and Bergamo: Comune di Bergamo, 1987.
Coquery, Emmanuel: "L'anatomie d'une Académie," in *L'Idéal classique: Les échanges artistiques entre Rome et Paris au temps de Bellori (1640–1700)*, ed. Olivier Bonfait, Paris: Somogy, 2002, pp. 140–60.
Corazzol, G.: *Livelli a Venezia nel 1591*, Pisa: Giardini, 1986.
Corbò, Anna Maria: "I pittori della Sagrestia Nuova di Santa Maria Maggiore a Roma," *Commentari*, XIX, 1968, pp. 320–26.
Corradini, Sandro: "La quadreria di Giancarlo Roscioli," *Antologia di Belle Arti*, III, no. 9–12, 1979, pp. 192–96.
Corradini, Sandro: "Nuove e false notizie sulla presenza del Caravag-

gio a Roma," in *Michelangelo Merisi da Caravaggio: La vita e le opere attraverso i documenti*, ed. Stefania Macioce, Rome: Logart, 1996, pp. 71–79.

Corsini, Andrea: "Un ritratto di Antonio Cocchi eseguito da Domenico Tempesti," *Rivista d'arte*, X, 1918, pp. 129–224.

Corti, Gino: "Contributi alla vita e alle opere di Francesco Furini," *Antichità viva*, X, no. 2, 1971, pp. 14–23.

Corti, Gino: "Il 'Registro de' mandati' dell'ambasciatore granducale Piero Guicciardini e la committenza artistica fiorentina a Roma nel secondo decennio del Seicento," *Paragone*, XL, no. 473, 1989, pp. 108–46.

Costanzi, Costanza and Marina Massa (eds.): *Claudio Ridolfi: Un pittore veneto nelle Marche del '600*, Ancona: Il Lavoro, 1994.

Costello, Jane: "The Twelve Pictures 'Ordered by Velasquez' and the Trial of Valguarnera," *Journal of the Warburg and Courtauld Institutes*, XIII, 1950, pp. 237–84.

Craievich, Alberto: "Antonio Molinari pittore di 'historie'," *Arte veneta*, LIV, 1999, pp. 32–53.

Craievich, Alberto: "Proposte per Silvestro Manaigo," *Arte in Friuli Arte a Trieste*, XXIII, 2004, pp. 39–50.

Craievich, Alberto: *Antonio Molinari*, Soncino: Edizioni del Soncino, 2005.

Crespi, Luigi: *La Certosa di Bologna: Descritta nelle sue pitture al molto venerando padre D. Sigismondo Guastuzzi degnissimo priore della suddetta e convisitatore della provincia di Toscana*, Bologna: A. S. Tommaso d'Aquino, 1772.

Crinò, Anna Maria: "Giuliano Periccioli senese, disegnatore, pittore, cartografo, incisore e illustratore," *Mitteilungen des Kunsthistorischen Institutes in Florenz*, XXXI, 1987, pp. 121–56.

Cropper, Elizabeth: *The Ideal of Painting: Pietro Testa's Düsseldorf Notebook*, Princeton: Princeton University Press, 1984.

Cropper, Elizabeth (ed.): *Pietro Testa 1612–1650: Prints and Drawings* (exh. cat., Philadelphia Museum of Art), Philadelphia: Philadelphia Museum of Art, 1988.

Cropper, Elisabeth: "New Documents for Artemisia Gentileschi's Life in Florence," *The Burlington Magazine*, CXXXV, 1993, pp. 760–61.

Currò, Roma: "Antonio Alberti detto il Barbalonga, pittore messinese del '600," *Siculorum Gymnasium*, XI, no. 1, 1958, pp. 1–66.

Curto, R.: "Da un'idea convenzionale di valore al valore rendimento: Estimi e significati della proprietà urbana tra '700 e '800 a Torino," *Storia urbana*, no. 71, 1995, pp. 67–87.

Da Canal, Vincenzo: *Vita di Gregorio Lazzarini*, ed. G. A. Moschini, Venice: Stamperia Palese, 1809.

Da Canal, Vincenzo: "Della maniera del dipingere moderno," *Mercurio filosofico letterario e poetico*, I, March 1810, pp. 3–20.

Da Silva, José-Gentil: *Banque et crédit en Italie au XVIIe siècle*, Paris: Klincksieck, 1969.

D'Addosio, Giambattista: "Documenti inediti di artisti napoletani del XVI e XVII secolo (I. Pittori)," *Archivio storico per le province napoletane*, XXXVII, 1912, pp. 593–616; XXXVIII, 1913, pp. 36–72, 232–59, 483–524, 578–83.

D'Afflitto, Chiara: *Lorenzo Lippi*, Florence: Edifir, 2002.

Dal Poggetto, Paolo: *Pietro Ricchi*, Rimini: Luisè, 1996.

Dal Pozzolo, Enrico Maria: "Cercar quadri e disegni nella Venezia del Cinquecento," in *Tra committenza e collezionismo: Studi sul mercato dell'arte nell'Italia settentrionale durante l'età moderna*, ed. Enrico Maria dal Pozzolo and Leonida Tedoldi, Vicenza: Terra ferma, 2003, pp. 49–65.

Dal Pozzolo, Enrico Maria and Leonida Tedoldi (eds.): *Tra committenza e collezionismo: Studi sul mercato dell'arte nell'Italia settentrionale durante l'età moderna*, Vicenza: Terra ferma, 2003.

D'Amelia, Marina: "La conquista di una dote: Regole del gioco e scambi femminili alla Confraternita dell'Annunziata (secc. XVII–XVIII)," in *Ragnatele di rapporti: Patronage e reti di relazione nella storia delle donne*, ed. L. Ferrante, M. Palazzi, and G. Pomata, Turin: Rosenberg and Sellier, 1988, pp. 305–43.

Damerini, Gino: *L'Isola e il Cenobio di San Giorgio Maggiore*, 2nd edition, Florence: Olschki, 1969.

D'Amico, Stefano, *Le contrade e la città: Sistema produttivo e spazio urbano a Milano fra Cinque e Seicento*, Milan: Giuffrè, 1994.

Dandelet, Thomas James: "Financing New Saint Peter's: 1506–1700," in *Sankt Peter in Rom, 1506–2006*, ed. Georg Satzinger and Sebastian Schütze, Munich: Hirmer, 1998, pp. 41–48.

Danesi Squarzina, Silvia: *La collezione Giustiniani*, Turin: Einaudi, 2003.

Danesi Squarzina, Silvia: "New Documents on Ribera, 'pictor in Urbe', 1612–16," *The Burlington Magazine*, CXLVIII, 2006, pp. 244–51.

Daniels, Jeffery: *Sebastiano Ricci*, Hove: Wayland, 1976.

D'Anza, Daniele: "Joseph Heintz il giovane 'pittore di più pennelli'," *Arte in Friuli Arte a Trieste*, XXIII, 2004a, pp. 13–26.

D'Anza, Daniele: "Pittori e mecenati: Joseph Heintz il Giovane artista dei Corner tra Venezia e Roma," *Arte veneta*, LXI, 2004b, pp. 97–109.

Davanzo Poli, Doretta: *I mestieri della moda a Venezia nei sec. XIII–XVIII: Documenti*, Venice: Gazzettino, 1984.

Davis, Robert: *Shipbuilders of the Venetian Arsenal: Workers and Workplace in the Preindustrial City*, Baltimore: The Johns Hopkins University Press, 1991.

De Boer, Waldemar: "Alcuni dipinti raffiguranti San Vincenzo di Alessandro Maganza e Francesco Maffei," *Arte veneta*, LIX, 2002, pp. 251–55.

De' Dominici, Bernardo: *Vite de' pittori, scultori ed architetti napoletani*, Naples: Ricciardi, 1742–45 (reprint, Bologna: Forni, 1971).

De Fuccia, Laura: "Residenti, viaggiatori e 'curieux' francesci," in *Il collezionismo d'arte a Venezia: Il Seicento*, ed. Linda Borean and Stefania Mason, Venice: Marsilio, 2007, pp. 125–40.

De Gennaro, Rosanna: *Per il collezionismo del Seicento in Sicilia: L'inventario di Antonio Ruffo Principe della Scaletta*, Pisa: Scuola Normale Superiore, 2003.

De Luca, Giuseppe: *Commercio del denaro e crescita economica a Milano tra Cinquecento e Seicento*, Milan: Il Polifilo, 1996.

De Maio, Romeo: *Pittura e controriforma a Napoli*, Rome: Laterza, 1983.

De Marchi, Neil: "The Role of Dutch Auctions and Lotteries in Shaping the Art Market(s) of 17th-century Holland," *Journal of Economic Behavior & Organization*, XXVIII, 1995, pp. 203–21.

De Marchi, Neil and Hans J. Van Miegroet: "Art, Value, and Market Practices in the Netherlands in the Seventeenth Century," *The Art Bulletin*, LXXVI, 1994, pp. 451–64.

De Marchi, Neil and Hans J. Van Miegroet: "Pricing Invention: 'Originals,' 'Copies,' and their Relative Value in Seventeenth Century Netherlandish Art Markets," in *Economics of the Arts: Selected Essays*, ed. Victor A. Ginsburgh and Pierre-Michel Menger, Amsterdam: Elsevier, 1996, pp. 27–70.

De Marchi, Neil and Hans J. Van Miegroet: "Novelty and Fashion Circuits in the Mid-Seventeenth-Century Antwerp–Paris Art Trade," *Journal of Medieval and Early Modern Studies*, XXVIII, 1998, pp. 201–46.

De Marchi, Neil and Hans J. Van Miegroet: "The History of Art Markets," in *Handbook of the Economics of Art and Culture*, vol. I, ed. Victor A. Ginsburgh and David Throsby, Amsterdam and Boston: Elsevier North-Holland, 2006a, pp. 69–122.

De Marchi, Neil and Hans J. Van Miegroet (eds.): *Mapping Markets for Paintings in Europe, 1450–1750*, Turnhout: Brepols, 2006b.

De Marchi, Neil, Hans J. Van Miegroet, and Matthew E. Raiff: "Dealer–Dealer Pricing in the 17th Century Antwerp–Paris Art Trade," in *Art Markets in Europe, 1400–1800*, ed. Michael North and David Ormrod, Aldershot: Ashgate, 1998, pp. 113–30.

De Marchi, Neil and Louisa C. Matthew: "I dipinti," in *Commercio e cultura mercantile* (vol. IV of *Il Rinascimento italiano e l'Europa*), ed. Franco Franceschi, Richard A. Goldthwaite, and Reinhold C. Mueller, Treviso: Angelo Colla, 2007, pp. 247–82.

De Piles, Roger: *Abregé de la vie des peintres*, Paris: François Muguet, 1699.

De Renzi, Salvatore: *Napoli nell'anno 1656*, Naples: Domenico di Pascale, 1867.

De Rosa, Erica: "Qualche traccia documentale per Giovan Battista Mariotti," *Arte/Documento*, X, 1996, pp. 83–91.

De Saint-Pierre de Rome à Aix-en-Provence: Un trésor de l'art italien retrouvé dans le patrimoine aixois (exh. cat., Musée du Vieil Aix), Aix-en-Provence: Musée du Vieil Aix, 2005.

De Vito, Giuseppe: "Il viaggio di lavoro di Luca Giordano a Venezia e alcune considerazioni per la scelta riberesca," in *Ricerche sul '600 napoletano: Saggi e documenti per la storia dell'arte: Dedicato a Luca Giordano*, Milan: L&T, 1991, pp. 33–122.

De Vito, Giuseppe: "Le tele di Luca Giordano nella Basilica di Santa Maria della Salute a Venezia," in *Richerche sul '600 napoletano: Saggi e documenti 1999*, Naples: Electa, 2000, pp. 118–29.

De Vito, Giuseppe: "Perifrasi fracanziane," in *Ricerche sul '600 napoletano, 2003–2004*, Naples: Electa, 2004, pp. 93–122.

De Vries, Jan: "Renaissance Cities," *Renaissance Quarterly*, XLII, 1989, pp. 781–93.

De Vries, Jan: "Art History," in *Art in History, History in Art: Studies in Seventeenth-Century Dutch Culture*, ed. David Freedberg and Jan de Vries, Santa Monica, CA: Getty Center for the History of Art and the Humanities, 1991, pp. 248–82.

De Vries, Jan: "Between Purchasing Power and the World of Goods: Understanding the Household Economy in Early Modern Europe," in *Consumption and the World of Goods*, ed. John Brewer and Roy Porter, London and New York: Routledge, 1993, pp. 85–132.

De Vries, Jan and Ad van der Woude: *The First Modern Economy: Success, Failure, and Perseverance of the Dutch Economy, 1500–1815*, Cambridge: Cambridge University Press, 1997.

Del Bravo, Carlo: "Su Cristofano Allori," *Paragone*, XVIII, no. 205, 1967, pp. 68–82.

Del Negro, Piero: "Dal mestiere alla professione di pittore nella Venezia di Giambattista Tiepolo: L'Arte, il Collegio e l'Accademia," in *Giambattista Tiepolo nel terzo centenario della rinascità*, ed. Lionello Puppi, Padua: Il Poligrafo, 1998, pp. 83–91.

Del Panta, Lorenzo: *Una traccia di storia demografica della Toscana nei secoli XVI–XVIII*, Florence: Dipartimento statistico-matematico, Università degli studi di Firenze, 1974.

Del Panta, Lorenzo et al.: *La popolazione italiana dal Medioevo a oggi*, Rome-Bari: Laterza, 1996.

Delfino, Antonio: "Nuovi documenti sulla chiesa e sul monastero di Donnaregina nel Seicento: Documenti inediti su alcuni pittori napoletani del Seicento," in *Ricerche sul '600 napoletano*, Milan: L&T, 1984, pp. 149–61.

Delfino, Antonio: "Documenti inediti tratti dall'Archivio Storico del Banco di Napoli," in *Ricerche sul '600 napoletano*, Milan: L&T, 1986, pp. 111–17.

Delfino, Antonio: "Documenti inediti sui pittori del '600 tratti dall'Archivio Storico del Banco di Napoli (A.S.B.N.) e dall'Archivio Storici di Napoli (A.S.N.)," in *Ricerche sul '600 napoletano*, Milan: L&T, 1987, pp. 79–98.

Delfino, Antonio: "Documenti inediti su Luca Giordano all'Archivio di Stato di Napoli," in *Ricerche sul '600 napoletano: Saggi e documenti 1998*, Naples: Electa, 1999, pp. 138–40.

Delille, Gérard: *Agricoltura e demografia nel regno di Napoli nei secoli XVIII e XIX*, Naples: Guida, 1977.

Della Pergola, Paola: *Galleria Borghese: I Dipinti*, Rome: Istituto Poligrafico dello Stato, 1955–59.

Della Valentina, Marcello: "I mestieri del pane a Venezia tra '600 e '700," *Atti dell'Istituto Veneto di Scienze, Lettere ed Arti*, CL, 1991–92, pp. 113–217.

Della Valentina, Marcello: "I tessitori di seta a Venezia nel Settecento," *Quaderni storici*, XXXVIII, 2003, pp. 399–418.

Della Volpe, Lisa: "Antonio Tanari e alcune vicende poco note sulla Chiesa di S. Pudenziana a Roma," *Storia dell'arte*, no. 111, 2005, pp. 139–50.

Delumeau, Jean: *La vie économique et sociale dans la seconde moitié du XVIe siècle*, Paris: E. de Boccard, 1957–59.

Dempsey, Charles: "Introduzione," in *Gli scritti dei Carracci: Ludovico, Annibale, Agostino, Antonio, Giovanni Antonio*, ed. Giovanna Perini, Bologna: Nuova Alfa, 1990, pp. 9–31.

Denunzio, Antonio Ernesto: "Una nota di pagamento per Guido Reni e qualche aggiunta per Domenichino, Carlo Saraceni e Lanfranco al servizio del Cardinale Odoardo Farnese," *Aurea Parma*, LXXXIV, 2000, pp. 365–86.

Derschau, Joachim von: *Sebastiano Ricci: Ein Beitrag zu den Unfängen der venezianischen Rococomalerei*, Heidelberg: C. Winter, 1922.

Di Dedda, Maria Teresa: "Volterrano, Rosa, Mehus, Dolci, Borgognone e la quadreria del Marchese Carlo Gerini (1616–1673): Documenti e dipinti inediti," *Storia dell'arte*, no. 119, 2008, pp. 31–96.

Di Macco, Michela: "Note su Antonio Mariani detto della Corgna: Pittore 'insigne nel copiare' e 'stimatore delle pitture'," in *Studi in onore di Giulio Carlo Argan*, Florence: La Nuova Italia, 1994, pp. 192–217.

Di Schino, June and Furio Luccichenti: *Viaggio di Papa Innocentio XII da Roma a Nettuno l'anno 1697*, Rome: Viviani, 2001.

DiFederico, Frank: "Documentation for the Paintings and Mosaics of the Baptismal Chapel in Saint Peter's," *The Art Bulletin*, L, 1968, pp. 194–98.

DiFederico, Frank: "Francesco Trevisani and the Decoration of the Crucifixion Chapel in San Silvestro in Capite," *The Art Bulletin*, LIII, 1971, pp. 52–67.

DiFederico, Frank: *The Mosaics of Saint Peter's*, University Park, PA: Pennsylvania State University Press, 1983.

Dizionario biografico degli italiani, dir. Alberto M. Ghisalberti, Rome: Istituto della Enciclopedia Italiana, 1960–.

Donati, Claudio: *L'idea di nobiltà in Italia, secoli XIV–XVIII*, Rome: Laterza, 1988.

Donazzolo, P. and M. Saibante: "Lo sviluppo demografico di Verona e della sua provincia dalla fine del secolo XV ai giorni nostri," *Metron*, VI, 1926, pp. 1–127.

D'Onofrio, Cesare: *Roma vista da Roma*, Rome: Liber, 1967.

Doria, G. and R. Savelli " 'Cittadini di governo' a Genova: Ricchezza e potere tra Cinque e Seicento," in *Gerarchie economiche e gerarchie sociali secoli XII–XVIII*, ed. Annalisa Guarducci, Florence: Le Monnier, 1990, pp. 445–534.

Douglas, Mary and Baron Isherwood: *The World of Goods: Towards an Anthropology of Consumption*, Harmondsworth: Penguin Books, 1980.

Drago, Gaetano and L. Salerno: *Ss. Ambrogio e Carlo al Corso* (Le chiese di Roma illustrate, no. 96), Rome: Marietti, 1967.

Dunn, Marilyn: "Father Sebastiano Resta and the Final Phase of the Decoration of S. Maria in Vallicella," *The Art Bulletin*, LXIV, 1982, pp. 601–22.

Ehrlich, Tracy L.: *Landscape and Identity in Early Modern Rome*, Cambridge: Cambridge University Press, 2002.

Elliott, John H.: "Royal Patronage and Collecting in Seventeenth-Century Spain," in *Economia e Arte secc. XIII–XVIII: Atti della Trentatreesima Settimana di Studi, 30 aprile–4 maggio 2001*, ed. Simonetta Cavaciocchi, Florence: Le Monnier, 2002, pp. 551–65.

Emiliani, Andrea (ed.): *La cupola della Madonna del Fuoco nella Cattedrale di Forlì*, Bologna: Alfa, 1979.

Emiliani, Andrea (ed.): *Simone Cantarini detto il Pesarese, 1612–1648* (exh. cat., Pinacoteca nazionale, Bologna), Milan: Electa, 1997.

Enggass, Robert: *The Painting of Baciccio, Giovanni Battista Gaulli 1639–1709*, University Park, PA: Pennsylvania State University Press, 1964.

Enggass, Robert and Jonathan Brown: *Italy and Spain 1600–1750: Sources and Documents*, Englewood Cliffs, NJ: Prentice-Hall, 1970.

Epe, Elisabeth: *Die Gemäldesammlungen des Ferdinando de' Medici, Erbprinz von Toskana (1663–1713)*, Marburg: Jonas, 1990.

Eskridge, Robert: "Attitude Toward Seventeenth-Century Landscape Painting in Rome" (M.A. thesis, Oberlin College, 1979).

Ewald, Gerhard: *Johann Carl Loth 1632–1698*, Amsterdam: Menno Hertzberger & Co, 1965.

Fabbri, Maria Cecilia: "Cappella Colloredo nella Santissima Annunziata," in *Cappelle barocche a Firenze*, ed. Mina Gregori, Cinisello Balsamo: Silvana Editoriale, 1990, pp. 79–98.

Fabbri, Maria Cecilia: "'La più grande e perfetta opera' del Volterrano: L'affresco nella tribuna della Santissima Annunziata," *Antichità viva*, XXXV, no. 2–3, 1996, pp. 43–58.

Facchinetti Bottai, Francesca: "Stanza della Stufa (scheda A.238)," in Marisa Forlani Conti, Francesca Facchinetti Bottai, and Laura Baldini Giusti, "Le mille stanze del Re. Firenze, Palazzo Pitti—Un organismo architettonico e le schede di catalogo," *Bollettino d'arte*, LXIV, 1979, no. 1, pp. 79–104.

Fagiolo dell'Arco, Maurizio, *Bernini*, Rome and Bari: Laterza, 2001.

Faini, Fiammetta: "Matteo Rosselli pittore" (Laurea thesis, University of Florence, 1965–66).

Falciai Prunai, Maria and Gabriella Orefice (eds.): *Un episodio del Seicento fiorentino: L'architetto Matteo Nigetti e la cappella Colloredo: Documenti e disegni* (exh. cat., Biblioteca Riccardiana, Florence), Florence: Centro Di, 1981.

Faldi, Italo: "Paolo Guidotti e gli affreschi della 'Sala del Cavaliere' nel palazzo di Bassano di Sutri," *Bollettino d'arte*, XLII, 1957, pp. 278–95.

Faldi, Italo: "I dipinti chigiani di Michele e Giovan Battista Pace," *Arte Antica e Moderna*, no. 34–36, 1966, pp. 144–50.

Faleoni, Celso: *Memorie historiche della chiesa bolognese e dei suoi pastori*, Bologna: Per Giacomo Monti 1649.

Falomir, Miguel: "The Value of Painting in Renaissance Spain," in *Economia e Arte secc. XIII–XVIII: Atti della Trentatreesima Settimana di Studi, 30 aprile–4 maggio 2001*, ed. Simonetta Cavaciocchi, Florence: Le Monnier, 2002, pp. 241–63.

Falomir, Miguel: "Artists' Responses to the Emergence of Markets for Paintings in Spain, c. 1600," in *Mapping Markets for Paintings in Europe, 1450–1750*, ed. Neil De Marchi and Hans J. Van Miegroet, Turnhout: Brepols, 2006, pp. 135–63.

Fanfani, Amintore: *Storia del lavoro in Italia dalla fine del sec. XV agli inizi del XVIII*, 2nd edition, Milan: Giuffrè, 1959.

Fano, Angiola: "La pala di San Giuseppe del pittore veneziano Giambattista Grone," *Arte veneta*, XLVII, 1995, pp. 102–5.

Fantelli, Pier Luigi: "Nicolo Renieri, pittor fiamengo," *Saggi e memorie di storia dell'arte*, IX, 1974, pp. 77–115.

Fanti, Mario: *San Procolo: La chiesa, l'abbazia; leggenda e storia*, Bologna: Cappelli, 1963.

Fanti, Mario: "Bologna nell'età Moderna (1506–1796)," in *Storia di Bologna*, ed. A. Ferri and G. Roversi, Bologna: Alfa, 1978, pp. 214–49.

Fanti, Mario: *I macellai bolognesi: Mestiere, politica e vita civile nella storia di una categoria attraverso i secoli*, Bologna: Sindacato esercenti macellerie, 1980.

Fantoni, Marcello: *La corte del granduca: Forme e simboli del potere mediceo fra Cinque e Seicento*, Rome: Bulzoni, 1994.

Fantoni, Marcello: "Architettura, corte ed economia: Alcune riflessioni sul caso mediceo," in *La Corte di Toscana dai Medici ai Lorena* (Atti delle giornate di studio, Archivio di Stato e Palazzo Pitti, 15–16 dicembre 1997), ed. Anna Bellinazzi and Alessandra Contini, Rome: Ministero per i beni e le attività culturali, Direzione Generale per gli Archivi, 2002, pp. 110–28.

Fantoni, Marcello and Lisa Goldenberg Stoppato: "Suttermans, Painter and Courtier of the Medici," *Italian History & Culture*, IX, 2003, pp. 31–42.

Fantoni, Marcello, Louisa C. Matthew, and Sara F. Matthews-Grieco (eds.): *The Art Market in Italy 15th–17th Centuries / Il mercato dell'arte in Italia secc. XV–XVII*, Ferrara: Franco Cosimo Panini, 2003.

Faraglia, Nunzio Federigo: *Storia dei prezzi in Napoli dal 1130 al 1860*, Naples: Pei Tipi del commendatore G. Novile Tipografico, 1878.

Faraglia, Nunzio Federigo: "Notizie di alcuni artisti che lavoravano nella Chiesa di S. Martino e nel Tesoro di S. Gennaro," *Archivio Storico per le province napoletane*, X, 1885, pp. 435–61.

Faraglia, Nunzio Federigo: "Notizie di alcuni artisti che lavoravano nella Chiesa di S. Martino e nel Tesoro di S. Gennaro," *Archivio Storico per le province napoletane*, XVII, 1892, pp. 657–78.

Farina, Viviana: *Giovan Carlo Doria, promotore delle arti a Genova nel primo Seicento*, Florence: Edifir, 2002.

Farinati, Paolo: *Giornale (1573–1606)*, ed. Lionello Puppi, Florence: Olschki, 1968.

Favaro, Elena: *L'Arte dei Pittori in Venezia e i suoi statuti*, Florence: Olschki, 1975.

Favero, Giovanni et al.: "Le anime dei demografi: Fonti per la rilevazione dello stato della popolazione di Venezia nei secoli XVI e XVII," *Bollettino di demografia storica*, XV, 1991, pp. 23–110.

Favilla, Massimo and Ruggero Rugolo: "Un pittore 'reale': Riflessioni su Louis Dorigny," *Studi Veneziani*, L, 2005, pp. 137–71.

Favilla, Massimo and Ruggero Rugolo: *Venezia 1688: La bibbia dei pittori*, Venice: Venezia Barocca, and Verona: Cierre Edizioni, 2006.

Feigenbaum, Gail: "Practice in the Carracci Academy," in *The Artist's Workshop*, ed. Peter M. Lukehart, Washington, D.C: National Gallery of Art, 1993, pp. 59–76.

Feigenbaum, Gail: "Per una storia istituzionale dell'arte bolognese, 1399–1650: Nuovi documenti sulla corporazione dei pittori, i suoi membri, le sue cariche e sull'Accademia dei Carracci," in *Il restauro del Nettuno, la statua di Gregorio XIII e la sistemazione di piazza Maggiore nel Cinquecento: Contributi anche documentari alla conoscenza della prassi e dell'organizzazione delle arti a Bologna prima dei Carracci*, Bologna: Minerva, 1999, pp. 353–77.

Feinblatt, Ebria: "The Roman Work of Domenico Maria Canuti," *The Art Quarterly*, XV, 1952, pp. 45–65.

Feinblatt, Ebria: "Angelo Michele Colonna: A Profile," *The Burlington Magazine*, CXXI, 1979, pp. 618–30.

Félibien, André: *Conferences de l'Académie Royale de Peinture et de Sculpture pendant l'année 1667*, Paris: Fréderic Leonard, 1668.

Félibien, André: *Entretiens sur les vies et sur les ouvrages des plus excellens peintres anciens et modernes*, Paris: Mabre-Cramoisy, 1666–88 (reprint, Paris: Trevoux, 1725).

Ferrante Lucia: "L'onore ritrovato: Donne nella Casa del Soccorso di San Paolo a Bologna," *Quaderni storici*, XVIII, 1983, pp. 449–527.

Ferrante, Lucia: "Il valore del corpo, ovvero la gestione economica della sessualità femminile," in *Il lavoro delle donne*, ed. A. Groppi, Bari: Laterza, 1996, pp. 206–28.

Ferrari, Daniela (ed.): *Giulio Romano: Repertorio di fonti documentarie*, Rome: Ministero per i Beni Culturali e Ambientali, 1992.

Ferrari, Oreste: "Una 'vita' inedita di Luca Giordano," *Napoli Nobilissima*, V, no. 3, 1966, pp. 89–96, 129–38.

Ferrari, Oreste and Giuseppe Scavizzi: *Luca Giordano: L'opera completa*, Naples: Electa, 1992.

Ferrari, Oreste and Giuseppe Scavizzi: *Luca Giordano: Nuove ricerche e inediti*, Naples: Electa, 2003.

Ferraro, Richard J.: *The Nobility of Rome, 1560–1700: A Study of Its Composition, Wealth, and Investment* (Ph.D. diss., University of Wisconsin, 1994), Ann Arbor: U.M.I., 1994.

Ferrières, Madeleine: *Les biens des pauvres en terre d'Eglise–Avignon 1610–1800*, Paris: Champ Vallon, 2004.

Filangieri di Candia, Antonio (ed.): *Diario di Annibale Caccavello scultore napoletano del XVI secolo*, Naples: L. Pierro, 1896.

Fileti Mazza, Miriam (ed.): *Il Cardinal Leopoldo, volume primo: Rapporti con il mercato veneto (Archivio del Collezionismo Mediceo)*, Milan: R. Ricciardi, 1987.

Findlen, Paula: *Possessing Nature: Museums, Collecting, and Scientific Culture in Early Modern Europe*, Berkeley: University of California Press, 1994.

Findlen, Paula: "Ereditare un museo: Collezionismo, strategie familiari e pratiche culturali nell'Italia del XVI secolo," *Quaderni storici*, XXXIX, 2004, pp. 45–81.

Fiorelli Malesci, Francesca: *La chiesa di Santa Felicita a Firenze*, Florence: Giunti, 1986.

Fletcher, Jennifer: "Marco Boschini and Paolo Del Sera Collectors and Connoisseurs of Venice," *Apollo*, CX, 1979, pp. 416–24.

Fogolari, Gino: "L'Accademia veneziana di pittura e scultura," *L'Arte*, XVI, 1913, pp. 241–72, 365–94.

Fogolari, Gino: "Lettere pittoriche del Gran Principe Ferdinando di Toscana a Niccolò Cassana (1698–1709)," *Rivista del R. Istituto d'Archeologia e Storia dell'Arte*, VI, no. 1–2, 1937, pp. 143–86.

Fontana, Vincenzo: "Venezia: Trasformazioni delle residenze signorili tra '600 e '700," in *L'uso dello spazio privato nell'età dell'Illuminismo*, ed. G. Simoncini, Florence: Olschki, 1995, pp. 141–64.

Fortini Brown, Patricia: "Le antichità," in *Commercio e cultura mercantile* (vol. IV of *Il Rinascimento italiano e l'Europa*), ed. Franco Franceschi, Richard A. Goldthwaite, and Reinhold C. Mueller, Treviso: Angelo Colla, 2007, pp. 309–37.

Fosi, Irene and Maria Antonietta Visceglia, "Marriage and Politics at the Papal Court in the Sixteenth and Seventeenth Centuries," in *Marriage in Italy, 1300–1650*, ed. Trevor Dean and K. J. P. Lowe, Cambridge: Cambridge University Press, 1998, pp. 197–226.

Fossaluzza, Giorgio: "Nota su Giovanni Antonio Fumiani," *Arte veneta*, XLII, 1988, pp. 112–18.

Fossaluzza, Giorgio: "Ambientarsi a Venezia: Tracce di Lodovico Antonio David da Lugano," in *I David: Due pittori tra Sei e Settecento (Lugano, Milano, Venezia, Parma e Roma)* (exh. cat., Pinacoteca Cantonale Giovanni Züst, Rancate), ed. Andrea Spiriti and Simona Capelli, Milan: Electa, 2004, pp. 33–59.

Fragnito, G.: "Cardinals' Courts in Sixteenth-Century Rome," *The Journal of Modern History*, LXV, no. 1, 1993, pp. 26–56.

Franceschi, Franco, Richard A. Goldthwaite, and Reinhold C. Mueller (eds.): *Commercio e cultura mercantile* (vol. IV of *Il Rinascimento italiano e l'Europa*), Treviso: Angelo Colla, 2007.

Francesco Cozza (1605–1682): Un calabrese a Roma tra Classicismo e Barocco (exh. cat., Palazzo Venezia, Rome), Soveria Mannelli: Rubbettino, 2007.

Francescutti, Elisabetta: "Maffeo Verona nella chiesa delle Zitelle di Udine," *Arte veneta*, LVIII, 2001, pp. 117–42.

Frank, Martina: "Zu einer kaum bekannten Vita des Ludovico Dorigny," *Wiener Jahrbuch für Kunstgeschichte*, XL, 1987, pp. 103–6.

Frank, Martina: *Virtù e fortuna: Il mecenatismo e le committenze artistiche della famiglia Manin tra Friuli e Venezia nel XVII e XVIII secolo*, Venice: Istituto Veneto di Scienze, Lettere ed Arti, 1996.

Frank, Martina: *Baldassarre Longhena*, Venice: Istituto Veneto di Scienze, Lettere ed Arti, 2004.

Franklin, David: "Guido Reni, Guercino, Matteo Rosselli and an Altarpiece for SS. Annunziata in Arezzo," *The Burlington Magazine*, CXIII, 1991, pp. 446–49.

Fregna, Roberto: *La pietrificazione del denaro: Studi sulla proprietà urbana tra XVI e XVII secolo*, Bologna: CLUEB, 1990.

Friedlaender, Walter: *Caravaggio Studies*, Princeton: Princeton University Press, 1955.

Frigo, Daniela: *Il padre di famiglia: Governo della casa e governo civile nella tradizione dell'economica tra Cinque e Seicento*, Rome: Bulzoni, 1985.

Fubini Leuzzi, Maria: *'Condurre a onore': Famiglia, matrimonio e assistenza dotale a Firenze in età moderna*, Florence: Olschki, 1999.

Fumagalli, Elena: "La villa Médicis au XVIIe siècle," in *La Villa Médicis*, vol. 2, ed. André Chastel and Philippe Morel, Rome: Académie de France à Rome and École Française de Rome, 1991, pp. 568–86.

Fumagalli, Elena: *Palazzo Borghese, committenza e decorazione privata*, Rome: De Luca, 1994.

Fumagalli, Elena: "Dipinti di natura morta tra Firenze e Roma," in *La natura morta al tempo di Caravaggio* (exh. cat., Musei Capitolini, Rome), Naples: Electa, 1995, pp. 67–71.

Fumagalli, Elena: "Le 'ambiguità' di Pietro da Cortona e la prima attività di Ciro Ferri," *Paragone*, XLVIII, no. 567, 1997, pp. 34–82.

Fumagalli Elena: "Giovanna Garzoni a Parigi," in *Giovanna Garzoni: Natures mortes*, ed. Silvia Meloni and Elena Fumagalli, Paris: Bibliothèque de l'image, 2000, pp. 11–13.

Fumagalli, Elena: "Padre Cosimo Cappuccino a Roma," in *Paolo Piazza: Pittore cappuccino dell'età della Controriforma tra conventi e corti d'Europa*, ed. Sergio Marinelli and Angelo Mazza, Verona: Bortolazzi Stei for the Banco Popolare di Verona e Novara, 2002, pp. 189–239.

Fumagalli, Elena: "Decorazione barocca tra Roma e Napoli: scambi di artisti e di modelli," *Paragone*, LVIII, no. 71, 2007a, pp. 61–79.

Fumagalli, Elena: "Napoli a Firenze nel Seicento" in *"filosofico umore" e "maravigliosa speditezza": Pittura napoletana del Seicento dalle collezioni medicee*, (exh. cat., Galleria degli Uffizi, Florence), ed. Elena Fumagalli, 2007b, pp. 27–135.

Fumagalli, Elena: "Prime indagini sui rapporti economici tra pittori e corte medicea nel Seicento," in *Vivere d'arte: Carriere e finanze nell'Italia moderna*, ed. Raffaella Morselli, Rome: Carocci, 2007c, pp. 135–66.

Fumagalli, Elena (ed.): *"filosofico umore" e "maravigliosa speditezza": Pittura*

napoletana del Seicento dalle collezioni medicee (exh. cat., Galleria degli Uffizi, Florence), Florence: Giunti, 2007d.
Fumagalli, Elena: "Conti e libri di conti di ritrattisti a Firenze nel Seicento," *Ricerche di storia dell'arte*, no. 102, forthcoming.
Furlan, C. (ed.): *Antonio Carneo nella pittura veneziana del Seicento* (exh. cat., Palazzo Vescovile, Portogruaro), Milan: Electa, 1995.
Furlotti, Barbara: *Le collezioni Gonzaga: Il carteggio tra Roma e Mantova (1587–1612)*, Cinisello Balsamo: Silvana Editoriale, 2003a.
Furlotti, Barbara: "'Lo splendore è un accidente inseparabile dalla Corte': Gli acquisti d'arte dei Gonzaga tra Cinque e Seicento a confronto con le 'Considerazioni sulla pittura' di Giulio Mancini," *Schifanoia*, XXIV–XXV, 2003b, pp. 259–66.
Gady, Bénédicte: "L'étrange Monsieur de La Teulière," in *L'Idéal classique: Les échanges artistiques entre Rome et Paris au temps de Bellori (1640–1700)*, ed. Olivier Bonfait, Paris: Somogy, 2002, pp. 161–85.
Gaehtgens, Barbara: *Adriaen van der Werff: Ein Beitrag zum Stilwandel der holländischen Malerei um 1700*, Munich: Deutscher Kunstverlag, 1987.
Gaier, Martin: "Mecenatismo e collezionismo della nuova nobilità veneziana nel Seicento. L'esempio di Girolamo Cavazza," in *Il collezionismo a Venezia e nel Veneto ai tempi della Serenissima*, ed. Bernard Aikema, Rosella Lauber, and Max Seidel, Venice: Marsilio, 2005, pp. 181–208.
Galán, Rocío Bruquetas and Marta Presa Cuesta: "Estudio de algunos materiales pictoricos utilizados por Zuccaro en las obras de San Lorenzo de El Escorial," *Archivo Español de Arte*, LXX, 1997, pp. 163–76.
Galasso, Giuseppe: *Napoli spagnola dopo Masaniello: Politica, cultura, società*, Florence: Sansoni, 1982.
Galazzi, Maria Clelia: "Gli anni dell'affermazione genovese tra committenze pubbliche e quadri da stanza," in *Bernardo Strozzi: Genova 1581/82–Venezia 1644* (exh. cat., Palazzo Ducale, Genoa), ed. Ezia Gavazza, Giovanna Nepi Sciré, and Giovanna Rotondi Terminiello, Milan: Electa, 1995, pp. 39–55.
Galli, Romeo: *Lavinia Fontana pittrice 1552–1604*, Imola: Paolo Galeati, 1940.
Gallo, Marco: "Ulteriori dati sulla Chiesa dei SS. Luca e Martina e sugli esordi di Jusepe De Ribera," *Storia dell'arte*, no. 93–94, 1998, pp. 312–36.
García-Frías Cecha, Carmen: "Análisis histórico-artístico del Martirio de San Lorenzo tras su restauración," in *Tiziano y el Martirio de San Lorenzo de El Escorial*, ed. Carmen García-Frías Cecha and Esperanza Rodríguez-Arana Muñoz, Madrid: Patrimonio Nacional, 2003, pp. 11–54.
Gardner von Teuffel, Christa: "From Polyptych to Pala: Some Structural Considerations," in *La pittura nel XIV e XV secolo: Il contributo dell'analisi tecnica alla storia dell'arte*, ed. H. W. van Os and J. R. J. van Asperen de Boer, Bologna: CLUEB, 1983, pp. 323–44.
Garms, Jörg (ed.): *Quellen aus dem Archiv Doria-Pamphilj zur Kunsttätigkeit in Rom unter Innocenz X*, Rome and Vienna: Hermann Böhlaus, 1972.
Garrard, Mary: *Artemisia Gentileschi: The Image of the Female Hero in Italian Baroque Art*, Princeton: Princeton University Press, 1989.
Garzoni, Tomaso: *La piazza universale di tutte le professioni del mondo*, Venice: Gio. Battista Somasco, 1585 (reprint, ed. Paolo Cherchi and Beatrice Collina, Turin: Einaudi, 1996).
Gatta, Francesco and Guendalina Serafinelli: "Attorno all'identificazione del Casino di Giovanni Lanfranco con l'attuale 'Casale Consorti': scoperte e documenti," *Bollettino d'arte*, XCII, no. 140, 2007, pp. 137–48.
Gavazza, Ezia, Giovanna Nepi Sciré, and Giovanna Rotondi Terminiello (eds.): *Bernardo Strozzi: Genova 1581/82–Venezia 1644* (exh. cat., Palazzo Ducale, Genoa), Milan: Electa, 1995.
Gaynor, J. S. and I. Toesca: *S. Silvestro in Capite* (Le chiese di Roma illustrate, no. 73), Rome: Marietti, 1963.
Geddo, Cristina: "Ritrovamenti sul marchese Cesare Pagani committente del pittore Paolo Pagani," *Paragone*, XLVI, no. 543–45, 1995, pp. 125–55.
Gentilcore, D.: "I Protomedicati come organismi professionali in Italia durante la prima età moderna," in *Avvocati, medici, ingegneri: Alle origini delle professioni moderne*, ed. M. L. Betri and A. Pastore, Bologna: CLUEB, 1997, pp. 93–104.
Georgelin, Jean: *Venise au siècle des lumières*, Paris: École des hautes études en sciences sociales, 1978.
Geremek, Bronislaw: *La pietà e la forca: Storia della miseria e della carità in Europa*, Rome: Laterza, 1986.
Gérin-Jean, Pierre: *Prix des oeuvres d'art et hiérarchie des valeurs artistiques au temps des Médicis* (Ph.D. diss., Université Paris IV–Sorbonne, 1998), Villeneuve d'Ascq: Presses Universitaires du Septentrion, 2001.
Germond, Suzan Major: "Orazio Gentileschi and S. Giovanni dei Fiorentini," *The Burlington Magazine*, CXXXV, 1993, pp. 754–59.
Ghelfi, Barbara (ed.): *Il libro dei conti del Guercino 1629–1666*, Bologna: Nuova Alfa, 1997.
Gheza Fabbri, Lia: "Drappieri, strazzaroli, zavagli: una compagnia Bolognese fra il XVI e il XVII secolo," *Il Carrobbio: Rivista di studi bolognesi*, VI, 1980, pp. 163–80.
Gheza Fabbri, Lia (ed.): *L'organizzazione del lavoro in una economia urbana: Le Società d'Arti a Bologna nei secoli XVI e XVII*, Bologna: CLUEB, 1989.
Ghidiglia Quintavalle, Augusta: "Premesse giovanili di Sebastiano Ricci," *Rivista dell'Istituto Nazionale d'Archeologia e Storia dell'Arte*, V–VI, 1956–57, pp. 395–415.
Ghidiglia Quintavalle, Augusta: "Jacopo Palma il Giovane nel modenese e nel reggiano," *Arte veneta*, X, 1957, pp. 129–42.
Ghidiglia Quintavalle, Augusta: "Alessandro Tiarini alla corte dei Farnese," *Paragone*, XVII, no. 197, 1966, pp. 37–44.
Ghio, Lilli and Edi Baccheschi: *Antonio Balestra*, Bergamo: Poligrafiche Bolis, 1989.
Gigli, Giacinto: *Diario Romano (1608–1670)*, ed. Giuseppe Ricciotti, Rome: Tumminelli, 1958.
Gigli, Giulio Cesare: *La pittura trionfante*, Venice, 1615 (edition cited, ed. Barbara Agosti and Silvia Ginzburg, Porretta Terme: I Quaderni del Battello Ebbro, 1996).
Giglioli, Odoardo H.: "Di una lunetta del Poccetti nel chiostro grande della SS. Annunziata (Da un documento inedito)," *Rivista d'arte*, VII, 1910, pp. 63–66.
Giglioli, Odoardo H.: *Giovanni da San Giovanni (Giovanni Mannozzi 1592–1636): Studi e ricerche*, Florence: Istituto di Edizioni Artistiche, 1949.
Giles, Laura M.: *The Paintings and Related Drawings of Giacomo Cavedone (1577–1660)* (Ph.D. diss., Harvard University, 1986), Ann Arbor: U.M.I., 1986.
Gilio da Fabriano, Giovanni Andrea: *Due dialoghi, nel primo de' quali si ragiona de le parti morali e civili appartenenti a' letterati cortigiani . . . nel secondo si ragiona degli errori de' pittori circa l'historie*, Camerino: A. Gioioso, 1564.
Giusti, Annamaria (ed.): *Splendori di pietre dure: L'arte di corte nella Firenze dei Granduchi* (exh. cat., Palazzo Pitti, Florence) Florence: Giunti, 1988.
Goffen, Rona: *Renaissance Rivals: Michelangelo, Leonardo, Raphael, Titian*, New Haven and London: Yale University Press, 2002.

Goi, Paolo: "Carneo e carneadi," in *Antonio Carneo e il suo tempo*, ed. Giuseppe Bergamini and Paolo Goi, Portogruaro: Città di Portogruaro, 1995, pp. 135–58.

Goldberg, Edward L.: *Patterns in Late Medici Art Patronage*, Princeton: Princeton University Press, 1983.

Goldenberg Stoppato, Lisa: "Giusto Suttermans, ritrattista di casa Medici, e la mostra allestita in suo onore dal granduca Cosimo III," in *Il viaggio a Compostela di Cosimo III de' Medici* (exh. cat., Museo Diocesano, Santiago de Compostela), Santiago de Compostela: Xunta de Galicia, 2004a, pp. 71–97.

Goldenberg Stoppato, Lisa: "Per Domenico e Valore Casini, ritrattisti fiorentini," *Mitteilungen des Kunsthistorischen Institutes in Florenz*, XLVIII, 2004b, pp. 165–210.

Goldenberg Stoppato, Lisa and Maria Pia Mannini: "Domenico e Valore Casini, ritrattisti: Un giornale di bottega ritrovato," in *Scritti per l'Istituto Germanico di Storia dell'Arte di Firenze*, eds. Cristina Acidini Luchinat, Luciano Bellosi, Miklos Boskovits, Pier Paolo Donati, and Bruno Santi, Florence: Le Lettere, 1997, pp. 349–354.

Goldthwaite, Richard A.: *Wealth and the Demand for Art in Italy, 1300–1600*, Baltimore and London: The Johns Hopkins University Press, 1993.

Goldthwaite, Richard A.: "Economic Parameters of the Italian Art Market (15th to 17th Centuries)," in *The Art Market in Italy 15th–17th Centuries: Il mercato dell'arte in Italia secc. XV–XVII*, ed. Marcello Fantoni, Louisa C. Matthew, and Sara F. Matthews-Grieco, Ferrara: Panini, 2003, pp. 423–44.

Goldthwaite, Richard A.: "L'economia del collezionismo," in *L'Età di Rubens: Dimore, committenti e collezionisti genovesi* (exh. cat., Palazzo Ducale, Palazzo Rosso, and Palazzo Spinola, Genoa), ed. Piero Boccardo, Milan: Skira, 2004, pp. 13–21.

Goldthwiate, Richard A.: *The Economy of Renaissance Florence*, Baltimore: The Johns Hopkins University Press, 2009.

Golzio, Vincenzo: *Documenti artistici sul Seicento nell'archivio Chigi*, Rome: Palombi, 1939.

Golzio, Vincenzo: "Mario de' Fiori e la natura morta," *L'Urbe*, XXVIII, 1965, pp. 1–9.

Gottardo, Ketty: "'Non voglio che li beni . . . Si possino mai vendere: Alienare, permutar'," in *Il collezionismo d'arte a Venezia: Il Seicento*, ed. Linda Borean and Stefania Mason, Venice: Marsilio, 2007, pp. 233–63.

Gozzano, Natalia: *La quadreria di Lorenzo Onofrio Colonna: Prestigio nobiliare e collezionismo nella Roma barocca*, Rome: Bulzoni, 2004.

Gozzano, Natalia: "Il conto di Claude Lorrain presso il Banco di Santo Spirito: Reddito e investimenti di un pittore nella Roma del Seicento," *Roma moderna e contemporanea*, XIII, 2005, pp. 277–316.

Gozzano, Natalia: "La vita economica di Claude Lorrain: Conti bancari, investimenti in luoghi di monte e pagamenti inediti," *Studiolo*, no. 5, 2007, pp. 149–72.

Granata, Belinda: "Appunti e ricerche d'archivio per il Cardinal Alessandro Montalto," in *Decorazione e collezionismo a Roma nel Seicento: Vicende di artisti, committenti, mercanti*, ed. Francesca Cappelletti, Rome: Gangemi, 2003, pp. 37–63.

Granata, Belinda: "'È giovane di buon aspetto, di grate maniere et di buon giudizio . . .': Il Cardinale Andrea Baroni Peretti, avveduto collezionista di pitture e antichità," *Annali dell'Università di Ferrara: Sezione storia*, no. 3, 2006, pp. 97–125.

Granata, Belinda: "Le passioni virtuose: Collezionismo e committenze artistiche del cardinale Alessandro Peretti Montalto (1571–1623)," Ph.D. diss., Università degli Studi di Roma "Sapienza," 2008–9.

Graziani, Irene: "Regestum," in *Lavinia Fontana: 1552–1614* (exh. cat., Museo Civico Archeologico, Bologna), ed. Vera Fortunati, Milan: Electa, 1994, pp. 212–15.

Graziani, Irene: "Il cenacolo di Elisabetta Sirani," in *Elisabetta Sirani: "pittrice eroina" 1638–1665* (exh. cat., Museo Civico Archeologico, Bologna), ed. Jadranka Bentini and Vera Fortunati, Bologna: Compositori, 2004, pp. 119–35.

Grazzini, Anton Francesco: *Le rime burlesche*, ed. Carlo Verzone, Florence: Sansoni, 1882.

Gregori, Mina (ed.): *Cappelle barocche a Firenze*, Cinisello Balsamo: Silvana Editoriale, 1990.

Gregori, Mina: "Divagazioni su un quadro di pesci di Antonio Tanari," *Paragone*, LVII, no. 65–66, 2006, pp. 3–48.

Gregori, Mina and Johann Georg Prinz von Hohenzollern (eds.): *Natura morta italiana tra Cinquecento e Settecento* (exh. cat., Kunsthalle der Hypo-Kulturstiftung, Munich), Milan: Electa, 2002.

Grendi, Edoardo: *I Balbi: Una famiglia genovese fra Spagna e Impero*, Turin: Einaudi, 1997.

Grenier, Jean-Yves: *L'économie d'Ancien Régime: Un monde de l'échange et de l'incertitude*, Paris: A. Michel, 1996.

Gronau, Giorgio: *Documenti artistici urbinati*, Florence: Sansoni, 1936.

Groppi, Angela: "Il diritto del sangue: Le responsabilità familiari nei confronti delle vecchie e delle nuove generazioni (Roma, secoli XVIII–XIX)," *Quaderni storici*, XXXI, 1996a, pp. 305–34.

Groppi, Angela: *Il lavoro delle donne*, Rome: Laterza, 1996b.

Groppi, Angela: "Une ressource légale pour une pratique illégale: Les juifs et les femmes contre la corporation des tailleurs dans la Rome pontificale (XVIIe–XVIIIe siècles)," in *The Value of the Norm: Legal Disputes and the Definition of Rights*, ed. Renata Ago, Rome: Biblink, 2002, pp. 137–61.

Gualandi, Michelangelo: *Memorie originali risguardanti le Belle Arti*, Bologna, 1840–45.

Gualandi, Michelangelo: *Nuova raccolta di lettere sulla pittura, scultura ed architettura*, Bologna: Sassi, 1844–56.

Gualdo, Jr., Girolamo: *1650: Giardino di Chà Gualdo*, ed. Lionello Puppi, Florence: Olschki, 1972.

Guarducci, Annalisa (ed.): *Gerarchie economiche e gerarchie sociali secoli XII–XVIII*, Florence: Le Monnier, 1990.

Guenzi, Alberto: "Un mercato regolato: Pane e fornai a Bologna in età moderna," *Quaderni storici*, XIII, 1978, pp. 371–97.

Guenzi, Alberto: "Il frumento e la città: Il caso di Bologna in età moderna," *Quaderni storici*, XVI, 1981, pp. 153–87.

Guenzi, Alberto and Carlo Poni: "Sinergia di due innovazioni: Chiaviche e mulini da seta a Bologna," *Quaderni storici*, XXII, 1987, pp. 110–27.

Guenzi, Alberto, Paola Massa, and Fausto Piola Caselli (eds.): *Guilds, Markets and Work Regulations in Italy, 16th–19th Centuries*, Aldershot: Ashgate, 1998.

Guerra, Camillo: "Pitture della Cappella del Tesoro di S. Gennaro, nella Cattedrale di Napoli," in *Memorie originali italiane risguardanti le belle arti*, vol. 5, ed. Michelangelo Gualandi, Bologna: 1844, pp. 128–77.

Guerzoni, Guido: *Apollo e Vulcano: I mercati aritistici in Italia (1400–1700)*, Venice: Marsilio, 2006.

Guerzoni, Guido: "The Social World of Price Formation: Prices and Consumption in Sixteenth-Century Ferrara," in *The Material Renaissance*, ed. Michelle O'Malley and Evelyn Welch, Manchester and New York: Manchester University Press, 2007, pp. 71–84.

Guicciardini Corsi Salviati, Alessandra: *Affreschi di Palazzo Corsini a Firenze 1650–1700*, Florence: Centro Di, 1989.

Guidicini, Giuseppe: *Cose notabili della città di Bologna*, Bologna: Tipografia delle Scienze di Giuseppe Vita, 1869.

Guido Reni, 1575–1642 (exh. cat., Pinacoteca nazionale, Bologna), Bologna: Nuova Alfa, 1988.

Gutton, J.-P.: *La société et les pauvres en Europe (XVIe–XVIIIe siècles)*, Paris: Presses universitaires de France, 1974.

Guzzo, Enrico Maria: "Documenti per la storia dell'arte a Verona in epoca barocca," *Atti e Memorie della Accademia di Agricoltura Scienze e Lettere di Verona*, XLII, 1990–91, pp. 247–79.

Guzzo, Enrico Maria: "Documenti per Biagio Falcieri (1627–1703) ed il suo 'entourage'," *Studi Storici Veronesi Luigi Simeoni*, XLV, 1995, pp. 195–208.

Guzzo, Enrico Maria: "Quadrerie Barocche a Verona: Le Collezioni Turco e Gazzola," *Studi Storici Veronesi Luigi Simeoni*, XLVIII, 1998, pp. 143–67.

Hammond, Frederick: *Music and Spectacle in Baroque Rome*, New Haven and London: Yale University Press, 1994.

Härth-Ragaller, Isolde: "Kirche und Kloster 'Madonna della Pace' in Florenz," in *Kunst des Barock in der Toskana: Studien zur Kunst unter den letzten Medici*, 1976, pp. 289–95.

Haskell, Francis: *Patrons and Painters: A Study in the Relations Between Italian Art and Society in the Age of the Baroque*, New York: Knopf, 1963 (revised ed., New Haven and London: Yale University Press, 1980).

Haskell, Francis: "The Patronage of Painting in Seicento Naples," in *Painting in Naples from Caravaggio to Giordano* (exh. cat., Royal Academy of Arts, London), ed. Clovis Whitfield and Jane Martineau, London: Royal Academy, 1982, pp. 60–64.

Hatfield, Rab: *The Wealth of Michelangelo*, Rome: Edizioni di storia e letteratura, 2002.

Heikamp, Detlef: "Il 'libro di debitori e creditori' di Andrea Boscoli," in Anna Forlani, "Andrea Boscoli," *Proporzioni*, IV, 1963, pp. 177–208.

Hendriks, Carla: *Northern Landscapes on Roman Walls: The Frescoes of Matthijs and Paul Bril*, Florence: Centro Di, 2003.

Hibbard, Howard: "Palazzo Borghese studies–II: The Galleria," *The Burlington Magazine*, CIV, 1962, pp. 9–20.

Hibbard, Howard: *Carlo Maderno and Roman Architecture, 1580–1630*, London: Zwemmer, 1971.

Hicks, John, A.: *Theory of Economic History*, Oxford: Oxford University Press, 1969.

Hill, John Walter: *Roman Monody, Cantata, and Opera from the Circles around Cardinal Montalto*, Oxford: Clarendon Press, 1997.

Hill, Paul: "Tintoretto's Marketing," in *Venedig und Oberdeutschland in der Renaissance*, ed. Bernd Roeck, Klaus Bergdolt, and Andrew John Martin, Simaringen: Jan Thorbecke, 1993, pp. 107–20.

Hochmann, Michel: "Les annotations marginales de Federico Zuccaro à un exemplaire des Vies de Vasari: La reaction anti-vasarienne à la fin du XVIe siècle," *Revue de l'art*, no. 80, 1988, pp. 64–71.

Hochmann, Michel: "Le mécénat de Marino Grimani: Tintoret, Palma le Jeune, Jacopo Bassano, Giulio del Moro et le décor du palais Grimani; Véronèse et Vittoria à San Giuseppe," *Revue de l'art*, no. 95, 1992a, pp. 41–51.

Hochmann, Michel: *Peintres et Commanditaires à Venise (1540–1628)*, Rome: École Française de Rome, 1992b.

Hochmann, Michel: "Les collections des familles 'papalistes' à Venise et à Rome du XVIe au XVIIIe siècle," in *Geografia del collezionismo: Italia e Francia tra il XVI e il XVIII secolo*, ed. Olivier Bonfait et al., Rome: École Française de Rome, 2001, pp. 203–23.

Hochmann, Michel: *Venise et Rome 1500–1600: Deux écoles de peinture et leurs échanges*, Geneva: Droz, 2004.

Hochmann, Michel, Rosella Lauber, and Stefania Mason (eds.): *Il collezionismo d'arte a Venezia: Dalle origini al Cinquecento*, Venice: Marsilio, 2008.

Hollanda, Francisco de: *Four Dialogues on Painting*, trans. Aubrey Bell, London: Oxford University Press, 1928.

Hollanda, Francisco de: *Diálogos em Roma (1538): Conversations on Art with Michelangelo Buonarroti*, ed. Grazia Dolores Folliero-Metz, Heidelberg: Winter, 1998.

Hollanda, Francisco de: *I Trattati d'arte*, ed. Grazia Modroni, Livorno: Sillabe, 2003.

Holmes, Megan: "Copying Practices and Marketing Strategies in a Fifteenth-Century Florentine Painter's Workshop," in *Artistic Exchange and Cultural Translation in the Italian Renaissance City*, ed. Stephen J. Campbell and Stephen J. Milner, Cambridge: Cambridge University Press, 2004, pp. 38–74.

Honig, Elizabeth, "Art, Honor, and Excellence in Early Modern Europe," in *Beyond Price: Value in Culture, Economics and the Arts*, ed. Michael Hutter and David Throsby, Cambridge: Cambridge University Press, 2008, pp. 89–105.

Hoogewerff, Godefridus Joannes: *De Bentvueghels*, 's-Gravenhage: Martinus Nijhoff, 1952.

Hope, Charles: *Titian*, London: Jupiter Books, 1980.

Hopkins, Anthony: *Santa Maria della Salute: Architecture and Ceremony in Baroque Venice*, Cambridge and New York: Cambridge University Press, 2000.

Huber, Hans Dieter: *Paolo Veronese: Kunst als soziales System*, Munich: W. Fink, 2005.

Humfrey, Peter: "The Venetian Trade Guilds as Patrons of Art in the Renaissance," *The Burlington Magazine*, CXXVIII, 1986, pp. 317–30.

Humfrey, Peter: *The Altarpiece in Renaissance Venice*, New Haven and London: Yale University Press, 1993.

Hutter, Michael and David Throsby, "Value and Valuation in Art and Culture: Introduction and Overview," in *Beyond Price: Value in Culture, Economics and the Arts*, ed. Michael Hutter and David Throsby, Cambridge: Cambridge University Press, 2008, pp. 1–19.

Ibsen, Monica: "Due 'provvisioni' salodiane per Andrea Celesti," *Arte veneta*, LI, 1997, pp. 103–7.

Ibsen, Monica: *Il Duomo di Salò*, Salò: Vannini, 1999.

Ilchman, Frederick: "Venetian Painting in an Age of Rivals," in Frederick Ilchman et al., *Titian, Tintoretto, Veronese: Rivals in Renaissance Venice* (exh. cat., Museum of Fine Arts, Boston, and Musée du Louvre, Paris, 2009–10), Farnham: Lund Humphries, 2009, pp. 21–38.

Ivanoff, Nicola: "Lodovico David da Lugano e la sua Accademia veneziana," *Emporium*, LXIII, 1957, pp. 248–53.

Ivanoff, Nicola: "Girolamo Pellegrini," *Emporium*, CXXVII, 1958, pp. 99–106.

Ivanoff, Nicola and Pietro Zampetti: *Giacomo Negretti, detto Palma il Giovane*, Bergamo: Poligrafiche Bolis, 1980.

Jansen, D. J.: "Jacopo Strada et le commerce de l'art," *Revue de l'Art*, no. 77, 1987, pp. 11–21.

Jansen, Guido and Peter C. Sutton (eds.): *Michael Sweerts (1618–1664)* (exh. cat., Amsterdam, San Francisco, Hartford), Zwolle: Waanders, 2002.

Jestaz, Bertrand: "Les collections de peinture à Venise au XVIe siècle," in *Geografia del collezionismo: Italia e Francia tra il XVI e il XVIII secolo*, ed. Olivier Bonfait et al., Rome: École Française de Rome, 2001, pp. 185–201.

Johns, Christopher: "The Entrepôt of Europe: Rome in the Eighteenth

Century," in *Art in Rome in the Eighteenth Century* (exh. cat., Philadelphia Museum of Art), ed. Edgar Peters Bowron and Joseph J. Rishel, Philadelphia: Philadelphia Museum of Art, 2000, pp. 17–45.

Junius, Franciscus: *The Painting of the Ancients: De Pictura Veterum according to the English Translation* (1638), ed. Keith Aldrich, Philipp Fehl, and Raina Fehl, Berkeley: University of California Press, 1991.

Karsten, Arne: *Bernini: Il creatore della Roma barocca*, Rome: Salerno, 2007.

Kindleberger, C. P.: "The Economic Crisis of 1619–1623," *Journal of Economic History*, LI, 1991, pp. 149–75.

Kirby, Jo: "The Price of Quality: Factors Influencing the Cost of Pigments during the Renaissance," in *Revaluing Renaissance Art*, ed. Gabriele Neher and Rupert Shepherd, Aldershot: Ashgate, 2000, pp. 19–42.

Kirby, Jo and David Saunders: "Sixteenth- to Eighteenth-Century Green Colours in Landscape and Flower Paintings: Composition and Deterioration," in *Painting Techniques: History, Materials and Studio Practice: Contributions to the Dublin Congress 7–11 September 1998*, ed. Ashok Roy and Perry Smith, London: International Institute for Conservation of Historic and Artistic Works, 1998, pp. 155–59.

Kirkendale, Warren: *The Court Musicians in Florence during the Principate of the Medici: With a Reconstruction of the Artistic Establishment*, Florence: Olschki, 1993.

Kirwin, William Chandler: *Christofano Roncalli (1551/52–1626): An Exponent of the Proto-Baroque: His Activity through 1605* (Ph.D. diss., Stanford University, 1972), Ann Arbor: U.M.I., 1972.

Klessmann, Rudiger: *Johann Liss*, Doornspijk: Davaco, 1999.

Klinge, Margret: "David Teniers and the Theatre of Painting," in *David Teniers and the Theatre of Painting* (exh. cat., London, Courtauld Institute of Art Gallery, 2006), ed. Ernst Vegelin van Claerbergen, London: Holberton, 2006, pp. 10–39.

Knöpfel, Dagmar: "Sui dipinti di Tintoretto per il coro della Madonna dell'Orto," *Arte veneta*, XXXVIII, 1984, pp. 149–54.

Knox, George: *Antonio Pellegrini, 1675–1741*, Oxford: Clarendon Press, 1995.

Kowalczyk, Bozena Anna: "Il Bellotto veneziano nei documenti," *Arte veneta*, XLVII, 1995, pp. 69–77.

Kowalczyk, Jerzy: "Sui quadri di Domenico Tintoretto ordinati da Jan Zamoyski," *Archivio Veneto*, CV, 1974, pp. 88–103.

Kranendonk, Wim: "La vista dalla casa veneziana di Giambattista Tiepolo," *Arte veneta*, XLII, 1988, pp. 154–56.

Krischel, Roland: "Zur Geschichte des Venezianischen Pigmenthandels: Das Sortiment des 'Jacobus De Benedictis A Coloribus'," *Wallraf-Richartz-Jahrbuch*, LXIII, 2002, pp. 93–158.

Krückmann, Peter: *Federico Bencovich 1677–1753*, Hildesheim and New York: Georg Olms, 1988.

Kubersky-Piredda, Susanne: "Immagini devozionali nel Rinascimento fiorentino: Produzione, commercio, prezzi," in *The Art Market in Italy 15th–17th Centuries: Il mercato dell'arte in Italia secc. XV–XVII*, ed. Marcello Fantoni, Louisa C. Matthew, and Sara F. Matthews-Grieco, Ferrara: Panini, 2003, pp. 115–25.

Kubersky-Piredda, Susanne: *Kunstwerke-Kunstwerte: Die Florentiner Maler der Renaissance und der Kunstmarkt ihrer Zeit*, Norderstedt: Books on Demand, 2005.

Kunert, Silvio de: "Notizie e documenti su Pietro Liberi," *Rivista d'arte*, XIII, 1931, pp. 539–75.

Kunst des Barock in der Toskana: Studien zur Kunst unter der letzen Medici, Munich: Bruckmann, 1976.

Labatut, Jean-Pierre: *Les noblesses européennes de la fin du XVe siècle à la fin du XVIIIe siècle*, Paris: Presses universitaires de France, 1978.

Labrot, Gérard: *Baroni in città: Residenze e comportamenti dell'aristocrazia napoletana, 1530–1734*, Naples: Società Editrice Napoletana, 1979.

Labrot, Gérard: *Collections of Paintings in Naples, 1600–1780* (Documents for the History of Collecting: Italian Inventories I, The Provenance Index of the Getty Information Institute), Munich: K. G. Saur, 1992.

Labrot, Gérard: *Palazzi napoletani: Storie di nobili e cortigiani 1520–1750*, Naples: Electa, 1993.

Labrot, Gérard: "Un marché dynamique: La peinture de série à Naples, 1606–1775," in *Economia e Arte secc. XIII–XVIII: Atti della Trentatreesima Settimana di Studi, 30 aprile–4 maggio 2001*, ed. Simonetta Cavaciocchi, Florence: Le Monnier, 2002, pp. 261–83.

Labrot, Gérard and Renato Ruotolo: "Pour une étude historique de la commande aristocratique dans le rouyaume de Naples espagnol," *Revue Historique*, I, 1980, pp. 25–48.

Lammertse, Friso and Jaap van der Veen: *Ulyenburgh & Sons: Art and Commerce from Rembrandt to De Lairesse, 1625–1675*, Zwolle: Waanders, 2006.

Landau, David and Peter Parshall: *The Renaissance Print, 1470–1550*, New Haven and London: Yale University Press, 1994.

Lanfranchi Strina, Bianca (ed.): *Libretto dei conti del pittore Tiberio Tinelli (1618–1633)*, Venice: Comitato, 2000.

Lanfranconi, Matteo: "Da Vouet a Poussin: La communità artistica francese nell'Accademia di San Luca," in *L'Idéal classique: Les échanges artistiques entre Rome et Paris au temps de Bellori (1640–1700)*, ed. Olivier Bonfait, Paris: Somogy, 2002, pp. 211–22.

Lankheit, Klaus: "Die Corsini-Kapelle in der Carmine-Kirche zu Florenz und ihre Reliefs," *Mitteilungen des Kunsthistorischen Institutes in Florenz*, VIII, 1957, pp. 35–60.

Lanzi, Luigi: *Storia pittorica dell'Italia dal risorgimento delle belle arti fin presso la fine del XVIII secolo*, Bassano: 1789 (reprint, ed. Martino Capucci, Florence: Sansoni, 1968–70).

Lauber, Rosella: "Per un ritratto di Gabriele Vendramin: Nuovi contributi," in *Figure di collezionisti a Venezia tra Cinque e Seicento*, ed. Linda Borean and Stefania Mason, Udine: Forum, 2002, pp. 25–75.

Laureati, Laura: "Painting Nature: Fruit, Flowers and Vegetables," in *The Genius of Rome* (exh. cat., Royal Academy of Arts, London, and Palazzo Venezia, Rome), ed. Beverly Louise Brown, London: Royal Academy of Arts, 2001, pp. 68–88.

Lavin, Irving: "Decorazioni barocche in San Silvestro in Capite a Roma," *Bollettino d'arte*, XLII, 1957, pp. 44–49.

Lavin, Marilyn Aronberg: "A Seventeenth-Century Painter's Supplies: Document of Payment to Andrea Camassei," *The Art Bulletin*, LII, 1970, pp. 192–94.

Lavin, Marilyn Aronberg: *Sevententh-Century Barberini Documents and Inventories of Art*, New York: New York University Press, 1975.

Lemoine, Annick: "Nicholas Régnier et son entourage: Nouvelles propositions biographiques," *Revue de l'Art*, no. 117, 1997, pp. 54–63.

Lemoine, Annick: "La pittura al naturale dans la Rome des années 1610–1620, entre tradition et innovation," in *Nicolas Tournier et la peinture caravagesque en Italie, en France et en Espagne*, ed. Pascal-François Bertrand, Toulouse: Framespa-CNRS France méridionale et Espagne, 2003, pp. 45–63.

Lemoine, Annick: *Nicolas Régnier (alias Niccolò Renieri) ca. 1588–1667: Peintre, collectionneur et marchand d'art*, Paris: Arthéna, 2007.

Leoncini, Giovanni: "Una 'vita di Jacopo Chiavistelli pittore di figure et eccellente nell'architettura a fresco'," *Rivista d'arte*, XXXVII, 1984, pp. 269–346.

Leoncini, Giovanni: "Gli affreschi del refettorio," in *La chiesa di Santa*

Trinita a Firenze, ed. Giuseppe Marchini and Emma Micheletti, Florence: Giunti, 1987, pp. 197–203.
Leoncini, Giovanni: "Cappella Franceschi ai Santi Michele e Gaetano," in *Cappelle barocche a Firenze*, ed. Mina Gregori, Cinisello Balsamo: Silvana Editoriale, 1990, pp. 17–30.
Leoncini, Luca (ed.): *Palazzo Reale di Genova: Studi di restauri, 1993–1994*, Genoa: Tormena, 1997.
Leone de Castris, Pierluigi: *La pittura del Cinquecento a Napoli 1573–1606: L'ultima maniera*, Naples: Electa, 1991.
Leoni, G. B.: *Delle lettere famigliari*, Venice, 1593.
Leoni, G. B.: *La falsa riputatione della Fortuna: Favola morale*, Venice, 1596.
Leopardi, Valeria: "Contributo per Bortolo Litterini," *Arte veneta*, XXXI, 1977, pp. 119–25.
Levi, D. and L. Tongiorgio Tomasi: "Testo e immagine in una rivista veneziana tra Sei e Settecento: La Galleria di Minerva," *Annali della Scuola Normale Superiore di Pisa*, XX, 1990, pp. 185–210.
Limentani Virdis, Caterina: "I Fiamminghi e la Serenissima: Pittori e generi," in *Fiamminghi: Arte fiammingha e olandese del Seicento nella Repubblica Veneta* (exh. cat., Palazzo della Ragione, Padua), ed. Caterina Limentani Virdis and Davide Banzato, Milan: Electa, 1990, pp. 13–24.
Limentani Virdis, Caterina: "Artisti della 'Nation fiamenga': Pittori e opere a Venezia," in *La pittura fiamminga nel Veneto e nell'Emilia*, ed. Caterina Limentani Virdis, Verona: Banca Popolare di Verona, 1997, pp. 36–66.
Limentani Virdis, Caterina and Davide Banzato (eds.): *Fiamminghi: Arte fiamminga e olandese del Seicento nella Repubblica Veneta* (exh. cat., Palazzo della Ragione, Padua), Milan: Electa, 1990.
Lo Bianco, Anna: "I dipinti sei-settecenteschi degli altari del Pantheon: Bonzi, Camassei, Maioli, Labruzzi," *Bollettino d'arte*, LXXII, 1987, no. 42, pp. 91–116.
Lo Bianco, Anna (ed.): *Pietro da Cortona, 1597–1669* (exh. cat., Palazzo Venezia, Rome), Milan: Electa, 1997.
Logan, Anne-Marie: *The "Cabinet" of Brothers Jan and Gerard Reynst*, Amsterdam: North Holland Publishing Co., 1979.
Loh, Maria: "Originals, Reproductions, and a 'Particular Taste' for Pastiche in the Seventeenth-Century Republic of Painting," in *Mapping Markets for Paintings in Europe, 1450–1750*, ed. Neil De Marchi and Hans J. Van Miegroet, Turnhout: Brepols, 2006, pp. 237–62.
Loire, Stéphane: *École italienne, XVIIe siècle, 1: Bologne* (Musée du Louvre, Département des peintures), Paris: Réunion des Musées Nationaux, 1996.
Lomazzo, Giovan Paolo: *Rabisch*, Milan, 1589 (edition cited: ed. D. Isella, Turin, 1993).
Longhi, Alessandro: *Compendio delle vite de' pittori veneziani istorici più rinomati del presente secolo*, Venice: Appresso l'Autore, 1762.
Longo, Lucia: "Le pitture di Antonio Triva nella 'Camera dell'alcova' della Residenza di Monaco," *Arte veneta*, XXXVIII, 1984, pp. 87–96.
Longo, Lucia: "Das Testament des Daniel Heintz vom 26 November 1709," *Jahrbuch des Zentralinstitutes für Kunstgeschichte*, I, 1985, pp. 419–22.
Longo, Lucia: "Joseph Heintz d. J. und Pietro Vecchia in der Kirche S. Antonino in Venedig," *Jahrbuch des Zentralinstitutes für Kunstgeschichte*, II, 1986, pp. 317–27.
Longo, Lucia: "Testimonianze documentarie su Antonio Triva 'pittore di corte' in Baviera (1669–1699)," *Arte veneta*, XLI, 1987, pp. 188–99.
Longo, Lucia: *Antonio Triva pittore (1626–1699)*, Trent: University of Trent, 1990.
Lopez, Robert S.: "Hard Times and Investment in Culture," in Wallace K. Ferguson et al., *The Renaissance*, New York: Metropolitan Museum of Art, 1953, pp. 29–54.
Loredano, Gian Francesco and Pietro Michiel: *Il Cimiterio: Epitafi giocosi*, Venice, 1645 (edition cited: Venice, 1680).
Lorenzi, Giovanni Battista: *Monumenti per servire alla storia del Palazzo Ducale di Venezia*, Venice: M. Visentini, 1868.
Lorizzo, Loredana: "Cardinal Ascanio Filomarino's Purchases of Works of Art in Rome: Poussin, Caravaggio, Vouet and Valentin," *The Burlington Magazine*, CXLIII, 2001, pp. 404–11.
Lorizzo, Loredana: "Documenti inediti sul mercato dell'arte: I testamenti e l'invertario della bottega del genovese Pellegrino Peri 'rivenditore di quadri' a Roma nella seconda metà del Seicento," in *Decorazione e collezionismo a Roma nel Seicento: Vicende di artisti, committenti, mercanti*, ed. Francesca Cappelletti, Rome: Gangemi, 2003a, pp. 159–74.
Lorizzo, Loredana: "Il mercato dell'arte a Roma nel XVII secolo: 'Pittori bottegari' e 'rivenditori di quadri' nei documenti dell'-Archivio Storico dell'Accademia di San Luca," in *The Art Market in Italy 15th–17th Centuries: Il mercato dell'arte in Italia secc. XV–XVII*, ed. Marcello Fantoni, Louisa C. Matthew, and Sara F. Matthews-Grieco, Ferrara: Panini, 2003b, pp. 325–36.
Lorizzo, Loredana: "People and Practices in the Paintings Trade in Seventeenth-Century Rome," in *Mapping Markets for Paintings in Europe, 1450–1750*, ed. Neil De Marchi and Hans J. Van Miegroet, Turnhout: Brepols, 2006, pp. 343–58.
Lotto, Lorenzo: *Il "Libro delle spese diverse": Con aggiunta di lettere e altri documenti*, ed. Pietro Zampetti, Venice-Rome: Istituto per la collaborazione culturale, 1969.
Lucchetta, Riccardo: "Girolamo Brusaferro: Precisazioni ed aggiunte al catalogo," *Arte veneta*, XLI, 1987, pp. 74–88.
Lucco, Mauro: "Il Cinquecento," in *Le pitture del Santo di Padova*, ed. Camillo Semenzato, Vicenza: Neri Pozza, 1984, pp. 145–63, 167–74.
Lucco, Mauro: "'Foresti' a Venezia nel Seicento," in *La pittura nel Veneto: Il Seicento*, vol. 2, ed. Mauro Lucco, Milan: Electa, 2001, pp. 485–522.
Lukehart, Peter: "Contending Ideals: The Nobility of Giovanni Battista Paggi and the Nobility of Painting" (Ph.D. diss., The Johns Hopkins University, 1987).
Lukehart, Peter: "Delineating the Genoese Studio: Giovani Accartati or Sotto Padre?" in *The Artist's Workshop*, ed. Peter Lukehart (Studies in the History of Art, 38), Washington, D.C.: National Gallery of Art, 1993, pp. 37–58.
Lukehart, Peter: "Parallel Lives: The Example of Taddeo Zuccaro in Late-Sixteenth-Century Rome," *Taddeo and Federico Zuccaro: Artist-Brothers in Renaissance Rome* (exh. cat., The J. Paul Getty Museum), ed. Julian Brooks, Los Angeles: The J. Paul Getty Museum, 2007, pp. 105–12.
Lunadoro, Girolamo: *The Court of Rome*, trans. H. C. Gent, London: Henry Herringman, 1654.
Lupis, Antonio: *Il plico*, Milan: Vigone, 1675.
Lupis, Antonio: *Il corriere*, Venice: Brigna, 1680.
Lupis, Antonio: *Il chiaro scuro di pittura morale*, Venice: Brigna, 1685.
Lutz, Georg: "Zur Papstfinanz von Klemens IX. bis Alexander VIII (1667–1691)," *Römische Quartal Schrift für christliche Altertumskunde und Kirchengeschichte*, LXXIII, 1973, pp. 32–90.
Luzio, Alessandro: *La galleria dei Gonzaga venduta all'Inghilterra nel 1627–28*, Milan: Cogliati, 1913.
Lydecker, John Kent: "The Domestic Setting of the Arts in Renaissance Florence" (Ph.D. diss, The Johns Hopkins University, 1987).
McCants, A.: "Goods at Pawn: The Overlapping Worlds of Material

Possessions and Family Finances in Early Modern Amsterdam," *Social Science History*, XXXI, no. 2, 2007, pp. 213–38.
Maccherini, Michele: "Caravaggio nel carteggio familiare di Giulio Mancini," *Prospettiva*, no. 86, 1997, pp. 71–92.
Maccherini, Michele: "Novità su Bartolomeo Manfredi nel carteggio familiare di Giulio Mancini: Lo 'Sdegno di Marte' e i quadri di Cosimo II granduca di Toscana," *Prospettiva*, no. 93–94, 1999, pp. 131–41.
Maccherini, Michele: "Giulio Mancini: Committenza e commercio di opera d'arte fra Siena e Roma," in *Siena & Roma: Raffaello, Caravaggio e i protagonisti di un legame antico* (exh. cat., S. Maria della Scala and Palazzo Squarcialupi, Siena), Siena: Protagon, 2005, pp. 393–401.
Macco, Michela di: "Note su Antonio Mariani detto della Corgna: Pittore 'insigne nel copiare' e 'stimatore delle pitture'," in *Studi in onore di Giulio Carlo Argan*, Scandicci: La Nuova Italia, 1994, pp. 192–217.
McCray, W. Patrick: *Glassmaking in Renaissance Venice: The Fragile Craft*, Aldershot: Ashgate, 1999.
MacKenney, Richard: *Tradesmen and Traders: The World of the Guilds in Venice and Europe c.1250–c.1650*, London and Sydney: Croom Helm, 1987.
McTighe, Sheila: "The End of Caravaggio" (exh. review), *The Art Bulletin*, LXXXVIII, 2006, pp. 583–89.
Maffei, Scipione: *Verona illustrata*, Verona: Jacopo Vallarsi e Pierantonio Berno, 1731.
Magagnato, Licisco: "La cappella intitolata ai Santi Zeno e Daniele del Collegio dei Notai nel Palazzo del Comune in Verona," in *Il Notariato Veronese attraverso i secoli*, ed. Giulio Sancassani, M. Carrara, and L. Magagnato, Verona: Valdonega, 1966, pp. 47–76.
Magalotti, Lorenzo: *Diario di Francia dell'anno 1668*, ed. Maria Louisa Doglio, Palermo: Sellerio, 1991.
Magani, Fabrizio: *Il collezionismo e la committenza artistica della famiglia Widmann, patrizi veneziani, dal Seicento all'Ottocento* (Memorie Classe di Scienze Morali Lettere ed Arti, XLI, no. 3), Venice: Istituto Veneto di Scienze, Lettere ed Arti, 1989.
Magani, Fabrizio: "Andrea Celesti decoratore in Palazzo Conti a Padova: La serie di ritratti di famiglia," *Bollettino del Museo Civico di Padova*, LXXX, 1991, pp. 197–221.
Magani, Fabrizio: *Antonio Bellucci: Catalogo ragionato*, Rimini: Stefano Patacconi, 1995.
Magani, Fabrizio: "Lucrezia, Clorinda, Angelica, Anna Renieri," in *Le tele svelate: Pittrici venete dal Cinquecento al Novecento*, ed. Caterina Limentani Virdis, Mirano: Eidos, 1996, pp. 78–92.
Magani, Fabrizio: "I pittori di Vincenzo da Canal: Liberi, Dorigny, Lazzarini, Molinari e Bellucci," in *Pittura veneziana dal Quattrocento al Settecento: Studi di storia dell'arte in onore di Egidio Martini*, ed. Giuseppe Maria Pilo, Venice: Arsenale, 1999, pp. 169–73.
Maginnis, Hayden B. J.: *Painting in the Age of Giotto: A Historical Reevaluation*, University Park, PA: Pennsylvania State University Press, 1997.
Mahoney, Michael: *The Drawings of Salvator Rosa* (Ph.D. diss., Courtauld Institute of Art, 1965), New York: Garland, 1977.
Makrykostas, Haris: *Antonio Vassilacchi called Aliense 1556–1629: A Melian Painter in Venice*, Athens: Silver & Baryte Ores Mining Co., 1993.
Malaguzzi Valeri, Francesco: "L'arte dei pittori a Bologna nel secolo XVI," *Archivio storico dell'arte*, III, 1897, pp. 309–14.
Malaguzzi Valeri, Francesco: "Un collezionista bolognese del Seicento," *L'Archiginnasio*, XIII, 1918, pp. 29–48.
Malanima, Paolo: *I Ricciardi di Firenze: Una famiglia e un patrimonio nella Toscana dei Medici*, Florence: Olschki, 1977.
Malanima, Paolo: *La decadenza di un'economia cittadina: L'industria di Firenze nei secoli XVI–XVIII*, Bologna: Il Mulino, 1982.
Malanima, Paolo: "L'economia toscana nell'età di Cosimo III," in *La Toscana nell'età di Cosimo III*, ed. Franco Angiolini, Vieri Becagli, and Marcello Verga, Florence: Edifir, 1993, pp. 3–17.
Malanima, Paolo: *La fine del primato: Crisi e riconversione nell'Italia del Seicento*, Milan: Bruno Mondadori, 1998.
Malanima Paolo: "L'economia toscana dalla peste nera alla fine del Seicento," in *Storia della Toscana, 3: Dal 1350 al 1700*, ed. Elena Fasano Guarini, Giuseppe Petralia, and Paolo Pezzino, Bari: Laterza, 2001, pp. 51–70.
Malanima, Paolo: *L'economia italiana: Dalla crescita medievale alla crescita contemporanea*, Bologna: Il Mulino, 2002.
Malanima, Paolo: "Measuring the Italian Economy, 1300–1861," *Rivista di Storia Economica*, XIX, 2003, pp. 265–95.
Malvasia, Carlo Cesare: *Felsina pittrice: Vite de' pittori bolognesi*, Bologna, 1678 (reprint, ed. Giampietro Zanotti et al., Bologna: Guidi all'Ancora, 1841).
Malvasia, Carlo Cesare: *Le pitture di Bologna*, Bologna: Monti, 1686 (reprint, ed. Giampietro Zanotti, Bologna: Nella stamperia del Longhi, 1732).
Malvasia, Carlo Cesare: *The Life of Guido Reni*, trans. Catherine Enggass and Robert Enggass, University Park, PA: Pennsylvania State University Press, 1980.
Malvasia, Carlo Cesare: *Scritti originali del conte Carlo Cesare Malvasia spettanti alla Felsina Pittrice*, ed. Lea Marzocchi, Bologna: Alfa, 1982.
Mampieri, Antonella: "Ludovico Lana," in *La Scuola di Guido Reni*, ed. Emilio Negro and Massimo Pirondini, Modena: Artioli, 1992, pp. 277–94.
Mancini, Francesco Federico (ed.): *Gian Domenico Cerrini: Il Cavalier Perugino tra classicismo e barocco* (exh. cat., Palazzo Baldeschi al Corso, Perugia), Cinisello Balsamo: Silvana Editoriale, 2005.
Mancini, Giulio: *Considerazioni sulla pittura*, ed. Adriana Marucchi and Luigi Salerno, Rome: Accademia nazionale dei Lincei, 1956–57.
Mancini, Vincenzo: "I colori della bottega: Sui commerci di Tiziano e Orazio Vecellio con la corte di Spagna," *Venezia Cinquecento*, VI, no. 11, 1996, pp. 163–73.
Mancini, Vincenzo: "Pittura del Seicento a Padova: Un 'Francese' pittore di 'bagatele'," *Bollettino del Museo Civico di Padova*, XC, 2001, pp. 39–48.
Mandich, G.: "Formule monetarie veneziane del periodo 1619–1650," *Il Risparmio*, V, 1957, pp. 634–82.
Manni, Domenico Maria (ed.): *Ricordanze della vita e pitture di Cosimo Ulivelli cittadino fiorentino e dipintor rinomato lasciate scritte da un suo contemporaneo*, Florence: Giovanni Risaliti, 1772.
Mannini, Maria Pia: *La decorazione in villa tra Sesto e Castello nel XVI e XVII secolo (grottesche, allegorie, emblemi)*, Sesto Fiorentino: Nova, 1979.
Mannini, Maria Pia: "Giovanni da San Giovanni," in *Il Seicento Fiorentino: Arte a Firenze da Ferdinando I a Cosimo III* (exh. cat., Palazzo Strozzi, Florence), vol. 3, Florence: Cantini, 1986, pp. 100–3.
Mantovanelli, Stefani: "Giovanni Battista Langetti: Profilo dell'artista e catalogo ragionato delle sue opere," *Saggi e memorie di storia dell'arte*, XVII, 1990, pp. 43–105.
Mantovanelli, Stefani: "Strozzi 'ingegnere' nella Repubblica di Venetia, e Langetti: Novità su due artisti genovesi e il milieu culturale della Serenissima," *Arte documento*, V, 1991, pp. 186–95.
Manzato, Davide: "Il soffitto dell'oratorio della SS. Trinità di Chioggia," *Arte veneta*, XXVI, 1975, pp. 111–20.
Marabottini, Alessandro: *Jacopo di Chimenti da Empoli*, Rome: De Luca, 1988.
Marcato, Gianna: "Istituzioni scolastiche, modelli culturali e scelte

politiche della Serenissima," in *Società, economia, istituzioni: Elementi per la conoscenza della Repubblica Veneta, II: Società e cultura*, Verona: Cierre, 2002, pp. 95–136.

Marchini, Gian Paolo: "Le origini dell'Accademia di Pittura di Verona," *Atti e Memorie dell'Accademia di Agricoltura, Scienze e Lettere di Verona*, XXVII, 1976, pp. 243–75.

Marchini, Gian Paolo: "Il collezionismo d'arte a Verona nel Settecento: La pinacoteca Mosconi," *Studi Storici Veronesi Luigi Simeoni*, XXX–XXXI, 1980–81, pp. 222–49.

Marchini, Giuseppe and Emma Micheletti (eds.): *La chiesa di Santa Trinita a Firenze*, Florence: Giunti, 1987.

Marcolini, Giuliana: "Cesare d'Este, Caravaggio e Annibale Carracci: Un duca, due pittori e una committenza 'a mal termine'," in *Sovrane passioni: Studi sul collezionismo estense*, ed. Jadranka Bentini, Milan: Federico Motta, 1998, pp. 9–35.

Marin, Brigitte: "Milieu professionnel et réseaux d'échanges intellectuels: Les médecins à Naples dans la seconde moitié du XVIIIe siècle," in *Naples, Rome, Florence: Une histoire comparée des milieux intellectuels italiens (XVIIe–XVIIIe siècles)*, ed. Jean Boutier, Brigitte Marin, and Antonella Romano, Rome: École Française de Rome, 2005, pp. 123–67.

Marinelli, Sergio: "Note da Felice Brusasorci a Pietro Ricchi," *Verona illustrata*, VII, 1994, pp. 65–76.

Marinelli, Sergio and Angelo Mazza (eds.): *Paolo Piazza: Pittore cappuccino nell'età della Controriforma tra conventi e corti d'Europa*, Verona: Banco Popolare di Verona e Novara, 2002.

Marini, Giorgio, Paola Marini, and Francesca Rossi (eds.): *Paolo Farinati 1524–1606: Dipinti, incisioni e disegni per l'architettura* (exh. cat., Museo di Castelvecchio, Verona), Venice: Marsilio, 2005.

Marino, J. A.: "La crisi di Venezia e la New Economic History," *Studi storici*, XIX, 1978, pp. 79–107.

Marshall, Christopher R.: "'Causa di Stravaganze': Order and Anarchy in Domenico Gargiulo's Revolt of Masaniello," *The Art Bulletin*, LXXX, 1998, pp. 478–97.

Marshall, Christopher R.: "'Senza il minimo scrupolo': Artists as Dealers in Seventeenth Century Naples," *Journal of the History of Collections*, XII, 2000, pp. 15–34.

Marshall, Christopher R.: "Appagare il pubblico: The Marketing Strategies of Luca Giordano (1673–1684)," in *The Art Market in Italy 15th–17th Centuries: Il mercato dell'arte in Italia secc. XV–XVII*, ed. Marcello Fantoni, Louisa C. Matthew, and Sara F. Matthews-Grieco, Ferrara: Panini, 2003, pp. 263–72.

Marshall, Christopher R.: "Markets, Money and Artistic Manoeuvres: Bernardo Cavallino and the Grand Manner," in *The Italians in Australia: Studies in Renaissance and Baroque Art*, ed. David R. Marshall, Florence: Centro Di with the University of Melbourne, 2004, pp. 41–48.

Marshall, Christopher R.: "The Spirit of Caesar in this Soul of a Woman: Artemisia Gentileschi and the Will to Succeed, 1629–54," *Melbourne Art Journal*, no. 8, 2005, pp. 4–27.

Marshall, Christopher R.: "Dispelling Negative Perceptions: Dealers Promoting Artists in Seventeenth-Century Naples," in *Mapping Markets for Paintings in Europe, 1450–1750*, ed. Neil De Marchi and Hans J. Van Miegroet, Turnhout: Brepols, 2006, pp. 363–80.

Martinat, Monica: *Le juste marché: Le système annonaire romain aux XVIe et XVIIe siècles*, Rome: École Française de Rome, 2004.

Martineau, Jane and Andrew Robison (eds.): *The Glory of Venice: Art in the Eighteenth Century* (exh. cat., Royal Academy of Arts, London, and National Gallery of Art, Washington, D.C.), New Haven and London: Yale University Press, 1994.

Martinelli Braglia, Graziella: "Matteo Loves: Ritratto di Francesco I d'Este, Ritratto di Maria Farnese d'Este," in *Sovrane Passioni: Le raccolte d'arte della Ducale Galleria Estense* (exh. cat., Galleria Estense, Palazzo dei Musei, Modena), ed. Jadranka Bentini, Milan: Federico Motta, 1998, pp. 288–89, cat. 82–83.

Martinetti, Giovanni: *S. Ignazio* (Le chiese di Roma illustrate, no. 97), Rome: Marietti, 1967.

Martini, Angelo: *Manuale di metrologia ossia misure, pesi e monete*, Turin: Ermanno Loescher, 1883.

Martini, Antonio: *Arti mestieri e fede nella Roma dei papi*, Bologna: Cappelli, 1965.

Martini, Georg Christoph: *Viaggio in Toscana (1725–1745)*, trans. Oscar Trumpy, Modena: Artioli, 1969.

Marzocchi, Lea: *Le carte di Carlo Cesare Malvasia: Le "vite" di Guido Reni e di Simone Cantarini dal manoscritto B 16–17 della Biblioteca Comunale dell'Archiginnasio di Bologna* (Rapporti della Soprintendenza per i Beni artistici e storici per le province di Bologna, Ferrara, Forlì e Ravenna), Bologna: Alfa, 1980.

Mascalchi, Silvia: "Vincenzo Mannozzi," in *Il Seicento Fiorentino: Arte a Firenze da Ferdinando I a Cosimo III* (exh. cat., Palazzo Strozzi, Florence), vol. 3, Florence: Cantini, 1986, pp. 111–12.

Maschio, R.: "La casa di Marco Boschini," *Atti dell'Istituto Veneto di Scienze, Lettere ed Arti*, CXXXIV, 1976, pp. 115–42.

Masetti, Anna Rosa: *Cecco Bravo pittore toscano del Seicento*, Venice: Pozza, 1962a.

Masetti, Anna Rosa: "Il Casino Mediceo e la pittura fiorentina del Seicento," *Critica d'arte*, IX, 1962b, part 1, no. 50, pp. 1–27, and part 2, no. 53–54, pp. 77–109.

Masetti Zannini, Gian Ludovico: "Ebrei, artisti, oggetti d'arte (documenti romani dei secoli XVI e XVII)," *Commentari*, XXV, 1974a, pp. 281–301.

Masetti Zannini, Gian Ludovico: *Pittori della seconda metà del Cinquecento in Roma*, Rome: De Luca, 1974b.

Masini, Antonio: *Bologna perlustrata*, Bologna: Benacci, 1666.

Mason Rinaldi, Stefania: "Precisazioni cronologiche su due dipinti di Palma il Giovane," *Arte veneta*, XXVIII, 1974, pp. 248–54.

Mason Rinaldi, Stefania: "Francesco Bassano e il soffitto del Maggior Consiglio in Palazzo Ducale," *Arte veneta*, XXXIV, 1980, pp. 214–19.

Mason Rinaldi, Stefania: *Palma il Giovane: L'opera completa*, Milan: Electa, 1984.

Mason, Stefania (Stefania Mason Rinaldi prior to 1996): "Per il collezionismo a Venezia nel Seicento: Conservatorismo nostalgico e aperture al contemporaneo," in *Geografia del collezionismo: Italia e Francia tra il XVI e il XVIII secolo*, ed. Olivier Bonfait et al., Rome: École Française de Rome, 2001, pp. 225–37.

Mason, Stefania: "Ritratti, perizie, acquisti e vendite: L'artista nel collezionismo e nel mercato del Cinquecento," in *Il collezionismo d'arte a Venezia: Dalle origini al Cinquecento*, ed. Michel Hochmann, Rosella Lauber, and Stefania Mason, Venice: Marsilio, 2008, pp. 107–20.

Matteoli, Anna: "Documenti su Cecco Bravo," *Rivista d'arte*, XLII, 1990, pp. 96–146.

Matteucci, Anna Maria and Giuseppina Raggi: "Agostino Mitelli a Palazzo Pitti: Un problema aperto" and "I documenti," in *Studi di storia dell'arte in onore di Mina Gregori*, Cinisello Balsamo: Silvana Editoriale, 1994, pp. 269–78.

Matteucci, Anna Maria and Giuseppina Raggi: "Angelo Michele Colonna e Agostino Mitelli al Casino di via della Scala a Firenze," in *Scritti per l'Istituto Germanico di Storia dell'Arte di Firenze: Settanta *studiosi italiani*, eds. Cristina Acidini Luchinat, Luciano Bellosi, Miklos Boskovits, Pier Paolo Donati, and Bruno Santi, Florence: Le Lettere, 1997, pp. 395–400.

Matteucci, Anna Maria and Rossella Ariuli: *Giovanni Francesco Grimaldi*, Bologna: CLUEB, 2002.

Matthew, Louisa: "The Painters' Presence: Signatures in Venetian Renaissance Pictures," *The Art Bulletin*, LXXX, 1998, pp. 616–48.

Matthew, Louisa: "'Vendecolori a Venezia': The Reconstruction of a Profession," *The Burlington Magazine*, CXLIV, 2002, pp. 680–86.

Matthew, Louisa: "Were There Open Markets for Pictures in Renaissance Venice?" in *The Art Market in Italy 15th–17th Centuries: Il mercato dell'arte in Italia secc. XV–XVII*, ed. Marcello Fantoni, Louisa C. Matthew, and Sara F. Matthews-Grieco, Ferrara: Franco Cosimo Panini, 2003, pp. 253–62.

Matthew, Louisa: "Painters Marketing Paintings in Fifteenth and Sixteenth-Century Florence and Venice," in *Mapping Markets for Paintings in Europe, 1450–1750*, ed. Neil De Marchi and Hans J. Van Miegroet, Turnhout: Brepols, 2006, pp. 307–28.

Mattozzi, Ivo: "Crisi, stagnazione e mutamento nello Stato veneziano sei-settecento: Il caso del commercio e della produzione olearia," *Studi Veneziani*, IV, 1980, pp. 199–276.

Mattozzi, Ivo, Francesco Bolelli, Carmen Chiasera, and Daniela Sabbioni: "Il politico e il pane a Venezia (1570–1650): Calmieri e governo della sussistenza," *Società e storia*, XX, 1983, pp. 271–303.

Mazza, Angelo: "La Madonna del Rosario . . . ," in *Guido Reni, 1575–1642* (exh. cat., Pinacoteca nazionale, Bologna), Bologna: Nuova Alfa, 1988, pp. 136–38, cat. 57.

Mazza, Cristiana: *I Sagredo: Committenti e collezionisti d'arte nella Venezia del Sei e Settecento*, Venice: Istituto Veneto di Scienze, Lettere ed Arti, 2003.

Mazzetti di Pietralata, Cecilia: "Giusti Antonio," in *Dizionario biografico degli italiani*, vol. LVII, Rome: Istituto della Enciclopedia italiana, 2001, pp. 168–70.

Megna, Laura: "Comportamenti abitativi del patriziato veneziano (1582–1740)," *Studi Veneziani*, XXII, 1991, pp. 253–323.

Megna, Tommaso: "Gherardo delle Notti a Roma: Le commissioni pubbliche, il 'patronage' Giustiniani e nuovi elementi documentari," in *Decorazione e collezionismo a Roma nel Seicento: Vicende di artisti, committenti, mercanti*, ed. Francesca Cappelletti, Rome: Gangemi, 2003, pp. 87–100.

Melchiori, Nadal: *Notizie di pittori e altri scritti, 1720*, ed. Giampaolo Bordignon Favero, Venice and Rome: Istituto per la collaborazione culturale, 1964.

Meloni, Silvia and Elena Fumagalli (eds.): *Giovanna Garzoni: Natures mortes*, Paris: Bibliothèque de l'image, 2000.

Menniti Ippolito, A.: *Fortuna e sfortune di una famiglia veneziana nel Seicento: Ottoboni al tempo dell'aggregazione al patriziato*, Venice: Istituto Veneto di Scienze, Lettere ed Arti, 1996.

Merling, Mitchell: *Marco Boschini's 'La carta del navegar pitoresco': Art Theory and Virtuoso Culture in Seventeenth-Century Venice* (Ph.D. diss., Brown University, 1992), Ann Arbor: U.M.I., 1992.

Merz, Jörg Martin: *Pietro da Cortona: Der Aufstieg zum führender Maler im barocken Rom*, Tübingen: Ernst Wasmuth, 1991.

Merz, Jörg Martin: *Pietro da Cortona und sein Kreis: Die Zeichnungen in Düsseldorf*, Munich and Berlin: Deutscher Kunstverlag, 2005.

Mezzetti, Amalia: "Contributi a Carlo Maratti," *Rivista dell'Istituto Nazionale d'Archeologia e Storia dell'Arte*, IV, 1955, pp. 253–354.

Migliorini, Maurizia and Alfonso Assini: *Pittori in tribunale: Un processo per copie e falsi alla fine del Seicento*, Nuoro: Ilisso, 2000.

Miller, Dwight C.: *Marcantonio Franceschini and the Liechtensteins*, Cambridge and New York: Cambridge University Press, 1991.

Miller, Dwight C.: *Marcantonio Franceschini*, trans. Cristina Casali and Fabio Chiodini, Turin: Artema, 2001.

Miller, Peter: "Friendship and Conversation in Seventeenth-Century Venice," *Journal of Modern History*, LXXIII, 2001, pp. 1–31.

Mira, G.: *Vicende economiche di una famiglia italiana dal XIV al XVIII secolo*, Milan: Vita e pensiero, 1940.

Mirto, Alfonso: *Lucas Holstenius e la corte medicea: Carteggio (1629–1660)*, Florence: Olschki, 1999.

Missirini, Melchoir: *Memorie per servire alla storia della romana Accademia di S. Luca fino alla morte di Antonio Canova*, Rome: De Romanis, 1823.

Modesti, Adelina: "Patrons as Agents and Artists as Dealers in Seicento Bologna," in *The Art Market in Italy 15th–17th Centuries: Il mercato dell'arte in Italia secc. XV–XVII*, ed. Marcello Fantoni, Louisa C. Matthew, and Sara F. Matthews-Grieco, Ferrara: Panini, 2003, pp. 367–88.

Modesti, Adelina: *Elisabetta Sirani, una virtuosa del Seicento bolognese*, Bologna: Compositori, 2004.

Mojana, Marina: *Valentin de Boulogne*, Milan: Eikonos, 1989.

Molli, Giovanna Baldissin: "Le pale d'altare 'bresciane' di Paolo Farinati," *Arte Documento*, XIII, 1999, pp. 183–87.

Molmenti, Pompeo: *G. B. Tiepolo, la sua vita e le sue opere*, Milan: U. Hoepli, 1909.

Monconys, Balthasar de: *Journal des voyages*, Lyon: Boissat, 1666.

Monducci, Elio: "Regesto e documenti," in *Alessandro Tiarini (1577–1668)*, ed. Massimo Pirondini et al., Manerba: Merigo, 2000, pp. 337–59.

Monducci, Elio: "Regesto e documenti," in *Leonello Spada (1576–1622)*, ed. Massimo Pirondini et al., Manerba: Merigo, 2002, pp. 155–78.

Montagu, Jennifer: *Roman Baroque Sculpture*, New Haven and London: Yale University Press, 1989.

Montaigne, Michel de: *The Complete Works*, trans. Donald M. Frame, New York: Everyman's Library, 2003.

Montalto, Lina: "Francesco Cozza nella libreria Pamphilj a Piazza Navona," *Commentari*, VII, 1956, pp. 41–52.

Montanari, Tomaso: "Bellori and Christina of Sweden," in *Art History in the Age of Bellori*, ed. Janis Bell and Thomas Willette, Cambridge: Cambridge University Press, 2002, pp. 94–126.

Montecuccoli degli Erri, Federico: "Venezia 1745–1750: Case (e botteghe) di pittori mercanti di quadri, incisori, scultori, architetti, stampatori e altri personaggi veneziani," *Ateneo Veneto*, CLXXXVI, 1998, pp. 63–140.

Montecuccoli degli Erri, Federico: "Il mercato dei quadri a Venezia nel XVIII secolo," in *Michele Marieschi: La vita, l'ambiente, l'opera*, ed. Federico Montecuccoli degli Erri and Filippo Pedrocco, Milan: Bocca, 1999, pp. 11–21.

Montecuccoli degli Erri, Federico and Filippo Pedrocco (eds.): *Michele Marieschi: La vita, l'ambiente, l'opera*, Milan: Bocca, 1999.

Montias, John Michael: "The Influence of Economic Factors on Style," *De Zeventiende eeuw*, VI, 1990, pp. 49–57.

Montias, John Michael: *Le marché de l'art aux Pays-Bas (XVe–XVIIe siècles)*, Paris: Flammarion, 1996.

Montias, John Michael: *Art at Auction in 17th Century Amsterdam*, Amsterdam: Amsterdam University Press, 2002.

Morandotti, Alessandro: *Paolo Pagani e i Pagani di Castello Valsolda*, Lugano: Fidia, 2000.

Morandotti, Alessandro: "Milano tra età spagnola e dominio austriaco: Componenti sociali e circolazione artistica," in *Geografia del collezionismo: Italia e Francia tra il XVI e il XVIII secolo*, ed. Olivier Bonfait et al., Rome: École Française de Rome, 2001, pp. 163–83.

Morassi, Antonio: *A Complete Catalogue of the Paintings of G. B. Tiepolo*, London: Phaidon, 1962.
Morassi, Antonio: "A 'Scuola del Nudo' by Tiepolo," *Master Drawings*, IX, 1971, pp. 43–50.
Morello, Federica: "I Caldogno committenti di Giulio Carpioni," *Arte veneta*, LV, 1999, pp. 162–78.
Moretti, Lino: "Documenti e appunti su Sebastiano Ricci (con qualche cenno su altri pittori del Settecento)," *Saggi e memorie di storia dell'arte*, XI, 1978, pp. 95–125.
Moretti, Lino: "Antonio Molinari rivisitato," *Arte veneta*, XXXIII, 1979, pp. 59–69.
Moretti, Lino: "Novità documentarie su Nicola Grassi," in *Nicola Grassi e il Rococò europeo: Atti del Congresso Internationale di Studi*, Udine: Istituto per l'Enciclopedia del Friuli Venezia Giulia, 1984, pp. 15–23.
Moretti, Lino: "L'eredità del pittore: L'inventario dei quadri 'al tempo della sua morte'," in *Bernardo Strozzi: Genova 1581/82–Venezia 1644* (exh. cat., Palazzo Ducale, Genoa), ed. Ezia Gavazza, Giovanna Nepi Sciré, and Giovanna Rotondi Terminiello, Milan: Electa, 1995, pp. 376–78.
Morper, Johann Joseph: "Johann Friedrich Graf von Waldstein und Claude Lorrain," *Münchner Jahrbuch der bildenden Kunst*, XII, 1961, pp. 203–17.
Morselli, Raffaella: "Enrico Kaiel," in *La Scuola di Guido Reni*, ed. Emilio Negro and Massimo Pirondini, Modena: Artioli, 1992a, pp. 275–76.
Morselli, Raffaella: "Guido Reni: I collezionisti, gli allievi, le copie," in *La Scuola di Guido Reni*, ed. Emilio Negro and Massimo Pirondini, Modena: Artioli, 1992b, pp. 17–25.
Morselli, Raffaella: "Ludovico e allievi nelle collezioni bolognesi del Seicento," in *La scuola dei Carracci: Dall'Accademia alla bottega di Ludovico*, ed. Emilio Negro and Massimo Pirondini, Modena: Artioli, 1994, pp. 13–20.
Morselli, Raffaella: "Alessandro Tiarini e l'iconografia di Santa Francesca Romana: Un modello per la scuola pittorica bolognese del Seicento," in *L'Istituto Rizzoli in San Michele in Bosco: Il patrimonio artistico del monastero e vicende storiche di cento anni di chirurgia ortopedica*, ed. Alfredo Cioni and Anna Maria Bertoli, Bologna: IOR, 1996, pp. 203–11.
Morselli, Raffaella: *Repertorio per lo studio del collezionismo bolognese del Seicento*, Bologna: Pàtron, 1997.
Morselli, Raffaella: *Collezionisti e quadrerie nella Bologna del Seicento: Inventari 1640–1707* (Documents for the History of Collecting, The Provenance Index of the Getty Information Institute), Los Angeles: The J. Paul Getty Trust, 1998a.
Morselli, Raffaella: "Protettori, mercanti, collezionisti: La Bologna di Simone Cantarini," in *Simone Cantarini detto il Pesarese, 1612–1648* (exh. cat., Pinacoteca nazionale, Bologna), ed. Andrea Emiliani, Milan: Electa, 1998b, pp. 50–69.
Morselli, Raffaella: *Il flavo delle stelle: Una sera di giugno dell'anno 1623 alla corte dei Gonzaga*, Mantua: Tre Lune, 1999.
Morselli, Raffaella: *Le collezioni Gonzaga: L'elenco dei beni del 1626–1627*, Cinisello Balsamo: Silvana Editoriale, 2000.
Morselli, Raffaella: "Vincenzo Gonzaga, Domenico Tintoretto e altri artisti veneziani: Intrecci e microstrie di committenze e di commercio artistico tra Venezia e Mantova al volgere del Cin-quecento," in *Figure di collezionisti a Venezia tra Cinque e Seicento*, ed. Linda Borean and Stefania Mason, Udine: Forum, 2002, pp. 77–116.
Morselli, Raffaella: "Le occasioni di Guido: Profitti e sperperi nella carriera di un pittore 'un poco extraordinario'," in *Vivere d'arte: Carriere e finanze nell'Italia moderna*, ed. Raffaella Morselli, Rome: Carocci, 2007.
Mortari, Luisa: *Bernardo Strozzi*, Rome: De Luca, 1995.
Moryson, Fynes: *An Itinerary Containing his Ten Yeeres Travell through the Twelve Dominions of Germany, Bohmerland, Sweitzerland, Netherland, Denmarke, Poland, Italy, Turky, France, England, Scotland & Ireland*, London, 1617 (reprint, Glasgow: James MacLehose and Sons, 1907).
Moryson, Fynes: *Shakespeare's Europe: Unpublished Chapters of Fynes Moryson's Itinerary*, London: Sherratt and Hughes, 1903.
Moschetti, A.: "La Scuola di San Rocco e i suoi recenti restauri," *Padova: Rivista comunale dell'attività cittadina*, IV, no. 1, 1930, pp. 15–67.
Moücke, Francesco: *Serie di ritratti degli eccellenti pittori dipinti di propria mano che esistono nell'Imperial Galleria di Firenze, colle vite in compendio de' medesimi descritte da Francesco Moücke*, Florence: Nella Stamperia Moückiana, 1752–62.
Mozzato, Andrea and Reinhold Mueller: "Prezzi e monete nella vacchetta di Tiberio Tinelli," in *Libretto dei conti del pittore Tiberio Tinelli (1618–1633)*, ed. Bianca Lanfranchi Strina, Venice: Comitato, 2000, pp. xxvii–xlv.
Mucchi, Antonio Maria and C. Della Croce: *Il pittore Andrea Celesti*, Cinisello Balsamo: Silvana Editoriale, 1954.
Muraro, Michelangelo: "I conti in tasca a Lorenzo Lotto," *Notizie da Palazzo Albani*, XIII, 1984, pp. 144–64.
Muraro, Michelangelo: *Il Libro secondo di Francesco e Jacopo dal Ponte*, Bassano: G. B. Verci, 1992.
Muzzarelli, Maria Giuseppina: *La legislazione suntuaria: Secoli XIII–XVI: Emilia-Romagna*, Rome: Pubblicazioni degli Archivi di Stato, 2002.
Nacamulli, Flavia: "Notizie su alcuni pittori operanti a Venezia nella seconda metà del Seicento," *Arte veneta*, XLI, 1987, pp. 184–88.
Nannelli, Francesca: "Antonio Franchi e la sua 'vita' scritta da Francesco Saverio Baldinucci," *Paradigma*, I, 1977, pp. 317–69.
Nappi, Eduardo: *Aspetti della società e dell'economia napoletana durante la peste del 1656: Dai documenti dell'Archivio Storico del Banco di Napoli*, Naples: Banco di Napoli, 1980.
Nappi, Eduardo: "I vicere e l'arte a Napoli," *Napoli Nobilissima*, XXII, 1983a, pp. 41–57.
Nappi, Eduardo: "Pittori del '600 a Napoli: Notizie inedite dai documenti dell'Archivio Storico del Banco di Napoli," in *Ricerche sul '600 napoletano: Saggi vari*, Milan: L&T, 1983b, pp. 73–80.
Nappi, Eduardo: "Le chiese di Giovan Giacomo Conforto (dai documenti dell'Archivio Storico del Banco di Napoli," in *Ricerche sul '600 napoletano*, Milan: L&T, 1988, pp. 129–52.
Nappi, Eduardo: "Un regesto di documenti editi ed inediti, tratti prevalentemente dall'Archivio Storico del Banco di Napoli, riguardanti Giuseppe Ribera e una conferma della presenza a Napoli nel novembre 1630 di Velázquez," in *Ricerche sul '600 napoletano*, Milan: L&T, 1990, pp. 177–86.
Nappi, Eduardo: "Momenti della vita di Luca Giordano nei documenti dell'Archivio Storico del Banco di Napoli," in *Ricerche sul '600 napoletano*, Milan: L&T, 1991, pp. 157–82.
Nappi, Eduardo (ed.): *Ricerche sul '600 napoletano: Catalogo delle pubblicazioni edite dal 1883 al 1990, riguardanti le opere di architetti, pittori, scultori, marmorari ed intagliatori per i secoli XVI e XVII, pagate tramite gli antichi banchi pubblici napoletani*, Milan: L&T, 1992.
Nappi, Eduardo: "La chiesa delle Anime del Purgatorio ad Arco nei secoli XVII–XVIII," in *Ricerche sul '600 napoletano, 1996–1997*, Naples: Electa, 1998, pp. 155–76.
Nappi, Eduardo: "La cappella del Tesoro e la Guglia di San Gennaro:

Nuovi documenti e nuove fonti," in *Ricerche sul '600 napoletano, 2001*, Milan: L&T, 2002, pp. 91–99.
Narducci, Enrico: "Artisti dimoranti in Roma nel rione di Campo Marzio l'anno 1656," *Il Buonarotti*, V, 1870, pp. 122–26.
Nasini, Giuseppe: *Della vita e delle opere del Cav. Giuseppe Nasini pittore del secolo XVII: Notizie raccolte ed ordinate dal Cav. G. N.*, Prato: Bruzzi, 1872.
Natale, Mauro: *Peintures Italiennes du XIV au XVIII Siècle* (Catalogue du Musée d'Art et d'Histoire, Genève), Geneva: Musée d'Art et d'Histoire, 1979.
Navarro, Fausta: "L'amico fiorentino di Gian Domenico Cerrini," in *Gian Domenico Cerrini: Il Cavalier Perugino tra classicismo e barocco* (exh. cat., Palazzo Baldeschi al Corso, Perugia), ed. Francesco Federico Mancini, Cinisello Balsamo: Silvana Editoriale, 2005, pp. 87–91.
Negro, Angela: *Il giardino dipinto del Cardinal Borghese*, Rome: Àrgos, 1996.
Negro, Angela: *La collezione Rospigliosi*, Rome: Àrgos, 1999.
Negro, Emilio and Massimo Pirondini (eds.): *La Scuola di Guido Reni*, Modena: Artioli, 1992.
Negro, Emilio and Nicosetta Roio: *Giacomo Cavedone 1577–1660*, Modena: Artioli, 1996.
Negro, Emilio and Nicosetta Roio: *Bartolomeo Schedoni 1578–1615*, Modena: Artioli, 2000.
Neppi, Lionello: *Palazzo Spada*, Rome: Editalia, 1975.
Nesi, Alessandro: "Nuovi argomenti e inediti documentari per Andrea Boscoli," *Storia dell'arte*, no. 110, 2005, pp. 105–12.
Niccoli, Ottavia: *Storie di ogni giorno in una città del Seicento*, Rome: Laterza, 2000.
Nichols, Tom: *Tintoretto: Tradition and Identity*, London: Reaktion, 1999.
Nicoletti, G.: "Per la storia dell'arte veneziana: Lista di nomi di artisti tolta dai libri di tanse o luminarie della fraglia dei pittori," *Ateneo Veneto*, XIV, 1980, pp. 378–82.
Noris, Fernando: "'Aver almeno impedito che Bergamo fosse raggiunta dall'ondata barocca' (il 'caso' S. Maria Maggiore)," in *Il Seicento a Bergamo* (exh. cat., Palazzo della Ragione, Bergamo), ed. Simonetta Coppa and Francesco Rossi, Cariplo: Cassa di Risparmio delle Provincie Lombarde and Bergamo: Comune di Bergamo, 1987, pp. 137–49.
North, Michael: "Auctions and the Emergence of an Art Market in Eighteenth-Century Germany," in *Mapping Markets for Paintings in Europe, 1450–1750*, ed. Neil De Marchi and Hans J. Van Miegroet, Turnhout: Brepols, 2006, pp. 285–304.
North, Michael and David Ormrod (eds.): *Art Markets in Europe, 1400–1800*, Aldershot: Ashgate, 1998.
Novelli, M.: "Nuovi accertamenti sul soggiorno bolognese di Sebastiano Ricci e suoi rapporti col Peruzzini," *Arte veneta*, XXXII, 1978, pp. 346–51.
Novelli Radice, Magda: "Contributi alla conscenza di Andrea e Onofrio de Leone," *Napoli Nobilissima*, XV, 1976, pp. 162–69.
Novelli Radice, Magda, "Notizie d'archivio sulla Chiesa di S. Maria la Nova in Napoli," *Campania Sacra*, XIII, no. 14, 1982–83, pp. 145–85.
Novelli Radice, Magda: "Andrea de Leone frescante e ipotesi sulla sua bottega," *Napoli Nobilissima*, XXVII, 1988, pp. 41–53.
Nussdorfer, Laurie: *Civic Politics in the Rome of Urban VIII*, Princeton: Princeton University Press, 1992.
Nussdorfer, Laurie: "Politics and the People of Rome," in *Rome–Amsterdam: Two Growing Cities in Seventeenth-Century Europe*, ed. Peter van Kessel and Elisja Schulte, Amsterdam: Amsterdam University Press, 1997, pp. 146–55.
Nuttall, Paula: *From Flanders to Florence: The Impact of Netherlandish Painting, 1400–1500*, New Haven and London: Yale University Press, 2004.
Olivari, Mariolina: catalogue entry for Antonio Zanchi, *Birth of the Virgin* (Sombreno, Santuario della Natività di Maria), in *Il Seicento a Bergamo* (exh. cat., Palazzo della Ragione, Bergamo), ed. Simonetta Coppa and Francesco Rossi, Cariplo: Cassa di Risparmio delle Provincie Lombarde and Bergamo: Comune di Bergamo, 1987, p. 103.
Olivato, Loredana: *Provvedimenti della Repubblica Veneta per la salvaguardia del patrimonio pittorico nei secoli XVII e XVIII*, Venice: Istituto Veneto di Scienze, Lettere ed Arti, 1974.
Oliveti, Chiara: "Contributo alla riscoperta di Giovanni Montini," *Proporzioni: Annali della Fondazione Roberto Longhi*, II–III, 2001–2, pp. 139–63.
O'Malley, Michelle: "Late Fifteenth- and Early Sixteenth-Century Painting Contracts and the Stipulated Use of the Painter's Hand," in *With and Without the Medici: Studies in Tuscan Art and Patronage 1434–1530*, ed. Eckart Marchand and Alison Wright, Aldershot: Ashgate, 1998, pp. 155–78.
O'Malley, Michelle: "Commissioning Bodies, Allocation Decisions and Price Structures for Altarpieces in Fifteenth- and Early Sixteenth-Century Italy," in *The Art Market in Italy 15th–17th Centuries: Il mercato dell'arte in Italia secc. XV–XVII*, ed. Marcello Fantoni, Louisa C. Matthew, and Sara F. Matthews-Grieco, Ferrara: Panini, 2003, pp. 163–80.
O'Malley, Michelle: *The Business of Art: Contracts and the Commissioning Process in Renaissance Italy*, New Haven and London: Yale University Press, 2005.
O'Malley, Michelle: "Pietro Perugino and the Contingency of Value," in *The Material Renaissance*, ed. Michelle O'Malley and Evelyn Welch, Manchester and New York: Manchester University Press, 2007, pp. 106–30.
O'Neil, Maryvelma Smith: *Giovanni Baglione*, Cambridge: Cambridge University Press, 2002.
Orbaan, J.: *Documenti sul Barocco in Roma*, Rome: Società alla Biblioteca Vallicelliana, 1920.
Oretti, Marcello: *Descrizione delle pitture che sono state esposte nelle Strade di Bologna per la festa del SS. Sacrimento*, Biblioteca Comunale dell'Archiginnasio, Bologna, ms B105.
Orlandi, Pellegrino Antonio: *Abcedario [sic] pittorico*, Bologna: Per Costantino Pisarri, 1719.
Orlandi, Pellegrino Antonio: *Abecedario pittorico*, ed. Pietro Guarienti, Venice: G. B. Pasquali, 1753.
Orlandi Balzari, Vittoria: "Alessandro Verri antiquario in Roma," *Quaderni storici*, XXXIX, 2004, pp. 495–528.
Ottani Cavina, Anna: *Carlo Saraceni*, Milan: Mario Spagnol, 1968.
Ottonelli, Giovanni Domenico and Pietro Berrettini [da Cortona]: *Trattato della pittura e scultura, uso et abuso loro*, Florence: Gio. Antonio Bonardi, 1652 (reprint, ed. Vittorio Casale, Treviso: Canova, 1973).
Pacelli, Vincenzo: "Affreschi storici in Palazzo Reale," in *Seicento napoletano: Arte, costume, ambiente*, ed. Roberto Pane, Milan: Edizioni di comunità, 1984a, pp. 158–79.
Pacelli, Vincenzo: "Testimonianze, considerazioni e problemi di restauro sui dipinti seicenteschi dell'Annunziata di Capua," in *Ricerche sul '600 napoletano: Saggi vari in memoria di Raffaello Causa*, Milan: L&T, 1984b, pp. 85–119.
Pacini, Piero: "Dipinti di Ciro Ferri e di Luca Giordano nella cappella maggiore della Chiesa di Santa Maria Maddalena de' Pazzi a Firenze," *Antichità viva*, XXXVI, no. 2–3, 1997, pp. 148–59.
Pacini, Piero: "L'oro e i simboli della fede per la glorificazione di Santa Maria Maddalena de' Pazzi," *Mitteilungen des Kunsthistorischen Institutes in Florenz*, IL, 2005, pp. 152–216.

Palagi, Giuseppe: *Di Lorenzo Cerrini pittore fiorentino del secolo XVII*, Florence: Le Monnier, 1873.

Palazzo Capponi sul Lungarno Guicciardini e gli affreschi restaurati di Bernardino Poccetti, ed. Litta Medri, text by Stefania Vasetti, Florence: Centro Di, 2001.

Pallucchini, Rodolfo: *La pittura veneziana del Seicento*, Venice: Alfieri, 1981.

Pallucchini, Rodolfo and Paola Rossi: *Tintoretto: Le opere sacre e profane*, Milan: Electa, 1982.

Palumbo, Margherita: "È nella Santa mente del Pontefice: Commercio e pratica alimentare negli editti e bandi pontifici," in *I Fasti del Banchetto Barocco*, ed. June di Schino, Rome: Diomeda Centro Studi e Ricerche, 2005, pp. 59–71.

Palumbo Fossati, Isabella: "L'interno della casa dell'artigiano e dell'artista nella Venezia del Cinquecento," *Studi Veneziani*, VIII, 1984, pp. 109–53.

Palumbo Fossati, Isabella: "Maisons et ateliers vénetiens (XVIe–XVIIIe siècles)," in *La maison de l'artiste: Construction d'un espace de representations entre réalité et imaginaire (XVIIe–XXe siècles)*, ed. Jean Gribenski, Véronique Meyer, and Solange Vernois, Rennes: Presses universitaires de Rennes, 2007, pp. 13–21.

Pampalone, Antonella: *La cappella della famiglia Spada nella Chiesa Nuova*, Rome: Poligrafico e Zecca dello Stato, 1993.

Pampalone, Antonella: "Parrocchia di Sant'Andrea delle Fratte: Rione Colonna," in *Artisti e Artigiani a Roma, I: Dagli Stati delle Anime del 1700, 1725, 1750, 1775*, Rome: Bonsignori, 2004, pp. 11–125.

Pampalone, Antonella: *Inquietudine e malinconia in Francesco Cozza calabrese*, Rome: Campisano, 2008.

Pancheri, Roberto: "'Accademie' di Pietro Vecchia," *Arte veneta*, LVIII, 2001, pp. 111–16.

Panofsky, Erwin: *The Life and Art of Albrecht Dürer*, Princeton: Princeton University Press, 1964.

Pantanella, Rossella: "Regesto documentario," in *Giovanni Battista Gaulli: Il Baciccio, 1639–1709* (exh. cat., Palazzo Chigi, Ariccia), ed. M. Fagiolo dell'Arco, D. Graf, and F. Petrucci, Milan: Skira, 1999, pp. 331–38.

Papadopoli Aldobrandini, Nicolò: *Le monete di Venezia*, Venice: Libreria Emiliana, 1893–1919.

Papi, Gianni: "Finson e altre congiunture di precoce naturalismo a Napoli," *Paragone*, LII, no. 39, 2001, pp. 35–47.

Parenti, Giuseppe: *Prime ricerche sulla rivoluzione dei prezzi in Firenze*, Florence: CYA, 1939.

Parenti, Giuseppe: "Prezzi e salari a Firenze dal 1520 al 1620," in *I prezzi in Europa dal XIII secolo a oggi*, ed. Ruggiero Romano, Turin: Einaudi, 1966, pp. 203–47.

Pascoli, Lione: *Vite de' pittori, scultori, ed architetti moderni*, Rome: Antonio de Rossi, 1730–36 (reprint, Amsterdam: Israel, 1965, and critical edition, ed. Alessandro Marabottini, Perugia: Electa Editori Umbri, 1992).

Pascoli, Lione: *Vite de' pittori, scultori ed architetti viventi dai manoscritti 1383 e 1743 della Biblioteca Comunale "Augusta" di Perugia*, ed. Valentino Martinelli and Francesco Federico Mancini, Treviso: Canova, 1981.

Passeri, Giovanni Battista: *Die Künstlerbiographien von Giovanni Battista Passeri*, ed. Jacob Hess, Leipzig and Vienna: Heinrich Keller, 1934 (reprint, Worms: Wernersche Verlagsgesellschaft, 1995).

Passeri, Niccola: *Del Metodo di studiare la pittura, e delle cagioni di sua decadenza*, Naples: Flauto, 1795.

Pastor, Ludwig von: *The History of the Popes*, St. Louis and London: 1938–1961 (editions and imprints vary).

Pavanello, G.: "I Rezzonico: Committenza e collezionismo fra Venezia e Roma," *Arte veneta*, LII, 1998, pp. 87–111.

Pears, Iain: *The Discovery of Painting: The Growth of Interest in the Arts in England, 1680–1768*, New Haven and London: Yale University Press, 1988.

Pedrocchi, Anna Maria: *Le Stanze del Tesoriere: La Quadreria Patrizi: Cultura senese nella storia del collezionismo romano del Seicento*, Milan: Alcon, 2000.

Pellicciari, Armanda: "La bottega di Guido Reni," *Accademia Clementina: Atti e Memorie*, no. 22, 1988, pp. 119–41.

Pepper, D. Stephen: "Guido Reni's Early Style: His Activity in Bologna, 1595–1601," *The Burlington Magazine*, CXI, 1969, pp. 472–83.

Pepper, D. Stephen: "Guido Reni's Roman Account Book: I–II," *The Burlington Magazine*, CXIII, 1971, pp. 309–17, 372–86.

Pepper, D. Stephen: "A New Late Work by Guido Reni for Edinburgh and his Late Manner Re-evaluated," *The Burlington Magazine*, CXXI, 1979, pp. 418–24.

Pepper, D. Stephen: *Guido Reni: A Complete Catalogue of his Works with an Introductory Text*, New York: New York University Press, 1984.

Pepper, D. Stephen: *Guido Reni: L'opera completa*, Novara: Istituto geographico de Agostini, 1988.

Pepper, D. Stephen: "New Documents for the Pietà dei Mendicanti," *The Burlington Magazine*, CXXXIII, 1991, pp. 441–45.

Pérez Sánchez, Alfonso Emilio and Nicola Spinosa: *L'opera completa del Ribera*, Milan: Rizzoli, 1978.

Pérez Sánchez, Alfonso Emilio and Nicola Spinosa (eds.): *Jusepe de Ribera, 1591–1652* (exh. cat., Metropolitan Museum of Art, New York), New York: Metropolitan Museum of Art, 1992.

Peri, Gio Domenico: *Il negotiante*, Genoa: 1639 (subsequent editions, Venice: Presso Gio. Giacomo Hertz, 1682, and Venice: Hertz, 1708; reprint of 1639 edition, Turin: Bottega d'Erasmo, 1972).

Petraccone, Claudia: *Napoli dal '500 all '800: Problemi di storia demografica e sociale*, Naples: Guida, 1974.

Petraccone, Claudia: "Manifattura e artigianato tessile a Napoli nella prima metà del XVII secolo," *Atti dell'Accademia di Scienze Morali e Politiche*, LXXXIX, 1978a, pp. 101–57.

Petraccone, Claudia: "Bottegai e piccoli commercianti a Napoli nella prima metà del XVII secolo," *Archivio storico per le province napoletane*, XVII, 1978b, pp. 171–202.

Petrocchi, Massimo: *Roma nel Seicento*, Bologna: Cappelli, 1970.

Petrucci, Francesco: "Nuovi contributi sulla committenza Chigi nel XVII secolo: Alcuni dipinti inediti nel Palazzo di Ariccia," *Bollettino d'arte*, LXXVII, no. 73, 1992, pp. 107–26.

Petrucci, Francesco: *Ferdinand Voet (1639–1689) detto Ferdinando de' Ritratti*, Rome: Ugo Bozzi, 2005.

Petrucci, Francesco: *Pittura di ritratto a Roma: Il Seicento*, Rome: Andreina & Valneo Budai, 2008.

Pezzolo, Luciano: *Il fisco dei veneziani: Finanza pubblica ed economia tra XV e XVII secolo*, Verona: Cierre, 2003.

Piacentini, Michelangiolo: "Richerche Archivistiche per la storia dell'arte: Documenti per l'arte barocca: Gli Artisti in Roma nel 1634," *Archivi: Archivi d'Italia e Rassegna internazionale degli Archivi*, VI, no. 3, 1939, pp. 156–83.

Piccinelli, Roberta: *Le collezioni Gonzaga: Il carteggio tra Firenze e Mantova (1554–1626)*, Cinisello Balsamo: Silvana Editoriale, 2000.

Pickrel, Thomas: "The Case of Domenico Castiglione, mercante di Quadri," *The Art Bulletin*, LXVI, 1984, pp. 311–12.

Piereth, Uta: *Bambocciade: Bild und Abbild des römischen Volkes im Seicento*, Bern: Peter Lang, 1997.

Pietropolli, Anna: *Gerolamo Brusaferro dipinti e disegni*, Padua: Il prato, 2002.

Pignatti, Terisio: *Veronese: L'opera completa*, Venice: Alfieri, 1976.

Pigozzi, Marinella: *Bologna al tempo di Cavazzoni: Approfondimenti*, Bologna: CLUEB, 1999.

Pilo, Giuseppe Maria: *Giulio Carpioni*, Venice: Alfieri, 1961.

Pinchera, Valeria: "Arte e consumo della nobilità fiorentina nel Sei e Settecento," in *Economia e Arte secc. XIII–XVIII: Atti della Trentatreesima Settimana di Studi, 30 aprile–4 maggio 2001*, ed. Simonetta Cavaciocchi, Florence: Le Monnier, 2002, pp. 635–48.

Piñeiro, Manuel Vaquero: "Ricerche sui salari nell'edilizia romana (1500–1650)," *Rivista Storica del Lazio*, IV, 1996, pp. 131–58.

Pinetti, Angelo: "La decorazione pittorica secentesca di S. Maria Maggiore," *Bollettino della Civica Biblioteca di Bergamo*, X, no. 3, 1916, pp. 113–42.

Pinetti, Angelo: "Notizie e documenti sopra alcuni quadri della Parrocchiale di Alzano," *Bollettino della Civica Biblioteca di Bergamo*, XV, no. 2, 1921, pp. 17–30.

Pino, Paolo: *Dialogo di pittura*, Venice: Pauolo Gherardo, 1548 (critical edition, *Trattati d'arte del Cinquecento, I*, ed. P. Barocchi, Bari: G. Laterza, 1960).

Piola Caselli, Fausto: "Aspetti del debito pubblico nello Stato pontificio: Gli uffici vacabili," *Annali della Facoltà di Scienze Politiche dell'Università di Perugia*, XI, 1973, pp. 101–74.

Piola Caselli, Fausto: "La diffusione dei luoghi di monte della Camera apostolica alla fine del XVI secolo: Capitali, investimenti e rendimenti," in *Credito e sviluppo economico in Italia dal Medioevo all'età contemporanea: Atti del convengo nazionale, 4–6 giugno 1987*, Verona: Arti grafiche, 1988, pp. 191–225.

Piola Caselli, Fausto: "Il ruolo dei banchi privati nella gestione del debito pubblico pontificio a Roma tra XVI e XVII secolo," in *Banchi pubblici, banchi privati e monti di pietà nell'Europa pre-industriale: Atti del Convegno, Genova, 1–6 ottobre 1990*, Genoa: Società ligure di storia patria, 1990, pp. 463–95.

Piola Caselli, Fausto: "Merci per dogana e consumi alimentari a Roma nel Seicento," in *La popolazione italiana nel Seicento: Relazioni presentate al convengo di Firenze, 28–30 novembre, 1996*, Bologna: CLUEB, 1999, pp. 387–409.

Piro, Franco: "Sistema fiscale, struttura e congiuntura in una economia preindustriale: Il caso di Bologna, 1546–1666," *Annali Istituto storico italo-germanico*, II, 1976, pp. 117–82.

Pirondini, Massimo: "Guido Reni: La bottega e la scuola," in *La Scuola di Guido Reni*, ed. Emilio Negro and Massimo Pirondini, Modena: Artioli, 1992, pp. 11–16.

Pirondini, Massimo et al.: *Alessandro Tiarini (1577–1668)*, Manerba: Merigo, 2000.

Pitacco, Francesca: "Alessandro Savorgnan," in *Il collezionismo d'arte a Venezia: Il Seicento*, ed. Linda Borean and Stefania Mason, Venice: Marsilio, 2007a, pp. 316–17.

Pitacco, Francesca: "Dal secolo d'oro ai secoli d'oro: I collezionisti stranieri e i loro agenti," in *Il collezionismo d'arte a Venezia: Il Seicento*, ed. Linda Borean and Stefania Mason, Venice: Marsilio, 2007b, pp. 103–24.

Pizzo, M.: "'Far Galleria': Collezionismo e mercato artistico tra Venezia e Roma nelle lettere di Quintiliano Rezzonico a Livio Odescalchi (1676–1709)," *Bollettino del Museo Civico di Padova*, LXXXIX, 2000, pp. 43–84.

Pizzo, M: "Livio Odescalchi e i Rezzonico: Documenti su arte e collezionismo alla fine del XVII secolo," *Saggi e memorie di storia dell'arte*, XXVI, 2002, pp. 119–53.

Pizzorusso, Claudio: *Ricerche su Cristofano Allori*, Florence: Olschki, 1982.

Pliny the Elder: *The Elder Pliny's Chapters on the History of Art*, trans. K. Jex-Blake, Chicago: Ares, 1982.

Poggi, Giovanni: "La Cappella Calderini in Santa Croce e gli affreschi di Giovanni da San Giovanni," *Rivista d'arte*, VII, 1910, pp. 36–41.

Pollak, Oskar: "Italienische Künstlerbriefe aus der Barockzeit," *Jahrbuch der königlich preuszischen Kunstsammlungen*, XXXIV, Beiheft, 1913, pp. 1–77.

Pollak, Oskar: "Ausgewählte Akten zur Geschichte der römischen Peterskirche (1535–1621)," *Jahrbuch der königlich preuszischen Kunstsammlungen*, XXXVI, Beiheft, 1915, pp. 21–117.

Pollak, Oskar: *Die Kunsttätigkeit unter Urban VIII*, Vienna: Filser, 1928–31.

Pomian, Krzysztof: *Collectors and Curiosities: Paris and Venice, 1500–1800*, trans. Elizabeth Wiles-Portier, Cambridge: Polity Press, 1990.

Poni, Carlo: "Norms and Disputes: The Shoemakers' Guild in Eighteenth-Century Bologna," *Past and Present*, no. 123, 1989, pp. 80–108.

Poni, Carlo: "Per una storia del distretto industriale serico di Bologna (secoli XVI–XIX)," *Quaderni storici*, XXV, 1990, pp. 93–167.

Poos, L. R.: "The Historical Demography of Renaissance Europe: Recent Research and Current Issues," *Renaissance Quarterly*, XLII, 1989, pp. 794–811.

Portier, François: "Prices Paid for Italian Pictures in the Stuart Age," *Journal of the History of Collections*, VIII, 1996, pp. 53–69.

Portogruaro, Davide da: *Paolo Piazza ossia P. Cosmo da Castelfranco pittore cappuccino (1560–1620)*, Venice: Libreria Emiliana, 1936.

Porzio, Francesco (ed.): *La natura morta in Italia*, Milan: Electa, 1989.

Posner, Donald: "Spada, Reni, and Roncalli at Loreto," *Arte antica e moderna*, no. 23, 1963, pp. 254–57.

Prati, Giovanni: *Il Genio divertito poesie liriche*, Venice: Poleti, 1690.

Predelli, R.: "Le memorie e le carte di Alessandro Vittoria," *Archivio Trentino*, XXIII, 1908, pp. 57–74, 129–229.

Preto, Paolo: *Peste e società a Venezia nel 1576*, Vicenza: N. Pozza, 1978.

Procacci, Ugo: "Di Iacopo di Antonio e delle compagnie di pittori del Corso degli Adimari nel XV secolo," *Rivista d'arte*, XXXV, 1960, pp. 3–70.

Procacci, Ugo: *La Casa Buonarroti a Firenze*, Milan: Electa, 1965.

Prota Giurleo, Ulisse: *Pittori montemurresi del '600*, Naples: Comune di Montemurro, 1952.

Prota Giurleo, Ulisse: *Pittori napoletani del Seicento*, Naples: Fausto Fiorentino, 1953.

Prota Giurleo, Ulisse: "Notizie su Massimo Stanzione e sul presunto manoscritto falsificato dal De Dominici," *Napoli-Rivista Municipale*, LXXXI, no. 11, 1955, pp. 17–32.

Proto Pisani, Rosanna Caterina: "Il ciclo affrescato del primo chiostro di San Marco: Una galleria della pittura fiorentina del Seicento," in *La chiesa e il convento di San Marco a Firenze, II*, Florence: Giunti, 1990, pp. 321–46.

Proto Pisani, Rosanna Caterina, A. Natali, C. Sisi, and E. Testaferrata (eds.): *Jacopo da Empoli 1551–1640: Pittore d'eleganza e devozione* (exh. cat., Chiesa di Santo Stefano and Convento degli Agostiniani, Empoli, 2004), Cinisello Balsamo: Silvana Editoriale, 2004.

Puglisi, Catherine R.: *Francesco Albani*, New Haven and London: Yale University Press, 1999.

Pulini, Massimo: *Ginevra Cantofoli: La nuova nascita di una pittrice nella Bologna del Seicento*, Bologna: Compositori, 2006.

Pullan, Brian: "Service to the Venetian State: Aspects of Myth and Reality in the Early Seventeenth Century," *Studi secenteschi*, V, 1964a, pp. 95–148.

Pullan, Brian: "Wage-Earners and the Venetian Economy, 1550–1630," *Economic History Review*, XVI, 1964b, pp. 407–26.
Pullan, Brian: "Introduction," in *Crisis and Change in the Venetian Economy in the Sixteenth and Seventeenth Centuries*, ed. Brian Pullan, London: Methuen, 1968, pp. 1–21.
Pullan, Brian: *Rich and Poor in Renaissance Venice: The Social Institutions of a Catholic State to 1620*, Cambridge, MA: Harvard University Press, 1971.
Pullan, Brian: "Poveri, mendicanti e vagabondi (secoli XIV–XVIII)," in *Dal feudalesimo al capitalismo* (Storia d'Italia, Annali, I), Turin: Einaudi, 1978, pp. 981–1047.
Puncuh, Dino: "Collezionismo e commercio di quadri nella Genova sei-settecentesca: Note archivistiche dai registri contabili Durazzo," *Rassegna degli Archivi di Stato*, XLIV, 1984, pp. 164–218.
Puppi, Lionello: "Revisioni e divagazioni archivistiche sul rinnovamento seicentesco dell'Oratorio di San Nicola di Vicenza," *Rivista dell'Istituto Nazionale di Archeologia e Storia dell'Arte*, XV, 1968, pp. 125–60.
Puppi, Lionello: "Copie, falsi, pastiches: Riflessioni preliminari intorno al mercato dell'arte come economia del gusto," in *Tra committenza e collezionismo: Studi sul mercato dell'arte nell'Italia settentrionale durante l'età moderna*, ed. Enrico Maria dal Pozzolo and Leonida Tedoldi, Vicenza: Terra ferma, 2003, pp. 23–34.
Puppi, Lionello: *Per Tiziano*, Milan: Skira, 2004.
Puppi, Lionello: "Tre eteronimi per Giovanni e Giacomo van Veerle: Collezionismo e mercato nascosto di qudri tra Venezia e le Fiandre nel Seicento," in *Il collezionismo d'arte a Venezia: Il Seicento*, ed. Linda Borean and Stefania Mason, Venice: Marsilio, 2007, pp. 173–80.
Puppi, Lionello and R. Rugolo: "'Un'ordinaria forma non alletta': Arte, riflessione sull'arte e società," in *Storia di Venezia, VII: La Venezia barocca*, ed. Gino Benzoni and Gaetano Cozzi, Rome: Istituto della Enciclopedia Italiana, 1997, pp. 595–699.
Quondam, Amedeo: "Il Barocco e la letteratura: Genealogie del mito della decadenza italiana," in *I capricci di Proteo: Percorsi e linguaggi del barocco: Atti del convengo internazionale di Lecce 23–26 ottobre 2000*, Rome: Salerno, 2002, pp. 111–76.
Radassao, Roberto: "Nicolo Bambini 'pittore pronto, spedito ed universale'," *Saggi e memorie di storia dell'arte*, XXII, 1998, pp. 131–287.
Ragosta Portioli, R.: "Specializzazione produttiva a Napoli nei secoli XVI e XVII," in *La seta in Europa, secc. XIII–XX*, ed. S. Cavaciocchi, Florence: Le Monnier, 1999, pp. 339–49.
Ramella, Franco: *Terra e telai: Sistemi di parentela e manifattura nel Biellese dell'Ottocento*, Turin: Einaudi, 1984.
Rao, A. M.: "Tra amministrazione e politica: Gli ambienti intellettuali napoletani," in *Naples, Rome, Florence: Une histoire comparée des milieux intellectuels italiens (XVIIe–XVIIIe siècles)*, ed. Jean Boutier, Brigitte Marin, and Antonella Romano, Rome: École Française de Rome, 2005, pp. 35–88.
Rapp, Richard: *Industry and Economic Decline in Seventeenth Century Venice*, Cambridge, MA: Harvard University Press, 1976.
Rapp, Richard: *Industria e decadenza economica a Venezia nel XVII secolo*, Rome: Il Veltro, 1986.
Raule, Angelo: "La parrocchia di Santa Maria della Pietà celebra il suo decennale," *L'Avvenire d'Italia*, 17 June 1829.
Ravà, Aldo: *G. B. Piazzetta*, Florence: Fratelli Alinari, 1921.
Ravelli, Lanfranco: *Stanchi dei Fiori*, Bergamo: Grafica & Arte, 2005.
Rearick, W. R.: "Bernardo Strozzi: Un Aggiornamento," *Saggi e memorie di storia dell'arte*, XX, 1996, pp. 229–75.
Redigonda, P. I.: "Il compimento dei Misteri del Rosario e l'affermazione malvasiana su Bartolomeo Cesi," *Arte Antica e Moderna*, no. 10, 1960, pp. 201–3.
Regesti di bandi editti notificazioni e provvedimenti diversi relativi alla Città di Roma ed allo Stato Pontificio, Rome: Cuggiani, 1920.
Reinhard, Wolfgang: *Papstfinanz und Nepotismus unter Paul V. (1605–1621)*, Stuttgart: A. Hiersemann, 1974.
Reinhard, Wolfgang: "Papal Power and Family Strategy in the Sixteenth and Seventeenth Centuries," in *Princes, Patronage, and the Nobility: The Court at the Beginning of the Modern Age, c.1450–1650*, ed. Ronald G. Asch and Adolf M. Birke, Oxford: Oxford University Press, 1991, pp. 329–56.
Reinhardt, Volker: *Überleben in der frühneuzeitlichen Stadt: Annona und Getreideversorgung in Rom, 1563–1797*, Tübingen: Niemeyer, 1991.
Reinhardt, Volker: "Annona and Bread Supply in Rome," in *Rome–Amsterdam: Two Growing Cities in Seventeenth-Century Europe*, ed. Peter van Kessel and Elisja Schulte, Amsterdam: Amsterdam University Press, 1997, pp. 209–20.
Reinhardt, Volker: "The Roman Art Market in the Sixteenth and Seventeenth Centuries," in *Art Markets in Europe, 1400–1800*, ed. Michael North and David Ormrod, Aldershot: Ashgate, 1998, pp. 81–92.
Restagno, Josepha Costa: "Ottavio Costa (1554–1639)," in *L'Età di Rubens: Dimore, committenti e collezionisti genovesi* (exh. cat., Palazzo Ducale, Palazzo Rosso, and Palazzo Spinola, Genoa), ed. Piero Boccardo, Milan: Skira, 2004, pp. 425–32.
Reuss, Matthias: *Antonio Belluccis Gemäldefolge für das Stadpalais Liechtenstein in Wien*, Hildesheim and New York: Georg Olms, 1998.
Revel, Jacques: "A Capital City's Privileges: Food Supplies in Early-Modern Rome," in *Food and Drink in History*, ed. Robert Forster and Orest Ranum, trans. Elborg Forster and Patricia Ranum, Baltimore: The Johns Hopkins University Press, 1979, pp. 37–49.
Riccio, Bianca: "Vita di Filippo Lauri di Francesco Saverio Baldinucci," *Commentari*, X, 1959, pp. 3–15.
Riccomini, Eugenio: "I pittori del coro di San Paolo in Bologna," *Arte antica e moderna*, no. 20, 1962, pp. 448–55.
Rice, Louise: *The Altars and Altarpieces of New St. Peter's*, Cambridge: Cambridge University Press, 1997.
Ridolfi, Carlo: *Le Maraviglie dell'arte, ovvero le vite degli illustri pittori veneti e dello stato*, Venice: Gio. Battista Sgaua, 1648 (critical edition, ed. Detlev von Hadeln, Rome: Società multigrafica editrice Somu, 1965).
Riedl, Helmut Philipp: *Antiveduto della Grammatica (1570/71–1626): Leben und Werk*, Munich and Berlin: Deutscher Kunstverlag, 1998.
Rigoni, C.: "La galleria di Palazzo Leoni Montanari a Vicenza," *Verona illustrata*, VI, 1993, pp. 69–85.
Rinehart, Sheila: "Cassiano Dal Pozzo (1588–1657): Some Unknown Letters," *Italian Studies*, XVI, 1961, pp. 35–59.
Rizzo, Vincenzo: "Documenti su Cavallino, Corenzio, De Matteis, Giordano, Lanfranco, Solimena, Stanzione, Zamperi ed altri, del 1636 al 1715," in *Seicento napoletano: Arte, costume, ambiente*, ed. Roberto Pane, Milan: Edizioni di comunità, 1984, pp. 314–33.
Rizzo, Vincenzo: "Altre notizie su pittori, scultori ed architetti napoletani del Seicento (dai documenti dell'Archivio Storico del Banco di Napoli)," in *Ricerche sul '600 napoletano*, Milan: L&T, 1987, pp. 153–75.
Robbin, Carmen Roxanne: "Ottavio Leoni as a Painter: New Evidence from an Inventory of his House on via del Babuino," *Storia dell'arte*, no. 99, 2000, pp. 84–93.
Roche, David: "Modelli economici del mecenatismo," *Intersezioni*, VI, 1986, pp. 5–14.

Rodriguez Canevari, Bruna: "La casa di Pietro Liberi sul Canal Grande," *Saggi e memorie di storia dell'arte*, IX, 1974, pp. 117–36, 199–208.

Roeck, Bernd: "La collocazione economica e sociale di artisti veneziani e della Germania meridionale attorno al 1600," in *Venedig und oberdeutschland in der Renaissance*, ed. Bernd Roeck, Ulars Bergdolt, and Andrew John Martin, Sigmaringen: Jan Thorbecke, 1993, pp. 53–76.

Rognini, Luciano: "Giuseppe della Corte da Cima, Pittore e Flagellante," *Studi Storici Veronesi Luigi Simeoni*, XXVI–XXVII, 1976–77, pp. 130–51.

Rohlmann, Michael: "Arte da lontano: Pittura fiamminga nella Firenze rinascimentale," in *The Art Market in Italy 15th–17th Centuries: Il mercato dell'arte in Italia secc. XV–XVII*, ed. Marcello Fantoni, Louisa C. Matthew, and Sara F. Matthews-Grieco, Ferrara: Panini, 2003, pp. 401–12.

Roli, Renato: "Giacomo Cavedoni 1577–1660" (Laurea thesis, University of Bologna, 1953–54).

Roli, Renato: *Pittura bolognese 1650–1800: Dal Cignani ai Gandolfi*, Bologna: Alfa, 1977.

Roma 1630: Il trionfo del pennello (exh. cat., Villa Medici, Rome), Milan: Electa, 1995.

Roman, Joseph: *Le Livre de raison du peintre Hyacinthe Rigaud publié avec une introduction et des notes*, Paris: Laurens, 1919.

Romani, Mario: *Pellegrini e viaggiatori nell'economia di Roma dal XIV al XVII secolo*, Milan: Vita e Pensiero, 1948.

Romano, G. B.: "Scuola di pittori in Udine e nel secolo XVII," *Pagine Friulane*, XII, no. 1, 1899, pp. 2–3.

Romano, Ruggiero: "La vita economica," in *Storia di Napoli*, vol. 6, pt. 1, Naples: Soc. Ed. Storia di Napoli, 1970, pp. 537–606.

Romano, Ruggiero: "La storia economica: Dal secolo XIV al Settecento," in *Storia d'Italia*, vol. 2, pt. 2, Turin: Einaudi, 1974, pp. 1813–1931.

Romei, Francesca: "Il Carosello notturno di Stefano della Bella," in *Stefano della Bella: Un dipinto riemerso dal buio dei secoli*, ed. Mina Gregori, Francesca Romei, and Gabriele Capecchi, Florence: Alessandro Falciani, 1997, pp. 21–40.

Ronchi, Oliviero: "Documenti inediti intorno al pittore Dario Varotari," *Bollettino del Museo Civico di Padova*, LVI, 1967, pp. 13–21.

Rosa, Salvator: *Satire*, ed. Danilo Romei, Milan: 1995.

Rosa, Salvator: *Lettere*, ed. L. Festa and Gian Giotto Borrelli, Naples: Il Mulino, 2003.

Rosand, David: *Painting in Cinquecento Venice: Titian, Veronese, Tintoretto*, New Haven and London: Yale University Press, 1982.

Rosenberg, Pierre and Louis-Antoine Prat: *Nicolas Poussin, 1594–1665* (exh. cat., Grand Palais, Paris), Paris: Réunion des Musées Nationaux, 1994.

Rossi, Adamo: "Autobiografia di Atanasio Bimbacci, pittore fiorentino," *Giornale di erudizione artistica*, IV, 1875, pp. 97–101.

Rossi, Elisabetta Antoniazzi: "Filippo Esengren, 'Pittore, di poi sensale di pitture' e i libri di disegni del Museo d'Arte," *Bollettino del Museo Civico di Padova*, XCII, 2003, pp. 149–60.

Rossi, Massimiliano: "Il tempo ritrovato di Sebastiano Mazzoni," *Paragone*, LI, no. 603, 2000, pp. 64–78.

Rossi, Paola: *Jacopo Tintoretto: I ritratti*, Venice: Alfieri, 1974.

Rossi, Paola: "Precisazioni cronologiche su alcuni dipinti della Chiesa di S. Rocco," *Atti dell'Istituto Veneto di Scienze, Lettere ed Arti*, CXXXV, 1976–77, pp. 427–46.

Rossi, Paola: "La Scuola Grande di San Rocco committente di artisti (Antonio Smeraldi, Enrico Merengo, Antonio Molinari, Giovanni Antonio Fumiani, Ambrogio Bon, Santo Piatti)," *Arte veneta*, XXXIX, 1985, pp. 194–203.

Rossi, Paola: "L'altare di Francesco Morosini di San Pietro di Castello e la sua decorazione: Qualche precisazione e aggiunta per il catalogo di Francesco Cavrioli," *Arte veneta*, XLII, 1988, pp. 163–69.

Rossi, Paola: *Francesco Maffei*, Milan: Berenice, 1991.

Rossi, Paola: "Notizie d'archivio su Girolamo Pellegrini, Antonio Zanchi e Michiel Maes intagliatore fiammingo," *Venezia Arti*, VII, 1993, pp. 170–72.

Rossi, Paola: "I cartoni di Jacopo e Domenico Tintoretto per i mosaici della basilica di San Marco," *Arte veneta*, XXXXVIII, 1996a, pp. 45–55.

Rossi, Paola: "Lavori settecenteschi a Palazzo Ducale nella Sala delle Quattro Porte," *Arte veneta*, XXXXIX, 1996b, pp. 107–19.

Röthlisberger, Marcel: *Claude Lorrain: The Paintings*, New Haven: Yale University Press, 1961.

Röttgen, Herwarth: *Il Cavalier Giuseppe Cesari D'Arpino*, Rome: Ugo Bozzi, 2002.

Roversi, Giancarlo: "Le opere d'arte della famiglia Gozzadini nella Basilica dei Servi di Bologna," *L'Archiginnasio*, LXII, 1967, pp. 15–263.

Roversi, Giancarlo: "Schede storiche," in Giampiero Cupini and Giancarlo Roversi, *I palazzi senatorii a Bologna: Architettura come immagine del potere*, Bologna: Zanichelli, 1974, p. 280.

Roworth, Wendy Wassyng: *Pictor Succensor: A Study of Salvator Rosa as Satirist, Cynic, and Painter* (Ph.D. diss., Bryn Mawr College, 1977), New York: Garland, 1978.

Ruby, Louisa Wood: *Paul Bril: The Drawings*, Turnhout: Brepols, 1999.

Rudolph, Stella: "Carlo Maratti figurista per pittori di nature morte," *Antichità viva*, XVIII, no. 2, 1979, pp. 12–20.

Ruffo, Vincenzo: "Galleria Ruffo nel secolo XVII in Messina (con lettere di pittori ed altri documenti inediti)," *Bollettino d'arte*, X, 1916, pp. 21–64, 95–128, 165–192, 237–256, 284–320, 369–88.

Ruggeri, Ugo: "Alessandro Varotari detto il Padovanino," *Saggi e memorie di storia dell'arte*, XVI, 1988, pp. 101–65.

Ruggeri, Ugo: *Il Padovanino*, Soncino: Edizioni del Soncino, 1993.

Ruggeri, Ugo: *Pietro e Marco Liberi: Pittori nella Venezia del Seicento*, Rimini: Luisè, 1996.

Saccardo, M.: *Notizie d'arte e di artisti vicentini*, Vicenza: Neri Pozza, 1981.

Safarik, Eduard: "Per la pittura veneta del Seicento: Girolamo Forabosco," *Arte illustrata*, VI, 1973, pp. 353–63.

Safarik, Eduard: "Per la pittura veneta del Seicento: Sebastiano Mazzoni," *Arte veneta*, XXVIII, 1974, pp. 157–68.

Safarik, Eduard: "Johann Anton Eismann," *Saggi e memorie di storia dell'arte*, X, 1976a, pp. 63–78.

Safarik, Eduard: "Per la pittura veneziana del Seicento: Francesco Ruschi," *Römisches Jahrbuch für Kunstgeschichte*, XVI, 1976b, pp. 305–44.

Safarik, Eduard: "Pietro Negri," *Saggi e memorie di storia dell'arte*, V, 1978, pp. 83–93.

Safarik, Eduard (ed.): *Catalogo summario della Galleria Colonna in Roma*, Rome: Bramante, 1981.

Safarik, Eduard: *Fetti*, Milan: Electa, 1990.

Sagrestani, Giovanni Camillo: "Le vite di artisti dei secoli XVII e XVIII di Giovanni Camillo Sagrestani [ca. 1720]," ed. Anna Matteoli, *Commentari*, XXII, 1971, pp. 187–240.

Salerno, Luigi: *Salvator Rosa*, Milan: Club del Libro, 1963.

Salerno, Luigi: *La Natura Morta Italiana / Still Life Painting in Italy, 1560–1805*, trans. Robert Erich Wolf, Rome: Ugo Bozzi, 1984.

Salmazo, Nicolo: "La catalogazione del patrimonio artistico del XVII secolo," *Bollettino del Museo Civico di Padova*, LXII, 1973, pp. 19–103.
Salvagni, Isabella: "Gli 'aderenti al Caravaggio' e la fondazione dell'Accademia di San Luca: Conflitti e potere (1593–1627)" and "Appendice documentaria," in *Intorno a Caravaggio*, ed. Margherita Fratarcangeli, Rome: Campisano, 2008, pp. 41–74, 83–124.
Salvioni, Giovanni Battista: *Il valore della lira bolognese dalla sua origine alla meta del secolo XVII*, Turin: Bottega d'Erasmo, 1961.
Sandrart, Joachim von: *Academie der Bau-, Bild- und Mahlerey-Künste von 1675*, ed. A. R. Peltzer, Munich: Hirth, 1925.
Sani, Bernardina (ed.): *Rosalba Carriera: Lettere, diari, frammenti*, Florence: Olschki, 1985.
Sani, Bernardina: *La fatica virtuosa di Ottavio Leoni*, Turin: Allemandi, 2005.
Sansovino, Francesco: *Le cose meravigliose dell'inclita città di Venezia*, with additions by Giovanni Nicolò Doglioni, Venice: Domenico Imberti, 1603.
Sansovino, Francesco: *Venetia: Città nobilissima et singolare descritta in XIIII libri*, with additions by Giustiniano Martinioni, Venice: Steffano Curti, 1663.
Santi, Bruno (ed.): *Zibaldone baldinucciano: Scritti di Filippo Baldinucci, Francesco Saverio Baldinucci, Luca Berrettini, Bernardo De Dominici, Giovanni Camillo Sagrestani e altri [sec. XVIII]*, Florence: SPES, 1980.
Sarti, Raffaella: *Europe at Home: Family and Material Culture 1500–1800*, New Haven and London: Yale University Press, 2002.
Sartori, Antonio: "Regesto di S. Giustina," in *La basilica di Santa Giustina: Arte e storia*, Castelfranco Veneto: Grifone, 1970, pp. 429–62.
Sartori, Antonio: *Documenti per la storia dell'arte a Padova*, ed. Clemente Fillarini, Vicenza: Neri Pozza, 1976.
Sartori, Antonio: *Archivio Sartori: Documenti di storia e arte francescana, I: Basilica e convento del Santo*, ed. Giovanni Luisetto, Padua: Biblioteca antoniana, Basilica del Santo, 1983.
Savini Branca, Simona: *Il collezionismo veneziano nel '600*, Padua: CEDAM, 1965.
Saxl, Fritz: "The Battle Scene without a Hero: Aniello Falcone and his Patrons," *Journal of the Warburg and Courtauld Institutes*, III, 1939–40, pp. 70–87.
Scaramuccia, Luigi: *Le finezze de' pennelli italiani*, Pavia: Gio. Andrea Magri, 1674 (reprint, ed. Guido Giubbini, Milan: Labor, 1965).
Scarpa, Annalisa: *Sebastiano Ricci*, Milan: Bruno Alfieri, 2006.
Scarpa, Jacopo: "Opere veneziane di Girolamo Pilotti," *Arte/Documento*, VII, 1993, pp. 49–56.
Schiavo, Armando: *The Altieri Palace*, Rome: Italian Bankers' Association [ca. 1964].
Schleier, Erich (ed.): *Giovanni Lanfranco: Un pittore barocco tra Parma, Roma e Napoli* (exh. cat., Reggia di Colorno, Parma, Castel Sant'Elmo, Naples, and Palazzo Venezia, Rome), Milan: Electa, 2002.
Schleier, Erich: "Lanfrancos Vigna und Casino in den Monti di Bravetta vor den Toren Roms. Mit biographischen Notizen," in *Jacobs-Weg auf den Spuren eines Kunsthistorikers: Hommage an den Forscherfreund und Lehrer Fritz Jacobs zum 70. Geburtstag*, ed. Karen Buttler and Felix Krämer, Weimar: VDG, 2007, pp. 123–32.
Schnapper, Antoine: *Le métier de peintre au Grand Siècle*, Paris: Gallimard, 2004.
Schumpeter, Joseph Alois: *History of Economic Analysis*, New York: Oxford University Press, 1954.
Schütze, Sebastian: "Pittura parlante e poesia taciturna–Il ritorno di Giovan Battista Marino a Napoli, il suo concetto di imitazione e una mirabile interpretazione pittorica," in *Documentary Culture: Florence and Rome from Grand-Duke Ferdinand I to Pope Alexander VII: Papers from a Colloquium Held at the Villa Spellman, Florence, 1990*, ed. Elizabeth Cropper, Giovanna Perini, and Francesco Solinas, Bologna: Nuova Alfa, 1992, pp. 209–26.
Schütze, Sebastian: "The Vita S. Brunonis Cartusianorum Patriarchae and its Interpretation by Massimo Stanzione in the Certosa di S. Martino in Naples," in *Parthenope's Splendor: Art of the Golden Age in Naples*, ed. Jeanne Chenault Porter, University Park, PA: Pennsylvania State University Press, 1993, pp. 194–229.
Schütze, Sebastian: "Il nuovo parnaso napoletano: Arti figurative e ambiente letterario nel primo Seicento," in *Napoli viceregno spagnolo: Una capitale della cultura alle origini dell'Europa moderna (sec. XVI–XVII)*, vol. 2, ed. Monika Bosse and André Stoll, Naples: Vivarium, 2001, pp. 407–34.
Schütze, Sebastian: *Kardinal Maffeo Barberini später Papst Urban VIII. und die Entstehung des römischen Hochbarock*, Munich: Hirmer, 2007.
Schütze, Sebastian and Thomas C. Willette: *Massimo Stanzione: L'opera completa*, Naples: Electa, 1992.
Scoppola, Francesco (ed.): *Palazzo Altemps*, Rome: De Luca, 1987.
Scott, John Beldon: *Images of Nepotism: The Painted Ceilings of Palazzo Barberini*, Princeton: Princeton University Press, 1991.
Scott, John Beldon: "The Art of the Painter's Scaffold: Pietro da Cortona in the Barberini Salone," *The Burlington Magazine*, CXXXV, 1993, pp. 327–37.
Scott, Jonathan: *Salvator Rosa: His Life and Times*, New Haven and London: Yale University Press, 1995.
Il Seicento Fiorentino: Arte a Firenze da Ferdinando I a Cosimo III (exh. cat., Palazzo Strozzi, Florence), Florence: Cantini, 1986.
Selfridge-Field, Eleanor: *Pallade Veneta: Writings on Music in Venetian Society 1650–1750*, Venice: Fondazione Levi, 1985.
Sella, Domenico: *Italy in the Seventeenth Century*, London: Longman, 1997.
Seravalli, Angelo: *Scoprimento del mondo umano di Lucio Agatone Prisco*, Siena: Bonetti, 1696.
Serpetro, Giovanni: *Mercato delle meraviglie*, Venice: Tomasini, 1653.
Sestieri, Giancarlo: *Repertorio della pittura romana della fine del Seicento e del Settecento*, Turin: Allemandi, 1994.
Sestieri, Giancarlo and Brigitte Daprà: *Domenico Gargiulo detto Micco Spadaro: La vita e l'opera*, Rome: Jandi Sapi, 1994.
Shakeshaft, P.: "'To much bewiched with thoes intysing things': The Letters of James Third Marquis of Hamilton and Basil, Viscount Fielding, concerning Collecting in Venice, 1635–1639," *The Burlington Magazine*, CXXVIII, 1986, pp. 114–31.
Shaw, James: "Institutional Controls and the Retail of Paintings: The Painters' Guild of Early Modern Venice," in *Mapping Markets for Paintings in Europe, 1450–1750*, ed. Neil De Marchi and Hans J. Van Miegroet, Turnhout: Brepols, 2006, pp. 107–24.
Sickel, Lothar: "Guido Reni: Portrait du cardinal Giacomo Sannesi," in Véronique Damian and Lothar Sickel, *Deux tableaux de la collection Sannesi: Tableaux des écoles émilienne et lombarde*, Paris: Galerie Canesso, 2006, pp. 6–15.
Signorotto, Gianvittorio and Maria Antonietta Visceglia (eds.): *La corte di Roma tra Cinque e Seicento "Teatro" della politica europea*, Rome: Bulzoni, 1998.
Silingardi, Luca: "Regesto," in *L'amorevole maniera: Ludovico Lana e la pittura emiliana del primo Seicento* (exh. cat., Chiesa del Voto and Galleria Estense, Modena), ed. Daniele Benati and Lucia Peruzzi, Cinisello Balsamo: Silvana Editoriale, 2003.
Sivori Porro, Gabriella: "Costi di costruzione e salari edili a Genova

nel secolo XVII," *Atti della società ligure di storia patria*, XXIX, 1989, pp. 339–423.
Sohm, Philip: "A New Document on Giambattista Tiepolo's Santa Fosca Residence," *Arte veneta,* XXXIX, 1986, pp. 242–44.
Sohm, Philip: *Pittoresco: Marco Boschini, his Critics and their Critiques of Painterly Brushwork in Seventeenth- and Eighteenth-Century Italy*, Cambridge: Cambridge University Press, 1991.
Sohm, Philip: "Seicento Mannerism: Eighteenth-Century Definitions of a Venetian Style," in *Treasures of Venice: Paintings from the Museum of Fine Arts, Budapest*, ed. George Keyes et al., Minneapolis: Minneapolis Institute of Art, 1995, pp. 51–66.
Sohm, Philip: *Style in the Art Theory of Early Modern Italy*, Cambridge: Cambridge University Press, 2001.
Sohm, Philip: "La critica d'arte del Seicento: Carlo Ridolfi and Marco Boschini," in *La pittura nel Veneto: Il Seicento*, ed. Mauro Lucco, Milan: Electa, 2002, pp. 725–56.
Sohm, Philip: *The Artist Grows Old: The Aging of Art and Artists in Italy, 1500–1800*, New Haven and London: Yale University Press, 2007.
Soli, Bernardo: *La veneranda confraternità di Santa Maria degli Angioli in Spilamberto e l'Assunta di Guido Reni*, Modena: G. Ferraguti, 1930.
Sonnino, Eugenio: "The Population in Baroque Rome," in *Rome–Amsterdam: Two Growing Cities in Seventeenth-Century Europe*, ed. Peter van Kessel and Elisja Schulte, Amsterdam: Amsterdam University Press, 1997, pp. 50–70.
Spagnoletti, Angelantonio: *Stato, aristocrazie e Ordine di Malta nell'Italia moderna*, Rome: École Française de Rome, 1988.
Sparti, Donatella Livia: "Appunti sulle finanze di Nicolas Poussin," *Storia dell'arte*, no. 79, 1993, pp. 341–50.
Sparti, Donatella Livia: *La casa di Pietro da Cortona*, Rome: Palombi, 1997.
Sparti, Donatella Livia: "Ciro Ferri and Luca Giordano in the Gallery of Palazzo Medici Riccardi," *Mitteilungen des Kunsthistorischen Institutes in Florenz*, XLVII, 2003, pp. 159–221.
Spear, Richard E.: *Renaissance and Baroque Paintings from the Sciarra and Fiano Collections*, University Park, PA: Pennsylvania State University Press, 1972.
Spear, Richard E.: *Domenichino*, New Haven and London: Yale University Press, 1982.
Spear Richard E.: "Re-viewing the 'Divine' Guido," *The Burlington Magazine*, CXXXI, 1989, pp. 367–72.
Spear, Richard E.: "Guercino's 'Prix-Fixe': Observations on Studio Practices and Art Marketing in Emilia," *The Burlington Magazine*, CXXXVI, 1994, pp. 592–602.
Spear, Richard E.: *The "Divine" Guido: Religion, Sex, Money and Art in the World of Guido Reni*, New Haven and London: Yale University Press, 1997.
Spear, Richard E.: "Lanfranco" (exh. review), *The Burlington Magazine*, CXLIV, 2002, pp. 126–29.
Spear, Richard E.: "Scrambling for Scudi: Notes on Painters' Earnings in Early Baroque Rome," *The Art Bulletin*, LXXXV, 2003, pp. 310–20.
Spear, Richard E.: "Claude and the Economics of Landscape Painting in Seicento Rome," *Konsthistorisk Tidskrift*, LXXIII, 2004a, pp. 147–57.
Spear, Richard E.: "What is an Original?" in *The Italians in Australia: Studies in Renaissance and Baroque Art*, ed. David R. Marshall, Florence: Centro Di with the University of Melbourne, 2004b, pp. 15–32.
Spear, Richard E.: "Money Matters: The Economic Lives of Artemisia and Orazio Gentileschi," in *Artemisia Gentileschi: Taking Stock*, ed. Judith W. Mann, Turnhout: Brepols, 2005, pp. 147–59.
Spear, Richard E.: "A Database of Prices Paid to Painters in Seventeenth-Century Rome," *Getty Research Journal*, no. 2, 2010, pp. 147–50.
Spear, Richard E.: "A Century of Pigment Prices: Seventeenth-Century Italy," in *Trade in Artists' Materials: Markets and Commerce in Europe to 1700*, ed. Jo Kirby, Susie Nash, and Joanna Cannon, London: Archetype Publications (in press).
Spezzaferro, Luigi: "Mola e il mercato artistico romano: Atteggiamenti e valutazioni," in *Pier Francesco Mola, 1612–1666* (exh. cat., Museo Cantonale d'Arte, Lugano, and Musei Capitolini, Rome, 1989–90), Milan: Electa, 1989, pp. 40–59.
Spezzaferro, Luigi: "Per il collezionismo dei Bamboccianti a Roma nel Seicento: Qualche appunto e qualche riflessione," in *Da Caravaggio a Ceruti* (exh. cat., Museo di Santa Giulia, Brescia), ed. Francesco Porzio, Milan: Skira, 1998, pp. 83–88.
Spezzaferro, Luigi: "Caravaggio accettato: Dal rifiuto al mercato," in *Caravaggio nel IV Centenario della Cappella Contarelli*, ed. Caterina Volpi, Città di Castello: Peruzzi, 2002, pp. 23–50.
Spezzaferro, Luigi: "Le contraddizioni del pittore: Note sulle trasformazioni del lavoro artistico nella prima metà del '600," *Quaderni storici*, XXXIX, 2004, pp. 329–51.
Spiazzi, A. M.: "Contributi alla pittura veneta del '600," *Notizie da Palazzo Albani*, IV, no. 1, 1975, pp. 29–33.
Spike, John T.: "L'inventario dello studio di Guido Reni (11 ottobre 1642)," *Atti e memorie dell'Accademia Clementina*, no. 22, 1988, pp. 43–48.
Spinelli, Riccardo: "Ricognizione su Giuseppe Broccetti (1684–1733)," *Annali della Fondazione di Studi di Storia dell'arte Roberto Longhi*, II, 1989, pp. 101–23.
Spinelli, Riccardo: "Cappella Niccolini in Santa Croce," in *Cappelle barocche a Firenze*, ed. Mina Gregori, Cinisello Balsamo: Silvana Editoriale, 1990, pp. 99–134.
Spinelli, Riccardo: "Una precisazione e qualche aggiunta a Domenico Tempesti," *Paragone*, XLII, no. 493–95, 1991, pp. 30–48.
Spinelli, Riccardo: "Il Pantheon privato tra Rinascimento e Barocco: La cappella Niccolini," in *Il Pantheon di Santa Croce a Firenze*, ed. Luciano Berti, Florence: Giunti, 1993, pp. 83–143.
Spinelli, Riccardo: "Baldassarre Franceschini detto il Volterrano in Palazzo Niccolini a Firenze e in Palazzo del Bufalo a Roma: nuovi documenti," *Antichità viva*, XXXVII, no. 1, 1998, pp. 25–40.
Spinelli, Riccardo (ed.): *Il Gran Principe Ferdinando de' Medici e Anton Domenico Gabbiani: Mecenatismo e committenza artistica ad un pittore fiorentino della fine del Seicento* (exh. cat., Museo Villa Medicea, Poggio a Caiano), Florence: Noèdizioni, 2003.
Spinelli, Riccardo: "Precisazioni e novità su alcune opere toscane di Angelo Michele Colonna e Agostino Mitelli," in *L'architettura dell'inganno: Quadraturismo e grande decorazione nella pittura di età barocca* (symposium acts, Rimini, 28–30 November 2002), ed. Fauzia Farneti and Deanna Lenzi, Florence: Alinea, 2004, pp. 49–58.
Spinosa, Nicola: "Aggiunte a Hendrick van Somer, 'alias' Enrico Fiammingo," in *Napoli, l'Europa: Ricerche di Storia dell'Arte in onore di Ferdinando Bologna*, ed. Francesco Abbate and Fiorella Sricchia Santoro, Catanzaro: Meridiana Libri, 1995, pp. 223–30.
Spinosa, Nicola: *Ribera: L'opera completa*, Naples: Electa, 2003.
Spiriti, Andrea: "Impegno finanziario e scelte strategiche: costo e valore dell'arte nella Milano di secondo Seicento," *Quaderni storici*, XXXIX, 2004, pp. 403–19.

Stefani, Chiara: "Considerazioni intorno al viaggio del Cavalier d'Arpino a Venezia," *Paragone*, LI, no. 599, 2000, pp. 67–77.

Stefani Mantovanelli, M.: "Giovanni Battista Langetti," *Saggi e memorie di storia dell'arte*, XVII, 1990, pp. 41–105.

Steinhoff, Judith, *Sienese Painting after the Black Death: Artistic Pluralism, Politics and the New Art Market*, Cambridge: Cambridge University Press, 2007.

Stone, David: "Bad Habit: Scipione Borghese, Wignacourt, and the Problem of Cigoli's Knighthood," in *Celebratio Amicitiae: Essays in Honour of Giovanni Bonello*, ed. Maroma Camillieri and Theresa Vella, Valletta (Malta): Fondazzjoni Patrimonju, 2006, pp. 207–29.

Storey, Tessa: *Carnal Commerce in Counter-Reformation Rome*, Cambridge: Cambridge University Press, 2008.

Stoughton, Michael: "The Paintings of Giovan Battistello Caracciolo" (Ph.D. diss., University of Michigan, Ann Arbor, 1973).

Stoughton, Michael: "Giovanni Battista Caracciolo: New Biographical Documents," *The Burlington Magazine*, CXX, 1978, pp. 204–15.

Strazzullo, Franco: *Documenti inediti per la storia dell'arte a Napoli (pittori)*, Naples: Il Fuidoro, 1955.

Strazzullo, Franco: "La peste del 1656 a Napoli," *Il Fuidoro*, IV, 1957, pp. 7–16.

Strazzullo, Franco: *La Real Cappella del Tesoro di S. Gennaro: Documenti inediti*, Naples: Società Editrice Napoletana, 1978.

Strazzullo, Franco: "Belisario Corenzio in tribunale: Affreschi perduti nel Carmine Maggiore di Napoli," in *Ricerche sul '600 napoletano*, Milan: L&T, 1985, pp. 139–48.

Strocchi, Maria Letizia: "Pratolino alla fine del Seicento e Ferdinando di Cosimo III," *Paradigma*, no. 2, 1978, pp. 419–38.

Strunck, Christina: *Berninis unbekanntes Meisterwerk: Die Galleria Colonna in Rom und die Kunstpatronage des römischen Uradels*, Munich: Hirmer, 2007.

Stumpo, Enrico: *Il capitale finanziario a Roma fra Cinque e Seicento: Contributo alla storia della fiscalità pontificia in età moderna (1570–1660)*, Milan: Giuffrè, 1985.

Succi, Dario: "Carlevarijs, van Wittel, Venezia," in *Luca Carlevarijs e la veduta veneziana del Settecento* (exh. cat., Palazzo della Ragione, Padua), ed. Isabella Reale and Dario Succi, Milan: Electa, 2004, pp. 35–58.

Summerscale, Anne: *Malvasia's Life of the Carracci: Commentary and Translation*, University Park, PA: Pennsylvania State University Press, 2000.

Supino, Igino Benvenuto (ed.): *I ricordi di Alessandro Allori* (Biblioteca della Rivista d'arte), Florence: Barbèra, 1908.

Sutherland Harris, Ann: *Andrea Sacchi*, Princeton: Princeton University Press, 1977.

Syre, Cornelia: *Tintoretto: The Gonzaga Cycle* (exh. cat., Alte Pinakothek, Munich), Ostfildern-Ruit: Hatje Cantz, 2000.

Szanto, Mickaël: "Libertas artibus restituta: La foire Saint-Germain et le commerce des tableaux, des frères Goetkindt à Jean Valdor (1660–1660)," in *Economia e Arte secc. XIII–XVIII: Atti della Trentatreesima Settimana di Studi, 30 aprile–4 maggio 2001*, ed. Simonetta Cavaciocchi, Florence: Le Monnier, 2002, pp. 149–85.

Szanto, Mickaël: "The Fortunes of a Northern Artist in Seventeenth-Century Paris: The Forgotten Years of Herman van Swanevelt," *The Burlington Magazine*, CXLV, 2003a, pp. 199–205.

Szanto, Mickaël: "Gli itinerari delle pitture dall'Italia alla Francia nel primo Seicento: dalle vie diplomatiche ai circuiti bancari," in *The Art Market in Italy 15th–17th Centuries: Il mercato dell'arte in Italia secc. XV–XVII*, ed. Marcello Fantoni, Louisa C. Matthew, and Sara F. Matthews-Grieco, Ferrara: Panini, 2003b, pp. 413–21.

Tagliaferri, Amelio: *Consumi e tenore di vita di una famiglia borghese del '600*, Milan: Giuffrè, 1968.

Tagliaferro, Laura: *La magnificenza privata: "Argenti, gioie, quadri e altri mobili" della famiglia Brignole-Sale, secoli XVI–XIX*, Genoa: Marietta, 1995.

Targioni Tozzetti, Giovanni: *Notizie degli aggrandimenti delle scienze fisiche accaduti in Toscana nel corso di anni LX del secolo XVII*, Florence: Si vende da Giuseppe Bouchard, 1780 (reprint, Bologna: Forni, 1967).

Il Teatro della Crudeltà praticata nelli più severi Tormenti del Mondo, cioè sin dalla Crocifissione di nostro Signore Giesu Cristo: Adornato con 104 figure di rame, inventate, e delineate da Giovanni Luychen Olandese, e dedicate al Molt'Illustre Signor Antonio Zanchi, pittore celeberrimo, Venice: Girolamo Albrizzi, 1696.

Tebbutt, Melanie: *Making Ends Meet: Pawnbroking and Working-Class Credit*, London: Methuen, 1984.

Tedoldi, Leonida: "Il mestiere del pittore a Brescia nel Cinquecento: Prime indagini," in *Tra committenza e collezionismo: Studi sul mercato dell'arte nell'Italia settentrionale durante l'età moderna*, ed. Enrico Maria dal Pozzolo and Leonida Tedoldi, Vicenza: Terra ferma, 2003, pp. 67–75.

Temanza, Tommaso: *Zibaldon*, 1732 (critical edition, ed. Nicola Ivanoff, Venice and Rome: Istituto per la collaborazione culturale, 1963).

Ternois, Daniel: *L'art de Jacques Callot*, Paris: De Nobele, 1962.

Terzaghi, Maria Cristina, *Caravaggio, Annibale Carracci, Guido Reni tra le ricevute del Banco Herrera & Costa*, Rome: "L'Erma" di Bretschneider, 2007.

Tessin the Younger, Nicodemus: *Travel Notes 1673–77 and 1687–88* (Sources, Works, Collections), ed. Merit Laine and Börje Magnusson, Stockholm: Nationalmuseum, 2002.

Thielemann, Andreas: "Klage-Klugheit-Standhaftigkeit: Künstlertopik von Vitruv und Alberti bis Elsheimer und Poussin," in *Adam Elsheimer in Rom: Werk-Kontext-Wirkung*, ed. Andreas Thielemann and Stefan Gronert, Munich: Hirmer, 2008, pp. 15–50.

Thuillier, Jacques: *Vouet* (exh. cat., Galeries nationales du Grand Palais, Paris), Paris: Réunion des Musées Nationaux, 1990.

Tiraboschi, Girolamo: *Notizie de' pittori, scultori, incisori, e architetti natii degli stati del Serenissimo Signor Duca di Modena*, Modena: Soc. Tipografia, 1786.

Todeschini, Giacomo: *I mercanti e il tempio: La società cristiana e il circolo virtuoso della ricchezza fra Medioevo ed età moderna*, Bologna: Il Mulino, 2002.

Tordella, Piera Giovanna: "Sui disegni di Pietro da Cortona e Ciro Ferri per Palazzo Pitti," in *Palazzo Pitti: La Reggia rivelata* (exh. cat., Palazzo Pitti, Florence), ed. Gabriele Capecchi, Amelio Fara, Detlef Heikamp, and Vincenzo Saladino, Florence: Giunti 2003, pp. 278–99.

Torresan, Chiara: "Per 'Treviso scomparsa': Nuovi documenti su artisti sei-settecenteschi attivi nelle chiese conventuali," *Arte veneta*, XLI, 1987, pp. 199–201.

Toscano, Bruno (ed.): *Arte e immagine del papato Borghese (1605–1621)*, San Casciano Val di Pesa: Libro Co. Italia, 2005.

Travaglini, Carlo M.: "Il ruolo del Banco di Santo Spirito e del monte di pietà nel mercato finanziario romano del Settecento," in *Banchi pubblici, banchi privati e monti di pietà nell'Europa pre-industriale: Atti del Convegno, Genova, 1–6 ottobre 1990*, Genoa: Società ligure di storia patria, 1990, pp. 617–39.

Travaglini, Carlo M.: "Rigattieri e società romana nel Settecento," *Quaderni storici*, XXVII, 1992, pp. 415–48.

Trebeschi, M.: "Note d'archivio sui pittori Andrea Celesti, Abramo e Nicola Grisiani," *Brixia Sacra*, XXXIII, 1988, pp. 57–60.

Trevisan, Antonio: "Monete Pesi e Misure," in *Il Libro Secondo di*

Francesco e Jacopo dal Ponte, ed. Michelangelo Muraro, Bassano: G. B. Verci, 1992, pp. 389–92.
Trivellato, Francesca: "Salaires et justice dans les corporations vénitiennes au 17e siècle: Le cas des manufactures de verre," *Annales: Histoire, Sciences Sociales*, LIV, 1999, pp. 245–73.
Trivellato, Francesca: *Fondamenta dei vetrai: Lavoro, tecnologia e mercato a Venezia tra Sei e Settecento*, Rome: Donzelli, 2000.
Tucci, Ugo: "Carriere popolane e dinastie di mestiere a Venezia," in *Gerarchie economiche e gerarchie sociali secoli XII–XVIII*, ed. Annalisa Guarducci, Florence: Le Monnier, 1990, pp. 817–52.
Turbolo, Gian Donato: *Discorso sopra le monete del regno di Napoli*, Naples: 1629.
Ulvioni, P.: "Stampatori e librai a Venezia nel Seicento," *Archivio Veneto*, CVIII, 1977, pp. 93–124.
Vaes, Maurice: "Corneille De Wael (1592–1667)," *Bulletin de l'Institut Historique Belge de Rome*, V, 1925, pp. 137–247.
Van Kessel, Peter and Elisja Schulte (eds.): *Rome–Amsterdam: Two Growing Cities in Seventeenth-Century Europe*, Amsterdam: Amsterdam University Press, 1997.
Van Mander, Karel: *The Lives of the Illustrious Netherlandish and German Painters, from the First Edition of the Schilder-boeck (1603–1604)*, ed. Hessel Miedema, Doornspijk: Davaco, 1994–99.
Van Os, H. W.: "Traditions and Innovation in Some Altarpieces by Bartolo di Fredi," *The Art Bulletin*, LXVII, 1985, pp. 50–66.
Van Zanden, Jan: "Wages and the Standard of Living in Europe, 1500–1800," *European Review of Economics*, II, 1999, pp. 175–97.
Vannugli, Antonio: "Due note documentarie per Mao Salini," *Paragone*, LVII, no. 70, 2006, pp. 67–71.
Varese, C.: "Momenti e implicazioni del romanzo libertino nel Seicento italiano", in *Il libertinismo in Europa*, ed. S. Bertelli, Milan and Naples: Ricciardi, 1980, pp. 239–69.
Vargas, Carmela: *Teodoro d'Errico: La maniera fiamminga del Viceregno*, Naples: Electa, 1988.
Varriano, John: *Caravaggio: The Art of Realism*, University Park, PA: Pennsylvania State University Press, 2006.
Vasari, Giorgio, *Der litterarische Nachlass Giorgio Vasari*, ed. Karl Frey, Munich: Georg Müller, 1923.
Vasari, Giorgio: *Lives of the Artists*, vol. 1, trans. George Bull, Harmondsworth: Penguin Books, 1965.
Vasari, Giorgio: *Le Vite de' più eccellenti pittori scultori e architettori nelle redazioni del 1550 e 1568*, ed. Rosanna Bettarini and Paola Barocchi, Florence: Studio per Edizioni Scelte, 1966–87.
Vasetti, Stefania: *Bernardino Poccetti e gli Strozzi: Committenze a Firenze nel primo decennio del Seicento*, Florence: Opus Libri, 1994.
Vasetti, Stefania: "Alcune puntualizzazioni sugli allievi di Bernardino Poccetti e un inedito ciclo di affreschi," *Annali della Fondazione di Studi di Storia dell'arte Roberto Longhi*, III, 1996, pp. 69–98.
Venturino, Alce O. P. : "Cronologia delle opere d'arte della Cappella di San Domenico in Bologna dal 1597 al 1619," *Arte Antica e Moderna*, no. 1, 1958, pp. 395–99.
Verberne, Judith: "The Bentvueghels (1620/21–1720) in Rome," in *Drawn to Warmth: 17th-Century Dutch Artists in Rome* (exh. cat., Rijksmuseum, Amsterdam), ed. Peter Schatborn, Amsterdam and Zwolle: Rijksmuseum and Waanders, 2001, pp. 22–32.
Verdi, Orietta: "Le fonti documentarie," in *Quaderni di Palazzo Venezia II: Il voltone di Pietro da Cortona in Palazzo Barberini*, Rome: De Luca, 1983, pp. 91–98.
Vergerio, Francesco: *Storia dell'antica Contea di Cesana, ora comune di Lentiai nel Feltrino*, Alassio: Pozzi, 1931.
Vernarecci, D. A.: *Di tre artisti fossombronesi: Gianfrancesco Guerrieri, Camilla Guerrieri, Giuseppe Diamantini*, Fossombrone: Monacelli, 1892.
Vertue, George: *Notebooks, IV* (Anecdotes of Painting in England), Oxford: Walpole Society, 1936.
Vianello, Andrea: *L'Arte dei calegheri e zavateri di Venezia tra XVII e XVIII secolo*, Venice: Istituto Veneto di Scienze, Lettere ed Arti, 1993.
Vielli, Maria Giovanna: "Nuovi documenti per Giovanni Segala," *Arte veneta*, LIII, 1998, pp. 176–79.
Vigo, Giovanni: "Real Wages of the Working Class in Italy: Building Workers' Wages (14th to 18th Century)," *The Journal of European Economic History*, III, 1974, pp. 378–99.
Villari, Rosario: *La rivolta antispagnola a Napoli: Le origini, 1585–1647*, Bari: Laterza, 1967.
Villari, Rosario: *The Revolt of Naples*, trans. James Newell, Cambridge: Polity Press, 1993.
Vio, Gastone: *Le Scuole Piccole nella Venezia dei Dogi: Note d'archivio per la storia delle confraternite veneziane*, Costabissara: A. Colla, 2004.
Visceglia, Maria Antonietta: "I consumi in Italia in età moderna," in *Storia dell'economia italiana, II: L'età moderna: Verso la crisi*, ed. Ruggiero Romano, Turin: Einaudi, 1991, pp. 211–41.
Visceglia, Maria Antonietta: "Burocrazia, mobilità sociale e patronage alla corte di Roma tra Cinque e Seicento: Alcuni aspetti del recente dibattito storiografico e prospettive di ricerca," *Roma moderna e contemporanea*, III, 1995, pp. 11–55.
Visonà, Mara: *Carlo Marcellini: Accademico "Spiantato" nella cultura fiorentina tardo-barocca*, Ospedaletto: Pacini, 1990.
Vitali, S.: "A New Document for the Carracci and Ruggero Bascapè at the Palazzo Magnani in Bologna," *The Burlington Magazine*, CXLIII, 2001, pp. 604–13.
Vliegenthart, Adriaan Willem: *La Galleria Buonarroti: Michelangelo e Michelangelo il Giovane*, Florence: Istituto Universitario Olandese di Storia dell'Arte, 1976.
Völkel, Markus: *Römische Kardinalshaushalte des 17. Jahrhunderts: Borghese-Barberini-Chigi*, Tübingen: Niemeyer, 1993.
Von Ludwig, Gustav: "Archivalische Beiträge zur Geschichte der Venezianischen Kunst," *Jahrbuch der königlich preussischen Kunstsammlungen*, XXIV, Beiheft, 1903, pp. 1–109.
Von Ludwig, Gustav: *Archivalische Beiträge zur Geschichte der venezianischen Kunst*, ed. W. Bode, G. Gronau, and D. v. Hadeln (Italienische Forschungen des Kunsthistorischen Institutes in Florenz, IV), Berlin: B. Cassirer, 1911.
Waldman, Louis: "Raffaellino del Garbo and his World: Commissions, Patrons, Associates," *Artibus et Historiae*, no. 54, 2006, pp. 51–94.
Warnke, Martin: *Artisti di corte: Preistoria dell'artista moderno*, trans. Renato Pedio, Rome: Istituto della Enciclopedia Italiana, 1991.
Warwick, Genevieve: *The Arts of Collecting: Padre Sebastiano Resta and the Market for Drawings in Early Modern Europe*, Cambridge: Cambridge University Press, 2000.
Welch, Evelyn: *Shopping in the Renaissance: Consumer Cultures in Italy, 1400–1600*, New Haven and London: Yale University Press, 2005.
Westin, Jean K. and Robert H. Westin: *Carlo Maratti and his Contemporaries: Figurative Drawings from the Roman Baroque* (exh. cat., Museum of Art, Pennsylvania State University), University Park, PA: Pennsylvania State University Press, 1975.
Wethey, Harold E.: "The Spanish Viceroy, Luca Giordano, and Andrea Vaccaro," *The Burlington Magazine*, CIX, 1967, pp. 678–87.
Wethey, Harold E.: *The Paintings of Titian, III: The Mythological and Historical Paintings*, London: Phaidon, 1975.
Wheeler, Joseph: "Neighbourhoods and Local Loyalties in Renaissance

Venice," in *Mediterranean Urban Culture 1400–1700*, ed. Alexander Cowan, Exeter: University of Exeter Press, 2000, pp. 31–42.

Whistler, Catherine: "Life Drawing in Venice from Titian to Tiepolo," *Master Drawings*, XLII, 2004, pp. 370–96.

Whitfield, Clovis: "Prospero Orsi, interprète du Caravage," *Revue de l'art*, no. 155, 2007, pp. 9–19.

Whitfield, Clovis and Jane Martineau (eds.): *Painting in Naples from Caravaggio to Giordano* (exh. cat., Royal Academy of Art, London), London: Royal Academy, 1982.

Wibiral, Norbert: "Contribuiti alle ricerche sul cortonismo in Roma: I pittori della Galleria di Alessandro VII nel Palazzo del Quirinale," *Bollettino d'arte*, XLV, 1960, pp. 123–65.

Williams, Robert: "The Vocation of the Artist as seen by Giovanni Battista Armenini," *Art History*, XVIII, 1995, pp. 518–36.

Williams, Robert: "The Artist as Worker in Sixteenth-Century Italy," in *Taddeo and Federico Zuccaro: Artist-Brothers in Renaissance Rome* (exh. cat., The J. Paul Getty Museum), ed. Julian Brooks, Los Angeles: The J. Paul Getty Museum, 2007, pp. 94–104.

Winckelmann, J. J.: *Abhandlung von der Fähigkeit der Empfindung des Schönen in der Kunst und dem Unterrichte in derselben*, Dresden: Walther, 1763.

Wine, Humphrey: *The Seventeenth Century French Paintings*, London: National Gallery, 2001.

Wright, A. D.: *The Early Modern Papacy: From the Council of Trent to the French Revolution, 1564–1789*, Harlow: Longman, 2000.

Wright, Alison: "Between the Patron and the Market: Production Strategies in the Pollaiuolo Workshop," in *The Art Market in Italy 15th–17th Centuries: Il mercato dell'arte in Italia secc. XV–XVII*, ed. Marcello Fantoni, Louisa C. Matthew, and Sara F. Matthews-Grieco, Ferrara: Panini, 2003, pp. 225–36.

Zacchia, Lanfranco: *De salario seu operariorum mercede tractatus in tres partes distinctus*, Rome: Nicolai Angeli Tinassi, 1658.

Zacchia, Lanfranco: *Centuria decisionum ad materiam tractatus de salario et operariorum mercede*, Venice: Turrinum, 1659.

Zampetti, Pietro: "Il Testamento di Sebastiano Ricci," *Arte veneta*, XIII–XIV, 1959–60, pp. 229–31.

Zampetti, Pietro: *Antonio Zanchi*, Bergamo: Poligrafiche Bolis, 1988.

Zanatta, F.: "L'inventario come fonte per lo studio della storia della ricchezza privata: Venezia 1661," *Studi Veneziani*, XXXIV, 1997, pp. 199–225.

Zandri, Giuliana: *S. Nicola da Tolentino* (Le chiese di Roma illustrate, no. 19), Rome: Palombi, 1987.

Zanetti, Anton Maria: *Descrizione di tutte le pubbliche pitture della città di Venezia*, Venice: Pietro Bassaglio, 1733.

Zangheri, Luigi: *Gli Accademici del Disegno: Elenco alfabetico*, Florence: Olschki, 2000.

Zannini, Andrea: *Burocrazia e burocrati a Venezia in età moderna: I cittadini originari (sec. XVI–XVIII)*, Venice: Istituto Veneto di Scienze, Lettere ed Arte, 1993a.

Zannini, Andrea: "Un censimento inedito del primo Seicento e la crisi demografica ed economica di Venezia," *Studi Veneziani*, XXVI, 1993b, pp. 87–116.

Zannini, Andrea: "L'impiego pubblico," in *Storia di Venezia, IV: Il Rinascimento*, ed. A. Tenenti and U. Tucci, Rome: Istituto della Enciclopedia Italiana, 1997, pp. 415–63.

Zannini, Andrea: "L'economia veneta nel Seicento: Oltre il paradigma della 'crisi generale'," in *Società Italiana di Demografia Storica: La popolazione nel Seicento*, Bologna: CLUEB, 1999, pp. 473–502.

Zapperi, Roberto: "Per la storia della Galleria Farnese: Nuove ricerche e precisazioni documentarie," *Bollettino d'arte*, LXXXIV, 1999, no. 109–10, pp. 87–102.

Zarri Giovanna: "Istituzioni ecclesiastiche e vita religiosa a Bologna," in *Storia illustrata di Bologna II*, ed. W. Tega, Milan: 1989, pp. 161–200.

Zava Boccazzi, Franca: "Nicolò Cassana a Venezia," *Atti dell'Istituto Veneto di Scienze, Lettere ed Arti*, CXXXVII, 1978–79, pp. 611–34.

Zava Boccazzi, Franca: *Pittoni*, Venice: Alfieri, 1979.

Zava Boccazzi, Franca: "Contributo alla ritrattistica di Nicolò Cassana," *Arte veneta*, XXXVIII, 1984, pp. 97–106.

Zava Boccazzi, Franca: "Battista Zelotti a Praglia," in *L'Abbazia di S. Maria di Praglia*, ed. Callisto Carpanese and Francesco Trolese, Cinisello Balsamo: Silvana Editoriale, 1985, pp. 149–59.

Zava Boccazzi, Franca: "I Veneti della Galleria Conti di Lucca (1704–1707)," *Saggi e memorie di storia dell'arte*, 17, 1990, pp. 109–52.

Zicarelli, Emanuela: "Demografia artistica: Ricerche negli stati delle anime, 2: Per un censimento degli artisti nella parrocchia di San Lorenzo in Lucina," in *Arte e immagine del papato Borghese (1605–1621)*, ed. Bruno Toscano, San Casciano Val di Pesa: Libro Co. Italia, 2005, pp. 33–48.

Zorzi, Marino: *La Libreria di San Marco: Libri, lettori, società nella Venezia dei Dogi*, Milan: Mondadori, 1987.

Zuccari, Alessandro: "Aggiornamenti sulla decorazione cinquecentesca di alcune cappelle del Gesù," *Storia dell'arte*, no. 50, 1984, pp. 27–33.

Zuccaro, Federico: "Il Lamento della pittura sul l'onde venete," in *Lettera a prencipi e signori amatori del dissegno, pittura, scultura et architettura*, Mantua: Francesco Osanna, 1605 (reprint, *Scritti d'arte*, ed. Detlef Heikamp, Florence: Olschki, 1961).

Zuccaro, Federico: *Il Passaggio per Italia, con la Dimora di Parma*, Bologna: Bartolomeo Cocchi, 1608 (reprint, *Scritti d'arte*, ed. Detlef Heikamp, Florence: Olschki, 1961).

Zuccaro, Federico: *R. P. D. Zarate Romana fideicommissi de Zuccaris: PRO Illustriss D. Constantia Toscanella CONTRA DD. de Zuccaris: 2.ª Facti*, Rome: Camerae Apost., 1655 (Archivio di Stato di Roma, Archivio dell'Archiconfraternità dell'Annunziata, 1609, vol. 38).

Notes on the Authors

Renata Ago (Laurea University of Rome "La Sapienza," 1970) is Professor of Early Modern History at the University of Rome "La Sapienza." She has published on various aspects of the economic and social history of Rome in the seventeenth century. Her books include *Carriere e clientele nella Roma barocca* (1990), *Economia barocca: Mercato e istituzioni nella Roma del Seicento* (1998), and *Il gusto delle cose: Una storia degli oggetti nella Roma del Seicento* (2006). She also is the editor of *Diritti di proprietà* (1995) and *The Value of the Norm: Legal Disputes and the Definition of Rights* (2002). Currently she is studying the definition of property rights in the *ancien régime* and the cultural meanings attached to the transmission of goods.

Elena Fumagalli (Ph. D. University of Rome "La Sapienza," 1992) is Associate Professor of Art History at the University of Modena and Reggio Emilia. She has published on various aspects of art history, patronage, and collecting in Florence, Rome, and Naples from the sixteenth to the eighteenth centuries. She was curator of the exhibitions *L'arme e gli amori: Ariosto, Tasso, Guarini e l'arte fiorentina del Seicento* (2001) and *"filosofico umore" e "maravigliosa speditezza": Pittura napoletana del Seicento dalle collezioni medicee* (2007). She is preparing a book on the social history of art in Florence during the seventeenth century.

Richard A. Goldthwaite (Ph. D. Columbia University, 1965) is Professor of History Emeritus of The Johns Hopkins University. He has published on various aspects of the economic history of Florence in the Renaissance; his general overview of the subject, *The Economy of Renaissance Florence*, appeared in 2009. In his *Wealth and the Demand for Art in Italy, 1300–1600* (1993) he studied the art market from the demand side, and his contribution to this volume continues a series of articles in which he attempts to evaluate the production and marketing of art in late medieval and early modern Italy as economic activities.

Christopher R. Marshall (Ph. D. University of Melbourne, 1994) is a Senior Lecturer in Art History and Museum Studies at the University of Melbourne in Australia. His studies of Neapolitan baroque patronage, collecting, and the art market have appeared in *The Art Bulletin*, *The Burlington Magazine*, the *Journal of the History of Collections*, and other journals. Recent publications in his parallel research specialization in contemporary museology include contributions to *Reshaping Museum Space* (2005) and *Making Art History* (2007). He is working on a book-length study of the Neapolitan baroque art world and an edited volume on the topic of sculpture and the museum.

Raffaella Morselli (Ph. D. University of Bologna, 1993) is Professor of Art History at the University of Teramo in Italy. She is author of *Repertorio per lo studio del collezionismo bolognese del Seicento* (1997), *Collezioni e quadrerie nella Bologna del Seicento* (1998), *Le collezioni Gonzaga: L'elenco dei beni del 1626–1627* (2000), *Gonzaga: La celeste galeria: Le raccolte* (2002), and *Le collezioni Gonzaga: La quadreria nell'elenco dei beni del 1626–1627* (2006). During the past years her research has focused on the economics of painting in seventeenth-century Bologna and the Gonzaga collections of European paintings. She is preparing a book, *Il portafoglio del pittore*, on the social history of art in Bologna during the seventeenth century.

Philip Sohm (Ph. D. The Johns Hopkins University, 1978) is University Professor at the University of Toronto. His books include *Pittoresco: Marco Boschini, his Critics, and their Critiques of Painterly Brushwork in Seventeenth- and Eighteenth-Century Italy* (1991), *Style in the Art Theory of Early Modern Italy* (2001), and most recently *The Artist Grows Old: The Aging of Art and Artists in Italy* (2007).

Richard E. Spear (Ph. D. Princeton University, 1965) is Affiliate Research Professor at the University of Maryland, College Park, and Jay Professor of Art History Emeritus, Oberlin College. His books include *Caravaggio and His Followers* (1971), *Domenichino* (1982), *The "Divine Guido": Religion, Sex, Money and Art in the World of Guido Reni* (1997), and *From Caravaggio to Artemisia: Essays on Painting in Seventeenth-Century Italy and France* (2002). Lately his articles have focused on the economics of painting in seventeenth-century Rome and the Tata collections of European paintings in the Prince of Wales Museum, Mumbai, India.

Index

Note: Page references in *italics* indicate illustrations.